Business and Administrative Communication

EIGHTH EDITION

Business and Administrative Communication

KITTY O. LOCKER
The Ohio State University

DONNA S. KIENZLER
Iowa State University

McGraw-Hill Irwin

Boston   Burr Ridge, IL   Dubuque, IA   New York   San Francisco   St. Louis
Bangkok   Bogotá   Caracas   Kuala Lumpur   Lisbon   London   Madrid   Mexico City
Milan   Montreal   New Delhi   Santiago   Seoul   Singapore   Sydney   Taipei   Toronto

BUSINESS AND ADMINISTRATIVE COMMUNICATION

Published by McGraw-Hill/Irwin, a business unit of The McGraw-Hill Companies, Inc., 1221 Avenue of the Americas, New York, NY, 10020. Copyright © 2008, 2006, 2003, 2000, 1998, 1995, 1992, 1989 by The McGraw-Hill Companies, Inc. All rights reserved. No part of this publication may be reproduced or distributed in any form or by any means, or stored in a database or retrieval system, without the prior written consent of The McGraw-Hill Companies, Inc., including, but not limited to, in any network or other electronic storage or transmission, or broadcast for distance learning.

Some ancillaries, including electronic and print components, may not be available to customers outside the United States.

This book is printed on acid-free paper.

1 2 3 4 5 6 7 8 9 0 WCK/WCK 0 9 8 7

ISBN   978-0-07-128311-3
MHID   0-07-128311-0

To my beloved husband Jim and closest friend Kitty

Kitty O. Locker was an Associate Professor of English at The Ohio State University in Columbus, Ohio, where she coordinated the Writing Center and taught courses in business and technical discourse and in research methods. She also taught as Assistant Professor at Texas A&M University and the University of Illinois.

She also wrote *The Irwin Business Communication Handbook: Writing and Speaking in Business Classes* (1993), coauthored *Business Writing Cases and Problems* (1980, 1984, 1987), and co-edited *Conducting Research in Business Communication* (1988). She twice received the Alpha Kappa Psi award for Distinguished Publication in Business Communication for her article "'Sir, This Will Never Do': Model Dunning Letters 1592–1873" and for her article " 'As Per Your Request': A History of Business Jargon." In 1992 she received the Association for Business Communication's Outstanding Researcher Award.

Her research included work on collaborative writing in the classroom and the workplace, and the emergence of bureaucratic writing in the correspondence of the British East India Company from 1600 to 1800.

Her consulting work included conducting tutorials and short courses in business, technical, and administrative writing for employees of URS Greiner, Ross Products Division of Abbott Laboratories, Franklin County, the Ohio Civil Service Employees Association, AT&T, the American Medical Association, Western Electric, the Illinois Department of Central Management Services, the Illinois Department of Transportation, the A. E. Staley Company, Flo-Con, the Police Executive Leadership College, and the Firemen's Institute. She developed a complete writing improvement program for Joseph T. Ryerson, the nation's largest steel materials service center.

She served as the Interim Editor of *The Bulletin of the Association for Business Communication* and, in 1994–95, as President of the Association for Business Communication (ABC). She edited ABC's *Journal of Business Communication* from 1998 to 2000.

In 1998, she received ABC's Meada Gibbs Outstanding Teacher Award.

Donna S. Kienzler is a Professor of English at Iowa State University in Ames, Iowa, where she teaches in the Rhetoric and Professional Communication program. She is the Director of Advanced Communication and oversees more that 150 sections of business and technical communication annually. She is also an Assistant Director of the university's Center for Excellence in Learning and Teaching, where she teaches classes, seminars, and workshops on pedagogy; directs graduate student programming; and directs the Preparing Future Faculty program.

Her research focuses on pedagogy and ethics. Her article with Helen Ewald, "Speech Act Theory and Business Communication Conventions," won an Association for Business Communication (ABC) Alpha Kappa Psi Foundation Award for distinguished publication in business communication. Her article with Carol David, "Towards an Emancipatory Pedagogy in Service Courses and User Departments" was part of a collection that won a National Council of Teachers of English (NCTE) Award for Excellence in Technical and Scientific Communication: Best Collection of Essays in Technical or Scientific Communication.

She has done consulting work for the Air Force, Tracor Consulting, Green Engineering, Northwestern Bell, Iowa Merit Employment, the Iowa Department of Transportation, and her local school district.

She is active in the Association for Business Communication (ABC), where she currently serves on the Business Practices and the Teaching Practices Committees. She also served on ABC's Ad Hoc Committee on Professional Ethics, which developed a Professional Ethics Statement for the national organization.

In 2002, she received ABC's Meada Gibbs Outstanding Teacher Award.

Donna and Kitty became close friends in graduate school at the University of Illinois, Urbana-Champaign, where they shared the same major professor. They remained close friends, and indeed considered each other family, until Kitty's death. During those wonderful years, their favorite topic of conversation was *Business and Administrative Communication;* they discussed content for the original book proposal, content for the first edition, changes for subsequent editions, and future plans for the book. Everything from new sidebars and footnotes to major organizational changes made its way into those long, frequent conversations. Donna looks forward to carrying on Kitty's tradition of excellence.

Welcome to *Business and Administrative Communication* (BAC). This textbook can make learning about business communication easier and more enjoyable.

You'll find that this edition of BAC is as flexible, specific, interesting, comprehensive, and up-to-date as its predecessors. The features users particularly like have been retained: the anecdotes and examples, the easy-to-follow lists, the integrated coverage of ethics and international business communication, the analyses of sample problems, the wealth of exercises and assignments. But a good book has become even better. This edition of BAC includes major changes.

Major Changes to the Eighth Edition

Eleven major changes make the eighth edition even better:

- New topics such as information overload, data security, and internships have been included.
- More emphasis has been added on communications that are not paper documents.
  - Expanded treatment of e-mail.
  - New material on electronic channels such as instant messaging, blogs, and wikis.
- New material has been added on popular topics such as the costs of business communication, legal problems stemming from careless communications, and technology.
- The discussions of document design and visuals have been expanded and combined.
- Chapter openers are real-world business examples that show the use of or need for the principles in the specific chapter.
- More evidence is included that businesses actually use the standard business communication practices taught in the textbooks.
- New and revised sidebars, many with discussion questions, keep the text up-to-date.
- New examples include a student proposal and report, plus new résumés and job letters.
- More discussion on the role of conventions in business communication is included throughout.
- The eighth edition includes new study aids:
  - Learning objectives.
  - Review questions paired to learning objectives.
  - A new section in chapter 1 on how to best use this textbook.
  - Additional grammar exercises.
  - An on-going case which is the last problem in every chapter.
- New content in the job chapters, which are now the second unit in the book, includes material on portfolios, blogs, social networking, videos, honesty, career fairs, campus interviews, phone interviews, and how to succeed in that all-important first job after college. Expanded coverage is included on topics such as electronic résumés, web resources, behavioral interviews, situational interviews, and follow-up messages.

Features Retained

BAC retains the features that have made it the number one book in business communication:

- **BAC is flexible.** Choose the chapters and exercises that best fit your needs. Choose from in-class exercises, messages to revise, problems with hints, and cases presented as they'd arise in the workplace. Many problems offer several options: small group discussions, individual writing, group writing, or oral presentations.

- **BAC is specific.** BAC provides specific strategies, specific guidelines, and specific examples. BAC takes the mystery out of creating effective messages.

- **BAC is interesting.** Anecdotes from a variety of fields show business communication at work. The lively side columns from the *Wall Street Journal* and a host of other sources provide insights into the workplace.

- **BAC is comprehensive.** BAC includes international communication, communicating across cultures in this country, ethics, collaborative writing, organizational cultures, graphs, and technology as well as traditional concerns such as style and organization. Assignments offer practice dealing with international audiences or coping with ethical dilemmas.

- **BAC is up-to-date.** The eighth edition of BAC incorporates the latest research and practice so that you stay on the cutting edge.

Supplements

The stimulating, user-friendly supplements package has been one of the major reasons that BAC is so popular.

1. The **Instructor's Resource Manual** contains

   - **Answers to all exercises,** an overview and difficulty rating for each problem, and, for several of the problems in the book, a detailed analysis, discussion questions, and a good solution.
   - **Additional transparency masters** with ready-to-duplicate examples and lecture points.
   - **Additional exercises and cases for** diagnostic and readiness tests, grammar and style, and for letters, memos, and reports.
   - **Lesson plans and class activities for each chapter.** You'll find discussion guides for transparencies, activities to reinforce chapter materials and prepare students for assignments, and handouts for group work, peer editing, and other activities.
   - **Sample syllabi** for courses with different emphases and approaches.

2. The **Test Bank** contains approximately 1,200 test items with answers, a difficulty rating for each, page references, and AAWB rating.

3. The **Instructor's CD-Rom** collects many features of the Instructor's Resource Manual, videos, PowerPoint slides, and lecture material in an electronic format.

4. The **BAC Web site** at www.mhhe.com/bac8e identifies sites for business, personal business, research, ethics, and job hunting. Additional exercises and quizzes are available to help students improve their writing and communication skills.

5. A **Computerized Test Bank** is available to qualified adopters in both Macintosh and Windows formats, and allows professors to generate and edit their own test questions.

6. **Managers Hot Seat for Business Communication** is now online at www.mhhe.com/MHS. This interactive video-based software puts students in the manager's hot seat where they have to apply their knowledge to make decisions on the spot on hot issues.

Continuing the Conversation

This edition incorporates the feedback I've received from instructors who used earlier editions. Tell me about your own success stories teaching *Business and Administrative Communication*. I look forward to hearing from you!

Donna S. Kienzler

All writing is in some sense collaborative. This book in particular builds upon the ideas and advice of teachers, students, and researchers. The people who share their ideas in conferences and publications enrich not only this book but also business communication as a field.

Many people reviewed the 7th edition, suggesting what to change and what to keep. Additional reviewers commented on drafts of the 8th edition or completed in-depth surveys, helping to further improve the book. We thank all of these reviewers for their attention to detail and their promptness!

Lenette Baker, *Valencia Community College*

Laura Barelman, *Wayne State College*

Fiona Barnes, *University of Florida*

Cathie Bishop, *Parkland College*

Melanie Bookout, *Greenville Technical College*

Donna Cox, *Monroe Community College*

Christine Leigh Cranford, *East Carolina University*

Marilyn Easter, *San Jose State University*

Susan Fiechtner, *Texas A&M University*

Susan Finnerty, *John Carroll University*

Melissa Fish, *American River College*

Mildred Franceschi, *Valencia Community College—West Camp*

Linda Fraser, *California State University, Fullerton*

Mary Greene, *Prince George's Community College*

Deborah Herz, *Salve Regina University*

Jeremy Kemp, *San Jose State University*

Newton Lassiter, *Florida Atlantic University*

Sally Lawrence, *East Carolina University*

Cheryl Ann Laws, *City University*

Margaret Mahoney, *Iowa State University*

Virginia Melvin, *Southwest Tennessee Community College*

Robert Von der Osten, *Ferris State University*

Greg Pauley, *Moberly Area Community College*

Melinda Phillabaum

Brenda Price, *Bucks County Community College*

David Ramsey, *Southeastern Louisiana University*

Betty Robbins, *University of Oklahoma*

Mary Jane Ryals, *Florida State University*

Don Soucy

Bruce Todd Strom, *University of Indianapolis*

Jie Wang, *University of Illinois—Chicago*

Marsha Daigle Williamson, *Spring Arbor University*

Bennie Wilson, *University of Texas-San Antonio*

In addition, the book continues to benefit from people who advised me on earlier editions:

Bill Allen, *University of LaVerne*

Vanessa Arnold, *University of Mississippi*

Lynn Ashford, *Alabama State University*

Dennis Barbour, *Purdue University—Calumet*

Jan Barton-Zimerman, *University of Nebraska, Kearney*

Jaye Bausser, *Indiana University—Purdue University at Fort Wayne*

Sallye Benoit, *Nicholls State University*

Raymond W. Beswick, *formerly of Synerude, Ltd.*

Carole Bhakar, *The University of Manitoba*

Randi Meryl Blank, *Indiana University*

Bennis Blue

John Boehm, *Iowa State University*

Maureen S. Bogdanowicz, *Kapi'olani Community College*

Kendra S. Boggess, *Concord College*

Christy Ann Borack, *California State University, Fullerton; Orange Coast College, Costa Mesa*

Charles P. Bretan, *Northwood University*

Vincent Brown, *Battelle Memorial Institute*

John Bryan, *University of Cincinnati*

Phyllis Bunn, *Delta State University*

Janice Burke, *South Suburban College of Cook County*

Robert Callahan, *The University of Texas, San Antonio*

Andrew Cantrell, *University of Illinois*

Danny Cantrell, *West Virginia State College*

Susan Carlson

John Carr, *The Ohio State University*

Kathy Casto

Jay Christiansen, *California State University, Northridge*

Lynda Clark, *Maple Woods Community College*

Brendan G. Coleman, *Mankato State University*

John Cooper, *University of Kentucky*

Tena Crews, *State University of West Georgia*

Carla Dando, *Idaho State University*

Susan H. Delagrange, *The Ohio State University*

Mark DelMaramo, *Thiel College*

Moira E. W. Dempsy, *Oregon State University*

Gladys DeVane, *Indiana University*

Jose A. Duran, *Riverside Community College*

Dorothy J. Dykman, *Point Loma Nazarene College*

Anna Easton, *Indiana University*

Mary Ann Firmin, *Oregon State University*

W. Clark Ford, *Middle Tennessee State University*

Louisa Fordyce, *Westmoreland County Community College*

Paula J. Foster, *Foster Communication*

Silvia Fuduric, *Wayne State University*

Robert D. Gieselman, *University of Illinois*

Cheryl Glenn, *Pennsylvania State University*

Jane Greer

Daryl Grider, *West Virginia State College*

Peter Hadorn, *Virginia Commonwealth University*

Ed Hagar, *Belhaven College*

Elaine Hage, *Forsythe Technical Community College*

Barbara Hagler, *Southern Illinois University*

Robert Haight, *Kalamazoo Valley Community College*

Les Hanson, *Red River Community College, Canada*

Kathy Harris, *Northwestern State University*

Mark Harstein, *University of Illinois*

Maxine Hart, *Baylor University*

Vincent Hartigan, *New Mexico State University*

David Hawes, *Owens Community College*

Charles Hebert, *The University of South Carolina*

Ruth Ann Hendrickson

Paulette Henry, *Howard University*

Robert Hill, *University of LaVerne*

Kenneth Hoffman, *Emporia State University*

Elizabeth Hoger, *Western Michigan University*

Carole A. Holden, *County College of Morris*

Carlton Holte, *California State University, Sacramento*

Glenda Hudson, *California State University, Bakersfield*

Elizabeth Huettman, *Cornell University*

Melissa Ianetta, *University of Southern Indiana*

Susan Isaacs, *Community College of Philadelphia*

Daphne A. Jameson, *Cornell University*

Elizabeth Jenkins, *Pennsylvania State University*

Lee Jones, *Shorter College*

Paula R. Kaiser, *University of North Carolina at Greensboro*

Robert W. Key, *University of Phoenix*

Joy Kidwell, *Oregon State University*

Donna Kienzler, *Iowa State University*

Susan E. Kiner, *Cornell University*

Lisa Klein, *The Ohio State University*

Gary Kohut, *University of North Carolina, Charlotte*

Sarah McClure Kolk, *Hope College*

Keith Kroll, *Kalamazoo Valley Community College*

Milton Kukon, *Southern Vermont College*

Linda M. LaDuc, *University of Massachusetts, Amherst*

Suzanne Lambert, *Broward Community College*

Barry Lawler, *Oregon State University*

Gordon Lee, *University of Tennessee*

Kathy Lewis-Adler, *University of North Alabama*

Luchen Li, *Iowa State University*

Dana Loewy, *California State University, Fullerton*

Andrea A. Lunsford, *Stanford University*

Elizabeth Macdonald, *Thunderbird Graduate School of International Management*

John T. Maguire, *University of Illinois*

Michael D. Mahler, *Montana State University*

Gianna Marsella

Pamela L. Martin, *The Ohio State University*

Iris Washburn Mauney, *High Point College*

Patricia McClure, *West Virginia State College*

Nancie McCoy-Burns, *University of Idaho*

Brian R. McGee, *Texas Tech University*

Yvonne Merrill, *University of Arizona*

Julia R. Meyers, *North Carolina State University*

Paul Miller, *Davidson College*

Scott Miller

Jayne Moneysmith, *Kent State University—Stark*

Josef Moorehead, *California State University, Sacramento*

Evelyn Morris, *Mesa Community College*

Frederick K. Moss, *University of Wisconsin—Waukesha*

Frank P. Nemecek, Jr., *Wayne State University*

Cheryl Noll, *Eastern Illinois University*

Nancy Nygaard, *University of Wisconsin, Milwaukee*

Carole Clark Papper

Jean E. Perry, *University of Southern California*

Linda N. Peters, *University of West Florida*

Florence M. Petrofes, *University of Texas at El Paso*

Evelyn M. Pierce, *Carnegie Mellon University*

Cathy Pleska, *West Virginia State College*

Susan Plutsky, *California State University, Northridge*

Virginia Polanski, *Stonehill College*

Janet Kay Porter, *Leeward Community College*

Susan Prenzlow, *Minnesota State University, Mankato*

Brenner Pugh, *Virginia Commonwealth University*

Kathryn C. Rentz, *University of Cincinnati*

Janetta Ritter, *Garland County Community College*

Naomi Ritter, *Indiana University*

Jeanette Ritzenthaler, *New Hampshire College*

Ralph Roberts, *University of West Florida*

Carol Roever, *Missouri Western State College*

Alisha Rohde

Mary Jane Ryals, *Florida State University*

Mary Saga, *University of Alaska-Fairbanks*

Betty Schroeder, *Northern Illinois University*

Nancy Schullery, *Western Michigan University*

Kelly Searsmith, *University of Illinois*

Sherry Sherrill, *Forsythe Technical Community College*

Frank Smith, *Harper College*

Pamela Smith, *Florida Atlantic University*

Janet Starnes, *University of Texas, Austin*

Ron Stone, *DeVry University*

Judith A. Swartley, *Lehigh University*

Christine Tachick, *University of Wisconsin, Milwaukee*

Mel Tarnowski, *Macomb Community College*

Bette Tetreault, *Dalhousie University*

Barbara Z. Thaden, *St. Augustine's College*

Linda Travis, *Ferris State University*

Lisa Tyler, *Sinclair Community College*

Donna Vasa, *University of Nebraska—Lincoln*

David A. Victor, *Eastern Michigan University*

Catherine Waitinas, *University of Illinois, Champaign-Urbana*

Vicky Waldroupe, *Tusculum College*

Randall Waller, *Baylor University*

George Walters, *Emporia State University*

Linda Weavil, *Elon College*

Judy West, *University of Tennessee—Chattanooga*

Paula Weston

Gail S. Widner, *University of South Carolina*

Andrea Williams

Rosemary Wilson, *Washtenaw Community College*

Janet Winter, *Central Missouri State University*

Bonnie Thames Yarbrough, *University of North Carolina at Greensboro*

Sherilyn K. Zeigler, *Hawaii Pacific University*

I'm pleased to know that the book has worked so well for so many people and appreciative of suggestions for ways to make it even more useful in this edition. I especially want to thank the students who have allowed me to use their letters and memos, whether or not they allowed me to use their real names in the text.

I am grateful to all the business people who have contributed. The companies where I have done research and consulting work have given me insights into the problems and procedures of business and administrative communication. Special acknowledgment is due Joseph T. Ryerson & Son, Inc., where Kitty created the Writing Skills program that ultimately became the first draft of this book. And I thank the organizations that permitted McGraw-Hill/Irwin to reproduce their documents in this book and in the ancillaries.

Many thanks to the six graduate students who helped with the eighth edition: Karen Bovenmyer, Rachelle Greer, Karen Gulbrandsen, Matthew Search, Christopher Toth, and Jennifer Veltsos. They updated sidebars and footnotes and added new exercises. Matt and Christopher provided much extra help with visual and technology components; Rachelle and Karen B. performed research wonders to find new materials. Rachelle and Christopher wrote new job letters and résumés; Matt wrote many chapter openers. Christopher rewrote the new student proposal and report; he also wrote the Mosaic case that appears in the exercises for all chapters. And most of all I am grateful to Karen B. and Christopher for their hours of extra help as the deadline approached. When the schedule seemed all but impossible to meet, they supported me with their time, editing talents, and encouragement. And they remained far more cheerful under sleep deprivation than I did.

More thanks for Rachelle Greer and Christopher Toth, who prepared the Instructor's Manual and the PowerPoint slides, and Christine Jonick, who prepared the TestBank. Thanks to Roxanne Clemens, who also wrote some chapter openers, and Heather Eddy and Austin Buelt, who helped with research.

The publisher, McGraw-Hill/Irwin, provided strong editorial and staff support. I am particularly grateful to Paul Ducham for providing extra support, Anna Chan and Kelly Pekelder for answering innumerable questions, and Sarah Evertson for finding such wonderful photos.

I also wish to thank Mary Conzachi, Artemio Ortiz, and Greg Bates for the appearance of the book.

And, finally, I thank my husband Jim, who provided support, research, editorial assistance, and, when deadlines loomed, meals.

A Guided Tour

Business and Administrative Communication, by Kitty O. Locker and Donna S. Kienzler, is a true leader in the business communications field. The 8th edition is designed to teach students how to think critically, communicate effectively, and improve written and oral business communication skills. These skills will successfully prepare students to meet a variety of challenges they may face in their future careers.

Beyond covering the broad scope of topics in both oral and written business communication, this text uses a student-friendly writing style and strong design element to hold student attention. In addition, real-world examples and real business applications underscore key material within the text.

We invite you to learn about this new edition and its features by paging through this visual guide.

CHAPTER PEDAGOGY

LEARNING OBJECTIVES

Each chapter begins with Learning Objectives to guide students as they study. The first exercise for each chapter, Reviewing the Chapter, poses questions specifically linked to the chapter's learning objectives.

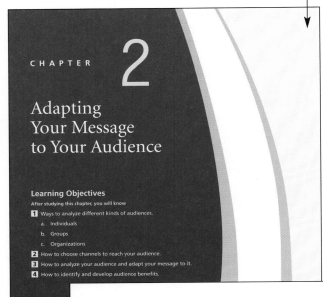

CHAPTER 2

Adapting Your Message to Your Audience

Learning Objectives

After studying this chapter, you will know

1 Ways to analyze different kinds of audiences.
   a. Individuals
   b. Groups
   c. Organizations
2 How to choose channels to reach your audience.
3 How to analyze your audience and adapt your message to it.
4 How to identify and develop audience benefits.

CHAPTER 2   Exercises and Problems

2.1   Reviewing the Chapter

1. Who are the five different audiences your message may need to address? (LO 1)
2. What are some characteristics to consider when analyzing individuals? (LO 1)
3. What are some characteristics to consider when analyzing groups? (LO 1)
4. What are some questions to consider when analyzing organizational culture? (LO 1)
5. What is a discourse community? Why will discourse communities be important in your career? (LO 1)
6. What are standard business communication channels? (LO 2)
7. What kinds of electronic channels seem most useful to you? Why? (LO 2)
8. What are considerations to keep in mind when selecting channels? (LO 2)
9. What are 12 questions to ask when analyzing your audience? (LO 3)
10. What are four characteristics of good audience benefits? (LO 4)
11. What are three ways to identify and develop audience benefits? (LO 4)
12. What are considerations to keep in mind when addressing multiple audiences? (LO 3)

2.2   Reviewing Grammar

Good audience analysis requires careful use of pronouns. Review your skills with pronoun usage by doing grammar exercise B.5, Appendix B.

2.3   Identifying Audiences

In each of the following situations, label the audiences as gatekeeper, primary, secondary, auxiliary, or watchdog:
1. Kent, Carol, and Jose are planning to start a Web site design business. However, before they can get started, they need money. They have developed a business plan and are getting ready to seek funds from financial institutions for starting their small business.

AN INSIDE PERSPECTIVE

Each chapter is introduced with current news articles relevant to the chapter's concepts. These opening articles set the stage for the chapter's content and allow students a glimpse at how the material applies in the business world.

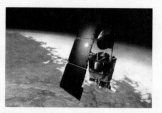

SIDEBARS

These novel and interesting examples effectively enhance student understanding of key concepts. Featured in the margins of every chapter, these sidebars cover topic areas that include International, Legal/Ethical, Just for Fun, Technology, and On the Job. In addition, gold stars identify "Classic" sidebars.

INSITE LINKS

These helpful URLs point to Web sites that include organizations and resources of effective business communication. These examples underscore the role of the Web in business communication and serve to motivate and enrich the student learning experience. These Web sites cover a wide range of reference sources, including corporate, small business, nonprofit, and government Web sites.

FULL-PAGE EXAMPLES

A variety of visual examples featuring full-sized letters, memos, e-mails, reports, and résumés are presented in the text. These examples include the authors' "handwritten" annotations, explaining communication miscues while offering suggestions for improvement.

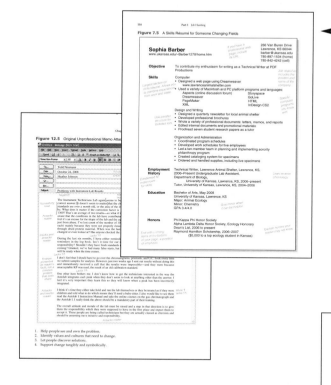

GOOD AND BAD EXAMPLES

Paired effective and ineffective communication examples are presented so students can pinpoint problematic ways to phrase messages to help improve their communication skills. Commentaries in red and blue inks indicate poor or good methods of message communication and allow for easy comparison.

CHECKLISTS

Checkpoints for important messages appear throughout the book. These helpful lists serve as a handy reference guide of items to keep in mind when composing and editing messages.

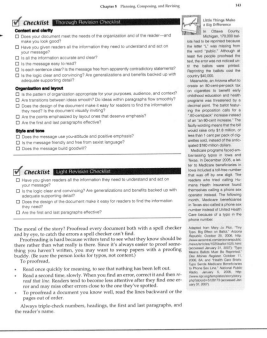

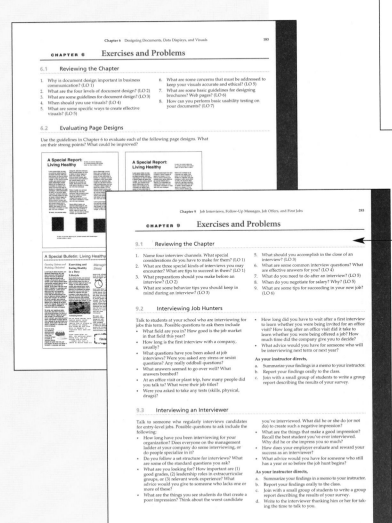

EXERCISES AND PROBLEMS

These hands-on exercises are flexible and can be used as in-class discussions or as individual and group assignments. These workplace exercises allow students to assume a role or perform a task in a variety of realistic business scenarios. Helpful "hints" provide structure and guidance to students for them to complete the exercises.

The first exercise is always a collection of chapter review questions connected to the learning objectives. The last exercise is always part of the ongoing Mosaic case, offering students a rich business scenario, complete with daily complications.

A WEALTH OF SUPPLEMENTS

INSTRUCTOR'S RESOURCE CD-ROM

This valuable teaching resource includes Instructor's Manual, Test Bank, and a 4-color PowerPoint presentation for each chapter. Included are: sample syllabi, teaching tips and questions for class discussions, as well as a computerized EZTest test generator.

MANAGER'S HOT SEAT PROGRAM

This interesting interactive video-based software captures real-life business managers responding to critical workplace situations. These videos provide an opportunity for students to see learned concepts in action and serve as excellent discussion starters. To access the videos go to www.mhhe.com/MHS

NEW ONLINE LEARNING CENTER

Numerous resources available for both instructors and students are online at www.mhhe.com/bac8e. Instructor resources include downloadable versions of the Instructor's Manual and PowerPoint. Student resources include practice exercises; memo, letter, and résumé templates; and links to business communication resources.

CONTENTS

PART TWO   Job Hunting

PART THREE   Basic Business Messages

PART FOUR   Interpersonal Communication

PART FIVE Reports

Business and Administrative Communication

1

Business Communication, Management, and Success

Learning Objectives

After studying this chapter, you will know:

1 Why you need to be able to communicate well.

2 What the costs of communication are.

3 What the costs of poor communication are.

4 What the trends in business communication are.

5 What role conventions play in business communication.

6 How to solve business communication problems.

Business Communication Lessons from Mars

Business communication problems occur everywhere, even in the depths of space. On September 23, 1999, NASA mission control lost contact with the *Mars Climate Orbiter* spacecraft just after it arrived at the planet Mars. The satellite vanished, and a subsequent investigation revealed that the main problem was a minor software programming error. So how is that a business communication problem? Because, according to the *Mars Climate Orbiter* Mishap Investigation Board report, that software error sent the satellite off course, but communication errors sent the software off course.

Like many business projects, the *Mars Climate Orbiter* involved a wide range of people doing a range of jobs, in a range of locations. In this case, the programmers who wrote the software that controlled the spacecraft's engines worked in Great Britain, and used metric measurements in their calculations, while the engineers who made the satellite's engines worked in the United States, and used English measurements. Both teams assumed that they were using the same measurement standards, neither team made any attempt to check, and no one else caught the error. With that failure, NASA lost a $125 million satellite and years of effort but gained a major public embarrassment.

> *"In a professional setting, everything you do involves communication."*

It wasn't just a case of two teams who didn't talk to each other: the Investigation Board found communication problems throughout the project. Teams didn't share information with each other or with management, and team members didn't receive adequate training on critical equipment and processes. Those problems have proved difficult to fix: as of January 2007, NASA's contractors were still communicating using different measurements. So for upcoming lunar missions, the moon base will use metric measures but the spaceships going to the moon won't—and NASA will have to keep even more careful watch over communication between its project teams.

In a professional setting, everything you do involves communication. Good business communication is about sharing information in ways that are useful to your co-workers, business partners, and clients: if the programmers, engineers, and managers at NASA had shared information, they could have saved the *Mars Climate Orbiter*. Good business communication is about building relationships and goodwill to create successful ventures: if the *Mars Orbiter* project teams had communicated more closely, they would have known what their co-workers needed for success.

Sources: NASA MCO Mission Failure Mishap Investigation Board, "*Mars Climate Orbiter* Mishap Investigation Board Phase I Report," ftp://ftp.hq.nasa.gov/pub/pao/reports/1999/MCO_report.pdf (accessed May 11, 2007); and A. J. Hosteler, "Going the Metric Mile: After Loss of Mars Orbiter, NASA Ready to Use Decimal Unit System for Lunar-Base Surface Operations," *Knight Ridder Tribune Business News*, January 15, 2007.

Chapter Outline

Communication Ability = Promotability

"I'll Never Have to Write Because . . ."

Communicating on the Job
- The Importance of Listening, Speaking, and Interpersonal Communication
- The Documents That Employees Write

The Cost of Communication

Costs of Poor Communication
- Wasted Time
- Wasted Efforts
- Lost Goodwill
- Legal Problems

Benefits of Improving Communication

Criteria for Effective Messages

Trends in Business and Administrative Communication
- Technology
- Focus on Quality and Customers' Needs
- Entrepreneurship
- Teamwork
- Diversity
- Globalization and Outsourcing
- Legal and Ethical Concerns
- Balancing Work and Family
- Job Flexibility
- Rapid Rate of Change

Following Conventions

Understanding and Analyzing Business Communication Situations

How to Solve Business Communication Problems
- Answer the Six Questions for Analysis.
- Organize Your Information to Fit Your Audiences, Your Purposes, and the Situation.
- Make Your Document Visually Inviting.
- Revise Your Draft to Create a Friendly, Businesslike, Positive Style.
- Edit Your Draft for Standard English; Double-Check Names and Numbers.
- Use the Response You Get to Plan Future Messages.

How to Use This Book

Summary of Key Points

Business depends on communication. People must communicate to plan products and services; hire, train, and motivate workers; coordinate manufacturing and delivery; persuade customers to buy; and bill them for the sale. Indeed, for many businesses and nonprofit and government organizations, the "product" is information or services rather than something tangible. Information and services are created and delivered by communication. In every organization, communication is the way people get their points across and get work done.

Communication takes many forms: face-to-face or phone conversations, informal meetings, presentations, e-mail messages, letters, memos, reports, blogs, text messaging, and Web sites. All of these methods are forms of **verbal communication,** or communication that uses words. **Nonverbal communication** does not use words. Pictures, computer graphics, and company logos are nonverbal. Interpersonal nonverbal signals include how people sit at meetings, how large offices are, and how long someone keeps a visitor waiting.

Communication Ability = Promotability

Even in your first job, you'll communicate. You'll read information; you'll listen to instructions; you'll ask questions; you may solve problems with other workers in teams. In a manufacturing company, workers may be updating assembly or safety procedures. In an insurance company, clerks answer customers' letters. Even "entry-level" jobs require high-level skills in reasoning, mathematics, and communicating. As a result, communication ability consistently ranks first among the qualities that employers look for in college graduates.[1]

The advantage of communication skills became acutely important in this decade, after the booming economy of the 1990s and the expansion of Internet technology gave way to a more sober business environment. Robert O. Best, Chief Information Officer of UNUMProvident, an insurance corporation, cautions, "You used to be able to get away with being a technical nerd. . . . Those days are over."[2] As more people compete for fewer jobs, the ones who will build successful careers are those who can communicate well with customers and colleagues—using words to teach, motivate, and build positive business relationships.

The National Commission on Writing surveyed 120 major corporations, employing nearly 8 million workers. Almost 70% of respondents said that at least two-thirds of their employees have writing responsibilities included in their position descriptions. E-mail and presentations with visuals (such as PowerPoint slides) were universal. Over half the respondents also reported other forms of communication as frequently required: memos and correspondence, 70%; formal reports, 62%; and technical reports, 59%. Respondents also noted that communication functions were least likely to be outsourced.[3]

Because communication skills are so important, good communicators earn more. Linguist Stephen Reder has found that among people with two- or four-year degrees, workers in the top 20% of writing ability earn, on average, more than three times as much as workers whose writing falls into the worst 20%.[4] Jeffrey Gitomer, business consultant and author of best-selling business books, says there are three secrets to getting known in the business world; all these are communication skills:

1. Writing: "Writing leads to wealth."
2. E-zine: "I reach more than 130,000 subscribers each week."
3. Speaking: "The secret is being prepared."[5]

"I'll Never Have to Write Because . . ."

Some students think that a secretary will do their writing, that they can use form letters if they do have to write, that only technical skills matter, or that they'll call rather than write. Each of these claims is fundamentally flawed.

Claim 1: Secretaries will do all my writing.

Reality: Because of automation and restructuring, job responsibilities in offices have changed. Today, secretaries and administrative assistants are likely to handle

Communication Is Key to Pay

How can you make more money at your job?

The number one way, according to the *Wall Street Journal*, is to "listen to your boss." Specifically, do the work your boss wants done, follow directions, work hard, and let your boss know what you have accomplished. Employees who follow this method collect raises at a rate of 9.9%, while average performers receive 3.6% and poor performers get 1.3%, according to one survey.

Just as important is to make sure you ask your manager to define expectations. Don't assume you know what your manager wants. Make sure you understand what your manager considers an outstanding performance in your position.

Adapted from Perri Capell, "10 Ways to Get the Most Pay out of Your Job," *Wall Street Journal*, September 18, 2006, R1.

Columbia Disaster Communication Failures

In 2003, the *Columbia* space shuttle disintegrated on re-entry, resulting in the deaths of all seven crew members. The independent research team investigating the disaster found communication problems to be the root cause of the accident. The researchers concluded that organizational barriers prevented effective communication of critical safety information and restrained communication of professionals.

The report identified the following communication problems:

- Communication flow between managers and subordinates: Managers did not heed the concerns of the engineers regarding debris impacts on the shuttle. Throughout the project, communication did not flow effectively up to or down from program managers.

- Circulation of information among teams: Although engineers were concerned about landing problems and therefore conducted experiments on landing procedures, the concerns were not relayed to managers or to system and technology experts who could have addressed the concerns.

- Communication sources: Managers received a large amount of their information from informal channels, which blocked relevant opinions and conclusions from engineers.

Source: *Columbia* Accident Investigation Board, "Report of *Columbia* Accident Investigation Board, Volume I," in *NASA Home, Mission Sections, Space Shuttle, Columbia,* http://www.nasa.gov/columbia/home /CAIB_Vol1.html (accessed May 16, 2007).

complex tasks such as training, research, and database management for several managers. Managers are likely to take care of their own writing, data entry, and phone calls.

Claim 2:   I'll use form letters or templates when I need to write.

Reality: A **form letter** is a prewritten, fill-in-the-blank letter designed to fit standard situations. Using a form letter is OK if it's a good letter. But form letters cover only routine situations. The higher you rise, the more frequently you'll face situations that aren't routine, that demand creative solutions.

Claim 3:   I'm being hired as an accountant, not a writer.

Reality: Almost every entry-level professional or managerial job requires you to write e-mail messages, speak to small groups, write documents, and present your work for annual reviews. People who do these things well are likely to be promoted beyond the entry level. Employees in jobs as diverse as firefighters, security professionals, and construction project managers are all being told to polish their writing and speaking skills.[6]

Claim 4:   I'll just pick up the phone.

Reality: Important phone calls require follow-up letters, memos, or e-mail messages. People in organizations put things in writing to make themselves visible, to create a record, to convey complex data, to make things convenient for the reader, to save money, and to convey their own messages more effectively. "If it isn't in writing," says a manager at one company, "it didn't happen." Writing is an essential way to make yourself visible, to let your accomplishments be known.

Communicating on the Job

Communication—oral, nonverbal, and written—goes to both internal and external audiences. **Internal audiences** (Figure 1.1) are other people in the same organization: subordinates, superiors, peers. **External audiences** (Figure 1.2) are people outside the organization: customers, suppliers, unions, stockholders, potential employees, government agencies, the press, and the general public.

The Importance of Listening, Speaking, and Interpersonal Communication

Informal listening, speaking, and working in groups are just as important as writing formal documents and giving formal oral presentations. As a newcomer in an organization, you'll need to listen to others both to find out what you're supposed to do and to learn about the organization's values and culture. Informal chitchat, both about yesterday's game and about what's happening at work, connects you to the **grapevine,** an informal source of company information. You may be asked to speak to small groups, either inside or outside your organization. Networking with others in your office and in town and working with others in workgroups will be crucial to your success.

These skills remain important as you climb the corporate ladder. Good managers interact with their employees. They listen to lunch room conversations; they chat with employees over coffee. They polish their speaking skills on audiences varying in size from one to hundreds, and sometimes thousands. Such interactions are even more critical to success in light of the drive to make organizations more efficient and customer-focused. Managers today often report to more than one boss—for example, the leader of their function (such as sales or finance) and the leader of their project or customer group. At

Figure 1.1 The Internal Audiences of the Sales Manager—West

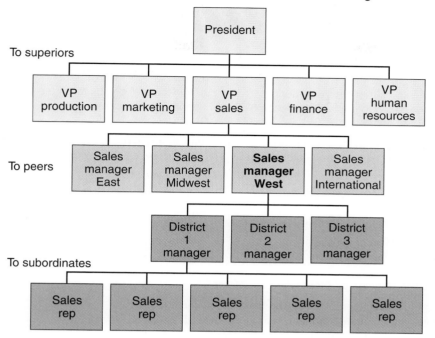

Figure 1.2 The Corporation's External Audiences

Source: Daphne A. Jameson

Succeeding against the Odds

I developed my communication skills as a technique of survival. I was born in poverty and spent two years on the welfare rolls, and I learned early that I had to communicate or die. And so I talked my way out of poverty—I communicated my way to the top. . . .

I read and re-read books on self-improvement, success and communication. The most important lesson I learned from these books is what I call "other focusing." This means, among other things, that if we want to communicate with employees, managers, and even competitors we must ask ourselves not what we want but what they want.

This rule made me a millionaire. For the only way I got to where I am today was by persuading thousands of blacks and whites, some of whom were very prejudiced, that the only way they could get what they wanted was by helping me get what I wanted. All the law and prophecy of communication theory can be found in that formula.

John H. Johnson, owner and publisher of *Ebony* magazine, quoted in Gloria Gordon, "EXCEL Award Winner John H. Johnson Communicates Success," *IABC Communication World* 6, no. 6 (May 1989): 18–19.

Figure 1.3   Internal Documents Produced in One Organization

Document	Description of document	Purpose(s) of document
Transmittal	Memo accompanying document, telling why it's being forwarded to the receiver	Inform; persuade reader to read document; build image and goodwill
Monthly or quarterly report	Report summarizing profitability, productivity, and problems during period. Used to plan activity for next month or quarter	Inform; build image and goodwill (report is accurate, complete; writer understands company)
Policy and procedure bulletin	Statement of company policies and instructions (e.g., how to enter orders, how to run fire drills)	Inform; build image and goodwill (procedures are reasonable)
Request to deviate from policy and procedure bulletin	Persuasive memo arguing that another approach is better for a specific situation than the standard approach	Persuade; build image and goodwill (request is reasonable; writer seeks good of company)
Performance appraisal	Evaluation of an employee's performance, with recommended areas for improvement or recommendation for promotion	Inform; persuade employee to improve
Memo of congratulations	Congratulations to employees who have won awards, been promoted, or earned community recognition	Build goodwill

international consulting firms, consultants may report to a director of their area of specialty and the head of their geographic region. Their communication must not only flow in several directions but cross cultural barriers as well.

The Documents That Employees Write

People in organizations produce a large variety of documents. Figures 1.3 and 1.4 list a few of the specific documents produced at Ryerson Tull. The company, which fabricates and sells steel, aluminum, other metals, and plastics to a wide

Figure 1.4   External Documents Produced in One Organization

Document	Description of document	Purpose(s) of document
Quotation	Letter giving price for a specific product, fabrication, or service	Inform; build goodwill (price is reasonable)
Claims adjustment	Letter granting or denying customer request to be given credit for defective goods	Inform; build goodwill
Job description	Description of qualifications and duties of each job. Used for performance appraisals, setting salaries, and hiring	Inform; persuade good candidates to apply; build goodwill (job duties match level, pay)
10-K report	Report filed with the Securities and Exchange Commission detailing financial information	Inform
Annual report	Report to stockholders summarizing financial information for year	Inform; persuade stockholders to retain stock and others to buy; build goodwill (company is a good corporate citizen)
Thank-you letter	Letter to suppliers, customers, or other people who have helped individuals or the company	Build goodwill

Business communication involves paper documents, electronic communications, but most of all, interpersonal abilities.

variety of industrial clients, has processing centers and sales offices across the United States and Canada.

All of the documents in Figures 1.3 and 1.4 have one or more of the **three basic purposes of organizational writing:** to inform, to request or persuade, and to build goodwill. When you **inform,** you explain something or tell readers something. When you **request or persuade,** you want the reader to act. The word *request* suggests that the action will be easy or routine; *persuade* suggests that you will have to motivate and convince the reader to act. When you **build goodwill,** you create a good image of yourself and of your organization—the kind of image that makes people want to do business with you.

Most messages have multiple purposes. When you answer a question, you're informing, but you also want to build goodwill by suggesting that you're competent and perceptive and that your answer is correct and complete. In a claims adjustment, whether your answer is *yes* or *no,* you want to portray that the reader's claim has been given careful consideration and that the decision is fair, businesslike, and justified.

The Cost of Communication

Writing costs money. Besides the cost of computers, software, printers, paper, and sometimes postage, there is the major expense: employees' time. Even short e-mails take time, especially now that employees write so many of them.

Document cycling processes also increase costs. In many organizations, all external documents must be approved before they go out. A document may **cycle** from writer to superior to writer to another superior to writer again 10 or more times before final approval.

Longer documents can involve large teams of people and take months to write. An engineering firm that relies on military contracts for its business calculates that it spends $500,000 to put together an average proposal and $1 million to write a large proposal.[7]

Good communication is worth every minute it takes and every penny it costs. In 2005/2006, the consulting firm Watson Wyatt conducted a study of

Hurricane Katrina Storms Communication Lines

On August 29, 2005, Hurricane Katrina swept through Mississippi and Louisiana leaving massive destruction. During the storm, communication failures between local, state, and federal officials left its own harm.

Communication difficulties began with the definition of the problem: If water flooded over the top, a general calamity, local government would respond. If the levees had been breached by Katrina's storm surge, a severe catastrophe, the federal government (FEMA) would take action.

Communication problems continued after the broken levees were determined to be the responsibility of FEMA. The main communication problems included:

- Lack of communication: Agencies used different radio frequency bands which led to lack of coordination and communication.

- Inconsistent messages: State and local agency teams were confused by conflicting messages.

- Ineffective communication: The Army Corps of Engineers confirmed the breach of the levees in confusing language that was buried in a six-page report.

Adapted from Christopher Cooper and Robert Block, "Behind the Katrina Imbroglio: New Book on Hurricane Describes How U.S. Confusion over Levees Slowed Federal Disaster Response," *Wall Street Journal,* July 27, 2006, B1; and Patrick Stuver, "Maximizing Emergency Communication," *Risk Management,* 53 (May 2006): 30–34.

Poor Customer Service Becomes Costly

A customer called AOL to cancel his service. The phone call lasted 21 minutes, including automated answering, waiting in a queue, and a five-minute conversation with a customer service representative. During the conversation, the customer service representative refused to comply with the customer's request to close his account despite 21 requests to "cancel" his service and approximately 9 "I-don't-need-it, I-don't-want-it, and I-don't-use-it" statements. To express his dissatisfaction, the customer posted the recorded conversation on the Web as a digital "documentary," which was heard by 300,000 visitors and highlighted on the *Today* show on NBC. Following the post, an AOL executive vice president e-mailed employees notifying them of the post and warning them that any of their customer interactions could be similarly posted. In addition, because of similar earlier violations, AOL agreed to pay a fine of $1.25 million and to use a third-party verification system.

Another customer service incident occurred when a customer welcomed a Comcast technician into his home to replace a faulty modem. When the technician called the central office, he was placed on hold and proceeded to fall asleep on the couch after an hour of waiting. In response, the customer recorded a short documentary, "A Comcast Technician Sleeping on My Couch" and posted it to YouTube where 500,000 viewers watched the customer service blunder.

Adapted from Randall Stross, "AOL Said, 'If You Leave Me I'll Do Something Crazy,'" *New York Times*, July 2, 2006, E3.

335 US and Canadian companies with an average of 13,000 employees each and median annual revenues of $1.8 billion. The study found that those companies who best communicated with their employees enjoyed "greater employee engagement and commitment, higher retention and productivity, and—ultimately—better financial performance. . . .

- They boasted a 19.4% higher market premium (the degree to which the company's market value exceeds the cost of its assets).
- They were 4.5 times more likely to report high levels of employee engagement.
- They were 20% more likely to report lower turnover rates."[8]

Another significant cost of communication is e-mail storage. In addition to the exponential increase in frequency, e-mails are also growing in size. Furthermore, about a fifth of them come with attachments. And businesses are storing much of this huge load on their servers. But the cost of the hardware is only about 20% of the storage cost; the remainder is for administering and maintaining the archives. These costs include downtime when storage systems crash and time spent retrieving lost or corrupted messages. Chevron estimates its employees spend 1½ to 3 days a month searching for needed information.[9]

Costs of Poor Communication

Poor communication can cost billions of dollars. We all can think of examples.

- As the chapter opener and the sidebar on page 6 show, the space industry has had billion dollar mistakes—mistakes where miscommunications were major contributing factors as confirmed by official government investigations.
- Hurricane Katrina caused billions of dollars of damage—damage that was worsened by horrendous miscommunications between federal, state, and private relief organizations (see sidebar on page 9).
- Amtrak cited communication failure for its loss of millions of dollars when it had to take the Acela trains out of service for weeks. Poorly written inspection instructions led to inadequate checks on brake discs.[10]
- The National Commission on Writing reported to Congress that states spend almost a quarter billion dollars annually on remedial writing instruction for their employees, and that indirect costs of that poor writing—from the confusions and errors caused—are probably even higher.[11]
- From figures provided by the members of the Business Roundtable, the National Commission on Writing calculated the annual private sector costs of writing training at $3.1 billion.[12] These figures do not include the retail and wholesale trade businesses.

Not all communication costs are so dramatic. When communication isn't as good as it could be, you and your organization pay a price in wasted time, wasted effort, lost goodwill, and legal problems.

Wasted Time

Bad writing takes longer to read as we struggle to understand what we're reading. How quickly we can do this is determined by the difficulty of the subject matter and by the document's organization and writing style.

Second, bad writing may need to be rewritten. Many managers find that a disproportionate amount of their time is taken trying to explain to subordinates how to revise a document. Poorly written documents frequently cycle to other people for help.

Third, ineffective communication may obscure ideas so that discussions and decisions are needlessly drawn out.

Fourth, unclear or incomplete messages may require the receiver to gather more information and some receivers may not bother to do so; they may make a wrong decision or refuse to act.

Wasted Efforts

Ineffective messages don't get results. A receiver who has to guess what the sender means may guess wrong. A reader who finds a letter or memo unconvincing or insulting simply won't do what the message asks.

One company sent out past-due bills with the following language:

> Per our conversation, enclosed are two copies of the above-mentioned invoice. Please review and advise. Sincerely, . . .

The company wanted money, not advice, but it didn't say so. The company had to write third and fourth reminders. It waited for its money, lost interest on it—and kept writing letters.

Lost Goodwill

Whatever the literal content of the words, every letter, memo, or report serves either to build or to undermine the image the reader has of the writer.

Part of building a good image is taking the time to write correctly. Even organizations that have adopted casual dress still expect writing to appear professional and to be free from typos and grammatical errors.

Messages can also create a poor image because of poor audience analysis and inappropriate style. The form letter printed in Figure 1.5 failed because it was stuffy and selfish. Four different customers called to complain about it. When you think how often you are annoyed by something—a TV commercial, a rude clerk—but how rarely you call or write the company to complain, you can imagine the ill will this letter generated.

As the comments in red show, several things are wrong with the letter in Figure 1.5.

1. **The language is stiff and legalistic.** Note the sexist "Gentlemen:" and obsolete "Please be advised," "herein," and "expedite."
2. **The tone is selfish.** The letter is written from the writer's point of view; there are no benefits for the reader. (The writer says there are, but without a shred of evidence, the claim isn't convincing.)
3. **The main point is buried** in the middle of the long first paragraph. The middle is the least emphatic part of a paragraph.
4. **The request is vague.** How many references does the supplier want? Are only vendor references OK, or would other credit references, like banks, work too? Is the name of the reference enough, or is it necessary also to specify the line of credit, the average balance, the current balance, the years credit has been established, or other information? What "additional financial information" does the supplier want? Annual reports?

The Cost Was Classified

A single hyphen omitted by a supervisor at a government-run nuclear installation may hold the cost record for punctuation goofs. He ordered rods of radioactive material cut into "10 foot long lengths"; he got 10 pieces, each a foot long, instead of the 10-foot lengths required. The loss was so great it was classified [as secret by the federal government].

Quoted from William E. Blundell, "Confused, Overstuffed Corporate Writing Often Costs Firms Much Time—and Money," *Wall Street Journal*, August 21, 1980, 21.

Figure 1.5   A Form Letter That Annoyed Customers

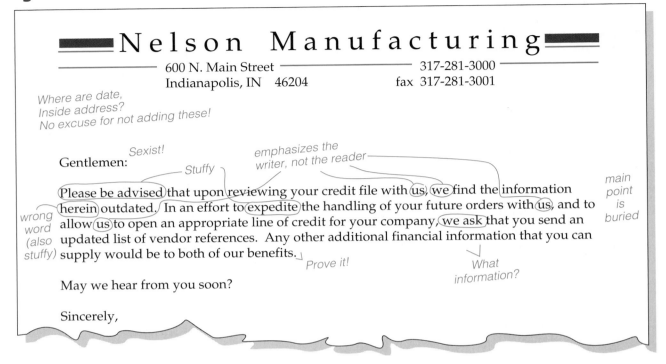

Bank balance? Tax returns? The request sounds like an invasion of privacy, not a reasonable business practice.

5. **Words are misused** (*herein for therein*), suggesting either an ignorant writer or one who doesn't care enough about the subject and the reader to use the right word.

Legal Problems

Poor communication choices can lead to legal problems for individuals and organizations. The news is full of examples. US Representative Mark Foley resigned after his instant messages to House pages were published. E-mails helped bring about the fall of senior Enron executives, Boeing CEO Harry Stonecipher, Credit Suisse First Boston banker Frank Quattrone, Merrill Lynch analyst Henry M. Blodgett, Hewlett-Packard Chairperson Patricia Dunn, and Wal-Mart Vice Presidents Julie Roehm and Sean Womack. One San Francisco law firm says that 70% of their routine evidence now comes from e-mails.[13]

In particular, letters, memos, e-mails, and instant messages create legal obligations for organizations. When a lawsuit is filed against an organization, the lawyers for the plaintiffs have the right to subpoena documents written by employees of the organization. These documents may then be used as evidence, for instance that an employer fired an employee without adequate notice or that a company knew about a safety defect but did nothing to correct it.

These documents may also be used as evidence in contexts the writer did not intend. This means that a careless writer can create obligations that the organization does not mean to assume. For instance, a letter from a manager telling a scout troop they may not visit a factory floor because it is too dangerous could be used in a worker's compensation suit.[14]

Careful writers and speakers think about the larger social context in which their words may appear. What might those words mean to other people in the field? What might they mean to a judge and jury?

Benefits of Improving Communication

Better communication helps you to

- **Save time.** Eliminate the time now taken to rewrite badly written materials. Reduce reading time, since comprehension is easier. Reduce the time taken asking, "What did you mean?"
- **Make your efforts more effective.** Increase the number of requests that are answered positively and promptly—on the first request. Present your points—to other people in your organization; to clients, customers, and suppliers; to government agencies; to the public—more forcefully.
- **Communicate your points more clearly.** Reduce the misunderstandings that occur when the audience has to supply missing or unclear information. Make the issues clear, so that disagreements can surface and be resolved more quickly.
- **Build goodwill.** Build a positive image of your organization. Build an image of yourself as a knowledgeable, intelligent, capable person.

Criteria for Effective Messages

Good business and administrative communication meets five basic criteria: it's clear, complete, and correct; it saves the audience's time; and it builds goodwill.

1. **It's clear.** The meaning the audience gets is the meaning the communicator intended. The audience doesn't have to guess.
2. **It's complete.** All of the audience questions are answered. The audience has enough information to evaluate the message and act on it.
3. **It's correct.** All of the information in the message is accurate. The message is free from errors in spelling, grammar, word order, and sentence structure.
4. **It saves the receiver's time.** The style, organization, and visual or aural impact of the message help the receiver read, understand, and act on the information as quickly as possible.
5. **It builds goodwill.** The message presents a positive image of the communicator and his or her organization. It treats the receiver as a person, not a number. It cements a good relationship between the communicator and the receiver.

Whether a message meets these five criteria depends on **the interactions among the communicator, the audience, the purposes of the message, and the situation.** No single set of words will work in all possible situations.

Trends in Business and Administrative Communication

Both business and business communication are changing. Ten trends in business, government, and nonprofit organizations affect business and administrative communication: Technology changes, including information overload and data

BlackBerry Orphans

"Children are exasperated by their parents' obsession with their [BlackBerrys]. . . .

"Hohlt Pecore, 7, and his sister, Elsa, 4, have complicated relationships with their mother's BlackBerry. . . . Elsa has hidden the BlackBerry on occasion—Hohlt says she tried to flush it down the toilet last year. . . . But Elsa also seems to recognize that it brings her mom comfort, not unlike a pacifier or security blanket. Recently, seeing her mom slumped on the couch after work, Elsa fished the BlackBerry from her mother's purse and brought it to her. 'Mommy,' she asked, 'will this make you feel better?' . . .

"Emma Colonna wishes her parents would behave, at least when they're out in public. The ninth-grade student . . . says she has caught her parents typing emails . . . during her eighth-grade awards ceremony, at dinner and in darkened movie theaters. 'During my dance recital, I'm 99% sure they were emailing except while I was on stage,' she says. 'I think that's kind of rude.' . . .

"Safety is another issue. Will Singletary, a 9-year-old, doesn't approve of his dad's proclivity for typing while driving. 'It makes me worried he's going to crash,' he says. 'He only looks up a few times.'"

Quoted from Katherine Rosman, "BlackBerry Orphans," *Wall Street Journal*, December 8, 2006, W1.

security versus privacy; a focus on quality and customers' needs; entrepreneurship; teamwork; diversity; globalization and outsourcing; legal and ethical concerns; balancing work and family; job flexibility; and the rapid rate of change.

Technology

In the current technological age, different forms of media are encompassing all parts of life. For instance, in 2007, the average American spends

- 1,555 hours watching television.
- 974 hours listening to the radio.
- 195 hours using the Internet.
- 86 hours playing video games.

These numbers of hours spent with media are expected to rise significantly in future years.[15]

The business world is no exception when it comes to technology. It continually embraces all forms that help increase productivity and save money. Technology advancements provide instant communication with the click of a button. Moreover, technology makes communications across the globe seem much closer. Almost all office employees are expected to know how to navigate through the Web and to use word processing, e-mail, spreadsheet, database, and presentation software.

The following sections—electronic tools, information overload, and data security versus privacy—discuss some key issues of technology use in professional organizations.

Electronic Tools

Businesses are quick to adopt new forms of technology that can enhance the experience of workers and improve the bottom line. New software programs and devices continually enter the market to help businesses. However, acquiring new technology and helping workers master it entails an enormous capital investment. Learning to use new-generation software and improved hardware takes time and may be especially frustrating for people who were perfectly happy with old software. Some of the most popular workplace devices that improve productivity are wikis, social-networking tools, portable media players, personal digital assistants (PDAs), and telepresences.

Wikis   With the popularity of Web sites like Wikipedia, the business world has been quick to follow suit. Many organizations are using wikis, an online form of content knowledge management, in which users can post information or collaborate on projects. The access to these wikis is limited to employees of the particular organization using them, much like intranets. One way for employees to use the wikis is to bookmark Web pages with a short summary and upload the entry to the system. Once there, other employees can quickly search for information using keywords. In addition, wikis reduce the amount of e-mailing of drafts among employees who are collaborating on a project. As an added bonus, every change made to documents on a wiki is tracked.

Social-networking tools   Following in the footsteps of MySpace and Facebook, larger organizations are adapting social-networking tools designed specifically for businesses. The software allows users to post a profile, blog, or useful links which allow workers to interact on a more personal level. Moreover, employees can share client information, and the social-networking tools may promote collaboration. The access to the social network is usually limited to an organization's employees.

Portable media players Portable media players (like iPods, MP3 players, and compatible cell phones) feature the ability to broadcast streaming video and audio. Some organizations give these devices to their employees loaded with recordings of meetings, new product information, or general announcements. These devices help keep employees connected, even when they're not always in the office.

Personal digital assistant PDAs, such as Treo or BlackBerry (sometimes called Smartphones or wireless handheld devices), allow users to send and receive e-mail, access Web sites, conduct word processing, and make telephone calls. Many of these devices also have touch screens. Like portable media players, these devices also can broadcast streaming video and audio. With the full functionality of these devices, employees can literally be connected to their work 24/7.

Telepresence Telepresence is the new high-end videoconferencing that puts older versions to shame by using 50-inch plasma screens and broadcast-quality cameras to create virtual meetings that are almost lifelike. These video meetings can occur across different time zones or between different nations instantaneously. However, state-of-the-art telepresence rooms cost anywhere from $150,000 up to $1,000,000. Some of the cost is associated with the actual equipment necessary to create a room, but most of the cost comes from the large amounts of bandwidth required for the conferencing. While the initial price seems high, some organizations, and the makers of these systems, quickly counter that the system will pay for itself within a few months as the amount of national or international travel is greatly reduced. Moreover, meetings never have to be delayed or postponed because of late flights or weather problems. Some estimates suggest that by 2010 telepresence rooms will see a 22% increase in sales from the $1.15 billion they grossed in 2006.[16]

Information Overload

New technology saves time, but it also leads to a new problem: information overload. Workers are becoming overwhelmed with all the information available to

Information overload is increasing worldwide.

As the Old Song Says, "I Got Rhythm"

One of the newest electronic security methods is keystroke authentication. It turns out that your typing pattern, the pressure of your fingers on the keys and your typing speed, is unique. It allows you to prove electronically that you are who you say you are.

Keystroke patterning has a long history. The military began using it over a hundred years ago to identify individual senders of Morse code by their tapping rhythms. As the location of those senders shifted, military trackers got data on enemy movements.

Currently, the biggest users of keystroke patterning are banks and credit unions, who are employing it in addition to standard password authentication. Since identity theft has become such a major problem, banks and credit unions are under a federal mandate to use stronger authentication measures to protect online customers.

Adapted from Kathleen Kingsbury, "Telltale Fingertips: With Biometrics, How You Type Can Allow Websites to Know Who You Are—Or Aren't," *Time Bonus Section*, January 2007, A10.

them. Cable, RSS feeds, Web sites, listservs, and blogs increase access to news at all levels, including news in one's professional field. The ease of desktop publishing has increased the flow of newsletters, reports, and flyers even from individual units within a business. The amount of information is becoming unmanageable:

- A Google search for information on *e-mail* offers over 2 million entries as of May 2007. A search for *listserv* offers over 32 million.
- One big legal case can use over 2 million pages of documents.[17]
- DuPont has a document warehouse with over 200,000 boxes, each box containing about 2,500 pages.[18]
- Chevron processes 2 million e-mails daily. The company estimates it now has 1,250 terabytes of data, where one terabyte equals the data of 1 million books.[19]

Perhaps the biggest problem for many employees is the amount of e-mail. IDC, a research consulting firm, estimates 84 billion e-mails are sent daily.[20] Spam clutters mailboxes—or leads to filters that stop some needed e-mail. Spam also means that many people do not open e-mail if they do not recognize either the sender or the topic. On a smaller level, workers forward unwanted jokes, pictures, and URLs. Workers who become e-mail addicts, sending too many e-mails with too little content, find that their e-mails are being opened last, if at all. Too many people forward too many messages to uncaring receivers, and the "Reply to All" button is getting a notorious reputation. A study conducted by Basex, another research firm, discovered that more people (31%) labeled normal e-mail as "most disruptive" than did so for spam (27%).[21]

Data security versus privacy

As electronic information increases, so do concerns about data theft. Just as individuals take steps—like not providing important identification numbers by e-mail—to prevent identity theft, so do organizations take steps to protect their data. Organizations are now monitoring many different kinds of electronic interactions. According to a 2005 survey by the American Management Association of 526 companies,

- 76% monitor Internet usage.
- 55% store and review e-mail.
- 51% use video surveillance.
- 50% store and review computer files.
- 36% monitor computer usage.
- 22% record phone calls.[22]

The same study also showed that 35% track keystrokes (and time spent at the computer).[23] Because of findings from such monitoring, some companies are blocking access to particular Web sites, especially Facebook, MySpace, YouTube, and online shopping sites. The companies claim that heavy usage of these sites slows down company business such as file transfers and e-mail.[24]

Other surveillance techniques use GPS (global positioning system) chips to monitor locations of company vehicles, as well as arrival and departure times at job sites. Data from Smart Tags on cars, showing exactly when a particular vehicle was at a particular toll station, are being used in court cases. Cell phones give approximate location signals that are accurate enough to help law enforcement officials locate suspects.[25]

Cellular phone technology is spreading worldwide.

Still other security measures include bans on electronic devices such as Palm Pilots, BlackBerrys, and MP3 players. Some companies are even disabling extra USB connections to ensure employees cannot attach these devices. Others are performing random checks of laptops to look for unauthorized or unsecured files and using scans of fingerprints, eyes, or faces to limit and track access to specific computers.[26]

The surveillance does not necessarily stop when employees leave their offices or cars. It can continue to the company parking areas, and even employees' personal blogs. Companies such as Google and Delta Air Lines have fired workers for content on their personal blogs. Although many workers believe their blogs are protected by the first amendment, the truth is that in most states, companies can fire employees for almost any reason except discrimination.[27]

Focus on Quality and Customers' Needs

After declining during the late 1990s, customer satisfaction among American consumers has been generally on the rise. This trend has a real payoff for businesses; higher levels of the American Customer Satisfaction Index are associated with stronger sales.[28] James Rosenfield, an expert in direct marketing, provides some numbers that help explain the relationship between satisfaction and sales:

> Unhappy customers in industrialized countries historically tell 15 people about their experiences. [On the Internet] with one keystroke, you can now tell 150 or 1,500 or 15,000![29]

Not only does superior customer service sell, it also increases business performance. A University of Michigan study showed that companies with high customer satisfaction scores outperformed the S&P 500, producing higher stock prices and less volatile stock values and cash flows.[30]

Offering superior customer service doesn't always mean spending extra money. Southwest Airlines customer service agent Sharron Mangone convinced an entire gate area to join in a "biggest hole in the sock" contest while they waited for their plane.[31] To notify customers of new merchandise, Nordstrom added RSS feeds to it Web site.[32] To attract patients, hospitals and health care facilities are improving communication, including accurate estimates of wait times and improved explanations of medical procedures, exams, and tests.[33]

Communication is at the center of the focus on quality and customers' needs. Brainstorming and group problem solving are essential to develop more efficient ways to do things. Then the good ideas have to be communicated throughout the company. Innovators need to be recognized. And only by listening to what customers say—and listening to the silences that may accompany their actions—can an organization know what its customers really want.

Entrepreneurship

Since 1980, the number of businesses in the United States has risen faster than the civilian labor force. The US Census Bureau counted 15 million individual proprietorships (self-employed workers without employees) in 2002.[34] Entrepreneurship is so popular that many business schools now offer courses, internships, or whole programs in starting and running a business.

Some established companies are trying to match the success and growth rate of start-ups by nurturing an entrepreneurial spirit within their organizations. Innovators who work within organizations are sometimes called **intrapreneurs.** A classic article in the *Harvard Business Review* made famous the examples of 3M (where researchers can spend 15 percent of their time on ideas that don't need management approval), Thermo Electron (where managers can "spin out" promising new businesses), and Xerox (where employees write business proposals competing for corporate funds to develop new technologies).[35]

Entrepreneurs have to handle all the communication in the organization: hiring, training, motivating, and evaluating employees; responding to customer complaints; drafting surveys; writing business plans; making presentations to venture capitalists and marketing the product or service.

Teamwork

More and more companies are getting work done through teams. Teamwork brings together people's varying strengths and talents to solve problems and make decisions. Often, teams are cross-functional (drawing from different jobs or functions) or cross-cultural (including people from different nations or cultural groups served by the company). Teams, including cross-functional teams, helped Sarasota Memorial Hospital resolve major problems with customer and employee satisfaction. For example, team members from the emergency room recorded every step in the process from pulling into the parking lot through decisions about patient care, and then they eliminated unnecessary steps. The ER team worked with the laboratory staff to improve the process of getting test results. At Michelin, the French tire maker, teams bring together people from the United States and Europe. According to the company's chemical purchasing manager for Europe, the exchange between the two continents helps employees on both sides of the Atlantic understand each other's perspectives and needs.[36]

A diverse workforce makes good business sense. It provides a larger pool of people and ideas for employers and more opportunities for employees.

Don't Be Fooled by IMs

It's now a given that e-mail is saved on your computer. E-mail is even saved on a server somewhere after it is deleted. However, employees are less likely to believe the same rules apply to Instant Message (IM) systems. When sending an IM, users may think the conversation is lost after they log out or the IM window is closed. Ultimately, that's not the case. For example, Florida Congressman Mark Foley lost his position for holding sexual and inappropriate IM conversations with underage pages.

Businesses are starting to monitor all IM conversations with growing frequency. In 2006, at least 2% had fired employees as the result of IM conversations.

Currently, Google Talk automatically stores chat sessions. Other IM services like AIM, Yahoo, and Window's Live Messenger offer services that easily save conversations. And some IM service providers are tailoring their products to businesses by offering more tracking capabilities, such as keyword searches of IM conversations.

Adapted from Amol Sharma and Jessica E. Vascellaro, "Those IMs Aren't as Private as You Think," *Wall Street Journal*, October 4, 2006, D1, D2.

The prevalence of teams puts a premium on learning to identify and solve problems, to share leadership, to work *with* other people rather than merely delegating work *to* other people, to resolve conflicts constructively, and to motivate everyone to do his or her best job. To learn more about working in teams, see Chapter 14 ➠.

Diversity

Teams put a premium on being able to work with other people—even if they come from different backgrounds.

Women, people of color, and immigrants have always been part of the US workforce. But for most of our country's history, they were relegated to clerical, domestic, or menial jobs. Even when men from working-class families began to get college degrees in large numbers after World War II, and large numbers of women and minorities entered the professions in the 1960s and 1970s, only a few made it into management. Now, US businesses realize that barriers to promotion hurt the bottom line as well as individuals. Success depends on using the brains and commitment as well as the hands and muscles of every worker.

In the last decade, we have also become aware of other sources of diversity beyond those of gender and race: age, religion, class, regional differences, sexual orientation, physical disabilities. Helping each worker reach his or her potential requires more flexibility from managers as well as more knowledge about intercultural communication. And it's crucial to help

Online Acronyms

E-mail writers often use the following abbreviations. The quick pace of instant messaging has made these even more popular.

ASAP	As soon as possible
BRB	Be right back
BTW	By the way
CU	See you
CWOT	Complete waste of time
EML	E-mail me later
F2F	Face to face
FAQ	Frequently asked questions
GMTA	Great minds think alike
IAE	In any event
IMHO	In my humble opinion
IOW	In other words
LOL	Laughing out loud
NRN	No reply necessary
OTOH	On the other hand
ROTFL	Rolling on the floor laughing
THX	Thanks
TTYL	Talk to you later

For a more complete listing of electronic abbreviations, check out the following Web site: http://searchcrm.techtarget.com/sDefinition/0,,sid11_gci211776,00.html.

workers from different backgrounds understand each other—especially when continuing layoffs make many workers fear that increased opportunities for someone else will come only at a cost to themselves.

Treating readers with respect has always been a principle of good business and administrative communication. The emphasis on diversity simply makes it an economic mandate as well. To learn more about diversity and the workforce, read Chapter 13 ➡.

Globalization and Outsourcing

In the global economy, importing and exporting are just a start. More and more companies have offices and factories around the world:

- Starbucks is serving coffee in China.
- McDonald's is serving veggie burgers in India, where cattle are sacred.
- Alcoa, Inc., an aluminum producer, has expanded its operations in Brazil, Russia, and China.
- 3M decided to increase its operations to include China, India, Korea, and Poland.[37]

The site of the store, factory, or office may not be the site of all the jobs. A data center in Washington can support many workers in India as businesses are outsourcing domestically and globally. Outsourcing means going outside the company for products and services that once were produced by the company's employees. Companies can outsource technology services, customer service, tax services, legal services, accounting services, benefit communications, manufacturing, and marketing. Outsourcing is often a win–win solution: the company saves money or gets better service, and the outsourcers make a profit. In *The World Is Flat,* Thomas Friedman says "the accountant who wants to stay in business in America will be the one who focuses on designing creative, complex strategies. . . . It means having quality-time discussions with

Many businesses are outsourcing their customer service operations, as well as accounting, legal services, and manufacturing.

clients."[38] He sees the work of the future as customization, innovation, service, and problem solving.[39]

All the challenges of communicating in one culture and country increase exponentially when people communicate across cultures and countries. Succeeding in a global market requires **intercultural competence,** the ability to communicate sensitively with people from other cultures and countries, based on an understanding of cultural differences. To learn more about international communication, see Chapter 13 ➡.

Legal and Ethical Concerns

Legal fees cost US businesses millions of dollars. The price of many simple items, such as ladders, is inflated greatly by the built-in reserve to protect the manufacturer against lawsuits. Companies are finding that clear, open communication can reduce lawsuits by giving all the parties a chance to shape policies and by clarifying exactly what is and isn't being proposed.

Ethical concerns don't carry the same clear dollar cost as legal fees. But when the Internet stock bubble burst at the beginning of this decade, the plunging stock prices and an overall economic slowdown were accompanied by a wave of news stories about unethical and illegal corporate practices. As investors and consumers heard the accusations of accounting fraud at World-Com, HealthSouth Corporation, Enron, and Adelphia Communications, many felt distrustful of businesses in general. At other companies, including ImClone and Tyco International, executives were accused of enriching themselves at their companies' expense. Such breaches of financial ethics at the top of a company have tainted, and even destroyed, entire organizations. The public outcry motivated Congress to pass the Sarbanes-Oxley Act, requiring corporations to engage in much more careful control and reporting of their financial activities.[40]

The public distrust and government regulation that followed the recent scandals have renewed attention to corporate ethics. One of the newer ethical and legal concerns involves backdating of executive stock options, a process which was used to change stock-sale proceeds (subject to ordinary income taxes) to capital gains, which were taxed at roughly half the rate. Since the proceeds being taxed can be millions of dollars, the difference is significant. SEC (Securities & Exchange Commission) investigations into backdating have led to companies correcting tax filings and restating financial result.[41]

As Figure 1.6 suggests, language, graphics, and document design—basic parts of any business document—can be ethical or manipulative. Persuasion and gaining compliance—activities at the heart of business and organizational life—can be done with respect or contempt for customers, co-workers, and subordinates.

Ethical concerns start with telling the truth and offering good value for money. Organizations must be concerned about broader ethical issues as well: being good environmental citizens, offering a good workplace for their employees, contributing to the needs of the communities in which they operate.

Balancing Work and Family

To reduce turnover, respond to a declining labor force, and increase employee satisfaction, companies are trying to be more family friendly by proving flextime, telecommuting, or some other type of flexible option. The balance of work and family is becoming such a popular topic that the *Wall Street Journal* now runs a regular column called "Work and Family." A 2005 National Study of Employers (NSE) found that employers are increasingly offering employees

Rule No. 1: Don't Copy
Rule 34: Don't Plagiarize

"Do not plagiarize" should have been included in *Unwritten Rules of Management*, the book by William Swanson, CEO of Raytheon. In 2004, Raytheon gave employees free copies of the book, which contained 33 rules. The book quickly became widely read by professionals and executives because of its humorous approach. However, an engineer at Hewlett-Packard discovered that 13 of the rules had been previously published by W. J. King in his 1944 best-seller, *The Unwritten Laws of Engineering*. Further findings uncovered that the additional rules were obtained from Defense Secretary Rumsfeld and humor editorial writer Dave Barry.

Swanson apologized for the mistake, which, he states, began when he asked employees to create a presentation from a file. The presentation was a great hit, which led to the creation of the 33 rules—one for each year he worked for Raytheon. Unfortunately, the rules were not original and the sources were not properly cited.

How can you avoid plagiarism?

Adapted from Lisa Takeuchi Cullen, "Rule No. 1: Don't Copy," *Time*, May 15, 2006, 41.

http://www.ethicsinaction.com/

The Ethics in Action Awards recognize businesses and individuals in British Columbia who are "doing the right thing." Log on to see winners from this year and years past. What services or products that made the list do you use? What components of the winners' organizations contributed to the label "ethical"?

Figure 1.6   Ethical Issues in Business Communication

Manner of conveying the message	Qualities of the message	Larger organizational context of the message
Language, Graphics, and Document Design • Is the message audience-friendly? Does it respect the audience? • Do the words balance the organization's right to present its best case with its responsibility to present its message honestly? • Do graphics help the audience understand? Or are graphics used to distract or confuse? • Does the design of the document make reading easy? Does document design attempt to make readers skip key points? **Tactics Used to Shape Response** • Are the arguments logical? Are they supported with adequate evidence? • Are the emotional appeals used fairly? Do they supplement logic rather than substituting for it? • Does the organizational pattern lead the audience without undue manipulation? • Are the tactics honest? That is, do they avoid deceiving the audience?	• Is the message an ethical one that treats all parties fairly and is sensitive to all stakeholders? • Have interested parties been able to provide input into the decision or message? • Does the audience get all the information it needs to make a good decision? • Is information communicated in a timely way, or is information withheld to reduce the audience's power? • Is information communicated so the audience can grasp it or are data "dumped" without any context?	• How does the organization treat its employees? How do employees treat each other? • How sensitive is the organization to stakeholders such as the people who live near its factories, stores, or offices and to the general public? • Does the organization support employees' efforts to be honest, fair, and ethical? • Do the organization's actions in making products, buying supplies, and marketing goods and services stand up to ethical scrutiny? • Is the organization a good corporate citizen, helpful rather than harmful to the community in which it exists? • Are the organization's products or services a good use of scarce resources?

options such as flexible work hours, time off for family and personal needs, and extended career breaks for caregiving.[42]

At McGraw-Hill, 60% of the employees work at home at least some of the time and can choose a shortened week with a compressed schedule, part-time work, job sharing, or telecommuting. Aflac allows employees to adjust and compress their work day to include both on- and off-site schedules. PricewaterhouseCoopers created the "Full Circle" program which allows women to leave the company for five years while keeping in touch with current employees. During the five years, employees have the option to return to the company at any time.[43]

At times, employees find ways other than physical presence to demonstrate their commitment and enthusiasm for organizational goals. Due to technology advances, employees can use laptops, BlackBerrys, e-mail, or cell phones to do work at any time, including weekends and evenings. The downside of this trend is that sometimes work and family life are not so much balanced as blurred. For instance, many employers are giving portable media players to workers for training courses, language lessons, and general organizational announcements to hear on their own time. Some employees are also expected to conduct business 24-hours a day because of different time zones of workplaces. The flexibility of employees is necessary in an age of downsizing and globalization, but it means that families are being impacted.

Job Flexibility

In traditional jobs, people did what they were told to do. Now, they do whatever needs to be done, based on the needs of customers, colleagues, and anyone else who depends on their work. They help team members finish individual work; they assist office mates with pressing deadlines. They are resourceful: they know how to find information and solution ideas. They work extra hours when the task demands it. They are ready to change positions and even locations when asked to do so. They need new skill sets even when they don't change jobs.

At Sarasota Memorial Hospital, food service workers do more than bring food to patients; they open containers, resolve problems with meals, help patients read their menus, and adjust orders to meet patients' preferences. This attentiveness not only serves the patients; it is part of a team-spirited approach to patient care that in this case frees nurses to do other work.[44] The experience at Sarasota Memorial is backed up by research suggesting that the most effective workers don't see work as assigned tasks. Instead, they define their own goals based on the needs of customers and clients.[45]

With flatter organizations, workers are doing a much wider variety of tasks. Today's secretaries, as mentioned earlier, are likely to be researching, planning meetings, and keeping records of the department's expenses. Even as more bank customers use ATMs for deposits and withdrawals, banks keep tellers on hand to help with more complicated problems and to sell financial products.

Your parents may have worked for the same company all their lives. You may do that, too, but you have to be prepared to job-hunt—not only when you finish your degree but also throughout your career. That means continuing to learn—keeping up with new technologies, new economic and political realities, new ways of interacting with people.

Rapid Rate of Change

The flexibility required for the modern job market is just one area in which change is defining the workplace. Jobs that are routine can readily be done in other countries at lower cost. Many US jobs have already been subject to such "offshoring," and more are sure to follow. The work that remains in the United States is more likely to be complex work requiring innovation, flexibility, and adaptation to new learning.[46]

As any employee who has watched his or her job go overseas can testify, change—even change for the better—is stressful. Many people, especially those who have felt battered by changes in the workplace, fear that more change will further erode their positions. Even when change promises improvements, people have to work to learn new skills, new habits, and new attitudes. To reduce the stress of change, scholars suggest reducing the number of major, radical changes and relying more on frequent, small, incremental changes.[47]

Rapid change means that no college course or executive MBA program can teach you everything you need to know for the rest of your working life. You'll need to stay abreast of professional changes by reading trade journals as well as professional Web sites and blogs, participating in professional listservs, and attending professional events. Continue to refine your skills and learn new ones. Take advantage of your company's training courses and materials; volunteer for jobs that will help you gain new skills and knowledge. Pay particular attention to your communication skills; they become even more important as you advance up your career ladder. A survey of 1,400 financial executives found that 75% considered oral, written, and interpersonal skills even more important for finance professionals now than they were just five years ago.[48]

Café Etiquette: Order Once an Hour

"A teleworker 'touchdown' spot is any place with wireless access that isn't a home or office. Most folks gravitate toward local or chain eateries, which provide both real and social nourishment. As with any public setting, rules do apply, even if they are largely unspoken:

- Tip big and eat often. Think of those hourly lattes or scones as rent for your table, payment of which is crucial for the survival of any business welcoming busy squatters.

- Take it outside. Keep cellphones and PDAs on vibrate, and when they do buzz, head straight for the door.

- Don't be a hog. It's fine to keep your things piled on a table when you step out for a breath of fresh air, but not if you plan to be away a while.

- Keep your eyes to yourself. Resist the temptation to sneak a look at neighboring laptops. With this crowd, it's considered as egregious as stealing company secrets.

- Cords get right of way. All electrical outlets are fair game, so expect to accommodate the odd power cord as it snakes past your dominion.

- Look for the high sign. Even though mere inches can separate you from a fellow teleworker, realize that only when both parties issue a mutual greeting is it OK to invade those invisible offices."

Quoted from Marco R. della Cava, "Computers, Quiche, and Quiet," *USA Today*, October 5, 2006, D1, D2. Reprinted with permission.

Big Companies Saving the World

American big businesses have recently adopted slogans and behaviors to change their negative image by showing their dedication to help the world. Why? Because customers and employees appreciate the goodwill gestures of large companies benefiting the environment and society.

For example, some of the new slogans include

- Ford   "Better World"
- Wal-Mart   "Change a light. Change the world"
- GE   "Solving some of the world's toughest problems"

Even better than slogans, companies are also modifying some of their behaviors. Starbucks, for example, is buying "fair trade" coffee above market prices to assist poor farmers. Gap and Nike are monitoring global outsourcing manufacturers to ensure good working conditions. Dell and Hewlett-Packard are recycling used computers.

Have you recently heard news about other attempts by big businesses to make the world a better place? To what extent do these goodwill attempts by big companies change your opinion of them? To what extent do they have ulterior motives?

Adapted from Geoff Colvin, "The 500 Gets Religion: Why Big Companies Are in the Business of Solving the World's Woes," in *CNNMoney,* http://money.cnn.com/magazines/fortune/fortune_archive/2007/04/30/8405462/index.htm (accessed April 17, 2007).

Technology plays a large role in the changing face of business communication. Tools such as intranets, extranets, faxes, and e-mail have contributed to the efficiency of workplace communication. Meeting rooms are frequently equipped with laptops, pagers, and video-conferencing equipment, making it possible for people to have meetings across continents and time zones.

The skills you learn can stand you in good stead for the rest of your life: critical thinking, computer savvy, problem solving, and the ability to write, to speak, and to work well with other people. It's almost a cliché, but it is still true: the most important knowledge you gain in college is how to learn.

Following Conventions

Conventions are widely accepted practices you routinely encounter. For example, a traditional classroom convention is for instructors to distribute a course syllabus to students near the beginning of the semester. The document wouldn't make much sense if distributed during the final week because the appropriate context would have passed. Moreover, the document would not function correctly if it did not include conventional elements such as due dates or required readings.

Organizational settings also have conventions particular to specific organizations. You wouldn't write an analytical report to your boss who only wanted a "yes" or "no" on whether you could make the scheduled meeting with potential clients. You would send the more appropriate and conventional response—an e-mail.

Similarly, common business communications have conventions. These conventions help people recognize, produce, and interpret different kinds of communications. Each chapter in this textbook presents conventions of traditional business documents. For example, Chapter 8 discusses conventions of job application letters, Chapter 12 highlights conventions of persuasive messages, and Chapter 17 talks about conventions of delivering oral presentations.

The key to using conventions effectively is to remember that they always need to fit the rhetorical situation—they always need to be adjusted for the particular audience, context, and purpose. For instance, Chapter 11 provides

Identity theft is such a growing concern that some companies make it the main focus of their business.

guidelines on constructing negative messages. However, you will need to adapt these guidelines based on the way your organization presents their negative messages. Some organizations will use a more formal tone than others; some present negative news bluntly, while others ease into it more gently.

Since every organization will be unique in the conventions they follow, the information presented in this text will provide a basic understanding of common elements for particular genres. You will always need to adjust the basics for your particular needs.

The best way to learn conventions in a particular workplace is to see what other workers are doing. How do they communicate with each other? Do their practices change when they communicate with superiors? What kinds of letters

Team Communication Saves Lives

Communication breakdowns during patient transfers between units or personnel shifts are the largest source of medical error. The hospital accreditation board is now requiring hospitals to establish standards for transfer communications. To help hospitals, the Institute for Healthcare Improvement is working with hospitals on a communication rubric known as SBAR:

- Situation: describe briefly, get attention.
- Background: offer enough to provide context for the problem.
- Assessment: your assessment of overall condition.
- Recommendation: your specific recommendations.

Kaiser Permanente, the large health care organization, pioneered using the model, which helps doctors and nurses convey the most critical information in just 60 seconds. The model increases communication between doctors who don't want nurses' opinions and nurses who are reluctant to provide their opinions.

One Kaiser physician administrator says, "In almost all serious avoidable episodes of patient harm, communication failure plays a central role. . . . By teaching caregivers new models of 'structured communication,' . . . we can make sure that we are all in the same movie."

Adapted from Laura Landro, "Hospitals Combat Errors at the 'Hand-Off': New Procedures Aim to Reduce Miscues as Nurses and Doctors Transfer Patients to Next Shift," *Wall Street Journal*, June 28, 2006, D1, D2.

Records of e-mails, instant messages, telephone records, and Web searches can be tracked by your employer and used in lawsuits. You should always observe professional practices while in the workplace.

and memos do they send? How much do they e-mail? What tone is preferred? Close observation will help your communications fit in with the conventions of your employer.

Understanding and Analyzing Business Communication Situations

The best communicators are conscious of the context in which they communicate; they're aware of options.

Ask yourself the following questions:

- **What's at stake—to whom?**   Think not only about your own needs but also about the concerns your boss and your audience will have. Your message will be most effective if you think of the entire organizational context—and the larger context of shareholders, customers, and regulators. When the stakes are high, you'll need to take into account people's feelings as well as objective facts.
- **Should you send a message?**   Sometimes, especially when you're new on the job, silence is the most tactful response. But be alert for opportunities to learn, to influence, to make your case. You can use communication to build your career.
- **What channel should you use?**   Paper documents and presentations are formal and give you considerable control over the message. E-mail, phone calls, and stopping by someone's office are less formal. Oral channels are better for group decision making, allow misunderstandings to be cleared up more quickly, and seem more personal. Sometimes you may need more than one message, in more than one channel.
- **What should you say?**   Content for a message may not be obvious. How detailed should you be? Should you repeat information that the audience already knows? The answers will depend on the kind of message, your purposes, audiences, and the corporate culture. And you'll have to figure these things out for yourself, without detailed instructions.
- **How should you say it?**   How you arrange your ideas—what comes first, second, and last—and the words you use shape the audience's response to what you say.

How to Solve Business Communication Problems

When you're faced with a business communication problem, you need to develop a solution that will both solve the organizational problem and meet the psychological needs of the people involved. The strategies in this section will help you solve the problems in this book. Almost all of these strategies can also be applied to problems you encounter on the job.

- **Gather knowledge.**   What are the facts? What can you infer from the information you're given? What additional information might be helpful? Where could you get it? What emotional complexities are involved?
- **Use the six questions for analysis in Figure 1.7 to analyze your audience, your purposes, and the situation.**   Try to imagine yourself in the situation, just as you might use the script of a play to imagine what kind of people the characters are. The fuller an image you can create, the better.
- **Brainstorm solutions.**   In all but the very simplest problems, there are *several* possible solutions. The first one you think of may not be best. Consciously develop several solutions. Then measure them against your audience and purposes: Which solution is likely to work best?
- **If you want to add or change information, get permission first.**   You can add facts or information to the problems in this book only if the information (1) is realistic, (2) is consistent with the way real organizations work, and (3) does not change the point of the problem. If you have any questions about ideas you want to use, *ask your instructor.* He or she can tell you *before* you write the message.

Sometimes you may want to use a condition that is neither specified in the problem nor true in the real world. For example, you may want to assume you're sending a letter in April even though you're really writing it in October. Change facts *only with your instructor's approval.*

Use this process to create good messages:

Answer the six questions for analysis in Figure 1.7.

Organize your information to fit your audiences, your purposes, and the context.

Make your document visually inviting.

Revise your draft to create a friendly, businesslike, positive style.

Edit your draft for standard spelling, punctuation, and grammar; double-check names and numbers.

Use the response you get to plan future messages.

Answer the Six Questions for Analysis.

The six questions in Figure 1.7 help you analyze your audience(s), purpose(s), and the organizational context.

1. **Who is (are) your audience(s)? What audience characteristics are relevant for this particular message? If you are writing or speaking to more than one person, how do the people in your audience differ?**

    How much does your audience know about your topic? How will they respond to your message? Some characteristics of your audience will be irrelevant; focus on ones that matter *for this message.* Whenever you address several people or a group, try to identify the economic, cultural, or situational differences that may affect how various subgroups may respond to what you have to say.

Figure 1.7   Questions for Analysis

1. Who is (are) your audience(s)? What audience characteristics are relevant for this particular message? If you are writing or speaking to more than one person, how do the people in your audience differ?
2. What are your purposes in communicating?
3. What information must your message include?
4. How can you build support for your position? What reasons or audience benefits will your audience find convincing?
5. What objection(s) can you expect your audience to have? What negative elements of your message must you de-emphasize or overcome?
6. What aspects of the total situation may affect the audience's response? The economy? The time of year? Morale in the organization? The relationship between the audience and the communicator? Any special circumstances?

**Just a Deadline.
No Directions**

School assignments are spelled out, sometimes even in writing. In the workplace, workers are less likely to get details about what a document should include. The transition can be disorienting. One intern reported, "I was less prepared than I thought. . . . I was so used to professors basically telling you what they want from you that I expected to be, if not taught, then told, what exactly it was that they wanted these brochures to accomplish. . . . They have not taken the time to discuss it—they just put things on my desk with only a short note telling me when they needed it done. No directions or comments were included."

Intern's quotation from Chris M. Anson and L. Lee Forsberg, "Moving Beyond the Academic Community," *Written Communication* 7, no. 3 (April 1990): 211.

2. **What are your purposes in communicating?**

What must this message do to solve the organizational problem? What must it do to meet your own needs? What do you want your audience to do? To think or feel? List all your purposes, major and minor. Specify *exactly* what you want your audience to know or think or do. Specify *exactly* what kind of image of yourself and of your organization you want to project.

Even in a simple message, you may have several related purposes: to announce a new policy, to make the audience aware of the policy's provisions and requirements, and to have them feel that the policy is a good one, that the organization cares about its employees, and that you are a competent communicator and manager.

3. **What information must your message include?**

Make a list of the points that must be included; check your draft to make sure you include them all. To include information without emphasizing it, put it in the middle of a paragraph or document and present it as briefly as possible.

4. **How can you build support for your position? What reasons or audience benefits will your audience find convincing?**

Brainstorm to develop reasons for your decision, the logic behind your argument, and possible benefits to the audience if they do as you ask. Reasons and audience benefits do not have to be monetary. Making the audience's job easier or more pleasant is a good audience benefit. In an informative or persuasive message, identify at least five audience benefits. In your message, use those that you can develop most easily and most effectively.

Be sure the benefits are adapted to your audience. Many people do not identify closely with their organizations; the fact that the organization benefits from a policy will help the individual only if the saving or profit is passed directly on to the employees. Instead, savings and profits are often eaten up by returns to stockholders, bonuses to executives, and investments in plants and equipment or in research and development.

5. **What objection(s) can you expect your audience to have? What negative elements of your message must you de-emphasize or overcome?**

Some negative elements can only be de-emphasized. Others can be overcome. Be creative: Is there any advantage associated with (even though not caused by) the negative? Can you rephrase or redefine the negative to make the audience see it differently?

6. **What aspects of the total situation may affect audience response? The economy? The time of year? Morale in the organization? The relationship between the audience and the communicator? Any special circumstances?**

Audiences may like you or resent you. You may be younger or older than they are. The organization may be prosperous or going through hard times; it may have just been reorganized or may be stable. All these different situations will affect what you say and how you say it.

Think about the news, the economy, the weather. Think about the general business and regulatory climate, especially as it affects the organization specified in the problem. Use the real world as much as possible. Think about interest rates, business conditions, and the economy. Is the industry in which the problem is set doing well? Is the government agency in which the problem is set enjoying general support? Think about the time of year. If it's fall when you write, is your business in a seasonal slowdown after a busy summer? Gearing up for the Christmas shopping rush? Or going along at a steady pace unaffected by seasons?

To answer these questions, draw on your experience, your courses, and your common sense. Read *The Wall Street Journal* or look at a company's Web site. Sometimes you may even want to phone a local business person to get information. For instance, if you needed more information to think of audience benefits for a problem set in a bank, you could call a local bank to find out what services it offers customers and what its rates are for loans.

Organize Your Information to Fit Your Audiences, Your Purposes, and the Situation.

You'll learn several different psychological patterns of organization later in this book. For now, remember these three basic principles:

1. Put good news first.
2. In general, put the main point or question first. In the subject line or first paragraph, make it clear that you're writing about something that is important to the reader.
3. Disregard point 2 and approach the subject indirectly when you must persuade a reluctant audience.

Make Your Document Visually Inviting.

A well-designed document is easier to read and builds goodwill. To make a document visually attractive

- Use subject lines to orient the reader quickly.
- Use headings to group related ideas.
- Use lists and indented sections to emphasize subpoints and examples.
- Number points that must be followed in sequence.
- Use short paragraphs—usually six typed lines or fewer.

If you plan these design elements before you begin composing, you'll save time and the final document will probably be better.

The best physical form for a document depends on how it will be used. For example, a document that will be updated frequently needs to be in a looseleaf binder so the reader can easily throw away old pages and insert new ones.

Classroom versus Workplace Contexts

Professors Aviva Freedman and Christine Adam found in a research study that students have to relearn ways to acquire basic knowledge when trying to mesh with their employer's organization once they enter the workforce.

School is structured to help students learn. On the other hand, the workplace is structured to get results, not help the learner/new employee. New college graduate hires frequently don't understand the context of communications. For example, new employees have to figure out which co-workers are trustworthy and can be a guide while not pushing away others.

Moreover, the roles of participants in each situation are different. While school settings have an instructor as the voice of authority, workplace settings are comprised of people with varying degrees of relevant and useful knowledge.

What has been your experience with internships? Have you noticed other ways in which workplace settings differ from classroom expectations?

Adapted from Aviva Freedman and Christine Adam, "Learning to Write Professionally: 'Situated Learning' and the Transition from University to Professional Discourse," *Journal of Business and Technical Communication* 10, no. 4 (October 1996): 395–427.

Help Your Customers (to) Fish

Fish, a business best seller for over a decade, presents the Fish philosophy. Under this philosophy, managers and employees use a friendly, businesslike, positive style with these basic elements:

- **Choose your attitude.** Employees at any job can choose the attitude toward the work they perform. Not all jobs are glamorous: the work of a fish seller is difficult, but the employees at Pike Place Fish choose to have "playful, cheerful" attitudes toward work. Choose your responses to the work you perform.

- **Play.** Work is serious business, but you can have fun while you work. At Pike Place Fish, employees throw fish. At First Guaranteed, employees turn on small lights when they have a good idea. The benefits to playing at work are low turnover, pride in the work, increased sales, and energy toward the work.

- **Make their day.** Customers should be included in the fun. Pike Place Fish selects customers to help catch the thrown fish. Respectfully engage customers to create positive energy and goodwill.

- **Be present.** Employees should be focused and engaged at work so they can help their colleagues and customers.

How can you adapt the Fish philosophy in your workplace and life?

Adapted from Stephen C. Lundin, Harry Paul, and John Christensen, *Fish: A Remarkable Way to Boost Morale and Improve Results* (New York: Hyperion, 2000), 78.

Revise Your Draft to Create a Friendly, Businesslike, Positive Style.

In addition to being an organizational member or a consumer, your reader has feelings just as you do. Writing that keeps the reader in mind uses **you-attitude.** Read your message as if you were in your reader's shoes. How would you feel if *you* received it?

Good business and administrative writing is both friendly and businesslike. If you're too stiff, you put extra distance between your reader and yourself. If you try to be too chummy, you'll sound unprofessional. When you write to strangers, use simple, everyday words and make your message as personal and friendly as possible. When you write to friends, remember that your message will be filed and read by people you've never even heard of: avoid slang, clichés, and "in" jokes.

Sometimes you must mention limitations, drawbacks, or other negative elements, but don't dwell on them. People will respond better to you and your organization if you seem confident. Expect success, not failure. If you don't believe that what you're writing about is a good idea, why should they?

You emphasize the positive when you

- Put positive information first, give it more space, or set it off visually in an indented list.
- Eliminate negative words whenever possible.
- Focus on what is possible, not what is impossible.

Edit Your Draft for Standard English; Double-Check Names and Numbers.

Business people care about correctness in spelling, grammar, and punctuation. If your grasp of mechanics is fuzzy, if standard English is not your native dialect, or if English is not your native language, you'll need to memorize rules and perhaps find a good book or a tutor to help you. Even software spelling and grammar checkers require the writer to make decisions. If you know how to write correctly but rarely take the time to do so, now is the time to begin to edit and proofread to eliminate careless errors. Correctness in usage, punctuation, and grammar is covered in Appendix B ➡.

Always proofread your document before you send it out. Double-check the reader's name, any numbers, and the first and last paragraphs.

Use the Response You Get to Plan Future Messages.

Evaluate the **feedback,** or response, you get. The real test of any message is "Did you get what you wanted, when you wanted it?" If the answer is *no,* then the message has failed—even if the grammar is perfect, the words elegant, the approach creative, the document stunningly attractive. If the message fails, you need to find out why.

Analyze your successes, too. You know you've succeeded when you get the results you want, both in terms of objective, concrete actions and in terms of image and goodwill. You want to know *why* your message worked. Often, you'll find that the principles in this book explain the results you get. If your results are different, why? There has to be a reason, and if you can find what it is, you'll be more successful more often.

How to Use This Book

This book has many aids to help you learn the material.

- Chapter outlines, learning objectives, and headings all provide previews of the contents. They can give you hooks on which to hang the information you are reading.

- Examples of written documents provide illustrations of effective and ineffective communications. Comments in red ink highlight problems; those in blue ink note effective practices.

- Words and phrases in bold are defined in the glossary at the end of the book.

- Sidebars provide workplace examples of ideas discussed in the text. They are categorized for you by the icons that appear beside them. A gold star with any icon signifies a classic example.
  - On-the-job examples have flip chart icons.
  - Ethics and legal examples have scale icons.
  - Web sites have a hand holding an @ sign.
  - Technology examples have laptop icons.
  - International examples have globe icons.
  - Fun examples have balloon icons.

- Chapter summaries at the end of each chapter, and review questions at the beginning of each set of chapter exercises, help you review the chapters for retention.

The last problem in each set of chapter exercises is an ongoing case to provide you with a richer context for problem solving. It involves the home store chain Mosaic, and various characters.

Mosaic, headquartered in Des Moines, Iowa, is a nationwide home store chain that sells furniture, bedding, kitchenware, and bath accessories targeted at middle-class households. Its main competitors are IKEA, Crate & Barrel, and Pottery Barn. Mosaic has stores in 32 of the continental United States and is always looking to expand nationally and possibly even internationally. The chain also offers customers the convenience of shopping for merchandise online without ever leaving their homes.

The organization fosters a diverse work environment and places high emphasis on collaboration among workers. Moreover, it is nationally ranked in the Top 100 Best Places to Work.

The three main characters in the case are Yvonne, Demetri, and Sarah. Yvonne heads the Communications Department at Mosaics headquarters and oversees two junior managers, Demetri and Sarah, who are also responsible for one or two other workers. Demetri is responsible for the communication publications for the physical stores, while Sarah is in charge of communications for the Web site. Yvonne's Communication Department oversees publication of routine mass correspondences with customers, production of Mosaic's annual report, and assemblage of training manuals for store managers/employees. It also hosts training sessions on Mosaic's style of professional communication.

Summary of Key Points

- Communication helps organizations and the people in them achieve their goals. The ability to write and speak well becomes increasingly important as you rise in an organization.

They Needed to Proofread

- One woman mailed out a cover letter for a $750,000 contract asking the reader "to take a moment not to read and sign this contract."

- One man mailed a letter to a male colleague with the salutation, "Dear Ms. Weeks."

- A common error made by job applicants is to discuss their experience as "mangers."

- In 1990, just hours before the graduation ceremony, the head of the U.S. Naval Academy discovered that the 1,600 diplomas conferred degrees from the "U.S. Navel Academy."

- People put things in writing to create a record, to convey complex data, to make things convenient for the reader, to save money, and to convey their own messages more effectively.
- **Internal documents** go to people inside the organization. **External documents** go to audiences outside: clients, customers, suppliers, stockholders, the government, the media, and the general public.
- The three basic purposes of business and administrative communication are **to inform, to request or persuade, and to build goodwill.** Most messages have more than one purpose.
- Poor writing wastes time, wastes effort, and jeopardizes goodwill.
- Good business and administrative writing meets five basic criteria: it's **clear, complete,** and **correct; it saves the reader's time;** and it **builds goodwill.**
- To evaluate a specific document, we must know the interactions among the writer, the reader(s), the purposes of the message, and the content. No single set of words will work for all readers in all situations.
- Ten trends affecting business and administrative communication are technology changes, including information overload and data security versus privacy; a focus on quality and customers' needs; entrepreneurship; teamwork; diversity; globalization and outsourcing; legal and ethical concerns; balancing work and family; job flexibility; and the rapid rate of change.
- To understand business communication situations, ask the following questions:
  - What's at stake—to whom?
  - Should you send a message?
  - What channel should you use?
  - What should you say?
  - How should you say it?
- The following process helps create effective messages:
  - Answer the analysis questions in Figure 1.7.
  - Organize your information to fit your audiences, your purposes, and the context.
  - Make your document visually inviting.
  - Revise your draft to create a friendly, businesslike, positive style.
  - Edit your draft for standard English; double-check names and numbers.
  - Use the response you get to plan future messages.
- Use these six questions to analyze business communication problems:
  1. Who is (are) your audience(s)? What characteristics are relevant to this particular message? If you are writing or speaking to more than one person, how do the people in your audience differ?
  2. What are your purposes in communicating?
  3. What information must your message include?
  4. How can you build support for your position? What reasons or benefits will your audience find convincing?
  5. What objection(s) can you expect your audience to have? What negative elements of your message must you de-emphasize or overcome?
  6. What aspects of the total situation may affect audience response? The economy? The time of year? Morale in the organization? The relationship between the audience and communicator? Any special circumstances?

- A solution to a business communication problem must both solve the organization's problem and meet the needs of the writer or speaker, the organization, and the audience.

CHAPTER 1   Exercises and Problems

1.1   Reviewing the Chapter

1. Why do you need to be able to communicate well? (LO 1)

2. What are some myths about workplace communication? What is the reality for each myth? (LO 1)

3. What are the costs of communication? (LO 2)

4. What are the costs of poor communication? (LO 3)

5. What are the 10 trends in business communication? What do these trends mean for you? (LO 4)

6. What role do conventions play in business communication? (LO 5)

7. What are the components of a good problem-solving method for business communication opportunities? (LO 6)

1.2   Assessing Your Punctuation and Grammar Skills

To help you see where you need to improve in grammar and punctuation, take the Diagnostic Test, B.1, Appendix B.

1.3   Letters for Discussion—Landscape Plants

Your nursery sells plants not only in your store but also by mail order. Today you've received a letter from Pat Sykes, complaining that the plants (in a $572 order) did not arrive in a satisfactory condition. "All of them were dry and wilted. One came out by the roots when I took it out of the box. Please send me a replacement shipment immediately."

The following letters are possible approaches to answering this complaint. How well does each message meet the needs of the reader, the writer, and the organization? Is the message clear, complete, and correct? Does it save the reader's time? Does it build goodwill?

1.

Dear Sir:

I checked to see what could have caused the defective shipment you received. After ruling out problems in transit, I discovered that your order was packed by a new worker who didn't understand the need to water plants thoroughly before they are shipped. We have fired the worker, so you can be assured that this will not happen again.

Although it will cost our company several hundred dollars, we will send you a replacement shipment.

Let me know if the new shipment arrives safely. We trust that you will not complain again.

2.

Dear Pat:

Sorry we screwed up that order. Sending plants across country is a risky business. Some of them just can't take the strain. (Some days I can't take the strain myself!) We'll send you some more plants sometime next week and we'll credit your account for $572.

3.

Dear Mr. Smith:

I'm sorry you aren't happy with your plants, but it isn't our fault. The box clearly says, "Open and water immediately." If you had done that, the plants would have been fine. And anybody who is going to buy plants should know that a little care is needed. If you pull by the leaves, you will pull the roots out. Since you don't know how to handle plants, I'm sending you a copy of our brochure, "How to Care for Your Plants." Please read it carefully so that you will know how to avoid disappointment in the future.

We look forward to your future orders.

4.

Dear Ms. Sykes:

Your letter of the 5th has come to the attention of the undersigned.

According to your letter, your invoice #47420 arrived in an unsatisfactory condition. Please be advised that it is our policy to make adjustments as per the Terms and Conditions listed on the reverse side of our Acknowledgment of Order. If you will read that document, you will find the following:

> ". . . if you intend to assert any claim against us on this account, you shall make an exception on your receipt to the carrier and shall, within 30 days after the receipt of any such goods, furnish us detailed written information as to any damage."

Your letter of the 5th does not describe the alleged damage in sufficient detail. Furthermore, the delivery receipt contains no indication of any exception. If you expect to receive an adjustment, you must comply with our terms and see that the necessary documents reach the undersigned by the close of the business day on the 20th of the month.

5.

Dear Pat Sykes:

You'll get a replacement shipment of the perennials you ordered next week.

Your plants are watered carefully before shipment and packed in specially designed cardboard containers. But if the weather is unusually warm, or if the truck is delayed, small root balls may dry out. Perhaps this happened with your plants. Plants with small root balls are easier to transplant, so they do better in your yard.

The violas, digitalis, aquilegias, and hostas you ordered are long-blooming perennials that will get even prettier each year. Enjoy your garden!

1.4   Online Messages for Discussion—Responding to Rumors

The Acme Corporation has been planning to acquire Best Products, and Acme employees are worried about how the acquisition will affect them. Ed Zeplin, Acme's human resource manager, has been visiting the message boards on job search sites and sees a dramatic rise in the number of messages posted by people claiming to be Acme employees. Many of the messages are spreading rumors about layoffs, and most of the rumors are false.

The following messages are possible responses that Ed can post to the message boards. How well does each message meet the needs of the reader, the writer, and the organization? Is the message clear, complete, and correct? Does it save the reader's time? Does it build goodwill?

1.

It Will Be Great!
Author: L. Ed Zeplin, HR
Date: Tuesday, May 23

I am happy to tell you that the HR news is good. Two months ago, the CEO told me about the merger, and I have been preparing a human resource plan ever since.

I want you to know about this because morale has been bad, and it shouldn't be. You really should wait for the official announcements, and you'll see that the staffing needs will remain strong. My department has been under a lot of pressure, but if you'll be patient, we'll explain everything—the staffing, the compensation.

Our plan should be ready by Monday, and then if you have any questions, just contact your HR rep.

2.

HR Staffing
Author: HR Boss
Date: Tuesday, May 23

The rumors are false. Just ask anyone in HR. There will be no layoffs.

3.

Don't Believe the Rumors
Author: lezeplin@acme.com
Date: Tuesday, May 23

Acme has 475 employees, and Best Products has 132 employees. Our human resource plan for next year calls for 625 employees. If you do the math, you can see that there will be no layoffs. Rather, we will be hiring 20 employees. Of course, as we consolidate operations with Best, there will be some redeployments. However, our plan indicates that we will be able to retain our current staff. All employees are valued at Acme, as our current benefits package testifies.

Our HR plan is based on the best analytic techniques and a business forecast by a top consulting firm. If you're an employee, you should review our business plan, at the Our Goals page on Acme's intranet. Everyone should read Acme's mission statement on our home page, www.acme.com/homepage.html.

4.

Layoff Rumors Do Acme a Disservice
Author: Zeplin in HR
Date: Tuesday, 23 May

If you come here to get your company information, you aren't getting the straight story. The people posting to this discussion board are spreading false rumors, not the truth. If you want to know the truth about Acme, ask the people who have access to the information.

As HR manager, I can assure you we won't be laying off employees after the merger with Best Products. I'm the one who approves the staffing plan, so I should know. If people would ask me, instead of reading the negative, whining lies at this site, they would know the facts, too.

If people really cared about job security, they would be meeting and exceeding their work goals, rather than wasting their time in rumor-mongering on message boards. Hard work: that's the key to success!

5.

The True Story about Lay-Offs
Author: lezeplin@acme.com
Date: Tuesday, 23 May

Whenever there is a merger or acquisition, rumors fly. It's human nature to turn to rumors when a situation seems uncertain. The case of Acme acquiring Best Products is no exception, so I'm not surprised to see rumors about layoffs posted on this message board.

Have no fear! I am working closely with our CEO and with the CEO and human resource manager at Best Products, and we all agree that our current staff is a valuable asset to Acme, to Best, and to our combined companies in the future. We have no plans to lay off any of our valued people. I will continue monitoring this message board and will post messages as I am able to disclose more details about our staffing plans. In the meantime, employees should watch for official information in the company newsletter and on our intranet.

We care about our people! If employees ever have questions about our plans and policies, they should contact me directly.

L. Ed Zeplin, HR Manager

1.5   Discussing Communication Barriers

With a small group, discuss some of the communication barriers you have witnessed in the workplace or classroom. What confuses audiences? What upsets them? What creates ill will? What causes loss of interest? Try to pinpoint exactly how the communication broke down. How closely do the problems you've identified coincide with the content from Chapter 1?

1.6   Identifying Poor Communicators

Almost everyone has come in contact with someone who is a poor communicator. With a small group, discuss some of your experiences with poor communicators either in the workplace or in the classroom. Why was the communicator ineffective? What would have made communication clearer? After your discussion, develop a list of poor communication traits and what can be done to overcome them.

1.7   Identifying Emerging Trends in Business Communication

With a small group, discuss current trends in business communication. Which of the trends outlined in this chapter seem most prominent in your workplace or classroom experiences? Discuss some of the implications of each trend.

When finished with your discussion, type a memo to your instructor that discusses your involvement with a business communication trend. Your memo should describe the trend and include a specific example. Moreover, you should predict what impact this trend will have in the future. Use complete memo format with appropriate headings. (See Appendix A ➡ for examples of memo format.) Use a conversational writing style; check your draft to polish the style and edit for mechanical and grammatical correctness.

1.8 Understanding the Role of Communication in Your Organization

Interview your supervisor to learn about the kinds and purposes of communication in your organization. Your questions could include the following:

- What channels of communication (e.g., memos, e-mail, presentations) are most important in this organization?
- What documents or presentations do you create? Are they designed to inform, to persuade, to build goodwill—or to do a combination?
- What documents or presentations do you receive? Are they designed to inform, to persuade, to build goodwill—or to do a combination?
- Who are your most important audiences within the organization?
- Who are our most important external audiences?
- What are the challenges of communicating in this organization?
- What kinds of documents and presentations does the organization prefer?

As your instructor directs,

a. Share your results with a small group of students.
b. Present your results in a memo to your instructor.
c. Join with a group of students to make a group presentation to the class.
d. Post your results online to the class.

1.9 Introducing Yourself to Your Instructor

Write a memo (at least 1½ pages long) introducing yourself to your instructor. Include the following topics:

Background: Where did you grow up? What have you done in terms of school, extracurricular activities, jobs, and family life?

Interests: What are you interested in? What do you like to do? What do you like to think about and talk about?

Achievements: What achievements have given you the greatest personal satisfaction? List at least five. Include things that gave *you* a real sense of accomplishment and pride, whether or not they're the sort of thing you'd list on a résumé.

Goals: What do you hope to accomplish this term? Where would you like to be professionally and personally five years from now?

Use complete memo format with appropriate headings. (See Appendix A ➠ for examples of memo format.) Use a conversational writing style; check your draft to polish the style and edit for mechanical and grammatical correctness. A good memo will enable your instructor to see you as an individual. Use specific details to make your memo vivid and interesting. Remember that one of your purposes is to interest your reader!

1.10 Introducing Yourself to Your Collaborative Writing Group

Write a memo (at least 1½ pages long) introducing yourself to the other students in your collaborative writing group. Include the following topics:

Background: What is your major? What special areas of knowledge do you have? What have you done in terms of school, extracurricular activities, jobs, and family life?

Previous experience in groups: What groups have you worked in before? Are you usually a leader, a follower, or a bit of both? Are you interested in a quality product? In maintaining harmony in the group? In working efficiently? What do you like most about working in groups? What do you like least?

Work and composing style: Do you like to talk out ideas while they're in a rough stage or work them out on paper before you discuss them? Would you rather have a complete outline before you start writing or just a general idea? Do you want to have a detailed schedule of everything that has to be done and who

will do it, or would you rather "go with the flow"? Do you work best under pressure, or do you want to have assignments ready well before the due date?

Areas of expertise: What can you contribute to the group in terms of knowledge and skills? Are you good at brainstorming ideas? Researching? Designing charts? Writing? Editing? Word processing? Managing the flow of work? Maintaining group cohesion?

Goals for collaborative assignments: What do you hope to accomplish this term? Where does this course fit into your priorities?

Use complete memo format with appropriate headings. (See Appendix A for examples of memo format.) Use a conversational writing style; edit your final draft for mechanical and grammatical correctness. A good memo will enable others in your group to see you as an individual. Use details to make your memo vivid and interesting. Remember that one of your purposes is to make your readers look forward to working with you!

1.11   Describing Your Experiences in and Goals for Writing

Write a memo (at least 1½ pages long) to your instructor describing the experiences you've had writing and what you'd like to learn about writing during this course.

Answer several of the following questions:

- What memories do you have of writing? What made writing fun or frightening in the past?
- What have you been taught about writing? List the topics, rules, and advice you remember.
- What kinds of writing have you done in school? How long have the papers been?
- How has your school writing been evaluated? Did the instructor mark or comment on mechanics and grammar? Style? Organization? Logic? Content? Audience analysis and adaptation? Have you gotten extended comments on your papers? Have instructors in different classes had the same standards, or have you changed aspects of your writing for different classes?

- What voluntary writing have you done—journals, poems, stories, essays? Has this writing been just for you, or has some of it been shared or published?
- Have you ever written on a job or in a student or volunteer organization? Have you ever edited other people's writing? What have these experiences led you to think about real-world writing?
- What do you see as your current strengths and weaknesses in writing skills? What skills do you think you'll need in the future? What kinds of writing do you expect to do after you graduate?

Use complete memo format with appropriate headings. (See Appendix A ➡ for examples of memo format.) Use a conversational writing style; edit your final draft for mechanical and grammatical correctness.

1.12   Mosaic Case

Yvonne, who manages Mosaic's Communications Department, holds routine staff meetings so that she can assign tasks and team members can update her about their progress on larger projects. (Refer back to page 31 for a general overview of Mosaic.)

Based on your initial reading of Chapter 1, consider the following questions:

- What types of situations do you think members of Yvonne's communication team face on a regular basis?
- What kinds of ethical concerns does Yvonne face with the workers in her department?

- What are the biggest challenges Yvonne has to deal with both internally and externally?
- What kinds of communication training do you think Yvonne gives the junior managers of Mosaic?
- How do you think the communication department impacts the quality of interaction customers have with Mosaic?
- How important is this department to the overall success of Mosaic?
- Scan the table of contents of this textbook. What kinds of problems do you think the team will run into during your semester?

2

Adapting Your Message to Your Audience

Learning Objectives

After studying this chapter, you will know:

1 Ways to analyze different kinds of audiences.

   a. Individuals

   b. Groups

   c. Organizations

2 How to choose channels to reach your audience.

3 How to analyze your audience and adapt your message to it.

4 How to identify and develop audience benefits.

Audience Analysis Is Always in Fashion

Kay Krill was the vice president of merchandising for Ann Taylor Stores' successful Ann Taylor Loft line of business casual fashions. When sales of the Ann Taylor business-formal brand sagged in 2004, the company asked her to take over both fashion lines. The problem: how to promote both lines, when both have different looks and appeal to different customers in different ways. The solution: focus on audience.

Step one was to research the target audience for each line. Krill's team interviewed Ann Taylor customers, observed them while they shopped, and visited their homes. They found two very different styles and motivations among their customers: Ann Taylor customers were focused on business wear that was appropriate to specific business settings, while Ann Taylor Loft customers bought clothes as expressions of personal identity.

"Audience analysis gives you the tools you need to shape your product and your message."

Step two was to envision the target audience for each fashion line as separate people—named "Ann" and "Loft"—and make decisions about each line based on the ideas and values that appealed to each of these "customers." Ann was characterized as "refined," "approachable," and "sophisticated." Loft was "relaxed," "casual," "lighthearted," "active," and "spirited." For the Ann Taylor staff, understanding their audience was the key to building fashion lines that resonated with each set of customers' needs and styles. The result? By 2006, net income at Ann Taylor stores was up 500% from 2004.

Audience analysis is the first step in any communication process: it gives you the tools you need to shape your product and your message. In order to communicate effectively with your audience, you need to understand who they are, what groups they belong to, and what values they hold.

Adapted from Amy Merrick, "Asking 'What Would Ann Do?'" *Wall Street Journal*, September 15, 2006, B1, B3.

Chapter Outline

Identifying Your Audiences

Ways to Analyze Your Audience
- Analyzing Individuals
- Analyzing Members of Groups
- Analyzing the Organizational Culture and the Discourse Community

Choosing Channels to Reach Your Audience

Using Audience Analysis to Adapt Your Message
1. How Will the Audience Initially React to the Message?
2. How Much Information Does the Audience Need?
3. What Obstacles Must You Overcome?
4. What Positive Aspects Can You Emphasize?
5. What Are the Audience's Expectations about the Appropriate Language, Organization, and Form of Messages?
6. How Will the Audience Use the Document?

Audience Analysis Works

Audience Benefits
- Characteristics of Good Audience Benefits
- Ways to Identify and Develop Audience Benefits
- Audience Benefits Work

Writing or Speaking to Multiple Audiences with Different Needs

Summary of Key Points

Knowing who you're talking to is fundamental to the success of any message. You need to identify your audiences, understand their motivations, and know how to reach them.

Identifying Your Audiences

The first step in analyzing your audience is to decide who your audience is. Organizational messages have multiple audiences:

1. A **gatekeeper** has the power to stop your message instead of sending it on to other audiences. The gatekeeper therefore controls whether your message even gets to the primary audience. Sometimes the supervisor who assigns the message is also the gatekeeper; sometimes the gatekeeper is higher in the organization. In some cases, gatekeepers may exist outside the organization.

2. The **primary audience** will decide whether to accept your recommendations or will act on the basis of your message. You must reach the primary audience to fulfill your purposes in any message.

3. The **secondary audience** may be asked to comment on your message or to implement your ideas after they've been approved. Secondary audiences also include lawyers who may use your message—perhaps years later—as evidence of your organization's culture and practices.

4. An **auxiliary audience** may encounter your message but will not have to interact with it. This audience includes the "read-only" people.

5. A **watchdog audience**, though it does not have the power to stop the message and will not act directly on it, has political, social, or economic power. The watchdog pays close attention to the transaction between you

Dow Chemical is aware that an audience is composed of individual people. Their advertising campaign—"The Human Element"—"is intended to make a high-level emotional connection with people and help them see Dow as a responsible and involved citizen of the world," according to Patti Temple Rocks, Dow's Vice President of Global Communications and Reputations.

Source: "Human Element Ad Campaign Jump Starts Reputation Initiative," *Around Dow* 12, no. 6 (July 2006): 1.

and the primary audience and may base future actions on its evaluation of your message.

As the following examples show, one person can be part of two audiences. Frequently, a supervisor is both the primary audience and the gatekeeper.

Dawn is an assistant account executive in an ad agency. Her boss asks her to write a proposal for a marketing plan for a new product the agency's client is introducing. Her **primary audience** is the executive committee of the client company, who will decide whether to adopt the plan. The **secondary audience** includes the marketing staff of the client company, who will be asked for comments on the plan, as well as the artists, writers, and media buyers who will carry out details of the plan if it is adopted. Her boss, who must approve the plan before it is submitted to the client, is the **gatekeeper.** Her office colleagues who read her plan are her **auxiliary audience.**

Joe works in the data processing unit of a bank. He must write a monthly progress report describing his work. This month, he has worked on implementing a centralized system for handling customers' checks. His boss is a **primary audience.** His boss will write a performance appraisal evaluating his work, so Joe wants to present his own efforts positively. The boss may also include paragraphs from Joe's progress report in a memo to the president of the bank, who wants to know when the bugs in the system will be worked out. The president is thus also a **primary audience.** The **secondary audience** includes the bank's customer service representatives, who must answer customer questions and deal with complaints about the new system, and sales representatives from the computer company that sold the hardware to the bank, who want to be sure that bank personnel are able to use the equipment effectively.

Ways to Analyze Your Audience

The most important tools in audience analysis are common sense and empathy. **Empathy** is the ability to put yourself in someone else's shoes, to feel with that person. Use what you know about people and about organizations to predict likely responses.

Analyzing Individuals

When you write or speak to people in your own organization and in other organizations you work closely with, you may be able to analyze your audience as individuals. You may already know your audience. It will usually be easy to get additional information by talking to members of your audience, talking to people who know your audience, and observing your audience. You may learn that one manager may dislike phone calls, so you will know to write

---

Accommodating Audiences

For years Wal-Mart has dominated the retail industry by offering a variety of products at "everyday low prices." But Wal-Mart's strategy of standardization and the resulting economies of scale that helped the company become a retailing giant may now have become its Achilles heel. In trying to be all things to all people, explains Eduardo Castro-Wright, the company's new CEO, "you end up underserving everyone because you don't have an offering that is specific to that customer segment."

To counter slipping sales and make the company even more competitive, Castro-Wright has introduced six demographic groups that will allow regional managers to localize their stores' product mix to better suit their customers.

- Stores in Hispanic markets will include large farmers-market events offering fresh foods and will feature displays for *quinceaneras.*

- Stores in areas with large "empty nest" populations will have smaller children's sections and a larger pharmacy area.

- A new urban-style store outside of Chicago quadrupled its display of gospel, rhythm and blues, and hip-hop music and added baby clothes and supplies designed for premature babies to meet the needs of local shoppers.

In addition to localizing its merchandise, Wal-Mart is also localizing its staff: regional executives, who once lived in company headquarters at Bentonville, AR, will now be required to live within their regions to better understand their customer base.

Adapted from Ann Zimmerman, "To Boost Sales, Wal-Mart Drops One-Size-Fits-All Approach," *Wall Street Journal*, September 7, 2006, A1.

One of the most relevant demographic measures for writers is the literacy level of their audience. Unfortunately, writers even in advanced economies have to ask how well their audience can read. In the United States, the answer may be "Not very well." An international study by Educational Testing Service recently found that US adults ranked 10th out of 17 industrialized countries in their ability to understand texts, interpret documents, and use basic math skills. Young adults lagged further behind their international counterparts than adults over 35.

Overall, 45 percent of the US adults tested had reading levels below that of a high school graduate. For business writers, this poses a challenge. When composing a message for a broad readership of employees or customers, writers may have to keep sentences short and words simple. They may also have to use graphics effectively to clarify meaning.

Adapted from Aaron Bernstein, "The Time Bomb in the Workforce: Illiteracy," *BusinessWeek*, February 25, 2002, 122.

your request in an e-mail. Another manager may have a reputation for denying requests made on a Friday, so you will know to get yours in earlier.

A useful schema for analyzing people is the **Myers-Briggs Type Indicator.**® This instrument uses four pairs of dichotomies to identify ways that people differ.[1] One of these dichotomies is well known: Extraversion-Introversion, measuring how individuals prefer to focus their attention and get energy. Extraverted types are energized by interacting with other people. Introverted types get their energy from within.

The other three dichotomies in Myers-Briggs® typology are Sensing-Intuition, Thinking-Feeling, and Judging-Perceiving. The Sensing-Intuition dichotomy measures the way an individual prefers to take in information. Sensing types gather information through their senses, preferring what is real and tangible. Intuitive types prefer to gather information by looking at the big picture, focusing on the relationships and connections between facts.

The Thinking-Feeling dichotomy measures the way an individual makes decisions. Thinking types prefer to use Thinking in decision making to consider the logical consequences of a choice or action to base their decisions. Feeling types make decisions based on the impact to people, considering what is important to them and to others involved.

The Judging-Perceiving dichotomy measures how individuals orient themselves to the external world. Judging types like to live in a planned, orderly way, seeking closure. Perceiving types prefer to live in a flexible, spontaneous way, enjoying possibilities.

The descriptors on each of the scales dichotomies represent a preference, just as we have a preference for using either our right or our left hand to write. If necessary, we can use the opposite style, but we have less practice in it and use it less easily.

You can find out your own personality type by taking the Myers-Briggs Type Indicator® instrument at your college's counseling center or student services office. Some businesses administer the Myers-Briggs Type Indicator® instrument to all employees to assist with team building and/or personal growth and development.

As Figure 2.1 suggests, you'll be most persuasive if you play to your audience's strengths. Indeed, many of the general principles of business communication reflect the types most common among managers. Putting the main point up front satisfies the needs of judging types, and some 75% of US managers are judging. Giving logical reasons satisfies the needs of the nearly 80% of US managers who are thinking types.[2]

Analyzing Members of Groups

In many organizational situations, you'll analyze your audience not as individuals but as members of a group: "taxpayers who must be notified that they owe more income tax," "customers who use our accounting services," or "employees with small children." Focus on what group members have in common. Although generalizations won't be true for all members of the group, generalization is necessary when you must appeal to a large group of people with one message. In some cases, no research is necessary: It's easy to guess the attitudes of people who must be told they owe more taxes. In other cases, databases may yield useful information. In still other cases, you may want to do original research.

If you know where your audience lives, databases enable you to map demographic and psychographic profiles of customers or employees. **Demographic characteristics** are measurable features that can be counted objectively: age, sex, race, religion, education level, income, and so on.

Figure 2.1   Using Myers-Briggs Types in Persuasive Messages

If your audience is	Use this strategy	Because
Introverted type	Write a memo and let the reader think about your proposal before responding.	Introverts prefer to think before they speak. Written documents give them the time they need to think through a proposal carefully.
Extraverted type	Try out your idea orally, in an informal setting.	Extraverts like to think on their feet. They are energized by people; they'd rather talk than write.
Sensing type	Present your reasoning step-by-step. Get all your facts exactly right.	Sensing types usually reach conclusions step-by-step. They want to know why something is important, but they trust their own experience more than someone else's say-so. They're good at facts and expect others to be, too.
Intuitive type	Present the big picture first. Stress the innovative, creative aspects of your proposal.	Intuitive types like solving problems and being creative. They can be impatient with details.
Thinking type	Use logic, not emotion, to persuade. Show that your proposal is fair, even if some people may be hurt by it.	Thinking types make decisions based on logic and abstract principles. They are often uncomfortable with emotion.
Feeling type	Show that your proposal values the people needs of the organization as well as the dollars-and-cents needs of the organization.	Feeling types are very aware of other people and their feelings. They are sympathetic and like harmony
Perceiving type	Show that you've considered all the alternatives. Ask for a decision by a specific date.	Perceiving types want to be sure they've considered all the options. They may postpone coming to closure.
Judging type	Present your request quickly.	Judging types are comfortable making quick decisions. They like to come to closure so they can move on to something else.

Source: Further information is available at www.cpp.com where you will find the full range of introduction to Type®. Modified and reproduced by special permission of the publisher, CPP, Inc., Palo Alto, CA, from *Introduction to Type*® 6th Ed. By Isabel Briggs Myers. Copyright 1998 by CPP, Inc. All rights reserved. Further reproduction is prohibited without the publisher's written consent.

Sometimes demographic information is irrelevant; sometimes it's important. Does education matter? Well, the fact that the reader has a degree from Eastern State rather than from Harvard may not matter, but how much the reader knows about accounting may. Does family structure matter? Sometimes. Noticing that almost half of US marriages today are the partners' second unions, with many involving children, some hotels and resorts are offering newlyweds "familymoon" packages that include baby-sitting, multiple bedrooms, and other family-friendly amenities.[3] Another trend that affects some marketing messages is the growing number of older Americans.

Psychographic characteristics are qualitative rather than quantitative: values, beliefs, goals, and lifestyles. Many marketers use the Values and Life Styles (VALS) profiles developed by the SRI research firm in California. VALS profiles divide US buyers into eight categories according to their primary motivation (ideals, achievement, or self-expression), the amount of resources they have, and the extent to which they innovate. For instance,

**Culture: Words
and Deeds**

Culture is more than a values statement on a Web site. A company's true culture is evident in the way people behave. Consider these examples of cultural mismatches:

A major international corporation hung signs in its hallways proclaiming that "trust" was one of its driving principles. Yet that same company searched employees' belongings each time they entered or exited the building.

At one company, Employee Appreciation Day featured morning bagels, a blast e-mail of thanks from the company president, and an afternoon gathering with food and refreshments. A flier promoting the event instructed employees to "please see your supervisor for a ticket. Cost: $15."

A multinational corporation that claimed to be committed to work/life values drew up an excellent plan to help managers incorporate work/life balance into the business. The company gathered its top 80 officers to review the plan—but scheduled the meetings on a weekend.

Quoted from Pamela Babcock, "Is Your Company Two-Faced?" *HR Magazine*, January 2004, 42.

**www.2h.com/
personality-tests.html**

Before analyzing your audience, log onto this Web site to discover and analyze your own personality. How will knowing your own personality traits better help you communicate with diverse audiences? How will it help you when establishing reader benefits?

Many organizations promote virtual offices, which allow employees to work from home.

Strivers are motivated by achievement and are relatively low in resources and innovation. These conspicuous consumers may not have a lot of money, but they do try to be in style. The other VALS categories are called Innovators, Thinkers, Believers, Achievers, Experiencers, Makers, and Survivors.[4] To see where you fit, follow the VALS link from the BAC Web site.

Knowing what your audience finds important allows you to organize information in a way that seems natural to your audience and to choose appeals that the audience will find persuasive. An electric utility increased participation in a conservation program by using VALS to define two target segments and locate the zip codes in which those segments were concentrated. The utility prepared two different mailings, one appealing to each segment, and saw a 25% increase in conservation participation.[5]

Other organizations also use group analysis. Toyota is pushing its expensive hybrid Lexus harder in Japan and Europe than in the United States. While wealthy Japanese look for fuel economy, wealthy American buyers are more interested in performance. The editors of *Grit*, a home gardening magazine, changed the look of the magazine by exchanging its newsprint format for full-color glossy pages in order to appeal to new and younger audiences. Even the content of their articles changed. In addition to articles about crops, animals and small-town life, the magazine began to include topics like organic gardening.[6]

Analyzing the Organizational Culture and the Discourse Community

Be sensitive to the culture in which your audiences work and the discourse community of which they are a part. **Organizational culture** is a set of values, attitudes, and philosophies. An organization's culture is revealed verbally in the organization's myths, stories, and heroes, as well as in documents such as employee manuals. It is revealed nonverbally in the allocation of space,

Some companies are beginning to accept visible body art and long hair in traditional workplace cultures.

Source: Mielikki Org, "The Tattooed Executive: Body Art Gains Acceptance in Once-Staid Office Settings," *Wall Street Journal,* August 28, 2003, sec D1.

money, and power. A **discourse community** is a group of people who share assumptions about what channels, formats, and styles to use for communication, what topics to discuss and how to discuss them, and what constitutes evidence.

In an organization that values equality and individualism, you can write directly to the CEO and address him or her as a colleague. In other companies, you'd be expected to follow a chain of command. Even if you know the name of the real decision maker, you'd be expected to send your message through your boss—and to be deferential to your superiors. Some organizations prize short messages; some expect long, thorough documents. Some cultures expect people to float trial balloons; others prefer that people work out all the details before they propose a change. Messages that are consistent with the organization's culture have a greater chance of succeeding.

You can begin to analyze an organization's culture by asking the following questions:

- Is the organization tall or flat? Are there lots of levels between the CEO and the lowest worker, or only a few?

- How do people get ahead? Are the organization's rewards based on seniority, education, being well-liked, saving money, or serving customers? Are rewards available only to a few top people, or is everyone expected to succeed?

- Does the organization value diversity or homogeneity? Does it value independence and creativity or being a team player and following orders?

- What stories do people tell? Who are the organization's heroes and villains?

- How important are friendship and sociability? To what extent do workers agree on goals, and how intently do they pursue them?

- How formal are behavior, language, and dress?

Whole Foods Values People AND Profits

Since 1980, Whole Foods has been a market leader in organic food. John Mackey, co-founder and CEO, credits his company's success, in part, to its corporate culture. "We have this empowered, decentralized culture, and a high percentage of [store managers] are trying to figure out how to make their stores better, how to improve customer experience. . . . We've got 189 stores. They're all faced with their own unique competitive environments. It's not necessary for me to know everything that's going on everywhere."

Across the country, Mackey empowers his team leaders and store managers to select products and set prices that are right for their unique locations. In order to meet the needs of local customers and to compete with mass-market retailers like Wal-Mart, Whole Foods encourages store managers to customize their product mixes, feature locally produced goods when possible, and aggressively match competitor's prices. The latter task is the trickiest because organic foods are often of higher quality, and more expensive, than nonorganic ones. Mackey acknowledges that most Americans value low prices, but as the population becomes wealthier, he believes that organic foods will penetrate more deeply into American kitchens. Mackey, a vegan, believes that the recent interest in natural and organic foods is "a value system, a belief system. It's penetrating into the mainstream."

Adapted and quoted from Steven Gray, "Natural Benefits," *Wall Street Journal*, December 4, 2006, B1, B3.

- What does the work space look like? Do employees work in offices, cubbies, or large rooms?
- What are the organization's goals? Making money? Serving customers and clients? Advancing knowledge? Contributing to the community?

To analyze an organization's discourse community, ask the following questions:

- What media, formats, and styles are preferred for communication?
- What do people talk about? What topics are not discussed?
- What kind of and how much evidence is needed to be convincing?

Corporate cultures can vary widely. Some West Coast computer companies are known for company gyms, pool and ping-pong tables, well-stocked snack rooms, and casual work attire. Ad agency Crispin Porter + Bogusky has a stuffed elephant and a firepole, plus some teepees to use as conference rooms. Personnel get around on bikes and skateboards. Whole Foods features a collaborative environment. Each department, such as meats or vegetables, is a decentralized team, and performance bonuses go to teams, not individuals. Sun Microsystems is known for its emphasis on its virtual office and flextime.[7]

Two companies in the same field may have very different cultures. When Procter & Gamble bought Gillette, they expected a smooth marriage between the world's number one toothbrush, Oral-B, and the world's number two toothpaste, Crest. But cultural differences caused problems. Gillette employees found P&G's culture rigid, its decision making slow. Gillette employees also had to learn P&G's famous acronyms, such as CIB (consumer is boss) and FMOT (first moment of truth, when consumers notice the product). P&G people sent memos, Gillette people called meetings.[8]

International differences also impact corporate culture. Many Asian businesses are conservative: they value face time in the office over telecommuting and group effort over individual initiative. Late nights at the office and even weekend work in the office are expected.[9]

Obtaining information about corporate culture—by checking Web sites, asking about communication practices, and observing employees when visiting a company—will help you decide if the organization is one you want to

Some employees at the New York office of Naked Communications use exercise balls as desk chairs. The balls require employees to use abdominal and lower back muscles to maintain posture. Employees say they are also fun because they can bounce.

Source: Anjali Athavaley, "The Ball's in Your Cubicle: New Workplace Trend Replaces Office Chairs with Gym Balls," *Wall Street Journal*, February 27, 2007, D1, D3.

work for. Such considerations are important, since new hires who fit the company's culture are more satisfied than those who do not.

Choosing Channels to Reach Your Audience

A **communication channel** is the means by which you convey your message. Communication channels vary in speed, accuracy of transmission, cost, number of messages carried, number of people reached, efficiency, and ability to promote goodwill. Depending on the audience, your purposes, and the situation, one channel may be better than another.

A written message makes it easier to

- Present extensive or complex data.
- Present many specific details.
- Minimize undesirable emotions.

Messages on paper are more formal than e-mail messages.

Oral messages make it easier to

- Use emotion to help persuade the audience.
- Focus the audience's attention on specific points.
- Resolve conflicts and build consensus.
- Modify plans.
- Get immediate action or response.

Choosing the right channel can be tricky sometimes. Even in the office, you will have to decide if your message will be more effective as an e-mail, phone

CLOSE TO HOME

©2006 JOHN McPHERSON / DIST. BY UNIVERSAL PRESS SYNDICATE

The others in the office send a poignant message to Frank to stop leaving dirty dishes in the break room.

It's Simple: Keep Employees, Keep Customers

Mother, a London advertising agency, created a corporate culture that centers on employees. In creating the unique culture, the company ensures employees know how their services help customers, spells out every employee's responsibility, and offers timely, meaningful, and unusual rewards.

The main features of this fun culture include a casual dress code (flip-flops and jeans), open work environment with no doors or offices, and "self-improvement bonuses" redeemable for gym memberships, massages, hot lunches, a winter ski trip, or three-month sabbaticals. Employees also receive the day after Mother's Day and birthdays off.

The result—Mother's revenue more than tripled between 2002 and 2005 to $267.1 million, turnover is minimal as fewer than 10% leave in a year, and loss of accounts is rare. The company attracts and retains top talent. In addition, customers appreciate Mother's corporate culture because they feel that they get better work from this highly motivated, happy workforce.

Adapted from Joann S. Lublin, "Keeping Clients by Keeping Workers: Unique Efforts to Encourage Employee Loyalty Pay Off for U.K. As Shop Mother," *Wall Street Journal*, November 20, 2006, B3.

Market research firm Claritas, Inc., combines demographic and psychographic data to identify 66 lifestyle clusters, including "Young Digerati" (tech-savvy young adults), "Close-In Couples" (older, African-American couples), and "Blue-Chip Blues" (young families with well-paying blue-colar jobs). Both the catchy names and drawings are copyrighted by Claritas, Inc., 2007.

call, visit, or sticky note posted on a colleague's computer. In nonstandard situations, choosing a channel can be challenging. If you are the head of a small, nonprofit literacy agency which helps adults learn to read, how do you reach your clients? You cannot afford TV ads, and they cannot read print channels such as flyers. If you are a safety officer for a manufacturer, how do you send out product recall notifications? Who ever files the contact-information cards when they purchase an item? If you are the benefits manager in a large manufacturing plant, how will you get information about your new benefits plan out to the thousand people on the floor? They don't use computers at work and may not have computer access at home.

The good news is that you will have many alternatives to choose from. The fastest-growing channels are electronic.

- To make a case for bioengineered crops, Monsanto filmed testimonials from farmers around the world and posted them on a Web site.[10]
- General Motors also uses online videos—to communicate with dealerships.[11]
- To sell more romance novels, HarperCollins sponsored an online writing contest. Other publishers are relying on independent bloggers to spread the word about new titles.[12]
- Companies such as Estée Lauder are setting up interactive Web sites to provide information and online forums where their customers can chat with each other about products and services.[13]
- Nationwide Insurance has a Web site where people can leave a "life" story for posting on Nationwide's Times Square giant screen billboard.[14]
- As part of its Shrek nutrition promotion, McDonald's created a Web site where children can play Shrek games, earning points for digital downloads, including screen savers.[15]
- Paramount Pictures has used widgets to advertise new movies. Widgets are small computer programs that let you install on your desktop or Web page items like clocks, calculators, news updates, and weather information; the items are framed by or placed next to the promotional material.[16]
- Vienna, Austria, is raising money for the main public library with a phone sex hotline. Pay by the minute and you get to hear a famous Austrian actress reading passages from the library's collection of erotic fiction from the 18th through 20th centuries.[17]

Creative channels abound. Ads are appearing on hotel shower curtains, the bellies of pregnant women, airport luggage conveyor belts, grocery checkout conveyors, and toilet stall doors. One company prints ads on cardboard shirt hangers which are distributed free to cleaners. The hangers are touted as a good way to reach male consumers. The US Post Office used shrink wrap to turn selected mail-collection boxes into R2-D2 clones in honor of their Star Wars anniversary stamp.[18]

Using Audience Analysis to Adapt Your Message

Zeroing in on the right audience with the right message is frequently a formula for success. Mike McNamara, a Texas attorney, aims for the spring break crowd at South Padre Island. His flyer reads, "Got drunk? Got caught? Call Mike. He won't tell your mama!" His Web site includes a picture of him in beach wear with a beer in his hand. Fees for representing someone for a misdemeanor run hundreds of dollar; felony fees run thousands of dollars.[19]

If you know your audience well and if you use words well, much of your audience analysis and adaptation will be unconscious. If you don't know your audience or if the message is very important, take the time to analyze your audience formally and to revise your message with your analysis in mind. The questions in Figure 2.2 will help guide a careful analysis.

As you answer these questions for a specific audience, think about the organizational culture in which the person works. At every point, your audience's reaction is affected not only by his or her personal feelings and preferences but also by the political environment of the organization, the economy, and current events.

Finding Your Niche

William B. Ziff, Jr., made millions by selling to niche markets rather than the masses. In the 1950s and 1960s, when national magazines like *Life*, *Time*, and *The Saturday Evening Post* reached millions of households, Ziff decided to take a different route to success. He created magazines for small groups of readers with disposable incomes and specialized interests. Today Ziff's magazines, such as *Car & Driver*, *Yachting*, and *PC Magazine* are some of the best-known special-interest magazines in the country. Ziff's practice of profiling his readers to fine-tune his magazines has become an industry-wide practice.

Adapted from Stephen Miller, "Finding His Niche: Magazine Empire Built on Specialties," *Wall Street Journal*, September 16, 2006, A4.

1. How Will the Audience Initially React to the Message?

a. Will the audience see this message as highly important?

Audiences will read and act on messages they see as important to their own careers; they may ignore messages that seem unimportant to them.

When the audience may see your message as unimportant, you need to

- Use a subject line or first paragraph that shows your reader this message is important and relevant.
- Make the action as easy as possible.
- Suggest a realistic deadline for action.
- Keep the message as short as possible.

b. How will the fact that the message is from you affect the audience's reaction to the words you use?

The audience's experience with you, your organization, and the subject you're writing about shapes the way they respond to this new message. Someone who thinks well of you and your organization will be prepared to receive your message favorably; someone who thinks poorly of you and the organization will be quick to find fault with what you say and the way you say it.

When your audience has negative feelings about your organization, your position, or you personally, you need to

- Make a special effort to avoid phrases that could seem condescending, arrogant, rude, hostile, or uncaring.
- Use positive emphasis (➡ p. 80) to counteract the natural tendency to sound defensive.
- Develop logic and benefits fully.

2. How Much Information Does the Audience Need?

a. How much does the audience already know about this subject?

It's easy to overestimate the knowledge an audience has. People outside your own immediate unit may not really know what it is you do. Even people who once worked in your unit may have forgotten specific details now that their daily work is in management. People outside your organization won't know how *your* organization does things.

Figure 2.2   Analyzing Your Audience

These questions will help you analyze your audience:
1. How will the audience initially react to the message?
2. How much information does the audience need?
3. What obstacles must you overcome?
4. What positive aspects can you emphasize?
5. What are the audience's expectations about the appropriate language, organization, and form of messages?
6. How will the audience use the document?

When some of your information is new to the audience, you need to

- Make a special effort to be clear. Define terms, explain concepts, use examples, avoid acronyms.
- Link new information to old information that the audience already knows.
- Use paragraphs and headings to break up new information into related chunks so that the information is easier to digest.
- Test a draft of your document with your reader or a subset of your intended audience to see whether the audience can understand and use what you've written.

b. Does the audience's knowledge need to be updated?

Our personal experience guides our expectations and actions. If you're trying to change someone's understanding of something, you need to

- Acknowledge the audience's initial understanding early in the message.
- Use examples or statistics to show the need for the change, or to show that the audience's experience is not universal.
- Allow the audience to save face by suggesting that changed circumstances call for new attitudes or action.

c. What aspects of the subject does the audience need to be aware of to appreciate your points?

When the audience must think of background or old information to appreciate your points, you can

- Preface information with "As you know" or "As you may remember" to avoid suggesting that you think the audience does not know what you're saying.
- Put old or obvious information in a subordinate clause.
- Put lengthy background or reminder information in a separate section with an appropriate heading or in an attachment to your letter or memo.

3. What Obstacles Must You Overcome?

a. Is your audience opposed to what you have to say?

People who have already made up their minds are highly resistant to change. When the audience will oppose what you have to say, you need to

- Start your message with any areas of agreement or common ground that you share with your audience.
- Make a special effort to be clear and unambiguous. Points that might be clear to a neutral audience can be misinterpreted by someone opposed to the message.
- Make a special effort to avoid statements that will anger the audience.
- Limit your statement or request to the smallest possible area. If parts of your message could be delivered later, postpone them.
- Show that your solution is the best solution currently available, even though it isn't perfect.

The Audiences for a CPA Audit Report

An audit report may be used by at least five different audiences:

The client, who may resent any report that isn't fully favorable.

Bankers, investors, and creditors, who make decisions based on audit reports and who may hold the CPA financially responsible for the report with a "third-party" lawsuit.

Colleagues, who use the reports, but who may have different ethical or theoretical positions.

Attorneys, who will use the reports as evidence for or against the CPA if a suit is filed.

The AICPA (American Institute of Certified Public Accountants), which sets the standards for accounting reports.

Good audit reports meet the needs and overcome the possible objections of all of these audiences.

Adapted from Aletha S. Hendrickson, "How to Appear Reliable without Being Liable: C.P.A. Writing in Its Rhetorical Context," *Worlds of Writing: Teaching and Learning in Different Discourse Communities,* ed. Carolyn Matalene (New York: Random House, 1989), 323.

b. Will it be easy for the audience to do as you ask?

Everyone has a set of ideas and habits and a mental self-image. If we're asked to do something that violates any of those, we first have to be persuaded to change our attitudes or habits or self-image—a change we're reluctant to make.

When your request is time-consuming, complicated, or physically or psychologically difficult, you need to

- Make the action as easy as possible. Provide a form that can be filled out quickly; provide a stamped, self-addressed envelope if you are writing to someone in another organization.
- Break down complex actions into a list, so the audience can check off each step as it is completed. This list will also help ensure complete responses.
- Show that what you ask is consistent with some aspect of what the audience believes.
- Show how the audience (not just you or your organization) will benefit when the action is completed.

4. What Positive Aspects Can You Emphasize?

a. From the audience's point of view, what are the benefits of what you have to say?

Benefits help persuade the audience that your ideas are good ones. Make the most of the good points inherent in the message you want to convey.

- Put good news first.
- Use audience benefits that go beyond the basic good news.

b. What experiences, interests, goals, and values do you share with the audience?

A sense of solidarity with someone can be an even more powerful reason to agree than the content of the message itself. When everyone in your audience shares the same experiences, interests, goals, and values, you can

- Consider using a vivid anecdote to remind the audience of what you share. The details of the anecdote should be interesting or new; otherwise, you may seem to be lecturing the audience.
- Use a salutation and close that remind the audience of their membership in this formal or informal group.

5. What Are the Audience's Expectations about the Appropriate Language, Organization, and Form of Messages?

a. What style of writing does the audience prefer?

Good writers adapt their style to suit the reader's preferences. A reader who sees contractions as too informal needs a different style from one who sees traditional business writing as too stuffy. As you write,

- Use what you know about your reader to choose a more or less distant, more or less friendly style.

- Use the reader's first name in the salutation only if you use that name when you talk to him or her in person or on the phone.

b. Are there hot buttons or "red flag" words that may create an immediate negative response?

You don't have time to convince the audience that a term is broader or more neutral than his or her understanding. When you need agreement or approval, you should

- Avoid terms that carry emotional charges for many people: for example, *criminal, un-American, feminist, fundamentalist, liberal.*
- Use your previous experience with individuals to replace any terms that have particular meanings for them.

c. How much detail does the audience want?

A message that does not give the audience the amount of or kind of detail they want may fail. When you know the members of your audience, ask them how much detail they want. When you write to people you do not know well, you can

- Provide all the detail they need to understand and act on your message.
- Group chunks of information under headings so that readers can go directly to the parts of the message they find most interesting and relevant.
- Imitate the level of detail in similar documents to the same audience. If those documents have succeeded, you're probably safe in using the same level of detail that they do.

d. Does the audience prefer a direct or indirect organization?

Individual personality or cultural background may lead someone to prefer a particular kind of structure. You'll be more effective if you use the structure and organization your audience prefers.

e. Does the audience have expectations about formal elements such as length, visuals, or footnotes?

A document that meets the reader's expectations about length, number of visuals, and footnote format is more likely to succeed. If you can't meet those expectations, you need to

- Revise your document carefully. Be sure that a shorter-than-usual document covers the essential points; be sure that a longer-than-usual document is free from wordiness and repetition.
- Pretest the message on a subset of your audience to see if the format enhances or interferes with comprehension and action.

6. How Will the Audience Use the Document?

a. Under what physical conditions will the audience use the document?

Reading a document in a quiet office calls for no special care. But suppose the reader will be reading your message on the train commuting home, or on a

Rx for Profits

Mr. Ost owns three of the smallest drugstores you ever saw, all located in the most bombed-out and burned-out section of [Philadelphia]. But he is doing $5 million of business a year, more than twice the average drugstore rate. . . .

[H]e noticed an assistant labeling a prescription by typewriter instead of by computer. She was translating it, she explained, because to many Spanish-speaking customers, English labels were gibberish. Afraid of confusing dosage, some wouldn't take their medicine.

With a few lines of programming code, Mr. Ost expanded a simple commitment to service into a powerful marketing weapon. He loaded some 1,000 common regimens in Spanish, any of which could be printed instead of the English equivalent with a single keystroke. Business took off. . . .

When an Asian influx hit, he leaped forward again, labeling in Vietnamese. Soon he was writing 400 prescriptions a day at his second location—half in English, 30% in Spanish and 20% in Vietnamese.

Quoted from Thomas Petzinger, Jr., "Druggist's Simple Rx: Speak the Language of Your Customers," *Wall Street Journal*, June 16, 1995, B1.

Visual Manpower

A Japanese advertising agency, Asatsu, invited a European car manufacturer to their Tokyo office to pitch a sales presentation in an effort to earn their business. Workers believed, however, that their European clientele would probably not be pleased by seeing the restrooms as soon as they stepped off the elevator in the building where the advertising agency's offices were located.

Some workers had the idea to put up a gold screen to block the unsightly view; management decided this expense was too high at $2,000 an hour. Instead, the employees formed a wall of people to block the restrooms when the Europeans stepped off the elevator. The car manufacturers were so impressed with the visual manpower—and the later presentation—that they decided to go with Asatsu for their advertising needs.

Adapted from Brian Moeran, *Ethnography at Work* (Oxford, UK: Berg, 2006), 42.

ladder as he or she attempts to follow instructions. Then the physical preparation of the document can make it easier or harder to use.

When the reader will use your document outside an office,

- Use lots of white space.
- Make the document small enough to hold in one hand.
- Number items so the reader can find his or her place after an interruption.
- Consider using plastic to protect the document.

b. Will the audience use the document as a general reference? As a specific guide? As the basis for a lawsuit?

Understanding how your audience will use the document will enable you to choose the best pattern of organization and the best level of detail. A great deal of detail is needed in an Environmental Protection Agency inspection report that will be used to determine whether to bring suit against a company for violating pollution control regulations. A memo within a company urging the adoption of pollution control equipment would need less information. Different information would be needed for instructions by the manufacturer of the equipment explaining how to install and maintain it.

If the document will serve as a general reference,

- Use a subject line to aid in filing and retrieval. If the document is online, consider using several keywords to make it easy to find the document in a database search program.
- Use headings within the document so that readers can skim it.
- Give the office as well as the person to contact so that the reader can get in touch with the appropriate person some time from now.
- Spell out details that may be obvious now but might be forgotten in six months or a year.

If the document will be a detailed guide or contain instructions,

- Check to be sure that all the steps are in chronological order.
- Number steps or provide check-off boxes so that readers can easily see which steps they've completed.
- Group steps into five to seven subprocesses if there are many individual steps.
- Put any warnings at the beginning of the document; then repeat them just before the specific step to which they apply.

If the document will be used as the basis for a lawsuit,

- Give specific observations with dates and exact measurements as well as any inferences you've drawn from those observations.
- Give a full report with all the information you have. The lawyer can then decide which parts of the information to use in preparing the case.

Audience Analysis Works

Audience analysis is a powerful tool. Amazon.com tracks users' online histories to make suggestions on items they might like. Nintendo believes that much of its success is extending its concept of audience. An important part of its audience is hard-core gamers, a very vocal group—they love to blog. But if

Nintendo listened just to them, they would be the only audience Nintendo had. Instead, Nintendo extended its audience by creating the Wii, a new system that the hard-core gamers had not imagined and one that is collecting new users who never imagined owning a system at all.[20]

Match.com has become the largest US online subscription dating site by appealing to singles over 50. Its audience research showed that this group was more likely to pay subscription fees than were younger users. Match.com targets itself as a site for those who want serious relationships, and it has made the site easier to navigate for people who are not Internet-savvy.[21]

Pulte Homes construction company surveys its customers when they buy—and checks back with them several years later to make sure they are still happy. They say this process has increased the percentage of their repeat and referral business from 20% to 45% in five years.[22]

Tesco PLC, Britain's largest retailer, is beating Wal-Mart in England by signing up customers for its Clubcard. The card gives customers discounts, and it gives Tesco audience data. When Tesco added Asian herbs and ethnic foods in Indian and Pakistani neighborhoods, the data showed the products were also popular with affluent white customers, so Tesco expanded its rollout. When customers buy diapers the first time, they get coupons for usual baby products such as wipes and toys. They also get coupons for beer, because the data show that new fathers buy more beer.[23]

Audience Benefits

Use your analysis of your audience to create effective **audience benefits,** advantages that the audience gets by using your services, buying your products, following your policies, or adopting your ideas. In informative messages, benefits give reasons to comply with the information you announce and suggest that the information is good. In persuasive messages, benefits give reasons to act and help overcome audience resistance. Negative messages do not use benefits.

Characteristics of Good Audience Benefits

Good benefits meet four criteria. Each of these criteria suggests a technique for writing good benefits.

1. Adapt benefits to the audience.

When you write to different audiences, you may need to stress different benefits. Suppose that you manufacture a product and want to persuade dealers to carry it. The features you may cite in ads directed toward customers—stylish colors, sleek lines, convenience, durability, good price—won't convince dealers. Shelf space is at a premium, and no dealer carries all the models of all the brands available for any given product. Why should the dealer stock your product? To be persuasive, talk about the features that are benefits from the dealer's point of view: turnover, profit margin, the national advertising campaign that will build customer awareness and interest, the special store displays you offer that will draw attention to the product.

The *Wall Street Journal* wanted subscribers to renew their subscriptions for two more years rather than just for one. The cost of the second year was 66% of the cost of the first year. The mailing admitted that renewing for two years would tie up the money but presented the cost of the second year as "a 34% tax-free return on your money." The benefit was highly appropriate for an audience concerned about returns on investments and aware of the risk that normally accompanies high returns. *Garbage* magazine urged subscribers to respond to the

Male Models

Adapting to your audience is big business when it comes to increasing sales figures. The fashion industry has recently noticed this trend and has developed an approach to targeting "regular" guys.

For the past few years, the trend in male modeling has been to use pale skinny boys or the complete opposite, buffed and tanned masculine men. These men were used to appeal mostly to women who were buying clothes for the men in their lives.

Since more men are shopping for themselves, the fashion industry is trying to target the regular guy. Beginning with 2007 fashion shows, designers such as Versace, Perry Ellis, Dsquared, Duckie Brown, and others used models that were more the down-to-earth guy-next-door look. The trend of "regular" guy models helps make shopping less intimidating for average guys.

Adapted from Ray A. Smith, "You Should Be So 'Average': Male Models Get a New Look as Fashion Targets Regular Guys," *Wall Street Journal,* February 2, 2007, B1.

first renewal notice to save the paper that an additional mailing would take. This logic was appropriate for an audience concerned about the disposal of solid waste.

2. Stress intrinsic as well as extrinsic motivators.

Intrinsic motivators come automatically from using a product or doing something. **Extrinsic motivators** are "added on." Someone in power decides to give them; they do not necessarily come from using the product or doing the action. Figure 2.3 gives examples of extrinsic and intrinsic motivators for three activities.

Intrinsic motivators or benefits are better than extrinsic motivators for two reasons:

1. There just aren't enough extrinsic motivators for everything you want people to do. You can't give a prize to every customer every time he or she places an order or to every subordinate who does what he or she is supposed to do.
2. Research shows that extrinsic motivators may actually make people *less* satisfied with the products they buy or the procedures they follow.

In a groundbreaking study of professional employees, Frederick Herzberg found that the things people said they liked about their jobs were all intrinsic motivators—pride in achievement, an enjoyment of the work itself, responsibility. Extrinsic motivators—pay, company policy—were sometimes mentioned as things people disliked, but they were never cited as things that motivated or satisfied them. People who made a lot of money still did not mention salary as a good point about the job or the organization.[24] Some surveys have found that employees prefer being rewarded with time off or flexible scheduling, helping them balance work demands with family needs and outside interests. Other motivation experts have found that motivators can vary with employees' ages; for example, young salespeople are more likely to enjoy travel rewards, whereas older salespeople might prefer to remain close to home and family, enjoying cash or merchandise as their rewards for high performance.[25]

Steak 'n Shake restaurant chain wanted to find out what motivated its employees to do their best at work. The company learned that what employees want more than money is respect and the feeling that management listens to them and values their input. Celadon, a trucking company, discovered that addressing drivers by name rather than their truck's number made a big difference in the drivers' satisfaction with the company.[26]

Figure 2.3   Extrinsic and Intrinsic Motivators

Activity	Extrinsic motivator	Intrinsic motivator
Making a sale	Getting a commission	Pleasure in convincing someone; pride in using your talents to think of a strategy and execute it
Turning in a suggestion to a company suggestion system	Getting a monetary reward when the suggestion is implemented	Solving a problem at work; making the work environment a little more pleasant
Writing a report that solves an organizational problem	Getting praise, a good performance appraisal, and maybe a raise	Pleasure in having an effect on an organization; pride in using your skills to solve problems; solving the problem itself

3. Prove benefits with clear logic and explain them in adequate detail.

An audience benefit is a claim or assertion that the audience will benefit if they do something. Convincing the audience, therefore, involves two steps: making sure that the benefit really will occur, and explaining it to the audience.

If the logic behind a claimed benefit is faulty or inaccurate, there's no way to make that particular benefit convincing. Revise the benefit to make it logical.

Faulty logic:	Moving your account information into Excel will save you time.
Analysis:	If you have not used Excel before, in the short run it will probably take you longer to work with your account information using Excel. You may have been pretty good with your old system!
Revised benefit:	Moving your account information into Excel will allow you to prepare your monthly budget pages with a few clicks of a button.

If the logic is sound, making that logic evident to the audience is a matter of providing enough evidence and showing how the evidence proves the claim that there will be a benefit. Always provide enough detail to be vivid and concrete. You'll need more detail in the following situations:

a. The audience may not have thought of the benefit before.
b. The benefit depends on the difference between the long run and the short run.
c. The audience will be hard to persuade, and you need detail to make the benefit vivid and emotionally convincing.

Until recently, Islamic women who wanted to go swimming had a problem. To meet their customers' needs, the Australian company Ahiida now makes hooded full-bodied bathing suits, called Burqinis, for Muslim women who wish to go swimming while still maintaining the Islamic customs of full body coverage.

Source: Lisa Miller, "Belief Watch: Surf's Up!" *Newsweek,* January 29, 2007, 15.

Retailers Analyze Online Consumers

Ever wonder if you are being watched on-line? Internet merchants are watching consumer Internet behavior and tastes, then targeting strategies to increase sales. The result is variable pricing, discounts, or free shipping offers based on shopper behavior and demographics.

- Overstock.com Inc. boasts that they can determine the gender and time zone of a consumer in five clicks; these categories then help determine what promotional offers a consumer may receive.

- eBay uses different displays on homepages based on previous view habits and geography.

- Ice.com is testing the results of different offers in different parts of the country.

- Yoox gives frequent customers early notification of discounts and a special site with reduced prices just for them.

- Delightful Deliveries gives customers different discount offers based on the search term they used to find the site. For example, a customer who searches for "gift baskets" may receive a 5% discount while someone who indirectly found the site may receive a free-shipping offer.

- Kiyonna Clothing shows customers different offers based on real-time information about their sessions. For instance, if a customer keeps going back and forth between the checkout page and an item the site often generates a free shopping offer valid only for the day of the Internet shopping event.

Adapted from Jessica E. Vascellaro, "Online Retailers Are Watching You," *Wall Street Journal,* November 28, 2006, D1.

Does the following statement have enough detail?

You'll save money by using our shop-at-home service.

Audiences always believe their own experiences. People who have never used a shop-at-home service may think, "If somebody else does my shopping for me, I'll have to pay that person. I'll save money by doing it myself." They aren't likely to think of savings from not having to pay for gas and parking, from having less car wear and tear, and from not losing the time it would take to travel to several different stores to get the selection you offer. People who already use shop-at-home services may believe you if they compare your items and services with another company's to see that your cost is lower. Even then, you could make saving money seem more forceful and more vivid by showing how much they could save and mentioning some of the ways they could use your service.

4. Phrase benefits in you-attitude.

If benefits aren't in you-attitude (➠ p. 76), they'll sound selfish and won't be as effective as they could be. It doesn't matter how you phrase benefits while you're brainstorming and developing them, but in your final draft, check to be sure that you've used you-attitude.

Lacks you-attitude: We have the lowest prices in town.
You-attitude: At Havlichek Cars, you get the best deal in town.

Psychological description (➠ Chapter 12) can help you make benefits vivid.

Ways to Identify and Develop Audience Benefits

Brainstorm lots of benefits—perhaps twice as many as you'll need. Then you can choose the ones that are most effective for your audience, or that you can develop most easily. The first benefit you think of may not be the best.

Sometimes benefits will be easy to think of and to explain. When they are harder to identify or to develop, use the following steps to identify and then develop good benefits:

1. Identify the feelings, fears, and needs that may motivate your audience.
2. Identify the objective features of your product or policy that could meet the needs you've identified.
3. Show how the audience can meet their needs with the features of the policy or product.

One way to think about benefits is by imagining your audience asking, "What's in it for me?" FedEx, the international shipping company, became a powerhouse by promising to deliver packages overnight and giving customers the ability to track packages along the route to their destinations. "We thought we were selling transportation of goods," explained Frederick W. Smith, Chairman, President, and CEO, "in fact, we were selling peace of mind."[27]

1. Identify the feelings, fears, and needs that may motivate your audience.

One of the best-known analyses of needs is Abraham H. Maslow's hierarchy of needs.[28] Physiological needs are the most basic, followed by needs for safety and security, for love and a sense of belonging, for esteem and recognition, and finally for self-actualization or self-fulfillment. All of us go back and forth between higher- and lower-level needs. Whenever lower-level needs make themselves felt, they usually take priority.

Maslow's model is a good starting place to identify the feelings, fears, and needs that may motivate your audience. Figure 2.4 shows organizational motivations for each of the levels in Maslow's hierarchy. Often a product or idea can meet needs on several levels. Focus on the ones that audience analysis suggests are most relevant for your audience, but remember that even the best analysis may not reveal all of a reader's needs. For example, a well-paid manager may be worried about security needs if her spouse has lost his job or if the couple is supporting kids in college or an elderly parent.

2. Identify the objective features of your product or policy that could meet the needs you've identified.

Sometimes just listing the audience's needs makes it obvious which feature meets a given need. Sometimes several features together meet the need. Try to think of all of them.

Suppose that you want to persuade people to come to the restaurant you manage. It's true that everybody needs to eat, but telling people they can satisfy their hunger needs won't persuade them to come to your restaurant rather than going somewhere else or eating at home. Depending on what

Figure 2.4 Organizational Motivations for Maslow's Hierarchy of Needs

Self-actualization
- Using your talents and abilities.
- Finding solutions to problems.
- Serving humanity.
- Having self-respect and pride.
- Being the best you can be.

Esteem, recognition
- Being publicly recognized for achievements.
- Being promoted or gaining authority.
- Having status symbols.
- Having a good personal reputation.
- Having a good corporate reputation.

Love, belonging
- Having friends, working with people you like.
- Cooperating with other people on a project.
- Conforming to a group's norms.
- Feeling needed.
- Being loyal or patriotic.
- Promoting the welfare of a group you identify with or care about.

Safety, security
- Earning enough to afford a comfortable standard of living.
- Having pleasant working conditions.
- Having good health insurance and pension plan.
- Understanding the reasons for actions by supervisors.
- Being treated fairly.
- Saving time and money.
- Conserving human and environmental resources.

Physical
- Earning enough to pay for basic food, clothing, shelter, and medical care.
- Having safe working conditions.

A Healthy Alternative to Blaming

Companies struggling with the rising cost of health care benefits are understandably concerned about the impact of obesity and smoking on their employees' health. According to a recent report by the US Department of Health and Human Services, illness linked to obesity costs the nation at least $69 billion a year, and the health costs of smoking are about $138 billion a year. Human resource specialists realize that employees can help lower the cost of health insurance by adopting a healthy lifestyle. Promoting healthy habits requires a positive message that motivates employees to take care of themselves—and refrain from blaming others.

Companies typically offer health education programs that encourage employees to make good choices about health care and healthful behaviors. The challenge arises when employees hear the company say, "Health care costs more because of people who don't have a healthy lifestyle." Employees may look around to see who is smoking or overweight or "too busy" to exercise, and they may be tempted to blame those coworkers rather than looking for ways to improve their own health.

The solution is careful definition of the benefits in wellness messages. Messages should emphasize concern for employees, not a desire to save money. The benefits should describe how good health affects employees personally. Feeling better and living longer are more motivating and positive than cost savings. Finally, rewards for group (not individual) health improvements can inspire employees to encourage one another.

Adapted from Linda Wasmer Andrews, "Defusing the Discontent," *HRMagazine*, December 2003, 82.

Audience Benefits or Bottom Line?

features your restaurant offered, you could appeal to one or more of the following subgroups:

Subgroup	Features to meet the subgroup's needs
People who work outside the home	A quick lunch; a relaxing place to take clients or colleagues
Parents with small children	High chairs, child-size portions, and things to keep the kids entertained while they wait for their order
People who eat out a lot	Variety both in food and in decor
People on tight budgets	Economical food; a place where they don't need to tip (cafeteria or fast food)
People on special diets	Low-sodium and low-carb dishes; vegetarian food; kosher food
People to whom eating out is part of an evening's entertainment	Music or a floor show; elegant surroundings; reservations so they can get to a show or event after dinner; late hours so they can come to dinner after a show or game

To develop your benefits, think about the details of each one. If your selling point is your relaxing atmosphere, think about the specific details that make the restaurant relaxing. If your strong point is elegant dining, think about all the details that contribute to that elegance. Sometimes you may think of features that do not meet any particular need but are still good benefits. In a sales letter for a restaurant, you might also want to mention the nonsmoking section, your free coatroom, the fact that you are close to a freeway or offer free parking or a drive-up window, and how fast your service is.

Whenever you're communicating with customers or clients about features that are not unique to your organization, it's wise to present both benefits of the features themselves and benefits of dealing with your company. If you talk about the benefits of dining in a relaxed atmosphere but don't mention your own restaurant, people may go somewhere else!

3. Show how the audience can meet their needs with the features of the policy or product.

Features alone rarely motivate people. Instead, link the feature to the audience's needs—and provide details to make the benefit vivid.

Weak: We have placemats with riddles.

Better: Answering all the riddles on Monical's special placemats will keep the kids happy till your pizza comes. If they don't have time to finish (and they may not, since your pizza will be ready so quickly), just take the riddles home—or answer them on your next visit.

Make your benefits specific.

Weak: You get quick service.

Better: If you only have an hour for lunch, try our Business Buffet. Within minutes, you can choose from a variety of main dishes, vegetables, and a make-your-own-sandwich-and-salad bar. You'll have a lunch that's as light or filling as you want, with time to enjoy it—and still be back to the office on time.

Audience Benefits Work

Appropriate audience benefits work so well that organizations spend much time and money identifying them and then developing them. Procter & Gamble studies customers' cleaning processes to promote its industrial cleaners. After observing launderers at the Millennium Hotel in Cincinnati, P&G researchers suggested cutting the products used from five to two, thus shortening the hotel's washing machine cycle five to seven minutes and reducing laundry wear on the linens from 4% to 1%. After observing staff at Wendy's, P&G calculated exactly how much product was needed to clean a table and then found a nozzle that would deliver exactly that much in one spritz.[29]

Other organizations are also paying attention to their audience benefits:

- State governments are offering incentives to attract teachers for disciplines experiencing teacher shortages, especially physics, chemistry, and mathematics. Those incentives include scholarships to instate students who will commit to teaching in the state and payment of student loans after the required years of teaching.[30]
- In the competition to acquire new customers, banks are offering college students gifts such as plane tickets, iPods, and lava lamps.[31]
- To improve customer service, offshore call centers are offering top agents benefits such as small electronics like iPods, cash prizes, and scholarships. One company has an annual Oscar-like ceremony where top workers are honored in front of thousands of employees and their families.[32]
- Hotels study which benefits are worth the money, and which are not. Holiday Inn keeps restaurants and bars in all their hotels, even though they are not money makers, but does not have bellhops. Staybridge Suites cleans less often but has "Sundowner receptions" which give guests a free meal and a chance to socialize.[33]

They Looked at the Audience and Saw Themselves

Before a bank took a survey of its customers, employees were asked to describe the bank's typical customer.

The CEO answered: "About 60, upper-income, community leader." The middle managers said: "About 40, with grown children. On the way up; good, solid citizen." The tellers said: "Twenties or thirties, newly married, just starting out. Lots of energy and drive."

According to the survey, the typical customer was in the mid-30s, had been married a few years, earned $20,000 a year, had 1½ cars and 2 children.

People looked at customers but saw only themselves.

Adapted from Ray Considine and Murray Raphel, *The Great Brain Robbery* (Pasadena, CA: The Great Brain Robbery, 1982), 68–69.

Writing or Speaking to Multiple Audiences with Different Needs

Many business and administrative messages go not to a single person but to a larger audience. When the members of your audience share the same interests and the same level of knowledge, you can use the principles outlined above for individual readers or for members of homogeneous groups. But often different members of the audience have different needs.

Researcher Rachel Spilka has shown that talking to readers both inside and outside the organization helped corporate engineers adapt their documents successfully. Talking to readers and reviewers helped writers involve readers in the planning process, understand the social and political relationships among readers, and negotiate conflicts orally rather than depending solely on the document. These writers were then able to think about content as well as about organization and style, appeal to common grounds (such as reducing waste or increasing productivity) that several readers shared, and reduce the number of revisions needed before documents were approved.[34]

When it is not possible to meet everyone's needs, meet the needs of gatekeepers and decision makers first.

Content and choice of details

- Provide an overview or executive summary for readers who want just the main points.

- In the body of the document, provide enough detail for decision makers and for anyone else who could veto your proposal.
- If the decision makers don't need details that other audiences will want, provide those details in appendixes—statistical tabulations, earlier reports, and so forth.

Organizing the document

- Use headings and a table of contents so readers can turn to the portions that interest them.
- Organize your message based on the decision makers' attitudes toward it.

Level of formality

- Avoid personal pronouns. *You* ceases to have a specific meaning when several different audiences use a document.
- If both internal and external audiences will use a document, use a slightly more formal style than you would in an internal document.
- Use a more formal style when you write to international audiences.

Use of technical terms and theory

- In the body of the document, assume the degree of knowledge that decision makers will have.
- Put background information and theory under separate headings. Then readers can use the headings and the table of contents to read or skip these sections, as their knowledge dictates.
- If decision makers will have more knowledge than other audiences, provide a glossary of terms. Early in the document, let readers know that the glossary exists.

Summary of Key Points

- The **primary audience** will make a decision or act on the basis of your message. The **secondary audience** may be asked by the primary audience to comment on your message or to implement your ideas after they've been approved. The **auxiliary audience** encounters the message but does not have to interact with it. A **gatekeeper** controls whether the message gets to the primary audience. A **watchdog audience** has political, social, or economic power and may base future actions on its evaluation of your message.
- Common sense and empathy are crucial to good audience analysis.
- A communication channel is the means by which you convey your message to your audience.
- The following questions provide a framework for audience analysis:
  1. What will the audience's initial reaction be to the message?
  2. How much information does the audience need?
  3. What obstacles must you overcome?
  4. What positive aspects can you emphasize?
  5. What expectations does the audience have about the appropriate language, organization, and format for messages?
  6. How will the audience use the document?

- **Audience benefits** are advantages that the audience gets by using your services, buying your products, following your policies, or adopting your ideas. Benefits can exist for policies and ideas as well as for goods and services.
- Good benefits are adapted to the audience, based on **intrinsic** rather than **extrinsic motivators,** supported by clear logic and explained in adequate detail, and phrased in you-attitude. Extrinsic benefits simply aren't available to reward every desired behavior; further, they reduce the satisfaction in doing something for its own sake.
- To create audience benefits,
  1. Identify the feelings, fears, and needs that may motivate your audience.
  2. Identify the features of your product or policy that could meet the needs you've identified.
  3. Show how the audience can meet their needs with the features of the policy or product.
- When you write to multiple audiences, use the primary audience to determine level of detail, organization, level of formality, and use of technical terms and theory.

CHAPTER 2   # Exercises and Problems

2.1   Reviewing the Chapter

1. Who are the five different audiences your message may need to address? (LO 1)
2. What are some characteristics to consider when analyzing individuals? (LO 1)
3. What are some characteristics to consider when analyzing groups? (LO 1)
4. What are some questions to consider when analyzing organizational culture? (LO 1)
5. What is a discourse community? Why will discourse communities be important in your career? (LO 1)
6. What are standard business communication channels? (LO 2)

7. What kinds of electronic channels seem most useful to you? Why? (LO 2)
8. What are considerations to keep in mind when selecting channels? (LO 2)
9. What are 12 questions to ask when analyzing your audience? (LO 3)
10. What are four characteristics of good audience benefits? (LO 4)
11. What are three ways to identify and develop audience benefits? (LO 4)
12. What are considerations to keep in mind when addressing multiple audiences? (LO 3)

2.2   Reviewing Grammar

Good audience analysis requires careful use of pronouns. Review your skills with pronoun usage by doing grammar exercise B.5, Appendix B.

2.3   Identifying Audiences

In each of the following situations, label the audiences as gatekeeper, primary, secondary, auxiliary, or watchdog:

1. Kent, Carol, and Jose are planning to start a Web site design business. However, before they can get started, they need money. They have developed a business plan and are getting ready to seek funds from financial institutions for starting their small business.

2. Barbara's boss asked her to write a direct mail letter to potential customers about the advantages of becoming a preferred member of their agency's travel club. The letter will go to all customers of the agency who are over 65 years old.

3. Paul works for the mayor's office in a big city. As part of a citywide cost-cutting measure, a blue-ribbon panel has recommended requiring employees who work more than 40 hours in a week to take compensatory time off rather than being paid overtime. The only exceptions will be the police and fire departments. The mayor asks Paul to prepare a proposal for the city council, which will vote on whether to implement the change. Before they vote, council members will hear from (1) citizens, who will have an opportunity to read the proposal and communicate their opinions to the city council; (2) mayors' offices in other cities, who may be asked about their experiences; (3) union representatives, who may be concerned about the reduction in income that will occur if the proposal is implemented; (4) department heads, whose ability to schedule work might be limited if the proposal passes; and (5) the blue-ribbon panel and good-government lobbying groups. Council members come up for reelection in six months.

4. Many customers have written complaint letters to Paws Food Inc. about their pets becoming ill after eating the company's pet foods. The CEO asked Rebecca, who is in charge of public relations, to draft a press release for newspapers notifying customers about the tainted food. The release should also encourage pet owners to avoid feeding their animals canned food until the issue is resolved.

2.4   Choosing a Channel to Reach a Specific Audience

Suppose that your business, government agency, or non-profit group had a product, service, or program targeted for each of the following audiences. What would be the best channel(s) to reach people in that group in your city? Would that channel reach all group members?

a. Renters.
b. African-American owners of small businesses.
c. People who use wheelchairs.
d. Teenagers who work part-time while attending school.
e. Competitive athletes.
f. Parents whose children play soccer.
g. Hispanics.
h. People willing to work part-time.
i. Financial planners.
j. Hunters.

2.5   Identifying and Developing Audience Benefits

Listed here are several things an organization might like its employees to do:

1. Use less paper.
2. Attend a brown-bag lunch to discuss ways to improve products or services.
3. Become more physically fit.
4. Volunteer for community organizations.
5. Ease a new hire's transition into the unit.

As your instructor directs,

a. Identify the motives or needs that might be met by each of the activities.
b. Take each need or motive and develop it as an audience benefit in a full paragraph. Use additional paragraphs for the other needs met by the activity. Remember to use you-attitude!

2.6   Identifying Objections and Audience Benefits

Think of an organization you know something about, and answer the following questions for it:

1. Your organization is thinking about creating a training wiki. What objections might people have? What benefits could wikis offer your organization? Who would be the easiest to convince? Who would be the hardest?

2. The advisory council at Midwest University recommends that business communication students have a three-month internship with an organization to get a feel for how communication functions in the workplace. What objections might people in your organization have to bringing in interns? What benefits might your organization receive? Who

would be easiest to convince? Who would be the hardest?

3. Your organization is thinking of outsourcing its customer service department. Contractors in another country would handle phone calls and e-mail from customers with questions and problems. What fears or objections might people have? What benefits might your organization receive? Who would be easiest to convince? Who would be hardest?

As your instructor directs,

a. Share your answers orally with a small group of students.

b. Present your answers in an oral presentation to the class.

c. Write a paragraph developing the best audience benefit you identified. Remember to use you-attitude.

2.7 Identifying and Developing Audience Benefits for Different Audiences

Assume that you want to encourage people to do one of the activities listed below:

1. Becoming more physically fit.
   Audiences: College students on the job market.
   Workers whose jobs require heavy lifting.
   Sedentary workers.
   People diagnosed as having high blood pressure.
   Managers who travel frequently on business.
   Older workers.

2. Getting advice about interior decorating.
   Audiences: Young people with little money to spend.
   Parents with small children.
   People upgrading or adding to their furnishings.
   Older people moving from singlefamily homes into smaller apartments or condominiums.
   Builders furnishing model homes.

3. Getting advice on investment strategies.
   Audiences: New college graduates.
   People earning more than $100,000 annually.
   Treasurers of religious congregations.
   Parents with small children.
   People within 10 years of retirement.

4. Gardening.
   Audiences: People with small children.
   People in apartments.
   People concerned about reducing pesticide use.
   People on tight budgets.
   Retirees.
   Teenagers.

5. Buying a laptop computer.
   Audiences: College students.
   Financial planners who visit clients at home.
   Sales representatives who travel constantly.
   People who make PowerPoint presentations.

6. Teaching adults to read.
   Audiences: Retired workers.
   Business people.
   Students who want to become teachers.
   High school and college students.
   People concerned about poverty.

7. Vacationing at a luxury hotel.
   Audiences: Stressed-out people who want to relax.
   Tourists who like to sight see and absorb the local culture.
   Business people who want to stay in touch with the office even on vacation.
   Parents with small children.
   Weekend athletes who want to have fun.

As your instructor directs,

a. Identify needs that you could meet for the audiences listed here. In addition to needs that several audiences share, identify at least one need that would be particularly important to each group.

b. Identify a product or service that could meet each need.

c. Write a paragraph or two of audience benefits for each product or service. Remember to use you-attitude.

2.8   Addressing Your Audience's Need for Information

"Tell me about yourself."

This may be the most popular opening question of job interviews, but it's also a question that you'll encounter in nearly any social situation when you meet someone new. Although the question may be the same, the answer you give will change based upon the rhetorical situation: the audience, purpose, and context of the question.

For each of the following situations in a–f, ask yourself these questions to help create a good response:

- How will the audience react to your answer? Will the audience see the message as important? What information will you need to include in your answer to keep their attention?

- How will the audience use your answer? Why is the audience asking the question? What information is relevant to the audience and what information can you leave out?

- How much information does the audience need? What information do they already know about you? What level of detail do they need?

- What are the audience's expectations about your answer? What are the appropriate word choices and

tone for your answer? What topics should you avoid (at least for now)?

- What are the physical conditions that will affect your answer? Where are you (e.g., Are you outside, in a noisy room, chatting via IM, on the phone)? How much time do you have to give your response?

Write your response to the statement "Tell me about yourself." Assume that the question is being asked by

a. A recruiter at a career fair in your university's auditorium.

b. A recruiter in a job interview in a small interview or conference room.

c. An attractive male or female at a popular weekend nightspot.

d. Your instructor on the first day of class.

e. Your new roommate on your first day in the dormitory.

f. The new religious leader after services at your place of worship.

2.9   Analyzing Individuals

The Myers-Briggs Type Indicator is a test that uses four pairs of personality traits to describe how people behave. For example, someone with an ESTJ (Extraverted, Sensing, Thinking, Judging) personality probably notices details, is logical and orderly, and makes quick decisions.

Take the free The Mental Muscle Diagram Indicator, a personality test based upon the Myers-Briggs Type Indicator®. (You can find the test at http://www.teamtechnology.co.uk/mmdi-re/mmdi-re.htm.)

Read about your personality type and consider how accurate the description may be. Print your results.

As your instructor directs,

- Share your results orally with a small group of students and discuss how accurately the Type

Indicator describes you. Identify some of the differences among your personality types and consider how the differences would affect efforts to collaborate on projects.

- Identify other students in the classroom with the same combination of personality traits. Create a brief oral presentation to the class that describes your Type Indicator and explains how the pros and cons of your personality will affect group dynamics in collaborative work.

- Write a brief memo to your instructor describing your results, assessing how well the results reflect your personality, and suggesting how your personality traits might affect your work in class and in the workplace.

2.10   Announcing Holiday Diversity

To better respect the religious and ethnic diversity of your employees, your organization will now allow employees to take any 10 days off during the year. Any religious, ethnic, or cultural holiday is acceptable. (Someone who wants to take off Cinco de Mayo or Bastille Day can do so.) As Vice President for Human Resources, you need to announce the policy.

Pick a specific organization you know something about, and answer the following questions about it:

1. What religious and ethnic groups do the employees come from?

2. How much do various groups know about each others' holidays?

3. What is the general climate for religious and ethnic tolerance? Should the message have a secondary purpose of educating people about less-common holidays?

4. Is the organization open every day of the year, or will it be closed on some holidays (e.g., Christmas, New Year's Day)? If an employee chooses to work on a day when offices or factories are closed, what should he or she do? Work at home? Get a key? (How? From whom?) What kinds of tasks could a person working alone do most profitably?

2.11   Announcing a New Employee Benefit

Your company has decided to pay employees for doing charity work. Employees can spend one hour working with a charitable or nonprofit group for every 40 hours they work. As Vice President of Human Resources, you need to announce this new program.

Pick a specific organization you know something about, and answer the following questions about it:

1. What proportion of the employees are already involved in volunteer work?

2. Is community service or "giving back" consistent with the organization's corporate mission?

3. Some employees won't be able or won't want to participate. What is the benefit for them in working for a company that has such a program?

4. Will promoting community participation help the organization attract and retain workers?

2.12   Announcing a Tuition Reimbursement Program

Assume that your organization has decided to reimburse workers for tuition and fees for job-related courses. As Director of Education and Training, you want to write a memo about the program to answer employees' questions and build support for the program. Pick a specific organization that you know something about, and answer the following questions about it.

1. What do people do on the job? What courses or degrees could help them do their current jobs even better?

2. How much education do people already have? How do they feel about formal schooling?

3. How busy are employees? Will most have time to take classes and study in addition to working 40 hours a week (or more)?

4. Is it realistic to think that people who get more education would get higher salaries? Or is money for increases limited? Is it reasonable to think that most people could be promoted? Or does the organization have many more low-level than high-level jobs?

5. What hassles do people encounter in their daily work? What could be done to alleviate one or more of those hassles? If the work environment were less stressful, how would their lives be easier or more pleasant?

6. How much loyalty do employees have to this particular organization? Is it "just a job," or do they care about the welfare of the organization?

7. How competitive is the job market? How easy is it for the organization to find and retain qualified employees?

8. Is knowledge needed to do the job changing, or is knowledge learned five or ten years ago still up-to-date?

9. How competitive is the economic market? Is this company doing well financially? Can its customers or clients easily go somewhere else? Is it a government agency dependent on tax dollars for funding? What about the current situation makes this an especially good time to hone the skills of the employees you have?

2.13   Sending a Question to a Web Site

Send a question or other message that calls for a response to a Web site. You could

- Ask a question about a product.
- Apply for an internship or a job (assuming you'd really like to work there).
- Ask for information about an internship or a job.
- Ask a question about an organization or a candidate before you donate money or volunteer.
- Offer to volunteer for an organization or a candidate. You can offer to do something small and

one-time (e.g., spend an afternoon stuffing envelopes, put up a yard sign), or you can, if you want to, offer to do something more time-consuming or even ongoing.

Pick a specific organization you might use, and answer the following questions about it:

1. Does the organization ask for questions or offers? Or will yours come out of the blue?

2. How difficult will it be for the organization to supply the information you're asking for or to do what you're asking it to do? If you're applying for an internship or offering to volunteer, what skills can you offer? How much competition do you have?

3. What can you do to build your own credibility so that the organization takes your question or request seriously?

2.14   Analyzing an Organization's Culture

W. L. Gore & Associates, the makers of GORE-TEX®, was ranked the fifth-best company to work for by *Fortune* magazine in 2006. While the company is famous for high-quality products like fabric, guitar strings, and even dental floss, much of the company's success lies in its innovative corporate structure. Instead of creating a traditional hierarchy, Gore uses a "flat lattice" organization in which every employee can (and does) communicate with everyone else.

Visit the company's Web site at http://www.gore.com/en_xx/aboutus/culture/index.html.

- What does the term "flat lattice" organization mean? Why has W. L. Gore & Associates chosen to structure the company this way?

- Identify a company that you would like to work for or that is well known in your field of study. Visit the company's Web site and research its corporate culture.

- What information are you able to learn about your target company from its Web site text?

- What type of images does the company use on its Web site? Do these support the information it uses to describe itself and its culture?

- What type of organizational structure does your target company use?

- What other information is available about the culture at your target company?

- To find information about a company's culture, try visiting business web sites like www.inc.com, www.fastcompany.com, or www.businessweek.com. You can also type the company name and "opinion" into a search engine to find unofficial reports of corporate culture.

2.15   Persuading Students to Use Credit Cards Responsibly

Many college students carry high balances on credit cards, in addition to student and car loans. You want to remind students on your campus to use credit cards responsibly.

Answer the following questions about students on your campus:

1. What socioeconomic groups do students on your campus come from?

2. Do students on your campus frequently receive credit card solicitations in the mail? Do groups set up tables or booths inviting students to apply for credit cards?

3. What resources exist on campus or in town for people who need emergency funds? For people who are overextended financially?

4. What channel will best reach students on your campus?

5. What tone will work best to reach the students who are overextended and really need to read the document?

2.16   Analyzing Your Boss

What goals matter most to your boss? What pressures is he or she under? Does your boss want details or just the big picture? What are his or her pet peeves? Is punctuality more important than creativity and thoroughness, or vice versa? If you have a question, would your boss rather answer in person, by e-mail, or by phone? Is he or she more approachable in the morning or the afternoon?

As your instructor directs,

a. Share your answers orally with a small group of students.

b. Present your answers in an oral presentation to the class.

c. Present your answers in a memo to your instructor.

d. Share your answers with a small group of students and write a joint memo reporting the similarities and differences you found.

2.17   Analyzing Your Co-Workers

What do your co-workers do? What hassles and challenges do they face? To what extent do their lives outside work affect their responses to work situations? What do your co-workers value? What are their pet peeves? How committed are they to organizational goals? How satisfying do they find their jobs? Are the people you work with quite similar to each other, or do they differ from each other? How?

As your instructor directs,

a. Share your answers orally with a small group of students.

b. Present your answers in an oral presentation to the class.

c. Present your answers in a memo to your instructor.

d. Share your answers with a small group of students and write a joint memo reporting the similarities and differences you found.

2.18   Analyzing the Audiences of Non-Commercial Web Pages

Analyze the implied audiences of two Web pages of two non-commercial organizations with the same purpose (combating hunger, improving health, influencing the political process, etc.). You could pick the home pages of the national organization and a local affiliate, or the home pages of two separate organizations working toward the same general goal.

Answer the following questions:

• Do the pages work equally well for surfers and for people who have reached the page deliberately?

• Possible audiences include current and potential volunteers, donors, clients, and employees. Do the pages provide material for each audience? Is the material useful? Complete? Up-to-date? Does new material encourage people to return?

• What assumptions about audiences do content and visuals suggest?

• Can you think of ways that the pages could better serve their audiences?

As your instructor directs,

a. Share your results orally with a small group of students.

b. Present your results in an oral presentation to the class.

c. Present your results in a memo to your instructor. Attach copies of the Web pages.

d. Share your results with a small group of students, and write a joint memo reporting the similarities and differences you found.

e. Post your results in an e-mail message to the class. Provide links to the two Web pages.

2.19   Analyzing an Organization's Culture

Interview several people about the culture of their organization. Possible organizations include

• Businesses, government agencies, and nonprofit organizations.

• Sports teams.

• Sororities, fraternities, and other social groups.

• Churches, mosques, synagogues, and temples.

• Departments in a community college, college, or university.

To learn about the corporate culture, use your own experiences, interviews with employees, published sources, or the Web. Interview questions include the following:

• Tell me about someone in this organization you admire. Why is he or she successful?

• Tell me about someone who failed in this organization. What did he or she do wrong?

• What ceremonies and rituals does this organization have? Why are they important?

- Why would someone join this group rather than a competitor?

To research corporate culture on the Web, check

- The company's site (usually under "about XYZ" or "working at XYZ"). In addition to explicit descriptions of corporate culture, check the mission and values statements and pages about employee benefits and regulations.
- Independent sites, especially job sites. Some job sites give information about corporate cultures. Some post company recruiting videos. (What kind of employees does the company seem to be looking for?)
- Opposition sites put up by unhappy employees and customers. To find these in a search engine, type in the company name and "opinion."

- Articles published about the company on www.inc.com, www.fastcompany.com, www.businessweek.com, or other business Web sites.

As your instructor directs,

a. Share your results orally with a small group of students.
b. Present your results orally to the class.
c. Present your results in a memo to your instructor.
d. Share your results with a small group of students, and write a joint memo reporting the similarities and differences you found.

2.20   Analyzing a Discourse Community

Analyze the way a group you are part of uses language. Possible groups include

- Work teams.
- Sports teams.
- Sororities, fraternities, and other social groups.
- Churches, mosques, synagogues, and temples.
- Geographic or ethnic groups.
- Groups of friends.

Questions to ask include the following:

- What specialized terms might not be known to outsiders?
- What topics do members talk or write about? What topics are considered unimportant or improper?
- What channels do members use to convey messages?
- What forms of language do members use to build goodwill? to demonstrate competence or superiority?

- What strategies or kinds of proof are convincing to members?
- What formats, conventions, or rules do members expect messages to follow?
- What are some nonverbal ways members communicate?

As your instructor directs,

a. Share your results orally with a small group of students.
b. Present your results in an oral presentation to the class.
c. Present your results in a memo to your instructor.
d. Share your results with a small group of students, and write a joint memo reporting the similarities and differences you found.

2.21   Mosaic Case

At today's staff meeting, Yvonne informed Sarah, who is in charge of communications for the online sector of Mosaic, that a recent study showed 20% of all Internet shopping is done by senior citizens.

"Part of the reason," noted Yvonne "is that this group of baby boomers makes up such a large amount of the population. And they don't want to get left behind," she said while making quote marks in the air with her index and middle fingers around the words *left behind.* "They are rapidly adapting to become savvy Internet shoppers."

"But the Web site isn't adapted to them," replied Sarah. "Currently, there are sections of the Web site that

offer product groupings by type. And we have product suggestion sections targeted for kids; college students; young, urban professionals; and families. But there is no area directly targeting senior citizens."

"Exactly! Without catering to their needs, we could potentially be losing hundreds of thousands of customers," said Yvonne.

"You're right. This is a huge opportunity that needs immediate attention. I'll have Trey brainstorm some initial ideas of how to target senior citizens with Mosaic's Web site. In fact, we could even have a whole section that is just for senior citizens to click on from Mosaic's homepage. The furniture showcased there could be adapted to their specific needs."

Take Trey's communication task of doing an audience analysis for senior citizens. Begin by identifying the feelings, fears, and needs that motivate this audience to purchase products online at Mosaic. What kinds of products would they buy? How would their purchases differ from those of other audiences already targeted by Mosaic?

Identify how the Web site could meet the needs of this particular audience. In addition, what are some Web site design choices that would be appropriate for this audience?

Building Goodwill

Learning Objectives

After studying this chapter, you will know how to:

1 Create you-attitude.

2 Create positive emphasis.

3 Improve tone in business communications.

4 Reduce bias in business communications.

Karma Capitalism

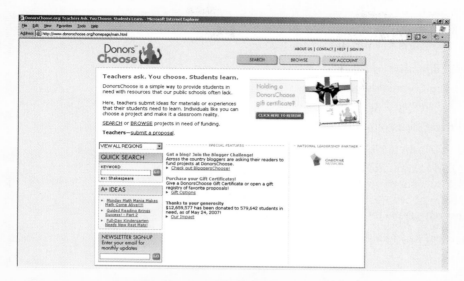

When Crate & Barrel, the upscale furniture retailer, set out to support education with donations, they didn't just give money to needy schools. Instead, they sent out coupons in their mailers inviting their customers to use the DonorsChoose.org Web site to decide how and where Crate & Barrel would donate its money.

The response? Customers loved the program. Not only did the coupons inspire a high rate of customer involvement—11% of the coupons were redeemed, compared to 2% in a normal mass mailing—but the coupons also improved customers' perceptions of the company: 75% of the customers who used the DonorsChoose coupons said they now considered Crate & Barrel a company with a positive attitude toward the community, while 82% said they'd be more likely to buy the company's products in the future.

So, is winning everything? Is greed good? In the 1980s and 1990s, when business managers liked to quote Sun Tzu's ancient Chinese classic

> *"You-attitude and goodwill involve showing your audience that you understand and care about their needs, concerns, and problems."*

The Art of War, those ideas seemed to describe the most successful way to run an organization. Today, when business scandals and the increasingly complex demands of a globalized economy dominate the headlines, people are finding good business ideas in another ancient Asian book: the *Bhagvad Gita*.

This "new" ancient wisdom isn't just about business trends—it's good advice. In the global marketplace, no organization exists in a vacuum and no one works alone: we all have business partners and customers we rely on for information, goods and services, and revenue. In "Karma Capitalism," successful businesses focus on creating relationships that build success. You-attitude and goodwill involve showing your audience that you understand and care about their needs, concerns, and problems. If you can demonstrate to your audience that you're interested in communicating about things they care about, in ways that they appreciate, they'll respond by paying attention to you, your message, your product, and your organization.

Sources: Pete Engardio, "Karma Capitalism," *BusinessWeek*, October 30, 2006, 84–91; and Emily Steel, "Novel Program Blends Charity and Marketing," *Wall Street Journal*, December 20, 2006, B1, B5; www.donorschoose.org.

Chapter Outline

You-Attitude

- How to Create You-Attitude
- You-Attitude Beyond the Sentence Level

Positive Emphasis

- How to Create Positive Emphasis
- How to Check Positive Emphasis

Tone, Power, and Politeness

Reducing Bias in Business Communication

- Making Language Nonsexist
- Making Language Nonracist and Nonagist
- Talking about People with Disabilities and Diseases
- Choosing Bias-Free Photos and Illustrations

Summary of Key Points

Goodwill smooths the challenges of business and administration. Companies have long been aware that treating customers well pays off in more sales and higher profits. Linda Thaler and Robin Koval built The Kaplan Thaler Group into an advertising agency with nearly $1 billion in billings using goodwill, you-attitude, and positive tone.[1] General Motors has found that customers who get good service from their dealers are five times more likely to buy another GM car than those who had poor service.[2] Government organizations now realize that they need citizen support—goodwill—to receive funding.

Goodwill is important internally as well as externally. More and more organizations are realizing that treating employees well is financially wise as well as ethically sound. Happy employees create less staff turnover, thus reducing hiring and training costs. A University of Pennsylvania study of 3,000 companies found that investing 10% of revenue on capital improvement boosted company productivity 3.9%, but spending the money on employees increased productivity 8.5%, or more than twice as much.[3]

You-attitude, positive emphasis, and bias-free language are three ways to help build goodwill. Messages that show you-attitude use the audience point of view, not the writer's or speaker's. Positive emphasis means focusing on the positive rather than the negative aspects of a situation. Bias-free language does not discriminate against people on the basis of sex, physical condition, race, age, or any other category. All three help you achieve your purposes and make your messages friendlier, more persuasive, more professional, and more humane. They suggest that you care not just about money but also about the needs and interests of your customers and employees.

You-Attitude

Putting what you want to say in you-attitude is a crucial step both in thinking about your audience's needs and in communicating your concern to your audience.

How to Create You-Attitude

You-attitude is a style of communication that looks at things from the audience's point of view, emphasizing what the audience wants to know, respecting the audience's intelligence, and protecting the audience's ego.

To apply you-attitude, use the following five techniques:

1. **Talk about the audience, not about yourself.**
2. **Refer to the audience's request or order specifically.**
3. **Don't talk about feelings, except to congratulate or offer sympathy.**
4. **In positive situations, use *you* more often than *I*. Use *we* when it includes the audience.**
5. **In negative situations, avoid the word *you*. Protect the audience's ego. Use passive verbs and impersonal expressions to avoid assigning blame.**

Revisions for you-attitude do not change the basic meaning of the sentence. However, revising for you-attitude often makes sentences longer because the revision is more specific and has more information. Long sentences need not be wordy. **Wordiness** means having more words than the meaning requires. We can add information and still keep the writing concise.

1. Talk about the audience, not about yourself.

Your audience wants to know how they benefit or are affected. When you provide this information, you make your message more complete and more interesting.

Lacks you-attitude:	I have negotiated an agreement with Apex Rent-a-Car that gives you a discount on rental cars.
You-attitude:	As a Sunstrand employee, you can now get a 20% discount when you rent a car from Apex.

Any sentence that focuses on the communicator's work or generosity lacks you-attitude, even if the sentence contains the word *you*. Instead of focusing on what you are giving, focus on what your audience can now do. To do that, you may need to change the grammatical subject.

Lacks you-attitude:	We are shipping your order of September 21 this afternoon.
You-attitude:	The two dozen Corning Ware starter sets you ordered will be shipped this afternoon and should reach you by September 28.

Emphasize what the audience wants to know. Your audience is less interested in when you shipped the order than in when it will arrive. Note that the phrase "should reach you by" leaves room for variations in delivery schedules. If you can't be exact, give your audience the information you do have: "A UPS shipment from California to Texas normally takes three days." If you have absolutely no idea, give your audience the name of the carrier, so then he or she knows whom to contact if the order doesn't arrive promptly. You might also provide the tracking number.

2. Refer to the customer's request or order specifically.

Refer to the customer's request, order, or policy specifically, not as a generic *your order* or *your policy*. If your customer is an individual or a small business, it's friendly to specify the content of the order. If you're dealing with a company with which you do a great deal of business, give the invoice or purchase order number.

Lacks you-attitude:	Your order . . .
You-attitude (to individual):	The desk chair you ordered . . .
You-attitude (to a large store):	Your invoice #783329 . . .

Exercising Empathy for Employees and Customers

Although the concept of happy employees leading to happy customers is not new, it is experiencing a resurgence in many different industries. For example, call centers are allowing seasoned employees to work at home while a grocery chain is giving employees a profit-sharing plan that rewards them for excellent customer service.

Companies are finding creative ways to help employees identify with customers. USAA, an insurance agency for the military, provides new employees with MREs (meals ready to eat) during orientation so they will better understand the lifestyle of the members they serve. Cabela's, an outdoor outfitter, encourages employees to use products they sell by loaning items free of charge in exchange for writing reviews on a company system. The loans are good perks for employees, and they help staff understand the issues customers may have with the products. At Four Seasons Hotels, employees receive free overnight stays and meals at the hotel for themselves and a guest. They gain a customer's perspective on the hotel, but they also grade the hotel on various services. The companies exercising empathy for employees and customers believe their customer service helps set them apart from other organizations.

Have you experienced empathy from a customer service representative recently? What did he or she do to build goodwill?

Adapted from Jena McGregor, "Customer Service Champs," *BusinessWeek*, March 5, 2007, 52.

3. Don't talk about feelings, except to congratulate or offer sympathy.

In most business situations, your feelings are irrelevant and should be omitted.

Lacks you-attitude:	We are happy to extend you a credit line of $5,000.
You-attitude:	You can now charge up to $5,000 on your American Express card.

Your audience doesn't care whether you're happy, bored stiff at granting a routine application, or worried about granting so much to someone who barely qualifies. All your audience cares about is the situation from their point of view.

It *is* appropriate to talk about your own emotions in a message of congratulations or condolence.

You-attitude:	Congratulations on your promotion to district manager! I was really pleased to read about it.

In internal e-mails, it may be appropriate to comment that a project has been gratifying or frustrating. In the letter of transmittal that accompanies a report, it is permissible to talk about positive feelings about doing the work. But even other audiences in your own organization are primarily interested in their own concerns, not in your feelings.

Don't talk about your audience's feelings, either. It's distancing to have others tell us how we feel—especially if they are wrong.

Lacks you-attitude:	You'll be happy to hear that Open Grip Walkway Channels meet OSHA requirements.
You-attitude:	Open Grip Walkway Channels meet OSHA requirements.

Maybe the audience expects that anything you sell would meet government regulations (OSHA—the Occupational Safety and Health Administration—is a federal agency). The audience may even be disappointed if they expected higher standards. Simply explain the situation or describe a product's features; don't predict the audience's response.

When you have good news, simply give the good news.

Lacks you-attitude:	You'll be happy to hear that your scholarship has been renewed.
You-attitude:	Congratulations! Your scholarship has been renewed.

4. In positive situations, use *you* more often than *I*. Use *we* when it includes the audience.

Talk about the audience, not you or your company.

Lacks you-attitude:	We provide health insurance to all employees.
You-attitude:	You receive health insurance as a full-time Procter & Gamble employee.

Most readers are tolerant of the word *I* in e-mail messages, which seem like conversation. But edit paper documents to use *I* rarely if at all. *I* suggests that you're concerned about personal issues, not about the organization's problems, needs, and opportunities. *We* works well when it includes the reader. Avoid *we* if it excludes the reader (as it would in a letter to a customer or supplier or as it might in a memo about what *we* in management want *you* to do).

5. In negative situations, avoid the word *you*. Protect your audience's ego. Use passive verbs and impersonal expressions to avoid assigning blame.

When you report bad news or limitations, use a noun for a group of which your audience is a part instead of *you* so people don't feel that they're singled out for bad news.

Lacks you-attitude:	You must get approval from the director before you publish any articles or memoirs based on your work in the agency.
You-attitude:	Agency personnel must get approval from the director to publish any articles or memoirs based on their work at the agency.

Use passive verbs and impersonal expressions to avoid blaming people. **Passive verbs** describe the action performed on something, without necessarily saying who did it. (See Chapter 4 ➡ for a full discussion of passive verbs.) **Impersonal expressions** omit people and talk only about things. In most cases, active verbs are better. But when your audience is at fault, passive verbs may be useful to avoid assigning blame.

Normally, communication is most lively when it's about people—and most interesting to audiences when it's about them. When you have to report a mistake or bad news, however, you can protect your audience's ego by using an impersonal expression, one in which things, not people, do the acting.

Lacks you-attitude:	You made no allowance for inflation in your estimate.
You-attitude (passive):	No allowance for inflation has been made in this estimate.
You-attitude (impersonal):	This estimate makes no allowance for inflation.

A purist might say that impersonal expressions are illogical: An estimate, for example, is inanimate and can't "make" anything. In the pragmatic world of business writing, however, impersonal expressions help you convey criticism tactfully.

You-Attitude Beyond the Sentence Level

Good messages apply you-attitude beyond the sentence level by using content and organization as well as style to build goodwill.

To create goodwill with content,

- Be complete. When you have lots of information to give, consider putting some details in an appendix, which may be read later.
- Anticipate and answer questions your audience is likely to have.
- When you include information your audience didn't ask for, show why it is important.
- Show your audience how the subject of your message affects them.

To organize information to build goodwill,

- Put information your audience is most interested in first.
- Arrange information to meet your audience's needs, not yours.
- Use headings and lists so readers can find key points quickly.

Consider the letter in Figure 3.1. As the red marginal notes indicate, many individual sentences in this letter lack you-attitude. Fixing individual sentences could improve the letter. However, it really needs to be totally rewritten.

You-Attitude with International Audiences

When you communicate with international audiences, look at the world from their point of view.

The United States is in the middle of most of the maps sold in the United States. It isn't in the middle of maps sold elsewhere in the world.

The United States clings to a measurement system that has been abandoned by most of the world. When you write for international audiences, use the metric system.

Even pronouns and direction words need attention. *We* may not feel inclusive to readers with different assumptions and backgrounds. *Here* won't mean the same thing to a reader in Bonn as it does to one in Boulder.

Figure 3.1   A Letter Lacking You-Attitude

450 INDUSTRIAL PARK
CLEVELAND, OH 44120
(216) 555-4670
FAX: (216) 555-4672

December 11, 2008

Ms. Carol McFarland
Rollins Equipment Corporation
18438 East Night Hawk Way
Phoenix, AZ 85043-7800

Dear Ms. McFarland:

Legalistic

Not you-attitude — We are now ready to issue a check to Rollins Equipment in the amount of $14,207.02. To receive said check, you will deliver to me a release of the mechanic's liens in the amount of $14,207.02.   *Sounds dictatorial*

Lacks you-attitude

Focuses on negative — Before we can release the check, we must be satisfied that the release is in the proper form. We must insist that we be provided with a stamped original of the lien indicating the document number in the appropriate district court where it is filed. Also, either the release must be executed by an officer of Rollins Equipment, or we must be provided with a letter from an officer of Rollins Equipment authorizing another individual to execute the release.

Hard to read, remember

Please contact the undersigned so that an appointment can be scheduled for this transaction.   *Jargon*

Sincerely,

Kelly J. Pickett

Kelly J. Pickett

Figure 3.2 shows a possible revision of this letter. The revision is clearer, easier to read, and friendlier.

Positive Emphasis

Some negatives are necessary. When you have bad news to give—announcements of layoffs, product defects and recalls, price increases—straightforward negatives build credibility. (See Chapter 11 ➡ on how to present bad news.) Sometimes negatives are needed to make people take a problem seriously. In some messages, such as disciplinary notices and negative

Figure 3.2   A Letter Revised to Improve You-Attitude

SIMMONS
STRUCTURAL STEEL

450 INDUSTRIAL PARK
CLEVELAND, OH 44120
(216) 555-4670
FAX: (216) 555-4672

December 11, 2008

Ms. Carol McFarland
Rollins Equipment Corporation
18438 East Night Hawk Way
Phoenix, AZ 85043-7800

Dear Ms. McFarland:

Starts with main point from the reader's point of view

Let's clear up the lien in the Allen contract.

Focuses on what reader gets

Rollins will receive a check for $14,207.02 when you give us a release for the mechanic's lien of $14,207.02. To assure us that the release is in the proper form,

List makes it easy to see that reader needs to do two things—and that the second can be done in two ways.

1. Give us a stamped original of the lien indicating the document's district court number, and

2. Either
    a. Have an officer of Rollins Equipment sign the release
            or
    b. Give us a letter from a Rollins officer authorizing someone else to sign the release.

Call me to tell me which way is best for you. *Emphasizes reader's choice*

Sincerely,

Kelly J. Pickett

Kelly J. Pickett   *Extension number makes it easy for reader to phone.*
Extension 5318

---

performance appraisals, one of your purposes is to make the problem clear. Even here, avoid insults or attacks on your audience's integrity or sanity. Being honest about the drawbacks of a job reduces turnover.

Sometimes negatives create a "reverse psychology" that makes people look favorably at your product. German power tool manufacturer Stihl advertises that its chain saws and other tools are *not* sold by chains like Lowe's or Home Depot. Instead, the company emphasizes that its products are sold through independent retailers. While the campaign risks offending potential customers by implying that shopping at big box stores means that they don't appreciate quality, Stihl insists that its high-end products are worth the prices that are charged by specialty stores.[4] New York marketing consultant Michael Fanuele says that purity is dull; ads that emphasize only the positive are viewed suspiciously by today's consumers. He advises companies to sell their imperfections. For instance, Ragu accepted the fact that its sauce was not as thick as Prego's. It marketed its sauce to young children, most of whom do not like chunky sauces.[5]

But in most situations, it's better to be positive. Researchers Annette N. Shelby and N. Lamar Reinsch, Jr., found that business people responded more positively to positive than to negative language and were more likely to say they would act on a positively worded request.[6] Martin Seligman's research for Met Life found that optimistic salespeople sold 37% more insurance than pessimistic colleagues. As a result, Met Life began hiring optimists even when they failed to meet the company's other criteria. These "unqualified" optimists outsold pessimists 21% in their first year and 57% in the next.[7]

Positive emphasis is a way of looking at things. Is the bottle half empty or half full? You can create positive emphasis with the words, information, organization, and layout you choose.

How to Create Positive Emphasis

Create positive emphasis by using the following five techniques:

1. Avoid negative words and words with negative connotations.
2. Focus on what the audience can do rather than on limitations.
3. Justify negative information by giving a reason or linking it to an audience benefit.
4. If the negative is truly unimportant, omit it.
5. Put the negative information in the middle and present it compactly.

Choose the technique that produces the clearest, most accurate sentence.

Businesswoman Ellen Elleman creates signs to encourage positive emphasis. These signs are available in multiple languages at www.nocant.com.

Source: Julie R. Bailey, "Gahanna Resident Spreads Positive Attitude with Her Signs," *Columbus Dispatch,* July 14, 2003, B1.

1. Avoid negative words and words with negative connotations.

Figure 3.3 lists some common negative words. If you find one of these words in a draft, try to substitute a more positive word. When you must use a negative, use the *least negative* term that will convey your meaning.

The following examples show how to replace negative words with positive words.

Negative: We have failed to finish taking inventory.

Better: We haven't finished taking inventory.

Still better: We will be finished taking inventory Friday.

Negative: If you can't understand this explanation, feel free to call me.

Better: If you have further questions, just call me.

Still better: Omit the sentence.

Omit double negatives.

Negative: Never fail to back up your documents.

Better: Always back up your documents.

When you must use a negative term, use the least negative word that is accurate.

Negative: Your balance of $835 is delinquent.

Better: Your balance of $835 is past due.

Getting rid of negatives has the added benefit of making what you write easier to understand. Sentences with three or more negatives are very hard to understand.[8]

Beware of **hidden negatives:** words that are not negative in themselves but become negative in context. *But* and *however* indicate a shift, so, after a positive statement, they are negative. *I hope* and *I trust that* suggest that you aren't sure. *Patience* may sound like a virtue, but it is a necessary virtue only when things are slow. Even positives about a service or product may backfire if they suggest that in the past the service or product was bad.

Figure 3.3 Negative Words to Avoid

afraid	error	lacking	trivial
anxious	except	loss	trouble
avoid	fail		wait
bad	fault	**Some mis- words:**	weakness
careless	fear	misfortune	worry
damage	hesitate	missing	wrong
delay	ignorant	mistake	
delinquent	ignore	neglect	**Many un- words:**
deny	impossible	never	unclear
difficulty		no	unfair
	Many in- words:	not	unfortunate
Some dis- words:	inadequate	objection	unfortunately
disapprove	incomplete	problem	unpleasant
dishonest	inconvenient	reject	unreasonable
dissatisfied	insincere	sorry	unreliable
eliminate	injury	terrible	unsure

Truth Can Be Spoken in Different Ways

One Iranian told a fable of an ancient king who had an ominous dream. In the dream the king saw himself aged and afflicted, with decaying and falling teeth. Calling together his court astrologers for an interpretation, the shaken king heard the first say, "Your Majesty, I regret to tell you that the interpretation must be bad. The dream means that you will die within a year." In a rage the king threw the brash astrologer out of his court and turned to the second man.

The second astrologer said, "Your Majesty, it is good news, the very best. It means that all your programs and projects will live on after you, and all your sons and daughters will survive you." The king, who was old and knew he might die soon, nevertheless was pleased with this interpretation and richly rewarded the astrologer.

Quoted from John P. Fieg and John G. Blair, *There Is a Difference: 12 Intercultural Perspectives* (Washington, DC: Meridian House International, 1975), 83.

Negative:	I hope this is the information you wanted. [Implication: I'm not sure.]
Better:	Enclosed is a brochure about road repairs scheduled for 2007–09.
Still better:	The brochure contains a list of all roads and bridges scheduled for repair during 2007–09. Call Gwen Wong at 555-3245 for specific dates when work will start and stop and for alternate routes.
Negative:	Please be patient as we switch to the automated system. [Implication: You can expect problems.]
Better:	If you have questions during our transition to the automated system, call Melissa Morgan.
Still better:	You'll be able to get information instantly about any house on the market when the automated system is in place. If you have questions during the transition, call Melissa Morgan.
Negative:	Now Crispy Crunch tastes better. [Implication: it used to taste terrible.]
Better:	Now Crispy Crunch tastes even better.

Removing negatives does not mean being arrogant or pushy.

Negative:	I hope that you are satisfied enough to place future orders.
Arrogant:	I look forward to receiving all of your future business.
Better:	Call Mercury whenever you need computer chips.

When you eliminate negative words, be sure to maintain accuracy. Words that are exact opposites will usually not be accurate. Instead, use specifics to be both positive and accurate.

Negative:	The exercycle is not guaranteed for life.
Not true:	The exercycle is guaranteed for life.
True:	The exercycle is guaranteed for 10 years.
Negative:	Customers under 60 are not eligible for the Prime Time discount.
Not true:	You must be over 60 to be eligible for the Prime Time discount.
True:	If you're 60 or older, you can save 10% on all your purchases with Right-Way's Prime Time discount.

Legal phrases also have negative connotations for most readers and should be avoided whenever possible. The idea will sound more positive if you use normal English.

Negative:	If your account is still delinquent, a second, legal notice will be sent to you informing you that cancellation of your policy will occur 30 days after the date of the legal notice if we do not receive your check.
Better:	Even if your check is lost in the mail and never reaches us, you still have a 30-day grace period. If you do get a second notice, you will know that your payment hasn't reached us. To keep your account in good standing, stop payment on the first check and send a second one.

2. Focus on what the audience can do rather than on limitations.

When there are limits, or some options are closed, focus on the alternatives that remain.

Negative:	We will not allow you to charge more than $1,500 on your VISA account.
Better:	You can charge $1,500 on your new VISA card.
or:	Your new VISA card gives you $1,500 in credit that you can use at thousands of stores nationwide.

As you focus on what will happen, check for **you-attitude.** In the last example, "We will allow you to charge $1,500" would be positive, but it lacks you-attitude.

Some stores might say, "Put books you don't want here." But bookseller Joseph Best in Lexington, KY, uses positive emphasis.

Four Ways to Say "Yes" Instead of "No"

"Yes, I want to help."
Even if you have to say no personally, there is usually an alternative yes. By helping to solve someone's problem—say, by referring them to someone who might be able to help them—you keep the positive energy in motion.

"Yes, you can do better."
Rather than say, "This is terrible," it's a lot more motivating to say, "You do such terrific work. I'm not sure this is up to your caliber."

"Yes, I see you."
It only takes a minute to send a thank-you note or respond to an unsolicited résumé.

"Yes, your talents lie elsewhere."
Warren Buffet says that he's never fired anyone. He has just helped them to find the right job.

Quoted from Linda Kaplan Thaler and Robin Koval, *The Power of Nice: How to Conquer the Business World with Kindness* (New York: Currency, 2006), 84–87.

When you have a benefit and a requirement the audience must meet to get the benefit, the sentence is usually more positive if you put the benefit first.

Negative: You will not qualify for the student membership rate of $25 a year unless you are a full-time student.

Better: You get all the benefits of membership for only $25 a year if you're a fulltime student.

3. Justify negative information by giving a reason or linking it to an audience benefit.

A reason can help your audience see that the information is necessary; a benefit can suggest that the negative aspect is outweighed by positive factors. Be careful, however, to make the logic behind your reason clear and to leave no loopholes.

Negative: We cannot sell individual report covers.

Loophole: To keep down packaging costs and to help you save on shipping and handling costs, we sell report covers in packages of 12.

Suppose the customer says, "I'll pay the extra shipping and handling. Send me seven." If you truly sell only in packages of 12, you need to say so:

Better: To keep down packaging costs and to help customers save on shipping and handling costs, we sell report covers only in packages of 12.

If you link the negative element to a benefit, be sure it is a benefit your audience will acknowledge. Avoid telling people that you're doing things "for their own good." They may have a different notion of what their own good is. You may think you're doing customers a favor by limiting their credit so they don't get in over their heads and go bankrupt. They may think they'd be better off with more credit so they could expand in hopes of making more sales and more profits.

4. If the negative is truly unimportant, omit it.

Omit negatives only when

* The audience does not need the information to make a decision.
* You have already given the audience the information and they have access to the previous communication.
* The information is trivial.

The following examples suggest the kind of negatives you can omit:

Negative: A one-year subscription to *PC Magazine* is $49.97. That rate is not as low as the rates charged for some magazines.

Better: A one-year subscription to PC Magazine is $49.97.

Still better: A one-year subscription to PC Magazine is $49.97. You save 43% off the newsstand price of $87.78.

Negative: If you are not satisfied with Interstate Fidelity Insurance, you do not have to renew your policy.

Better: Omit the sentence.

5. Put the negative information in the middle and present it compactly.

Put negatives at the beginning or end only if you want to emphasize the negative. To deemphasize a written negative, put it in the middle of a paragraph rather than in the first or last sentence and in the middle of the message rather than in the first or last paragraphs.

When a letter or memo runs several pages, remember that the bottom of the first page is also a position of emphasis, even if it is in the middle of a paragraph, because of the extra white space of the bottom margin. (The first page gets more attention because it is on top and the reader's eye may catch lines of the message even when he or she isn't consciously reading it; the tops and bottoms of subsequent pages don't get this extra attention.) If possible, avoid placing negative information at the bottom of the first page.

Giving a topic lots of space emphasizes it. Therefore, you can de-emphasize negative information by giving it as little space as possible. Give negative information only once in your message. Don't list negatives vertically on the page since lists take space and emphasize material.

How to Check Positive Emphasis

All five of the strategies listed above help create positive emphasis. However, you should always check to see that the positive emphasis is appropriate, sincere, and realistic.

As you read at the beginning of this section, positive emphasis is not always appropriate. Some bad news is so serious that presenting it with positive tone is insensitive, if not unethical. Layoffs, salary cuts, and product defects are all topics in this category.

Some positive emphasis is so overdone that it seems insincere. The used-car sales rep selling a rusting auto is one stereotype of insincerity. A more common example for most business people is the employee who gushes praise through gritted teeth over your promotion. Most of us have experienced something similar, and we know how easy it is to see through the insincerity.

Positive emphasis can also be so overdone that it clouds the reality of the situation. If your company has two finalists for a sales award, and only one award, the

loser does not have second place, which implies a second award. On the other hand, if all sales reps win the same award, top performers will feel unappreciated. Too much praise can also make mediocre employees think they are doing great.

Restraint can help make positive emphasis more effective. Conductor Otto Klemperer was known for not praising his orchestra. One day, pleased with a particularly good rehearsal, he spoke a brusque "good." His stunned musicians broke into spontaneous applause. Klemperer rapped his baton on his music stand to silence them and said, "Not *that* good."[9]

Tone, Power, and Politeness

Tone is the implied attitude of the communicator toward the audience. If the words of a document seem condescending or rude, tone is a problem. Norms for politeness are cultural and generational; they also vary from office to office.

Tone is tricky because it interacts with power. Language that is acceptable within one group may be unacceptable if used by someone outside the group. Words that might seem friendly from a superior to a subordinate may seem uppity if used by the subordinate to the superior. Similarly, words that may be neutral among peers may be seen as negative if sent by a superior to subordinate.

Paul Goward, the former police chief of Winter Haven, Florida, discovered this lesson about the connection between power and tone. Goward sent an e-mail to about 75 employees asking "Are You a Jelly Belly?" In the e-mail, he provided 10 reasons why his employees should be in better shape; the reasons ranged from health risks to department image. The e-mail added, "If you are unfit, do yourself and everyone else a favor. . . . See a professional about a proper diet. . . . Stop making excuses. . . . We didn't hire you unfit and we don't want you working unfit." The e-mail so offended employees that Goward was forced to resign.[10]

Using the proper tone with employees can have huge economic impact for a business. A Litigation Trends Survey, based on reports from 310 in-house counsel, found employee lawsuits to be the top litigation concern of corporate lawyers. Disgruntled employees are suing more than ever before, and disputes over wages or hours frequently can be brought as class actions, making them even more expensive.[11]

The desirable tone for business writing is businesslike but not stiff, friendly but not phony, confident but not arrogant, polite but not groveling. The following guidelines will help you achieve the tone you want.

Solving an Ethical Dilemma Using Goodwill

Most ethical dilemmas boil down to people, balancing the needs or desires of one constituency against those of another: Management versus staff, stockholders versus customers.

Toro, maker of lawnmowers, faced such a dilemma. One of its popular riding mowers is very hard to overturn, but when it does, it can seriously injure the driver. Toro decided to install roll bars behind the driver's seat on new machines but not raise the price because the bars were added for safety.

Then an even harder issue arose. Shouldn't the same ethical treatment be offered on machines already owned? Those owners would be protected but the cost would adversely affect shareholders.

What would you do? Toro installed the bars for all mowers, new and used, a decision they believed would best serve users and shareholders in the long term.

Adapted from Kevin Cashman. "What Exactly Is Ethics?" in *Leadership: Consulting Cashman,* Forbes.com, http://www.forbes.com/leadership/2007/03/03/leadership-cashman-ethics-leadership-citizen-cx_kc_0305ethics.html (accessed May 11, 2007).

- **Use courtesy titles for people outside your organization whom you don't know well.** Most US organizations use first names for everyone, whatever their age or rank. But many people don't like being called by their first names by people they don't know or by someone much younger. When you talk or write to people outside your organization, use first names only if you've established a personal relationship. If you don't know someone well, use a courtesy title:

Dear Mr. Reynolds:

Dear Ms. Lee:

- **Be aware of the power implications of the words you use.** "Thank you for your cooperation" is generous coming from a superior to a subordinate; it's not appropriate in a message to your superior.

As researchers Margaret Graham and Carol David have found, different ways of asking for action carry different levels of politeness.[12]

Order: (lowest politeness)	Turn in your time card by Monday.
Polite order: (midlevel politeness)	Please turn in your time card by Monday.

Hallmark is producing a new line of cards for common situations such as depression or chemotherapy. For example, "Get Well Soon," is not appropriate for someone who is battling cancer. Hallmark has changed the tone of their Journey's Collection to reflect the needs of their dual audiences—buyers and receivers of cards.

Source: David Twiddy, "Hallmark Tackles Real-Life Situations," *Chicago Tribune,* February 19, 2007, sec. Business.

| Indirect request: (higher politeness) | Time cards should be turned in by Monday. |
| Question: (highest politeness) | Would you be able to turn in your time card by Monday? |

Higher levels of politeness may be unclear. In some cases, a question may seem like a request for information to which it's acceptable to answer, "No, I can't." In other cases, it will be an order, simply phrased in polite terms.

You need more politeness if you're asking for something that will inconvenience the audience and help you more than the person who does the action. Generally, you need less politeness when you're asking for something small, routine, or to the audience's benefit. Some discourse communities, however, prefer that even small requests be made politely.

| Lower politeness: | To start the scheduling process, please describe your availability for meetings during the second week of the month. |
| Higher politeness: | Could you let me know what times you'd be free for a meeting the second week of the month? |

Generally, requests sound friendliest when they use conversational language.

| Poor tone: | Return the draft with any changes by next Tuesday. |
| Better tone: | Let me know by Tuesday whether you'd like any changes in the draft. |

- **When the stakes are low, be straightforward.**   Messages that beat around the bush sound pompous and defensive.

| Poor tone: | Distribution of the low-fat plain granola may be limited in your area. May we suggest that you discuss this matter with your store manager. |
| Better tone: | Our low-fat granola is so popular that there isn't enough to go around. We're expanding production to meet the demand. Ask your store manager to keep putting in orders, so that your grocery is on the list of stores that will get supplies when they become available. |

- **When you must give bad news, consider hedging your statement.**   Researchers John Hagge and Charles Kostelnick have shown that auditors' suggestion letters rarely say directly that firms are using unacceptable accounting practices. Instead, they use three strategies to be more diplomatic: specifying the time ("currently, the records are quite informal"), limiting statements ("it appears," "it seems"), and using impersonal statements that do not specify who caused a problem or who will perform an action.[13]
- **When you give bad news to your supervisor, display self-confidence and competency while respecting and being sensitive to your supervisor.**   Using politeness strategies in work situations can be tricky for subordinates reporting negative messages as researchers Rogers and Lee-Wong discovered. Their study found that subordinates need to balance the display of self-confidence and competence with showing understanding of the supervisor; the sender of negative messages must demonstrate the ability to suggest or make needed changes while also giving superiors respect and helping them save face. The subordinate should ask questions, request resources and provide feedback while not imposing on the supervisor's areas of expertise or self-worth.[14]

Reducing Bias in Business Communication

Bias-free language is language that does not discriminate against people on the basis of sex, physical condition, race, age, religion or any other category. It includes all readers, helps to sustain goodwill, is fair and friendly, and complies with the law.

Check to be sure that your language is bias-free. When you talk about people with disabilities or diseases, talk about the people, not the condition.

Goodwill Can't Be Bought

Asian multinational companies have encountered problems in merging and acquiring companies in the United States. Scholars speculate that one of the reasons is their inability to create goodwill with the media, activist groups, and politicians. To create goodwill with American companies, Asian businesses are discovering the importance of strategic communication. Goodwill communication practices needed include

1.   Targeting audiences: media and corporations.

2.   Demonstrating global nature.

3.   Building key stakeholder relationships including the government, politicians, unions, employees, local communities, customers, financial analysts, and media of both countries.

4.   Outlining benefits to the US economy.

5.   Becoming conscious of the culture, concerns, and perceptions of the company and the acquisition.

Adapted from Arun Sudhaman, "When Money Alone Can't Buy Goodwill," *Media*, April 2006, 10A.

When you produce newsletters or other documents with photos and illustrations, choose a sampling of the whole population, not just part of it.

Making Language Nonsexist

Nonsexist language treats both sexes neutrally. Check to be sure that your messages are free from sexism in four areas: job titles, courtesy titles, pronouns, and other words and phrases.

Job titles

Use neutral titles which do not imply that a job is held only by men or only by women. Many job titles are already neutral: *accountant, banker, doctor, engineer, inspector, manager, nurse, pilot, secretary, technician,* to name a few. Other titles reflect gender stereotypes and need to be changed.

Instead of	Use
Businessman	A specific title: executive, accountant, department head, owner of a small business, men and women in business, business person
Chairman	Chair, chairperson, moderator
Fireman	Firefighter
Foreman	Supervisor
Mailman	Mail Carrier
Salesman	Salesperson, sales representative
Waitress	Server
Woman lawyer	Lawyer
Workman	Worker, employee. Or use a specific title: crane operator, bricklayer, etc.

Courtesy titles

Memos normally use first and last names without courtesy titles. Letters, however, require courtesy titles in the salutation *unless* you're on a first-name basis with your reader. (See Appendix A ➡ for examples of memo and letter formats.)

- When you know your reader's name and gender, use courtesy titles that do not indicate marital status: *Mr.* for men and *Ms.* for women. There are, however, two exceptions:
  1.   If the woman has a professional title, use that title if you would use it for a man.

      Dr. Kristen Sorenson is our new company physician.

      The Rev. Elizabeth Townsley gave the invocation.
  2.   If the woman prefers to be addressed as *Mrs.* or *Miss,* use the title she prefers rather than *Ms.* (You-attitude takes precedence over nonsexist language: address the reader as she—or he—prefers to be addressed.) To find out if a woman prefers a traditional title,

      a.   Check the signature block in previous correspondence. If a woman types her name as *(Miss) Elaine Anderson* or *(Mrs.) Kay Royster,* use the title she designates.

      b.   Notice the title a woman uses in introducing herself on the phone. If she says, "This is Robin Stine," use *Ms.* when you write to her. If she says, "I'm Mrs. Stine," use the title she specifies.

c.   Check your company directory. In some organizations, women who prefer traditional titles can list them with their names.

d.   When you're writing job letters or crucial correspondence, call the company and ask the receptionist which title your reader prefers.

Ms. is particularly useful when you do not know what a woman's marital status is. However, even when you happen to know that a woman is married or single, **you still use *Ms.*** unless you know that she prefers another title.

In addition to using parallel courtesy titles, use parallel forms for names.

Not Parallel	Parallel
Members of the committee will be Mr. Jones, Mr. Yacone, and Lisa.	Members of the committee will be Mr. Jones, Mr. Yacone, and Ms. Melton.
	or
	Members of the committee will be Irving, Ted, and Lisa.

- When you know your reader's name but not the gender, either
  1.   Call the company and ask the receptionist, or
  2.   Use the reader's full name in the salutation:
       Dear Chris Crowell:
       Dear J. C. Meath:
- When you know neither the reader's name nor gender, you have three options:
  1.   Omit the salutation and use a subject line in its place. (See Figure A.3, AMS Simplified Format.)
       SUBJECT: RECOMMENDATION FOR BEN WANDELL
  2.   Use the reader's position or job title:
       Dear Loan Officer:
       Dear Registrar:
  3.   Use a general group to which your reader belongs:
       Dear Investor:
       Dear Admissions Committee:

Pronouns

When you refer to a specific person, use the appropriate gender pronouns:

In his speech, John Jones said that . . .

In her speech, Judy Jones said that . . .

When you are referring not to a specific person but to anyone who may be in a given job or position, traditional gender pronouns are sexist.

Sexist: a. Each supervisor must certify that the time sheet for his department is correct.

Sexist: b. When the nurse fills out the accident report form, she should send one copy to the Central Division Office.

Business communication uses four ways to eliminate sexist generic pronouns: use plurals, use second-person *you*, revise the sentence to omit the pronoun, or use pronoun pairs. Whenever you have a choice of two or more ways to make a phrase or sentence nonsexist, choose the alternative that is the smoothest and least conspicuous.

The following examples use these methods to revise sentences *a* and *b* above.

1.   Use plural nouns and pronouns.

   Nonsexist: a. Supervisors must certify that the time sheets for their departments are correct.

R-E-S-P-E-C-T

Most major airlines and hotel chains provide disability training to employees. . . . I recognize when someone has been trained—to offer me a Braille menu, use my name when addressing me, or take a moment to orient me to a new environment. What I appreciate even more, though, is . . . simple, common courtesy.

I don't care how many pages in an employee manual somewhere are devoted to . . . the dos and don'ts of interacting with someone who is deaf, blind, or mentally retarded. Among hundreds of experiences in airports and hotels, the one distinction that separates the (mostly) pleasing from the (occasionally) painful in my encounters has been the honest friendliness and respect with which I have or have not been treated.

Ask me where I'd like to sit, whether I need help getting there, and what other kinds of help I need.

Please, assume that I know more about my disability than anyone else ever could.

Respect me as you do any other customer who is paying for the same service, and have the grace to apologize if something does go wrong.

Too many companies, it seems to me, are busy shaking in their boots over the imagined high cost of accommodating people with disabilities when, in many instances, a good old-fashioned refresher course in manners would cover most bases.

Quoted from Deborah Kendrick, "Disabled Resent Being Patronized," *Columbus Dispatch*, July 21, 1996, 3B.

Attempts To Create a Unisex Pronoun

For more than 150 years, people have attempted to coin a unisex pronoun. None of the attempts has been successful.

Date	he or she	his or her	him or her
1850	ne	nis	nim
1884	le	lis	lim
1938	se	sim	sis
1970	ve	vis	ver
1977	e	e's	em
1988	ala	alis	alum

Adapted from Dennis E. Baron, "The Epicene Pronoun: Word That Failed," *American Speech* 56 (1981): 83–97; and Ellen Graham, "Business Bulletin," *Wall Street Journal*, December 29, 1988, A1.

Note: When you use plural nouns and pronouns, other words in the sentence may need to be made plural too. In the example above, plural supervisors have plural time sheets and departments.

Avoid mixing singular nouns and plural pronouns.

Nonsexist but lacks agreement: a. Each supervisor must certify that the time sheet for their department is correct.

Since *supervisor* is singular, it is incorrect to use the plural *their* to refer to it. The resulting lack of agreement is acceptable orally but is not yet acceptable in writing. Instead, use one of the four grammatically correct ways to make the sentence nonsexist.

2. Use *you.*

   Nonsexist: a. You must certify that the time sheet for your department is correct.

   Nonsexist: b. When you fill out an accident report form, send one copy to the Central Division Office.

You is particularly good for instructions and statements of the responsibilities of someone in a given position. Using *you* also may shorten sentences, since you write "Send one copy" instead of "You should send one copy." It also makes your writing more direct.

3. Substitute an article (*a, an,* or *the*) for the pronoun, or revise the sentence so that the pronoun is unnecessary.

   Nonsexist: a. The supervisor must certify that the time sheet for the department is correct.

   Nonsexist: b. The nurse will
      1. Fill out the accident report form.
      2. Send one copy of the form to the Central Division Office.

4. When you must focus on the action of an individual, use pronoun pairs.

   Nonsexist: a. The supervisor must certify that the time sheet for his or her department is correct.

   Nonsexist: b. When the nurse fills out the accident report form, he or she should send one copy to the Central Division Office.

Other words and phrases

If you find any of the terms in the first column in Figure 3.4 in your messages or your company's documents, replace them with terms from the second column.

Not every word containing *man* is sexist. For example, *manager* is not sexist. The word comes from the Latin *manus* meaning *hand*; it has nothing to do with maleness.

Avoid terms that assume that everyone is married or is heterosexual.

   Biased: You and your husband or wife are cordially invited to the dinner.

   Better: You and your guest are cordially invited to the dinner.

Making Language Nonracist and Nonagist

Language is **nonracist** and **nonagist** when it treats all races and ages fairly, avoiding negative stereotypes of any group. Use these guidelines to check for bias in documents you write or edit:

- **Give someone's race or age only if it is relevant to your story.** When you do mention these characteristics, give them for everyone in your

Figure 3.4 Getting Rid of Sexist Terms and Phrases

Instead of	Use	Because
The girl at the front desk	The woman's name or job title: "Ms. Browning," "Rosa," "the receptionist"	Call female employees *women* just as you call male employees *men*. When you talk about a specific woman, use her name, just as you use a man's name to talk about a specific man.
The ladies on our staff	The women on our staff	Use parallel terms for males and females. Therefore, use *ladies* only if you refer to the males on your staff as *gentlemen*. Few businesses do, since social distinctions are rarely at issue.
Manpower Manhours Manning	Personnel Hours or worker hours Staffing	The power in business today comes from both women and men.
Managers and their wives	Managers and their guests	Managers may be female; not everyone is married.

story—not just the non-Caucasian, non-young-to-middle-aged adults you mention.

- **Refer to a group by the term it prefers. As preferences change, change your usage.** Fifty years ago, *Negro* was preferred as a more dignified term than *colored* for African Americans. As times changed, *Black* and *African American* replaced it. Surveys in the mid-1990s showed that almost half of blacks aged 40 and older preferred *Black,* but those 18 to 39 preferred *African American*.[15] Currently, the National Association for the Advancement of Colored People (NAACP) uses African American on its Web page.

  Oriental has now been replaced by *Asian*.

  The term *Latino* is the most acceptable group term to refer to Mexican Americans, Cuban Americans, Puerto Ricans, Dominicans, Brazilianos, and other people with Central and Latin American backgrounds. (*Latina* is the term for an individual woman.) Better still is to refer to the precise group. The differences among various Latino groups are at least as great as the differences among Italian Americans, Irish Americans, Armenian Americans, and others descended from various European groups.

  Baby boomers, older people, and *mature customers* are more generally accepted terms than *Senior Citizens* or *Golden Agers*.

- **Avoid terms that suggest that competent people are unusual.** The statement "She is an intelligent black woman" suggests that the writer expects most black women to be stupid. "He is an asset to his race" suggests that excellence in the race is rare. "He is a spry 70-year-old" suggests that the writer is amazed that anyone that old can still move.

Talking about People with Disabilities and Diseases

A disability is a physical, mental, sensory, or emotional impairment that interferes with the major tasks of daily living. According to the US Census Bureau, 18% of Americans currently have a disability; of those, about 56% who were 21–64 were employed.[16] The number of people with disabilities will rise as the population ages.

Positive Emphasis Is Good for Your Health

The latest trend in therapy is happiness. "Positive psychology" helps patients focus on the things that are right in their lives rather than the things that are wrong. For years traditional therapy has encouraged patients to focus on their families to discover how their problems may be based upon past experiences and relationships. By contrast, positive psychology encourages patients to focus on the patient's strengths and interests; homework from the sessions may include writing letters of forgiveness or essays about favorite rituals, taking a class, reflecting on art, or even changing jobs.

The goal of positive psychology is to help patients feel more optimistic. The practice is not recommended for people with severe mental illnesses like bipolar disorder or schizophrenia, but it has shown some promise with people who suffer from depression or post-traumatic stress disorder, such as veterans and survivors of Hurricane Katrina.

Adapted from Elizabeth Bernstein, "Therapy that Keeps on the Sunny Side of Life," *Wall Street Journal*, September 26, 2006, D1.

Technology helps blind people contribute fully as members of the workforce. This Braille keyboard allows a computer engineer to key in commands and data. Specialized computer programs such as JAWS can read computer screens out loud.

- *People-first language* **focuses on the person, not the condition.**   **People-first language** names the person first, then adds the condition. Use it instead of the traditional noun phrases that imply the condition defines the person.

Instead of	Use	Because
The mentally retarded	People with mental retardation	The condition does not define the person or his or her potential.
Cancer patients	People being treated for cancer	

- **Avoid negative terms, unless the audience prefers them.**   You-attitude takes precedence over positive emphasis: use the term a group prefers. People who lost their hearing as infants, children, or young adults often prefer to be called *deaf,* or *Deaf* in recognition of Deafness as a culture. But people who lose their hearing as older adults often prefer to be called *hard of hearing,* even when their hearing loss is just as great as that of someone who identifies him- or herself as part of the Deaf culture.

Using the right term requires keeping up with changing preferences. If your target audience is smaller than the whole group, use the term preferred by that audience, even if the group as a whole prefers another term.

Some negative terms, however, are never appropriate. Negative terms such as *afflicted, suffering from,* and *struck down* also suggest an outdated view of any illness as a sign of divine punishment.

Instead of	Use	Because
Confined to a wheelchair	Uses a wheelchair	Wheelchairs enable people to escape confinement.
AIDS victim	Person with AIDS	Someone can have a disease without being victimized by it.
Abnormal	Atypical	People with disabilities are atypical but not necessarily abnormal.

Choosing Bias-Free Photos and Illustrations

When you produce a document with photographs or illustrations, check the visuals for possible bias. Do they show people of both sexes and all races? Is there a sprinkling of various kinds of people (younger and older, people using wheelchairs, etc.)? It's OK to have individual pictures that have just one sex or one race; the photos as a whole do not need to show exactly 50% men and 50% women. But the general impression should suggest that diversity is welcome and normal.

Check relationships and authority figures as well as numbers. If all the men appear in business suits and the women in maids' uniforms, the pictures are sexist even if an equal number of men and women are pictured. If the only blacks and Latinos pictured are factory workers, the photos support racism even when an equal number of people from each race are shown.

In 1997, as Marilyn Dyrud has shown, only 22% of the images of humans in clip art files were women, and most of those showed women in traditional roles. An even smaller percent pictured members of minority groups.[17] Don't use biased clip art or stock photos: create your own bias-free illustrations.

Summary of Key Points

- **You-attitude** is a style of communication that looks at things from the audience's point of view, emphasizing what the audience wants to know, respecting the audience's intelligence, and protecting the audience's ego.
  1. Talk about the audience, not about yourself.
  2. Refer to the audience's request or order specifically.
  3. Don't talk about feelings except to congratulate or offer sympathy.
  4. In positive situations, use *you* more often than *I*. Use *we* when it includes the audience.
  5. In negative situations, avoid the word *you*. Protect the audience's ego. Use passive verbs and impersonal expressions to avoid assigning blame.
- Apply you-attitude beyond the sentence level by using organization and content as well as style to build goodwill.
- **Positive emphasis** means focusing on the positive rather than the negative aspects of a situation. To create positive emphasis
  1. Avoid negative words and words with negative connotations.
  2. Focus on what the audience can do rather than on limitations.
  3. Justify negative information by giving a reason or linking it to an audience benefit.

4. If the negative is truly unimportant, omit it.
5. Put the negative information in the middle and present it compactly.

- Check to see that your positive emphasis is appropriate, sincere, and clear.
- The desirable tone for business communication is businesslike but not stiff, friendly but not phony, confident but not arrogant, polite but not groveling. The following guidelines will help you achieve the tone you want:
  - Use courtesy titles for people outside your organization whom you don't know well.
  - Be aware of the power implications of the words you use.
  - When the stakes are low, be straightforward.
  - When you must give bad news, consider hedging your statement.
  - Communication should be free from sexism in four areas: job titles, courtesy titles, pronouns, and others words and phrases.
  - *Ms.* is the nonsexist courtesy title for women. Whether or not you know a woman's marital status, use *Ms. unless* the woman has a professional title or unless you know that she prefers a traditional title.
  - Traditional pronouns are sexist when they refer to a class of people, not to specific individuals. Four ways to make the sentence nonsexist are to use plurals, to use *you,* to revise the sentence to omit the pronoun, and to use pronoun pairs.
  - Bias-free language is fair and friendly; it complies with the law. It includes all members of your audience; it helps to sustain goodwill.
  - Check to be sure that your language is nonsexist, nonracist, and nonagist. When you talk about people with disabilities or diseases, use the term they prefer. When you produce newsletters or other documents with photos and illustrations, picture a sampling of the whole population, not just part of it.

CHAPTER 3 Exercises and Problems

3.1   Reviewing the Chapter

1. What are five ways to create you-attitude? (LO1)
2. What are five ways to create positive emphasis? (LO2)
3. How can you improve the tone of business messages? (LO3)
4. What are different categories to keep in mind when you are trying to reduce bias in business messages? (LO4)
5. What techniques can you use when you are trying to reduce bias in business messages? (LO4)

3.2   Evaluating the Ethics of Positive Emphasis

The first term in each line is negative; the second is a positive term that is sometimes substituted for it. Which of the positive terms seem ethical? Which seem unethical? Briefly explain your choices.

cost	investment	nervousness	adrenaline
second mortgage	home equity loan	problem	challenge
tax	user fee	price increase	price change
		for-profit hospital	tax-paying hospital
		used car	pre-owned car
		credit card fees	usage charges

3.3   Eliminating Negative Words and Words with Negative Connotations

Revise each of the following sentences to replace negative words with positive ones. Be sure to keep the meaning of the original sentence.

1. You will lose customer goodwill if you are slow in handling returns and issuing refunds.
2. Do not put any paper in this box that is not recyclable.
3. When you write a report, do not make claims that you cannot support with evidence.
4. Don't drop in without an appointment. Your counselor or case worker may be unavailable.
5. I am anxious to discuss my qualifications in an interview.

3.4   Using Passives and Impersonal Expressions to Improve You-Attitude and Positive Emphasis

Revise each of these sentences to improve you-attitude and positive emphasis, first using a passive verb, then using an impersonal expression (one in which things, not people, do the action). Are both revisions equally good? Why or why not?

1. You did not supply all of the information necessary to process your claim.
2. The credit card number you supplied has expired.
3. You did not send us your check.
4. You did not include all the necessary information in your letter.
5. By failing to build a fence around your pool, you have allowed your property to violate city regulations against health hazards.

3.5   Focusing on the Positive

Revise each of the following sentences to focus on the options that remain, not those that are closed off.

1. Housing applications that arrive December 1 or later cannot be processed.
2. You cannot use flextime unless you have the consent of your supervisor.
3. As a first-year employee, you are not eligible for dental insurance.
4. I will be out of the country October 25 to November 10 and will not be able to meet with you then.
5. You will not get your first magazine for at least four weeks.

3.6   Identifying Hidden Negatives

Identify the hidden negatives in the following sentences and revise to eliminate them. In some cases, you may need to add information to revise the sentence effectively.

1. The seminar will help you become a better manager.
2. Thank you for the confidence you have shown in us by ordering one of our products. It will be shipped to you soon.
3. This publication is designed to explain how your company can start a recycling program.
4. I hope you find the information in this brochure beneficial to you and a valuable reference as you plan your move.
5. In thinking about your role in our group, I remember two occasions where you contributed something.

3.7   Improving You-Attitude and Positive Emphasis

Revise these sentences to improve you-attitude and positive emphasis. Eliminate any awkward phrasing. In some cases, you may need to add information to revise the sentence effectively.

1. You'll be happy to learn that the cost of tuition will not rise next year.
2. Although I was only an intern and didn't actually make presentations to major clients, I was required to prepare PowerPoint slides for the meetings and to answer some of the clients' questions.
3. At DiYanni Homes we have more than 30 plans that we will personalize just for you.

4. Please notify the publisher of the magazine of your change of address as soon as possible to prevent a disruption of subscription service.

5. I'm sorry you were worried. You did not miss the deadline for signing up for a flexible medical spending account.

6. We are in the process of upgrading our Web site. Please bear with us.

7. You will be happy to hear that our cell phone plan does not charge you for incoming calls.

8. The employee discount may only be used for purchases for your own use or for gifts; you may not buy items for resale. To prevent any abuse of the discount privilege, you may be asked to justify your purchase.

9. I apologize for my delay in answering your inquiry. The problem was that I had to check with our suppliers to see whether we could provide the item in the quantity you say you want. We can.

10. If you mailed a check with your order, as you claim, we failed to receive it.

3.8   Improving You-Attitude and Positive Emphasis

Revise these sentences to improve you-attitude and positive emphasis. Eliminate any awkward phrasing. In some cases, you may need to add information to revise the sentence effectively.

1. Your signature block in an e-mail message should not exceed more than four lines.

2. We have added a 24-hour-a-day seven-days-a-week ATM for your convenience.

3. There may be a slight delay while our Web site validates your order information. Please be patient while you wait.

4. The services on our Web site will enable job seekers to identify the areas where their skills are needed.

5. Don't forget that museum memberships make great gifts.

6. Please fill out our online survey. The survey will not be available after 5 PM October 10.

7. To prevent problems, when installing a new software program, don't click "OK" if the program asks you a question you don't understand.

8. Starting January 1, we are offering you a new employee benefit.

9. As a government employee, you must fill out the Financial Disclosure form so that you prove that your decisions are not biased.

10. Although I have had only one course in business communication, I could possibly be of some help as an intern. Please give me a chance.

3.9   Improving You-Attitude and Positive Emphasis

Revise these sentences to improve you-attitude and positive emphasis. Eliminate any awkward phrasing. In some cases, you may need to add information to revise the sentence effectively.

1. Don't put your visual on the screen until you are ready to talk about it.

2. We can arrange for our services to reach you within 24 hours.

3. Starting January 1, the company will create a new program that lets full-time employees volunteer one hour a week on company time.

4. APA style doesn't capitalize the major words in the titles of journal and newspaper articles.

5. I hope this answers your question. If you still do not understand, do not fail to ask for more information.

6. If you reserve your space online by November 27, we will extend to you a special rate of $1,295, which is $300 off the registration fee. You must enter DE35 in the priority code field to avoid being charged the regular rate.

7. Next Tuesday will not be a problem. Our service crew is not overbooked and will not have trouble fitting you in.

8. I realize that Wednesday at 10 AM is not a convenient time for everyone, but I was unable to arrange a time that is good for everyone.

9. You cannot accept gifts from anyone with whom you, as an employee of the Environmental Protection Agency, deal, because some citizen might suspect that your enforcement decision had been subject to undue influence.

10. If you supplied receipts with your request for reimbursement, as you claim, they have been lost.

3.10 Eliminating Biased Language

Explain the source of bias in each of the following, and revise to remove the bias.

1. We recommend hiring Jim Ryan and Elizabeth Shuman. Both were very successful summer interns. Jim drafted the report on using rap music in ads, and Elizabeth really improved the looks of the office.

2. All sales associates and their wives are invited to the picnic.

3. Although he is blind, Mr. Morin is an excellent group leader.

4. Unlike many blacks, Yvonne has extensive experience designing Web pages.

5. Chris Renker
   Pacific Perspectives
   6300 West Corondad Blvd.
   Los Angles, CA
   Gentlemen:

6. Enrique Torres has very good people skills for a man.

7. *Parenting 2007* shows you how to persuade your husband to do his share of child care chores.

8. Mr. Paez, Mr. O'Connor, and Tonya will represent our office at the convention.

9. Sue Corcoran celebrates her 50th birthday today. Stop by her cubicle at noon to get a piece of cake and to help us sing "The Old Grey Mare Just Ain't What She Used to Be."

10. Because older customers tend to be really picky, we will need to give a lot of details in our ads.

3.11 Advising a Hasty Subordinate

Three days ago, one of your subordinates forwarded to everyone in the office a bit of e-mail humor he'd received from a friend. Titled "You know you're Southern when . . . ," the message poked fun at Southern speech, attitudes, and lifestyles. Today you get this message from your subordinate:

Subject: Should I Apologize?

I'm getting flamed left and right because of the Southern message. I thought it was funny, but some people just can't take a joke. So far I've tried not to respond to the flames, figuring that would just make things worse. But now I'm wondering if I should apologize. What do you think?

Answer the message.

3.12 Responding to a Complaint

You're Director of Corporate Communications; the employee newsletter is produced by your office. Today you get this e-mail message from Caroline Huber:

Subject: Complaint about Sexist Language

The article about the "Help Desk" says that Martina Luna and I "are the key customer service representatives 'manning' the desk." I don't MAN anything! I WORK.

Respond to Caroline. And send a message to your staff, reminding them to edit newsletter stories as well as external documents to replace biased language.

3.13   Exploring the Positive Effects of Negative Messages

In 2004, Gap Inc. (Gap, Old Navy, and Banana Republic) released a social responsibility report that acknowledged wage, health, and safety violations in many of its overseas factories. Rather than hiding this information, Gap chose to go public and address the problem. In 2006, Ford Motor Company released a series of online documentaries about the company's turnaround efforts which included a film about the company stock receiving a "sell" rating from industry analysts (see sidebar on page 86).

Find an example of a company that has shared its problems and its plans to solve those problems with the public. What went wrong? How did the company respond? How did the company report the problem?

Can you find the current status of the company and its recovery?

As your instructor directs,

a.   Share your findings orally with a small group of students.

b.   Post your findings in an e-mail to the class.

c.   Summarize your findings in a memo to your instructor.

d.   Join with a group of students to create a written report summarizing negative corporate news.

Adapted from Cheryl Dahl, "Gap's New Look: The See-Through," *Fast Company,* September 2004, 69–70.

3.14   Evaluating Bias in Visuals

Evaluate the portrayals of people in one of the following:

- Ads in one issue of a business magazine
- A company's annual report
- A company's Web page

Do the visuals show people of both sexes and all races? Is there a sprinkling of people of various ages and physical conditions? What do the visuals suggest about who has power?

As your instructor directs,

a.   Share your findings orally with a small group of students.

b.   Post your findings in an e-mail to the class.

c.   Summarize your findings in a memo to your instructor.

d.   Present your findings in an oral presentation to the class.

e.   Join with a small group of students to create a written report.

3.15   Revising a Memo for Positive Tone

Revise the following memo to improve positive tone.

TO: All Staff

SUBJECT: Decorating Your Work Area

With the arrival of the holiday season, employees who wish to decorate their work areas should do so only with great caution. Don't do something stupid that might burn down the entire office. If you wish to decorate, don't forget the following guidelines:

1.   If using decorative lights, don't place them in obstructive places.

2.   Do not overload your workstation with decorations that will interfere with your daily duties.

3.   Don't forget to turn off and/or unplug all lights at the end of your workday.

4.   Do not use hot lights; they can burn your countertop so it is imperative that everyone take care in selecting your lights.

5.   Do not use decorations which will offend people of other religions.

6.   Absolutely no candles are allowed.

Don't forget these guidelines, and we'll have a great holiday season. Thank you for your cooperation.

3.16   Revising a Form Letter

You've taken a part-time job at a store that sells fine jewelry. In orientation, the manager tells you that the store photographs jewelry it sells or appraises and mails the photo as a goodwill gesture after the transaction.

However, when you see the form letter, you know that it doesn't build much goodwill—and you say so. The manager says, "Well, you're in college. Suppose you rewrite it."

Rewrite the letter. Use square brackets for material (like the customer's name) that would have to be inserted in the form letter to vary it for a specific customer. Add information that would help build goodwill.

> Dear Customer:
>
> We are most happy to enclose a photo of the jewelry that we recently sold you or appraised for you. We feel that this added service, which we are happy to extend to our fine customers, will be useful should you wish to insure your jewelry or need to identify it should you have the misfortune of suffering a loss.
>
> We trust you will enjoy this additional service. We thank you for the confidence you have shown by coming to our store.
>
> Sincerely,
> Your Sales Associate

3.17   Evaluating You-Attitude and Positive Emphasis in Brochures

Collect three brochures from organizations on your campus or from businesses in your city. Identify sentences in each brochure that demonstrate (or should demonstrate) you-attitude and positive emphasis.

As your instructor directs,

- Turn in a memo that identifies sentences with good you-attitude and positive emphasis. Include the original and a revision of sentences that should incorporate you-attitude and/or positive emphasis but did not.

- Share your findings with a small group of students. What patterns do you see? How would others revise the problematic sentences you found?

3.18   Evaluating You-Attitude and Positive Emphasis in University Web Sites

As they plan their college visits, many students begin by visiting university Web sites. Imagine you are a high school senior and a prospective student. Go to the "Prospective Students" part of your school's Web site and read about housing, course offerings, and student life. Evaluate the information you find for you-attitude and positive emphasis. Compare the text for prospective students with the text on several sites targeted for current students. Does the tone change? In what ways?

Now visit the Web site of another university. Review the same type of information for prospective students and compare it to that of your own school.

As your instructor directs,

- Share your findings orally with a small group of students.
- Share your findings orally with the class.
- Post your findings in an e-mail to the class.
- Summarize your findings in a memo to your instructor.

3.19   Mosaic Case

"Great job on brainstorming the needs of senior citizens, Trey," said Sarah, who was standing at the entrance to his cubicle.

"Thanks. I'm sure that targeting them specifically will increase our sales figures," replied Trey.

"Definitely. And Yvonne has another idea to let senior citizens know about the updates to the Web site," said Sarah.

"Oh, really? What do I have to do now?" asked Trey.

"Well," said Sarah with a big smile, "she wants a letter that we can send to all senior citizens who are currently on Mosaic's mailing list. She wants to get the word out. Or, as Yvonne would say "get the word out," this time mimicking air quotes that Yvonne often uses during their staff meetings.

They both chuckled at Sarah's imitation. "But seriously, Trey, this should be a pretty easy task."

"Yeah, it sounds like a piece of cake," Trey remarked sarcastically.

"If you could get a draft to me by later today, we can both look through the letter before I pass it on to Yvonne for final revisions."

After tinkering around with the letter for most of the day, Trey took his draft to Sarah to look over. However, she was gone for the day and only had a chance to look over it the next morning. When she did read the letter, she was shocked.

Here is the draft Trey wrote:

Dear Sir or Madam:

We at Mosaic are happy to inform you that we have now provided a section of the Web site that is just for you to make your life a little less stressful. We understand you get easily frazzled when things don't work the way you think they should. The new section of the Web site will help ease all your worries.

We have hand-selected and highlighted pieces of furniture that will fit an old lifestyle. For example, there are some stylish couches that sit higher off the ground so you won't to strain your bad back when you take a seat or stand.

In addition, we realize that you're old and have issues navigating through Web pages. Further, we want to make sure you can actually read the text on our Web pages, so we've taken the initiative to increase the size of the font to one that is appropriate for people with bad eyes.

Finally, Mosaic has decided to team up with AARP to give you a great benefit. If you're an AARP card-holding member, you now receive 5% off all online purchases on the checkout page.

We are fully committed to you as a customer of our store and are always thinking about your needs. If you have other ideas about improving the Web site, please don't hesitate to contact us.

Sincerely,

Mosaic

Although grammatically correct, Trey's letter stunned Sarah by its content. What happened to all the ideas he generated during the analysis of the audience's needs?

He called in sick today, so Sarah couldn't tell him directly what was wrong with the letter. Instead, she decided to write him a memo about areas where the letter needs to be improved. And since Yvonne wanted to see a draft of this letter by yesterday afternoon and Sarah doesn't know when Trey will be back to work, she decided to make the necessary changes to the letter herself.

Take on Sarah's communication tasks:

- Write a memo to Trey in which you provide some specific areas where Trey's letter could be improved and reasons for making changes. In addition, let him know the potential effects of sending out his version of the letter.

- Re-write the letter incorporating you-attitude, positive emphasis, goodwill, and unbiased language.

4

Making Your Writing Easy to Read

Learning Objectives

After studying this chapter, you will know:

1 New guidelines for effective word choice.

2 New sentence and paragraph construction techniques.

3 Ways to select stylistic techniques appropriate for a particular audience and context.

Doublespeak Translations

Death tax	Estate tax
Debriefings	Interrogations
Food insecurity	Hunger
Imperative security detainee	Terrorist
Self-injurious behavior incidents	Suicide by captive
Transfer tube	Body bag

During the years that American troops have fought in Iraq, President Bush has exhorted Americans to *stay the course; redeploying our troops,* he claims, would cause us to lose the *struggle for hearts and minds* of Iraqis. Back in the United States, politicians debate whether or not to eliminate the *death tax,* because everyone dies but only the rich leave estates, while millions of Americans are facing *food insecurity.* We try not to think about the *imperative security detainees* at Guantanamo Bay and the reports of *self-injurious behavior incidents* that occur within the prison.

What does all this mean?

The term *rhetoric* means skill in communicating effectively. Yet the word may often conjure thoughts of political rhetoric, in which language is used to obscure meaning as much as it is used to inform and persuade. The examples above demonstrate how euphemisms are often used to mask or soften the real meaning of a message. Former Secretary of Defense Donald Rumsfeld described the use of torture at Abu Ghraib as "the excesses of human nature that humanity suffers," a less offensive term than *torture.*

Of course, euphemisms are not restricted to politics. The military is famous for its colorful examples. *Body bags* of the Vietnam War became *human remains pouches* for the Gulf War and are now *transfer tubes* that are to be kept out of sight of the media. Many companies address *challenges* when they really mean *problems* and *downsize* rather than *lay off employees.* Manufacturing processes may cause *runoff* rather than *pollution;* car dealers may offer *pre-owned vehicles* rather than *used cars.* Stores sell canola oil rather than rapeseed oil, orange roughy rather than slimehead. Most of us have our own favorite euphemisms, especially for body functions.

What euphemisms can you identify? Which ones do you use?

When composing your documents, think about how the words you choose reveal or hide the message. While creative phrasing isn't illegal, is it ethical? How will your readers interpret your words?

> *"Euphemisms are often used to mask or soften the real meaning of a message."*

Adapted from NCTE Public Language Committee, *The Doublespeak Awards (1975–2006)* (accessed March 26, 2007); available from http://webserve.govst.edu /pa/Introduction/doublespeak_awards.htm; and Calvin Woodward, "Washington's 'Doublespeak' Lingo Needs Translation," *Des Moines Register,* November 27, 2006, 3A.

Chapter Outline

Good business and administrative writing should sound like a person talking to another person. Unfortunately, much of the writing produced in organizations today seems to have been written by faceless bureaucrats rather than by real people.

Using an easy-to-read style makes the reader respond more positively to your ideas. You can make your writing easier to read in two ways. First, you can make individual sentences and paragraphs easy to read, so that skimming the first paragraph or reading the whole document takes as little work as possible. Second, you can make the document look visually inviting and structure it with signposts to guide readers through it. This chapter focuses on ways to make words, sentences, and paragraphs easier to read. Chapter 6 will discuss ways to make the document as a whole easier to read.

Good Style in Business and Administrative Writing

Good business and administrative writing is closer to conversation and less formal than the style of writing that has traditionally earned high marks in college essays and term papers. (See Figure 4.1.)

Most people have several styles of talking, which they vary instinctively depending on the audience. Good writers have several styles, too. An e-mail to your boss complaining about the delays from a supplier will be informal, perhaps even chatty; a letter to the supplier demanding better service will be more formal.

Reports tend to be more formal than letters and memos, since they may be read many years in the future by audiences the writer can barely imagine. In reports, avoid contractions, spell out acronyms and abbreviations the first time you use them, and avoid personal pronouns. Since so many people read reports, *you* doesn't have much meaning. See Chapter 16 for more about report style.

Keep the following points in mind as you choose a level of formality for a specific document:

Figure 4.1 Different Levels of Style

Feature	Conversational style	Good business style	Traditional term paper style
Formality	Highly informal	Conversational; sounds like a real person talking	More formal than conversation would be, but retains a human voice
Use of contractions	Many contractions	OK to use occasional contractions	Few contractions, if any
Pronouns	Uses /, first- and second-person pronouns	Uses /, first- and second-person pronouns	First- and second-person pronouns kept to a minimum
Level of friendliness	Friendly	Friendly	No effort to make style friendly
How personal	Personal; refers to specific circumstances of conversation	Personal; may refer to reader by name; refers to specific circumstances of audiences	Impersonal; may generally refer to *readers* but does not name them or refer to their circumstances
Word choice	Short, simple words; slang	Short, simple words but avoids slang	Many abstract words; scholarly, technical terms
Sentence and paragraph length	Incomplete sentences; no paragraphs	Short sentences and paragraphs	Longer sentences and paragraphs
Grammar	Can be ungrammatical	Uses standard English	Uses more formal standard English
Visual impact	Not applicable	Attention to visual impact of document	No particular attention to visual impact

- Use a friendly, informal style to someone you've talked with.
- Avoid contractions, slang, and even minor grammatical lapses in paper documents to people you don't know. Abbreviations are OK in e-mail messages if they're part of the group's culture.
- Pay particular attention to your style when you write to people you fear or when you must give bad news. Reliance on nouns rather than on verbs and a general deadening of style increase when people are under stress or feel insecure.[1] Confident people are more direct. Edit your writing so that you sound confident, whether you feel that way or not.

More and more organizations are simplifying their communications.

- Alan Greenspan, former chair of the Federal Reserve, was infamously known for his lack of clarity in communications, but his successor is striving to bring about new clarity in the board's communications (see sidebar).
- Various local and state police departments are banishing their 10-codes and moving to plain English instead. The 10-codes vary by locale. In Virginia, a 10–50 denotes an auto accident; in Maryland it denotes a downed officer. The change is motivated by pressure from the Homeland Security Department to improve communications between agencies.[2]
- In the financial world, the US Securities and Exchange Commissions's *A Plain English Handbook: How to Create Clear SEC Disclosure Documents* asks for short sentences, everyday words, and active voice. It cautions against legal and highly technical terms.[3]

Communication consultants like Gerard Braud urge clients to say what they mean. He distinguishes between keeping communication easy to understand and "dumbing it down." Braud warns, "All communication affects [the] bottom

To Clarify or Not to Clarify

Former Federal Board Chair Alan Greenspan was known for his lack of clarity. After one speech, a headline in the *Washington Post* read "Greenspan Hints Fed May Cut Interest Rates," while the corresponding headline in the *New York Times* read "Doubt Voiced by Greenspan on a Rate Cut." Even his wife joked that he had to propose twice before she understood what he was saying.

The new chair, Ben Bernanke, has a different style. As he aims for more transparent communications, he plans to make the Fed clearer about goals for inflation and economic growth.

Adapted from Greg Ip, "'Transparent' Vision: New Fed Chairman Hopes to Downplay Impact of His Words," *Wall Street Journal*, (2006): A1; and Daniel Kadlec, "5 Ways the New Fed Chairman Will Be Different," *Time*, November 7, 2005, 49–50.

Figure 4.2　　Jeffrey Immelt's Letter Uses the Standard Business Style

Dear Fellow Stakeholders,

We made GE a stronger Company in 2003. Our businesses performed solidly despite downturns in aviation and energy, high oil prices and slack industrial demand. We grew operating cash flow 28% and strengthened our balance sheet. We invested more than $4 billion in technology and launched dozens of leading-edge products. We grew our services revenues 10% and global revenues 14%. We reorganized our businesses around markets to simplify our operations and deepen our relationships with customers. And we committed more than $30 billion to portfolio moves to create faster-growth industrial businesses and improve our returns from financial services.

Overall, we made tremendous progress on the strategy for long-term growth that I outlined in our last annual report. As you will see in this report, our actions in 2003 addressed the key question investors asked us last year: **How will you grow in an uncertain world?**

Short sentences and action verbs mark the standard business style.

For visual impact, the boldface type highlights the theme of growth.

(RIGHT TO LEFT)

JEFFREY R. IMMELT
Chairman of the Board
and Chief Executive Officer

ROBERT C. WRIGHT
Vice Chairman of the Board
and Executive Officer

DENNIS D. DAMMERMAN
Vice Chairman of the Board
and Executive Officer

Source: General Electric, Letter to Stakeholders, *General Electric 2003 Annual Report*, at www.ge.com/ar2003/chairman/index.jsp. Copyright © General Electric Company. Reprinted with Permission.

line. . . . When a reader, listener, viewer or member of a live audience has to take even a nanosecond to decipher what you are saying because you are making it more complicated than it needs to be, you may lose that person."[4]

Good business style allows for individual variation. Figures 4.2 and 4.3 show the opening paragraphs from the CEO letters in two different annual reports. Jeffrey Immelt's use of action verbs in Figure 4.2 conveys an image of energy and drive. Warren Buffett's direct, folksy style in Figure 4.3 suggests straightforwardness and integrity.

Half-Truths about Style

Many generalizations about style are half-truths and must be applied selectively, if at all.

Figure 4.3 Warren Buffett's Letter Uses a More Individual Style

BERKSHIRE HATHAWAY INC.

To the Shareholders of Berkshire Hathaway Inc.:

Paragraph 1 uses standard business style.

Our gain in net worth during 2003 was $13.6 billion, which increased the per-share book value of both our Class A and Class B stock by 21%. Over the last 39 years (that is, since present management took over) per-share book value has grown from $19 to $50,498, a rate of 22.2% compounded annually.*

The contraction "It's" and the movie-related "morphed" give a lighter tone in spite of the technical topic.

It's per-share intrinsic value that counts, however, not book value. Here, the news is good: Between 1964 and 2003, Berkshire morphed from a struggling northern textile business whose intrinsic value was less than book into a widely diversified enterprise worth far more than book. Our 39-year gain in intrinsic value has therefore somewhat exceeded our 22.2% gain in book. (For a better understanding of intrinsic value and the economic principles that guide Charlie Munger, my partner and Berkshire's vicechairman, and me in running Berkshire, please read our Owner's Manual, beginning on page 69.)

Despite their shortcomings, book value calculations are useful at Berkshire as a slightly understated gauge for measuring the long-term rate of increase in our intrinsic value. The calculation is less relevant, however, than it once was in rating any single year's performance versus the S&P 500 index (a comparison we display on the facing page). Our equity holdings, including convertible preferreds, have fallen considerably as a percentage of our net worth, from an average of 114% in the 1980s, for example, to an average of 50% in 2000-03. Therefore, yearly movements in the stock market now affect a much smaller portion of our net worth than was once the case.

Nonetheless, Berkshire's long-term performance versus the S&P remains all-important. Our shareholders can buy the S&P through an index fund at very low cost. Unless we achieve gains in per-share intrinsic value in the future that outdo the S&P's performance, Charlie and I will be adding nothing to what you can accomplish on your own.

Folksy reference to the firm's partners as "Charlie and I."

If we fail, we will have no excuses. Charlie and I operate in an ideal environment. To begin with, we are supported by an incredible group of men and women who run our operating units. If there were a Corporate Cooperstown, its roster would surely include many of our CEOs. Any shortfall in Berkshire's results will not be caused by our managers.

Additionally, we enjoy a rare sort of managerial freedom. Most companies are saddled with institutional constraints. A company's history, for example, may commit it to an industry that now offers limited opportunity. A more common problem is a shareholder constituency that pressures its manager to dance to Wall Street's tune. Many CEOs resist, but others give in and adopt operating and capital allocation policies far different from those they would choose if left to themselves.

At Berkshire, neither history nor the demands of owners impede intelligent decision-making. When Charlie and I make mistakes, they are – in tennis parlance – unforced errors.

*All figures used in this report apply to Berkshire's A shares, the successor to the only stock that the company had outstanding before 1996. The B shares have an economic interest equal to 1/30th that of the A.

Source: Berkshire Hathaway, "Warren Buffett's Letter to Berkshire Shareholders," Annual Report 2003, at www.berkshirehathaway.com/. Reproduced from copyrighted material with the permission of the author.

The Boss Won't Let Me Write That Way

When a writing consultant urged them to use *I*, the engineers in Research and Development (R&D) at one firm claimed they couldn't: "Our boss won't let us." The consultant checked with their boss, the vice president for Research and Development. He said, "I don't care what words they use. I just want to be able to understand what they write."

The vice president had a PhD and had once done experiments in R&D himself, but he'd spent several years in management. He no longer knew as many technical details as did his subordinates. Their efforts to impress him backfired: he was annoyed because he couldn't understand their reports and had to tell subordinates to rewrite them.

Moral 1: If you think your boss doesn't want you to use a word, ask. A few bosses do prize formal or flowery language. Most don't.

Moral 2: Even if your boss has the same background you do, he or she won't necessarily understand what you write. Revise your memos and reports so they're clear and easy to read.

Moral 3: What's in the file cabinet isn't necessarily a guide to good writing for your organization.

Half-Truth 1: "Write as You Talk."

Most of us use a coloquial, conversational style in speech that is too informal for writing. We use slang, incomplete sentences, and even grammatical errors.

Unless our speech is exceptionally fluent, "writing as we talk" can create awkward, repetitive, and badly organized prose. It's OK to write as you talk to produce your first draft, but edit to create a good written style.

Half-Truth 2: "Never Use *I*."

Using *I* too often can make your writing sound self-centered; using it unnecessarily will make your ideas seem tentative. However, when you write about things you've done or said or seen, using *I* is both appropriate and smoother than resorting to awkward passives or phrases like *this writer*.

Half-Truth 3: "Never Begin a Sentence with *And* or *But*."

Beginning a sentence with *and* or *also* makes the idea that follows seem like an afterthought. That's OK when you want the effect of spontaneous speech in a written document, as you may in a sales letter. If you want to sound as though you have thought about what you are saying, put the *also* in the middle of the sentence or use another transition: *moreover, furthermore*.

But tells the reader that you are shifting gears and that the point which follows not only contrasts with but also is more important than the preceding ideas. Presenting such verbal signposts to your reader is important. Beginning a sentence with *but* is fine if doing so makes your paragraph read smoothly.

Half-Truth 4: "Never End a Sentence with a Preposition."

Prepositions are those useful little words that indicate relationships: *with, in, under, at*. The prohibition against ending sentences with them is probably based on two facts: (1) The end of a sentence (like the beginning) is a position of emphasis. A preposition may not be worth emphasizing. (2) When the reader sees a preposition, he or she expects something to follow it. At the end of a sentence, nothing does.

In job application letters, reports, and important presentations, avoid ending sentences with prepositions. Most messages are less formal; it's OK to end an occasional sentence with a preposition. Noting exceptions to the rule, Sir Winston Churchill famously scolded an editor who had presumptuously corrected a sentence ending with a preposition, "This is the kind of impertinence up with which I will not put."[5] Analyze your audience and the situation, and use the language that you think will get the best results.

Half-Truth 5: "Big Words Impress People."

Learning an academic discipline requires that you master its vocabulary. After you get out of school, however, no one will ask you to write just to prove that you understand something. Instead, you'll be asked to write or speak to people who need the information you have.

Sometimes you may want the sense of formality or technical expertise that big words create. But much of the time, big words just distance you from your audience and increase the risk of miscommunication. When people misuse big words, they look foolish. If you feel you need to use big words, make sure you use them correctly.

Evaluating "Rules" about Writing

Some "rules" are grammatical conventions. For example, standard edited English requires that each sentence have a subject and verb, and that the subject and verb agree. Business writing normally demands standard grammar, but exceptions exist. Promotional materials such as brochures, advertisements, and sales and fund-raising letters may use sentence fragments to mimic the effect of speech.

Other "rules" may be conventions adopted by an organization so that its documents will be consistent. For example, a company might decide to capitalize job titles (e.g., *Production Manager*) even though grammar doesn't require the capitals, or always to use a comma before *and* in a series, even though a sentence can be grammatical without the comma. A different company might make different choices.

Still other "rules" are attempts to codify "what sounds good." "Never use *I*" and "use big words" are examples of this kind of "rule." To evaluate these "rules," you must consider your audience, the discourse community and organizational culture, (◀ p. 46), your purposes, and the situation. If you want the effect produced by an impersonal style and polysyllabic words, use them. But use them only when you want the distancing they produce.

Building a Better Style

To improve your style,

- Try WIRMI: *What I Really Mean Is.*[6] Then write the words.
- Try reading your draft out loud to someone sitting about three feet away—about as far away as you'd sit in casual conversation. If the words sound awkward, they'll seem awkward to a reader, too.
- Ask someone else to read your draft out loud. Readers stumble because the words on the page aren't what they expect to see. The places where that person stumbles are places where your writing can be better.
- Read widely and write a *lot*.
- Study revised sentences, like those in Figure 4.4.
- Use the 10 techniques in Figure 4.5 to polish your style.

Ten Ways to Make Your Writing Easier to Read

Direct, simple writing is easier to read. One study tested two versions of a memo report. The "high-impact" version had the "bottom line" (the purpose of the report) in the first paragraph, simple sentences in normal word order, active verbs, concrete language, short paragraphs, headings and lists, and first- and second-person pronouns. The high-impact version took 22% less time to read. Readers said they understood the report better, and tests showed that they really did understand it better.[7] Another study showed that high-impact instructions were more likely to be followed.[8] We'll talk about layout, headings, and lists in Chapter 6.

As You Choose Words

The best word depends on context: the situation, your purposes, your audience, the words you have already used.

Figure 4.4   Mutual Fund Prospectuses Revised to Meet the SEC's Plain English Guidelines

	Old prospectus	New prospectus
John Hancock Sovereign Balanced Fund	The fund utilizes a strategy of investing in those common stocks which have a record of having increased their shareholder dividend in each of the preceding ten years or more.	The fund's stock investments are exclusively in companies that have increased their dividend payout in each of the last ten years.
State Street Research Equity Income Fund	The applicability of the general information and administrative procedures set forth below accordingly will vary depending on the investor and the record-keeping system established for a shareholder's investment in the Fund. Participants in 401(k) and other plans should first consult with appropriate persons at their employer or refer to the plan materials before following any of the procedures below.	If you are investing through a large retirement plan or other special program, follow the instructions in your program materials.
State Street Research Equity Income Fund	The net asset value of the fund's shares will fluctuate as market conditions change.	The fund's shares will rise and fall in value.

Source: Toddi Gutner, "At Last, the Readable Prospectus," *BusinessWeek,* April 13, 1998, 100E10. Reprinted by special permission. Copyright © 1998 by The McGraw-Hill Companies, Inc.

Figure 4.5   Ten Ways to Make Your Writing Easier to Read

As you choose words,
1. Use words that are accurate, appropriate, and familiar.
2. Use technical jargon only when it is essential and known to the reader. Eliminate business jargon.

As you write and revise sentences,
3. Use active verbs most of the time.
4. Use verbs—not nouns—to carry the weight of your sentence.
5. Eliminate wordiness.
6. Vary sentence length and sentence structure.
7. Use parallel structure. Use the same grammatical form for ideas that have the same logical function.
8. Put your readers in your sentences.

As you write and revise paragraphs,
9. Begin most paragraphs with topic sentences so that readers know what to expect in the paragraph.
10. Use transitions to link ideas.

1. Use words that are accurate, appropriate, and familiar.

Accurate words mean what you want to say. Appropriate words convey the attitudes you want and fit well with the other words in your document. Familiar words are easy to read and understand.

Sometimes choosing the accurate word is hard. Most of us have word pairs that confuse us. Grammarian Richard Lederer tells Toastmasters that these 10 pairs are the ones you are most likely to see or hear confused.[9]

Affect/Effect	Disinterested/Uninterested
Among/Between	Farther/Further
Amount/Number	Fewer/Less
Compose/Comprise	Imply/Infer
Different from/Different than	Lay/Lie

For help using the pairs correctly, see Appendix B.

Some meanings have already evolved before we join the conversation. We may learn the meaning of words or actions by being alert and observant. We learn some meanings by formal and informal study: the importance of "generally accepted accounting principles" or what the trash can on a computer screen symbolizes. Some meanings are negotiated as we interact one-on-one with another person, attempting to communicate.

Individuals are likely to have different ideas about value-laden words like *fair* or *empowerment*. The *Wall Street Journal* notes that the Securities and Exchange Commission has upped the ante on the definition of "rich" as it regulates the net worth requirement for those eligible to invest in hedge funds, a dividing line that "has often been used as a proxy for the government's definition of 'rich':

> The SEC . . . says investors need to have investible assets of at least $2.5 million, excluding equity in any homes or businesses, to be eligible to sign on a hedge fund's dotted line. That's a huge jump from the current requirement, which says individuals have to have a net worth of at least $1 million, including the value of primary residences, or an annual income of $200,000 for the previous two years for individuals or $300,000 for couples."[10]

Some word choices have legal implications. The US Labor Department has recently been reviewing rules for classifying workers as "professionals" or "administrators." As of 1992, computer analysts, programmers, and software engineers were considered professionals. Now representatives of these workers dispute the classification, on the grounds that these workers' jobs tend to be routine and mechanical. The debate affects the workers' paychecks, because under labor laws, employers are exempt from paying extra when professionals and administrators work overtime.[11]

Some meanings are voted on. Take, for example, the term *minority-owned business.* For years, the National Minority Supplier Development Council (NMSDC) defined the term as a business in which at least 51% of the owners were members of racial or ethnic minorities. But that made it hard for businesses to attract major capital or to go public, since doing so would give more ownership to European American investors. In 2000, the NMSDC redefined *minority-owned business* as any business with minority management and at least 30% minority ownership.[12]

Accurate denotations. To be accurate, a word's denotation must match the meaning the writer wishes to convey. **Denotation** is a word's literal or dictionary meaning. Most common words in English have more than one denotation. The word *pound,* for example, means, or denotes, a unit of weight, a place where stray animals are kept, a unit of money in the old British system, and the verb *to hit.* Coca-Cola spends millions each year to protect its brand names so that *Coke* will denote only that brand and not just any cola drink.

When two people use the same word or phrase to mean, or denote, different things, **bypassing** occurs. For example, a large mail-order drug company notifies clients by e-mail when their prescription renewals get stopped because the

What's in a Name (1)

The honeymoon is an ancient tradition. Following their wedding ceremony, a new husband and wife spend a few days or weeks alone together as they settle into their new life together. Now retailers and travel agents are cashing in on the honeymoon tradition, with a twist, by inventing new "traditions" to mark the stages in a couple's life:

- **Anniversarymoons:** repeated honeymoons to celebrate wedding anniversaries.

- **Divorcemoons:** vacations, taken separately, to celebrate the end of a marriage.

- **Familymoons:** postwedding trips for blended families who want to include the children in the vacation.

- **Conceptionmoons:** vacations for couples who are trying to conceive a child.

- **Recoverymoons:** vacations for the mother of the bride.

Adapted from Jeffrey Zaslow, "Moving On: After a Honeymoon, a Conceptionmoon?" *Wall Street Journal,* November 11, 2006, D2.

What's in a Name? (2) or When Is a Sandwich Not a Sandwich? When It's a Burrito.

How would you define a sandwich? Most of us picture two slices of bread with some type of filling in between them. But not the Panera Bread Co.

When Qdoba Mexican Grill tried to move into a shopping center in Massachusetts last year, Panera tried to stop it. The chain has a clause in its lease that protects it from competition by restricting the shopping center from leasing space to another sandwich shop. That clause might keep Subway or Quizno's out, but when Qdoba Mexican Grill moved in, Panera tried to claim that the Mexican restaurant's burritos were sandwiches, and thus the shopping center had violated the agreement. To Panera, a tortilla is equivalent to bread and bread with stuffing in between is a sandwich.

Not so, says Massachusetts Superior Court Judge Jeffrey Locke. Using testimony from chefs as well as a dictionary definition, Locke ruled that the key difference is the shell: a single tortilla is not equivalent to two slices of bread.

Adapted from "Panera Loses Fight Over Status of Burrito," *Des Moines Register*, November 12, 2006, 22A.

doctor has not verified the prescription. Patients are advised to call their doctors and remind them to verify. However, the company's Web site posts a sentence telling clients that the prescription is *being processed*. The drug company means the renewal is in the system, waiting for the doctor's verification. The patients believe the doctor has checked in and the renewal is moving forward. The confusion results in extra phone calls to the company's customer service number, delayed prescriptions, and general customer dissatisfaction.

Careless use of technical terms can produce a kind of bypassing. For instance, behavioral scientists who research conflict management have identified a category of solutions they call "win–win," in which the parties actively work together to devise an outcome that gives both parties what they want. Such an outcome is difficult to achieve, but appealing. General business publications quickly latched onto the term *win–win*, which began appearing in more and more articles. However, a search of books and magazines found that their authors usually used the term to refer to a completely different category of conflict resolution, namely, *compromise*. A compromise requires both parties to make concessions in exchange for reaching a mutually acceptable agreement, so neither party really "wins."[13] Today if a negotiator proposes working toward a "win–win solution," the other party may misunderstand what kind of solution this would be.

Problems also arise when writers misuse words.

The western part of Ohio was transferred from Chicago to Cleveland.[14]

(Ohio did not move. Instead, a company moved responsibility for sales in western Ohio.)

Three major associations of property-liability companies are poised to strike out in opposite directions.[15]

(Three different directions can't be opposite each other.)

[Engulf & Devour] has grown dramatically over the past seven years, largely through the purchase of many smaller, desperate companies.[16]

This quote from a corporate news release probably did not intend to be so frank. More likely, the writer relied on a computer's spell checker, which had no way to know it should replace *desperate* with *disparate*, meaning "fundamentally different from one another."

Accurate denotations can make it easier to solve problems. In one production line with a high failure rate, the largest category of defects was *missed operations*. At first, the supervisor wondered if the people on the line were lazy or irresponsible. But some checking showed that several different problems were labeled *missed operations*: parts installed backward, parts that had missing screws or fasteners, parts whose wires weren't connected. Each of these problems had a different solution. Using accurate words redefined the problem and enabled the production line both to improve quality and to cut repair costs.[17]

Appropriate connotations.   Words are appropriate when their **connotations,** that is, their emotional associations or colorings, convey the attitude you want. A great many words carry connotations of approval or disapproval, disgust or delight. Words in the first column below suggest approval; words in the second column suggest criticism.

Positive word	Negative word
assume	guess
curious	nosy
cautious	fearful
firm	obstinate
flexible	wishy-washy

A supervisor can "tell the truth" about a subordinate's performance and yet write either a positive or a negative performance appraisal, based on the connotations of the words in the appraisal. Consider an employee who pays close attention to details. A positive appraisal might read, "Terry is a meticulous team member who takes care of details that others sometimes ignore." But the same behavior might be described negatively: "Terry is hung up on trivial details."

Advertisers carefully choose words with positive connotations. Expensive cars are never *used*; instead, they're *pre-owned, experienced,* or even *previously adored.*[18] Insurers emphasize what you want to *protect* (your home, your car, your life), rather than the losses you are insuring against (fire damage, auto accident, death). Credit card companies tell about what you can do with the card (charge a vacation), not the debt, payments, and fees involved.

Words may also connote categories. Some show status. Both *salesperson* and *sales representative* are nonsexist job titles. But the first sounds like a clerk in a store; the second suggests someone selling important items to corporate customers. Some words connote age: *adorable* generally connotes young children, not adults. Other words, such as *handsome* or *pretty,* connote gender.

Connotations change over time. The word *charity* had acquired such negative connotations by the 19th century that people began to use the term *welfare* instead. Now, *welfare* has acquired negative associations. Most states have *public assistance programs* instead.

Ethical implications of word choice.   How positively can we present something and still be ethical? *Pressure-treated lumber* sounds acceptable. But naming the material injected under pressure—*arsenic-treated lumber*—may lead the customer to make a different decision. We have the right to package our ideas attractively, but we have the responsibility to give the public or our superiors all the information they need to make decisions.

Word choices have ethical implications in other contexts as well. For example, as the racial and ethnic makeup of the US workforce has changed, more companies have adopted the language of "managing diversity." People tend to view this language as positive, because it presumes employees' differences can be an asset to their employer, not a source of difficulty. However, referring to employees as resources to be managed places corporate financial interests above employees' human interests. The risk is that managers may forget ethical dimensions of how they treat their diverse employees.[19]

Familiar words.   Use familiar words, words that are in almost everyone's vocabulary. Use the word that most exactly conveys your meaning, but whenever you can choose between two words that mean the same thing, use the shorter, more common one. Try to use specific, concrete words. They're easier to understand and remember.[20]

A series of long, learned, abstract terms makes writing less interesting, less forceful, and less memorable. When you have something simple to say, use simple words.

The following list gives a few examples of short, simple alternatives:

Formal and stuffy	Short and simple
ameliorate	improve
commence	begin
enumerate	list
finalize	finish, complete
prioritize	rank
utilize	use
viable option	choice

Selling Success in Plain English

If you've opened a mutual fund lately, you might notice something different in the disclosure documents: there's less to read. Several leading Wall Street financial service firms are simplifying their documentation.

James Gorman, retail-brokerage chief at Morgan Stanley, described the reason why his firm reduced the documentation from 136 pages in 14 documents to a single 48-page booklet. He noted that he did not understand all of the longer documentation, and the average person does not need that amount of information. Other financial services companies are also streamlining their documents. Smith Barney, for instance, now offers clients a customized welcome package that includes a table of contents, instruction pages, and only the disclosure information that is relevant to their funds. Banc of America Investment Services and Wachovia Securities are also rewriting their disclosure statements to reduce the amount of legalese and make the documents easier to understand.

The purpose of the streamlining is to encourage clients to read the information. In the past, some clients were reluctant to invest because they didn't understand the information or were simply overwhelmed with paperwork, including prospectuses. Bill Lutz, a consultant on plain English, also suggests that clearer language can help protect the firms from liability by reducing the number of clients who claim that they didn't understand what they were signing.

Adapted from Jaime Levy Pessin, "Wall Street Aims to Simplify Disclosures for Clients," *Wall Street Journal,* October 31, 2006, D2.

There are some exceptions to the general rule that "shorter is better":

1. Use a long word if it is the only word that expresses your meaning exactly.
2. Use a long word if it is more familiar than a short word. *Send out* is better than *emit* and *a word in another language for a geographic place or area* is better than *exonym* because more people know the first item in each pair.
3. Use a long word if its connotations are more appropriate. *Exfoliate* is better than *scrape off dead skin cells*.
4. Use a long word if your audience prefers it.

2. Use technical jargon sparingly; eliminate business jargon.

There are two kinds of **jargon.** The first kind of jargon is the specialized terminology of a technical field. *LIFO* and *FIFO* are technical terms in accounting; *byte* and *baud* are computer jargon; *scale-free* and *pickled and oiled* designate specific characteristics of steel. A job application letter is the one occasion when it's desirable to use technical jargon: using the technical terminology of the reader's field helps suggest that you're a peer who also is competent in that field. In other kinds of messages, use technical jargon only when the term is essential and known to the reader.

If a technical term has a "plain English" equivalent, use the simpler term. It is especially important to replace jargon with plain English when the specialized meaning of the technical term is not in fact being used. Consider this example:

Jargon: Additional parameters for price exception reporting were established for non-stock labor buy costs.

Better: We decided to include nonstock labor buys of over $_____ in the price exception report.

Parameters is a term that is essential in mathematics and statistics, but it is rarely used properly in general business and administrative writing. As the revision shows, the real meaning here was simple; no technical term was needed.

The second kind of jargon is the **businessese** that some writers still use: *as per your request, enclosed please find, please do not hesitate.* None of the words in this second category of jargon are necessary. Indeed, some writers call these terms *deadwood,* since they are no longer living words. If any of the terms in the first column of Figure 4.6 show up in your writing, replace them with more modern language.

Cornered   by Mike Baldwin

"I need an interpreter. Send in someone who speaks jargon."

Figure 4.6 Getting Rid of Business Jargon

Instead of	Use	Because
At your earliest convenience	The date you need a response	If you need it by a deadline, say so. It may never be convenient to respond.
As per your request; 65 miles per hour	As you requested; 65 miles an hour	*Per* is a Latin word for *by* or *for each*. Use *per* only when the meaning is correct; avoid mixing English and Latin.
Enclosed please find	Enclosed is; Here is	An enclosure isn't a treasure hunt. If you put something in the envelope, the reader will find it.
Forward same to this office.	Return it to this office.	Omit legal jargon.
Hereto, herewith	Omit	Omit legal jargon.
Please be advised; Please be informed	Omit—simply start your response	You don't need a preface. Go ahead and start.
Please do not hesitate	Omit	Omit negative words.
Pursuant to	According to; or omit	*Pursuant* does not mean *after.* Omit legal jargon in any case.
Said order	Your order	Omit legal jargon.
This will acknowledge receipt of your letter.	Omit—start your response	If you answer a letter, the reader knows you got it.
Trusting this is satisfactory, we remain	Omit	Eliminate *-ing* endings. When you are through, stop.

As You Write and Revise Sentences

At the sentence level, you can do many things to make your writing easy to read.

3. Use active verbs most of the time.

"Who does what" sentences with active verbs make your writing more forceful.

A verb is **active** if the grammatical subject of the sentence does the action the verb describes. A verb is **passive** if the subject is acted upon. Passives are usually made up of a form of the verb *to be* plus a past participle. *Passive* has nothing to do with *past.* Passives can be past, present, or future:

were received	(in the past)
is recommended	(in the present)
will be implemented	(in the future)

To spot a passive, find the verb. If the verb describes something that the grammatical subject is doing, the verb is active. If the verb describes something that is being done to the grammatical subject, the verb is passive.

Active	**Passive**
The customer received 500 widgets.	Five hundred widgets were received by the customer.
I recommend this method.	This method is recommended by me.
The state agencies will implement the program.	The program will be implemented by the state agencies.

Writing for the Web

Writers preparing content for a Web site should keep in mind the physical demands of reading a computer screen. Reading a screen is more tiring than reading a printed page, so readers tend to scan. Internet users also tend to be in a hurry to find whatever they are looking for. Writing for the Web is therefore most effective when it follows these guidelines:

- Write concisely.
- Put the main point first; then provide details.
- Break up the text with headings that describe the content.
- Choose easy-to-read type fonts.
- Use informal and direct language; don't try to be cute and clever.
- Keep hyperlinks to a minimum.

Adapted from Change Sciences Group, "Writing for the Web: Best Practices," Change Sciences Research Brief (Irvington, NY: Change Sciences Group, 2003), downloaded at www. changesciences.com.

Verbs can be changed from active to passive by making the direct object (in the oval) the new subject (in the box). To change a passive verb to an active one, you must make the agent ("by_____ " in <>) the new subject. If no agent is specified in the sentence, you must supply one to make the sentence active.

Active	**Passive**
The plant manager approved the request.	The request was approved by the <plant manager.>
The committee will decide next month.	A decision will be made next month. No agent in sentence.
[You] Send the customer a letter informing her about the change.	A letter will be sent informing the customer of the change. No agent in sentence.

If the sentence does not have a direct object in its active form, no passive equivalent exists.

Active	**No passive exists**
I would like to go to the conference.	
The freight charge will be about $1,400.	
The phone rang.	

Passive verbs have at least three disadvantages:

1. If all the information in the original sentence is retained, passive verbs make the sentence longer. Passives take more time to understand.[21]
2. If the agent is omitted, it's not clear who is responsible for doing the action.
3. Using many passive verbs, especially in material that has a lot of big words, can make the writing boring and pompous.

Passive verbs are desirable in these situations:

1. Use passives to emphasize the object receiving the action, not the agent.

   Your order was shipped November 15.

   The customer's order, not the shipping clerk, is important.

2. Use passives to provide coherence within a paragraph. A sentence is easier to read if "old" information comes at the beginning of a sentence. When you have been discussing a topic, use the word again as your subject even if that requires a passive verb.

   The bank made several risky loans in the late 1990s. These loans were written off as "uncollectible" in 2001.

   Using *loans* as the subject of the second sentence provides a link between the two sentences, making the paragraph as a whole easier to read.

3. Use passives to avoid assigning blame.

   The order was damaged during shipment.

   An active verb would require the writer to specify *who* damaged the order. The passive here is more tactful.

   According to PlainLanguage.gov, changing writing to active voice is the most powerful change that can be made to government documents.[22]

4. Use verbs—not nouns—to carry the weight of your sentence.

Put the weight of your sentence in the verb to make your sentences more forceful and up to 25% easier to read.[23] When the verb is a form of the verb *to be,* revise the sentence to use a more forceful verb.

Korean Air's ad plays delightfully on connotations of relaxation.

Weak: The financial advantage of owning this equipment instead of leasing it is 10% after taxes.

Better: Owning this equipment rather than leasing it will save us 10% after taxes.

Nouns ending in *-ment, -ion,* and *-al* often hide verbs.

~~make an adjustment~~	adjust
~~make a payment~~	pay
~~make a decision~~	decide
~~reach a conclusion~~	conclude
~~take into consideration~~	consider
~~make a referral~~	refer
~~provide assistance~~	assist

Use verbs to present the information more forcefully.

Weak: We will perform an investigation of the problem.

Better: We will investigate the problem.

Weak: Selection of a program should be based on the client's needs.

Better: Select the program that best fits the client's needs.

5. Eliminate wordiness.

Writing is **wordy** if the same idea can be expressed in fewer words. Unnecessary words increase writing time, bore your reader, and make your meaning more difficult to follow, since the reader must hold all the extra words in mind while trying to understand your meaning. Don Bush, the "friendly editor" columnist for *intercom,* calls wordiness the most obvious fault of technical writing.[24]

Using Your Computer to Improve Style

Laser copies look so perfect that it can be hard to edit them. But your computer can be an ally, not an enemy, as you revise and edit.

- Use the "search" or "find" command to find potential errors. One student replaces every "is" and "are" with capital letters ("IS" and "ARE") so that he can easily check his draft. Another replaces periods with several asterisks to check sentence integrity.

- Change the font or size. Putting your text in an unusual font or 24-point type can help you really see what you've said. (Just remember to change back to a standard font in a standard size before printing out the final version!)

- Ask a friend to edit, putting changes in all caps, so you can easily find them.

Adapted from Todd Taylor, "'Soft Copy' and the Illusion of Laser-Printed Text," *Technical Communication* 42, no. 1 (February 1995): 169–70.

Good writing is concise, but it may still be lengthy. Concise writing may be long because it is packed with ideas. In Chapter 3, we saw that revisions to create you-attitude and positive emphasis (◄▥ pp. 76, 80, respectively) and to develop benefits were frequently *longer* than the originals because the revision added information not given in the original.

Sometimes you may be able to look at a draft and see immediately how to condense it. When the solution isn't obvious, try the following strategies to condense your writing:

a. Eliminate words that add nothing.
b. Use gerunds (the *-ing* form of verbs) and infinitives (the *to* form of verbs) to make sentences shorter and smoother.
c. Combine sentences to eliminate unnecessary words.
d. Put the meaning of your sentence into the subject and verb to cut the number of words.

You eliminate unnecessary words to save the reader's time, not simply to see how few words you can use. You aren't writing a telegram, so keep the little words that make sentences complete. (Incomplete sentences are fine in lists where all the items are incomplete.)

The following examples show how to use these methods.

a. Eliminate words that add nothing.   Cut words if the idea is already clear from other words in the sentence. Substitute single words for wordy phrases.

Wordy: Keep this information on file for future reference.

Better: Keep this information for reference.

or: File this information.

Wordy: Ideally, it would be best to put the billing ticket just below the monitor and above the keyboard.

Better: If possible, put the billing ticket between the monitor and the keyboard.

Phrases beginning with *of, which,* and *that* can often be shortened.

Wordy: the question of most importance

Better: the most important question

Wordy: the estimate which is enclosed

Better: the enclosed estimate

Wordy: We need to act on the suggestions that our customers offer us.

Better: We need to act on customer suggestions.

Sentences beginning with *There are* or *It is* can often be tighter.

Wordy: There are three reasons for the success of the project.

Tighter: Three reasons explain the project's success.

Wordy: It is the case that college graduates advance more quickly in the company.

Tighter: College graduates advance more quickly in the company.

Check your draft. If you find these phrases, or any of the unnecessary words shown in Figure 4.7, eliminate them.

b. Use gerunds and infinitives to make sentences shorter and smoother.
A **gerund** is the *-ing* form of a verb; grammatically, it is a verb used as a noun. In the sentence, "Running is my favorite activity," *running* is the subject of the sentence. An **infinitive** is the form of the verb that is preceded by *to: to run* is the infinitive.

Figure 4.7   Words to Cut

Cut the following words	Cut redundant words	Substitute a single word for a wordy phrase	
quite	~~a period of~~ three months	~~at the present time~~	now
really	during ~~the course of~~ the negotiations	~~due to the fact that~~	because
very	during ~~the year of~~ 2004	~~in order to~~	to
	maximum ~~possible~~	~~in the event that~~	if
	~~past~~ experience	~~in the near future~~	soon (or give the date)
	plan ~~in advance~~	~~on a regular basis~~	regularly
	refer ~~back~~	~~prior to the start of~~	before
	~~the color~~ blue	~~until such time as~~	until
	~~the state of~~ Texas		
	~~true~~ facts		

In the revision below, a gerund *(purchasing)* and an infinitive *(to transmit)* tighten the sentence.

Wordy: A plant suggestion has been made where they would purchase a QWIP machine for the purpose of transmitting test reports between plants.

Tighter: The plant suggests purchasing a QWIP machine to transmit test reports between plants.

Even when gerunds and infinitives do not greatly affect length, they often make sentences smoother and more conversational.

c. Combine sentences to eliminate unnecessary words.   In addition to saving words, combining sentences focuses the reader's attention on key points, makes your writing sound more sophisticated, and sharpens the relationship between ideas, thus making your writing more coherent.

Wordy: I conducted this survey by telephone on Sunday, April 21. I questioned two groups of upperclassmen—male and female—who, according to the Student Directory, were still living in the dorms. The purpose of this survey was to find out why some upperclassmen continue to live in the dorms even though they are no longer required by the University to do so. I also wanted to find out if there were any differences between male and female upperclassmen in their reasons for choosing to remain in the dorms.

Tighter: On Sunday, April 21, I phoned upperclassmen and women living in the dorms to find out (1) why they continue to live in the dorms even though they are no longer required to do so, and (2) whether men and women gave the same reasons for staying in the dorms.

d. Put the meaning of your sentence into the subject and verb to cut the number of words.   Put the core of your meaning into the subject and verb of your main clause. Think about what you *mean* and try saying the same thing in several different ways. Some alternatives will be tighter than others. Choose the tightest one.

The Benefits of Plain English

Allen-Bradley spent two years converting its manuals to plain English. The work is paying off in five ways. (1) Phone calls asking questions about the products have dropped from 50 a day to only 2 a month. (2) The sales force is selling more systems because people can learn about them more quickly. (3) Distributors spend less time on site teaching customers about products. (4) The clearer documents are easier to translate into Japanese, German, and French for international sales. (5) The tighter documents cost less to print, especially when translated into Arabic and German, which require 125% more space than the same content in English.

Adapted from Barry Jereb, "Plain English on the Plant Floor," *Plain Language: Principles and Practice,* ed. Edwin R. Steinberg (Detroit: Wayne State University Press, 1991), 213.

Wordy: The reason we are recommending the computerization of this process is because it will reduce the time required to obtain data and will give us more accurate data.

Better: Computerizing the process will give us more accurate data more quickly.

Wordy: The purpose of this letter is to indicate that if we are unable to mutually benefit from our seller/buyer relationship, with satisfactory material and satisfactory payment, then we have no alternative other than to sever the relationship. In other words, unless the account is handled in 45 days, we will have to change our terms to a permanent COD basis.

Better: A good buyer/seller relationship depends upon satisfactory material and payment. You can continue to charge your purchases from us only if you clear your present balance in 45 days.

6. Vary sentence length and sentence structure.

Readable prose mixes sentence lengths and varies sentence structure. A really short sentence (under 10 words) can add punch to your prose. Really long sentences (over 30 or 40 words) are danger signs.

You can vary sentence patterns in several ways. First, you can mix simple, compound, and complex sentences. (See Appendix B ➡ for more information on sentence structure.) **Simple sentences** have one main clause:

We will open a new store this month.

Compound sentences have two main clauses joined with *and, but, or,* or another conjunction. Compound sentences work best when the ideas in the two clauses are closely related.

We have hired staff, and they will complete their training next week.

We wanted to have a local radio station broadcast from the store during its grand opening, but the DJs were already booked.

Complex sentences have one main and one subordinate clause; they are good for showing logical relationships.

When the stores open, we will have specials in every department.

Because we already have a strong customer base in the northwest, we expect the new store to be just as successful as the store in the City Center Mall.

You can also vary sentences by changing the order of elements. Normally the subject comes first.

We will survey customers later in the year to see whether demand warrants a third store on campus.

To create variety, occasionally begin the sentence with some other part of the sentence.

Later in the year, we will survey customers to see whether demand warrants a third store on campus.

To see whether demand warrants a third store on campus, we will survey customers later in the year.

Use these guidelines for sentence length and structure:

- Always edit sentences for conciseness. Even a 17-word sentence can be wordy.
- When your subject matter is complicated or full of numbers, make a special effort to keep sentences short.

- Use long sentences:
  To show how ideas are linked to each other.
  To avoid a series of short, choppy sentences.
  To reduce repetition.
- Group the words in long and medium-length sentences into chunks that the reader can process quickly.
- When you use a long sentence, keep the subject and verb close together.

Let's see how to apply the last three principles.

- **Use long sentences to show how ideas are linked to each other, to avoid a series of short, choppy sentences, and to reduce repetition.** The following sentence is hard to read not simply because it is long but because it is shapeless. Just cutting it into a series of short, choppy sentences doesn't help. The best revision uses medium-length sentences to show the relationship between ideas.

Too long: It should also be noted in the historical patterns presented in the summary, that though there were delays in January and February which we realized were occurring, we are now back where we were about a year ago, and that we are not off line in our collect receivables as compared to last year at this time, but we do show a considerable over-budget figure because of an ultraconservative goal on the receivable investment.

Choppy: There were delays in January and February. We knew about them at the time. We are now back where we were about a year ago. The summary shows this. Our present collect receivables are in line with last year's. However, they exceed the budget. The reason they exceed the budget is that our goal for receivable investment was very conservative.

Better: As the summary shows, although there were delays in January and February (of which we were aware), we have now regained our position of a year ago. Our present collect receivables are in line with last year's, but they exceed the budget because our goal for receivable investment was very conservative.

- **Group the words in long and medium-length sentences into chunks.** The "better" revision above has seven chunks. At 27 and 24 words, respectively, these sentences aren't short, but they're readable because no chunk is longer than 10 words. Any sentence pattern will get boring if it is repeated sentence after sentence. Use different sentence patterns—different kinds and lengths of chunks—to keep your prose interesting.
- **Keep the subject and verb close together.** Often you can move the subject and verb closer together if you put the modifying material in a list at the end of the sentence. For maximum readability, present the list vertically.

Hard to read: Movements resulting from termination, layoffs and leaves, recalls and reinstates, transfers in, transfers out, promotions in, promotions out, and promotions within are presently documented through the Payroll Authorization Form.

Better: The Payroll Authorization Form documents the following movements:
- Termination
- Layoffs and leaves
- Recalls and reinstates
- Transfers in and out
- Promotions in, out, and within

Writing for International Audiences

When you're writing for readers in another country, be careful to adjust your writing style to the new culture. Even the English language changes when you leave the United States. American spelling in documents for audiences who have learned British English can be annoying to readers. Remember that spelling is cultural, so adjust your writing to suit your readers, even if that means writing *grey, analyse, colour, centre, familiarise,* and *catalogue.* Adjusting your style and your spelling for international audiences demonstrates respect for their cultures.

If you're adapting your text for an international audience, go beyond a dictionary. Localize your document by asking a native speaker from your target country (or countries) to read the document and note any problematic words, phrases, images, or examples.

Adapted from James Calvert Scott, "American and British Business-Related Spelling Differences," *Business Communication Quarterly* 67, no. 3 (2004): 153–67.

Sometimes you will need to change the verb and revise the word order to put the modifying material at the end of the sentence.

Hard to read: The size sequence code that is currently used for sorting the items in the NOSROP lists and the composite stock lists is not part of the online file.

Smoother: The online file does not contain the size sequence code used for sorting the items in the composite stock lists and the NOSROP lists.

7. Use parallel structure.

Parallel structure puts words, phrases, or clauses in the same grammatical and logical form. In the following faulty example, *by reviewing* is a gerund, while *note* is an imperative verb. Make the sentence parallel by using both gerunds or both imperatives.

Faulty: Errors can be checked by reviewing the daily exception report or note the number of errors you uncover when you match the lading copy with the file copy of the invoice.

Parallel: Errors can be checked by reviewing the daily exception report or by noting the number of errors you uncover when you match the lading copy with the file copy of the invoice.

Also

parallel: To check errors, note

1. The number of items on the daily exception report.

2. The number of errors discovered when the lading copy and the file copy are matched.

Note that a list in parallel structure must fit grammatically into the umbrella sentence that introduces the list.

Words must also be logically parallel. In the following faulty example, *juniors, seniors,* and *athletes* are not three separate groups. The revision groups words into nonoverlapping categories.

Faulty: I interviewed juniors and seniors and athletes.

Parallel: I interviewed juniors and seniors. In each rank, I interviewed athletes and nonathletes.

Parallel structure is a powerful device for making your writing tighter, smoother, and more forceful. As Figure 4.8 shows, parallelism often enables you to tighten your writing. To make your writing as tight as possible, eliminate repetition in parallel lists; see Figure 4.9.

8. Put your readers in your sentences.

Use second-person pronouns (*you*) rather than third-person (*he, she, one*) to give your writing more impact. *You* is both singular and plural; it can refer to a single person or to every member of your organization.

Figure 4.8   Use Parallelism to Tighten Your Writing.

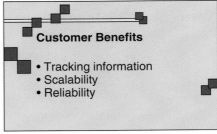

Faulty   Parallel

Figure 4.9   Eliminate Repeated Words in Parallel Lists.

PowerPoint Reports

- They work best when the audience is well-defined.
- They work best when visuals can carry the message.
- They work best when oral comments can explain and connect ideas.

Wordy

PowerPoint reports work best when

- The audience is well-defined.
- Visuals can carry the message.
- Oral comments can explain and connect ideas.

Concise

Reader-Friendly Topic Sentences

The best topic sentences have a you-attitude. They reflect the reader's interests and feelings.

If you are selling an idea to management, this means your topic sentences will emphasize the business benefits of your idea. Managers will want to know whether your idea will add to sales or cut costs. The details following your topic sentence should tell how your idea will provide these benefits. If possible, test your idea ahead of time, so you can back up your statement with facts, not just opinions.

If you are selling an idea to employees, each topic sentence should focus on benefits to them. For example, if you are writing about a new computer system, the order clerk will want to know how it will make the work easier or improve his or her performance. The clerk is less interested in financial statistics like inventory turnover and gross profits.

The same principles apply to answering objections. If an employee objects to a change by saying, "I've never done that before," a wise supervisor might reply, "Exactly. It's an opportunity to gain experience."

Adapted from Ted Pollock, "How to Sell an Idea," *Supervision* 64, no.6 (June 2003): 15–16.

Third-person: Funds in a participating employee's account at the end of each six months will automatically be used to buy more stock unless a "Notice of Election Not to Exercise Purchase Rights" form is received from the employee.

Second-person: Once you begin to participate, funds in your account at the end of each six months will automatically be used to buy more stock unless you turn in a "Notice of Election Not to Exercise Purchase Rights" form.

Be careful to use *you* only when it refers to your reader.

Incorrect: My visit with the outside sales rep showed me that your schedule can change quickly.

Correct: My visit with the outside sales rep showed me that schedules can change quickly.

As You Write and Revise Paragraphs

Paragraphs are visual and logical units. Use them to chunk your sentences.

9. Begin most paragraphs with topic sentences.

A good paragraph has **unity;** that is, it discusses only one idea, or topic. The **topic sentence** states the main idea and provides a scaffold to structure your document. Your writing will be easier to read if you make the topic sentence explicit and put it at the beginning of the paragraph.[25]

Hard to read (no topic sentence):   In fiscal 2001, the company filed claims for refund of federal income taxes of $3,199,000 and interest of $969,000 paid as a result of an examination of the company's federal income tax returns by the Internal Revenue Service (IRS) for the years 1997 through 1999. It is uncertain what amount, if any, may ultimately be recovered.

Better (paragraph starts with topic sentence):   The company and the IRS disagree about whether the company is responsible for back taxes. In fiscal 2001, the company filed claims for a refund of federal income taxes of $3,199,000 and interest of $969,000 paid as a result of an examination of the company's federal income tax returns by the Internal Revenue Service (IRS) for the years 1997 through 1999. It is uncertain what amount, if any, may ultimately be recovered.

A good topic sentence forecasts the structure and content of the paragraph.

Plan B also has economic advantages.

(Prepares the reader for a discussion of B's economic advantages.)

Figure 4.10 Transition Words and Phrases

To show addition or continuation of the same idea	To introduce an example	To show that the contrast is more important than the previous idea	To show time
and	for example (e.g.)	but	after
also	for instance	however	as
first, second, third	indeed	nevertheless	before
in addition	to illustrate	on the contrary	in the future
likewise	namely	**To show cause and effect**	next
similarly	specifically	as a result	then
To introduce another important item	**To contrast**	because	until
furthermore	in contrast	consequently	when
moreover	on the other hand	for this reason	while
	or	therefore	**To summarize or end**
			finally
			in conclusion

We had several personnel changes in June.

(Prepares the reader for a list of the month's terminations and hires.)

Employees have complained about one part of our new policy on parental leaves.

(Prepares the reader for a discussion of the problem.)

When the first sentence of a paragraph is not the topic sentence, readers who skim may miss the main point. Move the topic sentence to the beginning of the paragraph. If the paragraph does not have a topic sentence, you will need to write one. If you can't think of a single sentence that serves as an "umbrella" to cover every sentence, the paragraph lacks unity. To solve the problem, either split the paragraph into two or eliminate the sentence that digresses from the main point.

10. Use transitions to link ideas.

Transition words and sentences signal the connections between ideas to the reader. Transitions tell whether the next sentence continues the previous thought or starts a new idea; they can tell whether the idea that comes next is more or less important than the previous thought. Figure 4.10 lists some of the most common transition words and phrases.

Readability Formulas and Good Style

Readability formulas attempt to measure objectively how easy something is to read. However, since they don't take many factors into account, the formulas are at best a very limited guide to good style.

Computer packages that analyze style may give you a readability score. Some states' "plain English" laws require consumer contracts to meet a certain readability score. Some companies require that warranties and other consumer documents meet certain scores.

Readability formulas depend heavily on word length and sentence length. But as researchers Janice C. Redish and Jack Selzer have shown,[26] using shorter words and sentences will not necessarily make a passage easy to read. Short words are not always easy to understand, especially if they have technical meanings (e.g., *waive, bear market, liquid*). Short, choppy sentences and sentence fragments are actually harder to understand than well-written medium-length sentences.

No reading formula yet devised takes into account three factors that influence how easy a text is to read: the complexity of the ideas, the organization of the ideas, and the layout and design of the document.

Instead of using readability formulas to measure style, the Document Design Center recommends that you test your draft with the people for whom it is designed. How long does it take them to find the information they need? Do they make mistakes when they try to use the document? Do they think the document is easy to use? Answers to these questions can give us much more accurate information than any readability score.

Organizational Preferences for Style

Different organizations and bosses may legitimately have different ideas about what constitutes good writing. If the style the company prefers seems reasonable, use it. If the style doesn't seem reasonable—if you work for someone who likes flowery language or wordy paragraphs, for example—you have several choices.

- Go ahead and use the techniques in this chapter. Sometimes seeing good writing changes people's minds about the style they prefer.
- Help your boss learn about writing. Show him or her this book or the research cited in the notes to demonstrate how a clear, crisp style makes documents easier to read.
- Recognize that a style may serve other purposes than communication. An abstract, hard-to-read style may help a group forge its own identity. James Suchan and Ronald Dulek have shown that Navy officers preferred a passive, impersonal style because they saw themselves as followers. An aircraft company's engineers saw wordiness as the verbal equivalent of backup systems. A backup is redundant but essential to safety, because parts and systems do fail.[27] When big words, jargon, and wordiness are central to a group's self-image, change will be difficult, since changing style will mean changing the corporate culture.
- Ask. Often the documents that end up in files aren't especially good; later, other workers may find these and copy them, thinking they represent a corporate standard. Bosses may in fact prefer better writing.

Building a good style takes energy and effort, but it's well worth the work. Good style can make every document more effective; good style can help make you the good writer so valuable to every organization.

Summary of Key Points

- Good style in business and administrative writing is less formal, more friendly, and more personal than the style usually used for term papers.
- To improve your style,
  - Try WIRMI: *What I Really Mean Is.* Then write the words.
  - Try reading your draft out loud to someone. If the words sound awkward, they'll seem awkward to a reader, too.
  - Ask someone else to read your draft out loud. Readers stumble because the words on the page aren't what they expect to see. The places where that person stumbles are places where your writing can be better.
  - Write a *lot.*

Gifts Defined

"[Wal-mart corporate headquarters meeting rooms have] nothing on a wall save a poster labeled 'Gifts and Gratuities.' It reads:

It is our policy that associates of the Company, regardless of their capacity, do not accept for their personal benefits, gratuities, tips, cash, samples, etc., from anyone buying from us or selling to us, or in any way serving our company.

In case anyone misses the point, the poster goes on to define gifts and gratuities as including: tickets to entertainment events, kickbacks in the form of money or merchandise, special discounts, sample merchandise, Christmas gifts, or meals. There is no 'de minimis' rule; even a cup of coffee is forbidden."

What do you think of Wal-mart's definition of "gifts and gratuities"? Is the definition too restrictive? What benefits does it offer employees?

Quoted from Alan Murray, "Wal-Mart's Lesson for Wall Street," *Wall Street Journal*, December 13, 2006, A2.

- Use the following techniques to make your writing easier to read.

  As you choose words,

  1. Use words that are accurate, appropriate, and familiar. Denotation is a word's literal meaning; connotation is the emotional coloring that a word conveys.
  2. Use technical jargon only when it is essential and known to the reader. Eliminate business jargon.

  As you write and revise sentences,

  3. Use active verbs most of the time. Active verbs are better because they are shorter, clearer, and more interesting.
  4. Use verbs—not nouns—to carry the weight of your sentence.
  5. Eliminate wordiness. Writing is wordy if the same idea can be expressed in fewer words.
     a. Eliminate words that add nothing.
     b. Use gerunds and infinitives to make sentences shorter and smoother.
     c. Combine sentences to eliminate unnecessary words.
     d. Put the meaning of your sentence into the subject and verb to cut the number of words.
  6. Vary sentence length and sentence structure.
  7. Use parallel structure. Use the same grammatical form for ideas that have the same logical function.
  8. Put your readers in your sentences.

  As you write and revise paragraphs,

  9. Begin most paragraphs with topic sentences so that readers know what to expect in the paragraph.
  10. Use transitions to link ideas.

- Readability formulas are not a sufficient guide to style. They imply that all short words and all short sentences are equally easy to read; they ignore other factors that make a document easy or hard to read: the complexity of the ideas, the organization of the ideas, and the layout and design of the document.
- Different organizations and bosses may legitimately have different ideas about what constitutes good writing.

CHAPTER 4   Exercises and Problems

4.1   Reviewing the Chapter

1. What are some half-truths about style? (LO 1 and 2)
2. How do I evaluate writing rules? (LO 3)
3. What are some ways I can make my sentences more effective? (LO 1 and 2)
4. What are some ways I can make my paragraphs more effective? (LO 2)
5. How can I adapt good style to organization preferences? (LO 3)

4.2   Identifying Words with Multiple Denotations

a. Each of the following words has several denotations. How many can you list without going to a dictionary? How many additional meanings does a good dictionary list?

browser	log
court	table

b. List five words that have multiple denotations.

4.3   Explaining Bypassing

Show how different denotations make bypassing possible in the following examples.

a.   France and Associates: Protection from Professionals

b.   We were not able to account for the outstanding amount of plastic waste generated each year.

c.   I scanned the résumés when I received them.

4.4   Evaluating Connotations

a.   Identify the connotations of each of the following metaphors for a multicultural nation.

melting pot

mosaic

tapestry

crazy quilt

garden salad

stew

tributaries

b.   Which connotations seem most positive? Why?

4.5   Evaluating the Ethical Implication of Connotations

In each of the following pairs, identify the more favorable term. When is its use justifiable?

1.   wasted/sacrificed
2.   illegal alien/immigrant
3.   friendly fire/enemy attack
4.   terminate/fire
5.   inaccuracy/lying
6.   budget/spending plan
7.   feedback/criticism

4.6   Correcting Errors in Denotation and Connotation

Identify and correct the errors in denotation or connotation in the following sentences:

1.   In our group, we weeded out the best idea each person had thought of.
2.   She is a prudent speculator.
3.   The three proposals are diametrically opposed to each other.
4.   While he researched companies, he was literally glued to the Web.
5.   Our backpacks are hand sewn by one of roughly 16 individuals.

4.7   Using Connotations to Shape Response

Write two sentences to describe each of the following situations. In one sentence, use words with positive connotations; in the other, use negative words.

1.   Chris doesn't spend time on small talk.
2.   Chris often starts work on a new project without being told to do so.
3.   As a supervisor, Chris gives very specific instructions to subordinates.

4.8   Choosing Levels of Formality

Identify the more formal word in each pair. Which term is better for most business documents? Why?

1.   adapted to   geared to
2.   befuddled   confused
3.   assistant   helper
4.   pilot project   testing the waters
5.   cogitate   think

4.9   Eliminating Jargon and Simplifying Language

Revise these sentences to eliminate jargon and to use short, familiar words.

1. When the automobile company announced its strategic downsizing initiative, it offered employees a career alternative enhancement program.
2. Any alterations must be approved during the 30-day period commencing 60 days prior to the expiration date of the agreement.
3. As per your request, the undersigned has obtained estimates of upgrading our computer system. A copy of the estimated cost is attached hereto.
4. Please be advised that this writer is in considerable need of a new computer.
5. Enclosed please find the proposed draft for the employee negative retention plan. In the event that you have alterations which you would like to suggest, forward same to my office at your earliest convenience.

4.10   Changing Verbs from Passive to Active

Identify the passive verbs in the following sentences and convert them to active verbs. In some cases, you may need to add information to do so. You may use different words as long as you retain the basic meaning of the sentence. Remember that imperative verbs are active, too.

1. For a customer to apply for benefits, an application must be completed.
2. The cost of delivering financial services is being slashed by computers, the Internet, and toll-free phone lines.
3. When the vacation schedule is finalized it is recommended that it be routed to all supervisors for final approval.
4. As stated in my résumé, I have designed Web pages for three student organizations.
5. Material must not be left on trucks outside the warehouse. Either the trucks must be parked inside the warehouse or the material must be unloaded at the time of receiving the truck.

4.11   Using Strong Verbs

Revise each of the following sentences to replace hidden verbs with active verbs.

1. An understanding of stocks and bonds is important if one wants to invest wisely.
2. We must undertake a calculation of expected revenues and expenses for the next two years.
3. The production of clear and concise documents is the mark of a successful communicator.
4. We hope to make use of the company's Web site to promote the new product line.
5. If you wish to be eligible for the Miller scholarship, you must complete an application by January 31.
6. When you make an evaluation of media buys, take into consideration the demographics of the group seeing the ad.
7. We provide assistance to clients in the process of reaching a decision about the purchase of hardware and software.

4.12   Reducing Wordiness

1. Eliminate words that say nothing. You may use different words.
    a. There are many businesses that are active in community and service work.
    b. The purchase of a new computer will allow us to produce form letters quickly. In addition, return on investment could be calculated for proposed repairs. Another use is that the computer could check databases to make sure that claims are paid only once.
    c. Our decision to enter the South American market has precedence in the past activities of the company.
2. Use gerunds and infinitives to make these sentences shorter and smoother.
    a. The completion of the project requires the collection and analysis of additional data.
    b. The purchase of laser printers will make possible the in-house production of the newsletter.

c. The treasurer has the authority for the investment of assets for the gain of higher returns.

3. Combine sentences to show how ideas are related and to eliminate unnecessary words.

   a. Some customers are profitable for companies. Other customers actually cost the company money.

   b. If you are unable to come to the session on HMOs, please call the human resources office.

   You will be able to schedule another time to ask questions you may have about the various options.

   c. Major Japanese firms often have employees who know English well. US companies negotiating with Japanese companies should bring their own interpreters.

4.13 Improving Parallel Structure

Revise each of the following sentences to create parallelism.

1. The orientation session will cover the following information:

   • Company culture will be discussed.
   • How to use the equipment.
   • You will get an overview of key customers' needs.

2. Five criteria for a good Web page are content that serves the various audiences, attention to details, and originality. It is also important to have effective organization and navigation devices. Finally, provide attention to details such as revision date and the Webmaster's address.

3. When you leave a voice-mail message,

   • Summarize your main point in a sentence or two.
   • The name and phone number should be given slowly and distinctly.
   • The speaker should give enough information so that the recipient can act on the message.
   • Tell when you'll be available to receive the recipient's return call.

4.14 Putting Readers in Your Sentences

Revise each of the following sentences to put readers in them. As you revise, use active verbs and simple words.

1. Mutual funds can be purchased from banks, brokers, financial planners, or from the fund itself.

2. I would like to take this opportunity to invite you back to Global Wireless. As a previous customer we have outstanding new rate plans to offer you and your family. We invite you to review the rate plans on the attached page and choose the one that best fits your needs. All our customers are important to us.

3. Another aspect of the university is campus life, with an assortment of activities and student groups to participate in and lectures and sports events to attend.

4.15 Editing Sentences to Improve Style

Revise these sentences to make them smoother, less wordy, and easier to read. Eliminate jargon and repetition. Keep the information; you may reword or reorganize it. If the original is not clear, you may need to add information to write a clear revision.

1. There are many different topics that you will read about on a monthly basis once you subscribe to *Inc.*

2. With the new organic fertilizer, you'll see an increase in the quality of your tomatoes and the number grown.

3. New procedure for customer service employees: Please be aware effective immediately, if a customer is requesting a refund of funds applied to their account a front and back copy of the check must be submitted if the transaction is over $500.00. For example, if the customer is requesting $250.00 back, and the total amount of the transaction is $750.00, a front and back copy of the check will be needed to obtain the refund.

4. The county will benefit from implementing flextime.

   • Offices will stay open longer for more business.
   • Staff turnover will be lower.
   • Easier business communication with states in other time zones.
   • Increased employee productivity.

5. There is a seasonality factor in the workload, with the heaviest being immediately prior to quarterly due dates for estimated tax payments.

4.16   Practicing Plain Language

Working with a partner, create three sentences that feature problematic elements that mask meaning.

- Sentence 1: wordiness and/or euphemisms
- Sentence 2: jargon from your field of study
- Sentence 3: words with multiple denotations or connotations

Then exchange your sentences with another team and rewrite their sentences into plain language.

4.17   Using Topic Sentences

Make each of the following paragraphs more readable by opening each paragraph with a topic sentence. You may be able to find a topic sentence in the paragraph and move it to the beginning. In other cases, you'll need to write a new sentence.

1. At Disney World, a lunch put on an expense account is "on the mouse." McDonald's employees "have ketchup in their veins." Business slang flourishes at companies with rich corporate cultures. Memos at Procter & Gamble are called "reco's" because the model P&G memo begins with a recommendation.

2. The first item on the agenda is the hiring for the coming year. George has also asked that we review the agency goals for the next fiscal year. We should cover this early in the meeting since it may affect our hiring preferences. Finally, we need to announce the deadlines for grant proposals, decide which grants to apply for, and set up a committee to draft each proposal.

3. Separate materials that can be recycled from your regular trash. Pass along old clothing, toys, or appliances to someone else who can use them. When you purchase products, choose those with minimal packaging. If you have a yard, put your yard waste and kitchen scraps (excluding meat and fat) in a compost pile. You can reduce the amount of solid waste your household produces in four ways.

4.18   Revising Paragraphs

Revise each paragraph to make it easier to read. Change, rearrange, or delete words and sentences; add any material necessary.

a. Once a new employee is hired, each one has to be trained for a week by one of our supervisors at a cost of $1,000 each which includes the supervisor's time. This amount also includes half of the new employee's salary, since new hires produce only half the normal production per worker for the week. This summer $24,000 was spent in training 24 new employees. Absenteeism increased in the department on the hottest summer days. For every day each worker is absent we lose $200 in lost production. This past summer there was a total of 56 absentee days taken for a total loss of $11,200 in lost production. Turnover and absenteeism were the causes of an unnecessary expenditure of over $35,000 this summer.

b. One service is investments. General financial news and alerts about companies in the customer's portfolio are available. Quicken also provides assistance in finding the best mortgage rate and in providing assistance in making the decision whether to refinance a mortgage. Another service from Quicken is advice for the start and management of a small business. Banking services, such as paying bills and applying for loans, have long been available to Quicken subscribers. The taxpayer can be walked through the tax preparation process by Quicken. Someone considering retirement can use Quicken to ascertain whether the amount being set aside for this purpose is sufficient. Quicken's Web site provides seven services.

4.19   Writing Paragraphs

As you instructor directs, write a paragraph on one or more of the following topics.

a. Discuss your ideal job.
b. Summarize a recent article from a business magazine or newspaper.
c. Explain how technology is affecting the field you plan to enter.
d. Explain why you have or have not decided to work while you attend college.
e. Write a profile of someone who is successful in the field you hope to enter.

As your instructor directs,

a. Label topic sentences, active verbs, and parallel structure.
b. Edit a classmate's paragraphs to make the writing even tighter and smoother.

4.20   Mosaic Case

As the junior manager of the communications for the physical Mosaic's stores, Demetri constantly receives emails from the accounting department. For example, he needs to know the furniture pieces that have the best selling status so he can create appropriate promotional sales materials.

Unfortunately, there is a new accountant—Steve—who constantly uses bureaucratic jargon and awkward sentence construction in his e-mails.

Here is the latest e-mail Demetri received this morning:

To:	DemetriW@mosaic.com
From:	SteveR@mosaic.com
Subject:	Unspecified

Dear Mr. Demetri,

Pursuant to our conversation yesterday on the telephone, enclosed please find the needed sales figure for the past quarter of the current year. It should be noted that the figures presented herein include numbers on the most recent sales data for this quarter minus this past week prior to the official ending of the quarter.

At the request of the conversation that occurred with you, I have taken the liberty to commence prioritizing the furniture pieces that seemed to have the most impressive routine sales during the initial and final weeks of the sales quarter.

Should you have any further questions on this important and high priority issue that I need to take into consideration, please don't hesitate to contact me about your concerns at your earliest convenience so that we can discuss them at length until both parties can reach an agreed upon resolution.

Sincerely Yours,
Steve R.

All of the e-mails Demetri receives from Steve are similar to this one. Sometimes Demetri has to read the e-mails three or four times before he can even figure out what Steve is trying to say, which ultimately is a factor in productivity for Demetri and everyone else at Mosaic who has to read Steve's e-mails.

After reading this latest e-mail this morning, Demetri printed it out and showed his boss, Yvonne. "Can I do something about this?" he asked.

"Sure. He should know better! Send him an e-mail letting him know what he can do to improve his writing and how his level of formality is inappropriate. You have my green light," Yvonne said, while making her infamous imaginary quote marks in the air when she said "green light."

Take on the communication task of Demetri and send an e-mail to Steve that offers some ways he can improve his writing style based on the techniques outlined in this chapter.

5

Planning, Composing, and Revising

Learning Objectives

After studying this chapter, you will know:

1 More about the activities involved in the composing process, and how to use these activities to your advantage.

2 New techniques to revise, edit, and proofread your communications.

3 Ways to combat writer's block.

Always the Same, Always Different

We call it a "process" because, when we write, there are certain steps we always take. There's always an element of planning and research, always a step where we actually put words together, and always some kind of editing and revision.

Jane Garrard, the Vice President for investor and media relations at Tupperware Brands Corporation is responsible for producing an earnings release statement for the company Web site, every quarter. Every quarter, that task requires the same steps. She gathers facts and data about Tupperware's business and earnings; summarizes that information for Tupperware's shareholders and investors; produces the tables, graphs, and balance sheets that are part of the standard earnings release "boilerplate," or template; and circulates the document for review. That's a *writing* process, and it's the same every quarter.

But it's also a *communication* process, because it's different every quarter. Every quarter brings different numbers, different directions for the company, different market conditions with different investor expectations. Every quarter, it's a different message, requiring a different approach and different interpretations. Garrard and her team must decide the best ways to balance their responsibility to Tupperware's customers with regulatory requirements and company interests. They have to interpret the data, analyze their audience, consult with their co-workers, and then compose an earnings release statement that meets everyone's goals. That's a challenging job, and a "boilerplate" won't help with it.

It's important to have a process to follow when you communicate, because a process will help you organize your time, information, and priorities. But communication isn't just about doing the same thing in the same way, every time. Every communication task is different, so the first step in the "process" is to decide which steps in the process to follow, and how.

> *"The first step in the 'process' is to decide which steps in the process to follow, and how."*

Adapted from Assaf Kadem, "Facts and Interpretation," *Communication World*, December 2006, 30.

Chapter Outline

Ethics and the Writing Process

As you plan a message,
- Be sure you have identified the real audiences and purposes of the message.
- In difficult situations, seek allies in your organization and discuss your options with them.

As you compose,
- Provide accurate and complete information.
- Use reliable sources of material. Document when necessary.
- Warn your readers of limits or dangers in your information.
- Promise only what you can deliver.

As you revise,
- Check to see that your language does not use words that show bias.
- Use feedback to revise text and visuals that your audience may misunderstand.
- Check your sources.
- Assume that no document is confidential. E-mail documents can be forwarded and printed out without your knowledge; both e-mails and paper documents can be subpoenaed for court cases.

Skilled performances look easy and effortless. In reality, as every dancer, musician, and athlete knows, they're the products of hard work, hours of practice, attention to detail, and intense concentration. Like skilled performances in other arts, writing rests on a base of work.

The Ways Good Writers Write

No single writing process works for all writers all of the time. However, good writers and poor writers seem to use different processes.[1] Good writers are more likely to

- Realize that the first draft can be revised.
- Write regularly.
- Break big jobs into small chunks.
- Have clear goals focusing on purpose and audience.
- Have several different strategies to choose from.
- Use rules flexibly.
- Wait to edit until after the draft is complete.

The research also shows that good writers differ from poor writers in identifying and analyzing the initial problem more effectively, understanding the task more broadly and deeply, drawing from a wider repertoire of strategies, and seeing patterns more clearly. Good writers also are better at evaluating their own work.

Thinking about the writing process and consciously adopting the processes of good writers will help you become a better writer.

Activities in the Composing Process

Composing can include many activities: planning, brainstorming, gathering, organizing, writing, evaluating, getting feedback, revising, editing, and proofreading. The activities do not have to come in this order. Not every task demands all activities.

Planning

- Analyzing the problem, defining your purposes, and analyzing the audience.
- Brainstorming information, benefits, and objections to include in the document.
- Gathering the information you need—from the message you're answering, a person, a book, or the Web.
- Choosing a pattern of organization, making an outline, creating a list, writing headings.

Writing

- Putting words on paper or on a screen. Writing can be lists, fragmentary notes, stream-of-consciousness writing, incomplete drafts, and ultimately a formal draft.

Revising

- Evaluating your work and measuring it against your goals and the requirements of the situation and audience. The best evaluation results from *re-seeing* your draft as if someone else had written it. Will your audience understand it? Is it complete? Convincing? Friendly?
- Getting feedback from someone else. Is your pattern of organization appropriate? Does a revision solve an earlier problem? Are there any typos in the final copy?
- Adding, deleting, substituting, or rearranging. Revision can be changes in single words or in large sections of a document.

Editing

- Checking the draft to see that it satisfies the requirements of standard English. Here you'd correct spelling and mechanical errors and check word choice and format. Unlike revision, which can produce major changes in meaning, editing focuses on the surface of writing.
- Proofreading the final copy to see that it's free from typographical errors.

Note the following points about these activities:

- **The activities do not have to come in this order.** Some people may gather data *after* writing a draft when they see that they need more specifics to achieve their purposes.
- **You do not have to finish one activity to start another.** Some writers plan a short section and write it, plan the next short section and write it, and so on through the document. Evaluating what is already written may cause a writer to do more planning or to change the original plan.
- **Most writers do not use all activities for all the documents they write.** You'll use more activities when you write more complex or difficult documents about new subjects or to audiences that are new to you.

Research about what writers really do has destroyed some of the stereotypes we used to have about the writing process. Consider planning. Traditional advice stressed the importance of planning and sometimes advised writers to make formal outlines for everything they wrote. But we know now that not all good documents are based on outlines.

For many workplace writers, pre-writing is not a warm-up activity to get ready to write the "real" document. It's really a series of activities designed to gather and organize information, take notes, brainstorm with colleagues, and plan a document before writing a complete draft. And for many people, these activities do not include outlining. Traditional outlining may lull

When Words Hurt

In the summer of 2006, Iowa State University was gearing up to host the first national Special Olympics, a competition featuring people with intellectual disabilities. Visitors would be arriving from all over the country, and the small university town wanted to put on its best face for the crowds. The student newspaper, the *Iowa State Daily*, created a 14-page, full-color visitors' guide to the city of Ames and inserted it into the campus paper. Unfortunately, they named it "Ames for Dummies" after the popular book series.

The editor-in-chief quickly apologized for the insensitive choice of wording, while the *Daily* removed the inserts and replaced them with reprinted publications featuring a new headline.

Adapted from Lisa Rossi, "Olympics Section Goof Sends Paper Running," *Des Moines Register*, July 1, 2006, 1A, 4A.

The Art of Brainstorming

"Do you want good ideas? Do you want to spark more good ideas with others? [Researchers, managers, and inventors say:] Relax. Play music. Break bread with a colleague. Read a poem. Open yourself to eccentricity. Listen to someone else's story. Laugh. Resist the tyranny of drones. Seek catharsis. Get vulnerable. Do something risky. Be a rebel, with self-confidence. And, yes, with love."

Quoted from Robert Parker, "The Art of Brainstorming," *BusinessWeek*, August 26, 2002, 169.

writers into a false sense of confidence about their material and organization, making it difficult for them to revise their content and structure if they deviate from the outline developed early in the process.[2]

Using Your Time Effectively

To get the best results from the time you have, spend only one-third of your time actually "writing." Spend at least another one-third of your time analyzing the situation and your audience, gathering information, and organizing what you have to say. Spend the final third evaluating what you've said, revising the draft(s) to meet your purposes and the needs of the audience and the organization, editing a late draft to remove any errors in grammar and mechanics, and proofreading the final copy.

Do realize, however, that different writers and documents may need different time divisions to produce quality communications.

Brainstorming, Planning, and Organizing Business Documents

Spend significant time planning and organizing before you begin to write. The better your ideas are when you start, the fewer drafts you'll need to produce a good document. Start by using the analysis questions from Chapter 1 ◀▦ to identify purpose and audience. Use the strategies described in Chapter 2 to analyze audience and identify reader benefits. Gather information you can use for your document.

Sometimes your content will be determined by the situation. Sometimes, even when it's up to you to think of benefits or topics to include in a report, you'll find it easy to think of ideas. If ideas won't come, try the following techniques:

- **Brainstorming.** Think of all the ideas you can, without judging them. Consciously try to get at least a dozen different ideas before you stop. Good brainstorming depends on generating many ideas.

- **Freewriting.**[3] Make yourself write, without stopping, for 10 minutes or so, even if you must write "I will think of something soon." At the end of 10 minutes, read what you've written, identify the best point in the draft, then set it aside, and write for another 10 uninterrupted minutes. Read this draft, marking anything that's good and should be kept, and then write again for another 10 minutes. By the third session, you will probably produce several sections that are worth keeping—maybe even a complete draft that's ready to be revised.

- **Clustering.**[4] Write your topic in the middle of the page and circle it. Write down the ideas the topic suggests, circling them, too. (The circles are designed to tap into the nonlinear half of your brain.) When you've filled the page, look for patterns or repeated ideas. Use different colored pens to group related ideas. Then use these ideas to develop reader benefits in a memo, questions for a survey, or content for the body of a report. Figure 5.1 presents the clusters that one writer created about business communication in the United States and France.

- **Talk to your audiences.** As research shows, talking to internal and external audiences helps writers to involve readers in the planning process and to understand the social and political relationships among readers. This preliminary work helps reduce the number of revisions needed before documents are approved.[5]

Figure 5.1 Clustering Helps Generate Ideas

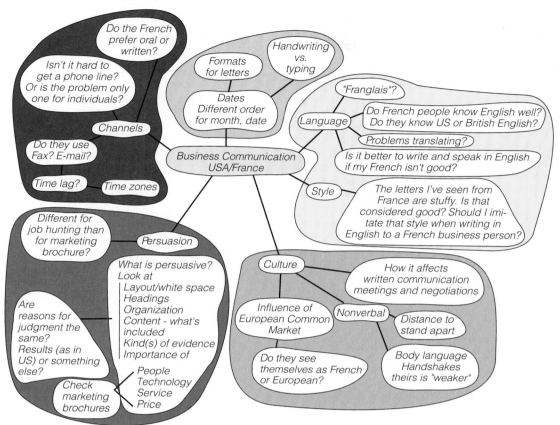

Thinking about the content, layout, or structure of your document can also give you ideas. For long documents, write out the headings you'll use. For short documents, jot down key points—information to include, objections to answer, reader benefits to develop. For an oral presentation, a meeting, or a document with lots of visuals, try creating a **storyboard,** with a rectangle representing each page or unit. Draw a box with a visual for each main point. Below the box, write a short caption or label.

Letters and memos will go faster if you choose a basic organizational pattern before you start. Chapters 10, 11, and 12 give detailed patterns of organization for the most common kinds of letters and memos. You may frequently customize those patterns to fit particular situations. Figure 5.2 shows planning guides developed for specific kinds of documents.

As you plan your document, pay attention to signals from your boss and the organization's culture. For example, if the organization has a style manual that specifies whether *data* is singular or plural, follow its guidelines. If the organization has an ethics counselor, think about consulting him or her as you decide what to write in a situation with ethical implications. Talk to people in the organization who will be affected by what you are announcing or proposing, to better understand their concerns. In some organizations, your boss may want to see an early planning draft to see that you're on the right track. In other organizations, you may be expected to do a great deal of revising on your own before anyone else sees the document.

Writing with Information

Good writers write with information. Michelle Russo writes reports appraising how much a hotel is worth. Gathering information is a big part of her composing process.

She visits the site. She talks to the general manager. She gets occupancy rates, financial statements, and tax forms. She talks to the tax assessor and all the managers of competing hotels. If it's a convention hotel, she talks to the convention bureau and gets the airlines' passenger traffic counts. Gathering all this information takes about four days. When she gets back to the office, she uses databases for even more information.

Adapted from Michelle S. Russo, telephone conversation with Kitty Locker, December 8, 1993.

When Roxanne Clemens was asked by a professor to edit an article about meat packing for the World Book Encyclopedia (WBE), she readily agreed to help. As a technical writer, Roxanne saw the project as an opportunity to make technical text accessible to a nontechnical audience. The author did not supply any style guidelines, so Roxanne researched similar articles in the WBE and created her own style guide for the article. Here's how Roxanne describes to the professor her edits to the article:

You may look at this and think, "this is not what I wrote." As you know, the challenge lies in explaining such complex concepts at a 6th-grade level. . . . I based most changes on the examples of WBE entries found on the Internet. Major style choices are the following:

- WBE uses short, concise sentences (almost what we would consider choppy). They use very few compound sentences, so I have broken up compound sentences where I thought the meaning would not be lost.

- Instead of using "however," WBE tends to use two sentences and to start the second sentence with "but."

- WBE uses a terminal comma in a series (e.g. red, white, and blue).

I did some reorganizing at the sentence level, except for moving livestock marketing ahead of meat because that's the way the heading reads and it also follows the process of turning animals into meat.

Let me know if you want me to do more or something different to the text.

Adapted and quoted from Roxanne Clemens, e-mail to Donna Kienzler, August 30, 2006.

Figure 5.2   Customized Planning Guides for Specific Documents

Planning guide for a trip report	**Planning guide for a proposal**
• The Big Picture from the Company's Point of View: We Can Go Forward on the Project. • Criteria/Goals • What We Did • Why We Know Enough to Go Forward • Next Steps	• Customer's Concern #1 Our Proposal/Answer • Customer's Concern #2 Our Proposal/Answer • Customer's Concern #3 Our Proposal/Answer • Customer's Concern #4 Our Proposal/Answer • Ask for Action
Planning guide for an e-mail message	**Planning guide for a credit rejection**
• My Purpose • Points I Want to Make • Document(s) to Attach • Next Steps	• Reason • Refusal • Alternative (Layaway/ Co-signer/Provide more information) • Goodwill Ending

Source: E-mail and proposal guides based on Fred Reynolds, "What Adult Work-World Writers Have Taught Me About Adult Work-World Writing," *Professional Writing in Context: Lessons from Teaching and Consulting in Worlds of Work* (Hillsdale, NJ: Lawrence Erlbaum Associates, 1995), 18, 20.

Revising, Editing, and Proofreading

A popular myth is that Abraham Lincoln wrote the Gettysburg address, perhaps the most famous American presidential speech, on the back of an envelope on the train as he traveled to the battlefield's dedication. The reality is that Lincoln wrote at least a partial draft of the speech before leaving for the trip and continued to revise it up to the morning of the speech. Furthermore, the speech was on a topic he passionately believed in, one he had been pondering for years.[6]

Like Lincoln, good writers work on their drafts; they make their documents better by judicious revising, editing, and proofreading.

- **Revising** means making changes that will better satisfy your purposes and your audience.

- **Editing** means making surface-level changes that make the document grammatically correct.

- **Proofreading** means checking to be sure the document is free from typographical errors.

What to Look for When You Revise

When you're writing to a new audience or have to solve a particularly difficult problem, plan to revise the draft at least three times. The first time, look for content and clarity. The second time, check the organization and layout. Finally, check you-attitude, positive emphasis, style, and tone (◀ Chapters 3 and 4). The Thorough Revision Checklist on page 143 summarizes the questions you should ask.

Often you'll get the best revision by setting aside your draft, getting a blank page or screen, and redrafting. This strategy takes advantage of the thinking you did on your first draft without locking you into the sentences in it. Use WIRMI ("what I really mean is") to replace awkward phrasing with what you really want to say.

As you revise, be sure to read the document through from start to finish. This is particularly important if you've composed in several sittings or if you've used text from other documents. Such documents tend to be choppy, repetitious, or inconsistent. You may need to add transitions, cut repetitive parts, or change words to create a uniform level of formality throughout the document.

If you're really in a time bind, do a light revision, as outlined in the Light Revision Checklist. The quality of the final document may not be as high as with a thorough revision, but even a light revision is better than skipping revision altogether.

What to Look for When You Edit

Even good writers need to edit, since no one can pay attention to surface correctness while thinking of ideas. Editing should always *follow* revision. There's no point in taking time to fix a grammatical error in a sentence that may be cut when you clarify your meaning or tighten your style. Some writers edit more accurately when they print out a copy of a document and edit the hard copy.

Check to be sure that the following are accurate:

- Sentence structure.
- Subject–verb and noun–pronoun agreement.
- Punctuation.
- Word usage.
- Spelling—including spelling of names.
- Numbers.

Punctuation errors are frequently difficult for writers to correct. Nancy Mann offers a useful decision tree for punctuating clauses correctly (see Figure 5.3).

To catch typos use a spell checker. But you still need to proofread by eye. In a University of Pittsburgh study, graduate students were asked to proofread a

Figure 5.3   The Punctuation Decision Algorithm

Is there a linking word?

If no   If yes
↓   ↘
. or ;   Can this linker move around within a statement?

            If yes   If no
            ↓   ↘
            . or ;   Can a statement using this linker move within the statement pair?

                        If no   If yes
                        ↓   ↘
                        . or ,   Is the second statement in thsi pair essential to the first?

                                    If no   If yes
                                    ↓   ↘
                                    ,   [no punctuation]

Note: For readability, the algorithm is depicted here as moving in a straight line; note that it actually "bends" at stage two, where the positions of *no* and *yes* reverse.

Nancy Mann offers a diagram for punctuating clauses. She believes it "comes close to articulating the rules of thumb that practiced adult writers unconsciously use in making normal punctuation choices."

Source: Nancy Mann, "Point Counterpoint: Teaching Punctuation as Information Management," *College Composition and Communication* 54, no. 3 (February 2003): 365.

one-page business letter. Students who were not allowed to use the spell checker tool in the word processor found an average of five more errors than those who were allowed to use the tool.[7]

Spell checkers work by matching words; they will signal any group of letters not listed in their dictionaries. However, they cannot tell you when you've used the wrong word but spelled it correctly.

You also need to know the rules of grammar and punctuation to edit. Errors such as sentence fragments and run-on sentences disturb most educated readers. Errors in punctuation can change the meaning of a sentence. Lynne Truss, author of the *New York Times* bestseller on punctuation *Eats, Shoots & Leaves*, offers "a popular 'Dear Jack' letter" to show the need for care:[8]

> Dear Jack,
>
> I want a man who knows what love is all about. You are generous, kind, thoughtful. People who are not like you admit to being useless and inferior. You have ruined me for other men. I yearn for you. I have no feelings whatsoever when we're apart. I can be forever happy—will you let me be yours?
>
> Jill

> Dear Jack,
>
> I want a man who knows what love is. All about you are generous, kind, thoughtful people, who are not like you. Admit to being useless and inferior. You have ruined me. For other men I yearn! For you I have no feelings whatsoever. When we're apart I can be forever happy. Will you let me be? Yours,
>
> Jill

Writers with a good command of grammar and mechanics can do a better job than the computer grammar checkers currently available. But even good writers sometimes use a good grammar handbook for reference. On the other hand, even good editors—such as Bill Walsh, Copy Desk Chief for the Business Desk of the *Washington Post*—warn writers that handbooks should be used with a clear goal of clarifying text, not blindly following rules.[9]

Appendix B ➠ reviews grammar and punctuation, numbers, and words that are often confused.

Most writers make a small number of errors over and over. If you know that you have trouble with dangling modifiers or subject–verb agreement, for example, specifically look for them in your draft. Also look for any errors that especially bother your boss and correct them.

How to Catch Typos

Don't underestimate the harm that spelling errors can create. For instance, a police officer who responded to a traffic accident wrapped a blanket around the female victim as she lay on the side of the road waiting for an ambulance. In court, the defendant's lawyer asked the officer if everything in his written report was accurate, and the officer confirmed that it was. The lawyer then pointed out that the officer had written that he "raped the woman on the side of the road." Reminding the officer that he had just sworn that everything in his report was correct, the lawyer cast doubt upon the officer's entire report.[10]

✔ *Checklist* Thorough Revision Checklist

Content and clarity

☐ Does your document meet the needs of the organization and of the reader—and make you look good?

☐ Have you given readers all the information they need to understand and act on your message?

☐ Is all the information accurate and clear?

☐ Is the message easy to read?

☐ Is each sentence clear? Is the message free from apparently contradictory statements?

☐ Is the logic clear and convincing? Are generalizations and benefits backed up with adequate supporting detail?

Organization and layout

☐ Is the pattern of organization appropriate for your purposes, audience, and context?

☐ Are transitions between ideas smooth? Do ideas within paragraphs flow smoothly?

☐ Does the design of the document make it easy for readers to find the information they need? Is the document visually inviting?

☐ Are the points emphasized by layout ones that deserve emphasis?

☐ Are the first and last paragraphs effective?

Style and tone

☐ Does the message use you-attitude and positive emphasis?

☐ Is the message friendly and free from sexist language?

☐ Does the message build goodwill?

✔ *Checklist* Light Revision Checklist

☐ Have you given readers all the information they need to understand and act on your message?

☐ Is the logic clear and convincing? Are generalizations and benefits backed up with adequate supporting detail?

☐ Does the design of the document make it easy for readers to find the information they need?

☐ Are the first and last paragraphs effective?

Little Things Make a Big Difference

In Ottawa County, Michigan, 170,000 ballots had to be reprinted because the letter "L" was missing from the word "public." Although at least five people proofread the text, the error was not noticed until the ballots were printed. Reprinting the ballots cost the country $40,000.

Meanwhile, an Arizona effort to create an 80-cent-per-pack tax on cigarettes to benefit early childhood education and health programs was threatened by a decimal point. The ballot featuring the proposition calls for a ".80-cent/pack" increase instead of an "an 80-cent increase." The faulty wording means that the bill would raise only $1.8 million, or less than 1 cent per pack of cigarettes sold, instead of the anticipated $180 million dollars.

Medicare programs faced embarrassing typos in Iowa and Texas. In December 2005, a letter to Medicare beneficiaries in Iowa included a toll-free number that was off by one digit. The readers who tried calling Humana Health Insurance found themselves calling a phone sex operator instead. The following month, Medicare beneficiaries in Texas also called a phone sex number instead of United Health Care because of a typo in the phone number.

Adapted from Mary Jo Pitzi, "Tiny Typo, Big Effect on Ballot," *Arizona Republic*, October 25, 2006, http://www.azcentral.com/arizonarepublic/news/articles/1025ballot1025.html (accessed January 31, 2007); "Typo Means Ballots Must Be Reprinted," *Des Moines Register*, October 11, 2006, 8A; and "Health Care Briefs: Typo Sends Medicare Beneficiaries to Phone Sex Line," *National Public Radio*, January 5, 2006, http://www.npr.org/templates/story/story.php?storyId=5128173 (accessed January 31, 2007).

The moral of the story? Proofread every document both with a spell checker and by eye, to catch the errors a spell checker can't find.

Proofreading is hard because writers tend to see what they know should be there rather than what really is there. Since it's always easier to proof something you haven't written, you may want to swap papers with a proofing buddy. (Be sure the person looks for typos, not content.)

To proofread,

* Read once quickly for meaning, to see that nothing has been left out.

* Read a second time, slowly. When you find an error, correct it and then *re-read that line.* Readers tend to become less attentive after they find one error and may miss other errors close to the one they've spotted.

* To proofread a document you know well, read the lines backward or the pages out of order.

Always triple-check numbers, headings, the first and last paragraphs, and the reader's name.

Writing the College Admission Essay

When college admissions officers review applications, part of the information they consider is the personal essay. Now students are getting help on those essays.

A thriving industry has grown up around the college essay. Numerous books, Web sites, and training seminars have been developed to help students write college essays that will win them admission into their college of choice. None of the sources actually write the essay, but all offer advice, suggestions, and examples to help students craft their own papers.

People in the new industry claim they are doing nothing wrong. After all, parents have always been able to help their children write and revise their applications. The authors also blame the universities themselves for creating the demand for writing assistance. Yet admissions officers worry that the college essay industry is doing more harm than good. They note that the prep services lead to formulaic essays that look prepped and may not match the information on the application form. Outstanding essays may not be matched by writing and verbal skills scores. Plagiarism site Turnitin.com says 11% of the admissions essays it checked contained at least one-quarter un-original material. Other critics claim that the costly services put students who cannot afford the extra help at a disadvantage.

What do you think? Are the essay prep services ethical?

Adapted from June Kronholz, "Perfect College Essay Takes Lots of Practice–and Extra Help," *Wall Street Journal*, July 11, 2005, A1, A8; and "The Admissions Police," *Wall Street Journal*, April 6, 2007, W1, W10.

Getting and Using Feedback

Getting feedback almost always improves a document. In many organizations, it's required. All external documents must be read and approved before they go out. The process of drafting, getting feedback, revising, and getting more feedback is called **cycling.** One researcher reported that documents in her clients' firms cycled an average of 4.2 times before reaching the intended audience.[11] Another researcher studied a major 10-page document whose 20 drafts made a total of 31 stops on the desks of nine reviewers on four different levels.[12] Being asked to revise a document is a fact of life in businesses, government agencies, and nonprofit organizations.

You can improve the quality of the feedback you get by telling people which aspects you'd especially like comments about. For example, when you give a reader the outline or planning draft, you probably want to know whether the general approach and content are appropriate, and if you have included all major points. After your second draft, you might want to know whether the reasoning is convincing. When you reach the polishing draft, you'll be ready for feedback on style and grammar. The Checklist on page 145 lists questions to ask.

It's easy to feel defensive when someone criticizes your work. If the feedback stings, put it aside until you can read it without feeling defensive. Even if you think that the reader hasn't understood what you were trying to say, the fact that the reader complained usually means the section could be improved. If the reader says "This isn't true" and you know the statement is true, several kinds of revision might make the truth clear to the reader: rephrasing the statement, giving more information or examples, or documenting the source.

Reading feedback carefully is a good way to understand the culture of your organization. Are you told to give more details or to shorten messages? Does your boss add headings and bullet points? Look for patterns in the comments, and apply what you learn in your next document.

Using Boilerplate

Boilerplate is language—sentences, paragraphs, even pages—from a previous document that a writer includes in a new document. In academic papers, material written by others must be quoted and documented. However, because businesses own the documents their employees write, old text may be included without attribution.

In some cases, boilerplate may have been written years ago. For example, many legal documents, including apartment leases and sales contracts, are almost completely boilerplated. In other cases, writers may use boilerplate they wrote for earlier documents. For example, a section from a proposal describing the background of the problem could also be used in the final report after the proposed work was completed. A section from a progress report describing what the writer had done could be used with only a few changes in the methods section of the final report.

Writers use boilerplate both to save time and energy and to use language that has already been approved by the organization's legal staff. However, research has shown that using boilerplate creates two problems.[13] First, using unrevised boilerplate can create a document with incompatible styles and tones. Second, boilerplate can allow writers to ignore subtle differences in situations and audiences.

To effectively incorporate old language in a new document,

- Check to see that the old section is well written.
- Consciously look for differences between the two situations, audiences, or purposes that may require different content, organization, or wording.

✓ *Checklist*   Questions to Ask Readers

Outline or planning draft

☐ Does the plan seem on the right track?

☐ What topics should be added? Should any be cut?

☐ Do you have any other general suggestions?

Revising draft

☐ Does the message satisfy all its purposes?

☐ Is the message adapted to the audience(s)?

☐ Is the organization effective?

☐ What parts aren't clear?

☐ What ideas need further development and support?

☐ Do you have any other suggestions?

Polishing draft

☐ Are there any problems with word choice or sentence structure?

☐ Did you find any inconsistencies?

☐ Did you find any typos?

☐ Is the document's design effective?

Your Edits May Be Showing

When SCO Group, a litigious Lindon (Utah) software company, filed a breach of contract suit in Michigan against DaimlerChrysler[, . . . a] CNET News reporter, poking through the Microsoft Word filing, discovered that the case had originally been drawn up as a suit against Bank of America in a California court. . . .

[H]idden in a Word, Excel, or PowerPoint file may [be] the names of the author and anyone who edited the document, reviewers' comments, . . . and deleted text. . . .

A *Wired News* analysis of a Word document circulated by California Attorney General Bill Lockyer urging other attorneys to crack down on file-sharing showed that the text had been edited or reviewed by an official of the Motion Picture Association of America. . . .

Nearly every business exchanges electronic documents with partners, competitors, and customers. . . . [To remove sensitive information,] select "Track Changes" from the tools menu and view the document as "Final Showing Markup." Make sure that all your changes have been either accepted or rejected by the program—a step that removes the tracking information. And make sure all versions but the last have been deleted.

Quoted from Stephen H. Wildstrom, "Don't Let Word Give Away Your Secrets," *BusinessWeek*, April 19, 2004, 26.

- Read through the whole document at a single sitting to be sure that style, tone, and level of detail are consistent in the old and new sections.

Overcoming Writer's Block

According to psychologist Robert Boice, who has made a career study of writer's block, these actions help overcome writer's block:[14]

1. **Prepare for writing.** Collect and arrange material. Talk to people; interact with some of your audiences. The more you learn about the company, its culture, and its context, the easier it will be to write—and the better your writing will be.

2. **Practice writing regularly and in moderation.** Try to write almost daily. Keep sessions to a moderate length; Boice suggests an hour to an hour and a half. Many successful writers plan to write at the same hour each day.

3. **Talk positively to yourself:** "I can do this." "If I keep working, ideas will come." "It doesn't have to be perfect; I can make it better later." Good writers think more about the document than about their feelings.

4. **Talk to other people about writing.** Value the feedback you get from your boss. Talk to your boss about writing. Ask him or her to share particularly good examples—from anyone in the organization. Find colleagues at your own level and talk about the writing you do. Do different bosses value different qualities? Which aspects of your own boss's preferences are individual, and which are part of the discourse community of the organization? Talking to other people expands your repertoire of strategies and helps you understand your writing community.

Other researchers have found that noise can distract writers and interfere with the "inner voice" that helps them compose their texts.[15] If you are having difficulty drafting your document, try eliminating distractions. Turn off music that has lyrics. Try to find a quiet room where you can't hear the voices of your co-workers.

Summary of Key Points

- Processes that help writers write well include not expecting the first draft to be perfect, writing regularly, modifying the initial task if it's too hard or too easy, having clear goals, knowing many different strategies, using rules as guidelines rather than as absolutes, and waiting to edit until after the draft is complete.

- Writing processes can include many activities: planning, gathering, brainstorming, organizing, writing, evaluating, getting feedback, revising, editing, and proofreading. **Revising** means changing the document to make it better satisfy the writer's purposes and the audience. **Editing** means making surface-level changes that make the document grammatically correct. **Proofreading** means checking to be sure the document is free from typographical errors. The activities do not have to come in any set order. It is not necessary to finish one activity to start another. Most writers use all activities only when they write a document whose genre, subject matter, or audience is new to them.

- To think of ideas, try **brainstorming, freewriting** (writing without stopping for 10 minutes or so), and **clustering** (brainstorming with circled words on a page).

- You can improve the quality of the feedback you get by telling people which aspects of a draft you'd like comments about. If a reader criticizes something, fix the problem. If you think the reader misunderstood you, try to figure out what caused the misunderstanding and revise the draft so that the reader can see what you meant.

- If the writing situation is new or difficult, plan to revise the draft at least three times. The first time, look for content and completeness. The second time, check the organization, layout, and reasoning. Finally, check style and tone.

- **Boilerplate** is language from a previous document that a writer includes in a new document. Using unrevised boilerplate can create a document with incompatible styles and tones and can encourage writers to see as identical situations and audiences that have subtle differences.

- To overcome writer's block,
    1. Prepare for writing.
    2. Practice writing regularly and in moderation.
    3. Talk positively to yourself.
    4. Talk about writing to other people.
    5. Eliminate distractions.

CHAPTER 5   ## Exercises and Problems

5.1   Reviewing the Chapter

1. What are some techniques of good writers? Which ones do you use regularly? (LO 1)

2. What activities are part of the composing process? Which one should you be doing more often or more carefully in your writing? (LO 1)

3. What are ways to get ideas for a specific communication? (LO 1)

4. What is the difference between revising, editing, and proofreading? Which one do you personally need to do more carefully? (LO 2)

5. How can you get better feedback on your writing? (LO 2)

6. What can you do to help yourself if you get writer's block? (LO 3)

5.2 Interviewing Writers about Their Composing Processes

Interview someone about the composing process(es) he or she uses for on-the-job writing. Questions you could ask include the following:

- What kind of planning do you do before you write? Do you make lists? formal or informal outlines?
- When you need more information, where do you get it?
- How do you compose your drafts? Do you dictate? Draft with pen and paper? Compose on screen? How do you find uninterrupted time to compose?
- When you want advice about style, grammar, and spelling, what source(s) do you consult?
- Does your superior ever read your drafts and make suggestions?
- Do you ever work with other writers to produce a single document? Describe the process you use.

- Describe the process of creating a document where you felt the final document reflected your best work. Describe the process of creating a document you found difficult or frustrating. What sorts of things make writing easier or harder for you?

As your instructor directs,

a. Share your results orally with a small group of students.

b. Present your results in an oral presentation to the class.

c. Present your results in a memo to your instructor.

d. Share your results with a small group of students and write a joint memo reporting the similarities and differences you found.

5.3 Analyzing Your Own Writing Processes

Save your notes and drafts from several assignments so that you can answer the following questions:

- Which practices of good writers do you follow?
- Which of the activities discussed in Chapter 5 do you use?
- How much time do you spend on each of the activities?
- What kinds of revisions do you make most often?
- Do you use different processes for different documents, or do you have one process that you use most of the time?
- What parts of your process seem most successful? Are there any places in the process that could be improved? How?

- What relation do you see between the process(es) you use and the quality of the final document?

As your instructor directs,

a. Discuss your process with a small group of other students.

b. Write a memo to your instructor analyzing in detail your process for composing one of the papers for this class.

c. Write a memo to your instructor analyzing your process during the term. What parts of your process(es) have stayed the same throughout the term? What parts have changed?

5.4 Checking Spelling and Grammar Checkers

Each of the following paragraphs contains errors in grammar, spelling, and punctuation. Which errors does your spelling or grammar checker catch? Which errors does it miss? Does it flag as errors any words that are correct?

a. Answer to an Inquiry
Enclosed are the tow copies you requested of our pamphlet, "Using the Internet to market Your products. The pamphelt walks you through the steps of planning the Home Page (The first page of the web cite, shows examples of other Web pages we have designed, and provide a questionaire that you can use to analyze audience the audience and purposes.

b. Performance Appraisal
Most staff accountants complete three audits a month. Ellen has completed 21 audits in this past six months she is our most productive staff accountant. Her technical skills our very good however some clients feel that she could be more tactful in suggesting ways that the clients accounting practices courld be improved.

c. Brochure
Are you finding that being your own boss crates it's own problems? Take the hassle out of working at home with a VoiceMail Answering System. Its almost as good as having your own secratery.

d. Presentation Slides
How to Create a Web Résumé
- Omit home adress and phone number
- Use other links only if they help an employer evalaute you.
    - Be Professional.
    - Carefully craft and proof read the phrase on the index apage.

How to Create a Scannable Résumé
- Create a "plain vanilla" document.
- Use include a "Keywords" section. Include personality traits sas well as accomplishments.
- Be specific and quantifyable.

5.5   Revising Text for Non-Native Speakers

The following terms are common idioms used in American business. For each term, write an explanation that would help a non-native speaker understand the meaning of the term.

- Across the board
- Ballpark figure
- Banker's hours
- Captain of industry
- Write off
- Turnaround
- Red ink
- Downhill/uphill
- Number-cruncher
- In the black
- Give someone the green light
- Cut corners
- Cold call
- Big gun/cheese/wheel/wig
- Sell like hotcakes
- Strike while the iron is hot

Now imagine that the non-native speaker wants to understand the origin of the idiom to help remember its meaning. Pick one term from the list and research its origin and its evolution to the contemporary usage.

As your teacher instructs,

a. Share your research results orally with a small group of students.

b. Present your research results orally to the class.

c. Write a memo to your instructor describing the meaning and evolution of the idiom.

5.6   Revising Documents using "Track Changes"

"Track Changes" is a feature in some word processors that records alterations made to a document. It is particularly useful when you are collaborating with a colleague to create, edit, or revise documents. Track Changes will highlight any text that has been added or deleted to your document but it also allows you to decide, for each change, whether to accept the suggestion or reject it and return to your original text. In addition to Track Changes, many word processors include a comment feature that allows you to ask questions or make suggestions without altering the text itself.

For this exercise, you will exchange a document with one of your classmates. With the Track Changes feature turned on, you will review each other's documents, make comments or ask questions, insert additions, and make deletions to improve the writing, and then revise your work based upon the changes and comments.

As your instructor directs, select the electronic file of the document you created for exercise 4.19 "Writing Paragraphs" or another document that you have created for this class. Exchange this file with your peer review partner.

- Open the file in Microsoft Word.
- In the Tools menu, select Track Changes to turn the feature on.

- Review the document and make suggestions that will help your peer improve the writing. For instance, you can
  - Look for accurate, appropriate, and ethical wording as well as instances of unnecessary jargon.
  - Look for active verbs, gerunds, and infinitives; try to eliminate words that say nothing.
  - Look for structural issues like topic sentences, tightly written paragraphs, varied sentence structure and length, and focus upon the thesis statement. Suggest where sentences can be combined or where sentences need parallel structure.
  - Look for you-attitude.
  - Ask questions (using comments) when the text isn't clear or make suggestions to tighten the writing or improve word choices.
- Return the document to its author and open yours to review the changes and comments your partner added to your document.
- For each change, decide whether to Accept or Reject the suggestion.

Continue to revise the document. Then submit a copy of your original version and the revised version to your instructor.

5.7   Mosaic Case

"OK folks," said Yvonne to the Communication Department during their staff meeting, "it's that time of year again for the annual Mosaic headquarters employee picnic. Since we rotate the honor of creating the invitation every year within the Communication Department," she said while making air quotes around *honor*, "who made the invitation last year?"

"I did!" shouted Demetri and Sarah simultaneously.

"Wait a minute, you both didn't do it," said Yvonne.

"Well, I did it last year when the picnic was at Grey's Lake Park," said Sarah.

"No, no, no," retorted Demetri. "That was two years ago. Last year the picnic was at Waterworks Park, and I made the invitation."

"Oh, yeah. You're right. Sorry," said Sarah. "Then I guess that means it is Trey's turn to create the invitation this year."

"I knew this was coming," Trey mumbled to himself.

"Ok, I can do it. It's only an invitation, so it shouldn't take too much effort. Where is the picnic at this year?" asked Trey to no one in particular.

"It's going to be at Blank Park Zoo in two weeks from tomorrow," answered Yvonne. "Corporate has arranged free admission for all employees and their guests from noon to 5pm. The event will also be catered this year. Food will be available from 12–2:30pm. In addition, the zoo is setting up a special giraffe petting area from to 2–4pm."

"Don't forget about the door prizes," chimed Demetri. "And there will be free camel rides for kids of Mosaic employees all afternoon. Oh, and there's the plasma TV raffle at the end."

"However, be sure to remind employees that they need to sign up ahead of time to get tickets if they're planning on attending. Carol in Human Resources is handling that," said Sarah to Trey.

One hour later, Trey gave his invitation to Sarah for approval before he passed it onto Yvonne.

"What do you think?" he asked Sarah, "Great job, right? This task is by far the easiest I've completed here!"

"Trey, just because something is short doesn't necessarily mean it's easy. You should know better," said Sarah. "Let's have a look."

The content of the invitation was on the minimal side. It had a picture of giraffe on the front and the following text was found inside:

Mosaic Employee Picnic

Blank Prak Zoo

Fun starts at 12pm.

Pet the Giraffes starring at 1pm.

Free Camel Rides For Kids!

see Carol in HR for details.

"Trey, I mean this in the nicest way possible . . . but this invitation is absolutely horrible!" said Sarah. "You've left out vital information, have inaccurate information, and have grammatical mistakes."

"Oh," said Trey, a bit embarrassed.

"Don't rush through writing tasks, even when they appear to be simple," said Sarah. "Yvonne would never send something like this out; the Communications Department would be the laughing joke at Mosaic! You need to re-do this invitation. Bring another version back for me to approve later today."

Take on the communication task of Trey. Revise, edit, and proofread the employee picnic invitation. Refer to Chapter 5 for distinctions of each.

Designing Documents, Data Displays, and Visuals

Learning Objectives

After studying this chapter, you will know:

1 Why document design is important in business communication.

2 The four levels of document design, and how they can help you critique documents.

3 Guidelines for document design.

4 When to use visuals.

5 How to create effective visuals.

6 How to design brochures and Web pages.

7 How to do basic usability testing on your documents.

Design at the *Wall Street Journal*

Document design is just about making your work pretty, isn't it? The publishers of the *Wall Street Journal* didn't see it that way. They spent two years researching, creating, and testing designs for the *Journal*'s new look before they unveiled it in 2007. After getting advice from their customers in the form of surveys, focus groups, and test marketing, the *Journal*'s publishers chose to redesign their newspaper in specific ways:

- They expanded their use of headings and white space, to make it easier for readers to find articles in the paper and to follow articles from page to page. People are more likely to read, and not skim, if they have clear navigational cues to follow.

- They created a hierarchy, through headline size and story placement, to indicate relative importance of news.

- They changed to a new, narrower paper size that would make the *Journal* more convenient to hold, fold, and read. The more convenient size decreases the time readers spend folding the paper into a manageable shape—which gives them more time to read.

> *"Everything that you put on the page is a choice that guides your readers' attention."*

- They added more color to help highlight important topics and help readers find information more easily. They also replaced the *Journal*'s traditional gray shading with soft color pastels, to brighten the paper's overall "look" and make it easier to read text printed in shaded sidebars.

- They also created a new font named Exchange for the *Journal*. Exchange was specifically designed to be easy to read, even when printed in a small size, in tight columns, on a narrow page. People are more likely to spend time reading text that's easy on the eyes.

Document design isn't just about making your work "pretty." Everything that you put on the page is a choice: the appearance of a document can guide your readers' attention, build goodwill, and establish rapport with them, just as much as the text on the page can.

Adapted from L. Gordon Crovitz, "What Is Changing—and What Isn't—in the *Wall Street Journal*," *Wall Street Journal*, December 4, 2006, A17; L. Gordon Crovitz, "What to Expect in Your *Journal*, Starting on Jan. 2," *Wall Street Journal*, December 30–31, 2006, A11; and Mario R. Garcia, "The Relevance of Good Design," *Wall Street Journal*, January 2, 2007, G8.

Chapter Outline

The Importance of Effective Design

Design as Part of Your Writing Process(es)

Design and Conventions

Levels of Design

Guidelines for Page Design

1. Use White Space.
2. Use Headings.
3. Limit the Use of Words Set in All Capital Letters.
4. Use No More Than Two Fonts in a Single Document.
5. Decide Whether to Justify Margins.
6. Put Important Elements in the Top Left and Lower Right Quadrants.
7. Use a Grid to Unify Graphic Elements.
8. Use Highlighting, Decorative Devices, and Color in Moderation.

Adding Visuals

When to Use Visuals

Guidelines for Visual Design

1. Check the Quality of the Data.
2. Determine the Story You Want to Tell.
3. Choose the Right Visual for the Story.
4. Follow the Conventions for Designing Typical Visuals.
5. Use Color and Decoration with Restraint.
6. Be Sure the Visual Is Accurate and Ethical.

Integrating Visuals in Your Text

Designing Data Displays and Images

Tables
Pie Charts
Bar Charts
Line Graphs
Gantt Charts
Photographs
Drawings
Maps

Designing Brochures

Designing Web Pages

Testing the Design for Usability

Summary of Key Points

Good document design saves time and money, reduces legal problems, and builds goodwill. A well-designed document looks inviting, friendly, and easy to read. Effective design also groups ideas visually, making the structure of the document more obvious so the document is easier to read. Research shows that easy-to-read documents also enhance your credibility and build an image of you as a professional, competent person.[1] In addition, many workplaces expect you to be able to create designs that go beyond the basic templates you'll find in common business software programs.[2] Good design is important not only for reports, Web pages, and newsletters but also for announcements and one–page letters and memos.

The Importance of Effective Design

When document design is poor, both organizations and society suffer. The *Challenger* space shuttle blew up because its O-rings failed in the excessive cold. Poor communication—including charts that hid, rather than emphasized, the data—contributed to the decision to launch. More recently, after the *Columbia* space shuttle disintegrated during reentry, poor communication was again implicated in NASA's failure to ensure the spacecraft was safe. Mission leaders insisted that engineers had not briefed them on the seriousness of the damage to the shuttle when a piece of foam struck it on takeoff. But after studying transcripts of meetings, Edward R. Tufte, who specializes in visual presentations of evidence, concludes that engineers did offer their concerns and supporting statistics. However, they did so using visuals that obscured the seriousness.[3] In 2000, the badly designed "butterfly ballot" confused enough voters to change the outcome of the US presidential election.[4]

Design as Part of Your Writing Process(es)

Design isn't something to "tack on" when you've finished writing. Indeed, the best documents, slides, and screens are created when you think about design at each stage of your writing process(es).

- As you plan, think about your audience. Are they skilled readers? Are they busy? Will they read the document straight through or skip around in it?

- As you write, incorporate lists and headings. Use visuals to convey numerical data clearly and forcefully.

- Get feedback from people who will be using your document. Do they find the document hard to understand? Do they need additional visuals?

- As you revise, check your draft against the guidelines in this chapter.

Design and Conventions

Like all aspects of communication, effective design relies heavily on conventions. These conventions provide a design language. For instance, most graphical interfaces are organized around the desktop metaphor, where we use files, folders, tabs, and trashcans. Commercial Web sites use the metaphor of the shopping cart. We have a mental image of the way brochures, business letters, or business cards are supposed to look.

Conventions may vary by audience, geographic area, industry, company, or even department, but they do exist. Some conventions work well with some audiences but not with others, so careful audience analysis is necessary. The British and Americans prefer serif typefaces; the French and Dutch prefer sans serif. Instruction pictures for office equipment generally show feminine hands using the equipment. Some female readers will relate more readily to the instructions; others will be offended at the implied assumption that only women perform such low-level office jobs.[5]

Conventions also change over time. Résumés used to be typed documents; now more and more companies ask for electronic ones. Today we rarely use

Good Document Design Saves Money, I

Much of the research on document design was done in the 1980s and early 1990s and was accompanied by impressive accounts of organizational savings:

- The British government began reviewing its forms in 1982. After 10 years, it had eliminated 27,000 forms, redesigned 41,000, and saved over $28 million.

- Revising the British lost-baggage form for airline passengers cut a 55% error rate to 3%.

- In Australia, rewriting one legal document saved the Victorian government the equivalent of $400,000 a year in staff salaries.

- In the Netherlands, revising the form for educational grants reduced by two-thirds the number of forms applicants filled out incompletely or incorrectly. The government saved time and money; the applicants got decisions more quickly.

Adapted from Karen Schriver, "Quality in Document Design: Issues and Controversy," *Technical Communication* 40, no. 2 (1993), 250–51.

Courier font; we italicize magazine titles rather than underlining them, and we space once rather than twice after periods at ends of sentences.

Violating conventions is risky: violations may not be interpreted correctly, or they may signal that the author or designer is unreliable or unknowledgeable. Brochures with text that does not fit properly into the folded panels, freehand drawings in a set of installation instructions, or bar charts with garish color designs can destroy the reader's trust.[6]

Levels of Design

Communications Professor Charles Kostelnick distinguishes four levels of design (see Figure 6.1). These levels of design give you an organized way to think about the design choices you can make in your own documents, presentations, and visuals. They're also useful when you analyze the documents you encounter in a professional setting: one of the best ways to get ideas for your own document designs is to analyze the design elements in successful documents.

When you look at communication design, look for Kostelnick's four levels:[7]

- Intra—Design choices for individual letters and words. The font and its size you choose; whether you use bold, italics, or color changes to emphasize key words; and the way you use capital letters are intra-level design choices.

   The serif font used for body text on this page is an intra-level choice, as is the sans serif font used for headings.

- Inter—Design choices for blocks of text. The ways you use headings, white space, indents, lists, and even text boxes are inter-level design choices.

   The headings and bulleted lists that organize information on this page are inter-level choices.

- Extra—Design choices for graphics that go with the text. The way you use pictures, photographs, data displays, charts, and graphs, and the ways in which you emphasize information on those graphics are extra-level design choices.

   The data displays in this chapter are extra-level design choices.

- Supra—Design choices for entire documents. The paper size you choose, headers and footers, and the index and table of contents are supra-level

Figure 6.1   Four Levels for Examining Visual Language

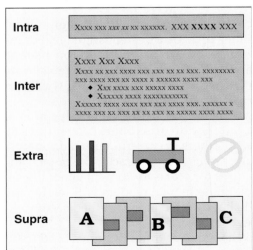

Source: Charles Kostelnick and David Roberts, *Designing Visual Language* (Boston: Allyn & Bacon, 1998), 85.

design choices, as are color schemes and layout grids that define the look of all sections of a document.

The placement of the page numbers in this book, the two-column layout grid on all of the pages in this chapter, and the navigation text in the header on this page are supra-level choices.

When you design a document or visual, think about each level of design. What choices are you making at each level of design? What design elements will help your audience?

Guidelines for Page Design

Use the guidelines in Figure 6.2 to create visually attractive documents.

1. Use White Space.

White space—the empty space on the page—makes material easier to read by emphasizing the material that it separates from the rest of the text. To create white space,

- Use headings.
- Use a mix of paragraph lengths (most no longer than seven typed lines). It's OK for a paragraph to be just one sentence. First and last paragraphs, in particular, should be short.
- Use lists.
  - Use tabs or indents—not spacing—to align items vertically.
  - Use numbered lists when the number or sequence of items is exact.
- Use **bullets** (large dots or squares like those in this list) when the number and sequence don't matter.

When you use a list, make sure that all of the items in it are parallel (p. 124) and fit into the structure of the sentence that introduces the list.

Faulty:	The following suggestions can help employers avoid bias in job interviews:
	1. Base questions on the job description.
	2. Questioning techniques.
	3. Selection and training of interviewers.
Parallel:	The following suggestions can help employers avoid bias in job interviews:
	1. Base questions on the job description.
	2. Ask the same questions of all applicants.
	3. Select and train interviewers carefully.

Figure 6.2 Guidelines for Page Design

1. Use white space to separate and emphasize points.
2. Use headings to group points and lead the reader through the document.
3. Limit the use of words set in all capital letters.
4. Use no more than two fonts in a single document.
5. Decide whether to justify margins based on the situation and the audience.
6. Put important elements in the top left and lower right quadrants of the page.
7. Use a grid of imaginary columns to unify visuals and other elements in a document.
8. Use highlighting, decorative devices, and color in moderation.

Good Document Design Saves Money, II

Document design changes are not just cosmetic. Infomap, a communications consulting company, reports these savings among its customers:

- A leading credit card company reduced the average length of phone calls to its customer service center by 60 seconds each after improving the design of its reference materials. This time reduction reduced costs by 20%.

- A leading health care provider redesigned its customer claims manual and saw the number of calls to the help desk decrease by 50%.

- A major government agency struggling with information overload used Information Mapping to create "uniform information architecture" agency wide. Newly trained "mappers" changed over 60,000 pages, and the agency reported over $17 million dollars of cost savings.

Their Web site quotes these results for other clients:

- 54% decrease in error rates.
- 83% decrease in first draft development time.
- 30% reduction in reading time.
- 80% decrease in customer service calls.

Adapted from Information Mapping, "Financial Services: Making Business Work," http://infomap.com/documents/Financialservices-ss.pdf (accessed April 15, 2007); and Information Mapping, "Customer Service Success Stories: Motorola Uses Information Mapping to Improve Customer Service," in *Expertise,* http://infomap.com/index.cfm/Expertise/Customer_Service_Success_Stories_ (accessed April 15, 2007).

Figure 6.3   A Document with Poor Visual Impact

Full capital letters make title hard to read

MONEY DEDUCTED FROM YOUR WAGES TO PAY CREDITORS

Long para-graph is visually uninviting

When you buy goods on credit, the store will sometimes ask you to sign a Wage Assignment form allowing it to deduct money from your wages if you do not pay your bill. When you buy on credit, you sign a contract agreeing to pay a certain amount each week or month until you have paid all you owe. The Wage Assignment Form is separate. It must contain the name of your present employer, your social security number, the amount of money loaned, the rate of interest, the date when payments are due, and your signature. The words "Wage Assignment" must be printed at the top of the form and also near the line for your signature. Even if you have signed a Wage Assignment agreement, Roysner will not withhold part of your wages unless all of the following conditions are met: 1. You have to be more than forty days late in payment of what you owe; 2. Roysner has to receive a correct statement of the amount you are in default and a copy of the Wage Assignment form; and 3. You and Roysner must receive a notice from the creditor at least twenty days in advance stating that the creditor plans to make a demand on your wages. This twenty-day notice gives you a chance to correct the problems yourself. If these conditions are all met, Roysner must withhold 15% of each paycheck until your bill is paid and give this money to your creditor.

If you think you are not late or that you do not owe the amount stated, you can argue against it by filing a legal document called a "defense." Once you file a defense, Roysner will not withhold any money from you. However, be sure you are right before you file a defense. If you are wrong, you have to pay not only what you owe but also all legal costs for both yourself and the creditor. If you are right, the creditor has to pay all these costs.

Important information is hard to find

Also parallel: Employers can avoid bias in job interviews by

1. Basing questions on the job description.
2. Asking the same questions of all applicants.
3. Selecting and training interviewers carefully.

Figure 6.3 shows an original typed document. In Figure 6.4, the same document has been improved by using shorter paragraphs, lists, and headings. These devices take space. When saving space is essential, it's better to cut the text and keep white space and headings. To see how to set up subheadings, see Figure 16.5 (p. 557 ➡) in Chapter 16.

2. Use Headings.

As George Miller has shown, our short-term memories can hold only seven plus or minus two bits of information.[8] Only after those bits are processed and put into long-term memory can we assimilate new information. Large amounts of information will be easier to process if they are grouped into three to seven chunks rather than presented as individual items.

Headings are words, short phrases, or short sentences that group points and divide your document into sections. Headings enable your reader to see at a

Figure 6.4 A Document Revised to Improve Visual Impact

Money Deducted from Your Wages to Pay Creditors

First letter of each main word capitalized— Title split onto two lines

When you buy goods on credit, the store will sometimes ask you to sign a Wage Assignment form allowing it to deduct money from your wages if you do not pay your bill.

Have You Signed a Wage Assignment Form?

Headings divide document into chunks

When you buy on credit, you sign a contract agreeing to pay a certain amount each week or month until you have paid all you owe. The Wage Assignment Form is separate. It must contain

- The name of your present employer,
- Your social security number,
- The amount of money loaned,
- The rate of interest,
- The date when payments are due, and
- Your signature.

List with bullets where order of items doesn't matter

Single-space list when items are short.

The words "Wage Assignment" must be printed at the top of the form and also near the line for your signature.

Headings must be parallel.

When Would Money Be Deducted from Your Wages to Pay a Creditor?

Here all are questions

Even if you have signed a Wage Assignment agreement, Roysner will not withhold part of your wages unless all of the following conditions are met:

White space between items emphasizes them

1. You have to be more than 40 days late in payment of what you owe;

2. Roysner has to receive a correct statement of the amount you are in default and a copy of the Wage Assignment form; and

Double-space between items in list when most items are two lines or longer.

Numbered list where number, order of items matter

3. You and Roysner must receive a notice from the creditor at least 20 days in advance stating that the creditor plans to make a demand on your wages. This 20-day notice gives you a chance to correct the problem yourself.

If these conditions are all met, Roysner must withhold fifteen percent (15%) of each paycheck until your bill is paid and give this money to your creditor.

What Should You Do If You Think the Wage Assignment Is Incorrect?

If you think you are not late or that you do not owe the amount stated, you can argue against it by filing a legal document called a "defense." Once you file a defense, Roysner will not withhold any money from you. However, be sure you are right before you file a defense. If you are wrong, you have to pay not only what you owe but also all legal costs for both yourself and the creditor. If you are right, the creditor has to pay all these costs.

What's on the Menu Tonight?

George Rapp is a "menu engineer" who helps restaurants around the world turn their menus into "profitable, user-friendly sales tools." His menus are attractive, full of savory detail, and carefully designed to lead the diner's eye to the high-profit items. Prices are nestled with food descriptions rather than aligned on the edge of the page so that readers can't scan the menu for the cheapest item. Expensive, profitable dishes are placed in the menu's prime real estate, the upper-right-hand corner; cheaper items are harder to locate. The longest, most mouthwatering descriptions are used for the most profitable items.

Adapted from Carolina A. Miranda, "The Menu Magician," *Time*, June 12, 2006, 86.

glance how the document is organized, to turn quickly to sections of special interest, and to compare and contrast points more easily. Headings also break up the page, making it look less formidable and more interesting.

- Make headings specific.
- Make each heading cover all the material until the next heading.
- Keep headings at any one level parallel: all nouns, all complete sentences, or all questions.

In a letter or memo, type main headings even with the left-hand margin in bold. Capitalize the first letters of the first word and of other major words; use lowercase for all other letters. (See Figure 6.4 for an example.) In single-spaced text, triple-space between the previous text and the heading; double-space between the heading and the text that follows.

If you need subdivisions within a head, use bold type and put a period after the subhead. Begin the paragraph on the same line. Use subheadings only when you have at least two subdivisions under a given main heading.

In a report, you may need more than two levels of headings. Figure 6.5 in (p. 557 ➡) Chapter 16 shows levels of headings for reports.

3. Limit the Use of Words Set in All Capital Letters.

We recognize words by their shapes.[9] (See Figure 6.5.) In capitals, all words are rectangular; letters lose the descenders and ascenders that make reading faster and more accurate.[10] In addition, many people interpret text in full capitals as "shouting," especially when that text appears in online documents. In those cases, full capitals might elicit a negative response from your audience. Use full capitals sparingly.

4. Use No More Than Two Fonts in a Single Document.

Fonts are unified styles of type. Each font comes in several sizes and usually in several styles (bold, italic, etc.). Typewriter fonts are **fixed;** that is, every letter takes the same space. An *i* takes the same space as a *w*. Courier and Prestige Elite are fixed fonts. Computers usually offer **proportional** fonts, where wider letters take more space than narrower letters. Times Roman, Palatino, Helvetica, and Arial are proportional fonts.

Serif fonts have little extensions, called serifs, from the main strokes. (In Figure 6.6, look at the feet on the *r*'s in New Courier and the flick on the top of the *d* in Lucinda.) New Courier, Elite, Times Roman, Palatino, and Lucinda Calligraphy are serif fonts. Serif fonts are easier to read since the serifs help the eyes move from letter to letter. Helvetica, Arial, Geneva, and Technical are **sans serif** fonts since they lack serifs (*sans* is French for *without*). Sans serif fonts are good for titles and tables.

You should choose the fonts you use carefully, because they shape reader response just as font size does. Research suggests that people respond positively to fonts that fit the genre and purpose of the document. For example, a font like Broadway (see Figure 6.6) is appropriate for a headline in a newsletter, but not for the body text of a memo.[11]

http://infomap.com/index .cfm/TheMethod/Demos

Information Mapping uses grids and tables to present complex information in an easy-to-find format. Review some of the online demos on the Information Mapping Web site, and notice how the 'after' documents make strong use of tables, lists, and white space to draw your attention to important points.

Try the fun demo at http://infomap.com/movies/demo.htm to see how they convert time savings to money savings.

Figure 6.5   Full Capitals Hide the Shape of a Word

Full capitals hide the shape of a word and slow reading 19%.

FULL CAPITALS HIDE THE SHAPE OF A WORD AND SLOW READING 19%.

Figure 6.6   Examples of Different Fonts

This sentence is set in 12-point Times Roman.

This sentence is set in 12-point Arial.

This sentence is set in 12-point New Courier.

This sentence is set in 12-point Lucinda Calligraphy.

This sentence is set in 12-point Broadway.

This sentence is set in 12-point Technical.

Most business documents use just one font—usually Times Roman, Palatino, Helvetica, or Arial. You can create emphasis and levels of headings by using bold, italics, and different sizes. Bold is easier to read than italics, so use bolding if you only need one method to emphasize text. In a complex document, use bigger type for main headings and slightly smaller type for subheadings and text.

Twelve-point Times Roman is ideal for letters, memos, and reports. Smaller type is harder to read, especially for readers older than 40.

If your material will not fit in the available pages, cut it. Putting some sections in tiny type will save space but creates a negative response—a negative response that may extend to the organization that produced the document.

5. Decide Whether to Justify Margins.

Computers often allow you to use **full justification** so that type on both sides of the page is evenly lined up. This paragraph justifies margins. Margins justified only on the left are sometimes called **ragged right margins.** Lines end in different places because words are of different lengths. The Sidebar columns in this book use ragged right margins.

Use full justification when you

- Can use proportional fonts.
- Want a more formal look.
- Want to use as few pages as possible.

Use ragged right margins when you

- Cannot use a proportional font.
- Want an informal look.
- Want to be able to revise an individual page without reprinting the whole document.
- Use very short line lengths.

6. Put Important Elements in the Top Left and Lower Right Quadrants.

Readers of English start in the upper left-hand corner of the page and read to the right and down. The eye moves in a Z pattern.[12] (See Figure 6.7.) Therefore, as Philip M. Rubens notes, the four quadrants of the page carry different visual

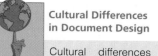

Cultural Differences in Document Design

Cultural differences in document design are based on reading practices and experiences with other documents. Language is one source of these differences. For example, English and other European languages are written in horizontal lines moving from left to right down the page. Hebrew and Arabic languages are read from left to right. This affects where readers of these languages look first when they see a page of text.

People in the United States focus first on the left side of a Web site. Middle Eastern people focus first on the right side, so Web sites in Arabic and Hebrew orient text, links, and graphics from right to left.

Translations also affect the layout of a document. To convey the same message, Spanish and French take up more room than English does. Writing concise text for brochures, packages, and Web pages is more challenging in the wordier languages. The problem is even more complex in designing bilingual or multilingual documents. For example, a company selling in Canada must use both English and French on its packages, and the French type must be printed at least as large as the English. On some products, such as a bottle of medicine or perfume, this requirement leaves little room for fancy graphics.

Adapted from Albert N. Badre, "The Effects of Cross Cultural Interface Design Orientation on World Wide Web User Performance," ftp://ftp.cc.gatech.edu/pub/gvu/tr/2001/01-03.html (accessed April 16, 2007); and Pan Demetrakakes, "Multilingual Labeling Broadens Product Appeal," in *Food and Drug Packaging,* http://www.findarticles.com/p/articles/mi_m0UQX/is_7_67/ai_106423172 (accessed April 16, 2007).

Figure 6.7   Put Important Elements in the Top Left and Bottom Right Quadrants

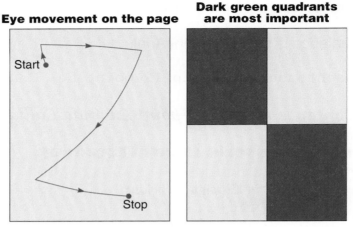

Source: Based on Russel N. Baird, Arthur T. Turnbull, and Duncan McDonald, *The Graphics of Communication: Typography, Layout, Design, Production,* 5th ed. (New York: Holt, Rinehart, and Winston, 1987), 37.

weights. The top left quadrant, where the eye starts, is the most important; the bottom right quadrant, where the eye ends, is next most important.[13] Titles should always start in the top left; reply coupons or another important element should be in the bottom right.

7. Use a Grid to Unify Graphic Elements.

For years, graphic designers have used a **grid system** to design pages. In its simplest form, a grid imposes two or three imaginary columns on the page. In more complex grids, these columns can be further subdivided. Then all the graphic elements—text indentations, headings, visuals, and so on—are lined up within the columns. The resulting symmetry creates a more pleasing page[14] and unifies long documents.

Figure 6.8 uses grids to organize a page with visuals, a newsletter page, and a résumé.

Figure 6.8   Examples of Grids to Design Pages

A page with visuals

Three-column grid.

A newsletter page

Six-column grid.

A résumé page

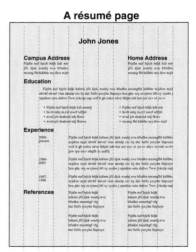

Twelve-column grid.

8. Use Highlighting, Decorative Devices, and Color in Moderation.

Many word-processing programs have arrows, pointing fingers, and a host of other **dingbats** that you can insert. Clip art packages and presentation software allow you to insert more and larger images into your text. The Document Design Center used icons as well as better page design when it revised Ford's warranty booklet. (See Figure 6.9.) Used in moderation, highlighting and decorative devices make pages more interesting. However, don't overdo them. A page or screen that uses every possible highlighting device just looks busy and hard to read.

Color works well to highlight points. Use color for overviews and main headings, not for small points.[15] Red is appropriate for warnings in North America. Since the connotations of colors vary among cultures, check with experts before you use color with international or multicultural audiences. (For more information on color, see the discussion on page 167.)

Adding Visuals

Visuals are a design element that helps make data meaningful. They help communicate your points in communications such as oral presentations, brochures, memos, letters, and reports.

Visuals can present numbers dramatically. Suppose you want to give investors information about various stocks' performance. They would not want to read paragraph after paragraph of statements about which stocks went up

Showing Trends and Changes

Jerry Atkinson gives his clients not only financial statements but also graphs of key trends. Atkinson is managing director of Atkinson and Company, a 62-employee CPA firm in Albuquerque, New Mexico.

Current-month or -year information isn't enough, he says. Clients need to see trends and changes. And graphs offer an easy way to show that.

Atkinson personalizes the graphs by using the colors of the company being profiled.

Adapted from John von Brachel, "Interpreting Financial Statements: How One Firm Uses the Language of Graphics," *Journal of Accountancy* 180, no. 2 (August 1995), 42–43.

Figure 6.9   "Before" and "After" Pages from Ford's Warranty Booklet

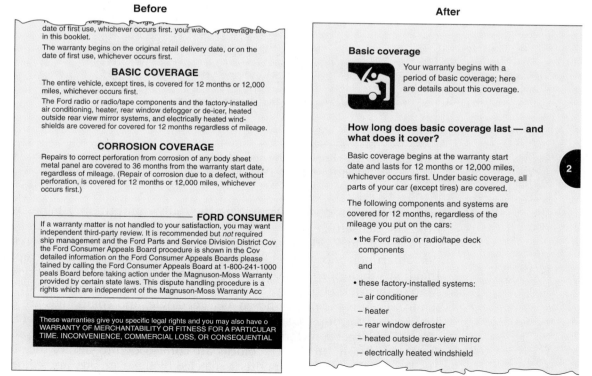

Source: Lee L. Gray, "Ford Offers a Readable Warranty Booklet," *Simply Stated . . . in Business*, no. 18 (March 1987): 12.

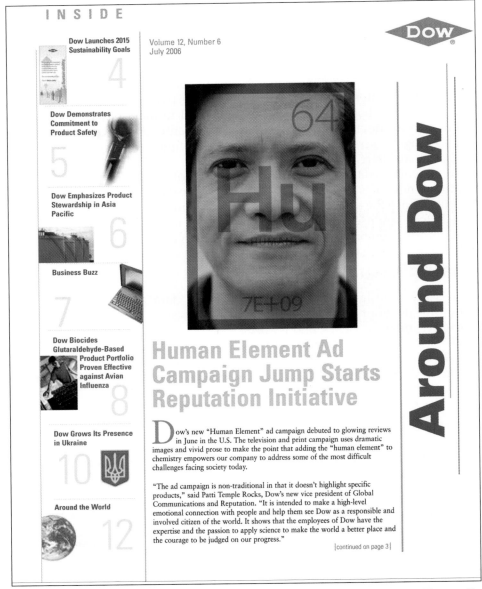

|continued on page 3|

Dow explains its "Human Elements" ad campaign in an employee newsletter. Three cells in the series were presented on page 43.

and which went down. Organizing the daily numbers into tables would be much more useful.

Tables of stock prices have been the norm until recently. Now, on the Internet, smartmoney.com offers subscribers Map of the Market, a graphics tool that helps them see the top performers. For 1,000 US and international stocks, Map of the Market displays visual information about each company's performance. Each company is shown as a rectangle, and companies are clustered into industry groups. Users can click on industry groups for a more detailed view. The larger a rectangle, the larger the company's market capitalization (total value of its stock). The blocks are color-coded to signify the size of the stock price change or other criteria selected by the user. Size and color provide easy cues for spotting the best and worst performers.[16]

When to Use Visuals

The ease of creating visuals by computer may make people use them uncritically. Use a visual only to achieve a specific purpose. Never put in numbers or visuals just because you have them; instead, use them to convey information the audience needs or wants.

In your rough draft, use visuals

- **To see that ideas are presented completely.** A table, for example, can show you whether you've included all the items in a comparison.
- **To find relationships.** For example, charting sales on a map may show that the sales representatives who made quota all have territories on the East or the West Coast. Is the central United States suffering a recession? Is the product one that appeals to coastal lifestyles? Is advertising reaching the coasts but not the central states? Even if you don't use the visual in your final document, creating the map may lead you to questions you wouldn't otherwise ask.

In the final presentation or document, use visuals

- **To make points vivid.** Readers skim memos and reports; a visual catches the eye. The brain processes visuals immediately. Understanding words—written or oral—takes more time.
- **To emphasize material** that might be skipped if it were buried in a paragraph. The beginning and end are places of emphasis. However, something has to go in the middle, especially in a long document. Visuals allow you to emphasize important material, wherever it logically falls.
- **To present material more compactly and with less repetition** than words alone would require. Words can call attention to the main points of the visual, without repeating all of the visual's information.

The number of visuals you will need depends on your purposes, the kind of information, and the audience. You'll use more visuals when you want to show relationships and to persuade, when the information is complex or contains extensive numerical data, and when the audience values visuals. Some audiences expect oral presentations and reports to use lots of visuals. Other audiences may see visuals as frivolous and time spent making visuals as time wasted. For these audiences, you'd sharply limit the number of visuals you use—but you'd still use them when your own purposes and the information called for them.

Guidelines for Visual Design

Use these six steps to create good visuals:

1. Check the quality of the data.
2. Determine the story you want to tell.
3. Choose the right visual for the story.
4. Follow the conventions for designing typical visuals.
5. Use color and decoration with restraint.
6. Be sure the visual is accurate and ethical.

Let's discuss each of these in more detail.

1. Check the Quality of the Data.

Your data display is only as good as the underlying data. Check to be sure that your data come from a reliable source. See "Identifying the Source of the

Trademark Cautions

Be careful when using names or trademarks of powerful organizations. Recently, companies like Starbucks Coffee, the Rock and Roll Hall of Fame, and the Virgin Group all went after little organizations who used similar-sounding names. In fact, in October of 2006, President Bush signed legislation that allows companies with famous trademarks to sue businesses with similar names "regardless of the presence or absence of actual or likely confusion, or competition, or of actual economic injury." Many would say this legislation sides in favor of the big guys. What do you think of the law? Is it fair? Should smaller businesses be sued for using the same name as a larger business even if there is no competition or direct economic gain?

Adapted from Ryan McCarthy, "Here Come the Trademark Bullies," *Inc.*, January 2007, 23.

Managing by Data

The best decisions are not necessarily the ones based on analyzing large amounts of data. Sometimes companies that manage with a bent toward numerical data are setting themselves up for failure because some important information isn't quantifiable. Employee morale, changing customer tastes, and new competition are examples.

Data can be called up almost effortlessly using dashboard displays. However, in some cases the recent hype of these data technology tools causes CEOs and other higher ups to rely on them. For example, when executives at Ford and GM were marketing SUVs, whose numbers looked great on the page, they failed to consider the largest factor and ultimately their biggest setback—gas prices.

Even when the numbers are complete, their interpretation can lead to bad calls. For instance, managers relying on data often assert correlations that aren't necessarily true. Furthermore, the way data are expressed can also shape interpretations. Notice the difference between saying 10% of employees will leave if management changes versus 90% will stay.

Adapted from David H. Freedman, "Do You Manage by the Numbers? Be Careful If You Do; Your Data May Be Playing Tricks on You," *Inc.*, November 2006, 59–60.

Data" in Chapter 16 ◂▥. Also check that you have data for all factors you should consider. Are some factors missing data from key locations or demographic areas? When Nielsen Media Research, the TV audience measuring organization, switched from paper diaries of TV viewing to "people meters," electronic recording devices, they discovered a marked rise in TV viewing by children and young adults.[17]

You may be able to use data based on assumptions and definitions in careful titles or notes: "Under the Fast-Growth Scenario, Sales Will Triple." "Over One-Fourth of Small Businesses Last Eight Years under Original Owners." If the data themselves are unreliable, you're better off not using visuals. The visual picture will be more powerful than verbal disclaimers, and the audience will be misled.

2. Determine the Story You Want to Tell.

Every visual should tell a story. Stories can be expressed in complete sentences that describe something that happens or changes. The sentence also serves as the title of the visual.

Not a story:	US Sales, 2000–2005
Possible stories:	Forty Percent of Our Sales Were to New Customers.
	Growth Was Highest in the South.
	Sales Increased from 2000 to 2005.
	Most Sales Representatives Have 2–5 Years' Experience.
	Sales Were Highest in the Areas with More Sales Representatives.

Stories that tell us what we already know are rarely interesting. Instead, good stories may

- Support a hunch you have.
- Surprise you or challenge so-called common knowledge.
- Show trends or changes you didn't know existed.
- Have commercial or social significance.
- Provide information needed for action.
- Be personally relevant to you and the audience.

To find stories,

1. Focus on a topic (where are the most SUVs bought, who likes jazz, etc.).
2. Simplify the data on that topic and convert the numbers to simple, easy-to-understand units.
3. Look for relationships and changes. For example, compare two or more groups: do men and women have the same attitudes? Look for changes over time. Look for items that can be seen as part of the same group. For example, to find stories about entertainers' incomes, you might compare the number of writers, actors, and musicians in three rankings.
4. Process the data to find more stories. Find the average and the median (▸ p. 541). Calculate the percentage change from one year to the next.

When you think you have a story, test it against all the data to be sure it's accurate.

Some stories are simple straight lines: "Computer Sales Increased." But other stories are more complex, with exceptions or outlying cases. Such stories will need more nuanced titles to do justice to the story. And sometimes the best story arises from the juxtaposition of two or more stories. In Figure 6.10, *BusinessWeek* uses four grouped visuals to tell a complex story.

Figure 6.10 A Complex Story Told Using Grouped Visuals

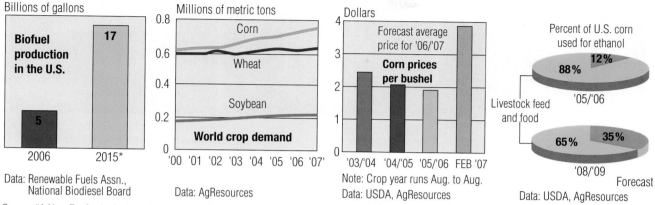

A New Era for Agriculture

What happens when farmers plant crops for energy as well as food

Source: "A New Era for Agriculture: What Happens When Farmers Plant Crops for Energy as Well as Food," *BusinessWeek*, February 5, 2007, 83.

Gene Zelazny points out that the audience should be able to *see* what the message *says:*

> [D]oes the chart support the title; and does the title reinforce the chart? So if I *say* in my title that "sales have increased significantly" I want to *see* a trend moving up at a sharp angle. If not, if the trend parallels the baseline, it's an instant clue that the chart needs more thinking.[18]

Almost every data set allows you to tell several stories. You must choose the story you want to tell. Dumps of uninterpreted data confuse and frustrate your audience; they undercut the credibility and goodwill you want to create.

Sometimes several stories will be important. When that's the case, you'll need a separate visual for each.

3. Choose the Right Visual for the Story.

Visuals are not interchangeable. Good writers choose the visual that best matches the purpose of presenting the data.

- Use a **table** when the reader needs to be able to identify exact values. (See Figure 6.11a.)
- Use a chart or graph when you want the reader to focus on relationships.
  - To compare a part to the whole, use a **pie chart**. (See Figure 6.11b.)
  - To compare one item to another item, use a **bar chart**. (See Figure 6.11c.)
  - To compare items over time, use a **bar chart** or a **line graph**. (See Figure 6.11d.)
  - To show frequency or distribution, use a **line graph** or **bar chart**. (See Figure 6.11e.)
  - To show correlations, use a **bar chart**, a **line graph**, or a **dot chart**. (See Figure 6.11f.)
- Use photographs to create a sense of authenticity or show the item in use. If the item is especially big or small, include something in the photograph that can serve as a reference point: a dime, a person.
- Use drawings to show dimensions, emphasize detail, or eliminate unwanted detail.

Figure 6.11   Choose the Visual to Fit the Story

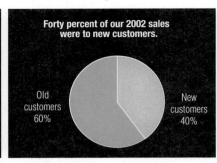

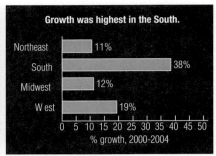

a. Tables show exact values.

b. Pie charts compare a component to the whole.

c. Bar charts compare items or show distribution or correlation.

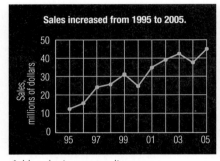

d. Line charts compare items over time or show distribution or correlation.

e. Bar charts can show frequency.

f. Dot charts show correlation.

- Use maps to emphasize location.
- Use **Gantt charts** to show timelines for proposals or projects.

4. Follow the Conventions for Designing Typical Visuals.

Every visual should contain six components:

1. A title telling the story that the visual shows.
2. A clear indication of what the data are. For example, what people *say* they did is not necessarily what they really did. An estimate of what a number will be in the future differs from numbers in the past that have already been measured.
3. Clearly labeled units.
4. Labels or legends identifying axes, colors, symbols, and so forth.
5. The source of the data, if you created the visual from data someone else gathered and compiled.
6. The source of the visual, if you reproduce a visual someone else created.

Formal visuals are divided into tables and figures. **Tables** are numbers or words arrayed in rows and columns; **figures** are everything else. In a document, formal visuals have both numbers and titles, e.g., "Figure 1. The Falling Cost of Computer Memory, 1990–2005." In an oral presentation, the title is usually used without the number: "The Falling Cost of Computer Memory, 1990–2005." The title should tell the story so that the audience knows what to look for in the visual and why it is important. **Spot visuals** are informal visuals that are inserted directly into the text; they do not have numbers or titles.

Figure 6.12 Colors and Their Common Connotations in Western Culture

Color	Positive	Negative
White	Clean, innocent, pure	Cold, empty, sterile
Red	Strong, brave, passionate	Dangerous, aggressive, domineering
Yellow	Happy, friendly, optimistic	Cowardly, annoying, brash
Brown	Warm, earthy, mature	Dirty, sad, cheap
Green	Natural, tranquil, relaxing	Jealous, inexperienced, greedy
Blue	Strong, trustworthy, authoritative	Cold, depressing, gloomy

Source: Katherine Nolan, "Color It Effective: How Color Influences the User," in *Microsoft Office Online, FrontPage 2003 Help and How-to: Working with Graphics,* http://office.microsoft.com/en-us/frontpage/HA010429371033.aspx (accessed April 15, 2007).

5. Use Color and Decoration with Restraint.

Color makes visuals more dramatic, but it also creates some problems. Colors may be interpreted positively or negatively depending on their context and the unique experiences of the people viewing them. Figure 6.12 gives some common positive and negative associations found in Western cultures. A good use of color occurs in the weather maps printed daily in many newspapers. Blue seems to fit cold; red seems to fit hot temperatures.

Meanings assigned to colors differ depending on the audience's national background and profession. Blue suggests masculinity in the United States, criminality in France, strength or fertility in Egypt, and villainy in Japan. Red is sometimes used to suggest danger or *stop* in the United States; it means *go* in China and is associated with festivities. Red suggests masculinity or aristocracy in France, death in Korea, blasphemy in some African countries, and luxury in many parts of the world.[19]

These general cultural associations may be superseded by corporate, national, or professional associations. Some people associate blue with IBM or Hewlett-Packard and red with Coca-Cola, communism, or Japan. People in specific professions learn other meanings for colors. Blue suggests *reliability* to financial managers, *water* or *coldness* to engineers, and *death* to health care professionals. Red means *losing money* to financial managers, *danger* to engineers, but *healthy* to health care professionals. Green usually means *safe* to engineers, but *infected* to health care professionals. Also avoid graphs that contrast red and green, because the colors will be indistinguishable to people with red-green colorblindness. Almost 10% of men and 2% of women are colorblind. Furthermore, as people get older, their ability to perceive colors also decreases.[20]

These various associations suggest that color is safest with a homogenous audience that you know well. In an increasingly multicultural workforce, color may send signals you do not intend. When you do use color in visuals, Eric Kenly and Mark Beach offer these cautions:[21]

- Check with your printer to determine the price of getting color documents printed.
- Paper choice will affect how much ink is absorbed, thus how vivid images appear.
- Be aware that colors on the computer screen will usually look different when printed on paper.

In any visual, use as little shading and as few lines as are necessary for clarity. Don't clutter up the visual with extra marks. When you design black-and-white

Medicine Shows Its Colors

One small, highly specialized, communication device is the hospital wristband. All patients have long been tagged with a band containing identifying information. Now hospitals are using colored bands to alert staff to special conditions such as medication allergies. Different colors represent different alerts. Sounds great, doesn't it?

The catch is that different hospitals use different colors for different alerts. One hospital may use red for allergy alerts and yellow for fall alerts (patients with a high risk of falling); another hospital may reverse the two. Since medical staff may work in more than one hospital, the colored bands are causing confusion and in some cases actually increasing risk.

To remedy the problem, hospital associations are trying to standardize the color codes. Some hospitals are switching to colored bands that also display a printed phrase such as "allergy" or "fall risk."

Adapted from Laura Landro, "Hospitals Target Risks of Color Wristbands," *Wall Street Journal,* April 4, 2007, D5.

Visuals That Translate Well

When preparing visuals, keep in mind cultural differences:

- Make sure any symbols in the visual will have the correct meaning in the culture of your audience. For example, a red cross symbolizes first aid in North America, but in Muslim countries the symbol with that meaning is typically a green crescent.

- If you use punctuation marks as symbols, be sure they are meaningful to your audience. A question mark [in English and certain other languages] might signal a help function or answers to questions. But in languages without this symbol, it has no meaning.

- In showing humans, respect the cultural norms of your audience. Europeans tend to accept images of nudity, but some cultures can be offended by images of even a bare leg or other body part.

- Organize the information according to the reading customs of the audience. North American and European audiences will tend to read visual information as they do text: from left to right. Asians view from right to left, and Middle Easterners in a rotation moving counterclockwise.

- Learn your audience's conventions for writing numbers. In the United States, a period indicates the decimal point, and commas separate groups of three digits. In much of Europe, a comma represents the decimal point, and a space goes between each group of three digits. For US and French readers, 3,333 would have different values.

Adapted from Gerald J. Alred, Charles T. Brusaw, and Walter E. Oliu, *The Business Writer's Handbook*, 8th ed. (New York: St. Martin's Press, 2006), 248–50, 558–62; and *The Chicago Manual of Style*, 15th ed. (Chicago: University of Chicago Press, 2003), 385.

graphs, use shades of gray rather than stripes, wavy lines, and checks to indicate different segments or items.

Resist the temptation to make your visual "artistic" or "relevant" by turning it into a picture or adding clip art. **Clip art** consists of predrawn images that you can import into your newsletter, sign, or graph. A small drawing of a car in the corner of a line graph showing the number of miles driven is acceptable in an oral presentation but out of place in a written report. Turning a line graph into a highway to show miles driven makes it harder to read: it's hard to separate the data line from lines that are merely decorative. Visuals authority Edward Tufte uses the term **chartjunk** for decorations that at best are irrelevant to the visual and at worst mislead the reader.[22] If you use clip art, be sure that the images of people show a good mix of both sexes, various races and ages, and various physical conditions.

6. Be Sure the Visual Is Accurate and Ethical.

Always double-check your visuals to be sure the information is accurate. Also, many visuals have accurate labels but misleading visual shapes. Visuals communicate quickly; audiences remember the shape, not the labels. If the reader has to study the labels to get the right picture, the visual is unethical even if the labels are accurate.

Cigarette warning labels are more severe in other countries. American audiences have not been receptive to such dire warnings.

Figure 6.13 is distorted by chartjunk and dimensionality. In an effort to make the visual interesting, the artist used a picture of a young man (presumably an engineer) rather than simple bars. By using a photograph rather than a bar, the chart implies that all engineers are young, nerdy-looking white men. The photograph also makes it difficult to compare the numbers. The number represented by the tallest figure is not quite 5 times as great as the number represented by the shortest figure, yet the tallest figure takes up 12 times as much space and appears even bigger than that. Two-dimensional figures distort data by multiplying the apparent value by the width as well as by the height—four times for every doubling in value. Perspective graphs are especially hard for readers to interpret and should be avoided.[23]

Even simple bar and line graphs may be misleading if part of the scale is missing, or truncated. **Truncated graphs** are most acceptable when the audience knows the basic data set well. For example, graphs of the stock market

Figure 6.13 Chartjunk and Dimensions Distort Data

How much is that engineer in the window?

Here's how much an employee in Silicon Valley was worth over the past year, determined by dividing the value of a sample acquisition by the number of employees acquired.

$5.6 million

$1.9 million

$1.3 million

Nov. 2000   July 2001   Nov. 2001

GETTY IMAGES (3)

Source: Adam Lashinsky, "Valley Horror Show: The Incredible Shrinking Engineer," *Fortune,* December 10, 2001, p. 40.

Slimming Down Couric

Always be careful about altering the appearance of photographs.

Katie Couric has two famous photographs. The first was snapped in May 2006 as an official media photo. The second, supposedly the same photo, appeared in the September 2006 issue of *Watch!,* a magazine distributed to CBS affiliates and to passengers on American Airline flights with a circulation around 400,000. In the second version Katie Couric dropped around 20 pounds and looked much younger. The magazine article which included the photo advertised Couric's move from NBC's *Today* to CBS's *Evening News.*

When asked about the doctored photo, Couric reportedly said that she liked the original because "there's more of me to love." Media experts suggest that whenever a photo is altered, the public deserves the right to be told about it.

What do you think? What are the ethics of altering photos so that subjects are slimmer and younger looking? How does this altering influence the public's obsession with beauty? How does Couric's photo hinder goodwill between CBS and the public?

Think about the photos you see in the media everyday. How many of them have been altered? How would you know? If you wanted to use an altered photo, what steps would you need to take to use it ethically?

Adapted from Buzzle Staff, "Katie Couric Magically Loses Weight in Photo Distributed to Media," in Buzzle.com, http://www.buzzle.com/editorials/9-1-2006-107383.asp (accessed April 15, 2007).

almost never start at zero; they are routinely truncated. This omission is acceptable for audiences who follow the market closely.

Since part of the scale is missing in truncated graphs, small changes seem like major ones. Figure 6.14 shows three different truncated graphs of US unemployment data. The first graph shows the trend in unemployment from May 2003 to January 2004. The curve falls from the fifth level of the graph to the second, resembling a 60% decline. But a close look at the numbers shows the decline is from a high of 6.3% to a low of 5.6% (a decline of 11%). The period chosen for the horizontal axis also is truncated. The first graph emphasizes the declining trend in unemployment since a tax cut was enacted in 2003, but the second graph uses the period November 2002–November 2003 to show unemployment wavering around 6%. The graph accompanies a news article about "cautious" employers and unemployment that "edged lower." The truncated scale on the vertical axis again makes the changes appear larger. The third graph takes a longer view (back to 1980) and puts the percentages on a scale starting at zero. On this scale, the changes in the unemployment rate seem less dramatic, and the recent decline looks as if it could be part of a regular pattern that follows recessions (the shaded areas). The graph starting with 1980 shows that the latest ("current") unemployment rate was lower than after past recessions.[24]

Data can also be distorted when the context is omitted. As Tufte suggests, a drop may be part of a regular cycle, a correction after an atypical increase, or a permanent drop to a new, lower plateau.[25] Consider the unemployment data shown in Figure 6.14. Putting the third graph in the context of data gathered since 1948, unemployment has often fallen lower than the 5.5% highlighted. The troughs on a longer unemployment curve include 5.7% (in 1979), 4.6% (1973), 3.4% (1968–1969), 4.8% (1960), 3.7% (1957), 2.5% (1953), and 3.4% (1948). The peak unemployment rate in Figure 6.14 (10.8% in 1982) is the highest since 1948; usually the unemployment rate has peaked between 6% and 8%. Therefore, the impression of an overall declining pattern of unemployment is not accurate before the period shown.

To make your data displays more accurate,

- Differentiate between actual and estimated or projected values.
- When you must truncate a scale, do so clearly with a break in the bars or in the background.
- Avoid perspective and three-dimensional graphs.
- Avoid combining graphs with different scales.
- Use images of people carefully in histograms to avoid sexist, racist, or other exclusionary visual statements.

Photographs in particular have received close attention for accuracy and ethics concerns. The doctored Katie Couric photo is a current example (see sidebar). However, the problem is not new. Photographers have always been able to frame their pictures in ways that cut objects they do not want. Pictures of homes for real estate sales can omit the collapsing garage; shots of collapsed homeless people can omit the image of social workers standing by to give aid.

Now Adobe Photoshop has added a new dimension to the discussion with its easy aid for altering photos. A classic example is the *Time* magazine cover

Figure 6.14   Truncated Scales Distort Data

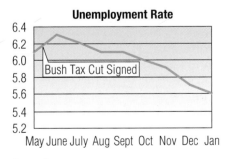
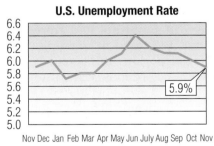
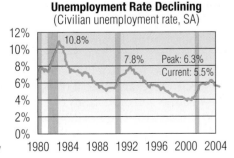

Source: Economy.com

Source: Bureau of Labor Statistics
Gray bars denote recessions

Sources: From Jerry Bowyer, "In Defense of the Unemployment Rate," National Review Online, March 5, 2004, www.nationalreview.com; Mark Gongloff, "Payroll Growth Disappoints," CNN Money, December 5, 2003, http://money.cnn.com; and Joint Economic Committee, "Charts: Economy," http://jec.senate.gov, last updated August 27, 2004.

of O.J. Simpson. On June 27, 1994, the cover of *Time* showed O.J.'s LAPD mug shot. In the photo, Simpson looked unshaven and surrounded by deep shadows: he looked like a criminal. However, *Time*'s art department had digitally altered that image. They'd used a computer to darken the photo and give Simpson a sinister look. That same day, the cover of *Newsweek* featured the original, unaltered photo, and when people saw the two images side-by-side on newsstands, they accused *Time* of biased, unethical journalism.

More recent discussions have involved the use of digital alterations to increase the beauty of ad models to unnatural degrees. You can watch the short video at http://www.campaignforrealbeauty.com/flat4.asp?id=6909 to see an illustration. First the model's looks are greatly enhanced with makeup and hairstyling. But even that gorgeous result is not good enough. The video shows the made-up model having her brows raised and her neck thinned and elongated with digital alterations for her billboard display.

In his discussion of photography ethics, John Long notes that it's easy to think of small changes to photographs as harmless. He argues that any change to the picture is deceptive, because when people see a photo, they assume that it's a true record of a real event. When you change a photo, you use that assumption to deceive.[26]

Integrating Visuals in Your Text

Refer to every visual in your text. Normally one gives the table or figure number in the text but not the title. Put the visual as soon after your reference as space and page design permit. If the visual must go on another page, tell the reader where to find it:

> As Figure 3 shows (page 10), . . .
>
> (See Table 2 on page 14.)

Summarize the main point of a visual *before* you present the visual itself. Then when readers get to it, they'll see it as confirmation of your point.

> Weak: Listed below are the results.
>
> Better: As Figure 4 shows, sales doubled in the last decade.

The weak statement mirrors the thought processes that occur as the writer processes data: one first categorizes the data in a very general way ("results"); one next looks at the data; and one finally decides what the data mean. But when this mental process becomes the writer's organizing pattern, the reader is forced to duplicate the whole process by which the writer reached a conclusion. Most readers, understandably, are unwilling to do work which the writer is supposed to do, so they will skim or skip the data presented in this unsatisfactory fashion. When the writer finally comes to the point, readers may be unconvinced because they haven't recognized the significance of the evidence in the table.

How much discussion a visual needs depends on the audience, the complexity of the visual, and the importance of the point it makes. If the material is new to the audience, you'll need a fuller explanation than if similar material is presented to this audience every week or month. If the visual is complex, you may want to help the reader find key points in it. If the point is important, you'll want to discuss its implications in some detail. In contrast, one sentence about a visual may be enough when the audience is already familiar with the topic and the data, when the visual is simple and well designed, and when the information in the visual is a minor part of your proof.

Two-Timing Pictures

Thanks to the spread of digital photo libraries, companies—sometimes competing ones—have been discovering that they are using the same photo in their advertisements. Both Bank of America and Key Bank used the same photo of a father showing something on his computer to his daughter. MetLife used the same male that Pfizer used in its Viagra ad. Dell and Washington Mutual used the same picture of a young Asian woman.

The duplication happens when companies buy photos from stock agencies without paying the high premiums for exclusive use. The problem intensifies when companies want pictures of minorities.

Adapted from "When Marketers See Double: As Digital Libraries Spread the Use of Stock Photography, Some Ad Images Are Recycled," *Wall Street Journal*, November 28, 2006, B1.

When you discuss visuals, spell out numbers that fall at the beginning of a sentence. If spelling out the number or year is cumbersome, revise the sentence so that it does not begin with a number.

Forty-five percent of the cost goes to pay wages and salaries.

In 2002, euronotes and coins became legal tender.

Put numbers in parentheses at the end of the clause or sentence to make the sentence easier to read:

Hard to read: As Table 4 shows, teachers participate (54%) in more community service groups than do members of the other occupations surveyed; dentists (20.8%) participate in more service groups than do members of five of the other occupations.

Better: As Table 4 shows, teachers participate in more community service groups than do members of the other occupations surveyed (54%); dentists participate in more service groups than do five of the other occupations (20.8%).

Designing Data Displays and Images

Once you know your story—once you know what you're saying, how you're saying it, and how you want text and visuals to combine to say it—then you're in a position to choose and create visuals. Each type of visual can do different things for you. Here are some of the most common types of visuals (data displays and images), and here's when, where and how they're most effective.

Tables

Use tables only when you want the audience to focus on specific numbers. Graphs convey less specific information but are more memorable. Figure 6.15 illustrates the basic structure of tables. The **boxhead** is the variable whose label is at the top; the **stub** is the variable listed on the side. When constructing tables,

- Use common, understandable units. Round off to simplify the data (e.g., 35% rather than 35.27%; 44.5 million rather than 44,503,276).
- Provide column and row totals or averages when they're relevant.
- Put the items you want readers to compare in columns rather than in rows to facilitate mental subtraction and division.
- When you have many rows, shade alternate rows (or pairs of rows) or double-space after every five rows to help readers line up items accurately.

Pie charts

Pie charts force the audience to measure area. However, people can judge position or length (which a bar chart uses) more accurately than they judge area, thus making information in pie charts more difficult for an audience to understand accurately.[27] The data in any pie chart can be put in a bar chart. Therefore, use a pie chart only when you are comparing one segment to the whole. When you are comparing one segment to another segment, use a bar chart, a line graph, or a map—even though the data may be expressed in percentages.

Figure 6.15 Tables Show Exact Values

Table Number – Title

Boxhead

Stub

Top 10 Search Providers for May 2007, Ranked by Searches (U.S.)

Provider	Searches (000)	YOY Growth	Share of Searches
1. Google Search	4,033,277	44.9%	56.3%
2. Yahoo! Search	1,540,949	18.6%	21.5%
3. MSN/Windows Live Search	605,400	0.8%	8.4%
4. AOL Search	381,961	5.1%	5.3%
5. Ask.com Search	142,418	−2.8%	2.0%
6. My Web Search	61,784	N/A	0.9%
7. Comcast Search	34,908	N/A	0.5%
8. EarthLink Search	33,461	21.7%	0.5%
9. BellSouth Search	30,122	N/A	0.4%
10. Dogpile.com Search	26,295	−10.6%	0.4%

Sources: http://www.netratings.com/pr/pr_070620.pdf (accessed August 11, 2007).

- Start at 12 o'clock with the largest percentage or the percentage you want to focus on. Go clockwise to each smaller percentage or to each percentage in some other logical order.
- Make the chart a perfect circle. Avoid 3D circles; they distort the data.
- Limit the number of segments to no more than seven. If your data have more divisions, combine the smallest or the least important into a single "miscellaneous" or "other" category.
- Label the segments outside the circle. Internal labels are hard to read.

Bar charts

Bar charts are easy to interpret because they ask people to compare distance along a common scale, which most people judge accurately. Bar charts are useful in a variety of situations: to compare one item to another, to compare items over time, and to show correlations. Use horizontal bars when your labels are long; when the labels are short, either horizontal or vertical bars will work. When constructing bar charts,

- Order the bars in a logical or chronological order.
- Put the bars close enough together to make comparison easy.
- Label both horizontal and vertical axes.

Tiny Photos That Speak Volumes

In planning visuals for a Web site, keep in mind that large and complicated images will download too slowly for many users. Small photographs will download faster than large ones, and visitors can have the option to click on a photo for a link to see details in a larger image.

Using small photos presents its own set of challenges. It is important to select and crop images carefully so that they are easy to see and understand. A photo should be simple, with just one or two objects on an uncomplicated background. Close-up shots without background clutter work best.

For contrasting examples of small photographs that fail and succeed, visit Jakob Nielsen's Alertbox message of December 2003 (at www.useit.com/alertbox/20031222.html). A photo from the White House Web site shows three tiny people walking on a road. The image is too small for site users to see who the people are and where they are walking, yet that information is what makes the image relevant. In another photo, CNN represents a story of flooding by showing a car stranded in deep water. The meaning of the photo is obvious, so it is an effective visual in this context.

Adapted from Jakob Nielsen, "Top Ten Web Design Mistakes of 2003" in *Alertbox*, useit.com, http://www.useit.com/alertbox/20031222.html (accessed April 15, 2007).

- Put all labels inside the bars or outside them. When some labels are inside and some are outside, the labels carry the visual weight of longer bars, distorting the data.
- Make all the bars the same width.
- Use different colors for different bars only when their meanings are different: estimates as opposed to known numbers, negative as opposed to positive numbers.
- Avoid using 3D perspective; it makes the values harder to read and can make comparison difficult.

Several varieties of bar charts exist. See Figure 6.16 for examples.

- **Grouped bar charts** allow you to compare either several aspects of each item or several items over time. Group together the items you want to compare. Figure 6.16a shows that sales were highest in the west each year. If we wanted to show how sales had changed in each region, the bars should be grouped by region, not by year.
- **Segmented, subdivided, or stacked bars** sum the components of an item. It's hard to identify the values in specific segments; grouped bar charts are almost always easier to use.
- **Deviation bar charts** identify positive and negative values, or winners and losers.
- **Paired bar charts** show the comparison between two items.
- **Histograms or pictograms** use images to create the bars.

Line graphs

Line graphs are also easy to interpret. Use line graphs to compare items over time, to show frequency or distribution, and to show possible correlations. When construsting line graphs,

Figure 6.16   Varieties of Bar Charts

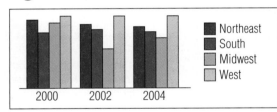

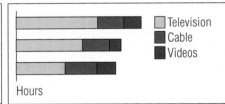

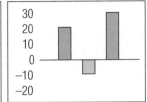

a. Grouped bar charts compare several aspects of each item, or several items over time.

b. Segmented, subdivided, or **stacked bars** sum the components of an item.

c. Deviation bar charts identify positive and negative values.

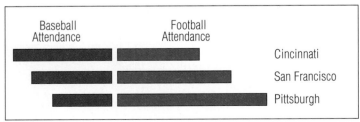

d. Paired bar charts show the comparison between two items.

e. Histograms or **pictograms** use images to create the bars.

- Label both horizontal and vertical axes. When time is a variable, it is usually put on the horizontal axis.
- Avoid using more than three different lines on one graph. Even three lines may be too many if they cross each other.
- Avoid using perspective. Perspective makes the values harder to read and can make comparison difficult.

Gantt charts

Gantt charts are bar charts used to show schedules. They're most commonly used in proposals. Figure 6.17 is a Gantt chart for a marketing plan. From the chart, it is easy to see which activities must be completed first in order to finish the total plan on time. When using Gantt charts,

- Color-code bars to indicate work planned and work completed.
- Use a red outline to indicate **critical activities,** which must be completed on time if the project is to be completed by the due date.
- Use diamonds to indicate progress reports, major achievements, or other accomplishments.

Photographs

Photographs convey a sense of authenticity. The photo of a prototype helps convince investors that a product can be manufactured; the photo of a devastated area can suggest the need for government grants or private donations.

Figure 6.17   Gantt Charts Show the Schedule for Completing a Project

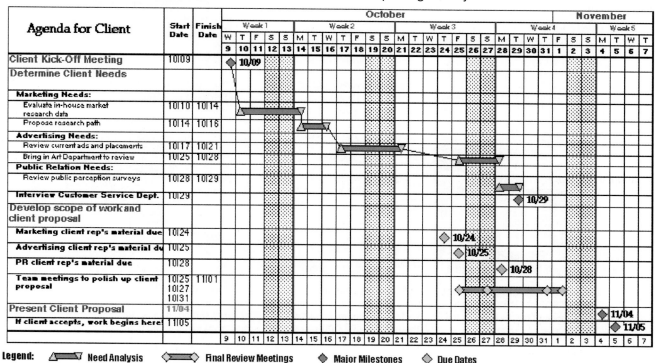

You may need to **crop,** or trim, a photo for best results. If someone else is doing the production, mark the places for cropping in the margins of the photo or attach nonsticky paper. Never write or mark on the photo or the negative.

A growing problem with photos is that they may be edited or staged, purporting to show something as reality even though it never occurred. See the discussion of ethics and accuracy starting on page 170.

Drawings

The richness of detail in photos makes them less effective than drawings for focusing on details. With a drawing, the artist can provide as much or as little detail as is needed to make the point; different parts of the drawing can show different layers or levels of detail. Drawings are also better for showing structures underground, undersea, or in the atmosphere.

In the drawings in Figure 6.18, no attempt is made to show the details of warehousing and transportation facilities. Such details would distract from the main point. Here, the drawings show how UPS Logistics handles the various activities required to move Birkenstock sandals from the shoe company's German factories to thousands of stores in the United States.

Figure 6.18   Sketches Can Show Processes

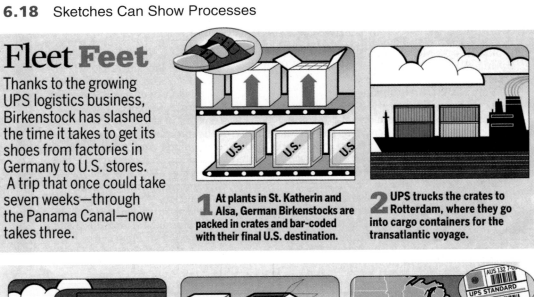

Source: Dean Foust, "Big Brown's New Bag," *BusinessWeek,* July 19, 2004, 54–56.

Maps

Use maps to emphasize location or to compare items in different locations. Figure 6.19 shows the prevalence of childhood asthma by state. A map is appropriate because the emphasis is on the distribution of asthma in various regions. Several computer software packages now allow users to generate local, state, national, or global maps, adding color or shadings, and labels. When using maps,

* Label states, provinces, or countries if it's important that people be able to identify levels in areas other than their own.
* Avoid using perspective. Perspective makes the values harder to read and can make comparison difficult.

Figure 6.19 The State of Childhood Asthma

Current asthma prevalence among children 0–17 years of age, by state, annual average for the period 2001–2005

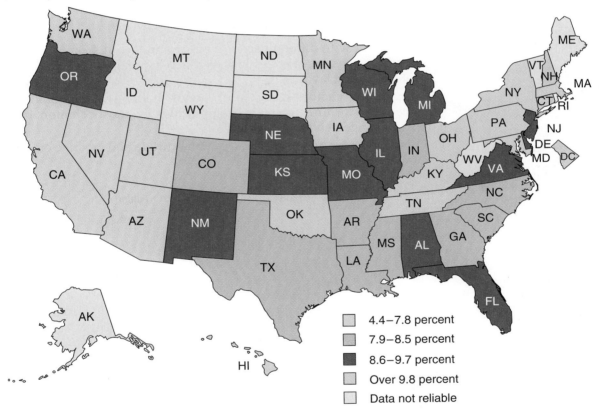

NOTES: Ranges are based on approximate quartiles among states with available estimates. Differences portrayed in this map should be interpreted with caution. The 95 percent confidence intervals for many states overlap. Current asthma prevalence estimates are based on the questions "Has a doctor or other health professional ever told you that (child's name) had asthma?" and "Does (child's name) still have asthma?" Estimates for Delaware, the District of Columbia, Mississippi, Nebraska, Nevada, and New Hampshire have a relative standard error greater than 30 percent and less than or equal to 50 percent and should be interpreted with caution as they do not meet the standard of reliability or precision. The estimates for Alaska, Idaho, Maine, Montana, North Dakota, South Dakota, Vermont, West Virginia, and Wyoming have a relative standard error greater than 50 percent and therefore are not represented in this figure.
SOURCE: CDC/NCHS, National Health Interview Survey.

Source: Lara J. Akinbami, "The State of Childhood Asthma, United States, 1980–2005," in *Advance Data from Vital and Health Statistics* (Hyattsville, MD: National Center for Health Statistics, 2006). (http://www.cdc.gov/nchs/data/ad/ad381.pdf)

Designing Brochures

To design brochures and newsletters, first think about audience and purpose. An "image" brochure designed to promote awareness of your company will have a different look than an "information" brochure telling people how to do something and persuading them to do it.

Use this process to create effective brochures.

1. Determine your objective(s).
2. Identify your target audience(s).
3. Identify a **central selling point:** one overarching benefit the audience will get.
4. Choose the image you want to project. (Clean and clear? Postmodern and hip?)
5. Identify objections and brainstorm ways to deal with them.
6. Draft text to see how much room you need. Do tighten your writing (◄▬ Chapter 4). But when you really need more room, use a bigger brochure layout or a series of brochures.
7. Select visuals to accompany text.
8. Experiment with different sizes of paper and layout. Consider how readers will get the brochure—must it fit in a standard rack? Use thumbnail sketches to test layouts.
9. Make every choice—color, font, layout, paper—a conscious one. The three-fold brochure shown in Figure 6.20 is the most common, but many other arrangements are possible.
10. Polish the prose and graphics. Use you-attitude and positive emphasis.

Figure 6.20   Three-Fold Brochure on 8 1/2-by-11-Inch Paper

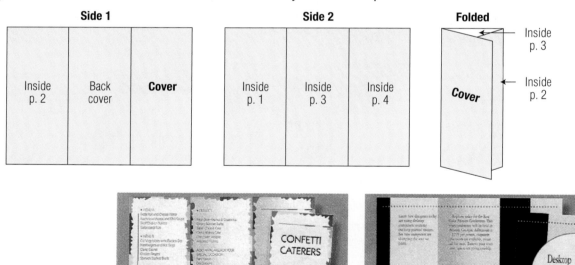

Special stationery is available to use with your laser printer or photocopier to produce brochures.

Follow these design principles to enhance your brochure:

- Use the cover effectively.
  - Put your central selling point on the cover.
  - Use a visual that tells a story. Remember that the visual has to work for the audience. A photo of a campus landmark may not mean much to an audience thinking about attending a summer program on campus.
- Use a grid to align the elements within the panels. Make sure that the Z pattern emphasizes important points for each spread the reader sees. In a three-fold brochure, the Z pattern needs to work for the cover alone, for inside pages 1 and 2 (as the reader begins to unfold the brochure), and for inside pages 1, 3, and 4 (when the brochure is fully opened).
- Effective brochures not only repeat design elements (headings, small photos) across panels to create a unified look but also contain contrast (between text and visuals, between a larger font for headings and a smaller one for text).
- Use color effectively.
  - Restraint usually works best for informative brochures. To get the effect of color with the least expense, use black print on colored paper.
  - If you use four-color printing, use glossy paper.
- Make the text visually appealing.
  - Use no more than two fonts—just one may be better.
  - Use proportional fonts.
  - Avoid italic type and underlining, which make text hard to read. To emphasize text, use bold (sparingly).
  - Use small tab indents.
  - Make sure that you have enough white space in your copy. Use lists and headings. Use short paragraphs with extra space between paragraphs.
  - Ragged right margins generally work better with short line lengths.
- If you use a reply coupon, make sure its back side doesn't have crucial information the reader needs to keep.

Research suggests that people hold on to brochures and other small documents when they see something that engages their attention. When you design a brochure:

- Try using humor in your central selling point or headline. Interesting headlines are not just informative: they're attention-grabbing, funny, or out-of-the-ordinary.
- Use sidebars with testimonial quotes, examples, or vignettes. Interesting stories can hold your readers' attention.
- Try using an unusual paper size, or try making your brochure look like something else: a postcard, a menu, an insert for a CD jewel box.
- Add something to get your readers involved with your brochure, such as a coupon for a free or discount offer, a quiz, or a puzzle.[28]

Say It with Color

In *Bulletproof Presentations*, consultant G. Michael Campbell says color is a useful tool for coding information and affecting the reader's reaction. Here are some of his ideas for using color:

- Identify ideas according to common associations with color—red for stop or danger, green for go or money.
- Use distinctive colors when you need to refer to something: "In the graph, the green bar shows how much our water quality has improved since Commissioner Jones took office."
- Match colors to the moods they tend to evoke. Red demands attention (but is easy to overuse); yellow is cheery. Blue and green tend to have a calming effect.
- Avoid color combinations that would confuse people who are colorblind. About 10 percent of men and 0.5 percent of women cannot distinguish between red and green.
- When you use a corporate logo, follow the company's color specifications exactly. Companies tend to be very protective of their logos.

Adapted from G. Michael Campbell, *Bulletproof Presentations* (Franklin Lakes, NJ: Career Press, 2002): 190–93.

Making Your Web Page Accessible

Users with hearing impairments need captions for audio material on the Web.

Blind users need words, not images. Words can be voiced by a screen reader or translated into Braille text. To make your Web page accessible for people with vision impairments,

- Put a link to a text-only version of the site in the upper-left-hand corner.
- Put navigation links, a site map, and search box at the top of the screen, preferably in the upper-left-hand corner.
- Arrange navigation links alphabetically so that blind users can use a screen reader to jump to the links they want.
- Provide alternative text (an "Alt tag") for all images, applets, and submit buttons.
- Provide a static alternative to flash or animation.
- In hypertext links, use text that makes sense when read alone. A person listening to the audio will not understand "Click here." "Click to order a copy" or "Click for details" offers a better clue.

The Web Accessibility Initiative (www.w3.org) points out that accessible Web sites are easier for a variety of people to use—not just those with obvious impairments.

Designing Web Pages

Good Web pages have both good content and an interesting design.

Your opening screen is crucial. Not only must it open quickly, but visitors must be able to find what they want quickly. Studies show that users grow impatient after waiting 15 seconds for a page to load, and Jakob Nielsen says users spend less than two minutes figuring out a site before deciding to leave. In addition, users tend not to scroll down beyond the first screen of text.[29] To keep visitors around long enough to find (and buy) what they want, make using the first screen extremely easy.

- Provide an introductory statement or graphic orienting the surfing reader to the organization sponsoring the page.
- Offer an overview of the content of your page, with links to take readers to the parts that interest them. Provide navigation bars vertically on the left of the screen or horizontally on the top and bottom. A site index and an internal search engine are valuable tools.
- Put information that will be most interesting and useful to most readers near the top of the first screen.
- Make it clear what readers will get if they click on a link.

Ineffective phrasing:	Employment. Openings and skill levels are determined by each office.
Better phrasing:	Employment. Openings listed by skill level and by location.

As you design pages,

- Use a white or light background for easy scanning.[30]
- Keep graphics small. Specify the width and height so that the text can load while the graphics are still coming in.
- Provide visual variety. Use indentations, bulleted or numbered lists, and headings.
- Unify multiple pages with a small banner, graphic, or label so surfers know who sponsors each page.
- On each page, provide a link to the home page, the name and e-mail address of the person who maintains the page, and the date when the page was last revised.
- Keep animation to a minimum, and allow viewers to control its use. If you have an animated site introduction page, include an easy-to-spot Skip Intro button.
- If your Web pages include music or sound effects, put an Off button where the user can see it immediately. Computer users may be at work, in a library or at another location where your brand's theme song would be disruptive—or embarrassing.

In Jakob Nielsen's Alertbox 2005 survey for the worst Web design mistakes, bad fonts won "by a landslide." Voters also panned small font sizes and low contrast between text and background. Nielsen urges his readers to get back to design basics. He reminds designers that users want quality basics; in his words, those basics are[31]

- Text they can read.
- Content that answers their questions.
- Navigation and search tools that help them find what they want.

- Short and simple forms.
- No bugs, typos, or corrupted data; no linkrot; no outdated content.

Appropriately enough, the Web has many Web pages on Web page design, as well as technical pages on HTML and Java.

Testing the Design for Usability

A design that looks pretty may or may not work for the audience. To know whether your design is functional, test it with your audience.

According to Jakob Nielsen, testing a draft with five users will reveal 85% of the problems with the document.[32] If time and money permit additional testing, revise the document and test the new version with another five users. Test the document with the people who are most likely to have trouble with it: very old or young readers, people with little education, people who read English as a second language.

Three kinds of tests yield particularly useful information:

- Watch someone as he or she uses the document to do a task. Where does the user pause, re-read, or seem confused? How long does it take? Does the document enable the user to complete the task accurately?
- Ask the user to "think aloud" while completing the task, interrupt the user at key points to ask what he or she is thinking, or ask the user to describe the thought process after completing the document and the task. Learning the user's thought processes is important, since a user may get the right answer for the wrong reasons. In such a case, the design still needs work.
- Ask users to put a plus sign (+) in the margins by any part of the document they like or agree with, and a minus sign (−) by any part of the document that seems confusing or wrong. Then use interviews or focus groups to find out the reasons for the plus and minus judgments.

Summary of Key Points

- An attractive document looks inviting, friendly, and easy to read. The visual grouping of ideas also makes the structure of the document more obvious so it is easier to read.
- Good document design can save time and money, and can prevent legal problems.
- The best documents are created when you think about design at each stage of the writing process.
  - As you plan, think about the needs of your audience.
  - As you write, incorporate lists, headings, and visuals.
  - Get feedback from people who will be using your document.
  - As you revise, check your draft against the guidelines in this chapter.
- Effective design relies heavily on conventions, which vary by audience.
- The four levels of design help you organize and analyze design choices:
  - Intra—letters and words.
  - Inter—blocks of text.
  - Extra—visuals.
  - Supra—features that serve the entire document.

Well-Designed Web Sites Keep Customers

Imagine going to a supermarket where three-fourths of the customers abandon their carts half full in the aisles because they are so frustrated they decide to shop somewhere else. It would be a lot like shopping online. In a recent poll, almost half the online retailers said they don't know what percentage of their customers abandon shopping carts. Among the rest, 87 percent reported abandonment rates above 20 percent. Because the Internet makes it easy for shoppers to go to other sites, Jakob Nielsen says, "People don't have to use bad sites."

What keeps online shoppers happy? Other polls ask customers what they look for when they shop on the Internet. Recent answers indicate they want pages that load quickly and make it easy to find what they want. They like basics such as search tools and clear labels. Few online shoppers care about bells and whistles like personalized recommendations.

These features are just what Change Sciences Group looks for when it tests Web sites. For example, to test credit card sites, it tries filling out applications. Some of these sites distract users with free offers, something they find more annoying than rewarding.[33]

- These guidelines help writers create visually attractive documents:
    1. Use white space.
    2. Use headings.
    3. Limit the use of words set in all capital letters.
    4. Use no more than two fonts in a single document.
    5. Decide whether to justify margins.
    6. Put important elements in the top left and lower right quadrants.
    7. Use a grid to unify visuals and other graphic elements.
    8. Use highlighting, decorative devices, and color in moderation.
- Visuals help make data meaningful for your audience.
- In the rough draft, use visuals to see that ideas are presented completely and to see what relationships exist. In the final report, use visuals to make points vivid, to emphasize material that the reader might skip, and to present material more compactly and with less repetition than words alone would require.
- You'll use more visuals when you want to show relationships and to persuade, when the information is complex or contains extensive numerical data, and when the audience values visuals.
- Always check the quality of your data.
- Pick data to tell a story, to make a point.
- To find stories,
    1. Focus on a topic.
    2. Simplify the data.
    3. Look for relationships and changes.
- Choose the right visual for the story.
- Visuals are not interchangeable. The best visual depends on the kind of data and the point you want to make with the data.
- Tables are numbers or words arrayed in rows and columns; figures are everything else. Formal visuals have both numbers and titles that indicate what to look for in the visual or why the visual is included and is worth examining.
- Visuals must present data accurately and ethically. **Chartjunk** denotes decorations that at best are irrelevant to the visual and at worst mislead the reader. **Truncated graphs** omit part of the scale and visually mislead readers. Graphs and charts with 3D mislead readers.
- Summarize the main point of a visual before it appears in the text.
- To design brochures, first think about audience and purpose. Use a consistent design for a series of brochures or for issues of a newsletter.
- Good Web pages have both good content and interesting design.
    - Orient the surfing reader to the organization sponsoring the page.
    - Offer an overview of the content of your page, with links to take readers to the parts that interest them.
    - Make it clear what readers will get if they click on a link.
    - Keep graphics small.
    - Provide visual variety.
- To test a document, observe people reading the document or using it to complete a task.

CHAPTER 6   Exercises and Problems

6.1   Reviewing the Chapter

1. Why is document design important in business communication? (LO 1)
2. What are the four levels of document design? (LO 2)
3. What are some guidelines for document design? (LO 3)
4. When should you use visuals? (LO 4)
5. What are some specific ways to create effective visuals? (LO 5)
6. What are some concerns that must be addressed to keep your visuals accurate and ethical? (LO 5)
7. What are some basic guidelines for designing brochures? Web pages? (LO 6)
8. How can you perform basic usability testing on your documents? (LO 7)

6.2   Evaluating Page Designs

Use the guidelines in Chapter 6 to evaluate each of the following page designs. What are their strong points? What could be improved?

As your instructor directs,

a. Discuss the design elements you see on these sample pages with a small group of classmates.

b. Write a memo to your instructor evaluating the design elements on each of the sample pages. Be sure to address the four levels of design, as well as the guidelines for page and visual design, discussed in this chapter.

c. In an oral presentation to the class, explain the process you'd use to redesign one of the sample pages. What design elements would make the page stronger or weaker? What design elements would you change, and how? Given the title of the document, what audience characteristics might your design take into account?

6.3   Recognizing Typefaces

Some companies commission a unique typeface, or wordmark, for their logos. Other companies use a standard font. When a logo is used consistently and frequently, it becomes associated with the organization. Can you name the brands that go with each letter of the alphabet below?

As your instructor directs,

a. Discuss the visual design of these brand visuals with a small group of classmates. What features distinguish them from other, similar brands? What makes them so recognizable?

b. Select one of the brand visuals represented and research it to determine its history. How has the visual changed over time? Write a memo to your instructor evaluating those changes, and identifying some of the design strategies (and business strategies) involved in each change.

Source: "Alphabet Soup," © *Issue: The Journal of Business and Design* 3, no. 2 (Fall 1997): 24–25.

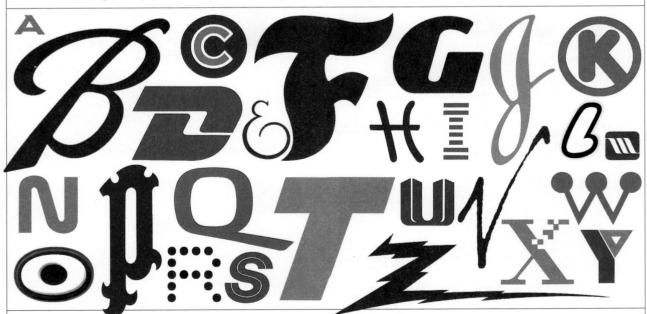

@ISSUE!

Alphabet Soup You don't always need to see the whole word to recognize the name of the brand. One letter will do. Used effectively, a distinctive logotype becomes the corporate signature. That is why many companies commission the design of a unique typeface, or wordmark, that incorporates clues to their line of business or operating philosophy. Other companies have adopted an off-the-shelf typeface that they have made their own through the use of designated corporate colors, upper or lower case styling, condensed or expanded leading and other techniques. As with any branding tool, a logotype must be used consistently and frequently to work. Test your familiarity with some of the best-known logotypes by naming the brand that goes with each letter in this alphabet.

Source: "Alphabet Soup." Reprinted with permission from © *Issue: The Journal of Business & Design*, Vol. 3, No. 2 (Fall 1997) 24–25. Published by Corporate Design Foundation and sponsored by Potlatch Corporation.

6.4   Evaluating the Ethics of Design Choices

Indicate whether you consider each of the following actions ethical, unethical, or a gray area. Which of the actions would you do? Which would you feel uncomfortable doing? Which would you refuse to do?

1. Putting the advantages of a proposal in a bulleted list, while discussing the disadvantages in a paragraph.
2. Using a bigger type size so that a résumé visually fills a whole page.
3. Using tiny print and very little white space on a credit card contract to make it less likely that people will read it.
4. Putting important information on the back of what looks like a one-page document.
5. Putting the services that are not covered by your health plan in full caps to make it less likely that people will read the page.
6. Using photos of Hawaiian beaches in advertising for Bermuda tourism, without indicating the location of the beaches.
7. Editing a photo by inserting an image of a young black person into a picture of an all-white group, and using that photo in a recruiting brochure designed to attract minority applicants to a university.
8. Altering people in your photographs so that they look skinnier and younger. (Watch the short video mentioned in the ethics discussion of this chapter.)
9. Modifying real estate photos by changing the physical appearance of houses or stores.
10. Including pictures in restaurant menus that are exaggerated in presentation quality, color appearance, and portion size.

6.5   Using Headings

Reorganize the items in each of the following lists, using appropriate headings. Use bulleted or numbered lists as appropriate.

a. Rules and Procedures for a Tuition Reimbursement Plan
1. You are eligible to be reimbursed if you have been a full-time employee for at least three months.
2. You must apply before the first class meeting.
3. You must earn a "C" or better in the course.
4. You must submit a copy of the approved application, an official grade report, and a receipt for tuition paid to be reimbursed.
5. You can be reimbursed for courses related to your current position or another position in the company, or for courses which are part of a degree related to a current or possible job.
6. Your supervisor must sign the application form.
7. Courses may be at any appropriate level (high school, college, or graduate school).

b. Activities in Starting a New Business
- Getting a loan or venture capital.
- Getting any necessary city or state licenses.
- Determining what you will make, do, or sell.
- Identifying the market for your products or services.
- Pricing your products or services.
- Choosing a location.
- Checking zoning laws that may affect the location.
- Identifying government and university programs for small business development.
- Figuring cash flow.
- Ordering equipment and supplies.
- Selling.
- Advertising and marketing.

6.6   Evaluating Visuals

Evaluate each of the following visuals.

- Is visual's message clear?
- Is it the right visual for the story?
- Is the visual designed appropriately? Is color, if any, used appropriately?
- Is the visual free from chartjunk?
- Does the visual distort data or mislead the reader in any way?

In problem 6.6, visuals 1 and 2 are the former and current food pyramids. Which pyramid is clearer? More informative? Which pyramid do you prefer? Why?

1.

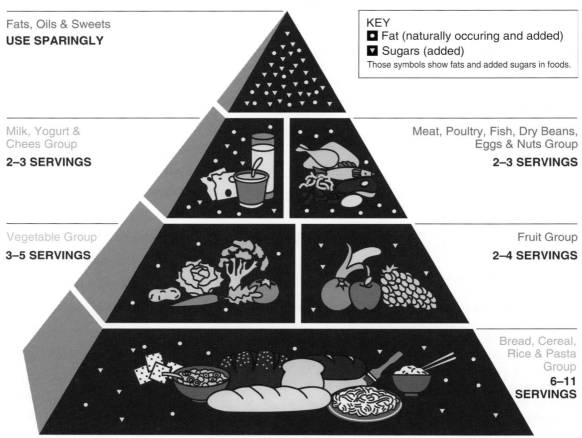

Former food pyramid

Fats, Oils & Sweets
USE SPARINGLY

KEY
◨ Fat (naturally occuring and added)
▼ Sugars (added)
Those symbols show fats and added sugars in foods.

Milk, Yogurt &
Chees Group
2–3 SERVINGS

Meat, Poultry, Fish, Dry Beans,
Eggs & Nuts Group
2–3 SERVINGS

Vegetable Group
3–5 SERVINGS

Fruit Group
2–4 SERVINGS

Bread, Cereal,
Rice & Pasta
Group
**6–11
SERVINGS**

Source: http://www.nal.usda.gov/fnic/Fpyr/pmap.htm (accessed April 18, 2007).

2.

Anatomy of MyPyramid

One size doesn't fit all

USDA's new MyPyramid symbolizes a personalized approach to healthy eating and physical activity.The symbol has been designed to be simple. It has been developed to remind consumers to makehealthy food choices and to be active every day. The different parts of the symbol are described below.

Current Food Pyramid

MyPyramid.gov
STEPS TO A HEALTHIER YOU

Activity
Activity is represented by the steps and the person climbing them, as a reminder of the importance of daily physical activity.

Moderation
Moderation is represented by the narrowing of each food group from bottom to top. The wider base stands for foods with little or no solid fats or added sugars. These should be selected more often. The narrower top area stands for foods containing more added sugars and solid fats. The more active you are, the more of these foods can fit into your diet.

Personalization
Personalization is shown by the person on the steps, the slogan and the URL. Find the kinds and amounts of food to eat each day at Mypyramid.gov.

Proportionality
Proportionality is shown by the different widths of the food group bands. The widths suggest how much food a person should choose from each group. The width are just a general guide, not exact proportions. Check the Web site for how much is right for you.

Variety
Variety is symbolized by the 6 color bands representing the 5 food groups of the Pyramid and oils. This illustrates that foods from all groups are needed each day for good health.

Gradual Improvement
Gradual improvement is encouraged by the slogan. It suggests that individuals can benefit from taking small steps to improve their diet and lifestyle each day.

USDA U.S. Department of Agriculture
Center for Nutrition Policy
and Promotion
April 2005 CNPP-16
USDA is an equal opportunity provider and employer

GRAINS   VEGETABLES   FRUITS   OILS   MILK   MEAT& BEANS

Source: United States Department of Agriculture, "Steps to a Healthier You," in MyPyramid.gov, http://www.mypyramid.gov (accessed April 16, 2007).

3.

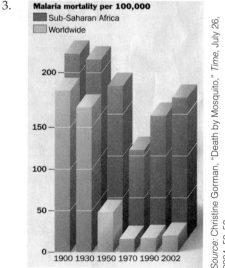

Malaria mortality per 100,000
- Sub-Saharan Africa
- Worldwide

200 —
150 —
100 —
50 —
0 —
1900 1930 1950 1970 1990 2002

Source: Christine Gorman, "Death by Mosquito," *Time*, July 26, 2004, 50–52.

4.

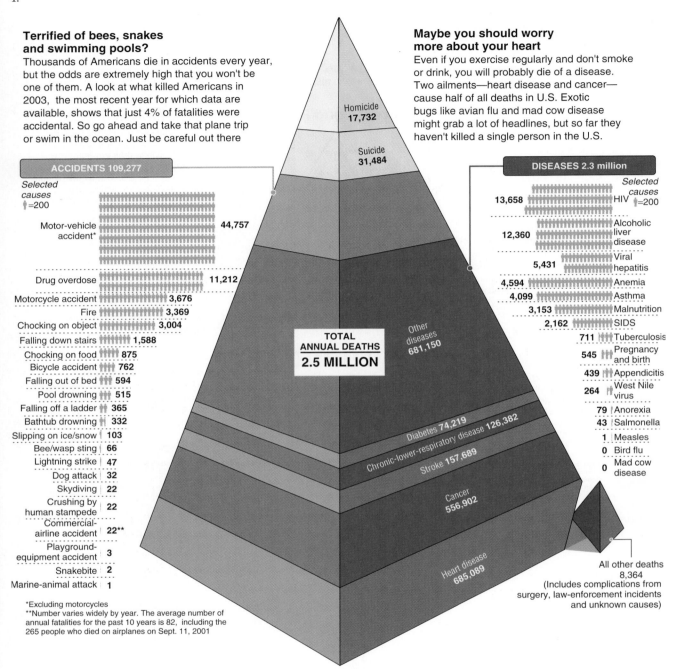

Terrified of bees, snakes and swimming pools?

Thousands of Americans die in accidents every year, but the odds are extremely high that you won't be one of them. A look at what killed Americans in 2003, the most recent year for which data are available, shows that just 4% of fatalities were accidental. So go ahead and take that plane trip or swim in the ocean. Just be careful out there

Maybe you should worry more about your heart

Even if you exercise regularly and don't smoke or drink, you will probably die of a disease. Two ailments—heart disease and cancer— cause half of all deaths in U.S. Exotic bugs like avian flu and mad cow disease might grab a lot of headlines, but so far they haven't killed a single person in the U.S.

Homicide 17,732

Suicide 31,484

ACCIDENTS 109,277

Selected causes 👤=200

Motor-vehicle accident*	44,757
Drug overdose	11,212
Motorcycle accident	3,676
Fire	3,369
Choking on object	3,004
Falling down stairs	1,588
Choking on food	875
Bicycle accident	762
Falling out of bed	594
Pool drowning	515
Falling off a ladder	365
Bathtub drowning	332
Slipping on ice/snow	103
Bee/wasp sting	66
Lightning strike	47
Dog attack	32
Skydiving	22
Crushing by human stampede	22
Commercial-airline accident	22**
Playground-equipment accident	3
Snakebite	2
Marine-animal attack	1

*Excluding motorcycles
**Number varies widely by year. The average number of annual fatalities for the past 10 years is 82, including the 265 people who died on airplanes on Sept. 11, 2001

DISEASES 2.3 million

Selected causes 👤=200

Deaths	Cause
13,658	HIV
12,360	Alcoholic liver disease
5,431	Viral hepatitis
4,594	Anemia
4,099	Asthma
3,153	Malnutrition
2,162	SIDS
711	Tuberculosis
545	Pregnancy and birth
439	Appendicitis
264	West Nile virus
79	Anorexia
43	Salmonella
1	Measles
0	Bird flu
0	Mad cow disease

TOTAL ANNUAL DEATHS 2.5 MILLION

Other diseases 681,150

Diabetes 74,219
Chronic-lower-respiratory disease 126,382
Stroke 157,689
Cancer 556,902
Heart disease 685,089

All other deaths 8,364 (Includes complications from surgery, law-enforcement incidents and unknown causes)

Sources: Jeffrey Kluger, "Why We Worry about the Things We Shouldn't . . . and Ignore the Things We Should," *Time*, December 4, 2006, 68. Copyright 2006 Time Inc. Reprinted by permission. Centers for Disease Control and Prevention; National Transportaion Safety Board.

5.

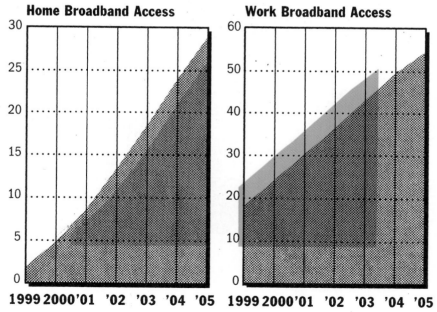

THROUGH GOOD AND BAD ECONOMIES, MINORITIES HAVE HAD HIGHER RATES OF UNEMPLOYMENT

Percent employed, by race and ethnic origin, 1975-1999.

□ Black
■ Hispanic
■ White

Source: U.S. Bureau of Labor Statistics

Source: Reprinted with permission from the June 2000 issue of *American Demographics.*
Copyright © 2000 Crain Communications Inc.

6. # Half Full...

Both at home and at work, more and more consumers enjoy broad-band access to the Web, which makes online entertainment a better experience (projections, in millions)

Home Broadband Access

1999 2000 '01 '02 '03 '04 '05

Work Broadband Access

1999 2000 '01 '02 '03 '04 '05

Source: Media Metrix

Source: The Wall Street Journal, March 26, 2001, R6. Media Metrix. Reprinted with permission.

7.

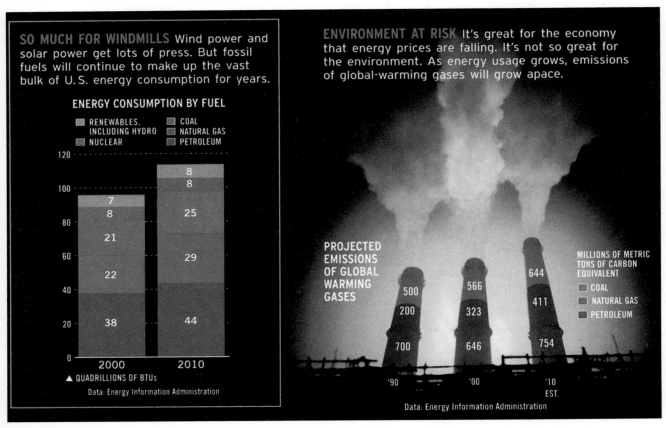

Source: BusinessWeek, August 27, 2001, 97.

8.

Worldwide alcohol causes 1.8 million deaths (3.2% of total) and 58.3 million (4% of total) of Disability
-Adjusted Life Years (DALYs). Unintentional injuries alone account for about one third of the 1.8 million
deaths, while neuro-psychiatric conditions account for close to 40% of the 58.3 million DALYs.
The burden is not equally distributed among the countries, as is shown on the map.

Source: World Health Organization, "Alcohol," in *Management of Substance Abuse,* http://www.who.int/substance_abuse/facts/alcohol/en/index.html
(accessed April 16, 2007).

6.7   Creating a Web Guide to Graphs

Create a Web page explaining how to create good visuals. Offer general principles and at least seven links to examples of good and poor visuals. (More is better.) At the top of the page, offer an overview of what the page covers. At the bottom of the page, put the creation/update date and your name and e-mail address.

As your instructor directs,

a. Turn in one copy of your page(s). On another page, give the URLs for each link.

b. Electronically submit your Web page files or submit them on a CD.

c. Write a memo to your instructor (1) identifying the audience for which the page is designed and explaining (2) the search strategies you used to find material on this topic, (3) why you chose the pages and information you've included, and (4) why you chose the layout and graphics you've used.

d. Present your page orally to the class.

Hints:

• Searching for words (*graphs, maps, Gantt charts, data*) will turn up only pages with those words. Also check pages on topics that may use graphs to explain their data: finance, companies' performance, sports, cost of living, exports, and so forth.

• In addition to finding good and bad visuals on the Web, you can also scan in examples you find in newspapers, magazines, and textbooks.

• If you have more than nine links, chunk them in small groups under headings.

6.8   Creating Visuals

As your instructor directs,

a. Identify visuals that you might use to help analyze each of the following data sets.

b. Identify and create a visual for one or more of the stories in each set.

c. Identify additional information that would be needed for other stories related to these data sets.

1. Active Internet home users.

Worldwide Active Internet Home Users, April 2007				
Country	**March 2007**	**April 2007**	**Growth (%)**	**Difference**
Australia	10,840,450	10,981,529	1.30	141,079
Brazil	16,257,348	15,867,826	−2.40	−389,522
France	21,528,789	21,390,880	−0.64	−137,909
Germany	32,757,877	32,566,632	−0.58	−191,245
Italy	18,220,139	16,830,493	−7.63	−1,389,646
Japan	45,774,229	44,714,273	−2.32	−1,059,956
Spain	13,196,513	13,730,296	4.04	533,783
Switzerland	3,765,304	3,681,476	−2.23	−83,828
U.K.	24,683,762	24,832,552	0.60	148,790
U.S.	146,817,112	146,343,718	−0.32	−473,394
Totals	333,841,523	330,939,675	−0.87	−2,901,848

Source: Enid Burns, "Active Home Internet Users by Country, April 2007," in *Trends & Statistics: The Web's Richest Source,* ClickZ.com, http://www.clickz.com/showPage.html?page=3626136 (accessed July 11, 2007). Reprinted with permission.

2.   Daily Change in Traffic to NCAA-Related Sports Web Sites, during "March Madness" (U.S., Home and Work).

Site	Wed: 3/15 UA (000)	Thurs: 3/16 UA (000)	Fri: 3/17 UA (000)	Wed-Fri Growth
CBS Sportsline.com Network	1,958	3,603	3,135	84%
AOL Sports (Web-only)	761	999	1,006	31%
FOX Sports on MSN	1,510	1,953	2,237	29%
Yahoo! Sports	2,121	2,601	2,377	23%
SI.com	724*	819*	773*	13%*
ESPN	3,074	3,312	2,941	8%
Total Unduplicated UA (Unique Audience)	**8,005**	**9,659**	**9,573**	**21%**

*These estimates are calculated on smaller sample sizes and are subject to increased statistical variability as a result.
http://www.nielsen-netratings.com/pr/pr_060321.pdf accessed July 1, 2007. From Enid Burns, "March Madness Invades Office Life," *Trends & Statistics: The Web's Richest Source,* Clickz.com. Reprinted with permission.

3.   Customer satisfaction with airlines.

	Baseline	Q1 1997	Q1 1998	Q1 1999	Q1 2000	Q1 2001	Q1 2002	Q1 2003	Q1 2004	Q1 2005	Q1 2006	Previous Year % Change	First Year % Change
Airlines	72	67	65	63	63	61	66	67	66	66	65	−1.5	−9.7
All Others	NM	70	62	67	63	64	72	74	73	74	74	0.0	5.7
Southwest Airlines Co.	78	76	74	72	70	70	74	75	73	74	74	0.0	−5.1
Continental Airlines, Inc.	67	64	66	64	62	67	68	68	67	70	67	−4.3	0.0
Delta Air Lines, Inc.	77	69	65	68	66	61	66	67	67	65	64	−1.5	−16.9
United Airlines (UAL Corporation)	71	68	65	62	62	59	64	63	64	61	63	3.3	−11.3
US Airways Group, Inc.	72	68	65	61	62	60	63	64	62	57	62	8.8	−13.9
American Airlines (AMR Corporation)	70	62	67	64	63	62	63	67	66	64	62	−3.1	−11.4
Northwest Airlines Corporation	69	64	63	53	62	56	65	64	64	64	61	−4.7	−11.6

Source: "First Quarter Scores," in *American Customer Satisfaction Index, May 16, 2006,* http://www.theacsi.org/ (accessed April 16, 2007).

6.9   Interpreting Data

As your instructor directs,

a. Identify at least five stories in one or more of the following data sets.

b. Create visuals for three of the stories.

c. Write a memo to your instructor explaining why you chose these stories and why you chose these visuals to display them.

d. Write a memo to some group that might be interested in your findings, presenting your visuals as part of a short report. Possible groups include career counselors, radio stations, advertising agencies, and Mothers Against Drunk Driving.

e. Brainstorm additional stories you could tell with additional data. Specify the kind of data you would need.

1. Data on tipping.

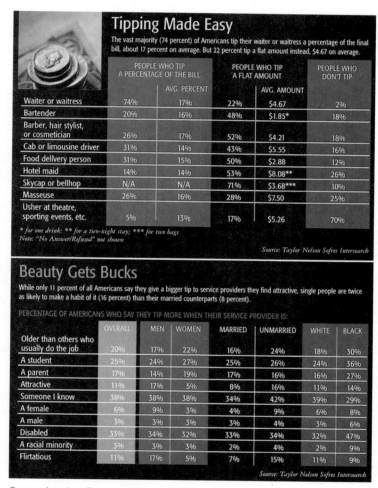

Tipping Made Easy

The vast majority (74 percent) of Americans tip their waiter or waitress a percentage of the final bill, about 17 percent on average. But 22 percent tip a flat amount instead, $4.67 on average.

	PEOPLE WHO TIP A PERCENTAGE OF THE BILL	AVG. PERCENT	PEOPLE WHO TIP A FLAT AMOUNT	AVG. AMOUNT	PEOPLE WHO DON'T TIP
Waiter or waitress	74%	17%	22%	$4.67	2%
Bartender	20%	16%	48%	$1.85*	18%
Barber, hair stylist, or cosmetician	26%	17%	52%	$4.21	18%
Cab or limousine driver	31%	14%	43%	$5.55	16%
Food delivery person	31%	15%	50%	$2.88	12%
Hotel maid	14%	14%	53%	$8.08**	26%
Skycap or bellhop	N/A	N/A	71%	$3.68***	10%
Masseuse	26%	16%	28%	$7.50	25%
Usher at theatre, sporting events, etc.	5%	13%	17%	$5.26	70%

* for one drink; ** for a two-night stay; *** for two bags
Note: "No Answer/Refused" not shown

Source: Taylor Nelson Sofres Intersearch

Beauty Gets Bucks

While only 11 percent of all Americans say they give a bigger tip to service providers they find attractive, single people are twice as likely to make a habit of it (16 percent) than their married counterparts (8 percent).

PERCENTAGE OF AMERICANS WHO SAY THEY TIP MORE WHEN THEIR SERVICE PROVIDER IS:

	OVERALL	MEN	WOMEN	MARRIED	UNMARRIED	WHITE	BLACK
Older than others who usually do the job	20%	17%	22%	16%	24%	18%	30%
A student	25%	24%	27%	25%	26%	24%	36%
A parent	17%	14%	19%	17%	16%	16%	27%
Attractive	11%	17%	5%	8%	16%	11%	14%
Someone I know	38%	38%	38%	34%	42%	39%	29%
A female	6%	9%	3%	4%	9%	6%	8%
A male	3%	3%	3%	3%	4%	3%	6%
Disabled	33%	34%	32%	33%	34%	32%	47%
A racial minority	3%	3%	3%	2%	4%	2%	9%
Flirtatious	11%	17%	5%	7%	15%	11%	9%

Source: Taylor Nelson Sofres Intersearch

Source: American Demographics, May 2001, 11. Copyright © 2001 Crain Communication Inc. Reprinted with permission.

2.   Alcohol consumption, 1997–2004.

Characteristic	Both sexes			Male			Female		
	1997	**2003**	**2004**	**1997**	**2003**	**2004**	**1997**	**2003**	**2004**
Age			Percent current drinkers among all adults						
All persons:									
18–44 years	68.5	66.4	65.7	73.8	72.3	72.4	63.3	60.7	59.2
18–24 years	61.3	59.5	58.0	65.5	64.6	63.6	57.0	54.5	52.5
25–44 years	70.6	68.7	68.3	76.3	74.9	75.4	65.2	62.8	61.5
45–64 years	62.7	60.4	61.7	69.8	65.7	66.4	55.9	55.4	57.4
45–54 years	66.5	63.8	64.4	73.0	68.0	69.1	60.3	59.9	59.9
55–64 years	56.7	55.5	57.9	64.8	62.4	62.4	49.2	49.0	53.9
65 years and over	42.8	42.4	43.6	52.0	51.1	52.8	36.0	36.0	36.9
65–74 years	47.9	46.5	49.5	56.1	53.7	58.1	41.4	40.6	42.4
75 years and over	36.0	37.8	37.0	45.9	47.6	45.8	29.7	31.4	31.4
Race									
White only	65.3	63.3	63.6	71.0	69.1	69.4	60.1	58.0	58.2
Black or African American only	46.7	47.4	46.6	55.5	54.7	55.7	40.0	41.8	39.7
American Indian or Alaska Native only	52.2	46.5	48.8	64.6	47.8	50.2	43.4	45.2	46.7
Asian only	45.7	39.1	43.8	59.8	49.4	56.9	31.6	30.3	30.8
Native Hawaiian or Other Pacific Islander only	—	—	—	—	—	—	—	—	—
2 or more races	—	54.5	62.0	—	62.4	68.2	—	48.4	57.3
Hispanic origin and race									
Hispanic or Latino	52.9	49.5	49.6	63.9	61.7	63.7	41.9	37.3	35.7
Mexican	52.7	47.5	47.8	66.3	60.9	62.4	38.7	33.4	32.8
Not Hispanic or Latino	63.3	62.1	62.4	69.3	67.4	67.9	58.0	57.4	57.6
White only	66.7	65.7	66.0	71.7	70.3	70.4	62.2	61.6	62.0
Black or African American only	46.7	47.2	46.3	55.7	54.3	55.4	39.8	41.8	39.3
Geographic region									
Northeast	67.9	67.8	67.7	73.4	73.7	73.8	63.3	62.9	62.2
Midwest	65.7	64.5	66.3	71.6	68.8	71.5	60.3	60.7	61.9
South	55.5	54.3	54.2	63.0	61.7	61.5	48.7	47.6	47.5
West	64.4	60.4	59.9	71.2	67.0	67.2	58.1	54.1	52.9

Source: "Alcohol Consumption by Adults 18 Years of Age and Over," in *National Center for Health Statistics*, http://www.cdc.gov/nchs/fastats/alcohol.htm (accessed March 4, 2007).

3. Top Celebrities, 2005.

Forbes magazine's Web site provides the full list of 100 top celebrities, explains the methodology, and re-ranks the list on any column. For example, you can click on "pay rank" and get a list ordered by earnings. You can also find lists for other years.

Power Rank	Name	Pay Rank	Web Rank	Press Rank	TV Rank
1	Oprah Winfrey	2	2	8	4
2	Tiger Woods	4	12	2	11
3	Mel Gibson	3	13	33	15
4	George Lucas	1	3	41	34
5	Shaquille O'Neal	26	26	5	12
6	Steven Spielberg	5	11	34	22
7	Johnny Depp	21	16	36	31
8	Madonna	11	5	30	19
9	Elton John	15	10	19	24
10	Tom Cruise	30	7	24	16
11	Brad Pitt	51	8	22	17
12	Dan Brown	6	27	39	61
13	Will Smith	24	15	27	20
14	David Letterman	16	61	26	7
15	Lance Armstrong	41	39	9	8
16	Michael Jordan	27	34	16	25
17	Michael Schumacher	8	37	29	81
18	Will Ferrell	16	71	55	36
19	Kobe Bryant	39	47	4	2
20	P Diddy	23	51	38	14
21	Jay Leno	34	33	28	5
22	J. K. Rowling	9	24	69	65
23	Metallica	20	9	50	69
24	Jennifer Lopez	63	6	25	18
25	Desperate Housewives	92	20	10	6

Source: "The Celebrity 100," in *Forbes*, http://www.forbes.com/lists/2005/53/Rank_1.html (accessed March 4, 2007). Reprinted by permission of *Forbes Magazine*, © 2007 Forbes Media LLC.

4. Statistics on high school graduates.

a. Curriculum levels completed, by gender

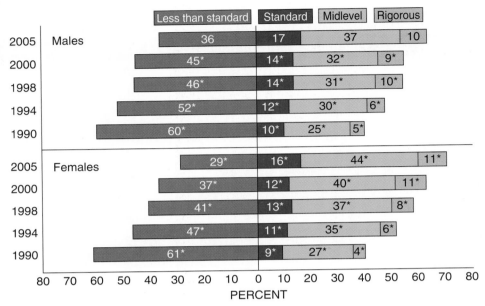

*Significantly different from 2005.
Source: "Curriculum Levels Completed, by Gender," in *U.S. Department of Education, Institute of Education Sciences, National Center for Education Statistics, High School Transcript Study (HSTS), various years, 1990–2005,* http://nationsreportcard.gov/hsts_2005/hs_stu_5b_2.asp (accessed April 13, 2007).

b. Trend in grade point average by gender

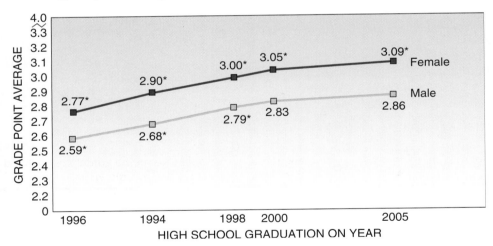

*Significantly different from 2005.
Source: "Trend in Grade Point Average, by Gender," in *U.S. Department of Education, Institute of Education Sciences, National Center for Education Statistics, High School Transcript Study (HSTS), various years, 1990–2005,* http://nationsreportcard.gov/hsts_2005/hs_stu_5b_3.asp (accessed April 13, 2007).

c. Trend in twelfth-grade average NAEP reading scores

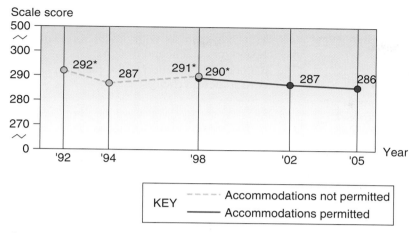

*Significantly different from 2005.

Source: "Trend in Twelfth-Grade Average NAEP Reading Scores," in *U.S. Department of Education, Institute of Education Sciences, National Center for Education Statistics, High School Transcript Study (HSTS), various years, 1990–2005,* http://nationsreportcard.gov/reading_math_grade12_2005/s0202.asp (accessed April 13, 2007).

6.10   Graphing Data from the Web

Find data on the Web about a topic that interests you. Sites with data include the following:

Catalyst
  http://www.catalyst.org/knowledge/research.shtml

ClickZ Internet Statistics and Demographics
  http://www.clickz.com/showPage.html?page=stats

FEDSTATS (links to 70 US government agencies)
  www.fedstats.gov

United Nations Environment Program
  http://grid2.cr.usgs.gov/

White House Briefing Room (economic issues)
  www.whitehouse.gov/fsbr/esbr.html

As your instructor directs,

a. Identify at least five stories in the data.

b. Create visuals for three of the stories.

c. Write a memo to your instructor explaining why you chose these stories and why you chose these visuals to display them.

d. Write a memo to some group which might be interested in your findings, presenting your visuals as part of a short report.

e. Print out the data and include it with a copy of your memo or report.

6.11   Creating a Visual Argument

With a partner, research one of the following topics:

• Having English-only laws in the workplace.

• Introducing new technology into the marketplace.

• Drinking at social functions for work.

• Requiring employers to offer insurance plans.

• Banning smoking in the workplace for insurance purposes.

• Hiring/recruiting and diversity in the workplace.

• Current hot business topic.

Then, prepare a four-minute slideshow presentation to share with your peers. The presentation should include only visual elements and contain no words. With the visuals, you should take a stand and present an argument about one of the topics. Recall the guidelines outlined in this chapter about effectively using visuals.

Remember that your presentation needs to be captivating to the audience and effectively convey your purpose. Finally, don't forget to cite all source material.

As your instructor directs,

a. Submit a copy of your slideshow presentation, including both hard and electronic versions.

b. Write a brief memo in which you explain in words the argument you were trying to make.

c. Submit a list of works cited for each of the visuals you used.

6.12   Gorilla Talk

Analyze the following newsletter:

1. Who is the audience? How does the newsletter appeal to that audience?
2. What is the purpose of the newsletter?
3. What story is the newsletter telling?
4. How does the newsletter use design elements to appeal to its audience and to achieve its purpose? Discuss for the four levels of design. In particular, how does the newsletter use color?

As your instructor directs,

a. Write a memo to your instructor explaining the choices for content and design.

b. In an oral presentation to the class, explain the content and design choices.

Gorilla Talk

THE GORILLA FOUNDATION NEWSLETTER / SUMMER 2006

APE ART

On June 20, 2005, at prestigious Bonhams auction house in London, paintings by Renoir, Warhol and Congo were offered to the public. Neither the Renoir nor the Warhol sold. The Congo, however, which had been expected to bring between $1000 and $1500, sold for a surprising $26,352 (including a buyer's premium).

Congo was a chimpanzee.

So is this all some sort of a joke?

At one time it was thought man was separated from the apes by his ability to make and use tools. This has been proven to be an incorrect assumption. Surely art must be that separation then. Art after all is the highest expression of the human psyche. Are the apes expressing themselves through the medium of paint or are they simply making a mess? There's no way to know.

No way unless, of course, you asked them.

And that brings us to the Gorilla Foundation, where the apes are more than happy to tell you what they are thinking.

We find that a great deal of the art Koko and Michael have produced is expressionism and reflects the emotions that they feel. The wild red and green strokes of *Anger* portray the essence of a gorilla's display. This contrasts dramatically with the large dark and light brown plays of paint depicting the *Earthquake*. Michael was asked to paint how the earthquake felt. In creating the painting Michael forcefully and repeatedly pounded dark brown paint onto the canvas with the brush. This

WORK IN PROGRESS

During the painting process Koko returned to study her subject matter: two banana slugs in her windowbox, eating a strawberry and a tomato that had been put out to attract them.

Note how large the delicious strawberry appears in the painting.

Koko indicated to Penny, her art assistant, that she would like to use some yellow acrylic paint next. She then proceeded to paint the bright yellow banana slug.

"Polite Lip (girl) Koko Love, Gorilla Love"

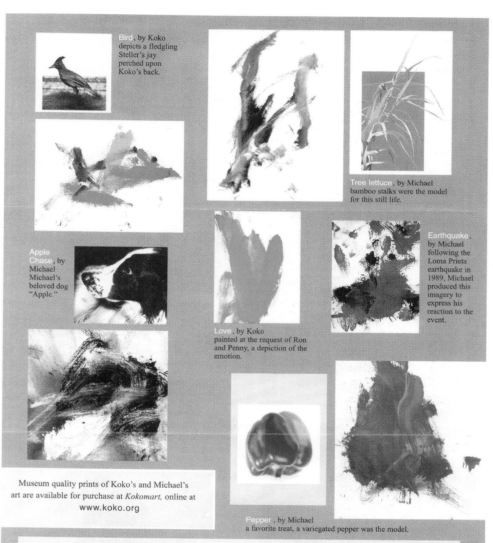

Bird, by Koko
depicts a fledgling
Steller's jay
perched upon
Koko's back.

Tree lettuce, by Michael
bamboo stalks were the model
for this still life.

Apple
Chase, by
Michael
Michael's
beloved dog
"Apple."

Earthquake,
by Michael
following the
Loma Prieta
earthquake in
1989, Michael
produced this
imagery to
express his
reaction to the
event.

Love, by Koko
painted at the request of Ron
and Penny, a depiction of the
emotion.

Museum quality prints of Koko's and Michael's
art are available for purchase at *Kokomart*, online at
www.koko.org

Pepper, by Michael
a favorite treat, a variegated pepper was the model.

seemed to represent the banging force of the quake. Then he took the light brown and gently painted over the dark, apparently representing the calm after the earthquake was over.

More remarkable, on many levels, are Koko and Michael's forays into impressionism. It is almost beyond comprehension that a nonhuman would possess the ability to depict the world they live in on canvas. Yet, there they are, titled by the gorillas themselves to leave no doubt as to what the subjects are.

Love, *by Koko, acrylic on canvas*. When a friend suggested that we ask the gorillas to paint emotions Koko selected bright pink and orange to paint her interpretation of the emotion love.

Bird, *by Koko, acrylic on canvas*. Koko seems to have painted her pet fledgling Steller's jay from memory. We rescued the bird from the nearby highway after a storm. Koko named the bird *Tongue* because of its protuberant tongue - the scrawny bird was always hungry and Koko enjoyed feeding it.

Tree lettuce, *by Michael, acrylic on canvas*. Outside the windows of the gorillas' apartments grow elegant stands of bamboo that rustle in the evening breezes. Called "tree lettuce" by Michael, young bamboo stalks are a tasty treat for gorillas.

Me, myself, good, *by Michael, acrylic on canvas*. Some people assumed that Michael was referring to his handprint when he named this piece. But when a 16-year-old autistic boy, who was associated with the Jane Goodall Institute in Israel, sketched the gorilla he could clearly see to the left of the handprint, it became obvious that this was a self-portrait. Michael liked to paint gorillas in rainbow colors.

Apple chase, *by Michael, acrylic on canvas*. Apple the dog (named by Koko) was a herding dog of a different ilk. Apple herded gorillas rather than sheep, and did so much to the gorillas' delight. Michael painted Apple in the midst of such an exuberant "chase" as they would run back and forth on either side of the gorilla enclosure. While painting Apple, Michael had available to him a full range of colors but intentionally limited his palette to accurately portray his dear friend.

Pepper, *by Michael, acrylic on canvas*. Although no one would ever call them "starving artists" food has always been a "consuming" topic of interest for gorillas both in conversation and in art.

Toy dinosaur, *by Michael, acrylic on canvas*. A favorite toy, a plastic T Rex, this painting is of special interest in terms of technique because to add texture (the spikes on this toy were fascinating to him) Michael placed his fresh painting face down on the floor and then carefully pulled it off again. Michael never repeated this action.

Stink gorilla more, *by Michael, acrylic on canvas*. Translated from gorilla speak to standard English the word "stink" means a flower and "more" is in reference to a large bouquet of wild flowers that Michael had been presented with.

Throughout the summer and into November of 2006 our friends at the Sternberg Museum of Natural History in Hays, Kansas will be hosting **Gorilla Art: Creative Works by Koko and Friends.** We hope to be able to share these beautiful works of art and interspecies communication with other natural history museums across the nation. We will keep you posted about up-coming shows at www.koko.org.

Sketch by 16-year-old

Me, myself, good a self-portrait by Michael with carefully placed handprint "signature."

6.13   Evaluating Page Designs

1. Collect several documents that you receive as a consumer, a student, or an employee: forms, letters, memos, newsletters, e-mail, announcements, ads, flyers, and reports. Use the guidelines in this chapter to evaluate each of them.
2. Compare these documents in a specific category to the documents produced by competing organizations. Which documents are more effective? Why?

As your instructor directs,

a. Discuss the documents with a small group of classmates.

b. Write a memo to your instructor evaluating three or more of the documents, and comparing them to similar documents produced by competitors. Include originals or photocopies of the documents you discuss in an appendix to your memo.

c. Write a letter to one of the originating organizations, recommending ways it can improve the design of the documents.

d. In an oral presentation to the class, explain what makes one document strong and another one weak. If possible, use transparencies so that classmates can see the documents as you evaluate them.

6.14   Evaluating Web Pages

Compare three Web pages in the same category (for example, helping the homeless, organizations, car companies, university departments, sports information). Which page(s) are most effective? Why? What weaknesses do the pages have?

As your instructor directs,

a. Discuss the pages with a small group of classmates.

b. Write a memo to your instructor evaluating the pages. Include URLs of the pages in your memo.

c. In an oral presentation to the class, explain what makes one page good and another one weak. If possible, put the pages on screen so that classmates can see the pages as you evaluate them.

d. Post your evaluation in an e-mail message to the class. Include the URLs so classmates can click to the pages you discuss.

6.15   Creating a Brochure

Create a brochure for a campus, nonprofit, government or business organization. As you work

- Analyze your intended audience. What are their needs? What factors are most likely to persuade them to read your brochure?
- Choose a story: What's the important information? What idea do you want your audience to take away?
- Make page design choices that create a usable document and generate a positive response from your audience.

- Make visual design choices that enhance and expand on your text without being simply decorative.

As your instructor directs,

a. Write a memo to your instructor explaining your choices for content and design.

b. In an oral presentation to the class, display your brochure and explain your content and design choices. If possible, display images of the brochure so that classmates can see the brochure as you describe it.

6.16   Creating a Web Page

Create a Web page for a campus, nonprofit, government or business organization that does not yet have one. As you work:

- Analyze your intended audience. What are their needs? What factors are most likely to persuade them to use this site?

- Choose a story: What's the important information? What action do you want them to take while they're browsing this site?
- Make page design choices that create a usable site and generate a positive response from your audience.

- Make visual design choices that enhance and expand on your text without being distracting.

As your instructor directs,

a. Write a memo to your instructor explaining your choices for content and design.

b. In an oral presentation to the class, display your site and explain your page and visual design choices. Provide the URL, or display images of the site as presentation visuals, so that classmates can evaluate your design as you present it.

6.17   Testing a Document

Ask someone to follow a set of instructions or to fill out a form. (Consider consumer instructions, forms for financial aid, and so forth.)

- Time the person. How long does it take? Is the person able to complete the task?
- Observe the person. Where does he or she pause, reread, seem confused?
- Interview the person. What parts of the document were confusing?

As your instructor directs,

a. Discuss the changes needed with a small group of classmates.

b. Write a memo to your instructor evaluating the document and explaining the changes that are needed. Include the document as an appendix to your memo.

c. Write to the organization that produced the document recommending necessary improvements.

d. In an oral presentation to the class, evaluate the document and explain what changes are needed. If possible, display the document so that classmates can see it.

6.18   Improving a Financial Aid Form

You've just joined the financial aid office at your school. The director gives you the following form and asks you to redesign it. The director says:

> We need this form to see whether parents have other students in college besides the one requesting aid. Parents are supposed to list all family members that the parents support—themselves, the person here, any other kids in college, and any younger dependent kids.
>
> Half of these forms are filled out incorrectly. Most people just list the student going here; they leave out everyone else.
>
> If something is missing, the computer sends out a letter and a second copy of this form. The whole process starts over. Sometimes we send this form back two or three times before it's right. In the meantime, students' financial aid is delayed—maybe for months. Sometimes things are so late that they can't register for classes, or they have to pay tuition themselves and get reimbursed later.
>
> If so many people are filling out the form wrong, the form itself must be the problem. See what you can do with it. But keep it to a page.

As your instructor directs,

a. Analyze the current form and identify its problems.

b. Revise the form. Add necessary information; re-order information; change the chart to make it easier to fill out.

c. Write a memo to the director of financial aid pointing out the changes you made and why you made them.

Hints:

- Where are people supposed to send the form? What is the phone number of the financial aid office? Should they need to call the office if the form is clear?
- Does the definition of *half-time* apply to all students or just those taking courses beyond high school?
- Should capital or lowercase letters be used?
- Are the lines big enough to write in?
- What headings or subdivisions within the form would remind people to list all family members whom they support?
- How can you encourage people to return the form promptly?

Please complete the chart below by listing all family members for whom you (the parents) will provide more than half support during the academic year (July 1 through June 30). Include yourselves (the parents), the student, and your dependent children, even if they are not attending college.

EDUCATIONAL INFORMATION, 200_ – 200_						
FULL NAME OF FAMILY MEMBER	AGE	RELATIONSHIP OF FAMILY MEMBER TO STUDENT	NAME OF SCHOOL OR COLLEGE THIS SCHOOL YEAR	FULL-TIME	HALF-TIME* OR MORE	LESS THAN HALF-TIME
STUDENT APPLICANT						

*Half-time is defined as 6 credit hours or 12 clock hours a term.

When the information requested is received by our office, processing of your financial aid application will resume. Please sign and mail this form to the above address as soon as possible. Your signature certifies that this information and the information on the FAF is true and complete to the best of your knowledge. If you have any questions, please contact a member of the need analysis staff.

_____   _____
Signature of Parent(s)   Date

6.19   Mosaic Case

Today, Yvonne received the following e-mail message from the Human Resource Department:

To: YvonneK@mosaic.com

From: SallyJ@mosaic.com

Subject: Policy Manual Help

Yvonne,

We outsourced the employee policy manual project this year instead of asking your department to do it. However, the final product is atrocious and extremely difficult to read.

As you know, on Monday, all employees of Mosaic received the employee policy manual. However, since then, our phone has been ringing non-stop with complaints and questions.

While I realize now how much of an asset your team is to Mosaic, it's probably too late to ask for your help. But if you have any team members that could use an extra project, could they redesign Mosaic's policy manual? All of the information is correct, but the layout is impossible for anyone to easily navigate and the font is horrible.

Please let me know.

Thanks,

Sally

At the weekly staff meeting, Yvonne asked for a volunteer to reformat the manual. "I know you're all really busy right now, but I also understand how important this policy manual is to our organization. The manual contains policies about sick leave, vacation time, smoking, health insurance, and discrimination among many others. Here are sample pages of the policy manual concerning discrimination and harassment," she said as she passed around copies to the group.

Non-Discrimination and Harassment Policy Overview: Mosaic's continual commitment to diversity provides an office environment that is free from all prohibited discrimination and bias activity, in particular when such actions are directed at a Mosaic employee or group of Mosaic's employees because of that individual's or group's age, color, faith, disability, ethnicity, gender, gender identity or expression, marital status, national origin, race, religion, sexual orientation, status as a veteran, or any combination of the above. Acts of prohibited discrimination and protected status (including sexual) harassment constitute violations of Title VII of the Civil Rights Act of 1964, amended in 1991. Any bias activity is prohibited by state and local law. Mosaic equally condemns bias activity and responds to such incidents appropriately.
Accordingly, this policy prohibits all Mosaic employees from engaging in prohibited discrimination and protected status harassment and expects all Mosaic employees to refrain from sexual harassment. What Is Sexual Harassment? Unwelcome sexual advances, requests for sexual favors, and other verbal or physical conduct of a sexual nature constitute sexual harassment when: 1) An employment decision affecting that individual is made because the individual submitted to or rejected the unwelcome conduct; or 2) The unwelcome conduct unreasonably interferes with an individual's work performance or creates an intimidating, hostile, or abusive work environment. Certain behaviors, such as conditioning promotions, awards, training or other job benefits upon acceptance of unwelcome actions of a sexual nature, are always wrong.
Unwelcome actions such as the following are inappropriate and, depending on the circumstances, may in and of themselves meet the definition of sexual harassment or contribute to a hostile work environment: Sexual pranks, or repeated sexual teasing, jokes, or innuendo, in person or via e-mail; Verbal abuse of a sexual nature; Touching or grabbing of a sexual nature; Repeatedly standing too close to or brushing up against a person; Repeatedly asking a person

to socialize during off-duty hours when the person has said no or has indicated he or she is not interested (supervisors in particular should be careful not to pressure their employees to socialize); Giving gifts or leaving objects that are sexually suggestive; Repeatedly making sexually suggestive gestures; Making or posting sexually demeaning or offensive pictures, cartoons or other materials in the workplace; Off-duty, unwelcome conduct of a sexual nature that affects the work environment.

A victim of sexual harassment can be a man or a woman. The victim can be of the same sex as the harasser. The harasser can be a supervisor, co-worker, other Mosaic employee, or a non-employee who has a business relationship with Mosaic.

Employees' Rights and Responsibilities under This Policy: Any employee who believes he or she has been the target of sexual harassment is encouraged to inform the offending person orally or in writing that such conduct is unwelcome and offensive and must stop. If the employee does not wish to communicate directly with the offending person, or if such communication has been ineffective, the employee has multiple avenues for reporting allegations of sexual harassment and/or pursuing resolution.

Employees are encouraged to report the unwelcome conduct as soon as possible to a responsible Mosaic human resource official. It is usually most effective—although it is not required—that the official be within the employee's supervisory chain.

"Good grief, that's absolutely awful!" replied Demetri when he was finished reading it.

"I can't figure out what information goes together or how to even read this," noted Sarah.

"Exactly! I would really like a volunteer," Yvonne said, while making her customary quote marks in the air when she said the word *volunteer*. "If no one volunteers, I'll be forced to assign one."

"I can do it," said Trey.

"Thanks!" said Sarah and Demetri simultaneously, who both knew how many other tasks they were responsible for right now.

"Great, Trey," said Yvonne. "Start with this Non-Discrimination and Harassment Policy. Reformat it, and we will use the new design to show Sally the kinds of changes we can make for her."

Take on Trey's communication task to revise the format of the policy manual. Use the above discrimination and harassment policy to showcase your knowledge about document design from reading Chapter 6. When you are finished with the revision, write a memo to Yvonne that explains how you changed the document design and why you made your changes.

NOTE: Parts of this harassment policy have been adapted from: "Sexual Harassment Policy," U.S. Department of State, http://www.state.gov/s/ocr/c14800.htm (accessed June 29, 2007).

Résumés

Learning Objectives

After studying this chapter, you will know how to:

1 Prepare a detailed time line for your job search.

2 Prepare a résumé that makes you look attractive to employers.

3 Deal with common difficulties that arise during job searches.

4 Handle the online portion of job searches.

5 Keep your résumé honest.

Voices of Experience—Finding the Right Career

Still don't know what you want to do when you graduate? Or, maybe you've discovered that your chosen career doesn't really suit you. Finding the right career isn't always a straightforward process, and not everyone makes the best choice of first job. The experience and advice of successful professionals who have found a rewarding career provide insight for the rest of us.

Oprah Winfrey, herself one of America's greatest success stories, devoted a show to individuals "who have found their true calling and have made millions doing what they love." Among Oprah's guests was Jeff Bezos, multibillionaire and founder of Amazon.com, who believes that failure *is* an option for a successful career. "Trying and failing is okay," says Mr. Bezos, who "pretends he is 80 years old and asks if he will regret not trying." Another guest, Lonnie Johnson, an engineer and inventor of the Super Soaker, advised "perseverance, don't take 'no' for an answer."

"Don't underestimate the importance of job satisfaction."

Of course, not everyone who finds a true calling makes millions. Anne Fisher, a senior writer for *Fortune,* invited readers to share their experiences in choosing careers and changes they would make if they could go back and make different decisions. Readers provided the following advice.

- *Choose your own career.* "Don't let anyone else choose your career for you," says an attorney-turned-teacher whose father and grandfather were lawyers. "My family assumed I would become a lawyer too, so I did. What a mistake."

- *Try out different jobs; take advantage of internships.* "I got into the retailing industry entirely by accident, thanks to a summer internship. . . . If anyone had told me I'd end up doing this, I'd have said they were nuts," says a senior buyer for a department store chain.

- *Be open to changes in your career plans.* "You can always change gears as you go," says a corporate trainer. "I started out as a graphic designer, moved into Web design, and now work with a corporate-training company. . . . I've found all my incarnations interesting. . . . "

- *Don't overestimate the importance of making money.* Fisher found that most readers "who now feel they made the wrong choice" say they made that choice for money. An attorney who made this mistake reports, "You will end up spending every penny you make just to try and console yourself for having a job you hate. . . . Life is too short to spend ten hours every day being miserable."

- *Don't underestimate the importance of job satisfaction.* Many people who changed careers also changed their definition of success. The attorney-turned-teacher notes that, "After 16 years in what I knew almost from Day One was not the right field for me, I finally got up the courage to do something about it. . . . The money isn't so great, but now I can't wait to get to work in the morning. Life is good."

Sources: Anne Fisher, "How to Choose the Right Career for You," in *CNNMoney.com: Fortune: Commentary: Ask Annie,* http://money.cnn.com/2005/10/10/news/economy/annie/fortune_annie101005/index.htm (accessed May 30, 2007); and "Finding Your Calling and Your Fortune," in *The Oprah Winfrey Show Archive,* http://www.oprah.com/tows/pastshows/tows_1999/tows_past_19991101.jhtml (accessed May 30, 2007).

Chapter Outline

A Time Line for Job Hunting

Evaluating Your Strengths and Interests

Using the Internet in Your Job Search

How Employers Use Résumés

Guidelines for Résumés

- Length
- Emphasis
- Details
- Writing Style
- Layout and Design

Kinds of Résumés

What to Include in a Résumé

- Name and Contact Information
- Career Objective
- Summary of Qualifications
- Education
- Honors and Awards
- Experience
- Other Skills
- Activities
- Portfolio

References

What Not to Include in a Résumé

Dealing with Difficulties

- "All My Experience Is in My Family's Business."
- "I've Been Out of the Job Market for a While."
- "I Want to Change Fields."
- "I Was Fired."
- "I Don't Have Any Experience."

Electronic Résumés

- Creating a Scannable Résumé
- Sending Your Résumé by E-mail
- Posting Your Résumé on the Web

A Caution about Blogs and Social Networking Sites

Honesty

Summary of Key Points

A **résumé** is a persuasive summary of your qualifications for employment. If you're on the job market, having a résumé is a basic step in the job hunt. When you're employed, having an up-to-date résumé makes it easier to take advantage of opportunities that may come up for an even better job. If you're several years away from job hunting, preparing a résumé now will help you become more conscious of what to do in the next two or three years to make yourself an attractive candidate. Writing a résumé may also be an ego-building experience: The person who looks so good on paper is **you**!

This chapter covers paper, Web, and scannable résumés. Job application letters (sometimes called cover letters) are discussed in Chapter 8. Chapter 9 discusses interviews and communications after the interview. All three chapters focus on job hunting in the United States. Conventions, expectations, and criteria differ from culture to culture: different norms apply in different countries.

All job communications should be tailored to your unique qualifications and the specifications of the job you want. Adopt the wording or layout of an example if it's relevant to your own situation, but don't be locked into the forms in this book. You've got different strengths; your résumé will be different, too.

A Time Line for Job Hunting

Many employers consider the way you do your job hunt to be evidence of the way you will work for them. Therefore, you should start preparing yourself several years ahead of your formal applications. Informal preparation for job hunting should start soon after you arrive on campus. Check out the services of your college placement and advising offices. Join extracurricular organizations on campus and in the community to increase your knowledge and provide a network for learning about jobs. Find a job that gives you experience. Note which courses you like—and why you like them. If you like thinking and learning about a subject, you're more likely to enjoy a job in that field. Select course projects and paper topics that will help you prepare for a job—and look good on your résumé.

Once you have selected a major, start reading job ads, particularly those posted on your professional organization's Web site. What kinds of jobs are available? Do you need to change your course selections to better fit them? What kinds of extras are employers seeking? Do they want communication skills? Spreadsheet familiarity? Extra statistics courses? International experience? Learn this information early while you still have time to add to the knowledge and skill sets you are acquiring. Attend job seminars and job fairs. Join your professional association and its listserv.

Formal preparation for job hunting should begin a full year *before you begin interviewing.* Enroll for the services of your campus placement office. Ask friends who are on the job market about their experiences in interviews; find out what kinds of job offers they get. Check into the possibility of getting an internship or a co-op job that will give you relevant experience before you interview.

The year you interview, register with your Placement Office early. An active job search takes significant chunks of time, so plan accordingly. If you plan to graduate in the spring, prepare your résumé and plan your interview strategy early in the fall. Initial campus interviews occur from October to February for May or June graduation. In January or February, write to any organization you'd like to work for that hasn't interviewed on campus. From February to April, you're likely to visit one or more offices for a second interview.

Try to have a job offer lined up *before* you get the degree. People who don't need jobs immediately are more confident in interviews and usually get better job offers. If you have to job-hunt after graduation, plan to spend at least 30 hours a week on your job search. The time will pay off in a better job that you find more quickly.

What Employers Want, I

You can increase your odds of getting an interview by understanding what hiring managers are thinking while they evaluate your résumé. The following are questions managers ask themselves:

Can this applicant fill the needs of the company? Your résumé should stress all of your most relevant skills and experience which match the position opening. Rather than submitting a generic résumé for every position you apply for, create a customized résumé based on your review of the job opening.

Will this applicant stay with the company long-term? Managers seek employees who are most likely to stay with a company long-term because the hiring process is long, difficult, and costly. The cost of replacing an employee averages $13,355 according to a study conducted by the Employment Policy Foundation. To avoid costly turnover, managers look at your résumé to see if you have a stable work history.

Will this applicant be professional? Your résumé represents your ability to communicate. Unfortunately, managers will eliminate résumés for the slightest problems since they may receive hundreds of résumés for one position. Make sure your résumé is easy to follow and does not contain typos or grammatical mistakes.

Employers are also looking for your dedication to your profession. To illustrate your professional interests, include related professional associations that you have joined, certificates you possess, or professional seminars you have taken.

Adapted from Robert Half International, "What Employers Think When They Read Your Résumé," in *Career builder.com: Career Advice: Job Search,* http://www.careerbuilder.com/ JobSeeker/careerbytes/CBArticle.aspx? articleID=427 (accessed May 30, 2007).

What Employers Want, II

Careerbuilder.com's 2006 hiring survey asked hiring managers what the top attribute is when they hire new graduates.

1. **Relevant experience** (23%): Managers look for a candidate's ability to make his/her job experience relevant to the company—and find this ability lacking. Most managers (63%) say they view volunteer activities as relevant experience.

2. **Fit with the company culture** (21%): This trait is frequently evaluated by the small talk at the interview, talk that many candidates mistakenly consider "unimportant."

3. **Educational background** (19%): Managers consider the school, degree earned, major, minor, GPA, and relevant courses.

4. **Enthusiasm** (19%): Managers want to see job applicants who are passionate about their company and jobs, because such employees tend to be more productive.

5. **Preparation** (8%): Managers want to see applicants prepared for interviews by being ready to discuss qualifications and how they can contribute to the success of the company.

How can you adapt your résumé, cover letter, and interview style to align with these findings?

Adapted from Laura Morsch, "Five Must-Haves for New Grads," in *Career builder.com: Career Advice: Job Search*, http://careerbuilder.com/JobSeeker/careerbytes/CBArticle.aspx?articleID =418 (accessed May 30, 2007).

Evaluating Your Strengths and Interests

A self-assessment is the first step in producing a good résumé. Each person could do several jobs happily. Richard Bolles, a nationally recognized expert in career advising for over a third of a century and author of the *What Color Is Your Parachute* books, says most people who don't find a job they like fail because they lack information about themselves.[1] Personality and aptitude tests can tell you what your strengths are, but they won't say, "You should be a _____." You'll still need to answer questions like these:

- What skills and strengths do you have?
- What achievements have given you the most satisfaction? *Why* did you enjoy them?
- Would you rather have firm deadlines or a flexible schedule? Do you prefer working independently or with other people? Do you prefer specific instructions and standards for evaluation or freedom and uncertainty? How comfortable are you with pressure? How much challenge do you want?
- Are you willing to take work home? To work weekends? To travel? How important is money to you? Prestige? Time to spend with family and friends?
- How fast do you want to move up? Are you willing to pay your dues for several years before you are promoted?
- Where do you want to live? What features in terms of weather, geography, cultural and social life do you see as ideal?
- Is it important to you that your work achieve certain purposes or values, or do you see work as just a way to make a living? Are the organization's culture and ethical standards important to you?

Once you know what is most important to you, analyze the job market to see where you could find what you want. For example, Peter's greatest interest is athletics, but he isn't good enough for the pros. Studying the job market might suggest several alternatives. He could teach sports and physical fitness as a high school coach or a corporate fitness director. He could cover sports for a newspaper, a magazine, or a TV station. He could go into management or sales for a professional sports team, a health club, or a company that sells sports equipment. Each possibility will require somewhat different training and course selection, underscoring the need for Peter to begin considering his job search process early in his college career.

Using the Internet in Your Job Search

In addition to searching for ads, every job candidate should check the Internet for information about writing résumés and application letters, researching specific companies and jobs, and preparing for interviews. Many comprehensive sites give detailed information that will help you produce more effective documents and be a better-prepared job candidate.

As you search the Web, remember that not all sites are current and accurate. In particular, be careful of .com sites: some are good, others are not. Check your school's career site for help. Check the sites of other schools: Stanford and Berkeley have particularly excellent career sites. And even good sources can have advice that is bad for you. When advice conflicts—and it will—choose the advice which is best for you.

Figure 7.1 lists some of the best sites.

Figure 7.1   Comprehensive Web Job Sites Covering the Entire Job Search Process

America's Job Bank
   www.ajb.dni.us
Campus Career Center
   www.campuscareercenter.com
CareerBuilder
   www.careerbuilder.com
College Central
   www.collegecentral.com
College Grad Job Hunter
   www.collegegrad.com
The Five O'Clock Club
   www.fiveoclockclub.com
JobHuntersBible.com (Dick Bolles)
   www.jobhuntersbible.com
JobStar Central
   http://jobstar.org
Monster.com
   www.monster.com
MonsterTrak
   www.monstertrak.monster.com
Quintessential Careers
   www.quintcareers.com
The Riley Guide
   www.rileyguide.com
The Rockport Institute
   www.rockportinstitute.com
Spherion Career Center
   www.spherion.com/careers/career_center_home.jsp
Snag a Job
   www.snagajob.com

How Employers Use Résumés

Understanding how employers use résumés will help you create a résumé that works for you.

1. **Employers use résumés to decide whom to interview.**   (The major exceptions are on-campus interviews, where the campus placement office has policies that determine who meets with the interviewer.) Since résumés are used to screen out applicants, omit anything that may create a negative impression. See Figure 7.2.
2. **Résumés are scanned or skimmed.**   At many companies, résumés are scanned into an electronic job applicant tracking system. Only résumés that match keywords are skimmed by a human being. A human may give a résumé 3 to 30 seconds before deciding to keep or toss it. You must design your résumé to pass both the "scan test" and the "skim test."
3. **Employers assume that your letter and résumé represent your best work.** Neatness, accuracy, and freedom from typographical errors are essential.

What Employers Want, III

Good communication skills, including both writing and speaking, and honesty and integrity are what employers want most when hiring new employees according to the 2007 Job Outlook survey. Unfortunately, communication skills were also the skills employers found most lacking in college graduates.

Other desired attributes which ranked high in the survey included honesty, interpersonal skills, motivation/initiative, strong work ethic, and teamwork skills.

Adapted from National Association of Colleges and Employers, "What Are You Doing After Graduation? What Employers Want (And You Need to Have)," in *JobWeb: Job Outlook 2007,* www.JobWeb.com/joboutlook/2007/student2.htm (accessed May 30, 2007).

Figure 7.2 Employers Rate the Importance of Specific Qualities/Skills

Qualities	Rating
Communication Skills	4.7
Honesty/integrity	4.7
Interpersonal skills (relates well to others)	4.5
Motivation/initiative	4.5
Strong work ethic	4.5
Teamwork skills (works well with others)	4.5
Computer skills	4.4
Analytical skills	4.3
Flexibility/adaptability	4.3
Detail-oriented	4.2
Organizational skills	4.0
Leadership skills	4.0
Self-confidence	4.0
Friendly/outgoing personality	3.9
Tactfulness	3.9
Well-mannered/polite	3.8
Creativity	3.7
GPA (3.0 or better)	3.6
Entrepreneurial skills/risk-taker	3.3
Sense of humor	3.2
Bilingual skills	2.3

(5-point scale, where 1 = not important, 2 = not very important; 3 = somewhat important; 4 = very important, and 5 = extremely important)

Source: Chart from National Association of Colleges and Employers, "What Are You Doing After Graduation? What Employers Want (And You Need To Have)," in *JobWeb: Job Outlook 2007*, http://www.JobWeb.com/joboutlook/2007/student2.htm (accessed May 30, 2007).

4. **Interviewers usually reread your résumé before the interview to refresh their memories.** Be ready to offer fuller details about everything on your résumé.
5. **After an employer has chosen an applicant, he or she submits the applicant's résumé to people in the organization who must approve the appointment.** These people may have different backgrounds and areas of expertise. Spell out acronyms. Explain awards, Greek-letter honor societies, unusual job titles, or organizations that may be unfamiliar to the reader.

Guidelines for Résumés

Writing a résumé is not an exact science. What makes your friend look good does not necessarily help you. If your skills are in great demand, you can violate every guideline here and still get a good job. But when you must compete against many applicants, these guidelines will help you look as good on paper as you are in person.

Length

A one-page résumé is sufficient, but do fill the page. Less than a full page suggests that you do not have very much to say for yourself.

If you have more good material than will fit on one page, use a second page. It is a myth that all résumés must fit on one page. According to surveys conducted by international staffing firm Accountemps of managers at the 1,000 largest companies in this country, approval of the one-page résumé is dropping. Ten years ago only 28% said one page was the ideal length; now the percentage has dropped to 7%.[2] An experiment that mailed one- or two-page résumés to recruiters at major accounting firms showed that even readers who said they preferred short résumés were more likely to want to interview the candidate with the longer résumé.[3] The longer résumé gives managers a better picture of how you will fit in.

If you do use more than one page, the second page should have at least 10 to 12 lines. Use a second sheet of paper; do not print on the back of the first page. Leave less important information for the second page. Put your name and "Page 2" on the page. If the pages are separated, you want the reader to know who the qualifications belong to and that the second page is not your whole résumé.

Emphasis

Emphasize the things you've done that (a) are most relevant to the position for which you're applying, (b) show your superiority to other applicants, and (c) are recent.

Show that you're qualified by giving relevant details on course projects, activities, and jobs where you've done similar work. Be brief about low-level jobs that simply show dependability. To prove that you're the best candidate for the job, emphasize items that set you apart from other applicants: promotions, honors and achievements, experience with computers or other relevant equipment, foreign languages, and so on.

If you're getting a two-year or a four-year degree, you should generally omit high school jobs, activities, and honors unless they are particularly relevant to a specific job, you need them to show geographic flexibility, or you need them to fill the page. Focus on achievements in the last three to five years. Whatever your age at the time you write a résumé, you want to suggest that you are now the best you've ever been.

Include full-time work after high school before you entered to college and work during college to support yourself or to earn expenses. If the jobs you held then were low-level ones, present them briefly or combine them:

> 2002–06 Part-time and full-time jobs to support family

You can emphasize material by putting it at the top or the bottom of a page, by giving it more space, and by setting it off with white space. The beginning and end—of a document, a page, a list—are positions of emphasis. When you have a choice (e.g., in a list of job duties), put less important material in the middle, not at the end, to avoid the impression of "fading out."

Weak order: Coordinated weekly schedules, assigned projects to five staff members, evaluated their performance, and submitted weekly time sheets.

Emphatic order: Coordinated weekly schedules and submitted weekly time sheets. Assigned projects to five staff members and evaluated their performance.

You can also emphasize material by presenting it in a vertical list, by using a phrase in a heading, and by providing details. For example, rather than presenting your internship work in long paragraphs, use bulleted lists to make your accomplishments stand out.

Templates: Use Caution

Do not use résumé templates that come with word-processing software.

Many Web sites also have templates for paper and online résumés. If you choose to use one of them, print out a copy before you submit your résumé. Less sophisticated programs use fixed spacing before headings. If you skip the objective, or have less experience than the template allows, you may get blank space—hardly a way to build a good impression.

Almost certainly, you can create a better résumé by adapting a basic style you like to your own unique qualifications.

Details

Details provide evidence to support your claims, convince the reader, and separate you from other applicants. Numbers make good details. Tell how many people you trained or supervised, how much money you budgeted or raised. Describe the interesting aspects of the job you did.

Too vague: Sales Manager, *The Daily Collegian*, University Park, PA, 2005–08. Supervised staff; promoted ad sales.

Good details: Sales Manager, *The Daily Collegian*, University Park, PA, 2005–08. Supervised 22-member sales staff; helped recruit, interview, and select staff; assigned duties and scheduled work; recommended best performers for promotion. Motivated staff to increase paid ad inches 10% over previous year's sales.

Omit details that add nothing to a title, that are less impressive than the title alone, or that suggest a faulty sense of priorities (e.g., listing hours per week spent filing). Either use strong details or just give the office or job title without any details.

Writing Style

Without sacrificing content, be as concise as possible.

Wordy: Member, Meat Judging Team, 2004–05

Member, Meat Judging Team, 2005–06

Member, Meat Judging Team, 2006–07

Captain, Meat Judging Team, 2007–08

Tight: Meat Judging Team, 2004–05; Captain 2007–08

Wordy: Performed foundation load calculations

Tight: Calculated foundation loads

Résumés normally use phrases and sentence fragments. Complete sentences are acceptable if they are the briefest way to present information. To save space and to avoid sounding arrogant, never use *I* in a résumé. *Me* and *my* are acceptable if they are unavoidable or if using them reduces wordiness.

Verbs or gerunds (the *-ing* form of verbs) create a more dynamic image of you than do nouns, so use them on résumés that will be read by people. (Rules for scannable résumés to be read by computers come later in this chapter.) In the following revisions of job responsibilities, nouns, verbs, and gerunds are in bold type:

Nouns: Chair, Income Tax Assistance Committee, Winnipeg, MB, 2007–08. Responsibilities: **recruitment** of volunteers; flyer **design, writing,** and **distribution** for **promotion** of program; **speeches** to various community groups and nursing homes to advertise the service.

Verbs: Chair, Income Tax Assistance Committee, Winnipeg, MB, 2007–08. **Recruited** volunteers for the program. **Designed, wrote,** and **distributed** a flyer to promote the program; **spoke** to various community groups and nursing homes to advertise the service.

Gerunds: Chair, Income Tax Assistance Committee, Winnipeg, MB, 2007–08. Responsibilities included **recruiting** volunteers for the program; **designing, writing,** and **distributing** a flyer to promote the program; and **speaking** to various community groups and nursing homes to advertise the service.

Note that the items in the list must be in parallel structure (◀▥ p. 124).

Layout and Design

Experiment with layout, fonts, and spacing to get an attractive résumé. Web sites listed in Figure 7.1 will give you many examples of résumés for ideas. Consider creating a letterhead that you use for both your résumé and your application letter.

One of the major decisions you will make is how to treat your headings. Do you want them on the left margin, with text immediately below them, as in Figure 7.3? Do you want them alone in the left column, with text in a column to the right, as in Figure 7.5? Would you like them boxed, as in Figure 7.6? Generally, people with more text on their résumés use the first or third option. Putting headings in their own column on the left takes space and thus helps spread a thinner list of accomplishments over the page. But be careful not to make the heading column too wide, or it will make your résumé look unbalanced and empty.

Work with fonts, bullets, and spacing to highlight your information. Do be careful, however, not to make your résumé look "busy" by using too many fonts. Generally three fonts should be the top limit, and you should avoid unusual fonts. Keep fonts readable by using at least 10-point type for large fonts such as Arial and 11-point for smaller fonts such as Times New Roman. Use enough white space to group items and make your résumé easy to read, but not so much that you look as if you're padding.

Use color sparingly, if at all. If a company is scanning paper résumés into its data files, colored text and shaded boxes can prevent accurate scanning. Similarly, white 8$\frac{1}{2}$- by 11-inch paper is standard, but do use a good-quality paper.

All of these guidelines are much more flexible for people in creative fields such as advertising and design.

Kinds of Résumés

Two basic categories of résumés are chronological and skills. A **chronological résumé** summarizes what you did in a time line (starting with the most recent events, and going backward in **reverse chronology**). It emphasizes degrees, job titles, and dates. It is the traditional résumé format. Figures 7.3 and 7.6 show chronological résumés.

Use a chronological résumé when

- Your education and experience are a logical preparation for the position for which you're applying.
- You have impressive job titles, offices, or honors.

A **skills résumé** emphasizes the skills you've used, rather than the job in which you used them or the date of the experience. Figure 7.5 (➡ pp. 224) shows a skills résumés. Use a skills résumé when

- Your education and experience are not the usual route to the position for which you're applying.
- You're changing fields.
- You want to combine experience from paid jobs, activities, volunteer work, and courses to show the extent of your experience in administration, finance, speaking, and so on.

The two kinds differ in what information is included and how that information is organized. You may assume that the advice in this chapter applies to both kinds of résumés unless there is an explicit statement that the two kinds of résumés would handle a category differently.

Résumé Blunders

"[CareerBuilders surveyed hiring managers to] find out the wackiest résumé items they've seen lately. Out of 2,627 responses, here are the top ten:
A job candidate . . .

1. . . . attached a letter from her mother.

2. . . . used pale blue paper with teddy bears printed around the border.

3. . . . explained a three-month gap in employment by saying that he was getting over the death of his cat.

4. . . . specified that his availability to work Fridays, Saturdays or Sundays is limited because the weekends are 'drinking time.'

5. . . . included a picture of herself in a cheerleading uniform.

6. . . . drew a picture of a car on the outside of the envelope and said the car would be a gift to the hiring manager.

7. . . . listed hobbies that included sitting on a levee at night watching alligators.

8. . . . mentioned the fact that her sister had once won a strawberry-eating contest.

9. . . . stated that he works well in the nude.

10. . . . explained an arrest record by stating, 'We stole a pig, but it was a really small pig.'"

Quoted from Anne Fisher, "10 Dumbest Résumé Blunders," in *CNNMoney.com: Fortune: Commentary: Ask Annie*, http://money.cnn.com/2007/04/25/news/economy/resume.blunders.fortune/index.htm (accessed May 30, 2007).

Figure 7.3   A Community College Chronological Résumé to Use for Career Fairs and Internships

Abhishek Ankit
aankit@mcc.edu

Vary font sizes. Use larger size for name and main headings.

Campus Address
1524 E. Main St
Boone, IA 50036
515-432-1997

Using both addresses ensures continuous contact information.

Permanent Address
2526 Prairie Lane
Omaha, NE 68235
402-442-7793

Education
Midwest Community College
AA in Financial Management, June 2008
GPA: 3.0/4.0 *Give your grade average if it's 3.0 or higher.*

Summary of Qualifications

Use keywords employers might seek.

List 3–7 qualifications.

- Self-motivated, detail-minded, results-oriented
- Consistently successful track record in sales
- Effectively developed and operated entrepreneurial business

Sales Experience
Financial Sales Representative, ABC Inc., Des Moines, IA, February 2006–present
- Establish client base.
- Develop investment strategy plans for clients.
- Research and recommend specific investments.

Other Experience
Entrepreneur, A-Plus T-Shirt Company, Omaha, NE, September 2004–January 2006

One way to handle self-employment.

- Created a saleable product (graphic T-shirts).
- Secured financial support.
- Located a manufacturer.
- Supervised production.
- Sold T-shirts to high school students.
- Realized a substantial profit to pay for college expenses.

Cook, Hamburger Shack, Omaha, NE, Summers 2001–2005
- Learned sales strategies.
- Ensured customer satisfaction.
- Worked cooperatively with a team of 25.

Collector and Repair Worker, ACN, Inc., Omaha, NE, Summer 1996–2001
- Collected and counted approximately $10,000 a day. *Specify large sums of money.*
- Worked with technicians troubleshooting and repairing coin mechanisms.

Other Skills
Computer: Outlook, HTML, Excel, Dreamweaver, Frontpage, GoLive
Language: Fluent in Spanish *Many employers appreciate a second language.*

What to Include in a Résumé

Although the résumé is a factual document, its purpose is to persuade. In a job application form or an application for graduate or professional school, you answer every question even if the answer is not to your credit. In a résumé, you cannot lie, but you can omit anything that does not work in your favor.

Résumés commonly contain the following information. The categories marked with an asterisk are essential.

*Name and Contact Information

Career Objective

Summary of Qualifications

*Education

Honors and Awards

*Experience

Other skills

Activities

Portfolio

You may choose other titles for these categories and add categories that are relevant for your qualifications, such as computer skills or foreign languages.

Education and Experience always stand as separate categories, even if you have only one item under each head. Combine other headings so that you have at least two long or three short items under each heading. For example, if you're in one honor society and two social clubs, and on one athletic team, combine them all under Activities and Honors.

If you have more than seven items under a heading, consider using subheadings. For example, a student who had a great many activities might divide them into Campus Activities and Community Service.

Put your strongest categories near the top and at the bottom of the first page. If you have impressive work experience, you might want to put that category first and Education second.

A résumé is your most important document at career fairs.

Objectionable Objectives

"[These job objectives did not help their writers:]

- 'Carrier Objective: To become a manager.' A man on the move.
- 'I want to play a major part in watching a company advance.' We'll put a Barcalounger next to your desk.
- 'To hopefully associate with a millionaire one day.' We'll keep our fingers crossed for you.
- 'I am seeking a second job to supplement my income and support my shopping habit.' We may have a job for you in purchasing.
- 'I would like to work for a company that is very lax when it comes to tardiness.' We'll get back to you.
- 'To obtain an entry-level position after I get my beachler's degree.' Will you also have a minor in surfing?
- 'A position that allows me to keep my sanity.' Seems like a reasonable request.
- 'I want to increase my career goals.' Don't let us stop you.
- 'I am looking for a change of scenery.' Have you tried the theater?
- 'To mature in the field of human behavior.' Good luck with that.
- 'My dream job would be as a professional baseball player, but since I can't do that, I'll settle on being an accountant.' Your enthusiasm is overwhelming.
- 'See challenges that test my mind and body, since the two are usually inseparable.' Glad to hear it."

Quoted from Robert Half International, "Resumania Archive," http://www.resumania.com/arcindex.html (accessed May 30, 2007).

Name and Contact Information

Use your full name, even if everyone calls you by a nickname. You may use an initial rather than spelling out your first or middle name. Put your name in big type.

If you use only one address, consider centering it under your name. If you use two addresses (office and home, campus and permanent, until _____ / after_____) set them up side by side to balance the page visually. Place a comma after the city and before the state. Use either post office (two-letter, full caps, no period) abbreviations for the state or spell out the state name, but do be consistent throughout your résumé.

Urbana, IL 61801

Wheaton, Illinois 60187

Provide an e-mail address. Some job candidates set up a new e-mail address just for job hunting.

Give a complete phone number, including the area code. Some job candidates give both home and cell phone numbers. Do provide a phone number where you can be reached during the day. Employers usually call during business hours to schedule interviews and make job offers. Do not give lab or dorm phone numbers unless you are sure someone there will take an accurate message for you at all times. Also, be sure that all answering machines have a professional-sounding message.

Career Objective

Career objective statements should sound like the job descriptions an employer might use in a job listing. Keep your statement brief—two or three lines at most. Tell what you want to do, what level of responsibility you want to hold. The best career objectives are tailored to a specific job.

Ineffective career objective:	To offer a company my excellent academic foundation in hospital technology and my outstanding skills in oral and written communication
Better career objective:	Hospital and medical sales requiring experience with state-of-the-art equipment

Good career objectives are hard to write. If you talk about entry-level work, you won't sound ambitious; if you talk about where you hope to be in 5 or 10 years, you won't sound as though you're willing to do entry-level work. When you're applying for a job that is a natural outgrowth of your education and experience, you may omit this category and specify the job you want in your cover letter.

Often you can avoid writing a career objective statement by putting the job title or field under your name:

Joan Larson Ooyen	Terence Edward Garvey	David R. Lunde
Marketing	Technical Writer	Corporate Fitness Director

Note that you can use the field you're in even if you're a new college graduate. To use a job title, you should have some relevant work experience.

If you use a separate heading for a career objective, put it immediately after your address, before the first major heading.

Summary of Qualifications

A section summarizing the candidate's qualifications seems to have first appeared in scannable résumés, where its keywords helped to increase the number of matches a résumé produced. But the section proved useful for human readers as well and now is a standard part of most résumés. The best summaries show your knowledge of the specialized terminology of your field and offer specific, quantifiable achievements.

Weak: Staff accountant

Better: Experience with accounts payable, accounts receivable, audits, and month end closings. Prepared monthly financial reports.

Weak: Presentation skills

Better: Gave 20 individual and 7 team presentations to groups ranging from 5 to 100 people.

Education

Education can be your first major category if you've just earned (or are about to earn) a degree, if you have a degree that is essential or desirable for the position you're seeking, or if you can present the information briefly. Put your Education section later if you need all of page 1 for another category or if you lack a degree that other applicants may have (see Figure 7.5 ➠).

Under Education, provide information about your undergraduate and graduate degrees, including the location of institutions and the year you received or expect your degree.

Use the same format for all schools. List your degrees in reverse chronological order (most recent first).

> Master of Accounting Science, May 2009, Arizona State University, Tempe, AZ
> Bachelor of Arts in Finance, May 2007, New Mexico State University, Las Cruces, NM
>
> BS in Personnel Management, June 2009, Georgia State University, Milledgeville, GA
> AS in Office Management, June 2007, Georgia Community College, Atlanta, GA

When you're getting a four-year degree, include community college only if it will interest employers, such as by showing an area of expertise different from that of your major. You may want to include your minor and any graduate courses you have taken. Include study abroad, even if you didn't earn college credits. If you got a certificate for international study, give the name and explain the significance of the certificate. Highlight proficiency in foreign or computer languages by using a separate category.

To punctuate your degrees, do not space between letters and periods:

A.S. in Office Administration

B.S. in Accounting

Ed.D. in Business Education

Current usage also permits you to omit the periods:

MBA

PhD in Finance

Be consistent with the usage you choose.

Professional certifications can be listed under Education or in a separate category.

If your GPA is good, include it. Because grade point systems vary, specify what your GPA is based on: "3.4/4.0" means 3.4 on a 4.0 scale. If your GPA is under 3.0 on a 4.0 scale, use words rather than numbers: "B— average." If your GPA isn't impressive, calculate your average in your major and your average for your last 60 hours. If these are higher than your overall GPA, consider using them. The National Association of Colleges and Employers, in its Job Outlook 2007 survey, found the 66% of employers do screen job applicants by GPA.[4] If you leave your GPA off your résumé, most employers will automatically assume that it is below a 3.0. If yours is, you will need to rely on internships, work experience, and skills acquired in activities to make yourself an attractive job candidate.

After giving the basic information (degree, field of study, date, school, city, state) about your degree, you may wish to list courses, using short descriptive titles rather than course numbers. Use a subhead like "Courses Related to Major" or "Courses Related to Financial Management" that will allow you to list all the courses (including psychology, speech, and business communication) that will help you in the job for which you're applying. Don't say "Relevant Courses," as that implies your other courses were irrelevant.

Bachelor of Science in Management, May 2008, Illinois State University, Normal, IL
GPA: 3.8/4.0
Courses Related to Management:

Personnel Administration	Business Decision Making
Finance	International Business
Management I and II	Marketing
Accounting I and II	Legal Environment of Business
Business Report Writing	Business Speaking

Listing courses is an unobtrusive way to fill a page. You may also want to list courses or the number of hours in various subjects if you've taken an unusual combination of courses that uniquely qualify you for the position for which you're applying.

BS in Marketing, May 2009, California State University at Northridge
30 hours in marketing
15 hours in Spanish
9 hours in Chicano studies

Honors and Awards

It's nice to have an Honors and Awards section, but not everyone can do so. If you have fewer than three and therefore cannot justify a separate heading, consider a heading Honors and Activities to get that important word in a position of emphasis.

Include the following kinds of entries in this category:

- Academic honor societies. Specify the nature of Greek-letter honor societies so the reader doesn't think they're just social clubs.

- Fellowships and scholarships, including honorary scholarships for which you received no money and fellowships you could not hold because you received another fellowship at the same time.

- Awards given by professional societies.

- Major awards given by civic groups.

- Varsity letters; selection to all-state or all-America teams; finishes in state, national, or Olympic meets. (These could also go under Activities but may look more impressive under Honors. Put them under one category or the other—not both.)

Identify honor societies ("national journalism honorary," "campus honorary for top 2% of business majors") for readers who are not in your discipline.

If your fellowships or scholarships are particularly selective or remunerative, give supporting details:

> Clyde Jones Scholarship: four-year award covering tuition, fees, room, and board.
>
> Marilyn Terpstra Scholarship: $25,000 annually for four years.
>
> Heemsly Fellowship: 50 awarded nationally each year to top Information Science juniors.

Be careful of listing Dean's List for only one or two semesters. Such a listing reminds readers that in these days of grade inflation you were off the list many more times than you were on it. Omit honors like "Miss Congeniality" or "Muscle Man Star" that work against the professional image you want your résumé to create.

As a new college graduate, try to put Honors on page 1. In a skills résumé, put Honors on page 1 if they're major (e.g., Phi Beta Kappa, Phi Kappa Phi). Otherwise, save them until page 2—Experience will probably take the whole first page.

Experience

You may use other headings if they work better: Work Experience, Summer and Part-Time Jobs, Military Experience, Marketing Experience. In a skills résumé, headings such as "Marketing Experience" allow you to include accomplishments from activities and course projects.

What to include

Under this section, include the following information for each job you list: position or job title, organization, city and state (no zip code), dates of employment, and other details, such as full- or part-time status, job duties, special responsibilities, or the fact that you started at an entry-level position and were promoted. Use the verbs in Figure 7.4 to brainstorm what you've done. Include any internships and co-ops you have had. Also, include unpaid jobs and self-employment if they provided relevant skills (e.g., supervising people, budgeting, planning, persuading).

Normally, go back as far as the summer after high school. Include earlier jobs if you started working someplace before graduating from high school but

But I Haven't Done Anything!

Some students have trouble coming up with details. "I've never really done anything." That's too negative. *Everybody* has done *something.* How have you spent the last five years?

One woman's only job was as a part-time salesclerk in the lighting department of a department store. Her official duties weren't important. But when she focused on what she'd actually done, she had evidence of skills employers want.

She had done research. To answer customers' questions, she read about lighting, vision, and energy consumption. She visited competitors and noticed their products and displays.

She had demonstrated creativity. In August, she rigged up a mannequin to look like a student—slouched in a chair, holding textbook and pop bottle, surrounded by clothes, a football, and a guitar. On the table was a lamp positioned to provide good study light with a sign, "At least he won't ruin his eyes."

Her display worked. The store sold four times as many lamps that August as it ever had, including the month before Christmas.

A résumé entry could give these details to support claims for experience in research and persuading. And she had increased sales in her unit 400%.

Adapted from John L. Munschauer, *Jobs for English Majors and Other Smart People* (Princeton, NJ: Peterson's Guides, 1986), 36–37.

Figure 7.4   Action Verbs for Résumés

analyzed	directed	led	reviewed
budgeted	earned	managed	revised
built	edited	motivated	saved
chaired	established	negotiated	scheduled
coached	examined	observed	simplified
collected	evaluated	organized	sold
conducted	helped	persuaded	solved
coordinated	hired	planned	spoke
counseled	improved	presented	started
created	increased	produced	supervised
demonstrated	interviewed	recruited	trained
designed	introduced	reported	translated
developed	investigated	researched	wrote

Résumé resources

These two Web sites provide extensive lists of action verbs that can be used for résumés:

- http://www.eresumes.com/action-verb-list.html
- http://www.quintcareers.com/action_alpha.html

What action verbs can you use to make your résumé stand out?

continued working there after graduation. However, give minimal detail about high school jobs. If you worked full-time after high school, make that clear.

The details you give about your experience are some of the most vital information on your résumé. As you provide these details, use bulleted lists (easy to read) rather than paragraphs which are harder to read and may be skipped over. Remember that items in lists need to have parallel structure; see Chapter 4, page 124 for a refresher. Focus on results rather than duties; employers are far more interested in what you accomplished than in what you had to do. Use numbers to support your results wherever possible:

Supervised crew of nine.

Managed $120,000 budget.

Wrote monthly four-page newsletter.

Use past tense verbs for jobs you held in the past, and present tense verbs for jobs you still have. Do not list minor duties such as distributing mail or filing documents. If your duties were completely routine, say, at your summer job at McDonald's, do not list them.

If as an undergraduate you've earned a substantial portion of your college expenses with jobs and scholarship, say so in a separate sentence either under Experience or in the section on personal data. (Graduate students are expected to support themselves.)

> These jobs paid 40% of my college expenses.

> Paid for 65% of expenses with jobs, scholarships, and loans.

Paying for school expenses just with loans is generally not considered noteworthy.

Formats for setting up Experience

There are two basic ways to set up the Experience section of your résumé. In **indented format,** items that are logically equivalent begin at the same space, with carryover lines indented. Indented format emphasizes job titles. It provides work information in this order:

Job title, name of organization, city, state, dates. Other information.

> Experience
>
> **Engineering Assistant,** Sohio Chemical Company, Lima, Ohio, Summers 2007 and 2008.
> - Tested wastewater effluents for compliance with Federal EPA standards.
> - Helped chemists design a test to analyze groundwater quality and seepage around landfills.
> - Presented weekly oral and written progress reports to Director of Research and Development.
>
> **Animal Caretaker,** Animalcare, Worthington, Ohio, Summers 2003–2006.

Two-margin or **block format** emphasizes *when* you worked, so it is appropriate if you've held only low-level jobs. Don't use two-margin format if your work history has gaps or if you've worked as an intern or held another job directly relevant to the position you're applying for.

EXPERIENCE	
Summers, 2006–08	Repair worker, Bryant Heating and Cooling, Providence, RI.
2006–07	Library Clerk, Boston University Library, Boston, MA. Part time during school year.
2004–06	Food Service Worker, Boston University, Boston, MA. Part-time during school year.
Summer, 2005	Delivery person, Domino's Pizza, Providence, RI.

Use a hyphen to join inclusive dates:

March-August, 2008 (or write out March to August, 2008)
2003-2006
2008-09

If you use numbers for dates, do not space before or after the slash:

10/07-5/08

Skills résumés

Skills résumés stress the skills you have acquired rather than specific jobs and show employers that you do have the desired skill set even if you lack the traditional employment background. They allow you to include skills acquired from activities and course projects in addition to jobs. On the other hand, they are also a clue to employers that you do lack that traditional background, or that you have gaps in your job history, so you will need to make your skill set convincing.

In a skills résumé, the heading of your main section usually changes from "Experience" to "Skills." Within the section, the subheadings will be replaced with the skills used in the job you are applying for, rather than the title or the dates of the jobs you've held (as in a chronological résumé). For entries under each skill, combine experience from paid jobs, unpaid work, classes, activities, and community service.

Use headings that reflect the jargon of the job for which you're applying: *logistics* rather than *planning* for a technical job; *procurement* rather than *purchasing* for a job with the military. Figure 7.5 shows a skills résumé for someone who is changing fields.

A job description can give you ideas for headings. Possible headings and subheadings for skills résumés include

Administration	Communication
Budgeting	Conducting Meetings
Coordinating	Editing
Evaluating	Fund-Raising
Implementing	Interviewing
Negotiating	Oral Skills
Planning	Negotiating
Scheduling	Persuading
Solving Problems	Proposal Writing
Supervising	Report Writing

Many jobs require a mix of skills. Try to include the skills that you know will be needed in the job you want. You need at least three subheadings in a skills résumé; six or seven is not uncommon. Give enough detail under each

I Do Good Work

[Create an "I Do Good Work" folder to] back up your claims of top performance with solid evidence.

Before you leave the office this Friday, write down five things you—not necessarily others—believe you did well this week, even if they represent common tasks. Perhaps you returned all phone calls, leaving no loose ends to tie at the end of the week. Or maybe the details you provide in your sales reports enabled you to find additional product fits for the client. Any letters from happy customers or e-mails thanking you for solving a problem should go right in your folder. . . .

Tuck that list away and continue this weekly exercise for the entire month. At the end of the month, narrow the four or five lists to 10 accomplishments that stand out to you. At the end of the year, review the 120 items and cull them to 25. Formalize the language that describes those 25 achievements and print them out in an organized manner . . . along with your references.

"When someone asks, 'What do you bring to this organization?' you won't merely reply, 'I'm good with people,' you'll hand that sales manager or HR person proof," says professional trainer Carol Price.

Quoted from Julie Sturgeon, "All About You," *Selling Power*, September 2000, 57.

Figure 7.5   A Skills Résumé for Someone Changing Fields

Sophia Barber
www.ukansas.edu/~Barber1278/home.htm

If you have a professional web page, include its URL.

266 Van Buren Drive
Lawrence, KS 66044
barber@ukansas.edu
785-897-1534 (home)
785-842-4242 (cell)

Objective   To contribute my enthusiasm for writing as a Technical Writer at PDF Productions

Job objective includes the position and name of the company.

Skills

Largest section on skills résumé. Allows you to combine experiences from work and class.

Computer
• Designed a web page using Dreamweaver
    www.lawrenceanimalshelter.com
• Used a variety of Macintosh and PC platform programs and languages:
    Aspects (online discussion forum)   Storyspace
    Dreamweaver   GoLive
    PageMaker   HTML
    XML   InDesign CS2

Specify computer programs you know well.

Use parallel structure for bulleted lists.

Design and Writing
• Designed a quarterly newsletter for local animal shelter
• Developed professional brochures
• Wrote a variety of professional documents: letters, memos, and reports
• Edited internal documents and promotional materials
• Proofread seven student research papers as a tutor

Organization and Administration
• Coordinated program schedules
• Developed work schedules for five employees
• Led a ten-member team in planning and implementing sorority philanthropy program
• Created cataloging system for specimens
• Ordered and handled supplies, including live specimens

Employment History

Condensed to make room for skills.

Technical Writer, Lawrence Animal Shelter, Lawrence, KS, 2006–Present Undergraduate Lab Assistant, Department of Biology,
        University of Kansas, Lawrence, KS, 2006–present
Tutor, University of Kansas, Lawrence, KS, 2004–2006

Uses reverse chronology.

Education   Bachelor of Arts, May 2008
University of Kansas, Lawrence, KS
Major: Animal Ecology
Minor: Chemistry
GPA 3.4/4.0

Give minor when it can be helpful.

Honors   Phi Kappa Phi Honor Society
Alpha Lambda Delta Honor Society, Ecology Honorary
Dean's List, 2006 to present
Raymond Hamilton Scholarship, 2006–2007
        ($5,000 to a top ecology student in Kansas)

Explain honors your reader may not know.

End with a strong items at the bottom of your page, a position of emphasis.

subheading so the reader will know what you did. Put the most important category from the reader's point of view first.

In a skills résumé, list your paid jobs under Work History or Employment Record near the end of the résumé (see Figure 7.5). List only job title, employer, city, state, and dates. Omit details that you have already used under Experience.

Other Skills

You may want a brief section in a chronological résumé where you highlight skills not apparent in your work history. These skills may include items such as foreign languages or programming languages. You might want to list software you have used or training on expensive equipment (electron microscopes, NMR machines). As always on your résumé, be completely honest: "four years of high school German," or "elementary speaking knowledge of Spanish." Any knowledge of a foreign language is a plus. It means that a company desiring a second language in its employees would not have to start from scratch in training you. See Figure 7.6 for an example.

Activities

Employers may be interested in your activities if you're a new college graduate because they can demonstrate leadership roles, management abilities, and social skills as well as the ability to juggle a schedule. If you've worked for several years after college or have an advanced degree (MBA, JD), you can omit Activities and include Professional Activities and Affiliations or Community and Public Service. If you went straight from college to graduate school but have an unusually strong record demonstrating relevant skills, include this category even if all the entries are from your undergraduate days.

Include the following kinds of items under Activities:

- Volunteer work. Include important committees, leadership roles, and communication activities.
- Membership in organized student activities. Include important subcommittees, leadership roles. Include minor offices only if they're directly related to the job for which you're applying or if they show growing responsibility (you held a minor office one year, a bigger office the following year). Include so-called major offices (e.g., vice president) even if you did very little. Provide descriptive details if (but only if) they help the reader realize how much you did and the importance of your work.
- Membership in professional associations. Many of them have special low membership fees for students, so you should join one or more.
- Participation in varsity, intramural, or independent athletics. However, don't list so many sports that you appear not to have had adequate time to study.
- Social clubs, if you held a major leadership role or if social skills are important for the job for which you're applying.
- Religious organizations if you held a major leadership role and you're applying for jobs with religious organizations.

As you list activities, add details that will be relevant for your job. Did you handle a six-figure budget for your Greek organization? Plan all the road trips for your soccer club? Coordinate all the publicity for the campus blood drive? Design the posters for homecoming? Major leadership, financial, and creative roles and accomplishments may look more impressive if they're listed under Experience instead of under Activities.

What to Know about Job References

Many job reference myths exist that may undermine your job search:

Myth: I don't have to mention a job that didn't work out, especially if I worked there only a short while.

Fact: Employers can check jobs through Social Security, and they will believe the worst of omissions.

Myth: Companies are not legally allowed to give damaging information about applicants.

Fact: Although many companies have formal policies of providing only bare-bones data, many employees within those organizations still engage in providing additional, negative information about applicants. Voice tone, or mentioning that you may not be eligible for rehire, may speak volumes.

Myth: References do not matter once you are hired.

Fact: References may still be checked after you are hired and can be used for grounds for termination.

Myth: If you sue an employer, that information may not be disclosed.

Fact: Employers indirectly release negative information by stating such things as, "Please hold while I discuss with our legal department on what we are allowed to say about this applicant."

Myth: References are not needed after you have a job.

Fact: Stay in contact with your references. You never know when you may want to change jobs.

Adapted from Anne Fisher, "The Seven Deadly Myths of Job References," in *CNNMoney.com: Fortune: Commentary: Ask Annie*, http://money.cnn.com/2005/10/25/news/economy/annie/fortune_annie102505/index.htm (accessed May 30, 2007).

Figure 7.6   A Two-Page Chronological Résumé

Uses a little more formatting than the other résumés. Goes well with architecture degree.

Maria Sanchez

sanchez@unl.edu ▪ 1535 Mission Way ▪ Lincoln, NE 68501 ▪ 402.975.6992

Summary of Qualifications

- Two architecture internships
- International experience in study abroad program
- Managed $100,000 budget
- Fluent in Spanish and Italian   *Note language facility.*
- Proficient in AutoCAD

Education

2003–2008

Bachelor of Arts Degree
University of Nebraska–Lincoln, NE

- Major: Architecture
- Major GPA: 3.4/4.0

Course lists are good if you have unusual ones or ones that show you are particularly well-prepared.

Design Coursework

Renaissance Design	Conceptual Design	Principles of Construction
Medieval Design	History of Design	Building Structures
Postmodern Design	Theory of Landscape Structures	Architectural Aesthetics

Professional Experience

June 2006–Present

Architecture Intern
Cutting Edge Architecture Firm–Lincoln, NE

- Conduct safety site surveys for four residential areas
- Research code requirements and prepare survey reports
- Prepare remodeling drawings using AutoCAD 2007 to remedy concerns
- Collaborate with various organizations and professionals to complete reports

Use present tense when you are doing the job now.

Sept. 2005–Dec. 2005

Study Aboard Participant
Nebraska Study Abroad Program–Turin and Rome, Italy

- Studied the varied architecture of Italy
- Participated in artistic and cultural traditions of Italy
- Engaged in intensive language learning of Italian

Use past tense for jobs that are over.

June 2005–Sept. 2005

Architecture Intern
Debalt Architects–Minneapolis, MN

- Generated construction drawings and details
- Created designs using AutoCAD 2006
- Developed and maintained client relationships

Figure 7.6 *Continued*

Maria Sanchez
sanchez@unl.edu
Page 2

If you use two pages, be sure to put your name, e-mail, and "Page 2" on the second page.

April 2003–Sept. 2004 **Publicist/Laborer**
Harman Contractors–Lincoln, NE

- Installed fixtures in new residential homes
- Filled cracks with plaster and sanded patches
- Finished painted work surfaces
- Designed publicity brochures and business cards

Leadership Experience

May 2005–Present **Assistant Director of Volunteer Recruitment**
Habitat for Humanity–Lincoln, NE

- Supervise four office volunteers
- Publicize volunteer opportunities to local community and university
- Develop a recruitment action plan

Sept. 2007–Present **President**
Chi Omega Sorority–U of Nebraska–Lincoln, NE

- Oversee operation of 65 member sorority
- Call and preside over all executive meetings
- Manage $100,000 annual budget

Quantify your experiences where possible.

Volunteer Experience

June 2006 **Swimming Official**
Special Olympics Semi-National Games–Lincoln, NE

- Encouraged athletes while timing relays
- Promoted positive environment

Other Skills

AutoCAD 2007
Sketch-up
Adobe Photoshop, Illustrator, and InDesign CS2
Fluent in Spanish and Italian

Affiliations

American Institute of Architecture Students
Interfraternity Council
Intramural Council

Keep lists of extras short. Focus them to appeal to employers.

Portfolio Available at Password Protected Web Site

One way to make your professional work available to interested employers.

Portfolio

If you have samples of your work available, you may want to end your résumé by stating "Portfolio (or writing samples) available on request."

References

References are generally no longer included on résumés. Nor do you say "References Available on Request," since no job applicant is going to refuse to supply references. However, you will probably be asked for references at some point in your application process, so it is wise to be prepared.

You will need at least three, usually no more than five, never more than six. As a college student or a new graduate, include at least one professor and at least one employer or adviser—someone who can comment on your work habits and leadership skills. If you're changing jobs, include your current superior. For a skills résumé, choose references who can testify to your abilities in the most important skills areas. Omit personal or character references who cannot talk about your work. Don't use relatives, friends, or roommates, even if you've worked for them, because everyone will believe they are biased in your favor.

Always ask permission to use the person as a reference. Instead of the vague "May I list you as a reference?" use, "Can you speak specifically about my work?" Jog the person's memory by taking along copies of work you did for him or her and a copy of your current résumé. Tell the person what points you'd like stressed in a letter. Keep your list of references up to date. If it's been a year or more since you asked someone, ask again—and tell the person about your recent achievements.

On your list of references, provide name, title or position, organization, city, state, phone number, and e-mail for each of your references. If their connection to you is not clear, add an identifying line (former academic advisor; former supervisor at Careltons) so they do not look like personal references. You could also give the full mailing address if you think people are more likely to write than to call. Use courtesy titles (*Dr., Mr., Ms.*) for all or for none. By convention, all faculty with the rank of assistant professor or above may be called *Professor.*

References that the reader knows are by far the most impressive. In fact, employers may ask about you among people they already know: a former classmate may now work for them; a professor in your major department may consult for them. It is wise to be well thought of by as many people in your department as possible.

Include the name and address of your placement office if you have written recommendations on file there.

What Not to Include in a Résumé

Résumés should not include personal information such as marital status, number of children, race, sex, date of birth, health, or national origin. For safety reasons, they should never include your Social Security number. Including this kind of information shows you have not researched the job-hunting process. Since many employers take your performance on the job hunt as an indication of the quality of work you will do for them, résumé lapses indicate that you may not be the best employee.

Since résumés are used to eliminate a large pool of job candidates down to the handful that will be interviewed, do not include controversial activities or associations. This category generally includes work for specific religious or political groups. (If the work is significant, you can include it generically: Wrote campaign publicity for state senator candidate.)

High school facts are generally omitted once you are a junior in college unless you have good reasons for keeping them. These reasons might include showing you have local connections or showing skill in a needed area not covered by college activities (perhaps you are applying for coaching jobs where a variety of team sports will help you, and you played basketball in high school and volleyball in college). The fact that you have good high school activities but few if any college activities is not a good reason. In this case, listing high school activities will show you are on a downward trend at a very early age!

Do not pad your résumé with trivial items; they are easily recognized as padding and they devalue the worth of your other items. For instance, except under the most unusual circumstances, graduate students should not list grants for travel to conferences as honors, since such travel grants are ubiquitous. Some community groups, especially churches, list all college graduates in their group-specific "honorary." Since everyone who graduates will belong, these are not considered honors.

Dealing with Difficulties

Some job hunters face special problems. This section gives advice for five common problems.

"All My Experience Is in My Family's Business."

In your résumé, simply list the company you worked for. For a reference, instead of a family member, list a supervisor, client, or vendor who can talk about your work. Since the reader may wonder whether "Jim Clarke" is any relation to the owner of "Clarke Construction Company," be ready to answer interview questions about why you're looking at other companies. Prepare an answer that stresses the broader opportunities you seek but doesn't criticize your family or the family business.

"I've Been Out of the Job Market for a While."

You need to prove to a potential employer that you're up-to-date and motivated:

- Create a portfolio of your work to show what you can do for the employer.
- Be active in professional organizations. Attend meetings.
- Attend local networking events.
- Read the journals and trade publications of your field.
- Learn the software that professionals use in your field.
- Be up-to-date with electronic skills such as IMing, text messaging, and computer searching.

"I Want to Change Fields."

Have a good reason for choosing the field in which you're looking for work. "I want a change" or "I need to get out of a bad situation" does not convince an employer that you know what you're doing.

Think about how your experience relates to the job you want. Sam wants a new career as a pharmaceutical sales representative. He has sold woodstoves,

The Cost of a Typo

Typos can cost you a job.

A survey developed by temporary staffing firm OfficeTeam found that 47% of U.S. executives would disqualify a candidate for a single typo, while 84% would remove a candidate from consideration if the résumé contained two errors.

"Candidates who submit application materials with typographical or grammatical errors may be seen as lacking professionalism and attention to detail, and thus spoil their chances for an interview or further consideration," says OfficeTeam's Diane Domeyer.

Domeyer added that after running a computer spell-check, it is still crucial for job candidates to proofread their résumés and also ask friends and family members to do so.

"I've often seen simple errors—such as a job seeker applying for the position of 'office manger'—derail even the most talented applicants," she says.

Source: "Beware the Typo, It Could Cost You a Job," in *Ottawa Business Journal*, http://www.ottawa businessjournal.com/29404529363 8272.php (accessed May 30, 2007).

Should I Create a Video Résumé?

What is a video résumé?

Job hunters post short videos as part of their job applications through services such as YouTube and Google video.

Who uses video résumés?

Anyone can. Currently, most video résumés are produced by applicants interested in entertainment and media, but job seekers in other industries are starting to use video postings.

Are there risks?

Yes, embarrassment. One Yale student applying for an international investment-banking job made national news when his video became a YouTube favorite. He did not get the job.

What are the benefits to employers?

Employers get an opportunity to screen applicants before asking for an interview. This may save an employer from conducting an interview.

If you decide to create a video posting, you may want to consider these tips for your video résumé:

1. Be brief and concise. Your video should be less than three minutes.

2. Be prepared. Avoid reading a script. You should be conversational and natural in your presentation

3. Tailor the video to the specific employer and position.

4. Be careful where you post your video. Remember anyone can watch it.

5. Be professional. Post a video that is clear, audible, and free from background noise.

Adapted from Anjali Athavaley, "Posting Your Résumé on YouTube: Young Job Hunters Try Using Video Clips to Stand Out; The Risk of Humiliation," *Wall Street Journal*, December 6, 2006, D1.

served subpoenas, and worked on an oil rig. A chronological résumé makes his work history look directionless. But a skills résumé could focus on persuasive ability (selling stoves), initiative and persistence (serving subpoenas), and technical knowledge (courses in biology and chemistry).

Learn about the skills needed in the job you want: learn the buzzwords of the industry. Figure 7.5 shows a skills résumé of someone changing fields from animal ecology to technical writing. Her reason for changing could be that she found she enjoyed the writing duties of her jobs more than she enjoyed the ecology field work.

"I Was Fired."

First, deal with the emotional baggage. You need to reduce negative feelings to a manageable level before you're ready to job-hunt.

Second, take responsibility for your role in the termination.

Third, try to learn from the experience. You'll be a much more attractive job candidate if you can show that you've learned from the experience—whether your lesson is improved work habits or that you need to choose a job where you can do work you can point to with pride.

Fourth, suggests Phil Elder, an interviewer for an insurance company, call the person who fired you and say something like this: "Look, I know you weren't pleased with the job I did at _____. I'm applying for a job at _____ now and the personnel director may call you to ask about me. Would you be willing to give me the chance to get this job so that I can try to do things right this time?" All but the hardest of heart, says Elder, will give you one more chance. You won't get a glowing reference, but neither will the statement be so damning that no one is willing to hire you.[5]

Fifth, be honest. Do not lie about your termination at an interview or on a job application. The application usually requires you to sign is statement that the information you are providing is true and that false statements can be grounds for dismissal.

"I Don't Have Any Experience."

If you have a year or more before you job hunt, you can get experience in several ways:

- Take a fast-food job—and keep it. If you do well, you'll be promoted to a supervisor within a year. Use every opportunity to learn about the management and financial aspects of the business.

- Join a volunteer organization that interests you. If you work hard, you'll quickly get an opportunity to do more: manage a budget, write fund-raising materials, and supervise other volunteers.

- Freelance. Design brochures, create Web pages, do tax returns for small businesses. Use your skills—for free, if you have to at first.

- Write. Create a portfolio of ads, instructions, or whatever documents are relevant for the field you want to enter. Ask a professional—an instructor, a local business person, someone from a professional organization—to critique them. Volunteer your services to local fund-raising organizations and small businesses.

If you're on the job market now, think carefully about what you've really done. Complete sentences using the action verbs in Figure 7.4. Think about what you've done in courses, in volunteer work, in unpaid activities. Especially focus on skills in problem solving, critical thinking, teamwork, and communication. Solving a problem for a hypothetical firm in an accounting class, thinking critically about a report problem in business communication, working with a group in a marketing class, and communicating with people at the senior center where you volunteer are experience, even if no one paid you.

If you're not actually looking for a job but just need to create a résumé for this course, ask your instructor whether you may assume that you're a senior and add the things you hope to do between now and your senior year.

Electronic Résumés

According to a study by Taleo Research, 94% of the top 500 US corporations solicit electronic résumés and use software to sort them and make matches with jobs.[6] Pat Kendall, president of the National Résumé Writers' Association, says over 80% of résumés are searched for keywords.[7] Electronic searches mean that you will need electronic résumés in addition to your print résumé.

Creating a Scannable Résumé

Many large companies request scannable résumés. (See Figure 7.7 for an example of a scannable résumé.)

To increase the chances that your résumé is scanned correctly,

- Use a standard typeface such as Helvetica, Futura, Arial, Times New Roman, and Palatino.
- Use 12- or 14-point type.
- Keep line length to a maximum of 65 characters, including spaces.
- Start all lines at the left margin.
- Use a ragged right margin rather than full justification. Scanners can't always handle the extra spaces between words and letters that full justification creates.
- Don't italicize or underline words—even titles of books or newspapers that grammatically require such treatment.
- Don't bold text. You can use full caps for major headings if you wish, but don't overdo them.
- Don't use bullets or tabs. You can replace them with keyboard characters such as asterisks, hyphens, or spaces if you wish.
- If your paper scannable résumé is more than one page, put your name at the top of each page. You should not do this for electronic scannable résumés, which will appear as one continuous document.
- Save your résumé as a Text Only/Plain Text document so it is compatible with all computer systems.
- Print your résumé on a high-quality printer.
- Use standard size 8½ × 11 white or a very light color paper. Use high quality paper.
- Don't fold or staple your pages.
- Mail paper copies flat in a page-sized envelope.

Electronic résumés need to use **keywords**—words and phrases the employer will have the computer seek. Keywords are frequently nouns or noun phrases: database management, product upgrades, cost compilation/analysis. However, they can also be adjectives such as *responsible*. Keywords may include

- Software program names such as Excel.
- Job titles.

Résumé Blasting

Résumé blasting is the process of distributing your résumé to dozens, hundreds, or thousands of résumé sites and databases. Résumé blasting services typically cost between $49 to $199, depending on the type of service and distribution you choose.

ResumeDoctor.com surveyed over 5,000 recruiters and hiring managers about online job postings. Top complaints were

1. Large numbers of irrelevant responses (92%). Most participants indicated that they receive hundreds of responses per online job posting.

2. Résumés not matching the job description (71%).

3. Job candidates "blasting out" résumés (63%).

Adapted from Pat Kendall, "Marketing Your Résumé on the Net," http://www.jumpstartyourjobsearch.com/marketing.html (accessed May 30, 2007); and "The Truth About 'Résumé Blasting,'" in *ResumeDoctor.com Resource Center*, http://resumedoctor.com/ResourceCenter.htm (accessed May 30, 2007).

Figure 7.7 A Scannable Résumé

Abhishek Ankit
aankit@mcc.edu

Use 12 or 14-point type in standard typeface. Here, Times New Roman is used.

Campus Address
1524 E, Main St.
Boone, IA 50036
515-432-1997

Permanent Address
2526 Prairie Lane
Omaha, NE 68235
402-442-7793

Use white space to separate sections.

Seek a position as Sales Advisor with Prime Financial

In keywords, use labels and terms that employers might use in a job listing.

Keywords: sales, advisors, business, communication, entrepreneur, strategy plans

Education
Midwest Community College
A.A. in Financial Management
June 2008
GPA: 3.0/4.0

Don't use columns, bold, or italics. Scanners can't handle these.

Summary of Qualifications
Self-motivated, detail-minded, results-oriented
Consistently successful track record in sales
Effectively developed and operated entrepreneurial business

Sales Experience
Financial Sales Representative,
ABC Inc.
Des Moines, IA
February 2006–present
Establish client base
Develop investment strategy plans for clients
Research and recommend specific investments

Other Experience
Entrepreneur
A-Plus T-Shirt Company
Omaha, NE
September 2004–January 2006
Created a saleable product
Secured financial support
Located a manufacturer
Supervised production

Give as much information as you like. The computer doesn't care how long the document is.

Figure 7.7 *Continued*

Sold T-Shirts to high school students
Realized a substantial profit to pay for college expenses

Don't right-justify margins. Doing so creates extra spaces which confuse scanners.

Cook
Hamburger Shack
Omaha, NE
Summers 2001–2005
Learned scales strategies
Ensured customer satisfaction
Worked cooperatively with a team of 25

Collector and Repair Worker
ACN, Inc.
Omaha, NE
Summer 1996–2001
Collected and counted approximately $10,000 a day
Worked with technicians troubleshooting and repairing coin mechanisms

Computer Skills
Outlook
HTML
Dreamweaver
FrontPage
GoLive

Language
Fluent in Spanish

- Types of degrees.
- College or company names.
- Job-specific skills, buzzwords, and jargon.
- Professional organizations (spell out the name and then follow it with its abbreviation in parentheses to increase the number of matches).
- Honor societies (spell out Greek letters).
- Personality traits, such as creativity, dependability, team player.
- Area codes (for geographic narrowing of searches).

To find the keywords you need in your job search, look through job ads and employer job sites for common terminology. If many ads mention "communication skills," your résumé should too.

Use keywords liberally in your Summary of Qualifications section. However, to get an interview, your résumé will usually need to put keywords into a context proving you have the skills or knowledge. This means that keywords will also have to appear in the rest of your résumé, too. Since you will not know exactly what keywords are desired, it makes sense to use some synonyms and similar terms: *manager* and *management, Excel* and *spreadsheets, creative* and *creativity.*

Many companies give specific directions for how they want their scannable résumés. Check company Web sites and be sure to follow directions exactly.

Digital Dirt

Do you wonder if your employer can find out if you committed a crime, experienced financial difficulties, really attended college, or received a driving ticket? According to a survey of executive recruiters by ExecuNet, an executive job-search and networking organization, 77% of recruiters use search engines to uncover information about job candidates.

Prospective employers can use employment screening services to obtain records from private, state and federal agencies. Employers also check social networking sites such as Facebook, and Google names to find blogs and personal Web sites.

Remember that nothing on the Web is private. Do not post or write anything on the Internet that you do not want a prospective employer to see—starting today. How can you clean up your reputation online?

- Google yourself. If you find something you would rather your prospective employer did not see, contact the Web site and ask for it to be removed.

- Clean up your Facebook or personal Web site. Remove any pictures that may not present a professional image or may be misunderstood by an outsider, especially pictures showing you drinking or dressed inappropriately.

- Cover negative information by increasing your positive online presence, including creating a professional Web page with many links to your accomplishments.

Adapted from Jared Flesher, "How to Clean Up Your Digital Dirt Before It Trashes Your Job Search," in *Wall Street Journal: CareerJournal.com: Job Hunting Advice: Using the Net*, http://www.careerjournal.com/job-hunting/usingnet/20060112-flesher.html?mod=RSS_Career_Journal&cjrss=frontpage (accessed May 30, 2007); and Marcia A. Reed-Woodward, "What You Look Like Online," *Black Enterprise* 37, no. 6 (2007): 56.

Sending Your Résumé by E-mail

You will probably be asked at least some of the time to send your scannable résumé by e-mail. Here are some basic guidelines of e-mail job-hunting etiquette:

- Don't use your current employer's e-mail system for your job search. You'll leave potential employers with the impression that you spend company time on writing résumés and other nonwork-related activities.

- Set up a free, Internet-based e-mail account using services such as Hotmail or Yahoo! to manage correspondence related to your job hunt.

- Avoid using silly or cryptic e-mail addresses. Instead of bubbles@aol.com, opt for something business like: yourname@yahoo.com.

- Write a simple subject line that makes a good first impression: Résumé—Kate Sanchez. A good subject line will improve the chances that your résumé is actually read, since e-mail from unknown senders is often deleted without being opened. If you are responding to an ad, use the job title or job code listed.

- Send only one résumé, even if the firm has more than one position for which you qualify. Most recruiters have negative reactions to multiple résumés.

- Experts differ on whether candidates should phone to follow up. Phoning once to be sure your résumé arrived is probably fine.

It's important to heed the specific directions of employers that you are e-mailing. Many do not want attachments because of viruses. While a few may want a Microsoft Word or PDF attachment of your résumé, others may specify that you paste your scannable résumé directly into the body of your e-mail message. Name the document appropriately: Smith Robyn Résumé. Never name it Résumé.doc; you do not want it to get lost in a long directory of documents.

Include a brief cover letter in your message. In it, mention the types of files you've included. (See Figure 8.9. ➡)

Before sending your résumé into cyberspace, test to see how it will look when it comes out on the other end. E-mail it to yourself and a friend, then critique and fix it.

Posting Your Résumé on the Web

You will probably want to post your résumé online. Be selective when you do: stick with well-known sites for safety reasons. Choose one or two of the large popular sites such as Monster or CareerBuilder. Also choose one or two smaller sites, preferably ones specific to your desired occupation or location. A well-chosen niche site can show employers that you know your field. Do not succumb to **résumé blasting**—posting your résumé widely on the Web. Many employers consider such blasting to be akin to spam and they respond negatively to job candidates who do it.

If the Web sites you choose have you place your information into their résumé form, cut and paste from your scannable résumé to avoid typos. Do not use résumé templates unless you are asked to do so; they will rarely present you as well as the layout you have designed for yourself.

For safety reasons, use your e-mail address as contact information instead of your address and phone number. Make sure your e-mail address looks professional; you should not be HotLips@Yahoo.com. To foil identity thieves, some Web consultants also recommend that you remove all dates from your résumé, and that you replace employer names with generic descriptions (statewide information technology company). Identity thieves can take information directly from online résumés, or they can call employers and, claiming to be conducting background checks, get additional information. They then use the information to apply for credit cards and loans in the job seeker's name.[8]

Since many databases sort résumés by submission date, renew your résumé by making small changes to it at least every two weeks. If you don't get any response to your résumé after a month or two, post it on a different site.

When you have your new job, remove your résumé from all sites. Your new employer will probably take a dim view of finding your résumé on job sites. In fact, new employees have been fired for such lapses. With all the private e-mail accounts available, it is virtually impossible to block your online résumé from people at your current place of employment.

If you post your résumé on your personal Web site, be sure that all the links go to professional-looking pages, such as documents you have created. Now is not the time to link to pictures of you partying. Also, make sure the first screen includes a current job objective and Summary of Qualifications. One study found that résumés on personal Web sites were particularly useful for self-employed workers, for whom they attracted clients.[9]

A Caution about Blogs and Social Networking Sites

Many employers routinely Google job candidates, and many report they are totally turned off by what they find—especially on personal blogs and Web pages and social networking sites such as Facebook and MySpace. If you have a personal blog, Web page, or other electronic presence, check sites carefully before you go on the job market.

- Remove any unprofessional material such as pictures of you at your computer with a beer in your hand or descriptions of your last party.
- Remove negative comments about current or past employers and teachers. People who spread dirt in one context will probably do so in others, and no one wants to hire such people.
- Remove any personal information that will embarrass you on the job. If you blog about romance novels, but don't want to be teased about your choice in literature on your new job, make ruthless cuts on your blog.
- Check your blog for writing aptitude. Many employers will consider your blog an extended writing sample. If yours is full of grammatical and spelling errors, obviously you are not a good writer.

Even if you take your blog off-line while you are job searching, employers may still find it in cached data on search engines. The best advice is to plan ahead and post nothing unprofessional on the Web.

Honesty

Be absolutely honest on your résumé—and in the rest of your job search. Just ask Marilee Jones, former Dean of Admissions at Massachusetts Institute of Technology (MIT). In 1979, when she applied for an admissions job at MIT, her résumé listed bachelor's and master's degrees from Rensselaer Polytechnic Institute. In reality, she attended there only one year as a part-time student. By 1997, when she was promoted to the deanship, she did not

Beware of Spam Filters

Employers are using filters to keep out spam and damaging computer viruses. Unfortunately, legitimate e-mails, including résumés, are also getting blocked. Applicants who send résumés with an e-mail may be rejected by spam filters for various reasons such as "foul" language (B.S.) or over-used phrases (*responsible for* or *duties included*).

What can you do to avoid spam filters?

- Avoid acronyms or titles that may be considered "foul" language.
- Watch overusing words or phrases.
- Avoid words like *free, extend, unbelievable, opportunity, trial, mortgage*.
- Avoid using colored backgrounds.
- Be careful of using all capitals or exclamation points in subject lines.

What preventative steps can you take to avoid being caught by spam filters?

- Set your personal spam filter to high; then send your résumé to your own e-mail account
- Send your résumé to http://www.lyris.com/resources/contentchecker/. The Lyris content checker will let you know if your résumé can avoid a spam filter.

Adapted from "Good Grief What Next—Spam-Friendly Résumés!" in *Gayle's SoapBox (The Official Top Margin Blog)*, http://www.topmargin.blogspot.com/2006/08/good-grief-what-next-spam-friendly.html (accessed May 30, 2007); and Kris Maher, "Don't Let Spam Filters Snatch Your Résumé," in *Wall Street Journal: CollegeJournal: Job Hunting: Résumé Advice*, http://www.collegejournal.com/jobhunting/resumeadvice/20040426-maher.html (accessed May 30, 2007).

have the courage to correct her résumé. In April 2007, she was forced to resign, even though she was a nationally recognized leader in admissions, after an anonymous tip.[10]

According to the Society for Human Resource Management, 96% of all businesses now conduct some kind of background check on job applicants.[11] Even graduate schools, particularly business schools, are checking applicants.[12]

You can omit some material on your résumé, because obviously you cannot include everything about your life to date. For instance, it's still ethical to omit a low GPA, although most employers will assume it is very low indeed to be omitted. But what you do include must be absolutely honest. More and more employers are performing background checks or paying consulting companies to do them.

Some of the most frequent inaccuracies on résumés are inflated job titles and incorrect dates of employment. While these data are easy to fudge, they are also easy to catch in background checks. It is also possible that some of these particular inaccuracies come from careless records kept by job candidates. Do you remember the exact job title of that first job you held as a sophomore in high school? Keep careful records of your employment history!

Other areas where résumés are commonly inaccurate are

- Degrees: many people conveniently forget they were a few hours short of a degree.
- GPAs: inflating one's grade point seems to be a big temptation.
- Honors: people list memberships in fake honoraries, or fake memberships in real honoraries.
- Salary increases.
- Fake addresses: people create these to have the "local" advantage.
- Fake contact information: this information frequently leads to family members or friends who will give fake referrals.
- Technical abilities.
- Language proficiency.

All dishonesty on a résumé is dangerous, keeping you from being hired if discovered early, and causing you to be fired if discovered later. However, the last two bullets listed above are particular dangerous because your chances are good of being asked at an interview to demonstrate your listed proficiencies.

Summary of Key Points

- Informal preparation for job hunting should start soon after you arrive on campus. Formal preparation for job hunting should begin a full year before you begin interviewing. The year you interview, register with your placement office early.
- Employers skim résumés to decide whom to interview. Employers assume that the letter and résumé represent your best work. Interviewers normally reread the résumé before the interview. After the search committee has chosen an applicant, it submits the résumé to people in the organization who must approve the appointment.
- A résumé must fill at least one page. Use two pages if you have extensive activities and experience.
- Emphasize information that is relevant to the job you want, is recent (last three years), and shows your superiority to other applicants.

- To emphasize key points, put them in headings, list them vertically, and provide details.
- Résumés use sentence fragments punctuated like complete sentences. Items in the résumé must be concise and parallel. Verbs and gerunds create a dynamic image of you.
- A **chronological résumé** summarizes what you did in a time line (starting with the most recent events, and going backward in **reverse chronology**). It emphasizes degrees, job titles, and dates. Use a chronological résumé when
  - Your education and experience are a logical preparation for the position for which you're applying.
  - You have impressive job titles, offices, or honors.
- A **skills résumé** emphasizes the skills you've used, rather than the job in which or the date when you used them. Use a skills résumé when
  - Your education and experience are not the usual route to the position for which you're applying.
  - You're changing fields.
  - You want to combine experience from paid jobs, activities or volunteer work, and courses to show the extent of your experience in administration, finance, speaking, etc.
  - Your recent work history may create the wrong impression (e.g., it has gaps, shows a demotion, shows job-hopping, etc.).
- Résumés contain the applicant's contact information, education, and experience. Career objectives, summary of qualifications, honors and awards, other skills, activities, and a portfolio reference may also be included.
- To create a scannable résumé, create a "plain vanilla" text; use keywords.
- Many résumés are now sent by e-mail and are posted on the Web.
- Remove any unprofessional material from your personal Web page, blog, and social networking sites.
- Always be completely honest in your résumé —and job search.

CHAPTER 7   Exercises and Problems

7.1   Reviewing the Chapter

1. What should you do soon after starting college to prepare for your job search? (LO 1)
2. What should you do a full year before your job search? (LO 1)
3. How can you use writing components such as emphasis and details to help set yourself apart from other candidates? (LO 2)
4. What are factors you should consider when preparing your contact information? (LO 2)
5. Why are career objectives hard to write? (LO 2)
6. What are keywords? How do you use them in your summary of qualifications? In electronic résumés? (LO 2)
7. What kinds of details make your experience look most attractive to potential employers? (LO 2)
8. How can activities help make you look attractive to potential employers? (LO 2)
9. What can you do to help get the best references possible? (LO 2)
10. Pick one of the common problems job hunters may face and explain how you would deal with it if it happened to you during your career. (LO 3)
11. How does a scannable résumé differ from your paper résumé? (LO 4)
12. What are some basic guidelines of e-mail job-hunting etiquette? (LO 4)

13. What safety precautions do you need to take when you post your résumé online? (LO 4)
14. What roles are blogs and Facebook pages playing in the job search? (LO 4)
15. Why is it more important now than ever before to be completely honest on your résumé? (LO 5)

7.2   Reviewing Grammar

Most résumés use lists, and items in lists need to have parallel structure. Polish your knowledge of parallel structure by revising the sentences in Exercise B.7, Appendix B.

7.3   Analyzing Your Accomplishments

List the 10 accomplishments that give you the most personal satisfaction. These could be things that other people wouldn't notice. They can be things you've done recently or things you did years ago.

Answer the following questions for each accomplishment:
1. What skills or knowledge did you use?
2. What personal traits did you exhibit?
3. What about this accomplishment makes it personally satisfying to you?

As your instructor directs,

a. Share your answers with a small group of other students.
b. Summarize your answers in a memo to your instructor.
c. Present your answers orally to the class.

7.4   Remembering What You've Done

Use the following list to jog your memory about what you've done. For each, give three or four details as well as a general statement.

Describe a time when you
1. Used facts and figures to gain agreement on an important point.
2. Identified a problem that a group or organization faced and developed a plan for solving the problem.
3. Made a presentation or a speech to a group.
4. Won the goodwill of people whose continued support was necessary for the success of some long-term project or activity.
5. Interested other people in something that was important to you and persuaded them to take the actions you wanted.
6. Helped a group deal constructively with conflict.
7. Demonstrated creativity.
8. Took a project from start to finish.
9. Created an opportunity for yourself in a job or volunteer position.
10. Used good judgment and logic in solving a problem.

As your instructor directs,

a. Identify which job(s) each detail is relevant for.
b. Identify which details would work well on a résumé.
c. Identify which details, further developed, would work well in a job letter.

7.5   Developing Action Statements

Use 10 of the verbs from Figure 7.4 to write action statements describing what you've done in paid or volunteer work, in classes, in extracurricular activities, or in community service.

7.6   Changing Verbs to Nouns

Revise the action statements you created for Problem 7.5, changing the verbs to nouns so that you could use the same information in a scannable résumé.

7.7   Evaluating Career Objective Statements

None of the following career objective statements is effective. What is wrong with each statement as it stands? Which statements could be revised to be satisfactory? Which should be dropped?

1. To use my acquired knowledge of accounting to eventually own my own business.

2. A progressively responsible position as a MARKETING MANAGER where education and ability would have valuable application and lead to advancement.

3. To work with people responsibly and creatively, helping them develop personal and professional skills.

4. A position in international marketing which makes use of my specialization in marketing and my knowledge of foreign markets.

5. To bring Faith, Hope, and Charity to the American workplace.

6. To succeed in sales.

7. To design and maintain Web pages.

7.8   Deciding How Much Detail to Use

In each of the following situations, how detailed should the applicant be? Why?

1. Ron Oliver has been steadily employed for the last six years while getting his college degree, but the jobs have been low-level ones, whose prime benefit was that they paid well and fit around his class schedule.

2. Adrienne Barcus was an assistant department manager at a clothing boutique. As assistant manager, she was authorized to approve checks in the absence of the manager. Her other duties were ringing up sales, cleaning the area, and helping mark items for sales.

3. Lois Heilman has been a clerk-typist in the Alumni Office. As part of her job, she developed a schedule for mailings to alumni, set up a merge system, and wrote two of the letters that go out to alumni. The merge system she set up has cut in half the time needed to produce letters.

4. As a co-op student, Stanley Greene spends every other term in a paid job. He now has six semesters of job experience in television broadcasting. During his last co-op he was the assistant producer for a daily "morning magazine" show.

7.9   Evaluating Web Résumés

Evaluate 10 résumés you find on the Web. Many schools of business have places where students can post résumés online. You may find other résumés on job boards (see the list in Figure 7.1).

As your instructor directs,

a. Share your results with a small group of students.

b. Write an e-mail message analyzing what works and what doesn't. Provide URLs or links to the pages you discuss.

c. Write a memo analyzing what works and what doesn't. Attach printouts of each page you discuss.

d. Join with a small group of students to analyze the pages.

e. Make a short oral presentation to the class discussing the best (or worst) page you found.

7.10   Writing Job Search Goals

Write a list of goals and tasks you need to accomplish for a successful job search. Which ones are crucial? What steps do you need to start taking now to accomplish these goals and tasks? Make a tentative time line for the steps.

7.11   Writing a Job Description

Write a job description for your "dream position." Include the following:

• Position title

• Position description including tasks, special requirements

• Location

• Work hours

• Working conditions (for example, office space, scheduling, amount of supervision)

• Company culture

- Pay
- Experience and education requirements
- Personal competencies (for example, ability to communicate, work in teams, problem solve, etc.).

- Amount of travel
- Social, political, and ethical issues that may be involved

In small groups, share your descriptions. Did you get some ideas from the dream jobs of other students?

7.12   Creating a Web or Paper Portfolio

Create a Web or paper portfolio highlighting your professional and academic accomplishments. Include course projects, workplace samples, and other documents that support your professional accomplishments and goals.

7.13   Writing a Paper Résumé

Write a résumé on paper that you could mail to an employer or hand to an interviewer at an interview.

As your instructor directs,

a. Write a résumé for the field in which you hope to find a job.

b. Write two different résumés for two different job paths you are interested in pursuing. Write a memo to your instructor explaining the differences.

c. Adapt your résumé to a specific company you hope to work for. Write a memo to your instructor explaining the specific adaptations you make and why.

d. Write a résumé for the dream job you developed in Exercise 7.11.

7.14   Writing a Scannable Résumé

Take a résumé from problem 7.13 and create a scannable version of it.

7.15   Critiquing Your Résumé, I

Answer the following overview questions for your résumé:

1. Exactly what position are you applying for? How did you choose the position?
2. What are your concerns with applying for this position?
3. What could the concerns of your audience be with your application? How did you try to address these concerns?
4. How do you think the audience will perceive your résumé? Explain.
5. Does your résumé target your employer and position specifically?

Answer the following questions on your design choices:

1. Does the page look balanced?
2. Does the résumé look original or based on a template?
3. Does the length of your résumé fit your situation and position?
4. Does your résumé include clear headings, bullets, and white space?
5. Do you use fonts appropriate for the career level and industry?
6. Do you use consistent font sizes and spacing throughout the document?

7. Does the design reflect your personality and your career ambitions?

Answer the following questions on the content of your résumé.

1. Are the résumé sections clearly, correctly, and consistently labeled?
2. Does the order of the headings highlight your strongest qualifications?
3. Is the work history listed from most recent to past positions?
4. Do you omit high school information? If not, explain your choice.
5. Do you provide details for your best qualifications?
6. Do you use numbers to support your accomplishments?
7. Is the information provided relevant to the position?
8. Does the information support your claim that you are qualified and the best person for this position?
9. Does the information flow logically and easily?
10. Do you avoid grammar, punctuation, and spelling errors?

Variation: Review a class member's résumé using the same questions.

7.16   Critiquing Your Résumé, II

Rate your résumé using the résumé checklist in the page 228 sidebar. Write a one-page memo to your instructor stating how you believe your résumé rates. Explain and support your position.

7.17   Mosaic Case

At their weekly Wednesday staff meeting, Sarah said to Yvonne, "Trey needs help with his job. He's a great worker, but the Web site business is skyrocketing, and he can't seem to keep up. I've been trying to help him out when my load is a little lighter, but it's not enough. Could we hire someone else for the same position Trey holds?"

"I don't think that would be financially possible right now," replied Yvonne. "Upper management will never accept the expense of another full-time position."

Demetri chimed in, "How about if we bring on an intern? We wouldn't have to ask management to support a full-time paid position with benefits. If we still like the intern after a trial period, we may be able to hire them full-time. Also, since business for the online sales is continually growing, we may have a better case to convince management to front the costs a few months from now. As an added benefit, we'll also have a candidate who already knows the job and what we're all about here at Mosaic."

Both Yvonne and Sarah were thrilled with Demetri's idea. "I'm sure I can convince upper management to give some funding for an internship. Great idea!" stated Yvonne. Then she turned to Sarah and said, "By our staff meeting next week, I want to see a job ad description for the position."

Take on the role of Sarah and construct the job advertisement for next week's staff meeting. Research Web sites, like www.monster.com or www.careerbuilder.com, to learn about components of an effective job advertisement. Determine how the material you put into a job advertisement will directly relate to the types of people who apply. Remember that Sarah needs a candidate who will have great communication skills, is detail-oriented, has the ability to work well in teams, and can meet deadlines. In addition, try to capture Mosaic's organizational setting from the details in Chapters 1–6.

Job Application Letters

Learning Objectives

After studying this chapter, you will know how to:

1 Find the information you need to write a good job letter to a specific employer.

2 Write a job letter that makes you look attractive to employers.

Targeting Is a Two-Way Street

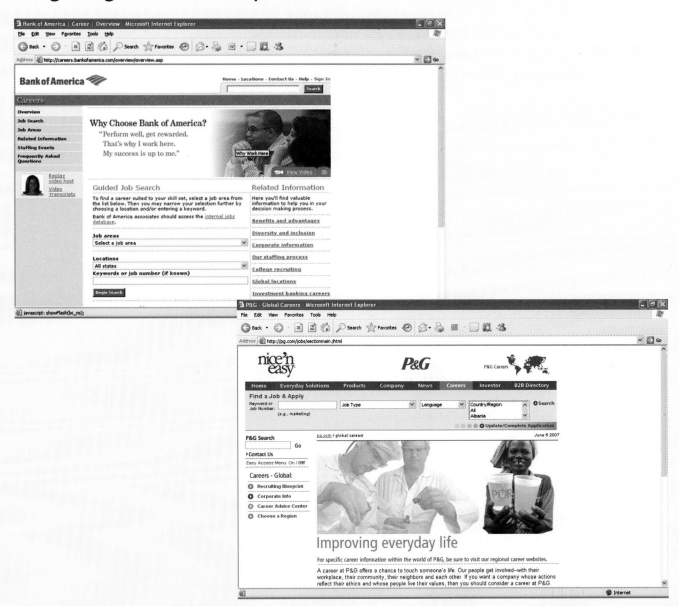

Employers are now targeting and using you-attitude when attracting new applicants. For example, Bank of America's Web site greets you with a representative who guides you through the application process. Procter & Gamble's site gives you career advice through free online classes to help you successfully apply for a position.

Which online career page grabs your attention more?

What topics could these employers add to assist you further?

Visit other employer Web sites.

Do they effectively target applicants?

How can they improve on appealing to prospective employees?

How can you target these employers?

How can you successfully target an employer in your job hunt documents?

Sources: Bank of America. "Why Choose Bank of America?" in *Bank of America Careers*, http://careers.bankofamerica.com/overview/overview.asp.
Procter & Gamble. "Find a Job & Apply," in *P&G Careers*, http://pg.com/jobs/sectionmain.jhtml.

The purpose of a job application letter is to get an interview. If you get a job through interviews arranged by your campus placement office or through contacts, you may not need to write a letter. Similarly, if you apply electronically through a company's Web site, a letter may not be part of the materials you submit. However, if you want to work for an organization that isn't interviewing on campus, or later when you change jobs, you may need a letter. Writing a letter is also a good preparation for a job interview, since the letter is your first step in showing a specific company what you can do for it.

Job letters are frequently seen as evidence of your written communication skills, so you want to do your best work in them. Flaws in your letter may well be seen as predicting shoddy job performance in the future.

How Job Letters Differ from Résumés

The job application letter accompanies your résumé and serves as its cover letter. Make the most of your letter; it is your chance to showcase the features that set you apart from the crowd. Here you bring to life the facts presented in your vita; here you can show some personality (don't overdo it). The cover letter is your opportunity to "sell" yourself into an interview.

Although résumés and job letters overlap somewhat, they differ in various ways:

- A résumé is adapted to a position. The letter is adapted to the needs of a particular organization.
- The résumé summarizes all your qualifications. The letter expands your best qualifications to show how you can help the organization meet its

needs, how you differ from other applicants, and that you have some knowledge of the organization.

- The résumé avoids controversial material. The job letter can explain in a positive way situations such as career changes or gaps in employment history.

- The résumé uses short, parallel phrases (← p. 124) and sentence fragments. The letter uses complete sentences in well-written paragraphs.

How to Find Out about Employers and Jobs

To adapt your letter to a specific organization, you need information both about the employer and about the job itself. You'll need to know

- **The name and address of the person who should receive the letter.** To get this information, check the ad, call the organization, check its Web site, or check with your job search contacts. An advantage of calling is that you can find out what courtesy title (← p. 90) a woman prefers and get current information.

- **What the organization does, and some facts about it.** Knowing the organization's larger goals enables you to show how your specific work will help the company meet its goals. Useful facts can include market share, new products or promotions, the kind of computer or manufacturing equipment it uses, plans for growth or downsizing, competitive position, challenges the organization faces, the corporate culture (← p. 46), and so forth.

  The Web sites listed in Figure 8.1 provide a wide range of information. More specific information about companies can be found on their Web sites. To get specific financial data (and to see how the organization presents itself to the public), get the company's annual report from your library, the Web, or the company itself. (Note: Only companies whose stock is publicly traded are required to issue annual reports. In this day of mergers and buyouts, many companies are owned by other companies. The parent company may be the only one to issue an annual report.) Recruiting notebooks at your campus placement office may provide information about training programs and career paths for new hires. To learn about new products, plans for growth, or solutions to industry challenges, read business newspapers such as the *Wall Street Journal*, business magazines such as *Fortune, BusinessWeek*, or *Forbes*, and trade journals.

Reach for Your Dream Job

"Can we truly love what we do and get paid for it?

"Recently, CareerBuilder.com and Disney Parks took a look at the idea of dream jobs. . . . According to their survey of over 6,000 workers nationwide, a staggering 84 percent of people say they aren't in their dream job. What's the biggest thing missing? Fun.

"'What defines a dream job is surprisingly reminiscent of childhood wishes for many workers. Workers said they want to enjoy their work experience, apply their talents and feel like they're making an impact,' says Richard Castellini, senior career advisor for CareerBuilder.com. 'Having fun at work was the most important attribute of a dream job for 39 percent of workers, which heavily outweighed the 12 percent who said salary was most important.' "

Quoted from Kate Lorenz. "Go Get your Dream Job," in *WomensWallStreet: Topics: Career*, http://www.womenswallstreet .com/topics/topic.aspx?aid=1177 (accessed May 30, 2007).

Figure 8.1   Web Sources for Facts about Companies

Company Facts	
http://www.jobsearch.org/	http://www.vault.com/
http://careernet.4jobs.com/	http://www.stockmarketyellowpages.com/
http://www.employmentspot.com/	http://www.prars.com/
http://www.financialjobs.com/	http://money.cnn.com/
http://www.job-hunt.org/	http://www.inc.com/resources/ inc500/2006/
http://www.jobweb.com/	http://www.bbb.org/
http://www.wetfeet.com/	http://allstocks.com/links/
http://www.forbes.com/	http://www.nypl.org/research/sibl/com pany/c2index.htm
http://www.talentzoo.com/website/ content/	http://www.lib.berkeley.edu/BUSI/
http://efinancialcareers.com/	**Salary Calculators**
http://www.irin.com/cgi-bin/main.cgi	http://www.careerjournal.com/
http://metamoney.com/w100/	http://salaryexpert.com/
http://www.hoovers.com/free/	http://www.indeed.com/salary
http://www.corporateinformation.com/	http://www.payscale.com/

So Many Job Sites, So Little Time

To use the Internet as the ultimate job-seeking tool, understand the kinds of employment sites it offers.

- Help wanted sites are developed and maintained by employers and act as electronic versions of postings in store windows. They are informative and provide detailed job descriptions.

- Classified sites are online versions of local newspapers' want ads.

- Résumé sites showcase applicants' skills and experience rather than employer profiles.

- Industry sites locate jobs in a specific industry. Most feature searchable lists as well as profiles of major industry employers and employment statistics.

- Career sites are operated by independent companies and can advertise hundreds of thousands of job listings in their searchable databases.

Adapted from Carolyn Gosselin, "Targeting a New Job: Where to Go in the Sea of Job Sites," *Chicago Tribune*, June 1, 2000.

- **What the job itself involves.** Campus placement offices and Web listings often have fuller job descriptions than appear in ads. Talk to friends who have graduated recently to learn what their jobs involve. Conduct information interviews to learn more about opportunities that interest you.

Using the Internet

As Figure 8.2 shows, many job listings are on the Web. Even better, the Web can be a fast way to learn about the company you hope to join. Check professional listservs and electronic bulletin boards. Employers sometimes post specialized jobs on them, and they're always a good way to get information about the industry you hope to enter.

Taking an Internship

Internships are becoming increasingly important as ways to find out about professions, employers, and jobs. Many companies use their internships to find full-time employees. Even if your internship does not lead to a full-time job, it can still give you valuable insight into the profession, as well as contacts you can use in your job search. An increasingly important side benefit is the work you do in your internship, which can become some of the best items in your professional portfolio.

Tapping into the Hidden Job Market

Many jobs are never advertised—and the number rises the higher on the job ladder you go. In fact, some authorities put the percentage of jobs that are not advertised as high as 80%.[1] Many new jobs come not from responding to an ad but from networking with personal contacts. Some of these jobs are created especially for a specific person. These unadvertised jobs are called the **hidden job market.** Information and referral interviews, organized methods of networking, offer the most systematic ways to tap into these jobs.

Information Interviews

In an **information interview** you talk to someone who works in the area you hope to enter to find out what the day-to-day work involves and how you can best prepare to enter that field. An information interview can let you know whether or not you'd like the job, give you specific information that you can use to present yourself effectively in your résumé and application letter, and create a good image of you in the mind of the interviewer. If you present yourself positively, the interviewer may remember you when openings arise.

Figure 8.2   Job Listings on the Web

Job listings	
America's Job Bank www.jobsearch.org	**Monster.com** www.monster.com
CareerBuilder.com www.careerbuilder.com	**MonsterTrak** www.monstertrak.monster.com
Careers.org www.careers.org	**Yahoo.com** www.hotjobs.yahoo.com
EmploymentGuide.com www.employmentguide.com	Job listings from the *Chicago Tribune, Detroit News, Los Angeles Times, Miami Herald, Philadelphia Inquirer, San Jose Mercury News,* and other city newspaper's Web sites.
Federal Jobs Career Central www.fedjobs.com	

Figure 8.3 E-mail Requesting an Information Interview

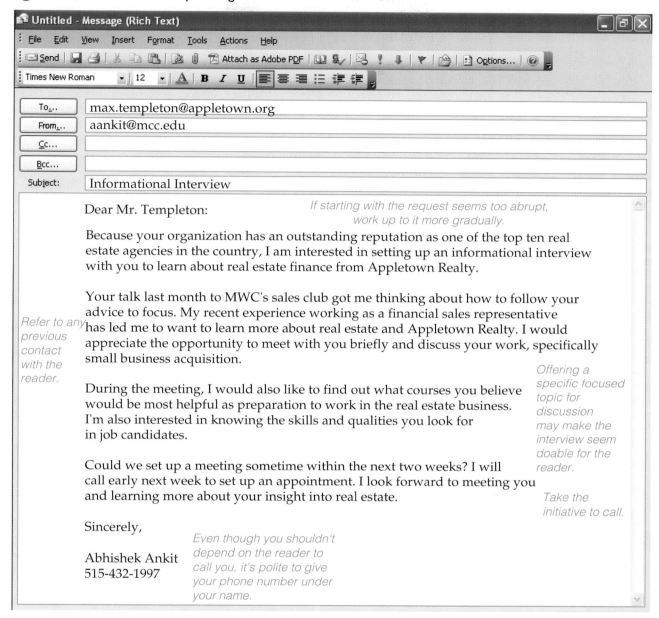

In an information interview, you might ask the following questions:

- How did you get started in this field?
- What have you been working on today?
- How do you spend your typical day?
- Have your duties changed a lot since you first started working here?
- What do you like best about your job? What do you like least?
- What do you think the future holds for this kind of work?
- What courses, activities, or jobs would you recommend as preparation for this kind of work?

To set up an information interview, you can phone or write an e-mail like the one in Figure 8.3. If you do e-mail, phone the following week to set up a specific time.

Networking Can Work

[One student describes her positive networking experience:]

"A student interested in attending law school was walking by the Justice Department building in Oakland. Curious, she walked into the building and struck up a conversation with a woman. They discussed the work of the Justice Department and issues the department was confronting. After a few minutes, the woman told the student, 'I'm the Director of the Office of Special Counsel. I'm very impressed that a Cal student would come in and ask questions as you've done. Send me a letter and résumé and we'll see what we can do to get you an internship in my department.' The student later told her career counselor, 'I was scared to death to do this kind of thing, but would not hesitate to do it again. As long as you've done a little homework on the subject and don't have your head in the clouds, it really works out.' "

Quoted from Berkeley Career Center, "The Job & Internship Search: Networking Success Story," in *Job Search Guide: 2006–2007,* University of California Berkeley, https://career.berkeley.edu/Guide/JobInternSearchSection.pdf (accessed May 30, 2007).

Referral interviews

Referral interviews are interviews you schedule to learn about current job opportunities in your field. Sometimes an interview that starts out as an information interview turns into a referral interview.

A referral interview should give you information about the opportunities currently available in the area you're interested in, refer you to other people who can tell you about job opportunities, and enable the interviewer to see that you could make a contribution to his or her organization. Therefore, the goal of a referral interview is to put you face-to-face with someone who has the power to hire you: the president of a small company, the division vice president or branch manager of a big company, the director of the local office of a state or federal agency.

Start by scheduling interviews with people you know who may know something about that field—professors, co-workers, neighbors, friends, former classmates. Use your alumni Web site to get the names and phone numbers of alumni who now work where you would like to work. Your purpose in talking to them is (ostensibly) to get advice about improving your résumé and about general job-hunting strategy and (really) to get referrals to other people. In fact, go into the interview with the names of people you'd like to talk to. If the interviewer doesn't suggest anyone, say, "Do you think it would be a good idea for me to talk to _____?"

Then, armed with a referral from someone you know, you call Mr. or Ms. Big and say, "So-and-so suggested I talk with you about job-hunting strategy." If the person says, "We aren't hiring," you say, "Oh, I'm not asking *you* for a job. I'd just like some advice from a knowledgeable person about the opportunities in banking [or desktop publishing, or whatever] in this city." If this person doesn't have the power to create a position, you seek more referrals at the end of *this* interview. (You can also polish your résumé, if you get good suggestions.)

Even when you talk to the person who could create a job for you, you *do not ask for a job.* But to give you advice about your résumé, the person has to look at it. When a powerful person focuses on your skills, he or she will naturally think about the problems and needs in that organization. When there's a match between what you can do and what the organization needs, that person has the power to create a position for you.

Some business people are cynical about information and referral interviewing; they know the real purpose of such interviews, and they resent the time needed. However, you can win over even the cynics by preparing as carefully for these interviews as you would for an interview when you know the organization is hiring. Think in advance of good questions; know something about the general field or industry; try to learn at least a little bit about the specific company.

Always follow up information and referral interviews with personal thank-you letters. Use specifics to show that you paid attention during the interview, and enclose a copy of your revised résumé.

Content and Organization for Job Application Letters

In your letter, focus on

- Your qualifications to meet major requirements of the job.
- Points that separate you from other applicants.
- Points that show your knowledge of the organization.
- Qualities that every employer is likely to value: the ability to write and speak effectively, to solve problems, to work well with people.

Figure 8.4   How to Organize a Solicited Job Application Letter

1. State that you're applying for the job (phrase the job title as your source phrased it). Tell where you learned about the job (ad, referral, etc.). Include any reference number mentioned in the ad. Briefly show that you have the major qualifications required by the ad: a college degree, professional certification, job experience, etc. Summarize your other qualifications briefly in the same order in which you plan to discuss them in the letter.

2. Develop your major qualifications in detail. Be specific about what you've done; relate your achievements to the work you'd be doing in this new job. Remember that readers know only what you tell them.

3. Develop your other qualifications, even if the ad doesn't ask for them. (If the ad asks for a lot of qualifications, pick the most important three or four.) Show what separates you from the other applicants who will also answer the ad. Demonstrate your knowledge of the organization.

4. Ask for an interview; tell when you'll be available to be interviewed and to begin work. End on a positive, forward-looking note.

Two different hiring situations call for two different kinds of application letters. Write a **solicited letter** when you know that the company is hiring: you've seen an ad, you've been advised to apply by a professor or friend, you've read in a trade publication that the company is expanding. This situation is similar to a direct request in persuasion (➠ p. 376): you can indicate immediately that you are applying for the position. Sometimes, however, the advertised positions may not be what you want, or you may want to work for an organization that has not announced openings in your area. Then you write a **prospecting letter.** (The metaphor is drawn from prospecting for gold.) The prospecting letter is like a problem-solving persuasive message (➠ p. 378).

Prospecting letters help you tap into the hidden job market. In some cases, your prospecting letter may arrive at a company that has decided to hire but has not yet announced the job. In other cases, companies create positions to get a good person who is on the market. Even in a hiring freeze, jobs are sometimes created for specific individuals.

In both solicited and prospecting letters you should

- Address the letter to a specific person (a must for a prospecting letter).
- Indicate the specific position for which you're applying.
- Be specific about your qualifications.
- Show what separates you from other applicants.
- Show a knowledge of the company and the position.
- Refer to your résumé (which you would enclose with the letter).
- Ask for an interview.

The following discussion follows the job letter from beginning to end. The two kinds of letters are discussed separately where they differ and together where they are the same. Letters for internships follow the same patterns: use a solicited letter to apply for an internship that has been advertised and a prospecting letter to create an internship with a company that has not announced one.

How to Organize Solicited Letters

When you know the company is hiring, use the pattern of organization in Figure 8.4. A sample solicited letter for a graduating senior is shown in Figure 8.5. A solicited letter following up from a career fair and requesting an internship is shown in Figure 8.8.

http://www.intel.com

Many Web sites give you all the information you need to write a good job letter. Intel's home page has links to jobs, current Intel news, and global responsibility. Follow links on "About Intel" to information on products or health care; that page also links to the annual report. Both the home page and "pressroom" give information about recent achievements. "Investor relations" has financial information.

Figure 8.5   A Solicited Letter from a Graduating Senior

Maria Sanchez

sanchez@unl.edu ▪ 1535 Mission Way ▪ Lincoln, NE 68501 ▪ 402.975.6992

February 5, 2009

Ms. Catherine Thomas
DaVinci Designs
2285 Michigan Avenue
Chicago, IL 67214

*Use the countesy title
the reader prefers*

Dear Ms. Thomas:

*Tell where you learned about the job.
If the job has a reference number, provide it.*

In paragraph 1, show you have the qualifications the ad lists.

I wish to apply for your Architect position announced on DaVinci Designs' Web site (A6782). This spring I will graduate from the University of Nebraska–Lincoln with a BA in Architecture and an emphasis in design. DaVinci's focus on international design and superior level of excellence are particularly attractive to me. My unique mix of architecture internships, senior design project, and international study make me an ideal candidate.

This summary sentence forecasts the structure of the rest of the letter.

Shows enthusiasm for the profession and picks up on the team work emphasis in the job ad.

While I always knew I enjoyed architecture, I realized my love for it the past two summers as I interned at Debalt in Minneapolis and Cutting Edge in Lincoln. Every single day I couldn't wait to go to work. Moreover, I would often be so immersed in a project that I would stay late to finish it. These internships also taught me the value of collaborating with fellow workers. Prior to my summer work, I had no idea just how much collaboration really goes on in an architecture firm. I can bring the lessons I learned about teamwork to DaVinci Design to help create the best projects.

Evidence of communication skills is a plus for almost any job.

Completing the senior design project, a redesign of Lincoln's main street, taught me the patience needed to carry a design through all planning stages. Moreover, the one-hour presentation I gave about my project to the design faculty at Nebraska helped increase my public speaking skills. I was well prepared for the presentation by monthly design critiques in my courses, where I had to present my work and then modify it on the basis of feedback I received. These skills will be beneficial as I interact and explain ideas to clients of DaVinci.

Many college courses provide concrete experiences.

Maria found out about DaVinci's international design emphasis from reading the company Web site.

Studying abroad in Italy honed my understanding of classical architecture. It's one thing to read about architecture in books; it's something entirely different to experience it firsthand. In addition, everywhere I traveled, I was also struck by the stylish women's fashion, which influenced my perception of and sparked creativity for design. Your firm can benefit from this international experience as I contribute ideas while working on international accounts.

Relates what she has done to what she could do for the company.

I would appreciate the opportunity to meet you and discuss the position. I will be in the Chicago area the week of March 13–17 and would be available for an interview. Your company has an excellent reputation for customer satisfaction, and I know that the combination of my experience and motivation to excel will make me an asset to your design department.

Sincerely,

Maria Sanchez

Maria Sanchez

Figure 8.6   How to Organize a Prospecting Letter

1. Catch the reader's interest.
2. Create a bridge between the attention-getter and your qualifications. Focus on what you know and can do. Since the employer is not planning to hire, he or she won't be impressed with the fact that you're graduating. Summarize your qualifications briefly in the same order in which you plan to discuss them in the letter. This summary sentence or paragraph then covers everything you will talk about and serves as an organizing device for your letter.
3. Develop your strong points in detail. Be specific. Relate what you've done in the past to what you could do for this company. Show that you know something about the company. Identify the specific niche you want to fill.
4. Ask for an interview and tell when you'll be available for interviews. (Don't tell when you can begin work.) End on a positive, forward-looking note.

How to Organize Prospecting Letters

When you don't have any evidence that the company is hiring, you cannot use the pattern for solicited letters. Instead, use the pattern of organization in Figure 8.6. A sample prospecting letter for a student desiring to change fields is shown in Figure 8.7.

First Paragraphs of Solicited Letters

When you know that the firm is hiring, announcing that you are applying for a specific position enables the firm to route your letter to the appropriate person, thus speeding consideration of your application. Identify where you learned about the job: "the position of junior accountant announced in Sunday's *Dispatch*," "William Paquette, our placement director, told me that you are looking for. . . ."

Note how the following paragraph picks up several of the characteristics of the ad:

Ad: Business Education Instructor at Shelby Adult Education. Candidate must possess a Bachelor's degree in Business Education. Will be responsible for providing in-house training to business and government leaders. . . . Candidate should have at least one year teaching experience.

Letter: I am applying for your position in Business Education that is posted on your school Web site. In December, I will receive a Bachelor of Science degree from North Carolina A & T University. I have two years' experience teaching word processing and computer accounting courses to adults and have developed leadership skills in the North Carolina National Guard.

Your **summary sentence** or **paragraph** covers everything you will talk about and serves as an organizing device for your letter.

I have a good background in standard accounting principles and procedures and a working knowledge of some of the special accounting practices of the oil industry. This working knowledge is based on practical experience in the oil fields: I have pumped, tailed rods, and worked as a roustabout.

My business experience, familiarity with DeVilbiss equipment, and communication skills qualify me to be an effective part of the sales staff at DeVilbiss.

Let me put my creative eye, artistic ability, and experience to work for McLean Design.

The Value of an Internship

Vault's Internship Survey found that 82% of the responding students said completing an internship was "extremely important" for their careers. In fact, 53% of students were completing two or more internships by the summer after graduation. Students found their internships from college career centers and on-campus recruiting efforts (43%), networking connections (28%), and cold calling (9%). For 64% of the students, internships led to full-time work offers from the companies where they interned.

Internships can be lucrative. According to the survey, 64% of the students were paid. Dollar amounts provided to the students ranged from $10/hr to $2600/week for 10 weeks. Students also mentioned such perks as a company car, free lunches, and tickets to concerts and sporting events.

What steps should you take to start finding your internship?

Adapted from Vault.com, "More Students Interning This Summer, Says New Vault Survey," in *Job Advice: Internships: News & Research*, http://www.vault.com/nr/newsmain.jsp?nr_page=3&ch_id=322&article_id=27063890 (accessed July 4, 2007).

Figure 8.7   A Prospecting Letter from a Career Changer

Sophia Barber
www.ukansas.edu/~Barber1278/home.htm

266 Van Buren Drive
Lawrence, KS 66044
barber@ukansas.edu
785-897-1534 (home)
785-842-4242 (cell)

Sophia uses a "letterhead" that hamonizes with her résumé. (see Figure 7.5)

March2, 2008

Mr. Pete Jenkins
PDF Productions
3232 White Castle Road
Minneapolis, MN 85434

Dear Mr. Jenkins:

In a prospecting letter, open with a sentence which (1) will seem interesting and true to the reader and (2) provides a natural bridge to talking about yourself.

The Wall Street Journal says that PDF Productions is expanding operations into Kansas, Minnesota, and Nebraska. My experience in technical writing, design, and computers would be an asset to your expanding organization.

Shows knowledge of the organization.

Briefly shows a variety of technical writing and computer skills.

While working at a local animal shelter, I used my technical writing skills to create a Web site that allows users to easily access information. To improve the Web site, I conducted usability tests which provided useful feedback that I incorporated to modify the overall design. In addition, I was also responsible for writing and editing the shelter's monthly newsletter, which was distributed to roughly 1,200 "Friends of the Shelter." I have extensive computer and design skills, which I am anxious to put to use for PDF Productions

Relates what she's done to what she could do for this company.

Coursework has also prepared me well for technical writing. I have written technical material on a variety of levels ranging from publicity flyers for the animal shelter to scientific reports for upper-level science courses. My coursework in statistics has shown me how to work with data and present it accurately for various audiences. Because of my scientific background, I also have a strong vocabulary in both life sciences and chemistry. This background will help me get up to speed quickly with clients such as ChemPro and Biostage. My background in science has also taught me just how important specific details can be.

Shows how her coursework is an asset.

Names specific clients, showing more knowledge of company.

In May, I will complete my degree from the University of Kansas and will be most interested in making a significant contribution to PDF Productions. I am available every Monday, Wednesday, and Friday for an interview (785-897-1534). I look forward to talking with you about technical writing I can do for PDF Productions.

Sincerely,

Sophia Barber

Figure 8.8   Letter Following Up from a Career Fair and Requesting an Internship

Abhishek Ankit
aankit@mcc.edu

Campus Address	**Permanent Address**	*Letterhead*
1524 E. Main Street	2526 Prairie Lane	*matches his*
Boone, 1A 50036	Omaha, NE 68235	*résumé.*
515-232-5718	402-442-7793	

January 23, 2008

Mr. Ron Pascel, HR Department
Prime Financial
Prime Park Place
Des Moines, IA 50023

Dear Mr. Pascel:

Uses his contact immediately.

Mary Randi at the Midwest Community College Career Fair suggested I send you my résumé for the Sales Advisor internship. My education combined with my past work experiences makes me a strong candidate for Prime Financial.

Shows he has been getting full value from his schooling.

While working toward my Associate of Arts degree in Financial Management from Midwest Community College, I have learned the value of fiscal responsibility. For example, in my social financial planning course, I developed a strategic plan to eliminate credit card debt for a one-income household with two children. Moreover, in my business communication course, I improved my oral communication ability so that I could effectively communicate my plans to potential clients. This ability will be an asset to Prime Financial as the organization works to maintain the strong relationship with the community and small business owners that Ms. Randi informed me about.

Refers to knowledge gained at career fair.

Paragraphs 2 and 3 show he has skills he can use immediately as an intern.

My financial education, combined with my previous work experiences in sales, will allow me to thoroughly analyze investment opportunities and establish a strong client base for Prime Financial. For example, I started the A-Plus T-Shirt Company that sold graphic T-shirts to high school students; it had a routine client base of over 150 customers. From managing this business, I know what it takes to be reliable and responsive to customer needs. I am looking forward to learning new approaches from Prime Financial's internship, particularly new ways to work with small businesses.

Provide details about his sales experience to interest his reader.

With my education and experience, I can provide the innovative and competitive edge necessary to be part of your team. I would welcome an interview to discuss your internship and the contributions I could make at Prime Financial.

Sincerely,

Abshishek Ankit

Jocks Rock in the Workplace

Some employers are seeking athletes to fill jobs because athletes possess qualities which lead to success in the workplace. For example Gretchen Tonnesen, former flying halfback captain for the Princeton University women's rugby team, now works at JP-Morgan Chase & Co. where she examines technology, media, and telecommunications companies for the investment bank. JPMorgan chose her because of her passionate involvement in sports.

Recruiters and employers recognize that college athletes provide leadership, competitiveness, and a sharp focus on goals. Athletes also understand team responsibility, time management, and dedication. In addition, athletes from top schools typically have the drive and stamina that matches the 80-hour high pressure workweeks found in many Wall Street jobs.

By the way, Tonnesen got her job through the Alumni Athlete Network, founded by a Harvard basketball captain. The carefully selected students in the Network's program have average GPAs of 3.6 and average SAT scores of 1320.

How can you capitalize on your extracurricular activities to help your job search?

Adapted from John DeBruicker, "If You're A Jock, You Rock," *BusinessWeek*, September 18, 2006, 67.

Good word choices can help set your letter apart from the scores or even hundreds of letters the company is likely to get in response to an ad. The following first paragraph of a letter in response to an ad by Allstate Insurance Company shows a knowledge of the firm's advertising slogan and sets itself apart from the dozens of letters that start with "I would like to apply for. . . ."

> The Allstate Insurance Company is famous across the nation for its "Good Hands Policy." I would like to lend a helping hand to clients as a financial analyst for Allstate, as advertised in the *Chicago Tribune*. I have a Masters of Accounting from Iowa State University and I have worked with figures, computers, and people.

Note that the last sentence forecasts the organization of the letter, preparing for paragraphs about the student's academic background and (in this order) experience with "figures, computers, and people."

First Paragraphs of Prospecting Letters

In a prospecting letter, asking for a job in the first paragraph is dangerous: unless the company plans to hire but has not yet announced openings, the reader is likely to throw the letter away. Instead, catch the reader's interest. Then in the second paragraph you can shift the focus to your skills and experience, showing how they can be useful to the employer and specifying the job you are seeking.

Here are some effective first and second paragraphs that provide a transition to the writer's discussion of his or her qualifications:

- First two paragraphs of a letter to the Director of Publications of Standard Oil:

> If scarcity of resources makes us use them more carefully, perhaps it would be a good idea to ration words. If people used them more carefully, internal communications specialists like you would have fewer headaches because communications jobs would be done right the first time.

> I have worked for the last six years improving my communications skills, learning to use words more carefully and effectively. I have taught business communication at a major university, worked for two newspapers, completed a Master's degree in English, and would like to contribute my skills to your internal communications staff.

- First two paragraphs of a letter applying to be a computer programmer for an insurance company:

> As you know, merging a poorly written letter with a database of customers just sends out bad letters more quickly. But you also know how hard it is to find people who can both program computers and write well.

> My education and training have given me this useful combination. I'd like to put my associate's degree in computer technology and my business experience writing to customers to work in State Farm's service approach to insurance.

Bruce Mau Design

Careers

If you are a superior thinker, strategist or designer and are ready to create MASSIVE CHANGE, send us your resumé along with your response to these three questions:

01 In the future, how will we communicate?
02 Will we shift from the service of war to the service of life?
03 How will we eradicate poverty?

jobs@brucemaudesign.com

Take action. Apply now.

Effective letters of application respond directly to the job description. This ad from BruceMauDesign.com makes it clear the firm is seeking good problem solvers with a social conscience. A good response would include evidence of creativity, problem solving, social action, and communication skills.

Notice how the second paragraph provides a transition to a discussion of qualifications.

- Questions work well only if the answers aren't obvious. The computer programmer above should *not* ask this question:

> Do you think that training competent and motivated personnel is a serious concern in the nuclear power industry?

If the reader says *yes,* the question will seem dumb. If the reader says *no,* the student has destroyed his common ground. The computer programmer, however, could pose this question:

> How often to you see a job candidate with both strong programming skills and good communication skills?

This question would give him an easy transition into paragraphs about his programming and communication skills.

Showing a Knowledge of the Position and the Company

If you could substitute another inside address and salutation and send out the letter without any further changes, it isn't specific enough. A job application letter is basically a claim that you could do a job. Use your knowledge of the position and the company to choose relevant evidence from what you've done to support your claims that you could help the company. (See Figures 8.5 and 8.7.)

The following paragraphs show the writer's knowledge of the company.

- A letter to PricewaterhouseCoopers's Minneapolis office uses information the student learned in a referral interview with a partner in an accounting firm. Because the reader will know that Herr Wollner is a partner in the Berlin office, the student does not need to identify him.

> While I was studying in Berlin last spring, I had the opportunity to discuss accounting methods for multinational clients of PricewaterhouseCoopers with Herr Fritz Wollner. We also talked about communication among PricewaterhouseCoopers's international offices.
>
> Herr Wollner mentioned that the increasing flow of accounting information between the European offices—especially those located in Germany, Switzerland, and Austria—and the US offices of PricewaterhouseCoopers makes accurate translations essential. My fluency in German enables me to translate accurately; and my study of communication problems in Speech Communication, Business and Professional Speaking, and Business and Technical Writing will help me see where messages might be misunderstood and choose words which are more likely to communicate clearly.

- A letter to KMPG uses information the student learned in a summer job.

> As an assistant accountant for Pacific Bell during this past summer, I worked with its computerized billing and record-keeping system, BARK. I had the opportunity to help the controller revise portions of the system, particularly the procedures for handling delinquent accounts. When the KMPG audit team reviewed Pacific Bell's transactions completed for July, I had the opportunity to observe your System 2170. Several courses in computer science allow me to appreciate the simplicity of your system and its objective of reducing audit work, time, and costs.

One or two specific details about the company usually are enough to demonstrate your knowledge. Be sure to use the knowledge, not just repeat it. Never present the information as though it will be news to the reader. After all, the reader works for the company and presumably knows much more about it than you do.

Showing What Separates You from Other Applicants

Your knowledge of the company separates you from other applicants. You can also use coursework, an understanding of the field, and experience in jobs and extracurricular events to show that you're unique. Stress your accomplishments, not your job responsibilities. Be specific but concise; usually three to five sentences will enable you to give enough specific supporting details.

This student uses both coursework and summer jobs to set herself apart from other applicants. Her research told her Monsanto had recently adopted new accounting methods for fluctuations in foreign currencies. Therefore, she mentions relevant simulations from her coursework.

> My college courses have taught me the essential accounting skills required to contribute to the growth of Monsanto. In two courses in international accounting, I compiled simulated accounting statements of hypothetical multinational firms in countries experiencing different rates of currency devaluation. Through these classes, I acquired the skills needed to work with the daily fluctuations of exchange rates and at the same time formulate an accurate and favorable representation of Monsanto.
>
> Both my summer jobs and my coursework prepare me to do extensive record keeping as well as numerous internal and external communications. As Office Manager for the steamboat *Julia Belle Swain,* I was in charge of most of the bookkeeping and letter writing for the company. I kept accurate records for each workday, and I often entered

over 100 transactions in a single day. In business and technical writing I learned how to write persuasive letters and memos and how to present extensive data in reports in a simplified style that is clear and easy to understand.

In your résumé, you may list activities, offices, and courses. In your letter, give more detail about what you did and show how those experiences will help you contribute to the employer's organization more quickly.

When you discuss your strengths, don't exaggerate. No employer will believe that a new graduate has a "comprehensive" knowledge of a field. Indeed, most employers believe that six months to a year of on-the-job training is necessary before most new hires are really earning their pay. Specifics about what you've done will make your claims about what you can do more believable and ground them in reality.

The Last Paragraph

In the last paragraph, indicate when you'd be available for an interview. If you're free anytime, you can say so. But it's likely that you have responsibilities in class and work. If you'd have to go out of town, there may be only certain days of the week or certain weeks that you could leave town for several days. Use a sentence that fits your situation.

> I could come to Albany for an interview any Wednesday or Friday.

> I'll be attending the Oregon Forestry Association's November meeting and will be available for interviews then.

> I could come to Memphis for an interview March 17–21.

Should you wait for the employer to call you, or should you call the employer to request an interview? In a solicited letter, it's safe to wait to be contacted: you know the employer wants to hire someone, and if your letter and résumé show that you're one of the top applicants, you'll get an interview. In a prospecting letter, call the employer. Because the employer is not planning to hire, you'll get a higher percentage of interviews if you're assertive.

If you're writing a prospecting letter to a firm that's more than a few hours away by car, say that you'll be in the area the week of such-and-such and could stop by for an interview. Companies pay for follow-up visits, but not for first interviews. A company may be reluctant to ask you to make an expensive trip when it isn't yet sure it wants to hire you.

End the letter on a positive note that suggests you look forward to the interview and that you see yourself as a person who has something to contribute, not as someone who just needs a job.

> I look forward to discussing with you ways in which I could contribute to The Limited's continued growth.

Do not end your letter with a variation of the tired cliché "Please do not hesitate to contact me." Why do you think they would hesitate?

Oh yes, one more thing. Don't forget to sign your letter—with blue or black ink—legibly.

Getting a Job with an *Inc.* 500 Company

Paul Moran decided he wanted to work for a small company. So he got the *Inc.* 500 list (the list of the 500 fastest-growing small companies, published each year by *Inc.* magazine). He sent letters to all 17 companies in the Los Angeles area, offering to work for free. "I am confident that any financial rewards will come later."

He included a reply coupon, asking employers to fill in a "preliminary job description" and check one of two boxes:

- Yes, we are interested in interviewing you for an UNPAID POSITION.
- Sorry, we are not interested in having you work for us WITHOUT PAY.

The coupon noted that Moran would call three finalists to set up interviews.

Paul Moran got a job with Collectech Systems. He's now regional president, and the firm is still on the *Inc.* 500 list.

Adapted from George Gendron, "FYI," *Inc.*, October 1995, 13.

Figure 8.9 An E-mail with Application Letter and Scannable Résumé

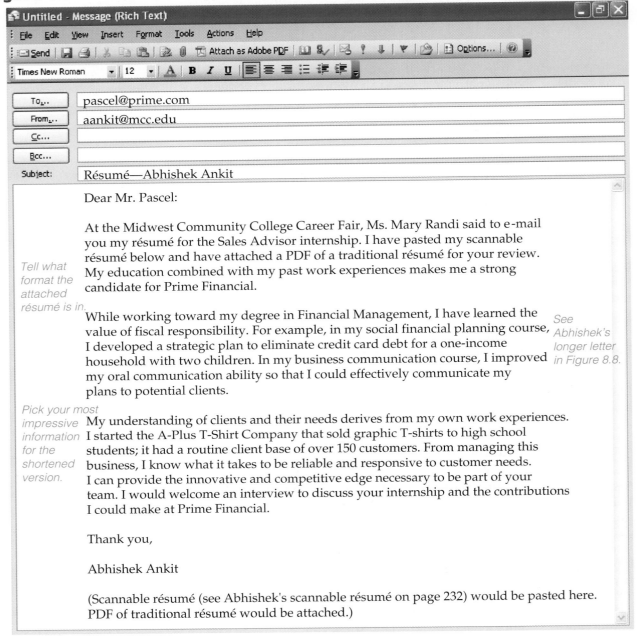

E-Mail Application Letters

Some Web ads give you a street address to submit applications but say "e-mail preferred." Other ads just give an e-mail address. It is becoming more likely all the time that you will e-mail some of your applications.

If your application is solicited, you can paste your traditional letter into your e-mail. If your application is prospecting, you need a shorter letter that will catch the reader's attention within the first screen (see Figure 8.9). Your first paragraph is crucial; use it to hook the reader.

More sources are starting to recommend a shorter letter for both situations, but many caution that you need to include enough information to make you seem to be the person for the job. Frequently that is hard to do in one screen.

When you submit an e-mail letter with an attached résumé,

- Tell what word-processing program your scannable résumé is saved in.
- Put the job number or title for which you're applying in your subject line and in the first paragraph.
- Prepare your letter in a word-processing program with a spell checker to make it easier to edit and proof the document.
- Don't send anything in all capital letters.
- Don't use smiley faces or other emoticons.
- Put your name at the end of the message.

Follow the e-mail advice given in the résumé chapter on issues such as line length and use of keywords. Follow all guidelines posted by the company. Do not add attachments unless you know doing so is OK. Test your letter by sending it to a friend; have your friend recheck it for appearance and correctness.

Creating a Professional Image

Every employer wants businesslike employees who understand professionalism. To make your application letter professional,

- Create your letter in a word-processing program so you can use features such as spell check. Use a standard font such as Times New Roman, Arial, or Helvetica in 12-point type.
- Address your letter to a specific person. If the reader is a woman, call the office to find out what courtesy title she prefers.
- Don't mention relatives' names. It's OK to use names of other people if the reader knows those people and thinks well of them, if they think well of you and will say good things about you, and if you have permission to use their names.
- Omit personal information not related to the job.
- Unless you're applying for a creative job in advertising, use a conservative style: few contractions; no sentence fragments, clichés, or slang.
- Edit the letter carefully and proof it several times to make sure it's perfect. Errors suggest that you're careless or inept. Double-check the spelling of the receiver's of name.
- Print on the same paper (both color and weight) you used for your résumé. Envelopes should match, too.
- Use a computer to print the envelope address.

Writing Style

Use a smooth, concise writing style (◀▥ p. 119). Use the technical jargon of the field to show your training, but avoid businessese and stuffy words like *utilize, commence,* and *transpire* (for *happen*). Use a lively, energetic style that makes you sound like a real person.

Avoid words that can be interpreted sexually. A model letter distributed by the placement office at a midwestern university included the following sentence:

> I have been active in campus activities and have enjoyed good relations with my classmates and professors.

One young woman incorporated this sentence in a letter she mailed. The recipient circled the sentence and then passed the letter around the office (and did not invite the woman for an interview). That's not the kind of attention you want your letter to get!

Email Horror Story

"I sent a digital resume and cover letter via email to apply for a position as a technical writer. Within a few hours, a message from the director in charge of hiring came via email. Full of anticipation, I opened the email to find a terse message: 'your resume is infected with a virus and has been quarantined.' A person cannot recover from an infected resume. I did not pursue the position further."

Quoted from "Interview Horror Stories," in *Resume Help for Recent Graduates: Career Center: Interview Center*, ResumeEdge.com, http://www.resumeedge.com/recent grads/careercenter/interviews/horror-stories.shtml (accessed May 30, 2007).

Study Abroad and Overseas Work Programs

Have you considered a studies abroad program or international job?

If so, a variety of resources are available. These Web sites offer assistance for students interested in study abroad programs:

http://www.ciee.org/

http://studyabroad.com/

http://iiepassport.org/

For information regarding full-time overseas opportunities, visit the following Web sites:

http://globalgateway.monster.com/

http://www.jobsabroad.com/search.cfm

http://transitionsabroad.com/

Positive Emphasis

Be positive. Don't plead ("Please give me a chance") or apologize ("I cannot promise that I am substantially different from the lot"). Most negatives should be omitted from the letter.

Avoid word choices with negative connotations (➡ p. 114). Note how the following revisions make the writer sound more confident.

Negative: I have learned an excessive amount about writing through courses in journalism and advertising.

Positive: Courses in journalism and advertising have taught me to recognize and to write good copy. My profile of a professor was published in the campus newspaper; I earned an "A + " on my direct mail campaign for the American Dental Association to persuade young adults to see their dentist more often.

Excessive suggests that you think the courses covered too much—hardly an opinion likely to endear you to an employer.

Negative: You can check with my references to verify what I've said.

Positive: Professor Hill can give you more information about my work on his national survey.

Verify suggests that you expect the employer to distrust what you've said.

Negative: I am anxious to talk with you about the opportunities for employment with Principal Financial.

Positive: I look forward to talking with you about opportunities at Principal Financial.

Anxious suggests that you're worried about the interview.

You-Attitude

Unsupported claims may sound overconfident, selfish, or arrogant. Create you-attitude (⬅ p. 76) by describing accomplishments and by showing how they relate to what you could do for this employer.

Lacks you-attitude: An inventive and improvising individual like me is a necessity in your business.

You-attitude: Building a summer house-painting business gave me the opportunity to find creative solutions to challenges. At the end of the first summer, for example, I had nearly 10 gallons of exterior latex left, but no more jobs. I contacted the home economics teacher at my high school. She agreed to give course credit to students who were willing to give up two Saturdays to paint a house being renovated by Habitat for Humanity. I donated the paint and supervised the students. I got a charitable deduction for the paint and hired the three best students to work for me the following summer. I could put these skills in problem solving and supervising to work as a personnel manager for Burroughs.

Show what you can do for them, not what they can do for you.

Lacks you-attitude: A company of your standing could offer the challenging and demanding kind of position in which my abilities could flourish.

You-attitude: Omit.

Remember that the word *you* refers to your reader. Using *you* when you really mean yourself or "all people" can insult your reader by implying that he or she still has a lot to learn about business:

Lacks you-attitude:	Running my own business taught me that you need to learn to manage your time.
You-attitude:	Running my own business taught me to manage my time.

Beware of telling readers information they already know as though they do not know it. This practice can also be considered insulting.

Lacks you-attitude:	Your company has just purchased two large manufacturing plants in France.
You-attitude:	My three college French courses would help me communicate in your newly acquired French manufacturing facilities.

Be sure your letter uses the exact language of the job ad and addresses all items included in the ad. If the ad mentions teamwork, your letter should give examples of teamwork; don't shift the vocabulary to collaboration. Many readers expect their job ad language in applicants' letters. If the language is not there, they may judge the applicant as not fitting the position. And so may their computer, since the vocabulary of the job ad probably contains crucial keywords for the computer to find.

Since you're talking about yourself, you'll use *I* in your letter. Reduce the number of *I*'s by revising some sentences to use *me* or *my*.

Under my presidency, the Agronomy Club . . .

Courses in media and advertising management gave me a chance to . . .

My responsibilities as a summer intern included . . .

In particular, avoid beginning every paragraph with *I*. Begin sentences with prepositional phrases or introductory clauses:

As my résumé shows, I . . .

In my coursework in media and advertising management, I . . .

As a summer intern, I . . .

While I was in Italy, . . .

Paragraph Length and Unity

Keep your first and last paragraphs fairly short—preferably no more than four or five typed lines. Vary paragraph length within the letter; it's OK to have one long paragraph, but don't use a series of eight-line paragraphs.

When you have a long paragraph, check to be sure that it covers only one subject. If it covers two or more subjects, divide it into two or more paragraphs. If a short paragraph covers several subjects, consider adding a topic sentence (p. 125) to provide paragraph unity.

Letter Length

Have at least three paragraphs. A short letter throws away an opportunity to be persuasive; it may also suggest that you have little to say for yourself or that you aren't very interested in the job.

Without eliminating content, tighten each sentence (p. 119) to be sure that you're using words as efficiently as possible. If your letter is a bit over a page, use slightly smaller margins or a type size that's one point smaller to get more on the page.

If you have excellent material that will not fit on one page, use it—as long as you have at least 6–12 lines of body text on the second page. The extra space gives you room to be more specific about what you've done and to add details about your experience that will separate you from other applicants. Employers don't *want* longer letters, but they will read them *if* the letter is well written

Worst Cover Letter

Forbes quotes the first three paragraphs from "one of the worst cover letters ever."

"I always dreamed of motivating a football crowd and bringing home a team victory. One evening late in my freshman year of high school, I had the chance to prove it. As I sat eagerly on the edge of my auditorium chair, I thought about winning. There were 108 young women competing for a spot on the [Central High] School varsity cheerleading squad. Only eight of us would win.

"Four months later, I achieved my goal. Standing out on the football field, I studied all the anxious faces peering down at me. My adrenaline flowed as I began cheering. Working the audience, I chanted spiritedly. My energy surged as the fans' enthusiasm accelerated. Minutes later, I had the crowd on their feet cheering the Eagles on to victory. In the end, the box score read Eagles 14, Wildcats 10.

"As a senior professional, I have spent 17 years motivating the crowd, inspiring wins and leading. My strongest assets include selling prospective clients, producing new company revenue, creating innovative market strategies and exceeding objectives."

Why this cover letter considered "one of the worst?"

• The story is too cute.

• The story focuses on the past, and even worse, on high school experiences.

Quoted from Scott Reeves, "Catastrophic Job Hunting Flubs," in *Forbes.com:Leadership: Careers: Business Basics*, http://www.forbes.com/careers/2006/01/25/work-jobs-careers-cx_sr_0126bizbasics.html (accessed May 30, 2007).

and *if* the applicant establishes early in the letter that he or she has the credentials the company needs. However, do remember that the trend is toward shorter letters.

Follow-Up

Follow up with the employer once if you hear nothing after two or three weeks. It is also OK to ask once after one week if e-mail materials were received. If your job letter was prospecting, it is fine to follow up two or three times. Do not make a pest of yourself, however, by calling or e-mailing too often; doing so could well eliminate you from further consideration.

Summary of Key Points

- Résumés differ from letters of application in the following ways:
    - A résumé is adapted to a position. The letter is adapted to the needs of a particular organization.
    - The résumé summarizes all your qualifications. The letter expands your best qualifications to show how you can help the organization meet its needs, how you differ from other applicants, and that you have some knowledge of the organization.
    - The résumé avoids controversial material. The letter can explain in positive ways situations such as gaps in employment history.
    - The résumé uses short, parallel phrases and sentence fragments. The letter uses complete sentences in well-written paragraphs.
- Use the Internet, annual reports, recruiting literature, business periodicals, trade journals, and internships to get information about employers and jobs to use in your letter.
- Information and referral interviews can help you tap into the **hidden job market**—jobs that are not advertised. In an **information interview** you find out what the day-to-day work involves and how you can best prepare to enter that field. **Referral interviews** are interviews you schedule to learn about current job opportunities in your field.
- When you know that a company is hiring, send a **solicited job letter.** When you want a job with a company that has not announced openings, send a **prospecting job letter.** In both letters, you should
    - Address the letter to a specific person.
    - Indicate the specific position for which you're applying.
    - Be specific about your qualifications.
    - Show what separates you from other applicants.
    - Show a knowledge of the company and the position.
    - Refer to your résumé (which you would enclose with the letter).
    - Ask for an interview.
- Organize a solicited letter in this way:
    1. State that you're applying for the job and tell where you learned about the job (ad, referral, etc.). Briefly show that you have the major qualifications required by the ad. Summarize your qualifications in the order in which you plan to discuss them in the letter.
    2. Develop your major qualifications in detail.
    3. Develop your other qualifications. Show what separates you from the other applicants who will also answer the ad. Demonstrate your knowledge of the organization.

4. Ask for an interview; tell when you'll be available to be interviewed and to begin work. End on a positive, forward-looking note.

- Organize a prospecting letter in this way:
  1. Catch the reader's interest.
  2. Create a bridge between the attention-getter and your qualifications. Summarize your qualifications in the order in which you plan to discuss them in the letter.
  3. Develop your strong points in detail. Relate what you've done in the past to what you could do for this company. Show that you know something about the company. Identify the specific niche you want to fill.
  4. Ask for an interview and tell when you'll be available for interviews. End on a positive, forward-looking note.

- Use your knowledge of the company, your coursework, your understanding of the field, and your experience in jobs and extracurricular activities to show that you're unique.

- Don't repeat information that the reader already knows; don't seem to be lecturing the reader on his or her business.

- Use positive emphasis to sound confident. Use you-attitude by supporting general claims with specific examples and by relating what you've done to what the employer needs.

- Have at least three paragraphs. It's desirable to limit your letter to one page, but use up to two pages if you need them to showcase all your credentials.

CHAPTER 8   Exercises and Problems

8.1   Reviewing the Chapter

1. What are four ways that job letters differ from résumés? (LO 2)
2. What are four ways to research specific employers? (LO 1)
3. What is the difference between information and referral interviews? (LO 1)
4. What are the differences between solicited and prospecting letters? (LO 2)
5. What are five tips for writing a job letter that makes you look attractive to employers? (LO 2)
6. What are 10 ways to create a professional image with your letter? (LO 2)

8.2   Reviewing Grammar

As you have read, it is crucial that your job letter be error-free. One common error in job letters, and one that spell-checking programs will not catch, is confusing word pairs like *affect/effect*. Practice choosing the correct word with Exercises B.12, B.13, and B.14 in Appendix B.

8.3   Analyzing First Paragraphs of Prospecting Letters

All of the following are first paragraphs in prospecting letters written by new college graduates. Evaluate the paragraphs on these criteria:

- Is the paragraph likely to interest readers and motivate them to read the rest of the letter?
- Does the paragraph have some content that the student can use to create a transition to talking about his or her qualifications?
- Does the paragraph avoid asking for a job?

1. For the past two and one-half years I have been studying turf management. On August 1, I will graduate from _____ University with a BA in Ornamental Horticulture. The type of job I will seek will deal with golf course maintenance as an assistant superintendent.

2. Ann Gibbs suggested that I contact you.

3. Each year, the Christmas shopping rush makes more work for everyone at Nordstrom's, especially for the Credit Department. While working for Nordstrom's Credit Department for three Christmas and summer vacations, the Christmas sales increase is just one of the credit situations I became aware of.

4. Whether to plate a two-inch eyebolt with cadmium for a tough, brilliant shine or with zinc for a rust-resistant, less expensive finish is a tough question. But similar questions must be answered daily by your salespeople. With my experience in the electroplating industry, I can contribute greatly to your constant need of getting customers.

5. What a set of tractors! The new 9430 and 9630 diesels are just what is needed by today's farmer with his ever-increasing acreage. John Deere has truly done it again.

6. Prudential Insurance Company did much to help my college career as the sponsor of my National Merit Scholarship. Now I think I can give something back to Prudential. I'd like to put my education, including a BS degree in finance from _____ University, to work in your investment department.

7. Since the beginning of Delta Electric Construction Co. in 1993, the size and profits have grown steadily. My father, being a stockholder and vice president, often discusses company dealings with me. Although the company has prospered, I understand there have been a few problems of mismanagement. I feel with my present and future qualifications, I could help ease these problems.

8.4   Improving You-Attitude and Positive Emphasis in Job Letters

Revise each of these sentences to improve you-attitude and positive emphasis. You may need to add information.

1. I understand that your company has had problems due to the mistranslation of documents during international ad campaigns.

2. Included in my résumé are the courses in Finance that earned me a fairly attractive grade average.

3. I am looking for a position that gives me a chance to advance quickly.

4. Although short on experience, I am long on effort and enthusiasm.

5. I have been with the company from its beginning to its present unfortunate state of bankruptcy.

8.5   Evaluating Rough Drafts

Evaluate the following drafts. What parts should be omitted? What needs to be changed or added? What parts would benefit from specific supporting details?

1.
Dear _____:

There is more to a buyer's job than buying the merchandise. And a clothing buyer in particular has much to consider.

Even though something may be in style, customers may not want to buy it. Buyers should therefore be aware of what customers want and how much they are willing to pay.

In the buying field, request letters, thank-you letters, and persuasive letters are frequently written.

My interest in the retail field inspired me to read The Gap's annual report. I saw that a new store is being built. An interview would give us a chance to discuss how I could contribute to this new store. Please call me to schedule an interview.

Sincerely,

2.

> Dear Sir or Madam:
>
> I am taking the direct approach of a personnel letter. I believe you will under stand my true value in the areas of practical knowledge and promotional capabilities.
>
> I am interested in a staff position with Darden in relation to trying to improve the operations and moral of the Olive Garden Restaurants, which I think that I am capable of doing. Please take a minute not to read my résumé (enclosed) and call to schedule an interview.
>
> Sincerely,

3.

> Dear _____:
>
> I would like to apply for the opening you announced for an Assistant Golf Course Superintendent. I have the qualifications you are asking for.
>
> Every year the Superintendent must go before the greens committee to defend its budget requests. To prepare myself to do this, I took courses in accounting, business and administrative writing, and speech.
>
> I have done the operations necessary to maintain the greens properly.
>
> I look forward to talking with you about this position.
>
> Sincerely,

8.6   Gathering Information about an Industry

Use six recent issues of a trade journal to report on three or four trends, developments, or issues that are important in an industry.

As your instructor directs,

a. Share your findings with a small group of other students.

b. Summarize your findings in a memo to your instructor. Include a discussion of how you could use this information in your job letter and résumé:

c. Present your findings to the class.

d. Join with a small group of other students to write a report summarizing the results of this research.

8.7   Gathering Information about Companies in Your Career Field

Use five different Web sites listed in Figure 8.1 to investigate three companies in your career field. Look at salary guides for your level of qualifications, product/service information, news articles about the companies, mission/vision statements, main competitors, annual reports, and financial reports.

As your instructor directs,

a. Share your findings with a small group of other students.

b. Summarize your findings in a memo to your instructor. Include a discussion of how you could use this information in your job letter and résumé.

c. Present your findings to the class.

d. Join with a small group of other students to write a report summarizing the results of this research.

8.8   Gathering Information about a Specific Organization

Gather information about a specific organization, using several of the following methods:

- Check the organization's Web site.
- Read the company's annual report.
- Pick up relevant information at the Chamber of Commerce.
- Read articles in trade publications and the *Wall Street Journal* or that mention the organization (check the indexes).
- Read recruiting literature provided by the company.

As your instructor directs,

a. Share your findings with a small group of other students.
b. Summarize your findings in a memo to your instructor. Include a discussion of how you could use this information in your job letter and résumé:
c. Present your findings orally to the class.
d. Write a paragraph for a job letter using (directly or indirectly) the information you found.

8.9   Conducting an Information Interview

Interview someone working in a field you're interested in. Use the questions listed on page 247 or the shorter list here:

- How did you get started in this field?
- What do you like about your job?
- What do you dislike about your job?
- What courses and jobs would you recommend as preparation for this field?

As your instructor directs,

a. Share the results of your interview with a small group of other students.
b. Write up your interview in a memo to your instructor. Include a discussion of how you could use this information in your job letter and résumé:
c. Present the results of your interview orally to the class.
d. Write to the interviewee thanking him or her for taking the time to talk to you.

8.10   Networking

a. Write to a friend who is already in the workforce, asking about one or more of the following topics:

- Are any jobs in your field available in your friend's organization? If so, what?
- If a job is available, can your friend provide information beyond the job listing that will help you write a more detailed, persuasive letter? (Specify the kind of information you'd like to have.)
- Can your friend suggest people in other organizations who might be useful to you in your

job search? (Specify any organizations in which you're especially interested.)

b. List possible networking contacts from your co-workers, classmates, fraternity/sorority members, friends, family friends, former employers and co-workers, neighbors, faculty members, and local business people. Who would be the most valuable source of information for you? Who would you feel most comfortable contacting?

8.11   Writing a Solicited Letter

Write a letter of application in response to an announced opening for a full-time job (not an internship) which a new college graduate could hold.

Turn in a copy of the listing. If you use option (a) or (b) below, your listing will be a copy. If you choose option (c), you will write the listing.

a. Respond to an ad in a newspaper, in a professional journal, in the placement office, or on the Web. Use an ad that specifies the company, not a blind ad. Be sure that you are fully qualified for the job.

b. Take a job description and assume that it represents a current opening. Use the Web to get the name of the person to whom the letter should be addressed.

c. If you have already worked somewhere, assume that your employer is asking you to apply for full-time work after graduation. Be sure to write a fully persuasive letter.

8.12 Writing a Prospecting Letter

Pick a company you'd like to work for and apply for a specific position. The position can be one that already exists or one that you would create if you could to match your unique blend of talents. Give your instructor a copy of the job description with your letter.

Address your letter to the person with the power to create a job for you: the president of a small company, or the area vice president or branch manager of a large company.

8.13 Critiquing a Job Letter

After you have written your job letter for Exercise 8.11 or 8.12, bring it to class and share it with a classmate.

- Read your cover letter aloud to your classmate noting any changes you would like to make and any areas that may not sound appropriate.

- Have your classmate reread your job letter and make suggestions to enhance it.
- Swap letters and go through the exercise again.

Write a memo to your instructor discussing the changes you will make to your job letter on the basis of this exercise.

8.14 Writing a Rhetorical Analysis of Your Job Letter

a. Examine the job letter you wrote for Exercise 8.11 or 8.12 and answer the following questions in a memo to your instructor:

- Who is your audience? Identify them beyond their name. What will they be looking for?
- How did you consider this audience when selecting information and the level of detail to use? What information did you exclude? How did you shape the information about you to address your audience's needs?
- How did you organize your information for this audience?

- How did you adapt your tone and style for this audience? How did you balance your need to promote yourself without bragging? Where did you use you-attitude, positive tone, and goodwill?
- How did you show knowledge of the company and the position without telling your audience what they already know?

b. Review a class member's cover letter using the same questions.

8.15 Applying Electronically

Write an e-mail application letter with a résumé in the text of the message. You may also attach a formal résumé.

8.16 Applying at Intel

Using the Intel sidebar on page 248, research possible jobs at Intel. Pick the one most appropriate for you and write an electronic job letter to Intel.

8.17 Writing an International Application Letter and Résumé

a. Write an application letter to an international company using the information in this chapter.

b. Write a short memo to your instructor explaining the differences between your international and domestic application letters.

8.18   Mosaic Case

"Mine is better!" shouted Sarah.

"No way, mine is much better!" retorted Demetri.

Yvonne came storming out of her office into the main employee work area. "What is going on out here?"

Demetri explained that they were arguing over who had found the better candidate to fill the intern position after going through stacks of cover letters and résumés.

"Well," said Yvonne, "from my office, it sounds like you're acting like children out here. I will not tolerate this kind of unprofessional behavior in this office! Got it?"

"Yes, Yvonne," replied Sarah and Demetri in unison.

"However," piped up Demetri, "I clearly have found the best candidate for the internship position. He meets everything we were looking for when we wrote the job advertisement."

"How about if you two put in writing who has found the better candidate, and I'll make the decision myself," said Yvonne.

Help resolve the disagreement between Sarah and Demetri. In a memo to Yvonne, identify who you believe has written the best cover letter and seems to be the best applicant for the job based on the excerpted paragraph from each letter.

Excerpt from Candidate A's Cover Letter

I spent four months taking business communication and marketing courses overseas in Barcelona, Spain. This international experience immersed me in a situation where I needed to fully understand how to communicate with a diverse group of people. In my courses, I created and implemented marketing strategies for energy drinks that met the needs of not only Spaniards, but all Europeans. My strengths as a communicator will benefit Mosaic through my ability to convey innovative ideas to diverse audiences as Mosaic explores the possibilities of expanding internationally.

Excerpt from Candidate B's Cover Letter

My internship experience at Swanson's Furniture Warehouse presented a stage for me to showcase my collaborative abilities. I helped the entire marketing team brainstorm for local promotional ideas and public relations. Moreover, once the brainstorming stage was complete, I worked closely with two full-time workers to carry out the production of publication materials and ensure the highest quality. My strong ability to complete projects while working cooperatively will be directly beneficial to Mosaic, which prides itself on the importance of collaboration.

Job Interviews, Follow-Up Messages, Job Offers, and First Jobs

Learning Objectives

After studying this chapter, you will know:

1 What kinds of interviews you may encounter.

2 What preparations to make before you start interviewing.

3 What to do during an interview.

4 How to answer common interview questions.

5 What to do after an interview.

6 What to do to settle in at your new job.

Whole New Mind for a Flat World

Interviewer: "Good morning, Mr. Allen. I'm Angela Macher—project engineering and human services at Consolidated Industries."

Senior: "Good morning, Ms. Macher—nice to meet you."

I: "So, I understand you're getting ready to graduate in May and you're looking for a position with Consolidated . . . and I also see you've got a 3.75 GPA coming into this semester—very impressive. What kind of position did you have in mind?"

S: "Well, I liked most of my engineering courses but especially the ones with lots of math and computer applications—I've gotten pretty good at Excel and Matlab and I also know some Visual Basic. I was thinking about control systems or design."

I: "I see. To be honest, we have very few openings in those areas—we've moved most of our manufacturing and design work to China and Romania and most of our programming to India. Got any foreign languages?"

S: "Um, a couple of years of Spanish in high school but I couldn't take any more in college—no room in the curriculum."

I: "How would you feel about taking an intensive language course for a few months and moving to one of our overseas facilities? If you do well you could be on a fast track to management."

S: "Uh . . . I was really hoping I could stay in the States. Aren't *any* positions left over here?"

I: "Sure, but not like ten years ago, and you need different skills to get them. Let me ask you a couple of questions to see if we can find a fit. First, what do you think your strengths are outside of math and computers?"

S: "Well, I've always been good in physics."

I: "How about social sciences and humanities?"

S: "I did all right in those courses—mostly A's—but I can't honestly say I enjoy that stuff."

I: "Right. And would you describe yourself as a people person?"

S: "Um . . . I get along with most people, but I guess I'm kind of introverted."

I: "I see. . . . " (Stands up.) OK, Mr. Allen—thanks. I'll forward your application to our central headquarters, and if we find any slots that might work we'll be in touch. Have a nice day."

> *"The American job market is changing, and to get and keep jobs future graduates will need skills beyond those that used to be sufficient."*

This hypothetical interview is not all that hypothetical. The American job market is changing, and to get and keep jobs future graduates will need skills beyond those that used to be sufficient.

How will globalization affect you in your career field?

Are you prepared for a global and diverse work force?

What skills, experiences and education would you recommend a new college student obtain before graduating to succeed in a global economy?

Source: Quoted from Richard M. Felder, "A Whole New Mind for a Flat World," *Chemical Engineer Education* 40, no. 2 (2006): 96–97. Reprinted with permission of Chemical Engineering Education.

Chapter Outline

Job interviews are scary, even when you've prepared thoroughly. But when you are prepared, you can harness the adrenaline to work for you, so that you put your best foot forward and get the job you want. The best way to prepare yourself is to know as much as possible about the process and the employer.

Interviewing in the 21st Century

Interviews are changing as interviewers respond to interviewees who are prepared to answer the standard questions. Today, many employers expect you to

- Be more assertive. Many employers expect you to call them to arrange interviews.
- Follow instructions to the letter. The owner of a delivery company tells candidates to phone at a precise hour. Failing to do so means that the person couldn't be trusted to deliver packages on time.[1]
- Participate in many interviews. Candidates may have one or more interviews by phone, computer, or video before they have an office interview.

- Take one or more tests, including drug tests, psychological tests, aptitude tests, computer simulations, and essay exams where you're asked to explain what you'd do in a specific situation.
- Be approved by the team you'll be joining. In companies with self-managed work teams, the team has a say in who is hired.
- Provide—at the interview or right after it—a sample of the work you're applying to do. You may be asked to write a memo or a proposal, calculate a budget on a spreadsheet, write computer code, or make a presentation.

All the phoning required in 21st-century interviews places a special emphasis on phone skills. Be polite to everyone with whom you speak, including administrative assistants and secretaries. Find out the person's name on your first call and use it on subsequent calls. "Thank you for being so patient. Can you tell me when a better time might be to try to reach Ms. X? I'll try again on [date]." Sometimes, if you call after 5 PM, executives answer their own phones since clerical staff have gone home. However, some of them resent interruptions at that time, so be particularly well prepared and focused.

If you get someone's voice mail, leave a concise message—complete with your name and phone number. Keep your voice pleasant. If you get voice mail repeatedly, call the main company number to speak with a receptionist. Ask whether the person you're trying to reach is in the building. If he or she is on the road, ask when the person is due in.

Developing an Interview Strategy

Develop an overall strategy based on your answers to these three questions:

1. **What about yourself do you want the interviewer to know?** Pick two to five points that represent your strengths for that particular job. These facts are frequently character traits (such as enthusiasm), achievements and experiences that qualify you for the job and separate you from other applicants, or unique abilities such as fluency in Spanish. For each strength, think of a specific accomplishment to support it. For instance, be ready to give an example to prove that you're hardworking. Be ready to show how you helped an organization save money or serve customers better.

   Then at the interview, listen to every question to see if you could make one of your key points as part of your answer. If the questions don't allow you to make your points, bring them up at the end of the interview.

2. **What disadvantages or weaknesses do you need to minimize?** Expect that you may be asked to explain weaknesses or apparent weaknesses in your record such as lack of experience, so-so grades, and gaps in your record.

   Plan how to deal with these issues if they arise. Decide if you want to bring them up yourself, particularly disadvantages or weaknesses that are easily discoverable. If you bring them up, you can plan the best context for them during the interview. Many students, for example, have been able to get good jobs after flunking out of school by explaining that the experience was a turning point in their lives and pointing out that when they returned to school they maintained a B or better grade point average. Although it is illegal to ask questions about marital status, married candidates with spouses who are able to move easily sometimes volunteer that information: "My husband is a dentist and is willing to relocate if the company wants to transfer me." See the suggestions later in this chapter under "Answering Traditional Interview Questions" and "Behavioral and Situational Interviews."

Career Fair Advice

Stanford University's Career Development Center offers the following tips for career fairs:

1. Prepare for the Career Fair. Answer the following questions before you attend:
   - What organizations are attending?
   - How will the employers be organized at the event?
   - What is the starting and ending time?
   - What attire is appropriate?

2. Write a résumé to hand out to potential employers. However, if you do not have a résumé, you can still attend the fair to gather information about organizations.

3. Set up a plan: Make a prioritized list of organizations you want to visit. However, be open to interesting organizations you run across at the fair; you might be surprised to find some new opportunities.

4. Create a one-minute presentation to give to potential employers outlining your background and qualifications which will meet the organization's needs.

5. Bring questions to ask.

6. Thank employers at the fair for materials you are given.

7. Collect business cards and write a fact on the back to remember when you write a thank you.

8. Write a thank-you note to those organizations you wish to pursue.

Adapted from Stanford University Career Development Center, "Before the Career Fair," in *Prepare for the Job Search: Career Fair Preparation,* http://cardinalcareers.stanford.edu/jobsearch/cfprep/before.htm (accessed June 5, 2007).

3. **What do you need to know about the job and the organization to decide whether or not you want to accept this job if it is offered to you?** Plan *in advance* the criteria on which you will base your decision (you can always change the criteria). Use "Deciding Which Offer to Accept" below to plan questions to elicit the information you'll need to rank each offer.

Preparing for the Interview

Preparing for your interviews can help you to feel more confident and make a better impression.

Final Research

Research the company interviewing you. Read their Web pages, company newsletters, annual reports. Read about them in trade journals and newspapers. Ask your professors, classmates, friends, family, and co-workers about them. If possible, find out who will interview you and research them, too.

Travel Planning

If your interview is not on campus, make sure you can find the building and the closest parking. Plan how much time you will need to get there. Leave time margins for stressors such as traffic jams or broken elevators. If you are fortunate enough to be flown to an interview, don't schedule too tightly. Allow for flight delays and cancellations. Plan how you will get from the airport to the interview site. Take enough cash and credit cards to cover emergencies.

Attire

The outfit you wear to an interview should meet your interviewer's expectations. The most conservative choice is the traditional dark business suit with a light blouse or shirt, plus tie shoes with matching dark socks for men and close-toed pumps with nude, unpatterned hose for women. Although this outfit is probably still the most common choice, you cannot count on it being the right choice.

For campus interviews, you should follow the dress code of your campus career center.

For office interviews, you should show that you understand the organization's culture. Try to find out from your career contacts what is considered appropriate attire. Some interviewers do not mind if you ask them what you should wear to the interview. (Others do mind, so be careful. They believe it means you have not done your homework.)

Paul Capelli, former public relations executive at Amazon.com and now vice president of public relations at CNBC, suggests that applicants find out what employees wear "and notch it up one step":

> If the dress is jeans and a T-shirt, wear slacks and an open collar shirt. . . . If it's slacks and an open collar shirt, throw on a sport coat. If it's a sport coat, throw on a suit. At least match it and go one step up.[2]

Choose comfortable shoes. You may do a fair amount of walking during an onsite interview. Check your heels to make sure they aren't run down; make sure your shoes are shined.

Make conservative choices. Have your hair cut or styled conservatively. Jewelry and makeup should be understated; face jewelry, such as eyebrow and nose studs, should be removed. If possible, cover tattoos. Personal hygiene

You can wear a wide range of apparel to interviews. Find out what is appropriate—and inappropriate—for each interview. Which of these outfits would you wear?

must be impeccable, with close attention paid to fingernails and breath. Make sure your clothes are clean and pressed. Avoid cologne and perfumed after-shave lotions.

What to Take to the Interview

Take extra copies of your résumé. If your campus placement office has already given the interviewer a data sheet, present the résumé at the beginning of the interview: "I thought you might like a little more information about me."

Take something to write on and something to write with. It's OK to carry a small notepad with the questions you want to ask on it.

Take copies of your work or a portfolio: an engineering design, a copy of a memo you wrote on a job or in a business writing class, an article you wrote for the campus paper. You don't need to present these unless the interview

The Stealth Job Interview

I flew to Bangor, ME, for an interview for the director of photography position with a well-known studio. . . . I was told that Mr. Olive, the company president, had been detained. . . .

A few minutes later, a well-dressed family of five walked in. Surprised, the receptionist said, "Why Mr. Smith, we had you down for an appointment to be photographed next Saturday. We don't have a photographer on duty today." . . . The embarrassed receptionist turned to me: "Mr. Williams, would you be able to help us out and photograph these people?"

I agreed. . . . Everything went well, although about three-fourths of the way through I noticed someone lurking in a small closet nearby. When I finished, I bid the Smiths goodbye and turned on the room lights. A distinguished-looking little man stepped out of the closet and said, "I like the way you handle yourself, kid. You've got the job!"

It was Mr. Olive. Later I learned that the "Smith family" was really Mr. Olive's daughter, son-in-law, and grandchildren. The entire session had been an elaborate test.

Quoted from Fred Williams, "Get the Picture?" *Selling Power*, March 2001, 20.

calls for them, but they can be very effective: "Yes, I have done a media plan. Here's a copy of a plan I put together in my advertising seminar last year. We had a fixed budget and used real figures for cost and rating points, just as I'd do if I joined Foote, Cone & Belding."

Take the names, addresses, and phone numbers of references. Take complete details about your work history and education, including dates and street addresses, in case you're asked to fill out an application form.

If you can afford it, buy a briefcase in which to carry these items. At this point in your life, an inexpensive vinyl briefcase is acceptable.

Interview Channels

Interviews use other channels in addition to the popular office setting. As a college student, you may well find yourself being interviewed on campus. You may also find you have a phone or video conference, as more and more companies use technology to keep hiring costs in check. Most of the interview advice in this chapter applies to all settings, but some channels do have unique particulars you should consider.

Campus Interviews

Most campus career offices have written protocols and expectations for campus interviews arranged through them. Be sure to follow these expectations so that you look informed.

However, because campus interviewers will see so many students who are all following the same protocols, it is important that you have good details and professional stories about your work to help you stand out from the crowd. Focus on three to four selling points you most want the interviewer to remember about you. If you have a choice, do not schedule your interview late in the day when interviewers are getting tired.

Phone Interviews

Some organizations use phone interviews to narrow the list of candidates they bring in for office visits. Phone interviews give you some advantages. Obviously, you do not have to dress up for them, or find an office. You can use all the materials you want as you speak. You can also take all the notes you want, although copious note-taking will probably impact your speaking quality, and you certainly don't want the sound of keyboard clicking to be heard by your interviewer.

On the other hand, phone interviews obviously deny you the important component of visual feedback. To compensate for this loss, you can ask your interviewer for verbal feedback (e.g., Is this sufficient detail? Would you like more on this topic?).

Although you always want to speak distinctly at an interview, doing so is even more crucial for a phone interview. And speech experts recommend that you smile, lean forward, and even gesture, although no one can see you. Such activities add warmth to your words. Be sure to eliminate all background noise such as music or TV. Finally, just as you did for a campus interview, focus on three to four selling points you most want the interviewer to remember about you.

Video Interviews

Video interviews are becoming more common. You may experience two different kinds. In one, the organization sends you a list of questions and you prepare a video which you send back to them. In the other, the organization conducts live interviews using videoconferencing equipment.

If you are preparing a video,

- Practice your answers so you are fluent. You don't want to stumble over your responses, but you also don't want to sound like you have memorized the answers.
- Capture a performance that represents you at your best. Retake as many times as necessary.
- Be thorough. Since the employer can't ask follow-up questions, you want to consider what those questions could be and then be sure to answer them.

If you are participating in a videoconference,

- Do a practice video of yourself ahead of time. Listen to your pronunciation and voice qualities. Watch your video with the sound turned off: check your posture, gestures, facial expressions, and clothing. Do you have nervous mannerisms you need to control?
- During the actual interview, keep your answers under two minutes. Then ask if interviewers want more information. People are generally more reluctant to interrupt a speaker in another location, and body language cues are limited, so ask for feedback ("Would you like to hear about that?").

Practicing for the Interview

Rehearse everything you can: Put on the clothes you'll wear and practice entering a room, shaking hands, sitting down, and answering questions. Ask a friend to interview you. Saying answers out loud is surprisingly harder than saying them in your head. If your department or career center offers practice interviews, take advantage of them.

Some campuses have videotaping facilities so that you can watch your own sample interview. Videotaping is particularly valuable if you can do it at least twice, so you can modify behavior the second time and check the tape to see whether the modification works.

During the Interview

Your interviewing skills will improve with practice. If possible, schedule a few interviews with other companies before your interview with the company that is your first choice. However, even if you're just interviewing for practice, you must still do all the research on that company. If interviewers sense that you aren't interested, they won't take you seriously and you won't learn much from the process. Also, interviewers talk to each other, sharing impressions and stories, sometimes with names attached.

Not all interviews are question and answer sessions. More employers are starting to use other screening devices; they are asking candidates to provide on-the-spot writing samples, or to take personality, critical thinking, or intelligence tests. For example, Securities America Inc., a securities broker-dealer, uses IQ tests, personality tests, and emotional intelligence tests.[3]

Behavior

How you act at the interview is as important as what you say.

When your mother told you that first impressions were important, she knew what she was talking about. Employers start judging you from the first second they see you. If you meet multiple people, first impressions will begin anew with each encounter. Always act professionally. Be polite to everyone, including people such as security agents, receptionists, and people in the restroom. Their input about you may be sought. Have a pleasant handshake; avoid the cold, limp, dead-fish hand.

Politeness extends to the interview itself:

- Practice active listening; it makes speakers feel appreciated and you will likely pick up clues you can use effectively during your interview.

- Do not monopolize the interview time with lengthy monologues. Generally your interviewer will have many questions to cover and will not appreciate an undue amount of time wasted on just one. Check the interviewer's verbal cues and body language for the amount of detail and depth desired. After two to three minutes, ask if the interviewer wants more detail. The best interviews are conversations in which you and your interviewer enjoy your interactions.

- Never say anything bad about current and former employers, a category that includes schools. Candidates who snipe about their employers and instructors will likely continue to do so on their new job and thus appear to be unattractive colleagues.

Be enthusiastic about the job. Enthusiasm helps convince people you have the energy to do the job well. Show how you are a good choice for their job by clearly presenting your carefully chosen accomplishments and strengths. If you are attending an onsite interview, where you could well be asked the same questions by different people, prepare to repeat yourself—with enthusiasm.

Should you be yourself? There's no point in assuming a radically different persona. If you do, you run the risk of getting into a job that you'll hate (though the persona you assumed might have loved it). Furthermore, as interviewers point out, you have to be a pretty good actor to come across convincingly if you try to be someone other than yourself. Yet keep in mind that all of us have several selves: we can be lazy, insensitive, bored, slow-witted, and tongue-tied, but we can also be energetic, perceptive, interested, intelligent, and articulate. Be your best self at the interview.

Interviews can make you feel vulnerable and defensive; to counter this, review your accomplishments—the things you're especially proud of having done. You'll make a better impression if you have a firm sense of your own self-worth.

Every interviewer repeats the advice that your mother probably gave you: sit up straight, don't mumble, look at people when you talk. It's good advice for interviews. Be aware that many people respond negatively to smoking. Remember to turn your cell phone off.

As much as possible, avoid nervous mannerisms: playing with your hair, jingling coins in your pocket, clicking your pen, or repeating verbal spacers such as "like" and "uh." These mannerisms distract your audience and detract from your presentation. It's OK to be a little nervous, however; it shows that you care.

Office visits that involve meals and semisocial occasions call for sensible choices. When you order, choose something that's easy to eat without being messy. Watch your table manners. Eat a light lunch, with no alcohol, so that you'll be alert during the afternoon. A survey by the Society for Human Resource Management found that 96% of human resources professionals believe job candidates should not drink at interview meals.[4] At dinner or an evening party, decline alcohol if you don't drink. If you do drink, accept just one drink—you're still being evaluated, and you can't afford to have your guard down. Be aware that some people respond negatively to applicants who drink hard liquor, even if it was offered to them (think of it as another test you have to pass).

The interview is also a time for you to see if you want to work for this organization. Look for signs of organizational culture (see page 46). How do people treat each other? Are offices or cubbies personalized? How many hours a week do the newest employees work? Is this the place where you want to become another new employee?

Note-Taking

During or immediately after the interview, write down

- The name of the interviewer (or all the people you talked to, if it's a group interview or an onsite visit).
- Tips the interviewer gave you about landing the job and succeeding in it.
- What the interviewer seemed to like best about you.
- Any negative points or weaknesses that came up that you need to counter in your follow-up messages or phone calls.
- Answers to your questions about the company.
- When you'll hear from the company.

The easiest way to get the interviewer's name is to ask for his or her card. You may be able to make all the notes you need on the back of the card.

Some interviewers say that they respond negatively to applicants who take notes during the interview. However, if you have several interviews back-to-back or if you know your memory is terrible, do take brief notes during the interview. That's better than forgetting which company said you'd be on the road every other week and which interviewer asked that *you* get in touch with him or her. Another approach is to ask your interviewers if they mind if you take notes. Try to maintain eye contact as much as possible while taking notes.

Interview Sections

Every interview has an opening, a body, and a close.

In the *opening* (two to five minutes), good interviewers will try to set you at ease. Some interviewers will open with easy questions about your major or interests. Others open by telling you about the job or the company. If this happens, listen so you can answer questions later to show that you can do the job or contribute to the company that's being described.

The *body* of the interview (10 to 25 minutes) is an all-too-brief time for you to highlight your qualifications and find out what you need to know to decide if you want to accept a site trip. Expect questions that give you an opportunity to showcase your strong points and questions that probe any weaknesses evident from your résumé. (You were neither in school nor working last fall. What were you doing?) Normally the interviewer will also try to sell you on the company and give you an opportunity to raise questions.

You need to be aware of time so that you can make sure to get in your key points and questions: "We haven't covered it yet, but I want you to know that I . . . " "I'm aware that it's almost 10:30. I do have some more questions that I'd like to ask about the company."

In the *close* of the interview (two to five minutes), the interviewer will usually tell you what happens next: "We'll be bringing our top candidates to the office in February. You should hear from us in three weeks." Make sure you know who to contact if the next step is not clearly spelled out or you don't hear by the stated time.

Handling Illegal Interview Questions

"Various federal, state, and local laws regulate the questions a prospective employer can ask you, the job candidate. An employer's questions—whether on the job application, in the interview, or during the testing process—must be related to the job you're seeking.

If asked an illegal question, you have three options:

- You can answer the question—you're free to do so, if you wish. However, if you choose to answer an illegal question, remember that you are giving information that isn't related to the job; in fact, you might be giving the 'wrong' answer, which could harm your chances of getting the job.

- You can refuse to answer the question, which is well within your rights. Unfortunately, . . . you run the risk of appearing uncooperative or confrontational—hardly words an employer would use to describe the 'ideal' candidate.

- You can examine the question for its intent and respond with an answer as it might apply to the job. For example, the interviewer asks, . . . 'What country are you from?' You've been asked an illegal question. You could respond, however, with 'I am authorized to work in the United States.' Similarly, let's say the interviewer asks, 'Who is going to take care of your children when you have to travel for the job?' You might answer, 'I can meet the travel and work schedule that this job requires.'"

Quoted from Rochelle Kaplan, "Handling Illegal Questions," in *Career Library: Interviews*, JobWeb.com, http://www.jobweb.com/Resources/Library/Interviews/Handling-Illegal_46_01.htm (accessed June 5, 2007), with permission of the National Association of Colleges and Employers.

The close of the interview is also the time for you to summarize your key accomplishments and strengths and to express enthusiasm for the job. Depending on the circumstances, you could say: "I've certainly enjoyed learning more about General Electric." "I hope I get a chance to visit your Phoenix office. I'd really like to see the new computer system you talked about." "This job seems to be a good match between what you're looking for and what I'd like to do."

"My short-term goal is to bluff my way through this job interview. My long-term goal is to invent a time machine so I can come back and change everything I've said so far."

Copyright 2007 Randy Glasbergen. www.glasbergen.com.

Answering Traditional Interview Questions

First interviews seek to screen out less qualified candidates rather than to find someone to hire. Negative information will hurt you less if it comes out in the middle of the interview and is preceded and followed by positive information. If you blow a question near the end of the interview, don't leave until you've said something positive—perhaps restating one of the points you want the interviewer to know about you.

As Figure 9.1 shows, successful applicants use different communication behaviors than do unsuccessful applicants. Successful applicants are more likely to use the company name during the interview, show they have researched the company, support their claims with specific details, use appropriate technical language, and ask specific questions about the company and industry. In addition to practicing the content of questions, try to incorporate these tactics.

The ultimate questions in your interviewers' minds are probably these three: What can you do for us? Why should we hire you instead of another candidate? Will you fit in our company/division/office? However, many interviewers do not ask these questions directly. Instead, they ask other questions to get their answers more indirectly. Some of the more common questions are discussed below. Do some unpressured thinking before the interview so that you'll have answers that are responsive, are honest, and paint a good picture of you. Choose answers that fit your qualifications and the organization's needs.

1. **Tell me about yourself.**

    Focus on several strengths that show you are a good candidate. Give examples with enough specifics to prove each strength. Don't launch into an autobiography, which will have too many details the interviewer will not care about. Provide professional, not personal, information.

2. **Walk me through your résumé.**

    Highlight your best features and offer reasons for major decisions. Why did you choose this college? Why did you take that job? Have professional reasons: You went to State U because it has a top-ranked accounting department, not because it is close to home; you took that summer job because it allowed some interaction with the company's accounting department, not because it was the only one you could find.

    Don't try to cover too much; your résumé walk should be no longer than three minutes. But do try to add some interesting detail that is not on your résumé. Above all, do maintain eye contact; do not read your résumé.

3. **What makes you think you're qualified to work for this company? Or, I'm interviewing 120 people for two jobs. Why should I hire you?**

Figure 9.1   The Communication Behaviors of Successful Interviewees

Behavior	Unsuccessful interviewees	Successful interviewees
Statements about the position	Have only vague ideas of what they want to do.	Specific and consistent about the position they want; are able to tell why they want the position.
Use of company name	Rarely use the company name.	Refer to the company by name.
Knowledge about company and position	Make it clear that they are using the interview to learn about the company and what it offers.	Make it clear that they have researched the company; refer to specific Web site, publications, or people who have given them information.
Level of interest, enthusiasm	Respond neutrally to interviewer's statements: "OK," "I see." Indicate reservations about company or location.	Express approval nonverbally and verbally of information provided by the interviewer; "That's great!" Explicitly indicate desire to work for this particular company.
Nonverbal behavior	Make little eye contact; smile infrequently.	Make eye contact often; smile.
Picking up on interviewer's cues	Give vague or negative answers even when a positive answer is clearly desired ("How are your writing skills?").	Answer positively and confidently—and back up the claim with a specific example.
Use of industry terms and technical jargon	Use almost no technical jargon.	Use technical jargon.
Use of specifics in answers	Give short answers—10 words or less, sometimes only one word; do not elaborate. Give general responses: "fairly well."	Support claims with specific personal experiences.
Questions asked by interviewee	Ask a small number of general questions.	Ask specific questions based on knowledge of the industry and the company. Personalize questions: "What would my duties be?"

Rescuing the Interview

A smart question made Deborah Brown realize she had flubbed an interview for a diversity consultant's spot at Organizational Resources Counselors, a New York human-resources consulting firm. She felt her interview with two ORC officials "was going really well." So, near the end, she asked whether they had any objections to her candidacy.

"They said, 'This is a job that requires getting top-level commitment to launch a diversity initiative. You seem very nice and low-key.' " . . .

Translation: She wasn't aggressive enough to sway captains of industry. . . .

Ms. Brown tried to recover with a rapidly dispatched missive that strongly refuted the officials' misperception. The letter detailed how she had spearheaded a high-level initiative at her then-employer, New York's Port Authority.

Equally importantly, Ms. Brown dressed and acted differently during her next interview with the same ORC staffers. . . .

She substituted a strikingly bright maroon suit for the conservative blue one worn the first time. She sat forward, projected her voice, spoke more animatedly and used additional gestures to dramatize her numerous ideas.

She got the coveted job.

Quoted from Joann S. Lublin, "You Blew the Interview, but You Can Correct Some of the Blunders," *Wall Street Journal*, December 5, 2000, B1.

This question may feel like an attack. Use it as an opportunity to state your strong points: your qualifications for the job, the things that separate you from other applicants.

4. **What two or three accomplishments have given you the greatest satisfaction?**

    Pick accomplishments that you're proud of, that create the image you want to project, and that enable you to share one of the things you want the interviewer to know about you. Focus not just on the end result, but on the problem-solving, thinking, and innovation skills that made the achievement possible.

5. **Why do you want to work for us? What is your ideal job?**

    Even if you're interviewing just for practice, make sure you have a good answer—preferably two or three reasons you'd like to work for that company. If you don't seem to be taking the interview seriously, the interviewer won't take you seriously, and you won't even get good practice.

    If your ideal job is very different from the ones the company has available, the interviewer may simply say there isn't a good match and end the interview. If you're interested in this company, do some research so that what you ask for is in the general ballpark of the kind of work the company offers.

6. **What college subjects did you like best and least? Why?**

    This question may be an icebreaker; it may be designed to discover the kind of applicant they're looking for. If your favorite class was something outside your major, prepare an answer that shows that you have qualities that can help you in the job you're applying for: "My favorite class was a seminar in the American novel. We got a chance to think on our own, rather than just regurgitate facts; we made presentations to the class every week. I found I really like sharing my ideas with other people and presenting reasons for my conclusions about something."

7. **What is your class rank? Your grade point? Why are your grades so low?**

    If your grades aren't great, be ready with a nondefensive explanation. If possible, show that the cause of low grades now has been solved or isn't relevant to the job you're applying for: "My father almost died last year, and my schoolwork really suffered." "When I started, I didn't have any firm goals. Once I discovered the field that was right for me, my grades have all been B's or better." "I'm not good at multiple-choice tests. But I am good at working with people."

8. **What have you read recently? What movies have you seen recently?**

    These questions may be icebreakers; they may be designed to probe your intellectual depth. The term you're interviewing, read at least one book or magazine (regularly) and see at least one movie that you could discuss at an interview. Make thoughtful selections.

9. **Show me some samples of your writing.**

    Many jobs require the ability to write well. Employers no longer take mastery of basic English for granted, even if the applicant has a degree from a prestigious university.

    The year you're interviewing, go through your old papers and select a few of the best ones, editing them if necessary, so that you'll have samples to present at the interview if you're asked for them.

10. **Describe a major problem you have encountered in your work and how you dealt with it.**

    Choose a problem that was not your fault: a customer's last-minute change to a large order, a flu outbreak during Christmas rush. In your solution, stress skills you know the company will be seeking.

11. **What are your interests outside work? What campus or community activities have you been involved in?**

    While it's desirable to be well-rounded, naming 10 interests is a mistake: the interviewer may wonder when you'll have time to work. Select activities that show skills and knowledge you can use on the job: "I have polished my persuasion skills by being a cabin counselor at a camp for troubled preteens."

    If you mention your fiancé, spouse, or children in response to this question ("Well, my fiancé and I like to go sailing"), it is perfectly legal for the interviewer to ask follow-up questions ("What would you do if your spouse got a job offer in another town?"), even though the same question would be illegal if the interviewer brought up the subject first.

12. **What have you done to learn about this company?**

    An employer may ask this to see what you already know about the company (if you've read the recruiting literature and the Web site, the interviewer doesn't need to repeat them). This question may also be used to see how active a role you're taking in the job search process and how interested you are in this job.

13. **What adjectives would you use to describe yourself?**

    Use only positive ones. Be ready to illustrate each with a specific example of something you've done.

14. **What is your greatest strength?**

    Employers ask this question to give you a chance to sell yourself and to learn something about your values. Pick a strength related to work, school, or activities: "I'm good at working with people." "I really can sell things." "I'm good at solving problems." "I learn quickly." "I'm reliable. When I say I'll do something, I do it." Be ready to illustrate each with a specific example of something you've done. It is important to relate your strength to the specific position.

15. **What is your greatest weakness?**

    Use a work-related negative, even if something in your personal life really is your greatest weakness. Interviewers won't let you get away with a "weakness" like being a workaholic or just not having any experience yet. Instead, use one of these strategies:

    a. Discuss a weakness that is not related to the job you're being considered for and will not be needed even when you're promoted. (Even if you won't work with people or give speeches in your first job, you'll need those skills later in your career, so don't use them for this question.) End your answer with a positive that *is* related to the job:

> [For a creative job in advertising:] I don't like accounting. I know it's important, but I don't like it. I even hire someone to do my taxes. I'm much more interested in being creative and working with people, which is why I find this position interesting.

> [For a job in administration:] I don't like selling products. I hated selling cookies when I was a Girl Scout. I'd much rather work with ideas—and I really like selling the ideas that I believe in.

> [For a job in architecture:] I hate fund-raising. It always seemed to me if people wanted to give, they would anyway. I'd much rather have something to offer people which will help them solve their own problems and meet their own needs.

Tattoos and Interviews

Should you hide tattoos for a job interview?

According to a study published in the *Journal of the American Academy of Dermatology*, about half of Americans in their 20s have either a tattoo or a body piercing other than traditional earrings. Out of the people who responded to the survey, 24% had at least one tattoo and 14% had a body piercing (not including the traditional earlobe).

Consequently, when candidates with tattoos and body piercing start to enter the work force, they need to be aware of how employers view body art. Employers vary considerably on the issue. The acceptance of body art depends on the workplace, industry, and managers. Some employers are imposing legal dress and body art codes, while other employers are loosening dress codes to attract younger applicants who may not feel comfortable in a conservative environment. Therefore, you should always find out the employer's policies and views towards body art before you interview.

What kind of careers and industries would be more likely to allow visible tattoos at work? Why do you think so?

Adapted from Madlen Read, "Body Art Taking a Bigger Role in the Workplace," in *Business*, Seattle Post–Intelligencer, http://seattlepi.nwsource.com/business/289570_tattoosatwork23.html (accessed June 5, 2007).

Amy's Ice Cream stores sell entertainment. To find creative, zany employees, Amy Miller gives applicants a white paper bag and a week to do something with it. People who produce something unusual are hired.

b. Discuss a weakness that you are working to improve:

> In the past, I wasn't a good writer. But last term I took a course in business writing that taught me how to organize my ideas and how to revise. I may never win a Pulitzer Prize, but now I'm a lot more confident that I can write effective reports and memos.

Choosing Employers

What are employees looking for in an employer?

Accenture, a global consulting company, asked 4,139 job seekers in 21 countries what they looked for in an employer. The respondents were both entry-level and experienced workers.

The top characteristic, named by 60%, was interesting work. Other desired characteristics were regular recognition and rewards; fast career growth and advancement; a financially strong, people-oriented environment; and flexible work arrangements. Interestingly, these categories, particularly recognition and rewards, were prominent for workers worldwide.

Do you know what you look for in an employer? What type of organization would make you feel productive? Where and what would help you develop a sense of accomplishment?

Adapted from Donna M. Airoldi, "What Workers Want," *Incentive*, October 22, 2006, 11.

16. **Why are you looking for another job?**

Stress what you're looking for in a new job, not why you want to get away from your old one: "I want more opportunity to work with clients." "I am looking for a sales job with more travel opportunities." If you are looking for a job with a bigger salary, it is better to use other points when answering this question.

If you were fired, say so. There are various acceptable ways to explain why you were fired:

a. It wasn't a good match. Add what you now know you need in a job, and ask what the employer can offer in this area.

b. You and your supervisor had a personality conflict. Make sure you show that this was an isolated incident, and that you normally get along well with people.

c. You made mistakes, but you've learned from them and are now ready to work well. Be ready to offer a specific anecdote proving that you have indeed changed.

17. **What questions do you have?**

This question gives you a chance to cover things the interviewer hasn't brought up; it also gives the interviewer a sense of your priorities and values. Now is not the time to bring up salary or fringe benefits (wait until you have a job offer). Instead, ask questions such as

- What would I be doing on a day-to-day basis?

- What kind of training program do you have? If, as I'm rotating among departments, I find that I prefer one area, can I specialize in it when the training program is over?

- How do you evaluate employees? How often do you review them? Where would you expect a new trainee (banker, staff accountant) to be three years from now?

- What happened to the last person who had this job?
- How are interest rates (a new product from competitors, imports, demographic trends, government regulations, etc.) affecting your company? Questions like these show you care enough to do your homework.
- How would you describe the company's culture?
- This sounds like a great job. What are the drawbacks?

You won't be able to anticipate every question you may get. Check with other people at your college or university who have interviewed recently to find out what questions are currently being asked in your field.

Kinds of Interviews

Many companies, dissatisfied with hires based on responses to traditional questions, are now using behavioral, situational, and stress interviews.

Behavioral Interviews

Using the theory that past behaviors predict future performance, **behavioral interviews** ask applicants to describe actual past behaviors, rather than future plans. Thus instead of asking "How would you motivate people?" the interviewer might ask, "Tell me what happened the last time you wanted to get other people to do something." Follow-up questions might include, "What exactly did you do to handle the situation? How did you feel about the results? How did the other people feel? How did your superior feel about the results?"

Additional behavioral questions may ask you to describe a situation in which you

1. Created an opportunity for yourself in a job or volunteer position.
2. Used writing to achieve your goal.
3. Went beyond the call of duty to get a job done.
4. Communicated successfully with someone you disliked.
5. Had to make a decision quickly.
6. Took a project from start to finish.
7. Used good judgment and logic in solving a problem.
8. Worked under a tight deadline.
9. Worked with a tough boss.
10. Worked with someone who wasn't doing his or her share of the work.

In your answer, describe the situation, tell what you did, and explain what happened. Think about the implications of what you did and be ready to talk about whether you'd do the same thing next time or if the situation were slightly different. For example, if you did the extra work yourself when a team member didn't do his or her share, does that fact suggest that you prefer to work alone? If the organization you're interviewing with values teams, you may want to go on to show why doing the extra work was appropriate in that situation but that you can respond differently in other situations. Figure 9.2 shows the poor responses to behavioral interview questions that cost candidates jobs at W. L. Gore & Associates.

Situational Interviews

Situational interviews put you in situations similar to those you will face on the job. They test your problem-solving skills, as well as your ability to handle problems under time constraints and with minimal preparation. While behavioral

STAR: An Interviewing Technique

"One strategy for preparing for behavioral interviews is to use the STAR Technique, as outlined below. (This technique is also referred to as the SAR and PAR techniques.)

Situation or Task

Describe the situation that you were in or the task that you needed to accomplish. You must describe a specific event or situation, not a generalized description of what you have done in the past. Be sure to give enough detail for the interviewer to understand. This situation can be from a previous job, from a volunteer experience, or any relevant event.

Action You Took

Describe the action you took and be sure to keep the focus on you. Even if you are discussing a group project or effort, describe what you did—not the efforts of the team. Don't tell what you might do, tell what you did.

Results You Achieved

What happened? How did the event end? What did you accomplish? What did you learn?"

Quoted from Randall Hansen, "STAR Interviewing Response Technique for Success in Behavioral Job Interviews," in *Quintessential Interviewing Resources*, Quintessential Careers, http://www.quintcareers.com/STAR_interviewing.html (accessed June 5, 2007).

Figure 9.2   Poor Responses to Behavioral Interview Questions

GORE-TEXT

Carolyn Murray (cmurray@wlgore.com), 37, a savvy recruiter at W.L. Gore & Associates, developers of Gore-Tex, pays little attention to a candidate's carefully scripted responses to her admittedly softball questions. Instead, she listens for a throwaway line that reveals the reality behind an otherwise benign reply. Herewith, Murray delivers a post-game analysis of how three job candidates whiffed during their interviews.

the PITCH	the SWING	the MISS
"Give me an example of a time when you had a conflict with a team member."	" 'Our leader asked me to handle all of the FedExing for our team. I did it, but I thought that FedExing was a waste of my time.' "	"At Gore, we work from a team concept. Her answer shows that she won't exactly jump when one of her teammates needs help."
"Tell me how you solved a problem that was impeding your project."	" 'One of the engineers on my team wasn't pulling his weight, and we were closing in on a deadline. So I took on some of his work. ' "	"The candidate may have resolved the issue for this particular deadline, but he did nothing to prevent the problem from happening again."
"What's the one thing that you would change about your current position?"	" 'My job as a salesman has become mundane. Now I want the responsibility of managing people.' "	"He's not maximizing his current position. Selling is never mundane if you go about it in the right way."

Source: Fast Company, January 1999, 156.

interviews asked how you handled something in the past, situational interviews focus on the future. For instance, for jobs with strong service components you could expect to be asked how you would handle an angry client. Frequently situational interviews contain actual tasks candidates are asked to perform. You may be asked to fix some computer coding, sell something to a client, prepare a brochure, or work with an actual spreadsheet. Two favorite tasks are to ask candidates to prepare and give a short presentation with visuals or to work through an online in-box. Both of these tasks test communication and organization skills, as well as the ability to perform under time constraints.

Stress Interviews

Obviously, if the task is complex, performing it at a job interview, particularly with time constraints, is stressful. Thus situational interviews can easily move into stress interviews. The higher up you move in your career, the more likely it is that you will have situational or stress interviews. **Stress interviews** deliberately put applicants under stress to see how they handle the pressure. The key is to stay calm; try to maintain your sense of humor.

Sometimes the stress is physical: for example, you're given a chair where the light is in your eyes. Speak up for yourself: ask if the position of the blind can be changed, or move to another chair.

Usually the stress is psychological. A group of interviewers may fire rapid questions. However, you can slow the pace down with deliberate answers. In another possibility, a single interviewer may probe every weak spot in your record and ask questions that elicit negatives. If you get questions that put you

Stress interviews can use physical conditions and people placement to see how candidates respond to uncomfortable situations. You have the option to change some uncomfortable conditions, such as lights shining in your eyes.

Body Language Sends Messages

"When you walk into a job interview, the first impression is made in three to seven seconds," notes Mary Dawne Arden, an executive coach. She adds, "One study found that a first impression is based on 7% spoken words, 38% tone of voice, and 55% body language."

Be aware of what your body language could be saying about you. Although actions can be interpreted differently, here are interpretations of common actions:

Closed arms	Defensive or uninterested
Hand in pockets	Unconfident
Legs crossed and wiggling foot	Nervous
Rubbing/ touching nose	Not being completely honest
Rubbing back of neck/head	Bored by conversation

Here are some tips to help you make a great first impression:

1. Choose to be too formal rather than sloppy or casual.
2. Watch your posture and plant your feet squarely on the floor.
3. Mirror your interviewer's major body language where appropriate, but don't mimic details.
4. Most importantly, be yourself, smile, and relax.

Adapted from Scott Reeves, "Is Your Body Betraying You in the Job Interview?" in *Leadership: Careers: Business Basics,* Forbes.com, http://www.forbes.com/careers/2006/02/15/employment-careers-interviews-cx_sr_0216bizbasics.html (accessed June 5, 2007).

on the defensive, rephrase them in less inflammatory terms, if necessary, and then treat them as requests for information.

Q: Why did you major in physical education? That sounds like a pretty Mickey Mouse major.

A: Are you wondering whether I have the academic preparation for this job? I started out in physical education because I've always loved team sports. I learned that I couldn't graduate in four years if I officially switched my major to business administration because the requirements were different in the two programs. But I do have 21 hours in business administration and 9 hours in accounting. And my sports experience gives me practical training in teamwork, motivating people, and management.

Respond assertively. The candidates who survive are those who stand up for themselves and who explain why indeed they *are* worth hiring.

Silence can also create stress. One woman walked into her scheduled interview to find a male interviewer with his feet up on the desk. He said, "It's been a long day. I'm tired and I want to go home. You have five minutes to sell yourself." Since she had planned the points she wanted to be sure interviewers knew, she was able to do this. "Your recruiting brochure said that you're looking for someone with a major in accounting and a minor in finance. As you may remember from my résumé, I'm majoring in accounting and have had 12 hours in finance. I've also served as treasurer of a local campaign committee and have worked as a volunteer tax preparer through the Accounting Club." When she finished, the interviewer told her it was a test: "I wanted to see how you'd handle it."

After the Interview

What you do after the interview can determine whether you get the job. Many companies expect applicants to follow up on their interviews within a week. If they don't, the company assumes that they wouldn't follow up with clients.

If the employer sends you an e-mail query, answer it promptly. You're being judged not only on what you say but on how quickly you repond. Have your list of references (see page 228) and samples of your work ready to send promptly if requested to do so.

Follow-Up Phone Calls and Messages

After a first interview, make follow-up phone calls to show enthusiasm for the job, to reinforce positives from the first interview, to overcome any negatives, and to provide information to persuade the interviewer to hire you.

A thank-you note, written within 24 hours of an onsite visit, is essential to thank your hosts for their hospitality as well as to send in receipts for your expenses. The note should

- Thank the interviewer for useful information and any helpful action.
- Remind the interviewer of what he or she liked in you.
- Use the jargon of the company and refer to specific things you learned during your interview or saw during your visit.
- Be enthusiastic about the position.
- Refer to the next move, whether you'll wait to hear from the employer or whether you want to call to learn about the status of your application.

Be sure the note is well written and error-free. Double-check the spelling of all names.

Figure 9.3 is an example of a follow-up letter after an office visit.

Negotiating for Salary and Benefits

The best time to negotiate for salary and benefits is after you have the job offer. Try to delay discussing salary early in the interview process, when you're still competing against other applicants.

Prepare for salary negotiations by finding out what the going rate is for the kind of work you hope to do. Cultivate friends who are now in the workforce to find out what they're making. Ask the campus placement office for figures on what last year's graduates got. Check trade journals and the Web.

This research is crucial. In one study, male students expected salaries in their first jobs that were 14% higher than the salaries female students expected. More than twice as many men as women expected to receive signing bonuses. Men were 16% more likely to expect annual bonuses, and the bonuses men expected were 16% higher than the bonuses women expected.[5] Knowing what a job is worth will give you the confidence to negotiate more effectively.

The best way to get more money is to convince the employer that you're worth it. During the interview process, show that you can do what the competition can't.

Figure 9.3   Follow-Up Letter after an Office Visit

405 West College, Apt. 201   *Single-space your address, date*
Thibodaux, LA 70301   *when you don't use letterhead.*
April 2, 2008

Mr. Robert Land, Account Manager
Sive Associates
378 Norman Boulevard
Cincinnati, OH 48528

Dear Mr. Land:

After visiting Sive Associates last week, I'm even more sure that writing direct mail is the career for me.

Refers to things she saw and learned during the interview.

I've always been able to brainstorm ideas, but sometimes, when I had to focus on one idea for a class project, I wasn't sure which idea was best. It was fascinating to see how you make direct mail scientific as well as creative by testing each new creative package against the control. I can understand how pleased Linda Hayes was when she learned that her new package for *Smithsonian* beat the control.

Seeing Kelly, Luke, and Gene collaborating on the Sesame Street package gave me some sense of the tight deadlines you're under. As you know, I've learned to meet deadlines, not only for my class assignments, but also in working on Nicholls' newspaper. The award I won for my feature on the primary election suggests that my quality holds up even when the deadline is tight!

Reminds interviewer of her strong points.

Thank you for your hospitality while I was in Cincinnati. You and your wife made my stay very pleasant. I especially appreciate the time the two of you took to help me find information about apartments that are accessible to wheelchairs. Cincinnati seems like a very livable city.

I'm excited about a career in direct mail and about the (possibility) of joining Sive Associates. I look forward to hearing from you soon!

Be positive, not pushy. She doesn't assume she has the job.

Refers to what will happen next.

Sincerely,

Gina Focasio

Gina Focasio
(504) 555-2948

Writer's phone number.

Puts request for reimbursement in P.S. to de-emphasize it; focuses on the job, not the cost of the trip.

P.S. My expenses totaled $454. Enclosed are receipts for my plane fare from New Orleans to Cincinnati ($367), the taxi to the airport in Cincinnati ($30), and the bus from Thibodaux to New Orleans ($57).

Encl.: Receipts for Expenses

After you have the offer, you can begin negotiating salary and benefits. You're in the strongest position when (1) you've done your homework and know what the usual salary and benefits are and (2) you can walk away from this offer if it doesn't meet your needs. Avoid naming a specific salary. Don't say you can't accept less. Instead, say you would find it difficult to accept the job under the terms first offered.

Remember that you're negotiating a package, not just a starting salary. A company that truly can't pay any more money now might be able to review you for promotion sooner than usual, or pay your moving costs, or give you a better job title. Some companies offer fringe benefits that may compensate for lower taxable income: use of a company car, reimbursements for education, child care or elder care subsidies, or help in finding a job for your spouse or partner. And think about your career, not just the initial salary. Sometimes a low-paying job at a company that will provide superb experience will do more for your career (and your long-term earning prospects) than a high salary now with no room to grow.

Work toward a compromise. You want the employer to be happy that you're coming on board and to feel that you've behaved maturely and professionally.

Deciding Which Offer to Accept

The problem with choosing among job offers is that you're comparing apples and oranges. The job with the most interesting work pays peanuts. The job that pays best is in a city where you don't want to live. The secret of professional happiness is taking a job where the positives are things you want and the negatives are things that don't matter much to you.

To choose among job offers, you need to know what is truly important to *you*. Start by answering questions like the following:

- Are you willing to work after hours? To take work home? To travel? How important is money to you? Prestige? Time to spend with family and friends?
- Would you rather have firm deadlines or a flexible schedule? Do you prefer working alone or with other people? Do you prefer specific instructions and standards for evaluation or freedom and uncertainty? How comfortable are you with pressure? How much variety and challenge do you want?
- What kinds of opportunities for training and advancement are you seeking?
- Where do you want to live? What features in terms of weather, geography, cultural and social life do you see as ideal?
- Is it important to you that your work achieve certain purposes or values, or do you see work as "just a way to make a living"? Are the organization's culture and ethical standards ones you find comfortable? Will you be able to do work you can point to with pride?

No job is perfect but some jobs will fulfill more of your major criteria than will others.

Some employers offer jobs at the end of the office visit. In other cases, you may wait for weeks or even months to hear. Employers may offer jobs orally. You must say something in response immediately, so it's good to plan some strategies in advance.

If your first offer is not from your first choice, express your pleasure at being offered the job, but do not accept it on the phone. "That's great! I assume I have two weeks to let you know?" Then *call* the other companies you're interested in. Explain, "I've just got a job offer, but I'd rather work for you. Can you tell me what the status of my application is?" Nobody will put that information in writing, but almost everyone will tell you over the phone. With this information, you're in a better position to decide whether to accept the original offer.

Companies routinely give applicants two weeks to accept or reject offers. Some students have been successful in getting those two weeks extended to several weeks or even months. Certainly if you cannot decide by the deadline, it is worth asking for more time: The worst the company can do is say *no*. If you do try to keep a company hanging for a long time, be prepared for weekly phone calls asking you if you've decided yet.

Make your acceptance contingent upon a written job offer confirming the terms. That letter should spell out not only salary but also fringe benefits and any special provisions you have negotiated. If something is missing, call the interviewer for clarification: "You said that I'd be reviewed for a promotion and higher salary in six months, but that isn't in the letter." Even well-intentioned people can forget oral promises. You have more power to resolve misunderstandings now than you will after six months or a year on the job. Furthermore, the person who made you the promise may no longer be with the company a year later.

When you've accepted one job, let the other places you visited know that you're no longer interested. Then they can go to their second choices. If you're second on someone else's list, you'll appreciate other candidates' removing themselves so the way is clear for you.

Your First Full-Time Job

Just like the step from high school to college, the step from college to your first full-time job brings changes that you must negotiate. As you go to being new kid on the block yet again, remember all the coping strategies you have developed as a newbie in middle school, high school, and college.

- Reread all your materials on the organization, its competition, and the industry.
- Network with people in the field.
- Talk to recent hires in the organization. Ask them what they found to be helpful advice when they were starting.
- Be observant. Watch what people wear, how they act, how they talk. Watch how they interact during meetings and in the break room. Look at the kinds of e-mails and letters people send.
- Find a successful person who is willing to mentor you.
- Ask lots of questions. It may feel embarrassing, but it will feel even worse to still be ignorant several months down the road.
- Be pleasant and polite to everyone, including support personnel.
- Be punctual. Arrive for work and meetings on time.
- Be dependable. Do what you say you will do—and by the deadline.
- Be organized. Take a few minutes to plan your daily work. Keep track of papers and e-mails.
- Be resourceful. Few work projects will come to you with the detailed instructions provided by your professors. Think projects through. Ask for suggestions from trusted colleagues. Have a plan before you go to your boss with questions.
- Be discreet. Be careful what you say, and where you say it. Above all, be careful what you put in e-mails; remember those company files!
- Go the extra mile. Help out even when you are not asked. Put in extra hours when your help is needed.
- Enjoy yourself. Enthusiasm for your new job and colleagues will have you part of the team in short order.

Job Seekers Make the Most Mistakes at Interviews

Successfully completing an interview is no easy task suggests a survey conducted by Robert Half Finance & Accounting, a financial recruitment service. The survey asked 1,400 chief financial officers to list the area in which job applicants make the most mistakes. According to the study, employers believe that job applicants make more mistakes during interviews than any other time in the hiring process.

Respondents cast their votes this way:

Interview	32%
Résumé	21%
Cover letter	9%
Reference checks	9%
Interview follow-up	7%
Screening call	6%
Other	2%
Don't know	14%

Interview mistakes frequently occur as a result of "not knowing enough about the company or position, displaying a bad attitude or inquiring about compensation prematurely," according to Max Messmer, Chairman of Robert Half Finance & Accounting and author of *Managing Your Career for Dummies*.

What steps can you take to better prepare yourself for an interview?

Adapted from Robert Half Finance & Accounting, "Tell Me About Yourself," in Press Room: 2005, http://www.roberthalffinance.com (accessed June 5, 2007).[6] For complete citation, see endnote 6.

Summary of Key Points

- Develop an overall strategy based on your answers to these three questions:
    1. What two to five facts about yourself do you want the interviewer to know?
    2. What disadvantages or weaknesses do you need to overcome or minimize?
    3. What do you need to know about the job and the organization to decide whether or not you want to accept this job if it is offered to you?
- Check on dress expectations before the interview.
- Rehearse everything you can. In particular, practice answers to common questions. Ask a friend to interview you. If your campus has practice interviewer on videotaping facilities, use them so that you can evaluate and modify your interview behavior.
- Be your best self at the interview.
- Bring an extra copy of your résumé, something to write on and write with, and copies of your work to the interview.
- Record the name of the interviewer, tips the interviewer gave you, what the interviewer liked about you, answers to your questions about the company, and when you'll hear from the company.
- Successful applicants know what they want to do, use the company name in the interview, have researched the company in advance, back up claims with specifics, use technical jargon, ask specific questions, and talk more of the time.
- **Behavioral interviews** ask the applicant to describe actual behaviors, rather than plans or general principles. To answer a behavioral question, describe the situation, tell what you did, and tell what happened. Think about the implications of what you did and be ready to talk about whether you'd do the same thing next time or if the situation were slightly different.
- **Situational interviews** put you in a situation that allows the interviewer to see whether you have the qualities the company is seeking.
- **Stress interviews** deliberately create physical or psychological stress. Change the conditions that create physical stress. Meet psychological stress by rephrasing questions in less inflammatory terms and treating them as requests for information.
- Use follow-up phone calls to reinforce positives from the first interview, and to provide information to persuade the interviewer to hire you.
- A follow-up message should
    - Thank the interviewer for useful information and any helpful actions.
    - Remind the interviewer of what he or she liked in you.
    - Use the jargon of the company and refer to specific things you learned during your interview or saw during your visit.
    - Be enthusiastic about the position.
    - Refer to the next move you'll make.
- The best time to negotiate for salary and benefits is after you have the job offer.
- If your first offer isn't from your first choice, call the other companies you're interested in to ask the status of your application.

CHAPTER 9   Exercises and Problems

9.1   Reviewing the Chapter

1. Name four interview channels. What special considerations do you have to make for them? (LO 1)
2. What are three special kinds of interviews you may encounter? What are tips to succeed in them? (LO 1)
3. What preparations should you make before an interview? (LO 2)
4. What are some behavior tips you should keep in mind during an interview? (LO 3)
5. What should you accomplish in the close of an interview? (LO 3)
6. What are some common interview questions? What are effective answers for you? (LO 4)
7. What do you need to do after an interview? (LO 5)
8. When do you negotiate for salary? Why? (LO 5)
9. What are some tips for succeeding in your new job? (LO 6)

9.2   Interviewing Job Hunters

Talk to students at your school who are interviewing for jobs this term. Possible questions to ask them include

- What field are you in? How good is the job market in that field this year?
- How long is the first interview with a company, usually?
- What questions have you been asked at job interviews? Were you asked any stress or sexist questions? Any really oddball questions?
- What answers seemed to go over well? What answers bombed?
- At an office visit or plant trip, how many people did you talk to? What were their job titles?
- Were you asked to take any tests (skills, physical, drugs)?

- How long did you have to wait after a first interview to learn whether you were being invited for an office visit? How long after an office visit did it take to learn whether you were being offered a job? How much time did the company give you to decide?
- What advice would you have for someone who will be interviewing next term or next year?

As your instructor directs,

a. Summarize your findings in a memo to your instructor.
b. Report your findings orally to the class.
c. Join with a small group of students to write a group report describing the results of your survey.

9.3   Interviewing an Interviewer

Talk to someone who regularly interviews candidates for entry-level jobs. Possible questions to ask include the following:

- How long have you been interviewing for your organization? Does everyone on the management ladder at your company do some interviewing, or do people specialize in it?
- Do you follow a set structure for interviews? What are some of the standard questions you ask?
- What are you looking for? How important are (1) good grades, (2) leadership roles in extracurricular groups, or (3) relevant work experience? What advice would you give to someone who lacks one or more of these?
- What are the things you see students do that create a poor impression? Think about the worst candidate

you've interviewed. What did he or she do (or not do) to create such a negative impression?
- What are the things that make a good impression? Recall the best student you've ever interviewed. Why did he or she impress you so much?
- How does your employer evaluate and reward your success as an interviewer?
- What advice would you have for someone who still has a year or so before the job hunt begins?

As your instructor directs,

a. Summarize your findings in a memo to your instructor.
b. Report your findings orally to the class.
c. Join with a small group of students to write a group report describing the results of your survey.
d. Write to the interviewer thanking him or her for taking the time to talk to you.

9.4   Preparing an Interview Strategy

Based on your analysis in Problems 7.3 and 7.4, prepare an interview strategy.

1. List two to five things about yourself that you want the interviewer to know before you leave the interview.
2. Identify any weaknesses or apparent weaknesses in your record and plan ways to explain them or minimize them.
3. List the points you need to learn about an employer to decide whether to accept an office visit or plant trip.

As your instructor directs,

a. Share your strategy with a small group of other students.
b. Describe your strategy in a memo to your instructor.
c. Present your strategy orally to the class.

9.5   Preparing Questions to Ask Employers

Prepare a list of questions to ask at job interviews.

1. Prepare a list of three to five general questions that apply to most employers in your field.
2. Prepare two to five specific questions for the three companies you are most interested in.

As your instructor directs,

a. Share the questions with a small group of other students.
b. List the questions in a memo to your instructor.
c. Present your questions orally to the class.

9.6   Preparing Answers to Questions You May Be Asked

Prepare answers to each of the interview questions listed in this chapter and to any other questions that you know are likely to be asked of job hunters in your field or on your campus.

As your instructor directs,

a. Write down the answers to your questions and turn them in.
b. Conduct mini-interviews in a small group of students. In the group, let student A be the interviewer and ask five questions from the list. Student B will play the job candidate and answer the questions, using real information about student B's field and qualifications. Student C will evaluate the content of the answer. Student D will observe the nonverbal behavior of the interviewer (A); student E will observe the nonverbal behavior of the interviewee (B).

After the mini-interview, let students C, D, and E share their observations and recommend ways that B could be even more effective. Then switch roles. Let another student be the interviewer and ask five questions of another interviewee, while new observers note content and nonverbal behavior. Continue the process until everyone in the group has had a chance to be "interviewed."

9.7   Writing a Follow-Up Message after an Onsite Visit

Write a follow-up e-mail message or letter after an office visit or plant trip. Thank your hosts for their hospitality; relate your strong points to things you learned about the company during the visit; allay any negatives that may remain; be enthusiastic about the company; and submit receipts for your expenses so you can be reimbursed.

9.8   Clarifying the Terms of a Job Offer

Last week, you got a job offer from your first choice company, and you accepted it over the phone. Today, the written confirmation arrived. The letter specifies the starting salary and fringe benefits you had negotiated. However, during the office visit, you were promised a 5% raise in six months. The job offer says nothing about the raise. You do want the job, but you want it on the terms you thought you had negotiated.

Write to your contact at the company, Damon Winters.

9.9   Researching a Geographic Area

Research a geographic area where you would like to work. Investigate the cost of living, industrial growth in the area, weather and climate, and attractions in the area you could visit. Factbook.com and the local Chamber of Commerce are good places to start your research.

As your instructor directs,

a.   Share your findings with a small group of other students.

b.   Describe your findings in a memo to your instructor.

c.   Present your findings orally to the class.

9.10   Listing Job Qualities

Write and rank a list of qualities you would like your future employer to possess (benefits, vacation policies, organizational culture traits, training programs, promotion schedules, and so forth).

As your instructor directs,

a.   Share your findings with a small group of other students.

b.   Describe your findings in a memo to your instructor.

c.   Present your findings orally to the class.

9.11   Mosaic Case

After a heated debate between Sarah and Demetri about who found the better candidate for the internship position (see Chapter 8, Exercise 8.18), Yvonne decided to interview both candidates for the communication specialist intern position.

On the day of the interview, candidate 1 arrived 10 minutes before his scheduled interview time. He wore a three-piece business suit with shiny shoes. His hair was well combed to the side, and he looked clean shaven. Demetri, positive this was the guy for the internship position, promptly greeted the candidate.

"Welcome!" he said while stretching out his hand. The candidate gave a firm handshake. "Nice to meet you," continued Demetri. "Follow me this way to our conference room. We'll begin in just a few moments as soon as Yvonne, the head of the Communication Department here at Mosaic, gets out of another meeting."

"That's fine," the candidate said and followed Demetri to the room.

Once the interview began, the candidate had some good credentials and experience that might come in handy for Mosaic. However, he spent a majority of the time talking about his past experiences and how great he was at all of them. Sarah got the impression the guy was really high on himself. For example, he mentioned multiple times that while working at a furniture warehouse, all three of his bosses routinely told him that he was the greatest employee they ever had work for them. At times, it also seemed like this internship at Mosaic would be merely a stepping stone for him to move on to bigger and better things.

Yvonne concluded by asking the candidate if he had any questions about Mosaic. "Nope. I understand everything about the job. I'm just ready to begin," said the candidate in a half-joking manner.

Sarah quickly thanked him and showed him to the door.

Candidate 2 arrived exactly at the time the interview was supposed to begin. When she walked into the communication wing of Mosaic, Demetri asked her, "Do you need any help or can I point you in the right direction?"

"Well, I'm here to interview for the internship position," she replied.

"Oh," said Demetri as he turned around so he wasn't facing her while holding back laughter. The candidate wore clothes that looked more like something that would be worn to a club on a Saturday night than to a professional interview. Her hair was a bit disheveled, and there were tattoos visible on her right ankle and neck.

When Demetri regained his composure, he turned around and said, "Right this way," and he led her into the conference room.

During the interview, she answered most of Yvonne's questions by discussing her skills and qualifications and how they would fit in with the team at Mosaic. The candidate had clearly done research about Mosaic and knew some of the major tasks the Communication Department accomplishes. For example, she asked if she would be part of preparing the annual report that was coming up soon. She also asked questions about her specific job duties and to whom she would report. Finally, she queried about the possibility of being hired full time if she proved herself to Mosaic.

Sarah, who was secretly rooting for this candidate, enthusiastically thanked her and escorted her out.

Consider the following questions for discussion:

- What risks is Mosaic taking by hiring either candidate?
- How much do appearances predict a worker's ability?
- How much do substantive answers predict a worker's ability?
- How might either candidate have approached the interview differently?
- Who should be hired for the internship position?

Informative and Positive Messages

Learning Objectives

After studying this chapter, you will know:

1 When to use common business media.

2 How to use the chosen channel effectively.

3 How to write letters and memos.

4 How to compose some of the common varieties of informative and positive messages.

All in a Day's (Communication) Work

Jim Donald, CEO and president of Starbucks, knows the value of informative and positive messages. His days are full of them. On the day of his *Fortune* magazine interview, around 6 AM he left a voice mail for 100 regional managers, wrote personal thank-you notes to 25 employees, and signed 500 birthday cards. He will sign more than 3,500 in the year. He gets 200–250 e-mails daily and responds personally to 75% of them.

> *"He gets 200–250 emails daily and responds personally to 75% of them."*

He is also known for visiting his stores, where he dons the green apron, goes behind the counter, and talks with employees. When he is in Seattle, he visits about 20 Starbucks a week; when he is traveling, about 10 a day.

Although you probably don't want his e-mail load, you might appreciate his meeting time limits. He books meetings for an hour and insists they be finished in 45 minutes, leaving everyone with 15 minutes to process ideas and maybe even cope with that e-mail load.

Source: Patricia Sellers, "A Double Shot of Productivity: Jim Donald, CEO and President, Starbucks," *Fortune*, October 16, 2006, 51.

Chapter Outline

Information Overload

Common Media
- Face-to-Face Contacts
- Phone Calls
- Instant Messages

Writing E-Mails, Letters, and Paper Memos

Organizing Informative and Positive Messages

Subject Lines for Informative and Positive Messages
- Making Subject Lines Specific
- Making Subject Lines Concise
- Making Subject Lines Appropriate for the Pattern of Organization
- Pointers for E-Mail Messages

Managing the Information in Your Messages

Using Benefits in Informative and Positive Messages

Ending Informative and Positive Messages

Humor in Informative Messages

Varieties of Informative and Positive Messages
- Transmittals
- Summaries
- Thank-You and Positive Feedback Notes
- Adjustments and Responses to Complaints

Solving a Sample Problem
- Problem
- Analysis of the Problem
- Discussion of the Sample Solutions

Summary of Key Points

Business messages must meet the needs of the sender (and the sender's organization), be sensitive to the audience, and accurately reflect the topic being discussed. Informative and positive messages are the bread-and-butter messages in organizations.

When we need to convey information to which the receiver's basic reaction will be neutral, the message is **informative**. If we convey information to which the receiver's reaction will be positive, the message is a **positive** or **good news message**. Neither message immediately asks the receiver to do anything. You usually do want to build positive attitudes toward the information you are presenting, so in that sense, even an informative message has a persuasive element. Chapter 11 will discuss messages where the receiver will respond negatively; Chapter 12 will discuss messages where you want the receiver to change beliefs or behavior.

Informative and positive messages include acceptances; positive answers to requests; information about procedures, products, services, or options; announcements of policy changes that are neutral or positive; and changes that are to the receiver's advantage.

Even a simple informative or good news message usually has several purposes:

Primary purposes:

To give information or good news to the receiver or to reassure the receiver.

To have the receiver view the information positively.

Secondary purposes:

To build a good image of the sender.

To build a good image of the sender's organization.

To cement a good relationship between the sender and the receiver.

To deemphasize any negative elements.

To reduce or eliminate future messages on the same subject.

Informative and positive messages are not necessarily short. Instead, the length of a message depends on your purposes, the audience's needs, and the complexity of the situation.

Information Overload

Although obviously some business communications must be longer, one of the realities of communication today is information overload. People are bombarded with junk mail, sales calls, spam, and other advertisements. On another level, even more routine communications are becoming overwhelming. With fast and cheap e-mails, plus the genuine belief in more transparent business procedures, businesses send more announcements of events, procedures, policies, services, and employee news. Departments send newsletters. Employees send announcements of and best wishes for births, birthdays, weddings, and promotions. Customers send comments about products, service, policies, and advertisements.

With this flood of information, you need to protect your communication reputation. You do not want to be the person whose e-mails or voice-mail messages are opened last because they take so long to get to the point, or even worse, the person whose messages are rarely opened at all.

Common Media

In the office, most informative and positive communications are made through five channels: face-to-face contacts, phone calls, instant messages, e-mails, and letters. Many people have personal preferences that need to be recognized. They may keep up with their e-mail but avoid listening to voice-mail messages; they may enjoy drop-in visitors but think instant messages are silly. Similarly, some channels seem better fitted for some situations than others.

Face-to-Face Contacts

Some businesses are encouraging their employees to write fewer e-mails and drop in each other's offices to conduct business.[1] Visits are a good choice when

- You know a colleague welcomes your visits.
- You are building a business relationship with a person.
- A real-time connection saves multiple phone calls or e-mails (e.g., setting a meeting agenda).
- Your business requires dialogue or negotiation.
- You need something immediately (like a signature).

**Phone Answering
Machine Pet Peeves**

- Callback numbers that are mumbled or given too quickly.
- Messages longer than 30 seconds.
- Messages that require serious note taking (when an e-mail would have been better).
- Too much or too little information.
- Demands to contact people without saying why.
- Messages expecting an immediate response.
- Angry messages.

- Discretion is vital and you do not want to leave a paper trail.
- The situation is complex enough that you want as many visual and aural cues as possible.

Use these tips for effective face-to-face contact:

- Ensure the timing is convenient for the recipient.
- If you are discussing something complex, have appropriate documents in hand.
- Don't usurp their space. Don't put your papers on top of their desk or table without their permission.
- Look for "time to go" signs. Some people have a limited tolerance for small talk, especially when they are hard at work on a task.

Phone Calls

Phone calls provide fewer contextual cues than face-to-face visits, but more cues that electronic or paper messages. Phone calls are a good choice when

- Tone of voice is important.
- A real-time connection saves multiple phone calls or e-mails (e.g., setting a meeting time).
- You need something immediately (like an OK).
- You do not want to leave a paper trail (but remember that phone records are easily obtained, as we all know from Hewlett-Packard's use of board member phone records).

Use these tips for effective phone calls:

- Ensure the timing is convenient for the recipient; promptly return calls to your machine.
- Speak clearly, especially when giving your name and phone number (even more important when leaving your name and phone number on an answering machine).
- Use an information hook: I am calling about. . . .
- Keep the call short and cordial. If you need to leave a message, keep it brief: 1–2 sentences.
- Focus on the call; do not do other work. Most people can tell if you are reading e-mail or Web pages while talking to them, and they get the message that their concern is not important to you.

Instant Messages

Formerly limited primarily to students, instant messages are beginning to gain acceptance in the business world. However, you will probably find more enthusiasm for them among your younger colleagues. But not always! Many parents have been initiated to instant messages by their children. Because they are less intrusive than phone calls or visits, instant messages are good for running commentary or questions on tasks you and your colleagues are working on simultaneously. Even here, audience is important. Some people will not recognize common abbreviations; others will not appreciate ones like OMG (oh my God). Remember that like e-mails, instant messages can be saved, forwarded, and printed. They too leave a paper trail.

Writing E-Mails, Letters, and Paper Memos

When people think of business communications, many think of e-mails, letters, and paper memos. **Letters** go to someone outside your organization; **paper** memos go to someone in your organization; e-mails can go anywhere. Today most memos are sent as e-mails rather than paper documents. A study by Rogen International reports that executives spend at least two hours a day on e-mail.[2]

E-mails, letters, and memos use different formats. The most common formats are illustrated in Appendix A. The AMS Simplified letter format is very similar to memo format: it uses a subject line and omits the salutation and the complimentary close. Thus, it is a good choice when you don't know the reader's name. Two obvious differences between the formats of e-mails and paper memos are that (1) paper memos frequently have a company name or logo, and (2) writers generally initial the "From" line on a paper memo.

The differences in audience and format are the only differences among these documents. All of these messages can be long or short, depending on how much you have to say and how complicated the situation is. All of these messages can be informal when you write to someone you know well, or more formal when you write to someone you don't know, to several audiences, or for the record. All of these messages can be simple responses that you can dash off in 15 minutes; they can also take hours of analysis and revision when you're facing a new situation or when the stakes are high.

E-mails are commonly used for these purposes:

- To accomplish routine, noncontroversial business activities (setting up meetings/appointments, reminders, notices, quick updates, information sharing).
- To save time: many people can look through 60–100 e-mails an hour.
- To save money: one e-mail can go to many people, including global teams.
- To allow readers to deal with messages at their convenience, when timing is not crucial.
- To communicate accurately.
- To provide readers with details for reference (meetings).
- To create a paper trail.

With the increasing volume of e-mails, writers need to be careful with their messages. In their research on e-mail overload, Professors Gail Fann Thomas and Cynthia L. King noted that length was not the problem: most e-mails in their study were short, four lines or less. Rather, they found three factors that contributed to the perception of e-mail overload. The first, unstable requests, included requests that got refined in the process of e-mail correspondence and frequently morphed into requests for more work. The second, pressure to respond, included requests for information within hours. People in the study noted that they were never away from their e-mail, and that these requests could come any time. The third factor, delegation of tasks and shifting interactants, included tasks that were indirectly delegated (Could anyone get me the figures on X for the noon meeting?) or that recipients of the group e-mail then gave to their own subordinates.[3]

An e-mail survey found yet another factor in overload: inappropriate e-mails. This group included jokes, personal information, and non-job-related e-mails, as well as e-mails that were unnecessarily long, trivial, and irrelevant.[4] However, another study found that as people became more comfortable working together on projects, their e-mails became more informal and personal and included such content as family commitments and personal health information. As their relationships developed, they also became more tolerant of spelling and grammar errors. When outsiders joined the project, however, e-mails went back to a formal, correct level.[5]

E-Mail Pet Peeves

- Missing or vague subject lines.
- Copying everyone rather than just the people that might find the information useful/interesting.
- Too much information/too little information.
- Too many instant messaging acronyms.
- Lack of capitalization and punctuation.
- Long messages without headings or bullets.
- Delayed response e-mails that don't include the original message. Sometimes readers have no idea what the e-mails are responding about.
- People who never respond to queries.
- People who expect an immediate answer.
- People who don't read their e-mail carefully enough to absorb a simple message.
- Superfluous images and attachments.
- Flaming.

In general, try to avoid another major problem with e-mail: using it for negative content. Negative critiques, bad news, and arguments generally have better outcomes when delivered in person. Sarcasm and irony are too frequently misinterpreted to be safely used. Similarly, avoid passing on gossip in your e-mails. The chances of having your gossip forwarded with your name attached are just too great.

Organizing Informative and Positive Messages

The patterns of organization in this chapter and others follow standard conventions of business. The patterns will work for 70 to 90% of the writing situations most people in business and government face. Using the appropriate pattern can help you compose more quickly, create a better final product, and demonstrate you know the conventions.

* Be sure you understand the rationale behind each pattern so that you can modify the pattern when necessary.
* Not every message that uses the basic pattern will have all the elements listed.
* Sometimes you can present several elements in one paragraph. Sometimes you'll need several paragraphs for just one element.

In real life, writing problems don't come with labels that tell you which pattern to use. Chapters 10, 11, and 12 offer advice about when to use each pattern.

Figure 10.1 shows how to organize informative and positive messages. Figures 10.2 and 10.3 illustrate two ways that the basic pattern can be applied.

The letter in Figure 10.2 announces a change in a magazine's ownership. Rather than telling subscribers that their magazine has been acquired, which sounds negative, the first two paragraphs describe the change as a merger that will give subscribers greater benefits from the combined magazine. Paragraph 3 provides details about how the arrangement will work,

Figure 10.1   How to Organize Informative and Positive Messages

1. **Start with good news or the most important information.** Summarize the main points. If the reader has already raised the issue, make it clear that you're responding.
2. **Give details, clarification, background.** Answer all the questions your reader is likely to have; provide all the information necessary to achieve your purposes. If you are asking or answering multiple questions, number them. Enumeration increases your chances of giving or receiving all the necessary information. Present details in the order of importance to the reader or in some other logical order.
3. **Present any negative elements—as positively as possible.** A policy may have limits; information may be incomplete; the reader may have to satisfy requirements to get a discount or benefit. Make these negatives clear, but present them as positively as possible.
4. **Explain any benefits.** Most informative memos need benefits. Show that the policy or procedure helps readers, not just the company. Give enough detail to make the benefits clear and convincing. In letters, you may want to give benefits of dealing with your company as well as benefits of the product or policy.

   In a good news message, it's often possible to combine a short benefit with a goodwill ending in the last paragraph.
5. **Use a goodwill ending: positive, personal, and forward-looking.** Shifting your emphasis away from the message to the specific reader suggests that serving the reader is your real concern.

Figure 10.2   A Positive Letter

eBusCompanyToday

P.O. Box 12345
Tampa, FL   33660
813-555-5555

Dear Ms. Locker,

Main point presented as good news —— We're excited to share some great news! *eBusCompanyToday* has merged with another business magazine, *High-Tech Business News*. This merged publication will be called *High-Tech Business News* and will continue to be edited and published by the *eBusCompanyToday* staff.

Details focus on benefits to the reader —— The "new" *High-Tech Business News* is a great tool for navigating today's relentlessly changing marketplace, particularly as it's driven by the Internet and other technologies. It reports on the most innovative business practices and the people behind them; delivers surprising, useful insights; and explains how to put them to work. Please be assured that you will continue to receive the same great editorial coverage that you've come to expect from *eBusCompanyToday*.

You will receive the "new" *High-Tech Business News* in about 4 weeks, starting with the combined August/September issue. If you already subscribe to *High-Tech Business News*, your subscription will be extended accordingly. And if you'd rather not receive this publication, please call 1-800-555-5555 within the next 3 weeks. —— *Option to cancel is offered but not emphasized*

Positive, personal, forward-looking ending —— Thank you for your continued loyalty to *eBusCompanyToday*; we're confident that you will enjoy reading *High-Tech Business News* every month.

Sincerely,

Alan Schmidt

Alan Schmidt, Editor and President

High-Tech Business News is published monthly except for two issues combined periodically into one and occasional extra, expanded or premium issues.

Figure 10.3   A Positive Memo, Sent to Chamber of Commerce Employees and Members

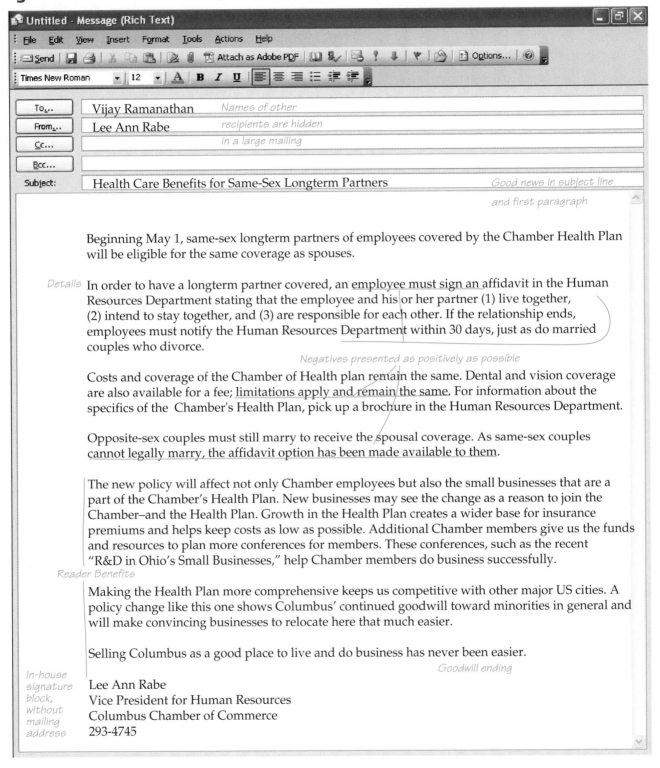

Untitled - Message (Rich Text)

File   Edit   View   Insert   Format   Tools   Actions   Help

Send | Attach as Adobe PDF | Options...

Times New Roman | 12 | A   B   I   U

To...   Vijay Ramanathan   *Names of other*
From...   Lee Ann Rabe   *recipients are hidden*
Cc...   *in a large mailing*
Bcc...
Subject: Health Care Benefits for Same-Sex Longterm Partners   *Good news in subject line*
                                                                        and first paragraph

Beginning May 1, same-sex longterm partners of employees covered by the Chamber Health Plan will be eligible for the same coverage as spouses.

Details In order to have a longterm partner covered, an <u>employee must sign an</u> affidavit in the Human Resources Department stating that the employee and his or her partner (1) live together, (2) intend to stay together, and (3) are responsible for each other. If the relationship ends, employees must notify the Human Resources Department within 30 days, just as do married couples who divorce.

Negatives presented as positively as possible

Costs and coverage of the Chamber of Health plan remain the same. Dental and vision coverage are also available for a fee; <u>limitations apply and remain the same</u>. For information about the specifics of the Chamber's Health Plan, pick up a brochure in the Human Resources Department.

Opposite-sex couples must still marry to receive the spousal coverage. As same-sex couples <u>cannot legally marry, the affidavit option has been made available to them</u>.

The new policy will affect not only Chamber employees but also the small businesses that are a part of the Chamber's Health Plan. New businesses may see the change as a reason to join the Chamber–and the Health Plan. Growth in the Health Plan creates a wider base for insurance premiums and helps keep costs as low as possible. Additional Chamber members give us the funds and resources to plan more conferences for members. These conferences, such as the recent "R&D in Ohio's Small Businesses," help Chamber members do business successfully.

Reader Benefits

Making the Health Plan more comprehensive keeps us competitive with other major US cities. A policy change like this one shows Columbus' continued goodwill toward minorities in general and will make convincing businesses to relocate here that much easier.

Selling Columbus as a good place to live and do business has never been easier.

Goodwill ending

In-house signature block, without mailing address

Lee Ann Rabe
Vice President for Human Resources
Columbus Chamber of Commerce
293-4745

along with a way to opt out. A possible negative is that readers who already have subscriptions to both magazines will now receive only one. The company addresses this positively by extending the subscription to the jointly published magazine. The goodwill ending has all the desired characteristics: it is positive ("we're confident"), personal ("your continued loyalty"), and forward-looking ("you will enjoy").

The memo in Figure 10.3 announces a new employee benefit. The first paragraph summarizes the policy. Paragraphs 2–4 give details. Negative elements are stated as positively as possible. The last section of the memo gives benefits and a goodwill ending.

Subject Lines for Informative and Positive Messages

A **subject line** is the title of a document. It aids in filing and retrieving the document, tells readers why they need to read the document, and provides a framework in which to set what you're about to say. Subject lines are standard in memos and e-mails. Letters are not required to have subject lines (see Appendix A, Formats for Letters, Memos, and E-Mail Messages).

A good subject line meets three criteria: it is specific, concise, and appropriate to the kind of message (positive, negative, persuasive).

Making Subject Lines Specific

The subject line needs to be specific enough to differentiate that message from others on the same subject, but broad enough to cover everything in the message.

Too general:	Training Sessions
Better:	Dates for 2008 Training Sessions
or:	Evaluation of Training Sessions on Conducting Interviews
or:	Should We Schedule a Short Course on Proposal Writing?

Making Subject Lines Concise

Most subject lines are relatively short. MailerMailer, a Web-based e-mail management service, found that e-mails whose subject lines were 35 characters or less were significantly more likely to be opened by readers than subject lines with more than 35 characters.[6]

Wordy:	Survey of Student Preferences in Regards to Various Pizza Factors
Better:	Students' Pizza Preferences

If you can't make the subject both specific and short, be specific.

Making Subject Lines Appropriate for the Pattern of Organization

Since your subject line introduces your reader to your message, it must satisfy the psychological demands of the situation; it must be appropriate to your purposes and to the immediate response you expect from your reader. In general, do the same thing in your subject line that you would do in the first paragraph.

When you have good news for the reader, build goodwill by highlighting it in the subject line. When your information is neutral, summarize it concisely for the subject line.

Use To/CC/BCC Lines to Your Advantage

To

Send your e-mail only to people who will really want or need it. If you are sending to multiple people, decide in which order to place the names. Is organizational rank important? Should you alphabetize the list? Don't hit "reply to all" unless all will appreciate your doing so.

CC

CC stands for "carbon copy," from the days of typewriters when carbon paper was used to make multiple copies. CC people who are not directly involved in the business of the e-mail but are interested in it. Marketing may not be helping you produce your new software, but they may want to stay abreast of the changes so they can start generating marketing ideas. A committee might CC a secretary who does not attend committee meetings but does maintain the committee's paper records.

Sometimes the CC line is used politically. For example, an administrative assistant doing routine business may CC the boss to give added weight to the e-mail.

BCC

BCC stands for "blind carbon copy," a copy that the listed receivers do not know is being sent. Blind copies can create ill will when they become known, so be careful in their use.

> Subject: Discount on Rental Cars Effective January 2
>
> Starting January 2, as an employee of Amalgamated Industries you can get a 15% discount on cars you rent for business or personal use from Roadway Rent-a-Car.

> Subject: Update on Arrangements for Videoconference with France
>
> In the last month, we have chosen the participants and developed a tentative agenda for the videoconference with France scheduled for March 21.

Pointers for E-Mail Messages

Many people skim through large lists of e-mails daily, so subject lines in e-mails are even more important than those in letters and memos. Subject lines must be specific, concise, and catchy. In these days of spam, some e-mail users get so many messages that they don't bother reading messages if they don't recognize the sender or if the subject doesn't catch their interest. Create a subject line that will help your e-mail get read:

- Use important information in the subject line. Many people delete blanks and generic tags such as "hello," "your message," "thank you," and "next meeting," if they don't recognize the sender, especially now that so much spam has common business tags.

- Put good news in the subject line.

E-mail messages are no longer received only on computers. The range of devices where users can access e-mail means creating messages that are clear, cordial, complete, concise, and correct is even more important.

- Name drop to make a connection: Our Director gave me your name.
- Make e-mail sound easy to deal with: Two Short Travel Questions.

The following subject lines would be acceptable for informative and good news e-mail messages:

Travel Plans for Sales Meeting
Your Proposal Accepted
Reduced Prices During February
Your Funding Request Approved

When you reply to a message, check to see that the automatic subject line "Re: [subject line of message to which you are responding]" is still appropriate. If it isn't, you may want to create a new subject line. And if a series of messages arises, you probably need a new subject line. "Re: Re: Re: Re: Question" is not an effective subject line.

Many people read their e-mails very quickly. They may read for only a few seconds or lines to decide if the e-mail is pertinent. Value your readers' time: Put the most important information in the first sentence. If your e-mail is more than one screen long, use headings and enumeration to help draw readers to successive screens.

Managing the Information in Your Messages

Information control is important. You want to give your audience the information they need, but you don't want to overwhelm them with information. Sometimes you will have good reasons for not providing all the information they want.

When you are the person in the know, it is easy to overestimate how much your audience knows. As a patient seeking medical treatment, you understand how much you would appreciate being told how long the wait is. When you leave a medical facility, you know how difficult it is to remember accurately those complicated instructions given to you orally by a doctor or nurse. Unfortunately, most of the huge medical industry seems to be just discovering these facts now. Medical offices are beginning to communicate waiting times and send patients home with written instructions for self-care and follow-up visits.[7]

But, of course, information management is not always that simple. Pharmaceutical companies struggle with how much information to provide about their drugs. In 2004, the FDA publicized an analysis showing that young people on antidepressants had a 2% risk of suicidal thoughts. There were no actual suicides reported in the studies, just suicidal thoughts. Nevertheless, the FDA put a Black Box warning—the strongest possible warning—on antidepressants. Parents and physicians began backing away from the medications. Use of SSRI (selective serotonin reuptake inhibitors) medications in young people declined 14%, and suicides increased 18% among young people the first year of the warnings.[8]

Other concerns about managing information are more prosaic. If you send out regularly scheduled messages on the same topic, such as monthly updates of training seminars, try to develop a system that lets people know immediately what is new. Use color for new or changed entries. Put new material at the top.

If you send messages with an attachment, put the most vital information in the e-mail too. Don't make readers open an attachment merely to find out the time or location of a meeting.

Check your message for accuracy and completeness. Remember all the e-mails you receive about meetings that forget to include the time, place, or

You—A Most Important Subject

On the job, one of the most important subjects you can communicate about is your own performance. Make sure your boss knows what you are doing. You don't have to brag; simply noting your accomplishments is usually enough, because many employees do not take the time to do so.

Remember that raises are based not on the hard work you actually do, but the hard work your boss knows about. Furthermore, bosses count the work they want done, which is not always the work employees emphasize.

Provide your boss with paper copies of your work; CC him/her on major e-mails, if appropriate. Have 30-second blurbs ready for times when you and your boss are alone in the elevator or break room: "We got the McCluskey contract ready a day early" or "the new G7 database is going to IT tomorrow."

Wacky Warnings

[In his book, *Remove Child before Folding: The 101 Stupidest, Silliest, and Wackiest Warning Labels Ever*, Bob Dorigo Jones provides these examples of wacky warnings:]

- "May cause drowsiness" (on a sleeping aid).
- "Never use when sleeping" (on a propane torch).
- "Do not eat toner" (on a printer cartridge).
- "Never iron clothes while they are being worn" (on a household iron).
- "Caution: This is not to be used by children under 3 years of age" (on a child's toy badge that proclaims "I am 2").
- "Harmful if swallowed" (on a fishing lure with a three-pronged hook).

"The most recent winner [is] a toilet-cleaning brush that comes with the warning, 'Do not use for personal hygiene.'"

Quoted from Ron Berthel, "Weird Warnings: Close Cover Before Striking This Book," *Des Moines Register*, February 4, 2007, 5op.

date, and don't let your e-mails fall in that incomplete category. Make a special effort to ensure that promised attachments really are attached. Be particularly careful with the last messages you send for the day or the week, when haste can cause errors.

Remember that e-mails are public documents, and may be widely forwarded. Save lowercase and instant message abbreviations for friends, if you use them at all. Never put anything in an e-mail that would embarrass you or harm your career if your employer, colleague, parent, or child saw it. An American employee responded to a request for floor mats from an American GI in Iraq by saying "We would NEVER ship to Iraq. If you were sensible, you and your troops would pull out of Iraq." The e-mail quickly circulated on the Internet, getting the employee fired and the business boycotted.[9] Starbucks had a different e-mail problem. An e-mail coupon for a free grande iced beverage was sent to some Atlanta employees to forward to family and friends. The coupon made its way to the Web, where it became an Internet star. It spread so widely that Starbucks stopped honoring the coupon.[10]

Using Benefits in Informative and Positive Messages

Not all informative and positive messages need benefits (p. 57). You don't need benefits when

- You're presenting factual information only.
- The audience's attitude toward the information doesn't matter.
- Stressing benefits may make the audience sound selfish.
- The benefits are so obvious that to restate them insults the audience's intelligence.

You do need benefits when

- You are presenting policies.
- You want to shape your audience's attitudes toward the information or toward your organization.
- Stressing benefits presents the audience's motives positively.
- Some of the benefits may not be obvious.

Messages to customers or potential customers sometimes include a sales paragraph promoting products or services you offer in addition to the product or service that the audience has asked about. Sales promotion in an informative or positive message should be low-key, not "hard sell."

Benefits are hardest to develop when you are announcing policies. The organization probably decided to adopt the policy because it appeared to help the organization; the people who made the decision may not have thought at all about whether it would help or hurt employees. Yet benefits are most essential in this kind of message so employees see the reason for the change and support it.

When you present benefits, be sure to present advantages *to the audience*. Most new policies help the organization in some way, but few workers will see their own interests as identical with these of the organization. Employees' benefits need to be spelled out, as do those of customers. To save money, an organization may change health care providers, but the notice to employees should spell out new benefits for employees and their families. Airlines announced their new check-in kiosks to customers as a way to avoid lines and save travelers' time.

To develop benefits for informative and positive messages, use the steps suggested in Chapter 3. Be sure to think about benefits that come from the activity or policy itself, apart from any financial benefits. Does a policy improve customers' experience or the hours employees spend at work?

Ending Informative and Positive Messages

Ending a letter or memo gracefully can be a problem in short informative and positive messages. In a one-page memo where you have omitted details and proof, you can tell readers where to get more information. In long messages, you can summarize your basic point. In persuasive messages, as you'll learn in Chapter 12, you can tell readers what you want them to do. In a short message containing all the information readers need, either write a goodwill paragraph that refers directly to the reader or the reader's organization, or just stop. In many short e-mails, just stopping is the best choice.

Goodwill endings should focus on the business relationship you share with your reader rather than on the reader's hobbies, family, or personal life. Use a paragraph that shows you see your reader as an individual. Possibilities include complimenting the reader for a job well done, describing a benefit, or looking forward to something positive that relates to the subject of the message.

When you write to one person, a good last paragraph fits that person so specifically that it would not work if you sent the same basic message to someone else or to a person with the same title in another organization. When you write to someone who represents an organization, the last paragraph can refer to your company's relationship to the reader's organization. When you write to a group (for example, to "All Employees"), your ending should apply to the whole group.

In the following example, a letter answered the question "When a patient leaves the hospital and returns, should we count it as a new stay?" For one company the answer was that if a patient was gone from the hospital overnight or longer, the hospital should start a new claim when the patient was readmitted.

Weak closing paragraph:	Should you have any questions regarding this matter, please feel free to call me.
Goodwill paragraph:	Many patients appreciate the freedom to leave the hospital for a few hours. It's nice working with a hospital which is flexible enough to offer that option.
Also acceptable:	Omit the paragraph; stop after the explanation.

Some writers end every message with a standard invitation:

If you have questions, please do not hesitate to ask.

That sentence implies both that your message did not answer all questions, and that readers will hesitate to contact you. Both implications are negative. But revising the line to say "feel free to call" is rarely a good idea. People in business aren't shrinking violets; they will call if they need help. Don't make more work for yourself by inviting calls to clarify simple messages.

Humor in Informative Messages

Some writers use humor to ensure their messages are read. Humor is a risky tool because of its tendency to rile some people. However, if you know your audience well, humor may help ensure that they read and remember your messages.

April Fool's Hoaxes: Famous (Mis) Information

"In 1996, the Taco Bell Corp. announced that it had bought the Liberty Bell from the federal government and was renaming it the Taco Liberty Bell. Hundreds of outraged citizens called up the National Historic Park in Philadelphia where the bell is housed to express their anger.

"In 1998 Burger King published a full page advertisement in *USA Today* announcing the introduction of a new item to their menu: a 'Left-Handed Whopper' specially designed for the 32 million left-handed Americans. According to the advertisement, the new whopper included the same ingredients as the original Whopper (lettuce, tomato, hamburger patty, etc.), but all the condiments were rotated 180 degrees for the benefit of their left-handed customers. The following day Burger King issued a follow-up release revealing that although the Left-Handed Whopper was a hoax, thousands of customers had gone into restaurants to request the new sandwich. Simultaneously, according to the press release, 'many others requested their own "right handed" version.'"

What benefits did these companies gain from their hoaxes? How could this misinformation backfire?

Hoaxes quoted from "The Top 100 April Fool's Day Hoaxes of All Time," http://www.museumofhoaxes.com/hoax/aprilfool/index (accessed April 27, 2007).

Adapted from Ellen Neuborne, "Making E-Mail Work: How to Enhance—Not Sabotage—Client Relationships with Electronic Newsletters," *Sales & Marketing Management*, February 2004, 18; and Rebecca Rohan, "The Messenger," *Black Enterprise*, July 2000, 55–56.

Welcome News

Many companies like to maintain ties with customers by sending out a regular newsletter via e-mail. Customers welcome this type of communication only if it is truly interesting and easy to read.

Here are a few pointers for publishing a successful electronic newsletter:

- **Be relevant.** Everyone gets plenty of cute humor online. The newsletter should be limited to information recipients can use.

- **Be brief.**

- **Be consistent.** Set up a regular schedule for the newsletter, and get it out on time. This conveys an image of dependability.

- **Be simple.** Skip the audio or video clips unless they are essential to your message. They tend to be distracting, and they slow down the process of opening e-mail.

- **Be considerate.** Set yourself apart from spammers by making it easy to unsubscribe as well as to subscribe. Lead off each mailing with an explanation like "*ABC Digest* is a monthly newsletter with hints for alphabet soup lovers, sent to subscribers who have requested it. If you would like to be removed from our mailing list, click on this link."

If you decide to use humor, these precautions will help keep it useful.

- Do not direct it against other people, even if you believe they will never see your message. The Internet abounds with proof that such certainties are false. In particular, never aim humor against a specific group of people.
- Political, religious, and sexual humor should always be avoided; it is against discrimination policies in many businesses.
- Use restraint with your humor; a little levity goes a long way.

Used with care, however, humor in carefully chosen situations can help your communications. An information technology person sent the following e-mail in his small, nonprofit organization:[11]

> My set of screw driver tips is missing. I may well have loaned them to someone, perhaps weeks ago. If you have them, please return them to me. I use them when someone reports that they have a screw loose.

He got his tips back promptly. Because he has a reputation for clever e-mails, people regularly read his messages.

Varieties of Informative and Positive Messages

Many messages can be informative, negative, or persuasive depending on what you have to say. A transmittal, for example, can be positive when you're sending glowing sales figures or persuasive when you want the reader to act on the information. A performance appraisal is positive when you evaluate someone who's doing superbly, negative when you want to compile a record to justify firing someone, and persuasive when you want to motivate a satisfactory worker to continue to improve. Each of these messages is discussed in the chapter of the pattern it uses most frequently. However, in some cases you will need to use a pattern from a different chapter.

Transmittals

When you send someone something, you frequently need to attach a memo or letter of transmittal explaining what you're sending. A transmittal can be as simple as a small yellow Post-it™ note with "FYI" ("for your information") written on it, or it can be a separate typed document.

Organize a memo or letter of transmittal in this order:

1. Tell the reader what you're sending.
2. Summarize the main point(s) of the document.
3. Indicate any special circumstances or information that would help the reader understand the document. Is it a draft? Is it a partial document that will be completed later?
4. Tell the reader what will happen next. Will you do something? Do you want a response? If you do want the reader to act, specify exactly what you want the reader to do and give a deadline.

Frequently transmittals have important secondary purposes. Consider the writer's purpose in Figure 10.4, a transmittal from a lawyer to her client. The primary purpose of this transmittal is to give the client a chance to affirm that his story and the lawyer's understanding of it are correct. If there's anything wrong, the lawyer wants to know *before* she files the brief. But an important secondary purpose is to build goodwill: "I'm working on your case; I'm earning my fee." The greatest number of complaints officially lodged against lawyers are for the lawyer's neglect—or what the client perceives as neglect—of the client's case.

Figure 10.4   A Transmittal

DREW & Associates

100 Barkley Plaza • Denver, CO 80210 • 303.555.4783 • Fax 303.555.4784

October 8, 2009

Mr. Charles Gibney
Personnel Manager
Roydon Interiors
146 East State Street
Denver, CO 80202

Dear Mr. Gibney:

Paragraph one tells reader what is enclosed and summarizes main points.

Here is a copy of the brief we intend to file with the Tenth Circuit Court in support of our position that the sex discrimination charge against Roydon Interiors should be dropped.

Will you please examine it carefully to make sure that the facts it contains are correct? If you have changes to suggest, please call my office by October 22nd, so that we can file the brief by October 24th.

Sincerely,

Diana Drew

Diana Drew

Last paragraph asks for action by a specific date.

Summaries

You may be asked to summarize a conversation, a document, or an outside meeting for colleagues or superiors. (Minutes of an internal meeting are usually more detailed. See ➡ Chapter 14 for advice on writing minutes of meetings.)

In a summary of a conversation for internal use, identify the people who were present, the topic of discussion, decisions made, and who does what next.

To summarize a document, start with the main point. Then go on to give supporting evidence or details. In some cases, your audience may also want you to evaluate the document. Should others in the company read this book? Should someone in the company write a letter to the editor responding to this newspaper article?

When you visit a client or go to a conference, you may be asked to share your findings and impressions with other people in your organization. Chronological accounts are the easiest to write but the least useful for the reader. Your company doesn't need a blow-by-blow account of what you did; it needs to know what *it* should do as a result of the meeting.

Electronic Feedback

In an attempt to boost business and promote discussion of products and services, small businesses are increasingly adding customer reviews to their Web sites. These reviews offer consumers a chance to weigh in on their experiences with a product or service. Over time, this review process has been shown to promote repeat and loyal business because consumers are more likely to trust word of mouth reviews than more traditional avenues of marketing.

A 2006 survey conducted by Forrester Research found that 71% of adults online (22 and over) and 81% of youth online (ages 13–21) use customer product ratings. The reviews not only help a small business know what's good about its organization, they also provide direct feedback on what could be improved or changed with a product or service.

Adapted from Kelly K. Spors, "How Are We Doing? Small Companies Find It Pays to Ask Customers That Question," *Wall Street Journal*, November 13, 2006, R9.

In 2006, Toyota launched an ad campaign to encourage safe driving among teenagers, who hold the highest rate for being in an accident. In the ads, Toyota attempts to inform the public about safety issues of driving recklessly, while appealing to the viewers' emotions.
Source: Toyota Advertisements, *Wall Street Journal*, October 4, 2006, A1, and September 27, 2006, A1.

Summarize a visit with a client or customer in this way:

1. Put the main point from your organization's point of view—the action to be taken, the perceptions to be changed—in the first paragraph.
2. Provide an **umbrella paragraph** to cover and foreshadow the points you will make in the report.
3. Provide necessary detail to support your conclusions and cover each point. Use lists and headings to make the structure of the document clear.

In the following example, the revised first paragraph summarizes the sales representative's conclusions after a call on a prospective client:
Original:

> On October 10th, Rick Patel and I made a joint call on Consolidated Tool Works. The discussion was held in a conference room, with the following people present:
> 1. Kyle McCloskey (Vice President and General Manager)
> 2. Bill Petrakis (Manufacturing Engineer)
> 3. Garett Lee (Process Engineering Supervisor)
> 4. Courtney Mansor-Green (Project Engineer)

Revised:

> Consolidated Tool Works is an excellent prospect for purchasing a Matrix-Churchill grinding machine. To get the order, we should
> 1. Set up a visit for CTW personnel to see the Matrix-Churchill machine in Kansas City;
> 2. Guarantee 60-day delivery if the order is placed by the end of the quarter; and
> 3. Extend credit terms to CTW.

Thank-You and Positive Feedback Notes

We all like to feel appreciated. Stress reduction expert Richard Carlson always recommended liberal applications of positive feedback in his popular books and lectures. As he reminded his audiences, employees who feel

Dear Professor Carlton,

Thank you for all your help this semester. My writing skills have improved greatly as have my organizational skills. The extra time you gave me really paid off. I've already had three job interviews due to the job packet I prepared for your course. I will miss your funny dog stories!!! Thanks again for everything!

Pat Robbins

Thank-you notes can be written on standard business stationery, using standard formats. But one student noticed that his professor really liked dogs and told funny dog stories in class. So the student found a dog card for a thank-you note.

appreciated are happier and work harder and better than those who feel taken for granted.[12]

Praising or congratulating people can cement good feelings between you and them and enhance your own visibility. Make your praise sound sincere by offering specifics and avoiding language that might seem condescending or patronizing. For example, think how silly it would sound to praise an employee for completing basic job requirements or to gush that one's professor or mentor has superior knowledge. In contrast, thanks for a kind deed and congratulations or praise on completing a difficult task are rewarding in almost any situation.

Sending a **thank-you note** will make people more willing to help you again in the future. Thank-you letters can be short but must be prompt. They need to be specific to sound sincere.

If you make it a habit to watch for opportunities to offer thanks and congratulations, you may be pleasantly surprised at the number of people who are extending themselves. Lawrence Fish, chief executive of Citizens Bank, tries to write a note of thanks or congratulations to one member of

Bad Words

Ruth King, who coaches building contractors, has advice for employees who handle customer complaints. When a customer complains, King says, avoid using the following words in your reply:

- **We're busy.** These words focus on your organization; you should focus on the customer. State the earliest possible time you can give your attention to the problem.

- **No.** When a customer is angry, the word *no* is like "gasoline on a fire." Instead, offer reasonable alternatives to choose from.

- **We can't.** These words are as infuriating as *no*. Again, specify what you *can* offer.

- **It's our policy.** Writing about the organization's policy takes the focus off the customer and is yet another way to say what you will not do. Customers aren't interested in policies, and they are likely to ask that the policy be changed or waived. Focus on alternatives that are available.

Adapted from Ruth King, "Five Things You Should Never Say to Customers," *Journal of Light Construction* 22, no. 1 (2003): 10.

his team every day. During his six-year term, Douglas Conant, Chief Executive of Campbell, sent over 16,000 handwritten thank-you notes to employees ranging from top executives to hourly workers. Linden Labs, a San Francisco virtual reality firm, has a "Love Machine" that allows employees to send other LL employees a note of thanks. These notes are tracked in a database, which is accessed during performance reviews.[13] As Kenneth Blanchard and Spencer Johnson, authors of the business best seller *The One Minute Manager*, note, "People who feel good about themselves produce good results."[14]

Adjustments and Responses to Complaints

A lot of consumers are angry these days, and organizations should be responsive to their complaints. In a recent study on customer rage by Customer Care Measurement and Consulting Firm, 70% of consumers report having bad customer-service experiences that left them "upset" or "extremely upset." Furthermore, 46% of consumers said they were dissatisfied with how a company handled their complaint. Most said they told their friends and family about their bad experience. This kind of bad publicity is risky in an Internet economy. The study suggests that the angriest customers have the power to influence about 18 other customers. That can be big money when it comes to business.[15]

Angry customers expect organizations to show that they are listening and want to resolve the problem. When you grant a customer's request for an adjusted price, discount, replacement, or other benefit to resolve a complaint, do so in the very first sentence.

> Your Visa bill for a night's lodging has been adjusted to $63. Next month a credit of $37 will appear on your bill to reimburse you for the extra amount you were originally asked to pay.

Don't talk about your own process in making the decision. Don't say anything that sounds grudging. Give the reason for the original mistake only if it reflects credit on the company. (In most cases, it doesn't, so the reason should be omitted.)

Solving a Sample Problem

Real-life problems are richer and less well defined than textbook problems and cases. But even textbook problems require analysis before you begin to write. Before you tackle the assignments for this chapter, examine the following problem. See how the analysis questions probe the basic points required for a solution. Study the two sample solutions to see what makes one unacceptable and the other one good. Note the recommendations for revision that could make the good solution excellent.[16] The checklist at the end of the chapter (p. 318) can help you evaluate a draft.

Problem

Interstate Fidelity Insurance (IFI) uses computers to handle its payments and billings. There is often a time lag between receiving a payment from a customer and recording it on the computer. Sometimes, while the payment is in line to be processed, the computer sends out additional notices: past-due notices, collection letters, even threats to sue. Customers are frightened or angry and write asking for an explanation. In most cases, if they just waited a little while, the situation would be straightened out. But policyholders are afraid that they'll be without insurance because the company thinks the bill has not been paid.

IFI doesn't have the time to check each individual situation to see if the check did arrive and has been processed. It wants you to write a letter that will persuade customers to wait. If something is wrong and the payment never reached IFI, IFI would send a legal notice to that effect saying the policy would be canceled by a certain date (which the notice would specify) at least 30 days after the date on the original premium bill. Continuing customers always get this legal notice as a third chance (after the original bill and the past-due notice).

Prepare a form letter that can go out to every policyholder who claims to have paid a premium for automobile insurance and resents getting a past-due notice. The letter should reassure readers and build goodwill for IFI.

Analysis of the Problem

1. **Who is (are) your audience(s)? What characteristics are relevant to this particular message? If you are writing to more than one reader, how do the readers differ?**

   Automobile insurance customers who say they've paid but have still received a past-due notice. They're afraid they're no longer insured. Since it's a form letter, different readers will have different situations: in some cases payments did arrive late, in some cases the company made a mistake, in some the reader never paid (check was lost in mail, unsigned, bounced, etc.).

2. **What are your purposes in writing?**

   To reassure readers that they're covered for 30 days. To inform them that they can assume everything is OK *unless* they receive a second notice. To avoid further correspondence on this subject. To build goodwill for IFI: (a) we don't want to suggest IFI is error-prone or too cheap to hire enough people to do the necessary work; (b) we don't want readers to switch companies; (c) we do want readers to buy from IFI when they're ready for more insurance.

3. **What information must your message include?**

   Readers are still insured. We cannot say whether their checks have now been processed (company doesn't want to check individual accounts). Their insurance will be canceled if they do not pay after receiving the second past-due notice (the legal notice).

4. **How can you build support for your position? What reasons or benefits will your reader find convincing?**

   Computers help us provide personal service to policyholders. We offer policies to meet all their needs. Both of these points would need specifics to be interesting and convincing.

5. **What objection(s) can you expect your reader(s) to have? What negative elements of your message must you deemphasize or overcome?**

   Computers appear to cause errors. We don't know if the checks have been processed. We will cancel policies if their checks don't arrive.

6. **What aspects of the total situation may affect reader response? The economy? The time of year? Morale in the organization? The relationship between the reader and writer? Any special circumstances?**

   The insurance business is highly competitive—other companies offer similar rates and policies. The customer could get a similar policy for about the same

One Tablespoon or Two?

The Internet has provided a means for information on just about any subject to be at your fingertips. For example, chefs are now communicating over the Internet to provide cooking tips to families just like yours. These chefs communicate through IM, e-mail, or chat boards—some services for free and some for a cost. This instant access to consumers provides just one more way chefs and restaurateurs can promote their businesses. Check out some of these sites from the following list and determine how effective they are at delivering informative messages:

- http://www.chefsline.com
- http://www.chefs.com
- http://www.cheftalk.com
- http://www.chefjoanna.com
- http://www.askachef.com

Adapted from Yuliya Cherrnova, "Soggy Stuffing, Dry Turkey? Now You Can IM a Chef," *Wall Street Journal*, November 22, 2006, D1.

http://www.thecoca-cola company.com/heritage/ stories/index.html

Stories are powerful ways to inform, teach, and persuade. Coca-Cola is one of several companies posting customer stories on its Web site. Log on to read some of the stories or submit your own memory involving Coca-Cola.

While reading the stories, consider how these positive messages help the organization build goodwill with its consumers. Why are these stories powerful? Out of all the mail Coca-Cola receives, why do you think these particular stories were chosen to appear on their Web site? Furthermore, why do you think interactive sites like these build brand loyalty with customers?

Personal Touch

E-mails are fine, but if you really want to thank a customer for his [or her] business, write a short note instead. Businesspeople get so few handwritten notes these days that your thank you is sure to stand out.

Quoted from "Networking Tip," *Sales & Marketing Management*, May 2004, 64.

money from someone else. Most people find that money is tight, so they'll want to keep insurance costs low. Yet the fact that prices are steady or rising means that the value of what they own is higher—they need insurance more than ever.

Many insurance companies are refusing to renew policies (car, liability, malpractice insurance). These refusals to renew have gotten lots of publicity, and many people have heard horror stories about companies and individuals whose insurance has been canceled or not renewed after a small number of claims. Readers don't feel very kindly toward insurance companies.

People need car insurance. If they have an accident and aren't covered, they not only have to bear the costs of that accident alone but also (depending on state law) may need to place as much as $50,000 in a state escrow account to cover future accidents. They have a legitimate worry.

Discussion of the Sample Solutions

The solution in Figure 10.5 is unacceptable. The red marginal comments show problem spots. Since this is a form letter, we cannot tell customers we have their checks; in some cases, we may not. The letter is far too negative. The explanation in paragraph 2 makes IFI look irresponsible and uncaring. Paragraph 3 is far too negative. Paragraph 4 is too vague; there are no reader benefits; the ending sounds selfish. A major weakness with the solution is that it lifts phrases straight out of the problem; the writer does not seem to have thought about the problem or about the words he or she is using. Measuring the draft against the answers to the questions for analysis suggests that this writer should start over.

The solution in Figure 10.6 is much better. The blue marginal comments show the letter's strong points. The message opens with the good news that is true for all readers. (Whenever possible, one should use the good

Figure 10.5   An Unacceptable Solution to the Sample Problem

Need date

Dear Customer:

This explanation makes company look bad.   Relax. We got your check.   *Not necessarily true. Reread problem.*

There is always a time lag between the time payments come in and the time they are processed. While payments are waiting to be processed, the computer with superhuman quickness is sending out past-due notices and threats of cancellation.

Too negative

Need to present this positively   Cancellation is not something you should worry about. No policy would be canceled without a legal notice to that effect giving a specific date for cancellation which would be at least 30 days after the date on the original premium notice.

If you want to buy more insurance, just contact your local Interstate Fidelity agent. We will be happy to help you.

Sincerely,

This paragraph isn't specific enough to work as a reader benefit. It lacks you-attitude and positive emphasis.

Figure 10.6   A Good Solution to the Sample Problem

Need date

Dear Customer: *Better: use computer to personalize. Put in name and address of a specific reader*

Your auto insurance is still in effect.   *Good ¶ 1. True for all readers*

Good to treat notice as information, tell reader what to do if it arrives

Past-due notices are mailed out if the payment has not been processed within three days after the due date. This may happen if a check is delayed in the mail or arrives without a signature or account number. When your check arrives with all the necessary information, it is promptly credited to your account.   *Good you-attitude*

Even if a check is lost in the mail and never reaches us, you still have a 30-day grace period. If you do get a second notice, you'll know that we still have not received your check. To keep your insurance in force, just stop payment on the first check and send a second one.

Benefits of using computers

IFI is always checking to ensure that you get any discounts you're eligible for: multicar, accident-free record, good student. If you have a claim, your agent uses computer tracking to find quality repair shops quickly, whatever car you drive. You get a check quickly—usually within 3 working days—without having to visit dealer after dealer for time-consuming estimates.   *Better to put in agent's name, phone number*

Too negative

Need to add benefits of insuring with IFI

Today, your home and possessions are worth more than ever. You can protect them with Interstate Fidelity's homeowners' and renters' policies. Let your local agent show you how easy it is to give yourself full protection. If you need a special rider to insure a personal computer, jewelry, a coin or gun collection, or a fine antique, you can get that from IFI, too.   *Good specifics*

Whatever your insurance needs—auto, home, life, or health—one call to IFI can do it all.   *Acceptable ending*

Sincerely,

---

news pattern of organization.) Paragraph 2 explains IFI's policy. It avoids assigning blame and ends on a positive note. The negative information is buried in paragraph 3 and is presented positively: the notice is information, not a threat; the 30-day extension is a "grace period." Telling the reader now what to do if a second notice arrives eliminates the need for a second exchange of letters. Paragraph 4 offers benefits for being insured by IFI. Paragraph 5 promotes other policies the company sells and prepares for the last paragraph.

As the red comments indicate, this good solution could be improved by personalizing the salutation and by including the name and number of the local agent. Computers could make both of those insertions easily. This good letter could be made excellent by revising paragraph 4 so that it doesn't end on a negative note and by using more reader benefits. For instance, do computers help agents advise clients of the best policies for them? Does IFI offer good service—quick, friendly, nonpressured—that could be stressed? Are agents well trained? All of these might yield ideas for additional reader benefits.

✓ *Checklist*   ▐ Checklist for Informative and Positive Messages ▐

☐ In positive messages, does the subject line give the good news? In either message, is the subject line specific enough to differentiate this message from others on the same subject?

☐ Does the first paragraph summarize the information or good news? If the information is too complex to fit into a single paragraph, does the paragraph list the basic parts of the policy or information in the order in which the memo discusses them?

☐ Is all the information given in the message? What information is needed will vary depending on the message, but information about dates, places, times, and anything related to money usually needs to be included. When in doubt, ask!

☐ In messages announcing policies, is there at least one benefit for each segment of the audience? Are all benefits ones that seem likely to occur in this organization?

☐ Is each benefit developed, showing that the benefit will come from the policy and why the benefit matters to this organization? Do the benefits build on the job duties of people at this organization and the specific circumstances of the organization?

☐ Does the message end with a positive paragraph—preferably one that is specific to the readers, not a general one that could fit any organization or policy?

And, for all messages, not just informative and positive ones,

☐ Does the message use you-attitude and positive emphasis?

☐ Is the tone friendly?

☐ Is the style easy to read?

☐ Is the visual design of the message inviting?

☐ Is the format correct?

☐ Does the message use standard grammar? Is it free from typos?

Originality in a positive or informative message may come from

- Creating good headings, lists, and visual impact.
- Developing reader benefits.
- Thinking about readers and giving details that answer their questions and make it easier for them to understand and follow the policy.

Summary of Key Points

- Good communicators need to thoughtfully select one of the five most common modes of office communications: face-to-face contact, phone calls, instant messages, letters, and memos/e-mails.
- Informative and positive messages normally use the following pattern of organization:
    1. Give any good news and summarize the main points.
    2. Give details, clarification, background.
    3. Present any negative elements—as positively as possible.
    4. Explain any benefits.
    5. Use a goodwill ending: positive, personal, and forward-looking.
- A **subject line** is the title of a document. A good subject line meets three criteria: it's specific; it's reasonably short; and it's adapted to the kind of message (positive, negative, persuasive). If you can't make the subject both specific and short, be specific.

- The subject line for an informative or positive message should highlight any good news and summarize the information concisely.
- Good messages provide the necessary information without overwhelming their audience.
- Use benefits in informative and positive messages when
  - You are presenting policies.
  - You want to shape your audience's attitudes toward the information or toward your organization.
  - Stressing benefits presents the audience's motives positively.
  - Some of the benefits may not be obvious.
- **Goodwill endings** should focus on the business relationship you share with your audience or the audience's organization. The last paragraph of a message to a group should apply to the whole group.
- Humor is a risky tool. Use it carefully in written messages, and only when you and your audience know each other well.
- Use the analysis questions listed in Chapter 1 to probe the basic points needed for successful informative and positive messages.

CHAPTER 10 Exercises and Problems

10.1 Reviewing the Chapter

1. What are the multiple purposes of informative and good news messages? (LO 1)
2. How does information overload impact your communications? (LO 1)
3. When do you use face-to-face contacts? Phone calls? Instant messages? Letters? Memos and e-mails? (LO 1)
4. What are some tips for effectively using face-to-face contacts? Phone calls? Instant messages? Letters? Memos and e-mails? (LO 2)

5. How do you organize informative and positive letters and memos/e-mails? (LO 3)
6. What are some concerns to consider when choosing and ordering the information in your message? (LO 3)
7. What are tips for composing some of the common varieties of informative and positive messages? (LO 4)

10.2 Reviewing Grammar

Do the exercises from Appendix B on correcting sentence errors (B.8) and editing for grammar and usage (B.9).

10.3 Offering Restaurant Nutrition Information

The Food and Drug Administration wants restaurants to provide more nutritional information, including calorie counts of offerings, so that customers can make more nutritious choices. You own a restaurant and are considering whether or not you should change your menu to comply. On the one hand, you know obesity is a national problem, and you might be able to attract health-conscious customers if you change your menu. On the other hand, the large majority of your customers do not seem to be counting calories. Their favorites on your menu are the comfort food selections such as fried chicken, mashed potatoes, pies, and cakes. Furthermore, it would cost you between $11,500 and $46,000 for a lab to test your menu items and provide nutritional content and calorie counts. In small groups, discuss whether or not your restaurant will comply. What are some compromises you can think of? Write a memo to your instructor summarizing your group's conclusions.

Adapted from Janet Adamy, "Restaurants Urged to Stress Nutrition: FDA-Funded Report Seeks Focus on Healthful Foods and More Data on Calories," *Wall Street Journal*, May 31, 2006, D4.

10.4   Letter for Discussion—Internal Revenue Service

Below is an actual complete letter that went to millions of taxpayers; only the address and identifying numbers are missing. Read the letter and then critique it in small groups. Here are some questions to get you started.

1. Can you tell what the purpose of the letter is? If not, what in the letter confuses the purpose?

2. What kinds of impressions are given readers by document design choices?

3. What kinds of impressions are given readers by the telephone help paragraph?

```
Department of the Treasury
Internal Revenue Service

STOP 33                                   In reply refer to:
KANSAS CITY MO 64999                                    LTR 12C  R
                                                        2 30 000
                                                           00840

AMES IA 50010


            Social Security Number:
            Document Locator Number:

Dear Taxpayer:

In processing your Federal income tax return for the year ended 19XX,
we find we need more information or do not have the fully completed
forms that are required. Please send us the information indicated or
fill out the necessary lines of forms mentioned below and return the
information and forms to us.

If this return is being filed by a parent for a minor child, A Power
of Attorney is not necessary. Please indicate if you are the childs
parent signing the return.

Please send us the information within 20 days from the date of this
letter so we can complete the processing of your return. Please
enclose only the information requested; DO NOT send a copy of your
return. It will take about 6 to 8 weeks from the time we receive your
response to issue any refund due you. If we do not hear from you, we
will have to use the information we have to process your return.
This may increase the tax you owe or reduce your refund because we
would not be able to give you proper credit.

If the item in question appeared in error on your return, please
note that on this letter when you reply. DO NOT file a corrected or
amended return because that will delay the processing of your
original return.

If you have any questions about this letter, please call Between
7:00a-7:00p at 816-926-5938. If the number is outside your local
calling area, there will be a long-distance charge to you. If you
prefer, you may call the IRS telephone number listed in your
local directory. An employee there may be able to help you, but the
```

```
office at the address shown on this letter is most familiar with
your case.

When you send the information or write to us, please provide your
telephone number and the most convenient time for us to call if we
need more information. Attach this letter to any correspondence to
help us identify your case. Keep the copy for your records.


Thank you for your cooperation.                          Page 2

                                    Sincerely yours,

                                    Juanita Benezette

                                    Juanita Benezette
                                    Chief, Document Perfection Branch

Enclosures:
Copy of this letter
Envelope
```

10.5   Memos for Discussion–Introducing a Suggestion System

Your organization has decided to institute a suggestion system. Employees on hourly pay scales will be asked to submit suggestions. (Managers and other employees on salary are not eligible for this program; they are supposed to be continually suggesting ways to improve things as part of their regular jobs.) If the evaluating committee thinks that the suggestion would save money, the employee will receive 10% of the first year's estimated annual savings. If the suggestion won't save money but will improve work conditions, service, or morale, the employee will get a check for $50.

The following memos are possible approaches. How well does each message meet the criteria in the checklist for informative and positive messages?

1.

Subject: Suggestion System (SS)

I want to introduce you to the Suggestion System (SS). This program enables the production worker to offer ideas about improving his job description, working conditions, and general company procedures. The plan can operate as a finely tuned machine, with great ideas as its product.

Operation will begin November 1. Once a week, a designate of SS will collect the ideas and turn them over to the SS Committee. This committee will evaluate and judge the proposed changes.

Only employees listed as factory workers are eligible. This excludes foremen and the rest of supervisory personnel. Awards are as follows:

1. $50 awards will be given to those ideas judged operational. These are awarded monthly.
2. There will be grand prizes given for the best suggestions over the six-month span.

Ideas are judged on feasibility, originality, operational simplicity, and degree of benefit to the worker and company. Evaluation made by the SS Committee is final. Your questions should be channeled to my office.

2.

Subject: Establishment of Suggestion System

We announce the establishment of a Suggestion System. This new program is designed to provide a means for hourly employees to submit suggestions to company management concerning operations and safety. The program will also provide an award system to compensate nonmanagement employees for implemented suggestions.

Here is how the program will work: beginning October 1, suggestions can be submitted by hourly workers to the company on Form 292, which will be furnished to all plants and their departments by October 1st. On the form, the submitting employee should include the suggestion, his or her name, and the department number. The form can be deposited in a suggestion drop box, which will be located near the personnel office in each plant.

Any suggestion dealing with the improvement of operations, safety, working conditions, or morale is eligible for consideration. The award structure for the program will be as follows:

1. For an implemented suggestion which improves safety or efficiency with no associated monetary benefits or cost reduction: $50.00.
2. For an implemented suggestion which makes or saves the company money: 10% of the first year's estimated annual savings or additional revenue.

It is hoped that we will have a good initial and continuous response from all hourly employees. This year, we are out to try to cut production costs, and this program may be the vehicle through which we will realize new savings and increased revenues. New ideas which can truly increase operational efficiency or cut safety problems will make the company a nicer place for all employees. A safer work environment is a better work environment. If department operations can be made more efficient, this will eventually make everyone's job just a little easier, and give that department and its employees a sense of pride.

3.

Subject: New Employee Suggestion System

Beginning October 1, all of you who are hourly employees of Video Adventures will be able to get cash awards when your suggestions for improving the company are implemented.

Ideas about any aspect of Video Adventures are eligible: streamlining behind-the-counter operations, handling schedule problems, increasing the life of videotapes.

■ If your idea cuts costs or increases income (e.g., increasing membership sales, increasing the number of movie rentals per customer), you'll receive 10% of the first year's estimated annual savings.

■ If the idea doesn't save money but does improve service, work conditions, or morale, you'll receive a check for $50.

To submit a suggestion, just pick up a form from your manager. On the form, explain your suggestion, describe briefly how it could be implemented, and show how it will affect Video Adventures. Return the completed form in the new suggestion box behind the back counter. Suggestions will be evaluated at the end of each month. Turn in as many ideas as you like!

Think about ways to solve the problems you face every day. Can we speed up the check-in process? Cut paperwork? Give customers faster service? Increase the percentage of customers who bring back their tapes on time? As you serve people at the counter, ask them what they'd like to see at Video Adventures.

Your ideas will keep Video Adventures competitive. Ten years ago, Video Adventures was the only video store on the west side of town. Now there are six other video stores within a two-mile radius. Efficiency, creativity, and service can keep Video Adventures ahead.

Employees whose ideas are implemented will be recognized in the regional Video Adventures newsletter. The award will also be a nice accomplishment to add to any college application or résumé. By suggesting ways to improve Video Adventures, you'll demonstrate your creativity and problem-solving abilities. And you'll be able to share the credit for keeping Video Adventures' reputation as the best video store in town.

10.6   E-Mails for Discussion—Saying Yes to a Subordinate

Today, you get this request from a subordinate.

> Subject: Request for Leave
>
> You know that I've been feeling burned out. I've decided that I want to take a three-month leave of absence this summer to travel abroad. I've got five weeks of vacation time saved up; I would take the rest as unpaid leave. Just guarantee that my job will be waiting when I come back!

You decide to grant the request. The following messages are possible responses. How well does each message meet the criteria in the checklist for informative and positive messages?

1.
> Subject: Re: Request for Leave
>
> I highly recommend Italy. Spend a full week in Florence, if you can. Be sure to visit the Brancacci Chapel—it's been restored, and the frescoes are breathtaking. And I can give you the names of some great restaurants. You may never want to come back!

2.
> Subject: Your Request for Leave
>
> As you know, we are in a very competitive position right now. Your job is important, and there is no one who can easily replace you. However, because you are a valued employee, I will permit you to take the leave you request, as long as you train a replacement before you leave.

3.
> Subject: Your Request for Leave Granted
>
> Yes, you may take a three-month leave of absence next summer using your five weeks of accumulated vacation time and taking the rest as unpaid leave. And yes, your job will be waiting for you when you return!
>
> I'm appointing Garrick to take over your duties while you're gone. Talk with him to determine how much training time he'll need, and let me know when the training is scheduled.
>
> Have a great summer! Let us know every now and then how you're doing!

10.7   Revising a Letter

You work for a credit card company and asked your assistant to draft a letter to new customers who have recently opened an account. The purpose of the letter is to inform clients of the services available to them, persuade them to use the services, and build goodwill.

> Subject: Credit Card
>
> Dear Sir or Madame,
>
> This letter will let you know about our organization and what we can do for you. We believe that you will like using our services, as we offer many convenient ones.
>
> Before we tell you about the great services we have to offer, we want to let you know how glad we our to have you as a new customer. We got out of our way to make sure you get the best benefits. 2% back on grocery purchases, no annual fee, and reward dollars—who could ask for anything more?! Shop, Shop, Shop and the rewards will pile up. Go online to sign up for rewards so you don't lose out. While your there, don't forget to enroll in e-mail alerts to remind you of upcoming due dates.
>
> We have been helping clients for almost a quarter of a century and are happy your apart of the family. Like a family member who just drops in, you get to chose your payment due date. Now how's that for convenience!
>
> Thank you for joining our service. We look forward to continuing our business relationship with you.
>
> Sincerely,

This draft definitely needs some work. It lacks you-attitude and needs attention to the organization. Moreover, the new services are not clearly explained, and there are many mechanical errors.

As your instructor directs,

a.   Write a memo to your subordinate, explaining what revisions are necessary.

b.   Revise the letter.

10.8   Responding to a Supervisor's Request

1.   You've received this e-mail message from your supervisor:

> Subject: Need "Best Practices"
>
> Please describe something our unit does well—ideally something that could be copied by or at least applied to other units. Our organization is putting together something on "Best Practices" so that good ideas can be shared as widely as possible.
>
> Be specific. For example, don't just say "serve customers"—explain exactly what you do and how you do it to be effective. Anecdotes and examples would be helpful.
>
> Also indicate whether a document, a videotape, or some other format would be the best way to share your practice. We may use more than one format, depending on the response.
>
> I need your answer ASAP so that I can send it on to my boss.

Answer the message, describing something that you or others in your unit do well.

2. You've received this e-mail message from your supervisor:

> Subject: Mistake of the Month
>
> Please describe a mistake you've made within the past month and explain what you learned from the mistake.
>
> I believe that sharing our mistakes will be as valuable as sharing our best practices. We can all learn from mistakes and improve the overall efficiency of the organization.
>
> Be specific. Explain exactly what you did and what you learned. An anecdote or clear example would be helpful. At the end of the week, we will all vote on the largest mistake. The staffer who made the biggest blunder will receive $50.
>
> Send your e-mail this week to all employees in the office.

Answer the message describing a mistake that you made while at work and what you learned from it.

Adapted from Jennifer Gill, "Strategies: The Mistake of the Month Award," *Inc.*, February 2005, 34.

10.9   Accommodating a Hearing-Impaired Employee

You're manager of Human Resources at your company. Two weeks ago, you got this e-mail message:

> Subject: Accommodations for Employee
>
> Our work team includes a hearing-impaired employee. She is our most productive team member on the floor, but at team meetings, she can't effectively contribute. I e-mailed her about my concerns, and she says the conversations are too hard to follow. What can we do so she can contribute her ideas?

One of your staffers has researched the issue for you and brought you several recommendations. Based on the staffer's research, you have determined that you will contract with a sign language interpreter to be present at the regular staff meetings. You will also have your staffer meet with the work team to share some basic guidelines for communicating, such as looking directly at the deaf team member when speaking, speaking slowly, using facial expressions when possible, and avoiding any statements not intended for the interpreter to translate (the interpreter will translate anything spoken during the meeting). These plans are part of your existing policy of complying with the Americans with Disabilities Act (ADA).

Write an e-mail message to the affected employees, telling them about the new practices for your employee.

10.10   Asking about a Product

Most Web sites offer a link called "Contact Us," but the quality of that contact varies substantially. Try contacting a company online, and evaluate the response you get.

Visit an e-commerce Web site. You might try a clothing retailer, a bank, an airline, or a site that sells tickets to concerts or movies. Identify a product that is out of stock or a type of product that does not seem to be offered at that site (but that might logically be found there).

Compose and send an e-mail message asking about the product. If the product is out of stock, ask when it is likely to become available. If you cannot find the product on the Web site, ask if it is somehow available.

Assuming you get a response, note how long the company took to reply. Evaluate the response. Does it seem to be an automated response, or does it sound personal? Is the response prompt and well written? Does it answer your question? If you do not get a reply, send a follow-up message. If you still do not get a reply, evaluate your own message: Could you have made it more effective?

Turn in a copy of your e-mail message and your evaluation of the company's response (or of your own message if you did not get a response).

10.11   Creating a Human Resources Web Page

As firms attempt to help employees balance work and family life (and as employers become aware that personal and family stresses affect performance at work), Human Resource departments sponsor an array of programs and provide information on myriad subjects. However, some people might be uncomfortable asking for help, either because the problem is embarrassing (who wants to admit needing help to deal with drug abuse, domestic violence, or addiction to gambling?) or because focusing on nonwork issues (e.g., child care) might lead others to think they aren't serious about their jobs. The Web allows organizations to post information that employees can access privately—even from home.

Create a Web page that could be posted by Human Resources to help employees with one of the challenges they face. Possible topics include

- Appreciating an ethnic heritage.
- Buying a house.
- Caring for dependents: child care, helping a child learn to read, living with teenagers, elder care, and so forth.
- Staying healthy: exercise, yoga, massage, healthy diet, and so forth.
- Dealing with a health problem: alcoholism, cancer, diabetes, heart disease, obesity, and so forth.
- Dressing for success or dressing for casual days.
- Financial management: basic budgeting, deciding how much to save, choosing investments, and so forth.
- Nourishing the spirit: meditation, religion.
- Getting out of debt.
- Planning for retirement.

- Planning vacations.
- Reducing stress.
- Resolving conflicts on the job or in families.

Assume that this page can be accessed from another of the organization's pages. Offer at least seven links. (More is better.) You may offer information as well as links to other pages with information. At the top of the page, offer an overview of what the page covers. At the bottom of the page, put the creation/update date and your name and e-mail address.

As your instructor directs,

a. Turn in one printed copy of your Web page(s). On another page, give the URLs for each link.

b. Electronically submit your Web page files, or submit them on a CD.

c. Write a memo to your instructor identifying the audience for which the page is designed and explaining (1) the search strategies you used to find material on this topic, (2) why you chose the pages and information you've included, and (3) why you chose the layout and graphics you've used.

d. Present your page orally to the class.

Hints:

- Pick a topic you know something about.
- Realize that audience members will have different needs. You could explain the basics of choosing day care or stocks, but don't recommend a specific day care center or a specific stock.
- If you have more than nine links, chunk them in small groups under headings.
- Create a good image of the organization.

10.12   Praising Work Done Well

Write an e-mail to a co-worker (with a copy to the person's supervisor) thanking him or her for helping you or complimenting him or her on a job well done. Use details to give your note sincerity.

10.13   Giving Good News

Write to a customer or client, to a vendor or supplier, or to your boss announcing good news. Possibilities include a product improvement, a price cut or special, an addition to your management team, a new contract, and so forth.

10.14   Correcting a Misconception

You're an assistant in the Governor's office. Today, the Press Secretary gives you this letter and asks you to answer it.

I see state employees driving BMWs and sports cars. These cars are a waste of tax-payer money!

Sincerely,

Rick Shipley

Rick Shipley

After checking with the Department of Public Safety, you find that some state employees do drive luxury cars. The vehicles were confiscated in criminal investigations, and the state uses them instead of buying other vehicles.

In the 10 years the policy has been in effect, the state has confiscated 43 vehicles—and thus bought 43 fewer vehicles than it would have otherwise needed.

Write to Mr. Shipley, responding to his criticism.

10.15 Reminding Guests about the Time Change

Twice a year in the United States, cities switch to day-light saving time and back again. The time change can be disruptive for hotel guests, who may lose track of the date, forget to change the clocks in their rooms, and miss appointments as a result.

Prepare a form letter to leave in each hotel room reminding guests of the impending time change. What should guests do?

Write the letter.

Hints:

* Use an attention-getting page layout so readers don't ignore the message.
* Pick a specific hotel or motel chain you know something about.
* Use the letter to build goodwill for your hotel or motel chain. Use specific references to services or features the hotel offers, focusing not on what the hotel does for the reader, but on what the reader can do at the hotel.

10.16 Announcing a New Employee Benefit

Your company has decided to pay employees for doing charity work. Employees can spend 1 hour working with a charitable on nonprofit group for every 40 they work. Employees will be paid for this hour, so their salaries will not fall. People who choose not to participate will work and be paid for the same number of hours as before. Supervisors are responsible for ensuring that essential business services are covered during business hours. Any employee who will be away during regular business hours (either to volunteer or to take off an hour in compensation for volunteering off-shift or on a weekend) will need to clear the planned absence with his or her supervisor. Your office is collecting a list of organizations that would welcome volunteers. People can work with an organized group or do something informal (such as tutoring at a local school or coaching kids at a local playground). People can volunteer 1 hour every week, 2 hours every other week, or a half-day each month. Volunteer hours cannot be banked from one month to the next; they must be used each month. The program starts January 1 (or June 1). The various groups that people work with will be featured in company publications.

As Vice President of Human Resources, write a memo to all employees announcing this new program.

Hints:

* Pick a business, government, or nonprofit organization that you know something about.
* What proportion of your employees are already involved in volunteer work?
* Is community service or "giving back" consistent with your corporate mission?
* Some employees won't be able or won't want to participate. What is the benefit for them in working for a company that has such a program?
* Will promoting community participation help your organization attract and retain workers?

10.17 Announcing an Additional Employee Benefit

Your organization has just created a benefit to help employees who are caring for elderly relatives. Now the Human Resources office will provide information and referral services for elder day care and long-term assisted-living or nursing care, and names and addresses of people willing to work part- or full-time as caregivers. However, your organization will not pay for any of the actual cost of hiring a caregiver or paying for a nursing home. In addition, you will sponsor seminars on a number of topics about dealing with elderly parents, such as choosing a nursing facility, deciding when to stop driving, and filling out medical forms.

As part of the new policy, the organization will allow employees to use personal time off and sick time to care for any family member. You will also allow employees to take time off during the workday to stay until a nurse arrives or to drive a parent to a doctor's appointment. Employees must notify their supervisors in advance that they will be away and must make up the time sometime during the next 30 days. Employees who need more time can take unpaid leaves of up to 15 months and can return to their present jobs and current salaries.

The policy takes effect the first of next month.

Nationally, one in four workers over 40 provides care for an aging parent or other relative; in some organizations, the figure is higher. People who care for aging parents without assistance often make more mistakes on the job and have higher absenteeism and higher medical claims due to increased stress. Even greater than the loss of time (9.3 hours a month, according to one study) may be the inability of caregivers to accept promotions and more responsibility in their jobs. Some of them even quit their jobs to care for their parents; thus, their skills are no longer available to the organization at all.

Assume that you're Director of Human Resources, and write a memo to all employees announcing the benefit.

Hints:

- Pick a business, government, or nonprofit organization you know well.
- What age groups do employees represent? How many of them are caring for elderly parents now?
- Specify the topic, date, and place of the first seminar you'll sponsor. If possible, give the schedule for the first three months.
- Be sure to provide benefits for employees who do not care for elderly parents as well as those who do.
- How easy is it for your organization to attract and retain skilled workers? Why is it important to your organization that people be alert and be willing to take more responsibility?

10.18   Announcing an Employee Fitness Center

Your company is ready to open an employee fitness center with on-site aerobics and yoga classes, exercycles tread mills, and weight machines. The center will be open 6 AM to 10 PM daily; at least one qualified instructor will be on duty at all times. Employees get first preference; if there is extra room, clients, spouses, and children may also use the facilities. Locker rooms and showers will also be available.

Your company hopes that the fitness center will help out-of-shape employees get the exercise they need to be more productive. Other companies have saved between $2.30 and $10.10 for every $1.00 spent on wellness programs. The savings come from lower claims on medical insurance, less absenteeism, and greater productivity.

Write the memo announcing the center.

Hints:

- Who pays the medical insurance for employees? If the employer pays, then savings from healthier employees will pay for the center. If another payment plan is in effect, you'll need a different explanation for the company's decision to open the fitness center.

- Stress benefits apart from the company's saving money. How can easier access to exercise help employees? What do they do? How can exercise reduce stress, improve strength, help employees manage chronic illnesses such as diabetes and high blood pressure, and increase productivity at work?
- What kind of record does the company have of helping employees be healthy? Is the fitness center a departure for the company, or does the company have a history of company sports teams, stop-smoking clinics, and the like?
- What is the company's competitive position? If the company is struggling, you'll need to convince readers that the fitness center is a good use of scarce funds. If the company is doing well, show how having fit employees can make people even more productive.
- Stress fun as a benefit. How can access to the center make employees' lives more enjoyable?

10.19   Announcing New Smoking Policy

During a recent board meeting, your organization's officers decided to respond to complaints from workers and clients about smokers who gather outside the main entrance to your office building. Complaints ranged from the effects of secondhand smoke to the message the smokers shed on the organization's image to outside clients who need to enter the building. The board decided that smoking will be allowed only in a designated area at the far end of the parking lot. Smokers can no longer congregate near the building's main entrance.

As vice president, write a memo to all employees announcing the immediate change in the smoking policy.

In addition, write a memo to your instructor that analyzes your rhetorical situation (context, audiences, and purposes) and the ethical decisions you had to make to construct this memo.

Hints:

- Pick a business, government, or nonprofit organization that you know something about.

- What benefits can you stress to employees about the new policy?
- Some employees, particularly those who smoke, may be disgruntled with the new policy. What benefits can you stress for them and how will you overcome their negative feelings?

10.20 Lining Up a Consultant to Improve Teamwork

As Director of Education and Training you oversee all in-house training programs. Five weeks ago, Pat Dyrud, Vice President for Human Resources, asked you to set up a training course on teams. After making some phone calls, you tracked down Sarah Reed, a business communication professor at a nearby college.

"Yes, I do workshops on teamwork," she told you on the phone. "I would want at least a day and a half with participants—two full days would be better. They need time to practice the skills they'll be learning. I'm free Mondays and Tuesdays. I'm willing to work with up to five teams at a time, as long as the total number of people is 30 or less. Tell me what kinds of teams they work in, what they already know, and what kinds of things you want me to emphasize. My fee is $2,500 a day. Of course, you'd reimburse me for expenses."

You told her you thought a two-day session would be feasible, but you'd have to get back to her after you got budget approval. You wrote a quick memo to Pat Dyrud explaining the situation and asking about what the session should cover.

Two weeks ago, you received this memo:

> I've asked the Veep for budget approval for $5,000 for a two-day session plus no more than $750 for all expenses. I don't think there will be a problem.
>
> We need some of the basics: strategies for working in groups, making decisions, budgeting time, and so forth. We especially need work on dealing with problem group members and on handling conflict—I think some of our people are so afraid that they won't seem to be "team players" that they agree too readily.
>
> I don't want someone to lecture. We've already had a lecture and frankly, it didn't do much good. Our people have even read some articles on teamwork, but somehow even with teams people are using old work habits. I don't want some ivory tower theorist. We need practical exercises that can help us acquire skills that we can put into effect immediately.
>
> Attached is a list of 24 people who are free Monday and Tuesday of the second week of next month. Note that we've got a good mix of people. If the session goes well, I may want you to schedule additional sessions.

Today, you got approval from the Vice President to schedule the session, pay Professor Reed the fee, and reimburse her for expenses to a maximum of $750. She will have to keep all receipts and turn in an itemized list of expenses to be reimbursed; you cannot reimburse her if she does not have receipts.

You also need to explain the mechanics of the session. You'll meet in the Conference Room, which has a screen and flip charts. You have an overhead projector, a slide projector, a laptop computer for showing PowerPoint slides, a video camera, a DVD player, and a TV, but you need to reserve these if she wants to use them.

Write to Professor Reed. You don't have to persuade her to come since she's already informally agreed, but you do want her to look forward to the job and to do her best work.

Hints:

- Choose an organization you know something about.
- What do teams do in this organization? What challenges do they face?
- Will most participants have experience working in teams? Will they have bad habits to overcome? What attitudes toward teams are they likely to have?
- Check the calendar to get the dates. If there's any ambiguity about what "the second week of next month" is, call Pat Dyrud to check.

10.21   Answering an International Inquiry

Your business, government, or nonprofit organization has received the following inquiries from international correspondents. (You choose the country the inquiry is from.)

1. Please tell us about a new product, service, or trend so that we can decide whether we want to buy, license, or imitate it in our country.

2. We have heard about a problem [technical, social, political, or ethical] that occurred in your organization. Could you please tell us what really happened and estimate how it is likely to affect the long-term success of the organization?

3. Please tell us about college programs in this field. We are interested in sending some of our managers to your country to complete a college degree.

4. We are considering setting up a plant in your city. We have already received adequate business information. However, we would also like to know how comfortable our nationals will feel. Do people in your city speak our language? How many? What opportunities exist for our nationals to improve their English? Does your town already have people

from a wide mix of nations? Which are the largest groups?

5. Our organization would like to subscribe to an English-language trade journal. Which one would you recommend? Why? How much does it cost? How can we order it?

As your instructor directs,

a. Answer one or more of the inquiries. Assume that your reader either reads English or can have your message translated.

b. Write a memo to your instructor explaining how you've adapted the message for your audience.

Hints:

- Even though you can write in English, English may not be your reader's native language. Write a letter that can be translated easily.
- In some cases, you may need to spell out background information that might not be clear to someone from another country.

10.22   Providing Information to Job Applicants

Your company is in a prime vacation spot, and as personnel manager you get many letters from students asking about summer jobs. Company policy is to send everyone an application for employment, a list of the jobs you expect to have open that summer with the rate of pay for each, a description of benefits for seasonal employees, and an interview schedule. Candidates must come for an interview at their own expense and should

call to schedule a time in advance. Competition is keen: Only a small percentage of those interviewed will be hired.

Write a form letter to students who've written to you asking about summer jobs. Give them the basic information about the hiring procedure and tell them what to do next. Be realistic about their chances, but maintain their interest in working for you.

10.23   Announcing a Premium Holiday

Rather than paying fees to an insurer, your company is self-insured. That is, you set aside corporate funds to pay for medical bills. If claims are light, the company saves money.

Employees pay a monthly fee for part of the amount of their health insurance. However, with one month to go in the fiscal year, you have more than enough set aside to cover possible costs. You're going to pass along some of the savings to employees (who, by staying

healthy, have kept medical costs down). Next month will be a "premium holiday." You will not deduct the monthly premium from employees' checks. As a result, they will have a slightly higher take-home pay next month. The holiday is just for one month; after it, the premium for health insurance will again be deducted each month.

Write a memo to all employees.

10.24   Announcing a Tuition Reimbursement Program

Your organization has decided to encourage employees to take courses by reimbursing each eligible employee a maximum of $3,500 in tuition and fees during any one calendar year. Anyone who wants to participate in the program must apply before the first class meeting; the application must be signed by the employee's immediate supervisor. The Office of Human Resources will evaluate

applications. That office has application forms; it also has catalogs from nearby schools and colleges.

The only courses employees may choose are those either related to the employee's current position (or to a position in the company that the employee might hold someday) or part of a job-related degree program. Again, the degree may be one that would help the employee's current position or that would qualify him or her for a promotion or transfer in the organization.

Only tuition and fees are covered, not books or supplies. People whose applications are approved will be reimbursed when they have completed the course with a grade of C or better. An employee cannot be reimbursed until he or she submits a copy of the approved application, an official grade report, and a statement of the tuition paid. If someone is eligible for other financial aid (scholarship, veterans benefits), the company will pay tuition costs not covered by that aid as long as the employee does not receive more than $3,500 and as long as the total tuition reimbursement does not exceed the actual cost of tuition and fees.

Part-time employees are not eligible; full-time employees must work at the company a year before they can apply to participate in the program. Courses may be at any appropriate level (high school, college, or graduate). However, the Internal Revenue Service currently requires workers to pay tax on any reimbursement for graduate programs. Undergraduate and basic education reimbursements of $5,250 a year are not taxed.

As Director of Human Resources, write a memo to all employees explaining this new benefit.

Hints:

- Pick an organization you know something about. What do its employees do? What courses or degrees might help them do their jobs better?
- How much education do employees already have? How do they feel about formal schooling?
- The information in the problem is presented in a confusing order. Put related items together.
- The problem stresses the limits of the policy. Without changing the provision, present them positively.
- How will having a better educated workforce help the organization? Think about the challenges the organization faces, its competitive environment, and so forth.

10.25 Summarizing Negative Feedback

Today, your in-basket contains this message from your boss:

> As you know, I'm leaving tomorrow for a vacation in New Zealand. While I'm gone, will you please scan the Internet each day for negative customer feedback and summarize any chat room threads that are relevant to our business? I'd like your summary in hard copy on my desk when I return.

As your instructor directs,

a. Choose one to three "anticorporate activism" Web sites or customer feedback Web sites where people discuss your company. (In a search engine, key in the company name and "customer opinion," or visit sites that specialize in this type of feedback—for example, PlanetFeedback, NetComplaints, eComplaints, or ePinions.) Scan the sites until you find three to five relevant chat room postings or threads for the company you have chosen.

b. Summarize the articles in a memo.

c. Compare summaries with a small group of students. Do summaries for different organizations focus on similar issues?

d. Present one of your summaries to the class.

Hints:

- Pick an organization you know something about. If the organization is large, focus on one division or department.
- Provide an overview to let your boss know whether the articles you've summarized are on a single topic or on several topics.
- Show how each posting or thread relates to the organization.
- Give the full citation (see Chapter 15) so that it's easy to track down postings if the boss wants to see the original.

10.26 Summarizing Information

Summarize one or more of the following:

1. An article from a recent edition of *BusinessWeek* or *Harvard Business Review*.
2. A tip from Jakob Nielsen's Alertboxes, http://www.alertbox.com.
3. An article about college, career development, or job searching from Quintessential Careers, http://www.quintcareers.com/articles.html.
4. Online information about options for recycling or donating used, outdated computers.
5. Options for consolidating student loans and other finances (visit http://www.consolidation-news.info).
6. An article or Web page assigned by your instructor.

As your instructor directs,

a. Write a summary of no more than 100 words.

b. Write a 250- to 300-word summary.

c. Write a one-page summary.

d. Compare your summary to those of a small group of students. How did the content of the summaries vary? How do you account for any differences?

10.27   Evaluating Web Pages

Today you get this e-mail from your boss:

> Subject: Evaluating Our Web Page
>
> Our CEO wants to know how our Web page compares to those of our competitors. I'd like you to do this in two steps. First, send me a list of your criteria. Then give me an evaluation of two of our competitors' and of our own pages. I'll combine your memo with others on other Web pages to put together a comprehensive evaluation for the next Executive Meeting.

As your instructor directs,

a. List the generic criteria for evaluating a Web page. Think about the various audiences for the page and the content that will keep them coming back, the way the page is organized, how easy it is to find something, the visual design, and the details, such as a creation/update date.

b. List criteria for pages of specific kinds of organizations. For example, a nonprofit organization might want information for potential and current donors, volunteers, and clients. A financial institution might want to project an image both of trustworthiness and as a good place to work.

c. Evaluate three Web pages of similar organizations. Which is best? Why?

10.28   Writing a Thank-You Letter

Write a thank-you letter to someone who has helped you achieve your goals.

As your instructor directs,

a. Turn in a copy of the letter.

b. Mail the letter to the person who helped you.

c. Write a memo to your instructor explaining the choices you made in writing the thank-you letter.

10.29   Ethics of Confidentiality Statements

> The information contained in this electronic message is confidential information intended for the use of the individual entity named above. If the reader of this message is not the intended recipient, or an employee responsible for delivering this electronic message to the intended recipient, you are hereby notified that any dissemination or copying of this communication is strictly prohibited. If this message contains nonpublic personal information about any customer of the sender or intended recipient, you are further prohibited under penalty of law from using or disclosing the information to any third party by provisions of the Gramm-Leach-Biley Act.

The above text is routinely attached to organizational e-mail correspondences. Using the Internet, research laws surrounding confidentiality statements in e-mail messages. Have there been many legal cases involving confidentiality statements that were attached to e-mails? What exactly does the law say about e-mail confidentiality statements? Consider your personal stance on these confidentiality statements. Have you ever received an e-mail with such a statement? Did you treat it differently than other e-mail correspondences? How effective do you think the confidentiality statements are when the medium in which these appear can be forwarded to multiple recipients with the click of the mouse?

As your instructor directs,

a. Write a memo to your instructor that discusses your answers to these questions.

b. Prepare a brief presentation of your findings for the class.

10.30 Mosaic Case

After being on the job as an intern for a little over two weeks, Martina really seems to like the job. Mostly she has been in charge of doing routine correspondences. Today, however, Sarah comes to her with a task that will require a considerable amount of time.

"In two weeks," Sarah tells Martina, who seems to always be eating a banana, "there is the annual convention of shareholders. During that time, all departments of Mosaic's headquarters showcase their best practices during a poster presentation. This year will not be an exception. Yvonne will stand by the poster and answer potential questions about the Communications Department during the official poster session. However, she doesn't have the time with everything else she needs to prepare for the convention to actually prepare the poster this year. Do you think you can handle it?"

Although a bit leery, Martina, after swallowing the last bite of her banana, answered, "Of course, I can!" She, of course, wants to make a good impression so that Yvonne and Sarah might hire her on at the end of the internship.

Take on the role of Martina and complete Sarah's communication request by designing a poster for the annual convention of shareholders. While there will be one session solely dedicated to the posters for which Yvonne will be present to answer questions, the poster will also be displayed throughout the entire convention. Since a person will not always be there to answer questions, the poster will have to be self explanatory.

The poster should showcase some best practices of the Communications Department. Use what you have learned from this chapter to decide what some of those practices will be.

As you create the poster, remember to use traditional poster conventions such as arrows, call-outs, and captions. Make sure the poster has a clearly identifiable point and recognizable flow of information. In other words, what is the main point you want the audience to take away from the poster after they look at it and how will they know in what order to look at the information? Consider the techniques outlined in Chapter 6 to assist in font, color, and overall layout and visual choices.

Negative Messages

Learning Objectives

After studying this chapter, you will know:

1 Different ways to organize negative messages.

2 Ways to construct the different parts of negative messages.

3 How to improve the tone of negative messages.

4 Ways to construct different kinds of negative messages.

Averting Crisis: Conveying the Right Message at the Right Time

JetBlue's infamous weather problems in the winter of 2007 illustrate how communication problems can exacerbate negative events.

On February 14, 2007, JetBlue, an airline with a reputation built on exceptional customer service, followed their normally aggressive customer service strategy by attempting to continue operations during an ice storm along parts of the East Coast. While other airlines canceled flights out of John F. Kennedy International airport in New York, JetBlue boarded passengers and rolled planes to runways for de-icing, betting that the planes eventually would be able to take off as the storm subsided.

The weather did not clear. Other planes were subsequently parked at terminal gates, preventing JetBlue planes from returning to the gates to unload passengers. Hundreds of passengers were held aboard planes, some for as long as 11 hours. Thousands more passengers and mounds of baggage were stranded inside JFK airport and at airports in other cities. Reports of JetBlue's problems were flashed around the country by news media.

JetBlue's problems were exacerbated by the company's failure to communicate critical messages at critical times.

Weather-related delays and cancellations are an unwelcome, but not unusual, situation for airlines and their passengers. In this case, however, JetBlue's problems were exacerbated by the company's failure to communicate critical messages at critical times.

• Posting flight delays rather than cancellations kept passengers waiting in airports for hours before the flights were finally canceled.

• Passengers stranded on planes reported they were not given information about their status because the flight crews were not being informed.

• JetBlue delayed asking for buses to evacuate passengers from the loaded planes.

• Discussions between airline agents and passengers became argumentative.

• The JetBlue phone number was overloaded. Callers experienced lengthy holds, and many could not get through at all.

• The airline's computer system and crew-scheduling software were inadequate for the task of scheduling crews after the storm, slowing the return to full service.

JetBlue issued a public apology and offered refunds, vouchers for free flights, and penalty-free rebooking services. Besides the damage to the company's reputation, estimated costs of the storm to JetBlue included $14 million in customer refunds, $16 million in travel vouchers, and $4 million in staff overtime. In addition, JetBlue created a Customer Bill of Rights and vowed to develop a recovery plan to prevent a recurrence of the ice storm crisis.

Sources: Allan Sloan, with Temma Ehrenfeld, "Skies Were Cloudy Before Jet Blew It," *Newsweek*, March 5, 2007, 26; Jesus Sanchez and Alana Semuels, "JetBlue Struggles to Get Past Last Week's Fiasco," *Chicago Tribune*, February 19, 2007; WABC-TV Eyewitness News Team, 2007, "JetBlue Trying to Make Up for Storm Fiasco," in *7Online.com: New York City and Metro Area Traffic on WABC-TV*, http://abclocal.go.com/wabc/story?section=traffic&id=5037072 (accessed March 15, 2007).

Chapter Outline

Organizing Negative Messages

- Giving Bad News to Clients and Customers
- Giving Bad News to Superiors
- Giving Bad News to Peers and Subordinates

The Parts of a Negative Message

- Subject Lines
- Buffers
- Reasons
- Refusals
- Alternatives
- Endings

Apologies

Tone in Negative Messages

Alternative Strategies for Negative Situations

- Recasting the Situation as a Positive Message
- Recasting the Situation as a Persuasive Message

Varieties of Negative Messages

- Rejections and Refusals
- Disciplinary Notices and Negative Performance Appraisals
- Layoffs and Firings

Solving a Sample Problem

- Problem
- Analysis of the Problem
- Discussion of the Sample Solutions

Summary of Key Points

In a **negative message,** the basic information we have to convey is negative; we expect the audience to be disappointed or angry.

For many business people, negative communications are among those they most love to hate. You just read "In the News" telling how miscommunications greatly worsened a negative situation for JetBlue. A medical study found that cardiac care units with nurses with negative attitudes had a death rate four times higher than that of comparable units.[1] One Silicon Valley company calculated the costs of negative communications from a sales person known for negative interpersonal skills and e-mails. Their costs included managerial time, HR time, anger management training and counseling, among others, and came to $160,000 for just one year. The company also deducted 60% of that cost from the employee's bonus. A British study estimated the costs of bullying in firms with 1,000 employees to be about $2 million a year per firm.[2]

The other side of the coin, and a classic illustration of how to handle negatives, is the Tylenol case. When Johnson and Johnson learned that seven people in the Chicago area had died from cyanide-laced Tylenol capsules, they immediately communicated their knowledge. They ordered the entire supply withdrawn from store shelves, and they offered to replace Tylenol capsules in people's homes with tablets. This decision cost the company tens of millions of dollars. But it was the right decision. When Tylenol was released again several months later in new, tamper-resistant containers, it recovered its market share. The company's forthright communications of the situation confirmed its integrity.[3] This chapter will follow the Tylenol path and look at some of the preferred ways to convey negative messages.

Negative messages include rejections and refusals, announcements of policy changes that do not benefit the audience, requests the audience will see as insulting or intrusive, negative performance appraisals, disciplinary notices, and product recalls or notices of defects.

A negative message always has several purposes:

Primary purposes:

- To give the audience the bad news.
- To have the audience read, understand, and accept the message.
- To maintain as much goodwill as possible.

Secondary purposes:

- To maintain, as much as possible, a good image of the communicator and the communicator's organization.
- To reduce or eliminate future communication on the same subject so the message doesn't create more work for the sender.

In many negative situations, the communicator and audience will continue to deal with each other. Even when further interaction is unlikely (for example, when a company rejects a job applicant or refuses to renew a customer's insurance), the firm wants anything the audience may say about the company to be positive or neutral rather than negative.

Some messages that at first appear to be negative can be structured to create a positive feeling. Even when it is not possible to make the audience happy with the news we must convey, we still want the audience to feel that

- They have been taken seriously.
- Our decision is fair and reasonable.
- If they were in our shoes, they would make the same decision.

Organizing Negative Messages

The best way to organize a negative message depends on your audience and on the severity of the negative information.

Giving Bad News to Clients and Customers

When you must give bad news to clients and customers, you need to be clear, but you also need to maintain goodwill. Compromises or alternatives can help you achieve both goals. See the first column in Figure 11.1.

Figure 11.2 illustrates one basic pattern for negative messages. This letter omits the reason, probably because the change benefits the company, not the customer. Putting the bad news first (though pairing it immediately with an alternative) makes it more likely that the recipient will read the letter. If this letter seemed to be just a routine renewal, or if it opened with the good news that the premium was lower, few recipients would read the letter carefully, and many would not read it at all. Then, if they had accidents and found that their coverage was reduced, they'd blame the company for not communicating clearly. Emphasizing the negative here is both good ethics and good business.

Listen!

Businesses often think they are listening to customers when they really aren't. Norm Brodsky is an entrepreneur with six businesses. His document destruction business received notification from an office manager that she was canceling their services. When Brodsky sent salespeople to see her, they "quickly realized that they had missed the real problem. Maybe they hadn't listened closely enough the first time or maybe she hadn't explained herself clearly and they hadn't asked enough questions. In any case, it turned out that the office manager didn't have complaints. Two other people did, and they'd taken their complaints to her. The complaints were fairly minor, and the other 48 people in the office were satisfied with our service, but the office manager didn't want to hear any complaints at all."

After resolving this issue, Brodsky writes how he "realized there were undoubtedly other accounts with similar issues. We had to understand that, when we signed up an office with 50 people in it, we had 50 customers not one." So Brodsky created a new position, service coordinator, who makes sure all customers, not just the office manager, can reach the company.

Adapted and quoted from Norm Brodsky, "We All Like to Think We Listen to Our Customers—But Do We Really Hear Them?" *Inc.*, July 2006, 56.

Figure 11.1 How to Organize Negative Messages

Negative messages to clients and customers	Negative messages to superiors	Negative messages to peers and subordinates
1. **When you have a reason that the audience will understand and accept, give the reason before the refusal.** A good reason prepares the audience to expect the refusal. 2. **Give the negative information or refusal just once, clearly.** Inconspicuous refusals can be missed altogether, making it necessary to say *no* a second time. 3. **Present an alternative or compromise, if one is available.** An alternative not only gives the audience another way to get what they want but also suggests that you care about them and helping them meet their needs. 4. **End with a positive, forward-looking statement.**	1. **Describe the problem.** Tell what's wrong, clearly and unemotionally. 2. **Tell how it happened.** Provide the background. What underlying factors led to this specific problem? 3. **Describe the options for fixing it.** If one option is clearly best, you may need to discuss only one. But if your superiors will think of other options, or if different people will judge the options differently, describe all the options, giving their advantages and disadvantages. 4. **Recommend a solution and ask for action.** Ask for approval so that you can go ahead to make the necessary changes to fix the problem.	1. **Describe the problem.** Tell what's wrong, clearly and unemotionally. 2. **Present an alternative or compromise, if one is available.** An alternative not only gives the audience another way to get what they want but also suggests that you care about them and helping them meet their needs. 3. **If possible, ask for input or action.** People in the audience may be able to suggest solutions. And workers who help make a decision are far more likely to accept the consequences.

Giving Bad News to Superiors

Your superior expects you to solve minor problems by yourself. But sometimes, solving a problem requires more authority or resources than you have. When you give bad news to a superior, also recommend a way to deal with the problem. Turn the negative message into a persuasive one. See the middle column in Figure 11.1.

Giving Bad News to Peers and Subordinates

When you must pass along serious bad news to peers and subordinates, use the variation in the last column in Figure 11.1.

No serious negative (such as being downsized or laid off) should come as a complete surprise, nor should it be delivered by e-mail. Researchers Timmerman and Harrison suggest that managers may be inclined to use electronic forms of communication to deliver bad news, but they should resist the temptation in most situations. Their study outlines four factors that should be considered when choosing a medium for delivering bad news: the severity of the message, the complexity of the explanation, the type of explanation, and the relationship between the superior and subordinates. Timmerman and Harrison suggest managers must always juggle the efficiency of delivering the message with its impact on receivers. Typically, managers who deliver bad news in face-to-face settings are more appreciated and accepted by employees.[4]

Managers can prepare for possible negatives by giving full information as it becomes available. It is also possible to let the people who will be affected by a decision participate in setting the criteria. Someone who has bought into the criteria for retaining workers is more likely to accept decisions using such criteria.

Figure 11.2   A Negative Letter

Insurance Company

3373 Forbes Avenue
Rosemont, PA 19010
(215) 572-0100

*Negative information
highlighted so reader won't
ignore message*

**Liability Coverage
Is Being Discontinued—
Here's How to Replace It!**

Negative

Alternative

Dear Policyholder:

Negative

When your auto insurance is renewed, it will no longer include liability coverage unless you select the new Assurance Plan. Here's why.

Liability coverage is being discontinued. It, and <u>the part of the premium which paid for it,</u> will be dropped from all policies when they are renewed.

*Positive
information
underlined
for emphasis*

This change could leave a gap in your protection. But you can replace the old Liability Coverage with Vickers' new Assurance Plan.

Alternative

No reason is given. The change probably benefits the company rather than the reader, so it is omitted.

With the new Assurance Plan, you receive benefits for litigation or awards arising from an accident—regardless of who's at fault. The cost for the Assurance Plan at any level is based on the ages of drivers, where you live, your driving record, and other factors. If these change before your policy is renewed, the cost of your Assurance Plan may also change. The actual cost will be listed in your renewal statement.

To sign up for the Assurance Plan, just check the level of coverage you want on the enclosed form and return it in the postage-paid envelope within 14 days. You'll be assured of the coverage you select.

*Forward-looking
ending emphasizes
reader's choice*

Sincerely,

C. J. Morgan

C. J. Morgan
President

Alternative

P.S. The Assurance Plan protects you against possible legal costs arising from an accident. Sign up for the Plan today and receive full coverage from Vickers.

And in some cases, the synergism of groups may make possible ideas that management didn't think of or rejected as "unacceptable." Some workplaces incorporate employee suggestion systems to help reduce excess costs and improve organizational effectiveness. In fact, a study by the Employee Involvement Agency showed that in 2003, ideas from employees saved organizations more than $624 million dollars.[5]

When the bad news is less serious, as in Figure 11.3, use the pattern in the first column of Figure 11.1 unless your knowledge of the audience suggests that another pattern will be more effective. The audience's reaction is influenced by the following factors:

- Do you and the audience have a good relationship?
- Does the organization treat people well?
- Has the audience been warned of possible negatives?
- Has the audience bought into the criteria for the decision?
- Do communications after the negative decision build goodwill?

Some organizations use "open book management," which provides employees with financial information of the organization in the hopes that open communication will foster ideas to improve productivity and cut costs. For example, Springfield Manufacturing, which was financially suffering, used

Figure 11.3   A Negative Memo to Subordinates

FIRSTBANK
Great Plains, Nebraska

Memo

Date: January 10, 2008
To: All Employees
From: Floyd E. Mattson   FEM

Subject: Limited Options for Group Dental Insurance

Reason

First Bank has always sought to provide employees with a competitive benefits package that meets the needs of our diverse workforce. At the same time, the costs of many benefits have risen rapidly, so at present we cannot offer as many benefits as we'd like. In the case of dental insurance, the company has concluded that at this time, we cannot expand the available coverage.

Alternatives considered but unavailable

Positive

In response to many requests, the Human Resource Deparment solicited bids for expanded dental coverage. None of the responses from insurers serving our area met our specifications. We continue to negotiate, but with costs rising at 20% per year, we don't see a high probability of success. Other banks in the area are in a similar situation, so our benefits package matches or exceeds what they offer.

Alternatives

Goodwill ending

First Bank continues to offer enrollment in an employee-funded group plan with ABC Dental. The coverage includes 37 dentists in our county and pays 50 percent of allowable fees. Many of our employees have found this coverage helpful. Employees also may use a medical savings account for dental care. Consider one of these options for the present, and First Bank will continue to investigate new opportunities for expanded coverage.

this approach to reduce a $3 million dollar debt and improve the state of the organization and lives of employees.[6]

The Parts of a Negative Message

This section provides more information about wording each part of a negative message.

Subject Lines

Many negative messages put the topic, but not the specific negative, in the subject line.

> Subject: Status of Conversion Table Program

Other negative message subject lines focus on solving the problem.

> Subject: Improving Our Subscription Letter

Use a negative subject line in messages when you think readers may ignore what they think is a routine message. Also use a negative subject line when the reader needs the information to make a decision or to act.

> Subject: Elevator to Be Out Friday, June 17

Many people do not read all their messages, and a neutral subject line may lead them to ignore the message.

Buffers

Traditionally, textbooks recommended that negative messages open with buffers. A **buffer** is a neutral or positive statement that allows you to delay the negative. Recent research suggests that buffers do not make readers respond more positively,[7] and good buffers are very hard to write. However, in special situations, you may want to use a buffer.

To be effective, a buffer must put the reader in a good frame of mind, not give the bad news but not imply a positive answer either, and provide a natural transition to the body of the letter. The kinds of statements most often used as buffers are good news, facts and chronologies of events, references to enclosures, thanks, and statements of principle.

1. **Start with any good news or positive elements the letter contains.**

> Starting Thursday, June 26, you'll have access to your money 24 hours a day at First National Bank.

Letter announcing that the drive-up windows will be closed for two days while automatic teller machines are installed

2. **State a fact or provide a chronology of events.**

> As a result of the new graduated dues schedule—determined by vote of the Delegate Assembly last December and subsequently endorsed by the Executive Council—members are now asked to establish their own dues rate and to calculate the total amount of their remittance.

Do You Have a Bad Boss?

A study from the Florida State University's College of Business found that many employees think they have a bad boss. More than 700 workers in various fields were asked how their bosses treat them. The study cites these findings:

- 39% of workers said their supervisor failed to keep promises.
- 37% said their supervisor failed to give credit when due.
- 31% said their supervisor gave them the "silent treatment" in the past year.
- 27% said their supervisor made negative comments about them to other employees or managers.
- 23% said their supervisors blamed others to cover up mistakes or to minimize embarrassment.

Employees who are not happy with their work environment are less productive, less concerned with the overall well-being of the organization, and more likely to look for other employment. The study recommends that workers stay optimistic in negative employment situations, since supervisor-subordinate relationships typically have a high turnover rate.

Adapted and quoted from Brent Kallestad, "Study: 2 in 5 Bosses Don't Keep Word," in *ABCNews.com*, n.d., http://abcnews.go.com/Business/print?id=2764148 (accessed January 2, 2007).

Announcement of a new dues structure that will raise most members' dues

3. **Refer to enclosures in the letter.**

> Enclosed is a new sticker for your car. You may pick up additional ones in the office if needed.

Letter announcing increase in parking rental rates

4. **Thank the reader for something he or she has done.**

> Thank you for scheduling appointments for me with so many senior people at First National Bank. My visit there March 14 was very informative.

Letter refusing a job offer

5. **State a general principle.**

> Good drivers should pay substantially less for their auto insurance. The Good Driver Plan was created to reward good drivers (those with five-year accident-free records) with our lowest available rates. A change in the plan, effective January 1, will help keep those rates low.

Letter announcing that the company will now count traffic tickets, not just accidents, in calculating insurance rates—a change that will raise many people's premiums

Some audiences will feel betrayed by messages whose positive openers delay the central negative point. Therefore, use a buffer only when the audience (individually or culturally) values harmony or when the buffer serves another purpose. For example, when you must thank the reader somewhere in the letter, putting the "thank you" in the first paragraph allows you to start on a positive note.

Buffers are hard to write. Even if you think the reader would prefer to be let down easily, use a buffer only when you can write a good one.

Reasons

Research shows that audiences who described themselves as "totally surprised" by negative news had many more negative feelings and described their feelings as being stronger than did those who expected the negative.[8] A clear and convincing reason prepares the audience for the negative, resulting in people who more easily accept it.

The following reason is inadequate.

Weak reason: The goal of the Knoxville CHARGE-ALL Center is to provide our customers faster, more personalized service. Since you now live outside the Knoxville CHARGE-ALL service area, we can no longer offer you the advantages of a local CHARGE-ALL Center.

If the reader says, "I don't care if my bills are slow and impersonal," will the company let the reader keep the card? No. The real reason for the negative is that the bank's franchise allows it to have cardholders only in a given geographical region.

Real reason: Each local CHARGE-ALL center is permitted to offer accounts to customers in a several-state area. The Knoxville CHARGE-ALL center serves customers east of the Mississippi. You can continue to use your current card until it expires. When that happens, you'll need to open an account with a CHARGE-ALL center that serves Texas.

Don't hide behind "company policy": your audience will assume the policy is designed to benefit you at their expense. If possible, show how your audience benefits from the policy. If they do not benefit, don't mention policy at all.

Weak reason:	I cannot write an insurance policy for you because company policy does not allow me to do so.
Better reason:	Gorham insures cars only when they are normally garaged at night. Standard insurance policies cover a wider variety of risks and charge higher fees. Limiting the policies we write gives Gorham customers the lowest possible rates for auto insurance.

Avoid saying that you *cannot* do something. Most negative messages exist because the communicator or company has chosen certain policies or cutoff points. In the example above, the company could choose to insure a wider variety of customers if it wanted to do so.

Often you as a middle manager will enforce policies that you did not design and announce decisions that you did not make. Don't pass the buck by saying, "This was a terrible decision." In the first place, carelessly criticizing your superiors is never a good idea. In the second place, if you really think a policy is bad, try to persuade your superiors to change it. If you can't think of convincing reasons to change the policy, maybe it isn't so bad after all.

If you have several reasons for saying *no,* use only those that are strong and watertight. If you give five reasons and readers dismiss two of them, readers may feel that they've won and should get the request.

Weak reason:	You cannot store large bulky items in the dormitory over the summer because moving them into and out of storage would tie up the stairs and the elevators just at the busiest times when people are moving in and out.
Way to dismiss the reason:	We'll move large items before or after the two days when most people are moving in or out.

If you do not have a good reason, omit the reason rather than use a weak one. Even if you have a strong reason, omit it if it makes the company look bad.

Reason that hurts company:	Our company is not hiring at the present time because profits are down. In fact, the downturn has prompted top management to reduce the salaried staff by 5% just this month, with perhaps more reductions to come.
Better:	Our company does not have any openings now.

Refusals

Deemphasize the refusal by putting it in the same paragraph as the reason, rather than in a paragraph by itself.

Sometimes you may be able to imply the refusal rather than stating it directly.

Direct refusal:	You cannot get insurance for just one month.
Implied refusal:	The shortest term for an insurance policy is six months.

Be sure the implication is crystal clear. Any message can be misunderstood, but an optimistic or desperate reader is particularly unlikely to understand a negative message. One of your purposes in a negative message is to close the door on the subject. You do not want to have to write a second letter saying that the real answer is *no.*

Straight Talk with Employees

Employees say they want organizations to be honest and open about bad news. In a survey by human resource specialists Towers Perrin, more than 90 percent of employees said they want the plain facts about their organization's performance and their jobs. They respect organizations for communicating honestly. Half said they think their employer tends to overdo putting a positive spin on the facts.

Adapted from Institute of Management & Administration (IMA), "The Best Policy Now: Less 'Spin' and More Honesty," *HR Focus* 81, no. 4 (2004): 4; and IMA, "Need to Deliver Bad News? How & Why to Tell It Like It Is," *HR Focus* 80, no. 11 (2003): 3.

Alternatives

Giving your audience an alternative or a compromise, if one is available, is a good idea for several reasons:

- It offers the audience another way to get what they want.
- It suggests that you really care about your audience and about helping to meet their needs.
- It enables your audience to reestablish the psychological freedom you limited when you said *no.*
- It allows you to end on a positive note and to present yourself and your organization as positive, friendly, and helpful.

When you give an alternative, give your audience all the information they need to act on it, but don't take the necessary steps. Let your audience decide whether to try the alternative.

Negative messages limit your audience's freedom. People may respond to a limitation of freedom by asserting their freedom in some other arena. Sharon and Jack W. Brehm calls this phenomenon **psychological reactance.**[9] Psychological reactance is at work when a customer who has been denied credit no longer buys even on a cash basis, a subordinate who has been passed over for a promotion gets back at the company by deliberately doing a poor job, or someone who has been laid off sabotages the company's computers.

An alternative allows your audience to react in a way that doesn't hurt you. By letting your audience decide for themselves whether they want the alternative, you allow them to reestablish their sense of psychological freedom.

The specific alternative will vary depending on the circumstances. In Figure 11.4, the company suggests using a different part. In different circumstances, the writer might offer different alternatives.

Endings

If you have a good alternative, refer to it in your ending: "Let me know if you can use A515 grade 70."

The best endings look to the future.

> Wherever you have your account, you'll continue to get all the service you've learned to expect from CHARGE-ALL, and the convenience of charging items at over a million stores, restaurants, and hotels in the United States and abroad—and in Knoxville, too, whenever you come back to visit!

Letter refusing to continue charge account for a customer who has moved

Avoid endings that seem insincere.

We are happy to have been of service, and should we be able to assist you in the future, please contact us.

This ending lacks you-attitude and would not be good even in a positive message. In a situation where the company has just refused to help, it's likely to sound sarcastic or sadistic.

Apologies

Not all negative messages need to include apologies. In business documents, apologize only when you are at fault. If you need to apologize, do it early,

Figure 11.4 A Refusal with an Alternative

Steel Fabrication

"Serving the needs of America since 1890"
1800 Olney Avenue • Philadelphia, PA 19140 • 215•555•7800 • Fax: 215•555•9803

April 27, 2008

Mr. H. J. Moody
Canton Corporation
2407 North Avenue
Kearney, NE 68847

Subject: Bid Number 5853, Part Number D-40040

Dear Mr. Moody:

Buffer Thank you for requesting our quotation on your Part No. D-40040.

Reason Your blueprints call for flame-cut rings 1/2" thick A516 grade 70. To use that grade, we'd have to grind down from 1" thick material. However, if you can use A515 grade 70, which we stock in 1/2" thick, you can cut the price by more than half.

Quantity	Description	Gross Weight	Price/Each
75	Rings Drawing D-40040, A516 Grade 70 1" thick x 6" O.D. x 2.8" I.D. ground to .5" thick.	12 lbs.	$15.08
75	Rings Drawing D-40040, A515 Grade 70 1/2" thick x 6" O.D. x 2.8" I.D.	6 lbs.	$6.91

Alternative (Depending on circumstances, different alternatives may exist.)

If you can use A515 grade 70, let me know. *Leaves decision up to reader to re-establish psychological freedom*

Sincerely,

Valerie Prynne

Valerie Prynne

VP:wc

briefly, and sincerely. Do so only once, early in the message. Do not dwell on the bad things that have happened. The reader already knows this negative information. Instead, focus on what you have done to correct the situation.

- **No explicit apology is necessary if the error is small and if you are correcting the mistake.**

Negative: We're sorry we got the nutrition facts wrong in the recipe.

Better: You're right. We're glad you made us aware of this. The correct amounts are 2 grams of fat and 4 grams of protein.

- **Do not apologize when you are not at fault.** The phrase "I'm sorry" is generally interpreted to mean the sorry person is accepting blame or responsibility. When you have done everything you can and when a delay or problem is due to circumstances beyond your control, you aren't at fault and don't need to apologize. It may, however, be appropriate to include an explanation so the reader knows you weren't negligent. In the previous example of a magazine's acknowledging an error, the editor might indicate the source of the error (such as a reference book or a government Web site the magazine uses for fact checking). If the news is bad, put the explanation first. If you have good news for the reader, put it before your explanation.

Negative:	I'm sorry that I could not answer your question sooner. I had to wait until the sales figures for the second quarter were in.
Better (neutral or bad news):	We needed the sales figures for the second quarter to answer your question. Now that they're in, I can tell you that . . .
Better (good news):	The new advertising campaign is a success. The sales figures for the second quarter are finally in, and they show that . . .

If the delay or problem is long or large, it is good you-attitude to ask the reader whether he or she wants to confirm the original plan or make different arrangements.

Negative:	I'm sorry that the chairs will not be ready by August 25 as promised.
Better:	Due to a strike against the manufacturer, the desk chairs you ordered will not be ready until November. Do you want to keep that order, or would you like to look at the models available from other suppliers?

There is an accelerating trend for apologies in the workplace. This cereal box mocks the genre of public apologies.

Source: The Denver Post and The Flip Side Staff, "Eating Crow," *Columbus Dispatch*, September 8, 2004, F8.

Figure 11.5   Avoid These Phrases in Negative Messages

Phrase	Because
I am afraid that we cannot	You aren't fearful. Don't hide behind empty phrases.
I am sorry that we are unable	You probably *are able* to grant the request; you simply choose not to. If you are so sorry about saying *no*, why don't you change your policy and say *yes?*
I am sure you will agree that	Don't assume that you can read the reader's mind.
Unfortunately	*Unfortunately* is negative in itself. It also signals that a refusal is coming.

Sometimes you will be in a fortunate position where you can pair your apology with a small appropriate benefit. Commercial Web sites offer good examples. After their site closed, Gap offered customers a 10% discount on their next purchase for a day.[10] Similarly, when the Hallmark Flowers Web site stopped taking orders the week before Mother's Day, Hallmark sent an e-mail asking customers to try again and offering free shipping for a day.[11]

Sincere apologies go hand in hand with efforts to rectify the problem.

Tone in Negative Messages

Tone—the implied attitude of the author toward the reader and the subject—is particularly important when you want readers to feel that you have taken their requests seriously. Check your draft carefully for positive emphasis (◄ p. 80) and you-attitude (◄ p. 76), both at the level of individual words and at the level of ideas.

Figure 11.5 lists some of the phrases to avoid in negative messages.

Even the physical appearance and timing of a letter can convey tone. An obvious form rejection letter suggests that the writer has not given much consideration to the reader's application. An immediate negative suggests that the rejection didn't need any thought. A negative delivered just before a major holiday seems especially unfeeling.

Copyright 2003 by Randy Glasbergen. www.glasbergen.com

"What fits your busy schedule better, exercising one hour a day or being dead 24 hours a day?"

Copyright 2007 Randy Glasbergen.

Alternative Strategies for Negative Situations

Whenever you face a negative situation, consider recasting it as a positive or persuasive message. Southwest Airlines, the low-cost airline, is famous for saying no to its customers. It says no to such common perks as reserve seats, meals, and interairline baggage transfers. But it recasts all those negatives into its two biggest positives, low-cost fares and conveniently scheduled frequent flights.[12]

Recasting the Situation as a Positive Message

If the negative information will directly lead to a benefit that you know readers want, use the pattern of organization for informative and positive messages:

Situation:	Your airline has been mailing out quarterly statements of frequent-flier miles earned. To save money, you are going to stop mailing statements and ask customers to look up that information at your Web site.
Negative:	Important Notice: This is your last Preferred Passenger paper statement.
Positive emphasis:	New, convenient online statements will replace this quarterly mailing. Now you can get up-to-the-minute statements of your miles earned. Choose e-mail updates or round-the-clock access to your statement at our Web site, www.aaaair.com. It's faster, easier, and more convenient.

Recasting the Situation as a Persuasive Message

Often a negative situation can be recast as a persuasive message. If your organization has a problem, ask readers to help solve it. A solution that workers have created will be much easier to implement.

When the Association for Business Communication raised dues, the Executive Director wrote a persuasive letter urging members to send in renewals early so they could beat the increase. The letter shared some of the qualities of any persuasive letter: using an attention-getting opener, offsetting the negative by setting it against the benefits of membership, telling the reader what to do, and ending with a picture of the benefit the reader received by acting. More recent increases, however, have been announced directly.

If you are criticizing someone, your real purpose may be to persuade the reader to act differently. Chapter 12 offers patterns for direct requests and problem-solving persuasive messages.

Varieties of Negative Messages

Three of the most difficult kinds of negative messages to write are rejections and refusals, disciplinary notices and negative performance appraisals, and layoffs and firings.

Rejections and Refusals

When you refuse requests from people outside your organization, try to use a buffer. Give an alternative if one is available. For example, if you are denying credit, it may still be possible for the reader to put an expensive item on layaway.

State Farm uses the unexpected to promote driving safety. Warnings like this are yet another form of delivering negative news. Third photo reads in part " Sounds Crazy, right? But it's true. Check out **sfagentfiles.com/chili** the next time you're online. You'll find other stuff that might surprise you."

Politeness and length help. In two different studies, job applicants preferred rejection letters that said something specific about their good qualities, that phrased the refusal indirectly, that offered a clear explanation of the procedures for making a hiring decision, that offered an alternative (such as another position the applicant might be qualified for), and that were longer.[13] Furthermore, businesses that follow this pattern of organization for rejection letters will retain applicants who still view the organization favorably, who will recommend the organization to others interested in applying there, and who will not file law suits.[14]

Double-check the words in a refusal to be sure the reason can't backfire if it is applied to other contexts. As Elizabeth McCord has shown, the statement that a plant is too dangerous for a group tour could be used as evidence against the company in a worker's compensation claim.[15] Similarly, writing resignation letters for a variety of reasons—leaving a job, stepping down from a committee, opting out of a fellowship—can be a delicate practice and can have serious future implications. As Shaun Fawcett has shown, a negative and poorly worded resignation letter can impact your chances for receiving a positive recommendation or reference in the future.[16]

When you refuse requests within your organization, use your knowledge of the organization's culture and of the specific individual to craft your message. In some organizations, it may be appropriate to use company slogans, offer whatever help already-established departments can give, and refer to the individual's good work (if you indeed know that it is good). In other, less personal organizations, a simple negative without embellishment may be more appropriate.

Disciplinary Notices and Negative Performance Appraisals

Performance appraisals are discussed in detail in Chapter 12. Performance appraisals will be positive when they are designed to help a basically good employee improve. But when an employee violates a company rule or fails to improve after repeated negative appraisals, the company may discipline the employee or build a dossier to support firing him or her.

Present disciplinary notices and negative performance appraisals directly, with no buffer. A buffer might encourage the recipient to minimize the message's importance—and might even become evidence in a court case that the employee had not been told to shape up "or else." Cite quantifiable observations of the employee's behavior, rather than generalizations or inferences based on it.

International Firing

"When doing business in another country, it is often easy to assume that things there are the same as in your country. . . . It is wise to know the proper way to dismiss an employee when working with other cultures. This is a difficult task to perform in a familiar territory but it is especially tricky when one is in a foreign country and does not always fully understand the local culture. An American manager stationed in Indonesia reportedly discovered this when he tried to fire an oilrig employee. Rather than notifying the employee privately of this dismissal, the manager publicly told the timekeeper to send the man 'packing.' In Indonesia, this public dismissal was considered unacceptable 'loss of face' which offended both the dismissed man and his friends. So, rather than leave quietly, the man grabbed fire axes and ran after the American manager. Reportedly, the American was barely rescued in time. Obviously, it is dangerous to ignore local management practices and customs!"

Quoted from David A. Ricks, *Blunders in International Business*, 4th ed. (Malden, MA: Blackwell Publishing, 2006), 105.

We fell. We got up. End of apology.

Schwinn needed a new product line to attract sophisticated cyclists. This apology for its old, boring line moves quickly to a discussion of its new technology. By evoking an experience every cyclist has had, the headline also suggests that falling is a minor event.

Weak:	Lee is apathetic about work.
Better:	Lee was absent 15 days and late by one hour 6 days in the quarter beginning January 1.
Weak:	Vasu is careless with her written documents.
Better:	Vasu had multiple spelling errors in her last three client letters; a fourth letter omitted the date of the mandatory federal training seminar.

If an employee is disciplined by being laid off without pay, specify the length of the suspension.

Not all disciplinary notices are as formal as performance appraisals. Blanchard and Johnson, of *One Minute Manager* fame, present what they call the One Minute Reprimand. Much of the effectiveness of these reprimands comes from the fact that supervisors tell their employees from the beginning, before any reprimands are needed, that there will be explicit communication about both positive and negative performances. The reprimand itself is to come immediately after negative behavior and specify exactly what is wrong. It distinguishes between positive feelings for the employee and negative feelings for his or her performance in the specific situation.[17]

Layoffs and Firings

If a company is in financial trouble, management needs to communicate the problem clearly. Sharing information and enlisting everyone's help in finding solutions may make it possible to save jobs. Sharing information also means that layoff notices, if they become necessary, will be a formality; they should not be new information to employees.

Give the employee an honest reason for the layoff or firing. Based on guidance from your organization's human resource experts, state the reasons in a way that is clear but does not expose the organization to legal liabilities. A study by researchers at the University of Florida found that employees are more cooperative and less likely to retaliate if bad news is excused in a way that is believable and indicates that the decision maker had no alternatives. They are more likely to criticize the decision if the message tries to justify it by showing it was the best decision in terms of some greater good.[18]

RadioShack made headlines when it fired 400 employees with a two-sentence e-mail.

Source: Tara Weiss, "You've Got Mail: You're Fired," in *Forbes.com*, http://www.forbes.com/leadership/2006/08/31/leadership-radio-shack-management-cx_tw_0831layoffs.html (accessed February 20, 2007).

Information about layoffs and firings is normally delivered orally but accompanied by a written statement explaining severance pay or unemployment benefits that may be available.

Solving a Sample Problem

Solving negative problems requires careful analysis. The checklist at the end of the chapter, on p. 355, can help you evaluate your draft.

Problem

You're Director of Employee Benefits for a Fortune 500 company. Today, you received the following memo:

From: Michelle Jagtiani
Subject: Getting My Retirement Benefits

Next Friday will be my last day here. I am leaving [name of company] to take a position at another firm.

Please process a check for my retirement benefits, including both the deductions from my salary and the company's contributions for the last six and a half years. I would like to receive the check by next Friday if possible.

You have bad news for Michelle. Although the company does contribute an amount to the retirement fund equal to the amount deducted for retirement from the employee's paycheck, employees who leave with less than seven years of employment get only their own contributions. Michelle will get back only the money that has been deducted from her own pay, plus 4 ½% interest

www.useit.com/alertbox
/20000123.html

General guidelines for saying no can be applied to specific situations. Computer expert Jakob Neilsen explains how to tell users that your Web site can't do what they want. Neilsen suggests telling users "no" upfront when your Web site cannot do something. Otherwise, users will spend too much time looking for the desired feature, and in the process will develop negative feelings for the site.

He also suggests if your site cannot meet a user's needs, that you direct them to another site that will. This referral builds goodwill and will make your site the starting point for the customer's next search. If an item will be available reasonably soon, you can allow customers to preorder or provide their e-mail for notification when the product or service becomes available. Log onto Neilsen's site and read the rest of his advice for telling users no. Can you think of other ways to tell Web site users no that Neilsen hasn't suggested?

compounded quarterly. Her payments and interest come to just over $17,200; the amount could be higher depending on the amount of her last paycheck, which will include compensation for any unused vacation days and sick leave. Furthermore, since the amounts deducted were not considered taxable income, she will have to pay income tax on the money she will receive.

You cannot process the check until after her resignation is effective, so you will mail it to her. You have her home address on file; if she's moving, she needs to let you know where to send the check. Processing the check may take two to three weeks.

Write a memo to Michelle.

Analysis of the Problem

Use the analysis questions in the first chapter to help you solve the problem.

1. Who is (are) your audience(s)? What characteristics are relevant to this particular message? If you are writing to more than one reader, how do the readers differ?

    Michelle Jagtiani. Unless she's a personal friend, I probably wouldn't know why she's leaving and where she's going.

    There's a lot I don't know. She may or may not know much about taxes; she may or may not be able to take advantage of tax-reduction strategies. I can't assume the answers because I wouldn't have them in real life.

2. What are your purposes in writing?

    To tell her that she will get only her own contributions, plus 4 ½% interest compounded quarterly; that the check will be mailed to her home address two to three weeks after her last day on the job; and that the money will be taxable as income.

    To build goodwill so that she feels that she has been treated fairly and consistently. To minimize negative feelings she may have.

    To close the door on this subject.

3. What information must your message include?

    When the check will come. The facts that her check will be based on her contributions, not the employer's, and that the money will be taxable income. How lump-sum retirement benefits are calculated. The fact that we have her current address on file but need a new address if she's moving.

4. How can you build support for your position? What reasons or benefits will your reader find convincing?

    Giving the amount currently in her account may make her feel that she is getting a significant sum of money. Suggesting someone who can give free tax advice (if the company offers this as a fringe benefit) reminds her of the benefits of working with the company. Wishing her luck with her new job is a nice touch.

5. What objection(s) can you expect your reader(s) to have? What negative elements of your message must you deemphasize or overcome?

    She is getting about half the amount she expected, since she gets no matching funds. She might have been able to earn more than 4½% interest if she had invested the money in the stock market. Depending on her personal tax situation she may pay more tax on the money as a lump sum than would have been due had she paid it each year as she earned the money.

Figure 11.6   An Unacceptable Solution to the Sample Problem

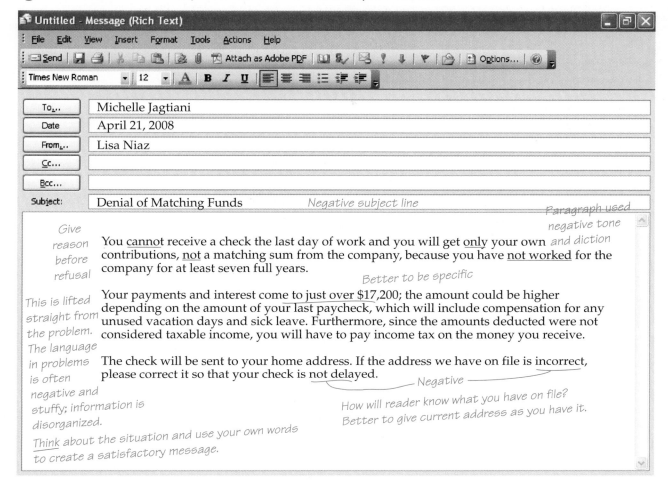

Discussion of the Sample Solutions

The solution in Figure 11.6 is not acceptable. The subject line gives a bald negative with no reason or alternative. The first sentence has a condescending tone that is particularly offensive in negative messages; it also focuses on what is being taken away rather than what remains. Paragraph 2 lacks you-attitude and is vague. The memo ends with a negative. There is nothing anywhere in the memo to build goodwill.

The solution in Figure 11.7, in contrast, is very good. The policy serves as a buffer and explanation. The negative is stated clearly but is buried in the paragraph to avoid overemphasizing it. Paragraph 2 emphasizes the positive by specifying the amount in the account and the fact that the sum might be even higher.

Paragraph 3 contains the additional negative information that the amount will be taxable but offers the alternative that it may be possible to reduce taxes. The writer builds goodwill by suggesting a specific person the reader could contact.

Paragraph 4 tells the reader what address is in the company files (Michelle may not know whether the files are up-to-date), asks that she update it if necessary, and ends with the reader's concern: getting her check promptly.

The final paragraph ends on a positive note. This generalized goodwill is appropriate when the writer does not know the reader well.

Figure 11.7   A Good Solution to the Sample Problem

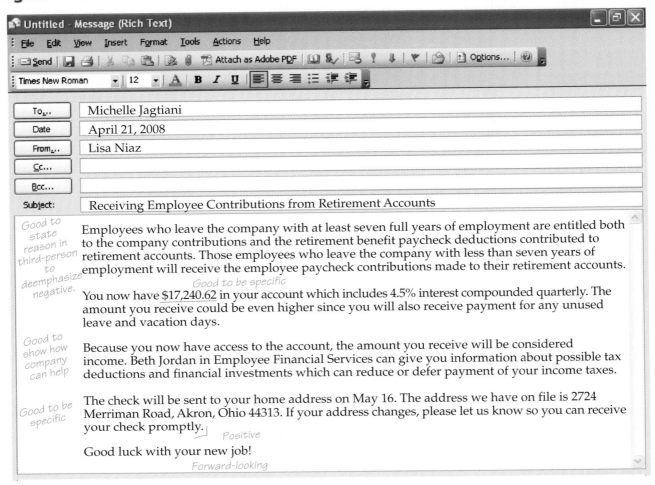

Summary of Key Points

- In a negative message, the basic information is negative; we expect the audience to be disappointed or angry.
- A good negative message conveys the negative information clearly while maintaining as much goodwill as possible. The goal is to make the audience feel that they have been taken seriously, that the decision is fair and reasonable, and that they would have made the same decision. A secondary purpose is to reduce or eliminate future communication on the same subject so that the message doesn't create more work for the communicator.
- Organize negative messages to customers and clients in this way:
  1. Give the reason for the refusal before the refusal itself when you have a reason that the audience will understand and accept.
  2. Give the negative just once, clearly.
  3. Present an alternative or compromise, if one is available.
  4. End with a positive, forward-looking statement.
- Organize negative memos to superiors in this way:
  1. Describe the problem.
  2. Tell how it happened.

✔ **Checklist**   Negative Messages

☐ Is the subject line appropriate?

☐ If a buffer is used, does it avoid suggesting either a positive or a negative response?

☐ Is the reason, if it is given, presented before the refusal? Is the reason watertight, with no loopholes?

☐ Is the negative information clear?

☐ Is an alternative given if a good one is available? Does the message provide all the information needed to act on the alternative but leave the choice up to the audience?

☐ Does the last paragraph avoid repeating the negative information?

☐ Is tone acceptable—not defensive, but not cold, preachy, or arrogant either?

Originality in a negative message may come from

☐ An effective buffer, if one is appropriate.

☐ A clear, complete statement of the reason for the refusal.

☐ A good alternative, clearly presented, which shows that you're thinking about what the audience really needs.

☐ Adding details that show you're thinking about a specific organization and the specific people in that organization.

---

3. Describe the options for fixing it.
4. Recommend a solution and ask for action.

- When you must pass along serious bad news to peers and subordinates, use a variation of the pattern to superiors:
  1. Describe the problem.
  2. Present an alternative or compromise, if one is available.
  3. If possible, ask for input or action.

- When the bad news is less serious, use the pattern for negative messages to clients and customers unless your knowledge of the audience suggests that another pattern will be more effective. Use a subject line appropriate for the pattern.

- A **buffer** is a neutral or positive statement that allows you to bury the negative message. Buffers must put the reader in a good frame of mind, not give the bad news but not imply a positive answer either, and provide a natural transition to the body of the letter. Use a buffer only when the reader values harmony or when the buffer serves a purpose in addition to simply delaying the negative.

- The kinds of statements most often used as buffers are (1) good news, (2) facts and chronologies of events, (3) references to enclosures, (4) thanks, and (5) statements of principle.

- A good reason prepares the audience for the negative and must be watertight. Give several reasons only if all are watertight and are of comparable importance. Omit the reason for the refusal entirely if it is weak or if it makes your organization look bad. Do not hide behind company policy.

- Make the refusal crystal clear.

- Giving the audience an alternative or a compromise
  - Offers the audience another way to get what they want.
  - Suggests that you really care about the audience and about helping to meet their needs.
  - Allows you to end on a positive note and to present yourself and your organization as positive, friendly, and helpful.

Effective Negative Letters

Researcher Catherine Schryer asked writers at an insurance company to evaluate the firm's letters denying claims. She found four differences between the letters judged effective and the letters judged ineffective:

- Good letters were easier to read. Poor letters contained more jargon; longer words and sentences; and stiff, awkward phrasing.

- Good letters gave fuller reasons for the rejection. Poor letters often used boilerplate and did not explain terms.

- Good letters were less likely to talk about the reader's emotions ("angry," "disappointed").

- Good letters were more likely to portray the writer and reader as active agents.

Adapted from Catherine Schryer, "Walking a Fine Line: Writing Negative Letters in an Insurance Company," *Journal of Business and Technical Communication* 14 (October 2000): 445–97.

- When you give an alternative, give the audience all the information they need to act on it, but don't take the necessary steps for them. Letting the audience decide whether to try the alternative allows the audience to reestablish a sense of psychological freedom.
- Many negative situations can be redefined to use the patterns of organization for informative and positive or for persuasive messages.

CHAPTER 11   # Exercises and Problems

11.1   Reviewing the Chapter

1. What are the reasons behind the patterns of organization for negative messages in different situations (Figure 11.1)? (L0 1)

2. What are the parts of negative messages? How may those parts be changed for different contexts? (LO 2)

3. When should you not use a buffer? (LO 2)

4. When should you not apologize? (LO 2)

5. What are some ways you can maintain a caring tone in negative messages? (LO 3)

6. What are some different varieties of negative messages? What are some examples from the chapter text and sidebars? (LO 4)

11.2   Reviewing Grammar

Negative news is frequently placed in dependent clauses to help de-emphasize it. Unfortunately, some dependent clauses and phrases are dangling or misplaced modifiers.

Do the exercise from Appendix B on improving modifiers (B.6) to help you learn to recognize this error.

11.3   Letters for Discussion—Credit Refusal

As director of customer service at C'est Bon, an upscale furniture store, you manage the store's credit. Today you are going to reject an application from Frank Steele. Although his income is fairly high, his last two payments on his college loans were late, and he has three bank credit cards, all charged to the upper limit, on which he's made just the minimum payment for the last three months.

The following letters are possible approaches to giving him the news. How well does each message meet the criteria in the checklist for negative messages?

1.

Dear Mr. Steele:

Your request to have a C'est Bon charge account shows that you are a discriminating shopper. C'est Bon sells the finest merchandise available.

Although your income is acceptable, records indicate that you carry the maximum allowable balances on three bank credit cards. Moreover, two recent payments on your student loans have not been made in a timely fashion. If you were given a C'est Bon charge account, and if you charged a large amount on it, you might have difficulty paying the bill, particularly if you had other unforeseen expenses (car repair, moving, medical emergency) or if your income dropped suddenly. If you were unable to repay, with your other debt you would be in serious difficulty. We would not want you to be in such a situation, nor would you yourself desire it.

Please reapply in six months.

Sincerely,

2.

Dear Frank:

No, you can't have a C'est Bon credit card—at least not right now. Get your financial house in order and try again.

Fortunately for you, there's an alternative. Put what you want on layaway. The furniture you want will be held for you, and paying a bit each week or month will be good self-discipline.

Enjoy your C'est Bon furniture!

Sincerely,

3.

Dear Mr. Steele:

Over the years, we've found that the best credit risks are people who pay their bills promptly. Since two of your student loan payments have been late, we won't extend store credit to you right now. Come back with a record of six months of on-time payments of all bills, and you'll get a different answer.

You might like to put the furniture you want on layaway. A $50 deposit holds any item you want. You have six months to pay, and you save interest charges.

You might also want to take advantage of one of our Saturday Seminars. On the first Saturday of each month at 11 AM, our associates explain one topic related to furniture and interior decorating. Upcoming topics are

How to Wallpaper a Room	February 5
Drapery Options	March 6
Persian Carpets	April 1

Sincerely,

11.4 E-Mails for Discussion—Saying *No* to a Colleague

A colleague in another state agency has e-mailed you asking if you would like to use the payroll software her agency developed. You wouldn't. Switching to a new program would take a lot of time, and what you have works well for you.

The following messages are possible approaches to giving her the news. How well does each message meet the criteria in the checklist for negative messages?

1.

Subject: Re: Use Our Software?

No.

2.

Subject: Re: Use Our Software?

Thanks for telling me about the payroll software your team developed. What we have works well for us. Like every other agency, we're operating on a bare-bones budget, and no one here wants to put time (that we really don't have) into learning a new program. So we'll say, no, thanks!

3.

Subject: Re: Use Our Software?

The payroll software your team developed sounds very good.

I might like to use it, but the people here are computer phobic. They HATE learning new programs. So, being a good little computer support person, I soldier on with the current stuff. (And people wonder why state government is SO INEFFICIENT! Boy, the stories I could tell!)

Anyway, thanks for the offer. Keep me posted on the next development—maybe it will be something so obviously superior that even the Neanderthals here can see its advantages!

11.5   Revising a Negative Message

Rewrite and reorganize the following negative message to make it more positive.

Account Number: 5555 5555 5555 5555

Dear Robert Jackson:

Due to the extended inactive status of your account, your credit card has not been reissued.

If you are interested in utilizing your account and would like to be considered for reissue, please contact us at the address listed above or the telephone number below.

Customer Service

1-888-555-6626

11.6   Firing Employees

In 2006, Radio Shack was having financial troubles and had closed about 500 of their stores. They also warned employees that more layoffs were probably on the horizon. Then, in August of 2006, Radio Shack sent layoff notices to 400 employees who worked at their headquarters in Fort Worth, Texas. The notices were sent in an e-mail. The message reads as follows:

"The work force reduction notification is currently in progress. Unfortunately, your position is one that has been terminated."

Based on your knowledge of negative messages, write a memo to your instructor which discusses why Radio Shack's layoffs e-mail is not effective. You should also offer alternative suggestions on how the termination news might be better presented. How does e-mail stand as a mode of communication for delivering this type of negative message? What are the disadvantages of firing employees in this way?

Adapted from Tara Weiss, "You've Got Mail: You're Fired," *Forbes.com*, August 31, 2006, http://www.forbes.com/leadership/2006/08/31/leadership-radio-shack-management-cx_tw_0831layoffs.html (accessed February 20, 2007).

11.7   Notifying Seniors That They May Not Graduate

State University asks students to file an application to graduate one term before they actually plan to graduate. The application lists the courses the student has already had and those he or she will take in the last two terms. Your office reviews the lists to see that the student will meet the requirements for total number of hours, hours in the major, and general education requirements. Some students have forgotten a requirement or not taken enough courses and cannot graduate unless they take more courses than those they have listed.

As your instructor directs,

Write form e-mail messages to the following audiences. Leave blanks for the proposed date of graduation and specific information that must be merged into the message:

a.   Students who have not taken enough total hours.

b.   Students who have not fulfilled all the requirements for their majors.

c.   Students who are missing one or more general education courses.

d.   Advisers of students who do not meet the requirements for graduation.

11.8   Correcting a Mistake

Today, as you reviewed some cost figures, you realized they didn't fit with the last monthly report you filed. You had pulled the numbers together from several sources, and you're not sure what happened. Maybe you miscopied, or didn't save the final version after you'd checked all the numbers. But whatever the cause, you've found errors in three categories. You gave your boss the following totals:

Personnel	$2,843,490
Office supplies	$43,500
Telephone	$186,240

E-mail your boss to correct the information.

As your instructor directs,

Write e-mail messages for the following situations:

a.   The correct numbers are

Personnel	$2,845,490
Office supplies	$34,500
Telephone	$186,420

b.   The correct numbers are

Personnel	$2,845,490
Office supplies	$84,500
Telephone	$468,240

Variations for each situation:

1.   Your boss has been out of the office; you know she hasn't seen the data yet.

2.   Your boss gave a report to the executive committee this morning using your data.

Hints:

- How serious is the mistake in each situation?
- In which situations, if any, should you apologize?
- Should you give the reason for the mistake? Why or why not?
- How do your options vary depending on whether your job title gives you responsibility for numbers and accounting?

11.9   Refusing to Pay an Out-of-Network Bill

Your employees' health insurance allows them to choose from one of three health maintenance organizations (HMOs). Once employees have selected an HMO, they must get all medical care (except for out-of-state emergency care) from the HMO. Employees receive a listing of the doctors and hospitals affiliated with each HMO when they join the company and pick an HMO and again each October when they have a one-month "open enrollment period" to change to another of the three HMOs if they choose.

As Director of Employee Benefits, you've received an angry e-mail from Alvin Reineke. Alvin had just received a statement from his HMO stating that it would not pay for the costs of his hernia operation two months ago at St. Catherine's Hospital in your city. Alvin is furious: one of the reasons he accepted a job with your company six months ago was its excellent health care coverage. He feels the company lied to him and should pay for his (rather large) hospital bill since the HMO refuses to do so.

The HMO which Alvin had selected uses two hospitals, but not St. Catherine's. When Alvin joined the company six months ago, he (like all new employees) received a thick booklet explaining the HMO options. Perhaps he did not take the time to read it carefully. But that's not your fault. Alvin can change plans during the next open enrollment, but even if he switched to an HMO that included St. Catherine's, that HMO wouldn't pay for surgery performed before he joined that HMO.

Write an e-mail message to Alvin giving him the bad news.

Hints:

*   What tone should you use? Should you be sympathetic? Should you remind him that this is his own fault?

*   Is there any help you can give Alvin (e.g., information about credit-union short-term loans or even information about negotiating payment terms with the hospital)?

*   What can you do to make Alvin feel that the company has not lied to him?

11.10   Announcing a Reduction in Benefits

In years past, your company has had a generous health insurance policy, fully funded by the employer. Employees pay only a $10 copayment for doctor visits and a $6 copayment for prescriptions. However, the cost of health insurance has risen much faster than the company's other expenses and much faster than the prices your company can charge its customers. Most other companies now expect their employees to contribute part of the cost of their health insurance through payroll deductions, and management has determined that your company must begin doing the same. For a group insurance policy similar to the one employees have received in the past, they will now have to pay $50 per month, and the copayment for doctor visits will rise to $15 per visit. The coverage for prescriptions will vary, with the $6 copayment applying only to generic drugs. For brand-name drugs, employees will have to pay more.

As your instructor directs,

Write an e-mail message to the employees of

a.   A large advertising agency in a big city. The agency's billings have fallen 30% in the last six months, and 10% of the staff have already been laid off.

b.   A manufacturing company. The company is still making a profit, but just barely. Unless the company saves money, layoffs may be necessary.

c.   A successful service business. The business is doing well, but most of the employees earn only the minimum wage. They do not own stock in the company.

11.11   Rejecting a Suggestion

Your company has a suggestion system that encourages workers to submit suggestions that will save the organization money or improve safety, customer service, or morale. If a suggestion is accepted that will save the company money, its proposer gets 10% of the estimated first year's savings. If a suggestion is accepted but will not save money, the proposer gets $25. You chair the committee which makes the decisions.

Today, you must tell Wayne Andersen that the committee has rejected his suggestion to buy a second photocopying machine for the sales department. Wayne pointed out that the sales department occupies a whole floor yet has only one copier. Although the copier is in the center of the room (by the coffee and vending machines), some people have to walk quite a distance to get to it. Of course, they often stop to talk to the people they pass. Wayne calculated how much time people waste walking to the copier and talking to co-workers multiplied by annual salaries compared to the shorter time needed to walk to one of two copiers, each located to serve half the floor. He calculated that the company could save the cost of a $10,000 machine in just six months, with a further $10,000 savings by the end of the first year.

No one on the committee liked Wayne's idea:

"I don't trust his numbers. After all, lots of people combine trips to the copier with a trip to get a cup of coffee or a cola. They'd do even more walking if they had to make two trips."

"He talks about people waiting in line to use the copier, but I'm in sales, and I know the copier really isn't used that much. Sure, there are some bottlenecks—especially when reports are due—but lots of the time the machine just sits there."

"I'm worried about the economy. I don't think this is the time to spend money we don't have to spend."

"I guess his system would be more efficient. But the real savings comes not from less walking but from less talking. And I think we *want* people to talk to each other. Informal conversations are great for relieving stress, sharing ideas, and strengthening our loyalty to each other and to the company."

"I agree. I think our company is built on informal interchange and a sense that you don't have to account for every single minute. Our people are almost all on salary; they stay overtime without any extra pay. If someone wants to take a break and talk to someone, I think that's OK."

"Well, sometimes we do waste time talking. But his idea isn't really new. Lots of people think we could save money by buying more of every kind of equipment. Even if we get a copier, I don't think he should get any money."

You pointed out that even if a new copier didn't save as much money as Wayne predicted, it would shorten the lines when lots of people have copying to do. You suggested adopting his suggestion but reducing the estimated savings and therefore the award. But the committee rejected your compromise and the suggestion. As chair of the committee, you vote only to break a tie.

Write an e-mail message to Wayne, reporting the committee's decision.

Hints:

* What reason(s) should you give for the committee's decision?

* Should you tell Wayne that you disagreed with the majority?
* How can you encourage Wayne to continue to submit suggestions?

11.12   E-Mailing Bad News about Lab Hours

You're the administrator of your university's computer labs. Many students have asked for longer lab hours, and you presented the request to your superiors. However, you've just been informed that, beginning next term, the hours for the computer labs are being reduced. The labs will open one hour later each morning as a cost-saving measure.

Write an e-mail message, including subject line, to all students, informing them of this change.

11.13   Telling Employees to Remove Personal Web Sites

You're Director of Management and Information Systems (MIS) in your organization. At your monthly briefing for management, a vice president complained that some employees have posted personal Web pages on the company's Web server.

"It looks really unprofessional to have stuff about cats and children and musical instruments. How can people do this?"

You took the question literally. "Well, some people have authorization to post material—price changes, job listings, marketing information. Someone who has authorization could put up anything."

Another manager said, "I don't think it's so terrible—after all, there aren't any links from our official pages to these personal pages."

A third person said, "But we're paying for what's posted—so we pay for server space and connect time. Maybe it's not much right now, but as more and more people become Web-literate, the number of people putting up unauthorized pages could spread. We should put a stop to this now."

The vice president agreed. "The Web site is carefully designed to present an image of our organization. Personal pages are dangerous. Can you imagine the flak we'd get if someone posted links to pornography?"

You said, "I don't think that's very likely. If it did happen, as system administrator, I could remove the page."

The third speaker said, "I think we should remove all the pages. Having any at all suggests that our people have so much extra time that they're playing on the Web. That suggests that our prices are too high and may make some people worry about quality. In fact, I think that we need a new policy prohibiting personal pages on the company's Web server. And any pages that are already up should be removed."

A majority of the managers agreed and told you to write a message to all employees. Create an e-mail message to tell employees that you will remove the personal pages already posted and that no more will be allowed.

Hint:

* Suggest other ways that people can post personal Web pages.
* Give only reasons that are watertight and make the company look good.

11.14   Refusing to Waive a Fee

As the Licensing Program Coordinator for your school, you evaluate proposals from vendors who want to make or sell merchandise with the school's name, logo, or mascot. If you find the product acceptable, the vendor pays a $250 licensing fee and then 6.5% of the wholesale cost of the merchandise manufactured (whether or not it is sold). The licensing fee helps to support the cost of your office; the 6.5% royalty goes into a student scholarship fund. At well-known universities or those with loyal students and alumni, the funds from such a program can add up to hundreds of thousands of dollars a year.

On your desk today is a proposal from a current student, Meg Winston.

I want to silk-screen and sell T-shirts printed with the name of the school, the mascot, and the words "We're Number One!" (A copy of the design I propose is enclosed.) I ask that you waive the $250 licensing fee you normally require and limit the 6.5% royalty only to those T-shirts actually sold, not to all those made.

I am putting myself through school by using student loans and working 30 hours a week. I just don't have $250. In my marketing class, we've done feasibility analyses, and I've determined that the shirts can be sold if the price is low enough. I hope to market these shirts in an independent study project with Professor Doulin, building on my marketing project earlier this term. However, my calculations show that I cannot price the shirts competitively if just one shirt must bear the 6.5% royalty for all the shirts produced in a batch. I will of course pay the 6.5% royalty on all shirts sold and not returned. I will produce the shirts in small batches (50–100 at a time). I am willing to donate any manufactured but unsold shirts to the athletic program so that you will know I'm not holding out on you.

By waiving this fee, you will show that this school really wants to help students get practical experience in business, as the catalog states. I will work hard to promote these shirts by getting the school president, the coaches, and campus leaders to endorse them, pointing out that the money goes to the scholarship fund. The shirts themselves will promote school loyalty, both now and later when we're alumni who can contribute to our alma mater.

I look forward to receiving the "go-ahead" to market these shirts.

The design and product are acceptable under your guidelines. However, you've always enforced the fee structure across the board, and you see no reason to make an exception now. Whether the person trying to sell merchandise is a student or not doesn't matter; your policy is designed to see that the school benefits whenever it is used to sell something. Students aren't the only ones whose cash flow is limited; many businesses would find it easier to get into the potentially lucrative business of selling clothing, school supplies, and other items with the school name or logo if they got the same deal Meg is asking for. (The policy also lets the school control the kinds of items on which its name appears.) Just last week, your office confiscated about 400 T-shirts and shorts made by a company that had used the school name on them without permission; the company has paid the school $7,500 in damages.

Write a letter to Meg rejecting her special requests. She can get a license to produce the T-shirts, but only if she pays the $250 licensing fee and the royalty on all shirts made.

11.15 Correcting Misinformation

You're the director of the city's Division of Water. Your mail today contains this letter:

When we bought our pool, the salesman told us that you would give us a discount on the water bill when we fill the pool. Please start the discount immediately. I tried to call you three times and got nothing but busy signals.

Sincerely,

Larry Shadburn-Butler

Larry Shadburn-Butler

The salesperson was wrong. You don't provide discounts for pools (or anything else). At current rates, filling a pool with a garden hose costs from $8.83 (for a 1,800-gallon pool) to $124.67 (for 26,000 gallons) in the city. Filling a pool from any other water source would cost more. Rates are 30% higher in the suburbs and 50% higher in unincorporated rural areas. And you don't have enough people to answer phones. You tried a voicemail system but eliminated it when you found people didn't have time to process all the messages that were left. But the city budget doesn't allow you to hire more people.

As your instructor directs,

a. Write a letter to Mr. Shadburn-Butler.

b. Write a letter to all the stores that sell swimming pools, urging them to stop giving customers misinformation.

c. Write a notice for the one-page newsletter that you include with quarterly water bills. Assume that you can have half a page for your information.

11.16 Analyzing Job Rejection Letters

1. Here are three rejections letters to an applicant who applied for an accounting position.

Letter 1

We realize that the application process for the accounting position at AlphaBank required a substantial amount of thought, time, and effort on your part. Therefore, we would like to express our sincere appreciation for your willingness to participate in the search process.

The task of selecting a final candidate was difficult and challenging due to the quality of the applicant pool. We regret to inform you that we selected another candidate who we believe will best meet the needs of AlphaBank.

We thank your for your interest in employment at AlphaBank and extend our best wishes as you pursue your professional goals.

Letter 2

Thank you for your interest in the accounting position at AlphaBank. I'm sorry to inform you that you were not one of the finalists. The position has now been filled.

The search committee and I wish you the best in your future employment searches.

Letter 3

Thank you for your interest in the accounting position at AlphaBank.

I'm sorry to inform you that the search committee has decided to offer the position to another candidate. This was an extremely difficult decision for us to make. We were all impressed with your résumé and credentials.

Again, thank you for your interest in AlphaBank.

Analyze these three job rejection letters by answering the following questions:

- Do these letters use buffers? If so, how effective are they?
- What reasons do the letters give, if any?
- Does the letter attempt to build goodwill with the audience? If yes, how so?
- Do any of the letters offer an alternative?
- How do you think recipients will react to each of the letters? Which (if any) are more preferable?

As your instructor directs,

a. Discuss your findings in a small group.

b. Present your findings orally to the class.

c. Present your findings in a memo to your instructor.

2. Collect job rejection letters mailed to seniors on your campus. Analyze the letters, answering the following questions:

- Do these letters use buffers? If so, how effective are they?
- What reasons do the letters give, if any?
- Do the letters attempt to build goodwill with the audience? If yes, how so?
- Do any of the letters offer an alternative?
- How do you think recipients will react to each of the letters? Which (if any) are more preferable?

As your instructor directs,

a. Discuss your finding in a small group.

b. Present your findings orally to the class.

c. Present your findings in a memo to your instructor.

d. Join with other students to write a report based on your findings.

11.17   Writing a Job Rejection Letter

After a job search at BAC Inc., your boss is pleased with the new candidate, Kimberly Lowery, selected for the Communications Coordinator position. There were over 75 well-qualified applicants, and it was an extremely difficult decision.

Today, your boss wants you to notify the other job candidates that they were not selected. He suggests that you "let them down easy. You never know when we might need these candidates again in the future."

As your instructor directs,

a. Write a form letter to the job applicants who were not hired for the position. Remember to maintain goodwill as much as possible so that applicants have a favorable opinion of BAC Inc.

b. Write a memo to your instructor that focuses on the ethical choices you had to make while constructing the negative message.

11.18   Turning Down a Faithful Client

You are Midas Investment Services' specialist in estate planning. You give talks to various groups during the year about estate planning. You ask nonprofit groups (churches, etc.) just to reimburse your expenses; you charge for-profit groups a fee plus expenses. These fees augment your income nicely, and the talks also are marvelous exposure for you and your company.

Every February for the last five years, Gardner Manufacturing Company has hired you to conduct an eight-hour workshop (two hours every Monday night for four weeks) on retirement and estate planning for its employees who are over 60 or who are thinking of taking early retirement. These workshops are popular and have generated clients for your company. The session last February went smoothly, as you have come to expect.

Today, out of the blue, you got a letter from Hope Goldberger, Director of Employee Benefits at Gardner, asking you to conduct the workshops every Tuesday evening *next* month at your usual fee. She didn't say whether this is an extra series or whether this will replace next February's series.

You can't do it. Your spouse, a microbiologist, is giving an invited paper at an international conference in Paris next month and the two of you are taking your children, ages 13 and 9, on a three-week trip to Europe. (You've made arrangements with school authorities to have the kids miss three weeks of classes.) Your spouse's trip will be tax-deductible, and you've been looking forward to and planning the trip for the last eight months.

Unfortunately, Midas Investment Services is a small group, and the only other person who knows anything about estate planning is a terrible speaker. You could suggest a friend at another financial management company, but you don't want Gardner to turn to someone else permanently; you enjoy doing the workshops and find them a good way to get leads.

Write the letter to Ms. Goldberger.

11.19   Pacifying Customers

Macy's, a New York–based department store and financer of the annual Macy's Thanksgiving Day Parade, launched a nationwide takeover of many long-standing department stores, such as Marshall Field's, Kauffmann's, and Meier & Frank. Beyond the name change, shoppers really began to notice when Macy's changed some long-standing holiday traditions.

For example in Portland, Oregon, the annual parade was shorter and the Santa Land monorail, a family tradition at Meier & Frank, was not in operation. In Chicago customers were disgruntled with losing their long-time Marshall Field's store; some customers refused to shop there during the holiday season. In fact, a survey by Deloitte & Touche suggested that 41% of Chicagoans were unhappy with the name change. Macy's is in a bind. Clearly, they want to keep loyal customers.

Take on the role of the Macy's Communication Department and write to angry Meier & Frank customers.

Hints:

- Remember to always maintain goodwill by analyzing how the audience feels about the situation.
- Point out the advantages of having a historically and nationally known department store take over smaller, less-known department stores.
- Keep in mind the monorail is only down for one year during the store renovation.
- Macy's also plans to add to the parade next year by including new inflatable characters for the kids and electrically powering the floats.

Based on Venessa O'Connell, "Macy's Brands the Holidays: As Marshall Field's, Kaufmann's, Others Take Chain's Name, Department Stores Try to Maintain Local Shoppers' Loyalty," *Wall Street Journal*, November 22, 2006, B1, B2.

11.20   Sending Negative Messages to Real Audiences

As your instructor directs, write a negative letter that responds to one of the following scenarios:

- Write a letter to the owner of a restaurant where you received poor service.
- Write a letter to a company whose product unsatisfactorily met your expectations or needs.
- Identify a current political topic on which you disagree with your congressional representative. Write a letter that outlines your views for him/her and calls for change.
- Identify a television advertisement with which you disagree. Write a letter to the company explaining

your position and request that the advertisement be altered or taken off the air.

Hints:

- For all of these scenarios, your main goal should be to promote change.
- Express your complaint as positively as possible.
- Remember to consider your audience's needs; how can you build support for your position?

11.21   Getting Information from a Co-worker

Your boss has been pressuring you because you are weeks late turning in a termination report. However, you cannot begin your section of the report until your colleague, Matt Churetta, finishes his section. Right now, he is the problem. Here is a series of e-mail exchanges between you and Matt:

7/25/2008

Matt,

The boss wants the termination report now. Send over your section as soon as you finish.

Thanks,

Matt's reply:

7/31/2008

My apologies about the report,

On another note, I'm waiting to see my oncology surgeon to see what the course of treatment will be for the esophageal cancer. I will keep you posted on the process.

Please let me know if there is anything else coming up.

Thanks,

8/15/2008

Matt,

I had no idea that you are dealing with esophageal cancer. Definitely keep me posted on your condition. Best wishes as you work through your treatment.

I need your section of the termination report as soon as you finish it. The boss has been waiting patiently for the finished version.

Thanks,

Matt's reply:

8/26/2008

Report is coming along. The last two weeks have been difficult dealing with all the tests, doctors' appointments, etc. I will beat this deal!!!

Take Care,

It is now September, and over a month has passed from the termination report's original due date. While you are sympathetic to Matt's situation, the boss is demanding the finished report.

As your instructor directs,

a. Write an e-mail to Matt telling him you have to have his portion of the report as soon as possible. You are concerned for your job security, as well as his, if this report is not finalized soon.

b. Write a memo to your boss explaining the situation.

c. Write a memo to your instructor that focuses on the ethical choices you had to make while constructing the two messages.

11.22   Mosaic Case

As the communications specialist for Mosaic's physical stores, Demetri received some bad news today from the Phoenix, Arizona, store. Apparently, shoppers have been complaining about the lousy customer service they have been receiving from the sales associates. These customers were so angry that they wrote their complaint letters to the headquarters in Des Moines, instead of just contacting the manager of the Phoenix store. The letters were passed to the Communications Department to deal with the issues. Sadly, the complaints are not from just one or two customers. Demetri has a stack of letters piled up on his desk. He estimates there must be 30 or 40.

Demetri realized he had to take immediate and swift action. However, he wanted to run the idea past Sarah first.

He walked across the office and handed Sarah a few of the letters to skim.

Here is what one customer had to say—

> I have been a loyal customer of Mosaic for the past ten years while I lived in Sacramento. I recently moved to the Phoenix area and was happy to learn there is a Mosaic just around the corner from my new house. However, I am appalled at the way the workers act in the store. While I was there, employees in two different parts of the store were verbally making fun of customers behind their backs.
>
> No one seemed to be available to answer questions. When I asked one worker a question about a sale item, she looked at me and said, "I don't know; I don't work here!" even though she was wearing the Mosaic uniform. When I walked away, I heard her whisper to another person dressed in a Mosaic uniform some insulting comments about my clothes.
>
> Although I have come to really like the products available at Mosaic, I question whether I can continue shopping in this unpleasant environment.

Here is what another customer wrote:

> On June 27th, I was shopping at the Mosaic store in Phoenix and could not believe how unkind the workers were. I'm a 70-year-old man and asked for help getting a heavy item from a shelf that I couldn't quite reach. One of the workers I asked said— "I'm not your lackey old geezer."
>
> The week before, my daughter was at Mosaic and overheard three workers, who were just standing around, having a contest for spotting the most unattractive customer.
>
> I will never shop at Mosaic again and have told everyone I know to boycott the store as well.

"Wow!" said Sarah. "Are they all like this?"

"Yes," answered Demetri. "I really need to do some damage control. And fast! I think I'm going to respond to these customer complaints by sending out a general apology," Demetri told Sarah. "I'm also going to add in a coupon for 10% off their next shopping experience."

"Well, normally, I wouldn't recommend the 10% coupon because it's an extrinsic motivator. However, in this case, it could be a good idea. It's going to be difficult to re-establish goodwill with them. Thirty or forty unhappy customers is a big deal and could definitely tarnish the Mosaic name. I once read that every customer who has a bad experience is likely to tell between 15–25 people, more than they tell about a good experience. You need to do some serious troubleshooting before Yvonne finds out about this."

"I know, I know. So I'm going to write to the customers and apologize as soon as possible."

"But what about the sales associates who are rude or inappropriately behaving? If you don't do anything to resolve the issue, the problem will still be there the next time the customers shop at Mosaic."

"Good point. I guess I'll also have to write a memo to managers at the Phoenix store to alert them about the customers' issues."

Take on the communication task of Demetri and write three correspondences.

- Write a letter to all of Mosaic's customers who wrote a letter about the Phoenix store. Make sure that you apologize for the sales associates' behaviors and let the customers know what is being done to correct the situation.
- Write a memo to the Phoenix Mosaic store manager, Lucas Pekelder, alerting him to the situation, as well as offering some alternatives on how to correct it.
- Write a memo to Yvonne. In the memo, explain the actions you took in writing the letter to customers and memo to Mr. Pekelder and how and why you said the things you did.

12

Persuasive Messages

Learning Objectives

After studying this chapter, you will know how to:

1 Analyze a persuasive situation.

2 Identify basic persuasive strategies.

3 Write persuasive direct requests.

4 Write persuasive problem-solving messages.

5 Write sales and fund-raising messages.

6 Use rational and emotional appeals to support persuasive messages.

The Art of Persuasion: Posters of World War II

The United States is involved in a protracted war effort. Gasoline is in short supply, and gas and food prices are rising. To strengthen public support for the war and encourage energy conservation, the government begins an aggressive propaganda campaign using images that symbolize American strength, democratic values, and the battle against evil to arouse patriotism and public support for American troops.

This scenario may bring the Iraq War to mind, but it actually describes U.S. involvement in World War II and posters that were used to persuade Americans to support the war effort.

We Can Do It!

Women were needed to help ease labor shortages, and recruiting campaigns focused on convincing women who had never worked outside their homes to take jobs. These campaigns glamorized working women while supporting the ideal of femininity, and no image personified both better than Rosie the Riveter. Dressed in overalls and a bandana, Rosie revised the American image of the feminine ideal.

"In World Ward II, posters were used to persuade Americans to support the war effort."

The Four Freedoms

On January 6, 1941, President Franklin D. Roosevelt delivered a speech outlining four essential human freedoms: freedom of speech and expression, the freedom of all people to worship God in their own way, freedom from want, and freedom from fear. Following the speech, artist Norman Rockwell portrayed the four freedoms as classic scenes of American life. These scenes were published in *The Saturday Evening Post* and were so well-received by the American public that they were used on posters to encourage people to purchase bonds to support the war effort.

Food Is a Weapon

In response to shortages of foods and supplies, the government asked Americans to conserve. Some foods were rationed, and people were urged to plant Victory Gardens so commercially produced foods could be sent to troops overseas. As this poster suggests, conserving food so the troops would have enough was as important as providing them with arms for winning the war.

Source: The National Archives, "Powers of Persuasion: Poster Art from World War II," http://www.archives.gov/exhibits/powers_of_persuasion/powers_of_persuasion_home.html (accessed June 11, 2007).

Chapter Outline

Persuasion is almost universal in good business communications. If you are giving people information, you are persuading them to consider it good information, or to remember it, or even to use it. If you are giving people negative news, you are trying to persuade them to accept it. But some messages seem more obviously persuasive to us than others. Employees try to persuade their supervisors to institute flex hours or casual Fridays; supervisors try to persuade workers to keep more accurate records, thus reducing time spent correcting errors; or to follow healthier lifestyles, thus reducing health benefit costs. You may find yourself persuading your colleagues to accept your ideas, your staff to work overtime on a rush project, and your boss to give you a raise.

Whether you're selling safety equipment or ideas, effective persuasion is based on accurate logic, effective emotional appeal, and credibility or trust. Reasons have to be ones the audience finds important; emotional appeal is based on values the audience cares about; credibility is in the eye of the beholder.

In the 21st century, businesses and other administrative agencies depend more and more on persuasion and buy-in to get quality work done. You can

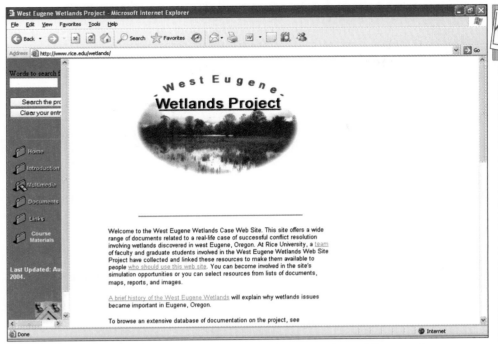

Difficult situations arise when multiple stakeholders in an issue have different and even contradictory points of view. This Web site, http://www.rice.edu/wetlands/, shows how a wetland was saved. It presents documents, maps, and reports that led to a successful resolution.

command people to make widgets. You can't command people to be creative. And even if you're making widgets, just going through the motions isn't enough. You want people to make high-quality widgets, while reducing scrap and other costs. Internal commitment is needed to make that happen.

External motivation doesn't last. Some people will buy a certain brand of pizza if they have a "2 for the price of 1" coupon. But if the coupon expires, or if another company offers the same deal, customers may leave. In contrast, if customers like your pizza better, if they are motivated internally to choose it, then you may keep your customers even if another company comes in with a lower price.

Persuasive messages include requests, proposals and recommendations, sales and fund-raising messages, job application letters, and efforts to change people's behavior, such as collection letters, criticisms or performance appraisals where you want the subordinate to improve behavior, and public-service ads designed to reduce drunk driving, drug use, and so on. Reports are persuasive messages if they recommend action.

This chapter gives general guidelines for persuasive messages. Chapter 15 discusses grants and proposals; reports are the subject of Chapter 16. Chapter 8 covers job application letters.

All persuasive messages have several purposes:

Primary purpose:

- To have the audience act.

Secondary purposes:

- To build a good image of the communicator.
- To build a good image of the communicator's organization.
- To cement a good relationship between the communicator and audience.

A More Persuasive Sales Force

When Pat Goepel took charge of Ceridian Corporation's sales and marketing operations, he was most concerned about communication. Ceridian, which provides human resource services to corporations, was sending the wrong message. "We were talking too much about what we do, rather than about what customers need and how we can help."

Goeple determined that Ceridian's salespeople needed to share a clear and persuasive message. He brought together a team of sales and marketing employees and charged them with creating one simple expression to explain the company to customers. The team's starting point was that Ceridian takes care of human resource tasks so that client organizations can concentrate on their own areas of expertise. The sales message would therefore be "Free to Focus."

For the Free to Focus theme, the team created a 15-second speech for salespeople to use to explain themselves quickly, gaining the prospect's interest. The team also identified four clear selling points related to the theme, with details to back up each one. Ceridian trained its salespeople to touch on all these points in their communications with clients and prospects.

The new sales message has improved Ceridian's opportunities to submit proposals and the share of contracts it wins. In addition, turnover among the sales force has fallen. After all, it's more fun to play on a winning team.

Adapted from Andy Cohen, "Turnaround Artist," *Sales & Marketing Management,* 155, no. 7 (2003): 40.

- To overcome any objections that might prevent or delay action.
- To reduce or eliminate future communication on the same subject so the message doesn't create more work for the communicator.

Analyzing Persuasive Situations

Choose a persuasive strategy based on your answers to four questions. Use these questions to analyze persuasive situations:

1. What do you want people to do?
2. What objections, if any, will the audience have?
3. How strong a case can you make?
4. What kind of persuasion is best for the organization and the culture?

1. What Do You Want People to Do?

Identify the specific action you want and the person who has the power to do it. If your goal requires several steps, specify what you want your audience to do *now*. For instance, your immediate goal may be to have people come to a meeting or let you make a presentation, even though your long-term goal is a major sale or a change in policy.

2. What Objections, If Any, Will the Audience Have?

If you're asking for something that requires little time, money, or physical effort and for an action that's part of the person's regular duties, the audience is likely to have few objections.

Often, however, you'll encounter some resistance. People may be busy and have what they feel are more important things to do. They may have other uses for their time and money. To be persuasive, you need to show your audience that your proposal meets their needs; you need to overcome any objections.

The easiest way to learn about objections your audience may have is to ask. Particularly when you want to persuade people in your own organization or your own town, talk to knowledgeable people. Phrase your questions nondefensively, in a way that doesn't lock people into taking a stand on an issue: "What concerns would you have about a proposal to do *x*?" "Who makes a decision about *y*?" "What do you like best about [the supplier or practice you want to change]?" Ask follow-up questions to be sure you understand: "Would you be likely to stay with your current supplier if you could get a lower price from someone else? Why?"

People are likely to be most aware of and willing to share objective concerns such as time and money. They will be less willing to tell you that their real objection is emotional. People have a **vested interest** in something if they benefit directly from keeping things as they are. People who are in power have a vested interest in retaining the system that gives them their power. Someone who designed a system has a vested interest in protecting that system from criticism. To admit that the system has faults is to admit that the designer made mistakes. In such cases, you'll need to probe to find out what the real reasons are.

Whether your audience is inside or outside your organization, they will find it easier to say *yes* when you ask for something that is consistent with the person's self-image. A manager, for example, is likely to have the self-image of being a careful decision maker who considers the company's best interests. When Lynda Ford, now a human resource consultant, was a business manager, she wanted to persuade her company's chief executive to change a policy for interviewing job candidates. Interviewing took place at headquarters, and some employees fit poorly with the cultures of the various work sites away from headquarters. Ford wanted recruiters to travel to the job sites, but the CEO complained, "I don't understand why we have to waste time with people out of the office." Responding to the executive's concern about waste, Ford presented her argument in terms of the savings from making more successful hiring decisions. Ford won the argument—and improved hiring efficiency.[1]

3. How Strong Is Your Case?

The strength of your case is based on three aspects of persuasion: argument, credibility, and emotional appeal.

Argument refers to the reasons or logic you offer. Sometimes you may be able to prove conclusively that your solution is best. Sometimes your reasons may not be as strong, the benefits may not be as certain, and obstacles may be difficult or impossible to overcome. For example, suppose that you wanted to persuade your organization to offer a tuition reimbursement plan for employees. You'd have a strong argument if you could show that tuition reimbursement would improve the performance of marginal workers or that reimbursement would be an attractive recruiting tool in a tight job market. However, if dozens of fully qualified workers apply for every opening you have, your argument would be weaker. The program might be nice for workers, but you'd have a hard job proving that it would help the company.

Credibility is the audience's response to you as the source of the message. Credibility in the workplace has three sources: expertise, image, and relationships.[2] Citing experts can make your argument more credible. In some organizations, workers build credibility by getting assigned to high-profile teams. You build credibility by your track record. The more reliable you've been in the past, the more likely people are to trust you now.

The Power of the Written Idea

Raymond Dreyfack credits his writing skills for his successful career at Faberge Perfumes. As he worked in supervisory and management jobs, he kept his eye open for opportunities to solve problems and improve performance. Then, when he had an idea, he wrote a memo to his boss.

Why a memo? The written format forced Dreyfack to organize his initial idea clearly and concisely. Editing memos trained Dreyfack to consider whether his messages reflected the reader's interests and viewpoints. The written format also gave Dreyfack's boss time to consider the idea and reflect on its merits. (If you spring an idea on your boss in the hallway, he or she might find it easier to blurt out a *no* than to give the idea fair consideration. Managers are extremely busy.)

Adapted from Raymond Dreyfack, "The Write Way to Jump-Start Your Career," *Supervision* 65, no. 4 (April 2004): 13–15.

Citibank's "Live Richly" ad campaign creates emotional appeal to those that seek a balance in life. The company found that the appeal for these "balance-seekers" had less to do with saving money and more with saving time. The ads strengthen the Citigroup brand by supporting the consumer's quest for financial and personal life goals.

Courtesy of Citigroup

Direct *and* Persuasive

Supervisors typically use direct requests as their persuasive strategy with employees. This pattern makes sense because the message is clear and employees consider their role in the company to include following their supervisor's directions. Even so, supervisors can be more persuasive if they follow these guidelines when making requests:

- Explain requests completely, even if the explanation includes bad news.

- If possible, when directing employees to correct a problem, give them some latitude in how to solve it. People are more committed to a solution they feel is their own.

- Be honest. If a task will be difficult, don't try to make it sound easy. Emphasize benefits without exaggerating them.

- When a request involves a significant change, allow time for employees to get used to the idea. Give information ahead of the change.

- Use a tone that is quiet and assertive, rather than demanding and aggressive.

- Recognize that if a request sounds difficult, employees may feel afraid or angry. Allow time for emotions to drain before countering objections rationally.

Adapted from W. H. Weiss, "Using Persuasion Successfully," *Supervision* 64, no. 1 (2003): 3–6.

We are also more likely to trust people we know. That's one reason that new CEOs make a point of visiting as many branch offices as they can. Building a relationship with someone—even if the relationship is based on an outside interest, like sports or children—makes it easier for that person to see you as an individual and to trust you.

When you don't yet have the credibility that comes from being an expert or being powerful, build credibility by the language and strategy you use:

- **Be factual.** Don't exaggerate. If you can test your idea ahead of time, do so, and report the results. Facts about your test are more convincing than opinions about your idea.

- **Be specific.** If you say "X is better," show in detail *how* it is better. Show the reader exactly where the savings or other benefits come from so that it's clear that the proposal really is as good as you say it is.

- **Be reliable.** If you suspect that a project will take longer to complete, cost more money, or be less effective than you originally thought, tell your audience *immediately*. Negotiate a new schedule that you can meet.

Emotional appeal means making the reader *want* to do what you ask. People don't make decisions—even business decisions—based on logic alone. Interns who find changes that could save their companies large sums of money may find that their bosses do not forward their suggestions. Why not? Those suggestions would require the supervisors to explain why a change so obvious an intern spotted it had not already been made.

De Tijd, a Belgian business newspaper, won a European Marketing Council award for its creative approach with getting human resource managers to use its pension brochure. Every manager who published a job ad in the newspaper received a handwritten letter from Cyriel, age 84, applying for the position. The message on the last page of Cyriel's application read, "Save your employees from having to do like Cyriel: to look for a job when they retire. Offer your employees our brochure." Sales of the brochure increased 24%.[3]

4. What Kind of Persuasion Is Best for the Organization and the Culture?

A strategy that works in one organization may not work somewhere else. One corporate culture may value no-holds-barred aggressiveness. In another organization with different cultural values, an employee who used a hard-sell strategy for a request would antagonize people.

Corporate culture (p. 46) isn't written down; it's learned by imitation and observation. What style do high-level people in your organization use? When you show a draft to your boss, are you told to tone down your statements or to make them stronger? Role models and advice are two ways organizations communicate their culture to newcomers.

Different kinds of persuasion also work for different social cultures. In North Carolina, police are using a new combination to persuade drug dealers to shut down. The combination includes iron-clad cases against the dealers, but also pressure from loved ones—mothers, grandmothers, mentors—along with a second chance. A study of symphony orchestras has surprised the classical music world by showing that traditional modes of persuading younger audiences to buy concert tickets do not work. Younger listeners enjoy the free concerts by jeans-clad musicians, but not enough to buy a concert ticket. Instead, the study showed that younger listeners do own classical CDs, and like to listen in their cars and homes, not concert halls, suggesting that symphonies should put more effort into selling their recordings.[4]

Different cultures also have different preferences for gaining compliance. In one study, students who were native speakers of American English judged direct statements ("Do this"; "I want you to do this") clearer and more effective than questions ("Could you do this?") or hints ("This is needed"). Students who were native speakers of Korean, in contrast, judged direct statements to be *least* effective. In the Korean culture, the clearer a request is, the ruder and therefore less effective it is.[5] Another study notes that communicators from countries such as China, Japan, and Korea prefer to establish personal relationships before they address business issues. They also show modesty and humility, debasing their egos in favor of collective relationships and disdaining personal profit.[6]

Latino marketing expert Chiqui Cartagena notes that for many Latinos, direct marketing materials have to be extra clear about exactly what the customer is getting, because many Latinos lack the direct marketing experiences of US customers. Also, companies have to be prepared to be paid with cash or money orders.[7]

Choosing a Persuasive Strategy

If your organization prefers a specific approach, use it. If your organization has no preference, or if you do not know your audience's preference, use the following guidelines to choose a strategy:

- Use the **direct request pattern** when
  - The audience will do as you ask without any resistance,
  - You need responses only from people who will find it easy to do as you ask, or
  - Busy people may not read all the messages they receive.
- Use the **problem-solving pattern** when the audience may resist doing as you ask and you expect logic to be more important than emotion in the decision.
- Use the **sales pattern** when the audience may resist doing as you ask and you expect emotion to be more important than logic in the decision.

Why Threats Are Less Effective than Persuasion

Sometimes people think they will be able to mandate change by ordering or threatening subordinates. Real managers disagree. Research shows that managers use threats only for obligatory duties such as coming to work on time. For more creative duties—like being part of a team or thinking of ways to save the company money—good managers persuade. Persuasion not only keeps the lines of communication open, it fosters better working relationships and makes future discussions go more smoothly.[8] When you set out to advocate change, consider the things that might motivate people to change. A survey found that salespeople in the United States and United Kingdom are most motivated by the potential to earn large incomes.[9] (In other countries, primary motivators included ability to use one's talents, the stimulation and challenge of the job, and freedom from routine.) And threats are even less effective in trying to persuade people whose salaries you don't pay.

A **threat** is a statement—explicit or implied—that someone will be punished if he or she does (or doesn't do) something. Various reasons explain why threats don't work:

1. **Threats don't produce permanent change.** Many people obey the speed limit only when a marked police car is in sight.

2. **Threats won't necessarily produce the action you want.** If you embarrass or punish people who take too much paper, they might write fewer reports—hardly the response you'd want!

3. **Threats may make people abandon an action—even in situations where it would be appropriate.** Criticizing workers for talking about nonbusiness topics such as sports may reduce communication about business topics as well.

4. **Threats produce tension.** People who feel threatened put their energies into ego defense rather than into productive work.

5. **People dislike and avoid anyone who threatens them.** A supervisor who is disliked will find it harder to enlist cooperation and support on the next issue that arises.

6. **Threats can provoke counteraggression.** Getting back at a boss can run the gamut from complaints to work slowdowns to sabotage.

In *The Tipping Point,* Malcolm Gladwell describes classic fear experiments conducted at Yale University. The point of the experiments was to get students to go to the health center for tetanus shots. Students were given high-fear or low-fear versions of booklets explaining why they should get the shots. The high-fear booklet included gruesome pictures and text; the low-fear booklet did not. As you might predict, more of the students reading the high-fear booklet said they would get the shots than those reading the low-fear version. But only 3% of students in either group actually did so. However, one small change upped the percentage to 28% (evenly spread across both groups). That change was including a campus map with the health center circled and the times shots were available listed. The map shifted the persuasion from abstract material about the dangers of tetanus to practical, personal advice.[10]

Making Persuasive Direct Requests

When you expect quick agreement, save your audience's time by presenting the request directly (see Figure 12.1). Also use the direct request pattern for busy people who do not read all the messages they receive and in organizations whose cultures favor putting the request first.

In written direct requests, put the request, the topic of the request, or a question in the subject line.

> Subject: Request for Updated Software
>
> My copy of HomeNet does not accept the nicknames for Eudora accounts.

Figure 12.1   How to Organize a Persuasive Direct Request

1. **Consider asking immediately for the information or service you want.** Delay the request if it seems too abrupt or if you have several purposes in the message.
2. **Give your audience all the information they will need to act on your request.** Number your questions or set them off with bullets so readers can check to see that all have been answered.
3. **Ask for the action you want.** Do you want a check? A replacement? A catalog? Answers to your questions? If you need an answer by a certain time, say so. If possible, show why the time limit is necessary.

Figure 12.2   A Direct Request

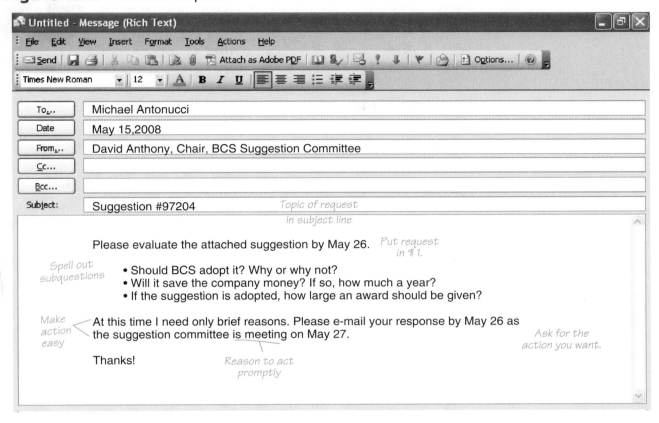

Subject: Status of Account #3548-003

Please get me the following information about account #3548-003.

Subject: Do We Need an Additional Training Session in October?

The two training sessions scheduled for October will accommodate 40 people. Last month, you said that 57 new staff accountants had been hired. Should we schedule an additional training session in October? Or can the new hires wait until the next regularly scheduled session in February?

Figure 12.2 illustrates a direct request. Note that a direct request does not contain benefits and does not need to overcome objections: it simply asks for what is needed.

Direct requests should be direct. Don't make people guess what you want.

Indirect request: Is there a newer version of the 1995 *Accounting Reference Manual?*

Direct request: If there is a newer version of the 1995 *Accounting Reference Manual,* please send it to me.

In a claim, a message asking for correction or compensation for goods or services, explain the circumstances so that the reader knows what happened. Be sure to include all the relevant details: date of purchase, model or invoice number, and so on.

In more complicated direct requests, anticipate possible responses. Suppose you're asking for information about equipment meeting certain specifications. Explain which criteria are most important so that the reader can recommend an alternative if no single product meets all your needs. You may also want to tell the reader what your price constraints are and ask whether the item is in stock or must be special-ordered.

Writing Persuasive Problem-Solving Messages

Use an indirect approach and the problem-solving pattern of organization when you expect resistance from your audience but can show that doing what you want will solve a problem you and your audience share. The pattern in Figure 12.3 allows you to disarm opposition by showing all the reasons in favor of your position before you give your audience a chance to say *no*.

Figure 12.4 uses the problem-solving pattern of organization. Benefits can be brief in this kind of message since the biggest benefit comes from solving the problem.

Subject Lines for Problem-Solving Messages

When you have a reluctant audience, putting the request in the subject line just gets a quick *no* before you've had a chance to give all your arguments. One option is to use a neutral subject line. In the following examples, the first is the most neutral. The remaining two increasingly reveal the writer's preference.

> Subject: A Proposal to Change the Formula for Calculating Retirees' Benefits
>
> Subject: Arguments for Expanding the Marysville Plant
>
> Subject: Why Cassano's Should Close Its West Side Store

Another option is to use common ground or a benefit—something that shows the audience that this message will help them.

> Subject: Reducing Energy Costs in the Louisville Office
>
> Energy costs in our Louisville office have risen 12% in the last three years, even though the cost of gas has fallen and the cost of electricity has risen only 5%.

Figure 12.3   How to Organize a Persuasive Problem-Solving Message

1. **Catch the audience's interest by mentioning a common ground.** Show that your message will be interesting or beneficial. You may want to catch attention with a negative (which you will go on to show can be solved).
2. **Define the problem you both share (which your request will solve).** Present the problem objectively: don't assign blame or mention personalities. Be specific about the cost in money, time, lost goodwill, and so on. You have to convince people that *something* has to be done before you can convince them that your solution is the best one.
3. **Explain the solution to the problem.** If you know that the audience will favor another solution, start with that solution and show why it won't work before you present your solution.

   Present your solution without using the words *I* or *my*. Don't let personalities enter the picture; don't let the audience think they should say *no* just because you've had other requests accepted recently.
4. **Show that any negative elements (cost, time, etc.) are outweighed by the advantages.**
5. **Summarize any additional benefits of the solution.** The main benefit—solving the problem—can be presented briefly since you described the problem in detail. However, if there are any additional benefits, mention them.
6. **Ask for the action you want.** Often your audience will authorize or approve something; other people will implement the action. Give your audience a reason to act promptly, perhaps offering a new benefit. ("By buying now, we can avoid the next quarter's price hikes.")

Figure 12.4   A Problem-Solving Persuasive Message

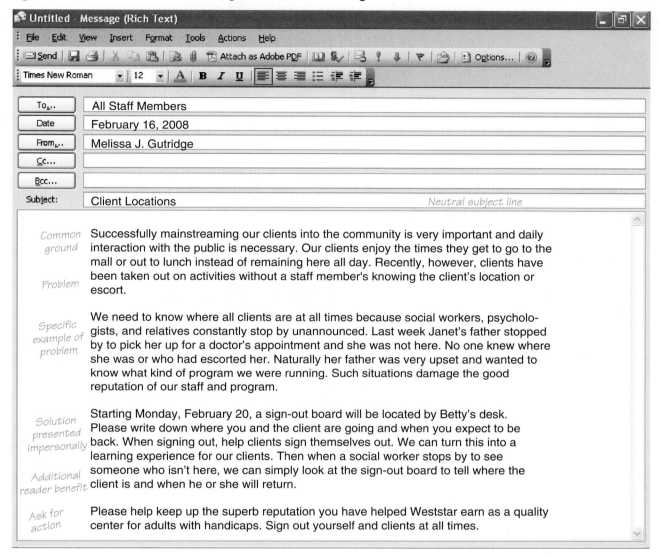

Although your first paragraph may be negative in a problem-solving message, your subject line should be neutral or positive.

Developing a Common Ground

A common ground avoids the me-against-you of some persuasive situations and suggests that both you and your audience have a mutual interest in solving the problems you face. To find a common ground, we analyze the audience; understand their biases, objections, and needs; and identify with them so that we can make them identify with us. This analysis can be carried out in a cold, manipulative way. It can also be based on a respect for and sensitivity to the audience's position.

Audiences are highly sensitive to manipulation. No matter how much you disagree with your audience, respect their intelligence. Try to understand why they believe or do something and why they may object to your position. If you can understand your audiences' initial positions, you'll be more effective—and you won't alienate your audience by talking down to them.

The best common grounds are specific. Often a negative—a problem the audience will want to solve—makes a good common ground.

| Vague common ground: | This program has had some difficulty finding enough individuals to volunteer their services for the children. As a result, we are sometimes unable to provide the one-on-one mentoring that is our goal. |
| Improved specific common ground: | On five Sundays in the last three months, we've had too few volunteers to provide one-on-one mentoring. Last Sunday, we had just two college students to take eight children to the Museum of Science and Industry. |

Generalizations are likely to bore the audience. Instead, use the idea behind the generalization to focus on something the audience cares about.

| Vague common ground: | We all want this plant to be profitable. |
| Improved specific common ground: | We forfeited a possible $1,860,000 in profits last month due to a 17% drop in productivity. |

In your common ground, emphasize the parts of your proposal that fit with what your audience already does or believes. Some HMOs are trying to improve patients' health (and cut the costs of providing care for them) by reaching out to individual patients and persuading them to take medications, get needed tests, and manage chronic conditions. Often, they first have to overcome patients' belief that HMOs want to limit their access to care. They do so by emphasizing the patients' needs and health.

Use audience analysis to evaluate possible common grounds. Suppose you want to install a system to play background music in a factory. To persuade management to pay for the system, a possible common ground would be increasing productivity. However, to persuade the union to pay for the system, you'd need a different common ground. Workers would see productivity as a way to get them to do more work for the same pay. A better common ground would be that the music would make the factory environment more pleasant.

Dealing with Objections

If you know that your audience will hear other points of view, or if your audience's initial position is negative, you have to deal with their objections to persuade them. The stronger the objection is, the earlier in your message you should deal with it.

The best way to deal with an objection is to eliminate it. When Norm Brodsky was starting a messenger service, the firms he called on were reluctant to switch to his company, even when he offered lower rates. Finally, an office manager gave him the clue he needed: She didn't care about lower prices, she wanted invoices that grouped charges according to her client accounts. The existing messenger services all presented lump-sum bills, so it was a lot of work for her to assign costs to clients. Brodsky set up his billing system to provide breakdowns by client, and his new company soon had a sizable share of the market.[11]

If an objection is false and is based on misinformation, give the response to the objection without naming the objection. (Repeating the objection gives it extra emphasis.) In a brochure, you can present responses with a "question/answer" format.

When objections have already been voiced, you may want to name the objection so that your audience realizes that you are responding to that specific objection. However, to avoid solidifying the opposition, don't attribute the objection to your audience. Instead, use a less personal attribution: "Some people wonder . . . "; "Some citizens are afraid that . . . "

If real objections remain, try one or more of the following strategies to counter objections:

1. Specify how much time and/or money is required—it may not be as much as the audience fears.

> Distributing flyers to each house or apartment in your neighborhood will probably take two afternoons.

2. Put the time and/or money in the context of the benefits they bring.

> The additional $252,500 will (1) allow the Open Shelter to remain open 24 rather than 16 hours a day, (2) pay for three social workers to help men find work and homes, and (3) keep the Neighborhood Bank open, so that men don't have to cash Social Security checks in bars and so that they can save up the $800 they need to have up front to rent an apartment.

3. Show that money spent now will save money in the long run.

> By buying a $1,000 safety product, you can avoid $5,000 in OSHA fines.

4. Show that doing as you ask will benefit some group or cause the audience supports, even though the action may not help the audience directly. This is the strategy used in fund-raising letters.

> By being a Big Brother or a Big Sister, you'll give a child the adult attention he or she needs to become a well-adjusted, productive adult.

Shrek has a new starring role—in a government-sponsored campaign against childhood obesity. In a series of ads, he and his friends urge children into active play. See http://www.healthierus.gov/ for other examples.

Shrek the Spokesogre

When you think of popular media characters, Shrek probably isn't your first choice for a health model. In fact, it may surprise you that he is the spokesogre for a new government campaign against obesity in children. In a series of ads, Shrek will be telling children to exercise, or more specifically, to play an hour a day.

Sometimes the key to persuasion is finding the right spokesperson to present the message to your audience. In this case, while Shrek—the animated star of a series of popular children's movies—isn't known for his commitment to exercise, he is a recognizable face and voice to the target audience for this message. The idea behind the campaign is that if the unfit Shrek can play an hour a day, anyone can.

If advertisers were trying to deliver a health-consciousness message to you or the other students in your class, whom would you suggest for the spokesperson? Would you make your recommendation based on their association with the message, on their popularity, or both?

Adapted from M. Marr, "Shrek, a Massive Beast, Stars in Campaign against Obesity," *Wall Street Journal,* February 1, 2007, D7.

5. Show the audience that the sacrifice is necessary to achieve a larger, more important goal to which they are committed.

> These changes will mean more work for all of us. But we've got to cut our costs 25% to keep the plant open and to keep our jobs.

6. Show that the advantages as a group outnumber or outweigh the disadvantages as a group.

> None of the locations is perfect. But the Backbay location gives us the most advantages and the fewest disadvantages.

7. Turn a disadvantage into an opportunity.

> With the hiring freeze, every department will need more lead time to complete its own work. By hiring another person, the Planning Department could provide that lead time.

Use the following steps when you face major objections:

1. **Find out why your audience members resist what you want them to do.** Sit down one-on-one with people and listen. Don't try to persuade them; just try to understand.

2. **Try to find a win–win solution.** People will be much more readily persuaded if they see benefits for themselves. Sometimes your original proposal may have benefits that the audience had not thought of, and explaining the benefits will help. Sometimes you'll need to modify your original proposal to find a solution that solves the real problem and meets everyone's needs.

3. **Let your audience save face.** Don't ask people to admit that they have been wrong all along. If possible, admit that the behavior may have been appropriate in the past. Whether you can do that or not, always show how changed circumstances or new data call for new action.

4. **Ask for something small.** When you face great resistance, you won't get everything at once. Ask for a month's trial. Ask for one step that will move toward your larger goal. For example, if your ultimate goal is to eliminate prejudice in your organization, a step toward that goal might be to convince managers to make a special effort for one month to recognize the contributions of women or members of minorities in group meetings.

5. **Present your arguments from your audience's point of view.** Offer benefits that help the audience, not just you. Take special care to avoid words that attack or belittle your audience. Present yourself as someone helping your audience achieve their goals, not someone criticizing or giving orders from above.

The draft in Figure 12.5 makes the mistake of attacking readers in a negative message; the division manager (Heather) berates the lab manager (Todd) for sending out inaccurate test results. Making the memo less accusatory would help, but the message doesn't need to be negative at all. Instead, the writer can take the information in paragraph 3 and use it as the attention-getter and common ground for a problem-solving persuasive message. Figure 12.6 shows a possible revision.

Organizational changes work best when the audience buys into the solution. And that happens most easily when they themselves find it. Management can

Figure 12.5 Original Unprofessional Memo Attacking Readers

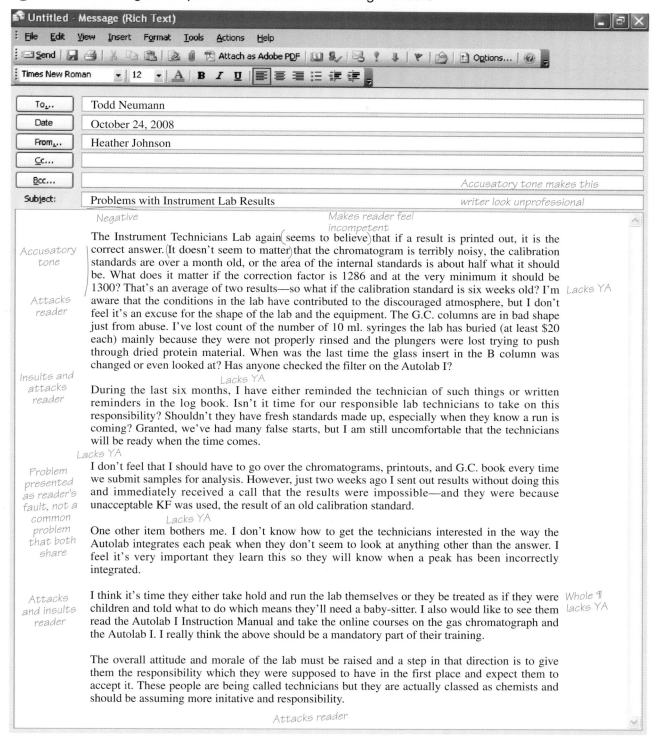

1. Help people see and own the problem.
2. Identify values and cultures that need to change.
3. Let people discover solutions.
4. Support change tangibly and symbolically.

Figure 12.6   Revised Memo Creating a Common Ground and a Professional Image

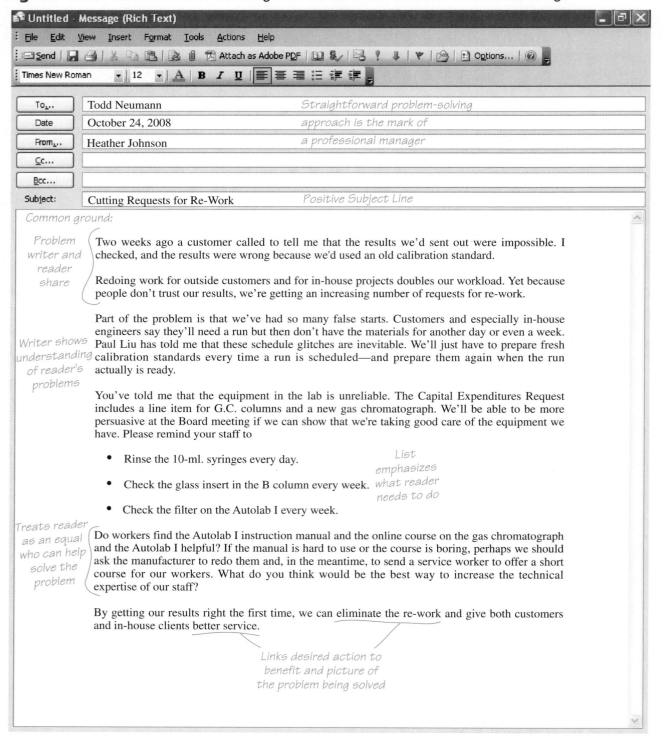

Offering a Reason for the Audience to Act Promptly

The longer people delay, the less likely they are to carry through with the action they had decided to take. In addition, you want a fast response so you can go ahead with your own plans.

Request action by a specific date. Try to give people at least a week or two: they have other things to do besides respond to your requests. Set deadlines in the middle of the month, if possible. If you say, "Please return this by March 1," people will think, "I don't need to do this till March." Ask for the response by February 28 instead. Similarly, a deadline of Friday, 5 PM, will frequently be seen as Monday morning. If such a shift causes you problems, if you were going to work over the weekend, set a Thursday deadline. If you can use a response even after the deadline, say so. Otherwise, people who can't make the deadline may not respond at all.

Your audience may ignore deadlines that seem arbitrary. Show why you need a quick response:

- **Show that the time limit is real.** Perhaps you need information quickly to use it in a report that has a due date. Perhaps a decision must be made by a certain date to catch the start of the school year, the Christmas selling season, or an election campaign. Perhaps you need to be ready for a visit from out-of-town or international colleagues.

- **Show that acting now will save time or money.** If business is slow and your industry isn't doing well, then your company needs to act now (to economize, to better serve customers) in order to be competitive. If business is booming and everyone is making a profit, then your company needs to act now to get its fair share of the available profits.

- **Show the cost of delaying action.** Will labor or material costs be higher in the future? Will delay mean more money spent on repairing something that will still need to be replaced?

Emotional appeals can be intense. The Save Darfur campaign used this ad to raise awareness of horrifying brutality and genocide. Do you think this graphic works to solicit support for this cause?

Getting Employees to Buy into Cost Cutting

Employees are in a position to see first-hand where the company is wasting money. Smart organizations involve their employees in deciding how to cut costs. That involvement also increases their commitment to the change.

Many employees are suspicious of cost-cutting efforts, so some persuasion may be necessary. Elizabeth Gibson, a consultant, says employee involvement in cost cutting is more likely to succeed if managers explain why cost cutting is necessary, tell employees how they will benefit from the effort, and describe what an ideal employee suggestion is like.

Communications consultant Jim Bolton says organizations that want employee ideas should take into account that different groups of employees will have different frames of reference. Therefore, the organization should modify its persuasive messages to address the concerns and knowledge of each group of employees.

Adapted from Lin Grensing Pophal, "Involve Your Employees in Cost Cutting," *HRMagazine* 48, no. 11 (November 2003): 52–56.

Creative Response to an Objection

Jim Young sold apples by direct mail order. One year, a hailstorm just before the harvest bruised the apples.

At first, the obstacle appeared insurmountable. For years, his selling point had been that his apples looked as good as they tasted.

But Jim was able to turn the disadvantage into an advantage.

He knew that cold weather (partially responsible for the hailstorm) improves the flavor of ripening apples. So he filled the orders, inserting a note in each box:

Note the hail marks which have caused minor skin blemishes in some of these apples. They are proof of their growth at a high mountain altitude where the sudden chills from hailstorms help firm the flesh, develop the natural sugars, and give these apples their incomparable flavor.

Not one customer asked for a refund. In fact, the next year, some people wrote on their orders, "Send the hail-marked apples if possible."

Adapted from Ray Considine and Murray Raphael, *The Great Brain Robbery* (Los Angeles: Rosebud Books, 1980), 95–96.

Building Emotional Appeal

Stories and psychological description are effective ways of building emotional appeal. Emotional appeal works best when people want to be persuaded.

Even when you need to provide statistics or numbers to convince the careful reader that your anecdote is a representative example, telling a story first makes your message more persuasive. In *Made to Stick,* Chip and Dan Heath report on research done at Carnegie Mellon supporting the value of stories. After a survey (completing the survey for money ensured all participants had cash for the real experiment), participants received an envelope with a letter requesting they donate to Save the Children. Researchers tested two letters: one was full of grim statistics about starving Africans. The other letter told the story of seven-year-old Rokia. Participants receiving the Rokia letter gave more than twice as much money as those receiving the statistics letter. A third group received a letter with both sets of information: the story and the statistics. This group gave a little more than the statistics group, but far less than the group that had the story alone. The researchers theorized that the statistics put people in an analytical frame of mind which canceled the emotional effect of the story.[12]

As with other appeals, the emotional appeal should focus on the reader. To describe its service of gathering up and renting good-quality used cardboard boxes, Boomerang Boxes could focus on its innovative thinking, but its Web site appeals to readers by telling them they can "Save time, save money and save trees!" The company tells its story with descriptive language: "No longer do you have to drive around aimlessly searching for good quality boxes behind supermarkets and liquor stores. No longer do you have to contribute to the destruction of strong healthy trees, just so more cardboard boxes can be made, used (often only once) and thrown away."[13] That story is likely to resonate

Emotional appeal is often used in advertisements concerning health issues. Here, the American Heart Association urges the public to prevent childhood obesity, while addressing the health risks of heart disease.

Reproduced with permission. © 2000, American Heart Association.

Figure 12.7   Business Ethics Resources on the Web

- **Business Ethics Resources on the Internet**
  http://www.ethicsweb.ca/resources/business
- **Defense Industry Initiative on Business Ethics and Conduct**
  http://dii.org
- **DePaul University's Institute for Business and Professional Ethics**
  http://commerce.depaul.edu/ethics
- **Ethics Effectiveness Quick Test**
  http://www.ethicsa.org.za/documents/pdf/EEQT-Short.pdf?
  PHPSESSID=b9c6651bf57e1980d5eebf2a91c59bc6
- **Ethics in International Business**
  http://library.lib.binghamton.edu/subjects/business/intbuseth.html
- **E-Business Ethics**
  http://www.e-businessethics.com
- **Various Codes of Conduct**
  http://www.ethicsweb.ca/resources/business/codes.html

**Hard Tests
for Persuasion**

How do you get your employees to agree to be tested for AIDS? This was a huge concern for SABMiller, a South African brewer who faced losing about 15% of its workforce within three years. Their first step was to hire an outside testing firm to allay fears that a positive HIV test would become company gossip or hurt careers. Participants also joined raffles for free radios and TVs. The company pays for anti-retroviral treatment for infected employees.

How do you get employees to leave their jobs? France Telecom's need for a major workforce reduction inspired them to be creative. In addition to traditional means such as early retirement plans and retirement bonuses, they developed a program to shift people to public sector jobs at other institutions. They also helped employees start their own businesses, offering assistance with writing business plans, applying for loans, and purchasing equipment. They paid for consultations with business people and new educational courses.

What other hard tests for businesses can you identify? What persuasive solutions can you imagine?

Adapted from William Echikson and Adam Coher, "SABMiller's AIDS Test Program Gets Results: Effort Benefits Business, Saves Employee Lives; Building Confidence Is Key," *Wall Street Journal*, August 18, 2006, A7; and Leila Abboud, "At France Telecom, Battle to Cut Jobs Breeds Odd Tactics: Company Offers Money, Advice on Starting New Business if Employees Will Leave," *Wall Street Journal*, August 14, 2006, A1.

with many an apartment-renting student who has scrounged boxes for a low-cost moving day.

Difficult situations sometimes have ethical implications. Figure 12.7 lists some of the Web resources that deal with business ethics.

Sense impressions—what the reader sees, hears, smells, tastes, feels—evoke a strong emotional response. **Psychological description** means creating a scenario rich with sense impressions so readers can picture themselves using your product or service and enjoying its benefits. You can also use psychological description to describe the problem your product will solve. Psychological description works best early in the message to catch readers' attention.

Feature:	Snooze alarm
Benefit:	If the snooze button is pressed, the alarm goes off and comes on again nine minutes later.
Psychological description:	Some mornings, you really want to stay in bed just a few more minutes. With the Sleepytime Snooze Alarm, you can snuggle under the covers for a few extra winks, secure in the knowledge that the alarm will come on again to get you up for that breakfast meeting with an important client. If you don't have to be anywhere soon, you can keep hitting the snooze alarm for up to an additional 63 minutes of sleep. With Sleepytime, you're in control of your mornings.

Someone who's already looking for a product may need only the feature or the benefit. Good psychological description uses vivid details and sensory imagery to motivate uncommitted readers. The flyer for a university's food services in Figure 12.8 gets your gastric juices flowing.

In psychological description, you're putting your audience in a picture. If the audience doesn't feel that the picture fits them, the technique backfires. To prevent this, psychological description often uses subjunctive verbs ("if you like . . . " "if you were . . . ") or the words *maybe* and *perhaps*.

Frequently the sensory impressions are more than words. Advertisers have been using visually tempting pictures for a long time, and perfumes scent entire issues of magazines. Now Kraft is using magazine ads that allow people to smell its products being advertised. By rubbing a spot on the ad, readers

Figure 12.8   Using Psychological Description to Develop Benefits

You–attitude psychological description

The Colonial Room

When you dine in the Illini Union Colonial Room, it's easy to imagine yourself a guest in a fine Virginian mansion. Light from the gleaming chandeliers reflects from a hand-carved mirror hanging over the dark, polished buffet. Here you can dine in quiet elegance amid furnishings adapted from 18th century Williamsburg and the Georgian homes of the James River Valley in Virginia.

Visual details

Perhaps you'd like a dinner of stuffed rainbow trout. Or the pork fricassee. The menu features a variety of complete meals which are changed daily, as well as the regular a la carte service. Whatever your choice, you'll enjoy an evening of fine dining at very reasonable prices.

The Illini Union Colonial Room is located on the northeast corner of the first floor. Dinners are served Monday through Friday from 5:30 to 7:30 p.m. Please call 333-0690 for reservations, and enjoy the flavor of the Colonies tonight.

Details appeal to sight, taste, smell

Emphasis on reader's choice— Not every reader will want the same thing

The Cafeteria

In the Illini Union Cafeteria, you start out with an empty tray and silverware. Then comes the food, several yards of it, all yours for the choosing. By the time you've finished, your empty tray has become a delicious meal.

In the morning, the warm aroma of breakfast fills the air. Feast your eyes and then your appetite on the array of eggs, bacon, pancakes, toast, sausage, rolls, juices, and coffee . . . They're all waiting to wake you up with good taste. Have a hearty breakfast or make it quick and tasty. The warm, freshly baked sweet rolls and coffeecakes practically beg to be smothered in butter and savored with a cup of hot coffee.

By 11 a.m. the breakfast menu has made way for lunch. Here come the plump Reuben sandwiches and the toasty grilled cheese. Soups and salads make their appearance. A variety of vegetables are dressed up to entice you and several main dishes lead the luncheon parade. Any number of complete meals can take shape as you move along.

What? Back for dinner? Well, no wonder! The Cafeteria sets out a wide selection of entrees and side dishes. Veal parmigiana steams for your attention but the roast beef right next to it is rough competition. Tomorrow the fried chicken might be up for selection. Choose the dinner combination that best fits your appetite and your pocket.

The newly remodeled Cafeteria is on the ground floor and is open for breakfast from 7 to 11 a.m. Monday through Saturday and 8 to 11 a.m. on Sunday. Lunch is served from 11 a.m. to 1:15 p.m. Monday through Saturday and 11 a.m. to 2 p.m. on Sunday. Dinner is served from 4:45 to 7 p.m. Monday through Friday.

A meal in a restaurant is expensive. A meal at home is a chore. But a meal at the Cafeteria combines good food and reasonable prices to make dining a pleasure.

---

can smell strawberry cheesecake, cinnamon coffee, or white chocolate. The ads have the further advantage of keeping the reader engaged with the ad for a longer time, thus increasing awareness of the product.[14]

Tone in Persuasive Messages

The best phrasing depends on your relationship to the your audience. When you ask for action from people who report directly to you, polite orders ("Please get me the Ervin file") and questions ("Do we have the third-quarter numbers yet?") will work. When you need action from co-workers, superiors, or people outside the organization, you need to be more forceful but also more polite.

How you ask for action affects whether you build or destroy positive relationships with other employees, customers, and suppliers. Avoiding messages that sound parental or preachy is often a matter of tone. Adding "Please" is a nice touch. Tone will also be better when you give reasons for your request or reasons to act promptly.

Parental: Everyone is expected to comply with these regulations. I'm sure you can see that they are commonsense rules needed for our business.

Better: Even on casual days, visitors expect us to be professional. So please leave the gym clothes at home!

When you write to people you know well, humor can work. Just make sure that the message isn't insulting to anyone who doesn't find the humor funny.

Writing to superiors is trickier. You may want to tone down your request by using subjunctive verbs and explicit disclaimers that show you aren't taking a *yes* for granted.

Arrogant: Based on this evidence, I expect you to give me a new computer.

Better: If department funds permit, I would like a new computer.

Passive verbs and jargon sound stuffy. Use active imperatives—perhaps with "Please" to create a friendlier tone.

Stuffy: It is requested that you approve the above-mentioned action.

Better: Please authorize us to create a new subscription letter.

It can be particularly tricky to control tone in e-mail messages, which tend to sound less friendly than paper documents or conversations. For important requests, compose your message offline and revise it carefully before you send it.

Major requests that require great effort or changes in values, culture, or lifestyles should not be made in e-mail messages.

Varieties of Persuasive Messages

Performance appraisals and letters of recommendation are two important kinds of persuasive messages.

Performance Appraisals

Good supervisors give their employees regular feedback on their performances. The feedback may range from a brief "Good job!" to a hefty bonus. And companies are recognizing the need to lavish more praise on their workers, especially younger ones. Land's End and Bank of America hired consultants to teach their supervisors how to compliment workers. The Scooter Store Inc. hired a "celebrations assistant," whose duties include handing out 100–500 celebration balloons and tossing 25 pounds of confetti—per week. (The celebrations assistant has become averse to confetti, so her praise comes in the form of text messaging.) Such companies see the praise as a way to maintain work quality and keep good workers.[15]

Performance appraisal documents are more formal ways by which supervisors evaluate, or appraise, the performance of their subordinates. In most organizations, employees have access to their files; sometimes they must sign the appraisal to show that they've read it. The superior normally meets with the subordinate to discuss the appraisal.

At Whirlpool Corp., those meetings are occurring quarterly, and both managers and employees are pleased with the results from the more frequent feedback. Companies such as Whirlpool and Texas Children's Hospital are

Saving Face Saves Money

Helping people save face can help them act in ways that can help your company. To customers who had fallen behind with their payments, a credit card company sent not the expected stern collection letter but a hand-addressed, hand-signed greeting card. The front of the card pictured a stream running through a forest. The text inside noted that sometimes life takes unexpected turns and asked people to call the company to find a collaborative solution. When people called the 800 number, they got credit counseling and help in creating a payment plan.

The project was successful. Instead of having to write off bad debts, the company received payments—and created goodwill.

Adapted from Scott Robinette, "Get Emotional," *Harvard Business Review* 79, no. 5 (May 2001): 24–25.

Performance Persuasion

More and more employees are finding that modest annual pay increases are far outweighed by performance-based pay raises and incentive bonuses. Companies like linking pay to performance because they can keep fixed expenses down while still rewarding their most valuable workers.

From bonuses to raises, your paycheck can depend on the results of your performance appraisals. As you prepare for your performance evaluation, look on it as an opportunity not only to describe your accomplishments and contributions, but also to practice your persuasive skills. Think about the people who will be performing your appraisal, choose a persuasive strategy, and describe yourself accordingly. What will work best? A direct request? A problem-solving request?

Adapted from Jeff D. Opdyke, "Companies Strive to Find True Stars for Raises, Bonus," *Wall Street Journal*, December 20, 2006, D3.

also asking employees to draft at least some of their own goals. Whirlpool asks for at least one ambitious goal that goes beyond regular job duties.[16]

As a subordinate, you should prepare for the appraisal interview by listing your achievements and goals. What have you accomplished during the appraisal period? What supporting details will you need? Where do you want to be in a year or five years? What training and experience do you need to reach your goals? If you need training, advice, or support from the organization to improve, the appraisal interview is a good time to ask for this help.

Appraisals need to both protect the organization and motivate the employee. Sometimes these two purposes conflict. Most of us will see a candid appraisal as negative; we need praise and reassurance to believe that we're valued and can do better. But the praise that motivates someone to improve can come back to haunt the company if the person does not eventually do acceptable work. An organization is in trouble if it tries to fire someone whose evaluations never mention mistakes.

When you are writing performance appraisals that need to document areas for improvement, avoid labels (*wrong*, *bad*) and inferences. Instead, cite specific observations that describe behavior.

Inference:	Sam is an alcoholic.
Vague observation:	Sam calls in sick a lot. Subordinates complain about his behavior.
Specific observation:	Sam called in sick a total of 12 days in the last two months. After a business lunch with a customer last week, Sam was walking unsteadily. Two of his subordinates have said that they would prefer not to make sales trips with him because they find his behavior embarrassing.

Sam might be an alcoholic. He might also be having a reaction to a physician-prescribed drug; he might have a mental illness; he might be showing symptoms of a physical illness other than alcoholism. A supervisor who jumps to conclusions creates ill will, closes the door to solving the problem, and may provide grounds for legal action against the organization.

Be specific in an appraisal.

Too vague:	Sue does not manage her time as well as she could.
Specific:	Sue's first three weekly sales reports have been three, two, and four days late, respectively; the last weekly sales report for the month is not yet in.

Without specifics, Sue won't know that her boss objects to late reports. She may think that she is being criticized for spending too much time on sales calls or for not working 80 hours a week. Without specifics, she might change the wrong things in a futile effort to please her boss.

It is also important that specifics be included in performance appraisals for good employees to help them continue to shine and also to receive their well-deserved raises and promotions.

Appraisals are more useful to subordinates if they make clear which areas are most important and contain specific recommendations for improvement. No one can improve 17 weaknesses at once. Which two should the employee work on this month? Is getting in reports on time more important than increasing sales?

Phrase goals in specific, concrete terms. The subordinate may think that "considerable progress toward completing" a report may mean that the project should be 15% finished. The boss may think that "considerable progress" means 50% or 85% of the total work.

Sometimes a performance appraisal reflects mostly the month or week right before the appraisal, even though it is supposed to cover six months or a year.

Many managers record specific observations of subordinates' behavior two or three times a month. These notes jog the memory so that the appraisal doesn't focus unduly on recent behavior.

Figure 12.9 shows a performance appraisal for a member of a collaborative business communication group.

Letters of Recommendation

You may write letters of recommendation when you want to recommend someone for an award or for a job. Letters of recommendation must be specific. General positives that are not backed up with specific examples and evidence are seen as weak recommendations. Letters of recommendation that focus on minor points also suggest that the person is weak.

Either in the first or the last paragraph, summarize your overall evaluation of the person. Early in the letter, perhaps in the first paragraph, show how well and how long you've known the person. In the middle of the letter, offer specific details about the person's performance. At the end of the letter, indicate whether you would be willing to rehire the person and repeat your overall evaluation. Figure A.3 in Appendix A ➡ shows a sample letter of recommendation.

Although experts are divided on whether you should include negatives, the trend is moving away from doing so. Negatives can create legal liabilities, and many readers feel that any negative weakens the letter. Other people feel that presenting but not emphasizing honest negatives makes the letter more convincing. In either case, you must ensure that your recommendation is honest and accurate.

In many discourse communities, the words "Call me if you need more information" in a letter of recommendation mean "I have negative information that I am unwilling to put on paper. Call me and I'll tell you what I really think."

In an effort to protect themselves against lawsuits, some companies state only how long they employed someone and the position that person held. Such bare-bones letters have themselves been the target of lawsuits when employers did not reveal relevant negatives.

Sales and Fund-Raising Messages

Sales and fund-raising messages are a special category of persuasive messages. They are known as **direct marketing** because they ask for an order, inquiry, or contribution directly from the audience. Direct marketing includes printed (direct mail), verbal (telemarketing), and electronic (e-mails, Web sites) channels.

Time-Life Books, CitiBank, American Express—these are only a few of the companies that use letters to persuade customers to buy their products and use their services. The American Cancer Society, the Republican National Committee, Habitat for Humanity—these are only a few of the organizations that use letters to persuade people to donate time or money to their causes. Microsoft is placing ads on the Web, in video games, on mobile phones, and alongside Internet search results. Those maligned subscription cards that fall out of magazines nevertheless account for 12% of the industry's new subscribers.[17]

This section focuses on two common channels of direct marketing: sales and fund-raising letters. Large organizations hire professionals to write their direct marketing materials. If you own your own business, you can save money by doing your firm's own direct marketing. If you are active in a local group that needs to raise money, writing the fund-raising letter yourself is

From Full Time to Part Time

Many employees dream about working fewer hours or even cutting back to part-time work. But managers agree that most employees ask their boss the wrong way. Too often employees focus on why *they* want part-time work; managers want to hear about advantages and disadvantages for the company.

You might use these persuasive arguments to convince your employer to let you work fewer hours:

- Demonstrate that you understand and appreciate corporate policies on part-time work. (Hint: read up on those policies in your company's employee manual or talk to human resources staff before you talk to your boss.)

- Stress that your dedication to your work won't fade when you start working fewer hours.

- Agree to be reached outside the office if your colleagues need you.

- Present a plan detailing how the rest of your work will get done.

- Above all, treat the situation as a persuasive message: develop a common ground with your employer, anticipate objections, and suggest solutions.

Adapted from Erin White, "Build a Case before Asking to Work Less," *Wall Street Journal*, October 24, 2006, B7.

Figure 12.9   A Performance Appraisal

February 13, 2009

To: Barbara Buchanan

From: Brittany Papper *BAP*

Subject: Your Performance Thus Far in Our Collaborative Group

Subject line indicates that memo is a performance appraisal

Overall evaluation

You have been a big asset to our group. Overall, our communications group has been one of the best groups I have ever worked with, and I think that only minor improvements are needed to make our group even better.

These headings would need to be changed in a negative performance appraisal.

What You're Doing Well

Specific observations provide dates, details of performance

You demonstrated flexibility and compatibility at our last meeting before we turned in our proposal on February 9 by offering to type the proposal since I had to study for an exam in one of my other classes. I really appreciated this because I definitely did not have the time to do it. I will definitely remember this if you are ever too busy with your other classes and cannot type the final report.

Another positive critical incident occurred February 2. We had discussed researching the topic of sexual discrimination in hiring and promotion at Midstate Insurance. As we read more about what we had to do, we became uneasy about reporting the information from our source who works at Midstate. I called you later that evening to talk about changing our topic to a less personal one. You were very understanding and said that you agreed that the original topic was a touchy one. You offered suggestions for other topics and had a positive attitude about the adjustment. Your suggestions ended my worries and made me realize that you are a positive and supportive person.

Other strengths

Your ideas are a strength that you definitely contribute to our group. You're good at brainstorming ideas, yet you're willing to go with whatever the group decides. That's a nice combination of creativity and flexibility.

Areas for Improvement

Two minor improvements could make you an even better member.

Specific recommendations for improvement

The first improvement is to be more punctual to meetings. On February 2 and February 5 you were about 10 minutes late. This makes the meetings last longer. Your ideas are valuable to the group, and the sooner you arrive (the sooner we can share in your suggestions.)

Positive cast to suggestion

Specific behavior to be changed

The second suggestion is one we all need to work on. We need to keep our meetings positive and productive. I think that our negative attitudes were worst at our first group meeting February 3. We spent about half an hour complaining about all the work we had to do and about our busy schedules in other classes. In the future if this happens, maybe you could offer some positive things about the assignment to get the group motivated again.

Overall Compatibility

Positive, forward-looking ending

I feel that this group has gotten along very well together. You have been very flexible in finding times to meet and have always been willing to do your share of the work. I have never had this kind of luck with a group in the past and you have been a welcome breath of fresh air. I don't hate doing group projects any more!

likely to be the only way your group can afford to use direct mail. If you can write an equally effective e-mail message, you can significantly cut the costs of a marketing campaign or supplement the success of your direct mail with direct e-mail. According to the Direct Marketing Association, the return on investment for a direct e-mail message is eight times higher than that of direct mail.[18]

The principles in this chapter will help you write solid, serviceable letters and e-mails that will build your business and help fund your group.

Sales, fund-raising, and promotional messages have multiple purposes:

Primary purpose:

- To have the reader act (order the product, send a donation).

Secondary purpose:

- To build a good image of the writer's organization (to strengthen the commitment of readers who act, and make readers who do not act more likely to respond positively next time).

Organizing a Sales or Fund-Raising Message

Use the sales persuasion pattern to organize your message (see Figure 12.10).

Opener

The opener of your message gives you 30 to 60 seconds to motivate your audience to read the rest of the message.

A good opener will make readers want to read the message and provide a reasonable transition to the body of the message. A very successful subscription letter for *Psychology Today* started out,

> Do you still close the bathroom door when there's no one in the house?

The question is both intriguing in itself and a good transition into the content of *Psychology Today:* practical psychology applied to the quirks and questions we come across in everyday life.

It's essential that the opener not only get attention but also be something that can be linked logically to the body of the message. A sales letter started,

> Can You Use $50 This Week?

Certainly that gets attention. But the letter only offered the reader the chance to save $50 on a product. Readers may feel disappointed or even cheated when they learn that instead of getting $50, they have to spend money to save $50.

To brainstorm possible openers, use the four basic modes: questions, narration, startling statements, and quotations.

Figure 12.10 How to Organize a Sales or Fund-Raising Message

1. Open by catching the audience's attention.
2. In the body, provide reasons and details.
3. End by telling the audience what to do and providing a reason to act promptly.

Unethical Sales Pitches

Here is a list of questionable tactics that some salespeople use to tailor their persuasive messages to you:

- Ask you to tell them about yourself, and pretend to be interested in the same things you are.
- Look for your weak spots: emotional appeals that you're less likely to resist.
- Tell you that they're offering a one-of-a-kind deal.
- Tell you that if you don't take their offer, someone else will.
- Give you a "free" gift for listening to their pitch, hoping that you'll feel obligated to buy their product.

What about these tactics makes them unethical? How can you craft persuasive messages using similar techniques—good psychological descriptions, for example—without being unethical?

Adapted from Jonathan Clements, "Don't Get Hit by the Pitch: How Advisers Manipulate You," *Wall Street Journal*, January 3, 2007, D1.

When Consumers Say "Enough!"

One thing most target audiences have in common is advertising fatigue. A study by Yankelovich Partners found that over half of consumers think the amount of marketing and advertising is "out of control," and almost two-thirds feel "constantly bombarded" by ads. The best solution is to write about what the audience cares about.

A regional bank tested this approach when it wanted to offer a top-of-the-line checking account. To half its list, it sent a standard letter about the new account. For the other half, the bank identified 11 groups, based on their interests and motivations. The bank wrote a separate letter to each of these groups. The response rate for the subgroups was 40% greater than for the standard group.

Other advice for getting readers' attention is subject to debate. After testing e-mail campaigns for six weeks, E-Post Direct found that responses were much higher for messages with a subject line that offered a "free direct mail encyclopedia" than for a subject line describing the benefits of its service. But Janet Libert of American Express has found that spam filters often intercept e-mail with *free* in the subject line.

Adapted from "How to Use the Killer App Without Getting Killed by Spam," *Circulation Management,* September 1, 2003, 9; Kris Oser, " 'Free' Performs Well in E-mail: Study," *Direct,* November 1, 2003; and Yankelovich Partners, "Yankelovich Study: Consumer Resistance to Marketing Techniques," http://www.the-dma.org (accessed April 26, 2004).

1. Questions

> Dear Writer:
>
> What is the best way to start writing?

This letter selling subscriptions to *Writer's Digest* goes on to discuss Hemingway's strategy for getting started on his novels and short stories. *Writer's Digest* offers practical advice to writers who want to be published. The information in the letter is useful to any writer, so the recipient keeps reading; the information also helps to prove the claim that the magazine will be useful.

Good questions are interesting enough that the audience want the answers, so they read the letter.

> Poor question: Do you want to make extra money?
>
> Better question: How *much* extra money do you want to make next year?

A series of questions can be an effective opener. Answer the questions in the body of the letter.

2. Narration, stories, anecdotes

> Dear Reader:
>
> She hoisted herself up noiselessly so as not to disturb the rattlesnakes snoozing there in the sun.
>
> To her left, the high desert of New Mexico. Indian country. To her right, the rock carvings she had photographed the day before. Stick people. Primitive animals.
>
> Up ahead, three sandstone slabs stood stacked against the face of the cliff. In their shadow, another carving. A spiral consisting of rings. Curious, the young woman drew closer. Instinctively, she glanced at her watch. It was almost noon. Then just at that moment, a most unusual thing happened.
>
> Suddenly, as if out of nowhere, an eerie dagger of light appeared to stab at the topmost ring of the spiral. It next began to plunge downwards—shimmering, laser-like.
>
> It pierced the eighth ring. The seventh. The sixth. It punctured the innermost and last. Then just as suddenly as it had appeared, the dagger of light was gone. The young woman glanced at her watch again. Exactly twelve minutes had elapsed.
>
> Coincidence? Accident? Fluke? No. What she may have stumbled across that midsummer morning three years ago is an ancient solar calendar. . . .

This subscription letter for *Science84* argues that it reports interesting and significant discoveries in all fields of science—all in far more detail than do other media. The opener both builds suspense so that the reader reads the subscription letter and suggests that the magazine will be as interesting as the letter and as easy to read.

3. Startling statements

> Dear Membership Candidate:
>
> I'm writing to offer you a job.
> It's not a permanent job, understand. You'll be working for only as much time as you find it rewarding and fun.
> It's not even a paying job. On the contrary, it will cost *you* money.

This fund-raising letter from Earthwatch invites readers to participate in its expeditions, subscribe to its journal, and donate to its programs. Earthwatch's volunteers help scientists and scholars dig for ruins, count bighorns, and monitor changes in water; they can work as long as they like; they pay their own (tax-deductible) expenses.

Variations of this mode include special opportunities, twists, and challenges.

4. Quotations

> "I never tell my partner that my ankle is sore or my back hurts. You can't give in to pain and still perform."
>
> —Jill Murphy
> Soloist

The series of which this letter is a part sells season tickets to the Atlanta Ballet by focusing on the people who work to create the season. Each letter quotes a different member of the company. The opening quote is used on the envelope over a picture of the ballerina and as an opener for the letter. The letters encourage readers to see the artists as individuals, to appreciate their hard work, and to share their excitement about each performance.

Body

The body of the message provides the logical and emotional links that move the audience from their first flicker of interest to the action that is wanted. A good body answers the audience's questions, overcomes their objections, and involves them emotionally.

All this takes space. One of the industry truisms is "The more you tell, the more you sell." Tests show that longer letters bring in more new customers or new donors than do shorter letters. A four-page letter is considered ideal for mailings to new customers or donors.

Can short letters work? Yes, when you're writing to old customers or when the mailing is supported by other media. One study showed that a one-page letter was just as effective as a two-page letter in persuading recent purchasers of a product to buy a service contract.[19] E-mail direct mail is also short—generally just one screen. The shortest message record may be the two-word postcard that a fishing lake resort sent its customers: "They're biting!"

Content for the body of the message can include

* Information the audience will find useful even if they do not buy or give.
* Stories about how the product was developed or what the organization has done.
* Stories about people who have used the product or who need the organization's help.
* Word pictures of people enjoying the benefits offered.

Costs are generally mentioned near the end of the body and are connected to specific benefits. Sometimes costs are broken down to monthly, weekly, or daily amounts: "For less than the cost of a cup of coffee a day, you can help see that Eren is no longer hungry."

Action Close

The action close in the message must do four things:

Donating to Operating Expenses?

Wouldn't you want to make sure that your charitable donations went to support worthwhile causes, rather than overhead expenses within a non-profit organization? Many people do, and so look for non-profits that either limit their spending on overhead or can guarantee that gifts will go toward specific programs, not overhead.

However, even non-profit organizations have bills to pay. As the *Wall Street Journal* reports, some non-profits are challenged with the tasks of soliciting donations while convincing donors that money spent on overhead is still money well spent. One solution? Some non-profits ask for donations specifically to cover their operating expenses by asking for money to support their teams or their business plans.

Philanthropy advisers suggest that donors also consider how effectively the charity uses its money. Some organizations that spend 70% of their funds on their core mission do a better job than those who spend 80%.

The very best way to judge a charity? Be one of their volunteers.

How would asking for a donation to pay for a non-profit's overhead be different than asking for donations to support a worthy cause? What persuasive strategies could you use to make that request?

Adapted from Rachel Emma Silverman and Sally Beatty, "Save the Children (but Pay the Bills, Too)," *Wall Street Journal*, December 26, 2006, D1, D2.

Prizes for Innovation

Research and innovation are expensive prospects. Prizes are one tool that some companies and nonprofit organizations are using to solve tough problems without investing in extra in-house infrastructure. Some examples:

- In 2004, the X-Prize Foundation gave $10 million to the first team to build and test a reusable spacecraft. Among their current projects: a prize for the first team that can build a machine to quickly and accurately sequence human DNA.

- Netflix, the movie-rental company, is offering a $1 million prize for a computer program that predicts customer preferences better than its current program.

- InnoCentive charges clients to post problems, and cash prizes for solving them, on their Web site. About 30% of their problems get solved. One surprising finding is that the problem posted is frequently not the solver's area of expertise.

These are large scale applications, designed to help solve difficult scientific or economic problems. How might a smaller company, a nonprofit organization, or even a government agency use this same technique? Think of some problems in your own school, workplace, or community that could be solved this way—how could you implement a prize for innovation?

Adapted from David Wessel, "Prizes for Solutions to Problems Play Valuable Role in Innovation," *Wall Street Journal*, January 25, 2007, A6.

1. **Tell the audience what to do:** Respond. Avoid *if* ("If you'd like to try . . . ") and *why not* ("Why not send in a check?"). They lack positive emphasis and encourage your audience to say *no*.

2. **Make the action sound easy:** Fill in the information on the reply card, sign the card (for credit sales), put the card and check (if payment is to accompany the order) in the envelope, and mail the envelope. If you provide an envelope and pay postage, stress those facts.

3. **Offer a reason for acting promptly.** People who think they are convinced but wait to act are less likely to buy or contribute. Reasons for acting promptly are easy to identify when a product is seasonal or there is a genuine limit on the offer—time limit, price rise scheduled, limited supply, and so on. Sometimes you can offer a premium or a discount if the your audience acts quickly. When these conditions do not exist, remind readers that the sooner they get the product, the sooner they can benefit from it; the sooner they contribute funds, the sooner their dollars can go to work to solve the problem.

4. **End with a positive picture** of the audience enjoying the product (in a sales message) or of the audience's money working to solve the problem (in a fund-raising message). The last sentence should never be a selfish request for money.

The action close can also remind people of central selling points, and mention when the customer will get the product.

Using a P.S.

In a direct mail letter or e-mail, the postscript, or P.S., occupies a position of emphasis by being the final part of the message. Direct mail often uses a deliberate P.S. after the signature block. It may restate the central selling point or some other point the letter makes, preferably in different words so that it won't sound repetitive when the reader reads the letter through from start to finish.

Here are four of the many kinds of effective P.S.'s.

- Reason to act promptly:

> P.S.   Once I finish the limited harvest, that's it! I do not store any SpringSweet Onions for late orders. I will ship all orders on a first-come, first-served basis and when they are gone they are gone. Drop your order in the mail today . . . or give me a call toll free at 800-531-7470! (In Texas: 800-292-5437)

Sales letter for Frank Lewis Alamo Fruit

- Description of a premium the reader receives for giving:

> P.S.   And . . . we'll be pleased to send you—as a *new* member—the exquisite, full-color Sierra Club Wilderness Calendar. It's our gift . . . absolutely FREE to you . . . to show our thanks for your membership at this critical time.

Fund-raising letter for Sierra Club

- Reference to another part of the package:

> P.S.   Photographs may be better than words, but they still don't do justice to this model. Please keep in mind as you review the enclosed brochure that your SSJ will look even better when you can see it firsthand in your own home.

Sales letter for the Danbury Mint's model of the Duesenberg SSJ

- Restatement of central selling point:

> P.S. It is not easy to be a hungry child in the Third World. If your parents' crops fail or if your parents cannot find work, there are no food stamps . . . no free government-provided cafeteria lunches.
>
> Millions of hungry schoolchildren will be depending on CARE this fall. Your gift today will ensure that we will be there—that CARE won't let them down.

Fund-raising letter for CARE

Strategy in Sales Messages and Fund-Raising Appeals

In both sales messages and fund-raising appeals, the basic strategy is to help your audience see themselves using your products/services or participating in the goals of your charity. Too often, communicators stress the new features of their gadgets, rather than picturing the audience using it, or the statistics about their cause, rather than stories about people helping that cause.

Sales Messages

The basic strategy in sales messages is satisfying a need. People buy to get something or to get rid of something. Your message must remind people of the need your product meets, prove that the product will satisfy that need, show why your product is better than similar products, and make people *want* to have the product. Use psychological description ( p. 387) to show people how the product will help them. Testimonials from other buyers can help persuade them that the product works; details about how the product is made can carry the message of quality.

Generally, the price is not mentioned until the last fourth of the message, after the content makes the audience *want* the product.

You can make the price more palatable with the following techniques:

1. **Link the price to the benefit the product provides.** "Your piece of history is just $39.95."
2. **Link the price to benefits your company offers.** "You can reach our customer service agents 24/7."
3. **Show how much the product costs each day, each week, or each month.** "You can have all this for less than the cost of a cup of coffee a day." Make sure that the amount seems small and that you've convinced people that they'll use this product all year long.
4. **Allow customers to charge sales or pay in installments.** Your bookkeeping costs will rise, and some sales may be uncollectible, but the total number of sales will increase.

Sales trainer Jeffrey Gitomer urges customer testimonials as one of the best ways to overcome price resistance.[20]

Fund-Raising Appeals

In a fund-raising appeal, the basic emotional strategy is **vicarious participation.** By donating money, people participate vicariously in work they are not able to do personally. This strategy affects the pronouns you use. Throughout the appeal, use *we* to talk about your group. However, at the end, talk about what *you* the audience will be doing. End positively, with a picture of the audience's dollars helping to solve the problem.

Fund-raising appeals require some extra strategy. To achieve both your primary and secondary purposes, you must give a great deal of information. This

---

Gimmicks in Business-to-Business Sales

Direct mail letters to business customers often use enclosures to get the attention of busy executives.

Phoneworks introduced its interactive marketing system, SmartSpiffs, by FedExing 100 ad agency heads wallets, each containing $3, an ID card with the agency head's name, and a note: "I found your wallet." Most of the items in the wallet promoted SmartSpiffs: a *Wall Street Journal* article, a to-do reminder to learn more about the system, a matchbook with SmartSpiffs' 800 number. The mailing cost $5,340 and brought in sales of nearly $5 million in the first eight months.

Packager Cryovac sent two sample bags to manufacturers of premium pet food. One bag held caramel corn; the other held an Omaha steak on dry ice. "K-9000 bags keep oxygen out and lock in freshness and taste." The mailing cost $111,000 and brought in $2.4 million in sales.

SRHD sent paint cans filled with tools and urged companies to "Paint Your Vision" with SRHD's expertise. The mailing brought in more than $10 million in new business.

Adapted from Josh Inch, " 'Quest for Denali' Uncovers DMA's Echo Diamond Award," *Advertising Age*, October 12, 1998, 56; and "McCann Tops Echo Winners," *Direct Marketing*, October 16, 2000, s18–s20.

Combining Charity with Marketing

When Crate & Barrel, the upscale furniture retailer, set out to support education with donations, they didn't just give money to needy schools. Instead, they sent out coupons in their mailers, inviting their customers to use the DonorsChoose website to decide how and where Crate & Barrel would donate its money.

The response? Customers loved the program. Not only did the coupons inspire a higher rate of customer involvement—11% of the coupons were redeemed, compared to 2% in a normal mass-mailing—but the coupons also improved customers' perceptions of the company: 75% of the customers who used the DonorsChoose coupons said they now considered Crate & Barrel a company with a positive attitude toward the community, while 82% said they'd be more likely to buy the company's products in the future.

Think about the non-profit organizations that you support: how might they convince local businesses to try the same approach?

Adapted from Emily Steel, "Novel Program Blends Charity and Marketing," *Wall Street Journal*, December 20, 2006, B1, B5.

information (1) helps to persuade people; (2) gives supporters evidence to use in conversations with others; and (3) gives people who are not yet supporters evidence that may make them see the group as worthwhile, even if they do not give money now.

In your close, in addition to asking for money, suggest other ways people can help: doing volunteer work, scheduling a meeting on the subject, writing letters to Congress or the leaders of other countries, and so on. By suggesting other ways to participate, you not only involve your audience but also avoid one of the traps of fund-raising appeals: sounding as though you are interested in only your audience for the money they can give.

Deciding How Much to Ask For

Most messages to new donors suggest a range of amounts, from $50 or $100 (for employed people) up to perhaps double what you *really* expect to get from a single donor. A second strategy is to ask for a small, set amount that nearly everyone can afford ($15 or $25).

One of the several reasons people give for not contributing is that a gift of $25 or $100 seems too small to matter. It's not. Small gifts are important both in themselves and to establish a habit of giving. The American Heart Association recently determined that first-time donors responding to direct mail give an average of $21.84 and give $40.62 over a lifetime. But multiplied by the 7.6 million donors who respond to the AHA's mailings, the total giving is large. Also, over $20 million of the money that the AHA receives from estate settlements after a person's death comes from people who have a relationship as direct-mail donors.[21]

You can increase the size of gifts by using the following techniques:

1. **Link the gift to what it will buy.** Tell how much money it costs to buy a brick, a hymnal, or a stained glass window for a church; a book or journal subscription for a college library; a meal for a hungry child. Linking amounts to specific gifts helps the audience feel involved and often motivates them to give more: instead of saying, "I'll write a check for $25," the person may say, "I'd like to give a _____" and write a check to cover it.

2. **Offer a premium for giving.** Public TV and radio stations have used this ploy with great success, offering books, umbrellas, and carryall bags for gifts at a certain level. The best premiums are things that people both want and will use or display, so that the organization will get further publicity when other people see the premium.

3. **Ask for a monthly pledge.** People on modest budgets could give $15 or $25 a month; more prosperous people could give $100 a month or more. These repeat gifts not only bring in more money than the donors could give in a single check but also become part of the base of loyal supporters, which is essential to the continued success of any organization that raises funds.

Annual appeals to past donors often use the amount of the last donation as the lowest suggested gift, with other gifts 25%, 50%, or even 100% higher.

Always send a thank-you message to people who respond to your appeal, whatever the size of their gifts. By telling about the group's recent work, a thank-you message can help reinforce donors' commitment to your cause.

Logical Proof in Fund-Raising Messages

The body of a fund-raising message must prove that (1) the problem deserves attention, (2) the problem can be solved or at least alleviated, (3) your organization is helping to solve it, (4) private funds are needed, and (5) your organization will use the funds wisely.

1. The problem deserves attention.   No one can support every cause. Show why your audience should care about solving this problem.

If your problem is life-threatening, give some statistics: Tell how many people are killed in the United States every year by drunk drivers, or how many children in the world go to bed hungry every night. Also tell about one individual who is affected.

If your problem is not life-threatening, show that the problem threatens some goal or principle your audience find important. For example, a fund-raising letter to boosters of a high school swim team showed that team members' chances of setting records were reduced because timers relied on stopwatches. The letter showed that automatic timing equipment was accurate and produced faster times, since the timer's reaction time was no longer included in the time recorded.

2. The problem can be solved or alleviated.   People will not give money if they see the problem as hopeless—why throw money away? Sometimes you can reason by analogy. Cures have been found for other deadly diseases, so it's reasonable to hope that research can find a cure for cancer and AIDS. Sometimes you can show that short-term or partial solutions exist. For example, a UNICEF letter showed that four simple changes could save the lives of millions of children: oral rehydration, immunization, promoting breast feeding, and giving mothers cardboard growth charts so they'll know if their children are malnourished. Those solutions don't affect the underlying causes of poverty, but they do keep children alive while we work on long-term solutions.

3. Your organization is helping to solve or alleviate the problem.   Prove that your organization is effective. Be specific. Talk about your successes in the past. Your past success helps readers believe that you can accomplish your goals.

4. Private funds are needed to accomplish your group's goals.   We all have the tendency to think that taxes, or foundations, or church collections yield enough to pay for medical research or basic human aid. If your group does get some tax or foundation money, show why more money is needed. If the organization helps people who might be expected to pay for the service, show why they cannot pay, or why they cannot pay enough to cover the full cost. If some of the funds have been raised by the people who will benefit, make that clear.

5. Your organization will use the funds wisely.   Prove that the money goes to the cause, not just to the cost of fund-raising.

Emotional Appeal in Fund-Raising Messages

Emotional appeal is needed to make people pull out their checkbooks. How strong should emotional appeal be? A mild appeal is unlikely to sway any one who is not already committed, but your audience will feel manipulated by appeals they find too strong and reject them. Audience analysis may help you decide how much emotional appeal to use. If you don't know your audience well, use the strongest emotional appeal *you* feel comfortable with.

Emotional appeal is created by specifics. It is hard to care about, or even to imagine, a million people; it is easier to care about one specific person. Details and quotes help us see that person as real. According to Bobby Dean, director of donor services for Cal Farley's Boys Ranch and Affiliates, the Texas

www.habitat.org

Habitat for Humanity's Web site provides information for potential and current donors, volunteers, and clients.

Enclosures In Fund-Raising Letters

Fund-raising letters sometimes use inexpensive enclosures to add interest and help carry the message.

Brochures are inexpensive, particularly if you photocopy them. Mailings to alumni have included "Why I Teach at Earlham" (featuring three professors) and letters from students who have received scholarships.

Seeds don't cost much. Mailings from both Care and the New Forests Fund include four or five seeds of the leucaena, a subtropical tree that can grow 20 feet in a year. Its leaves feed cattle; its wood provides firewood or building materials; its roots reduce soil erosion. (Indeed, the enclosure easily becomes the theme for the letter.)

Reprints of newspaper or magazine articles about the organization or the problem it is working to solve add interest and credibility. Pictures of people the organization is helping build emotional appeal.

Major campaigns may budget for enclosures: pictures of buildings, tapes of oral history interviews, even sea shells and Mason jars.

The Changing Role of Catalogs

If sales from mass-mailer catalogs have been declining in recent years, replaced by e-commerce sales through web sites, isn't it time to retire paper catalogs? Not necessarily: catalogs are still an excellent way for companies to build customer interest and persuade customers to make purchases—even if those purchases are online.

Catalogs can be an integral part of a company's marketing plan:

- Instead of showing a company's entire stock, a good catalog will save space (and costs!) by listing a representative sampling. The idea is to attract the widest possible range of customers, with the widest possible interests.

- Good catalogs increase customer involvement with the products, either by providing them with a shopping experience; "in hand," or by directing them to an interactive web site.

Think about the catalogs that you receive in the mail. How do you use them? What would you need to see in a catalog to convince you to visit its web site or a physical store?

Adapted from Louise Lee, "Catalogs, Catalogs, Everywhere," *BusinessWeek,* December 4, 2006, 32–34.

Catalogs are still an excellent way for companies to build customer interest and persuade customers to buy—even if the sales are made at the company's Web site.

provider of residential care for at-risk youth emphasizes stories about the children it has helped. Its mailings to donors include stories about the children's successes—and sometimes their setbacks, too, which make the stories more realistic. In ongoing correspondence, Cal Farley's brings donors up to date about the progress these now-grown-up people make in their lives. Similarly, in its work for children's hospitals, Newport Creative Communications has found that stories about patients are the most effective appeal in its fund-raising letters. Newport vice president Stephen Power reports that the effectiveness of an appeal was especially critical in the aftermath of the September 2001 terrorist attacks, when donations flowed heavily to the Red Cross and New York City charities, leaving many local nonprofits underfunded.[22]

Sample Fund-Raising Letter

The letter from The Gorilla Foundation shown in Figure 12.11 uses interesting details and color photos to lead the reader through the document.

Much of the appeal of this letter is its novelty: this isn't the standard environmental fund-raising letter. The poster of Koko and her kitten included in the package is cute and involves the reader with the package.

Strategy in Contact Messages

Contact messages do not ask directly for action; instead, they keep in touch with customers or donors.

Contact messages are low key and short—often less than a page. They take as their theme the seasons or a recent event. The end of the message refers to the relationship between reader and writer and looks to the future.

Some organizations routinely send contact messages to keep their names before clients and customers, particularly for items that are purchased infrequently. After the September 11, 2001, terrorist attacks, many organizations sent contact letters to customers and donors; the event seemed to cry out for comment. One of the best letters came from Amnesty International (see Figure 12.12).

Writing Style

Direct mail is the one kind of business writing where elegance and beauty of language matter; in every other kind, elegance is welcome but efficiency is all that finally counts. Direct mail imitates the word choice and rhythm of conversation.

Figure 12.11   A Fund-Raising Letter

Photos break up the text and provide visual interest.

THE GORILLA FOUNDATION
BOX 620-640 WOODSIDE, CA 94062
INTERNET SITE: www.gorilla.org

Dear Friend of Animals,

Not you-attitude

First paragraph is weak. It isn't really news (as paragraph 3 admits); the allusion to a "myth" doesn't work; the paragraph lacks specifics.

(I'm writing) to share with you an astonishing breakthrough in our understanding of the world. The news is that a very remarkable gorilla named Koko has changed myth into fact ... <u>by speaking to humans!</u>

Underlining is meant to look as though person had marked key points

Slightly revised, this ¶ would make an acceptable opener

It's true. After years of dedicated teaching, Koko has learned to use sign language--the gestural language used by the deaf. With her newfound vocabulary, Koko is now providing us with an astounding wealth of knowledge about the way animals view the world. *A detail would be nice.*

Builds credibility

If you read magazines such as *National Geographic, People,* and *Life,* or watch television programs like "I Witness Video, Day One and 20/20," then you already know about Koko and the fascinating things she is telling us. Through the media, more than 40 million Americans have discovered what this young female gorilla can teach you and me about *homo sapiens'* closest living relatives.

Builds credibility

My name is Penny Patterson, and I have been Koko's teacher since 1972. In this letter Koko and I would like to share with you what we are learning together. And, perhaps most importantly, we'd like to <u>invite you to become a member of the amazing world of speaking with animals</u> by joining the Gorilla Foundation as part of Koko's <u>extended family.</u>

Emotional appeal

Dangerous to assume reader's reaction

As you read this, I think you'll be astonished at what more than two decades of study here at the Gorilla Foundation have revealed. By using sign language, Koko has confirmed humanity's timeless intuitions about the nature of animal intelligence.

Indeed, I constantly marvel at the complex and all-encompassing spectrum of this gentle animal's emotions: joy and grief, hope and

Talking about your <u>own</u> responses, however, is OK.

Figure 12.11   A Fund-Raising Letter *(Continued)*

despair, patience and frustration, greed and generosity, guilt and remorse, confidence and fear, pride and shame, empathy and jealousy, love and hate ... all the emotions that you and I experience.

Let me tell you a particularly poignant story to illustrate what I mean.

Uses stories to engage reader interest

For years, Koko had expressed an interest in the cats she saw through her windows or in the pages of her magazines. Her dreams came true when she selected a tailless manx kitten from a litter to be her very own.

I was moved by the relationship that developed between the 230-pound gorilla and the roly-poly kitten she named "All Ball." On occasion we would witness the tragicomical scene of Koko pouting when tiny All Ball had bitten or scratched her.

Interesting details keep the reader reading.

But far more frequently the then 13-year-old Koko would tell us how much she adored her tiny kitten. Certainly there's no better example of the old maxim "A picture is worth 1,000 words" than the cover of the January 1985 *National Geographic* that showed Koko softly cradling the diminutive kitten in her arms.

This photo is on the poster included in the package.

Koko is not alone in teaching us about the remarkable intelligence of these gentle primates. Her gorilla companion Michael has his own stories to tell. Unlike Koko, who was born in the San Francisco Zoo, Michael was orphaned in his birthplace in Cameroon, Africa.

Using sign language, the 400-pound gorilla can relate how he was captured--"big trouble"--when he was only two years old. He and his mother were "chased" by native gorilla hunters, who then killed his mother. He uses startlingly violent gestures to explain how the men "hit" him and his mother. (There are verified stories of the centuries-old native practice of butchering and eating adult gorillas in front of their young.)

Whether they're telling us about their cats or providing us with a great ape's ideas about life and death, the gorillas are doing something more remarkable and profound than "just" communicating with humans.

Koko and Michael are changing the way we view our world; they're forcing us to reexamine everything we've ever thought about animals.

Figure 12.11 A Fund-Raising Letter *(Continued)*

The effects of our studies are nothing less than revolutionary. Just as Copernicus proved that the universe doesn't revolve around the earth, we're proving that all life on this planet doesn't revolve around humans.

Imagine what could happen when people realize that animals have memories ... thought processes ... even hopes and dreams. <u>The fight to end cruelty to animals will gain new momentum; the efforts to preserve animals from extinction will take on even greater importance when humanity realizes what the real stakes are.</u>

links this project to larger environmental concerns

Humans are already reaping the benefits of our work as well. I have received thousands of letters from parents and educators who cite Koko and Michael as inspirations to young children to learn all kinds of skills--from reading to toilet training. (Yes, Koko uses a bathroom just as we do ... and even likes to use that time to leaf through magazines!)

Details are both interesting in themselves and help answer question, "Why does this matter?"

The breakthroughs in non-verbal communication we've pioneered and the teaching methods we've developed with Koko and Michael have exciting and promising applications for reaching autistic children, the severely retarded, and other handicapped people who have difficulty communicating. The possibilities are endless.

More breakthroughs will surely come, for the work we're doing with Koko and Michael is a lifetime project. That's right: A gorilla's life expectancy is over 50 years ... and my colleagues and I have committed the rest of our lives to learning everything these gorillas have to tell us.

This commitment overrides everything else. If we fail, such a long-term project may never happen again.

But our greatest fear--the one grim possibility that lends the greatest urgency to our work--is one simple fact: one day there simply may be no more gorillas.

The fact is that all sub-species of these wonderful animals are in trouble. Only about 600 mountain gorillas survive today in Uganda, Zaire and war-torn Rwanda. <u>It's all too likely that these magnificent primates--all of whom live in a total of 113 square miles--will be extinct within 15 years.</u>

Wouldn't it be tragic if--just as we are learning to talk with these beautiful animals--there were no more to talk with?

general goal

<u>Some day, if you and hundreds of others help us, Koko and Michael will live in a large preserve with other gorillas where they will thrive in a natural setting, communicate with humans, and reproduce future generations.</u>

Specific needs

But many obstacles must be overcome before our dream can become reality. Just Koko and Michael's basics--housing, food, and staff to meet their basic needs--require the average income of two adults. And then there are the unique expenses of our revolutionary project: custom

Figure 12.11   A Fund-Raising Letter *(Concluded)*

educational tools, a well-trained teaching staff, special data collection and analysis hardware, custom-written computer programs and the weeks of computer time needed to run them, miles of videotape, and thousands of pieces of mail to answer every month from fascinated children and interested colleagues. Add to that the professional administrative support required to keep everything running efficiently and economically, and you can see that our breakthroughs have <u>cost</u> a great deal.

better to continue focus on new need that could be met with contributions

In fact, our work has cost much, much more than we've been able to afford--and so much needs to be done.

<u>That's why we're making this appeal to the general public: We want to invite you to become part of Koko and Michael's (extended family) as a member of the Gorilla Foundation.</u>

builds emotional appeal

When you do, you'll share in the excitement only "talking gorillas" can generate. As a member, you'll receive special updates on the latest developments in Koko and Michael's education. In addition, we'll send you our special reports--*The Gorilla Foundation Journal*--featuring transcriptions of our conversations with the gorillas; the latest reports on the state of the world's gorillas; and amazing, amusing photographs you'll find nowhere else.

largest amount mentioned is underlined

When I asked Koko "What do gorillas like to do most?" she replied "Gorilla love eat good." Your $50 contribution could buy the approximately 60 pounds of food Koko, Michael and their friend Ndume eat every day.

Good specifics

And you can help establish a sanctuary for gorillas. Your $35 donation could help pay for about two square feet of outdoor habitat in a new tropical preserve.

Amounts are both presented in descending order and linked to what they will buy

A $20 gift could help pay for an hour of videotaped documentation of our research, and $100 will help pay for a mailing to share vital information with every zoo in the world where gorillas are housed.

Highest amount should be first--but linked to something that will seem more important.

You know our work, how we've worked tirelessly for almost two decades to reveal some of nature's greatest secrets. Now we call on your dedication, too: Won't you please join the Gorilla Foundation?

Or, as Koko says, "Love gorilla."

Sincerely,

Penny Patterson

Penny Patterson, Ph.D.
President

Love,

[signature]

Koko
"Fine Animal Gorilla"

P.S. Please don't put this letter aside with the intention of responding later. <u>We need your help today.</u> Just make your check payable to Koko, and return it in the convenient postage-paid envelope we have enclosed. Our heartfelt thanks.

P.S. connects donations directly to Koko

Figure 12.12   A Contact Letter

WILLIAM F. SCHULZ
EXECUTIVE DIRECTOR

September 21, 2001

Dear Amnesty Member,

Repetition of "Sometimes death comes . . . But not this time" creates powerful opener.

alliteration

Sometimes death comes in the dark, in the dead of night. But not this time. This time the day could not have been brighter or more beautiful.

Sometimes death comes when we are by ourselves. But not this time. This time it came to those who were surrounded by friends and colleagues.

Sometimes death comes on a battlefield or in a prison cell. But not this time. This time it came in commercial airplanes and pleasant office buildings.

Transition from the event to the organization sending the letter

And sometimes death comes after a long struggle and much anticipation. But not this time. This time it came in an instant. And it appears to have swept in its wake family members of our staff and volunteers, friends of members of our Board and doubtless a good many Amnesty International members themselves.

In keeping with the organization's philosophy, the letter calls for a thoughtful, measured response.

Now that it has, you and I have work to do. Not the kind of work that sorts through rubble or loads up body bags, thank God. Those who do *that* work deserve a thousand tears of gratitude. Our work is of a different order but just as important nonetheless. The work of anger, to be sure, but an anger tempered by wisdom. The work of grieving, absolutely, but a grieving that pays homage to suffering. And the work of justice, no question about it, but a justice of which every one of us can be proud.

Rule of 3 with internal contrasts in each line.

alliteration

To get to grieving, we must go through anger. And to get to justice, we must go through grieving. Because, as the theologian Sam Keen so eloquently put it, "Every day we are not mourning is a day we will be taking vengeance" and vengeance is different from justice.

Repetition

Those who died on September 11 represent the best that is in us as human beings, as citizens and people. The best that is in us knows that individuals are responsible for this crime – not anonymous masses of people. The best that is in us knows that the guilty deserve to be punished – not those who share their names or their language, their skin color or their religion. It knows that blind hatred corrupts the hater. It knows that the greatest power evil has is to entice the innocent to mimic its practices. It knows that every action has unintended consequences. It knows that the truly strong never forget that in the heart of every stranger lurks a reflection of our own.

Rule of 3

Those who died on September 11 represent the best that is in us, the calling of our highest selves. We owe them anger; we owe them grieving; we owe them justice. But everything that we do now must reflect the best, not the lowest, of our humanity. We pay those precious souls their rightful tribute only by leveling a wise justice, only by exhibiting a tender righteousness. We pay them tribute only by understanding what brought about their deaths and hewing to those principles that call us to a more abundant life.

AMNESTY INTERNATIONAL USA • 322 EIGHTH AVENUE • NEW YORK, NY 10001
(212) 807-8400 • www.amnestyusa.org

Figure 12.12   A Contact Letter *(Concluded)*

Parallelism

Toward those ends, Amnesty International will mourn the victims; we will speak out against impunity for the perpetrators; we will demand that those innocent of crimes be protected and respected; and we will insist that justice is not justice if it fails to adhere to international human rights norms. Both the International Secretariat of Amnesty International and we in AIUSA have appointed Crisis Response Teams to work together in a coordinated, unified response to this tragedy and its aftermath. We will be determining as soon as possible how best our membership can help advance our common goals.

Short sentences ending in consonants bring a sense of closure.

For death has come in an instant. And now there is work to be done.

Repetition of sentence in ¶ 4

William F. Schulz
Executive Director

The best sales, fund-raising, and promotional writing is closer to the language of poetry than to that of academia: it shimmers with images, it echoes with sound, it vibrates with energy.

Many of the things that make writing vivid and entertaining *add* words because they add specifics or evoke an emotional response. Individual sentences should flow smoothly. The passage as a whole may be fun to read precisely because of the details and images that "could have been left out."

1. Make Your Writing Interesting.

If the style is long-winded and boring, the reader will stop reading. Eliminating wordiness is crucial. You've already seen ways to tighten your writing in Chapter 4. Direct mail goes further, breaking some of the rules of grammar. In the following examples, note how sentence fragments and ellipses (spaced dots) are used in parallel structure to move the reader along:

> So tiny, it fits virtually unnoticed in your pocket. So meticulously hand-assembled by unhurried craftsmen in Switzerland, that production may never exceed demand. So everyday useful, that you'll wonder how you ever got along without it.

Letter asking for inquiries about Dictaphone

> Dear Member-elect:
>
> If you still believe that there are nine planets in our solar system . . . that wine doesn't breathe . . . and that you'd recognize a Neanderthal man on sight if one sat next to you on the bus . . . check your score. There aren't. It does. You wouldn't.

Subscription letter for *Natural History*

2. Use Psychological Description.

Psychological description (p. 387) means describing your product or service in terms of benefits. In a sales letter, you can use psychological description to create a scenario so readers can picture themselves using your product or service and enjoying its benefits. You can also use psychological description to describe the problem your product will solve.

A *Bon Appétit* subscription letter uses psychological description in its opener and in the P.S., creating a frame for the sales letter:

> Dear Reader:
>
> First, fill a pitcher with ice.
> Now pour in a bottle of ordinary red wine, a quarter cup of brandy, and a small bottle of Club soda.
> Sweeten to taste with a quarter to half cup of sugar, garnish with slices of apple, lemon, and orange. . . .
> . . . then *move your chair to a warm, sunny spot.* You've just made yourself Sangria—one of the great glories of Spain, and the perfect thing to sit back with and sip while you consider this invitation. . . .
>
> P.S. One more thing before you finish your Sangria. . . .

It's hard to imagine any reader really stopping to follow the recipe before finishing the letter, but the scenario is so vivid that one can imagine the sunshine even on a cold, gray day.

3. Make Your Letter Sound Like a Letter, Not an Ad.

Maintain the image of one person writing to one other person that is the foundation of all letters. Use an informal style with short words and sentences, and even slang.

You can also create a **persona**—the character who allegedly writes the letter—to make the letter interesting and keep us reading. Use the rhythms of speech, vivid images, and conversational words to create the effect that the author is a "character."

The following opening creates a persona who fits the product:

> Dear Friend:
>
> There's no use trying. I've tried and tried to tell people about my fish. But I wasn't rigged out to be a letter writer, and I can't do it. I can close-haul a sail with the best of them. I know how to pick out the best fish of the catch, I know just which fish will make the tastiest mouthfuls, but I'll never learn the knack of writing a letter that will tell people why my kind of fish—fresh-caught prime-grades, right off the fishing boats with the deep-sea tang still in it—is lots better than the ordinary store kind.

Sales letter, Frank Davis Fish Company

Leave 'Em Laughing?

Not too many sales brochures and letters leave you holding your sides with laughter. There may be a good reason. A good joke may put you in a good mood, but it rarely gives the motivation to buy a product or make a donation.

The lack of jokes in sales letters and brochures may seem odd in contrast to the frequency of humor in advertising. The two kinds of writing generally serve different purposes, though. A great deal of advertising is designed to give the audience a positive image of a product or brand. Sales letters and brochures are focused on a more direct response—say, subscribing to a magazine or contributing to a cause. Humor can actually distract the audience from that purpose.

Still, some products use humor in their direct mail, perhaps because humor is part of what they are known for providing. Consider two examples of political humor. One of the most successful mailings by *The Nation* magazine featured a caricature of President George W. Bush wearing a crown, along with the words "Don't you just love this guy? If your answer is yes, don't open this envelope." And the *National Review* once sent out a mailing in an envelope carrying a definition of "Slickaphobia," alluding to conservatives' nickname for President Bill Clinton, Slick Willie. The possibility of offending some people with either of these references would not be a marketing problem because the offended individuals were unlikely to be in the magazine's target market.

Adapted from Beth Negus Viveiros, "No Laughing Matter: Use of Humor in Direct Mail Marketing," *Direct*, January 2003.

This letter, with its "Aw, shucks, I can't sell" persona, with language designed to make you see an unassuming fisherman ("rigged out," "close-haul"), was written by a professional advertiser.[23]

Solving a Sample Problem

Problem

In one room in the production department of Nakamura Electronics Company, employees work on TVs under conditions that are scarcely bearable due to the heat. Even when the temperature outside is only 75°, it is over 100° in the "set room." In June, July, and August, 24 out of 36 workers quit because they couldn't stand the heat. This turnover happens every summer.

In a far corner of the room sits a quality control inspector in front of a small fan (the only one in the room). The production workers, in contrast, are carrying 30-pound TV sets. As Production Supervisor, you tried to get air-conditioning two years ago, before Nakamura acquired the company, but management was horrified at the idea of spending $300,000 to insulate and air-condition the warehouse (it is impractical to air-condition the set room alone).

Inflation has pushed the price of insulation and air-conditioning up to $500,000, but with such high turnover, you're losing money every summer. Write a memo to Jennifer M. Kirkland, Operations Vice President, renewing your request.

Analysis of the Problem

Use the problem analysis questions in the first chapter to think through the problem.

1. Who is (are) your audience(s)? What characteristics are relevant to this particular message? If you are communicating to more than one audience, how do they differ?

    The Operations Vice President will be concerned about keeping costs low and keeping production running smoothly. Kirkland may know that the request was denied two years ago, but another person was Vice President then; Kirkland wasn't the one who said *no*.

2. What are your purposes in writing?

    To persuade Kirkland to authorize insulation and air-conditioning. To build a good image of myself.

3. What information must your message include?

    The cost of the proposal. The effects of the present situation.

4. How can you build support for your position? What reasons or benefits will your audience find convincing?

    Cutting turnover may save money and keep the assembly line running smoothly. Experienced employees may produce higher-quality sets. Putting in air-conditioning would relieve one of the workers' main complaints; it might make the union happier.

5. What objection(s) can you expect your audience to have? What negative elements of your message must you deemphasize or overcome?

    The cost. The time operations will be shut down while installation is taking place.

6. What aspects of the total situation may affect the response? The economy? The time of year? Morale in the organization? The relationship between the reader and writer? Any special circumstances?

> The electronics industry is having a shakeout; money is tight; the company will be reluctant to make a major expenditure. Filling vacancies in the set room is hard—we are getting a reputation as a bad place to work. Summer is over, and the problem is over until next year.

Discussion of the Sample Solutions

Solution 1, shown in Figure 12.13, is unacceptable. By making the request in the subject line and the first paragraph, the writer invites a *no* before giving all the arguments. The writer does nothing to counter the objections that any manager will have to spending a great deal of money. By presenting the issue in terms of fairness, the writer produces defensiveness rather than creating a common ground. The writer doesn't use details or emotional appeal to show that the problem is indeed serious. The writer asks for fast action but doesn't show why the reader should act now to solve a problem that won't occur again for eight months.

Solution 2, shown in Figure 12.14, is an effective persuasive message. The writer chooses a positive subject line. The opening sentence catches the reader's attention with a common ground problem. However, the paragraph makes it clear that the memo offers a solution to the problem. The problem is spelled out in detail. Emotional impact is created by taking the reader through the day as the temperature rises. The solution is presented impersonally. There are no *I*'s in the memo.

The memo stresses benefits: the savings that will result once the investment is recovered. The last paragraph tells the reader exactly what to do and links prompt action to a benefit. The memo ends with a positive picture of the problem solved.

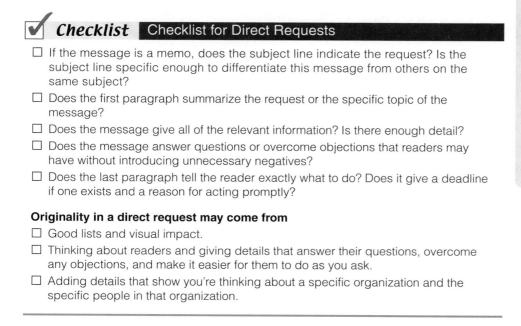

✓ *Checklist*   **Checklist for Direct Requests**

☐ If the message is a memo, does the subject line indicate the request? Is the subject line specific enough to differentiate this message from others on the same subject?

☐ Does the first paragraph summarize the request or the specific topic of the message?

☐ Does the message give all of the relevant information? Is there enough detail?

☐ Does the message answer questions or overcome objections that readers may have without introducing unnecessary negatives?

☐ Does the last paragraph tell the reader exactly what to do? Does it give a deadline if one exists and a reason for acting promptly?

Originality in a direct request may come from

☐ Good lists and visual impact.

☐ Thinking about readers and giving details that answer their questions, overcome any objections, and make it easier for them to do as you ask.

☐ Adding details that show you're thinking about a specific organization and the specific people in that organization.

Cell Phone Ads in China

"Mobile advertising in its simplest form—text message solicitations—has been around in Asia for years, and many have dismissed it as spam. But an increasing number of advertisers are taking to the medium, believing they can find new ways to reach Chinese consumers through what has become an indispensable accessory: cell phones.

"Coca-Cola China was one of the earliest companies to try its luck with mobile marketing. The company created a national campaign asking Beijing residents to send text messages guessing the high temperature in the city every day for a month, for a chance to win a one-year supply of Coke products. The campaign attracted more than four million messages over the course of 35 days.

"Mobile ads can be more targeted than other ads because advertisers can select their audiences based on user data from mobile operators. The kind of phone or service plan customers use, for example, can give an indication of their age or income."

One of the keys to mobile advertising's success in China is interactivity: engaging customers by asking them to respond to a message. What would convince you to respond to an ad delivered to your cell phone? How would you convince a customer to respond to an ad?

Quote from Loretta Chao, "Cellphone Ads Are Easier Pitch in China," *Wall Street Journal*, January 4, 2007, B5.

Figure 12.13   An Unacceptable Solution to the Sample Problem

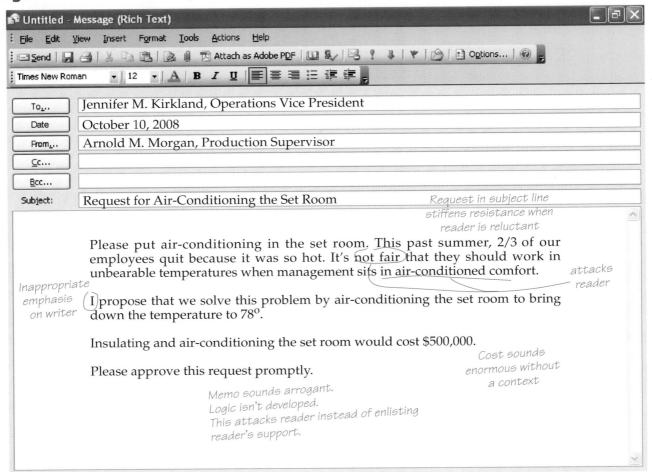

To: Jennifer M. Kirkland, Operations Vice President

Date October 10, 2008

From: Arnold M. Morgan, Production Supervisor

Cc...

Bcc...

Subject: Request for Air-Conditioning the Set Room   *Request in subject line stiffens resistance when reader is reluctant*

Inappropriate emphasis on writer

Please put air-conditioning in the set room. This past summer, 2/3 of our employees quit because it was so hot. It's not fair that they should work in unbearable temperatures when management sits in air-conditioned comfort.   *attacks reader*

I propose that we solve this problem by air-conditioning the set room to bring down the temperature to 78°.

Insulating and air-conditioning the set room would cost $500,000.   *Cost sounds enormous without a context*

Please approve this request promptly.

Memo sounds arrogant.
Logic isn't developed.
This attacks reader instead of enlisting reader's support.

Ethics and Direct Mail

Deception in direct mail is all too easy to find.

Some mailers have sent "checks" to readers. But the "check" can only be applied toward the purchase of the item the letter is selling.

Some mailings now have yellow Post-it notes with "handwritten" notes signed with initials or a first name only—to suggest that the mailing is from a personal friend.

One letter offers a "free" membership "valued at $675" (note the passive—who's doing the valuing?) but charges—up front—$157 for "maintenance fees."

Such deception has no place in well-written direct mail.

✓ *Checklist*   Checklist for Problem-Solving Persusive Messages

- ☐ If the message is a memo, does the subject line indicate the writer's purpose or offer a benefit? Does the subject line avoid making the request?
- ☐ Does the first sentence interest the audience?
- ☐ Is the problem presented as a joint problem both communicator and audience have an interest in solving, rather than as something the audience is being asked to do for the communicator?
- ☐ Does the message give all of the relevant information? Is there enough detail?
- ☐ Does the message overcome objections that the audience may have?
- ☐ Does the message avoid phrases that sound dictatorial, condescending, or arrogant?
- ☐ Does the last paragraph tell the audience exactly what to do? Does it give a deadline if one exists and a reason for acting promptly?

Originality in a problem-solving persuasive message may come from

- ☐ A good subject line and common ground.
- ☐ A clear and convincing description of the problem.
- ☐ Thinking about the audience and giving details that answer their questions, overcome objections, and make it easier for them to do as you ask.
- ☐ Adding details that show you're thinking about a specific organization and the specific people in that organization.

Figure 12.14   A Good Solution to the Sample Problem

Date: October 10, 2008

To: Jennifer M. Kirkland, Operations Vice President

From: Arnold M. Morgan, Production Supervisor   *AMM*

Subject: Improving Summer Productivity

Paper memo selected for problem this large

Reader benefit in subject line

Problem creates a common ground

Nakamura forfeited a possible $186,000 in profits last summer due to a 17% drop in productivity. That's not unusual: Nakamura has a history of low summer productivity. But we can reverse the trend and bring summer productivity in line with the rest of the year's.

Good to show problem can be resolved

Cause of problem

The problem starts in the set room. Due to high turnover and reduced efficiency from workers who are on the job, we just don't make as many TV sets as we do during the rest of the year. And when we don't have sets, we can't make sales quotes.

Additional reason to solve problem

Both the high turnover and reduced efficiency are due to the unbearable heat in the set room. Temperatures in the set room average 25° over the outside temperature. During the summer, when work starts at 8, it's already 85° in the set room. By 11:30, it's at least 105°. On six days last summer, it hit 120°. When the temperatures are that high, we are violating OSHA regulations.

Production workers are always standing, moving, or carrying 30-lb. TV sets. When temperatures hit 90°, they slow down. When no relief is in sight, many of them quit.

We replaced 24 of the 36 employees in the set room this summer. When someone quits, it takes an average of five days to find and train a replacement; during that time, the trainee produces nothing. For another five days, the new person can work at only half speed. And even "full speed" in the summer is only 90% of what we expect the rest of the year.

More details about problem

Here's where our losses come from:

Normal production = 50 units a person each day (upd)

Loss due to turnover:
| | |
loss of 24 workers for 5 days =   6,000 units
24 at $^1/_2$ pace for 5 days =   3,000 units
   Total loss due to turnover =   9,000 units

Shows detail— Set up like an arithmetic problem

Loss due to reduced efficiency:
loss of 5 upd x 12 workers x 10 days =   600 units
loss of 5 upd x 36 x 50 days =   9,000 units
   Total loss due to reduced efficiency =   9,600 units

Total Loss =   18,600 units

(continued)

Figure 12.14   A Good Solution to the Sample Problem *(Concluded)*

Jennifer M. Kirkland   2   October 10, 2008

According to the accounting department, Nakamura makes a net profit of $20 on every TV set we sell. And, as you know, with the boom in TV sales, we sell every set we make. Those 18,600 units we don't produce are costing us $372,000 a year.

Shows where numbers in paragraph 1 come from

Additional benefit

Bringing down the temperature to 78° (to meet federal guidelines) from the present summer average of 112° will require an investment of $500,000 to insulate and air-condition the set room. Extra energy costs for the air-conditioning will run about $30,000 a year. We'll get our investment back in less than two years. Once the investment is recouped, we'll be making an additional $340,000 a year—all without buying additional equipment or hiring additional workers.

Tells reader what to do

By installing the insulation and air-conditioning this fall, we can take advantage of lower off-season rates. Please authorize the Purchasing Department to request bids for the system. Then, next summer, our productivity can be at an all-time high.

Reason to act promptly

Ends on positive note of problem solved, reader enjoying benefit

---

Play before You Pay

For video game companies, one of the most persuasive "messages" is the playable demo. Many game developers make trial versions of their games available for download on the Internet, or on trial-version DVDs, so that potential customers can experience the graphics and gameplay first-hand. Downloadable game demos are abridged versions of a full game; they compare to song clips that let consumers sample music before they buy.

These demos generate real sales. According to research conducted by Microsoft through their Xbox Live online service, about 40% of users who download a game demo will play the final version of the game, which they will likely buy.

What other Internet or online services might benefit from the same sales model? How might you convince a skeptical boss to try this kind of promotion?

Adapted from Nick Wingfield, "Down-loadable Game Demos Get Test," *Wall Street Journal*, August 23, 2006, B3.

Summary of Key Points

- The primary purpose in a persuasive message is to have the audience act. Secondary purposes are to overcome any objections that might prevent or delay action, to build a good image of the communicator and the communicator's organization, to cement a good relationship between the communicator and audience, and to reduce or eliminate future communication on the same subject.
- **Credibility** is the audience's response to you as the source of the message. You can build credibility by being factual, specific, and reliable.
- Use the persuasive strategy your organization prefers.
- Use the **direct request pattern** when the audience will do as you ask without any resistance. Also use the direct request pattern for busy readers in your own organization who do not read all the messages they receive.
- Use the **problem-solving pattern** when the audience may resist doing what you ask and you expect logic to be more important than emotion in the decision.
- Use the **sales pattern** when the audience may resist doing as you ask and you expect emotion to be more important than logic in the decision.
- In a direct request, consider asking immediately for the information or service you want. Give your audience all the information they will need to act on your request. Ask for the action you want.
- Organize a problem-solving persuasive message in this way:
  1. Catch the audience's interest by mentioning a common ground.
  2. Define the problem you both share (which your request will solve).
  3. Explain the solution to the problem.
  4. Show that any negative elements (cost, time, etc.) are outweighed by the advantages.

5. Summarize any additional benefits of the solution.

6. Ask for the action you want.

- In a direct request, put the request, the topic of the request, or a question in the subject line. Do not put the request in the subject line of a problem-solving persuasive message. Instead, use a neutral subject line or a benefit. Use a positive or neutral subject line even when the first paragraph will be negative.

- Use one or more of the following strategies to counter objections that you cannot eliminate:

  - Specify how much time and/or money is required.
  - Put the time and/or money in the context of the benefits they bring.
  - Show that money spent now will save money in the long run.
  - Show that doing as you ask will benefit some group the audience identifies with or some cause the audience supports.
  - Show the audience that the sacrifice is necessary to achieve a larger, more important goal to which they are committed.
  - Show that the advantages as a group outnumber or outweigh the disadvantages as a group.
  - Turn the disadvantage into an opportunity.

- Threats don't produce permanent change. They won't necessarily produce the action you want, they may make people abandon an action entirely (even in situations where abandoning would be not appropriate), and they produce tension. People dislike and avoid anyone who threatens them. Threats can provoke counteraggression.

- Base persuasion in difficult persuasive situations on the following five steps:

  1. Find out why your audience members resist what you want them to do.
  2. Try to find a win–win solution.
  3. Find a way to let your audience save face.
  4. Ask for something small.
  5. Present your argument from your audience's point of view.

- To encourage people to act promptly, set a deadline. Show that the time limit is real, that acting now will save time or money, or that delaying action will cost more.

- Build emotional appeal with stories and psychological description.

- Performance appraisals should cite specific observations, not inferences. They should contain specific suggestions for improvement and identify the two or three areas that the worker should emphasize in the next month or quarter.

- Letters of recommendation must be specific and tell how well and how long you've known the person.

- A good opener makes readers want to read persuasion messages and provides a reasonable transition to the body of the message. Four modes for openers are questions, narration, startling statements, and quotations. A good body answers the audience's questions, overcomes their objections, and involves them emotionally. A good action close tells people what to do, makes the action sound easy, gives them a reason for acting promptly, and ends with a benefit or a picture of their money helping to solve the problem.

- Specify price near the end of the body of a sales message, after you've given your evidence and made the audience *want* the product.

Small Victories

You can change the culture of a company to make it more ethical and more inclusive. And you don't have to wait till you're the CEO. Do it by making small changes.

One man wanted to coach his kids' soccer teams—so he left work before his colleagues did. He didn't want phone calls about work between 6 and 8 P.M. As people stopped calling him, it became clear that others felt the same way. Gradually, the company culture changed to reserve early-evening hours for family time.

At PricewaterhouseCoopers, a woman partner changed pronouns. When she created example scenarios for other partners, she populated them with *she*'s. It was a step in creating a cultural shift.

At still another company, a superior asked an African American woman to unbraid her hair before a meeting with a client. She refused. Her immediate boss praised her courage and congratulated the organization on expanding its understanding of professionalism.

Successful radicals have allies, both inside the company and outside it. Networks of supporters provide emotional support, information, resources, and sounding boards. Small victories, over time, lead to worthwhile change.

Adapted from Keith H. Hammonds, "Practical Radicals," *Fast Company*, September 2000, 162–74.

- In a fund-raising appeal, the basic strategy is vicarious participation. By donating money, people participate vicariously in work they are not able to do personally.

- The primary purpose in a fund-raising appeal is to get money. An important secondary purpose is to build support for the cause so that people who are not persuaded to give will still have favorable attitudes toward the group and will be sympathetic when they hear about it again.

- The body of a fund-raising appeal must prove that (1) the problem deserves attention, (2) the problem can be solved or at least alleviated, (3) your organization is helping to solve it, (4) private funds are needed, and (5) your organization will use the funds wisely.

- To increase the size of gifts, link the gift to what it will buy; offer a premium for giving; and ask for a monthly pledge.

- **Contact letters** keep in touch with customers or donors.

- Good writing in direct mail is interesting. It uses psychological description, is specific, and relies on conversational tone.

CHAPTER 12   Exercises and Problems

12.1   Reviewing the Chapter

1. What are four questions you should answer when analyzing persuasive situations? Which question do you think is the most important? Why? (LO 1)

2. What are three basic persuasive strategies? In what kinds of situations is each preferred? (LO 2)

3. Why aren't threats effective persuasion tools? (LO 2)

4. How do you start the body of persuasive direct requests? Why? (LO 3)

5. How do you organize persuasive problem-solving messages? (LO 4)

6. How do you develop a common ground with your audience? (LO 4)

7. What are 10 ways to deal with objections? (LO 4 and LO 6)

8. What are ways to build emotional appeal? (LO 4 and LO 6)

9. What are four good beginnings for sales and fund-raising messages? (LO 5)

10. What are ways to de-emphasize costs or donation requests? (LO 5)

11. What kinds of rational evidence should you use to support your persuasion? (LO 6)

12. What kinds of emotional appeals should you use to support your persuasion? (LO 6)

12.2   Reviewing Grammar

Persuasion uses lots of pronouns. Correct the sentences in Exercise B.4, Appendix B, to practice making pronouns agree with their nouns, as well as practicing subject–verb agreement.

12.3   Writing Psychological Description

For one or more of the following groups, write two or three paragraphs of psychological description that could be used in a brochure, news release, or direct mail message directed to members of that group.

1. Having a personal trainer.
   Audiences: Professional athletes.
              Busy managers.
              Someone trying to lose weight.
              Someone making a major lifestyle change after a heart attack.

2. Buying a cellular phone.
   Audiences: People who do a lot of big-city driving.
              People who do a lot of driving in rural areas.
              People who do a lot of flying.

3. Using vending machines newly installed in school cafeterias and stocked with healthful snacks, such as yogurt, raisins, carrots with dip, and all-natural juices.

Audiences: High school students
 Parents
 High school faculty

4. Attending a fantasy sports camp (you pick the sport), playing with and against retired players who provide coaching and advice.
5. Attending a health spa where clients get low-fat and low-carb meals, massages, beauty treatments, and guidance in nutrition and exercise.

Hints:

- For this assignment, you can combine benefits or programs as if a single source offered them all.
- Add specific details about particular sports, activities, and so on, as material for your description.
- Be sure to use vivid details and sense impressions.
- Phrase your benefits with you-attitude.

12.4 Evaluating Subject Lines

Evaluate the following subject lines. Is one subject line in each group clearly best? Or does the "best" line depend on company culture, whether the message is a paper memo or an e-mail message, or on some other factor?

1. Subject: Request
 Subject: Why I Need a New Computer
 Subject: Increasing My Productivity
2. Subject: Who Wants Extra Hours?
 Subject: Holiday Work Schedule
 Subject: Working Extra Hours During the Holiday Season
3. Subject: Student Mentors
 Subject: Can You Be an E-Mail Mentor?
 Subject: Volunteers Needed
4. Subject: More Wine and Cheese
 Subject: Today's Reception for Japanese Visitors
 Subject: Reminder
5. Subject: Reducing Absenteeism
 Subject: Opening a Day Care Center for Sick Children of Employees
 Subject: Why We Need Expanded Day Care Facilities

12.5 Choosing a Persuasive Approach

For each of the following situations requiring a persuasive message, choose the persuasive approach that you feel would work best. Explain your reasoning; then give a short list of the types of information you'd use to persuade your audience.

1. Asking for an extension on a project.
2. Requesting a job interview.
3. Requesting a free trial of a service.
4. Inviting customers to a store opening.
5. Reporting a co-worker's poor work performance.
6. Requesting a new office computer.
7. Asking co-workers to participate in a charity event.

As your instructor directs,

a. Write a memo, letter, or e-mail that addresses one of the situations in this exercise, drawing on details from your personal experiences. (You might address a real problem that you've faced.)
b. Write a memo to your instructor listing the choices you've made and justifying your approach.

12.6 Identifying Observations

Susan has taken the following notes about her group's meetings. Which of the following are specific observations that she could use in a performance appraisal of group members? If she had it to do over again, what kinds of details would turn the inferences into observations?

1. Feb. 22: Today was very frustrating. Sam was totally out of it—I wonder if he's on something. Jim was dictatorial. I argued, but nobody backed me up. Masayo might just as well have stayed home. We didn't get anything done. Two hours, totally wasted.
2. February 24: Jim seems to be making a real effort to be less domineering. Today he asked Sam and me for our opinions before proposing his own. And he noticed that Masayo wasn't talking much and brought her into the conversation. She suggested some good ideas.
3. February 28: Today's meeting was OK. I thought Masayo wasn't really focusing on the work at hand. She needs to work on communicating her ideas to others. Sam was doing some active listening, but he needs to work at being on time. Jim was involved in the project. He has strong leadership skills. There were some tense moments, but we got a lot done, and we all contributed. I got to say what I wanted to say, and the group decided to use my idea for the report.
4. March 5: This week most of us had midterms, and Masayo had an out-of-town gymnastics trip. We couldn't find a time to meet. So we did stuff by e-mail. Sam and Jim found some great stuff at the library and on the Web. Jim created a tentative schedule that he sent to all of us and then revised. I wrote up a draft of the description of the problem.

Then Masayo and I put everything together. I sent my draft to her; she suggested revisions (in full caps so I could find them in the e-mail message). Then I sent the message to everyone. Masayo and Jim both suggested changes, which I made before we handed the draft in.

5. March 15: We were revising the proposal, using Prof. Jones's comments. When we thought we were basically done, Masayo noticed that we had not responded to all of the specific comments about our introductory paragraph. We then went back and thought of some examples to use. This made our proposal better and more complete.

As your instructor directs,

a. Based on Susan's notes, write a performance appraisal memo addressed to Prof. Jones. For each group member, including Susan, note specific areas of good performance and make specific suggestions for improvement.

b. Write a memo to your instructor describing the process you used to make your recommendations. Be sure to identify each of the observations you used to provide specific details, and each of the inferences that needed more information.

12.7   Revising a Form Memo

You've been hired as a staff accountant; one of your major duties will be processing expense reimbursements. Going through the files, you find this form memo:

> Subject: Reimbursements
>
> Enclosed are either receipts that we could not match with the items in your request for reimbursement or a list of items for which we found no receipts or both. Please be advised that the Accounting Department issues reimbursement checks only with full documentation. You cannot be reimbursed until you give us a receipt for each item for which you desire reimbursement. We must ask that you provide this information. This process may be easier if you use the Expense Report Form, which is available in your department.
>
> Thank you for your attention to this matter. Please do not hesitate to contact us with questions.

You know this memo is horrible. In addition to wordiness, a total lack of positive emphasis and you-attitude, and a vague subject line, the document design and organization of information bury the request.

Create a new memo that could be sent to people who do not provide all the documentation they need in order to be reimbursed.

12.8   Suggesting a Change in Your Organization's URL

You work for a small organization that operates a Web site, but has not purchased a customized domain name for their site: instead, your site's URL is a long, complicated string of text that references your Internet provider's name, not yours. It's difficult to remember, unwieldy for customers to use, and too long to include on business materials (stationery, business cards, invoices, product packaging, brochures, catalogs, voice-mail announcements, e-mail signatures, and promotional items such as pens, coffee cups, and mouse pads). Purchasing a custom domain name would increase your organization's visibility (and the visibility of its Web page).

As your instructor directs,

a. Identify the person in your organization with the power to authorize the purchase of a new Internet domain name and add that name to physical materials. Write an e-mail to that person, asking him or her to authorize that change.

b. Write an e-mail to all employees, asking them to add the URL and a brief message promoting the organization to their e-mail signature blocks. Include some sample promotional messages.

Hints:

- Pick a business, nonprofit, or government organization you know something about. What self-promotional materials does it produce? Which would benefit from the new URL?

- Will the reader know you? Has your organization asked for suggestions, or will this come out of the blue?

- What are the costs associated with registering and maintaining a custom domain name?
- What should be done with materials already printed or manufactured that lack the Web address, or that feature the old Web address? Should they be discarded, or should they be used until they run out?

- Who in your organization has the authority to authorize this change? What objections might they have to your suggestion? What persuasive approach would be most appropriate when you address them?
- What exactly do you want your reader(s) to do? What information does your reader need?

12.9   Asking for a Job Description

Your organization has gone through a lot of changes, and you suspect that the original job descriptions people were hired into are no longer accurate. So you'd like all employees to list their current job duties. You'd also like them to indicate which parts of their jobs they see as most important, and to indicate how much time they spend on each part of the job.

E-mail all employees, asking for the descriptions.

Hints:

- Pick a real business, government, or nonprofit group you know about.
- When is the next cycle of performance appraisals? Will these descriptions be used then?

- People will be reluctant to tell you they're spending lots of time on things that aren't important, and some people may honestly not know how they spend their time. How can you encourage accurate reporting? (If you ask people to keep logs for a week, be sure also to ask them if that week was typical—it may or may not be.)
- Some people will want to change their job descriptions—that is, to change their duties or the proportion of time they spend on each. Is that an option in your organization right now? If it isn't (or if it is an option for very few people), how can you make that clear to readers?

12.10   Asking for More Time and/or Resources

Today, this message from your boss shows up in your e-mail inbox:

Subject: Want Climate Report

This request has come down from the CEO. I'm delegating it to you. See me a couple of days before the board meeting—the 4th of next month—so we can go over your presentation.

I want a report on the climate for underrepresented groups in our organization. A presentation at the last board of directors' meeting showed that while we do a good job of hiring women and minorities, few of them rise to the top. The directors suspect that our climate may not be supportive and want information on it. Please prepare a presentation for the next meeting. You'll have 15 minutes.

Making a presentation to the company's board of directors can really help your career. But preparing a good presentation and report will take time. You can look at exit reports filed by Human Resources when people leave the company, but you'll also need to interview people—lots of people. And you're already working 60 hours a week on three major projects, one of which is behind schedule. Can one of the projects wait? Can someone else take one of the projects? Can you get some help? Should you do just enough to get by? Ask your boss for advice—in a way that makes you look like a committed employee, not a shirker.

12.11   Persuading Employees Not to Share Files

Your computer network has been experiencing slowdowns, and an investigation has uncovered the reason. A number of employees have been using the system to download and share songs and vacation photos. You are concerned because the bulky files clog the network, and downloading files opens the network to computer viruses and worms. In addition, management does not want employees to spend work time and resources on personal matters. Finally, free downloads of songs are often illegal, and management is worried that a recording firm might sue the company for failing to prevent employees from violating its copyrights.

As Director of Management Information Systems (MIS), you want to persuade employees to stop sharing files unrelated to work. You are launching a policy of regularly scanning the system for violations, but you prefer that employees voluntarily use the system properly.

Violations are hard to detect, and increasing scanning in an effort to achieve system security is likely to cause resentment as an intrusion into employees' privacy.

Write an e-mail message to all employees, urging them to refrain from downloading and sharing personal files.

12.12   Sending a Question to a Web Site

Send a question or other message that calls for a response to a Web site. You could

- Ask a question about a product.
- Apply for an internship or a job (assuming you'd really like to work there).
- Ask for information about an internship or a job.
- Ask a question about an organization or a candidate before you donate money or volunteer.
- Offer to volunteer for an organization or a candidate. You can either offer to do so something small and one-time (e.g., spend an afternoon stuffing envelopes, put up a yard sign) or offer to do something more time-consuming or even ongoing.

As your instructor directs,

a. Turn in a copy of your e-mail message and the response you received.

b. Critique messages written by other students in your class. Suggest ways the messages could be clearer and more persuasive.

c. Write a memo evaluating your message and the response, using the checklists in this chapter as a starting place for your evaluation. If you did not receive a response, did the fault lie with your message?

d. Make an oral presentation to the class, evaluating your message and the response and using the checklists in this chapter as a starting place for your evaluation. If you did not receive a response, did the fault lie with your message?

Hints:

- Does the organization ask for questions or offers? Or will yours come out of the blue?
- How difficult will it be for the organization to supply the information you're asking for or to do what you're asking it to do? If you're applying for an internship or offering to volunteer, what skills can you offer? How much competition do you have?
- What can you do to build your own credibility so that the organization takes your question or request seriously?

12.13   Not Doing What the Boss Asked

Today, you get this e-mail message:

To: All Unit Managers

Subject: Cutting Costs

Please submit five ideas for cutting costs in your unit. I will choose the best ideas and implement them immediately.

You think your boss's strategy is wrong. Cutting costs will be easier if people buy into the decision rather than being handed orders. Instead of gathering ideas by e-mail, the boss should call a meeting so that people can brainstorm, teaching each other why specific strategies will or won't be easy for their units to implement.

Reply to your boss's e-mail request. Instead of suggesting specific ways to cut costs, persuade the boss to have a meeting where everyone can have input and be part of the decision.

12.14   Asking for Volunteers

You have an executive position with one of the major employers in town. (Pick a business, nonprofit organization, or government office you know something about.) Two years ago, your company "adopted" a local school. You've provided computers and paid for Internet access; a small number of workers have signed up to be mentors. Today you get a call from the school's principal, a friend of yours.

Principal: I'd like to talk to you about the mentoring program. You're providing some mentors, and we're grateful for them, but we need ten times that number.

You: [You wince. This program has not been one of your successes.] I know that part of the program hasn't worked out as well as we hoped it would. But people are really busy here. Not all that many people have two or three hours a week to spend with a kid.

Principal: So you think the time it takes is really the problem.

You: [Maybe your friend will appreciate that you can't force people to do this.] Pretty much.

Principal: Do you think people would be willing to be mentors if we could find a way for it to take less time?

You: Maybe. [You sense that a hook is coming, and you're wary.]

Principal: Your people spend a lot of time on e-mail, don't they?

You: Yes. Two to three hours a day, for most of them.

Principal: What if we created a new mentoring structure, where people just e-mailed their mentees instead of meeting with

them? That way they could still provide advice and support, but they could do it at any time of the day. And it wouldn't have to take long.

You: [This sounds interesting.] So people would just have e-mail conversations. That would be a lot easier, and we'd get more people. But can they really have a relationship if they don't meet the kids?

Principal: Maybe we could have a picnic or go to a game a couple of times a year so people could meet face-to-face.

You: And all the kids have computers?

Principal: Not necessarily at home. But they all have access to e-mail at school. Writing e-mail to professionals will also give them more practice and more confidence. People like to get e-mail.

You: Not when they get 200 messages a day, they don't.

Principal: Well, our kids aren't in that category. What do you say?

You: I think it will work. Let's try it.

Principal: Great. Just send me a list of the people who are willing to do this, and we'll match them up with the kids. We'd like to get this started as soon as possible.

Write an e-mail message to all employees asking them to volunteer, while you're thinking about it right now.

12.15 Persuading the CEO to Attend Orientation

As the Director of Education and Training of your organization, you run orientation sessions for new hires. You're planning next quarter's session (new quarters start in January, April, July, and October) for a big group of new college graduates. You'd really like the organization's president and CEO to come in and talk to the group for at least 15 minutes. Probably most of the employees have seen the CEO, but they haven't had any direct contact. The CEO could come any time during the three-day session. Speaking just before or after lunch would be ideal, because then the CEO could also come to lunch and talk informally with at least a few people. Next best would be speaking just before or after either the midmorning or the midafternoon break. But the CEO is busy, and you'll take what you can get.

As your instructor directs,

a. Assume that your instructor is your CEO, and send an e-mail message persuading him or her to come to orientation.

b. Send an e-mail message to your instructor, asking him or her to address new members of a campus organization.

c. Address the CEO of your college or your workplace, asking him or her to speak to new employees.

As your instructor directs,

In 12.16 through 12.19,

a. Create a document or presentation to achieve the goal.

b. Write a memo to your instructor describing the situation at your workplace and explaining your rhetorical choices (medium, strategy, content selection, tone, wording, graphics or document design, and so forth).

12.16   Recommending a Co-Worker for a Bonus or an Award

Recommend someone at your workplace for a bonus or an award. The award can be something bestowed by the organization itself ("Employee of the Month," "Dealership of the Year," and so forth), or it can be a community or campus award ("Business Person of the Year," "Volunteer of the Year," an honorary degree, and so forth).

12.17   Justifying Your Position

Organizations facing downsizing have to decide which positions to keep and which to cut. Imagine that your organization is facing financial problems and that your supervisor, who wants to keep you, has asked you to draft something explaining why your position should be retained and why you are the best person to keep in the position. Create a memo or presentation to do the job.

Hints:

- Show how you contribute to the unit's and the organization's goals.
- Write your memo in the third person, so that your supervisor can send it upward without having to revise it.

12.18   Changing What's Wrong

No workplace is perfect. Pick one of the things you'd like to change about your workplace, identify the decision maker(s), and create a memo or presentation to start the persuasion process.

12.19   Asking for More Resources for Your Unit

Write a memo or prepare a presentation to persuade your organization to give more resources to your unit.

Hints:

- Who in the organization decides the level of resources your unit receives? What are the values of that person or group?
- How much do the decision makers know about your unit? How much evidence do you need to provide about your contribution to organization goals?
- What kind of evidence is most persuasive in your organization? Should you talk about customers or clients? About internal clients? Give numbers?
- Will you be more persuasive if you ask for funds to take on new tasks, or argue that additional resources will help you do current tasks better?

12.20   Persuading Guests to Allow Extra Time for Checkout

Your hotel has been the headquarters for a convention, and on Sunday morning you're expecting 5,000 people to check out before noon. You're staffing the checkout desk to capacity, but if everyone waits till 11:30 to check out, things will be a disaster.

So you want to encourage people to allow extra time. And they don't have to stand in line at all: by 4 AM, you'll put a statement of current charges under each guest's door. If that statement is correct and the guest is leaving the bill on the credit card used at check-in, the guest can just leave the key in the room and leave. You'll mail a copy of the final bill together with any morning charges by the end of the week.

Write a one-page message that can be put on pillows when the rooms are made up Friday and Saturday nights.

12.21   Asking for a Flexible Work Arrangement

Write a memo to your supervisor, requesting that you be allowed a flexible work arrangement in which you work part-time, do some or all of your work at home, or a combination of the two. Consider your work requirements, and identify which of them do not require your physical presence. In the case of part-time work, consider which of your duties you should retain, and how the remainder should be addressed. Explain how you will be able to demonstrate that you can work at least as effectively under the new arrangements, and how you can continue to demonstrate your dedication to your job. Your supervisor will have to be able to justify this arrangement to his or her own boss.

12.22 Convincing a Member to Become Active Again

In every organization, one of the ongoing problems is convincing inactive members to become active again. Sometimes members become inactive because of short-term pressures. Sometimes they are offended by something the organization has done or not done. Sometimes they fall through the cracks and are not included in events. Whatever the reason, once they've become less active, it's psychologically easy for them to drop out entirely. Persuading these members to become active again is important. Because they once supported the organization, it may be easier to persuade them than to seek new members. And if they remain disenchanted with the organization, they may convince other people that the organization has little to offer.

As your instructor directs,

a. Write to someone you know well, urging him or her to become active in the organization again.

b. Write notes for a phone conversation or meeting with your friend.

c. Join with a small group of students to write a form letter to go to inactive members in an organization.

d. Write a memo to your instructor explaining your audience analysis and your choice of strategy and appeals.

Hints:

- Pick a campus, professional, civic, social, or religious organization you know well.

- Be specific about what the organization is doing now, how readers can benefit from it, and why the organization needs them.

- If your audience objects to specific things the organization has done or not done, respond to these concerns in your message. Did a misunderstanding occur? Is change already under way? Is change possible if enough people (like your audience, perhaps) work for it?

- What are your audience's priorities? Can you show that this organization will help your audience meet its needs?

12.23 Requesting More Funds for the Writing Center

State University is facing major budget cuts. A popular idea is to reduce or eliminate funding for the Writing Center. As the Center's director, you're horrified by these ideas.

The Writing Center offers free tutoring in writing to any student or faculty member on campus. Your emphasis is not on fixing an individual paper, but on helping the writer develop strategies that he or she can use not only in this paper but in everything he or she writes.

The services you offer help students do better in classes. Your help is particularly important when budget cuts are leading to larger classes, so that faculty spend less time with each student. Furthermore, your operation is really quite efficient. You only have one paid regular faculty member on your staff; the rest are graduate teaching assistants (who are paid much less than faculty) or undergraduate peer tutors. Finally, the dollars involved aren't that great. Cutting the Center's budget in half would mean you would have to turn away most students. Yet the dollars are small in comparison with the budgets of large departments.

As your instructor directs,

a. Write a memo to all faculty urging them to support full funding for the Writing Center.

b. Write a news release for the campus newspaper about the problem.

c. Identify the person or group on your campus with the power to make budget decisions, and write to that group urging that it support a Writing Center on your campus. Use information about the center and the fiscal situation that fits your community college, college, or university.

Hints:

- Visit the Writing Center on campus to get information about its hours and policies. Sign up for an appointment. What happens in a session? What parts are especially helpful?

- Be sure to prove and limit your claims. Even if the Center is fully funded, some students will be turned away. Even if its funding is increased, not everyone will write well.

- Be sure to use you-attitude and to make sure that the writing in your message is a good advertisement for your own writing skills.

12.24 Handling a Sticky Recommendation

As a supervisor in a state agency, you have a dilemma. You received this e-mail message today:

From: John Inoye, Director of Personnel, Department of Taxation

Subject: Need Recommendation for Peggy Chafez

Peggy Chafez has applied for a position in the Department of Taxation. On the basis of her application and interview, she is the leading candidate. However, before I offer the job to her, I need a letter of recommendation from her current supervisor.

Could you please let me have your evaluation within a week? We want to fill the position as quickly as possible.

Peggy has worked in your office for 10 years. She designed, writes, and edits a monthly statewide newsletter that your office puts out; she designed and maintains the department Web site. Her designs are creative; she's a very hard worker; she seems to know a lot about computers.

However, Peggy is in many ways an unsatisfactory staff member. Her standards are so high that most people find her intimidating. Some find her abrasive. People have complained to you that she's only interested in her own work; she seems to resent requests to help other people with projects. And yet both the newsletter and the Web page are projects that need frequent interaction. She's out of the office a lot. Some of that is required by her job (she takes the newsletters to the post office, for example), but some people don't like the fact that she's out of the office so much. They also complain that she doesn't return voice-mail and e-mail messages.

You think managing your office would be a lot smoother if Peggy weren't there. You can't fire her: state employees' jobs are secure once they get past the initial six-month probationary period. Because of budget constraints, you can hire new employees only if vacancies are created by resignations. You feel that it would be pretty easy to find someone better.

If you recommend that John Inoye hire Peggy, you will be able to hire someone you want. If you recommend that John hire someone else, you may be stuck with Peggy for a long time.

As your instructor directs,

a. Write an e-mail message to John Inoye.
b. Write a memo to your instructor listing the choices you've made and justifying your approach.

Hints:

- Polarization may make this dilemma more difficult than it needs to be. What are your options? Consciously look for more than two.
- Is it possible to select facts or to use connotations so that you are truthful but still encourage John to hire Peggy? Is it ethical? Is it certain that John would find Peggy's work as unsatisfactory as you do? If you write a strong recommendation and Peggy doesn't do well at the new job, will your credibility suffer? Why is your credibility important?

12.25 Persuading Tenants to Follow the Rules

As resident manager of a large apartment complex, you receive free rent in return for collecting rents, doing simple maintenance, and enforcing the complex's rules. You find the following notice in the files:

Some of you are failing to keep any kind of standard of sanitation code, resulting in the unnecessary cost on our part to hire exterminators to rid the building of roaches.

Our leases state breach of contract in the event that you are not observing your responsibility to keep your apartment clean.

We are in the process of making arrangements for an extermination company to rid those apartments that are experiencing problems. Get in touch with the manager no later than 10 PM Monday to make arrangements for your apartment to be sprayed. It is a fast, odorless operation. You are also required to put your garbage in plastic bags. Do not put loose garbage or garbage in paper bags in the dumpster, as this leads to rodent or roach problems.

Should we in the course of providing extermination service to the building find that your apartment is a source of roaches, then you will be held liable for the cost incurred to rid your apartment of them.

The message is horrible. The notice lacks you-attitude, and it seems to threaten anyone who asks to have his or her apartment sprayed.

The annual spraying scheduled for your complex is coming up. Under the lease, you have the right to enter apartments once a year to spray. However, for spraying to be fully effective, residents must empty the cabinets, remove kitchen drawers, and put all food in the refrigerator. People and pets need to leave the apartment for about 15 minutes while the exterminator sprays.

Tell residents about the spraying. Persuade them to prepare their apartments to get the most benefit from it, and persuade them to dispose of food waste quickly and properly so that the bugs don't come back.

Hints:

- What objections may people have to having their apartments sprayed for bugs?
- Why don't people already take garbage out promptly and wrap it in plastic? How can you persuade them to change their behavior?
- Analyze your audience. Are most tenants students, working people, or retirees? What tone would be most effective for this group?

12.26   Evaluating the Persuasion on Social Networking Sites

Some companies, nonprofit organizations, and government agencies use public community sites such as MySpace.com and YouTube.com as advertising venues. In addition to purchasing traditional ads, they create and maintain "personal" profiles, media, and other resources designed to market to the people who use those sites.

As your instructor directs,

a.   Log on to www.MySpace.com or www.YouTube.com and locate an example of this type of advertising (see sidebar on page 408 for hints). Evaluate the persuasive strategies that the advertisements employ. Then compose an e-mail to the organization that's maintaining the ad and suggest improvements to their message. Be sure to identify any ethical challenges you see in their message, and recommend ways for them to improve.

b.   Write a memo to your instructor describing the process you used to make your recommendations.

Be sure to describe and evaluate the response you receive to your e-mail.

Hints:

- You can find this type of marketing on MySpace or YouTube by searching for profiles, blogs, channels, and other media that reference current films, advertising campaigns, or political campaigns.
- Who is the target audience for the ad? Write to the people who have listed this ad as "friends" or who have left comments on it. Collect their opinions to provide data for your evaluations, and to provide evidence for your recommendations.
- Examine other persuasive messages linked to the ads you find. For example, if you find a MySpace page for a character from a movie, look up the official movie site, the trailer, and advertising related to the film.

12.27   Getting Permission from Parents for a School Project

As part of a community cleanup program, all public-school students will spend the afternoon of the second Friday of April picking up trash. Younger students will pick up trash on school grounds, in parks, and in parking lots; older students will pick up trash downtown. Schoolteachers will supervise the students; where necessary, school buses will transport them. After students are finished, they'll return to their school's playground, where they'll be supervised until the end of the school day. Each school will maintain a study hall for any students whose parents do not give them permission to participate. Trash bags and snacks have been donated by local merchants.

Write a one-page cover letter that students can take home to their parents telling them about the project and

persuading them to sign the necessary permission form. You do not need to create the permission form, but do refer to it in your letter.

Hints:

- What objections may parents have? How can you overcome these?
- Where should parents who drive their kids to school pick them up?
- Should students wear their normal school clothing?
- When must the form be returned? Who gets it?
- Whom can parents call if they have questions before they sign the form?

12.28   Asking an Instructor for a Letter of Recommendation

You're ready for the job market, transfer to a four-year college, or graduate school, and you need letters of recommendation.

As your instructor directs,

a. Assume that you've orally asked an instructor for a recommendation, and he or she has agreed to write one. "Why don't you write up something to remind me of what you've done in the class? Tell me what else you've done, too. And tell me what they're looking for. Be sure to tell me when the letter needs to be in and to whom it goes."

b. Assume that you've been unable to talk with the instructor whose recommendation you want. When you call, no one answers the phone; you stopped by once and no one was in. Write asking for a letter of recommendation.

c. Assume that the instructor is no longer on campus. Write him or her a letter asking for a recommendation.

Hints:

• Be detailed about the points you'd like the instructor to mention.

• How well will this instructor remember you? How much detail about your performance in his or her class do you need to provide?

• Specify the name and address of the person to whom the letter should be written; specify when the letter is due. If there's an intermediate due date (for example, if you must sign the outside of the envelope to submit the recommendation to law school), say so.

12.29   Writing a Performance Appraisal for a Member of a Collaborative Group

During your collaborative writing group meetings, keep a log of events. Record specific observations of both effective and ineffective things that group members do. Then evaluate the performance of the other members of your group. (If there are two or more other people, write a separate appraisal for each of them.)

In your first paragraph, summarize your evaluation. Then in the body of your memo, give the specific details that led to your evaluation by answering the following questions:

• What specifically did the person do in terms of the task? Brainstorm ideas? Analyze the information? Draft the text? Suggest revisions in parts drafted by others? Format the document or create visuals? Revise? Edit? Proofread? (In most cases, several people will have done each of these activities together. Don't overstate what any one person did.) What was the quality of the person's work?

• What did the person contribute to the group process? Did he or she help schedule the work? Raise or

resolve conflicts? Make other group members feel valued and included? Promote group cohesion? What roles did the person play in the group?

Support your generalizations with specific observations. The more observations you have and the more detailed they are, the better your appraisal will be.

As your instructor directs,

a. Write a midterm performance appraisal for one or more members of your collaborative group. In each appraisal, identify the two or three things the person should try to improve during the second half of the term.

b. Write a performance appraisal for one or more members of your collaborative group at the end of the term. Identify and justify the grade you think each person should receive for the portion of the grade based on group process.

c. Give a copy of your appraisal to the person about whom it is written.

12.30   Evaluating P.S.'s

Evaluate the following P.S.'s. Will they motivate readers to read the whole messages if readers turn to them first? Do they create a strong ending for those who have already read the message?

1. P.S. It only takes <u>one</u> night's stay in a hotel you read about here, <u>one</u> discounted flight, <u>one</u> budget-priced cruise, or <u>one</u> low-cost car rental to make mailing back your Subscription Certificate well worth it.

P.P.S. About your free gift! Your risk-free subscription to CONSUMER REPORTS TRAVEL LETTER comes with a remarkable 314-page book as a FREE GIFT.

2. P.S. Help spread the tolerance message by using your personalized address labels on all your correspondence. And remember, you will receive a free *Teaching Tolerance* magazine right after your tax-deductible contribution arrives.

3. P.S. Every day brings more requests like that of Mr. Agyrey-Kwakey—for our "miracle seeds." And it's urgent that we respond to the emergency in Malaysia and Indonesia by replanting those forests destroyed by fire. Please send your gift today and become a

partner with us in these innovative projects around the world.

4. P.S. Even as you read this letter, a donated load of food waits for the ticket that will move it to America's hungry. Please give today!

12.31   Evaluating Sales and Fund-Raising Messages

Collect the sales and fund-raising messages that come to you, your co-workers, landlord, neighbors, or family. Use the following questions to evaluate each package:

- What mode does the opener use? Is it related to the rest of the message? How good is the opener?
- What central selling point or common ground does the message use?
- What kinds of proof does the message use? Is the logic valid? What questions or objections are not answered?
- How does the message create emotional appeal?
- Is the style effective?
- Does the close tell people what to do, make action easy, give a reason for acting promptly, and end with a positive picture?
- Does the message use a P.S.? How good is it?
- Is the message visually attractive? Why or why not?
- What other items besides the letter or e-mail are in the package?

As your instructor directs,

a. Share your analysis of one or more messages with a small group of your classmates.

b. Analyze one message in a presentation to the class. Make overhead transparencies or photocopies of the message to use as a visual aid in your presentation.

c. Analyze one message in a memo to your instructor. Provide a copy or photocopy of the message along with your memo.

d. With several other students, write a group memo or report analyzing one part of the message (e.g., openers) or one kind of letter (e.g., political messages, organizations fighting hunger, etc.). Use at least 10 messages for your analysis if you look at only one part; use at least 6 messages if you analyze one kind of message. Provide copies or photocopies as an appendix to your report.

12.32   Creating a Web Site

The Internet enables individuals and organizations to sell products, services, and causes. The cost can be much lower than that of other forms of marketing and, because the consumer chooses to go to the page and can interact with the material, Web pages may create a more positive response than other forms of marketing.

Create a Web site to sell a product or service, or to raise funds for an organization or candidate. Include persuasive material to catch your readers' attention, so that they are motivated to explore the site. Provide both a "snail mail" address to which funds can be sent and a form on which people can buy or contribute online by entering their credit card numbers. At the bottom of each page, put the creation/update date and your name and e-mail address.

As your instructor directs,

a. Turn in printed copies of the pages in your site. On a separate page, give the URLs for any links.

b. Turn in the electronic files on a CD, or submit the URL for your site to your instructor via e-mail.

c. Write a memo to your instructor (1) identifying the audience for whom the site is designed, and explaining (2) the search strategies you used to find materials on this topic, (3) why you chose the information you've included, and (4) why you chose the layout and graphics you've used.

d. Present your site to the class in an oral presentation.

Hints:

- Pick a product, service, candidate, or organization you know something about.
- Divide information logically over several pages.
- Interest readers so that they will stay with your site as long as possible.
- Include links to sites sponsored by other organizations only if they support your purposes.
- Offer a reason for people to return to your site after their initial visit.

12.33　Creating a Brochure

Create a brochure for a campus group or a nonprofit organization. Turn in two copies of your brochure and a memo to your instructor explaining your choices for strategy, content, and design. Would this brochure be part of a series? What are the purposes of the brochure? Who are the audiences? Where will the brochure be physically available? What is your central selling point? Why did you choose it? Why did you choose to be more or less formal, more or less complete, and so forth? Explain your choices for strategy, content, wording, layout, visuals (if any), and color (if any).

12.34　Writing a Fund-Raising Appeal

Write a 2½- to 4-page letter to raise money from *new donors* for an organization you support. You must use a real organization, but it does not actually have to be conducting a fund-raising drive now. Assume that your letter would have a reply card and postage-paid envelope. You do NOT have to write these, but DO refer to them in your letter.

Options for organizations include

- Tax-deductible charitable organizations—churches; synagogues; hospitals; groups working to feed, clothe, and house poor people.
- Lobbying groups—Mothers Against Drunk Driving, the National Abortion Rights Action League, the National Rifle Association, groups working against nuclear weapons, etc.

- Groups raising money to fight a disease or fund research.
- Colleges trying to raise money for endowments, buildings, scholarships, faculty salaries.
- Athletic associations raising money for scholarships, equipment, buildings, facilities.

For this assignment, you may also use groups which do not regularly have fund-raising drives but which may have special needs. Perhaps a school needs new uniforms for its band or an automatic timing device for its swimming pool. Perhaps a sorority or fraternity house needs repairs, remodeling, or expansion.

12.35　Writing a Fund-Raising Letter for a Political Candidate

One of the problems in running for office is financing the campaign. Direct mail is a primary means of raising money. A letter can give far more information about a candidate's views than a TV or radio spot; unlike those media, it can target a specific group of voters. For presidential elections, direct mail is essential: candidates must demonstrate national support to qualify for federal matching funds.

Choose a real candidate and write a letter to raise funds for him or her. Use real information about the candidate's positions and the issues in the race. Let readers know ways to help the campaign instead of or in addition to giving money. Assume that your letter would have a reply card and postage-paid envelope. You do NOT have to write these, but DO refer to them in your letter.

Choose a target audience that would be likely to support this candidate. In a memo to your instructor, describe the audience and explain your decisions about the content to include.

Hints:

- Read newspapers and pick up the candidate's literature to find out where the candidate stands on the issues. The League of Women Voters can help you find each candidate's headquarters. Read the candidate's Web site.
- Talk to some of the people who live in the district to see what their concerns are. Read material from other candidates so you'll know what you have to combat.

12.36　Attracting People to Your State, Province, or Country

Create a brochure or letter to attract people to your state, province, or country. Rather than trying to cover an entire state, province, or country, you may want to focus on one region, city, or tourist attraction. Possible audiences and purposes include the following:

a. Persuade people with high-tech skills to work in your state, province, or country.

b. Persuade growing businesses to move to your state, province, or country.

c. Persuade movie and TV producers to film in your state, province, or country.

d. Persuade retirees to move to your state, province, or country.

e. Persuade travelers to vacation in your state, province, or country.

12.37   Proposing a Prize for Innovation

Research and innovation are expensive prospects. Prizes are one tool that some companies and nonprofit organizations are using to solve tough problems without investing in extra in-house infrastructure. For example, the X-Prize Foundation gave $10 million in 2004 to the first team to build and test a reusable spacecraft. However, the same principle can be applied to smaller problems.

Write a letter to an organization, identifying a problem that they face and proposing a prize-based solution. Detail the nature of the problem (including a description of why it might be prohibitively difficult to solve in-house), identify potential prizes the organization might offer, and describe the method by which they could advertise and administer the contest.

Hints:

- Small businesses might offer goods or services as prizes, while nonprofit organizations or government agencies could reward prize winners with public recognition.
- Remember to treat this letter as a persuasive message: choose the best method to persuade your target audience; explain the problem and your proposed solution in simple, direct language; and anticipate any objections to your proposal.

This exercise based on David Wessel, "Prizes for Solutions to Problems Play Valuable Role in Innovation," *Wall Street Journal*, January 25, 2007, A6.

12.38   Combining Charitable Giving with Marketing

When Crate & Barrel, the upscale furniture retailer, set out to support education with donations, they didn't just give money to needy schools. Instead, they sent out coupons in their mailers, inviting their customers to use www.DonorsChoose.org to decide how and where Crate & Barrel would donate its money. Their customers responded enthusiastically to the program—and to Crate & Barrel.

Write a letter to a local business or organization recommending a similar program that combines charitable giving with a marketing opportunity. Detail the benefits to the organization, the benefits to the organization(s) receiving funds, and the process(es) by which they could ensure their customers' involvement.

Hints:

- Talk to a representative from the business you're targeting to find out what types of charitable giving they currently support.

- Look at targetable donation sites such as www.DonorsChoose.org, www.Kiva.org, www.ModestNeeds.org, and www.GlobalGiving.org for ideas about the types of charitable projects that your proposed program might fund.
- It might be easier to persuade businesses to support causes close to home. So, ask locally: many charities and nonprofits maintain lists to those Web sites of worthwhile causes in your local community.

This exercise based on Emily Steel, "Novel Program Blends Charity and Marketing," *Wall Street Journal*, December 20, 2006, B1, B5.

12.39   Mosaic Case

"All right. I need everyone in the conference room. Now!" shouted Yvonne across the Communication Department's cubicles.

Trey just glanced at Martina, who was just about to peel open a banana.

"What do you think this is all about?" she asked.

"I have no idea, but I'm sure somehow it'll end in me doing more work," Trey said sardonically.

As Trey and Martina strolled into the conference room, Demetri and Sarah were already taking their seats around the mahogany conference table, where everyone else was already sitting.

"Let's go, let's go. Take a seat," Yvonne said trying to hurry them.

"What's all this commotion about?" asked Sarah.

"Well, I've just finished my meeting with management. We talked about personnel issues and the policy manual."

"Great. They didn't like my design revision, did they? I can't believe this. I spent hours on it! And I have to say, not to toot my own horn or anything, but it looked much better than what was originally distributed to all employees. How could they possibly not like it?" babbled Trey. "I used all of the document design principles I could think of when redesigning. And one more thing . . . ".

"Trey, calm down!" interrupted Yvonne, "They loved it."

"Oh, I thought they would," said Trey half-assured.

"The problem is the Internet," said Yvonne.

"The Internet? You mean they're upset with something I did," asked Sarah, who manages online communications.

"No. They're not mad at any of you. Can you all just calm down for one second and let me explain?! Geesh!" said Yvonne.

"Sorry," a few of them mumbled in unison.

"So here's the deal. Management is upset with Internet usage at headquarters and in our stores. You see, employees have been abusing their Internet access. They are forwarding jokes or other junk mail that's clamming up our system, downloading music or other media files for personal use, shopping, surfing the Web, checking sports scores, and sending nonwork-related e-mail using their Mosaic account just to name a few. Now I know that none of the employees in *my* department would be doing these sorts of things . . . " said Yvonne in an accusatory tone.

"Of course not," they replied.

" . . . but there are others out there who are. Your Internet access at Mosaic should be used for doing work that's associated with your job. Do you all remember that new guy in accounting, Steve?" Yvonne asked.

"Oh, I do. He either sent horribly worded e-mails or inappropriate forwards that had nothing to do with work," chimed in Demetri.

"Well, it turns out, there will be a new, new guy in accounting starting next week. Steve has been let go after they found things on his hard drive that I don't even want to mention."

"What's computer use have to do with the policy manual?" asked Trey.

"Good question, Trey," answered Yvonne. "The problem is that currently, and maybe you noticed this as you were redesigning the manual, we have no computer policy in place. Since we can't print the employee policy manual again until next year due to cost, management wants us to send a persuasive memo to all employees, including those who work in our stores, encouraging appropriate use of the Internet at work. They want it to go out as soon as possible. I know we're all busy right now, but Trey and Martina, can you two take on this task?"

"Sure," answered Martina, while she looked across the table and smiled at Trey.

"Great. Thanks for your time. Back to work," said Yvonne.

"Told ya so," Trey said to Martina as they walked out of the conference room.

Take on the communication task given to Trey and Martina. With a partner, conduct research on the Internet where you examine the computer use policies of other organizations or universities. Then write a persuasive memo to all Mosaic employees which persuades them to use their Internet access appropriately. As you draft the memo, determine how to connect with your audience and establish credibility. How can you set guidelines for a policy that will seem fair to all workers? In addition, remember not to criticize or threaten your audience if you want them to take you seriously and respond favorably.

Communicating across Cultures

Learning Objectives

After studying this chapter, you will know:

1 Why global business is important.

2 Why diversity is becoming more important.

3 How our values and beliefs affect our responses to other people.

4 How nonverbal communication impacts cross-cultural communications.

5 How to adapt oral communication for cross-cultural communications.

6 How to adapt written communications for international audiences.

Marketing Disney to China

For many Americans, the mention of Disneyland brings to mind the image of Cinderella's castle, set in a land of fun and fantasy where every child's dreams can be fulfilled. Years of advertising and the continuous introduction of new products have made Disneyland an icon of American family entertainment. But, as officials at the Walt Disney Company have discovered, not everyone shares these cultural associations.

Only six months after Hong Kong Disneyland opened, Disney officials were scrambling to understand why attendance was so low at the new park. They turned to China's travel industry for answers, and Chinese travel agents who book tours were blunt in their assessment. Some of these agents believed Disney officials had not tried to understand the local market and Chinese culture.

After the disappointing start at the Hong Kong park, Disney officials were anxious to learn and ready to make changes. Using the travel industry feedback and other market research, Disney developed a new advertising campaign. Original ads had featured an aerial view of the park; new TV spots focused on people and showed guests riding attractions. A new print ad featuring a grandmother, mother, and daughter showed that Disneyland is a place where strong generational boundaries can be relaxed and families can have fun together.

Disney also worked to make visitors more comfortable inside the park. At an attraction offered in three different languages, guests had gravitated toward the shortest line—usually the line for English-speaking guests. Now, three separate signs clearly mark which language will be used to communicate with guests in that line. Greater use of Mandarin-speaking guides, Mandarin reading materials, and Mandarin subtitles helps guests better understand and enjoy shows and attractions. And, additional seating was added in dining areas because Chinese diners take longer to eat than do Americans. Disney is hoping such changes will attract more guests to the Hong Kong park.

"After the disappointing start at the Hong Kong park, Disney officials were anxious to learn and ready to make changes."

Source: Merissa Marr and Geoffrey A. Fowler, "Chinese Lessons for Disney," *Wall Street Journal,* June 12, 2006, B1, B5.

Chapter Outline

Our values, priorities, and practices are shaped by the culture in which we grow up. Understanding other cultures is crucial if you want to sell your products to other cultures in our country, sell to other countries, manage an international plant or office, or work in this country for a multinational company headquartered in another country.

The successful intercultural communicator is

- Aware of the values, beliefs, and practices in other cultures.
- Sensitive to differences among individuals within a culture.
- Aware that his or her preferred values and behaviors are influenced by culture and are not necessarily "right."
- Sensitive to verbal and nonverbal behavior.
- Flexible and open to change.

The first step in understanding another culture is to realize that it may do things very differently, and that the difference is not bad or inferior. The second step is understanding that people within a single culture differ.

When pushed too far, the kinds of differences summarized in this chapter can turn into stereotypes, which can be just as damaging as ignorance. Psychologists have shown that stereotypes have serious consequences and that they come into play even when we don't want them to. Asking African American students to identify their race before answering questions taken from the Graduate Record Examination, the standardized test used for admission to graduate schools, cut in half the number of items they got right. Similarly, asking students to identify their sex at the beginning of Advanced Placement (AP) calculus tests, used to give high school students college credits, lowered the scores of women. If the sex question were moved to the end of the test, about 5% more women would receive AP credit.[1]

Don't try to memorize the material in this chapter as a rigid set of rules. Instead, use the examples to get a sense for the kinds of things that differ from one culture to another. Test these generalizations against your experience. When in doubt, ask.

Global Business

As we saw in Chapter 1, exports are essential both to the success of individual businesses and to a country's economy as a whole. Most major businesses operate globally, and an increasing share of profits comes from outside the headquarters country. McDonald's has restaurants in over 100 countries and earns more than 66% of its income outside the United States. 3M has 61% of its sales internationally; Google 47%. Starbucks is expanding into Brazil, Egypt, and Russia, giving it sales in 40 countries. Eventually the company plans to have half its stores outside the United States. Wal-Mart's international stores earn "only" 20% of the company's total sales. However, if the international operations were an independent chain, it would be the world's fourth-largest retailer.[2]

Many companies—even service businesses—depend on vendors or operations in other countries. These international operations help companies spend more time with customers, focus more on innovation, and fund projects that otherwise would have been unaffordable. IBM has 43,000 employees in India staffing data centers, call centers, software development, and research. Over a billion dollars of finance and accounting jobs are being performed by India's Genpact for Wachovia Corporation. Eli Lilly does 20% of its chemistry work in China and is performing clinical trials in Brazil, Russia, China, and India.[3]

As they expand globally, US retailers are catering to local tastes and customs. Wal-Mart stores in China sell live fish from fish tanks and live tortoises and snakes; Johnson's Baby Oil is stocked next to moisturizers containing sheep placenta, a native wrinkle "cure." Wal-Mart lures customers on foot or bikes with free shuttle buses and home deliveries for large items. Perhaps the biggest change is Wal-Mart's acceptance of organized labor in China; in July 2006 it accepted its first union ever into its stores. Tommy Hilfiger made different changes as it opened its high-end stores in Europe. The company's signature cotton knit sweaters don't sell well in Europe, where men prefer wool sweaters, so Hilfiger began offering lamb's wool sweaters. Underwear packages received more seductive pictures. Baggy jeans, popular in the United States, were replaced with slimmer silhouettes to cater to European tastes.[4]

When plants, stores, and offices move overseas, people follow—top executives as well migrant workers. After the 2000 dot-com crash, many companies outsourced departments such as software development, data analysis, and research. Now top executives are also being relocated. Cisco Systems, a 50,000-person employer, seeks to locate 20% of senior managers at their Globalization Center in Bangalore, India, by 2010. The executives will represent the best talent from San Jose, California, and Bangalore. IBM currently has 150 executives working and living overseas including 35 in India and 89 in China. At Procter & Gamble, 17 of the top 30 executives have had international assignments. Such assignments give companies a pool of executives with intercultural skills and global awareness.[5]

For their own careers, managers often find they need international experience if they want top-level jobs. Neville Isdell, chief executive officer of Coca-Cola, rose in that company by helping Coke enter markets in India, eastern Europe, and elsewhere. After that experience, Isdell ran Coca-Cola Beverages, a European bottler. Doug Lipp built a successful career on his love of the Japanese language. Lipp studied Japanese in college, and coupled his language skill with a college internship at Disney to land a job in which he helped to open Tokyo Disney. He later moved to higher-level jobs with Disney before starting his own company.[6] Siemens, a German engineering and electronics firm, employs mostly Germans in its top management and local-country natives in its many overseas facilities (for example, American managers of its American business units). English has become the company's standard working language.[7]

Beyond Stereotypes

Learning about different cultures is important for understanding the different kinds of people we work with. However, leadership coaches Keith Caver and Ancella Livers caution that people are individuals, not just representatives of a cultural group. Based on their work with African American executives and middle managers, Caver and Livers have found that coworkers sometimes treat these individuals first as representatives of black culture, and only second as talented and experienced managers.

As an example, Caver and Livers cite the all-too-common situation of a newly hired black manager who participates in a management development activity. The new manager is prepared to answer questions about her area of business expertise, but the only questions directed toward her are about "diversity." African American clients of Caver and Livers have complained that they are often called upon to interpret the behavior of famous black Americans such as Clarence Thomas or Jesse Jackson, and they wonder whether their white colleagues would feel their race qualifies them to interpret the deeds of famous white Americans.

In this example, stereotypes make well-intentioned efforts at communication offensive. To avoid such offense, consider not only culture, but also people's individual qualities and their roles and experiences. A person who communicates one way in the role of son or daughter may communicate very differently as engineer or client.

Adapted from Keith A. Caver and Ancella B. Livers, "Dear White Boss," *Harvard Business Review* 80, no. 11 (November 2002): 76–81.

Let's Be Diverse

Some organizations know the importance of including diversity in their workforce. For example, IBM and Harley-Davidson have benefited by being inclusive.

IBM

IBM has extended diversity programs into all countries where it does business, and in so doing has increased its bottom line. Although not all countries are as open to diversity initiatives as the United States, IBM has continued its programs by seeking the best talent for positions. They explain to employees that, "We have corporate values that dictate how we're going to run business—and if that creates discomfort for you, you shouldn't work here." As a result, women and minorities are becoming managers for IBM in countries and positions where they have not had the opportunity before. For example, in South Africa, a black South African man is the general manager and in northeast Europe, a woman heads the operations.

Harley-Davidson, Inc.

Harley-Davidson, Inc. understands the importance of attracting minority employees and customers. The company has increased the number of women and minorities in all positions, including management, since 1995; the number of women and minorities holding vice-president, general manager, or senior manager positions is at 25%. As a result, Harley-Davidson's client base has also expanded past the traditional white male.

What is your employer's stance on diversity issues?

Adapted from Carol Hymowitz, "Diversity in a Global Economy—Ways Some Firms Get It Right," *Wall Street Journal*, November 16, 2005, B4.

A survey of multinational companies by Mercer Human Resource Consulting found that firms were increasing international assignments, and that more of those assignments were going to women. Cross-cultural training for the assignments was provided by 60% of the companies, but once abroad employees generally had to fend for themselves, including finding their own housing.[8]

The executives join a host of migrant workers already abroad. Migrant workers benefit the economies of both host and home countries. The money sent home by expatriate workers, more than $160 billion a year, is far more than the total aid spent by the developed world for developing countries (about $100 billion a year). Thus the money sent home is one of the major drivers of international development. India and China provide one-quarter of the global migrant population, and their contributions are significant. Indian managers and accountants are increasingly running businesses in the Gulf. The Chinese are a particularly strong presence in Africa.[9]

Thomas Friedman, Pulitzer Prize author and *New York Times* columnist, uses the metaphor of a flat world to describe the increasing globalization. In *The World Is Flat: A Brief History of the Twenty-First Century*, he says,

> What the flattening of the world means is that we are now connecting all the knowledge centers on the planet together into a single global network, which—if politics and terrorism do not get in the way—could usher in an amazing era of prosperity, innovation, and collaboration, by companies, communities, and individuals.[10]

Diversity in the United States and Canada

Even if you stay in the United States and Canada, you'll work with people whose backgrounds differ from yours. Residents of small towns and rural areas may have different notions of friendliness than do people from big cities. Californians may talk and dress differently than people in the Midwest. The cultural icons that resonate for baby boomers may mean little to members of Generation Y.

The last two decades have seen a growing emphasis on diversity, with more and more women and people of color joining the US workforce. But people outside the power structure have always worked. In the past, such people (including non-elite white males) may have been relegated to low-status and low-paying jobs, to agricultural or domestic work, or to staff rather than line work and management. This deployment is changing.

"Diversity" in the workplace comes from many sources:

- Gender.
- Race and ethnicity.
- Regional and national origin.
- Social class.
- Religion.
- Age.
- Sexual orientation.
- Physical ability.

Many young Americans are already multicultural. According to 2005 US census figures, almost 40% of Americans aged 15 to 24 are African American, Latino, Asian, or Native American.[11] Some of them are immigrants or descendants of immigrants. In recent years, the largest numbers of immigrants to the United States have come from Mexico, India, China, Philippines, Cuba, Vietnam, Dominican Republic, and Korea.[12] In 2002 Latinos became the largest minority group in the United States. The US Census Bureau predicts

Federal Bureau of Investigations (FBI) Equal Employment Opportunity Statement

We Are Committed to Be an Equal Opportunity Employer

The Federal Bureau of Investigation is an Equal Opportunity Employer. All qualified applicants will receive consideration. Except where otherwise provided by law, selection will be made without regard to, and there will be no discrimination because of race, religion, color, national origin, sex, political affiliations, marital status, nondisqualifying physical or mental disability, age, sexual orientation, membership or nonmembership in an employee organization, or on the basis of personal favoritism or other non-merit factors.

The FBI welcomes and encourages applications from persons with physical and mental disabilities, and will reasonably accommodate the needs of those persons. The decision on granting reasonable accommodation will be on a case-by-case basis. The FBI is firmly committed to satisfying its affirmative obligations under the Rehabilitation Act of 1973, to ensure that persons with disabilities have every opportunity to be hired and advanced on the basis of merit within the FBI.

Quoted from Federal Bureau of Investigation, "We Are Committed to Be an Equal Opportunity Employer," in *Careers: Diversity: Equal Opportunity Employer,* http://www.fbijobs.gov/1114.asp (accessed June 12, 2007).

that by 2050, the non-Hispanic white population will be only 50% of the country's total population.[13]

Bilingual Canada has long compared the diversity of its people to a mosaic. But now immigrants from Italy, Greece, and Hong Kong add their voices to the medley of French, English, and Inuit. Radio station CHIN in Toronto broadcasts in 32 languages.[14] According to 2000 US census figures, about 4.6 million people identified themselves as belonging to more than one race.[15] US Census figures also show that 18.7% of the population nationally and 41.3% in California speak a language other than English at home.[16] In cities such as Los Angeles and San Jose, over half the population speaks a language other than English at home; in El Paso, that percentage is 76.8.[17] Not surprisingly, immigrants' children tend to be more comfortable with English than the immigrants themselves are. Among Hispanics, for example, almost three-quarters speak Spanish as their primary language. Their children are about equally divided between those who use primarily English and those who use both languages equally. By the third generation, most Hispanic Americans are English dominant, though many are bilingual, and many continue to maintain a strong identity with Hispanic culture.[18]

Faced with these figures, organizations are making special efforts to diversify their workforces. Nike recruits minority students on college campuses and offers them summer internships; Clorox partners with professional organizations like the National Black M.B.A. Association. Microsoft has 44 different diversity advisory councils (DACs). The oldest, BAM—Blacks at Microsoft—has 500 members. Four are for employees with disabilities; still others are for employees from specific international regions. In addition to supporting the group members, DACs help recruit and integrate new employees and help Microsoft adapt their communications and products for diverse segments of the global economy.[19]

These companies are smart; new evidence shows that diversity can improve business. Cedric Herring, researcher at the University of Illinois at Chicago, analyzed the relationship between diversity levels and business performance of 250 US businesses. He found a correlation between diversity and business success; companies with high levels of racial and ethic minorities have the highest profits, the highest market shares, and highest number of customers. On the other hand, organizations with low levels of diversity have the lowest profits, the lowest market shares, and the lowest number of customers. Sam Sommers, psychologist at Tufts University, contends that diversity may improve businesses's success because minorities introduce new perspectives and catalyze new thinking among others.[20]

General Mills features a photograph of B. Smith, an African American Martha Stewart, on their cornbread mix packages in their effort to gain more of the cornbread market. The idea to include B. Smith was suggested by African American employees of General Mills to increase appeal to the product's target audience.

Source: Steven Gray, "Betty Crocker Adds B. Smith to Package for Cornbread Mix, and Sales Take Off," *Wall Street Journal,* November 14, 2006, B1.

Ways to Look at Culture

Each of us grows up in a **culture** that provides patterns of acceptable behavior and belief. We may not be aware of the most basic features of our own culture until we come into contact with people who do things differently. If we come from a culture where dogs are pets, that interpretation may seem "natural" until we learn that in other cultures, dogs, like chickens, are raised for food.

As anthropologist Edward Hall first described, we can categorize cultures as high-context or low-context. In **high-context cultures,** most of the information is inferred from the social relationships of the people and the context of a message; little is explicitly conveyed. Chinese, Japanese, Arabic, and Latin American cultures are high-context. In **low-context cultures,** context is less important; most information is explicitly spelled out. German, Scandinavian, and North American cultures are low-context.

High- and low-context cultures value different kinds of communication and have different attitudes toward oral and written communication. As

Figure 13.1   Views of Communication in High- and Low-Context Cultures

	High-context (Examples: Japan, Saudi Arabia)	Low-context (Examples: Germany, North America)
Preferred communication strategy	Indirectness, politeness, ambiguity	Directness, confrontation, clarity
Reliance on words to communicate	Low	High
Reliance on nonverbal signs to communicate	High	Low
Importance of relationships	High	Low
Importance of written word	Low	High
Agreements made in writing	Not binding	Binding
Agreements made orally	Binding	Not binding
Attention to detail	Low	High

Source: Robert T. Moran, Philip R. Harris, and Sarah V. Moran, *Managing Cultural Differences: Global Leadership Strategies for the 21st Century,* 7th ed. (Boston: Elsevier, 2007), 49–52.

Figure 13.2   National Culture, Organizational Culture, and Personal Culture Overlap

Figure 13.1 shows, low-context cultures like those of the United States favor direct approaches and may see indirectness as dishonest or manipulative. The written word is seen as more important than oral statements, so contracts are binding but promises may be broken. Details matter. Business communication practices in the United States reflect these low-context preferences.

The discussion that follows focuses on national and regional cultures. But business communication is also influenced by the organizational culture and by personal culture, such as gender, race and ethnicity, social class, and so forth. As Figure 13.2 suggests, all of these intersect to determine what kind of communication is needed in a given situation. In a study of the leadership styles of African American women executives, Patricia S. Parker found that they tended to share a distinctive style of communication that was open in ways that exposed important issues, invited ideas from others, and was free of "hidden agendas."[21] To the extent that this communication style is unique to this group of executives, it may reflect their cultural experiences as women, as African Americans, and as talented, well-educated managers.

Sometimes one kind of culture may be more important than another. For example, in a study of aerospace engineers in Europe, Asia, and the United States, researchers John Webb and Michael Keene found that the similarities of the professional discourse community outweighed differences in national cultures.[22] Such professional and cultural influences can change over time. A study of medical journal articles published over 65 years found differences in the ways that Spanish, French, and English articles expressed academic conflict: opinions were more indirect in English-language articles and were blunter and more authoritarian in French and Spanish articles. However, the differences among articles decreased over the last few years of the study, as the authors apparently adopted a shared writing style that was "professional, collegial and pragmatic."[23]

Values, Beliefs, and Practices

Values and beliefs, often unconscious, affect our response to people and situations. Most North Americans, for example, value "fairness." "You're not playing fair" is a sharp criticism calling for changed behavior. In some countries, however, people expect certain groups to receive preferential treatment. Most North Americans accept competition and believe that it produces better performance. Many Japanese, however, believe that competition leads to disharmony. US business people believe that success is based on individual achievement and is open to anyone who excels. In England and in France, success is more obviously linked to social class. In Ukraine, social status is important for determining how people interact, so people's titles are significant and

Does the Glass Ceiling Exist?

"**The news:** Men and women have different views on whether women face a 'glass ceiling' in financial professions, according to a survey of 363 financial executives by *CFO* magazine.

"**The numbers:** In the survey, 40% of women said they perceive limits to how far women can rise; only 10% of men believe women face a glass ceiling.

"**The differences:** Two-thirds of women, 66%, said women face one or more obstacles to success in finance, such as a lack of operational experience or an inability to negotiate effectively. But only 38% of men said women face such difficulties. Five times as many women as men said female executives have more trouble gaining the respect and trust of the CEO.

"**The background:** Few women hold top financial jobs in major U.S. corporations, even though women earn more undergraduate business degrees than men. Just 7% of Fortune 500 companies have female CFOs, according to recruiters Heidrick & Struggles International Inc."

Quoted from Jaclyne Badal, "Surveying the Field: Cracking the Glass Ceiling," *Wall Street Journal*, June 19, 2006, B3.

When Communication Styles Conflict

Some cultures differ in their ideas about how businesspeople should communicate. What if you want to close a deal with someone who expects business communications to be flowery or argumentative? If you rarely compose elegant prose, or if you dislike arguments, you may lose the business opportunity unless one of you adapts.

Business professor Nurit Zaidman studied how Israeli and Indian businesspeople handle this type of conflict. About two-thirds of attempts at Israeli-Indian deals fail, even though the countries share a common business language (English). Zaidman interviewed managers from the two countries and studied their written communications. He found cultural differences and, occasionally, creative efforts to bridge the communication gap.

Israeli businesspeople generally prefer communication to be simple and direct, even forceful. Israelis also value treating others as equals. Indian English emphasizes politeness, as shown through long, indirect, and poetic sentences. Another sign of politeness is humility.

The Indian businesspeople often interpreted correspondence from Israelis to be rude, signaling inability to collaborate appropriately. The Israelis were confused by the indirect wording of Indian messages. They felt unsure about what to expect. However, Zaidman also found examples of Israeli businesspeople trying to choose polite and elegant language, and of Indian businesspeople simplifying their style.

Adapted from Nurit Zaidman, "Cultural Codes and Language Strategies in Business Communication," *Management Communication Quarterly* 14, no. 3 (February 2001): 408–41.

Living and working in another country require being sensitive to cultural beliefs and practices. The Japanese holiday Shichi-go-san (seven-five-three) is celebrated on November 15th when boys (ages 3 and 5) and girls (ages 3 and 7) are taken by their parents to a Shinto shrine to give thanks for their health and growth, and to pray for their future. Shichi-go-san dates back to ancient times when the families of samurai and noblemen would mark milestones in their children's growth.

may be long. To address a Ukrainian person politely, one must learn and use the correct titles. When addressing a person of higher rank, a writer must use a formal style to signify respect. Other signals of respect include phrases like *as you may know* to introduce information, signaling that the writer does not presume to be more informed than the reader.[24]

Many people in the United States value individualism. Other countries may value the group. Japan's traditional culture emphasized the group, but there is evidence that this cultural value is changing. According to research and analysis by David Matsumoto, Japanese cultural norms such as the sacrifice of one's personal time for the company, avoidance of disagreements with one's boss, and the favoring of compliance over individual initiative have become part of Japan's business past. Modern business values in Japan place more emphasis on the individual person's goals and accomplishments.[25]

Values and beliefs are influenced by religion. Christianity coexists with a view of the individual as proactive. In some Muslim and Asian countries, however, it is seen as presumptuous to predict the future by promising action by a certain date. The Protestant work ethic legitimizes wealth by seeing it as a sign of divine favor. In other Christian cultures, a simpler lifestyle is considered to be closer to God.

Religion also affects business communication and business life. Observant Muslims, Jews, and Christians observe days of rest and prayer on Friday, Saturday, and Sunday, respectively. During the holy month of Ramadan, Muslims fast from sunup to sundown; scheduling a business luncheon with a Muslim colleague during Ramadan would be inappropriate. A sampling of international holidays, including Ramadan, appears in Figure 13.3.

Figure 13.3   A Sampling of International Holidays

Holiday	Date	Celebrated in	Commemorates
Chinese New Year (Spring Festival)	January or February (date varies)	Countries with Chinese residents	Beginning of lunar new year
Independence Day	March 6	Ghana	1957 independence from Great Britain
St. Patrick's Day	March 17	Ireland	Ireland's patron saint
Cinco de Mayo	May 5	Mexico	1867 victory over the French
St. Jean-Baptiste Day	June 24	Québec province of Canada	Québec's national holiday
Canada Day	July 1	Canada	1867 proclamation of Canada's status as dominion
Bastille Day	July 14	France	1789 fall of the Bastille prison during the French Revolution
Ramadan	Ninth month of lunar year	Countries with Muslim residents	Atonement; fasting from sunup to sundown
Respect for the Aged Day	September 15	Japan	Respect for elderly relatives and friends
Chun Ben	Last week of September	Cambodia, other Buddhist countries	The dead and actions for one's salvation
Yom Kippur	September or October (dates vary)	Countries with Jewish residents	Day of atonement
Diwali	October or November	Countries with Hindu residents	Festival of lights celebrating renewal of life
Guy Fawkes Day	November 5	England	Capture of Guy Fawkes, who plotted to blow up Parliament
Christmas	December 25	Countries with Christian residents	Birth of Jesus
Boxing Day	December 26	British Commonwealth	Tradition of presenting small boxed gifts to service workers

Even everyday practices differ from culture to culture. North Americans and Europeans put the family name last; Asians put it first. North American and European printing moves from top to bottom and from left to right; Arabic reads from right to left, but still from top to bottom. The Chinese language is traditionally written using characters signifying ideas, rather than letters signifying sounds. Opening the Internet to Chinese readers has been challenging because of the need to use the Chinese characters. Internet portal Yahoo gained access to the Chinese market by purchasing Zhou Hongyi's keyword-search firm called 3721 (the name represents ease of use, in the sense of being as easy as "3 times 7 equals 21"). Companies pay 3721 to register their Chinese names as keywords.[26]

Nonverbal Communication

Nonverbal communication—communication that doesn't use words—takes place all the time. Smiles, frowns, who sits where at a meeting, the size of an office, how long someone keeps a visitor waiting—all these communicate pleasure or anger, friendliness or distance, power and status. Most of the time

Mac and PC's Overseas Adventures

"When Apple Inc. wanted to bring its series of 'Mac vs. PC' ads to international markets, it faced a difficult issue: What's funny in one culture can seem ill-mannered in another.

"In the American ads . . . a nerdy PC guy keeps getting trumped by his hip Mac counterpart, who uses pointed banter that demonstrates how Macs are better. In one recent spot, PC is proudly having a camera taped to his head so he can do video chatting—only to discover that Mac already has a built-in camera. . . .

"But in Japanese culture, where direct-comparison ads have long been frowned upon, it's rude to brag about one's strengths. So for Japanese versions of the ads that rolled out last fall, two local comedians from a troupe called the Rahmens made subtle changes to emphasize that Macs and PCs are not that different. Instead of clothes that cast PC clearly as a nerd and Mac as a hipster, PC wears plain office attire and Mac weekend fashion, highlighting the work/home divide between the devices more than personality differences. . . .

"PC's body language is a big source of the humor in Japan: Mac looks embarrassed when the PC touches his shoulder, or hides behind Mac's legs to avoid viruses. . . .

"The international campaigns reflect a growing move by U.S. companies to refine their ad campaigns for overseas markets."

Quoted from Geoffrey A. Fowler, Brian Steinberg, and Aaron O. Patrick, "Mac and PC's Overseas Adventures: Globalizing Apple's Ads Meant Tweaking Characters, Clothing, Body Language," *Wall Street Journal*, March 1, 2007, B1.

we are no more conscious of interpreting nonverbal signals than we are conscious of breathing.

Yet nonverbal signals can be misinterpreted just as easily as can verbal symbols (words). And the misunderstandings can be harder to clear up because people may not be aware of the nonverbal cues that led them to assume that they aren't liked, respected, or approved.

Learning about nonverbal language can help us project the image we want to present and make us more aware of the signals we are interpreting. However, even within a single culture, a nonverbal symbol may have more than one meaning.

Body Language

The Japanese value the ability to sit quietly. They may see the US tendency to fidget and shift as an indication of lack of mental or spiritual balance. Even in North America, interviewers and audiences usually respond negatively to nervous gestures such as fidgeting with a tie or hair or jewelry, tapping a pencil, or swinging a foot.

People use body language to signal their interest level and emotional involvement. A typical posture for a Swedish listener is to fold the arms in front of the torso and to hold the back erect. This position is meant to be a sign of serious, respectful attention. An American speaker might interpret such body language as signaling boredom, annoyance, or disagreement.[27] Americans working in the Middle East are cautioned to avoid pointing their finger at people or showing the soles of their feet when seated. They also need to avoid misreading handholding among Arab men, for whom it is an expression of affection and solidarity.[28]

Eye contact

North American whites see eye contact as a sign of attention; in fact, lack of eye contact is slightly suspect. But in many cultures, dropped eyes are a sign of appropriate deference to a superior. Japanese children are taught to look at the neck. As adults, Japanese show respect by lowering their eyes when speaking to superiors. In some Latin American and African cultures, such as Nigeria, it

These SUBWAY stores in Saudi Arabia and Germany have adapted to an international culture.

is disrespectful for lower-status people to prolong eye contact with their superiors. Similarly, in the United States, staring is considered rude. For the English, however, polite people pay strict attention to speakers and blink their eyes to show understanding. In China, a widening of the eyes shows anger, in the United States—surprise. Among Arab men, eye contact is important; it is considered impolite not to face someone directly.[29] In Muslim countries, women and men are not supposed to have eye contact.

These differences can lead to miscommunication in the multicultural workplace. Superiors may feel that subordinates are being disrespectful when the subordinates are being fully respectful—according to the norms of their culture.

Smiling

The frequency of smiling and the way people interpret smiles may depend on the purpose smiles serve in a particular culture. In the United States, smiling varies from region to region. In Germany, Sweden, and the "less-smiley" US cultures, smiling is more likely to be reserved for close relationships and genuine joy. Frequent smiles in other situations would therefore seem insincere. For other people, including those in Thailand, smiling can be a way to create harmony and make situations pleasant. These people might interpret a lack of smiles to signal a lack of harmony and goodwill. Thais tend to smile in most situations, so the meaning of a smile depends on the context—for example, whether the smiling person is telling a joke or smoothing over difficulties.[30] Greeks may express anger with a smile.[31]

Gestures

Americans sometimes assume that they can depend on gestures to communicate if language fails. But the meanings of gestures vary widely in different cultures. Kissing is usually an affection gesture in the United States but is a greeting gesture in other countries. In Greece, people may nod their heads to signify *no* and shake their heads to signify *yes*.[32]

Gestures that mean approval in the United States may have very different meanings in other countries. The "thumbs up" sign, which means "good work" or "go ahead" in the United States and most of Western Europe, is a vulgar insult in Greece. The circle formed with the thumb and first finger that means *OK* in the United States is obscene in Southern Italy and can mean "you're worth nothing" in France and Belgium.[33]

The V-sign is another gesture with multiple meanings. Made with the palm facing out, it was famously used by Churchill during WWII and by the hippies in the 60s and 70s. Made with the palm facing in, it is the equivalent of giving someone the finger in countries such as the United Kingdom, Ireland, and Australia. An American president made interesting headlines when he inadvertently used the V-sign on a visit to Australia.

Space

Personal space is the distance someone wants between himself or herself and other people in ordinary, nonintimate interchanges. Observation and limited experimentation show that many North Americans, North Europeans, and Asians want a bigger personal space than do many Latin Americans, French, Italians, and Arabs. People who prefer lots of personal space are often forced to accept close contact on a crowded elevator or subway.

Even within a culture, some people like more personal space than do others. In many cultures, people who are of the same age and sex take less personal space than do mixed-age or mixed-sex groups.

Sweatshop Controversies

One of the most recent sweatshop controversies has involved the Bratz dolls, an urban-styled rival to Barbie. Allegedly, employees in Southern China worked 94 hours a week, which greatly exceeded the legal maximum of 36 hours of overtime per month.

Moreover, workers received 17 cents for each doll they made. In the US, each doll sells for around $16 or more. In addition, workers were denied paid sick leave and other benefits according to a US-based China Labor Watch and National Labor Committee reports.

What current policies, laws, and actions exist to ensure proper working conditions for international employees?

Adapted from Associated Press, "Activists Report Harsh Working Conditions at Bratz Dolls Factory in China," *Ponca City News*, December 22, 2006, C4.

Touch

Repeated studies have shown that babies need to be touched to grow and thrive and that older people are healthier both mentally and physically if they are touched. But some people are more comfortable with touch than others. Each kind of person may misinterpret the other. A person who dislikes touch may seem unfriendly to someone who's used to touching. A toucher may seem overly familiar to someone who dislikes touch.

Most parts of North America allow opposite-sex couples to hold hands or walk arm-in-arm in public but frown on the same behavior in same-sex couples. People in some other countries have the opposite expectation: male friends or female friends can hold hands or walk arm-in-arm, but it is slightly shocking for an opposite-sex couple to touch in public.

In US business settings, people generally shake hands when they meet, but little other touching is considered appropriate. In Mexico, greetings may involve greater physical contact. Men may embrace one another, and women may kiss one another. In many European settings, business colleagues may shake hands when they encounter one another throughout the day. In countries along the Mediterranean, hugs and shoulder pats are common as well. In some European countries, greetings include light kisses. The typical pattern is to kiss the person's right cheek and then the left (or to kiss the air near the cheek). In Italy this pattern stops with two kisses; Belgians continue for three, and the French for four.[34]

People who don't know each other well may feel more comfortable with each other if a piece of furniture separates them. For example, a group may work better sitting around a table than just sitting in a circle. Desks can be used as barricades to protect oneself from other people.

Spatial arrangements

In the United States, the size, placement, and privacy of one's office connotes status. Large corner offices have the highest status. An individual office with a door that closes connotes more status than a desk in a common area. Windows also may matter. An office with a window may connote more status than one without.

Time

Differences in time zones complicate international phone calls and video conferences. But even more important are different views of time and attitudes toward time. Organizations in the United States—businesses, government, and schools—keep time by the calendar and the clock. Being "on time" is seen as a sign of dependability. Other cultures may keep time by the seasons, the moon, the sun, internal "body clocks," or a personal feeling that "the time is right."

North Americans who believe that "time is money" are often frustrated in negotiations with people who take a much more leisurely approach. Part of the problem is that people in many other cultures want to establish a personal relationship before they decide whether to do business with each other.

The problem is made worse because various cultures mentally measure time differently. Many North Americans measure time in five-minute blocks. Someone who's five minutes late to an appointment or a job interview feels compelled to apologize. If the executive or interviewer is running half an hour late, the caller expects to be told about the likely delay upon arriving. Some people won't be able to wait that long and will need to reschedule their appointments. But in other cultures, half an hour may be the smallest block of time. To someone who mentally measures time in 30-minute blocks, being

45 minutes late is no worse than being 10 minutes late is to someone who is conscious of smaller units.

Different cultures have different lead times for scheduling events. In some countries, you need to schedule important meetings at least two weeks in advance. In other countries, not only are people not booked up so far in advance, but a date two weeks into the future may be forgotten.

Anthropologist Edward Hall distinguishes between **monochronic cultures,** which focus on clock time, and **polychronic cultures,** which focus on relationships. People in monochronic cultures tend to schedule their time and do one task at a time; people in polychronic cultures tend to want their time unstructured and do multiple tasks at the same time. When US managers feel offended because a Latin American manager also sees other people during "their" appointments, the two kinds of time are in conflict.[35]

Time issues complicate some employees' work schedules. Many workdays can now extend through so many time zones that 18-hours workdays are routine. As a result, employees are losing focus, burning out easily, and interrupting their family time. Unfortunately, the traditional flextime methods do not remedy the problem because calls from around the world can come any time. In response to the growing amount of employee exhaustion, employers are finding new time management solutions. For example, Dow Corning instituted "no-meeting-weeks," which cut all nonessential meetings and travel for one week each quarter. IBM established "ThinkFridays," a block of uninterrupted, free time on Friday afternoons for employees to focus on research, paperwork, and business-related activities other than meetings.[36]

Other Nonverbal Symbols

Many other symbols can carry nonverbal meanings: clothing, colors, age, and height, to name a few.

In North America, certain styles and colors of clothing are considered more "professional" and more "credible." Some clothing denotes not only status but also occupational group. Cowboy boots, firefighter hats, and judicial robes all may, or may not, signal specific occupations. Tool belts, coveralls, hard hats, and stethoscopes may signal broader occupational groupings.

Colors can also carry meanings in a culture. Chinese tradition associates red with good fortune. Korean Buddhists use red to announce death. Black is the color of joy in Japan, the color of death in the United States.[37] White is the color of funerals in eastern countries; in the United States it is the color of brides. UPS found its company color working against it when it entered the Spanish market. The brown trucks that distinguish the delivery company's brand in the United States are not a good image in Spain, where hearses are traditionally brown. When UPS realized its mistake, it altered its uniforms and truck colors in Spain, emphasizing the company logo rather than the color brown.[38]

In the United States, youth is valued. People color their hair and even have face-lifts to look as youthful as possible. In Japan, younger people generally defer to older people. Americans attempting to negotiate in Japan are usually taken more seriously if at least one member of the team is noticeably gray-haired.

Height connotes status in many parts of the world. Executive offices are usually on the top floors; the underlings work below. Even being tall can help a person succeed. A recent study found that white, non-Hispanic males of below-average height earned 10 percent less than males of above-average height. Each additional inch of height was linked to 2.5 percent greater income. Perhaps surprisingly, the measurement that produced this effect was the man's height when he was a teenager. Those who grew later in life did not enjoy the income benefits of greater height. For white women in the study, actual

Thinking Outside the Time Line

To organize a convincing argument, the typical European or North American will develop several points and present a case for them one by one. Negotiating a contract, this person might present a list of terms, such as price, quantity, and delivery date, expecting to discuss each one in turn, moving down the list. This approach seems obvious to a Westerner, because Westerners tend to think sequentially—that is, with ideas moving from a beginning to an end.

The typical Chinese negotiator, in contrast, rarely thinks in terms of a sequence or time line. Rather, the Chinese are more likely to engage in holistic thinking, considering all the details as part of a whole. They want to see a proposal in its full context and are likely to reconsider individual details repeatedly, as part of studying the entire proposal from various angles.

As a result of this difference, Americans negotiating with Chinese often doubt they are making progress. Worse, if they follow a Western-style negotiating strategy, they may make costly concessions. In a negotiation between Tandem Computers and China Telecom, the Tandem sales manager offered to reduce the price by 5 percent in exchange for China Telecom's commitment to sign an order for delivery within one month. The purchasing manager responded that there was no need to rush, but since the price was flexible, the price reduction would be acceptable.

Adapted from John L. Graham and N. Mark Lam, "The Chinese Negotiation," *Harvard Business Review,* October 2003, 82–91.

Wal-Mart is one of many companies that have expanded internationally, not, however, without some difficulty at first. For example, when expanding to China, Wal-Mart enraged consumers when they sold dead fish and meat packaged in Styrofoam, which shoppers saw as old merchandise. Wal-Mart quickly learned to compensate by leaving meat uncovered and installing fish tanks to sell live fish.

Source: Keith Naughton, "The Great Wal-Mart of China," *Newsweek*, October 30, 2006, 50–52.

adult height was associated with greater income. The researchers lacked sufficient data on other ethnic groups except to say that there seems to be a height–income effect for black males that resembles the effect for white males.[39]

Oral Communication

Effective oral communication requires cultural understanding. As Figure 13.4 shows, even an act as specific as a business introduction may differ across cultures. During business meetings, even words as distinct as *yes* and *no* may cause confusion. In some cultures where saying *no* is considered rude, a *yes* may mean merely "I heard you."

Learning at least a little of the language of the country where you hope to do business will help you in several ways. First, learning the language will give you at least a glimpse into the culture. In English, for example, we say

Figure 13.4   Cultural Contrasts in Business Introductions

	United States	**Japan**	**Arab countries**
Purpose of introduction	Establish status and job identity; network	Establish position in group, build harmony	Establish personal rapport
Image of individual	Independent	Member of group	Part of rich culture
Information	Related to business	Related to company	Personal
Use of language	Informal, friendly; use first name	Little talking	Formal; expression of admiration
Values	Openness, directness, action	Harmony, respect, listening	Religious harmony, hospitality, emotional support

Source: Adapted from Farid Elashmawi and Philip R. Harris, *Multicultural Management 2000: Essential Cultural Insights for Global Business Success* (Houston: Gulf, 1998), 113.

that a clock "runs." The French say "*Il marche*"—literally, "It is walking." Second, learning some of the language will help you manage the daily necessities of finding food and getting where you need to go while you're there. If you know enough, you'll even be able to sightsee and take advantage of the unique opportunities business travel can provide. Finally, in business negotiations, knowing a little of the language gives you more time to think. You'll catch part of the meaning when you hear your counterpart speak; you can begin thinking even before the translation begins.

Frequently you will need a good translator when you travel abroad on business. Brief him or her with the technical terms you'll be using; explain as much of the context of your negotiations as possible. A good translator can also help you interpret nonverbal behavior and negotiating strategies. Some translators can help their clients establish trust and credibility with international businesses.

Understatement and Exaggeration

To understand someone from another culture, you must understand the speaker's conversational style. The British have a reputation for understatement. Someone good enough to play at Wimbledon may say he or she "plays a little tennis." In many contexts, Americans accept exaggeration as a way to express positive thinking. Particularly in advertising, Americans expect some hype. Germans, in contrast, generally see exaggeration as a barrier to clear communication. German customers are likely to be intolerant of claims that seem logically unsupportable. An American writing for a German audience should ensure that any claims are literally true.[40]

Compliments

The kinds of statements that people interpret as compliments and the socially correct ways to respond to compliments also vary among cultures. Statements that seem complimentary in one context may be inappropriate in another. For example, women in business may be uncomfortable if male colleagues or superiors compliment them on their appearance: the comments may suggest that the women are being treated as visual decoration rather than as contributing workers.

Voice Qualities

Tone of voice refers to the rising or falling inflection that tells you whether a group of words is a question or a statement, whether the speaker is uncertain or confident, whether a statement is sincere or sarcastic. Anyone who has written dialog with adverbs ("he said thoughtfully") has tried to indicate tone of voice.

When tone of voice and the meaning of words conflict, people "believe" the tone of voice. If you respond to your friends' "How are you?" with the words "I'm dying, and you?" most of your friends will reply "Fine." If the tone of your voice is cheerful, they may not hear the content of the words.

Pitch measures whether a voice uses sounds that are low (like the bass notes on a piano) or high. Low-pitched voices are usually perceived as being more authoritative, sexier, and more pleasant to listen to than are high-pitched voices. Most voices go up in pitch when the speaker is angry or excited; some people raise pitch when they increase volume. Women whose normal speaking voices are high may need to practice projecting their voices to avoid becoming shrill when they speak to large groups.

Are You Gaining Weight?

The workplace culture in China varies considerably from that of the US because Chinese people draw the lines between personal and work space differently than do Americans. For example, coworkers in China may comment on your increasing waistline, the size of your apartment, or your salary, all of which are taboo topics in the US workplace.

Some Chinese office customs are a result of Chinese corporations "embracing the idea of company as surrogate family." Consequently, you may find a coworker napping during lunch, ladies in the office with slippers on, or a "tea lady," making tea and lunches for the office employees.

In contrast, American workplace culture can also create culture shock for Chinese employees. Although Chinese workplaces are family oriented, Chinese would not consider calling their supervisors by their first names or eating while talking with a senior manager during a lunch conference, all of which are common practices in the US.

How would you handle cultural differences?

What would you say if someone commented that you were getting fat?

How do you handle fellow coworkers asking you personal questions?

Adapted from Geoffrey A. Fowler, "In China's Offices, Foreign Colleagues Might Get an Earful," *Wall Street Journal*, February 13, 2007, B1.

Stress is the emphasis given to one or more words in a sentence. As the following example shows, emphasizing different words can change the meaning.

I'll give you a raise.

> [Implication, depending on pitch and speed: "Another supervisor wouldn't" or "I have the power to determine your salary."]

I'll **give** you a raise.

> [Implication, depending on pitch and speed: "You haven't **earned** it" or "OK, all right, you win. I'm saying 'yes' to get rid of you, but I don't really agree," or "I've just this instant decided that you deserve a raise."]

I'll give **you** a raise.

> [Implication: "But nobody else in this department is getting one."]

I'll give you **a** raise.

> [Implication: "But just one."]

I'll give you a **raise.**

> [Implication: "But you won't get the promotion or anything else you want."]

I'll give **you** a **raise.**

> [Implication: "You deserve it."]

I'll give you a **raise!**

> [Implication: "I've just this minute decided to act, and I'm excited about this idea. The raise will please both of us."]

Speakers who use many changes in tone, pitch, and stress as they speak usually seem more enthusiastic; often they also seem more energetic and more intelligent. Someone who speaks in a monotone may seem apathetic or unintelligent. Nonnative speakers whose first language does not use tone, pitch, and stress to convey meaning and attitude may need to practice varying these voice qualities when they give presentations in the United States.

Volume is a measure of loudness or softness. Very soft voices, especially if they are also breathy and high-pitched, give the impression of youth and inexperience. People who do a lot of speaking to large groups need to practice projecting their voices so they can increase their volume without shouting.

In some cultures, it is considered rude to shout; loud voices connote anger and imminent violence. In others, everyday conversations are loud.

Writing to International Audiences

Most cultures are more formal than the United States. When you write to international audiences, use titles, not first names; avoid contractions, slang, and sports metaphors. Do write in English unless you're extremely fluent in your reader's language. Be clear, but be adult. Don't write in second-grade English.

The patterns of organization that work for North American audiences may need to be modified in international correspondence. For most cultures, buffer negative messages and make requests more indirect. As Figures 13.5 and 13.6 suggest, the style, structure, and strategies that would motivate a US audience may need to be changed for international readers. A junior manager in a financial firm caused hard feelings when he e-mailed a direct question to a colleague at the Manila office: "Were the deal numbers checked against the source?" This question was taken by the employee in Manila as an accusation.[41]

Response time expectations may also need to be modified. US employees tend to expect fast answers to e-mails. However, other cultures with hierarchical

Figure 13.5 Cultural Contrasts in Written Persuasive Documents

	United States	Japan	Arab countries
Opening	Request action or get reader's attention	Offer thanks; apologize	Offer personal greetings
Way to persuade	Immediate gain or loss of opportunity	Waiting	Personal connections; future opportunity
Style	Short sentences	Modesty; minimize own standing	Elaborate expressions; many signatures
Closing	Specific request	Desire to maintain harmony	Future relationship, personal greeting
Values	Efficiency; directness; action	Politeness; indirectness; relationship	Status; continuation

Source: Adapted from Farid Elashmawi and Philip R. Harris, *Multicultural Management 2000: Essential Cultural Insights for Global Business Success* (Houston: Gulf, 1998), 139.

Figure 13.6 Cultural Contrasts in Motivation

	United States	Japan	Arab countries
Emotional appeal	Opportunity	Group participation; company success	Religion; nationalism; admiration
Recognition based on	Individual achievement	Group achievement	Individual status; status of class/society
Material rewards	Salary; bonus; profit sharing	Annual bonus; social services; fringe benefits	Gifts for self/family; salary
Threats	Loss of job	Loss of group membership	Demotion, loss of reputation
Values	Competition; risk taking; freedom	Group harmony; belonging	Reputation; family security; religion

Source: Adapted from Farid Elashmawi and Philip R. Harris, *Multicultural Management 2000: Essential Cultural Insights for Global Business Success* (Houston: Gulf, 1998), 169.

organization structures may need extra response time to allow for approval by superiors. Pressing for a quick response may alienate the people whose help is needed and may result in false promises.[42]

Business people from Europe and Japan who correspond frequently with North America are beginning to adopt US directness and patterns of organization. If you know that your reader understands North American behavior, you can write just as you would to someone in the United States or Canada. If you don't know your reader well, it may be safer to modify your message slightly.

In international business correspondence, list the day before the month:

Not: April 8, 2008

But: 8 April 2008

Spell out the month to avoid confusion. A US professor wrote to the British library to reserve the books he would need for his visit on April 10. However, he wrote "4/10," and the British assumed he wanted them on October 4.

http://www.cyborlink.com/
http://www.kwintessential.co.uk/

Cyborlink.com and Kwintessential.co.uk provide information on business communication in various countries. On both sites, choose a country to explore and you will get general information on topics such as negotiations, gift giving, personal space, and much more.

Don't Be Piggish

Recently, China banned all images and spoken references to pigs in commercials, including references to the Lunar New Year. Unfortunately, Nestlé's new advertising campaign to celebrate China's "Year of the Pig" featured a smiling, cartoon pig. The commercial was prohibited from air time by the China Central Television.

The reason for the ban was to avoid offending Muslims, who consider pigs unclean, even though they make up less than 2% of the population. In addition, the ban occurred after 18 Muslims were killed by Chinese police in January 2007.

Like Nestlé, Coca-Cola had a pig commercial ready for air. It decided to feature a panda instead.

Adapted from Gordon Fairclough and Geoffrey A. Fowler, "Pigs Get the Ax in China TV Ads, in Nod to Muslims," *Wall Street Journal*, January 25, 2007, A1, A16.

Learning More about International Business Communication

Learning to communicate with people from different backgrounds shouldn't be a matter of learning rules. Instead, use the examples in this chapter to get a sense for the kinds of factors that differ from one culture to another. Test these generalizations against your experience. And when in doubt, ask.

You can also learn by seeking out people from other backgrounds and talking with them. Many campuses have centers for international students. Some communities have groups of international business people who meet regularly to discuss their countries. By asking all these people what aspects of the dominant US culture seem strange to them, you'll learn much about what is "right" in their cultures.

Summary of Key Points

- **Culture** provides patterns of acceptable behavior and beliefs.
- The successful intercultural communicator is
  - Aware of the values, beliefs, and practices in other cultures.
  - Sensitive to differences among individuals within a culture.
  - Aware that his or her preferred values and behaviors are influenced by culture and are not necessarily "right."
  - Sensitive to verbal and nonverbal behavior.
  - Flexible and open to change.
- In **high-context cultures,** most of the information is inferred from the context of a message; little is explicitly conveyed. In **low-context cultures,** context is less important; most information is explicitly spelled out.
- **Nonverbal communication** is communication that doesn't use words. Nonverbal communication can include voice qualities, body language, space, time, and other miscellaneous matters such as clothing, colors, age, and height.
- Nonverbal signals can be misinterpreted just as easily as can verbal symbols (words).
- No gesture has a universal meaning across all cultures. Gestures that signify approval in North America may be insults in other countries, and vice versa.
- **Personal space** is the distance someone wants between him- or herself and other people in ordinary, nonintimate interchanges.
- North Americans who believe that "time is money" are often frustrated in negotiations with people who want to establish a personal relationship before they decide whether to do business with each other.
- The patterns of organization that work for North American audiences may need to be modified in international correspondence.

CHAPTER 13   ## Exercises and Problems

13.1   Reviewing the Chapter

1. Why is global business important? (LO 1)
2. What are the advantages of receiving an overseas assignment? (LO 1)
3. Why is diversity becoming more important than ever before? (LO 2)
4. What are low-context and high-context cultures? (LO 3)

5. How do our values and beliefs affect our responses to other people? (LO 3)

6. What are some forms of nonverbal communication? What variations would you expect to see in them among people of different cultures? (LO 4)

7. Why do people from monochronic cultures sometimes have trouble with people from polychronic cultures? (LO 4)

8. What are some characteristics of oral communications you should consider when communicating cross-culturally? (LO 5)

9. What are some cautions to consider when writing for international audiences? (LO 6)

13.2   Identifying Sources of Miscommunication

In each of the following situations, identify one or more ways that cultural differences may be leading to miscommunication.

1. Alan is a US sales representative in South America. He makes appointments and is careful to be on time. But the person he's calling on is frequently late. To save time, Alan tries to get right to business. But his hosts want to talk about sightseeing and his family. Even worse, his appointments are interrupted constantly, not only by business phone calls but also by long conversations with other people and even the customers' children who come into the office. Alan's first progress report is very negative. He hasn't yet made a sale. Perhaps South America just isn't the right place to sell his company's products.

2. To help her company establish a presence in Asia, Susan wants to hire a local interpreter who can advise her on business customs. Kana Tomari has superb qualifications on paper. But when Susan tries to probe about her experience, Kana just says, "I will do my best. I will try very hard." She never gives details about any of the previous positions she's held. Susan begins to wonder if the résumé is inflated.

3. Stan wants to negotiate a joint venture with an Asian company. He asks Tung-Sen Lee if the people have enough discretionary income to afford his product. Mr. Lee is silent for a time, and then says, "Your product is good. People in the West must like it." Stan smiles, pleased that Mr. Lee recognizes the quality of his product, and he gives Mr. Lee a contract to sign. Weeks later, Stan still hasn't heard anything. If Asians are going to be so nonresponsive, he wonders if he really should try to do business with them.

4. Elspeth is very proud of her participatory management style. On assignment in India, she is careful not to give orders but to ask for suggestions. But people rarely suggest anything. Even a formal suggestion system doesn't work. And to make matters worse, she doesn't sense the respect and camaraderie of the plant she managed in the United States. Perhaps, she decides gloomily, people in India just aren't ready for a woman boss.

13.3   Asking about Travel Arrangements

The CEO is planning a trip to visit colleagues in another country (you pick the country). As Executive Assistant to the CEO of your organization, it's your job to make travel plans. At this stage, you don't know anything except dates and flights. (The CEO will arrive in the country at 7 AM local time on the 28th of next month and stay for three days.) It's your job to find out what the plans are and communicate any of the CEO's requirements.

Write an e-mail message to your contact.

Hints:

- Pick a business, nonprofit organization, or government agency you know something about, making assumptions about the kinds of things its executive would want to do during an international visit.

- How much international traveling does your CEO do? Has he or she ever been to this country before? What questions will he or she want answered?

13.4   Studying International Communication at Your Workplace

Does your employer buy from suppliers or sell to customers outside the country? Get a sampling of international messages, or interview managers about the problems they've encountered.

As your instructor directs,

a. Share your results orally with a small group of students.

b. Present your findings orally to the class.

c. Summarize your findings in a memo to your instructor.

d. Join with other students in your class to write a group report.

13.5   Creating a Web Page

Create a Web page of international information for managers who are planning assignments in another country or who work in this country for a multinational company headquartered in another country.

Assume that this page can be accessed from another of the organization's pages. Offer at least seven links. (More is better.) You may offer information as well as links to other pages with information. At the top of the page, offer an overview of what the page covers. At the bottom of the page, put the creation/update date and your name and e-mail address.

As your instructor directs,

a.   Turn in a copy of your page(s). On another page, give the URLs for each link.

b.   Write a memo to your instructor (1) identifying the audience for which the page is designed and explaining (2) the search strategies you used to find material on this topic, (3) why you chose the pages and information you've included, and (4) why you chose the layout and graphics you've used.

c.   Present your page orally to the class.

Hints:

- Limit your page to just one country or one part of the world.

- You can include some general information about working abroad and culture, but most of your links should be specific to the country or part of the world you focus on.

- Consider some of these topics: history, politics, geography, culture, money, living accommodations, transport, weather, business practices, and so forth.

- Chunk your links into small groups under headings.

13.6   Comparing Company Web Pages for Various Countries

Many multinationals have separate Web pages for their operations in various countries. For example, Coca-Cola's pages include pages for Belgium, France, and Japan. Analyze three of the country pages of a company of your choice.

- Is a single template used for pages in different countries, or do the basic designs differ?

- Are different images used in different countries? What do the images suggest?

- If you can read the language, analyze the links. What information is emphasized?

- To what extent are the pages similar? To what extent do they reveal national and cultural differences?

As your instructor directs,

a.   Write a memo analyzing the similarities and differences you find. Attach printouts of the pages to your memo.

b.   Make an oral presentation to the class. Paste the Web pages into PowerPoint slides.

c.   Join with a small group of students to create a group report comparing several companies' Web pages in three specific countries. Attach printouts of the pages.

d.   Make a group oral presentation to the class.

13.7   Planning an International Trip

Assume that you're going to the capital city of another country on business two months from now. (You pick the country.) Use a search engine to find out

- What holidays will be celebrated in that month.

- What the climate will be.

- What current events are in the news.

- What key features of business etiquette you might consider.

- What kinds of gifts you should bring to your hosts.

- What sight-seeing you might include.

As your instructor directs,

a.   Write a memo to your instructor reporting the information you found.

b.   Post a message to the class analyzing the pages. Include the URLs as hotlinks.

c.   Make an oral presentation to the class.

d.   Join with a small group of students to create a group report on several countries in a region.

e.   Make a group oral presentation to the class.

13.8   Recommending a Candidate for an Overseas Position

Your company sells customized computer systems to businesses large and small around the world. The Executive Committee needs to recommend someone to begin a three-year term as Manager of Eastern European Marketing.

As your instructor directs,

a. Write a memo to each of the candidates, specifying the questions you would like each to answer in a final interview.

b. Assume that it is not possible to interview the candidates. Use the information here to write a memo to the CEO recommending a candidate.

c. Write a memo to the CEO recommending the best way to prepare the person chosen for his or her assignment.

d. Write a memo to the CEO recommending a better way to choose candidates for international assignments.

e. Write a memo to your instructor explaining the assumptions you made about the company and the candidates that influenced your recommendation(s).

Information about the candidates:

All the candidates have applied for the position and say they are highly interested in it.

1. **Deborah Gere,** 39, white, single. Employed by the company for eight years in the Indianapolis and New York offices. Currently in the New York office as Assistant Marketing Manager, Eastern United States; successful. University of Indiana MBA. Speaks Russian fluently; has translated for business negotiations that led to the setting up of the Moscow office. Good technical knowledge, acceptable managerial skills, excellent communication skills, good interpersonal skills. Excellent health; excellent emotional stability. Swims. One child, age 12. Lived in the then–Soviet Union for one year as an exchange student in college; business and personal travel in Europe.

2. **Claude Chabot,** 36, French, single. Employed by the company for 11 years in the Paris and London offices. Currently in the Paris office as Assistant Sales Manager for the European Economic Community; successful. No MBA, but degrees from MIT in the United States and l'Ecole Supérieure de Commerce de Paris. Speaks native French; speaks English and Italian fluently; speaks some German. Good technical knowledge, excellent managerial skills, acceptable communication skills, excellent interpersonal skills. Excellent health, good emotional stability. Plays tennis. No children. French citizen; lived in the United States for two years, in London for five years (one year in college, four years in the London office). Extensive business and personal travel in Europe.

3. **Linda Moss,** 35, African American, married. Employed by the company for 10 years in the Atlanta and Toronto offices. Currently Assistant Manager of Canadian Marketing; very successful. Howard University MBA. Speaks some French. Good technical knowledge, excellent managerial skills, excellent communication skills, excellent interpersonal skills. Excellent health; excellent emotional stability. Does Jazzercize classes. Husband is an executive at a US company in Detroit; he plans to stay in the States with their children, ages 11 and 9. The couple plans to commute every two to six weeks. Has lived in Toronto for five years; business travel in North America; personal travel in Europe and Latin America.

4. **Steven Hsu,** 42, of Asian American descent, married. Employed by the company for 18 years in the Los Angeles office. Currently Marketing Manager, Western United States; very successful. UCLA MBA. Speaks some Korean. Excellent technical knowledge, excellent managerial skills, good communication skills, excellent interpersonal skills. Good health, excellent emotional stability. Plays golf. Wife is an engineer who plans to do consulting work in eastern Europe. Children ages 8, 5, and 2. Has not lived outside the United States; personal travel in Europe and Asia.

Your committee has received this memo from the CEO.

To:	Executive Committee
From:	Ed Conzachi
Subject:	Choosing a Manager for the New Eastern European Office

Please write me a memo recommending the best candidate for Manager of East European Marketing. In your memo, tell me whom you're choosing and why; also explain why you have rejected the unsuccessful candidates.

This person will be assuming a three-year appointment, with the possibility of reappointment. The company will pay moving and relocation expenses for the manager and his or her family.

The Eastern European division currently is the smallest of the company's international divisions. However, this area is poised for growth. The new manager will supervise the Moscow office and establish branch offices as needed.

The committee has invited comments from everyone in the company. You've received these memos.

To:	Executive Committee
From:	Robert Osborne, US Marketing Manager *RO*
Subject:	Recommendation for Steve Hsu

Steve Hsu would be a great choice to head up the new Moscow office. In the past seven years, Steve has increased sales in the Western Region by 15%—in spite of recessions, earthquakes, and fires. He has a low-key, participative style that brings out the best in subordinates. Moreover, Steve is a brilliant computer programmer. He probably understands our products better than any other marketing or salesperson in the company.

Steve is clearly destined for success in headquarters. This assignment will give him the international experience he needs to move up to the next level of executive success.

To:	Executive Committee
From:	Becky Exter, Affirmative Action Officer *RRE*
Subject:	Hiring the New Manager for East European Marketing

Please be sensitive to affirmative action concerns. The company has a very good record of appointing women and minorities to key positions in the United States and Canada; so far our record in our overseas divisions has been less effective.

In part, perhaps, that may stem from a perception that women and minorities will not be accepted in countries less open than our own. But the experience of several multinational firms has been that even exclusionary countries will accept people who have the full backing of their companies. Another concern may be that it will be harder for women to establish a social support system abroad. However, different individuals have different ways of establishing support. To assume that the best candidate for an international assignment is a male with a stay-at-home wife is discriminatory and may deprive our company of the skills of some of its best people.

We have several qualified women and minority candidates. I urge you to consider their credentials carefully.

To: Executive Committee   *WED*

From: William E. Dortch, Marketing Manager, European Economic Community

Subject: Recommendation for Debbie Gere

Debbie Gere would be my choice to head the new Moscow office. As you know, I recommended that Europe be divided and that we establish an Eastern European division. Of all the people from the States who have worked on the creation of the new division, Debbie is the best. The negotiations were often complex. Debbie's knowledge of the language and culture was invaluable. She's done a good job in the New York office and is ready for wider responsibilities. Eastern Europe is a challenging place, but Debbie can handle the pressure and help us gain the foothold we need.

To: Ed Conzachi, President

From: Pierre Garamond, Sales Representative,
            European Economic Community   *PG*

Subject: Recommendation for Claude Chabot

Claude Chabot would be the best choice for Manager of Eastern European Marketing. He is a superb supervisor, motivating us to the highest level of achievement. He understands the complex legal and cultural nuances of selling our products in Europe as only a native can. He also has the budgeting and managerial skills to oversee the entire marketing effort.

You are aware that the company's record of sending US citizens to head international divisions is not particularly good. European Marketing is an exception, but our records in the Middle East and Japan have been poor. The company would gain stability by appointing Europeans to head European offices, Asians to head Asian offices, and so forth. Such people would do a better job of managing and motivating staffs which will be comprised primarily of nationals in the country where the office is located. Ending the practice of reserving the top jobs for US citizens would also send a message to international employees that we are valued and that we have a future with this company.

To: Executive Committee

From: Elaine Crispell, Manager, Canadian Marketing   *EC*

Subject: Recommendation for Linda Moss

Linda Moss has done well as Assistant Manager for the last two and a half years. She is a creative, flexible problem solver. Her productivity is the highest in the office. Though she could be called a "workaholic," she is a warm, caring human being.

As you know, the Canadian division includes French-Speaking Montreal and a large Native Canadian population; furthermore, Toronto is an international and intercultural city. Linda has gained intercultural competence both on a personal and professional level.

Linda has the potential to be our first woman CEO 15 years down the road. She needs more international experience to be competitive at that level. This would be a good opportunity for her, and she would do well for the company.

13.9   Analyzing EEO Statements

Find the EEO statements on the Web of three different companies. Do any of the statements have interesting features? How are the statements similar? How are the statements different? How do they compare to the EEO statement of the FBI (see the box on page 435)?

As your instructor directs,

a.   Present your analysis in a memo to your instructor.

b.   Share your findings in small groups. Using all the group's EEO statements, answer the questions above. Put your analysis in a memo to your instructor, or share your findings orally with the class.

13.10   Researching Diversity at Your School

Research your university's policies and practices regarding diversity. Conduct the following research:

- Locate your university's position statement on diversity for both employment and educational opportunities.
- Find diversity data for your university's student body.
- Gather pictures of the student body you can find from the Internet, brochures, and posters throughout your university.
- Analyze your findings. Do the pictures you find resemble the statistics you find?

As your instructor directs,

a.   Write an e-mail to your instructor explaining your findings, opinions, and conclusions.

b.   Share your results with a small group of students.

c.   Write an e-mail message to the president of the university outlining your opinion on how your university is achieving diversity and what, if anything, needs to be done to improve its efforts.

d.   Make a short oral presentation to the class discussing your findings and conclusions.

13.11   Researching Diversity Programs of Companies

Find three businesses that are successfully globalizing or outsourcing.

- Specify their successes. What actions, behaviors, and policies do they follow to be successful at globalizing and/or outsourcing their organization?
- Note what other organizations can learn from these examples.

Find three businesses that are having problems globalizing or outsourcing.

- Specify their problems. What actions, behaviors, and policies do they follow that are causing the problems?

- Note what other organizations can learn from these examples.

As your instructor directs,

a.   Write an e-mail to your instructor explaining your findings, opinions, and conclusions.

b.   Share your results with a small group of students.

c.   Make a short oral presentation to the class discussing your findings and conclusions.

13.12   Mosaic Case

"Based on recent sales figures, our Southern stores are booming because of Hispanic clientele," said Demetri to everyone during the weekly staff meeting. "But I'm concerned about how we're meeting this clientele's needs."

"What do you mean?" asked Martina between bites of her banana. "How can we better meet their needs? Aren't all our stores the same? Consistency is good."

"Well, let's not go making strict rules," said Demetri while imitating Yvonne's imaginary air quotes around the words *strict rules.*

Trey let a chuckle escape, but Yvonne didn't seem to notice what was going on.

"In fact," continued Demetri, "all of our stores shouldn't be the same. The increasing numbers of Hispanic customers mean that we should be changing to target their needs."

"Definitely, Demetri," said Yvonne. "I was just talking with Sonya over in the marketing department yesterday about these initial figures. She suggested there is a wealth of research on adapting to and targeting Hispanic needs and wants. She's going to send over two of her employees, Katie and Luke, I think, so that we can team up and tackle this issue."

"That's a great idea," said Demetri. "I would really like it if we could figure out new strategies for the Mosaic stores we have in Florida, Texas, New Mexico, Arizona, and Southern California."

"Martina, this would probably be a great project for you to work to get even more experience," said Sarah.

"Great!" she replied. "This'll be an awesome learning opportunity."

"And Trey, since you've just finished that computer persuasion memo with Martina, how about if you work with her again and these others from the marketing department?" said Sarah. "Hopefully you can learn some approaches that we can use for the Web site as well."

"Excellent," he said sarcastically. "What time will the rest of the team be over here?"

"Actually, here they are now," answered Yvonne, watching through the window of the conference room as Katie and Luke entered the Communication Department. "We'll end our meeting so you four can get started on the task. Good luck!"

With your group, take on the communication task of Martina, Trey, Katie, and Luke to complete Demetri's request. Conduct research on the Internet and in the library on how organizations are adapting their products and approaches to merchandising for Hispanic audiences. When you have completed your research, write a memo to Demetri explaining what you have found and offering some ways for Mosaic's southern stores to incorporate your research.

Working and Writing in Groups

Learning Objectives

After studying this chapter, you will know:

1 Ways to improve your listening skills.

2 Different kinds of productive and nonproductive roles in groups.

3 Group decision-making strategies.

4 Characteristics of successful groups.

5 Techniques for resolving conflict.

6 Techniques for making meetings effective.

7 Techniques for collaborative writing.

Corporate Annual Meetings

Corporate annual meetings have become more interesting as activists become more vocal. PETA representatives press restaurant operators on the ethical treatment of the animals slaughtered for them. Environmentalists pressure manufacturers about their water treatments. Shareholders confront executive compensation plans they believe to be out of line.

All the action is moving corporate officials to stage-manage their annual meetings. Companies have been assigning "escorts" to activists, requiring questions to be submitted ahead of time in writing, setting speaker time limits of 1–3 minutes, and using stationary microphones, rather than roving ones, to ensure orderly proceedings. Many companies are Googling the sponsors of shareholder resolutions. Some firms are moving meeting locations to out-of-the-way locations: U-Haul's parent company held one annual meeting in a tiny Nevada town. Home Depot hired several dozen beefy "greeters" to enforce speaker time limits. Some activists find they are greeted by an official who sits by them at the meeting and escorts them to the door afterwards.

Some companies are going too far. Wal-Mart had to apologize after a report that they had investigated some resolution sponsors. And some companies still believe in showing courtesy to shareholders as a way to generate goodwill.

> *"Companies have been assigning 'escorts' to activists, requiring questions to be submitted ahead of time in writing, setting speaker time limits of 1–3 minutes, and using stationary microphones, rather than roving ones, to ensure orderly proceedings."*

Source: Erin White, "Stage-Managing the Annual Meeting: Companies Keep Tight Rein on Activists, Limit Speeches; Beefy 'Greeters' at the Depot," *Wall Street Journal*, April 16, 2007, B1, B3.

Chapter Outline

Teamwork is crucial to success in an organization. Some teams produce products, provide services, or recommend solutions to problems. Other teams—perhaps in addition to providing a service or recommending a solution—also produce documents.

Interpersonal communication, communication between people, is crucial for good teamwork. It relies heavily on interpersonal skills such as listening and dealing with conflict. These skills will make you more successful in your job, social groups, community service, and volunteer work. In writing groups, giving careful attention to both group process and writing process (◄ p. 137) improves both the final product and members' satisfaction with the group.

Listening

Listening is crucial to building trust. However, listening on the job may be more difficult than listening in classes. Many classroom lectures are well organized, with signposts and repetition of key points to help hearers follow. But conversations usually wander. A key point about when a report is due may be sandwiched in among statements about other due dates for other projects. Finally, in a classroom you're listening primarily for information. In interchanges with friends and co-workers, you need to listen for feelings, too. Feelings such as being rejected or overworked need to be dealt with as they arise. But you can't deal with a feeling unless you are aware of it.

Listening errors also can result from being distracted by your own emotional response, especially when the topic is controversial. Listeners have to be aware of their emotional responses so that they can clarify the speaker's intent and also allow time for cooling off, if necessary. A "you" attitude is as helpful for listening as it is for writing. Listening is more effective if the listener focuses more on understanding than on formulating a reply. Thinking about your own response too often causes you to miss important information.

Some listening errors also happen because the hearer wasn't paying enough attention to a key point. Be aware of points you need to know and listen for them.

Inattention and emotions can cause listeners to misinterpret a speaker. To reduce listening errors caused by misinterpretation,

- Paraphrase what the speaker has said, giving him or her a chance to correct your understanding.
- At the end of the conversation, check your understanding with the other person. Especially check who does what next.
- After the conversation, write down key points that affect deadlines or how work will be evaluated.
- Don't ignore instructions you think are unnecessary. Before you do something else, check with the order giver to see if there is a reason for the instruction.
- Consider the other person's background and experiences. Why is this point important to the speaker? What might he or she mean by it?

Listening to people is an indication that you're taking them seriously. **Acknowledgment responses**—nods, *uh huhs,* smiles, frowns—help carry the message that you're listening. However, remember that listening responses vary in different cultures.

In **active listening,** receivers actively demonstrate that they've understood a speaker by feeding back the literal meaning, the emotional content, or both. These strategies create active responses:

- Paraphrase the content. Feed back the meaning in your own words.
- Mirror the speaker's feelings. Identify the feelings you think you hear.
- Ask for information or clarification.
- Offer to help solve the problem. ("What can I do to help?")

Instead of simply mirroring what the other person says, many of us immediately respond in a way that analyzes or attempts to solve or dismiss the problem. People with problems need first of all to know that we hear that they're having a rough time. Figure 14.1 lists some of the responses that block communication. Ordering and threatening both tell the other person that the speaker doesn't want to hear what he or she has to say. Preaching attacks the other person. Minimizing the problem suggests the other person's concern is misplaced. It can even attack the other person's competency by suggesting that other people are coping just fine with bigger problems. Even advising shuts off discussion. Giving a quick answer minimizes the pain the person feels and puts him or her down for not seeing (what is to us) the obvious answer. Even if it is a good answer from an objective point of view, the other person may not be ready to hear it. And too often, the off-the-top-of-the-head solution doesn't address the real problem.

Active listening takes time and energy. Even people who are skilled active listeners can't do it all the time. Active listening can reduce the conflict that results from miscommunication, but it alone cannot reduce the conflict that comes when two people want apparently inconsistent things or when one person wants to change someone else.

Choose and Listen Wisely

[Jim Collins, author of bestselling business books *Built to Last* and *Good to Great,* suggests that having great people on a team and top executives who will listen to the ideas of these great people contributes to successful businesses.]

[Often,] "the CEO has already made a decision, and his [her] definition of leadership is to get people to participate so that they feel good about the decision he's [she's] already made," [states Collins].

[The problem, however, is that] "you're ignoring people who might know a lot that would be useful in making the decision. You're accepting the idea that because you're in the CEO seat, you somehow know more or you're smarter than everyone else. But what you're really doing is cutting yourself off from hearing options or ideas that might be better. You have to recognize that your position can be a hindrance to getting the best information. And so can your personality."

Quoted from Jerry Useem, "Interview: Jim Collins on Tough Calls," *Fortune,* June 27, 2005, 90–93.

http://www.team technology.co.uk/

Log on to this Web site to find a wide range of articles and resources about interacting effectively in team settings. More specifically, click on "Team Roles" to find some interactive links to aid in assessing yourself as a team member as well as determining roles of your fellow group members.

Figure 14.1   Blocking Responses versus Active Listening

Blocking response	Possible active response
Ordering, threatening "I don't care how you do it. Just get that report on my desk by Friday."	**Paraphrasing content** "You're saying that you don't have time to finish the report by Friday."
Preaching, criticizing "You should know better than to air the department's problems in a general meeting."	**Mirroring feelings** "It sounds like the department's problems really bother you."
Minimizing the problem "You think *that's* bad. You should see what *I* have to do this week."	**Asking for information or clarification** "What parts of the problem seem most difficult to solve?"
Advising "Well, why don't you try listing everything you have to do and seeing which items are most important?"	**Offering to help solve the problem together** "Is there anything I could do that would help?"

Source: These responses that block communication are based on a list in Thomas Gordon and Judith Gordon Sands, *P.E.T. in Action* (New York: Wyden, 1976), 117–18.

Swift Start Action Teams

On July 19, 1989, at 3:16 pm, the engine of United Airlines Flight 232 exploded over western Iowa, eventually making all the hydraulic systems nonfunctional. As a result, the airplane could not be steered correctly, making a safe landing virtually impossible. However, through successful communication, the crew was able to save over half of the nearly 300 passengers, who normally wouldn't have survived such an impending disaster. The crew, which consisted of trained strangers within a single organization, used formalized interactions of signaling, expressed values nonverbally, and understood their own responsibility to the team. The combination of these skills enabled the crew to cope successfully with the high-risk situation. The same skills can be used by businesses to develop "swift start" teams for high-stakes situations.

Adapted from Earl H. McKinney Jr., James R. Baker, Kevin Davis, and Daryl Smith, "How Swift Starting Action Teams Get Off the Ground: What United Flight 232 and Airline Crews Can Tell Us about Team Communication," *Management Communication Quarterly* 19, no. 2 (November 2005): 198–237.

Group Interactions

Groups can focus on different dimensions. **Informational dimensions** focus on content: the problem, data, and possible solutions. **Procedural dimensions** focus on method and process. How will the group make decisions? Who will do what? When will assignments be due? **Interpersonal dimensions** focus on people, promoting friendliness, cooperation, and group loyalty.

Different kinds of communication dominate during these stages of the life of a task group: formation, coordination, and formalization.

During **formation,** when members meet and begin to define their task, groups need to develop some sort of social cohesiveness and to develop procedures for meeting and acting. Interpersonal and procedural comments reduce the tension that always exists in a new group. Insistence on information in this first stage can hurt the group's long-term productivity.

Groups are often most effective when they explicitly adopt ground rules. Figure 14.2 lists some of the most common ground rules used by workplace teams.

During **formation,** conflicts almost always arise when the group chooses a leader and defines the problem. Successful leaders make the procedure clear so that each member knows what he or she is supposed to do. Interpersonal communication is needed to resolve the conflict that surfaces during this phase. Successful groups analyze the problem thoroughly before they begin to search for solutions.

Coordination is the longest phase and the phase during which most of the group's work is done. While procedural and interpersonal comments help maintain direction and friendliness, most of the comments need to deal with information. Good information is essential to a good decision. Conflict may occur as the group debates alternate solutions. Successful groups carefully consider as many solutions as possible before choosing one.

In **formalization,** the group seeks consensus. The success of this phase determines how well the group's decision will be implemented. In this stage, the group seeks to forget earlier conflicts.

Figure 14.2   Possible Group Ground Rules

- Start on time; end on time.
- Attend regularly.
- Come to the meeting prepared.
- Focus comments on the issues.
- Avoid personal attacks.
- Listen to and respect members' opinions.
- Everyone speaks on key issues and procedures.
- Address problems as you become aware of them. If you have a problem with another person, tell that person, not everyone else.
- Do your share of the work.
- Communicate immediately if you think you may not be able to fulfill an agreement.
- Produce your work by the agreed-upon time.

http://www.quintcareers.com/team_player_quiz_scoring.html

Log on to Quint Careers.com and take a quiz that gauges how effective you are as a team player.

How did you do? Are you an effective team player? If not, consider the guidelines outlined in this chapter to become a better and more resourceful team member.

Roles in Groups

Individual members can play various roles within groups. These roles can be positive or negative.

Positive roles and actions that help the group achieve its task goals include the following.

- **Seeking information and opinions**—asking questions, identifying gaps in the group's knowledge.
- **Giving information and opinions**—answering questions, providing relevant information.
- **Summarizing**—restating major points, pulling ideas together, summarizing decisions.
- **Evaluating**—comparing group processes and products to standards and goals.
- **Coordinating**—planning work, giving directions, and fitting together contributions of group members.

Positive roles and actions that help the group build loyalty, resolve conflicts, and function smoothly include the following:

- **Encouraging participation**—demonstrating openness and acceptance, recognizing the contributions of members, calling on quieter group members.
- **Relieving tensions**—joking and suggesting breaks and fun activities.
- **Checking feelings**—asking members how they feel about group activities and sharing one's own feelings with others.
- **Solving interpersonal problems**—opening discussion of interpersonal problems in the group and suggesting ways to solve them.
- **Listening actively**—showing group members that they have been heard and that their ideas are being taken seriously.

Negative roles and actions that hurt the group's product and process include the following:

- **Blocking**—disagreeing with everything that is proposed.
- **Dominating**—trying to run the group by ordering, shutting out others, and insisting on one's own way.

Drum the Team Beat

Organizations and agencies are trying innovative approaches to encourage collaboration among their employees. Companies, such as UBS AG and Meredith Corporation, publisher of *Parents* and *Better Homes and Gardens*, hold sessions where employees beat drums for up to 90 minutes to establish team spirit. Drumming is an interactive task that doesn't require prior experience. Employers hope these drum sessions will add excitement to meetings, provide a springboard for collaboration, and help employees relate better to one another through a shared experience. Participants usually lower their inhibitions after drumming only a short while and are more likely to be engaged for the duration of the meeting.

Adapted from Erin White, "Theory & Practice: Firms Try Drumming Up Team Spirit," *Wall Street Journal*, October 23, 2006, B4.

Emotional Leaders

According to Kevin S. Groves, a management professor at California State University–Los Angeles, leaders should be selected based on emotional communication ability.

Groves conducted a study with 108 organizational leaders and 325 of their subordinates from various workplace settings. He discovered direct correlations between a leader's emotional communication skills (i.e. facial expressions, direct eye contact, tone of voice, etc.) and being evaluated as effective leaders by their subordinates.

Using "emotional expressivity" as an assessment tool for promotion of managers could improve job performance and the overall productivity of the organization.

Adapted from Kevin S. Groves, "Leader Emotional Expressivity, Visionary Leadership, and Organizational Change," *Leadership & Organizational Development Journal* 27, no. 7 (2006): 566–83.

Group efforts are becoming increasing important in the business world. Some work sessions are so productive they extend over meal times.

- **Clowning**—making unproductive jokes and diverting the group from the task.
- **Overspeaking**—taking every opportunity to be the first to speak; insisting on personally responding to everyone else's comments.
- **Withdrawing**—being silent in meetings, not contributing, not helping with the work, not attending meetings.

Some actions can be positive or negative depending on how they are used. Active participation by members helps groups move forward, but too much talking from one member blocks contributions from others. Criticizing ideas is necessary if the group is to produce the best solution, but criticizing every idea raised without ever suggesting possible solutions blocks a group. Jokes in moderation can defuse tension and make the group more fun. Too many jokes or inappropriate jokes can make the group's work more difficult.

Leadership in Groups

You may have noted that "leader" was not one of the roles listed above. Being a leader does *not* mean doing all the work yourself. Indeed, someone who implies that he or she has the best ideas and can do the best work is likely playing the negative roles of blocking and dominating.

Effective groups balance three kinds of leadership, which parallel the three group dimensions:

- Informational leaders generate and evaluate ideas and text.
- Interpersonal leaders monitor the group's process, check people's feelings, and resolve conflicts.
- Procedural leaders set the agenda, make sure that everyone knows what's due for the next meeting, communicate with absent group members, and check to be sure that assignments are carried out.

While it's possible for one person to assume all these responsibilities, in many groups, the three kinds of leadership are taken on by three (or more) different people. Some groups formally or informally rotate or share these responsibilities, so that everyone—and no one—is a leader.

Studies have shown that people who talk a lot, listen effectively, and respond nonverbally to other members in the group are considered to be leaders.[1]

Decision-Making Strategies

Probably the least effective decision-making strategy is to let the person who talks first, last, loudest, or most determine the decision. Most groups instead aim to air different points of view with the objective of identifying the best choice, or at least a choice that seems good enough for the group's purposes. The group discussion considers the pros and cons of each idea. In many groups, someone willingly plays "devil's advocate" to look for possible flaws in an idea. To give ideas a fair hearing, John Tropman recommends that group leaders also call upon an "angel's advocate" to speak up for an idea's positive aspects.[2]

After the group has considered alternatives, it needs a method for picking one to implement. Typical selection methods include voting and consensus. Voting is quick but may leave people in the minority unhappy with and un-committed to the majority's plan. Coming to **consensus** takes time but usually results in speedier implementation of ideas. Even in situations where consensus is not possible, good teams ensure everyone's ideas are considered. Most people will agree to support the group's decision, even if it was not their choice, as long as they feel they have been heard.

Business people in different nations have varying preferences about these two methods. An international survey of 15,000 managers and employees found that four-fifths of the Japanese respondents preferred consensus, but a lit-tle more than one-third of the Americans did. Other nations in which consensus was preferred included Germany, the Netherlands, Belgium, and France.[3]

Two strategies that are often useful in organizational groups are the stan-dard problem-solving process and dot planning.

The standard problem-solving process has multiple steps:

1. Understand what the group has to deliver, in what form, by what due date. Identify available resources.
2. Identify the task or problem. What is the group trying to do?
3. Gather information, share it with all group members, and examine it critically.
4. Establish criteria. What would the ideal solution include? Which elements of that solution would be part of a less-than-ideal but still acceptable solu-tion? What legal, financial, moral, or other limitations might keep a solu-tion from being implemented?
5. Generate alternate solutions. Brainstorm and record ideas for the next step.
6. Measure the alternatives against the criteria.
7. Choose the best solution.

Dot planning offers a way for large groups to choose priorities quickly. First, the group brainstorms ideas, recording each on pages that are put on the wall. Then each individual gets two strips of three to five adhesive dots in dif-ferent colors. One color represents high priority, the other lower priority. People then walk up to the pages and stick dots by the points they care most about. Some groups allow only one dot from one person on any one item; others al-low someone who is really passionate about an idea to put all of his or her dots on it. The dots make it easy to see which items the group believes are most and least important.

Characteristics of Successful Student Groups

Studies of student groups completing class projects have found that students in successful groups were not necessarily more skilled or more experienced than students in less successful groups. Instead, successful and less successful groups communicated differently.

Meeting Overload

A recent study by Steven G. Rogelberg from the University of North Carolina at Charlotte confirms what you always believed: too many meetings are bad for you, and for your employer.

Rogelberg distributed surveys to 980 professionals. He found that the more meetings task-oriented employees attended, the less of a positive attitude these employees had about their job and overall well-being. Of-ten these feelings surfaced from these task-oriented employees because they viewed meetings as interruptions to other work they could be completing. On the other hand, for people who had less ambition and motiva-tion about their work, meetings had a positive effect because they provided a structure to their work day.

Are you a goal-oriented person? Do meetings frustrate you?

Adapted from E. Packard, "Meetings Frustrate Task-Oriented Employees, Study Finds," *Monitor on Psychology* 37, no. 6 (June 2006): 10.

"Assertiveness" May Be a Matter of Conversational Style

"Rachel regularly led training groups with a male colleague. He always did all the talking, and she was always angry at him for dominating and not giving her a chance to say anything. . . . He would begin to answer questions from the group while she was still waiting for a slight pause to begin answering. And when she was in the middle of talking, he would jump in—but always when she had paused. So she tried pushing herself to begin answering questions a little sooner than felt polite, and not to leave long pauses when she was talking. The result was that she talked a lot more, and the man was as pleased as she was. Her supervisor complimented her on having become more assertive."

"Whether or not Rachel actually became more assertive is debatable. . . . [S]he solved her problem with a simple and slight adjustment of her way of speaking, without soul-searching, self-analysis, external intervention, and—most important—without defining herself as having an emotional problem or a personality defect: unassertiveness."

Quoted from Deborah Tannen, *That's Not What I Meant!* (New York: William Morrow, 1986), 177–78.

- Successful groups assign specific tasks, set clear deadlines, and schedule frequent meetings. In less successful groups, members are not sure what they are supposed to be doing or when it is needed. Less successful groups meet less often.
- Successful groups listen carefully to each other and respond to emotions as well as words. Less successful groups pay less attention to what is said and how it is said.
- In successful groups members work more evenly and actively on the project.[4] Successful groups even find ways to use members who don't like working in groups. For example, a student who doesn't want to be a "team player" can be a freelancer for her group, completing assignments by herself and e-mailing them to the group. Less successful groups have a smaller percentage of active members and frequently have some members who do very little on the final project.
- Successful groups make important decisions together. In less successful groups, a subgroup or an individual makes decisions.
- Successful groups listen to criticism and try to improve their performance on the basis of it. In less successful groups, criticism is rationalized.
- Successful groups deal directly with conflicts that emerge; unsuccessful groups try to ignore conflicts.[5]

Rebecca Burnett has shown that student groups produce better documents when they disagree over substantive issues of content and document design. The disagreement does not need to be angry: a group member can simply say, "Yes, and here's another way we could do it." Deciding among two (or more) alternatives forces the proposer to explain the rationale for an idea. Even when the group adopts the original idea, considering alternatives rather than quickly accepting the first idea produces better writing.[6]

As you no doubt realize, these characteristics of good groups actually apply to most groups, not just student groups. A survey of engineering project teams found that 95% of the team members thought that good communication was the reason for group success, and poor communication the reason for group failures.[7]

Peer Pressure and Groupthink

Groups that never express conflict may be experiencing groupthink. **Groupthink** is the tendency for groups to put such a high premium on agreement that they directly or indirectly punish dissent.

Many people feel so much reluctance to express open disagreement that they will say they agree even when objective circumstances would suggest the first speaker cannot be right. In a series of classic experiments in the 1950s, Solomon Asch showed the influence of peer pressure. People sitting around a table were shown a large card with a line and asked to match it to the line of the same length on another card. It's a simple test: people normally match the lines correctly almost 100% of the time. However, in the experiment, all but one of the people in the group had been instructed to give false answers for several of the trials. When the group gave an incorrect answer, the focal person accepted the group's judgment 36.8% of the time. When someone else also gave a different answer—even if it was another wrong answer—the focal person accepted the group's judgment only 9% of the time.[8]

The experimenters varied the differences in line lengths, hoping to create a situation in which even the most conforming subjects would trust their own senses. But some people continued to accept the group's judgment, even when one line was seven inches longer than the other.

A classic example of groupthink, and one illustrating the sometimes constraining influence of a powerful group leader, occurred during President Kennedy's administration. The deliberations of Kennedy and his advisers illustrated classic characteristics of groupthink such as premature agreement and suppression of doubts. Kennedy guided the discussions in a way that minimized disagreements. The result was the disastrous decision to launch the Bay of Pigs invasion, whose failure led to the Cuban Missile Crisis. However, Kennedy subsequently analyzed what had gone wrong with the decision process, and he had his advisers do likewise. He used these analyses to change the process for the Cuban Missile Crisis. Although the group again included Kennedy and many of the same advisers, it avoided groupthink. Kennedy ordered the group to question, allowed free-ranging discussions, used separate subgroup meetings, and sometimes left the room himself to avoid undue influence of the discussions.[9]

Groups that "go along with the crowd" and suppress conflict ignore the full range of alternatives, seek only information that supports the positions they already favor, and fail to prepare contingency plans to cope with foreseeable setbacks. A business suffering from groupthink may launch a new product that senior executives support but for which there is no demand. Student groups suffering from groupthink turn in inferior documents.

The best correctives to groupthink are to consciously search for additional alternatives, to test one's assumptions against those of a range of other people, and to protect the right of people in a group to disagree. When power roles are a factor, input may need to be anonymous.

Working in Diverse Groups

In any organization, you will work with people whose backgrounds and working styles differ from yours. Residents of small towns and rural areas have different notions of friendliness than do people from big cities. Marketing people tend to have different values and attitudes than researchers or engineers. In addition, differences arise from gender, class, race and ethnicity, religion, age, sexual orientation, and physical ability. Even people who share some of these characteristics are likely to differ in personality type.

Diverse teams can extend the range of group efforts and ideas.

These differences affect how people behave in groups and what they expect from groups. For example, in a business negotiation, people from Asia are more likely to see the goal of negotiation as development of a relationship between the parties. In contrast, American negotiators (especially the lawyers in the group) are more likely to see the purpose of a negotiation as to produce a signed contract.[10] Such differences are likely to affect what people talk about and how they talk. Some western cultures use direct approaches; other cultures, especially eastern cultures, consider such approaches rude and respond by withholding information.

Another pitfall of group differences is that people who sense a difference may attribute problems in the group to prejudice, when other factors may be responsible. In fact, a body of research shows that ethnically diverse teams produce more and higher quality ideas.[11] Research has also found that over time, as group members focus on their task, mission, or profession, cultural differences become less significant than the role of being a group member.[12]

As the second sidebar in the chapter shows, sometimes the culture to which the group belongs is a distinct asset, uniting strangers in positive ways and giving them strengths to use in high-stakes situations. With their group skills enhanced by the organizational culture, airline crews may perform heroically in a crisis.[13]

Savvy group members play to each other's strengths and devise strategies for dealing with differences. These efforts can benefit the whole group. A study of multicultural teams published in the *Harvard Business Review* found adaptation, acknowledging cultural gaps openly and cooperatively working through them, an ideal strategy for surmounting cultural differences. For example, a US and UK team used their differing approaches to decision making to create a higher-quality decision. The UK members used their slower approach to analyze possible pitfalls, and the US members used their "forge ahead" approach to move the project along. Both sides appreciated the contributions of the other members.[14]

Some potential sources of miscommunication to be prepared for include differences in conversational style and nonverbal communication.

Conversational Style

Deborah Tannen uses the term **conversational style** to denote our conversational patterns and the meaning we give to them: the way we show interest, politeness, appropriateness.[15] Your answers to the following questions reveal your own conversational style:

- How long a pause tells you that it's your turn to speak?
- Do you see interruption as rude? or do you say things while other people are still talking to show that you're interested and to encourage them to say more?
- Do you show interest by asking lots of questions? or do you see questions as intrusive and wait for people to volunteer whatever they have to say?

Tannen concludes that the following features characterize her own conversational style:

Fast rate of speech.

Fast rate of turn-taking.

Persistence—if a turn is not acknowledged, try again.

Preference for personal stories.

Tolerance of, preference for simultaneous speech.

Abrupt topic shifting.

Different conversational styles are not better or worse than each other, but people with different conversational styles may feel uncomfortable without knowing why. A subordinate who talks quickly may be frustrated by a boss who speaks slowly. People who talk more slowly may feel shut out of a conversation with people who talk more quickly. Someone who has learned to make requests directly ("Please pass the salt") may be annoyed by someone who uses indirect requests ("This casserole needs some salt").

In the workplace, conflicts may arise because of differences in conversational style. If people see direct questions as criticizing or accusing, they may see an ordinary question ("Will that report be ready Friday?") as a criticism of their progress. One supervisor might mean the question simply as a request for information. Another supervisor might use the question to mean "I want that report Friday."

Daniel N. Maltz and Ruth A. Borker believe that differences in conversational style (Figure 14.3) may be responsible for the miscommunication that often occurs in male–female conversations. Certainly conversational style is not the same for all men and for all women, but research has found several common patterns in the US cultures studied so far.[16] For example, researchers have found that women are much more likely to nod and to say *yes* or *mm hmm* than men are.[17] Maltz and Borker hypothesize that to women, these symbols mean simply "I'm listening; go on." Men, on the other hand, may decode these symbols as "I agree" or at least "I follow what you're saying so far." A man who receives nods and *mms* from a woman may feel that she is inconsistent and unpredictable if she then disagrees with him. A woman may feel that a man who doesn't provide any feedback isn't listening to her.

Nonverbal Communication

Posture and body movements connote energy and openness. North American **open body positions** include leaning forward with uncrossed arms and legs, with the arms away from the body. **Closed** or **defensive body**

Figure 14.3   Different Conversational Styles

	Debating	Relating
Interpretation of questions	See questions as requests for information.	See questions as way to keep a conversation flowing.
Relation of new comment to what last speaker said	Do not require new comment to relate explicitly to last speaker's comment. Ignoring previous comment is one strategy for taking control.	Expect new comments to acknowledge the last speaker's comment and relate directly to it.
View of aggressiveness	See aggressiveness as one way to organize the flow of conversation.	See aggressiveness as directed at audience personally, as negative, and as disruptive to a conversation.
How topics are defined and changed	Tend to define topics narrowly and shift topics abruptly. Interpret statements about side issues as effort to change the topic.	Tend to define topics gradually, progressively. Interpret statements about side issues as effort to shape, expand, or limit the topic.
Response to someone who shares a problem	Offer advice, solutions.	Offer solidarity, reassurance. Share troubles to establish sense of community.

Sources: Based on Daniel N. Maltz and Ruth A. Borker, "A Cultural Approach to Male-Female Miscommunication," *Language and Social Identity,* ed. John J. Gumperz (Cambridge: Cambridge University Press, 1982), 213; and Deborah Tannen, *Talking from 9 to 5: Women and Men in the Workplace: Language, Sex and Power* (New York: William Morrow, 1995).

positions include leaning back, sometimes with both hands behind the head, arms and legs crossed or close together, or hands in pockets. As the labels imply, open positions suggest that people are accepting and open to new ideas. Closed positions suggest that people are physically or psychologically uncomfortable, that they are defending themselves and shutting other people out.

People who cross their arms or legs often claim that they do so only because the position is more comfortable. But notice your own body the next time you're in a perfectly comfortable discussion with a good friend. You'll probably find that you naturally assume open body positions. The fact that so many people in organizational settings adopt closed positions may indicate that many people feel at least slightly uncomfortable in school and on the job.

As Chapter 13 explains, even within a culture, a nonverbal sign may have more than one meaning. A young woman took a new idea into her boss, who sat there and glared at her, brows together in a frown, as she explained her proposal. The stare and lowered brows symbolized anger to her, and she assumed that he was rejecting her idea. Several months later, she learned that her boss always "frowned" when he was concentrating. The facial expression she had interpreted as anger had not been intended to convey anger at all.

As we saw in Chapter 13, misunderstandings are even more common when people communicate with people from other cultures or other countries. Knowing something about other cultures may help you realize that a subordinate who doesn't meet your eye may be showing respect rather than dishonesty. But it's impossible to memorize every meaning that every nonverbal sign has in every culture. And in a multicultural workforce, you can't know whether someone retains the meanings of his or her ancestors or has adopted the dominant US meanings. The best solution is to ask for clarification.

(a)   (b)

(a)"THE REAL THING: A real smile involves the whole face, not just the mouth. While muscles pull the corners of the mouth up (1), an involuntary nerve causes the upper eyefold (2) to relax."

(b)"THE SOCIAL SMILE: When faking, the lips are pulled straight across (3). Though this creates cheek folds (4) similar to those of a real smile, the lack of eye crinkles (5) is a dead giveaway."

Quoted from: Andy Raskin, "A Face Any Business Can Trust," *Business 2.0* 4, no. 11 (December 2003): 60.

Body language can give big clues about our attitude to office visitors.

Conflict Resolution

Conflicts are going to arise in any group of intelligent people who care about the task. Yet many of us feel so uncomfortable with conflict that we pretend it doesn't exist. However, unacknowledged conflicts rarely go away: they fester, making the next interchange more difficult.

To reduce the number of conflicts in a group,

- Make responsibilities and ground rules clear at the beginning.
- Discuss problems as they arise, rather than letting them fester till people explode.
- Realize that group members are not responsible for each others' happiness.

In spite of these efforts, some conflict is a part of any group's life. Group members need to resolve the conflict. When a conflict is emotionally charged, people will need a chance to calm themselves before they can arrive at a well-reasoned solution. Meeting expert John Tropman recommends the "two-meeting rule" for emotional matters: Controversial items should be handled at two different meetings. The first meeting is a chance for everyone to air a point of view about the issue. The second meeting is the one at which the group reaches a decision. The time between the two meetings becomes a cooling-off period.[18]

Figure 14.4 suggests several possible solutions to conflicts that student groups often experience. Often the symptom arises from a feeling of not being respected or appreciated by the group. Therefore, many problems can be averted if people advocate for their ideas in a positive way. One way to do this is to devote as much effort to positive observations as possible. Another technique is to state analysis rather than mere opinions. Instead of "I wouldn't read an eight-page brochure," the member of a team could say, "Tests we did a couple of years ago found a better response for two-page brochures. Could we put some of that information on our Web site instead?" As in this example, an opinion can vary from person to person; stating an opinion does not provide a basis for the group to make a decision. In contrast, analysis provides objective information for the group to consider.[19]

Steps in Conflict Resolution

Dealing successfully with conflict requires attention both to the issues and to people's feelings. This technique will help you resolve conflicts constructively.

Power Talk

"A person who feels confident and in control will speak at length, set the agenda for a conversation, stave off interruptions, argue openly, make jokes, and laugh. Such a person is more inclined to make statements, less inclined to ask questions. They are more likely to offer solutions or a program or a plan. . . ."

"The power deficient drop into conversations, encourage other speakers, ask numerous questions, avoid argument, and rely on gestures such as smiling and nodding that suggest agreement. They tend to offer empathy rather than solutions. They often use unfinished sentences. . . ."

"The key is figuring out who gets listened to within your corporate culture. That can make you a more savvy user of language. Try to sit in on a meeting as a kind of researcher, observing conversational patterns. . . . Then try to determine who gets noticed and why."

Quoted from Sarah McGinty, "How You Speak Shows Where You Rank," *Fortune*, February 2, 1998, 156.

Figure 14.4   Troubleshooting Group Problems

Symptom	Possible solutions
We can't find a time to meet that works for all of us.	a. Find out why people can't meet at certain times. Some reasons suggest their own solutions. For example, if someone has to stay home with small children, perhaps the group could meet at that person's home. b. Assign out-of-class work to "committees" to work on parts of the project. c. Use e-mail to share, discuss, and revise drafts.
One person isn't doing his or her fair share.	a. Find out what is going on. Is the person overcommitted? Does he or she feel unappreciated? Those are different problems you'd solve in different ways. b. Early on, do things to build group loyalty. Get to know each other as writers and as people. Sometimes, do something fun together. c. Encourage the person to contribute. "Mary, what do you think?" "Jim, which part of this would you like to draft?" Then find something to praise in the work. "Thanks for getting us started." d. If someone misses a meeting, assign someone else to bring the person up to speed. People who miss meetings for legitimate reasons (job interviews, illness) but don't find out what happened may become less committed to the group. e. Consider whether strict equality is the most important criterion. On a given project, some people may have more knowledge or time than others. Sometimes the best group product results from letting people do different amounts of "work." f. Even if you divide up the work, make all decisions as a group: what to write about, which evidence to include, what graphs to use, what revisions to make. People excluded from decisions become less committed to the group.
I seem to be the only one in the group who cares about quality.	a. Find out why other members "don't care." If they received low grades on early assignments, stress that good ideas and attention to detail can raise grades. Perhaps the group should meet with the instructor to discuss what kinds of work will pay the highest dividends. b. Volunteer to do extra work. Sometimes people settle for something that's just OK because they don't have the time or resources to do excellent work. They might be happy for the work to be done—if they don't have to do it. c. Be sure that you're respecting what each person can contribute. Group members sometimes withdraw when one person dominates and suggests that he or she is "better" than other members.
People in the group don't seem willing to disagree. We end up going with the first idea suggested.	a. Appoint someone to be a devil's advocate. b. Brainstorm so you have several possibilities to consider. c. After an idea is suggested, have each person in the group suggest a way it could be improved. d. Have each person in the group write a draft. It's likely the drafts will be different, and you'll have several options to mix and match. e. Talk about good ways to offer criticism. Sometimes people don't disagree because they're afraid that other group members won't tolerate disagreement.
One person just criticizes everything.	a. Ask the person to follow up the criticism with a suggestion for improvement. b. Talk about ways to express criticism tactfully. "I think we need to think about x" is more tactful than "You're wrong." c. If the criticism is about ideas and writing (not about people), value it. Ideas and documents need criticism if we are to improve them.

1. Make sure the people involved really disagree.

Sometimes different conversational styles, differing interpretations of symbols, or faulty inferences create apparent conflicts when no real disagreement exists. Sometimes someone who's under a lot of pressure may explode.

But the speaker may just be venting anger and frustration; he or she may not in fact be angry at the person who receives the explosion. One way to find out if a person is just venting is to ask, "Is there something you'd like me to do?"

2. Check to see that everyone's information is correct.

Sometimes people are operating on outdated or incomplete information. People may also act on personal biases or opinions rather than data.

3. Discover the needs each person is trying to meet.

Sometimes determining the real needs makes it possible to see a new solution. The **presenting problem** that surfaces as the subject of dissension may or may not be the real problem. For example, a worker who complains about the hours he's putting in may in fact be complaining not about the hours themselves but about not feeling appreciated. A supervisor who complains that the other supervisors don't invite her to meetings may really feel that the other managers don't accept her as a peer. Sometimes people have trouble seeing beyond the presenting problem because they've been taught to suppress their anger, especially toward powerful people. One way to tell whether the presenting problem is the real problem is to ask, "If this were solved, would I be satisfied?" If the answer is *no*, then the problem that presents itself is not the real problem. Solving the presenting problem won't solve the conflict. Keep probing until you get to the real conflict.

4. Search for alternatives.

Sometimes people are locked into conflict because they see too few alternatives. People tend to handle complexity by looking for ways to simplify. In a group, someone makes a suggestion, so the group members discuss it as if it is the only alternative. The group generates more alternatives only if the first one is unacceptable. As a result, the group's choice depends on the order in which group members think of ideas. When a decision is significant, the group needs a formal process to identify alternatives before moving on to a decision.[20] Many groups use brainstorming when they search for alternatives.

5. Repair negative feelings.

Conflict can emerge without anger and without escalating the disagreement, as the next section shows. But if people's feelings have been hurt, the group needs to deal with those feelings to resolve the conflict constructively. Only when people feel respected and taken seriously can they take the next step of trusting others in the group.

Responding to Criticism

Conflict is particularly difficult to resolve when someone else criticizes or attacks us directly. When we are criticized, our natural reaction is to defend ourselves—perhaps by counterattacking. The counterattack prompts the critic to defend him- or herself. The conflict escalates; feelings are hurt; issues become muddied and more difficult to resolve.

Just as resolving conflict depends on identifying the needs each person is trying to meet, so dealing with criticism depends on understanding the real concern of the critic. Constructive ways to respond to criticism and get closer

Who Does What

Working successfully in a group depends on being open about preferences, constraints, and skills and then using creative problem-solving techniques.

A person who prefers to outline the whole project in advance may be in a group with someone who expects to do the project at the last minute. Someone who likes to talk out ideas before writing may be in a group with someone who wants to work on a draft in silence and revise it before showing it to anyone. By being honest about your preferences, you make it possible for the group to find a creative solution that builds on what each person can offer.

In one group, Rob wanted to wait to start the project because he was busy with other class work. David and Susan, however, wanted to go ahead now because their schedules would get busier later in the term. A creative solution would be for David and Susan to do most of the work on parts of the project that had to be completed first (such as collecting data and writing the proposal) and for Rob to do work that had to be done later (such as revising, editing, and proofreading).

What are your work preferences? What are the preferences of other people in your group? How can you work together to accommodate everyone's schedules and preferences?

http://3m.com/meeting network/readingroom/ index.html

Log onto 3M's Web site for articles offering advice about holding effective meetings. What advice offered in these articles do you think would be helpful for conducting meetings with your fellow group members?

to the real concern include paraphrasing, checking for feelings, checking inferences, and buying time with limited agreement.

Paraphrasing

To **paraphrase,** repeat in your own words the verbal content of the critic's message. The purposes of paraphrasing are (1) to be sure that you have heard the critic accurately, (2) to let the critic know what his or her statement means to you, and (3) to communicate the feeling that you are taking the critic and his or her feelings seriously.

> Criticism: You guys are stonewalling my requests for information.
>
> Paraphrase: You think that we don't give you the information you need.

Checking for feelings

When you check the critic's feelings, you identify the emotions that the critic seems to be expressing verbally or nonverbally. The purposes of checking feelings are to try to understand (1) the critic's emotions, (2) the importance of the criticism for the critic, and (3) the unspoken ideas and feelings that may actually be more important than the voiced criticism.

> Criticism: You guys are stonewalling my requests for information.
>
> Feeling check: You sound pretty angry.

Always *ask* the other person if you are right in your perception. Even the best reader of nonverbal cues is sometimes wrong.

Checking for inferences

When you check the inferences you draw from criticism, you identify the implied meaning of the verbal and nonverbal content of the criticism, taking the statement a step further than the words of the critic to try to understand *why* the critic is bothered by the action or attitude under discussion. The purposes of checking inferences are (1) to identify the real (as opposed to the presenting) problem and (2) to communicate the feeling that you care about resolving the conflict.

> Criticism: You guys are stonewalling my requests for information.
>
> Inference: Are you saying that you need more information from our group?

Inferences can be faulty. In the above interchange, the critic might respond, "I don't need more information. I just think you should give it to me without my having to file three forms in triplicate every time I want some data."

Buying time with limited agreement

Buying time is a useful strategy for dealing with criticisms that really sting. When you buy time with limited agreement, you avoid escalating the conflict (as an angry statement might do) but also avoid yielding to the critic's point of view. To buy time, restate the part of the criticism you agree to be true. (This is often a fact, rather than the interpretation or evaluation the critic has made of that fact.) *Then let the critic respond, before you say anything else.* The purposes of buying time are (1) to allow you time to think when a criticism really hits home and threatens you, so that you can respond to the criticism rather than simply reacting defensively, and (2) to suggest to the critic that you are trying to hear what he or she is saying.

> Criticism: You guys are stonewalling my requests for information.
>
> Limited agreement: It's true that the cost projections you asked for last week still aren't ready.

DO NOT go on to justify or explain. A "Yes, but . . . " statement is not a time-buyer.

You-Attitude in Conflict Resolution

You-attitude means looking at things from the audience's point of view, respecting the audience, and protecting the audience's ego. The *you* statements that many people use when they're angry attack the audience; they do not illustrate you-attitude. Instead, substitute statements about your own feelings. In conflict, *I* statements show good you-attitude!

Lacks you-attitude:	You never do your share of the work.
You-attitude:	I feel that I'm doing more than my share of the work on this project.
Lacks you-attitude:	Even you should be able to run the report through a spelling checker.
You-attitude:	I'm not willing to have my name on a report with so many spelling errors. I did lots of the writing, and I don't think I should have to do the proofreading and spell checking, too.

Effective Meetings

Meetings have always taken a large part of the average manager's week. Although e-mail has eliminated some meetings, the increased number of teams means that meetings are even more frequent. As the sidebar on page 463 suggests, meetings are not always good. Many workers see them as all too often a waste of time, interrupting valuable work.[21] However, meetings can easily be made more effective.

Meetings can have multiple purposes:

- To share information.
- To brainstorm ideas.
- To evaluate ideas.
- To develops plans.
- To make decisions.
- To create a document.
- To motivate members.

When meetings combine two or more purposes, it's useful to make the purposes explicit. For example, in the meeting of a university senate or a company's board of directors, some items are presented for information. Discussion is possible, but the group will not be asked to make a decision. Other items are presented for action; the group will be asked to vote. A business meeting might specify that the first half hour will be time for brainstorming, with the second half hour devoted to evaluation.

Formal meetings are run under strict rules, like the rules of parliamentary procedure summarized in *Robert's Rules of Order*. Motions must be made formally before a topic can be debated. Each point is settled by a vote. **Minutes** record each motion and the vote on it. Formal rules help the meeting run smoothly if the group is very large or if the agenda is very long. **Informal meetings,** which are much more common in the workplace, are run more loosely. Votes may not be taken if most people seem to agree. Minutes may not be kept. Informal meetings are better for team-building and problem solving.

Planning the agenda is the foundation of a good meeting. A good agenda indicates

- A list of items for consideration.
- Whether each item is presented for information, for discussion, or for a decision.

Being Taken Seriously

It's frustrating to speak in a meeting and have people ignore what you say. Here are some tips for being taken seriously:

- Link your comment to the comment of a powerful person, even if logic suffers a bit. For example, say, "John is saying that we should focus on excellence, AND I think we can become stronger by encouraging diversity."

- Show that you've done your homework. Laura Sloate, who is blind, establishes authority by making sure her first question is highly technical: "In footnote three of the 10K, you indicate . . . "

- Find an ally in the organization and agree ahead of time to acknowledge each other's contributions to the meeting, whether you agree or disagree with the point being made. Explicit disagreement signals that the comment is worth taking seriously: "Duane has pointed out . . . , but I think that. . . . "

- Use the style of language that powerful people in your organization use.

- Repeat your ideas. Put important ideas in a memo before the meeting.

Adapted from Joan E. Rigdon, "Managing Your Career," *Wall Street Journal,* December 1. 1993, B1; Cynthia Crossen, "Spotting Value Takes Smarts, Not Sight, Laura Sloate Shows," *Wall Street Journal,* December 10, 1987. A1, A14; and Anne Fisher, "Ask Annie: Putting Your Money Where Your Mouth Is," *Fortune,* September 3, 2001, 238.

Collaborating on "Remote" Teams

Technology can link team members who are located far apart. Members of these remote teams (sometimes called virtual teams) share work electronically and communicate via phone calls, e-mail, and instant messaging. Without the advantages of face-to-face communication, how do they keep working relationships strong and projects on track?

Writers Nancy Larbi and Susan Springfield have often been remote team members for SAS, a software company based in North Carolina. They and other SAS writers work from offices located throughout the United States and Canada, participating in team projects for up to 10 months.

Larbi and Springfield advise that especially on remote teams, team members must learn about each other, the client, and the type of project before the project begins. Remote team members also need to be precise about the project's plan. Someone must be responsible for each element of the plan, and deadlines must be established. Assumptions are especially dangerous on a remote team, because it is harder to notice when something is not getting done according to expectations. Numbering each version of a document helps people ensure they are seeing the same version. Word-processing software also offers a feature that creates a record of what is changing and who made the change. Finally, Larbi and Springfield say, e-mail works well for disseminating information, but if problems arise, there is no substitute for a face-to-face meeting.

Adapted from Nancy E. Larbi and Susan Springfield, "When No One's Home: Being a Writer on Remote Project Teams," *Technical Communication* 51, no. 1 (February 2004): 102–08.

- Who is sponsoring or introducing each item.
- How much time is allotted for each item.

The information on an agenda should be specific enough that participants can come to the meeting prepared with ideas, background information, and any other resources they need for completing each agenda item.

Many groups put first routine items on which agreement will be easy. Doing so gets the meeting off to a positive start. However, it may also waste the time when people are most attentive. Another approach is to put routine items at the end. If there's a long list of routine items, sometimes you can dispense with them in an omnibus motion. An **omnibus motion** allows a group to approve many items together rather than voting on each separately. A single omnibus motion might cover multiple changes to operational guidelines, or a whole slate of candidates for various offices, or various budget recommendations. It's important to schedule controversial items early in the meeting, when people's energy level is high, and to allow enough time for full discussion. Giving a controversial item only half an hour at the end of the day or evening makes people suspect that the leaders are trying to manipulate them.

Pay attention to people and process as well as to the task at hand. At informal meetings, a good leader observes nonverbal feedback and invites everyone to participate. If conflict seems to be getting out of hand, a leader may want to focus attention on the group process and ways that it could deal with conflict, before getting back to the substantive issues.

If the group doesn't formally vote, the leader should summarize the group's consensus after each point. At the end of the meeting, the leader should summarize all decisions and remind the group who is responsible for implementing or following up on each item. If no other notes are taken, someone should record the decisions and assignments. Long minutes will be most helpful if assignments are set off visually from the narrative.

If you're planning a long meeting, for example, a training session or a conference, recognize that networking is part of the value of the meeting. Allow short breaks at least every two hours and generous breaks twice a day so participants can talk informally to each other. If participants will be strangers, include some social functions so they can get to know each other. If they will have different interests or different levels of knowledge, plan concurrent sessions on different topics or for people with different levels of expertise.

Collaborative Writing

Whatever your career, it is likely that some of the documents you produce will be written with a group. Lisa Ede and Andrea Lunsford found that 87% of the 700 professionals in seven fields who responded to their survey sometimes wrote as members of a team or a group.[22] Collaboration is often prompted by one of the following situations:

1. The task is too big or the time is too short for one person to do all the work.
2. No one person has all the knowledge required to do the task.
3. A group representing different perspectives must reach a consensus.
4. The stakes for the task are so high that the organization wants the best efforts of as many people as possible; no one person wants the sole responsibility for the success or failure of the document.

Collaborative writing can be done by two people or by a much larger group. The group can be democratic or run by a leader who makes decisions alone. The group may share or divide responsibility for each stage in the writing process. There are several ways groups commonly divide the work. One person

Many important historical documents resulted from collaborative efforts. Thomas Jefferson may have written the foundation for the Declaration of Independence, but received many suggestions and changes from other key players, including John Adams and Benjamin Franklin. The document underwent 47 alterations before it was finalized and presented to Congress.

might do the main writing, with others providing feedback. Another approach is to divide the whole project into smaller tasks and to assign each task to a different group member. This approach shares the workload more evenly but is harder to coordinate. Sometimes group members work together simultaneously, discussing and responding to each other's ideas.[23]

Research in collaborative writing suggests strategies that produce the best writing. As noted earlier, research has found that student groups that voiced disagreements as they analyzed, planned, and wrote a document produced significantly better documents than those that suppressed disagreement, going along with whatever was first proposed.[24] A case study of two collaborative writing teams in a state agency found that the successful group distributed power in an egalitarian way, worked to soothe hurt feelings, and was careful to involve all group members. In terms of writing process, the successful group understood the task as a response to a rhetorical situation, planned revisions as a group, saw supervisors' comments as legitimate, and had a positive attitude toward revision.[25] Ede and Lunsford's detailed case studies of collaborative teams in business, government, and science create an "emerging profile of effective collaborative writers": "They are flexible; respectful of others; attentive and analytical listeners; able to speak and write clearly and articulately; dependable and able to meet deadlines; able to designate and share responsibility, to lead and to follow; open to criticism but confident in their own abilities; ready to engage in creative conflict."[26]

Planning the Work and the Document

Collaborative writing is most successful when the group articulates its understanding of the document's purposes, audiences, and contexts, and explicitly discusses the best way to achieve rhetorical goals. Businesses schedule formal planning sessions for large projects to set up a time line specifying intermediate and final due dates, meeting dates, who will attend each meeting, and who will do what. Putting the plan in writing reduces misunderstandings during the project.

When you plan a collaborative writing project,

- Make your analysis of the problem, audience, context, and purposes explicit so you know where you agree and where you disagree. It usually helps to put these in writing.
- Plan the organization, format, and style of the document before anyone begins to write to make it easier to blend sections written by different authors. Decide who is going to do what and when each piece of the project will be due.
- Consider your work styles and other commitments when making a timeline. A writer working alone can stay up all night to finish a single-authored document. But members of a group need to work together to accommodate each other's styles and to enable members to meet other commitments.
- Decide how you will give constructive feedback on each person's work.
- Build some leeway into your deadlines. It's harder for a group to finish a document when one person's part is missing than it is for a single writer to finish the last section of a document on which he or she has done all the work.

Composing the Drafts

Most writers find that composing alone is faster than composing in a group. However, composing together may reduce revision time later, since the group examines every choice as it is made.

When you draft a collaborative writing project,

- Carefully label and date drafts so everyone is working on the most current version. Consider if this is a document that can be posted on a server where everyone can work on it. Sometimes this method saves time, but not always.
- If the quality of writing is crucial, have the best writer(s) draft the document after everyone has gathered the necessary information.

Revising the Document

Revising a collaborative document requires attention to content, organization, and style. The following guidelines can make the revision process more effective:

- Evaluate the content and discuss possible revisions as a group. Brainstorm ways to improve each section so the person doing the revisions has some guidance.
- Recognize that different people favor different writing styles. If the style satisfies the demands of standard English and the conventions of business writing, accept it even if you wouldn't say it that way.
- When the group is satisfied with the content of the document, one person—probably the best writer—should make any changes necessary to make the writing style consistent throughout.

Editing and Proofreading the Document

Since writers' mastery of standard English varies, a group report needs careful editing and proofreading.

- Have at least one person check the whole document for correctness in grammar, mechanics, and spelling and for consistency in the way that format elements (particularly headings), names, and numbers are handled.
- Run the document through a spell checker.
- Even if you use a computerized spell checker, at least one human being should proofread the document too.

Like any member of the writing team, those handling the editing tasks need to consider how they express their ideas. In many situations, the editor plays the role of diplomat, careful to suggest changes in ways that do not seem to call the writer's abilities into question. Describing the reason for a change is typically more helpful than stating an opinion. Writers are more likely to allow editing of their prose if they know a sentence has a dangling modifier, or a paragraph needs work on parallel structure. Words like *could* and *should* to modify a direction can add a tone of politeness.[27]

Making the Group Process Work

All the information in this chapter can help your collaborative writing group listen effectively, run meetings efficiently, and deal with conflict constructively. The following suggestions apply specifically to writing groups:

- Give yourselves plenty of time to discuss problems and find solutions. Writing a group report may require hours of discussion time in addition to the time individuals spend doing research and writing drafts.
- Take the time to get to know group members and to build group loyalty. Group members will work harder and the final document will be better if the group is important to members.
- Be a responsible group member. Attend all the meetings; carry out your responsibilities on time.
- Be aware that people have different ways of experiencing reality and of expressing themselves.
- Because talking is "looser" than writing, people in a group can think they agree when they don't. Don't assume that because the discussion went smoothly, a draft written by one person will necessarily be acceptable.

Summary of Key Points

- **Interpersonal communication** is communication between people.
- To avoid listening errors,
  - Be conscious of the points you need to know and listen for them.
  - Paraphrase what the speaker has said, giving him or her a chance to correct your understanding.
  - At the end of the conversation, check your understanding with the other person.
  - After the conversation, write down key points that affect deadlines or how work will be evaluated.
  - Don't ignore instructions you think are unnecessary.
  - Consider the other person's background and experiences. Why is this point important to the speaker?
- In **active listening,** receivers actively demonstrate that they've heard and understood a speaker by feeding back either the literal meaning or the emotional content or both.

Using Informal Meetings to Advance Your Career

You'll see your supervisor several times a week. Some of these meetings will be accidental: you'll meet by the coffee pot or ride up the elevator together. Some of them will be deliberately initiated: your boss will stop by your work station, or you'll go to your boss's office to ask for something.

Take advantage of these meetings by planning for them. These informal meetings are often short. An elevator ride, for example, may last about three minutes. So plan 90-second scripts that you can use to give your boss a brief report on what you're doing, ask for something you need, or lay the groundwork for an important issue.

Planning scripts is especially important if your boss doesn't give you much feedback or mentoring. In this case, your boss probably doesn't see you as promotable. You need to take the initiative. Make statements that show the boss you're thinking about ways to work smarter. Show that you're interested in learning more so that you can be more valuable to the organization.

- Effective groups balance information leadership, interpersonal leadership, and procedural group management.
- Successful groups set clear deadlines, schedule frequent meetings, deal directly with conflict, have an inclusive decision-making style, and have a higher proportion of members who worked actively on the project.
- **Groupthink** is the tendency for groups to put such a high premium on agreement that they directly or indirectly punish dissent. The best correctives to groupthink are to consciously search for additional alternatives, to test one's assumptions against those of a range of other people, and to protect the right of each person in the group to disagree.
- **Conversational style** denotes our conversational patterns and the meaning we give to them: the way we show interest, politeness, and appropriateness.
- To resolve conflicts, first make sure that the people involved really disagree. Next, check to see that everyone's information is correct. Discover the needs each person is trying to meet. The **presenting problem** that surfaces as the subject of dissension may or may not be the real problem. Search for alternatives. Repair negative feelings.
- Constructive ways to respond to criticism include paraphrasing, checking for feelings, checking inferences, and buying time with limited agreement.
- Use statements about your own feelings to own the problem and avoid attacking the audience. In conflict, *I* statements are good you-attitude!
- To make meetings more effective,
  - State the purpose of the meeting at the beginning.
  - Distribute an agenda that indicates whether each item is for information, discussion, or action, and how long each is expected to take.
  - Allow enough time to discuss controversial issues.
  - Pay attention to people and process as well as to the task at hand.
  - If you don't take formal votes, summarize the group's consensus after each point. At the end of the meeting, summarize all decisions and remind the group who is responsible for implementing or following up on each item.
- **Collaborative writing** means working with other writers to produce a single document. Writers producing a joint document need to pay attention not only to the basic steps in the writing process but also to the processes of group formation and conflict resolution.

CHAPTER 14   # Exercises and Problems

14.1   Reviewing the Chapter

1. What are some ways to improve your listening skills? (LO 1)
2. What is active listening? (LO 1)
3. What are 10 kinds of productive roles in groups? Which roles do you prefer to play? (LO 2)
4. What are five kinds of nonproductive roles in groups? (LO 2)
5. What are some group decision-making strategies? (LO 3)
6. Name five characteristics of successful groups. (LO 4)
7. What is groupthink? Have you ever experienced it? (LO 3)
8. What are some techniques for resolving conflict? (LO 5)
9. What are some techniques for responding to criticism? (LO 5)
10. What are some techniques for making meetings effective? (LO 6)
11. What are some techniques for collaborative writing? (LO 7)
12. Have you ever been part of a group that wrote a document as a whole group rather than assigning out pieces? If so, how did the process work for your group? (LO 7)

14.2 Making Ethical Choices

Indicate whether you consider each of the following actions ethical, unethical, or a gray area. Which of the actions would you do? Which would you feel uncomfortable doing? Which would you refuse to do?

Discuss your answers with a small group of classmates. In what ways did knowing you would share with a group change your answers?

1. Taking home office supplies (e.g., pens, markers, calculators, etc.) for personal use.
2. Inflating your evaluation of a subordinate because you know that only people ranked *excellent* will get pay raises.
3. Making personal long-distance calls on the company phone.
4. Writing a feasibility report about a new product and de-emphasizing test results that show it could cause cancer.
5. Coming in to the office in the evening to use the company's word processor and computer for personal projects.
6. Designing an ad campaign for a cigarette brand.
7. Working as an accountant for a company that makes or advertises cigarettes.
8. Working as a manager in a company that exploits its nonunionized hourly workers.
9. Writing copy for a company's annual report hiding or minimizing the fact that the company pollutes the environment.
10. "Padding" your expense account by putting on it charges you did not pay for.
11. Writing a subscription letter for a sex magazine that glamorizes rape, violence, and sadism.
12. Doing the taxes of a client who publishes a sex magazine that glamorizes rape, violence, and sadism.
13. Telling a job candidate that the company "usually" grants cost-of-living raises every six months, even though you know that the company is losing money and plans to cancel cost-of-living raises for the next year.
14. Laughing at the racist or sexist jokes a client makes, even though you find them offensive.
15. Reading the *Wall Street Journal* on company time.

14.3 Identifying Responses That Show Active Listening

Which of the following responses show active listening? Which responses block communication?

1. Comment: Whenever I say something, the group just ignores me.

   Responses:
   a. That's because your ideas aren't very good. Do more planning before group meetings.
   b. Nobody listens to me, either.
   c. You're saying that nobody builds on your ideas.

2. Comment: I've done more than my share of work on this project. But the people who have been freeloading are going to get the same grade I've worked so hard to earn.

   Responses:
   a. Yes, we're all going to get the same grade.
   b. Are you afraid we won't do well on the assignment?
   c. It sounds like you feel resentful.

3. Comment: My parents are going to kill me if I don't have a job lined up when I graduate.

   Responses:
   a. You know they're exaggerating. They won't *really* kill you.
   b. Can you blame them? I mean, it's taken you six years to get a degree. Surely you've learned something to make you employable!
   c. If you act in interviews the way you do in our class, I'm not surprised. Companies want people with good attitudes and good work ethics.

14.4 Brainstorming Ways to Resolve Conflicts

Suggest one or more ways that each of the following groups could deal with the conflict(s) it faces.

1. Mike and Takashi both find writing hard. Elise has been getting better grades than either of them, so they offer to do all the research if she'll organize the document and write, revise, edit, and proofread it. Elise thinks that this method would leave her doing a disproportionate share of the work. Moreover, scheduling the work would be difficult, since she wouldn't know how good their research was until the last minute.

2. Because of their class and work schedules, Lars and Andrea want to hold group meetings from 8 to 10 PM,

working later if need be. But Juan's wife works the evening shift, and he needs to be home with his children, two of whom have to be in bed before 8. He wants to meet from 8 to 10 AM, but the others don't want to meet that early.

3. Lynn wants to divide up the work exactly equally, with firm due dates. Marcia is trying to get into medical school. She says she'd rather do the lion's share of the work so that she knows it's good.

4. Jessie's father is terminally ill. This group isn't very important in terms of what's going on in her life, and she knows she may have to miss some group meetings.

5. Sherry is aware that she is the person in her group who always points out the logical flaws in

arguments: she's the one who reminds the group that they haven't done all the parts of the assignment. She doesn't want her group to turn in a flawed product, but she wonders whether the other group members see her as too critical.

6. Jim's group missed several questions on their group quiz. Talking to Tae-Suk after class, Jim learns that Tae-Suk knew all the answers. "Why didn't you say anything?" Jim asks angrily. Tae-Suk responds quietly, "Todd said that he knew the answers. I did not want to argue with him. We have to work together, and I do not want anyone to lose face."

14.5   Comparing Meeting Minutes

As your instructor directs,

Have two or more people take minutes of each class or collaborative group meeting for a week. Compare the accounts of the same meeting.

- To what extent do they agree on what happened?

- Does one contain information missing in other accounts?
- Do any accounts disagree on a specific fact?
- How do you account for the differences you find?

In Problems 14.6 through 14.11, assume that your group has been asked to recommend a solution.

As your instructor directs,

- Send e-mail messages to group members laying out your initial point of view on the issue and discussing the various options.

- As a group, answer the message.
- Write a memo to your instructor telling how satisfied you are with
  a. The decision your group reached.
  b. The process you used to reach it.

14.6   Recommending a Policy on Student Entrepreneurs

Assume that your small group comprises the officers in student government on your campus. You receive this e-mail from the Dean of Students:

As you know, campus policy says that no student may use campus resources to conduct business-related activities. Students can't conduct business out of dorm rooms or use university e-mail addresses for business. They can't post business Web pages on the university server.

On the other hand, a survey conducted by the Kauffman Center for Entrepreneurial Leadership showed that 7 out of 10 teens want to become entrepreneurs.

Should campus policy be changed to allow students to use dorm rooms and university e-mail addresses for business? (And then what happens when roommates complain and our network can't carry the increased e-mail traffic?) Please recommend what support (if any) should be given to student entrepreneurs.

Write a group report recommending what (if anything) your campus should do for student entrepreneurs and supporting your recommendation.

Hints:

- Does your campus offer other support for entrepreneurs (courses, a business plan competition, a start-up incubator)? What should be added or expanded?

- Is it realistic to ask alumni for money to fund student start-ups?

- Are campus dorms, e-mail, phone, and delivery services funded by tax dollars? If your school is a public institution, do state or local laws limit business use?

14.7   Recommending a Fair Way to Assign Work Around the Holidays

Assume that your small group comprises your organization's Labor-Management Committee. This e-mail arrives from the general manager:

> Subject: Allocating Holiday Hours
>
> As you know, lots of people want to take extra time off around holidays to turn three-day weekends into longer trips. But we do need to stay open. Right now, there are allegations that some supervisors give the time off to their friends. But even "fair" systems, such as giving more senior workers first choice at time off, or requiring that workers with crucial skills work, also create problems. And possibly we need a different system around Christmas, when many people want to take off a week or more, than around lesser holidays, when most people take only an extra day or two.
>
> Please recommend an equitable way to decide how to assign hours.

Write a group response recommending the best way to assign hours and supporting your recommendation.

Hint:

Agree on an office, factory, store, hospital, or other workplace to use for this problem.

14.8   Recommending a Dress Policy

Assume that your small group comprises your organization's Labor-Management Committee
   This e-mail arrives from the CEO:

> In the last 10 years, we became increasingly casual. But changed circumstances seem to call for more formality. Is it time to reinstate a dress policy? If so, what should it be?

Write a group response recommending the appropriate dress for employees and supporting your recommendation.

Hint:

Agree on an office, factory, store, or other workplace to use for this problem.

14.9   Responding to an Employee Grievance

Assume that your small group comprises the Labor-Management committee at the headquarters of a chain of grocery stores. This e-mail arrives from the vice president for human resources:

> As you know, company policy requires that employees smile at customers and make eye contact with them. In the past 9 months, 12 employees have filed grievances over this rule. They say they are being harassed by customers who think they are flirting with them. A produce clerk claims customers have propositioned her and followed her to her car. Another says "Let *me* decide who I am going to say hello to with a big smile." The union wants us to change the policy to let workers *not* make eye contact with customers, and to allow workers to refuse to carry groceries to a customer's car at night. My own feeling is that we want to maintain our image as a friendly store that cares about customers, but that we also don't want to require behavior that leads to harassment. Let's find a creative solution.

Write a group response recommending whether to change the policy and supporting your recommendation.

14.10   Recommending Whether to Keep the Skybox

Assume that your small group composes the executive committee of a large company that has a luxury football skybox. (Depending on the stadium, a skybox for a professional football team may cost as little as $100,000 a year or 10 times that much. A portion—perhaps up to 30%—of the cost may be deductible as a business expense.) The CEO says, "Times are tight. We need to reevaluate whether we should retain the skybox."

Write a group response recommending whether to keep the skybox and supporting your recommendation.

Hints:

- Agree on a company to use for this problem.
- Does having a skybox match the values in the company's mission statement? If you keep the skybox, who should have priority in using it?
- How is the company doing financially? Is it laying off workers?

14.11   Answering an Ethics Question

Assume that your small group comprises your organization's Ethics Committee. You receive the following anonymous note:

> People are routinely using the company letterhead to write letters to members of Congress, senators, and even the president stating their positions on various issues. Making their opinions known is of course their right, but doing so on letterhead stationery implies that they are speaking for the company, which they are not.
>
> I think that the use of letterhead for anything other than official company business should be prohibited.

Determine the best solution to the problem. Then write a message to all employees stating your decision and building support for it.

14.12   Answering an Inquiry about Photos

You've just been named Vice President for Diversity, the first person in your organization to hold this position.

Today, you receive this memo from Sheila Lathan, who edits the employee newsletter.

Subject: Photos in the Employee Newsletter

Please tell me what to do about photos in the monthly employee newsletter. I'm concerned that almost no single issue represents the diversity of employees we have here.

As you know, our layout allows two visuals each month. One of those is always the employee of the month (EM). In the last year, most of those have been male and all but two have been white. What makes it worse is that people want photos that make them look good. You may remember that Ron Olmos was the EM two months ago; in the photo he wanted me to use, you can't tell that he's in a wheelchair. Often the EM is the only photo; the other visual is often a graph of sales or something relating to quality.

Even if the second visual is another photo, it may not look balanced in terms of gender and race. After all, 62% of our employees are men, and 78% are white. Should the pictures try to represent those percentages? The leadership positions (both in management and in the union) are even more heavily male and white. Should we run pictures of people doing important things, and risk continuing the imbalance?

I guess I could use more visuals, but then there wouldn't be room for as many stories—and people really like to see their names in print. Plus, giving people information about company activities and sales is important to maintaining goodwill. A bigger newsletter would be one way to have more visuals and keep the content, but with the cost-cutting measures we're under, that doesn't look likely.

What should I do?

As your instructor directs,

a. Work in a small group with other students to come up with a recommendation for Sheila.

b. Write a memo responding to her.

c. Write an article for the employee newsletter about the photo policy you recommend and how it relates to the company's concern for diversity.

14.13   Planning a Game

Many companies are using games and contests to solve problems in an enjoyable way. One company promised to give everyone $30 a month extra if they got the error rate below 0.5%. The rate improved immediately. After several successful months, the incentive went to $40 a month for getting it under 0.3% and finally to $50 a month for getting it under 0.2%. Another company offered workers two "well hours" if they got in by 7 AM every day for a month. An accounting and financial-services company divided its employees into two teams. The one that got the most referrals and new accounts received a meal prepared and served by the losing team (the firm paid for the food). Games are best when the people who will play them create them. Games need to make business sense and give rewards to many people, not just a few. Rewards should be small.

Think of a game or contest that could improve productivity or quality in your classroom, on campus, or in a workplace you know well.

As your instructor directs,

a. Write a message to persuade your instructor, boss, or other decision maker to authorize the game or contest.

b. Write a message announcing the game and persuading people to participate in it.

Source: Based on John Case, *The Open-Book Experience: Lessons from Over 100 Companies Who Successfully Transformed Themselves* (Reading, MA: Addison-Wesley, 1998), 129–201.

14.14   Creating Brochures

In a collaborative group, create a series of brochures for an organization and present your design and copy to the class in a group oral presentation. Your brochures should work well as a series but also be capable of standing alone if a reader picks up just one. They should share a common visual design and be appropriate for your purposes and audience. You may use sketches rather than photos or finished drawings. Text, however, should be as it will appear in the final copy.

As you prepare your series, talk to a knowledgeable person in the organization. For this assignment, as long as the person is knowledgeable, he or she does not have to have the power to approve the brochures.

In a manila folder, turn in

1. Two copies of each brochure.
2. A narrative explaining (a) how you responded to the wishes of the person in the organization who was your contact (b) how the brochures work together as a series, and (c) five of the choices you made in terms of content, visuals, and design, and why you made these choices.

14.15   Interviewing Workers about Listening

Interview someone who works in an organization about his or her on-the-job listening. Possible questions to ask include the following:

- Whom do you listen to as part of your job? Your superior? Subordinates? (How many levels down?) Customers or clients? Who else?
- How much time a day do you spend listening?
- What people do you talk to as part of your job? Do you feel they hear what you say? How do you tell whether or not they're listening?
- Do you know of any problems that came up because someone didn't listen? What happened?

- What do you think prevents people from listening effectively? What advice would you have for someone on how to listen more accurately?

As your instructor directs,

a. Share your information with a small group of students in your class.
b. Present your findings orally to the class.
c. Present your findings in a memo to your instructor.
d. Join with other students to present your findings in a group report.

14.16   Interviewing Workers about Collaborating

Interview someone who works in an organization about his or her on-the-job collaboration activities. Possible questions to ask include the following:

- How often do you work on collaborative projects?
- Do your collaborative projects always include people who are in your immediate office? How often do you collaborate with people via telephone or the Internet?
- How do you begin collaborative projects? What are the first steps you take when working with others?
- How do you handle disagreements?
- What do you do when someone isn't doing their share of the work on a collaborative project?
- What do you do to see every person meets group deadlines?

- How do you handle unexpected problems? Illness? Injury? Broken equipment?
- What advice can you give about effectively collaborating on projects?

As your instructor directs,

a. Share your information with a small group of students in your class.
b. Present your findings orally to the class.
c. Present your findings in a memo to your instructor.
d. Join with other students to present your findings in a group report.

14.17   Analyzing Instant Messaging Communication

Working in small groups, have two group members hold a conversation about one of the topics below for 6 to 10 minutes using an instant messaging system (i.e., Yahoo Messenger, AIM, MSN, etc.).

- Having English-only laws in the workplace.
- Introducing new technology into the marketplace.
- Drinking at social functions for work.
- Requiring employers to offer insurance plans.

- Smoking in the workplace.
- Diversity and hiring in the workplace.
- Surfing the Internet at work.
- Current "hot" business topics.

When the conversation is finished, print out a copy for all members of your group to review and analyze. Then, answer the following questions about instant messaging communication systems.

Questions to consider with your group:

- How is communication helped by an instant messaging system?
- How is communication hindered by an instant messaging system?
- How often did your group members use slang, abbreviations, emoticons, or acronyms in the conversation? Did these shorthand forms help or hinder effective communication?

- How does a synchronous chat affect the way each person's main ideas are received?
- How possible is it to employ a form of active listening using an instant messaging system?
- What role do you foresee instant messaging systems taking in professional settings?

14.18   Writing a Group Action Plan

Before you begin working on a team project, develop a group action plan to establish a framework that will hold your group members accountable for their work.

After reading the project assignment sheet and meeting your group, decide upon answers for the following questions:

- What are the tasks your group needs to accomplish? Be specific and set preliminary completion dates.
- Should you have a team leader? If so, who? Why is the person qualified? What is expected of him/her?
- What will be the roles of the other members of the group?
- When will meetings outside of class take place? Decide whether you can hold meetings if all group members are not present. How will you inform members of what occurred at meetings if they are not present?

- How will you resolve disagreements that may arise while working on the project?
- Define what an absence means for your group. Are all types equal?
- Create a policy dealing with people who don't attend class during your preparation days or the presentation, don't attend meetings outside of class, miss deadlines, or don't do their assigned work at all or in a timely manner. (You may consider loss of points, grade reductions, failure, a group firing, or a group intervention to name a few.)

After your group determines and agrees on an action plan, the group's secretary should send your answers in a memo to your instructor, who will keep the document on file in case a problem arises.

14.19   Writing Team Meeting Minutes

As you work in a collaborative group setting, designate a different member to take minutes for each meeting.

As your instructor directs, your minutes should include:

- Name of the group holding the meeting.
- Members who were present. Include first and last name.
- Members who were absent. Include first and last name.
- Place, time, and date of meeting.
- Work—Record work, and who did it, completed during the meeting.
- Actions—Record actions that need to be completed, the person responsible, and the due date.

- Decisions—Record all decisions made during the meeting.
- New Issues—Any issues raised at the meeting but not resolved should be recorded for future meetings.
- Signature of acting secretary.

Remember to keep your minutes brief and to the point. When it is your turn to take minutes, be prepared with a writing utensil and paper.

When the minutes are complete, e-mail them to your fellow group members and cc: them to your instructor.

14.20   Keeping a Journal about a Group

As you work in a collaborative writing group, keep a journal after each group meeting.

- What happened?
- What roles did you play in the meeting?

- What conflicts arose? How were they handled?
- What strategies could you use to make the next meeting go smoothly?
- Record one observation about each group member.

14.21   Writing for a Client

With a group of three or four other people, find a client on your campus or in your community who has a writing project you could construct. For example, you could write a routine sales letter, create a brochure or other promotional materials, build a Web site, write an instructional manual, and so forth.

Once you have a client who is willing to let you take on a project, be sure to spend time interviewing them about the project. Find out the specific purposes of the project and what they envision as the "look" of the end product. What do they see as potential pitfalls to avoid? In addition, remember to ask about the specific audience you should target with the project. What layers of audience will use the project and in what contexts?

To begin working on the project, your group should brainstorm some possible ideas for the final product and how you'll get there. When you all come to a consensus on what would be the best course of action, start drafting the project.

Create the project using the guidelines for various business genres found throughout this textbook. Make sure all members of your group contribute equally to the project. In addition, ask your client questions as they arise throughout the production stages.

Be sure to revise and edit all of your work. You may also considering testing whether your project functions for real audiences by soliciting feedback, which can help improve your design.

Turn in a copy of the project your group completed to the client and a copy to your instructor. Also give your instructor two different drafts of the project and a memo explaining changes made to each draft to reflect the client's audiences, purpose, and wishes.

In addition, in your group prepare a brief presentation to share with your class that summarizes your experience of working in a collaborative setting. Your presentations should also discuss member participation/roles and any challenges your group faced and how you overcame these difficulties.

14.22   Preparing Collaborative Presentations

With a group of peers, research one of the following topics:

- Having English-only laws in the workplace.
- Introducing new technology into the marketplace.
- Drinking at social functions for work.
- Requiring employers to offer insurance plans.
- Smoking in the workplace.
- Diversity and hiring in the workplace.
- Surfing the Internet at work.
- Current "hot" business topic.

Then, prepare a 12-minute slideshow presentation or movie to share your research findings with the rest of the class. Remember that all members of your group should contribute equally to the presentation, and it should be captivating to the audience. Finally, don't forget to cite all source material.

14.23   Analyzing the Dynamics of a Group

Analyze the dynamics of a task group of which you are a member. Answer the following questions:

1. Who was the group's leader? How did the leader emerge? Were there any changes in or challenges to the original leader?

2. Describe the contribution each member made to the group and the roles each person played.

3. Did any members of the group officially or unofficially drop out? Did anyone join after the group had begun working? How did you deal with the loss or addition of a group member, both in terms of getting the work done and in terms of helping people work together?

4. What planning did your group do at the start of the project? Did you stick to the plan or revise it? How did the group decide that revision was necessary?

5. How did your group make decisions? Did you vote? reach decisions by consensus?

6. What problems or conflicts arose? Did the group deal with them openly? To what extent did they interfere with the group's task?

7. Evaluate your group both in terms of its task and in terms of the satisfaction members felt. How did this group compare with other task groups you've been part of? What made it better or worse?

8. What were the strengths of the group? Weaknesses?

9. How did the group's strengths and weaknesses impact the quality of the work produced?

10. If you had the project to do over again, what would you do differently?

As you answer the questions,

- Be honest. You won't lose points for reporting that your group had problems or did something "wrong."

- Show your knowledge of good group dynamics. That is, if your group did something wrong, show that you know what *should* have been done. Similarly, if your group worked well, show that you know *why* it worked well.

- Be specific. Give examples or anecdotes to support your claims.

As your instructor directs,

a. Discuss your answers with the other group members.

b. Present your findings orally to the class.

c. Present your findings in an individual memo to your instructor.

d. Join with the other group members to write a collaborative memo to your instructor.

14.24   Mosaic Case

"The experience of researching Hispanic clientele has been awful, Yvonne," said Martina to her. "I don't understand how they get anything done over there in the Marketing Department."

"I agree," said Trey chiming in. "This project is never going to be completed on time if they don't step up their act."

"Well, what exactly seems to be the problem?" asked Yvonne of Trey and Martina, who both just finished eating a banana during their morning coffee break. "I mean, why don't you think you can make this work?"

"Basically," said Trey as Martina swallowed her last bite, "it seems to us that every time we set preliminary deadlines, things never happen. Martina and I usually have our stuff completed a day or two before the preliminary deadline. On the other hand, Luke and Katie usually don't have anything. They wait until the very last minute it seems before they even start to think about what they need to do. And I realize they are busy over there in the Marketing Department, but it's not like we sit around all day over here twiddling our thumbs hoping for something to do."

"Most of the time," said Martina, "they don't have their stuff done. For example, last week Luke showed up to our meeting and asked us what he was supposed to do again with the statistics we researched about Hispanic clientele. At this morning's meeting, Katie informed us the official deadline is not for another two weeks, so she

didn't see the need to focus her efforts on this project right now."

Yvonne just nodded at what Martina was telling her.

"And Katie always seems bitter," said Trey. "I'm not sure what anyone did or said to her, but she just always seems unhappy at our meetings. I try to crack a joke every once in a while, but she never seems to budge a smile. I hate feeling like she is somehow unhappy with us."

"Have you asked Katie about this? Or let her know how you feel about the situation?" asked Yvonne.

"No," answered Trey.

"Oh," said Martina as she continued thinking about the situation, "beyond the bitter issue, Katie's contribution during our meetings is almost non-existent. Most of the time she's on her cell phone talking to someone. I'm also not sure if it's always Mosaic related," said Martina, "I'm just really stressed out about how our final report will turn out."

"I see," said Yvonne. "Well, here are some suggestions . . . "

Take on the communication task of Yvonne. Based on your reading of Chapter 14, what advice can you offer Trey and Martina to resolve some of the conflict they appear to face while working with Katie and Luke from the Marketing Department? What can you suggest to make their meetings more productive?

Planning, Proposing, and Researching Reports

Learning Objectives

After studying this chapter, you will know how to:

1. Define report problems.
2. Write proposals.
3. Write progress reports.
4. Employ different research strategies.
5. Use and document sources.

Research and Innovation: Fun and Games at Hasbro

On Fridays, game designers and other employees at Hasbro, Inc., spend their lunchtime playing board games and thinking about ways to update games or create new ones. The Friday games are just one of the creative approaches to research and innovation used at the company that manufactures some of America's best-known board games, such as Monopoly, Scrabble, Sorry, and Clue.

In the world of board games, continuous innovation is necessary to fit games to changing consumer lifestyles and preferences. Hasbro invests in extensive market research, such as conducting online surveys, observing children and adults playing games in the company's Game-Works lab, and talking with people about how they want to spend leisure time. Hasbro also looks to game inventors outside the company for new ideas.

In response to information obtained through these strategies, Hasbro has modified several of its traditional games.

Friday games are just one of the creative approaches to research used at Hasbro.

- To accommodate consumers' tight schedules, Hasbro developed "express" versions of Monopoly, Sorry, and Scrabble that can be completed within 20 minutes.

- To address consumers' desire for more balanced lives, The Game of Life now includes life experience, education, and family life as elements of a successful life, rather than basing success only on making the most money.

- To update changing consumer preferences in tourist destinations, a revised version of Monopoly includes some different squares. Based on three million votes cast in response to an online survey, game designers replaced Boardwalk with Times Square and replaced Pacific Avenue with Las Vegas Boulevard.

- To attract customers who enjoy using technology to play games, game designers developed electronic versions of games such as the Clue DVD, which includes an electronic version of the original board game plus 10 additional murder plots.

Source: Adapted from Carol Hymowitz, "All Companies Need Innovation: Hasbro Finds a New Magic," *Wall Street Journal*, February 26, 2007, B1.

Chapter Outline

Varieties of Reports

A Timeline for Writing Reports

Defining Report Problems

Writing Proposals
- Proposals for Class Research Projects
- Proposals for Action
- Sales Proposals
- Proposals for Funding
- Figuring the Budget and Costs

Writing Progress Reports
- Chronological Progress Reports
- Task Progress Reports
- Recommendation Progress Reports

Research Strategies for Reports
- Finding Information Online and in Print
- Evaluating Web Sources
- Designing Questions for Surveys and Interviews
- Conducting Surveys and Interviews
- Observing Customers and Users

Using and Documenting Sources

Summary of Key Points

Proposals and reports depend on research. The research may be as simple as pulling up data with a computer program or as complicated as calling many different people, conducting focus groups and surveys, or even planning and conducting experiments. Care in planning, proposing, and researching reports is needed to produce reliable **data.**

In writing any report, there are five basic steps:

1. Define the problem.
2. Gather the necessary data and information.
3. Analyze the data and information.
4. Organize the information.
5. Write the report.

After reviewing the varieties of reports, this chapter focuses on the first two steps. Chapter 16 discusses the last three steps.

Varieties of Reports

Many kinds of documents are called *reports*. In some organizations, a report is a long document or a document that contains numerical data. In others, one- and two-page memos are called *reports*. In still others, *reports* consist of PowerPoint slides printed out and bound together. A short report to a client may use letter format. **Formal reports** contain formal elements such as a title page, a transmittal, a table of contents, and a list of illustrations. **Informal reports** may be letters and memos or even computer printouts of production or sales figures. But all reports, whatever their length or degree of formality,

Figure 15.1   Three Levels of Reports

Reports can provide

Information only

- **Sales reports** (sales figures for the week or month).
- **Quarterly reports** (figures showing a plant's productivity and profits for the quarter).

Information plus analysis

- **Annual reports** (financial data and an organization's accomplishments during the past year).
- **Audit reports** (interpretations of the facts revealed during an audit).
- **Make-good or pay-back reports** (calculations of the point at which a new capital investment will pay for itself).

Information plus analysis plus a recommendation

- **Feasibility reports** evaluate two or more alternatives and recommend which alternative the organization should choose.
- **Justification reports** justify the need for a purchase, an investment, a new personnel line, or a change in procedure.
- **Problem-solving reports** identify the causes of an organizational problem and recommend a solution.

provide the information that people in organizations need to make plans and solve problems.

Reports can just provide information, both provide information and analyze it, or provide information and analysis to support a recommendation (see Figure 15.1). Reports can be called **information reports** if they collect data for the reader, **analytical reports** if they interpret data but do not recommend action, and **recommendation reports** if they recommend action or a solution.

The following reports can be information, analytical, or recommendation reports, depending on what they provide:

- *Accident reports* can simply list the nature and causes of accidents in a factory or office. These reports can also recommend ways to make conditions safer.

- *Credit reports* can simply summarize an applicant's income and other credit obligations. These reports can also evaluate the applicant's collateral and creditworthiness.

- *Progress and interim reports* can simply record the work done so far and the work remaining on a project. These reports can also analyze the quality of the work and recommend that a project be stopped, continued, or restructured.

- *Trip reports* can simply share what the author learned at a conference or during a visit to a customer or supplier. These reports can also recommend action based on that information.

- *Closure reports* can simply document the causes of a failure or of possible products that are not economically or technically feasible under current conditions. They can also recommend action to prevent such failures in the future.

A Timeline for Writing Reports

When you write a report, plan to spend half your time analyzing your data, writing and revising the draft, and preparing visuals and slides. When you write a report for a class project, plan to complete at least one-fourth of your research before you write the proposal. Begin analyzing your data as you collect it; prepare your list of sources and drafts of visuals as you go along. Start writing your first draft before the research is completed. An early draft can help clarify where you need more research. Save at least one-fourth of your time at the end of the project to think and write after all your data are collected. For a collaborative report, you'll need even more time to write and revise.

Up-front planning helps you use your time efficiently. Start by thinking about the whole report process. Read the sample reports in Chapter 16 ➠ even before you write your proposal. Talk to your readers to understand how much detail and formality they want. In a company, look at earlier reports. List all the parts of the report you'll need to prepare. Then articulate— to yourself or your group members—the purposes, audiences, and generic constraints for each part. The fuller idea you have of the final product when you start, the fewer drafts you'll need to write and the better your final product will be.

Defining Report Problems

Good report problems grow out of real problems: disjunctions between reality and the ideal, choices that must be made. When you write a report as part of your job, the organization may define the topic. To think of problems for class reports, think about problems that face your college or university; housing units on campus; social, religious, and professional groups on campus and in your city; local businesses; and city, county, state, and federal governments and their agencies. Read your campus and local papers and newsmagazines; read the news on the internet, watch it on TV, or listen to it on National Public Radio.

A good report problem in business or administration meets the following criteria:

1. The problem is
   * Real.
   * Important enough to be worth solving.
   * Narrow but challenging.
2. The audience for the report is
   * Real.
   * Able to implement the recommended action.
3. The data, evidence, and facts are
   * Sufficient to document the severity of the problem.
   * Sufficient to prove that the recommendation will solve the problem.
   * Available to *you*.
   * Comprehensible to *you*.

Often problems need to be narrowed. For example, "improving the college experiences of international students studying in the United States" is far too broad. First, choose one college or university. Second, identify the specific problem. Do you want to increase the social interaction between US and international students? Help international students find housing? Increase the number of ethnic grocery stores and restaurants? Third, identify the specific audience that would have the power to implement your recommendations. Depending on the specific topic, the audience might be the Office of International Studies, the residence hall counselors, a service organization on campus or in town, a store, or a group of investors.

Alissa Kozuh analyzes the words customers type in on the search feature at www.nordstrom. com. She's found five patterns: customers key in particular items ("shoes"), trends ("leopard prints"), departments from the bricks-and-mortar stores ("Brass Plum," the juniors department), designer names, and special occasions ("prom"). The changes she suggested for the site based on her research increased Web sales 32%.

Source: Ron Lieber, "She Reads Customers' Minds," *Fast Company,* January 2001, 54.

Some problems are more easily researched than others. If you have easy access to the Chinese Student Association, you can survey them about their experiences at the local Chinese grocery. However, if you want to recommend ways to keep the Chinese grocery in business, but you do not have access to their financial records, you will have a much more difficult time solving the problem. Even if you have access, if the records are written in Chinese, you will have problems unless you read the language or have a willing translator.

Pick a problem you can solve in the time available. Six months of full-time (and overtime) work and a team of colleagues might allow you to look at all the ways to make a store more profitable. If you're doing a report in 6 to 12 weeks for a class that is only one of your responsibilities, limit the topic. Depending on your interests and knowledge, you could choose to examine the prices and brands carried, its inventory procedures, its overhead costs, its layout and decor, or its advertising budget.

How you define the problem shapes the solutions you find. For example, suppose that a manufacturer of frozen foods isn't making money. If the problem is defined as a marketing problem, the researcher may analyze the product's price, image, advertising, and position in the market. But perhaps the problem is really that overhead costs are too high due to poor inventory management, or that an inadequate distribution system doesn't get the product to its target market. Defining the problem accurately is essential to finding an effective solution.

Once you've defined your problem, you're ready to write a purpose statement. The purpose statement goes both in your proposal and in your final report. A good **purpose statement** makes three things clear:

- The organizational problem or conflict.
- The specific technical questions that must be answered to solve the problem.
- The rhetorical purpose (to explain, to recommend, to request, to propose) the report is designed to achieve.

The following purpose statements have all three elements:

> Current management methods keep the elk population within the carrying capacity of the habitat but require frequent human intervention. Both wildlife conservation specialists and the public would prefer methods that controlled the elk population naturally. This report will compare the current short-term management techniques (hunting, trapping and transporting, and winter feeding) with two long-term management techniques, habitat modification and the reintroduction of predators. The purpose of this report is to recommend which techniques or combination of techniques would best satisfy the needs of conservationists, hunters, and the public.

Report audience: The superintendent of Yellowstone National Park

> When banner ads on Web pages first appeared in 1994, the initial response, or "click-through" rate, was about 10%. However, as ads have proliferated on Web pages, the click-through rate has dropped sharply. Rather than assuming that any banner ad will be successful, we need to ask, What characteristics do successful banner ads share? Are ads for certain kinds of products and services or for certain kinds of audiences more likely to be successful on the Web? The purpose of this report is to summarize the available research and anecdotal evidence and to recommend what Leo Burnett should tell its clients about whether and how to use banner ads.

Report audience: Leo Burnett Advertising Agency

To write a good purpose statement, you must understand the basic problem and have some idea of the questions that your report will answer. Note, however, that you can (and should) write the purpose statement before researching the specific alternatives the report will discuss.

Writing Proposals

Proposals suggest a method for finding information or solving a problem.[1] Finding the information or solving the problem helps an organization decide whether to change, decide how to change, or implement a change that is agreed on. (See Figure 15.2.)

Proposals have two goals: to get the project accepted and to get you accepted to do the job. Proposals must stress audience benefits and provide specific supporting details. In a memo supporting a new technology fee for all students, a university's technology committee listed benefits for each suggested program that the fee would cover. For example, the committee recommended setting up undergraduate computing labs for specific disciplines. The related benefits listed for students were on-site software support and an improved sense of community for undergraduate majors.

Proposals may be competitive or noncompetitive. *Competitive proposals* compete against each other for limited resources. Applications for research funding are often very competitive. Many companies will bid for corporate or government contracts, but only one will be accepted. In 2005, the National Institutes of Health awarded more than $23 billion, including research grants, research training, and fellowships, to universities, hospitals, nonprofits, small

Figure 15.2 Relationship among Situation, Proposal, and Final Report

Company's current situation	The proposal offers to	The final report will provide
We don't know whether we should change.	Assess whether change is a good idea.	Insight, recommending whether change is desirable.
We need to/want to change, but we don't know exactly what we need to do.	Develop a plan to achieve desired goal.	A plan for achieving the desired change.
We need to/want to change, and we know what to do, but we need help doing it.	Implement the plan, increase (or decrease) measurable outcomes.	A record of the implementation and evaluation process.

Source: Adapted from Richard C. Freed, Shervin Freed, and Joseph D. Romano, *Writing Winning Proposals: Your Guide to Landing the Client, Making the Sale, Persuading the Boss* (New York: McGraw-Hill, 1995), 21.

businesses, and other organizations. The total sum may seem large, but at many universities hundreds of faculty write grant proposals, and the fate of those proposals plays a major role in the faculty member's career as well as the reputation of the institution. Of the NIH institutional grants in 2005, Johns Hopkins University ranked first, receiving more than $607 million; the University of Pennsylvania ranked second, receiving more than $471 million.[2]

Noncompetitive proposals have no real competition. For example, a company could accept all of the internal proposals it thought would save money or improve quality. And often a company that is satisfied with a vendor asks for a noncompetitive proposal to renew the contract.

To write a good proposal, you need to have a clear view of the problem you hope to solve and the kind of research or other action needed to solve it. A proposal must answer the following questions convincingly:

- **What problem are you going to solve?** Show that you understand the problem and the organization's needs. Define the problem as the audience sees it, even if you believe that the presenting problem (◄ p. 471) is part of a larger problem that must first be solved.

- **How are you going to solve it?** Prove that your methods are feasible. Show that a solution can be found in the time available. Specify the topics you'll investigate. Explain how you'll gather data.

- **When will you complete the work?** Provide a detailed schedule showing when each phase of the work will be completed.

- **Can you deliver what you promise?** Show that you have the knowledge, the staff, and the facilities to do what you say you will. Describe your previous work in this area, your other qualifications, and the qualifications of any people who will be helping you.

- **What benefits can you offer?** For many proposals, various organizations may be able to supply the goods, services, or research needed. Show why the company should hire you. Discuss the benefits—direct and indirect—that your firm can provide.

- **How much will you charge?** Provide a detailed budget that includes costs for materials, salaries, and overhead.

- **What exactly will you provide for us?** Specify the tangible products you'll produce; explain how you'll evaluate them.

Government agencies and companies often issue **requests for proposals,** known as **RFPs.** Use the exact headings, terminology, and structure of an RFP when responding to one. Competitive proposals are often scored by

Playing for Real Money

Not many college classes have cash prizes, but some students working toward MBA degrees can participate in business plan contests. Groups of students write a business plan and present it to real-world bankers and venture capitalists. The stakes are high. Major contests have big cash awards and a shot at really starting the business the students have been planning. Even the losers benefit from the writing practice and the feedback they can use to continue improving their plans.

Among the winners is Sarah Takesh, who took first place in the National Social Ventures Competition, earning $25,000 for a fashion company called Tarsian and Blinkley. In Takesh's business, which she has since launched, Afghan workers apply local handicrafts to produce clothing sold in boutiques in New York and San Francisco. Although the items are beautiful, Takesh's fashion sense was less important to the judges than her insights about international trade.

Another contest winner, KidSmart, is a plan for a company offering a new product: an alarm that alerts children with a recording of a parent's voice, rather than the earsplitting beeps of a traditional smoke alarm. The KidSmart business plan won the $100,000 grand prize in Moot Corp, sponsored by the University of Texas. The four-person KidSmart team supported its presentation with video footage showing that its smoke detector is better at waking children than the traditional beeps are.

Adapted from Patrick J. Sauer, "How to Win Big Money and Get Ahead in Business," *Inc.* 25, no. 9 (September 2003): 95–96+ .

giving points in each category. Evaluators look only under the heads specified in the RFP. If information isn't there, the proposal may get no points in that category.

Proposals for Class Research Projects

You may be asked to submit a proposal for a report that you will write for a class. Your instructor wants evidence that your problem is meaningful but not too big to complete in the allotted time, that you understand it, that your method will give you the information you need, that you have the knowledge and resources to collect and analyze the data, and that you can produce the report by the deadline.

A proposal for a student report usually has the following sections:

1. In your first paragraph (no heading), summarize in a sentence or two the topic and purposes of your report.

2. **Problem.**   What organizational problem exists? What is wrong? Why does it need to be solved? Is there a history or background that is relevant?

3. **Feasibility.**   Are you sure that a solution can be found in the time available? How do you know? (This section may not be appropriate for some class projects.)

4. **Audience.**   Who in the organization would have the power to implement your recommendation? What secondary audiences might be asked to evaluate your report? What audiences would be affected by your recommendation? Will anyone in the organization serve as a gatekeeper, determining whether your report is sent to decision makers? What watchdog audiences might read the report? Will there be other readers?

   For each of these audiences give the person's name, job title, and business address and answer the following questions:

   • What is the audience's major concern or priority? What "hot buttons" must you address with care?

   • What will the audience see as advantages of your proposal? What objections, if any, is the reader likely to have?

   • How interested is the audience in the topic of your report?

   • How much does the audience know about the topic of your report?

   List any terms, concepts, or assumptions that one or more of your audiences may need to have explained. Briefly identify ways in which your audiences may affect the content, organization, or style of the report.

5. **Topics to investigate.**   List the questions and subquestions you will answer in your report, the topics or concepts you will explain, the aspects of the problem you will discuss. Indicate how deeply you will examine each of the aspects you plan to treat. Explain your rationale for choosing to discuss some aspects of the problem and not others.

6. **Methods/procedure.**   How will you get answers to your questions? Whom will you interview or survey? What questions will you ask? What published sources will you use? Give the full bibliographic references.

   Your methods section should clearly indicate how you will get the information needed to answer questions posed in the other sections of the proposal.

7. **Qualifications/facilities/resources.**   Do you have the knowledge and skills needed to conduct this study? Do you have adequate access to the organization? Is the necessary information available to you? Are you aware of any supplemental information? Where will you turn for help if you hit an unexpected snag?

You'll be more convincing if you have already scheduled an interview, checked out books, or printed out online sources.

8. **Work schedule.** List both the total time you plan to spend on and the date when you expect to finish each activity. This is one list of possible activities; you may think of others for your project.

- Gathering information.
- Analyzing information.
- Organizing information.
- Preparing the progress report.
- Writing the draft.
- Revising the draft.
- Preparing the visuals.
- Editing the draft.
- Proofreading the report.

These steps frequently overlap. Many writers start analyzing and organizing information as it comes in. They start writing pieces of the final document early in the process.

Organize your work schedule in either a chart or calendar. A good schedule provides realistic estimates for each activity, allows time for unexpected snags, and shows that you can complete the work on time.

9. **Call to action.** In your final section, indicate that you'd welcome any suggestions your instructor may have for improving the research plan. Ask your instructor to approve your proposal so that you can begin work on your report.

Figure 15.3 shows a student proposal for a long report.

Proposals for Action

You can write a proposal for action or change in your organization. Normally, proposals for action recommend new programs or ways to solve organizational problems. As manager of compensation planning, Catherine Beck had to propose a compensation system when telephone companies Bell Atlantic and Nynex Corporation merged and again a few years later when Bell Atlantic merged with GTE to form Verizon. When two companies merge, each has its own pay scale, bonus policy, and so on; the problem is that the merged companies will need a single, unified system. In these two mergers, Beck had to recommend the system she thought would work best in the new company.[3]

Writing a proposal for action requires considerable research. When Catherine Beck had to propose a new compensation policy, she worked with a team of human resource and other managers plus compensation experts. Together they began by studying the existing policies of the merging organizations, including job titles, salary structures, bonus plans, and the system of performance appraisals. They compared the two systems, looking for their underlying principles. In the first merger, between Bell Atlantic and Nynex, they determined that the two plans were so different that they would have to create a completely new system. In the second merger, of Bell Atlantic and GTE, they concluded that the plans were similar enough to be modified and combined into a single system. After this internal research leading to an initial decision, preparing a proposal and implementing a system for tens of thousands of management employees took months in both mergers.[4]

Often, writing a proposal requires gathering information from outside the organization, too. Basic steps include reading articles in trade and professional journals, looking up data online, and talking to employees or customers.

Choosing Topics to Investigate

No report investigates all possible topics. Choose the ones that decision makers care most about and will find most useful.

Specific topics will relate to the topic of the report. General topics can include managerial, technical, and social criteria. Here are some examples:

Managerial Criteria

- Cost (e.g., acquisition, maintenance, disposal; taxes).
- Market demand.
- Staffing requirements.
- Organizational impact (distribution of resources; effect on personnel, other projects, and image).
- Consistency with organizational goals.

Technical Criteria

- Availability of technology, materials, parts.
- Compatibility with existing systems.
- Adaptability, flexibility, ability to be upgraded.
- Reliability, longevity, repair record.
- Compliance with legal codes (e.g., environment, Americans with Disabilities Act).

Social Criteria

- Human impact (jobs, morale, employment benefits).
- Environmental impact.
- Safety.
- Quality.
- Ethical issues (e.g., conflict of interest, use of resources, impact on stakeholders).

Adapted from Mary M. Lay, Billie J. Wahlstrom, Carolyn Rude, Cindy Selfe, and Jack Selzer, *Technical Communication*, 2nd ed. (Burr Ridge, IL: Irwin/McGraw-Hill, 2000), 510.

Figure 15.3   Proposal for a Student Group Report

March 29, 2007

To: Professor Chris Toth

From: JOABA Consulting

In the subject line ① indicate that this is a proposal ② specify the kind of report ③ specify the topic

Subject: Proposal to Research and Make a Recommendation on the Feasibility of Expanding Panera into Chile

Summarize topic and purpose of report. Panera Bread Company has recently approached our group to explore the feasibility of expanding into a foreign country. We believe Chile is a suitable country for this initial global expansion. This proposal provides a brief overview of Chile and outlines how we will conduct our research in preparation for the formal research report.

Problem   *If the "Problem" section is detailed and well-written you may be able to use it unchanged in your report.*

Panera Bread Company has saturated the US market with its stores and is now looking to expand its business to foreign markets. We need to find and research a location that will support and welcome an organization like Panera, while at the same time increasing the overall profits of the company.

Country Overview   *This section is a "Background" section for this proposal. Not all proposals include background.*

After some initial research, we believe the Republic of Chile, or Chile, would be a suitable country to research for the possible expansion. Chile has a population of approximately 15.9 million, with 35% of that population located in the capital city of Santiago. The official national language is Spanish ("Chile"). *Proposal uses in-text citations.*

Business hours in Chile typically run Monday through Friday from 8:30 a.m. to 6:00 p.m. Lunch varies between one and two hours, and in urban areas such as Santiago, it is rare for people to go home for lunch ("Chile"). Chile is a long country and extends over many tastes of food and drinks. In addition, it is well known for its seafood and wine. Among the many foods that Chileans enjoy are empanadas, seafood, sandwiches, and desserts. The Chilean diet also includes many dishes that use chicken and beef products ("Typical").

Chile has a booming and growing economy. It serves as a model country for other Latin American nations with a low inflation rate, increasing GDP, and decreasing unemployment rate. The nation has also signed several trade agreements with other countries and continues to liberalize its trade policies ("Chile"). These are all positive economic indicators that encourage foreign firms to invest in Chile. Since the country's economic growth is estimated to continue into future years, Panera should view it as an attractive market to enter.

Not all class reports will need a "Feasibility" section.

(continued)

Figure 15.3 Proposal for a Student Group Report *(Continued)*

Include a header on all additional pages.

Proposal to Research and Make a Recommendation on the Feasibility of Expanding Panera into Chile
March 29, 2007
Page 2

Audience

Our formal report has multiple layers of audiences:

List your major audiences. Identify their knowledge, interest, and concerns.

- *Gatekeeper*: Professor Toth. You have the power to accept or reject the formal report before it is passed on to the primary audience.

- *Primary*: Mr. Ronald M. Shaich, the CEO of Panera Bread Company, as well as other members of the executive committee. They will be the audience who decides whether to accept our recommendations found in the formal report.

- *Secondary*: The marketing and human resources departments at Panera, all employees of Panera who are affected by the message, as well as the Santiago Chamber of Commerce. The Santiago Chamber of Commerce may try to keep Panera out of the city if they believe the organization will be too much competition for local businesses.

- *Auxiliary*: Panera employees who may read the report, but who will not be directly affected by it.

- *Watchdog*: Other companies looking to expand into Chile, the Securities and Exchange Commission, and competitors of Panera who are looking to expand internationally.

Topics to Investigate

We plan to answer the following questions in detail:

Indicate what you'll discuss briefly and what you'll discuss in more detail. This list should match your audience's concerns.

1. What does the company need from the country?
    - Culture—How can Panera operate in this culture and still maintain Panera's identity?
    - Legal Restrictions—What hoops will Panera need to jump through in order to open a store for business?
    - Political Stability—How stable is the government to ensure that the store can stay in business for years to come?
    - Economic Feasibility—Under what prices and costs will Panera need to operate? Can it still be profitable? What is Panera's economic standing?

All items in list must be grammatically parallel. Here, all are questions.

2. What does the company need from the Chilean market?
    - Market Acceptability—How easily can Panera adapt its products to the Chilean culture?
    - Competitor Analysis—Who is our competition? (What is the competition in Chile? Look at both American restaurants and local cafes in Santiago.)
    - Location—What area or city will best serve the interests of Panera in the Chilean market?

(continued)

Figure 15.3   Proposal for a Student Group Report *(Continued)*

Proposal to Research and Make a Recommendation on the Feasibility of Expanding Panera into Chile
March 29, 2007
Page 3

3. What does the company need in terms of work force?

If it is well written, "Topics to Investigate" section will become the "Scope" section of the report—with minor revisions.

- Employees—What mix of local managers and American managers will best serve Panera? What will be the mix of store workers?
- Employment Outlook—What is the current work outlook in Chile? High unemployment? Does the country offer an available work force to staff the store?
- Employee Expectations—How will employee expectations be different than those of American employees? How do the work ethics of each group compare?

Methods and Resources

We expect to get the most information from: (1) various websites, (2) books, and (3) an interview with a native Chilean resident. The following Web sites and books appear useful:

If you'll administer a survey or conduct interviews, tell how many, subjects you'll have, how you'll choose them, and what you'll ask them. This group does not use a survey.

"Amcham Chile." <u>The Chilean American Chamber of Commerce</u>. 2005. 29 March 2007. <http://www.amchamchile.cl/english/default.asp>.

Blake, Charles H. <u>Politics in Latin America</u>. Boston: Houghton Mifflin, 2005.

If you're using library or Web research, list sources you hope to use. Use full bibliographic citations.

"Chile." <u>Central Intelligence Agency: The World Factbook</u>. 10 Jan. 2006. 29 March 2007. <https://www.cia.gov/library/publications/the-world-factbook/geos/ci.html>.

"Chile Foreign Investment Committee." 2005. State of Chile. 29 March 2007. <http://www.foreigninvestment.cl/index/index.asp>.

Hartlyn, Jonathan, and Samuel A. Morley. <u>Latin American Political Economy: Financial Crisis and Political Change</u>. Boulder, CO: Westview P., 1986.

Lustig, Nora. <u>Coping With Austerity</u>. Washington, D.C.: The Brookings Institution, 1995.

"Made in USA, Sold in Chile." <u>Buyusa.Gov</u>. 2006. U.S Commercial Service. 29 March 2007. <www.buyusa.gov/chile/en>.

This list uses MLA format.

Panera Bread. 2006. 29 March 2006. <http://www.panerabread.com/>.

Santiago—Chile. "Embassy of the USA." 2007. <u>U.S. Department of State</u>. 29 March 2007. <www.usembassy.cl>.

"The Global Coalition against Corruption." <u>Transparency International</u>. 2006. 29 March 2007. <http://www.transparency.org/>.

"Typical Chilean Food and Drink." <u>Woodward Chile</u>, 28 November 2005. Woodward: A Different Kind of Thinking. 30 March 2007 <http://woodward.cl.chilefood.html>.

Your list of sources should convince your instructor that you have made initial progress on the report.

(continued)

Figure 15.3 Proposal for a Student Group Report *(Concluded)*

Proposal to Research and Make a Recommendation on the Feasibility of Expanding Panera into Chile
March 29, 2007
Page 4

Qualifications *Cite knowledge and skills from other classes, jobs, and activities that will enable you to conduct the research and interpret your data.*

We are all students enrolled in a business communication course, and the variety of our majors—marketing, business, health and human performance—give us a broad perspective for this expansion project. Moreover, two members of our group are fluent in Spanish, which will aid in any language barriers we encounter. JOABA Consulting is committed to increasing our knowledge of international expansion and creating a quality report.

Work Schedule

The following schedule will enable us to finish this report on time.

Activity	Total Time	Completion Date
Gathering information	10 hours	March 31
Analyzing information	7 hours	April 3
Organizing information	4 hours	April 5
Writing draft/creating visuals	6 hours	April 8
Revising the draft	3 hours	April 9
Preparing presentation slides	3 hours	April 11
Editing the draft	2 hours	April 12
Proofreading the report	3 hours	April 14
Rehearsing presentation	2 hours	April 16

Time will depend on the length and topic of your report, your knowledge of the topic, and your writing skills.

Good reports need good revision, editing, and proofreading as well as good research.

Allow plenty of time!

Call to Action

We are confident we can complete the assigned task with the schedule listed above. We would appreciate your suggestions and ideas for strengthening our plan to make our report better. Please approve our proposal so that we can begin preparing our report.

It's tactful to indicate you'll accept suggestions. End on a positive, forward-looking note.

Sales Proposals

To sell expensive goods or services, you may be asked to submit a proposal.

Be sure that you understand the buyer's priorities. A phone company lost a $36 million sale to a university because it assumed the university's priority would be cost. Instead, the university wanted a state-of-the-art system. The university accepted a higher bid.

Don't assume that the buyer will understand why your product or system is good. For everything you offer, show the benefits of each feature. Be sure to present the benefits using you-attitude (◀▦ p. 76). Consider using psychological description (◀▦ p. 387) to make the benefits vivid.

Writing an Effective Business Plan

How do entrepreneurs raise the capital needed to launch a new business? They write a business plan. When you write one, you need to persuade an investor that your concept for an organization is solid and that you're the best person to carry it out. Venture capitalists and successful entrepreneurs give the following advice about writing a solid business plan:

- Keep it short and simple—a good business plan articulates what the company will do and how it will benefit the customer. Specify the product or service. Begin with an executive summary.

- Introduce the management team—a good business plan explains the people behind the product.

- Anticipate problems and challenges—a good business plan answers the tough questions about your idea. Venture capitalists will already know the problem; they want to be sure you do too.

- Show there is a market—a good business plan identifies a target market and demonstrates that people will use the product or service offered.

- Show a path to profit—a good business plan explains how the business will make money

- Make it personal—a good business plan is not a template; it shows passion about ideas.

Adapted from Greg Farrell, "Business Plans Should Be Simple, Passionate," *USA Today,* July 31, 2006, 5E.

Use language appropriate for your audience. Even if the buyers want a state-of-the-art system, they may not want the level of detail that your staff could provide; they may not understand or appreciate technical jargon.

Sales proposals, particularly for complicated systems costing millions of dollars, are often long. Provide a one-page cover letter to present your proposal succinctly. The best organization for this letter is a modified version of the sales pattern in Chapter 12:

1.   Catch the reader's attention and summarize up to three major benefits you offer.

2.   Discuss each of the major benefits in the order in which you mentioned them in the first paragraph.

3.   Deal with any objections or concerns the reader may have.

4.   Mention other benefits briefly.

5.   Ask the reader to approve your proposal and provide a reason for acting promptly.

Proposals for Funding

Proposals for funding include both **business plans** (documents written to raise capital for new business ventures) and proposals submitted to foundations, corporations, and government agencies, to seek money for public service projects. In a proposal for funding, stress the needs your project will meet and show how your project helps fulfill the goals of the organization you are asking for funds.

Proposals are a major part of nonprofits' fund-raising activity; they write grant proposals to governmental organizations, foundations, and individuals to raise money for their organization. The writing process involves considerable research and planning, and often is preceded by informal conversations and formal presentations to potential funders. The funding process is often seen as a relationship-building process that involves researching, negotiating with, and persuading funders that the proposal not only meets their guidelines, but also is a cause worthy of a grant.

Every funding source has certain priorities; some have detailed lists of the kind of projects they fund. The Foundation Center hosts *The Foundation Directory,* which indexes foundations by state and city as well as by field of interest. The Foundation Center also supports *The Foundation Grants Index Annual,* which lists grants of $5,000 or more made by the 425 biggest foundations. Check recent awards to discover foundations that may be interested in your project. The same company provides *Source Book Profiles* which describes 1,000 national and regional foundations. All three indexes may be searched online if you pay a subscription fee. *Philanthropic Research Inc.* publishes free information about grants and grantmakers at its *GuideStar* Web site (http://www.guidestar.org), though a more detailed database is available by subscription. For information about grants made by the US government, visit http://www.grants.gov/, a Web site published by the *Department of Health and Human Services.* The site offers information on grant programs of all federal grant-making agencies, as well as downloadable grant applications.

Figuring the Budget and Costs

For a class research project, you may not be asked to prepare a budget. However, many proposals do require budgets, and a good budget is crucial to making the winning bid.

In fact, your budget may well be the most carefully scrutinized part of your proposal.[5]

Ask for everything you need to do a quality job. Asking for too little may backfire, leading the funder to think that you don't understand the scope of the project. Include less obvious costs, such as overhead. Also include costs that will be paid from other sources. Doing so shows that other sources also have confidence in your work. Pay particular attention to costs that may appear to benefit you more than the sponsor such as travel and equipment. Make sure they are fully justified in the proposal.

Do some research. Read the RFP to find out what is and isn't fundable. Talk to the program officer (the person who administers the funding process) and read successful past proposals to find answers to the following questions:

- What size projects will the organization fund in theory?
- Does the funder prefer making a few big grants or many smaller grants?
- Does the funder expect you to provide in-kind or cost-sharing funds from other sources?

Think about exactly what you'll do and who will do it. What will it cost to get that person? What supplies or materials will he or she need? Also think about indirect costs for using office space, about retirement and health benefits as well as salaries, about office supplies, administration, and infrastructure.

Make the basis of your estimates specific.

Weak:	75 hours of transcribing interviews	$1,500
Better:	25 hours of interviews; a skilled transcriber can complete 1 hour of interviews in 3 hours; 75 hours @ $20/hour	$1,500

Figure your numbers conservatively. For example, if the going rate for skilled transcribers is $20 an hour, but you think you might be able to train someone and pay only $12 an hour, use the higher figure. Then, even if your grant is cut, you'll still be able to do the project well.

Writing Progress Reports

When you're assigned to a single project that will take a month or more, you'll probably be asked to file one or more progress reports. A progress report reassures the funding agency or employer that you're making progress and allows you and the agency or employer to resolve problems as they arise. Different readers may have different concerns. An instructor may want to know whether you'll have your report in by the due date. A client may be more interested in what you're learning about the problem. Adapt your progress report to the needs of the audience.

Christine Barabas's study of the progress reports in a large research and development organization found that poor writers tended to focus on what they had done and said very little about the value of their work. Good writers, in contrast, spent less space writing about the details of what they'd done but much more space explaining the value of their work for the organization.[6]

When you write progress reports, use what you know about emphasis, positive tone, and you-attitude. Don't present every detail as equally important. Use emphasis techniques to stress the major ones. Readers will generally not care that Jones was out of the office when you went to visit him and that you had to return a second time to catch him. In your report, try to exceed expectations in at least some small way. Perhaps your research is ahead of schedule, or needed equipment arrived earlier than expected. However, do not present

http://foundationcenter.org/

http://www.kn.pacbell.com/products/grants/index.html

Many nonprofits rely on foundation support to deliver programs and services to constituents. In support of the nonprofit sector, the Foundation Center was established in 1956 to "strengthen the nonprofit sector by advancing knowledge about US philanthropy."

As a leading authority on philanthropy, the Foundation Center offers many resources online to connect nonprofits and grant-makers, maintaining a database on US grant-makers and their grants. In addition, the Foundation Center conducts research, operates library/learning centers, and offers educational and training programs.

Another helpful resource for writing grants is the Pacific Bell Knowledge Network. The site lists resources for researching and writing grant proposals.

Where the Funds Are

Dr. Richard Klausner has a lot of money to give away. He holds the job of global-health executive director for the Bill & Melinda Gates Foundation, a charitable foundation whose assets total about $24 billion, making it perhaps the largest foundation in history. The Gates Foundation funds work in two main areas: education and global health. So far, the foundation has given $2.8 billion to health-related efforts.

Having so much money to give away poses its own set of problems. As diseases such as malaria, tuberculosis, and AIDS devastate regions of the world, someone has to set priorities. Klausner and his staff have developed principles for awarding grants. The health grants target one of three areas of concern: HIV/AIDS and tuberculosis, infectious diseases and vaccines, and reproductive and child health. Even these areas are broad, so the foundation's staff must rely on grant writers to make a convincing case. They look for programs that offer long-term solutions, rather than temporary fixes.

Klausner appreciates the process. He told a reporter, "A well-written grant is a beautiful thing. You have a really smart person saying, 'I have this idea.' It's a wonderful story." Together with his staff, Klausner evaluates these stories, looking for the best ideas. In Klausner's words, the process is "an opportunity to ask, 'What's our thinking about turning this [proposal] down? Are we missing something important here?'" When the foundation does fund a proposal, it stays involved, monitoring progress to be sure the program is delivering the promised benefits.

Adapted from Chuck Salter, "Richard Klausner Spends to Save Lives," *Fast Company*, November 2002, 128.

the good news by speculating on the reader's feelings; many readers find such statements offensive.

Poor: You will be happy to hear the software came a week early.

Better: The software came a week early, so Pat can start programming earlier than expected.

Remember that your audience for your report is usually in a position of power over you, so be careful what you say to them. Generally it is not wise to blame them for project problems even if they are at fault.

Poor: We could not proceed with drafting the plans because you did not send us the specifications for the changes you want.

Better: Chris has prepared the outline for the plan. We are ready to start drafting as soon as we receive the specifications. Meanwhile, we are working on. . . .

Subject lines for progress reports are straightforward. Specify the project on which you are reporting your progress.

> Subject: Progress on Developing a Marketing Plan for TCBY

> Subject: Progress on Group Survey on Campus Parking

If you are submitting weekly or monthly progress reports on a long project, number your progress reports or include the time period in your subject line. Include dates for the work completed since the last report and work to be completed before the next report.

Make your progress report as positive as you honestly can. You'll build a better image of yourself if you show that you can take minor problems in stride and that you're confident of your own abilities.

Negative: I have not deviated markedly from my schedule, and I feel that I will have very little trouble completing this report by the due date.

Positive: I am back on schedule and expect to complete my report by the due date.

Focus on your solutions to problems rather than the problems themselves:

Negative: Our group can't find the books we need at the library.

Positive: We have ordered the books we need from Interlibrary Loan; they are expected to arrive Monday, November 15.

Do remember to use judicious restraint with your positive tone. Without details for support, glowing judgments of your own work may strike readers as ill-advised bragging, or maybe even dishonesty.

Progress reports can be organized in three ways: by chronology, by task, and to support a recommendation.

Chronological Progress Reports

The chronological pattern of organization focuses on what you have done and what work remains.

1. **Summarize your progress in terms of your goals and your original schedule.** Use measurable statements.

    Poor: My progress has been slow.

    Better: The research for my report is about one-third complete.

2. **Under the heading "Work Completed," describe what you have already done.** Be specific, both to support your claims in the first paragraph and to allow the reader to appreciate your hard work. Acknowledge the people who have helped you. Describe any serious obstacles you've encountered and tell how you've dealt with them.

> Poor: I have found many articles about Procter & Gamble on the Web. I have had a few problems finding how the company keeps employees safe from chemical fumes.
>
> Better: On the Web, I found Procter & Gamble's home page, its annual report, and mission statement. No one whom I interviewed could tell me about safety programs specifically at P&G. I have found seven articles about ways to protect workers against pollution in factories, but none mentions P&G.

3. **Under the heading "Work to Be Completed," describe the work that remains.** If you're more than three days late (for school projects) or two weeks late (for business projects) submit a new schedule, showing how you will be able to meet the original deadline. You may want to discuss "Observations" or "Preliminary Conclusions" if you want feedback before writing the final report or if your reader has asked for substantive interim reports.

4. **Either express your confidence in having the report ready by the due date or request a conference to discuss extending the due date or limiting the project.** If you are behind your original schedule, show why you think you can still finish the project on time.

Even in chronological reports you need to do more than merely list work you have done. Show the value of that work and your prowess in achieving it, particularly your ability at solving problems. The student progress report in Figure 15.4 uses the chronological pattern of organization.

Task Progress Reports

In a task progress report, organize information under the various tasks you have worked on during the period. For example, a task progress report for a group report project might use the following headings:

> Finding Background Information on the Web and in Print
> Analyzing Our Survey Data
> Working on the Introduction of the Report and the Appendices

Under each heading, the group could discuss the tasks it has completed and those that remain.

Task progress reports are appropriate for large projects with distinct topics or projects.

Recommendation Progress Reports

Recommendation progress reports recommend action: increasing the funding for a project, changing its direction, canceling a project that isn't working out. When the recommendation will be easy for the reader to accept, use the direct request pattern of organization from Chapter 12 (◀▥ p. 376). If the recommendation is likely to meet strong resistance, the problem-solving pattern (◀▥ p. 378) may be more effective.

The Political Uses of Progress Reports

Progress reports can do more than just report progress. You can use progress reports to

- Enhance your image. Details about the number of documents you've read, people you've surveyed, or experiments you've conducted create a picture of a hardworking person doing a thorough job.

- Float trial balloons. Explain, "I could continue to do X [what you approved]; I could do Y instead [what I'd like to do now]." The detail in the progress report can help back up your claim. Even if the idea is rejected, you don't lose face because you haven't made a separate issue of the alternative.

- Minimize potential problems. As you do the work, it may become clear that implementing your recommendations will be difficult. In your regular progress reports, you can alert your boss or the funding agency to the challenges that lie ahead, enabling them to prepare psychologically and physically to act on your recommendations.

Figure 15.4   A Student Chronological Progress Report

November 10, 2008

To: Kitty O. Locker

From: David G. Bunnel *DGB*

Subject: Progress on CAD/CAM Software Feasibility Study for the Architecture Firm, Patrick
          and Associates, Inc.

*¶ 1:
Summarize
results in
terms of
purpose,
schedule.*

I have obtained most of the information necessary to recommend whether CADAM or CATIA is
better for Patrick and Associates, Inc. (P&A). I am currently analyzing and organizing this information and am on schedule.

Work Completed   *Underline headings
or bold.*

*Be very
specific
about
what
you've
done.*

To learn how computer literate P&A employees are, I interviewed a judgment sample of five
employees. My interview with Bruce Ratekin, the director of P&A's Computer-Aided Design
(CAD) Department on November 3 enabled me to determine the architectural drafting needs of
the firm. Mr. Ratekin also gave me a basic drawing of a building showing both two- and three-
dimensional views so that I could replicate the drawing with both software packages.

*Show how
you've
overcome
minor
problems.*

I obtained tutorials for both packages to use as a reference while making the drawings. First I
drew the building using CADAM, the package designed primarily for two-dimensional architectural drawings. I encountered problems with the isometric drawing because there was a mistake
in the manual I was using; I fixed the problem by trying alternatives and finally getting help from
another CADAM user. Next, I used CATIA, the package whose strength is three-dimensional
drawings, to construct the drawing. I am in the process of comparing the two packages based
on these criteria: quality of drawing, ease of data entry (lines, points, surfaces, etc.) for computer experts and novices, and ease of making changes in the completed drawings. Based on
my experience with the packages, I have analyzed the training people with and without experience in CAD would need to learn to use each of these packages.

Work to Be Completed   *Indicate changes in purpose, scope, or recommendations.
Progress report is a low-risk way to bring the readers on board.*

Making the drawings has shown that neither of the packages can do everything that P&A needs.
Therefore, I want to investigate the feasibility of P&A's buying both packages.

*Specify
the work
that
remains.*

As soon as he comes back from an unexpected illness that has kept him out of the office, I will
meet with Tom Merrick, the CAD systems programmer for The Ohio State University, to learn
about software expansion flexibility for both packages as well as the costs for initial purchase,
installation, maintenance, and software updates. After this meeting, I will be ready to begin the
first draft of my report.

Whether I am able to meet my deadline will depend on when I am able to meet with Mr. Merrick.
Right now, I am on schedule and plan to submit my report by the December 10th deadline.

End on a positive note.

Research Strategies for Reports

Research for a report may be as simple as getting a computer printout of sales for the last month; it may involve finding published material or surveying or interviewing people. **Secondary research** retrieves information that someone else gathered. Library research and online searches are the best known kinds of secondary research. **Primary research** gathers new information. Surveys, interviews, and observations are common methods for gathering new information for business reports.

Finding Information Online and in Print

You can save time and money by checking online and published sources of data before you gather new information. Many college and university libraries provide

- Workshops on research techniques.
- Handouts explaining how to use printed and computer-based sources.
- Free or inexpensive access to computer databases.
- Research librarians who can help you find and use sources.

  Categories of sources that may be useful include

- Specialized encyclopedias for introductions to a topic.
- Indexes to find articles. Most permit searches by keyword, by author, and often by company name.

Good research uses multiple media and sources.

- Abstracts for brief descriptions or summaries of articles. Sometimes the abstract will be all you'll need; almost always, you can tell from the abstract whether an article is useful for your needs.
- Citation indexes to find materials that cite previous research. Citation indexes thus enable you to use an older reference to find newer articles on the topic. The *Social Sciences Citation Index* is the most useful for researching business topics.
- Newspapers for information about recent events.
- US Census reports, for a variety of business and demographic information.

To use a computer database efficiently, identify the concepts you're interested in and choose keywords that will help you find relevant sources. **Keywords** or **descriptors** are the terms that the computer searches for. If you're not sure what terms to use, check the ABI/Inform Thesaurus for synonyms and the hierarchies in which information is arranged in various databases.

Specific commands allow you to narrow your search. For example, to study the effect of the minimum wage on employment in the restaurant industry, you might use a Boolean search (see Figure 15.5):

(minimum wage) *and* (restaurant or fast food) *and*
(employment rate *or* unemployment).

This descriptor would give you the titles of articles that treat all three of the topics in parentheses. Without *and,* you'd get articles that discuss the minimum wage in general, articles about every aspect of *restaurants,* and every article that refers to *unemployment,* even though many of these would not be relevant to your topic. The *or* descriptor calls up articles that use the term *fast food* or the term *restaurant.* Many Web search engines, including AltaVista and Google, allow you to specify words that cannot appear in a source.

Many words can appear in related forms. To catch all of them, use the database's **wild card** or **truncated code** for shortened terms and root words. To find this feature and others, go to the Advanced Search screen for the search engine you are using. Search engines vary in the symbols they use for searches, so be sure to check for accurate directions.

Web search engines are particularly effective for words, people, or phrases that are unlikely to have separate pages devoted to them. For general topics or famous people, directories like Yahoo! may be more useful. Figure 15.6 lists a few of the specialized sources available.

Figure 15.5   Example of a Boolean Search

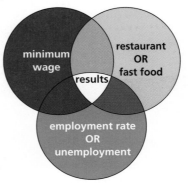

Evaluating Web Sources

Some of the material on the Web is excellent, but some of it is wholly unreliable. With print sources, the editor or publisher serves as a gatekeeper, so you can trust the material in good journals. To put up a Web page, all one needs is access to a server.

Figure 15.6 Sources for Web Research

Subject matter directories

SmartPros (accounting and corporate finance)
   http://smartpros.com/
Rutgers Accounting Research Center (RARC)
   http://www.accounting.rutgers.edu/
Education Index
   http://www.educationindex.com
Resources for Economists on the Internet
   http://www.aeaweb.org/RFE/
Human resource management resources on the Internet
   http://www.nbs.ntu.ac.uk/research/depts/hrm/links.php
Global Edge
   http://www.globaledge.msu.edu/
International Business Kiosk
   http://www.calintel.org/kiosk/
Management and entrepreneurship
   http://www.lib.lsu.edu/bus/managemt.html
KnowThis: Knowledge source for marketing
   http://www.knowthis.com
Internet marketing resources
   http://www.lib.lsu.edu/bus/marketin.html
Statistical Resources on the Web (University of Michigan Documents Center)
   http://www.lib.umich.edu/govdocs/stats.html

News sites

BusinessWeek
   http://www.businessweek.com
CNN/CNNFN
   http://www.cnn.com (news)
   http://money.cnn.com/ (financial news)
National Public Radio
   http://www.npr.org
NewsLink (links to US, Canadian, and international newspapers, magazines, and resources online)
   http://newslink.org
New York Times
   http://www.nytimes.com
Wall Street Journal
   http://online.wsj.com/
Washington Post
   http://www.WashingtonPost.com

(continued)

Not Necessarily True

Can you believe everything you read on the Internet? Here are a few examples of the kinds of Internet hoaxes that continue to circulate.

In 2006, one rumor in circulation claimed that ATMs have a hidden safety feature that lets users signal the police of robbery in progress. Users simply have to enter their personal identification number (PIN) backwards. While the reverse-PIN system does exist on paper (its inventor claims it would reduce crime), the technology has yet to be implemented on an actual ATM.

As of 2006, an eight-year old e-mail hoax supposedly from Microsoft founder Bill Gates was still going strong. As originally composed, the message promised $1,000 to every person who helped the company beta test its new email tracking software. All you had to do was forward the message to everyone you knew. Later versions included phony news reports claiming that AOL, Microsoft, and Intel were merging.

In 2005, 9-year-old Penny Brown had been "missing" for four years. A chain email asked readers to send information about her to the email address zicozicozico@hotmail.com. But, neither Penny Brown nor the e-mail address exists. Will this chain letter ever end?

Go to http://urbanlegends.about.com/ and http://www.scambusters.org for more information about Internet hoaxes and frauds.

Adapted from David Emery, "Top 10 Hoaxes and Legends of 2006," in *News & Issues: Urban Legends and Folklore: Internet/Web Hoaxes,* About.com, http://urbanlegends.about.com/od/internet/a/2006_top_ten.htm (accessed June 15, 2007).

Figure 15.6   Sources for Web Research *(Concluded)*

US government information

FedStats (links from over 100 federal agencies)
    http://www.fedstats.gov
Stat-USA/Internet (trade statistics from the Department of Commerce)
    http://www.stat-usa.gov/
US Government Printing Office
    http://www.gpoaccess.gov/index.html
Bureau of Economic Analysis
    http://www.bea.gov/
Bureau of Labor Statistics
    http://www.bls.gov/
Census Bureau (including a link to the *Statistical Abstract of the United States*)
    http://www.census.gov/
Securities and Exchange Commission Filings and Forms (EDGAR)
    http://sec.gov/edgar.shtml
Small Business Administration
    http://www.sbaonline.sba.gov/
White House Briefing Room (economic issues)
    http://www.whitehouse.gov/fsbr/esbr.html
White House Briefing Room (social statistics)
    http://www.whitehouse.gov/fsbr/ssbr.html

Reference collections

Hoover's Online (information on more than 13,000 public and private companies worldwide)
    http://www.hoovers.com/
Industry Research Desk
    http://www.virtualpet.com/industry/rdindex2.htm
My Virtual Reference Desk
    http://www.refdesk.com/
Tile.Net's guide to Internet discussion and information lists
    http://tile.net/lists/

Use four criteria to decide whether a Web site is good enough to use for a research project:

1. **Authors.** What person or organization sponsors the site? What credentials do the authors have?
2. **Objectivity.** Does the site give evidence to support its claims? Does it give both sides of controversial issues? Is the tone professional?
3. **Information.** How complete is the information? What is it based on?
4. **Revision date.** When was the site last updated?

Answers to these questions may lead you to discard some of the relevant sites you find. For example, if you find five different Web pages about the cell phones and car accidents that all cite the same Toronto study, you have one source, not five. Choose the most complete for your project.

Be warned that many course instructors and other professionals do not consider Wikipedia a legitimate source.

Designing Questions for Surveys and Interviews

A **survey** questions a large group of people, called **respondents** or **subjects.** The easiest way to ask many questions is to create a **questionnaire,** a written list of questions that people fill out. An **interview** is a structured conversation with someone who will be able to give you useful information. Surveys and interviews can be useful only if the questions are well designed.

Good questions ask only one thing, are phrased neutrally, avoid making assumptions about the respondent, and mean the same thing to different people. At a telecommunications firm, a survey asked employees to rate their manager's performance at "hiring staff and setting compensation." Although both tasks are part of the discipline of human resource management, they are different activities. A manager might do a better job of hiring than of setting pay levels, or vice versa. The survey gave respondents—and the company using the survey—no way to distinguish performance on each task.[7]

Phrase questions in a way that won't bias the response. In the political sphere, for example, opinions about rights for homosexuals vary according to the way questions are asked. More Americans oppose "allowing gays and lesbians to marry legally" than oppose "legal agreements giving many of the same rights as marriage." Furthermore, the order in which the questions are asked may matter. In a survey in which the order of questions varied, more people favored legal rights for gay and lesbian couples when they already had been asked about "gay marriage." Possibly, the order of questions encouraged them to draw a distinction between marriages and civil unions. With regard to homosexual relations, the number of people who say such behavior should be "illegal" is greater than the number who say "consenting adults engaged in homosexual activities in private should be prosecuted for a crime."[8]

Avoid questions that make assumptions about your subjects. The question "Does your wife have a job outside the home?" assumes that your respondent is a married man.

Use words that mean the same thing to you and to the respondents. If a question can be interpreted in more than one way, it will be. Words like *often* and *important* mean different things to different people. When a consulting firm called Employee Motivation and Performance Assessment helped Duke Energy assess the leadership skills of its managers, an early draft of the employee survey asked employees to rate how well their manager "understands the business and the marketplace." How would employees know what is in the manager's mind? Each respondent would have to determine what is reasonable evidence of a manager's understanding. The question was rephrased to identify behavior the employees could observe: "resolves complaints from customers quickly and thoroughly." The wording is still subjective ("quickly and thoroughly"), but at least all employees will be measuring the same category of behavior.[9]

Even questions that call for objective information can be confusing. For example, consider the owner of a small business confronted with the question "How many employees do you have?" Does the number include the owner as well as subordinates? Does it include both full- and part-time employees? Does it include people who have been hired but who haven't yet started work, or someone who is leaving at the end of the month? A better wording would be

How many full-time employees were on your payroll the week of May 16?

As discussed in Chapter 4, bypassing occurs (◀ p.113) when two people use the same words or phrases but interpret them differently. To reduce bypassing, avoid terms that are likely to mean different things to different people and pretest your questions with several people who are like those who will fill out

http://www.galluppoll .com

Designing survey questions is an important and difficult part of getting valid results. For examples of surveys, including information about their design, visit the Gallup Poll pages of the Gallup Organization's Web site. On the site, click on "Poll Topics A–Z" to examine the ways in which surveys and survey questions are designed. The Web site also includes a "Video Archives" page of Gallup's survey work. The videos discuss the results of particular polls; many also talk about the poll's audience and purpose, important factors in a survey's design. Watch several videos and examine several polls for the ways in which audience and purpose shape the questions in the survey.

Watch Your Language

In two decades of writing and using surveys, psychologist Palmer Morrel-Samuels has seen that the wording of a survey question can affect responses. For example, the connotation of a phrase can unintentionally skew the way people react to a question. He recalls a survey that a maker of photographic equipment used to learn about the leadership skills of its managers. A question asked employees whether their manager "takes bold strides" and "has a strong grasp" of complicated issues. Male managers tended to outscore female managers. Morrel-Samuels noted that, in a literal sense, males on average take longer strides and have more muscle strength than females. The company changed the wording of the survey. "Has a strong grasp of complex problems" became "discusses complex problems with precision and clarity." After this change, the difference in ratings of female and male managers disappeared. Employees apparently stopped mixing images of size and strength into their ratings of intellectual insight.

Another word-related bias is that respondents tend to agree more than disagree with statements. If a survey about managers asks employees whether their manager is fair, ethical, intelligent, knowledgeable, and so on, they are likely to assign all of these qualities to the manager—and to agree more and more as the survey goes along. To correct for this, some questions should be worded to generate the opposite response. For example, a statement about ethics can be balanced by a statement about corruption, and a statement about fairness can be balanced by a statement about bias or stereotypes.

Adapted from Palmer Morrel-Samuels, "Getting the Truth into Workplace Surveys," *Harvard Business Review*, 80, No. 2 (February 2002): 111–18.

the survey to catch questions that can be misunderstood. Even a small pretest with 10 people can help you refine your questions.

Kinds of questions

Questions can be categorized in several ways.

Closed questions have a limited number of possible responses. **Open questions** do not lock the subject into any sort of response. Figure 15.7 gives examples of closed and open questions. The second question in Figure 15.7 is an example of a Likert-type scale. Closed questions are faster for subjects to answer and easier for researchers to score. However, since all answers must fit into prechosen categories, they cannot probe the complexities of a subject. You can improve the quality of closed questions by conducting a pretest with open questions to find categories that matter to respondents. Analyzing the responses from open questions is usually less straightforward than analyzing responses from closed questions.

Use an "Other, Please Specify" category when you want the convenience of a closed question but cannot foresee all the possible responses. These responses can be used to improve choices if the survey is to be repeated.

> What is the single most important reason that you ride the bus?
> _____   I don't have a car.
> _____   I don't want to fight rush-hour traffic.
> _____   Riding the bus is cheaper than driving my car.
> _____   Riding the bus conserves fuel and reduces pollution.
> _____   Other (please specify): _____

Figure 15.7   Closed and Open Questions

Closed questions

Are you satisfied with the city bus service? (yes/no)

How good is the city bus service?

   Excellent   5   4   3   2   1   Terrible

Indicate whether you agree (A) or disagree (D) with each of the following statements about city bus service.

   A   D   The schedule is convenient for me.

   A   D   The routes are convenient for me.

   A   D   The drivers are courteous.

   A   D   The buses are clean.

Rate each of the following improvements in the order of their importance to you (1 = most important and 5 = least important).

_____   Buy new buses.

_____   Increase non-rush-hour service on weekdays.

_____   Increase service on weekdays.

_____   Provide earlier and later service on weekdays.

_____   Buy more buses with wheelchair access.

_____   Provide unlimited free transfers.

Open questions

How do you feel about the city bus service?

Tell me about the city bus service.

Why do you ride the bus? (or, Why don't you ride the bus?)

What do you like and dislike about the city bus service?

How could the city bus service be improved?

When you use multiple-choice questions, make the answer categories mutually exclusive and exhaustive. This means you make sure that any one answer fits only in one category and that a category is included for all possible answers. In the following example of overlapping categories, a person who worked for a company with exactly 25 employees could check either *a* or *b*. The resulting data would be hard to interpret.

Overlapping categories: Indicate the number of full-time employees in your company on May 16:

    _____ a. 0–25

    _____ b. 25–100

    _____ c. 100–500

    _____ d. over 500

Discrete categories: Indicate the number of full-time employees on your payroll on May 16:

    _____ a. 0–25

    _____ b. 26–100

    _____ c. 101–500

    _____ d. more than 500

Branching questions direct different respondents to different parts of the questionnaire based on their answers to earlier questions.

> 10. Have you talked to an academic adviser this year? yes no
> (If "no," skip to question 14.)

Use closed multiple-choice questions for potentially embarrassing topics. Seeing their own situation listed as one response can help respondents feel that it is acceptable. However, very sensitive issues are perhaps better asked in an interview, where the interviewer can build trust and reveal information about himself or herself to encourage the interviewee to answer.

Generally, put early in the questionnaire questions that will be easy to answer. Put questions that are harder to answer or that people may be less willing to answer (e.g., age and income) near the end of the questionnaire. Even if people choose not to answer such questions, you'll still have the rest of the survey filled out.

If subjects will fill out the questionnaire themselves, pay careful attention to the physical design of the document. Use indentations and white space effectively; make it easy to mark and score the answers. Label answer scales frequently so respondents remember which end is positive and which is negative. Include a brief statement of purpose if you (or someone else) will not be available to explain the questionnaire or answer questions. Pretest the questionnaire to make sure the directions are clear. One researcher mailed a two-page questionnaire without pretesting it. One-third the respondents didn't realize there were questions to answer on the back of the first page.

See Figure 15.8 for an example of a questionnaire for a student report.

Conducting Surveys and Interviews

Face-to-face surveys are convenient when you are surveying a fairly small number of people in a specific location. In a face-to-face survey, the interviewer's sex, race, and nonverbal cues can bias results. Most people prefer not to say things they think their audience will find unacceptable. For that reason,

If People Can Misunderstand the Question, They Will

Q: Give previous experience with dates.

A: Moderately successful in the past, but I am now happily married!

Q: How many autopsies have you performed on dead people?

A: All my autopsies have been on dead people.

Q: James stood back and shot Tommy Lee?

A: Yes.

Q: And then Tommy Lee pulled out his gun and shot James in the fracas?

A: (After hesitation) No sir, just above it.

Q: What is the country's mortality rate?

A: 100%. Everybody dies.

Q: Give numbers of employees broken down by sex.

A: None. Our problem is booze.

Q: Sex?

A: Once a week.

Adapted from James Hartley, *Designing Instructional Text* (London: Kogan Page, 1978), 109; Richard Lederer, *Anguished English* (New York: Wyrick, 1988); and surveys of college students.

Figure 15.8   Questionnaire for a Student Report Using Survey Research

An interesting title can help.

In your introductory ¶,
①*tell how to return the survey*
②*tell how the information will be used*

Survey: Why Do Students Attend Athletic Events?

The purpose of this survey is to determine why students attend sports events, and what might increase attendance. All information is to be used solely for a student research paper. Please return completed surveys to Elizabeth or Vicki in the Union. Thank you for your assistance!

Start with easy-to-answer questions

1. Gender (Please circle one)   M   F

2. What is your class year? (Please circle)   1   2   3   4   Grad   Other

Seeing a response in a survey can make respondents more willing to admit to feelings they may be embarrassed to volunteer.

3. How do you feel about women's sports? (Please circle)

1	2	3	4	5
I enjoy watching women's sports		I'll watch, but it doesn't really matter		Women's sports are boring/ I'd rather watch men's sports

The words below each number anchor responses, while still allowing you to average the data.

4. Do you like to attend MSU men's basketball games or watch them on TV? (Please circle)   Y   N

5. How often do you attend MSU women's basketball games? (Please circle)

1	2	3	4	5
All/most games	Few games a season	Once a season	Less than once a year	Never

6. If you do not attend all of the women's basketball games, why not? (Please check all that apply. If you attend all the games, skip to #7.)

__I've never thought to go.
__I don't like basketball.
__I don't like sporting events.
__The team isn't good enough.
__My friends are not interested in going.
__I want to go, I just haven't had the opportunity.
__The tickets cost too much ($3).
__Other (please specify) _____

Think about factors that affect the problem you're studying, and write survey questions to get information about them.

7. To what extent would each of the following make you more likely to attend an MSU women's basketball game? (please rank all)

1	2	3
Much more likely to attend	Possibley more likely	No effect

__Increased awareness on campus (fliers, chalking on the Oval, more articles in the *Gazette*)
__Marketing to students (give-aways, days for residence halls or fraternities/sororities)
__Student loyalty program (awarding points towards free tickets, clothing, food for attending games)
__Education (pocket guide explaining the rules of the game provided at the gate)
__Other (please specify) _____

Thank you!
Please return this survey to Elizabeth or Vicki in the Union.

Repeat where to turn in or mail completed surveys.

women will be more likely to agree that sexual harassment is a problem if the interviewer is also a woman. Members of a minority group are more likely to admit that they suffer discrimination if the interviewer is a member of the same minority.

Telephone surveys are popular because they can be closely supervised. Interviewers can read the questions from a computer screen and key in answers as the respondent gives them. The results can then be available just a few minutes after the last call is completed.

Phone surveys also have limitations. First, they reach only people who have phones and thus underrepresent some groups such as poor people. Answering machines, caller ID, and cell phones also make phone surveys more difficult. Since a survey based on a phone book would exclude people with unlisted numbers, professional survey-takers use automatic random-digit dialing. Decide in advance to whom you want to speak, and ask for that person rather than surveying whoever answers the phone.

To increase the response rate for a phone survey, call at a time respondents will find convenient. Avoid calling between 5 and 7 PM, a time when many families have dinner.

Mail surveys can reach anyone who has an address. Some people may be more willing to fill out an anonymous questionnaire than to give sensitive information to a stranger over the phone. However, mail surveys are not effective for respondents who don't read and write well. Further, it may be more difficult to get a response from someone who doesn't care about the survey or who sees the mailing as junk mail. Over the phone, the interviewer can try to persuade the subject to participate.

Online surveys deliver questions over the Internet. The researcher can contact respondents with e-mail containing a link to a Web page containing the survey or can ask people by mail or in person to log on and visit the Web site with the survey. Another alternative is to post a survey on a Web site and invite the site's visitors to complete the survey. This approach does not generate a random sample, so the results probably do not reflect the opinions of the entire population. Interactive technology makes it easy to use branching questions; the survey can automatically send respondents to the next question on a branch. However, many people worry about the privacy of online surveys, so they may be reluctant to participate. Researchers have found that a lower percentage of people are willing to complete online surveys than other kinds. To encourage participation, researchers should make online surveys as short as possible. A bank recently used a 32-screen survey; few customers are likely to bother finishing such an undertaking.[10]

A major concern with any kind of survey is the **response rate,** the percentage of people who respond. People who refuse to answer may differ from those who respond, and you need information from both groups to be able to generalize to the whole population. Low response rates pose a major problem, especially for phone surveys. Answering machines and caller ID are commonly used to screen incoming calls resulting in decreased response rates.

Widespread use of cell phones in recent years has also negatively affected the ability of telephone surveyors to contact potential respondents. A 2006 Pew Research Center Study found that 7% to 9% of the American general public is cell only. They are young, less affluent, unmarried, and less likely to own their own home. Politically, landline-only and cell-only groups tend to be Democrats more than those having both services. Surprisingly, cell phone users are as focused and cooperative as those reached by landlines.[11]

The problem of nonresponse has increased dramatically in recent years. The University of Michigan's Survey of Consumer Attitudes experienced only

Market Research Creates an Ad Campaign

[The tiny company that made Boker knives was considering dropping the brand. But before making the decision, executives and ad agency personnel talked to current and potential customers: people who hunt and fish.]

"They knew they were onto something when they ran into a longtime Boker customer who told them what he liked about the knife. He said that whenever he wants to make French fries, he just opens his Boker, puts it in the glove box of his four-by-four pickup with a bunch of potatoes, and drives over a rocky road in second gear. He added, 'Of course, for hash browns I use third gear.'

"As they began to collect stories like this, others poured in. The agency ran a print campaign featuring fanciful pictures of old-time Boker users. The title of the ad ran: IN EVERY LIE ABOUT THE BOKER THERE'S A LITTLE BIT OF TRUTH. The ads recounted the tall tales, which guaranteed high readership. Then the ads told the serious part of the Boker message. Within a year, both market share and profits had doubled."

Quoted from Robert H. Waterman, *The Renewal Factor* (Toronto: Bantam, 1987), 163.

Research on a Shoestring

Traditional market research can cost $20,000 to $50,000 or even more. What does a company do if its budget isn't that big?

Mark Bissel used diaries and observations to collect data about a European home-cleaning product he wanted to sell in the United States. In return for a $1,500 donation, his local Parent-Teacher Association let him make a presentation at a meeting. Twenty people agreed to try the product in their homes. Each kept a diary about experiences using the "Steam Gun," and Bissel's marketing director visited homes to watch people using the product.

The first lesson was that the product's name was a problem. Kids threatened to blow their siblings away with the "Steam Gun." And US consumers didn't believe that steam without soap or chemicals would get stuff clean. So the company changed the name to "Steam N' Clean."

People serious about cleaning liked the product best. The product was great for blasting dirt out of corners and crevices in the kitchen and bathroom. So the company developed infomercials touting the benefits of steam for cleaning. The product sold well both from the infomercials and in Kmart.

Adapted from Alison Stein Wellner, "Research on a Shoestring," *American Demographics*, April 2001, 38–39.

a small drop in response rate between 1979–1996, from 72% to 67%. But the deterioration in response rate has accelerated since then, and in 2003 the response rate had dropped to 48%.[12]

According to figures that researchers have reported to the Marketing Research Association, the response rate for door-to-door surveys was 53%, and the response rate for face-to-face surveys in malls and other central locations was 38%. The response rate for Web surveys averaged 34%.[13] To get as high a response rate as possible, good researchers follow up, contacting nonrespondents at least once and preferably twice to try to persuade them to participate in the survey. Sometimes money or other rewards are used to induce people to participate.

Selecting a sample for surveys and interviews

To keep research costs reasonable, usually only a sample of the total population is polled. How that sample is chosen and the attempts made to get responses from nonrespondents will determine whether you can infer that what is true of your sample is also true of the population as a whole.

A **sample** is a subset of the population. The **sampling units** are those actually sampled. Frequently, the sampling unit is an individual. If a list of individuals is not available then a household can be the sampling unit. The list of all sampling units is the **sampling frame**. For interviews, this could be a list of all addresses, or for companies a list of all Fortune 500 CEOs.[14] The **population** is the group you want to make statements about. Depending on the purpose of your research, your population might be all Fortune 1000 companies, all business students at your college, or all consumers of tea in the mid-Atlantic states.

A **convenience sample** is a group of subjects who are easy to get: students who walk through the union, people at a shopping mall, workers in your own unit. Convenience samples are useful for a rough pretest of a questionnaire and may be acceptable for some class research projects. However, you cannot generalize from a convenience sample to a larger group.

A purposive or **judgment sample** is a group of people whose views seem useful. Someone interested in surveying the kinds of writing done on campus might ask each department for the name of a faculty member who cared about writing, and then send surveys to those people.

In a **random sample,** each person in the population theoretically has an equal chance of being chosen. When people say they did something *randomly* they often mean *without conscious bias*. However, unconscious bias exists. Someone passing out surveys in front of the library will be more likely to approach people who seem friendly and less likely to ask people who seem intimidating, in a hurry, much older or younger, or of a different race, class, or sex. True random samples rely on random digit tables, published in statistics texts and books such as *A Million Random Digits*. An online random number table site can be found at http://ts.nist.gov/WeightsandMeasures/upload/AppendB-HB133-05-Z.doc. Computers can also be programmed to generate random numbers.

If you take a true random sample, you can generalize your findings to the whole population from which your sample comes. Consider, for example, a random phone survey that shows 65% of respondents approve of a presidential policy. Measures of variation should always be attached to survey-derived estimates like this one. Typically, a confidence interval provides this measure of variability. Using the confidence interval, we might conclude it is likely that between 58% and 72% of the population approve of the presidential policy when the confidence interval is ± 7%. The accuracy range is based on the size of the sample and the expected variation within the population. Statistics texts tell you how to calculate these figures.

Do not confuse sample size with randomness. A classic example is the 1936 Literary Digest poll which predicted Republican Alf Landon would beat Democrat and incumbent President Franklin Roosevelt. Literary Digest sent out 10 million ballots to its magazine subscribers as well as people who owned cars and telephones, all of whom in 1936 were richer than the average voter—and more Republican.[15]

Conducting research interviews

Schedule interviews in advance; tell the interviewee about how long you expect the interview to take. A survey of technical writers (who get much of their information from interviews) found that the best times to interview subject matter experts are Tuesdays, Wednesdays, and Thursday mornings.[16] People are frequently swamped on Mondays and looking forward to the weekend, or trying to finish their week's work on Fridays.

Interviews can be structured or unstructured. In a **structured interview,** the interviewer uses a detailed list of questions to guide the interview. Indeed, a structured interview may use a questionnaire just as a survey does.

In an **unstructured interview,** the interviewer has three or four main questions. Other questions build on what the interviewee says. To prepare for an unstructured interview, learn as much as possible about the interviewee and the topic. Go into the interview with three or four main topics you want to cover.

Interviewers sometimes use closed questions to start the interview and set the interviewee at ease. The strength of an interview, however, is getting at a person's attitudes, feelings, and experiences. Situational questions let you probe what someone would do in a specific circumstance. Hypothetical questions that ask people to imagine what they would do generally yield less reliable answers than questions about **critical incidents** or key past events.

Hypothetical question:	What would you say if you had to tell an employee that his or her performance was unsatisfactory?
Critical incident question:	You've probably been in a situation where someone who was working with you wasn't carrying his or her share of the work. What did you do the last time that happened?

A **mirror question** paraphrases the content of the last answer: "So you confronted him directly?" "You think that this product costs too much?" Mirror questions are used both to check that the interviewer understands what the interviewee has said and to prompt the interviewee to continue talking. **Probes** follow up an original question to get at specific aspects of a topic:

Question:	What do you think about the fees for campus parking?
Probes:	Would you be willing to pay more for a reserved space? How much more? Should the fines for vehicles parked illegally be increased? Do you think fees should be based on income?

Probes are not used in any definite order. Instead, they are used to keep the interviewee talking, to get at aspects of a subject that the interviewee has not yet mentioned, and to probe more deeply into points that the interviewee brings up.

If you read questions to subjects in a structured interview, use fewer options than you might in a written questionnaire.

I'm going to read a list of factors that someone might look for in choosing a restaurant. After I read each factor, please tell me whether that factor is Very Important to you, Somewhat Important to you, or Not Important to you.

Ethical Issues in Interviewing

If you're trying to get sensitive information, interviewees may give useful information when the interview is "over" and the tape recorder has been turned off. Is it ethical to use that information?

If you're interviewing a hostile or very reluctant interviewee, you may get more information if you agree with everything you can legitimately agree to, and keep silent on the rest. Is it ethical to imply acceptance even when you know you'll criticize the interviewee's ideas in your report?

Most people would say that whatever public figures say is fair game: they're supposed to know enough to defend themselves.

Many people would say that different rules apply when you'll cite someone by name than when you'll use the information as background or use a pseudonym so that the interviewee cannot be identified.

As a practical matter, if someone feels you've misrepresented him or her, that person will be less willing to talk to you in the future. But quite apart from practical considerations, interview strategies raise ethical issues as well.

And the Survey Says . . .

Increasingly, companies use surveys to measure their customer's satisfaction with their products or services. But are they really using that data? A survey by Bain & Company of 362 companies and their customers has revealed a discrepancy between the companies' and consumers' perceptions of customer satisfaction. The survey found that while 80% of the companies thought they were providing a "superior" consumer experience, only 8% of the customers described their experience that way.

Unfortunately, an even wider disconnect exists between measuring customer satisfaction and changing corporate business practices to achieve it. Getting data is one thing. But, circulating the findings and making sure the findings are put to use is another. So, when you go to the work of collecting data, make sure that you also make the data work for you.

Adapted from Christopher Meyer and Andre Schwager, "Understanding Customer Experience," *Harvard Business Review* 85, no. 2 (February 2007): 116–26.

If the interviewee hesitates, reread the scale.

Always tape the interview. Test your equipment ahead of time to make sure it works. If you think your interviewee may be reluctant to speak on tape, take along two tapes and two recorders; offer to give one tape to the interviewee.

Pulitzer Prize winner Nan Robertson offers the following advice to interviewers[17]:

- Do your homework. Learn about the subject and the person before the interview.
- To set a nervous interviewee at ease, start with nuts-and-bolts questions, even if you already know the answers.
- Save controversial questions for the end. You'll have everything else you need, and the trust built up in the interview makes an answer more likely.
- Go into an interview with three or four major questions. Listen to what the interviewee says and let the conversation flow naturally.
- At the end of the interview, ask for office and home telephone numbers in case you need to ask an additional question when you write up the interview.

Observing Customers and Users

Answers to surveys and interviews may differ from actual behavior—sometimes greatly. To get more accurate consumer information, many marketers observe users. For example, one problem with asking consumers about their television-watching behavior is that they sometimes underreport the number of hours they watch and the degree to which they watch programs they aren't proud of liking. Researchers have tried to develop a variety of measurement methods that collect viewing data automatically. Arbitron introduced the Portable People Meter (PPM), which receives an inaudible electronic signal from radio stations and broadcast and cable TV stations. Consumers simply carry the PPM, and it records their media exposure. One of the first results showed that consumers listened to radio more than they had indicated in diaries.[18] Nielsen Media Research has added commercial viewings to its famous TV show numbers; advertisers are naturally anxious to know how many people actually watch commercials instead of leaving to get a snack or fast-forwarding through them on digital video recorders.[19] Nielsen has also started tracking college students' viewing, installing its people meters in commons areas such as dorms. The new data boosted ratings for some shows, such as *Grey's Anatomy* and *America's Next Top Model* by more than 35%.[20]

Observation can tell marketers more about customers than the customers can put into words themselves. Intuit, a leader in observation studies, sends employees to visit customers and watch how they use Intuit products such as QuickBooks. Watching small businesses struggle with QuickBooks Pro told the company of the need for a new product, QuickBooks Simple Start.[21] Miller Lite beer hired OgilvyDiscovery to observe men drinking beer in bars. The researchers observed the group's social behaviors, such as how close they stood to one another and how they took turns telling stories. These details later found their way into commercials, giving the message greater authenticity.[22]

Observation can also be used for gathering in-house information such as how efficiently production systems operate and how well employees serve customers. Many businesses use "mystery shoppers." For instance, McDonald's has used mystery shoppers to check cleanliness, customer service, and food quality. The company posts store-by-store results online, giving store operators an incentive and the information they need to improve quality on measures where they are slipping or lagging behind the region's performance.[23]

Even health care facilities use mystery shoppers. The most commonly reported changes after the shoppers' reports are improved estimates of waiting times and better explanations of medical procedures. So many organizations use mystery shoppers that there is a Mystery Shopping Providers Association; it reported $600 million revenue for the industry in 2004.[24]

Observation is often combined with other techniques to get the most information. *Think-aloud protocols* ask users to voice their thoughts as they use a document or product: "First I'll try. . . . " These protocols are tape-recorded and later analyzed to understand how users approach a document or product. *Interruption interviews* interrupt users to ask them what's happening. For example, a company testing a draft of computer instructions might interrupt a user to ask, "What are you trying to do now? Tell me why you did that." *Discourse-based interviews* ask questions based on documents that the interviewee has written: "You said that the process is too complicated. Tell me what you mean by that."

Using and Documenting Sources

In a good report, sources are cited and documented smoothly and unobtrusively. **Citation** means attributing an idea or fact to its source *in the body of the report:* "According to the 2000 Census . . . " "Jane Bryant Quinn argues that . . . " Citing sources demonstrates your honesty and enhances your credibility. **Documentation** means providing the bibliographic information readers would need to go back to the original source. The two usual means of documentation are notes and lists of references.

Note that citation and documentation are used in addition to quotation marks. If you use the source's exact words, you'll use the name of the person you're citing and quotation marks in the body of the report; you'll indicate the source in parentheses and a list of references or in a footnote or endnote. If you put the source's idea into your own words, or if you condense or synthesize information, you don't need quotation marks, but you still need to tell whose idea it is and where you found it. See Figures 15.9 and 15.10 for examples of quoting and paraphrasing.

Long quotations (four typed lines or more) are used sparingly in business reports. Since many readers skip quotes, always summarize the main point of the quotation in a single sentence before the quotation itself. End the sentence with a colon, not a period, since it introduces the quote. Indent long quotations on the left and right to set them off from your text. Indented quotations do not need quotation marks; the indentation shows the reader that the passage is a quote.

To make a quotation fit the grammar of your report, you may need to change one or two words. Sometimes you may want to add a few words to explain something in the longer original. In both cases, use square brackets to indicate words that are your replacements or additions. Omit any words in the original source that are not essential for your purposes. Use ellipses (spaced dots) to indicate where your omissions are. See Figures 15.9 and 15.10 for examples.

Document every fact and idea that you take from a source except facts that are common knowledge. Historical dates and facts are considered common knowledge. Generalizations are considered common knowledge ("More and more women are entering the workforce") even though specific statements about the same topic (such as the percentage of women in the workforce in 1975 and in 2000) would require documentation.

The three most widely used formats for footnotes, endnotes, and bibliographies in reports are those of the American Psychological Association (APA), the

Looking with the Customers' Eyes

IDEO, a design firm based in Palo Alto, California, uses observational research to design work processes that improve the customer's experience. IDEO requires its customers to participate in the research so that they can see how it feels to be a customer. Clients may try using the company's product or go on shopping trips, or they may quietly observe customers. Following an initial observation phase, IDEO works with clients to use the observation data for brainstorming. IDEO then prepares and tests prototypes of the redesigned service, refines the ideas, and puts the revisions into action.

IDEO helped Kaiser Permanente revise its long-term growth plan to be more focused on clients' experiences with the health system. Working in teams with nurses, doctors, and managers from Kaiser, IDEO employees observed patients and occasionally role-played patient experiences. They saw that the check-in process was annoying, and waiting rooms were uncomfortable. Many of the patients arrived with a relative or friend for support, but they were often not allowed to remain together. Sitting alone in examination rooms was unpleasant and unnerving.

Based on these observations, Kaiser realized that it needed to focus more on improving patient experiences than on the original plan of modernizing buildings. The company created more comfortable areas in which patients could wait with family and friends, as well as examination rooms large enough to accommodate two people in addition to the patient. Instructions on where to go were made clearer as well.

Adapted from Bruce Nussbaum, "The Power of Design," *BusinessWeek,* May 17, 2004, 86.

Figure 15.9   Report Paragraphs with APA Documentation

Heading, ¶ numbers help readers find material in Web site without page numbers.

APA Format

Modern office buildings contain a surprising number of pollutants. Printing and copying documents creates particles which can be harmful to health. Office carpets and furniture emit chemical pollutants (Environmental Protection Agency, "Management of pollutant sources" section, ¶s 4-5). Indeed, the dyes and sealants used in many office chairs are considered hazardous waste. "Most people are sitting on chairs that are an amalgam of hundreds of chemicals that have never been [tested]. . . . The [more deeply] we look, [the more] we find . . . cancer-causing chemicals," says William McDonough, an architectural consultant who specializes in air-quality concerns (Conlin, 2003, p. 128).

Square brackets indicate a change from the original to make the quote fit into the structure of your sentence.

Ellipses (spaced dots) indicate some material has been omitted.

An extra dot serves as the period of the sentence.

The problem is compounded by inadequate ventilation. The American Society of Heating, Refrigeration, and Air-Conditioning Engineers recommends that a building's heating, ventilation, and cooling system deliver 20 cubic feet per minute of outside air for each occupant (Areas, 2004, "Ventilation rates" section, ¶ 5). But, Conlin reports (2003), some buildings provide only 5 cubic feet of fresh air per person a minute. And that "fresh air" may not be pure. Some buildings have fresh air vents over loading docks and parking garages. Revolving doors pull in second-hand smoke "like a chimney" (p. 117) from smokers who stand by the door.

All material from citation to end of ¶ is from a single source.

Use page number for direct quote (no need to repeate source when named earlier in ¶).

In the 1990s, responses to "sick buildings" often focused on the cost of solving the problem—a cost sometimes undertaken only after a lawsuit was filed (Nai, 1999). But recently, several companies have found that improving air quality pays for itself. Pennsylvania Power and Light's remodeling paid for itself in just 69 days by cutting absenteeism 25%, increasing productivity 13%, and reducing energy costs 69% (Aerias, 2004, "Why indoor air quality should be improved," ¶ 4).

Place author, date in parentheses (use page numbers only for a direct quote).

References

List all works (but only those works) cited in text.

Don't abbreviate month.

Aerias. (2004). Overview of IAQ problems in offices. Retrieved September 24, 2004 from the World Wide Web: http://www.aerias.org/office_overview.htm

List sources alphabetically.

Use URL of specific web page.

List source only once, even when it's used more than once.

Conlin, M. (with Carey, J.). (2003, June 5). Is your office killing you? *BusinessWeek*, 114-128.

Copyright/update date

Repeat hundreds.

Environmental Protection Agency. (2004, July 19). An office building occupant's guide to indoor air quality. Retrieved September 19, 2004, from the World Wide Web: http://www.epa.gov/iaq/pubs/occupgd.html

The URL of the specific Web page when possible.

← No punctuation at the end of a URL

Nai, A. K. (1999, October 26). Squabbles delay cure of "sick" office building. *The Wall Street Journal*, pp. B1, B3.

Modern Language Association (MLA), and the University of Chicago *Manual of Style* format, which this book uses. The APA format uses internal documentation with a list of references; it does not use footnotes or endnotes. **Internal documentation** provides the work and the page number where the reference was found in parentheses in the text. The work may be indicated by the author's last name (if that isn't already in the sentence), or by the last name plus the date of the work (if you're using two or more works by the same author, or if the dates of the works are important). The full bibliographical citation appears in a list of references or works cited at the end of the report. Figures 15.9 and 15.10 show a portion of a report in APA and MLA formats, respectively, with the list of references

Figure 15.10 Report Paragraphs with MLA Documentation

An extra dot serves as the period of the sentence. Put the ellipsis in brackets.

MLA Format

Modern office buildings contain a surprising number of pollutants. Printing and copying documents creates particles which can be harmful to health. Office carpets and furniture emit chemical pollutants (Environmental Protection Agency, "Management of Pollutant Sources" section, pars. 4-5). Indeed, the dyes and sealants used in many office chairs are considered hazardous waste. "Most people are sitting on chairs that are an amalgam of hundreds of chemicals that have never been [tested] [. . .] The [more deeply] we look, [the more] we find [. . .] cancer-causing chemicals," says William McDonough, an architectural consultant who specializes in air-quality concerns (Conlin 128).

Square brackets indicate a change from the original to make the quote fit into the structure of your sentence.

No comma between author, page number; no "p." before page number.

The problem is compounded by inadequate ventilation. The American Society of Heating, Refrigeration, and Air-Conditioning Engineers recommends that a building's heating, ventilation, and cooling system deliver 20 cubic feet per minute of outside air for each occupant (Aerias, 2004, "Ventilation Rates" section, par. 5). But, Michelle Conlin reports, some buildings provide only 5 cubic feet of fresh air per person a minute. And that "fresh air" may not be pure. Some buildings have fresh air vents over loading docks and parking garages. Revolving doors pull in second-hand smoke "like a chimney" (117) from smokers who stand by the door.

Use only page number since author identified in sentence.

In the 1990s, responses to "sick buildings" often focused on the cost of solving the problem—a cost sometimes undertaken only after a lawsuit was filed (Nai B1). But recently, several companies have found that improving air quality pays for itself. Pennsylvania Power and Light's remodeling paid for itself in just 69 days by cutting absenteeism 25%, increasing productivity 13%, and reducing energy costs 69% (Aerias, 2004, "Why Indoor Air Quality Should Be Improved," par. 4).

Heading, paragraph number or screen helps reader find material in Web sites without page numbers.

Give page number for facts, not just quotes.

Works Cited *Copyright/update date*

List all works cited in text.

Date you visited site

Aerias. "Overview of IAQ Problems in Offices." 2004. 24 Sept. 2004 <http://www.aerias.org/office_overview.htm>.

List sources alphabetically.

URL in angle brackets; period after angle bracket.

Conlin, Michelle with John Carey. "Is Your Office Killing You?" <u>BusinessWeek</u> 5 June 2000: 114-28.

Don't repeat hundreds.

Environmental Protection Agency. "An Office Building Occupant's Guide to Indoor Air Quality." 19 July 2004. 19 Sept. 2004 <http://www.epa.gov/iaq/pubs/occupgd.html>.

If URL is too long to fit on one line, break after a punctuation mark.

Use date month year; abbreviate month.

Nai, Amal Kumar. "Squabbles Delay Cure of 'Sick' Office Building." <u>The Wall Street Journal</u> 26 October 1999: B1.

(APA) or works cited (MLA). Figures 15.11 and 15.12 show the APA and MLA formats for the sources used most often in reports.

If you have used many sources that you have not cited, you may want to list both works cited and works consulted. The term *bibliography* covers all sources on a topic.

If you use a printed source that is not readily available, consider including it as an appendix in your report. For example, you could copy an ad or include an organization's promotional brochure.

Figure 15.11   APA Format for Sources Used Most Often in Reports

APA internal documentation gives the author's last name and the date of the work in parentheses in the text. A comma separates the author's name from the date (Gilsdorf & Leonard, 2004). The page number is given only for direct quotations (Cross, 2004, p. 74). If the author's name is used in the sentence, only the date is given in parentheses. (See Figure 15.9.) A list of references gives the full bibliographic citation, arranging the entries alphabetically by the first author's last name.

In the examples below, headings in green identify the kind of work being referenced. The green headings are not part of the actual citation itself.

In titles of articles and books capitalize only ① *first word,* ② *first word of subtitle,* ③ *proper nouns.*

comma   *last name first*   *No quotes around title of article*   *Year (period outside parenthesis).*

Article in a Periodical

Gilsdorf, J., & Leonard, D. (2004). Big stuff, little stuff: A decennial measurement of executives' and academics' reactions to questionable usage elements. *The Journal of Business Communication, 38*, 439-475.

no "pp." when journal has a volume number   *Italicize volume.*   *Capitalize all major words in title of journal, magazine, or newspaper.*

Article in a Newspaper

McCartney, S. (2003, December 27). Why a baseball superstar's megacontract can be less than it seems. *The Wall Street Journal*, p. B1, B3.

Separate discontinuous pages with comma and space.

Article in an Edited Book

Ampersands join names of co-authors, co-editors.

Killingsworth, M. J., & Jacobsen, M. (2002). The rhetorical construction of environmental risk narratives in government and activist websites: A critique. In J. M. Perkins & N. Blyler (Eds.), *Narrative and professional communication* (pp. 167-177). Stamford, CT: Ablex.

Editors' names have last names last.

Editors before book title   *Repeat "1" in 177.*   *Give state when city is not well known.*

Article from a Publication on the Web

Greengard, S. (2004, May). Scoring web wins. *Business Finance Magazine*. p. 37. Retrieved July 12, 2004, from http://www.businessfinancemag.com/archives/appfiles/Article.cfm? IssueID=348&ArticleID=13750

Give date you retrieved article.   *no punctuation after URL*

Initials only for first and middle names   *Italicize title of book.*

Book

Cross, G. A. (2004). *Forming the collective mind: A contextual exploration of large-scale collaborative writing in industry*. Creskill, NJ: Hampton Press.

Put in square brackets information known to you but not printed in document.

Book or Pamphlet with a Corporate Author

Citibank. (1998). *Indonesia: An investment guide*. [Jakarta:] Author.

Indicates organization authoring document also published it.

E-Mail Message

[Identify e-mail messages in the text as personal communications. Give name of author and as specific a date as possible. Do not list in References.]

Government Document

Senate Special Committee on Aging. (2004). *Long-term care: States grapple with increasing demands and costs*. Hearing before the Special Committee on Aging, Senate, One Hundred Seventh Congress, first session, hearing held in Washington, DC, July 11, 2004 (Doc ID: 75-038). Washington, DC: U.S. Government Printing Office.

No abbreviations in titles   *Document number*   *APA uses periods for "U.S."*

(continued)

Figure 15.11 APA Format for Sources Used Most Often in Reports *(Concluded)*

copyright or update date

Government Document Available on the Web from the GPO Access Database

U.S. General Accounting Office. (2004, September 20.) Aviation security: Terrorist acts demonstrate urgent need to improve security at the nation's airports. Testimony before the Committee on Commerce, Science, and Transportation, U.S. Senate (GAO-01-1162T). Retrieved December 19, 2004, from General Accounting Office Reports Online via GPO Access: http://www.gao.gov/new.items/d011162t.pdf

date you visited site

keep "http://"

Interview Conducted by the Researcher

[Identify interviews in the text as personal communications. Give name of interviewee and as specific a date as possible. Do not list in References.]

Posting to a Listserv

[Identify messages on listservs to which one must subscribe in the text as personal communications. Give name of author and as specific a date as possible. Do not list in References.]

Web Site

American Express. (2001). Creating an effective business plan. Retrieved December 20, 2004, from the World Wide Web: http://home3.americanexpress.com/smallbusiness/vtool/biz_plan/index.asp

comma

Break long web address at a slash or other punctuation mark.

no punctuation

Figure 15.12 MLA Format for Sources Used Most Often in Reports

MLA internal documentation gives the author's last name and page number in parentheses in the text for facts as well as for quotations (Gilsdorf and Leonard 470). Unlike APA, the year is not given, no comma separates the name and page number, and the abbreviation "p." is not used (Cross 74). If the author's name is used in the sentence, only the page number is given in parentheses. (See Figure 15.10.) A list of Works Cited gives the full bibliographic citation, arranging the entries alphabetically by the first author's last name.

In the examples below, headings in green identify the kind of work being referenced. The green headings are not part of the actual citation itself.

Article in a Periodical

first name first for second author

Put quotation marks around title of article.

Capitalize all major words in titles of articles, books, journals magazines, and newspapers.

Gilsdorf, Jeanette and Don Leonard. "Big Stuff, Little Stuff: A Decennial Measurement of Executives' and Academics' Reactions to Questionable Usage Elements." The Journal of Business Communication 38 (2004): 448-75.

omit "4" in "475"

McCartney, Scott. "Why a Baseball Superstar's Megacontract Can Be Less Than It Seems." The Wall Street Journal, 27 Dec. 2003: B1+.

Plus sign indicates article continues past first page.

Article from an Edited Book

Give authors', editors' full names as printed in the source.

Killingsworth, M. Jimmie and Martin Jacobsen. "The Rhetorical Construction of Environmental Risk Narratives in Government and Activist Websites: A Critique." Narrative and Professional Communication. Ed. Jane M. Perkins and Nancy Blyler. Stamford, CT: Ablex. 167-77.

Give state when city is not well known.

Spell out editors' names. Join with "and." Put last names last.

Put book title before editors' name.

Figure 15.12 MLA Format for Sources Used Most Often in Reports *(Concluded)*

Article from a Publication on the Web

Greengard, Samuel. "Scoring Web Wins." <u>Business Finance Magazine</u>. May 2004. 12 July 2004. <http://www.businessfinancemag.com/archives/appfiles/Article.cfm? IssueID=348&ArticleID=13750>.

Put Web address in angle brackets. End entry with a period.

Don't add any extra hyphens when you break a long Web address.

Book

Cross, Geoffrey A. <u>Forming the Collective Mind: A Contextual Exploration of Large-Scale Collaborative Writing in Industry</u>. Creskill, NJ: Hampton Press, 2004.

Put in square brackets information known to you but not printed in source.

Book or Pamphlet with a Corporate Author

Citibank. <u>Indonesia: An Investment Guide</u>. [Jakarta:] Citibank, 1998.

Date after city and publisher

Abbreviate long months.

E-Mail Message

Locker, Kitty O. "Could We Get a New Photo?" E-mail to Rajani J. Kamuth. 17 Dec. 2004.

day month year

Government Document

United States. Sen. Special Committee on Aging. <u>Long-Term Care: States Grapple with Increasing Demands and Costs.</u> 107th Cong., 1st sess. Washington: GPO, 2004.

Omit state when city is well known.

Abbreviate "Government Printing Office."

Government Document Available on the Web from the GPO Access Database

United States. General Accounting Office. <u>Aviation Security: Terrorist Acts Demonstrate Urgent Need to Improve Security at the Nation's Airports</u>. Testimony before the Committee on Commerce, Science, and Transportation, U.S. Senate (GAO-01-1162T). 20 Sept. 2004. 19 Dec. 2004 <http://www.gao.gov/new.items/d011162t.pdf>.

Give date you accessed site.

Interview Conducted by the Researcher

Drysdale, Andrew. Telephone interview. 12 Apr. 2005.

Posting to a Listserv

Dietrich, Dan. "Re: Course on Report and Proposal Writing." Online posting. 14 Feb. 2003. BizCom Discussion Group. 23 Dec. 2004 <bizcom@ebbs.English.vt.edu>.

Date of posting.

Date you accessed posting

If discussion group has a Web archive, give the Web address.

Web Site

American Express. <u>Creating an Effective Business Plan</u>. 2001. 20 Dec. 2004. <http://home3.americanexpress.com/smallbusiness/tool/biz_plan/index.asp>.

If it doesn't have a Web page, give the e-mail address of the list.

Summary of Key Points

- **Information reports** collect data for the reader; **analytical reports** present and interpret data; **recommendation reports** recommend action or a solution.
- A good purpose statement must make three things clear:
  - The organizational problem or conflict.
  - The specific technical questions that must be answered to solve the problem.

- The rhetorical purpose (to explain, to recommend, to request, to propose) that the report is designed to achieve.
- A proposal must answer the following questions:
  - What problem are you going to solve?
  - How are you going to solve it?
  - When will you complete the work?
  - Can you deliver what you promise?
  - What benefits can you offer?
  - How much will you charge?
  - What exactly will you provide for us?
- In a proposal for a class research project, prove that your problem is the right size, that you understand it, that your method will give you the information you need to solve the problem, that you have the knowledge and resources, and that you can produce the report by the deadline.
- Use the following pattern of organization for the cover letter for a sales proposal:
  1. Catch the reader's attention and summarize up to three major benefits you offer.
  2. Discuss each of the major benefits in the order in which you mentioned them in the first paragraph.
  3. Deal with any objections or concerns the reader may have.
  4. Mention other benefits briefly.
  5. Ask the reader to approve your proposal and provide a reason for acting promptly.
- In a project budget, ask for everything you will need to do a good job. Research current cost figures so yours are in line.
- In a proposal for funding, stress the needs your project will meet. Show how your project will help fulfill the goals of the organization you are asking for funds.
- Progress reports may be organized chronologically, by task, or to support a recommendation.
- Use positive emphasis in progress reports to create an image of yourself as a capable, confident worker.
- Use indexes and directories to find information about a specific company or topic.
- To decide whether to use a Web site as a source in a research project, evaluate the site's authors, objectivity, information, and revision date.
- A **survey** questions a large group of people, called **respondents** or **subjects.** A **questionnaire** is a written list of questions that people fill out. An **interview** is a structured conversation with someone who will be able to give you useful information.
- Good questions ask just one thing, are phrased neutrally, avoid making assumptions about the respondent, and mean the same thing to different people.
- **Closed questions** have a limited number of possible responses. **Open questions** do not lock the subject into any sort of response. **Branching questions** direct different respondents to different parts of the questionnaire based on their answers to earlier questions. A **mirror question** paraphrases the content of the last answer. **Probes** follow up an original question to get at specific aspects of a topic.

- Good researchers attempt to reach nonrespondents at least once and preferably twice.
- A **convenience sample** is a group of subjects who are easy to get. A **judgment sample** is a group of people whose views seem useful. In a **random sample,** each person in the population theoretically has an equal chance of being chosen. A sample is random only if a formal, approved random sampling method is used. Otherwise, unconscious bias exists.
- **Citation** means attributing an idea or fact to its source in the body of the report. **Documentation** means providing the bibliographic information readers would need to go back to the original source.

CHAPTER 15   Exercises and Problems

15.1   Reviewing the Chapter

1. What are some criteria for defining report problems? (LO 1)
2. What are six questions a good proposal should answer? (LO 2)
3. What are some guidelines for preparing a budget for a proposal? (LO 2)
4. What are the differences between chronological and task progress reports? (LO 3)
5. What are four criteria for evaluating Web sources? (LO 4)
6. What are some criteria for good survey questions? (LO 4)
7. What is a random sample? (LO 4)
8. Choose either APA or MLA. For that format, write a References entry or Works Cited entry for a book, journal article, and Web site. (LO 5)

15.2   Reviewing Grammar

Reports use lots of numbers. Test your knowledge about writing numbers by doing Exercise B.10 in Appendix B.

15.3   Identifying the Weaknesses in Problem Statements

Identify the weaknesses in the following problem statements.

- Is the problem narrow enough?
- Can a solution be found in a semester or quarter?
- What organization could implement any recommendations to solve the problem?
- Could the topic be limited or refocused to yield an acceptable problem statement?

1. One possible report topic I would like to investigate would be the differences in women's intercollegiate sports in our athletic conference.
2. How to market products effectively to college students.
3. Should Web banners be part of a company's advertising?
4. How can US and Canadian students get jobs in Europe?
5. We want to explore ways our company can help raise funds for the Open Shelter. We will investigate whether collecting and recycling glass, aluminum, and paper products will raise enough money to help.
6. How can XYZ University better serve students from traditionally underrepresented groups?
7. What are the best investments for the next year?

15.4 Writing a Preliminary Purpose Statement

Answer the following questions about a topic on which you could write a formal report. (See Problems 16.5, 16.9, 16.11, and 16.12.)

As your instructor directs,

a. Be prepared to answer the questions orally in a conference.

b. Bring written answers to a conference.

c. Submit written answers in class.

d. Give your instructor a photocopy of your statement after it is approved.

1. What problem will you investigate or solve?

    a. What is the name of the organization facing the problem?

    b. What is the technical problem or difficulty?

    c. Why is it important to the organization that this problem be solved?

d. What solution or action might you recommend to solve the problem?

e. List the name and title of the person in the organization who would have the power to accept or reject your recommendation.

2. Will this report use information from other classes or from work experiences? If so, give the name and topic of the class and/or briefly describe the job. If you will need additional information (that you have not already gotten from other classes or from a job), how do you expect to find it?

3. List the name, title, and business phone number of a professor who can testify to your ability to handle the expertise needed for this report.

4. List the name, title, and business phone number of someone in the organization who can testify that you have access to enough information about that organization to write this report.

15.5 Choosing Research Strategies

For each of the following reports, indicate the kinds of research that might be useful. If a survey is called for, indicate the most efficient kind of sample to use.

a. How can XYZ store increase sales?

b. What is it like to live and work in [name of country]?

c. Should our organization have a dress code?

d. Is it feasible to start a monthly newsletter for students in your major?

e. How can we best market to mature adults?

f. Can compensation programs increase productivity?

g. What skills are in demand in our area? Of these, which could the local community college offer courses in?

15.6 Identifying Keywords for Computer Searches

As your instructor directs,

Identify the keyword combinations that you could use in researching one or more of the following topics:

a. Ways to evaluate whether recycling is working.

b. Safety of pension funds.

c. Ethical issues in accounting.

d. Effects of advertising on sales of automobiles.

e. What can be done to increase the privacy of personal data.

f. Accounting for intellectual capital.

g. Advantages and problems of Web advertising.

15.7 Evaluating Web Sites

Choose 10 Web sites that are possible resources for a report. Evaluate them on the credibility and trustworthiness of their information. Consider the following questions and compare and contrast your findings.

- Who are the authors? Who is responsible for the information?

- Are other sources cited? Are you familiar with those sources?

- Is the site current? How current does the information need to be for your topic?

- What perspective does the site have about the issue you are studying?

Based on your findings, which sites are best for your report and why?

As your instructor directs,

a. Write a memo to your instructor summarizing your results.

b. Share your results with a small group of students.

c. Present your results to the class in an oral presentation.

15.8   Choosing Samples for Surveys and Interviews

For the following topics, indicate the types of sample(s) you would use in collecting survey data and in conducting interviews.

a.   How can your school improve access to computers for students?

b.   How can your favorite school organization attract more student members?

c.   How can your school improve communication with international students?

d.   How should your school deal with hate speech?

e.   How can instructors at your school improve their electronic presentations for students?

15.9   Evaluating Survey Questions

Evaluate each of the following questions. Are they acceptable as they stand? If not, how can they be improved?

a.   Survey of clerical workers:

Do you work for the government? □
or the private sector? □

b.   Questionnaire on grocery purchases:

1.   Do you *usually* shop at the same grocery store?
   a.   Yes
   b.   No
2.   Do you use credit cards to purchase items at your grocery store?
   a.   Yes
   b.   No
3.   How much is your average grocery bill?
   a.   Under $25
   b. $25–50
   c. $50–100
   d. $100–150
   e.   Over $150

c.   Survey on technology:

1.   Would you generally welcome any technological advancement that allowed information to be sent and received more quickly and in greater quantities than ever before?
2.   Do you think that all people should have free access to all information, or do you think that information should somehow be regulated and monitored?

d.   Survey on job skills:

How important are the following skills for getting and keeping a professional-level job in US business and industry today?

	Low				High
Ability to communicate	1	2	3	4	5
Leadership ability	1	2	3	4	5
Public presentation skills	1	2	3	4	5
Selling ability	1	2	3	4	5
Teamwork capability	1	2	3	4	5
Writing ability	1	2	3	4	5

15.10   Designing Questions for an Interview or Survey

Submit either a one- to three-page questionnaire or questions for a 20- to 30-minute interview AND the information listed below for the method you choose.

Questionnaire

1.   Purpose(s), goal(s).
2.   Subjects (who, why, how many).
3.   How and where to be distributed.
4.   Any changes in type size, paper color, etc., from submitted copy.
5.   Rationale for order of questions, kinds of questions, wording of questions.
6.   References, if building on questionnaires by other authors.

Interview

1.   Purpose(s), goal(s).
2.   Subjects (who, and why).
3.   Proposed site, length of interview.
4.   Rationale for order of questions, kinds of questions, wording of questions, choice of branching or follow-up questions.
5.   References, if building on questions devised by others.

As your instructor directs,

a.   Create questions for a survey on one of the following topics:

• Survey students on your campus about their knowledge of and interest in the programs and activities sponsored by a student organization.
• Survey workers at a company about what they like and dislike about their jobs.
• Survey people in your community about their willingness to pay more to buy products using

recycled materials and to buy products that are packaged with a minimum of waste.

- Survey two groups on a topic that interests you.

b. Create questions for an interview on one of the following topics:

- Interview an international student about the forms of greetings and farewells, topics of small talk, forms of politeness, festivals and holidays, meals at home, size of families, and roles of family members in his or her country.
- Interview a TV producer about what styles and colors work best for people appearing on TV.

- Interview a worker about an ethical dilemma he or she faced on the job, what the worker did and why, and how the company responded.
- Interview the owner of a small business about problems the business has, what strategies the owner has already used to increase sales and profits and how successful these strategies were, and the owner's attitudes toward possible changes in product line, decor, marketing, hiring, advertising, and money management.
- Interview someone who has information you need for a report you're writing.

15.11 Choosing Subject Lines for Memo Reports

Identify the strengths and weaknesses of each subject line, and choose the best subject line(s) from each group.

1. A proposal to conduct research.
   a. Membership Survey
   b. Proposal to Survey Former Members to Learn Their Reasons for Not Rejoining
   c. Proposal to Investigate Former Members' Reasons for Not Rejoining
2. A survey to find out why former members did not renew their memberships.

   a. 2009 Delinquency Survey
   b. Results of 2009 Former Member Survey
   c. Why Members Did Not Renew Their Memberships in 2009
3. A progress report.
   a. Progress Report
   b. Work Completed, October 15–November 5
   c. Status of the Survey of Former Members

15.12 Citing Sources

As your instructor directs,

a. Revise the following list of sources using MLA format.
b. Revise the following list of sources using APA format.

1. Author Christopher Marquis
   The New York Times
   "Reports on Attacks are Gripping, Not Dry"
   June 20, 2004
   A1
2. Keep online surveys short
   Jakob Nielsen
   Alertbox
   www.useit.com
   Downloaded February 2, 2004

3. Susan J. Wells
   HRMagazine
   "Merging Compensation Strategies"
   May 2004
   Pages 108–109
4. *Composition Research: Empirical Designs*
   Janice M. Lauer and J. William Asher
   Oxford University Press
   1986
   New York
   Oxford University Press
5. Bernard Wysocki Jr.
   "At Pitt, scientists decode the secret of getting grants"
   The Wall Street Journal
   6/28/04

15.13 Writing a Progress Report

As your instructor directs,
Send an e-mail message

a. To the other members of your group, describing your progress since the last group meeting.

b. To your instructor, describing your progress.
c. To your instructor, asking for help solving a problem you have encountered.

As your instructor directs,

In Problems 15.14 through 15.16,

a. Create a document or presentation to achieve the goal.

b. Write a memo to your instructor describing the situation at your workplace and explaining your rhetorical choices (medium, strategy, content, tone, wording, graphics or document design, and so forth).

15.14   Proposing a Change

No organization is perfect, especially when it comes to communication. Propose a change that would improve communication within your organization. The change can be specific to your unit or can apply to the whole organization; it can relate to how important information is distributed, to who has access to important information, how information is accessed, or any other change in communication practices that you see as having a benefit. Direct your proposal to the person or committee with the power to authorize the change.

15.15   Proposing to Undertake a Research Project

Pick a project you would like to study whose results could be used by your organization. (See Problem 16.5.) Write a proposal to your supervisor requesting time away from other duties to do the research. Show how your research (whatever its outcome) will be useful to the organization.

15.16   Writing a Progress Report to Your Superior

Describe the progress you have made this week or this month on projects you have been assigned. You may describe progress you have made individually, or progress your unit has made as a team.

15.17   Writing a Report Based on a Survey

As your instructor directs,

a. Survey 40 to 50 people on some subject of your choice.

b. Team up with your classmates to conduct a survey and write it up as a group. Survey 50 to 80 people if your group has two members, 75 to 120 people if it has three members, 100 to 150 people if it has four members, and 125 to 200 people if it has five members.

c. Keep a journal during your group meetings and submit it to your instructor.

d. Write a memo to your instructor describing and evaluating your group's process for designing, conducting, and writing up the survey. (See Chapter 14 on working and writing in groups.)

For this assignment, you do **not** have to take a random sample. Do, however, survey at least two different groups so that you can see if they differ in some way. Possible groups are men and women, business majors and English majors, Greeks and independents, first-year students and seniors, students and townspeople.

As you conduct your survey, make careful notes about what you do so that you can use this information when you write up your survey. If you work with a group, record who does what. Use complete memo format.

Your subject line should be clear and reasonably complete. Omit unnecessary words such as "Survey of." Your first paragraph serves as an introduction, but it needs no heading. The rest of the body of your memo will be divided into four sections with the following headings: Purpose, Procedure, Results, and Discussion.

In your first paragraph, briefly summarize (not necessarily in this order) who conducted the experiment or survey, when it was conducted, where it was conducted, who the subjects were, what your purpose was, and what you found out. You will discuss all of these topics in more detail in the body of your memo.

In your **Purpose** section, explain why you conducted the survey. What were you trying to learn? What hypothesis were you testing? Why did this subject seem interesting or important?

In your **Procedure** section, describe in detail *exactly* what you did. "The first 50 people who came through the Union on Wed., Feb. 2" is not the same as "The first 50 people who came through the south entrance of the Union on Wed., Feb. 2, and agreed to answer my questions." Explain any steps you took to overcome possible sources of bias.

In your **Results** section, first tell whether your results supported your hypothesis. Use both visuals and words to explain what your numbers show. (See Chapter 6 on how to design visuals.) Process your raw data in a way that will be useful to your reader.

In your **Discussion** section, evaluate your survey and discuss the implications of your results. Consider these questions:

1. What are the limitations of your survey and your results?

2. Do you think a scientifically valid survey would have produced the same results? Why or why not?

3. Were there any sources of bias either in the way the questions were phrased or in the way the subjects were chosen? If you were running the survey again, what changes would you make to eliminate or reduce these sources of bias?

4. Do you think your subjects answered honestly and completely? What factors may have intruded? Is the fact that you did or didn't know them, were or weren't of the same sex relevant? If your results seem to contradict other evidence, how do you account for the discrepancy? Were

your subjects shading the truth? Was your sample's unrepresentativeness the culprit? Or have things changed since earlier data were collected?

5. What causes the phenomenon your results reveal? If several causes together account for the phenomenon, or if it is impossible to be sure of the cause, admit this. Identify possible causes and assess the likelihood of each.

6. What action should be taken?

The discussion section gives you the opportunity to analyze the significance of your survey. Its insight and originality lift the otherwise well-written memo from the ranks of the merely satisfactory to the ranks of the above-average and the excellent.

The whole assignment will be more interesting if you choose a question that interests you. It does not need to be "significant" in terms of major political or philosophic problems; a quirk of human behavior that fascinates you will do nicely.

15.18　Writing a Proposal for a Student Report

Write a proposal to your instructor to do the research for a formal or informal report. (See Problems 16.5, 16.9, 16.11 and 16.12.)

The headings and the questions in the section titled "Proposals for Class Research Projects" are your RFP; be

sure to answer every question and to use the headings exactly as stated in the RFP. Exception: where alternate heads are listed, you may choose one, combine the two ("Qualifications and Facilities"), or treat them as separate headings in separate categories.

15.19　Writing a Proposal for Funding for a Nonprofit Group

Pick a nonprofit group you care about. Examples include professional organizations, a school sports team, a charitable group, a community organization, a religious group, or your own college or university.

As your instructor directs,

a. Check the Web or a directory of foundations to find one that makes grants to groups like yours. Brainstorm a list of businesses that might be willing to give money for specific projects. Check to see

whether state or national levels of your organization make grants to local chapters.

b. Write a proposal to obtain funds for a special project your group could undertake if it had the money. Address your proposal to a specific organization.

c. Write a proposal to obtain operating funds or money to buy something your group would like to have. Address your proposal to a specific organization.

15.20　Writing a Sales Proposal

Pick a project that you could do for a local company or government office. Examples include

- Creating a brochure or Web page.
- Revising form letters.
- Conducting a training program.
- Writing a newsletter or an annual report.
- Developing a marketing plan.
- Providing plant care, catering, or janitorial services.

Write a proposal specifying what you could do and providing a detailed budget and work schedule.

As your instructor directs,

a. Phone someone in the organization to talk about its needs and what you could offer.

b. Write an individual proposal.

c. Join with other students in the class to create a group proposal.

d. Present your proposal orally.

15.21   Writing a Progress Report

Write a memo to your instructor summarizing your progress on your report.

In the introductory paragraph, summarize your progress in terms of your schedule and your goals. Under a heading titled *Work Completed,* list what you have already done. (This is a chance to toot your own horn: if you have solved problems creatively, say so! You can also describe obstacles you've encountered that you have not yet solved.) Under *Work to Be Completed,* list what you still have to do. If you are more than two days behind the schedule you submitted with your proposal, include a revised schedule, listing the completion dates for the activities that remain.

In your last paragraph, either indicate your confidence in completing the report by the due date or ask for a conference to resolve the problems you are encountering.

15.22   Writing a Progress Report for a Group Report

Write a memo to your instructor summarizing your group's progress.

In the introductory paragraph, summarize the group's progress in terms of its goals and its schedule, your own progress on the tasks for which you are responsible, and your feelings about the group's work thus far.

Under a heading titled *Work Completed,* list what has already been done. Be most specific about what you yourself have done. Describe briefly the chronology of group activities: number, time, and length of meetings; topics discussed and decisions made at meetings.

If you have solved problems creatively, say so! You can also describe obstacles you've encountered that you have not yet solved. In this section, you can also comment on problems that the group has faced and whether or not they've been solved. You can comment on things that have gone well and have contributed to the smooth functioning of the group.

Under *Work to Be Completed,* list what you personally and other group members still have to do. Indicate the schedule for completing the work.

In your last paragraph, either indicate your confidence in completing the report by the due date or ask for a conference to resolve the problems you are encountering.

15.23   Analyzing Annual Reports

Locate two annual reports either in paper or electronic form. Use the following questions to analyze both reports:

- Who is the audience(s)?
- What is the purpose(s) of the report?
- How is the report organized and what does the order of information reflect about the company?
- How does the report validate/support the claims it makes? What type of evidence is used more often—textual or visual? What kinds of claims are used—logical, emotional, or ethical?
- How does the text establish credibility for the report?
- What can you tell about the company's financial situation from the report?
- What role do visuals play in the report? What image do they portray for the company? How do the visuals help establish credibility for the report? What do they imply about power distribution in the company?
- Does the report deal with any ethical issues?

As your instructor directs,

a.   Write a memo to your instructor comparing and contrasting the two reports according to your analysis answers. Explain which report you find more effective and why.

b.   Share your results orally with a small group of students.

c.   Present your results to the class.

15.24   Mosaic Case

"I'm pleased to say that the new strategies for targeting Hispanic customers have been greatly noticed," said Demetri, when Yvonne gave him the floor to talk at their routine staff meeting. "Many of the Mosaic store managers from the southern stores have taken the time to e-mail me about positive verbal feedback they've been getting from our customers."

"It's good to know our hard work is paying off, despite the *challenges,*" said Trey while letting out a fake cough, "we faced when working with the Marketing Department."

Martina just snickered at his remark.

Ignoring the exchange, Demetri said, "Here's the deal. While we've received some positive feedback from the store managers, I don't have any data from actual customers."

"Any ideas on how to get some?" asked Yvonne.

"Well, yes, actually," said Demetri, a tad bit pleased with himself. "I want to create a survey that Mosaic's employees could pass out with clipboards to Hispanic customers that come into our stores."

"That's a great idea." said Sarah, "Depending on what you're thinking about and come up with, I might also put the survey up on the Web site."

"I want to know how Hispanic customers are responding to the changes at Mosaic. Have they even noticed any? Have they been pleased with their shopping experience at Mosaic? What can we do to make their shopping experiences even better? What do they think about merchandise targeted specifically for them and their needs? Or how about our new bilingual Mosaic employees we've added to these southern stores? Are there differences in opinions of Hispanics based on age or annual household income? Etcetera, etcetera," said Demetri with a passionate flair. "I want real data that can tell us where to go from here."

"Trey and Martina, do you think you can handle putting this together?" asked Yvonne.

"Definitely!" Martina said while starting to peel a banana.

Take on the communication task of Trey and Martina using your newly acquired knowledge from Chapter 15.

- Create a 10-question survey that will effectively measure the information Demetri seeks to know. Make sure that your questions are phrased neutrally, ask only one thing, are not biased, and use words that mean the same to all respondents.

- Conduct a usability test of your survey with a convenience sample of 10 peers to make sure all your questions are comprehensible and clear.

- Determine what needs to be different if Sarah wants to also post the survey on the Mosaic Web site. In other words, if you put a paper-based survey on the Internet, do questions need to change in some way?

CHAPTER 16

Analyzing Information and Writing Reports

Learning Objectives

After studying this chapter, you will know:

1 Ways to analyze data, information, and logic.

2 How to choose information for reports.

3 Different ways to organize reports.

4 How to present information effectively in reports.

5 How to prepare the different components of formal reports.

"Seasonal Fluctuations": Facts, Spin, and Annual Reports

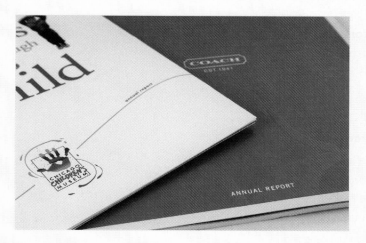

In 2005, the US Securities and Exchange Commission (SEC) started legal action against the former CEO and CFO of Kmart Corporation, because the Management's Discussion and Analysis (MD&A) portion of Kmart's 2001 annual report was misleading to stockholders. The report explained an increase in inventory by "seasonal fluctuations" (a natural part of doing business that stockholders wouldn't question) when the increase was really caused by one executive's poor decisions (which would reflect badly on the company). Did Kmart's CEO and CFO actually write that report themselves? Probably not, but they signed off on the information and certified it as factual, so the SEC found them liable for the lies.

Kmart isn't the only corporation whose annual report has come under heavy scrutiny: in the post-Enron business world, the SEC now watches corporate annual reports more closely than ever. The result? As ReportWatch notes in their 2006 *Annual Report on Annual Reports,* many US companies have replaced descriptive, easy-to-read MD&A sections with simple "10-K" statements: tables of financial data taken directly from the Form 10-K that all publicly held US companies must file with the SEC. These new MD&A's are factual and detailed, with no spin and no misleading information, but they don't provide much actual information about the companies' economic realities.

> "A good report . . . [combines] hard data with the explanations and details that are necessary for your readers to understand the numbers."

A good annual report should do both: it should combine hard data with the explanations and details that are necessary for your readers to understand the numbers and make good decisions about you and your organization. To write a good report, you'll need to know your audience(s)' needs, goals, and interests. You'll also need to gather data from a variety of sources, interpret and format that data—using graphics to increase usability—and collaborate with others to make sure the final product is factual and reflects your organization's goals.

Sources: Amy Borrus, "The SEC: Cracking Down on Spin," *BusinessWeek,* September 26, 2005, 94–97; and ReportWatch.net, "Annual Report on Annual Reports 2006," http://www.reportwatch.net/download/AnnualReport_on_AnnualReports2006.pdf (accessed May 18, 2007).

Chapter Outline

Using Your Time Efficiently

Analyzing Data and Information for Reports
- Identifying the Source of the Data
- Analyzing Numbers
- Analyzing Words
- Analyzing Patterns
- Checking Your Logic

Choosing Information for Reports

Organizing Information in Reports
- Basic Patterns for Organizing Information
- How to Organize Specific Varieties of Reports

Presenting Information Effectively in Reports
1. Use Clear, Engaging Writing.
2. Keep Repetition to a Minimum.
3. Introduce Sources and Visuals.
4. Use Forecasting, Transitions, Topic Sentences, and Headings.

Writing Formal Reports
- Title Page
- Letter or Memo of Transmittal
- Table of Contents
- List of Illustrations
- Executive Summary
- Introduction
- Background or History
- Body
- Conclusions and Recommendations

Summary of Key Points

Careful analysis, smooth writing, and effective document design work together to make effective reports, whether you're writing a 2½-page memo report or a 250-page formal report complete with all the report components.

Chapter 15 covered the first two steps in writing a report:

1. Define the problem.
2. Gather the necessary data and information.

This chapter covers the last three steps:

1. Analyze the data and information.
2. Organize the information.
3. Write the report.

Using Your Time Efficiently

To use your time efficiently, think about the parts of the report before you begin writing. Much of the introduction comes from your proposal, with only minor revisions. You can write six sections even before you've finished your research: Purpose, Scope, Assumptions, Methods, Criteria, and Definitions.

Mock up tables and figures early. Since they provide information on which you will base your arguments or explanations, it is important to arrange data logically and plan how you will use it in the report. As you tally and analyze the data, prepare your figures and tables, and a complete list of references. The background reading for your proposal can form the first draft of your list of references. Save a copy of your questionnaire or interview questions to use as an appendix. You can print appendixes before the final report is ready if you number their pages separately. Appendix A pages would be A-1, A-2, and so forth; Appendix B pages would be B-1, B-2, and so forth.

You can write the title page and the transmittal as soon as you know what your recommendation will be.

After you've analyzed your data, write the body, the conclusions and recommendations, and the executive summary. Prepare a draft of the table of contents and the list of illustrations.

When you write a long report, list all the sections (headings) that your report will have. Mark those that are most important to your reader and your logic, and spend most of your time on them. Write the important sections early. That way, you won't spend all your time on Background or History of the Problem. Instead, you'll get to the meat of your report.

Analyzing Data and Information for Reports

Good reports begin with good data. Analyzing the data you have gathered is essential to produce the tight logic needed for a good report. Analyze your data with healthy skepticism. Check to see that they correspond with expectations or other existing data. If they don't, check for well-supported explanations of the difference.

Spreadsheets can be particularly troublesome. Cell results derived by formulas can be subtly, or grossly, wrong by incorrectly defining ranges, for example. It is easy to generate results that are impossible, such as sums that exceed known totals. Always have an estimate of the result of a calculation. Using spreadsheets, you can easily be wrong by a factor of 10, 100, or 1,000. Results produced by this kind of error are wrong at best, and can be ludicrous and embarrassing. One study found that 30% of spreadsheets had errors, such as misplaced decimal points, transposed digits, and wrong signs, built into their rules.[1] Try to keep ball-park figures, estimates of what the numbers should be, in mind as you look at numerical data. Question surprises before accepting them.

Analyzing data can be hard even for experts. New techniques continually appear, allowing experts to challenge earlier conclusions. One example is the Number Needed to Treat (NNT), a new measure of drug effectiveness developed within the past 20 years. Most clinical trials answer the question, "Will patients on this drug do better than those taking a placebo?" For statins, drugs to reduce high cholesterol, the answer is yes: you may see 30% fewer heart attacks, depending on the particular trial. Sounds great, yes? But how many of those people would have had heart attacks in the first place? If the number is very small, 30% fewer isn't much decrease, particularly considering the cost of statins and possible side effects including liver damage. The NNT asks, "How many people have to take this drug to avoid one heart attack?" For statins, the answer is about 50, much different odds and more food for thought for America's aging population as it decides whether or not to take more prescriptions.[2]

Numerous studies exist in scholarly journals challenging the data-based conclusions of earlier articles. One example is the fate of unmarried, college-educated women over 30. A famous *Newsweek* cover story, "Too Late for Prince

Measure What Matters

It sounds obvious: Find out whether your customers are satisfied, because satisfied customers will buy from you again and again, helping your profits grow. It sounds so obvious that big companies pay generous fees to researchers who create sophisticated measures of customer satisfaction.

It sounds obvious, but it's wrong. Frederick Reichheld compared consumers' answers to questions about customer satisfaction and loyalty with measures of their actual purchases and their memory of referring others to the company. He found little relationship between stated satisfaction and repeat purchases. Instead, the best predictor of repeat purchases was a favorable response to "How likely is it that you would recommend [company X] to a friend or colleague?" People who would recommend the company were also likely to buy from it again.

Responses fall into three clusters: promoters, defined as the customers who were extremely likely to recommend (choosing 9 or 10 on a 10-point scale), those who were less likely ("passively satisfied," at 7 or 8), and the remainder of the customers. The greater the share of customers who are promoters, the faster a company's revenues grow. Over the three years studied, companies with many promoters included Southwest Airlines, Earthlink, and Enterprise Rent-A-Car, and all of them grew much faster than their competitors. Reichheld's advice to companies looking for growth: Skip the fancy questionnaires, and just ask customers if they will recommend your company.

Adapted from Frederick F. Reichheld, "The One Number You Need to Grow," *Harvard Business Review* 81, no. 12 (December 2003): 46–54.

Getting the Right Data

Surveys are often used to measure consumer satisfaction, asking people to rate products and services. However, does high customer satisfaction also mean that the quality of the product or service is also high? In a recent study, medical researchers found no correlation between patient-satisfaction and the quality of the care received. Those patients that rated the quality of their care as 10 (on a scale of 1 to 10) were no more likely to have received better care than those who gave it a 5.

This example shows some of the thorny issues associated with surveys. First, because surveys are easy to get and report, they are popular. But, people who respond to surveys tend to be those who are satisfied with the product or service. In addition, relying on survey data can exclude other important findings. As in the case in medical research, customer satisfaction can mean something very different than the quality of medical care received.

Given these complexities, how can surveys be used effectively?

Adapted from David Wessel, "In Health Care, Consumer Theory Falls Flat," *Wall Street Journal*, September 7, 2006, A2.

Charming?" reported the Yale and Harvard study that suggested such women had only a 20% chance of finding husbands, and only a 2.6% chance by the time they reached 40. Twenty years later an economist at the University of Washington examined 30 years of census data. Her figures for the decade of the original study showed that women aged 40–44 with advanced degrees were only 25% less likely to be married than comparably aged women with just high school diplomas. By 2000, those women with postcollege education were slightly more likely to be married than those who had finished only high school.[3]

Identifying the Source of the Data

Check to be sure that your data come from a reliable source. Use the strategies outlined in Chapter 15 to evaluate Web sources (◄ p. 509). When the source has a vested interest (◄ p. 372) in the results, scrutinize them with special care. To analyze a company's financial prospects, use independent information as well as the company's annual report and press releases.

If your report is based upon secondary data from library and online research, look at the sample, the sample size, and the exact wording of questions to see what the data actually measure. (See Chapter 15 for more information on sampling and surveying.) Does the sample have a built-in bias? A survey of city library users may uncover information about users, but it may not find what keeps other people away from the library.

For many kinds of research, a large sample is important for giving significant results. For example, polls found that citizens were closely divided about the 2004 presidential elections. The difference of a few percentage points was within the margin of error, meaning that the pollsters really did not know whether President George W. Bush or Senator John Kerry was in the lead; the difference in the numbers could have been mere chance. In that situation, a large sample was essential for the results to be meaningful. Nielsen Media Research collects about 2 million television viewing diaries annually to gather viewing data. The large numbers also allow it to provide viewing information for local stations and their advertisers.[4]

A survey that has been the target of much questioning in the press is the one behind the annual college rankings of *US News & World Report*. Critics charge that the rankings are based far too heavily on opinion (peer evaluations from other schools), uncorroborated data supplied by the schools themselves, and irrelevant data (such as rates of alumni giving). Critics also charge schools with gaming the system through practices such as heavy solicitation of students who have almost no chance of being accepted (low acceptance rates help schools' rankings).[5]

Identify exactly what the data measure. When advertisers began to place messages on the Internet, they soon realized that they had a measurement problem. The tools they used to measure viewer response counted the number of people who clicked on an ad that delivered them to the advertiser's Web site. In most cases, of course, advertisers want more than Web site visitors; they want people to buy from the company. Now more sophisticated tools can keep track of the percentage of people who click on the ad and then make a purchase at the company's Web site. Advertisers can use this information to test different versions of their advertising, so they use only the most profitable versions. At the same time, the companies that sell online advertising complain that these measures are unfair because they hold Internet advertising to a higher standard. Other media, such as magazines and television, merely estimate the number of people who see an ad, not the percentage who make a purchase.[6]

Identify the assumptions used in analyzing the data. When Nielsen Media Research estimates the number of people who view television stations, it must make a number of assumptions. The company has to determine how well its People Meter actually tracks whether people are watching, and it has to make decisions about how to count groups that are hard to measure. Nielsen has reported that 18- to 34-year-old males are watching less television, in part because they spend more time with videogames and DVDs. However, television networks complained that the company was underreporting this group's hours for a variety of reasons. For example, Nielsen was not counting young people who leave for college, and its sample did not include homes with TiVo or other personal video recorders (devices that make measurement more difficult). Because of such differences, the networks, Nielsen, and advertisers disagree about whether young men are losing interest in television programming.[7] Nielsen continually refines the ways it collects data. Since its original report on young men, for instance, it has started measures to track college students' viewing. Those efforts have increased ratings for some shows by more then 35%.[8]

Analyzing Numbers

Many reports analyze numbers—either numbers from databases and sources or numbers from a survey you have conducted. The numerical information, properly analyzed, can make a clear case in support of a recommendation. Suppose, for example, you are trying to make your company's Web site easier to use. In your report, you might want to include numbers from Jakob Nielsen that using Web sites is 206% harder for people with disabilities and 122% harder for elderly people.[9] These numbers are striking because they are large and because they are quite different. They make the case that some groups are having great difficulty with Web sites; if your company cares about serving these groups, it would be worthwhile to find out how to make your company's Web site easier for them to use. Also, depending on your group's objectives, you might decide to focus more on people with disabilities (because they have much more difficulty) or to focus more on elderly computer users (because they are a larger part of the population). The next steps would include finding out why these groups have trouble and how to make your company's Web site more user friendly. (The Web Accessibility Initiative provides excellent material on how to make Web sites accessible to the disabled: http://www.w3.org/WAI/intro/accessibility.php.)

Recognize that even authorities can differ on the numbers they offer, or on the interpretations of the same data sets. Researchers from the United Nations and Johns Hopkins University differed on their estimates of Iraqi deaths in the war by 500% (see sidebar on page 542).[10]

In their books, *The Tipping Point* and *Freakonomics,* Malcolm Gladwell and Steven D. Levitt and Stephen J. Dubner reach different conclusions about the data on dropping crime rates for New York City. Gladwell attributes the drop to the crackdown by the new police chief on even minor crimes such as graffiti and public drunkenness. Levitt and Dubner first explain why the cause was not a crackdown on crime (the years don't match well; other cities also experienced the drop) and attribute it to the legalization of abortion (at the time of the crime drop the first wave of children born after Roe v. Wade was hitting late teen years and thus prime crime time; that group was short on the category most likely to become criminal: unwanted children). They also provide corroborating evidence from other countries.[11]

If you've conducted a survey, your first step in analyzing your numbers is to transfer the responses on the survey form into numbers. For some categories, you'll assign numbers arbitrarily. For example, you might record men

---

Analyzing Numbers, I

True story. One of the Big Three Detroit Automakers put together a customer relationship management (CRM) system that helped it decide which cars to manufacture based on what was going on in dealers' lots. It worked great.

Well, except for one catch. According to Eric Almquist, VP at Mercer Management Consulting, the company's marketing team had just created sales incentives to get rid of a lot of lime-green cars, which no one wanted. As consumers snapped up the special deals on the cars, the CRM software noticed the surge of sales in lime-green cars and instructed the factory to produce more. The automaker lost millions of dollars before it caught the error.

Quoted from Brian Caulfield, "Facing Up to CRM," *Business 2.0,* August/September 2001, 149.

Analyzing Numbers, II

Beth Baldwin, Director of Marketing Information at Terra Lycos, the giant dotcom portal, knew the numbers didn't add up. Last November, New York–based Web audience measurement service Media Matrix reported that Lycos Zone—the portal's site for kids—had seen a 5 percent decline from the previous month. Baldwin's own numbers, however, showed that in fact the amount of traffic to the site had increased during that period.

Baldwin believed that her numbers, generated by Terra Lycos's site-metrics software, were probably right, but she had to prove it because Wall Street was more inclined to treat Media Matrix as the final word. It took two months, but she finally found the answer in a study, conducted by market research firm Roper Starch Worldwide, that reported on Web usage in schools and listed popular K–12 sites. Baldwin realized that many of the visitors to Lycos Zone were kids logging on from school, and that Media Matrix doesn't count those users. Her numbers were indeed correct.

Quoted from Brian Caulfield, "Why Your Site Traffic Numbers Are out of Whack," *Business 2.0*, March 2001, 122.

as 1 and women as 2—or vice versa. Such assignments don't matter, as long as you're consistent throughout your project. In these cases, you can report the number and percentage of men and women who responded to your survey, but you can't do anything else with the numbers.

When you have numbers for salaries or other figures, start by figuring the average (or mean), the median, and the range. The **average** or **mean** is calculated by adding up all the figures and dividing by the number of samples. The **mode** is the number that occurs most often. The **median** is the number that is exactly in the middle. When you have an odd number of observations, the median will be the middle number. When you have an even number, the median will be the average of the two numbers in the center. The **range** is the difference between the high and low figures for that variable.

Figure 16.1 shows the raw data that a student recorded in a report evaluating a hospital's emergency room procedures. To analyze the data, we could rearrange them, listing them from low to high (see Figure 16.2). The average waiting time is 26.6 minutes, but the median (the middle number) is only 22.

Finding the average takes a few more steps when you have different kinds of data. For example, it's common to ask respondents whether they find a feature "very important," "somewhat important," or "not important." You might code "very important" as "3," "somewhat important" as "2," and "not important" as "1." To find the average in this kind of data,

1. For each response, multiply the code by the number of people who gave that response.
2. Add up the figures.
3. Divide by the total number of people responding to the question.

For example, suppose you have the following data after selecting a random sample and surveying 50 people about the features they want in a proposed apartment complex:

	Very important (coded as "3")	Somewhat important (coded as "2")	Not important (coded as "1")
Party house	26	12	13
Extra parking for guests	26	23	1

Following step 1, to get the average for "party house," multiply $3 \times 26 = 78$; $2 \times 12 = 24$; and $1 \times 13 = 13$. Then add $78 + 24 + 13 = 115$. Divide by the

Figure 16.1   Raw Data from Observations for a Report

Amount of time (rounded off to the nearest minute) that patients wait in the emergency room before being examined in triage.

Patient	Wait	Patient	Wait	Patient	Wait
1	12	6	17	11	19
2	17	7	35	12	31
3	15	8	12	13	41
4	22	9	54	14	23
5	35	10	50	15	17

Figure 16.2   Rearranging Data to Find the Average (Mean), Mode, and Median

```
12, 12        Average: 26.6 minutes
15            Median: 22 minutes
17, 17, 17    Mode: 17 minutes
19            Range: 12 - 54 minutes
22
23
31
35, 35
41
50
54
```

When Estimates Collide

Why do married couples argue about money? One reason might be differences in what they think they have. In the National Longitudinal Studies, the Bureau of Labor Statistics looks at household measures over many years. Economist Jay Zagorsky found a problem with the financial data: husbands and wives differ in their estimates of income and assets.

On average, husbands report 5 percent more income and 10 percent more total wealth than wives do. In one way, though, spouses are consistent. Both report lower earnings for their spouses than the spouses report as their income. Their estimates differ by more than $3,000. When it comes to total wealth, husbands report more wealth than wives estimate.

Who is wrong? Zagorsky isn't sure. Couples do agree on which spouse pays most of the bills. For about 60 percent of the couples, that person is the wife.

Zagorsky's research tells others to be cautious in reviewing estimates of family earnings. For example, the federal government uses the Current Population Survey to calculate statistics about poverty. About two-thirds of respondents are women. Are poverty estimates too high? So far, we can only wonder.

Adapted from Jeff Grabmeier, "Husbands, Wives Don't Agree on Their Financial Status," *OnCampus*, June 12, 2003, 5–6.

number of people answering the question and you get the average for that factor: 115 divided by 50 = 2.3. Repeat the process for the next factor, "extra parking": 3 × 26 = 78; 2 × 23 = 46; 1 × 1 = 1. Adding 78 + 46 + 1 = 125; dividing by 50 = 2.5.

The average then gives an easy way to compare various features. If the party house averages 2.3 while extra parking for guests is 2.5, you know that your respondents would find extra parking more important than a party house. (Whether the difference is significant or not is a statistics question.) You can now arrange the factors in order of importance:

Table 4. "How Important Is Each Factor to You in Choosing an Apartment?"	
n = 50; 3 = "Very Important"	
Extra parking for guests	2.5
Party house	2.3
Pool	2.2
Convenient to bus line	2.0

Often it's useful to simplify numerical data: rounding it off, combining similar elements. Then you can see that one number is about 2½ times another. Charting it can also help you see patterns in your data. (See Chapter 6 for a full discussion of charts as a way of analyzing and presenting numerical data.) Look at the raw data as well as at percentages. For example, a 50% increase in shoplifting incidents sounds alarming. An increase from two to three shoplifting incidents sounds less so but is the same data stated differently.

Many people believe numbers are more "objective" than words. In reality, this belief is inaccurate; both numbers and words require interpretation and context to have meaning. Consider the data collected by the Department of Transportation's National Highway Traffic Safety Administration (NHTSA). For each year, the NHTSA gathers and reports statistics on the number of motor vehicle accident fatalities, breaking down the data by type of accident, type of vehicle, and state. In 2003 the agency determined that 42,643 people died in traffic accidents in the United States. When the data were ready, the NHTSA news release proclaimed, "DOT Announces Historic Low Highway Fatality Rate in 2003." The release quoted Transportation Secretary Norman Mineta as saying, "America's roads are safer than ever." The "historic low" was a rate of 1.48 per 100 million

Getting the Data Right

A 2006 report by Johns Hopkins University claimed that 655,000 Iraqis had died in the war in Iraq, a figure that diverged wildly from other estimates—sometimes more than 1,000%. The Hopkins figure is 500% more than that of the United Nations. Such a difference from other reports calls into question the accuracy of the Hopkins report.

To understand why the figure is so much higher than other research reports, it is important to consider how the data were gathered. The Hopkins researchers used cluster sampling for interviews, a methodology that makes sense given the country's war-zone status. Researchers randomly selected neighborhoods and then conducted door-to-door interviews with "clusters" of individuals from within those neighborhoods. Such a technique saves time and money and is common in research within developing countries.

But, the key to this kind of technique is to use enough cluster points. A lack of cluster points can mean that the population sampled isn't representative of the population in Iraq. The Hopkins researchers did not use enough cluster points. In addition, the Hopkins researchers didn't gather demographic data from their participants for comparison to census data. Doing so would have added to the believability of their results.

Getting the data right is important because numbers can have a significant impact on decisions and policies. In terms of casualties, the decisions made based on the numbers reported have an impact on millions of Iraqis and Americans.

Adapted from Stephen E. Moore, "655,000 War Dead?" *Wall Street Journal*, October 18, 2006, A20.

vehicle miles traveled, the first time that rate had been less than 1.5 since the NHTSA began gathering the data. A columnist for the *Wall Street Journal* acknowledged the good news but observed that the rate of decline was just 0.8%. The NHTSA news release emphasized reasons for the decline in fatalities (more seat belt use and stiffer drunk-driving laws), whereas the *Wall Street Journal* highlighted reasons for the small size of the decline (the popularity of SUVs and pickups, whose fatality rates are declining but are higher than for passenger cars).[12]

The same numbers can be presented in different ways to create very different impressions. In the case of the NHTSA data, the *Kansas City Star* and *Time* magazine prepared articles emphasizing not the overall decline in fatalities, but the difference between the fatality rates observed for passenger cars and SUVs. Both articles mentioned that passengers are "11% more likely to die" in a crash if they are driving an SUV rather than an automobile. A story in *Forbes* magazine, however, called SUVs "slightly more dangerous" but focused on additional data comparing various types of crashes. The *Forbes* article emphasized that in crashes between a light truck and a passenger car, if someone died, that person usually was an occupant of the car. The article listed the number of deaths recorded in each type of crash but not the percentage of fatalities (13%) in crashes between cars and light trucks.[13] In each of these examples, the publication used the same data to reach a conclusion that is more dramatic than a decline in fatalities of less than 1%.

A common myth associated with numbers is that numbers are more objective than words: "numbers don't lie."

Analyzing Words

If your data include words, try to find out what the words mean to the people who said them. An effort to measure the effectiveness of four TV commercials in Australia asked whether each commercial "encourages me to try/buy the brand product." The question is ambiguous. Some consumers might think the researcher wants to know whether the ad is obviously a sales pitch. (Is the ad "encouraging me to buy" or just trying to make me feel good?) Others might think the question is asking about how effective the ad is in persuading the consumer. (Did the ad succeed at encouraging me, or did it fail?) This question therefore might measure either the commercials' content or their ability to persuade, depending on how people interpret the words.[14]

Also try to measure words against numbers. When he researched possible investments, Peter Lynch found that people in mature industries were pessimistic, seeing clouds. People in immature industries saw pie in the sky, even when the numbers weren't great.[15]

Analyzing Patterns

Patterns can help you draw meaning from your data. If you have library sources, on which points do experts agree? Which disagreements can be explained by early theories or numbers that have now changed? Which disagreements are the result of different interpretations of the same data? Which are the result of having different values and criteria? In your interviews and surveys, what patterns do you see?

- Have things changed over time?
- Does geography account for differences?
- Do demographics such as gender, age, or income account for differences?
- What similarities do you see?
- What differences do you see?

- What confirms your hunches?
- What surprises you?

Checking Your Logic

State accurately what your data show. For example, suppose that you've asked people who use computers if they could be as productive without them and the overwhelming majority say *no*. This finding shows that people *believe* that computers make them more productive, but it does not prove that they in fact are more productive.

Don't confuse causation with correlation. *Causation* means that one thing causes or produces another. *Correlation* means that two things happening at the same time are positively or negatively related. One might cause the other, but both might be caused by a third. Correlation and causation are easy to confuse, but the difference is important. Consider studies showing that intelligence declines as birth order increases. Thus, the average first-born child is more intelligent than the average second-born, and IQs continue to fall for the third-, fourth-, and fifth-born. Does that mean having older siblings makes a person less intelligent? A more plausible explanation would be that a third factor makes large families different from small ones in a way that relates to intelligence measures. Similarly, the Census Bureau publishes figures showing that greater education levels are associated with greater incomes. A widely held assumption is that more education causes greater earnings. But might people from richer backgrounds seek more education? Or might some third factor, such as intelligence, lead to both greater education and higher income? The Census Bureau does not measure intelligence.[16]

Consciously search for at least three possible causes for each phenomenon you've observed and at least three possible solutions for each problem. The more possibilities you brainstorm, the more likely you are to find good options. In your report, mention all of the possibilities; discuss in detail only those that will occur to readers and that you think are the real reasons and the best solutions.

When you have identified causes of the problem or the best solutions, check these ideas against reality. Can you find support in quotes or in numbers? Can you answer claims of people who interpret the data in other ways?

Make the nature of your evidence clear to your reader. Do you have observations that you yourself have made? Or do you have inferences based on observations or data collected by others? Old data may not be good guides to future action.

If you can't prove the claim you originally hoped to make, modify your conclusions to fit your data. Even when your market test is a failure or your experiment disproves your hypothesis, you can still write a useful report.

- Identify changes that might yield a different result. For example, selling the product at a lower price might enable the company to sell enough units.
- Divide the discussion to show what part of the test succeeded.
- Discuss circumstances that may have affected the results.
- Summarize your negative findings in progress reports to let readers down gradually and to give them a chance to modify the research design.
- Remember that negative results aren't always disappointing to the audience. For example, the people who commissioned a feasibility report may be relieved to have an impartial outsider confirm their suspicions that a project isn't feasible. Marketing consultant Arthur Shapiro once worked with an executive who was disappointed when the results were *positive*. Shapiro tested a proposed advertising campaign and found that it performed as

http://www.pewinternet.org/

To see examples of the ways in which reports are written and disseminated, visit the Pew Internet & American Life Project at the above Web site.

The project produces reports on the impact of the Internet on American lives, collecting and analyzing data or real-world developments as they intersect with the virtual world. Following data collection, the results are written into the reports and posted as PDFs to the Web site.

Visit the Project's Web pages to see examples of the ways in which reports are first presented and then rewritten by the press for their audience and purpose.

intended. But after receiving the results, the executive responded that he could not be convinced because, he explained, "I hate the campaign."[17]

Choosing Information for Reports

Don't put information in reports just because you have it or just because it took you a long time to find it. Instead, choose the information that your reader needs to make a decision.

If you know your readers well, you may know what their priorities are. For example, the supervisor of a call center knows that management will be looking for certain kinds of performance data, including costs, workload handled and forecast, and customer satisfaction. To write regular reports, the supervisor would set up a format in which it is easy to see how well the center is doing in each of these areas. Using the same format month after month simplifies the reader's task. Presenting the actual performance alongside objectives helps managers focus on major successes and failures. The supervisor also would highlight and explain any unusual data, such as an unexpected surge in volume or a one-time expense.[18]

If you don't know your readers, you may be able to get a sense for what is important by showing them a tentative table of contents (a list of your headings) and asking, "Have I included everything?" When you cannot contact an external audience, show your draft to colleagues and superiors in your organization.

How much information you need to include depends on whether your audience is likely to be supportive, neutral, or skeptical. If your audience is likely to be pleased with your research, you can present your findings directly. If your audience will not be pleased, you will need to explain your thinking in a persuasive way and provide substantial evidence.

You must also decide whether to put information in the body of the report or in appendixes. Put material in the body of the report if it is crucial to your proof, if your most significant readers will want to see it there, or if it is short. (Something less than half a page won't interrupt the reader.) Frequently decision makers want your analysis of the data in the report body rather than the actual data itself. Supporting data that will be examined later by specialists such as accountants, lawyers, and engineers are generally put in an appendix.

Anything that a careful reader will want but that is not crucial to your proof can go in an appendix. Appendixes can include

- A copy of a survey questionnaire or interview questions.
- A tally of responses to each question in a survey.
- A copy of responses to open-ended questions in a survey.
- A transcript of an interview.
- Computer printouts.
- Complex tables and visuals.
- Technical data.
- Previous reports on the same subject.

Organizing Information in Reports

Most sets of data can be organized in several logical ways. Choose the way that makes your information easiest for the reader to understand and use. If you were compiling a directory of all the employees at your plant, for example, alphabetizing by last name would be far more useful than listing people by height, social security number, or length of service with the company, although those organizing principles might make sense in other lists for other purposes.

In one company, a young employee comparing the economics of two proposed manufacturing processes gave his logic and his calculations in full before getting to his conclusion. But his superiors didn't want to wade through eight single-spaced pages; they wanted his recommendation up front.[19]

The following three guidelines will help you choose the arrangement that will be the most useful for your reader:

1. **Process your information before you present it to your reader.** The order in which you became aware of information usually is not the best order to present it to your reader.

2. **When you have lots of information, group it into three to seven categories.** The average person's short-term memory can hold only seven chunks, though the chunks can be of any size.[20] By grouping your information into seven categories (or fewer), you make your report easier to read.

3. **Work with the reader's expectations, not against them.** Introduce ideas in the overview in the order in which you will discuss them.

Basic Patterns for Organizing Information

Seven basic patterns for organizing information are useful in reports:

1. Comparison/contrast.
2. Problem-solution.
3. Elimination of alternatives.
4. General to particular or particular to general.
5. Geographic or spatial.
6. Functional.
7. Chronological.

Any of these patterns can be used for a whole report or for only part of it.

1. Comparison/contrast

Many reports use comparison/contrast sections within a larger report pattern. Comparison/contrast can also be the purpose of the whole report. Feasibility studies usually use this pattern. You can focus either on the alternatives you are evaluating or on the criteria you use. See Figure 16.3 for examples of these two patterns in a report.

Focus on the alternatives when

- One alternative is clearly superior.
- The criteria are hard to separate.
- The reader will intuitively grasp the alternative as a whole rather than as the sum of its parts.

Focus on the criteria when

- The superiority of one alternative to another depends on the relative weight assigned to various criteria. Perhaps Alternative A is best if we are most concerned about Criterion 1, cost, but worst if we are most concerned about Criterion 2, proximity to target market.
- The criteria are easy to separate.
- The reader wants to compare and contrast the options independently of your recommendation.

Tell Them a Story

To persuade people, tell them a story or anecdote that proves your point.

Experiments with both high school teachers and quantitatively trained MBA students show that people are more likely to believe a point and more likely to be committed to it when points were made by examples, stories, and case studies. Stories alone were more effective than a combination of stories and statistics; the combination was more effective than statistics alone. In another experiment, attitude changes lasted longer when the audience had read stories than when they had only read numbers. Recent research suggests that stories are more persuasive because people remember them.

In many cases, you'll need to provide statistics or numbers to convince the careful reader that your anecdote is a representative example. But give the story first. It's more persuasive.

Adapted from Dean C. Kazoleas, "A Comparison of the Persuasive Effectiveness of Qualitative versus Quantitative Evidence," *Communication Quarterly* 41, no. 1 (Winter 1993): 40–50; and Joanne Martin and Melanie E. Powers, "Truth of Corporate Propaganda," in *Organizational Symbolism*, ed. Louis R. Pondy, et al. (Greenwich, CT: JAI Press, 1983), 97–107.

Figure 16.3　Two Ways to Organize a Comparison/Contrast Report

Focus on alternatives	
Alternative A	Opening a New Store on Campus
Criterion 1	Cost of Renting Space
Criterion 2	Proximity to Target Market
Criterion 3	Competition from Similar Stores
Alternative B	Opening a New Store in the Suburban Mall
Criterion 1	Cost of Renting Space
Criterion 2	Proximity to Target Market
Criterion 3	Competition from Similar Stores
Focus on criteria	
Criterion 1	Cost of Renting Space for the New Store
Alternative A	Cost of Campus Locations
Alternative B	Cost of Locations in the Suburban Mall
Criterion 2	Proximity to Target Market
Alternative A	Proximity on Campus
Alternative B	Proximity in the Suburban Mall
Criterion 3	Competition from Similar Stores
Alternative A	Competing Stores on Campus
Alternative B	Competing Stores in the Suburban Mall

A variation of the divided pattern is the **pro-and-con pattern.** In this pattern, under each specific heading, give the arguments for and against that alternative. A report recommending new plantings for a university quadrangle uses the pro-and-con pattern:

> Advantages of Monocropping
> 　High Productivity
> 　Visual Symmetry
> Disadvantages of Monocropping
> 　Danger of Pest Exploitation
> 　Visual Monotony

This pattern is least effective when you want to deemphasize the disadvantages of a proposed solution, for it does not permit you to bury the disadvantages between neutral or positive material.

2. Problem-solution

Identify the problem; explain its background or history; discuss its extent and seriousness; identify its causes. Discuss the factors (criteria) that affect the decision. Analyze the advantages and disadvantages of possible solutions. Conclusions and recommendation can go either first or last, depending on the preferences of your reader. This pattern works well when the reader is neutral.

A report recommending ways to eliminate solidification of a granular bleach during production uses the problem-solution pattern:

Recommended Reformulation for Vibe Bleach
Problems in Maintaining Vibe's Granular Structure
   Solidifying during Storage and Transportation
   Customer Complaints about "Blocks" of Vibe in Boxes
Why Vibe Bleach "Cakes"
   Vibe's Formula
   The Manufacturing Process
   The Chemical Process of Solidification
Modifications Needed to Keep Vibe Flowing Freely

3. Elimination of alternatives

After discussing the problem and its causes, discuss the *impractical* solutions first, showing why they will not work. End with the most practical solution. This pattern works well when the solutions the reader is likely to favor will not work, while the solution you recommend is likely to be perceived as expensive, intrusive, or radical.

   A report on toy commercials, "The Effect of TV Ads on Children," eliminates alternatives:

Alternative Solutions to Problems in TV Toy Ads
   Leave Ads Unchanged
   Mandate School Units on Advertising
   Ask the Industry to Regulate Itself
   Give FCC Authority to Regulate TV Ads Directed at Children

4. General to particular or particular to general

General to particular starts with the problem as it affects the organization or as it manifests itself in general and then moves to a discussion of the parts of the problem and solutions to each of these parts. Particular to general starts with the problem as the audience defines it and moves to larger issues of which the problem is a part. Both are good patterns when you need to redefine the reader's perception of the problem to solve it effectively.

   The directors of a student volunteer organization, VIP, have defined their problem as "not enough volunteers." After studying the subject, the writer is convinced that problems in training, supervision, and campus awareness are responsible for both a high dropout rate and a low recruitment rate. The general-to-particular pattern helps the audience see the problem in a new way:

Why VIP Needs More Volunteers
Why Some VIP Volunteers Drop Out
   Inadequate Training
   Inadequate Supervision
   Feeling That VIP Requires Too Much Time
   Feeling That the Work Is Too Emotionally Demanding
Why Some Students Do Not Volunteer
   Feeling That VIP Requires Too Much Time
   Feeling That the Work Is Too Emotionally Demanding
   Preference for Volunteering with Another Organization
   Lack of Knowledge about VIP Opportunities
How VIP Volunteers Are Currently Trained and Supervised
Time Demands on VIP Volunteers

Glass Ceilings?

Researchers not only write reports about their data, they also use reports to gather data. In a recent study, researchers from Dartmouth's Tuck School of Business and Loyola University–Chicago investigated proxy statements and Securities and Exchange Commission reports to gather data about the status of female CEOs.

Researchers categorized and ranked biographical data by gender, age, and tenure of executives from the largest 942 U.S. companies to predict the rate at which female executives will advance to become CEOs. In 2000, 0.6 % of board chairs and CEOs were women. By 2016, the proportion of females in those top positions is projected to be 6.2 percent. They concluded that "despite advances in the corporate sphere, it's still lonely at the top for female CEOs—and will be for at least another decade."

Adapted from Elizabeth Woyke, "Glass Ceilings: Corner Office Crawl," *BusinessWeek*, December 4, 2006, 14.

Emotional Demands on VIP Volunteers
Ways to Increase Volunteer Commitment and Motivation
   Improving Training and Supervision
   Improving the Flexibility of Volunteers' Hours
   Providing Emotional Support to Volunteers
   Providing More Information about Community Needs and VIP Services

5. Geographic or spatial

In a geographic or spatial pattern, you discuss problems and solutions by units by their physical arrangement. Move from office to office, building to building, factory to factory, state to state, region to region, etc.

A sales report uses a geographic pattern of organization:

Sales Have Risen in the European Community
Sales Are Flat in Eastern Europe
Sales Have Fallen Sharply in the Middle East
Sales Are Off to a Strong Start in Africa
Sales Have Risen Slightly in Asia
Sales Have Fallen Slightly in South America
Sales Are Steady in North America

6. Functional

In functional patterns, discuss the problems and solutions of each functional unit. For example, a small business might organize a report to its venture capitalists by the categories of research, production, and marketing. A government report might divide data into the different functions an agency performed, taking each in turn:

Major Accomplishments FY 09
   Regulation
   Education
   Research
   International coordination

7. Chronological

A chronological report records events in the order in which they happened or are planned to happen. Many progress reports are organized chronologically:

Work Completed in October
Work Planned for November

If you choose this pattern, be sure you do not let the chronology obscure significant points or trends.

How to Organize Specific Varieties of Reports

Informative, feasibility, and justification reports will be more successful when you work with the readers' expectations for that kind of report.

Informative and closure reports

Informative and **closure reports** summarize completed work or research that does not result in action or recommendation.

Informative reports often include the following elements:

* Introductory paragraph summarizing the problems or successes of the project.
* Purpose and scope section(s) giving the purpose of the report and indicating what aspects of the topic it covers.
* Chronological account of how the problem was discovered, what was done, and what the results were.
* Concluding paragraph with suggestions for later action. In a recommendation report, the recommendations would be based on proof. In contrast, the suggestions in a closure or recommendation report are not proved in detail.

Figure 16.4 presents this kind of informative closure report.

Closure reports also allow a firm to document the alternatives it has considered before choosing a final design and to prove its right to copyrights and patents.

Feasibility reports

Feasibility reports evaluate two or more alternatives and recommend one of them. (Doing nothing or delaying action can be one of the alternatives.)

Feasibility reports normally open by explaining the decision to be made, listing the alternatives, and explaining the criteria. In the body of the report, each alternative will be evaluated according to the criteria using one of the two comparison/contrast patterns. Discussing each alternative separately is better when one alternative is clearly superior, when the criteria interact, or when each alternative is indivisible. If the choice depends on the weight given to each criterion, you may want to discuss each alternative under each criterion.

Whether your recommendation should come at the beginning or the end of the report depends on your reader and the culture of your organization. Most readers want the "bottom line" up front. However, if the reader will find your recommendation hard to accept, you may want to delay your recommendation until the end of the report when you have given all your evidence.

Justification reports

Justification reports recommend or justify a purchase, investment, hiring, or change in policy. If your organization has a standard format for justification reports, follow that format. If you can choose your headings and organization, use this pattern when your recommendation will be easy for your reader to accept.

1. **Indicate what you're asking for and why it's needed.** Since the reader has not asked for the report, you must link your request to the organization's goals.
2. **Briefly give the background of the problem or need.**
3. **Explain each of the possible solutions.** For each, give the cost and the advantages and disadvantages.
4. **Summarize the action needed to implement your recommendation.** If several people will be involved, indicate who will do what and how long each step will take.
5. **Ask for the action you want.**

Failure Isn't Final

Researchers write closure reports when the company decides that the project they're working on isn't feasible. However, a few years later, new technologies, new conditions, or new ideas may make a "failed" idea feasible.

Post-It® notes use a "failed" adhesive because one 3M employee saw the weak adhesive as a solution to a problem:

I was singing in the choir in my church. . . . I would mark the pages with little pieces of paper normally. And sometimes they would fall out. . . . I thought what I really need is . . . a bookmark that's going to stick to those pages . . . and still not damage the book when I pull them off. . . . I knew that Spence Silver back in our laboratory had just developed an adhesive that would do that. And I made . . . rough samples of the bookmarks. . . . I had also made up some larger sizes and found, hey, these are really handy for notes.

An adhesive that failed in its original application was a spectacular success in a new and highly profitable product.

Adapted from John Nathan, *In Search of Excellence* (Waltham, MA: Nathan/Tyler Productions, 1985), 9.

Figure 16.4   An Informative Memo Report Describing How a Company Solved a Problem

March 14, 2008

To: Kitty O. Locker

From: Sara A. Ratterman *SAR*   *Informal short reports use*
                                                      letter or memo format.

First   Subject: Recycling at Bike Nashbar
paragraph
summarizes
main   Two months ago, Bike Nashbar began recycling its corrugated cardboard boxes. The program
points.   was easy to implement and actually saves the company a little money compared to our previous
                 garbage pickup.

Purpose   In this report, I will explain how and why Bike Nashbar's program was initiated, how the
and scope program works and what it costs, and why other businesses should consider similar programs.
of report.

                                      Bold or underline headings.

The Problem of Too Many Boxes and Not Enough Space in Bike Nashbar

                 Every week, Bike Nashbar receives about 40 large cardboard boxes containing bicycles and other
                 merchandise. As many boxes as possible would be stuffed into the trash bin behind the building,
Cause of   which also had to accommodate all the other solid waste the shop produces. Boxes that didn't fit
problem.   in the trash bin ended up lying around the shop, blocking doorways, and taking up space needed
                 for customers' bikes. The trash bin was only emptied once a week, and by that time, even more
                 boxes would have arrived.

                            Triple space before
                                    heading.
The Importance of Recycling Cardboard Rather than Throwing It Away
                                Double space after heading.
                 Arranging for more trash bins or more frequent pickups would have solved the immediate
                 problem at Bike Nashbar but would have done nothing to solve the problem created by throwing
                 away so much trash in the first place.
                            Double space between paragraphs within heading.
                 According to David Crogen, sales representative for Waste Management, Inc., 75% of all solid
                 waste in Columbus goes to landfills. The amount of trash the city collects has increased 150% in
Further   the last five years. Columbus's landfill is almost full. In an effort to encourage people and
seriousness businesses to recycle, the cost of dumping trash in the landfill is doubling from $4.90 a cubic yard
of problem. to $9.90 a cubic yard next week. Next January, the price will increase again, to $12.95 a cubic
                 yard. Crogen believes that the amount of trash can be reduced by cooperation between the
                 landfill and the power plant and by recycling.

                                                            Capitalize first letter of
How Bike Nashbar Started Recycling Cardboard   *major words in heading.*

                 Waste Management, Inc., is the country's largest waste processor. After reading an article about
                 how committed Waste Management, Inc., is to waste reduction and recycling, I decided to see
Solution.   whether Waste Management could recycle our boxes. Corrugated cardboard (which is what Bike
                 Nashbar's boxes are made of) is almost 100% recyclable, so we seemed to be a good candidate for
                 recycling.

(continued)

Figure 16.4   An Informative Memo Report Describing How a Company Solved a Problem
(Continued)

Kitty O. Locker   *Reader's name,*
March 14, 2008   *date,*
Page 2   *page number.*

To get the service started, I met with a friendly sales rep, David Crogen, that same afternoon to discuss the service.

Waste Management, Inc., took care of all the details. Two days later, Bike Nashbar was recycling its cardboard.

How the Service Works and What It Costs   *Talking heads tell reader what to expect in each section.*

Details of solution. Waste Management took away our existing 8-cubic-yard garbage bin and replaced it with two 4-yard bins. One of these bins is white and has "cardboard only" printed on the outside; the other is brown and is for all other solid waste. The bins are emptied once a week, with the cardboard being taken to the recycling plant and the solid waste going to the landfill or power plant.

Double space between paragraphs. Since Bike Nashbar was already paying more than $60 a week for garbage pickup, our basic cost stayed the same. (Waste Management can absorb the extra overhead only if the current charge is at least $60 a week.) The cost is divided 80/20 between the two bins: 80% of the cost pays for the bin that goes to the landfill and power plant; 20% covers the cardboard pickup. Bike Nashbar actually receives $5.00 for each ton of cardboard it recycles.

Each employee at Bike Nashbar is responsible for putting all the boxes he or she opens in the recycling bin. Employees must follow these rules:

- The cardboard must have the word "corrugated" printed on it, along with the universal recycling symbol.

Indented lists provide visual variety.

- The boxes must be broken down to their flattest form. If they aren't, they won't all fit in the bin and Waste Management would be picking up air when it could pick up solid cardboard. The more boxes that are picked up, the more money and space that will be made.

- No other waste except corrugated cardboard can be put in the recycling bin. Other materials could break the recycling machinery or contaminate the new cardboard.

- The recycling bin is to be kept locked with a padlock provided by Waste Management so that vagrants don't steal the cardboard and lose money for Waste Management and Bike Nashbar.

(continued)

Figure 16.4   An Informative Memo Report Describing How a Company Solved a Problem *(Concluded)*

Kitty O. Locker
March 14, 2008
Page 3

*Dis-
advantages
of
solution.*

Minor Problems with Running the Recycling Program

The only problems we've encountered have been minor ones of violating the rules. Sometimes employees at the shop forget to flatten boxes, and air instead of cardboard gets picked up. Sometimes people forget to lock the recycling bin. When the bin is left unlocked, people do steal the cardboard, and plastic cups and other solid waste get dumped in the cardboard bin. I've posted signs where the key to the bin hangs, reminding employees to empty and fold boxes and relock the bin after putting cardboard in it. I hope this will turn things around and these problems will be solved.

Advantages of the Recycling Program

*Advantages
of
solution.*

The program is a great success. Now when boxes arrive, they are unloaded, broken down, and disposed of quickly. It is a great relief to get the boxes out of our way, and knowing that we are making a contribution to saving our environment builds pride in ourselves and Bike Nashbar.

Our company depends on a clean, safe environment for people to ride their bikes in. Now we have become part of the solution. By choosing to recycle and reduce the amount of solid waste our company generates, we can save money while gaining a reputation as a socially responsible business.

Why Other Companies Should Adopt Similar Programs

*Argues
that her
company's
experience
is relevant
to other
companies.*

Businesses and institutions in Franklin County currently recycle less than 4% of the solid waste they produce. David Crogen tells me he has over 8,000 clients in Columbus alone, and he acquires new ones every day. Many of these businesses can recycle a large portion of their solid waste at no additional cost. Depending on what they recycle, they may even get a little money back.

The environmental and economic benefits of recycling as part of a comprehensive waste reduction program are numerous. Recycling helps preserve our environment. We can use the same materials over and over again, saving natural resources such as trees, fuel, and metals and decreasing the amount of solid waste in landfills. By conserving natural resources, recycling helps the U.S. become less dependent on imported raw materials. Crogen predicts that Columbus will be on a 100% recycling system by the year 2020. I strongly hope that his prediction will come true and the future may start to look a little brighter.

If the reader will be reluctant to grant your request, use this variation of the problem-solving pattern described in Chapter 12 (◀▦ p. 378):

1. **Describe the organizational problem (which your request will solve).** Use specific examples to prove the seriousness of the problem.
2. **Show why easier or less expensive solutions will not solve the problem.**

3. **Present your solution impersonally.**
4. **Show that the disadvantages of your solution are outweighed by the advantages.**
5. **Summarize the action needed to implement your recommendation.** If several people will be involved, indicate who will do what and how long each step will take.
6. **Ask for the action you want.**

How much detail you need to give in a justification report depends on the corporate culture and on your reader's knowledge of and attitude toward your recommendation. Many organizations expect justification reports to be short—only one or two pages. Other organizations may expect longer reports with much more detailed budgets and a full discussion of the problem and each possible solution.

Presenting Information Effectively in Reports

The advice about style in Chapter 4 also applies to reports, with three exceptions:

1. **Use a fairly formal style, without contractions or slang.**
2. **Avoid the word** *you***.** In a document with multiple audiences, it will not be clear who *you* is. Instead, use the company name.
3. **Include in the report all the definitions and documents needed to understand the recommendations.** The multiple audiences for reports include readers who may consult the document months or years from now; they will not share your special knowledge. Explain acronyms and abbreviations the first time they appear. Explain as much of the history or background of the problem as necessary. Add as appendixes previous documents on which you are building.

The following points apply to any kind of writing, but they are particularly important in reports:

1. Use clear, engaging writing.
2. Keep repetition to a minimum.
3. Introduce sources and visuals.
4. Use forecasting, transitions, topic sentences, and headings to make your organization clear to your reader.

Let's look at each of these principles as they apply to reports.

1. Use Clear, Engaging Writing.

Most people want to be able to read a report quickly while still absorbing its important points. You can help them do this by using accurate diction. Not-quite-right word choices are particularly damaging in reports, which may be skimmed by readers who know very little about the subject. Occasionally you can simply substitute a word:

Incorrect:	With these recommendations, we can overcome the solutions to our problem.
Correct:	With these recommendations, we can overcome our problem.
Also correct:	With these recommendations, we can solve our problem.

Sometimes you'll need to completely recast the sentence.

The Importance of Annual Reports

A 2006 survey, conducted by WithumSmith & Brown and MGT Design Inc., found that the annual report is the most important publication that a company produces. To understand the value of annual reports, the survey asked individual investors, portfolio managers, and securities analysts (the primary audiences for annual reports) about the ways that they read and use the reports to make decisions.

Here are some of their findings:

- 77% said the annual report is the most important publication that a company produces.
- 33% read most of the report.
- Nearly 64% read the report's Financial Highlights first.
- 47% said that poorly done annual reports are a sign that the organization is not performing well.
- 90% said that important concerns facing the industry, such as environment issues and corporate governance, should be addressed in the report.
- 81% prefer a print version over electronic versions. Respondents said the print documents were easier to read, highlight, annotate, and file.

Taken together, these findings suggest that the annual report is an important communication for organizations and well worth the time spent creating it.

Adapted from WithumSmith & Brown and MGT Design Inc., "AR Survey + Findings," in *News & Financial Tools: WS+B Press Releases: WS+B In The News: Survey Reveals Importance of Corporate Annual Reports,* http://www.withum.com/pressRelease Files/Annual%20Report%20Survey% 20Results.pdf (accessed June 17, 2007).

Who Did What?

The passive verbs and impersonal constructions in US reports of coal mine disasters ("coal dust was permitted to accumulate" and "an accident occurred") suggest that accidents are inevitable. Who permitted the coal dust to accumulate? What could have been done to prevent the accumulation? Mine disaster reports contain sentences like the following: "The . . . fatality occurred when the victim proceeded into an area . . . before the roof was supported." *Why* did the man who was killed go into the area? Had a supervisor checked to see that the roof was supported? Who ordered what?

British reports of mine disasters, in contrast, focus on people and what they did to limit the damage from the disaster. Perhaps as a result, British mines have a much lower incidence of disasters than do US coal mines.

Adapted from Beverly A. Sauer, "Sense and Sensibility in Technical Documentation: How Feminist Interpretation Strategies Can Save Lives in the Nation's Mines," *Journal of Business and Technical Communication* 7 (January 1993): 63–83.

Incorrect:	The first problem with the incentive program is that middle managers do not use good interpersonal skills in implementing it. For example, the hotel chef openly ridicules the program. As a result, the kitchen staff fear being mocked if they participate in the program.
Better:	The first problem with the incentive program is that some middle managers undercut it. For example, the hotel chef openly ridicules the program. As a result, the kitchen staff fear being mocked if they participate in the program.

A strong writing style is especially important when you are preparing a report that relies on a wealth of statistics. Most people have difficulty absorbing number after number. To help your readers, use text to highlight the message you want the statistics to convey. Examples and action-oriented details keep the reader engaged. An example that has this level of clarity is the 2004 report of the US government's commission investigating the terrorist attacks of September 11, 2001. The report was praised for its "solid, clear narrative that provides a sense of drama" and was described as being "richly detailed and colorful" and using language that is "precise, economical and highly authoritative." The commission's executive director, Philip D. Zelikow, said the report was intentionally made readable because the commission's leadership wanted people to read and act on it.[21]

2. Keep Repetition to a Minimum.

Some repetition in reports is legitimate. The conclusion restates points made in the body of the report; the recommendations appear in the transmittal, the abstract or executive summary, and in the recommendations sections of the report. However, repetitive references to earlier material ("As we have already seen") may indicate that the document needs to be reorganized. Read the document through at a single sitting to make sure that any repetition serves a useful purpose.

3. Introduce Sources and Visuals.

The first time you cite an author's work, use his or her full name: "Rosabeth Moss Kanter points out. . . . " In subsequent citations, use only the last name: "Kanter shows. . . . " Use active rather than passive verbs.

The verb you use indicates your attitude toward the source. *Says* and *writes* are neutral. *Points out, shows, suggests, discovers,* and *notes* suggest that you agree with the source. Words such as *claims, argues, contends that, believes,* and *alleges* distance you from the source. At a minimum, they suggest that you know that not everyone agrees with the source; they are also appropriate to report the views of someone with whom you disagree.

The report text should refer to all visuals:

As Table 1 shows, . . .
See Figure 4.

4. Use Forecasting, Transitions, Topic Sentences, and Headings.

Forecasts are overviews that tell the reader what you will discuss in a section or in the entire report. Make your forecast easy to read by telling the reader how many points there are and using bullets or numbers (either words or figures). In the following example, the first sentence in the revised paragraph tells the reader to look for four points; the numbers separate the four points clearly. This overview paragraph also makes a contract with readers, who now expect to read about tax benefits first and employee benefits last.

Paragraph without numbers:	Employee stock ownership programs (ESOPs) have several advantages. They provide tax benefits for the company. ESOPs also create tax benefits for employees and for lenders. They provide a defense against takeovers. In some organizations, productivity increases because workers now have a financial stake in the company's profits. ESOPs are an attractive employee benefit and help the company hire and retain good employees.
Revised paragraph with numbers:	Employee stock ownership programs (ESOPs) provide four benefits. First, ESOPs provide tax benefits for the company, its employees, and lenders to the plan. Second, ESOPs help create a defense against takeovers. Third, ESOPs may increase productivity by giving workers a financial stake in the company's profits. Fourth, as an attractive employee benefit, ESOPs help the company hire and retain good employees.

Legal Liability and Report Drafts

During civil litigation (such as a tort case charging that a product has injured a user), rough drafts may be important to establish the state of mind and intent of a document's drafters.

To protect the company, one lawyer recommends labeling all but the final draft "Preliminary Draft: Subject to Change." That way, if there's ever a lawsuit, the company will be able to argue that only the final report, not the drafts, should be used as evidence.

Adapted from Elizabeth McCord, "'But What You Really Meant Was . . . Multiple Drafts and Legal Liability," paper presented at the Association for Business Communication Midwest Regional Conference, Akron, OH, April 3–5, 1991.

Transitions are words, phrases, or sentences that tell readers whether the discussion is continuing on the same point or shifting points.

There are economic advantages, too.
(Tells the reader that we are still discussing advantages but that we have now moved to economic advantages.)
An alternative to this plan is . . .
(Tells reader that a second option follows.)
The second factor . . .
(Tells reader that the discussion of the first factor is finished.)
These advantages, however, are found only in A, not in B or C.
(Prepares reader for a shift from A to B and C.)

A topic sentence introduces or summarizes the main idea of a paragraph. Readers who skim reports can follow your ideas more easily if each paragraph begins with a topic sentence.

Hard to read (no topic sentence):	Another main use of ice is to keep the fish fresh. Each of the seven kinds of fish served at the restaurant requires one gallon twice a day, for a total of 14 gallons. An additional 6 gallons a day are required for the salad bar.
Better (begins with topic sentence):	Twenty gallons of ice a day are needed to keep food fresh. Of this, the biggest portion (14 gallons) is used to keep the fish fresh. Each of the seven kinds of fish served at the restaurant requires one gallon twice a day ($7 \times 2 = 14$). An additional 6 gallons a day are required for the salad bar.

Headings (see Chapter 6 p. 156) are single words, short phrases, or complete sentences that indicate the topic in each section. A heading must cover all of the material under it until the next heading. For example, *Cost of Tuition* cannot include the cost of books or of room and board. You can have just one paragraph under a heading or several pages. If you do have several pages between headings you may want to consider using subheadings. Use subheadings only when you have two or more divisions within a main heading.

Topic headings focus on the structure of the report. As you can see from the following example, topic headings give very little information.

Topic headings are vague.
Recommendation
Problem
Situation 1
Situation 2
Causes of the Problem
Background
Cause 1
Cause 2
Recommended Solution

Talking heads, in contrast, tell the reader what to expect. Talking heads, like those in the examples in this chapter, provide an overview of each section and of the entire report.

Talking heads are specific.
Recommended Reformulation for Vibe Bleach
Problems in Maintaining Vibe's Granular Structure
Solidifying during Storage and Transportation
Customer Complaints about "Blocks" of Vibe in Boxes
Why Vibe Bleach "Cakes"
Vibe's Formula
The Manufacturing Process
The Chemical Process of Solidification
Modifications Needed to Keep Vibe Flowing Freely

Headings must be parallel (◄ p. 124); that is, they must use the same grammatical structure. Subheads must be parallel to each other but do not necessarily have to be parallel to subheads under other headings.

> Not parallel: Are Students Aware of VIP?
>
>   Current Awareness among Undergraduate Students
>
>   Graduate Students
>
>   Ways to Increase Volunteer Commitment and Motivation
>
>   We Must Improve Training and Supervision
>
>   Can We Make Volunteers' Hours More Flexible?
>
>   Providing Emotional Support to Volunteers
>
>   Provide More Information about Community Needs and VIP Services

Parallel: Campus Awareness of VIP

                    Current Awareness among Undergraduate Students

                    Current Awareness among Graduate Students

                Ways to Increase Volunteer Commitment and Motivation

                Improving Training and Supervision

                Improving the Flexibility of Volunteers' Hours

                Providing Emotional Support to Volunteers

                Providing More Information about Community Needs and VIP Services

In a very complicated report, you may need up to three levels of headings. Figure 16.5 illustrates one way to set up headings. Follow these standard conventions for headings:

Figure 16.5   Setting Up Headings in a Single-Spaced Document

Center the title; use bold and a bigger font.

Typing Titles and Headings for Reports *14-point type.*

For the title of a report, use a bold font two point sizes bigger than the largest size in the body of the report. You may want to use an even bigger size or a different font to create an attractive title page. Capitalize the first word and all major words of the title.

Heading for main divisions   ↕ *Two empty spaces (triple space)*

Typing Headings for Reports *12-point type.*
↕ *One empty space (double space)*

12-point type for body text

Center main headings, capitalize the first and all major words, and use bold. In single-spaced text, leave two empty spaces before main headings and one after. Also leave an extra space between paragraphs. You may also want to use main headings that are one point size bigger than the body text.

This example provides just one example of each level of heading. However, in a real document, use headings only when you have at least two of them in the document. In a report, you'll have several.

↕ *Two empty spaces (triple space)*

Typing Subheadings *Bold; left margin*
↕ *One empty space*

Most reports use subheadings under some main headings. Use subheadings only if you have at least two of them under a given heading. It is OK to use subheadings in some sections and not in others. Normally you'll have several paragraphs under a subheading, but it's OK to have just one paragraph under some subheadings.

12-point type

Subheadings in a report use the same format as headings in letters and memos. Bold subheadings and set them at the left margin. Capitalize the first word and major words. Leave two empty spaces before the subheading and one empty space after it, before the first paragraph under the subheading. Use the same size font as the body paragraphs.

Period after heading

↕ *One empty space (normal paragraph spacing)*

Typing Further Subdivisions. For a very long report, you may need further subdivisions under a subheading. Bold the further subdivision, capitalizing the first word and major words, and end the phrase with a period. Begin the text on the same line. Use normal spacing between paragraphs. Further subdivide a subheading only if you have at least two such subdivisions under a given subheading. It is OK to use divisions under some subheadings and not under others.

Tantalizing Titles

Two titles define two reports that look at business through very different lenses, one with a rosy glow and one in a bleaker light.

The darker images are in Sydney Finkelstein's book, *Why Smart Executives Fail.* Finkelstein has earned a reputation as a management expert by studying business failures. For example, he has looked in depth at the collapse of Internet start-up Webvan Group and the inability of Barney's New York to sell clothing in the Midwest. Finkelstein uses problems as a tool to help managers learn what *not* to do.

A pair of writers from McKinsey and Company, Tom Peters and Robert Waterman, compiled a best-seller when they wrote *In Search of Excellence* over two decades ago. Peters now admits that their book started as a marginal project at the consulting giant. While others were immersed in quantitative data, he and Waterman visited organizations where people worked together effectively; they summarized what they saw. They identified eight principles (for example, "Close to the Customer" and "Productivity through People") as a way to make "pounds of transcripts" digestible by clients. Peters downplays the significance of their methods but insists that the eight principles were important for their time. Also, the coauthors never claimed that following the eight principles would guarantee success. Rather, businesspeople are supposed to continue seeking principles that contribute to excellence in today's environment.

Adapted from Jennifer Merritt, "The ABCs of Failure," *BusinessWeek,* June 9, 2003, 126; and Tom Peters, "Tom Peters's True Confessions," *Fast Company,* December 2001, 78–81+.

- Although the figure shows only one example of each level of headings, in an actual report you would not use a subheading unless you had at least two subsections under the next higher heading.
- Whatever the format for headings, avoid having a subhead come immediately after a heading. Instead, some text should follow the main heading before the subheading. (If you have nothing else to say, give an overview of the division.)
- Avoid having a heading or subheading all by itself at the bottom of the page. Instead, have at least one line (preferably two) of type. If there isn't room for a line of type under it, put the heading on the next page.
- Don't use a heading as the antecedent for a pronoun. Instead, repeat the noun.

Writing Formal Reports

Formal reports are distinguished from informal letter and memo reports by their length and by their components. A full formal report may contain the following components (see Figures 16.6 and 16.7):

Cover
Title Page
Letter or Memo of Transmittal
Table of Contents
List of Illustrations
Executive Summary
Report Body
Introduction (Orients the reader to the report. Usually has subheadings for Purpose and Scope; depending on the situation, may also have Limitations, Assumptions, Methods, Criteria, and Definitions.)

Figure 16.6   The Components in a Report Can Vary

More formal ⟵	⟶ Less formal	
Cover	Title Page	Introduction
Title Page	Table of Contents	Body
Transmittal	Executive Summary	Conclusions
Table of Contents	Body	Recommendations
List of Illustrations	Introduction	
Executive Summary	Body	
Body	Conclusions	
Introduction	Recommendations	
Body		
Conclusions		
Recommendations		
References/Works Cited		
Appendixes		
Questionnaires		
Interviews		
Computer Printouts		
Related Documents		

Figure 16.7 A Formal Report

Center all text on the title page.

Viva Panera!

Use a large font size for the main title.

Expanding Panera into Chile

Use a slightly smaller font size for the sub-heading.

Prepared for

No punctuation

Mr. Ronald M. Shaich, CEO
Panera Bread Company
Richmond Heights, MO 63117

The rest of the document should use 12-point font size.

Name of reader, job title, organization, city, state, and zip code.

Prepared by

No punctuation

JOABA Consulting
April Hoffmeyer
Betsy Hertz
Andrea Keeney
Jessica Oney
Omar Romero
Iowa State University
Ames, IA 50011

Name of writer(s), organization, city, state, and zip code.

April 16, 2007

Date report is released

(continued)

Figure 16.7   A Formal Report *(Continued)*

This student group designed their own letterhead, assuming they were doing this report as consultants.

This letter uses Block format.

JOABA Consulting
131 Ross Hall
Ames, IA 50011

April 17, 2006

Mr. Ronald M. Shaich, CEO
Panera Bread Company
6710 Clayton Road
Richmond Heights, MO 63117

In paragraph 1, release the report. note when and by whom the report was authorized. Note report's purpose.

Dear Mr. Shaich:

Here you will find the report you requested in March including information on the feasibility of expanding a Panera Bread facility into Chile and our recommendations for a plan of action.

During the market analysis, our team considered and researched various macro environment factors including location, customs and behaviors, economics and laws, and market possibilities and competition. Our findings show that Chile is an attractive market to invest in, and we recommend it as a location into which Panera Bread should expand. The research conducted about your business and Chile's consumer market leads us to recommend opening a corporate-owned facility in the capital city of Santiago.

Give recommendations or thesis of report.

The capital city of Santiago is already home to many successful American franchises, and to stay competitive with these franchises, we suggest you expand into this market. With the use of appropriate marketing campaigns and employment of locals with management experience, your business has the potential to penetrate the market in Santiago.

The analysis in this report came from several helpful resources. The U.S. Commercial Services, the Central Intelligence Agency's World Factbook, and the Santiago Chamber of Commerce were all very helpful and cooperative in answering our questions.

Note sources that were helpful.

Thank reader for the opportunity to do the research.

Thank you for allowing us to conduct this research. We have learned about Panera, the country of Chile, and the international business environment. If you have any questions, feel free to contact our firm at any time. We look forward to working with you in the future.

Offer to answer questions about the report.

Sincerely,

April Hoffmeyer

April Hoffmeyer
JOABA Team Leader

Center page number at the bottom of the page. Use a lowercase Roman numeral for initial pages of report.

i

(continued)

Figure 16.7   A Formal Report *(Continued)*

Headings or subheadings must be parallel with a section.

Table of contents does not list itself.

Table of Contents

Use lower-case Roman numerals for initial pages.

Introduction begins on page l.

Capitalize first letter of each major word in headings.

Indentions show level of heading at a glance.

Line up right margin (justify)

Add a "List of Illustrations" at the bottom of the page or on a separate page if the report has graphs and other visuals.

Figures and tables are numbered independently, so you could have both a Figure 1 and a Table 1.

List of Illustrations

(continued)

Figure 16.7   A Formal Report *(Continued)*

Viva Panera!

Report title.

Many audiences only read the Executive Summary, not the report. Include enough information to give readers the key points you make.

Expanding Panera into Chile

Executive Summary

Start with recommendation or thesis.

To remain competitive with an ever-expanding market, Panera should expand into Santiago, Chile's capital. Santiago is home to approximately 5.6 million people and is one of the most modern cities in South America because of its buildings, subway system, and green areas. Santiago is already home to many American franchises, several direct competitors of Panera, and remaining competitive with these chains would be beneficial to Panera.

Provide brief support for recommen -dation.

As far as our research shows, expanding into Chile is likely to be a profitable decision for a few reasons. For example, the country's foods are similar to those of Panera's and would not require extensive menu changes. In addition, the current economic situation is among the most stable in South America, and with an unemployment rate of 8%, there will likely be workers to fill positions at the restaurant. Moreover, the political standing and lack of legal barriers in Chile is beneficial to foreign-run businesses.

To ensure a successful expansion, JOABA recommends the following:

1. **Expand into one location in Santiago, Chile.** Opening one store in this large city will introduce the restaurant into the Chilean culture with minimal risk. The locals will have the opportunity to show their acceptance or rejection of Panera through their patronage.
   - Start a company-owned store (as opposed to a franchise).
   - Open the store with both an American and Chilean manager so the American can train the Chilean in the business to ensure Panera's identity is maintained.
   - Hire local people in Santiago as employees.

2. **Evaluate the success and expansion feasibility at the end of a 12 month period.**
   - Survey locals for their feedback on the restaurant.
   - Explore additional places in Santiago to expand to (if expansion is the result of the evaluation).

3. **After three years, investigate selling the company-owned stores to managers to transition the stores into franchises.**
   - Evaluate the success of the stores based on sales and community response.
   - Research the economic feasibility of this change of ownership.

Language in Executive Summary can come from report. Make sure any repeated language is well-written!

The abstract or Executive Summary contains the logical skeleton of the report: the recommendation(s) and evidence supporting it.

iii

(continued)

Figure 16.7   A Formal Report *(Continued)*

A running header is optional

Viva Panera!: Expanding Panera into Chile   1

Introduction   *Center main headings*

To stay competitive in the global market, Panera Bread has asked us to explore expanding into Chile. In order to make a wise and well-researched proposal, JOABA Consulting has researched Chilean data to see if Panera would be potentially prosperous and successful there.

"Purpose" and "Scope" can be separate sections if either is long

Purpose and Scope

Panera has experienced recent success and is growing rapidly within the United States. To stay competitive in the global market, they must look to expand into other countries. The purpose of this research is to propose a plan stating if and to what extent Panera should expand into Chile.

Tell what you discuss and how thoroughly you discuss each topic

Topics in "Scope" section should match those in the report.

This report will cover several topics about Chile including: location, customs and behaviors, politics, economics and laws, and market possibilities and competition. Throughout this report, we do not discuss topics dealing with the internal intricacies of Panera Bread Company. We also do not include any on-site research from local Chilean people.

Give topics in the order in which you'll discuss them

List any relevant topics you do not discuss.

Assumptions   *Assumptions cannot be proved. But if they are wrong, the report's recommendation may no longer be valid.*

Our recommendation is based on the assumption that Panera's expansion process will be similar to that of other American competitors who have successfully opened stores in Chile. We are also assuming that Chile's political outlook will remain stable and its economic situation will remain healthy.

If you collected original data (surveys, interviews, or observations), tell how you chose whom to study, what kind of sample you used, and when you collected the information. This report does not use original data; it just provides a brief discussion of significant sources.

Methods

The information from this report came from newspapers, library books, and online sources. We have found the U.S. Commercial Services, the Central Intelligence Agency's World Factbook, and Kwintessential Language and Cultural Specialists websites to be extremely useful resources to explore this expansion possibility.

Limitations   *If your report has limitations, state them.*

This research was limited to materials available via the Internet and from our university's library. In addition, only one of the five JOABA group members is a business major, and the other group members are somewhat unfamiliar with this type of business analysis. Time constraints have limited the possibility of an exhaustive search for information regarding the expansion of Panera Bread into Chile. Moreover, our group would have greatly benefited by actually traveling to Chile for on-location research.

Criteria

This section outlines the criteria used to make the overall recommendation.

JOABA Consulting established criteria, which we used during our investigation of Chile. These criteria included the location, customs, politics, economic climate and legal issues, market

(continued)

Figure 16.7   A Formal Report *(Continued)*

Viva Panera!: Expanding Panera into Chile   2

possibilities and competition. At least four of these five criteria needed to be favorable for us to give a positive recommendation.

Triple space before headings

Location

While Chile offers many possible cities for Panera to expand, we believe that Santiago would be the most prosperous. Santiago, the capital of Chile and home to approximately 5.6 million people, is one of the most modern cities of South America because of its buildings, subway system, and green areas ("Chile"). Expanding Panera Bread into Santiago would be ideal because of the large market.

It's ok to have subheadings under some headings and not others.

Begin most paragraphs with topic sentences.

Moreover, Santiago ranked first on AméricaEconomía's list of the *Best Cities for Doing Business in Latin America* in 2005. The study looked at the costs and benefits of different locations and was based on the recommendations of international consulting firms. Santiago was found to add the most value to a business and to offer the best combination of quality of life, business potential, and professional development. The ranking also points out the city's attention to transportation infrastructure, showing that it benefits both commuters and business visitors ("Business Environment"). In 2006, Santiago was ranked second behind Sao Paulo, Brazil.

Italicize titles.

The continued high ranking of Santiago reinforces it as one of the best cities for doing business in Latin America, and supports our belief that Santiago would make a great city in which Panera could expand.

Not every idea needs a source. Here, general population figures are readily available.

Chilean Customs and Behaviors

Panera must have a deep understanding of the approximately 16 million Chilean people if it is to effectively adapt products to its new audience. Panera representatives, who would implement the plan, must appreciate and respect Chilean customs and behavioral norms so they do not send negative signals to the native Chilean people.

In order to ensure a smooth expansion effort for Panera, we have researched food preferences, eating times, family life, greetings and address, body language, and religion. The following information presents the results of this research and can serve as a guide to understanding some of the customs and behaviors of Chilean people.

List subtopics in the order in which they are discussed.

Use subheadings only when you have two or more sections

Food Preferences

Chilean cuisine boasts a wide range of tastes, which vary from region to region. Seafood dishes are popular, including the use of eel, bass, scallops, clams and other shellfish. Although many assume Chilean food to be hot, spiciness is a rarity in this country. Chano en piedra and pebre are two common spices used in Chilean cooking. Chano en piedra is made by grinding tomato, garlic and onions with a stone. Pebre is made from tomatoes, onions, chili, coriander, and chives. Main dishes are commonly made from beef, chicken or pork and lots of vegetables ("Typical Chilean").

(continued)

Figure 16.7   A Formal Report *(Continued)*

Viva Panera!: Expanding Panera into Chile   3

Sandwiches and breads are also popular in Chile. Both cold and grilled sandwiches are served for the smaller meals during the day. The type of sandwiches eaten ranges from ham and chicken deli meat to hamburgers and hotdogs, usually topped with vegetables, especially tomatoes and avocados. Breads are also served at smaller meals. Pan amasado is a homemade bread and sopaipilla is a deep fried flat bread made using pumpkin and flour ("Typical Chilean").

Period goes outside of the parenthesis.

Many Chilean dishes correspond with Panera's menu. The popularity of vegetables suggests salads would work well. Sandwiches are well-liked in Chile both grilled and cold, often with deli meats. Panera could easily adapt their menu for the Chilean people by blending traditional Panera flavors with common Chilean flavors. Soups and stews are common in Chile and could also be adapted for a menu in Chile. A Panera in Chile could also offer more seafood dishes because of its popularity and availability. Panera's traditional coffees and teas would fit in to the culture and could be served, especially during the *once* meal.

Eating Times

In Chile, most people customarily eat four meals a day. Breakfast is a small meal consisting of fresh bread with jelly or manjar (a caramel-like spread). Lunch is the largest meal of the day, having several courses, usually a cazuela soup or stew, a main dish, and a vegetable side dish, often beans. *Once* (pronounced own-say) is served in the afternoon between 4:00 and 7:00 PM. It includes bread or a sandwich served with coffee or tea. Dinner is a smaller meal than lunch and is typically served late evening (Rawlinson).

Use author's name in parentheses when it isn't in the sentence introducing quote.

Family Life

Chilean life is family-centered, and people spend a lot of time with their extended family and distant relatives. Large family gatherings are common, and Panera restaurants in Chile would have to cater to the needs of large groups for such events. Family is also important in the business world, as many businesses in Chile are run by a single family (Nicol). A Panera franchise could potentially be owned and operated by a single family.

Greetings and Address

People in Chile are traditional as well as friendly. When greeting someone new, a firm handshake and good eye contact are usually expected. If a man is greeting a friend or family member, he would give them a hug, while a woman would kiss them on the cheek ("Chile: Society"). When engaged in conversation, Chileans speak close to one another and usually maintain eye contact. Common conversational topics are family and children (Nicol).

Addressing people by the proper name is important to build goodwill with people in business. In Chile, it is common for people to have two surnames, one from both the mother and the father. Most of the time the father's name is first and that is what most people will go by ("Chilean Culture").

Figure 16.7   A Formal Report *(Continued)*

Viva Panera!: Expanding Panera into Chile   4

Body Language
Body language is also important to keep in mind when interacting with someone from Chile. Hitting your fist into the other hand is usually considered obscene. Holding one's fist to the same height as their head is a sign of communism. In addition, a hand palm-up with fingers spread out signals you think something is stupid. Moreover, yawns should always be covered or stifled (Nicol). At meals, hands should always be above the table, with wrists resting on the edge of the table. Serving wine with the left hand is sometimes seen as disrespectful. ("Chile: Society").

Use first words of the title in quotation marks for sources with no author.

Religion
Roman Catholicism is the predominant religion in Chile, making up 89% of the population ("Chile"). The religion is integrated into the society, as it is taught in most public schools and is the reason for most public holidays. Even many of the country's laws are influenced by Catholic beliefs. For example, because of the Church's inherent disbelief in divorce, it was illegal until 2004 ("Chile: Society"). The religion of Chile would affect Panera's business, particularly during the Lenten season, because Catholics change their diet by refraining from eating meat on Fridays. The Catholic religion also affects holidays for the customers, as well as the employees.

Chilean Politics

Headings must cover everything under that heading until next one.

To comprehend the importance of the current political stability, Panera must understand some recent Chilean political history. Specifically, it should know about presidential power and trade agreements.

Capitalize all main words of headings and subheadings.

Presidential Power
In 1973, Augusto Pinochet led a military coup and declared himself president. His regime hurt the country and its economy, closing down the Chilean Parliament and banning all political and trade union activity. Pinochet was overthrown in 1990 and democracy was finally restored to Chile. (Franklin).

Chile is currently a republic with seven primary political parties, which are grouped into two main groups ("Why Chile?"). The Concertación coalition has been in power since the end of Pinochet's rule. In January 2006, the first female president in Chile's history, Michelle Bachelet, was elected. Bachelet is the fourth consecutive head of state from the center-left Concertación coalition ("Business Environment").

Trade Agreements
In addition to the positive political environment, the country is also taking positive steps to improve its stability through relations with other countries. The U.S. Chile Free Trade Agreement (FTA) has expanded U.S-Chilean trade ties and relations between the U.S. and Chile, and they are the best they have ever been (Santiago–Chile). The two governments regularly discuss issues

(continued)

Figure 16.7   A Formal Report *(Continued)*

Viva Panera!: Expanding Panera into Chile   5

of mutual concern including multilateral diplomacy, security, culture, and science. The strong relationship between the governments shows the political stability of Chile. The U.S. Embassy in Santiago will also be available to assist Panera through its involvement in strengthening the relationship between the two countries (Santiago–Chile).

Chilean Economics and Legal Concerns

We believe that Panera should know characteristics of the Chilean economy and other legal concerns before expanding. Ideally, Panera wants a stable economy before expanding there because economic instability might affect Panera's success. The local currency and its stability should be taken into account when considering how to price our products. The GDP per capita is also important because it is an indicator of the average income of an average citizen. Our analysis of Chile's economy shows us that it is well suited for the expansion of Panera Bread into its market because of its stable and growing economy and its willingness to allow foreign investment and free trade.

Refer to Figure in text before you show it. Tell what point it makes.

Economic Growth

By the end of 1999, exports and economic activity had begun to recover from the low growth levels seen for much of the 90s. By 2000, economic growth increased to 4.5%. However, growth once again dropped in 2001 to 3.4% and to 2.2% in 2002 as seen in Figure 1. The drop occurred largely because of low global growth, and the devaluation of the Argentine peso ("Business Environment").

Provide a heading for figures and tables.

Economic Growth in Chile 2000–2005

Label both axes. See Chapter 6 for more information on creating graphs and visuals.

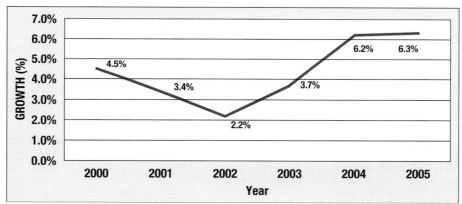

Figure 1. Recent economic growth rates in Chile ("Business Environment").

Number Figures and Tables independently

However, in 2003, Chile's economy began a recovery resulting in growth of 3.7% and increases to 6.2% and 6.3% in 2004 and 2005, respectively, while Chile maintained a low rate of inflation

(continued)

Figure 16.7   A Formal Report *(Continued)*

Viva Panera!: Expanding Panera into Chile   6

("Business Environment"). Over the last few years, GDP growth can be attributed to record high copper prices, solid export earnings, and increased foreign investment. The growth in GDP has reduced inflation but unemployment remains high at 8.0% ("Chile"), which indicates a large labor pool.

Currency and GDP

The currency of Chile is the Chilean Peso (CPL), and the current exchange rate between the U.S. dollar and the Chilean Peso is $1 to 514.90 CPL. In recent years, the Chilean Peso has strengthened significantly against the U.S. dollar and has remained stable. This can be attributed to the growing GDP of the country and increased trade with other countries ("Chile"). The stable currency will make Panera's expansion more favorable.

In 2005, the GDP was $180.6 billion, with a GDP per capita of approximately $11,300. In 2005, Chile had a current account balance of $309 million and external debt of $44.8 billion. As of 2002, Chile has not received economic aid from the IMF, the World Bank, or another country ("Chile"). Chile serves as an economic model for the rest of Latin America with its continued economic growth and is expected to continue growing into 2009 ("Business Environment").

Imports

The country's largest import partners are Argentina, United States, Brazil, and China. Chile is relatively open to trade and investment and has a Free Trade Agreement with the United States. When the U.S.-Chile Free Trade Agreement came into effect in January 1, 2004, 90% of tariffs on U.S. exports were eliminated. By 2015, all trade between the two countries will be duty free.

Typically, Chile has few barriers to imports. However, in the case of agriculture, some exceptions apply. If Panera is going to import processed food products, it will have to obtain permission from the Health Service Officer at the port of entry, who will take samples and perform necessary tests. Upon importation of products, there is some necessary documentation that will have to accompany the products. This documentation includes commercial invoices, certificates of origin, bills of lading, freight insurance and packing lists. Franchises are subject to regular trade laws. The withholding tax on royalties is 35% and all imports are subject to 19% value-added tax ("Made").

In addition, Chile has certain labeling requirements for imported products. The product must display the country of origin before being sold. Packaged goods must be marked with the quality, purity, ingredients, and the net weight or measure. The labeling must also be in Spanish and measurements should use the metric system. Foreign firms in Chile are allowed the same protection and operate under the same conditions as local firms. Trademarks, patents, industrial designs, models, and copyrights are protected in Chile under the Paris Convention because Chile belongs to the World Intellectual Property Organization. Trademark stockpiling is rather common in Chile, so U.S. companies are encouraged to register their trademark as soon as possible ("Made").

(continued)

Figure 16.7   A Formal Report *(Continued)*

Viva Panera!: Expanding Panera into Chile   7

This legal analysis provides Panera with a synopsis of the opportunities and restrictions available to the company when considering doing business in Chile. These legal restrictions will need to be followed if opening a facility in Chile so that any legal risk between the business and consumers or the government can be avoided.

Franchising

Chile has no franchising laws that might restrict the advancement of Panera. ("Chile"). The current franchise fee of a Panera store is $35,000 plus royalties of 4–5% of annual sales ("Panera Bread"). Because of this high startup cost, the Panera facility that would open in Chile would be company owned. After an evaluation of the success of the initial restaurant, the facility could change from being company owned to becoming a franchise with opportunities to expand in numbers of franchises.

Refer to Figure before it appears in report.

Market Possibilities and Competitors

Panera also needs to be aware of the Chilean market possibilities and current competitors, now there are about 50 franchise businesses operating in Chile with over 914 locations. As seen below in Figure 2, U.S.-run franchise operations account for 55% of the total Chilean markets mostly because of technology, convenience, and marketing strategies borrowed from the U.S.

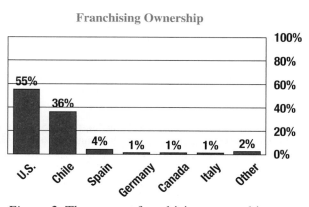

Be sure to proofread for errors such as incorrect words and comma splices.

Number Figures consecutively throughout the report.

Figure 2. The current franchising ownership in Santiago, Chile ("Franchising").

Note that spelling checkers would not catch this mistake.

American restaurant franchises currently present are Domino's Pizza, Kentucky Friend Chicken, Pizza Hut, Burger King, Dunkin Donuts, Bennigans, Chuck E. Cheese, TGI Fridays, Taco Bell, McDonalds, Au Bon Pain, and Ruby Tuesday. The local franchise competitors are Schop Dog,

(continued)

Figure 16.7   A Formal Report *(Continued)*

Viva Panera!: Expanding Panera into Chile   8

Lomito'n, and Doggis, all fast food restaurants, and Tavelli. These local competitors are in direct competition with American based franchises, especially in Santiago ("Can One Get a Decent"). This competition most likely will be positive for Panera because of the market awareness created by the competitors.

However, it should be noted that full service restaurants are listed among the best commercial opportunities because in general, they can compete with the inadequate amount of restaurants present ("Franchising"). Some café and bakery style restaurants such as Au Bon Pain, a North American chain marketed as a bakery/cafeteria serving a variety of sandwiches, salads, and breads, have done extremely well in Santiago. The marketability of Au Bon Pain restaurants and the chain's success in Chile is a key indicator that Panera could do the same ("Can One Get a Decent").

Moreover, other foreign restaurants have done equally well. For example, Doggendorf is a family-run German bakery in Santiago. The franchise began as a doughnut shop, and has now expanded into a larger commercial operation of four family-owned and run bakeries. The fact that Chileans have accepted this foreign bakery is a good indicator that Panera would also be well-accepted ("Your Complete Guide").

Conclusions repeat points made in the report. Recommendations are actions the readers should take.

Some companies ask for Conclusions and Recommendations at the beginning of the report.

Conclusions and Recommendations

Chile's unique culture and customs, progressive politics, and efficient business management along with its growing economy leads JOABA Consulting to suggest their market is ready for a new franchise. Therefore, we conclude that Panera should expand into Chile. We recommend the following process to ensure a successful expansion:

Numbering points makes it easy for readers to follow and discuss them.

1. **Expand into one location in Santiago, Chile.** Opening one store in this large city will introduce the restaurant into the Chilean culture with minimal risk. The locals will have the opportunity to show their acceptance or rejection of Panera through their patronage.
   - Start a company-owned store (as opposed to a franchise).
   - Open the store with both an American and Chilean manager so the American can train the Chilean in the business to ensure Panera's identity is maintained.
   - Hire local people in Santiago as employees.

Make sure all items in a list are parallel

2. **Evaluate the success and expansion feasibility at the end of a 12-month period.**
   - Survey locals in the area for their feedback on the restaurant.
   - Explore additional places in Santiago to expand to (if expansion is the result of the evaluation).

3. **After three years, investigate selling the company-owned stores to managers to transition the stores into franchises.**
   - Evaluate the success of the stores based on sales and community response.
   - Research the economic feasibility of this change of ownership.

Because many readers turn to the "Recommendations" first, provide enough information so that the reason is clear all by itself. The ideas in this section must be logical extensions of the points made and supported in the body of the report.

(continued)

Figure 16.7   A Formal Report *(Concluded)*

Viva Panera!: Expanding Panera into Chile   9

References   *This report uses MLA citation style*

"Business Environment." *Chile Foreign Investment Committee*. 2006. 30 March 2007.
     <http://www.cinver.cl/index/plantilla3.asp?id_seccion=7&id_subsectiones=32>.

Start with title of article or Web site when no author is given.

"Can One Get Decent Coffee in Santiago?" *Tourism Promotion Corporation of Chile*. 2006. 2 April 2006.
     <http://www.visit-chile.org/50faq/50faq-section-eng.phtml?id_secc=5>.

"Chile." *Central Intelligence Agency: The World Factbook*. 10 Jan. 2006. 29 March 2007
     <http://www.cia.gov/library/publications/the-world-factbook/geos/ci.html>.

Remove hyperlinks from URLs; enclose URLs in brackets.

"Chile: Culture and Customs." *San Marcos Church*. 30 July 2002. 30 March 2007.
     <http://www.sanmarcoschurch.cl/fr_culture.html>.

"Chile: Society, Language and Culture Guide." *Kwintessential Language and Cultural Specialists*.
     2006. 30 Mar. 2007. <http://www.kwintessential.co.uk/resources/global-etiquette/chile.html>.

"Franchising." *U.S. Commercial Service*. 2006. U.S.A. Department of Commerce. 2 April 2007.
     <www.buyusa.gov/chile>.

Franklin, Jonathan. "Chile Identified 35,000 Victims of Pinochet." *Guardian Unlimited*.
     15 November 2004. 16 June 2007.<http://www.guardian.co.uk/
     chile/story/0,13755,1351421,00.html>.

"Made in USA, Sold in Chile." *Buyusa.Gov*. 2006. U.S. Commercial Service. 29 March 2007.
     <www.buyusa.gov/chile/en>.

Nicol, Joni. "Chile." *International Business Center*. 2003. International-Business-
     Center.Com. 30 March 2007. <http://www.cyborlink.com/besite/chile.htm>.

Panera Bread. 2007. 29 Mar. 2007 <http://www.panerabread.com/>.

Rawlinson, Joe. "Chilean Food." *Pepe's Chile*. 1995-2006. Joe's Kitchen. 30 March 2007.
     <http://www.joeskitchen.com/chile/culture/food.htm>.

Santiago–Chile. "Embassy of the USA." 2007. U.S. Department of State. 29 March 2007.
     <www.usembassy.cl>.

"Typical Chilean Food and Drink." *Woodward Chile*. 28 November 2005. Woodward: A
     Different Kind of Thinking. 30 March 2007. <http://www.woodward.cl.chilefood.htm>.

"Your Complete Guide to Santiago." *Area Guides.Net*. 2006. 2 April 2007
     <http://santiagoch.ags.myareaguide.com/index.html?detailID=57577&SSC=413>.

*List all the printed and online sources cited in your report. Do not
list sources you used for background but did not cite.*

Compare this list of sources with those in the proposal. Notice how the authors had to adjust the list as they completed the research.

Background or History of the Problem (Orients the reader to the topic of the report. Serves as a record for later readers of the report.)

Body (Presents and interprets data in words and visuals. Analyzes causes of the problem and evaluates possible solutions. Specific headings will depend on the topic of the report.)

Conclusions (Summarizes main points of report.)

Recommendations (Recommends actions to solve the problem. May be combined with Conclusions; may be put at beginning of body rather than at the end.)

Notes, References, or Works Cited (Documents sources cited in the report.)

Appendixes (Provides additional materials that the careful reader may want: transcripts of interviews, copies of questionnaires, tallies of all the questions, complex tables, computer printouts, previous reports.)

As Figure 16.6 shows, not every formal report necessarily has all these components. In addition, some organizations call for additional components or arrange these components in a different order. As you read each section below, you may want to turn to the corresponding pages of the long report in Figure 16.7 to see how the component is set up and how it relates to the total report.

Title Page

The title page of a report usually contains four items: the title of the report, the person or organization for whom the report is prepared, the person or group who prepared the report, and the release date. Some title pages also contain a brief summary or abstract of the contents of the report; some title pages contain decorative artwork.

The title of the report should be as informative as possible. Like subject lines, report titles are straightforward.

Poor title: New Plant Site

Better title: Eugene, Oregon, Site for the New Kemco Plant

Large organizations that issue many reports may use two-part titles to make it easier to search for reports electronically. For example, US government report titles first give the agency sponsoring the report, then the title of that particular report.

> Small Business Administration: Management Practices Have Improved for the Women's Business Center Program

In many cases, the title will state the recommendation in the report: "Why the United Nations Should Establish a Seed Bank." However, the title should omit recommendations when

- The reader will find the recommendations hard to accept.
- Putting all the recommendations in the title would make it too long.
- The report does not offer recommendations.

If the title does not contain the recommendation, it normally indicates what problem the report tries to solve.

Eliminate any unnecessary words:

Wordy: Report of a Study on Ways to Market Life Insurance to Urban Professional People Who Are in Their Mid-40s

Better: Marketing Life Insurance to the Mid-40s Urban Professional

The identification of the receiver of the report normally includes the name of the person who will make a decision based on the report, his or her job title, the organization's name, and its location (city, state, and zip code). Government reports often omit the person's name and simply give the organization that authorized the report.

If the report is prepared primarily by one person, the *Prepared by* section will have that person's name, his or her title, the organization, and its location (city, state, and zip code). In internal reports, the organization and location are usually omitted if the report writer works at the headquarters office.

If several people write the report, government reports normally list all their names, using a separate sheet of paper if the group working on the report is large. Practices in business differ. In some organizations, all the names are listed; in others, the division to which they belong is listed; in still others, the name of the chair of the group appears.

The **release date,** the date the report will be released to the public, is usually the date the report is scheduled for discussion by the decision makers. The report is frequently due four to six weeks before the release date so that the decision makers can review the report before the meeting.

If you have the facilities and the time, try using type variations, color, and artwork to create a visually attractive and impressive title page. However, a plain typed page is acceptable. The format in Figure 16.7 will enable you to create an acceptable typed title page.

Letter or Memo of Transmittal

Use a letter of transmittal if you are not a regular employee of the organization for which you prepare the report; use a memo if you are a regular employee. See Appendix A for letter and memo formats.

The transmittal has several purposes: to transmit the report, to orient the reader to the report, and to build a good image of the report and of the writer. An informal writing style is appropriate for a transmittal even when the style in the report is more formal. A professional transmittal helps you create a good image of yourself and enhances your credibility. Personal statements are appropriate in the transmittal, even though they would not be acceptable in the report itself.

Organize the transmittal in this way:

1. **Transmit the report.** Tell when and by whom it was authorized and the purpose it was to fulfill.

2. **Summarize your conclusions and recommendations.** If the recommendations will be easy for the reader to accept, put them early in the transmittal. If they will be difficult, summarize the findings and conclusions before the recommendations.

3. **Mention any points of special interest in the report. Show how you surmounted minor problems you encountered in your investigation. Thank people who helped you.** These optional items can build goodwill and enhance your credibility.

4. **Point out additional research that is necessary, if any.** Sometimes your recommendation cannot be implemented until further work is done. If you'd be interested in doing that research, or if you'd like to implement the recommendations, say so.

5. **Thank the reader for the opportunity to do the work and offer to answer questions.** Even if the report has not been fun to do, expressing satisfaction in doing the project is expected. Saying that you'll answer questions about the report is a way of saying that you won't charge the reader your normal hourly fee to answer questions (one more reason to make the report clear!).

The letter of transmittal on page i of Figure 16.7 uses this pattern of organization.

Report Your Way to a Better Job

Joan was hired by a computer company to find references to the computer industry in current publications. To expand her job description, Joan wrote reports summarizing the data instead of just sending files of clippings. The receivers were delighted because she was saving them time.

Her second step was to meet with the people who got her reports to ask them what sorts of information they needed. Now she was able to target her reports to her readers' needs. People in each unit began to invite her to meetings discussing the projects she was researching.

As a member of the various groups within the company, Joan now had the information she needed to take a third step: drafting the report for decision makers. For example, if the sales department wanted information for a proposal to a client, she presented her information in a sales proposal. If the president wanted material for a speech, she arranged her information in a speech outline.

When the director of business communications resigned, Joan was the obvious choice for the job.

Adapted from Janice LaRouche, "I'm Stuck in a Dead-End Job," *Family Circle,* March 24, 1987, 121.

Table of Contents

In the table of contents, list the headings exactly as they appear in the body of the report. If the report is less than 25 pages, you'll probably list all the levels of headings. In a very long report, pick a level and put all the headings at that level and above in the table of contents.

Page ii of Figure 16.7 shows the table of contents.

List of Illustrations

A list of illustrations enables readers to refer to your visuals.

Report visuals comprise both tables and figures. *Tables* are words or numbers arranged in rows and columns. *Figures* are everything else: bar graphs, pie charts, flow charts, maps, drawings, photographs, computer printouts, and so on. Tables and figures may be numbered independently, so you may have both a Table 1 and a Figure 1. In a report with maps and graphs but no other visuals, the visuals are sometimes called Map 1 and Graph 1. Whatever you call the illustrations, list them in the order in which they appear in the report; give the name of each visual as well as its number.

See ◀▥ Chapter 6 for information about how to design and label visuals.

Executive Summary

An **executive summary** or **abstract** tells the reader what the document is about. It summarizes the recommendation of the report and the reasons for the recommendation or describes the topics the report discusses and indicates the depth of the discussion. It should be clear even to people who will read only the abstract.

A good abstract is easy to read, concise, and clear. Edit your abstract carefully to tighten your writing and eliminate any unnecessary words.

> Wordy: The report describes two types of business jargon, *businessese* and *reverse gobbledygook*. He gives many examples of each of these and points out how their use can be harmful.

> Tight: The report describes and illustrates two harmful types of business jargon, *businessese* and *reverse gobbledygook*.

It's OK to use exactly the same words in the abstract and the report.

Abstracts generally use a more formal style than other forms of business writing. Avoid contractions and colloquialisms. Try to avoid using the second-person *you*. Because reports may have many different readers, *you* may become inaccurate.

Summary abstracts present the logical skeleton of the article: the thesis or recommendation and its proof. Use a summary abstract to give the most useful information in the shortest space.

To market life insurance to mid-40s urban professionals, Interstate Fidelity Insurance should advertise in upscale publications and use direct mail.

Network TV and radio are not cost-efficient for reaching this market. This group comprises a small percentage of the prime-time network TV audience and a minority of most radio station listeners. They tend to discard newspapers and general-interest magazines quickly, but many of them keep upscale periodicals for months or years. Magazines with high percentages of readers in this group include *Architectural Digest, Bon Appetit, BusinessWeek, Forbes, Golf Digest, Metropolitan Home, Southern Living,* and

Smithsonian. Most urban professionals in their mid-40s are already used to shopping by mail and respond positively to well-conceived and well-executed direct mail appeals.

Any advertising campaign needs to overcome this group's feeling that they already have the insurance they need. One way to do this would be to encourage them to check the coverage their employers provide and to calculate the cost of their children's expenses through college graduation. Insurance plans that provide savings and tax benefits as well as death benefits might also be appealing.

One way to start composing an abstract is to write a sentence outline. A **sentence outline** not only uses complete sentences rather than words or phrases but also contains the thesis sentence or recommendation and the evidence that proves that point. Combine the sentences into paragraphs, adding transitions if necessary, and you'll have your abstract.

Descriptive abstracts indicate what topics the report covers and how deeply it goes into each topic, but they do not summarize what the report says about each topic. Phrases that describe the report ("this report covers," "it includes," "it summarizes," "it concludes") are marks of a descriptive abstract. An additional mark of a descriptive abstract is that the reader can't tell what the report says about the topics it covers.

This report recommends ways Interstate Fidelity Insurance could market insurance to mid-40s urban professionals. It examines demographic and psychographic profiles of the target market. Survey results are used to show attitudes toward insurance. The report suggests some appeals that might be successful with this market.

Introduction

The **Introduction** of the report always contains a statement of purpose and scope and may include all the parts in the following list.

- **Purpose.**   The purpose statement (◀ p. 493) identifies the organizational problem the report addresses, the technical investigations it summarizes, and the rhetorical purpose (to explain, to recommend).

- **Scope.**   The scope statement identifies how broad an area the report surveys. For example, Company XYZ is losing money on its line of computers. Does the report investigate the quality of the computers? The advertising campaign? The cost of manufacturing? The demand for computers? A scope statement allows the reader to evaluate the report on appropriate grounds. If the person who approved the proposal accepted a focus on advertising, then one cannot fault a report that considers only that factor.

- **Assumptions.**   Assumptions in a report are like assumptions in geometry: statements whose truth you assume, and which you use to prove your final point. If they are wrong, the conclusion will be wrong too.

   For example, to plan cars that will be built five years from now, an automobile manufacturer commissions a report on young adults' attitudes toward cars. The recommendations would be based on assumptions both about gas prices and about the economy. If gas prices radically rose or fell, the kinds of cars young adults wanted would change. If there were a major recession, people wouldn't be able to buy new cars.

   Almost all reports require assumptions. A good report spells out its assumptions so that readers can make decisions more confidently.

- **Methods.** If you conducted surveys, focus groups, or interviews, you need to tell how you chose your subjects, and how, when, and where they were interviewed. If the discussion of your methodology is more than a paragraph or two, you should probably make it a separate section in the body of the report rather than including it in the introduction. Reports based on scientific experiments usually put the methods section in the body of the report, not in the Introduction.

  If your report is based solely on library or online research, provide a brief description of significant sources. See ◄▦ Chapter 15 on how to cite and document sources.

- **Limitations.** Limitations make your recommendations less valid or valid only under certain conditions. Limitations usually arise because time or money constraints haven't permitted full research. For example, a campus pizza restaurant considering expanding its menu may ask for a report but not have enough money to take a random sample of students and townspeople. Without a random sample, the writer cannot generalize from the sample to the larger population.

  Many recommendations are valid only for a limited time. For instance, a campus store wants to know what kinds of clothing will appeal to college men. The recommendations will remain in force only for a short time: Three years from now, styles and tastes may have changed, and the clothes that would sell best now may no longer be in demand.

- **Criteria.** The criteria section outlines the factors or standards that you are considering and the relative importance of each. If a company is choosing a city for a new office, is the cost of office space more or less important than the availability of skilled workers? Check with your audience before you write the draft to make sure that your criteria match those of your readers.

- **Definitions.** Many reports define key terms in the introduction. For instance, a report on unauthorized Internet use by employees might define what is meant by "unauthorized uses." A report on the corporate dress code might define such codes broadly to include general appearance, so it could include items such as tattoos, facial piercings, and general cleanliness. Also, if you know that some members of your primary, secondary, or intermediate audience will not understand technical terms, define them. If you have only a few definitions, you can put them in the Introduction. If you have many terms to define, put a **glossary** in an appendix. Refer to it in the Introduction so that readers know that you've provided it.

Background or History

Formal reports usually have a section that gives the background of the situation or the history of the problem. Even though the current audience for the report probably knows the situation, reports are filed and consulted years later. These later audiences will probably not know the background, although it may be crucial for understanding the options that are possible.

In some cases, the history section may cover many years. For example, a report recommending that a US hotel chain open hotels in Romania may give the history of that country for at least several decades. In other cases, the history section is much briefer, covering only a few years or even just the immediate situation.

The purpose of most reports is rarely to provide a history of the problem. Do not let the background section achieve undue length.

Body

The body of the report is usually its longest section. Here you analyze causes of the problem and offer possible solutions. Here you present your argument with all its evidence and data. Data that are necessary to follow the argument are included with appropriate visuals and explanatory text. Extended data sets, such as large tables and long questionnaires, are generally placed in appendices. It is particularly important in the body that you use headings, forecasting statements, and topic sentences to help lead your readers through the body. Readers will also appreciate clear, concise, and engaging prose. Remember to cite your sources (see Chapter 15) and to refer in the text to all visuals and appendices.

Conclusions and Recommendations

Conclusions summarize points you have made in the body of the report; **Recommendations** are action items that would solve or ameliorate the problem. These sections are often combined if they are short: *Conclusions and Recommendations*. No new information should be included in this section.

Many readers turn to the recommendations section first; some organizations ask that recommendations be presented early in the report. Number the recommendations to make it easy for people to discuss them. If the recommendations will seem difficult or controversial, give a brief paragraph of rationale after each recommendation. If they'll be easy for the audience to accept, you can simply list them without comments or reasons. The recommendations will also be in the executive summary and perhaps in the title and the transmittal.

Summary of Key Points

- Good reports begin with good data. Make sure your data come from reliable sources.
- Analyze report numbers and text for accuracy and logic.
- Choose an appropriate organizational pattern for your information and purposes. The most common patterns are comparison/contrast, problem-solving, elimination, general to particular, particular to general, geographic or spatial, and functional.
- Reports use the same style as other business documents, with three exceptions:
  1. Reports use a more formal style than do many letters and memos.
  2. Reports rarely use the word *you.*
  3. Reports should include all the definitions and documents needed to understand the recommendations.
- To create good report style,
  1. Use clear, engaging writing.
  2. Keep repetition to a minimum.
  3. Introduce all sources and visuals.
  4. Use forecasting, transitions, topic sentences, and headings.

- **Headings** are single words, short phrases, or complete sentences that cover all of the material under it until the next heading. **Talking heads** tell the reader what to expect in each section.
- Headings must use the same grammatical structure. Subheads under a heading must be parallel to each other but do not necessarily have to be parallel to subheads under other headings.
- The title page of a report usually contains four items: the title of the report, whom the report is prepared for, whom it is prepared by, and the date.
- If the report is 25 pages or less, list all the headings in the table of contents. In a long report, pick a level and put all the headings at that level and above in the contents.
- Organize the transmittal in this way:
  1. Release the report.
  2. Summarize your conclusions and recommendations.
  3. Mention any points of special interest in the report. Show how you surmounted minor problems you encountered in your investigation. Thank people who helped you.
  4. Point out additional research that is necessary, if any.
  5. Thank the reader for the opportunity to do the work and offer to answer questions.
- **Summary abstracts** present the logical skeleton of the article: the thesis or recommendation and its proof. **Descriptive abstracts** indicate what topics the article covers and how deeply it goes into each topic, but do not summarize what the article says about each topic.
- A good abstract or executive summary is easy to read, concise, and clear. A good abstract can be understood by itself, without the report or references.
- The **Introduction** of the report always contains a statement of purpose and scope. The **Purpose** statement identifies the organizational problem the report addresses, the technical investigations it summarizes, and the rhetorical purpose (to explain, to recommend). The **Scope** statement identifies how broad an area the report surveys. The introduction may also include **Limitations,** problems or factors that limit the validity of your recommendations; **Assumptions,** statements whose truth you assume, and which you use to prove your final point; **Methods,** an explanation of how you gathered your data; **Criteria** used to weigh the factors in the decision; and **Definitions** of terms readers may not know.
- A **Background** or **History** section is usually included because reports are filed and may be consulted years later by people who no longer remember the original circumstances.
- The body of the report, usually the longest section, analyzes causes of the problem and offers possible solutions. It presents your argument with all evidence and data.
- **Conclusions** summarize points made in the body of the report; **Recommendations** are action items that would solve or ameliorate the problem. These sections are often combined if they are short.

CHAPTER 16   Exercises and Problems

16.1   Reviewing the Chapter

1. What are some criteria to check to ensure you have quality data? (LO 1)
2. What kinds of patterns should you look for in your data and text? (LO 1)
3. What are some guidelines for choosing information for reports? (LO 2)
4. Name seven basic patterns for organizing reports. For four of them, explain when they would be particularly effective or ineffective. (LO 3)
5. What are three ways that style in reports differs from conventional business communication style? (LO 4)
6. Name four good writing principles that are particularly important in reports. (LO 4)
7. How do you introduce sources in the text of the report? (LO 4)
8. Why should reports try to have a topic sentence at the beginning of each paragraph? (LO 4)
9. What are the characteristics of an effective report title? (LO 5)
10. What goes in the letter of transmittal? (LO 5)
11. What is the difference between summary and descriptive abstracts? (LO 5)
12. What goes in the introduction of a report? (LO5)
13. What is the difference between conclusions and recommendations? (LO 5)

16.2   Identifying Assumptions and Limitations

Indicate whether each of the following would be an assumption or a limitation in a formal report.

a. Report on Ways to Encourage More Students to Join XYZ Organization
   1. I surveyed a judgment sample rather than a random sample.
   2. These recommendations are based on the attitudes of current students. Presumably, students in the next several years will have the same attitudes and interests.
b. Report on the Feasibility of Building Hilton Hotels in Vietnam
   1. This report is based on the expectation that the country will be politically stable.
   2. All of my information is based on library research. The most recent articles were published two months ago; much of the information was published a year ago or more. Therefore some of my information may be out of date.
c. Report on Car-Buying Preferences of Young Adults
   1. These recommendations may change if the cost of gasoline increases dramatically or if there is another deep recession.
   2. This report is based on a survey of adults ages 20 to 24 in California, Texas, Illinois, Ontario, and Massachusetts.
   3. These preferences are based on the cars now available. If a major technical or styling innovation occurs, preferences may change.

16.3   Revising an Executive Summary

The following Executive Summary is poorly organized and too long. Rearrange information to make it more effective. Cut information that does not belong in the summary. You may use different words as you revise.

In this report I will discuss the communication problems which exist at Rolling Meadows Golf Club. The problems discussed will deal with channels of communication. The areas which are causing problems are internal. Radios would solve these internal problems.

Taking a 15-minute drive on a golf cart in order to find the superintendent is a common occurrence. Starters and rangers need to keep in touch with the clubhouse to maintain a smooth flow of players around the course. The rangers have expressed an interest in being able to call the clubhouse for advice and support.

Purchasing two-channel FM radios with private channels would provide three advantages. First, radios would make the golf course safer by providing a means of notifying someone in the event of an emergency. Second, radios would make the staff more efficient by providing a faster channel of communication. Third, radios would enable clubhouse personnel to keep in touch with the superintendent, the rangers, and the starters.

During the week, radios can be carried by the superintendent, the golf pro, and another course worker. On weekends and during tournaments, one radio will be used by the golf professional. The other two will be used by one starter and one ranger. Three radios is the minimum needed to meet basic communication needs. A fourth radio would provide more flexibility for busy weekends and during tournaments.

Tekk T-20 radios can be purchased from Page-Com for $129 each. These radios have the range and options needed for use on the golf course. Radios are durable and easy to service. It is possible that another brand might be even less expensive.

Rolling Meadows Golf Club should purchase four radios. They will cost under $600 and can be paid for from the current equipment budget.

16.4   Analyzing Data and Information

Every year, *Business Ethics* magazine releases its annual survey of the "100 Best Corporate Citizens." The survey measures a company's social responsibility to the environment and to their community and employees.

Go to the Web site http://www.business-ethics.com/what_new/100best.html and analyze the data and information used to create their list. Consider the following questions:

- Do the data come from a reliable source? Does the source have a vested interest in the results?
- What do the data actually measure?
- Are there any assumptions or limitations that need to be considered when analyzing these numbers?

As your instructor directs,

- Write a memo to your instructor summarizing your analysis.
- Share your analysis orally with a small group of students.
- Present your analysis to the class.

16.5   Recommending Action

Write a report recommending an action that your unit or organization should take. Possibilities include

- Buying more equipment for your department.
- Hiring an additional worker for your department.
- Making your organization more family-friendly.
- Making a change that will make the organization more efficient.
- Making changes to improve accessibility for customers or employees with disabilities.

Address your report to the person who would have the power to approve your recommendation.

As your instructor directs,

a. Create a document or presentation to achieve the goal.

b. Write a memo to your instructor describing the situation at your workplace and explaining your rhetorical choices (medium, strategy, tone, wording, graphics or document design, and so forth).

16.6   Evaluating a Report from Your Workplace

Consider the following aspects of a report from your workplace:

- Content. How much information is included? How is it presented?
- Emphasis. What points are emphasized? What points are deemphasized? What verbal and visual techniques are used to highlight or minimize information?
- Visuals and layout. Are visuals used effectively? Are they accurate and free from chartjunk? What image do the pictures and visuals create? Are color and white space used effectively? (See Chapter 6 on visuals.)

As your instructor directs,

a. Write a memo to your instructor analyzing the report.

b. Join with a small group of students to compare and contrast several reports. Present your evaluation in an informal group report.

c. Present your evaluation orally to the class.

16.7   Analyzing and Writing Reports

Reread the sidebar about the Pew Internet and American Life Project at http://www.pewinternet.org/. Go to the Web site and browse through the reports. Select a report and answer the following questions:

- Who is the report's audience?
- What is its purpose?
- How were the data collected?
- What did the data collection measure?
- Why was the data collection important?

Given your analysis of the report's audience, purpose, and data collection, consider the strategies used in the report to convey the information. Answer these questions:

- What tone did the writer adopt?
- How was the report organized and designed to meet the needs of the audience?
- What language choices did the writer make?

Finally, examine the press releases that are written about the report (the press releases for each report are included as links) for the ways the information in the report is adapted for a different audience and purpose. How do the content, organization, tone, and language choices differ from those of the original report? Do you see any ethical issues involved in condensing the report into a press release?

As your instructor directs,

- Write a report of your findings to your instructor.
- Present your findings to the class using presentation software.

16.8   Writing a Feasibility Study

Write a report evaluating the feasibility of two or more alternatives. Possible topics include the following:

1. Is it feasible to start a monthly newsletter for students in your major?

2. Is it feasible for your student organization to write an annual report? Would doing so help the next year's officers?

3. Is it feasible for your student organization to create a wiki, blog, or newsletter to facilitate communication with a constituency?

4. Is it feasible for your workplace to create a newsletter to communicate internally?

5. Is it feasible for a local restaurant to open another branch? Where should it be?

6. Is it feasible to open another student parking lot on or near campus? Where should it be?

In designing your study, identify the alternatives, define your criteria for selecting one option over others, carefully evaluate each alternative, and recommend the best course of action.

16.9   Writing an Informative or Closure Report

Write an informative report on one of the following topics.

1. What should a US or Canadian manager know about dealing with workers from _____ [you fill in the country or culture]? What factors do and do not motivate people in this group? How do they show respect and deference? Are they used to a strong hierarchy or to an egalitarian setting? Do they normally do one thing at once or many things? How important is clock time and being on time? What factors lead them to respect someone? Age?

Experience? Education? Technical knowledge? Wealth? Or what? What conflicts or miscommunications may arise between workers from this culture and other workers due to cultural differences? Are people from this culture similar in these beliefs and behaviors, or is there lots of variation?

2. What benefits do companies offer? To get information, check the Web pages of three companies in the same industry. Information about benefits is usually on the page about working for the company.

3. Describe an ethical dilemma encountered by workers in a specific organization. What is the background of the situation? What competing loyalties exist? In the past, how have workers responded? How has the organization responded? Have "whistle-blowers" been rewarded or punished? What could the organization do to foster ethical behavior?

4. Describe a problem or challenge encountered by an organization where you've worked. Describe the problem, show why it needed to be solved, tell who did what to try to solve it, and tell how successful the efforts were. Possibilities include

   - How the organization is implementing work teams, downsizing, or changing organizational culture.
   - How the organization uses e-mail or voice mail.
   - How the organization uses telecommuting.
   - How managers deal with stress, make ethical choices, or evaluate subordinates.
   - How the organization is responding to changing US demographics, the Americans with Disabilities Act, or international competition and opportunities.

16.10 Writing a Consultant's Report—Restaurant Tipping

Your consulting company has been asked to conduct a report for Diamond Enterprises, which runs three national chains: FishStix, The Bar-B-Q Pit, and Morrie's. All are medium-priced, family-friendly restaurants. The CEO is thinking of replacing optional tips with a 15% service fee automatically added to bills.

You read articles in trade journals, surveyed a random sample of 200 workers in each of the chains, and conducted an e-mail survey of the 136 restaurant managers. Here are your findings:

1. Trade journals point out that the Internal Revenue Service (IRS) audits restaurants if it thinks that servers underreport tips. Dealing with an audit is time-consuming and often results in the restaurant's having to pay penalties and interest.

2. Only one Morrie's restaurant has actually been audited by the IRS. Management was able to convince the IRS that servers were reporting tips accurately. No penalty was assessed. Management spent $1,000 on CPA and legal fees and spent over 80 hours of management time gathering data and participating in the audit.

3. Restaurants in Europe already add a service fee (usually 15%) to the bill. Patrons can add more if they choose. Local custom determines whether tips are expected and how much they should be. In Germany, for example, it is more usual to round up the bill (from 27 € to 30 €, for example) than to figure a percentage.

4. If the restaurant collected a service fee, it could use the income to raise wages for cooks and hosts and pay for other benefits, such as health insurance, rather than giving all the money to servers and bussers.

5. Morrie's servers tend to be under 25 years of age. FishStix employs more servers over 25, who are doing this for a living. The Bar-B-Q Pit servers are students in college towns.

6. In all three chains, servers oppose the idea. Employees other than servers generally support it.

	Retain tips	Change to service fee added to bill	Don't care
FishStix servers ($n = 115$)	90%	7%	3%
Bar-B-Q servers ($n = 73$)	95%	0%	5%
Morrie's servers ($n = 93$)	85%	15%	0%
Morrie's nonservers ($n = 65$)	25%	70%	5%
FishStix nonservers ($n = 46$)	32%	32%	37%
Bar-B-Q nonservers ($n = 43$)	56%	20%	25%

(Numbers do not add up to 100% due to rounding.)

7. Servers said that it was important to go home with money in their pockets (92%), that their expertise increased food sales and should be rewarded (67%), and that if a service fee replaced tips they would be likely to look for another job (45%). Some (17%) thought that if the manager distributed service-fee income, favoritism rather than the quality of work would govern how much tip income they got. Most (72%) thought that customers would not add anything beyond the 15% service fee, and many (66%) thought that total tip income would decrease and their own portion of that income would decrease (90%).

8. Managers generally support the change.

	Retain tips	Change to service fee added to bill	Don't care
FishStix managers ($n = 44$)	20%	80%	0%
Bar-B-Q managers ($n = 13$)	33%	67%	0%
Morrie's managers ($n = 58$)	55%	45%	0%

9. Comments from managers include: "It isn't fair for a cook with eight years of experience to make only $12 an hour while a server can make $25 an hour in just a couple of months," and "I could have my pick of employees if I offered health insurance."

10. Morale at Bar-B-Q seems low. This is seen in part in the low response rate to the survey.

11. In a tight employment market, some restaurants might lose good servers if they made the change. However, hiring cooks and other nonservers would be easier.

12. The current computer systems in place can handle figuring and recording the service fee. Since bills are printed by computer, an additional line could be added. Allocating the service-fee income could take extra managerial time, especially at first.

16.11   Writing a Library Research Report

Write a library research report.

As your instructor directs,

Turn in the following documents:

a. The approved proposal.

b. Two copies of the report, including

Cover.

Title Page.

Letter or Memo of Transmittal.

Table of Contents.

List of Illustrations.

Executive Summary or Abstract.

Body (Introduction, all information, recommendations). Your instructor may specify a minimum length, a minimum number or kind of sources, and a minimum number of visuals.

References or Works Cited.

c. Your notes and rough drafts.

Choose one of the following topics.

1. **Selling to College Students.**   Your car dealership is located in a university town, but the manager doubts that selling cars to college students will be profitable. You agree that college incomes are low to nonexistent, but you see some students driving late-model cars. Recommend to the dealership's manager whether to begin marketing to college students, suggesting some tactics that would be effective.

2. **Advertising on the Internet.**   You work on a team developing a marketing plan to sell high-end sunglasses. Your boss is reluctant to spend money for online advertising because she has heard that the money is mostly wasted. Also, she associates the ads with spam, which she detests. Recommend whether the company should devote some of its advertising budget to online ads. Include samples of online advertising that supports your recommendation.

3. **Improving Job Interview Questions.**   Turnover among the sales force has been high, and your boss believes the problem is that your company has been hiring the wrong people. You are part of a team investigating the problem, and your assignment is to evaluate the questions used in job interviews. Human resource personnel use tried-and-true questions like "What is your greatest strength?" and "What is your greatest weakness?" The sales manager has some creative alternatives, such as asking candidates to solve logic puzzles and seeing how they perform under stress by taking frequent phone calls during the interview. You are to evaluate the current interviewing approaches and propose changes where they would improve hiring decisions.

4. **Selling to Wal-Mart.**   Your company has a reputation for making high-quality lamps and ceiling fans sold in specialty stores. Although the company has been profitable, it could grow much faster if it sold through Wal-Mart. Your boss is excited about her recent discussions with that retailer, but she has heard from associates that Wal-Mart can be a demanding customer. She asked you to find out if there is a downside to selling through Wal-Mart and, if so, whether manufacturers can afford to say no to a business deal with the retail giant.

5. **Making College Affordable.**   The senator you work for is concerned about fast-rising costs of a college education. Students say they cannot afford their tuition bills. Colleges say they are making all the cuts they can without compromising the quality of education. In order to propose a bill that would help make college affordable for those who are qualified to attend, the senator has asked you to research alternatives for easing the problem. Recommend one or two measures the senator could include in a bill for the Senate to vote on.

6. With your instructor's permission, investigate a topic of your choice.

16.12   Writing a Recommendation Report

Write an individual or a group report.

As your instructor directs,

Turn in the following documents:

1. The approved proposal.
2. Two copies of the report, including
   Cover.
   Title Page.
   Letter or Memo of Transmittal.
   Table of Contents.
   List of Illustrations.
   Executive Summary or Abstract.
   Body (Introduction, all information, recommendations). Your instructor may specify a minimum length, a minimum number or kind of sources, and a minimum number of visuals.
   Appendixes if useful or relevant.
3. Your notes and rough drafts.

Pick one of the following topics.

1. **Improving Customer Service.**   Many customers find that service is getting poorer and workers are getting ruder. Evaluate the service in a local store, restaurant, or other organization. Are customers made to feel comfortable? Is workers' communication helpful, friendly, and respectful? Are workers knowledgeable about products and services? Do they sell them effectively? Write a report analyzing the quality of service and recommending what the organization should do to improve.

2. **Recommending Courses for the Local Community College.**   Businesses want to be able to send workers to local community colleges to upgrade their skills; community colleges want to prepare students to enter the local workforce. What skills are in demand in your community? What courses at what levels should the local community college offer?

3. **Improving Sales and Profits.**   Recommend ways a small business in your community can increase sales and profits. Focus on one or more of the following: the products or services it offers, its advertising, its decor, its location, its accounting methods, its cash management, or any other aspect that may be keeping the company from achieving its potential. Address your report to the owner of the business.

4. **Increasing Student Involvement.**   How could an organization on campus persuade more of the students who are eligible to join or to become active in its programs? Do students know that it exists? Is it offering programs that interest students? Is it retaining current members? What changes should the organization make? Address your report to the officers of the organization.

5. **Evaluating a Potential Employer.**   What training is available to new employees? How soon is the average entry-level person promoted? How much travel and weekend work are expected? Is there a "busy season," or is the workload consistent year-round? What fringe benefits are offered? What is the corporate culture? Is the climate nonracist and nonsexist? How strong is the company economically? How is it likely to be affected by current economic, demographic, and political trends? Address your report to the Placement Office on campus; recommend whether it should encourage students to work at this company.

6. With your instructor's permission, choose your own topic.

16.13   Mosaic Case

The Communications Department at Mosaic is getting ready to produce the organization's annual report that will be distributed to all investors and shareholders. Yvonne, who normally oversees the production and printing of this high-end report, is doing some reconnaissance work abroad. As a result, she passed the torch to complete this project to Sarah and Demetri, since they are responsible for Mosaic's physical stores and online communications.

For the past week, Sarah and Demetri have been frantic and on everyone's case. They know not only how important the annual report is to the image of the organization, but also the detrimental effect it could have on their jobs if they do a poor job.

Today while taking a coffee break, Sarah said to Demetri, "I'm not sure about the content of an annual report. I've seen them before, but Yvonne usually handles organizing it all. I'm not exactly sure what even needs to be included."

"I have a general idea about content," said Demetri but I'm not positive about how to arrange the visuals and layout the report in a way that will really mean something to shareholders."

Trey, who was also in the break room and overhead their conversation, suggested to them, "Why don't you just research Mosaic's past annual reports, as well as reports from similar competitors to become more comfortable with the look and conventions of the document?"

"That's a great idea, Trey," said Sarah and Demetri almost simultaneously. "I'll have Martina get right on that!" said Sarah.

Martina the intern, who coincidentally walked into the break room just then eating a banana and minding her own business, suddenly found herself as a key player in the production of Mosaic's annual report.

Take on the communication task of Martina. Research the annual reports of five major corporations (competitors) as Sarah and Demetri have asked her to do. When you are finished, write a memo to Sarah and Demetri that explains what sections are typically included in these organizations' annual reports and possible reasons for including them. If variation occurs in the typical content of corresponding sections, give Sarah and Demetri some idea of the range of variations and why you think the differences occur. In addition, figure out how the annual reports have incorporated visual displays and other pictures and how the visuals help convey information to the audience of the report (www.annualreports.com is a great place to start if you cannot locate hard copies of reports.)

Making Oral Presentations

Learning Objectives

After studying this chapter, you will know how to:

1. Plan effective presentations.

2. Select and organize information for effective presentations.

3. Deliver effective presentations.

4. Handle questions during presentations.

Toastmasters

Does public speaking make you nervous? Since 1924, Toastmasters International has been helping its members improve their public speaking abilities and deal with the challenges of oral communication. Toastmasters clubs, which exist in communities and organizations worldwide, provide forums where members can work on their speaking, networking, and leadership skills and get valuable feedback from veteran presenters.

A Toastmasters club provides a setting where you can practice speaking before a group without being under the pressure of a formal presentation setting. Most clubs have between 20 and 40 members, but no "teachers." Instead, members of the club provide feedback, support, and critiques of each others' presentations. Toastmasters doesn't focus only on public speaking, however: the clubs have resources to help you practice extemporaneous speaking, parliamentary procedure (the official rules of speaking used in formal meetings, such as government proceedings), debate, and group facilitation. You can locate a Toastmasters club near you through the Toastmasters International website: www.toastmasters.org.

"When you speak before a group, you showcase not only your communication skills, but also your ability to organize information, act as a leader, and facilitate a discussion."

Why is it important to develop public speaking skills? Because formal speaking opportunities are an important and challenging part of your professional life. When you speak before a group, you showcase not only your communication skills, but also your ability to organize information, act as a leader, and facilitate a discussion. In that regard, the same skills you develop for public speaking can also help you in difficult, one-on-one conversations such as job interviews, performance assessments, and sales pitches, where you're not only presenting your material: you're presenting yourself. It can be uncomfortable to have everyone's attention centered on you, but with practice, preparation, and attention to detail, you'll have nothing to be nervous about.

Source: Toastmasters International, "Public Speaking Skills Aren't Debatable," in *Information for Members: Press Releases*, http://www.toastmasters.org/artisan/member.asp?CategoryID=1&SubCategoryID=21&ArticleID=94&SearchText= (accessed June 16, 2007).

The power to persuade people to care about something you believe in is crucial to business success. Making a good oral presentation is more than just good delivery: it also involves developing a strategy that fits your audience and purpose, having good content, and organizing material effectively. The choices you make in each of these areas are affected by your purposes, the audience, and the situation.

Purposes in Oral Presentations

Oral presentations have the same three basic purposes that written documents have: to inform, to persuade, and to build goodwill. Like written messages, most oral presentations have more than one purpose.

Informative presentations inform or teach the audience. Training sessions in an organization are primarily informative. Secondary purposes may be to persuade new employees to follow organizational procedures, rather than doing something their own way, and to help them appreciate the organizational culture.

Persuasive presentations motivate the audience to act or to believe. Giving information and evidence is an important means of persuasion. Stories, visuals, and self-disclosure are also effective. In addition, the speaker must build goodwill by appearing to be credible and sympathetic to the audience's needs. The goal in many presentations is a favorable vote or decision. For example, speakers making business presentations may try to persuade the audience to approve their proposals, to adopt their ideas, or to buy their products. Sometimes the goal is to change behavior or attitudes or to reinforce existing attitudes. For example, a speaker at a meeting of factory workers may stress the importance of following safety procedures. A speaker at a church meeting may talk about the problem of homelessness in the community and try to build support for community shelters for the homeless.

Goodwill presentations entertain and validate the audience. In an after-dinner speech, the audience wants to be entertained. Presentations at sales meetings may be designed to stroke the audience's egos and to validate their commitment to organizational goals.

Make your purpose as specific as possible.

Weak: The purpose of my presentation is to discuss saving for retirement.

Better: The purpose of my presentation is to persuade my audience to put their 401k funds in stocks and bonds, not in money market accounts and CDs.

or: The purpose of my presentation is to explain how to calculate how much money someone needs to save in order to maintain a specific lifestyle after retirement.

Write down your purpose before you start preparing your presentation. Note that the purpose is *not* the introduction of your talk; it is the principle that guides your choice of strategy and content.

Comparing Written and Oral Messages

Giving a presentation is in many ways very similar to writing a message. All of the chapters up to this point—on using you-attitude and positive emphasis, developing benefits, analyzing your audience, designing slides, overcoming objections, doing research, and analyzing data—remain relevant as you plan an oral presentation.

A written message makes it easier to

- Present extensive or complex financial data.
- Present many specific details of a law, policy, or procedure.
- Minimize undesirable emotions.

Oral messages make it easier to

- Use emotion to help persuade the audience.
- Focus the audience's attention on specific points.
- Answer questions, resolve conflicts, and build consensus.
- Modify a proposal that may not be acceptable in its original form.
- Get immediate action or response.

Oral and written messages have many similarities. In both, you should

- Adapt the message to the specific audience.
- Show the audience how they would benefit from the idea, policy, service, or product.

Oral presentation skills are a big asset in the business world.

Selling Your Message

A lot of schools teach the "art" of advertising. But not one has a course or section devoted to the brutally important topic of presenting. Presentation skills are critical to an ad exec's career, especially in the creative department. And not just in pitches [selling a campaign to a client]. If you cannot sell yourself, how can you hope to sell anything? . . .

Being nervous is OK. It is not a sign of weakness. It's a sign of respect. Tell your clients that. I do this all the time. It works before speeches as well. People will warm up to you. Remember, some of the best performances begin with a healthy dose of stage fright. . . .

So many people try to cover up and play cool. . . . You know they know [you're afraid], and you end up stuttering and saying "basically" too much. Be honest about your nerves. Tell them this is the biggest meeting you've ever been in and of course you're nervous. Tell them it would be disrespectful if you weren't. Not only is it the truth, it's a great opener. . . .

When all is said and done, confidence tempered by respect is the most important trait a team can bring into the room. Second only to big ideas and a cashmere jacket from Barneys.

Quoted from Steffan Postaer, "The Rules of Presenting," *Adweek*, February 24, 2003, 19.

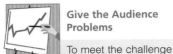

Give the Audience Problems

To meet the challenge of getting and keeping the audience's interest, some speakers are adapting a method used by teachers: problem-based learning. With this technique, students identify a problem and learn principles and methods for solving the problem, often working as a group.

For presentations, speakers apply problem-based learning in various ways:

- They might present the topic in terms of a problem to be solved. For example, if the topic is employee morale, the speaker might describe an employee who feels unappreciated.

- The speaker might ask audience members to work in pairs and brainstorm possible sources of the problem. This activity might last just five minutes, but it gets the audience alert, focused, and involved in the topic.

- The presentation should allow plenty of time for questions. Before replying to a question, the speaker might ask audience members to suggest solutions.

- The presenter should offer resources for further learning after the presentation is over. Motivating participants to continue learning is one of the goals of problem-based learning.

A common thread of the various techniques is that they shift the presenter's role. Not just a deliverer of information, the presenter aims to help the audience learn.

Adapted from Richard T. Kasuya, "Give Your Audience a Problem and They Will Learn," *Presentations* 18, no. 8 (August 2004): 46.

- Overcome any objections the audience may have.
- Use you-attitude and positive emphasis.
- Use visuals to clarify or emphasize material.
- Specify exactly what the audience should do.

Planning a Strategy for Your Presentation

A **strategy** is your plan for reaching your specific goals with a specific audience.

In all oral presentations, simplify what you want to say. Identify the one idea you want the audience to take home. Simplify your supporting detail so it's easy to follow. Simplify visuals so they can be taken in at a glance. Simplify your words and sentences so they're easy to understand. Researchers at Bell Labs are practicing these techniques. Where once they spent their days on basic research and academic papers, they now are condensing their scientific work into eight-minute PowerPoint presentations for potential corporate partners and venture capital as the Lab's new director seeks to make it profitable.[1]

An oral presentation needs to be simpler than a written message to the same audience. If readers forget a point, they can turn back to it and reread the paragraph. Headings, paragraph indentation, and punctuation provide visual cues to help readers understand the message. Listeners, in contrast, must remember what the speaker says. Whatever they don't remember is lost. Even asking questions requires the audience to remember which points they don't understand.

Analyze your audience for an oral presentation just as you do for a written message. If you'll be speaking to co-workers, talk to them about your topic or proposal to find out what questions or objections they have. For audiences inside the organization, the biggest questions are often practical ones: Will it work? How much will it cost? How long will it take? How will it impact me?

Think about the physical conditions in which you'll be speaking. Will the audience be tired at the end of a long day of listening? Sleepy after a big meal? Will the group be large or small? The more you know about your audience, the better you can adapt your message to them.

Choosing the Kind of Presentation

Choose one of three basic kinds of presentations: monologue, guided discussion, or interactive.

In a **monologue presentation,** the speaker speaks without interruption; questions are held until the end of the presentation, where the speaker functions as an expert. The speaker plans the presentation in advance and delivers it without deviation. This kind of presentation is the most common in class situations, but it's often boring for the audience. Good delivery skills are crucial, since the audience is comparatively uninvolved.

In a **guided discussion,** the speaker presents the questions or issues that both speaker and audience have agreed on in advance. Rather than functioning as an expert with all the answers, the speaker serves as a facilitator to help the audience tap its own knowledge. This kind of presentation is excellent for presenting the results of consulting projects, when the speaker has specialized knowledge, but the audience must implement the solution if it is to succeed. Guided discussions need more time than monologue presentations, but produce more audience response, more responses involving analysis, and more commitment to the result.

An **interactive presentation** is a conversation, even if the speaker stands up in front of a group and uses charts and overheads. Most sales presentations are interactive presentations. The sales representative uses questions to determine the buyer's needs, probe objections, and gain provisional and then final commitment to the purchase. Even in a memorized sales presentation, the buyer will talk a significant portion of the time. Top salespeople let the buyer do the majority of the talking.

Adapting Your Ideas to the Audience

Measure the message you'd like to send against where your audience is now. If your audience is indifferent, skeptical, or hostile, focus on the part of your message the audience will find most interesting and easiest to accept.

Don't seek a major opinion change in a single oral presentation. If the audience has already decided to hire an advertising agency, then a good presentation can convince them that your agency is the one to hire. But if you're talking to a small business that has always done its own ads, limit your purpose. You may be able to prove that an agency can earn its fees by doing things the owner can't do and by freeing the owner's time for other activities. Only after the audience is receptive should you try to persuade the audience to hire your agency rather than a competitor.

Make your ideas relevant to your audience by linking what you have to say to their experiences and interests. Showing your audience that the topic affects them directly is the most effective strategy. When you can't do that, at least link the topic to some everyday experience.

> When was the last time you were hungry? Maybe you remember being hungry while you were on a diet, or maybe you had to work late at a lab and didn't get back to the dorm in time for dinner.

Speech about world hunger to an audience of college students

Planning a Strong Opening and Closing

The beginning and the end of a presentation, like the beginning and the end of a written document, are positions of emphasis. Use those key positions to interest the audience and emphasize your key point. You'll sound more natural and more effective if you talk from notes but write out your opener and close in advance and memorize them. (They'll be short: just a sentence or two.)

Consider using one of the four modes for openers that appeared in Chapter 12 (pp. 394–95): startling statement, narration or anecdote, question, or quotation. The more you can do to personalize your opener for your audience, the better. Recent events are better than things that happened long ago; local events are better than events at a distance; people they know are better than people who are only names.

Startling statement

> Twelve of our customers have canceled orders in the past month.

This presentation to a company's executive committee went on to show that the company's distribution system was inadequate and to recommend a third warehouse located in the Southwest.

Strategy for a Corporate Speech

Security directors of the 50 most prominent international banks meet periodically to discuss common problems. BankAmerica's Bob Beck wanted to talk to the group about chemical dependency and BankAmerica's approach to the problem.

Audience's initial position: Resistant. Most favored testing, not treatment.

One point to leave with audience: Treatment is a practical alternative that works.

Adapting message to audience: Used terms from sports, banking, and security to make it easy for audience to identify with message. Backed up points with details and statistics. Explained problems of drug testing. Did not ask for action.

Opener: Hard-hitting statistics on how much chemical dependency costs US businesses—$26 billion a year.

Outline: (1) Chemical dependency as a disease; the size of the problem; testing as the usual response. (2) BankAmerica's treatment approach: policy, program design, and education in the workplace. (3) The business advantages of treatment: protects investment in trained people; confines business losses caused by chemical dependency.

Adapted from Robin Welling, *No Frills, No Nonsense, No Secrets* (San Francisco: International Association of Business Communicators, 1988), 290–93.

Narration or anecdote

When the salespeople for a company that sells storage of backed-up computer data give presentations to clients, they open by telling a story:

> A consultant asked a group of people how many of them had [a backup plan]. One brave soul from a bank raised his hand and said, "I've got a disaster recovery plan—complete and ready to go into action. It's real simple, just one page." And the consultant asked, "A one-page disaster plan? What would you do if your computer center blew up, or flooded, or caught on fire? How could you recover with just a one-page disaster plan?" He said, "Well, it's really very simple. It's a two-step plan. First, I maintain my résumé up-to-date at all times. And second, I store a backup copy off-site."[2]

This anecdote breaks the ice in introducing an uncomfortable subject: the possibility of a company losing valuable data. It uses humor to make major points—that a variety of disasters are possible, many firms are unprepared, and the consequences are great. The client will be more open to listening than if the salespeople started by questioning the client's own planning.

Even better than canned stories are anecdotes that happened to you. The best anecdotes are parables that contain the point of your talk.

Question

Asking the audience to raise their hands or reply to questions gets them actively involved in a presentation. Tony Jeary skillfully uses this technique in sessions devoted to training the audience in presentation skills. He begins by asking the audience members to write down their estimate of the number of presentations they give per week:

> "How many of you said one or two?" he asks, raising his hand. A few hands pop up. "Three, four, six, eight?" he asks, walking up the middle of the aisle to the back of the room. Hands start popping up like targets in a shooting gallery. Jeary's Texas drawl accelerates and suddenly the place sounds like a cattle auction. "Do I hear 10? Twelve? Thirteen to the woman in the green shirt! Fifteen to the gentlemen in plaid," he fires, and the room busts out laughing.[3]

Most presenters will not want to take a course in auctioneering, as Jeary did to make his questioning routine more authentic. However, Jeary's approach both engages the audience and makes the point that many jobs involve a multitude of occasions requiring formal and informal presentation skills.

Quotation

> According to Towers Perrin, the profits of Fortune 100 companies would be 25% lower—they'd go down $17 billion—if their earnings statements listed the future costs companies are obligated to pay for retirees' health care.

This presentation on options for health care for retired employees urges executives to start now to investigate options to cut the future costs.

Your opener should interest the audience and establish a rapport with them. Some speakers use humor to achieve those goals. However, an inappropriate joke can turn the audience against the speaker. Never use humor that's directed against the audience. For example, the following joke was effective in the context of an oil company executive addressing other industry members about government regulations—and would have been disastrous if told to a group that included environmentalists:

> [When regulations slowed the construction of a chemical plant,] I got to feeling a little like Moses crossing the Red Sea with the Egyptians in hot pursuit. When Moses asked God for help, God looked down and said, "I've got some good news and some bad news. The good news is that I'll part the Red Sea, let your people pass through, and then destroy the Egyptians." "That's great," said Moses. "What's the bad news?" God said, "First you have to file an environmental impact statement."[4]

When in doubt about humor, be sure it makes fun of yourself and your own group, not of others.

Humor isn't the only way to set an audience at ease. Smile at your audience before you begin; let them see that you're a real person and a nice one.

The end of your presentation should be as strong as the opener. For your close, you could do one or more of the following:

- Restate your main point.
- Refer to your opener to create a frame for your presentation.
- End with a vivid, positive picture.
- Tell the audience exactly what to do to solve the problem you've discussed.

When Mike Powell described his work in science to an audience of nonscientists, he opened and then closed with words about what being a scientist feels like. He opened humorously, saying, "Being a scientist is like doing a jigsaw puzzle . . . in a snowstorm . . . at night . . . when you don't have all the pieces . . . and you don't have the picture you are trying to create." Powell closed by returning to the opening idea of "being a scientist," but he moved from the challenge to the inspiration with this vivid story:

> The final speaker at a medical conference [I] attended . . . walked to the lectern and said, "I am a thirty-two-year-old wife and mother of two. I have AIDS. Please work fast."[5]

When you write out your opener and close, be sure to use oral rather than written style. As you can see in the example close above, oral style uses shorter sentences and shorter, simpler words than writing does. Oral style can even sound a bit choppy when it is read by eye. Oral style uses more personal pronouns, a less varied vocabulary, and more repetition.

Planning Presentation Visuals

Visuals can give your presentation a professional image and greater impact. One study found that in an informative presentation, multimedia (PowerPoint slides with graphics and animation) produced 5% more learning than overheads made from the slides and 16% more learning than text alone.[6]

Well-designed visuals can serve as an outline for your talk (see Figure 17.1), eliminating the need for additional notes. Visuals can help your audience follow along with you, and help you keep your place as you speak. Your visuals should highlight your main points, not give every detail. Elaborate on your visuals as you talk; most people find it boring to have slide after slide read to them.

Build Interest through Multimedia

One of the fastest ways to engage your audience is through a multimedia presentation that combines text, images, animation, video, and sound. Though multimedia was once an expensive, time-consuming option, you can incorporate simple multimedia techniques into your own presentations:

- Add video clips and sound clips to your *PowerPoint* presentations.
- Use a screen-capture program like *Camtasia* to create interactive demonstration movies.
- Create your own animated banner ads and product brochures using *Flash*.
- Convert your printed brochure into a website for your clients to visit.

The next time you surf the internet, pay close attention to your favorite websites. What examples of multimedia do you see? How do those sites use multimedia to grab your attention?

Adapted from Guy D. Ball, "Creating Multimedia Presentations for Training," *Intercom*, May 2005, 25–26.

Figure 17.1   Poorly Formatted Presentation Slides (Top) and Well-Formatted Slides (Bottom)

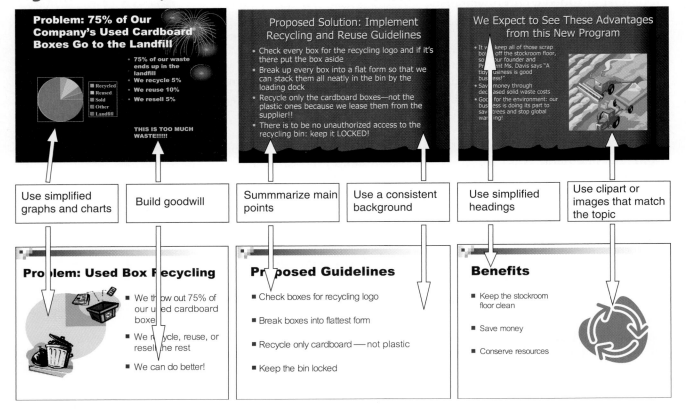

Designing presentation slides

As you design slides for PowerPoint and other presentation programs, keep the following guidelines in mind:

- Use a big font size: 44 or 50 point for titles, 32 point for subheads, and 28 point for examples. You should be able to read the smallest words easily when you print a handout version of your slides.
- Use bullet-point phrases rather than complete sentences.
- Use clear, concise language.
- Make only three to five points on each slide. If you have more, consider using two slides.
- Customize your slides with your organization's logo, and add visuals: charts, pictures, downloaded Web pages, and photos and drawings.

Use **animation** to make words and images appear and move during your presentation—but only in ways that help you control information flow and build interest. For example, in a sales presentation for Portola Packaging, a bar graph showing sales growth was redesigned to highlight the company's strong performance: instead of static bars, the graph featured upward-sloping arrows drawn from the initial sales level to the new, higher level. The presenter clicks the mouse once to display the graph title and labels; with the second mouse click, the arrow wipes up, emphasizing the growth pattern.[7] Avoid using animation or sound effects just to be clever; they will distract your audience.

Use **clip art** in your presentations only if the art is really appropriate to your points and only if you use nonsexist and nonracist images. In the 1990s,

Marilyn Dyrud found the major clip art packages to be biased.[8] Today, however, Internet sources have made such a wide variety of drawings and photos available that designers really have no excuse for failing to pick an inclusive and visually appealing image. Even organizations on tight budgets can find free and low-cost resources, such as the public domain (that is, not copyrighted) collections of the US Fish and Wildlife Service (http://images. fws.gov) and the National Oceanic and Atmospheric Administration (http:// www.photolib.noaa.gov/).

Choose a consistent **template,** or background design, for your entire presentation. Make sure that the template is appropriate for your subject matter and audience. For example, use a globe only if your topic is international business and palm trees only if you're talking about tropical vacations. One problem with PowerPoint is that the basic templates may seem repetitive to people who see lots of presentations made with the program. For an important presentation, you may want to consider customizing the basic template. You can also find many professionally designed templates available for free to download online to help lend your presentation a more unique look.

Choose a light **background** if the lights will be off during your presentation and a dark background if the lights will be on. Slides will be easier to read if you use high contrast between the words and backgrounds. See Figure 17.2 for examples of effective and ineffective color combinations.

Using visuals in your presentation

Visuals for presentations need to be simpler than visuals the audience reads on paper. For example, to adapt a printed data table for a presentation, you might cut out one or more columns or rows of data, round off the data to simplify them, or replace the chart with a graph or other visual. If you have many data tables or charts in your presentation, consider including them on a handout for your audience.

Your presentation visuals should include titles, but don't need figure numbers. As you prepare your presentation, be sure to know where each visual is so that you can return to it easily if someone asks about it during the question period. Rather than reading from your slides, or describing visuals to your audience in detail, summarize the story contained on each slide and elaborate on what it means for your audience.

Figure 17.2 Effective and Ineffective Colors for Presentation Slides

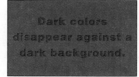

http://norvig.com/ Gettysburg

Not every speech needs visuals. As Peter Norvig shows, Lincoln's Gettysburg Address is hurt, not helped, by adding bland PowerPoint slides.

Using technology to involve your audience

Projected visuals work only if the technology they depend on works. When you give presentations in your own workplace, check the equipment in advance. When you make a presentation in another location or for another organization, arrive early so that you'll have time to not only check the equipment but also track down a service worker if the equipment isn't working. Be prepared with a backup plan to use if you're unable to show your visuals.

Keep in mind how you will use your presentation slides. Most likely, they will provide visual support for an oral presentation in a face-to-face meeting or videoconference. The slides should visually identify the key points of your presentation in a way that allows you to interact with your audience. Your oral presentation should always include more material than the text on your slides. If the audience can read the entire presentation for themselves, why are you there?

Consider ways to stimulate your audience's curiosity, invite questions, and build enthusiasm. For instance, instead of saying, "Sales grew 85% with this program," you could show a graph that shows sales declining up to the introduction of the program; invite the audience to consider what this program might do; and finally, after explaining the program, reveal the full sales graph with an animation that highlights the spike using a dramatic magenta line.

You can also involve the audience in other ways. Demonstrations are effective, especially to teach a process and to show how a product works or what it can do for the audience. Hewlett-Packard has developed a series of presentations that show consumers how to use its products for applications that may be unfamiliar. In one presentation, demonstrators teach how to use an HP computer to prepare digital photographs. A specialist showed how to restore a 50-year-old photograph of a football team. When she was done, she commented that the picture included her father, who had died two years earlier, and she planned to give the restored photo to her mother. The personal information made her presentation memorable and brought home the value of learning the skill she was teaching.[9]

In another presentation, the speaker used himself as an illustration. Sam Reese, then vice president of sales at Kinko's, wanted to fire up a sales force he thought had grown complacent with past successes. Reese wanted to shift their attention from the past to the challenges of the future. During the company's national sales meeting, he stated this position and proclaimed, "We're planning on being successful, and I'm not letting up." Then he took off his shoes and his shirt. Reese continued with his speech and then removed his pants. Underneath were a singlet and shorts—the track suit Reese had worn as a star runner at Colorado University. Reese explained that as silly as it was for him, in his midthirties, to boast of being "one of the fastest guys in the country," it was equally misguided for the salespeople to continue "living in the past." The audience laughed but took the message to heart. That year, sales at Kinko's shot up again.[10]

Choosing Information to Include in a Presentation

Choose the information that is most interesting to your audience and that answers the questions your audience will have. Limit your talk to three main points. In a long presentation (20 minutes or more) each main point can have subpoints. Your content will be easier to understand if you clearly show the relationship between each of the main points. Turning your information into a story also helps. For example, a presentation about a plan to reduce scrap rates on the second shift can begin by setting the scene and defining the problem: Production expenses have cut profits in half. The plot unfolds as the speaker describes the facts that helped her trace the problem to scrap rates on the second shift. The resolution to the story is her group's proposal.

One way to keep the choice of supporting information focused on what the audience needs to know is to start by writing the conclusion. Then move backward, identifying the main points that lead to this conclusion.

As part of choosing what to say, you should determine what data to present, including what to show in visuals. Any data you mention should be related to the points you are making. Databases and presentation software (such as PowerPoint) have given employees direct access to ready-made and easy-to-create slides. The temptation is to choose these and sprinkle them throughout the presentation, rather than starting with decisions about what the audience needs to know. Corporate trainer Pam Gregory observes, "What presentations are supposed to do is save the audience time in sifting through data themselves. But often presentations are overloaded with data; there may be an argument but it is buried."[11]

Statistics and numbers can be convincing if you present them in ways that are easy to hear. Simplify numbers by reducing them to two significant digits.

Hard to hear: Crude petroleum and natural gas extraction in the United States produced $85,906,216,000 in sales revenues in 2002.

Easy to hear: Crude petroleum and natural gas extraction in the United States produced almost $86 billion in sales revenues in 2002.[12]

In an informative presentation, link the points you make to the knowledge your audience has. Show the audience members that your information answers their questions, solves their problems, or helps them do their jobs. When you explain the effect of a new law or the techniques for using a new machine, use specific examples that apply to the decisions they make and the work they do. If your content is detailed or complicated, give people a written outline or handouts. The written material both helps the audience keep track of your points during the presentation and serves as a reference after the talk is over.

To be convincing, you must answer the audience's questions and objections.

> Some people think that working women are less reliable than men. But the facts show that women take fewer sick days than men do.

Trade show entries use visuals and oral presentations to convey information.

Sharing the Stage with Visuals

The audience can look at the speaker or the visual, but not both at the same time. An effective speaker directs the audience's attention to the visual and then back to the speaker, rather than trying to compete with the visual.

When Steve Mandel coaches clients on public speaking, he teaches them to use brief silences for visuals, so the audience has time to pay attention. For example, a speaker might say, "I've just talked to you about several problems you might experience. Now I'd like you to see a possible solution." Then the speaker shows the slide without talking for several seconds. This gives the audience time to absorb the contents of the slide. The presenter can regain attention by stepping toward the audience as he or she begins to speak again.

At its sales workshops, Communispond teaches a technique called "think-turn-talk." The presenter stands next to the visual and points to it with an open hand, thinking of what he or she intends to say. Then the presenter turns and makes eye contact with a person in the audience. Finally, the presenter talks. Communispond also teaches presenters to walk toward the audience when giving details from a visual. The connection is between presenter and audience, not presenter and slide.

Adapted from Dave Zielinski, "Perfect Practice," *Presentations* 17, no. 5 (2003): 30–36; and Julia Chang, "Back to School," *Sales and Marketing Management* 156, no. 7 (2004): 28–31.

However, don't bring up negatives or inconsistencies unless you're sure that the audience will think of them. If you aren't sure, save your evidence for the question phase. If someone does ask, you'll have the answer.

Quotations work well as long as you cite authorities whom your audience genuinely respects. Often you'll need to paraphrase a quote to put it into simple language that's easy to understand. Be sure to tell whom you're citing: "According to Al Gore," "An article in *BusinessWeek points* out that," and so forth.

Demonstrations can prove your points dramatically and quickly. During the investigation of the space shuttle *Challenger* disaster, the late physicist Richard Feynman asked for a glass of water. When it came, he put a piece of the space shuttle's O-ring into the cold water. After less than a minute, he took it out and pinched it with a small clamp. The material kept the pinched shape when the clamp came off. The material couldn't return to its original shape.[13] A technical explanation could have made the same point: the O-ring couldn't function in the cold. But the demonstration was fast and easy to understand. It didn't require that the audience follow complex chemical or mathematical formulas. In an oral presentation, seeing is believing.

Demonstrations can also help people remember your points. Dieticians had long known that coconut oil, used on movie popcorn, was bad for you. But no one seemed to care. Until, that is, the folks at the Center for Science in the Public Interest (CSPI) took up the cause. They called a press conference to announce that a medium (and who eats just a medium?) movie popcorn had more saturated fat than a bacon-and-eggs breakfast, a Big Mac and fries lunch, and a steak dinner with all the trimmings—combined. They provided the full buffet for TV cameras. The story played on all the major networks as well as the front pages of many newspapers. Even better, people remembered the story and popcorn sales plunged.[14]

In their book *Made to Stick: Why Some Ideas Survive and Others Die*, Chip Heath and Dan Heath say that ideas are remembered—and have lasting impact on people's opinions and behavior—when they have six characteristics:

1. **Simplicity:** they are short but filled with meaning; both demonstrations above could be comprehended in seconds.
2. **Unexpectedness:** they have some novelty for us: a bag of movie popcorn is worse than a whole day's meals of fatty foods.
3. **Concreteness:** the ideas must be explained with psychological description (see page 387) or in terms of human actions.
4. **Credibility:** ideas have to carry their own credibility if they do not come from an acknowledged expert. In both demonstrations above, people could see the effects for themselves.
5. **Emotions:** the ideas must make people feel some emotion, and it has to be the right emotion. Antismoking campaigns for teenagers have not been successful using fear, but they have had some success using resentment at the duplicity of cigarette companies.
6. **Stories:** the ideas have to tell stories.

The Heaths call the combination of these six factors stickiness. And the concept really works. Amounts of saturated fats are not exciting ideas, but CSPI changed movie popcorn with its demonstration.[15]

Organizing Your Information

Most presentations use a direct pattern of organization, even when the goal is to persuade a reluctant audience. In a business setting, the audience is in a hurry and knows that you want to persuade them. Be honest about your goal, and then prove that your goal meets the audience's needs too.

In a persuasive presentation, start with your strongest point, your best reason. If time permits, give other reasons as well and respond to possible objections. Put your weakest point in the middle so that you can end on a strong note.

Often one of five standard patterns of organization will work:

- **Chronological.** Start with the past, move to the present, and end by looking ahead. This pattern works best when the history helps show a problem's complexity or magnitude, or when the chronology moves people to an obvious solution.

- **Problem–causes–solution.** Explain the symptoms of the problem, identify its causes, and suggest a solution. This pattern works best when the audience will find your solution easy to accept.

- **Excluding alternatives.** Explain the symptoms of the problem. Explain the obvious solutions first and show why they won't solve the problem. End by discussing a solution that will work. This pattern may be necessary when the audience will find the solution hard to accept.

- **Pro–con.** Give all the reasons in favor of something, then those against it. This pattern works well when you want the audience to see the weaknesses in its position.

- **1–2–3.** Discuss three aspects of a topic. This pattern works well to organize short informative briefings. "Today I'll review our sales, production, and profits for the last quarter."

Make your organization clear to your audience. Written documents can be reread; they can use headings, paragraphs, lists, and indentations to signal levels of detail. In a presentation, you have to provide explicit clues to the structure of your discourse.

Early in your talk—perhaps immediately after your opener—provide an overview of the main points you will make.

> First, I'd like to talk about who the homeless in Columbus are. Second, I'll talk about the services The Open Shelter provides. Finally, I'll talk about what you—either individually or as a group—can do to help.

An overview provides a mental peg that hearers can hang each point on. It also can prevent someone from missing what you are saying because he or she wonders why you aren't covering a major point that you've saved for later.

Offer a clear signpost as you come to each new point. A **signpost** is an explicit statement of the point you have reached. Choose wording that fits your style. The following statements are four different ways that a speaker could use to introduce the last of three points:

> Now we come to the third point: what you can do as a group or as individuals to help homeless people in Columbus.

> So much for what we're doing. Now let's talk about what you can do to help.

> You may be wondering, what can I do to help?

> As you can see, the Shelter is trying to do many things. We could do more things with your help.

Being Interviewed by the Press

Business people and community leaders are often interviewed by the press. To appear your best on camera, on tape, or in a story,

- Try to find out in advance why you're being interviewed and what information the reporter wants.

- Practice answering possible questions in a single sentence. A long answer is likely to be cut for TV or radio news.

- Talk slowly. You'll have time to think, the audience will have more time to understand what you're saying, and a reporter taking notes will record your words more accurately.

- To reduce the possibility of being misquoted, make your own recording.

Adapted from James L. Graham, "What to Do When a Reporter Calls," *IABC Communication World*, April 1985, 15; and Robert A. Papper, Personal communication with Kitty Locker, March 17, 1991.

Delivering an Effective Presentation

Audiences want the sense that you're talking directly to them and that you care that they understand and are interested. They'll forgive you if you get tangled up in a sentence and end it ungrammatically. They won't forgive you if you seem to have a "canned" talk that you're going to deliver no matter who the audience is or how they respond. You can convey a sense of caring to your audience by making direct eye contact with them and by using a conversational style.

Dealing with Fear

Feeling nervous is normal. But you can harness that nervous energy to help you do your best work. As one student said, you don't need to get rid of your butterflies. All you need to do is make them fly in formation.

To calm your nerves before you give an oral presentation,

- Be prepared. Analyze your audience, organize your thoughts, prepare visual aids, practice your opener and close, check out the arrangements.
- Use only the amount of caffeine you normally use. More or less may make you jumpy.
- Avoid alcoholic beverages.
- Relabel your nerves. Instead of saying, "I'm scared," try saying, "My adrenaline is up." Adrenaline sharpens our reflexes and helps us do our best.

Just before your presentation,

- Consciously contract and then relax your muscles, starting with your feet and calves and going up to your shoulders, arms, and hands.
- Take several deep breaths from your diaphragm.

During your presentation,

- Pause and look at the audience before you begin speaking.
- Concentrate on communicating well.
- Use body energy in strong gestures and movement.

Using Eye Contact

Look directly at the people you're talking to. In one study, observers were more than twice as likely to notice and comment on poor presentation features, like poor eye contact, than good features, and tended to describe speakers with poor eye contact as disinterested, unprofessional, and poorly prepared.[16] In another study, subjects rated speakers who made more eye contact and longer eye contact as being friendlier and more engaged than speakers who had poor eye contact—especially when speakers combined good eye contact with friendly facial expressions.[17]

The point in making eye contact is to establish one-on-one contact with the individual members of your audience. People want to feel that you're talking to them. Looking directly at individuals also enables you to be more conscious of feedback from the audience, so that you can modify your approach if necessary.

Michael Campbell suggests some techniques to improve eye contact. Make eye contact before you start speaking. With each person, make eye contact for about five seconds. Then look at someone else for about five seconds. If you can, pick a few friendly faces in different parts of the room, so that you feel encouraged. Without the five-second eye contact, your gaze will appear to be roving aimlessly around the room. If you are reading notes or a speech, pause while you read, and then make eye contact while you speak.[18]

Developing a Good Speaking Voice

People will enjoy your presentation more if your voice is easy to listen to. To find out what your voice sounds like, tape-record it. Also tape the voices of people on TV or on campus whose voices you like and imitate them. In a few weeks, tape yourself again.

When you speak to a group, talk loudly enough so that people can hear you easily. If you're using a microphone, adjust your volume so you aren't shouting. When you speak in an unfamiliar location, try to get to the room early so you can check the size of the room and the power of the amplification equipment. If you can't do that, ask early in your talk, "Can you hear me in the back of the room?"

The bigger the group is, the more carefully you need to **enunciate,** that is, voice all the sounds of each word. Words starting or ending with *f, t, k, v,* and *d* are especially hard to hear. "Our informed and competent image" can sound like "Our informed, incompetent image."

You can reduce the number of *uhs* you use by practicing your talk several times. Filler sounds aren't signs of nervousness. Instead, say psychologists at Columbia University, they occur when speakers pause searching for the next word. Searching takes longer when people have big vocabularies or talk about topics where a variety of word choices are possible. Practicing your talk makes your word choices automatic, and you'll use fewer *uhs.* People become more conscious of fillers and less likely to use them when they record and listen to their voice or ask someone to listen and point out the fillers. This is one of the reasons it is important to rehearse delivering the speech—that is, literally say it out loud as if you have an audience. According to David Green, curriculum director for Dale Carnegie & Associates, presenters typically spend too much time thinking about what they will say and too little time rehearsing how they will say it. In Green's opinion, "if it were only about the material, we could simply e-mail our presentations to audiences and have them e-mail any questions back."[19]

Use your voice as you would use your facial expressions: to create a cheerful, energetic, and enthusiastic impression for your audience. Doing so can help you build rapport with your audience, and can demonstrate the importance of your material. If your ideas don't excite you, why should your audience find them exciting?

Standing and Gesturing

Stand with your feet far enough apart for good balance, with your knees flexed. Unless the presentation is very formal or you're on camera, you can walk if you want to. Some speakers like to come in front of the lectern to remove that barrier between themselves and the audience.

If you use slides or transparencies, stand beside the screen so that you don't block it.

Build on your natural style for gestures. Gestures usually work best when they're big and confident.

Avoid nervous gestures such as swaying on your feet, jingling coins in your pocket, or twisting a button. These mannerisms distract the audience.

Appearing on Camera

When you make a presentation on video, be informal and friendly. Look at the camera when you talk to create the effect of making eye contact with the audience.

Since the sound reproduction equipment may deaden voices, make a special effort to vary pitch and expression. Don't interrupt another speaker. Two people talking at the same time on camera produce gibberish.

Dress for the camera.

- Don't wear white. Only very expensive cameras can handle pure white.
- Don't wear bold stripes, checks, plaids, or polka dots.
- Don't wear large accessories.
- Blue and green photograph well.

Adapted from Robert A. Papper, Personal communication with Kitty Locker, March 17, 1991.

Coping with Interruptions

As "multitasking" has become a norm in business, speakers have more trouble holding attention. During a presentation, audience members are likely to be answering phone calls, sending text messages, and checking e-mail. Speakers have to figure out how to cut through all the mental clutter of these interruptions and hold the audience's attention.

The speaker must keep a sharp focus on the main point. The message should be clear, and the speaker should avoid tangents. The speaker should also concentrate on the presentation and the audience.

Storytelling is another way to keep the audience's attention. Expressing ideas with relevant anecdotes builds emotional involvement. A memorable story cuts through the clutter better than a wealth of data.

Multimedia tools, such as video and animation, can grab attention. However, loud music and bold videos will not necessarily hold attention for very long.

Some interruptions are too significant to ignore. Suppose you are presenting to a group of managers, and the chief executive visits. To keep everyone involved, you might invite a member of your audience to update the CEO on the main points. This technique also lets you check which of your main points the group has heard. Another way to involve the CEO without losing the rest of the group is to prepare in advance one or two questions to get the senior-level perspective and provoke discussion.

Adapted from Julie Hill, "The Attention Deficit," *Presentations* 17, no. 10 (October 2003): 26; and "Surprise, It's the CEO," *Sales & Marketing Management* 156, no. 3 (March 2004): 9.

Using Notes and Visuals

Put your notes on cards or on sturdy pieces of paper and number them. Most speakers like to use 4-by-6-inch or 5-by-7-inch cards because they hold more information than 3-by-5-inch cards. Your notes need to be complete enough to help you if you go blank, so use long phrases or complete sentences. Under each main point, jot down the evidence or illustration you'll use. Indicate where you'll refer to visuals.

Look at your notes infrequently. Most of your gaze time should be directed to members of the audience. Hold your notes high enough so that your head doesn't bob up and down as you look from the audience to your notes and back again.

If you have lots of visuals and know your topic well, you won't need notes. Face the audience, not the screen. Show the entire visual at once: don't cover up part of it. If you don't want the audience to read ahead, prepare several visuals that build up. In your overview, for example, the first visual could list your first point, the second the first and second, and the third all three points.

Keep the room lights on if possible; turning them off makes it easier for people to fall asleep and harder for them to concentrate on you.

Handling Questions

Prepare for questions by listing every fact or opinion you can think of that challenges your position. Treat each objection seriously and try to think of a way to deal with it. If you're talking about a controversial issue, you may want to save one point for the question period, rather than making it during the presentation. Speakers who have visuals to answer questions seem especially well prepared.

During your presentation, tell the audience how you'll handle questions. If you have a choice, save questions for the end. In your talk, answer the questions or objections that you expect your audience to have. Don't exaggerate your claims so that you won't have to back down in response to questions later.

During the question period, don't nod your head to indicate that you understand a question as it is asked. Audiences will interpret nods as signs that you agree with the questioner. Instead, look directly at the questioner. As you answer the question, expand your focus to take in the entire group. Don't say, "That's a good question." That response implies that the other questions have been poor ones.

If the audience may not have heard the question or if you want more time to think, repeat the question before you answer it. Link your answers to the points you made in your presentation. Keep the purpose of your presentation in mind, and select information that advances your goals.

If a question is hostile or biased, rephrase it before you answer it. Suppose that during a sales presentation, the prospective client exclaims, "How can you justify those prices?" A response that steers the presentation back to the service's benefits might be: "You're asking about our pricing. The price includes 24-hour, on-site customer support and. . . . " Then explain how those features will benefit the prospect. Michael Campbell writes that he admires the way the late Senator Paul Simon handled hostile questions. According to Campbell, Simon would reply, "There are two ways to consider that matter. The way you just mentioned—and a way that starts from a slightly different base." Then Senator Simon would politely explain his point of view. This kind of response respects the questioner by leaving room for more than one viewpoint.[20]

Occasionally someone will ask a question that is really designed to state the speaker's own position. Respond to the question if you want to. Another option is to say, "I'm not sure what you're asking," or even, "That's a clear statement of your position. Let's move to the next question now." If someone asks about something that you already explained in your presentation, simply answer the question without embarrassing the questioner. No audience will understand and remember 100% of what you say.

If you don't know the answer to a question, say so. If your purpose is to inform, write down the question so that you can look up the answer before the next session. If it's a question to which you think there is no answer, ask if anyone in the room knows. When no one does, your "ignorance" is vindicated. If an expert is in the room, you may want to refer questions of fact to him or her. Answer questions of interpretation yourself.

At the end of the question period, take two minutes to summarize your main point once more. (This can be a restatement of your close.) Questions may or may not focus on the key point of your talk. Take advantage of having the floor to repeat your message briefly and forcefully.

Making Group Presentations

Plan carefully to involve as many members of the group as possible in speaking roles.

The easiest way to make a group presentation is to outline the presentation and then divide the topics, giving one to each group member. Another member can be responsible for the opener and the close. During the question period, each member answers questions that relate to his or her topic.

In this kind of divided presentation, be sure to

- Plan transitions.
- Enforce time limits strictly.
- Coordinate your visuals so that the presentation seems a coherent whole.
- Practice the presentation as a group at least once; more is better.

The best group presentations are even more fully integrated: the group writes a very detailed outline, chooses points and examples, and creates visuals together. Then, within each point, voices trade off. This presentation is most effective because each voice speaks only a minute or two before a new voice comes in. However, it works only when all group members know the subject well and when the group plans carefully and practices extensively.

Whatever form of group presentation you use, be sure to introduce each member of the team to the audience and to pay close attention to each other. If other members of the team seem uninterested in the speaker, the audience gets the sense that that speaker isn't worth listening to.

Summary of Key Points

- **Informative presentations** inform or teach the audience. **Persuasive presentations** motivate the audience to act or to believe. **Goodwill presentations** entertain and validate the audience. Most oral presentations have more than one purpose.
- A written message makes it easier to present extensive or complex information and to minimize undesirable emotions. Oral messages make it easier to use emotion, to focus the audience's attention, to answer questions and resolve conflicts quickly, to modify a proposal that may not be acceptable in its original form, and to get immediate action or response.
- In both oral and written messages, you should
  - Adapt the message to the specific audience.
  - Show the audience how they benefit from the idea, policy, service, or product.

An Alternative to PowerPoint

Barbara Waugh is Worldwide Personnel Manager at Hewlett Packard Labs. [Several years ago, she was researching how to make HP Labs the best in the business. Waugh's data helped her narrow the problem to three areas needing improvement: programs (clearer priorities and fewer projects), people (elimination of poor performers and more freedom for good performers), and processes (better information sharing). Next, Waugh's challenge was to present these ideas to top managers in a way they could understand and accept.] The last thing she wanted was to preach through PowerPoint. So instead of creating bullet-point slides, she drew on her experience with street theatre and created a "play" about HP Labs. She worked passages from the surveys into dialogue and then recruited executives to act as staff members, and junior people to act as executives. The troupe performed for 30 senior managers. "At the end of the play, the managers were very quiet," Waugh remembers. "Then they started clapping. It was exciting. They really got it. They finally understood."

Quoted from Katherine Mieszkowski, "I Grew Up Thinking That Change Was Cataclysmic. The Way We've Done It Here Is to Start Slow and Work Small." *Fast Company*, December 1998, 152.

- Overcome any objections the audience may have.
- Use you-attitude and positive emphasis.
- Use visuals to clarify or emphasize material.
- Specify exactly what the audience should do.
- An oral presentation needs to be simpler than a written message to the same audience.
- In a **monologue presentation,** the speaker plans the presentation in advance and delivers it without deviation. In a **guided discussion,** the speaker presents the questions or issues that both speaker and audience have agreed on in advance. Rather than functioning as an expert with all the answers, the speaker serves as a facilitator to help the audience tap its own knowledge. An **interactive presentation** is a conversation using questions to determine needs, probe objections, and gain provisional and then final commitment to the objective.
- Adapt your message to your audience's beliefs, experiences, and interests.
- Use the beginning and end of the presentation to interest the audience and emphasize your key point.
- Use visuals to seem more prepared, more interesting, and more persuasive.
- Use a direct pattern of organization. Put your strongest reason first.
- Limit your talk to three main points. Early in your talk—perhaps immediately after your opener—provide an overview of the main points you will make. Offer a clear signpost as you come to each new point. A **signpost** is an explicit statement of the point you have reached.
- To calm your nerves as you prepare to give an oral presentation,
  - Be prepared. Analyze your audience, organize your thoughts, prepare visual aids, practice your opener and close, check out the arrangements.
  - Use only the amount of caffeine you normally use.
  - Avoid alcoholic beverages.
  - Relabel your nerves. Instead of saying, "I'm scared," try saying, "My adrenaline is up." Adrenaline sharpens our reflexes and helps us do our best.

  Just before your presentation,
  - Consciously contract and then relax your muscles, starting with your feet and calves and going up to your shoulders, arms, and hands.
  - Take several deep breaths from your diaphragm.

  During your presentation,
  - Pause and look at the audience before you begin speaking.
  - Concentrate on communicating well.
  - Use body energy in strong gestures and movement.
- Convey a sense of caring to your audience by making direct eye contact with them and by using a conversational style.
- Treat questions as opportunities to give more detailed information than you had time to give in your presentation. Link your answers to the points you made in your presentation.
- Repeat the question before you answer it if the audience may not have heard it or if you want more time to think. Rephrase hostile or biased questions before you answer them.
- The best group presentations result when the group writes a very detailed outline, chooses points and examples, and creates visuals together. Then, within each point, voices trade off.

CHAPTER 17 Exercises and Problems

17.1   Reviewing the Chapter

1. What are four major components of planning effective presentations? (LO 1)
2. What are four different kinds of presentation openers you can use? (LO 1)
3. Name 10 guidelines for creating effective visuals. (LO 1)
4. What are some major criteria for choosing the information for your presentation? (LO 2)
5. Provide a suitable topic for each of the five common patterns of organization for presentations. (LO 2)
6. What are some ways to deal with the common fear of public speaking? Which ways would work for you? (LO 3)
7. List some pointers for effectively handling questions during presentations. (LO 4)

17.2   Analyzing Openers and Closes

The following openers and closes came from class presentations on information interviews.

- Does each opener make you interested in hearing the rest of the presentation?
- Does each opener provide a transition to the overview?
- Does the close end the presentation in a satisfying way?

a. Opener: I interviewed Mark Perry at AT&T.
   Close: Well, that's my report.
b. Opener: How many of you know what you want to do when you graduate?
   Close: So, if you like numbers and want to travel, think about being a CPA. Ernst & Young can take you all over the world.

c. Opener: You don't have to know anything about computer programming to get a job as a technical writer at CompuServe.
   Close: After talking to Raj, I decided technical writing isn't for me. But it is a good career if you work well under pressure and like learning new things all the time.
d. Opener: My report is about what it's like to work in an advertising agency.
   Middle: They keep really tight security; I had to wear a badge and be escorted to Susan's desk.
   Close: Susan gave me samples of the agency's ads and even a sample of a new soft drink she's developing a campaign for. But she didn't let me keep the badge.

17.3   Developing Points of Interest

One of the keys to preparing an engaging presentation is finding interesting points to share with your audience, either in the form of personal anecdotes to create rapport and build goodwill, or in the form of interesting facts and figures to establish your ethos as a presenter. For each of the following topics, prepare one personal anecdote based on your own experience, and research one interesting fact to share with your audience.

1. Why people need to plan.
2. Dealing with change.
3. The importance of lifelong learning.
4. The value of good customer service.
5. The culture of an organization that you know well.

As your instructor directs,

a. Share your points of interest with a small group of students, and critique each other's work.
b. Turn in your stories in a memo to your instructor.
c. Make a short (1–2 minute) oral presentation featuring your story and fact(s) for one of the assignment topics.

17.4   Evaluating PowerPoint Slides

Evaluate the following drafts of PowerPoint slides.
- Are the slides' background appropriate for the topic?
- Do the slides use words or phrases rather than complete sentences?
- Is the font big enough to read from a distance?
- Is the art relevant and appropriate?
- Is each slide free from errors?

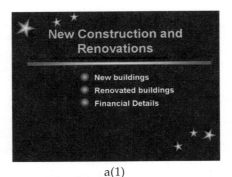

a(1)

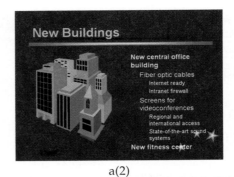

a(2)

Remodeling

Central Office Building
- Sound control
- Better modem and phone access
- Climate control

West office building
- New carpeting
- New office furniture

a(3)

Financial Details

New Construction
$12 million
- $6 million in prime rate mortgages (30 year)
- $3 million from cash reserves
- $3 million from bonds

Renovations
$10 million
- $5 million in prime rate mortgages (30 year)
- $3 million from cash reserves
- $3 million from bonds

a(4)

Niche Marketing

Understanding the Older Buyer

b(1)

Number of Older Buyers Grows

- Baby boomers swell over–50 ranks
- Older Americans live longer due to better health care
- Addults over 50 control most of discretionary wealth

45-64 / 65-79 / 80+
1990 1995 2000 2005

b(2)

Differences from Younger Buyers

- *Older buyers want more details and evidence.*
- *Older buyers may need larger fonts since eyesight may be dimmer. Also, type needs to be more legible–avoide light blue, which can be hard to read.*
- *Link to lifestyle–grandchildren, retirement.*

b(3)

Older Buyers and Technology

- Boomers
  - Adopt rapidly
  - Use for work, leisure
- Over 65's
  - Continue to use familiar products
  - Learn new products in social atmosphere

b(4)

Using PowerPoint

Tips for Creating Slides

c(1)

Simplify.

- Use bullets points.
  - Keep text short.
  - Keep points parallel.
- Use 3-7 lines of body type per slide.
- Use white space.
- Use as few levels of indentation as possible.

c(2)

Add Builds and Transitions.

- Direct audience's attention.
- Provide visual interest.
- Develop consistent "look."
  - Use same transition throughout.
  - Use build for a reason-not necessarily for every line.

c(3)

Use Strong Visuals.

- Choose art that is
  - Relevant.
  - Bias-free.
  - Fresh to the audience.
  - Adapted to the company and the audience.

c(4)

17.5   Making a Short Oral Presentation

As your instructor directs,

Make a short (three- to five-minute) presentation with PowerPoint slides on one of the following topics:

a. Explain how what you've learned in classes, in campus activities, or at work will be useful to the employer who hires you after graduation.

b. Profile someone who is successful in the field you hope to enter and explain what makes him or her successful.

c. Describe a specific situation in an organization in which communication was handled well or badly.

d. Make a short presentation based on another problem in this book.

   1. Introduce yourself to the class.
   2. Describe your boss's management style.
   3. Describe how your co-workers employ teamwork on the job.
   4. Explain a "best-practice" in your organization.
   5. Explain what a new hire in your organization needs to know to be successful.

6. Tell your boss about a problem in your unit.

7. Make a presentation to raise funds for a nonprofit organization.

8. Describe the content of a brochure for a nonprofit organization.

9. Tell the class in detail about one of your accomplishments.

10. Explain one of the challenges (e.g., technology, ethics, international competition) that the field you plan to enter is facing.

11. Profile a company that you would like to work for and explain why you think it would make a good employer.

12. Share the results of an information interview.

13. Share some advice for students currently on the job market.

14. Share what you learn when you interview an interviewer.

15. Explain your job interview strategy.

17.6   Making a Longer Oral Presentation

As your instructor directs,

Make a 5- to 12-minute presentation on one of the following. Use visuals to make your talk effective.

a. Show why your unit is important to the organization and either should be exempt from downsizing or should receive additional resources.

b. Persuade your supervisor to make a change that will benefit the organization.

c. Persuade your organization to make a change that will improve the organization's image in the community.

d. Persuade classmates to donate time or money to a charitable organization.

e. Persuade an employer that you are the best person for the job.

f. Use another problem in this book as the basis for your presentation.

   1. Analyze an organization's culture.
   2. Analyze a discourse community.

3. Describe the communication process of a person you've interviewed who is working in the field you plan to enter.

4. Evaluate the page design of one or more documents from a business setting.

5. Evaluate the design of a corporate Web page.

6. Present a Web page you have designed.

7. Analyze rejection letters that students on your campus have received.

8. Persuade an organization on your campus to make a change.

9. Analyze one or more sales or fund-raising letters.

10. Analyze international messages that your workplace has created or received.

11. Present the results of a survey you conduct.

12. Research the business practices of an organization you would like to work for and present the results to the class.

17.7   Making a Group Oral Presentation

As your instructor directs,

Make a 5- to 12-minute presentation on one of the following. Use visuals to make your talk effective.

1. Explain the role of communication in one or more organizations.

2. Create and present a fund-raising strategy for a nonprofit organization.

3. Report on another country.

4. Design brochures and other print materials for a business and present them to the class.

5. Interview the employees of an organization about their teamwork strategies and present the information to the class.

17.8   Evaluating Oral Presentations

Evaluate an oral presentation given by a classmate or given by a speaker on your campus. Use the following categories:

Strategy

1. Choosing an effective kind of presentation for the situation.
2. Adapting ideas to audience's beliefs, experiences, and interests.
3. Using a strong opening and close.
4. Using visual aids or other devices to involve audience.

Content

5. Using specific, vivid supporting material and language.
6. Providing rebuttals to counterclaims or objections.

Organization

7. Providing an overview of main points.
8. Signposting main points in body of talk.
9. Providing adequate transitions between points and speakers.

Visuals

10. Using an appropriate design or template.
11. Using standard edited English.
12. Being creative.

Delivery

13. Making direct eye contact with audience.
14. Using voice and gestures effectively.
15. Handling questions effectively.
16. Stance, position (not blocking screen)

As your instructor directs,

a. Fill out a form indicating your evaluation in each of the areas.
b. Share your evaluation orally with the speaker.
c. Write a memo to the speaker evaluating the presentation. Send a copy of your memo to your instructor.

17.9   Evaluating Team Presentations

Evaluate team presentations using the following questions:

1. How thoroughly were all group members involved?
2. Did members of the team introduce themselves or each other?
3. Did team members seem interested in what their teammates said?
4. How well was the material organized?
5. How well did the material hold your interest?
6. How clear did the material seem to you?
7. How effective were the visuals?
8. How well did the team handle questions?
9. What could be done to improve the presentation?
10. What were the strong points of the presentation?

As your instructor directs,

a. Fill out a form indicating your evaluation in each of the areas.
b. Share your evaluation orally with the team.
c. Write a memo to the team evaluating the presentation. Send a copy of your memo to your instructor.

17.10   Evaluating the Way a Speaker Handles Questions

Listen to a speaker talking about a controversial subject. (Go to a talk on campus or in town, or watch a speaker on a TV show like *Face the Nation* or *60 Minutes*.) Observe the way he or she handles questions.

- About how many questions does the speaker answer?
- What is the format for asking and answering questions?
- Are the answers clear? responsive to the question? something that could be quoted without embarrassing the speaker and the organization he or she represents?
- How does the speaker handle hostile questions? Does the speaker avoid getting angry? Does the speaker retain control of the meeting? How?

- If some questions were not answered well, what (if anything) could the speaker have done to leave a better impression?
- Did the answers leave the audience with a more or less positive impression of the speaker? Why?

As your instructor directs,

a. Share your evaluation with a small group of students.
b. Present your evaluation formally to the class.
c. Summarize your evaluation in a memo to your instructor.

17.11   Mosaic Case

"I can't believe it's over already," Martina said to Trey solemnly.

"Yeah, I know that I'm sure going to miss having you around to give all my difficult projects," Trey said while chuckling to help brighten Martina's spirits.

She smiled. After a whole semester, Martina's time at Mosaic, at least as an intern, was already coming to an end.

"And," said Trey, "rumor around here has it that Yvonne will be asking you to stay full-time as soon as she gets clearance from upper management."

"Well, I'm not going to get my hopes up," she responded. "But I also would love to work here. I do have one favor to ask of you, Trey."

"What's that?" he asked.

"Well, I need to report back to my internship supervisor and give a formal presentation report about my experiences at Mosaic to him and the rest of the students who enrolled in the internship course," said Martina.

"That'll be fun," said Trey sarcastically.

"I don't have a lot of time, only around seven minutes. Since I only have this short amount of time to present, I want to focus the content around things I've learned about business communication while working at Mosaic. Also, I'm a little unsure about getting up in front of people to deliver the presentation. Do you have any tips?" she asked.

Take on the role of Trey and answer Martina's favor request. Give her tips for being an effective oral communicator. What should she do during the presentation and what should she not do?

In addition, reflect on your experiences with this business communication textbook. What are the top-three things you are going to take with you as you leave this course? What recommendations would you give for the content of Martina's presentation?

Formats for Letters, Memos, and E-Mail Messages

Learning Objectives

After studying this appendix, you will know:

1 Formats for letters.

2 Formats for envelopes.

3 Formats for memos and e-mail messages.

Letters normally go to people outside your organization; **memos** go to other people in your organization. E-mails go to both audiences. Letters, memos, and e-mails do not necessarily differ in length, formality, writing style, or pattern of organization. However, letters, memos, and e-mails do differ in format. **Format** means the parts of a document and the way they are arranged on the page.

Formats for Letters

If your organization has a standard format for letters, use it.

Many organizations and writers choose one of three letter formats: **block format** (see Figure A.2), **modified block format** (see Figure A.3), or the **Administrative Management Society (AMS) Simplified format** (see Figure A.4). Your organization may make minor changes from the diagrams in margins or spacing.

Figure A.1 shows how the three formats differ.

Use the same level of formality in the **salutation,** or greeting, as you would in talking to someone on the phone: *Dear Glenn* if you're on a first-name basis, *Dear Mr. Helms* if you don't know the reader well enough to use the first name.

Some writers feel that the AMS Simplified format is better since the reader is not *Dear.* Omitting the salutation is particularly good when you do not know the reader's name or do not know which courtesy title (◀▥ p. 90) to use. (For a full discussion on nonsexist salutations and salutations when you don't know the reader's name, see Chapter 3.) However, readers like to see their names. Since the AMS Simplified omits the reader's name in the salutation, writers who use this format but who also want to be friendly often try to use the reader's name early in the body of the letter.

The Simplified letter format is good in business-to-business mail, or in letters where you are writing to anyone who holds a job (admissions officer, customer service representative) rather than to a specific person. It is too cold and distancing for cultures that place a premium on relationships.

Sincerely and *Yours truly* are standard **complimentary closes.** When you are writing to people in special groups or to someone who is a friend as well as a business acquaintance, you may want to use a less formal close. Depending on the circumstances, the following informal closes might be acceptable: *Yours for a better environment, Cordially, Thank you!,* or even *Ciao.*

In **mixed punctuation,** a colon follows the salutation and a comma follows the close. In a sales or fund-raising letter, it is acceptable to use a comma after the salutation to make the letter look like a personal letter rather than like a business letter. In **open punctuation,** omit all punctuation after the salutation and the close. Mixed punctuation is traditional.

Figure A.1　Comparing and Contrasting Letter Formats

	Block	Modified block	AMS Simplified
Date and signature block	Lined up at left margin	Lined up ½ or ⅔ of the way over to the right	Lined up at left margin
Paragraph indentation	None	Optional	None
Salutation and complimentary close	Yes	Yes	None
Subject line	Optional	Rare	Yes
Lists, if any	Indented	Indented	At left margin
Writer's signature	Yes	Yes	None
Writer's typed name	Upper- and lowercase	Upper- and lowercase	Full capital letters
Paragraph spacing	Single-spaced, double-space between	Single-spaced, double-space between	Single-spaced, double-space between

A **subject line** tells what the letter is about. Subject lines are required in memos and e-mails; they are optional in letters. Good subject lines are specific, concise, and appropriate for your purposes and the response you expect from your reader.

- When you have good news, put it in the subject line.
- When your information is neutral, summarize it concisely in the subject line.
- When your information is negative, use a negative subject line if the reader may not read the message or needs the information to act.
- When you have a request that will be easy for the reader to grant, put either the subject of the request or a direct question in the subject line.
- When you must persuade a reluctant reader, use a common ground, a benefit, or a neutral subject line.

For examples of subject lines in each of these situations, see Chapters 10, 11, and 12.

A **reference line** refers the reader to the number used on the previous correspondence this letter replies to, or the order or invoice number this letter is about. Very large organizations, like the IRS, use numbers on every piece of correspondence they send out so that it is possible to find quickly the earlier document to which an incoming letter refers.

All three formats can use headings, lists, and indented sections for emphasis.

Each of the three formats has advantages. Both block and AMS Simplified can be typed quickly since everything is lined up at the left margin. Block format is the format most frequently used for business letters; readers expect it. Modified block format creates a visually attractive page by moving the date and signature block over into what would otherwise be empty white space. Modified block is a traditional format; readers are comfortable with it.

The examples of the three formats in Figures A.2–A.4 show one-page letters on company letterhead. **Letterhead** is preprinted stationery with the organization's name, logo, address, and phone number. Figure A.5 shows how to set up modified block format when you do not have letterhead. (It is also acceptable to use block format without letterhead.)

When your letter runs two or more pages, use a heading on the second page to identify it. Using the reader's name helps the writer, who may be printing

Figure A.2   Block Format on Letterhead (mixed punctuation)

Line up everything at left margin

1–6 spaces depending on length of letter

Northwest Hardware Warehouse
100 Freeway Exchange   Provo, UT 84610   (801) 555-4683   www.northwesthardware.com

June 20, 2009

1"–1½"

Mr. James E. Murphy, Accounts Payable   *Title could be on a separate line*
Salt Lake Equipment Rentals
5600 Wasatch Boulevard
Salt Lake City, Utah 84121

Use first name in salutation if you'd use it on the phone

Dear Jim: *Colon in mixed punctuation*

The following items totaling $393.09 are still open on your account.   *¶ 1 never has a heading*

Invoice #01R-784391 *Bold or underline heading*

After the bill for this invoice arrived on May 14, you wrote saying that the material had not been delivered to you. On May 29, our Claims Department sent you a copy of the delivery receipt signed by an employee of Salt Lake Equipment. You have had proof of delivery for over three weeks, but your payment has not yet arrived.   *⅝"–1"*

Please send a check for $78.42.   *Single-space paragraphs*
Double-space between paragraphs (one blank space)

Triple-space before new heading (2 blank spaces)

Voucher #59351

Do not indent paragraphs

The reference line on your voucher #59351, dated June 16, indicates that it is the gross payment for invoice #01G-002345. However, the voucher was only for $1171.25, while the invoice amount was $1246.37. Please send a check for $75.12 to clear this item.

Voucher #55032

Voucher #55032, dated June 16, subtracts a credit for $239.55 from the amount due. Our records do not show that any credit is due on this voucher. Please send either an explanation or a check to cover the $239.55 immediately.

Total Amount Due   *Headings are optional in letters*

Please send a check for $393.09 to cover these three items and to bring your account up to date.

1–2 spaces

Sincerely,

2–4 spaces

Neil Hutchinson
Credit Representative

cc: Joan Stottlemyer, Credit Manager

Leave bottom margin of 3–6 spaces— more if letter is short

Figure A.3   Modified Block Format on Letterhead (mixed punctuation)

Bay City Information Systems
151 Bayview Road • San Francisco, CA 81153 • (650) 405-7849 • www.baycity.com

2–6 spaces

September 15, 2009
Line up date with signature block
$\frac{1}{2}$ or $\frac{2}{3}$ of the way over to the right

1–4 spaces

Ms. Mary E. Arcas
Personnel Director
Cyclops Communication Technologies
1050 South Sierra Bonita Avenue
Los Angeles, CA 90019   *Zip code on same line*

$1"-1\frac{1}{2}"$

Dear Ms. Arcas: *Colon in mixed punctuation*

$\frac{5}{8}"-1"$

Indenting ¶ is optional in modified block

Let me respond to your request for an evaluation of Colleen Kangas. Colleen was hired as a clerk-typist by Bay City Information Systems on April 4, 2007, and was promoted to Administrative Assistant on August 1, 2008. At her review in June, I recommended that she be promoted again. She is an intelligent young woman with good work habits and a good knowledge of computer software.

Single-space paragraphs

As an Adminstrative Assistant, Colleen not only handles routine duties such as processing time cards, ordering supplies, and entering data, but also screens calls for two marketing specialists, answers basic questions about Bay City Information Systems, compiles the statistics I need for my monthly reports, and investigates special assignments for me. In the past eight months, she has investigated freight charges, inventoried department hardware, and transferred files to CD-Roms. I need only to give her general directions: she has a knack for tracking down information quickly and summarizing it accurately.

Double-space between paragraphs (one blank line)

Although the department's workload has increased during the year, Colleen manages her time so that everything gets done on schedule. She is consistently poised and friendly under pressure. Her willingness to work overtime on occasion is particularly remarkable considering that she has been going to college part-time ever since she joined our firm.

At Bay City Information Systems, Colleen uses Microsoft Word and Access software. She tells me that she has also used PowerPoint in her college classes.

If Colleen were staying in San Francisco, we would want to keep her. She has the potential either to become an Executive Secretary or to move into line or staff work, especially once she completes her degree. I recommend her highly.

1–2 spaces

Sincerely,   *Comma in mixed punctuation*

Headings are optional in letters

2–4 spaces

Jeanne Cederlind

Jeanne Cederlind
Vice President, Marketing
jeanne_c@baycity.com

Line up signature block with date

1–4 spaces

Encl.: Evaluation Form for Colleen Kangas

Leave at least 3–6 spaces at bottom of page—more if letter is short

Figure A.4   AMS Simplified Format on Letterhead

1500 Main Street   Iowa City, IA 52232   (319) 555-3113

*Line up
everything
at left
margin*

↕ 2–4 spaces

August 24, 2010

↕ 1–4 spaces

◄—1"–1½"—►

Melinda Hamilton
Medical Services Division
Health Management Services, Inc.
4333 Edgewood Road, NE
Cedar Rapids, IA 52401

Triple space (2 blank spaces)   *Subject line in full capital letters*

REQUEST FOR INFORMATION ABOUT COMPUTER SYSTEMS

◄— No salutation

We're interested in upgrading our computer system and would like to talk to one of
your marketing representatives to see what would best meet our needs. We will use
the following criteria to choose a system:

1. Ability to use our current software and data files.   *Double-space (one blank space)*

between items in list if any items

2. Price, prorated on a three-year expected life.   *are more than one line long*

3. Ability to provide auxiliary services, e.g., controlling inventory of drugs and
    supplies, monitoring patients' vital signs, and faster processing of insurance
    forms.

4. Freedom from downtime.

Triple-space (two blank spaces) between list, next paragraph

*Do not
indent
paragraphs*

McFarlane Memorial Hospital has 50 beds for acute care and 75 beds for long-term
care. In the next five years, we expect the number of beds to remain the same while
outpatient care and emergency room care increase.

Could we meet the first or the third week in September? We are eager to have the
new system installed by Christmas if possible.

Please call me to schedule an appointment.

No close. No signature.   *Headings are
optional in letters*

HUGH PORTERFIELD   *Writer's name in full capital letters*
Controller

↕ 1–4 spaces

Encl.:   Specifications of Current System
         Databases Currently in Use

cc: Rene Seaburg

*↕ Leave 3–6 spaces at bottom
of page—more if letter is short*

Figure A.5   Modified Block Format without Letterhead (open punctuation)

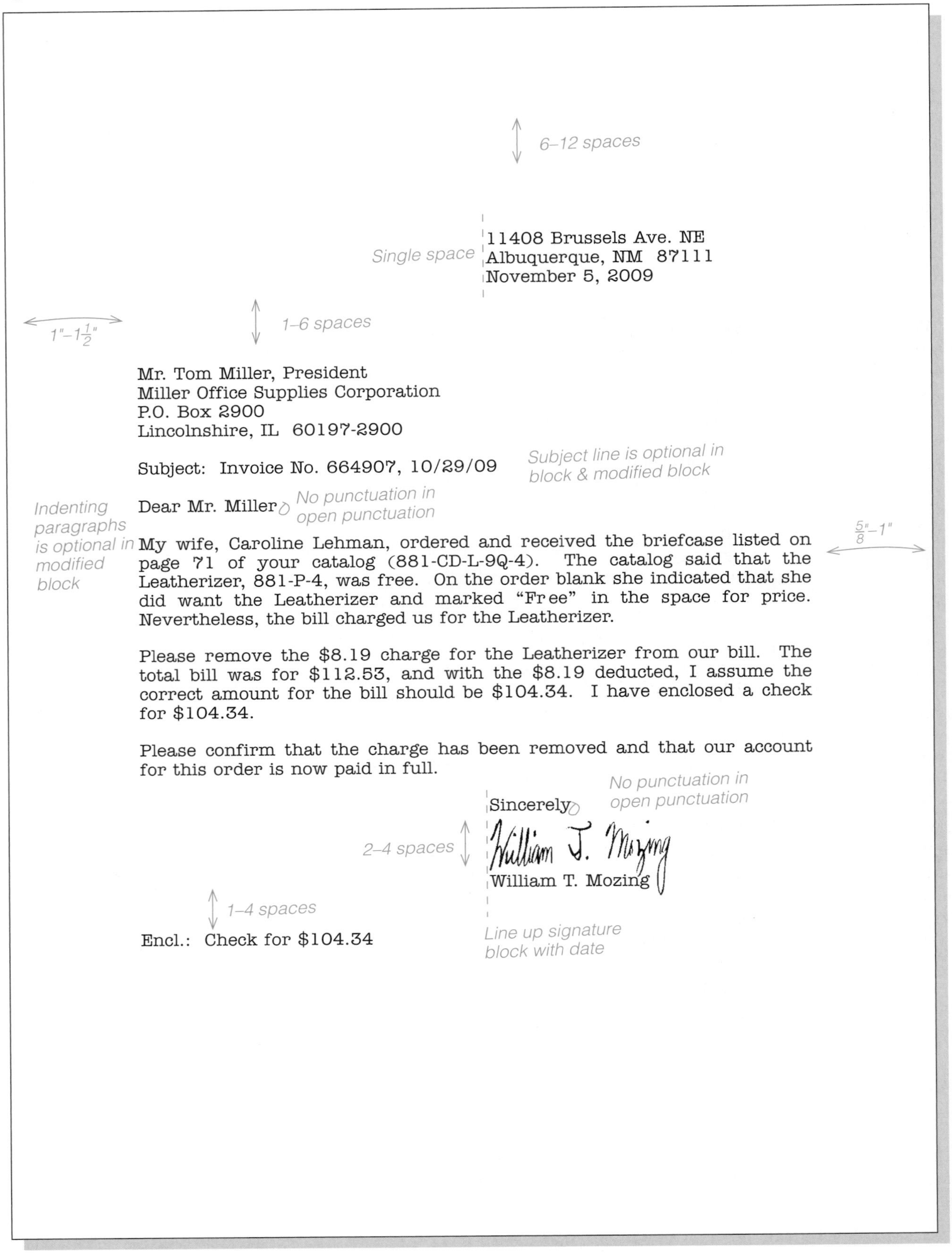

6–12 spaces

Single space
11408 Brussels Ave. NE
Albuquerque, NM 87111
November 5, 2009

1"–1½"

1–6 spaces

Mr. Tom Miller, President
Miller Office Supplies Corporation
P.O. Box 2900
Lincolnshire, IL 60197-2900

Subject: Invoice No. 664907, 10/29/09   *Subject line is optional in block & modified block*

Indenting paragraphs is optional in modified block

Dear Mr. Miller   *No punctuation in open punctuation*

My wife, Caroline Lehman, ordered and received the briefcase listed on page 71 of your catalog (881-CD-L-9Q-4).   The catalog said that the Leatherizer, 881-P-4, was free. On the order blank she indicated that she did want the Leatherizer and marked "Free" in the space for price. Nevertheless, the bill charged us for the Leatherizer.

Please remove the $8.19 charge for the Leatherizer from our bill.   The total bill was for $112.53, and with the $8.19 deducted, I assume the correct amount for the bill should be $104.34.   I have enclosed a check for $104.34.

Please confirm that the charge has been removed and that our account for this order is now paid in full.

⅝"–1"

Sincerely   *No punctuation in open punctuation*

2–4 spaces

William T. Mozing

1–4 spaces

Encl.: Check for $104.34

Line up signature block with date

out many letters at a time, to make sure the right second page gets in the envelope. The two most common formats are shown in Figures A.6, A.7, A.8, and below. Note even when the signature block is on the second page, it is still lined up with the date.

Reader's Name
Date
Page Number

or

Reader's Name   Page Number   Date

When a letter runs two or more pages, use letterhead only for page 1. (See Figures A.6, A.7, and A.8.) For the remaining pages, use plain paper that matches the letterhead in weight, texture, and color.

Set side margins of 1 inch to 1½ inches on the left and ⅝ inch to 1 inch on the right. If your letterhead extends all the way across the top of the page, set your margins even with the ends of the letterhead for the most visually pleasing page. The top margin should be three to six lines under the letterhead, or 2 inches down from the top of the page if you aren't using letterhead. If your letter is very short, you may want to use bigger side and top margins so that the letter is centered on the page.

To eliminate typing the reader's name and address on an envelope, some organizations use envelopes with cut-outs or windows so that the **inside address** (the reader's name and address) on the letter shows through and can be used for delivery. If your organization does this, adjust your margins, if necessary, so that the whole inside address is visible.

Many letters are accompanied by other documents. Whatever these documents may be—a multipage report or a two-line note—they are called **enclosures,** since they are enclosed in the envelope. The writer should refer to the enclosures in the body of the letter: "As you can see from my résumé, . . . " The enclosure line reminds the person who seals the letter to include the enclosures.

Sometimes you write to one person but send copies of your letter to other people. If you want the reader to know that other people are getting copies, list their names on the last page. The abbreviation *cc* originally meant *carbon copy* but now means *computer copy.* Other acceptable abbreviations include *pc* for *photocopy* or simply *c* for *copy.* You can also send copies to other people without telling the reader. Such copies are called **blind copies.** Blind copies are not mentioned on the original; they are listed on the copy saved for the file with the abbreviation *bc* preceding the names of people getting these copies.

You do not need to indicate that you have shown a letter to your superior or that you are saving a copy of the letter for your own files. These are standard practices.

Alternate Format for Letters That Are Not Individually Typed

Merge functions in word processing programs allow you to put in a reader's name and address even in a form letter. *If you use a specific name in the salutation,* also use the reader's name and address in the inside address.

Figure A.6   Second Page of a Two-Page Letter, Block Format (mixed punctuation)

State
University

4300 Gateway Boulevard
Midland, TX

August 11, 2009

1"–1½"

Ms. Stephanie Voght
Stephen F. Austin High School
1200 Southwest Blvd.
San Antonio, TX 78214

↕ 1 – 2 spaces

Dear Ms. Voght: *Colon in mixed punctuation.*

⅝"–1"

Enclosed are 100 brochures about State University to distribute to your students. The brochures describe the academic programs and financial aid available. When you need additional brochures, just let me know.

Videotape about State University

You may also want to show your students the videotape "Life at State University." This

*Plain paper
for page 2.*

↕ ½"–1"

Center

Stephanie Voght ← *Reader's
name*   2   August 11, 2009

*Also OK to line up page number and
date at left under reader's name.*

campus life, including football and basketball games, fraternities and sororities, clubs and organizations, and opportunities for volunteer work. The tape stresses the diversity of the student body and the very different lifestyles that are available at State.

*Triple space before
each new heading (two blank spaces).*

Scheduling the Videotape   *Bold or underline headings.*

*Same
margins
as p 1.*

To schedule your free showing, just fill out the enclosed card with your first, second, and third choices for dates, and return it in the stamped, self-addressed envelope. Dates are reserved in the order that requests arrive. Send in your request early to increase the chances of getting the date you want.

"Life at State University" will be on its way to give your high school students a preview of the college experience.

1–2 spaces ↕

Sincerely,   *Comma in mixed punctuation.*

*2–4
spaces ↕* Michael L. Mahler

*Headings are
optional in
letters.*

Michael L. Mahler
Director of Admissions

↕ 1–4 spaces

Encl.: Brochures, Reservation Form

cc: R. J. Holland, School Superintendent
      Jose Lavilla, President, PTS Association

Figure A.7   Second Page of a Two-Page Letter, Modified Block Format (mixed punctuation)

Glenarvon Carpets

1500 Summit Avenue   (612) 555-1002
Minneapolis, MN   Fax (612) 555-4032
                     www.glenarvon.biz

↕ 1–4 spaces

November 5, 2010

*Line up date with
signature block.*

Mr. Roger B. Castino
Castino Floors and Carpets
418 E. North Street
Brockton, MA 02410

*Indenting
paragraphs
is optional
in modified
block.*

Dear Mr. Castino:

Welcome to the team of Glenarvon Carpet dealers!

Your first shipment of Glenarvon samples should reach you within ten days. The samples include

↕ ½"–1"

*Plain paper
for page 2*   Mr. Roger B. Castino   *← Reader's
name*   Center   2   November 5, 2010

territory . In addition, as a dealer you receive

- Sales kit highlighting product features
- Samples to distribute to customers
- Advertising copy to run in local newspapers
- Display units to place in your store.

*Indent or center list
to emphasize it.*

The Annual Sales Meeting each January keeps you up-to-date on new products while you get to know other dealers and Glenarvon executives and relax at a resort hotel.

*Use
same
margins
as p 1.*   Make your reservations now for Monterey January 10-13 for your first Glenarvon Sales Meeting!

*2–4
spaces*   Cordially, *Comma in mixed punctuation*

Barbara S. Charbonneau

Barbara S. Charbonneau
Vice President, Marketing

*Line up signature block with
date in heading and on p1.*

↕ 1–4 spaces

Encl.: Organization Chart
        Product List
        National Advertising Campaigns in 2009
        1–4 spaces
cc: Nancy Magill, Northeast Sales Manager
     Edward Spaulding, Sales Representative

*↕ 3–6 spaces – more if
second page isn't a full page.*

Figure A.8   Second Page of a Two-Page Letter, AMS Simplified Format

Options for Living

115 State Street
Ames, IA 50014
515-292-8756
www.optionsforliving.org

↕ 1–4 spaces

January 20, 2010

↕ 1–2 spaces

Gary Sammons, Editor
Southeastern Home Magazine
253 North Lake Street
Newport News, VA 23612

Triple space (two blank spaces)   *Subject line in full caps*

MATERIAL FOR YOUR STORY ON HOMES FOR PEOPLE WITH DISABILITIES

No salutation

Apartments and houses can easily be designed to accommodate people with disabilities.
From the outside, the building is indistinguishable from conventional housing. But the
modifications inside permit people who use wheelchairs or whose sight or hearing is impaired
to do everyday things like shower, cook, and do laundry.

↕ ½"–1"   *Plain paper for page 2*

Gary Sammons   *← Reader's*
January 20, 2010   *name*
Page 2

Everything in hallways and showers and adjustable cabinets that can be raised or lowered. Cardinal says
lined up that the adaptations can run from a few dollars to $5000, depending on what the customer
at left selects.
margin

The Builders Association of South Florida will install many features at no extra cost: 36-inch
doorways—eight inches wider than standard—to accommodate wheelchairs and extra wiring
for electronic items for people whose sight or hearing is impaired.

Same If you'd like pictures to accompany your story, just let me know.
margins
as page 1

MARILYN TILLOTSON *No close, no signature*
Executive Director   *Writer's name in full caps*

Encl.: Blueprints for Housing for People with Disabilities

cc: Douglas Stringfellow, President, BASF
       Thomas R. Galliher, President, Cardinal Industries

↕ at least 3–6 spaces—more if page 2 is not a full page

If you cannot afford to type each reader's name and address individually on the page, you have two options. The first option is to omit the inside address and use a generic salutation: "Dear Voter." The second option is to omit the salutation and use the space where it and the inside address normally go for a benefit or attention-getter. Figure A.9 illustrates this option.

Formatting Envelopes

Business envelopes need to put the reader's name and address in the area that is picked up by the Post Office's Optical Character Readers (OCRs). Use side margins of at least 1 inch. Your bottom margin must be at least ⅜ inch but no bigger than 2¼ inches.

Most businesses use envelopes that already have the return address printed in the upper left-hand corner. When you don't have printed envelopes, type your name (optional), your street address, and your city, state, and zip code in the upper left-hand corner. Since the OCR doesn't need this information to route your letter, exact margins don't matter. Use whatever is convenient and looks good to you.

Format for Memos

Memos omit both the salutation and the close entirely. Memos rarely use indented paragraphs. Subject lines are required; headings are optional but useful in memos a full page or longer. Each heading must cover all the information until the next heading. Never use a separate heading for the first paragraph.

Figure A.10 illustrates the standard memo format typed on a plain sheet of paper. Note that the first letters of the reader's name, the writer's name, and the subject phrase are lined up vertically. Note also that memos are usually initialed by the To/From block. Initialing tells the reader that you have proofread the memo and prevents someone sending out your name on a memo you did not in fact write.

Some organizations have special letterhead for memos. When *Date/To/From/ Subject* are already printed on the form, main margin may be lined up vertically with the date, writer's and reader's names, and subject. (See Figure A.11.)

Some organizations alter the order of items in the Date/To/From/Subject block. Some organizations ask employees to sign memos rather than simply initialing them. The signature goes below the last line of the memo, starting halfway over on the page, and prevents anyone's adding unauthorized information.

If the memo runs two pages or more, set up the second and subsequent pages in one of the following ways (see Figure A.12):

Brief Subject Line
Date
Page Number

or

Brief Subject Line	Page Number	Date

Formats for E-Mail Messages

E-mail programs prompt you to supply the various parts of the memo format. See Chapters 10, 11, and 12 for information about designing e-mail subject lines. "Cc:" denotes computer copies; the recipient will see that these people are getting the message. "Bcc:" denotes blind computer copies; the recipient

Figure A.9   A Form Letter Whose Attention-Getter Mimics an Inside Address

COMPUTER SUPPORT
CORPORATION

2215 Midway Road • Carrollton, Texas 75006
(214) 661-8960 • Telex: 284831 CSCTX UR • Fax: (214) 661-1096

*"Johnson Box" used for emphasis
visual variety*

```
* * * * * * * * * * *
* Five FREE Libraries *
* Worth Up to $615!   *
* * * * * * * * * * *
```

*Date omitted so letter can be sent
out unchanged
Johnson Box visually substitutes
for date*

*Attention–getter
visually
substitutes
for inside
address,
salutation*

```
No Other Business
Graphics Software Can
Match the Versatility &
Flexibility of Diagraph!
```

Let us prove to you that Diagraph is a breakthrough in business
graphics software.

Use Diagraph to turn your ideas, concepts, plans, and data into
organization charts, signs, flow charts, diagrams, forms, and maps.
Diagraph comes with a money-back guarantee. Use it for 30 days and
we're certain that you will have discovered so many uses for
Diagraph that you won't want to part with it.

And now you have two choices: Diagraph/500 for only $99 or
Diagraph/2000 for $395.

Diagraph/500 files are fully compatible with Diagraph/2000 so you
can upgrade to Diagraph/2000 at any time. What's more, the cost of
Diagraph/500 is credited towards your purchase of Diagraph/2000.

See the enclosed data sheet for additional information or call us
today to see how the power of Diagraph can enhance everything you
write!

                              Sincerely,

4 sp.   *Gail McCannon*

                              Gail McCannon
                              Director, Customer Services

Initials of writer
Initials of typist
GM:ec

*Signature block lined up with
Johnson Box*

Encl.

P.S. As an added incentive, if you purchase Diagraph/2000 before
November 30, you can select five Diagraph libraries, worth up to
$615, absolutely free. Call for more details.

*Reader benefit saved for a P.S.
People's eyes go to P.S., which they may
read before returning to rest of letter*

Figure A.10   Memo Format (on plain paper)

*Everything
lined up at left*   *Plain paper*

*1–4
spaces*   October 7, 2009

Double space   To: Annette T. Califero   *Line up*
(one blank space)
          From: Kyle B. Abrams *KBA*   *Writer's initials added in ink*

1"–1½"   Subject: A Low-Cost Way to Reduce Energy Use   *Capitalize first letter of each
                                                          major word in subject line*

*No
heading
for ¶ 1*   As you requested, I've investigated low-cost ways to reduce our energy use. Reducing   *⅝"–1"*
the building temperature on weekends is a change that we could make immediately,
that would cost nothing, and that would cut our energy use by about 6%.

              Triple space before each new heading (two blank spaces)

The Energy Savings from a Lower Weekend Temperature   *Bold or underline headings*

*Single-space
paragraphs;*   Lowering the temperature from 68° to 60° from 8 p.m. Friday evening to 4 a.m.
double-space   Monday morning could cut our total consumption by 6%. It is not feasible to lower the
between   temperature on weeknights because a great many staff members work late; the cleaning
paragraphs   crew also is on duty from 6 p.m. to midnight. Turning the temperature down for only
(one blank   four hours would not result in a significant heat saving.
space)

Turning the heat back up at 4 a.m. will allow the building temperature to be back to
68° by 9 a.m. Our furnace already has computerized controls which can be set to
automatically lower and raise the temperature.

              Triple sp (two blank spaces)

How a Lower Temperature Would Affect Employees   *Capitalize first letter of
                                                     each major word of heading*

*Do not
indent*   A survey of employees shows that only 7 people use the building every weekend or
paragraphs   almost every weekend. Eighteen percent of our staff have worked at least one weekend
day in the last two months; 52% say they "occasionally" come in on weekends.

People who come in for an hour or less on weekends could cope with the lower
temperature just by wearing warm clothes. However, most people would find 60° too
cool for extended work. Employees who work regularly on weekends might want to
install space heaters.

Action Needed to Implement the Change

Would you also like me to check into the cost of buying a dozen portable space
heaters? Providing them would allow us to choose units that our wiring can handle and
would be a nice gesture towards employees who give up their weekends to work. I
could have a report to you in two weeks.

We can begin saving energy immediately. Just authorize the lower temperature, and I'll
see that the controls are reset for this weekend.

          *Memos are initialed by
          To/From/Subject block — no signature*   *Headings are optional in memos*

Figure A.11   Memo Format (on memo letterhead)

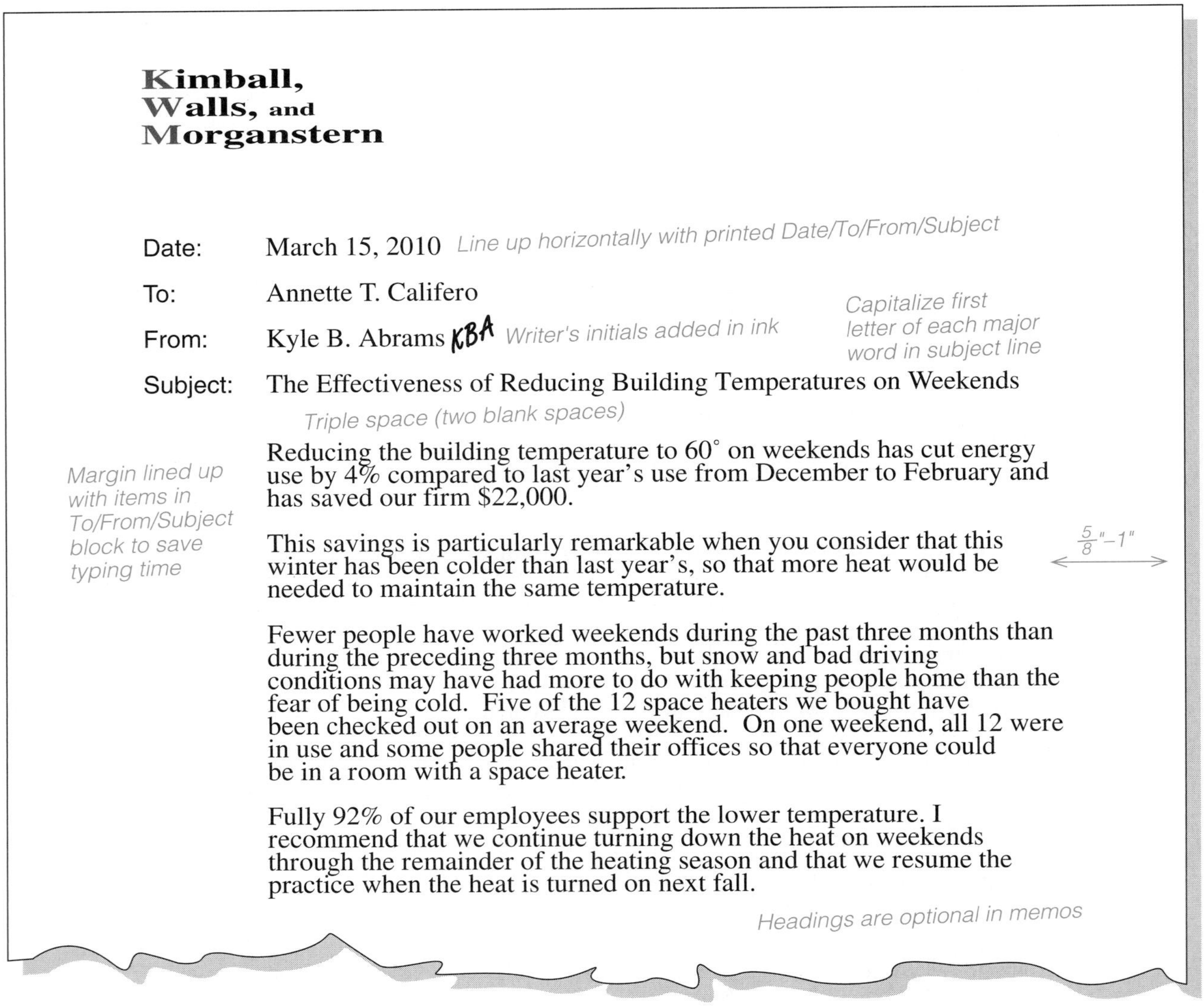

Kimball, Walls, and Morganstern

Date: March 15, 2010 *Line up horizontally with printed Date/To/From/Subject*

To: Annette T. Califero

From: Kyle B. Abrams **KBA** *Writer's initials added in ink*   *Capitalize first letter of each major word in subject line*

Subject: The Effectiveness of Reducing Building Temperatures on Weekends

Triple space (two blank spaces)

Margin lined up with items in To/From/Subject block to save typing time

Reducing the building temperature to 60° on weekends has cut energy use by 4% compared to last year's use from December to February and has saved our firm $22,000.

This savings is particularly remarkable when you consider that this winter has been colder than last year's, so that more heat would be needed to maintain the same temperature. $\frac{5}{8}" - 1"$

Fewer people have worked weekends during the past three months than during the preceding three months, but snow and bad driving conditions may have had more to do with keeping people home than the fear of being cold. Five of the 12 space heaters we bought have been checked out on an average weekend. On one weekend, all 12 were in use and some people shared their offices so that everyone could be in a room with a space heater.

Fully 92% of our employees support the lower temperature. I recommend that we continue turning down the heat on weekends through the remainder of the heating season and that we resume the practice when the heat is turned on next fall.

Headings are optional in memos

does not see the names of these people. Most e-mail programs also allow you to attach documents from other programs. The computer program supplies the date and time automatically.

Some aspects of e-mail format are still evolving. In particular, some writers treat e-mail messages as if they were informal letters; some treat them as memos. Even though the e-mail screen has a "To" line (as do memos), some writers still use an informal salutation, as in Figure A.13. The writer in Figure A.13 ends the message with a signature block. You can store a signature block in the e-mail program and set the program to insert the signature block automatically. In contrast, the writer in Figure A.14 omits both the salutation and his name. When you send a message to an individual or a group you have set up, the "From:" line will have your name and e-mail address.

If you post a message to a listserv, be sure to give at least your name and e-mail address at the end of your message, as some list-servs strip out identifying information when they process messages.

When you hit "reply," the e-mail program automatically uses "Re:" (Latin for *about*) and the previous subject line. The original message is set off, usually with

Figure A.12   Second Page of Two-Page Memo

1"–1½"

February 18, 2009

To: Dorothy N. Blasingham

Double-space (one blank space)   From: Roger L. Trout   **R.L.T.**   *Writer's initials added in ink*

Subject: Request for Third-Quarter Computer Training Sessions   *Capitalize first letter of all major words in subject line*

Triple space (two blank spaces)

¶ 1 never has a heading   Could you please run advanced training sessions on using Excel in April and May and basic training sessions for new hires in June?   *⅝"–1"*

Triple-space before a heading (two blank spaces)

Advanced Sessions on Excel
Bold or underline headings

Double-space between paragraphs (one blank space)   Once the tax season is over, Jose Cisneros wants to have his first- and second-year people take your advanced course on Excel. Plan on about 45-50 people in three sessions. The people in the course already use Excel for basic spreadsheets but need to learn the fine points of macros and charting.

If possible, it would be most convenient to have the sessions run for four afternoons rather

Plain paper for page 2   *½"–1"*

Dorothy N. Blasingham ← *Brief subject line or reader's name*   2   *Page number*   February 18, 2009

Also OK to line up page number, date at left under reader's name

Same margins as p 1.   before the summer vacation season begins.

Orientation for New Hires   *Capitalize first letter of all major words in heading*

With a total of 16 full-time and 34 part-time people being hired either for summer or permanent work, we'll need at least two and perhaps three orientation sessions. We'd like to hold these the first, second, and third weeks in June. By May 1, we should know how many people will be in each training session.

Would you be free to conduct training sessions on how to use our computers on June 9, June 16, and June 23? If we need only two dates, we'll use June 9 and June 16, but please block off the 23rd too in case we need a third session.

Triple-space before a heading (two blank spaces)

Request for Confirmation

Let me know whether you're free on these dates in June, and which dates you'd prefer. If you'll let me know by February 25, we can get information out to participants in plenty of time for the sessions.

Headings are optional in memos

Thanks!

Memos are initialed by To/From/Subject block

Figure A.13   A Basic E-Mail Message (direct request)

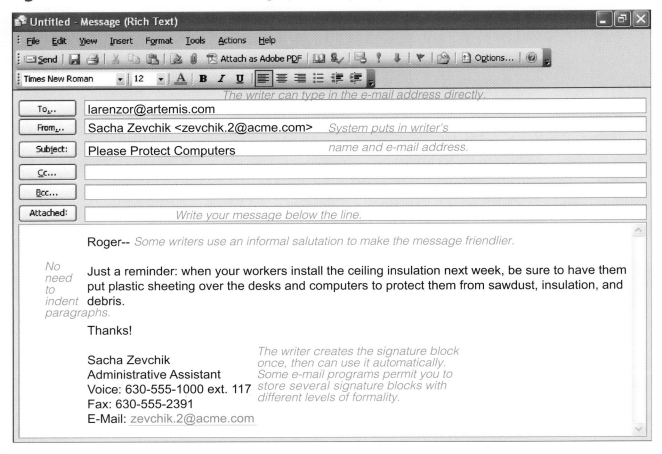

Figure A.14   An E-Mail Message with an Attachment (direct request)

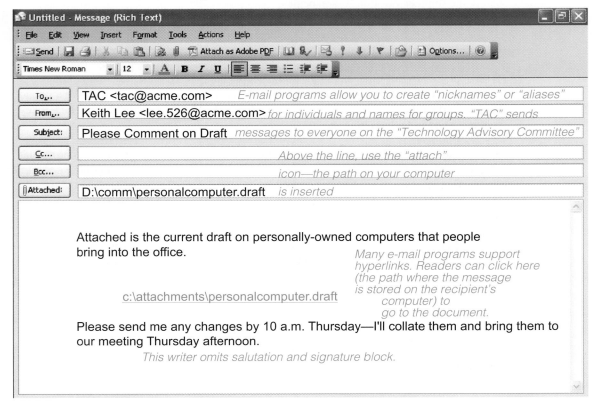

Figure A.15 An E-Mail Reply with Copies (response to a complaint)

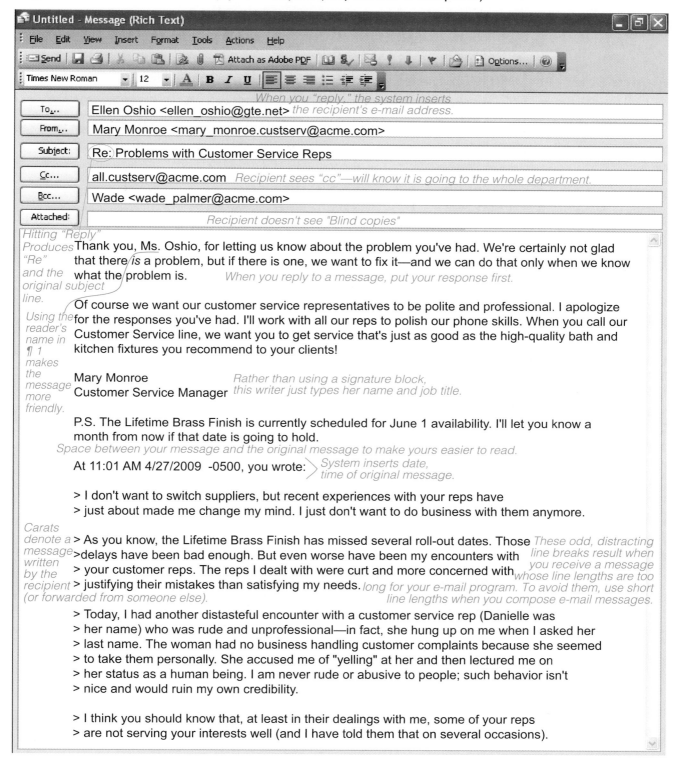

one or more vertical lines in the left margin or with carats (see Figure A.15). You may want to change the subject line to make it more appropriate for your message.

Use short line lengths in your e-mail message. If the line lengths are too long, they'll produce awkward line breaks, as in Figure A.15.

State and Province Abbreviations

States with names of more than five letters are frequently abbreviated in letters and memos. The Post Office abbreviations use two capital letters with no punctuation. See Figure A.16.

Figure A.16   Post Office Abbreviations for States, Territories, and Provinces

State name	Post Office abbreviation	State name	Post Office abbreviation
Alabama	AL	Missouri	MO
Alaska	AK	Montana	MT
Arizona	AZ	Nebraska	NE
Arkansas	AR	Nevada	NV
California	CA	New Hampshire	NH
Colorado	CO	New Jersey	NJ
Connecticut	CT	New Mexico	NM
Delaware	DE	New York	NY
District of Columbia	DC	North Carolina	NC
Florida	FL	North Dakota	ND
Georgia	GA	Ohio	OH
Hawaii	HI	Oklahoma	OK
Idaho	ID	Oregon	OR
Illinois	IL	Pennsylvania	PA
Indiana	IN	Rhode Island	RI
Iowa	IA	South Carolina	SC
Kansas	KS	South Dakota	SD
Kentucky	KY	Tennessee	TN
Louisiana	LA	Texas	TX
Maine	ME	Utah	UT
Maryland	MD	Vermont	VT
Massachusetts	MA	Virginia	VA
Michigan	MI	Washington	WA
Minnesota	MN	West Virginia	WV
Mississippi	MS	Wisconsin	WI
		Wyoming	WY

Territory name	Post Office abbreviation	Province name	Post Office abbreviation
Guam	GU	Alberta	AB
Puerto Rico	PR	British Columbia	BC
Virgin Islands	VI	Manitoba	MB
		New Brunswick	NB
		Newfoundland and Labrador	NL
		Northwest Territories	NT
		Nova Scotia	NS
		Nunavut	NU
		Ontario	ON
		Prince Edward Island	PE
		Quebec	PQ
		Saskatchewan	SK
		Yukon Territory	YT

Writing Correctly

Learning Objectives

After studying this appendix, you will know:

1 Common grammar usage.

2 Correct ways to use punctuation.

3 The right way to use words that are often confused.

Appendix Outline

Using Grammar

- Agreement
- Case
- Dangling Modifier
- Misplaced Modifier
- Parallel Structure
- Predication Errors

Understanding Punctuation

Punctuating Sentences

- Comma Splices
- Run-on Sentences
- Fused Sentences
- Sentence Fragments

Punctuation within Sentences

- Apostrophe
- Colon
- Comma
- Dash
- Hyphen
- Parentheses
- Period
- Semicolon

Special Punctuation Marks

- Quotation Marks
- Square Brackets
- Ellipses
- Underlining and Italics

Writing Numbers and Dates

Words That Are Often Confused

Proofreading Symbols

Too much concern for correctness at the wrong stage of the writing process can backfire: writers who worry about grammar and punctuation when they're writing a first or second draft are more likely to get writer's block. Wait till you have your ideas on paper to check your draft for correct grammar, punctuation, typing of numbers and dates, and word use. Use the proofreading symbols at the end of this appendix to indicate changes needed in a typed copy.

Most writers make a small number of grammatical errors repeatedly. Most readers care deeply about only a few grammatical points. Keep track of the feedback you get (from your instructors now, from your supervisor later) and put your energy into correcting the errors that bother the people who read what you write. A command of standard grammar will help you build the credible, professional image you want to create with everything you write.

Using Grammar

With the possible exception of spelling, grammar is the aspect of writing that writers seem to find most troublesome. Faulty grammar is often what executives are objecting to when they complain that college graduates or MBAs "can't write."

Agreement

Subjects and verbs agree when they are both singular or both plural.

Incorrect: The accountants who conducted the audit was recommended highly.

Correct: The accountants who conducted the audit were recommended highly.

Subject–verb agreement errors often occur when other words come between the subject and the verb. Edit your draft by finding the subject and the verb of each sentence.

American usage treats company names and the words *company* and *government* as singular nouns. British usage treats them as plural:

Correct (US):   State Farm Insurance trains its agents well.

Correct (Great Britain):   Lloyds of London train their agents well.

Use a plural verb when two or more singular subjects are joined by *and*.

Correct: Larry McGreevy and I are planning to visit the client.

Use a singular verb when two or more singular subjects are joined by *or, nor,* or *but.*

Correct: Either the shipping clerk or the superintendent has to sign the order.

When the sentence begins with *Here* or *There,* make the verb agree with the subject that follows the verb.

Correct: Here is the booklet you asked for.

Correct: There are the blueprints I wanted.

Note that some words that end in *s* are considered to be singular and require singular verbs.

Correct: A series of meetings is planned.

When a situation doesn't seem to fit the rules, or when following a rule produces an awkward sentence, revise the sentence to avoid the problem.

Problematic: The Plant Manager in addition to the sales representative (was, were?) pleased with the new system.

Better: The Plant Manager and the sales representative were pleased with the new system.

Problematic: None of us (is, are?) perfect.

Better: All of us have faults.

Errors in **noun–pronoun agreement** occur if a pronoun is of a different number or person than the word it refers to.

Incorrect: All drivers of leased automobiles are billed $300 if damages to his automobile are caused by a collision.

Correct: All drivers of leased automobiles are billed $300 if damages to their automobiles are caused by collisions.

Incorrect: A manager has only yourself to blame if things go wrong.

Correct: As a manager, you have only yourself to blame if things go wrong.

The following words require a singular verb and pronoun:

everybody	neither
each	nobody
either	a person
everyone	

Banished Words

Correct grammar and spelling are basic ways to signal careful, intelligent writing. Another fundamental is to choose words and phrases that say what you mean. Out of habit or carelessness, however, writers may sprinkle their work with meaningless words.

To highlight the problem, Lake Superior State University each January announces its "List of Words Banished from the Queen's English for Mis-Use, Over-Use and General Uselessness." A sample from 2003 and 2004:

- *Captured alive*—If someone is dead, it's too late to capture him or her.

- *Place stamp here* (on a return envelope)—This phrase states the obvious. Mail requires postage; we know where to put the stamp, don't we?

- *On the ground* (in news broadcasts)—With the exception of the occasional report from a helicopter or battleship, where else would the reporter be?

- *Extreme* (in advertisements)—This word has been attached to so many products, it no longer means anything. Extreme deodorants? Extremely what?

- *Make no mistake about it*—This phrase seems to insult the listener. It is a kind of filler that seems to mean only "Pay attention to what I will say."

Based on Lake Superior University, "Banished Words List," "The History of Word Banishment," "2004 List of Banished Words," and "2003 List of Banished Words," all http:// (accessed www.lssu.edu September 20, 2004.)

Correct: Everyone should bring his or her copy of the manual to the next session on changes in the law.

If the pronoun pairs necessary to avoid sexism seem cumbersome, avoid the terms in this list. Instead, use words that take plural pronouns or use second-person *you*.

Each pronoun must refer to a specific word. If a pronoun does not refer to a specific term, add a word to correct the error.

Incorrect: We will open three new stores in the suburbs. This will bring us closer to our customers.

Correct: We will open three new stores in the suburbs. This strategy will bring us closer to our customers.

Hint: Make sure *this* and *it* refer to a specific noun in the previous sentence. If either refers to an idea, add a noun ("this strategy") to make the sentence grammatically correct.

Use *who* and *whom* to refer to people and *which* to refer to objects. *That* can refer to anything: people, animals, organizations, and objects.

Correct: The new Executive Director, who moved here from Boston, is already making friends.

Correct: The information which she wants will be available tomorrow.

Correct: This confirms the price that I quoted you this morning.

Case

Case refers to the grammatical role a noun or pronoun plays in a sentence. Figure B.1 identifies the case of each personal pronoun.

Use **nominative case** pronouns for the subject of a clause.

Correct: Shannon Weaver and I talked to the customer, who was interested in learning more about integrated software.

Use **possessive case** pronouns to show who or what something belongs to.

Correct: Microsoft Office will exactly meet her needs.

Use **objective case** pronouns as objects of verbs or prepositions.

Figure B.1   The Case of the Personal Pronoun

	Nominative (subject of clause)	Possessive	Objective	Reflexive/ intensive
Singular				
1st person	I	my, mine	me	myself
2nd person	you	your, yours	you	yourself
3rd person	he/she/it	his/her(s)/its	him/her/it	himself/herself/itself
	one/who	one's/whose	one/whom	oneself/(no form)
Plural				
1st person	we	our, ours	us	ourselves
2nd person	you	your, yours	you	yourselves
3rd person	they	their, theirs	them	themselves

Correct: When you send in the quote, thank her for the courtesy she showed Shannon and me.

Hint: Use *whom* when *him* would fit grammatically in the same place in your sentence.

To (who/whom) do you intend to give this report?

You intend to give this report to him.

Whom is correct.

Have we decided (who, whom?) will take notes?

Have we decided he will take notes?

Who is correct.

Use **reflexive** and **intensive case** pronouns to refer to or emphasize a noun or pronoun that has already appeared in the sentence.

Correct: I myself think the call was a very productive one.

Do not use reflexive pronouns as subjects of clauses or as objects of verbs or propositions.

Incorrect: Elaine and myself will follow up on this order.

Correct: Elaine and I will follow up on this order.

Incorrect: He gave the order to Dan and myself.

Correct: He gave the order to Dan and me.

Note that the first-person pronoun comes after names or pronouns that refer to other people.

Dangling Modifier

A **modifier** is a word or phrase that gives more information about the subject, verb, or object in a clause. A **dangling modifier** refers to a word that is not actually in the sentence. The solution is to reword the modifier so that it is grammatically correct.

Incorrect: Confirming our conversation, the truck will leave Monday. [The speaker is doing the confirming. But the speaker isn't in the sentence.]

Incorrect: At the age of eight, I began teaching my children about American business. [This sentence says that the author was eight when he or she had children who could understand business.]

Correct a dangling modifier in one of these ways:

• Recast the modifier as a subordinate clause.

Correct: As I told you, the truck will leave Monday.

Correct: When they were eight, I began teaching my children about American business.

• Revise the main clause so its subject or object can be modified by the now-dangling phrase.

Correct: Confirming our conversation, I have scheduled the truck to leave Monday.

Correct: At the age of eight, my children began learning about American business.

Hint: Whenever you use a verb or adjective that ends in *-ing*, make sure it modifies the grammatical subject of your sentence. If it doesn't, reword the sentence.

The Fumblerules of Grammar

1. Avoid run-on sentences they are hard to read.
2. A writer must not shift your point of view.
3. Verbs has to agree with their subjects.
4. No sentence fragments.
5. Reserve the apostrophe for it's proper use and omit it when its not needed.
6. Proofread carefully to see if you any words out.
7. Avoid commas, that are unnecessary.
8. Steer clear of incorrect forms of verbs that have snuck in the language.
9. In statements involving two word phrases make an all out effort to use hyphens.
10. Last but not least, avoid clichés like the plague; seek viable alternatives.

Quoted from William Safire, "On Language: The Fumblerules of Grammar," *New York Times Magazine*, November 11, 1979, 16; and "On Language: Fumblerule Follow-up," *New York Times Magazine*, November 25, 1979, 14

Misplaced Modifier

A **misplaced modifier** appears to modify another element of the sentence than the writer intended.

Incorrect: Customers who complain often alert us to changes we need to make. [Does the sentence mean that customers must complain frequently to teach us something? Or is the meaning that frequently we learn from complaints?]

Correct a misplaced modifier by moving it closer to the word it modifies or by adding punctuation to clarify your meaning. If a modifier modifies the whole sentence, use it as an introductory phrase or clause; follow it with a comma.

Correct: Often, customers who complain alert us to changes we need to make.

Parallel Structure

Items in a series or list must have the same grammatical structure.

Not parallel: In the second month of your internship, you will
1. Learn how to resolve customers' complaints.
2. Supervision of desk staff.
3. Interns will help plan store displays.

Parallel: In the second month of your internship, you will
1. Learn how to resolve customers' complaints.
2. Supervise desk staff.
3. Plan store displays.

Also parallel: Duties in the second month of your internship include resolving customers' complaints, supervising desk staff, and planning store displays.

Hint: When you have two or three items in a list (whether the list is horizontal or vertical) make sure the items are in the same grammatical form. Put lists vertically to make them easier to see.

Predication Errors

The predicate of a sentence must fit grammatically and logically with the subject.

In sentences using *is* and other linking verbs, the complement must be a noun, an adjective, or a noun clause.

Incorrect: The reason for this change is because the SEC now requires fuller disclosure.

Correct: The reason for this change is that the SEC now requires fuller disclosure.

Make sure that the verb describes the action done by or done to the subject.

Incorrect: Our goals should begin immediately.

Correct: Implementing our goals should begin immediately.

Understanding Punctuation

Punctuation marks are road signs to help readers predict what comes next. (See Figure B.2.)

When you move from the subject to the verb, you're going in a straight line; no comma is needed. When you end an introductory phrase or clause, the comma tells readers the introduction is over and you're turning to the main clause. When words interrupt the main clause, like this, commas tell the reader when to turn off the main clause for a short side route and when to return.

Figure B.2   What Punctuation Tells the Reader

Mark	Tells the reader
Period	We're stopping.
Semicolon	What comes next is closely related to what I just said.
Colon	What comes next is an example of what I just said.
Dash	What comes next is a dramatic example of or a shift from what I just said.
Comma	What comes next is a slight turn, but we're going in the same basic direction.

What Bothers Your Boss?

Most bosses care deeply about only a few points of grammar. Find out which errors are your supervisor's pet peeves, and avoid them.

Any living language changes. New usages appear first in speaking. Here are four issues on which experts currently disagree:

1. Plural pronouns to refer to *everybody, everyone,* and *each.* Standard grammar says these words require singular pronouns.

2. Split infinitives. An infinitive is the form of a verb that contains *to: to understand.* An infinitive is split when another word separates the *to* from the rest of an infinitive: *to easily understand.*

3. *Hopefully* to mean *I hope that. Hopefully* means "in a hopeful manner." However, a speaker who says "Hopefully, the rain will stop" is talking about the speaker's hope, not the rain's.

4. *Verbal* to mean *oral. Verbal* means "using words." Both writing and speaking are verbal communication. Nonverbal communication (for example, body language) does not use words.

Ask your instructor and your boss whether they are willing to accept the less formal usage. When you write to someone you don't know, use standard grammar and usage.

Some people have been told to put commas where they'd take breaths. That's bad advice. How often you'd take a breath depends on how big your lung capacity is, how fast and how loud you're speaking, and the emphasis you want. Commas aren't breaths. Instead, like other punctuation, they're road signs.

Punctuating Sentences

A sentence contains at least one main clause. A **main** or **independent clause** is a complete statement. A **subordinate** or **dependent clause** contains both a subject and a verb but is not a complete statement and cannot stand by itself. A phrase is a group of words that does not contain both a subject and a verb.

Main clauses

   Your order will arrive Thursday.

   He dreaded talking to his supplier.

   I plan to enroll for summer school classes.

Subordinate clauses

   if you place your order by Monday

   because he was afraid the product would be out of stock

   since I want to graduate next spring

Phrases

   With our current schedule

   As a result

   After talking to my advisor

A clause with one of the following words will be subordinate:

after	if
although, though	when, whenever
because, since	while, as
before, until	

Using the correct punctuation will enable you to avoid three major sentence errors: comma splices, run-on sentences, and sentence fragments.

Comma Splices

A **comma splice** or **comma fault** occurs when two main clauses are joined only by a comma (instead of by a comma and a coordinating conjunction).

Incorrect: The contest will start in June, the date has not been set.

The Most Common Errors in First-Year Composition Papers

A survey of hundreds of student papers found that the following errors were most common:

1. No comma after introductory element
2. Vague pronoun reference
3. No comma in compound sentence
4. Wrong word
5. No comma in nonrestrictive clause
6. Wrong/missing inflected endings
7. Wrong or missing preposition
8. Comma splice
9. Possessive apostrophe error
10. Tense shift
11. Unnecessary shift in person
12. Sentence fragment
13. Wrong tense or verb form
14. Subject–verb agreement error
15. Lack of comma in series
16. Pronoun agreement error
17. Unnecessary comma with restrictive clause
18. Run-on or fused sentence
19. Dangling or misplaced modifier
20. Its/it's error

Based on Robert J. Connors and Andrea A. Lunsford, "Frequency of Formal Errors in Current College Writing, or Ma and Pa Kettle Do Research," *College Composition and Communication* 39, no. 4 (December 1988), 403.

Correct a comma splice in one of the following ways:

*   If the ideas are closely related, use a semicolon rather than a comma. If they aren't closely related, start a new sentence.

    Correct: The contest will start in June; the exact date has not been set.

*   Add a coordinating conjunction.

    Correct: The contest will start in June, but the exact date has not been set.

*   Subordinate one of the clauses.

    Correct: Although the contest will start in June, the exact date has not been set.

Remember that you cannot use just a comma with the following transitions:

however   nevertheless
therefore   moreover

Instead, either use a semicolon to separate the clauses or start a new sentence.

Incorrect: Computerized grammar checkers do not catch every error, however, they may be useful as a first check before an editor reads the material.

Correct: Computerized grammar checkers do not catch every error. However, they may be useful as a first check before an editor reads the material.

Run-on Sentences

A **run-on sentence** strings together several main clauses using *and, but, or, so,* and *for.* Run-on sentences and comma splices are "mirror faults." A comma splice *uses only* the comma and omits the coordinating conjunction, while a run-on sentence uses *only* the conjunction and omits the comma. Correct a short run-on sentence by adding a comma. Separate a long run-on sentence into two or more sentences. Consider subordinating one or more of the clauses.

Incorrect: We will end up with a much smaller markup but they use a lot of this material so the volume would be high so try to sell them on fast delivery and tell them our quality is very high.

Correct: Although we will end up with a much smaller markup, volume would be high since they use a lot of this material. Try to sell them on fast delivery and high quality.

Fused Sentences

A **fused sentence** results when two sentences or more are *fused*, or joined with neither punctuation nor conjunctions. To fix the error, add the punctuation, add punctuation and a conjunction, or subordinate one of the clauses.

Incorrect: The advantages of Intranets are clear the challenge is persuading employees to share information.

Correct: The advantages of Intranets are clear; the challenge is persuading employees to share information.

Also correct: Although the advantages of Intranets are clear, the challenge is persuading employees to share information.

Sentence Fragments

In a **sentence fragment,** a group of words that is not a complete sentence is punctuated as if it were a complete sentence.

Incorrect: Observing these people, I have learned two things about the program. The time it takes. The rewards it brings.

To fix a sentence fragment, either add whatever parts of the sentence are missing or incorporate the fragment into the sentence before it or after it.

Correct: Observing these people, I have learned that the program is time-consuming but rewarding.

Remember that clauses with the following words are not complete sentences. Join them to a main clause.

after	if
although, though	when, whenever
because, since	while, as
before, until	

Incorrect: We need to buy a new computer system. Because our current system is obsolete.

Correct: We need to buy a new computer system because our current system is obsolete.

Punctuation within Sentences

The good business and administrative writer knows how to use the following punctuation marks: apostrophes, colons, commas, dashes, hyphens, parentheses, periods, and semicolons.

Apostrophe

1. Use an apostrophe in a contraction to indicate that a letter or symbol has been omitted.

    We're trying to renegotiate the contract.

    The '90s were years of restructuring for our company.

2. To indicate possession, add an apostrophe and an *s* to the word.

    The corporation's home office is in Houston, Texas.

    Apostrophes to indicate possession are especially essential when one noun in a comparison is omitted.

    This year's sales will be higher than last year's.

    When a word already ends in an *s*, add only an apostrophe to make it possessive.

    The meeting will be held at New Orleans' convention center.

    With many terms, the placement of the apostrophe indicates whether the noun is singular or plural.

Incorrect: The program should increase the participant's knowledge. [Implies that only one participant is in the program.]

Correct: The program should increase the participants' knowledge. [Many participants are in the program.]

Hint: Use "of" in the sentence to see where the apostrophe goes.

The figures of last year = last year's figures

The needs of our customers = our customers' needs

Pity the Apostrophe

The apostrophe is so often misused that in England John Richards founded the Apostrophe Protection Society. The society's Web site, www.apostrophe.fisnet.co.uk, summarizes the basic rules for using apostrophes in English. The entertaining part of the Web site is its examples, photos of signs that have abused apostrophes in many ways, including overuse and omission. Here are some examples:

*   In a banquet hall's brochure: "The Ultimate Attraction for all sorts of Function's ranging from, Fair's, Carnival's, Bon Fire Display's, Music Concert's, Party's, Ball's, Corporate Function's and even Wedding's" (and that's just what the ideas range *from; imagine what they range to!*).

*   By a parking lot: "Resident's and Visitor's Only" (meaning something belonging to one resident and one visitor).

*   By a school parking lot: "Reserved for Principals Office" (a sign that will not enhance the school's reputation).

*   In a set of contest rules: "The judges decision is final." (Writer couldn't decide where to put the apostrophe, so he or she didn't try.)

*   At a government office building: "Disabled Access (All Depts's) via Dep. of Social Security" (trying all punctuation possibilities at once).

Based on John Richards, Apostrophe Protection Society Web site, home page and examples, www.apostrophe.fsnet.co.uk, (accessed September 20, 2004).

The History of Punctuation

WHENWRITING

BEGANTHERE

WERENOBREAKS

BETWEENWORDS

In inscriptions on monuments in ancient Greece, breaks were chosen to create balance and proportion.

WHENWRITI

NGBEGANTH

EREWERENO

BREAKSBET

WEENWORDS

In the third century BC, Aristophanes added a dot high in the line (like this •), after a complete thought, or *periodos*. For part of a complete thought, or *colon*, he used a dot on the line (like this •). For a comma, or subdivision of a colon, he used a dot halfway up (like this •).

The monks in the Middle Ages substituted a strong slash for the midway dot. As time went on, the strong slash was shortened and acquired a curl—becoming our comma today.

Based on Lionel Casson, "howandwhy punctuationevercametobeinvented," *Smithsonian* 19, no. 7 (October 1988), 216.

Note that possessive pronouns (e.g., *his, ours*) usually do not have apostrophes. The only exception is *one's*.

The company needs the goodwill of its stockholders.

His promotion was announced yesterday.

One's greatest asset is the willingness to work hard.

3. Use an apostrophe to make plurals that could be confused for other words.

I earned A's in all my business courses.

However, other plurals do not use apostrophes.

Colon

1. Use a colon to separate a main clause and a list that explains the last element in the clause. The items in the list are specific examples of the word that appears immediately before the colon.

Please order the following supplies:

Printer cartridges

Computer paper (20-lb. white bond)

Bond paper (25-lb., white, 25% cotton)

Company letterhead

Company envelopes

When the list is presented vertically, capitalize the first letter of each item in the list. When the list is run in with the sentence, you don't need to capitalize the first letter after the colon.

Please order the following supplies: printer cartridges, computer paper (20-lb. white bond), bond paper (25-lb., white, 25% cotton), company letterhead, and company envelopes.

Do not use a colon when the list is grammatically part of the main clause.

Incorrect:	The rooms will have coordinated decors in natural colors such as: eggplant, moss, and mushroom.
Correct:	The rooms will have coordinated decors in natural colors such as eggplant, moss, and mushroom.
Also correct:	The rooms will have coordinated decors in a variety of natural colors: eggplant, moss, and mushroom.

If the list is presented vertically, some authorities suggest introducing the list with a colon even though the words preceding the colon are not a complete sentence.

2. Use a colon to join two independent clauses when the second clause explains or restates the first clause.

Selling is simple: give people the service they need, and they'll come back with more orders.

Comma

1. Use commas to separate the main clause from an introductory clause, the reader's name, or words that interrupt the main clause. Note that commas both precede and follow the interrupting information.

R. J. Garcia, the new Sales Manager, comes to us from the Des Moines office.

A **nonessential clause** gives extra information that is not needed to identify the noun it modifies. Because nonessential clauses give extra information, they need extra commas.

Sue Decker, who wants to advance in the organization, has signed up for the company training program in sales techniques.

Do not use commas to set off information that restricts the meaning of a noun or pronoun. **Essential clauses** give essential, not extra, information.

Anyone who wants to advance in the organization should take advantage of on-the-job training.

The clause "who wants to advance in the organization" restricts the meaning of the pronoun *anyone.*

Do not use commas to separate the subject from the verb, even if you would take a breath after a long subject.

Incorrect: Laws requiring anyone collecting $5,000 or more on behalf of another person, apply to schools and private individuals as well to charitable groups and professional fund-raisers.

Correct: Laws requiring anyone collecting $5,000 or more on behalf of another person ☐ apply to schools and private individuals as well to charitable groups and professional fund-raisers.

2. Use a comma after the first clause in a compound sentence if the clauses are long or if they have different subjects.

This policy eliminates all sick-leave credit of the employee at the time of retirement, and payment will be made only once to any individual.

Do not use commas to join independent clauses without a conjunction. Doing so produces comma splices.

3. Use commas to separate items in a series. Using a comma before the *and* or *or* is not required by some authorities, but using a comma always adds clarity. The comma is essential if any of the items in the series themselves contain the word *and.*

The company pays the full cost of hospitalization insurance for eligible employees, spouses, and unmarried dependent children under age 23.

Dash

Use dashes to emphasize a break in thought.

Ryertex comes in 30 grades—each with a special use.

To type a dash, use two hyphens with no space before or after.

Hyphen

1. Use a hyphen to indicate that a word has been divided between two lines.

Attach the original receipts for lodging, meals, tips, transportation, and registration fees.

Divide words at syllable breaks. If you aren't sure where the syllables divide, look up the word in a dictionary. When a word has several syllables, divide it after a vowel or between two consonants. Don't divide words of one syllable (e.g., *used*); don't divide a two-syllable word if one of the syllables is only one letter long (e.g., *acre*).

2. Use hyphens to join two or more words used as a single adjective.

Order five 10- or 12-foot lengths.

The computer-prepared Income and Expense statements will be ready next Friday.

The hyphen prevents misreading. In the first example, five lengths are needed, not lengths of 5, 10, or 12 feet. In the second example, without the hyphen, the reader might think that *computer* was the subject and *prepared* was the verb.

Parentheses

1. Use parentheses to set off words, phrases, or sentences used to explain or comment on the main idea.

For the thinnest Ryertex (.015") only a single layer of the base material may be used, while the thickest (10") may contain over 600 greatly compressed layers of fabric or paper. By varying the fabric used (cotton, asbestos, glass, or nylon) or the type of paper, and by changing the kind of resin (phenolic, melamine, silicone, or epoxy), we can produce 30 different grades.

Any additional punctuation goes outside the second parenthesis when the punctuation applies to the whole sentence. It goes inside when it applies only to the words in the parentheses.

Please check the invoice to see if credit should be issued. (A copy of the invoice is attached.)

2. Use parentheses for the citations in a text. See Chapter 16 for examples.

Period

1. Use a period at the end of a sentence. Space once before the next sentence.
2. Use a period after some abbreviations. When a period replaces a person's name, leave one space after the period before the next word. In other abbreviations, no space is necessary.

R. J. Tebeaux has been named Vice President for Marketing.

The U.S. division plans to hire 300 new M.B.A.s in the next year.

The tendency is to reduce the use of punctuation. It would also be correct to write

The US division plans to hire 300 new MBAs in the next year.

Semicolon

1. Use semicolons to join two independent clauses when they are closely related.

We'll do our best to fill your order promptly; however, we cannot guarantee a delivery date.

Using a semicolon suggests that the two ideas are very closely connected. Using a period and a new sentence is also correct but implies nothing about how closely related the two sentences are.

2. Use semicolons to separate items in a series when the items themselves contain commas.

The final choices for the new plant are El Paso, Texas; Albuquerque, New Mexico; Salt Lake City, Utah; Eureka, California; and Eugene, Oregon.

Hospital benefits are also provided for certain specialized care services such as diagnostic admissions directed toward a definite disease or injury; normal maternity delivery, Caesarean section delivery, or complications of pregnancy; and inpatient admissions for dental procedures necessary to safeguard the patient's life or health.

Hint: A semicolon could be replaced by a period and a capital letter. It has a sentence on both sides.

Special Punctuation Marks

Quotation marks, square brackets, ellipses, and underlining are necessary when you use quoted material.

Quotation Marks

1. Use quotation marks around the names of brochures, pamphlets, and magazine articles.

   Enclosed are 30 copies of our pamphlet "Saving Energy."

   You'll find articles like "How to Improve Your Golf Game" and "Can You Keep Your Eye on the Ball?" in every issue.

   In US punctuation, periods and commas go inside quotation marks. Colons and semicolons go outside. Question marks go inside if they are part of the material being quoted.

2. Use quotation marks around words to indicate that you think the term is misleading.

   These "pro-business" policies actually increase corporate taxes.

3. Use quotation marks around words that you are discussing as words.

   Forty percent of the respondents answered "yes" to the first question.

   Use "Ms." as a courtesy title for a woman unless you know she prefers another title.

   It is also acceptable to italicize words instead of using quotation marks.

4. Use quotation marks around words or sentences that you quote from someone else.

   "The Fog Index," says its inventor, Robert Gunning, is "an effective warning system against drifting into needless complexity."

Square Brackets

Use square brackets to add your own additions to or changes in quoted material.

| Senator Smith's statement: | "These measures will create a deficit." |
| Your use of Smith's statement: | According to Senator Smith, "These measures [in the new tax bill] will create a deficit." |

The square brackets show that Smith did not say these words; you add them to make the quote make sense in your document.

International Punctuation

Cultures differ in their use of punctuation marks. US writers put periods and commas inside closing quotation marks; writers in England put them outside the quotation marks. Spanish writers also put sentence-ending punctuation outside. Also, in some regions Spanish writers use angled quotation marks: « and ». Angled quotation marks also are the norm in French writing.

In dialogue, French and Spanish writers traditionally signal a change of speakers by starting with a dash.

Chinese and Japanese use different punctuation marks with their writing systems. For example, a period is a small circle, set near the base line, and quotation marks are 90-degree angles that appear at the upper left and lower right. Because the characters cannot be italicized as Roman letters can, Chinese and Japanese use book title marks and chapter marks.

Some languages use accents as well as punctuation marks. Accents identify how a letter is to be pronounced, and they affect the meaning of a word. Sametz Blackstone Associates, a consulting firm, was wise to have a native speaker check a translation into Spanish. The proofreader caught a missing tilde (~). Without the tilde, the Spanish version didn't say "celebrating 35 years"; it said "celebrating 35 anuses."

Based on Complete Translation Services, "A History of Punctuation," http://www.completetranslation.com, (accessed September 20, 2004; and Mark Lasswell, "Lost in Translation," *Business 2.0*, 5, no. 7 (August 2004): 68.

Ellipses

Ellipses are spaced dots. In typing, use three spaced periods for an ellipsis. When an ellipsis comes at the end of a sentence, use a dot immediately after the last letter of the sentence for a period. Then add three spaced dots, with another space after the last dot.

1. Use ellipses to indicate that one or more words have been omitted in the middle of quoted material. You do not need ellipses at the beginning or end of a quote.

   The Wall Street Journal notes that Japanese magazines and newspapers include advertisements for a "$2.1 million home in New York's posh Riverdale section . . . 185 acres of farmland [and] . . . luxury condos on Manhattan's Upper East Side."

2. In advertising and direct mail, use ellipses to imply the pace of spoken comments.

   If you've ever wanted to live on a tropical island . . . cruise to the Bahamas . . . or live in a castle in Spain . . .

   . . . you can make your dreams come true with Vacations Extraordinaire.

Underlining and Italics

1. Underline or italicize the names of newspapers, magazines, and books.

   The Wall Street Journal   *The Wall Street Journal*

   Fortune   *Fortune*

   The Wealth of Nations   *The Wealth of Nations*

   Titles of brochures and pamphlets are put in quotation marks.

2. Underline or italicize words to emphasize them.

   Here's a bulletin that gives you, in handy chart form, workable data on over 50 different types of tubing and pipe.

   You may also use bold to emphasize words. Bold type is better than either underlining or italics because it is easier to read. (See Chapter 6. ◀▥)

Writing Numbers and Dates

Spell out **numbers** from one to nine. Use figures for numbers 10 and over in most cases. Always use figures for amounts of money.

Spell out any number that appears at the beginning of a sentence. If spelling it out is impractical, revise the sentence so that it does not begin with a number.

Fifty students filled out the survey.

In 2002, euro notes and coins entered circulation.

When two numbers follow each other, spell out the smaller number and use figures for the larger number.

In **dates,** use figures for the day and year. The month is normally spelled out. Be sure to spell out the month in international business communication. American usage puts the month first, so that *1/10/10* means *January 10, 2010.* European usage puts the day first, so that *1/10/10* means *October 1, 2010.* Modern punctuation uses a comma before the year only when you give both the month and the day of the month:

May 1, 2010

but

Summers 2007–10

August 2010

Fall 2009

No punctuation is needed in military or European usage, which puts the day of the month first: 13 July 2009. Do not space before or after the slash used to separate parts of the date: 10/05–5/09.

Use a hyphen to join inclusive dates.

March–August 2010 (or write out: March to August 2010)

'08–'09

1999–2001

Note that you do not need to repeat the century in the date that follows the hyphen: 2008–09.

Words That Are Often Confused

Here's a list of words that are frequently confused. Master them, and you'll be well on the way to using words correctly.

1. accede/exceed
   accede: to yield
   exceed: to go beyond, surpass
   I accede to your demand that we not exceed the budget.

2. accept/except
   accept: to receive; to agree to
   except: to leave out or exclude; but
   I accept your proposal except for point 3.

3. access/excess
   access: the right to use; admission to
   excess: surplus
   As supply clerk, he had access to any excess materials.

4. adapt/adopt
   adapt: adjust
   adopt: to take as one's own
   She would adapt her ideas so people would adopt them.

5. advice/advise
   advice: (noun) counsel
   advise: (verb) to give counsel or advice to someone
   I asked him to advise me, but I didn't like the advice I got.

6. affect/effect
   affect: (verb) to influence or modify
   effect: (verb) to produce or cause; (noun) result
   He hoped that his argument would affect his boss's decision, but so far as he could see, it had no effect.
   The tax relief effected some improvement for the citizens whose incomes had been affected by inflation.

The Knead for Approve Reed Her with a Spell Chequer

Who wood have guest The Spell Chequer would super seed The assent of the editor Who was once a mane figure? . . . Once, awl sought his council; Now nun prophet from him. How suite the job was; It was all sew fine. . . . Never once was he board As he edited each claws, Going strait to his deer work Where he'd in cyst on clarity. Now he's holy unacceptable, Useless and knot kneaded. . . . This is know miner issue, Fore he cannot urn a wage. Two this he takes a fence, Butt nose naught watt too due. He's wade each option Of jobs he mite dew, But nothing peaks his interest Like making pros clear. Sum will see him silly For being sew upset, But doesn't good righting Go beyond the write spelling?

Quoted from Jeff Lovill, "On the Uselessness of an Editor in the Presents of a Spell Chequer," *Technical Communication* 35, no. 4 (1988), 267; and Edward M. Chilton, "Various Comments on 4Q88," *Technical Communication* 36, no. 2 (1989), 173.

7. affluent/effluent

    affluent: (adjective) rich, possessing in abundance

    effluent: (noun) something that flows out

    > Affluent companies can afford the cost of removing pollutants from the effluents their factories produce.

8. a lot/allot

    a lot: many (informal)

    allot: divide or give to

    > A lot of players signed up for this year's draft. We allotted one first-round draft choice to each team.

9. among/between

    among: (use with more than two choices)

    between: (use with only two choices)

    > This year the differences between the two candidates for president are unusually clear.

    > I don't see any major differences among the candidates for city council.

10. amount/number

    amount: (use with concepts or items that can be measured but that cannot be counted individually)

    number: (use when items can be counted individually)

    > It's a mistake to try to gauge the amount of interest he has by the number of questions he asks.

11. attributed/contributed

    attributed: was said to be caused by

    contributed: gave something to

    > The rain probably contributed to the accident, but the police officer attributed the accident to driver error.

12. cite/sight/site

    cite: (verb) to quote

    sight: (noun) vision, something to be seen

    site: (noun) location, place where a building is or will be built

    > She cited the old story of the building inspector who was depressed by the very sight of the site for the new factory.

13. complement/compliment

    complement: (verb) to complete, finish; (noun) something that completes

    compliment: (verb) to praise; (noun) praise

    > The compliment she gave me complemented my happiness.

14. compose/comprise

    compose: make up, create

    comprise: consist of, be made up of, be composed of

    > The city council is composed of 12 members. Each district comprises an area 50 blocks square.

15. confuse/complicate/exacerbate

    confuse: to bewilder

    complicate: to make more complex or detailed

    exacerbate: to make worse

    > Because I missed the first 20 minutes of the movie, I didn't understand what was going on. The complicated plot exacerbated my confusion.

16. dependant/dependent

    dependant: (noun) someone for whom one is financially responsible

    dependent: (adjective) relying on someone else

    > IRS regulations don't let us count our 25-year-old son as a dependant, but he is still financially dependent on us.

17. describe/prescribe

    describe: list the features of something, tell what something looks like

    prescribe: specify the features something must contain

    > The law prescribes the priorities for making repairs. This report describes our plans to comply with the law.

18. different from/different than

    Almost always *different from* (try changing the adjective *different* to the verb *differs*)

    > Bob's job description is different from mine.

    The most common exception is the indirect comparison.

    > Susan has a different attitude than you and I [*do* is implied].

19. discreet/discrete

    discreet: tactful, careful not to reveal secrets

    discrete: separate, distinct

    > I have known him to be discreet on two discrete occasions.

20. disinterested/uninterested

    Disinterested: impartial

    Uninterested: unconcerned

    > Because our boss is uninterested in office spats, she makes a disinterested referee.

21. elicit/illicit

    elicit: (verb) to draw out

    illicit: (adjective) not permitted, unlawful

    > The reporter could elicit no information from the senator about his illicit love affair.

22. eminent/immanent/imminent

    eminent: distinguished

    immanent: existing in the mind or consciousness

    imminent: about to happen

    > The eminent doctor believed that death was imminent. The eminent minister believed that God was immanent.

23. farther/further

    Farther: use for physical difference

    Further: use for metaphoric difference; also use for *additional* or *additionally*

    > As I traveled farther from the destruction at the plant, I pondered the further evidence of sabotage presented to me today.

24. fewer/less

    fewer: (use for objects that can be counted individually)

    less: (use for objects that can be measured but not counted individually)

    > There is less sand in this bucket; there are probably fewer grains of sand, too.

25. forward/foreword

    forward: ahead

foreword: preface, introduction
>The author looked forward to writing the foreword to the book.

26. good/well
good: (adjective, used to modify nouns; as a noun, means something that is good)
well: (adverb, used to modify verbs, adjectives, and other adverbs)
>Her words "Good work!" told him that he was doing well.
>He spent a great deal of time doing volunteer work because he believed that doing good was just as important as doing well.

27. i.e./e.g.
i.e.: (*id est*—that is) introduces a restatement or explanation of the preceding word or phrase
e.g.: (*exempli gratia*—for the sake of an example; for example) introduces one or more examples
>Although he had never studied Latin, he rarely made a mistake in using Latin abbreviations, e.g., i.e., and etc., because he associated each with a mnemonic device (i.e., a word or image used to help one remember something). He remembered *i.e.* as *in effect*, pretended that *e.g.* meant *example given*, and used *etc.* only when *examples to continue* would fit.

28. imply/infer
imply: suggest, put an idea into someone's head
infer: deduce, get an idea out from something
>She implied that an announcement would be made soon. I inferred from her smile that it would be an announcement of her promotion.

29. it's/its
it's: it is, it has
its: belonging to it
>It's clear that a company must satisfy its customers to stay in business.

30. lectern/podium
lectern: raised stand with a slanted top that holds a manuscript for a reader or notes for a speaker
podium: platform for a speaker or conductor to stand on
>I left my notes on the lectern when I left the podium at the end of my talk.

31. lie/lay
lie: to recline; to tell a falsehood (never takes an object)
lay: to put an object on something (always takes an object)
>He was laying the papers on the desk when I came in, but they aren't lying there now.

32. loose/lose
loose: not tight
lose: to have something disappear
>If I lose weight, this suit will be loose.

33. moral/morale
moral: (adjective) virtuous, good; (noun: morals) ethics, sense of right and wrong
morale: (noun) spirit, attitude, mental outlook
>Studies have shown that coed dormitories improve student morale without harming student morals.

34. objective/rationale

objective: goal

rationale: reason, justification

> The objective of the meeting was to explain the rationale behind the decision.

35. personal/personnel

personal: individual, to be used by one person

personnel: staff, employees

> All personnel will get personal computers by the end of the year.

36. possible/possibly

possible: (adjective) something that can be done

possibly: (adverb) perhaps

> It is possible that we will be able to hire this spring. We can choose from possibly the best graduating class in the past five years.

37. precede/proceed

precede: (verb) to go before

proceed: (verb) to continue; (noun: proceeds) money

> Raising the money must precede spending it. Only after we obtain the funds can we proceed to spend the proceeds.

38. principal/principle

principal: (adjective) main; (noun) person in charge; money lent out at interest

principle: (noun) basic truth or rule, code of conduct

> *The Prince*, Machiavelli's principal work, describes his principles for ruling a state.

39. quiet/quite

quiet: not noisy

quite: very

> It was quite difficult to find a quiet spot anywhere near the floor of the stock exchange.

40. regulate/relegate

regulate: control

relegate: put (usually in an inferior position)

> If the federal government regulates the size of lettering on country road signs, we may as well relegate the current signs to the garbage bin.

41. respectfully/respectively

respectfully: with respect

respectively: to each in the order listed

> When I was introduced to the queen, the prime minister, and the court jester, I bowed respectfully, shook hands politely, and winked, respectively.

42. role/roll

role: part in a play or script, function (in a group)

roll: (noun) list of students, voters, or other members; round piece of bread; (verb) move by turning over and over

> While the teacher called the roll, George—in his role as class clown—threw a roll he had saved from lunch.

Spelling Demons

The words listed below (in order of increasing difficulty) are among the most frequently misspelled words in English. How many of them do you spell correctly?

1. Grammar
2. Argument
3. Surprise
4. Achieve
5. Definitely
6. Separate
7. Desirable
8. Development
9. Existence
10. Occasion
11. Assistant
12. Repetition
13. Privilege
14. Dependent
15. Consensus
16. Accommodate
17. Occurrence
18. Commitment
19. Allotted
20. Liaison
21. Proceed
22. Harass
23. Dissention
24. Prerogative
25. Inadvertent

Based on Bruce O. Boston, ed., *Stet!* (Alexandria, VA: Editorial Experts, 1986), 267–68

43.   simple/simplistic

simple: not complicated

simplistic: watered down, oversimplified

She was able to explain the proposal in simple terms without making the explanation sound simplistic.

44.   stationary/stationery

stationary: not moving, fixed

stationery: paper

During the earthquake, even the stationery was not stationary.

45.   their/there/they're

their: belonging to them

there: in that place

they're: they are

There are plans, designed to their specifications, for the house they're building.

46.   to/too/two

to: (preposition) function word indicating proximity, purpose, time, etc.

too: (adverb) also, very, excessively

two: (adjective) the number 2

The formula is too secret to entrust to two people.

47.   unique/unusual

unique: sole, only, alone

unusual: not common

I believed that I was unique in my ability to memorize long strings of numbers until I consulted *Guinness World Records* and found that I was merely unusual: someone else had equaled my feat in 1993.

48.   verbal/oral

verbal: using words

oral: spoken, not written

His verbal skills were uneven: his oral communication was excellent, but he didn't write well. His sensitivity to nonverbal cues was acute: he could tell what kind of day I had just by looking at my face.

Hint: Oral comes from the Latin word for mouth, *os*. Think of Oral-B Toothbrushes: for the mouth. Verbal comes from the Latin word for word, *verba*. Nonverbal language is language that does not use words (e.g., body language, gestures).

49.   whether/weather

whether: (conjunction) used to introduce possible alternatives

weather: (noun) state of the atmosphere: wet or dry, hot or cold, calm or storm

We will have to see what the weather is before we decide whether to hold the picnic indoors or out.

50.   your/you're

your: belonging to you

you're: you are

You're the top candidate for promotion in your division.

Proofreading Symbols

Use the proofreading symbols in Figure B.3 to make corrections on paper copies. Figure B.4 shows how the symbols can be used to correct a typed text.

Figure B.3 Proofreading Symbols

ℯ	delete	[	move to left
ℒ	insert a letter	]	move to right
ℂ	start a new paragraph here	⌐	move up
(stet)	stet (leave as it was before the marked change)	⌐	move down
(tr) ⌐	transpose (reverse)	#	leave a space
(lc)	lower case (don't capitalize)	⌒	close up
≡	capitalize	//	align vertically

Figure B.4 Marked Text

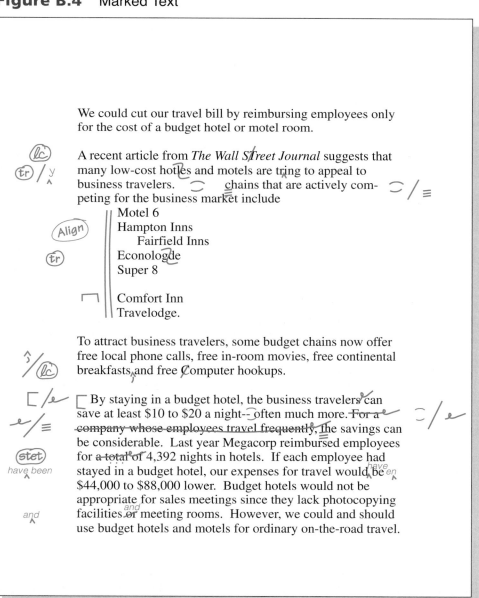

APPENDIX B   # Exercises and Problems

B.1   Diagnostic Test on Punctuation and Grammar

Identify and correct the errors in the following passages.

a.

> Company's are finding it to their advantage to cultivate their suppliers. Partnerships between a company and it's suppliers can yield hefty payoffs for both company and supplier. One example is Bailey Controls an Ohio headquartered company. Bailey make control systems for big factories. They treat suppliers almost like departments of their own company. When a Bailey employee passes a laser scanner over a bins bar code the supplier is instantly alerted to send more parts.

b.

> Entrepreneur Trip Hawkins appears in Japanese ads for the video game system his company designed. "It plugs into the future! he says in one ad, in a cameo spliced into shots of U.S kids playing the games. Hawkins is one of several US celebrieties and business people whom plug products on Japanese TV. Jodie Foster, harrison ford, and Charlie Sheen adverstises canned coffee beer and cigarettes respectively.

c.

> Mid size firms employing between 100 and 1000 peopole represent only 4% of companies in the U.S.; but create 33% of all new jobs. One observe attributes their success to their being small enough to take advantage of economic opportunity's agilely, but big enough to have access to credit and to operate on a national or even international scale. The biggest hiring area for midsize company's is wholesale and retail sales (38% of jobs), construction (20% of jobs, manufacturing (19% of jobs), and services (18 of jobs).

B.2   Providing Punctuation

Provide the necessary punctuation in the following sentences. Note that not every box requires punctuation.

1. The system □ s □ user □ friendly design □ provides screen displays of work codes □ rates □ and client information.

2. Many other factors also shape the organization □ s □ image □ advertising □ brochures □ proposals □ stationery □ calling cards □ etc.

3. Charlotte Ford □ author of □ Charlotte Ford □ s □ Book of Modern Manners □□ says □□ Try to mention specifics of the conversation to fix the interview permanently in the interviewer □ s □ mind and be sure to mail the letter the same day □ before the hiring decision is made □□

4. What are your room rates □ and charges for food service □

5. We will need accommodations for 150 people □ five meeting rooms □ one large room and four small ones □ □ coffee served during morning and afternoon breaks □ and lunches and dinners.

6. The Operational Readiness Inspection □ which occurs once every three years □ is a realistic exercise □ which evaluates the National Guard □ s □ ability to mobilize □ deploy □ and fight.

7. Most computer packages will calculate three different sets of percentages □ row percentages □ column percentages □ and table percentages □

8. In today □ s □ economy □ it □ s almost impossible for a firm to extend credit beyond it □ s regular terms.

9. The Department of Transportation does not have statutory authority to grant easements □ however □ we do have authority to lease unused areas of highway right □ of □ way.

10. The program has two goals □ to identify employees with promise □ and to see that they get the training they need to advance.

B.3   Providing Punctuation

Provide the necessary punctuation in the following sentences. Note that not every box requires punctuation.

1. Office work □□ especially at your desk □□ can create back □ shoulder □ neck □ or wrist strain.

2. I searched for □ vacation □ and □ vacation planning □ on Google and Alta Vista.

3. I suggest putting a bulletin board in the rear hallway □ and posting all the interviewer □ s □ photos on it.

4. Analyzing audiences is the same for marketing and writing □ you have to identify who the audiences are □ understand how to motivate them □ and choose the best channel to reach them.

5. The more you know about your audience □□ who they are □ what they buy □ where they shop □□ the more relevant and effective you can make your ad.

6. The city already has five □ two □ hundred □ bed hospitals.

7. Students run the whole organization □ and are advised by a board of directors from the community.

8. The company is working on three team □ related issues □ interaction □ leadership □ and team size.

9. I would be interested in working on the committee □ however □ I have decided to do less community work so that I have more time to spend with my family.

10. □ You can create you own future □□ says Frank Montaño □□ You have to think about it □ crystallize it in writing □ and be willing to work at it □ We teach a lot of goal □ setting and planning in our training sessions □□

B.4   Creating Agreement

Revise the following sentences to correct errors in noun–pronoun and subject–verb agreement.

1. If there's any tickets left, they'll be $17 at the door.

2. A team of people from marketing, finance, and production are preparing the proposal.

3. Image type and resolution varies among clip art packages.

4. Your health and the health of your family is very important to us.

5. If a group member doesn't complete their assigned work, it slows the whole project down.

6. Baker & Baker was offended by the ad agency's sloppy proposal, and they withdrew their account from the firm.

7. The first step toward getting out of debt is not to add any more to it. This means cutting up your old credit card.

8. Contests are fun for employees and creates sales incentives.

9. The higher the position a person has, the more professional their image should be.

10. A new employee should try to read verbal and nonverbal signals to see which aspects of your job are most important.

B.5   Correcting Case Errors

Revise the following sentences to correct errors in pronoun case.

1. I didn't appreciate him assuming that he would be the group's leader.

2. Myself and Jim made the presentation.

3. Employees which lack experience in dealing with people from other cultures could benefit from seminars in international business communication.

4. Chandra drew the graphs after her and I discussed the ideas for them.

5. Please give your revisions to Cindy, Tyrone, or myself by noon Friday.

B.6   Improving Modifiers

Revise the following sentences to correct dangling and misplaced modifiers.

1. Originally a group of four, one member dropped out after the first meeting due to a death in the family.

2. Examining the data, it is apparent that most of our sales are to people on the northwest side of the city.

3. As a busy professional, we know that you will want to take advantage of this special offer.

4. Often documents end up in files that aren't especially good.

5. By making an early reservation, it will give us more time to coordinate our trucks to better serve you.

B.7 Creating Parallel Structure

Revise the following sentences to create parallel structure.

1. To narrow a Web search,
   - Put quotation marks around a phrase when you want an exact term.
   - Many search engines have wild cards (usually an asterisk) to find plurals and other forms of a word.
   - Reading the instructions on the search engine itself can teach you advanced search techniques.
2. Men drink more alcoholic beverages than women.
3. Each issue of *Hospice Care* has articles from four different perspectives: legislative, health care, hospice administrators, and inspirational authors.
4. The university is one of the largest employers in the community, brings in substantial business, and the cultural impact is also big.

5. These three tools can help competitive people be better negotiators:
   1. Think win–win
   2. It's important to ask enough questions to find out the other person's priorities, rather than jumping on the first advantage you find.
   3. Protect the other person's self-esteem.
   These three questions can help cooperative people be better negotiators:
   1. Can you developing a specific alternative to use if negotiation fails?
   2. Don't focus on the bottom line. Spend time thinking about what you want and why you need it.
   3. Saying "You'll have to do better than that because . . . " can help you resist the temptation to say "yes" too quickly.

B.8 Correcting Sentence Errors

Revise the following sentences to correct comma splices, run-on-sentences, fused sentences, and sentence fragments.

1. Members of the group are all experienced presenters, most have had little or no experience using PowerPoint.
2. Proofread the letter carefully and check for proper business format because errors undercut your ability to sell yourself so take advantage of your opportunity to make a good first impression.
3. Some documents need just one pass others need multiple revisions.
4. Videoconferencing can be frustrating. Simply because little time is available for casual conversation.
5. Entrepreneurs face two main obstacles. Limited cash. Lack of business experience.

6. The margin on pet supplies is very thin and the company can't make money selling just dog food and the real profit is in extras like neon-colored leashes, so you put the dog food in the back so people have to walk by everything else to get to it.
7. The company's profits jumped 15%. Although its revenues fell 3%.
8. The new budget will hurt small businesses it imposes extra fees it raises the interest rates small businesses must pay.
9. Our phones are constantly being used. Not just for business calls but also for personal calls.
10. Businesses are trying to cut travel costs, executives are taking fewer trips and flying out of alternate airports to save money.

B.9 Editing for Grammar and Usage

Revise the following sentences to eliminate errors in grammar and usage.

1. The number of students surveyed that worked more than 20 hours a week was 60%.
2. Not everyone is promoted after six months some people might remain in the training program a year before being moved to a permanent assignment.
3. The present solutions that has been suggested are not adequate.
4. At times while typing and editing, the text on your screen may not look correct.
5. All employees are asked to cut back on energy waste by the manager.
6. The benefits of an online catalog are
   1. We will be able to keep records up-to-date;

   2. Broad access to the catalog system from any networked terminal on campus;
   3. The consolidation of the main catalog and the catalogs in the departmental and branch libraries;
   4. Cost savings.
7. You can take advantage of several banking services. Such as automatic withdrawal of a house or car payment and direct deposit of your pay check.
8. As a freshman, business administration was intriguing to me.
9. Thank you for the help you gave Joanne Jackson and myself.
10. I know from my business experience that good communication among people and departments are essential in running a successful corporation.

B.10   Writing Numbers

Revise the following sentences to correct errors in writing numbers.

1. 60% percent of the respondents hope to hold internships before they graduate.
2. 1992 marked the formal beginning of the European Economic Community.
3. In the year two thousand, twenty percent of the H-1B visas for immigrants with high-tech skills went to Indians.
4. More than 70,000,000 working Americans lack an employer-sponsored retirement plan.
5. The company's sales have risen to $16 million but it lost five million dollars.

B.11   Using Plurals and Possessives

Choose the right word for each sentence.

1. Many Canadian (companies, company's) are competing effectively in the global market.
2. We can move your (families, family's) furniture safely and efficiently.
3. The (managers, manager's) ability to listen is just as important as his or her technical knowledge.
4. A (memos, memo's) style can build goodwill.
5. (Social workers, social worker's) should tell clients about services available in the community.
6. The (companies, company's) benefits plan should be checked periodically to make sure it continues to serve the needs of employees.
7. Information about the new community makes the (families, family's) move easier.
8. The (managers, manager's) all have open-door policies.
9. (Memos, memo's) are sent to other workers in the same organization.
10. Burnout affects a (social workers, social worker's) productivity as well as his or her morale.

B.12   Choosing the Right Word

Choose the right word for each sentence.

1. Exercise is (good, well) for patients who have had open-heart surgery.
2. This response is atypical, but it is not (unique, unusual).
3. The personnel department continues its (roll, role) of compiling reports for the federal government.
4. The Accounting Club expects (its, it's) members to come to meetings and participate in activities.
5. Part of the fun of any vacation is (cite, sight, site)-seeing.
6. The (lectern, podium) was too high for the short speaker.
7. The (residence, residents) of the complex have asked for more parking spaces.
8. Please order more letterhead (stationary, stationery).
9. The closing of the plant will (affect, effect) house prices in the area.
10. Better communication (among, between) design and production could enable us to produce products more efficiently.

B.13   Choosing the Right Word

Choose the right word for each sentence.

1. The audit revealed a small (amount, number) of errors.
2. Diet beverages have (fewer, less) calories than regular drinks.
3. In her speech, she (implied, inferred) that the vote would be close.
4. We need to redesign the stand so that the catalog is eye-level instead of (laying, lying) on the desk.
5. (Their, There, They're) is some evidence that (their, there, they're) thinking of changing (their, there, they're) policy.
6. The settlement isn't yet in writing; if one side wanted to back out of the (oral, verbal) agreement, it could.
7. In (affect, effect), we're creating a new department.
8. The firm will be hiring new (personal, personnel) in three departments this year.
9. Several customers have asked that we carry more campus merchandise, (i.e., e.g.,) pillows and mugs with the college seal.
10. We have investigated all of the possible solutions (accept, except) adding a turning lane.

B.14   Choosing the Right Word

Choose the right word for each sentence.

1. The author (cites, sights, sites) four reasons for computer phobia.
2. The error was (do, due) to inexperience.
3. (Your, You're) doing a good job motivating (your, you're) subordinates.
4. One of the basic (principals, principles) of business communication is "Consider the reader."
5. I (implied, inferred) from the article that interest rates would go up.
6. Working papers generally are (composed, comprised) of working trial balance, assembly sheets, adjusting entries, audit schedules, and audit memos.
7. Eliminating time clocks will improve employee (moral, morale).
8. The (principal, principle) variable is the trigger price mechanism.
9. (Its, It's) (to, too, two) soon (to, too, two) tell whether the conversion (to, too, two) computerized billing will save as much time as we hope.
10. Formal training programs (complement, compliment) on-the-job opportunities for professional growth.

B.15   Tracking Your Own Mechanical Errors

Analyze the mechanical errors (grammar, punctuation, word use, and typos) in each of your papers.

- How many different errors are marked on each paper?
- Which three errors do you make most often?
- Is the number of errors constant in each paper, or does the number increase or decrease during the term?

As your instructor directs,

a. Correct each of the mechanical errors in one or more papers.

b. Deliberately write two new sentences in which you make each of your three most common errors. Then write the correct version of each sentence.

c. Write a memo to your instructor discussing your increasing mastery of mechanical correctness during the semester or quarter.

d. Briefly explain to the class how to avoid one kind of error in grammar, punctuation, or word use.

Video Cases to Accompany Manager's Hot Seat

Every business depends on communication. Good communication skills are crucial in relaying information, listening to instructions, and problem solving—important functions that contribute to success in any organization.

In the real world, miscommunication can cause you to lose a job, get passed up for a promotion, or just result in wasted time and efforts. The Manager's Hot Seat presents a range of situations that you may face as employees and managers in today's workplace. The chosen scenarios depict how good communicators must be conscious of the context in which they communicate and show the high costs of poor communication.

Part 1 Video Case

"Virtual Workplace: Out of the Office Reply"

An awareness of how business and business communication are changing is necessary to maintain success in any business. For example, technology is constantly changing the ways in which we access information or communicate with colleagues. Technological advances such as videophones, faxes, e-mail, PDAs, Blackberries, and Iphones provide employees the opportunity to work from home or another location rather than commuting to a central office.

Technology can make working from home easier, but it can also create specific communication challenges and leave room for misinterpretation. These are issues addressed in the video segment **Virtual Workplace: Out of the Office Reply.** After viewing the video, respond to the questions below.

Scenario: Three months ago, Ralph Ramos assigned a number of employees to work as telecommuters to alleviate the lack of space in their office building. Among them was Angela Zononi, an employee and friend for over four years, who was delighted to work from home since her commute to the office was particularly time-consuming. Although things went relatively smoothly for the first six weeks, since then communication and performance have taken a steady downturn. Angela has biweekly meetings with Ralph in his office. Lately they have had unprecedented arguments and frequent misunderstandings.

Back History: Angela was one of five employees who moved to home offices three months ago. She had volunteered right off the bat because she could spend more time with her family if she eliminated all that commuter time [on a bad day she was losing over three hours round-trip!]

The telecommuting has had its ups and downs but her relationship with Ralph is going downhill. They've been having frequent misunderstandings, and a few small arguments. Angela feels that Ralph's operating on an "out of sight out of mind" mentality. He doesn't even seem to read the e-mail reports very closely. They do meet every two weeks at the office as a check-in but it's a pure formality. To make matters worse, a colleague who works in the office told her about all the high stakes claims another investigator, Bob, has been working on. Angela hasn't had anything 'hot' in weeks.

Ralph is happy with the way things are working out. The office is no longer over-crowded or disturbingly noisy. The telecommuters are doing their work and reporting regularly. He is having more trouble staying on top of their reports and their projects but that's probably because he's so busy.

Scene Setup: Ralph and Angela are meeting to discuss their recent miscommunications and Angela reveals her dissatisfaction with her recent treatment.

Questions

1. What Trends in Business and Administrative Communication (from Chapter 1) are displayed in this scenario?

2. What specific communication challenges are addressed in this segment? What attempts prior to the meeting have been made by Angela to overcome these challenges? What attempts were made by Ralph?

3. Chapter 3 explains the importance of building goodwill in business communication. How effective is each speaker in employing the concepts below?

    *   Using you-attitude
    *   Avoiding negative words
    *   Justifying negative information
    *   Maintaining a polite tone

4. Describe the kinds of audience analysis Angela could have done to more effectively communicate with Ralph.

5. What does the company's telecommuting program say about the company's corporate culture? How does Ralph's preference of how Angela should report to him follow or not follow this culture?

6. As Angela, write a memo to Ralph convincing him to give you more important assignments and suggestions on what you can do to make checking in with him more efficient.

    Hint:

    *   Remember to employ the six questions for analysis of business communication problems (Chapter 1) prior to writing your memo.

7. As Ralph, write a memo to Angela to persuade her not to resign and explain why you chose to give Bob the high-stakes assignment. Include at least three audience benefits in your memo.

Part 2 Video Case

"Change: More Pain than Gain"

Clear and thoughtful communication is important to good business whether the message is positive or negative. When providing negative information, particular care needs to be taken to maintain goodwill and prevent or limit any negative feelings that may result. A persuasive strategy also needs to be considered if the negative information is paired with a follow-up request. This can be the case when it comes to countering objections or developing a problem-solving persuasive message.

In the video segment **Change: More Pain than Gain,** we see how employees handle a difficult situation after two companies merge and the conflicts that managers face in the aftermath. This case explores issues of dealing with a negative situation and navigating through a difficult change process. After viewing the video, respond to the questions below.

Overview: A national media communications company acquires a regional communications company. As a result of the merger the regional marketing department is reorganized, combining the staff of the two organizations. The manager, Carlos Alarcon, is overseeing the restructuring process and is having a lot of difficulty with people shifting roles, sharing assignments, and adapting to new hierarchies.

Alarcon meets with two department members, Rita Finch and Juan Rayes, who are very displeased with the new changes. The employees eventually ask the manager to leave the company and head a start-up—funding is already in place.

Back History: Carlos, Rita, and Juan have been working together at Franklin/Warner (now acquired by MediaWorld) for over eight years and have a very amicable working relationship. Since the merger, Rita and Juan are now sharing their roles with two employees from the merger company, Jackson and Peters. They both perceive Jackson and Peters to be incompetent and a hindrance to the productivity of their departments. Each has different issues, complaining of arrogance, condescension, slacking, and poor communication skills, but at the root of the problem, they are furious that they are in essence working under people who are less experienced and less knowledgeable than they.

Scene Setup: Carlos is having check-in meetings with all of the employees in his department, to assess the progress of the reorganization since the merger took place.

Questions

1.   Rita and Juan have been unhappy with the aftereffects of the merger for some time. The scenario indicates that Carlos has put off meeting with the two, and Rita and Juan's aggravation with the situation may have increased as a result of this lack of communication. Assume that the outcome of the scenario would have been different if Rita and Juan had conveyed their displeasure prior to this meeting. As Rita, write a memo to Carlos stating your grievance with the company's changes.
     Hints:
     - Identify your goal—are you still in consideration of how you can make the best of the situation or are you determined to walk away?
     - How can you build goodwill so that Carlos will take your side?
2.   Company mergers often affect the organizational structure in staffing. In this video scenario, we saw the restructuring process involved staff members sharing titles, assignments, and office space. As Carlos, write an e-mail message to the employees of Franklin/Warner, announcing the impending merger and the changes they might expect.
3.   Imagine that Carlos was not closed off to the idea of joining Rita and Juan in leaving the company. As Juan, write an e-mail to Carlos outlining your and Rita's plans to head a start-up and asking him to join you.
4.   Rita asserts that Peters does not respect her position and admits that she does not think highly of him in return. They've been forced to work together and the relationship has been rocky, to say the least. The following e-mail from Rita is representative of their working relationship.

> Peters,
>
> It's been several weeks since I asked for that report for the Simmons account. I'd assumed you'd been working on it, but this huge delay makes me suspect otherwise. I believe you know that this account is one of our largest and we are meeting with them next week. Have you made any progress at all?
>
> I was forced to share this account with you and the least you can do is shoulder your load. I don't feel that it's part of my job to watch over every task for our team. Please give me a status on that report ASAP or I'll speak to Carlos about this.

     This e-mail message is horrible. Rita's strategy is all wrong and she is clearly letting her frustration show. Rework this e-mail to request the information you need from Peters.

Hints:

- Pay attention to the tone of your message and determine what tone would work best in this situation.
- Suggest specific ways to get what you need using persuasion.
- Set a deadline for when you need the information.
- Remember that threats are less effective than persuasion.

5. Imagine that Rita and Juan have left Franklin/Warner and since have started their own media communications company. As Rita or Juan, write a contact letter to go to new clients and customers telling them about your new company. Write a separate contact letter to the client list you had established at Franklin/Warner, persuading the client to switch to your firm.

Part 3 Video Case

"Working in Teams: Cross-Functional Dysfunction"

Successful teamwork encourages ideas and capitalizes on the collective power of each individual's experiences and strengths. However, successful collaborative work must take into account the roles within a group and the interactions between the members. As we will see, the interpersonal communication between team members can ultimately make or break a project.

In the video segment **Working in Teams: Cross-Functional Dysfunction,** we look at how cross-functional teams pose unique challenges to a team leader and the group members. The "built-in" diversity of cross-functional teams is both an attribute and a difficulty when accomplishing group goals. After viewing the video, respond to the questions below.

Overview: The Executive Director of Operations has assigned Joe Tanney the role of Team Leader for a high-priority project. Each office is at different stages of computerization, with different teams preferring different technologies for particular tasks. This makes everything more complex—from collaboration to revisions to cost and time management—and is having a serious impact on the company's bottom line. The team includes Rosa Denson, Cheng Jing, and Simon Mahoney. These four account managers have been asked to get together by senior management to generate a proposal for streamlining the antiquated blueprint generation process.

Back History: W & W has been expanding at leaps and bounds over the past eight years or so. The growth has been spectacular and hurried—they have not always taken the time to implement change in the most efficient fashion, nor have they opened new offices with any sense of continuity of process or corporate culture. Business has been plateauing for about eight months now, and senior management has decided to take this opportunity to assess efficiencies and practices and make the necessary improvements across the board. Rumor has it that things may take a swift downturn in the months to come.

The team has been attempting to meet for a couple of weeks but has never been able to agree on a date. They all agreed to start generating ideas and breaking down the tasks in the meantime—nobody has done it except Joe, who has created a very thorough analysis of the project. This is their first meeting—they need to plan a course of action, assign tasks, and set deadlines. Simon is the manager with most seniority and everyone assumed he would lead the team.

Scene Setup: The group gathers to go over Joe's agenda regarding the team project.

Questions

1. The meeting does not go well in this scenario and the participants seem to have communication difficulties. Cheng, Rosa, and Simon seem to have little interest in the project. Identify the negative roles and actions for each of the three that indicate the absence of good interpersonal communication among the group.

2. As Joe, respond to each of the team's complaints with an active response.
   a. Jeng's comment: I'm getting transferred to the design department soon and I'm not sure how much I'll be able to contribute to the project.
   b. Rosa's comment: My mother-in-law is coming to town and I'll need a lot of help on this project.
   c. Simon's comment: This idea has been tried before and hasn't worked. I don't see the point of continuing this project.

3. Using the background information provided here and your observation of the video, identify five symptoms of group conflict in this scenario. Provide three possible solutions to resolve each of the conflicts you've identified.

4. A week after the meeting, Rosa sends Joe the following e-mail:

> Joe,
>
> I'm sorry, but things are crazy at home with my mother-in-law right now. I'm really unable to do any more than I have on this project. Simon has said he would pick up the slack, but he hasn't even been doing his fair share. I need help!

As Joe, respond to Rosa's e-mail by writing a memo to the team proposing a solution to this conflict.

5. Two weeks after the meeting, Joe sends out the following memo to the team:

> We're not making a lot of headway and I feel that I'm the only one that cares about this project. I understand that each of you has other commitments on your time, but our proposal can really help the company if we put forth our best efforts. How do you think we should proceed?

Write a group response stating whether this project should progress and give reasons supporting your recommendation.

Part 4 Video Case

"Project Management: Steering the Committee"

Documents in business often appear in the form of a report, whether they are long formal reports that include research and data, or short one- or two-page memos. Reports can be in a letter format or even a progress report in the form of an e-mail. Basically, reports are necessary to good business communication and are appropriate in a wide range of business situations.

In the video segment **Project Management: Steering the Committee,** we see how doing research and preparing a proposal and report can play a key role in an organization's communication. We see how report preparation can inform team members, solve problems, play a role in group dynamics, and affect the overall success of a project.

Overview: Three months ago, Patrick was given the goal of implementing a computerized tracking system on the factory floor with the expectations that it would raise quality control and workflow by a significant percentage. The team spends an enormous amount of time revising/fixing chips after they fail quality control testing—mostly due to lack of information. There would be a serious review of the project after the first phase is complete—that is now.

Patrick is called to a meeting with three top executives. The tracking system project is very costly and has not been proven, but the company was anxious to keep up with their competitors who are using computerized systems in their production facilities. Patrick has spent a little time writing a report, but is feeling generally confident.

Back History: TechBox produces a specialized computer chip for a large client base of high-end computer companies such as Dell, IBM, and HP. Within the TechBox compound are the manufacturing factories and the corporate headquarters.

Patrick Bennett is the new manager overseeing the production of the main component of the chip. He has started to implement a computerized tracking system to increase quality control and workflow. He supervises a floor of 50 workers. Patrick has been working at TechBox for two years and has been widely praised for numerous successes and improvements on the factory floor—improvements with very positive financial results.

Scene Setup: A meeting is held with key stakeholders of Patrick's project to discuss the status in terms of time and budget.

Questions

1.   The following Executive Summary (Chapter 16) is poorly organized and too long. Rearrange information to make it more effective. Cut out information that does not belong in the summary. You may use different words as you revise.

> In this report I will discuss the production problems of the Q-247 chip which exist at TechBox. This report will discuss how communication problems with the quality control process for the chips are causing internal problems and slowing production. I believe a new computerized tracking system would solve the communication problems.
>
> The main component of the chip is manufactured in-house. We produce approximately 100,000 chips in a day. The chips are then sent to quality control (QC), which is a 2-day process. Currently, 67% of those chips pass quality control in the first round. Any rejected chips are manually logged as defective by QC workers and resubmitted back to the Production department for revision. Production logs out the chips and resubmits chips back to QC the next day.
>
> The manual tracking system for these chips is inefficient and results in an average of 5,000 lost chips monthly. A computerized tracking system would track the location of each chip much more efficiently, resulting in fewer lost chips. This tracking system would be a direct communication channel between Production and Quality Control.
>
> This system could be developed and implemented within a year. Please refer to the outlined schedule below.

> I propose we develop the budget by pooling reserves from Production, Distribution, Product Management, and Operations budgets, since these are the departments that would benefit from this new system.

2. You've been asked to write a proposal to implement the new computerized tracking system. Indicate what kinds of research would be useful. Provide two examples each of primary and secondary research sources.

3. Write a proposal for funding for the computerized tracking system. Direct it to the departments involved. Stress the needs the system will meet and show how the project will help improve efficiency in each department.

4. Patrick is confident going into this meeting, unaware of the other executives' concerns regarding the project. As Patrick, prepare a justification report with the necessary information that would address these concerns. What is the background history for this new tracking system? What problems or successes has this new system faced? What are the results and progress of the project so far? What financial and production benefits will result from this new tracking system? What future actions are planned to finish out the project?

   Hints:
   - Provide a timeline to track the progress of the project.
   - Address budget allocations and the costs involved.
   - Use a persuasive strategy to justify continuation of the project.

5. As Sam, write a recommendation progress report (see Chapter 15) to the other executives to cancel the project. Explain why you think the project isn't working out and propose alternatives to the project.

6. As Patrick, write a progress report to the other executives, describing your progress since the last group meeting.
   Hints:
   - Use positive emphasis. Take this opportunity to enhance your image (research you've done, specific tasks to get the project back on track).
   - Try to minimize potential problems. Use your progress report to inform the executives of upcoming hurdles and propose possible solutions.

Part 5 Video Case

"Interviewing: Best Foot Forward or One Step Back?"

Entering the job market can be daunting, but you will find that preparation and organization can make all the difference in a successful job search. To make yourself an attractive candidate, there are three essential things that should be part of your job hunting strategy. To look well organized and prepared, you must prepare a résumé, create an interesting application letter, and present your best self at the job interview and follow-up.

In the video segment **Interviewing: Best Foot Forward or One Step Back?** we examine the interviewing styles of two qualified candidates competing for the same position.

Overview: Robert Gedaliah has been interviewing candidates to fill the new Customer Outreach Representative position for his delivery services company, and he has narrowed it down to two, Jacqueline Coleman and Sonya Jennings. He has invited Paul Munez, the customer service team leader, for the second interview of these two candidates.

Back History: Beck 'n Call was founded by Robert eight years ago. It was one of the first "we deliver anything" services in this city and completely cornered the market. Initially there was a bike messenger team of 10 running around from cleaners to banks to movie stores, doing errands for those who'd rather pay than go. Over eight years, it has grown to a staff of 50, with many fleets of transportation, warehousing an eclectic inventory of products from videos to popcorn to printer ink to black pantyhose, as well as establishing concrete partner relationships with service vendors throughout town. Beck 'n Call is growing at a rapid rate—Robert knows it's wise to take a precise and cautious approach toward growth, and scrutinizes all aspects. He has interviewed 15 people for the new Customer Outreach Representative and has narrowed it down to two very qualified young women. As is his policy, he has invited the team leader in for the follow-up interview. He also has a preference for group interviews because the dynamics are richer and therefore better reflect reality.

Scene Setup: Robert and Paul interview both candidates to determine who will be the best fit for the company.

Questions

1. Robert posted the following ad for the Customer Outreach Representative position. As Jacqueline, respond to the ad with a traditional letter of application.

> Beck 'N Call, a rapidly expanding citywide delivery service, is looking for a customer outreach representative. The representative will work with team members in the customer satisfaction department, as well as with vendors and customers in the community. As we expand our customer base, the representative will work closely with the new neighborhoods and communities to build relationships and ensure customer satisfaction.
>
> This is a full-time position. Salary is commensurate with experience. The candidate should have graduated from college, customer service experience preferred. The ideal candidate will enjoy working with people and have excellent interpersonal skills.

2. As Sonya, respond to the same ad with a one-screen application letter to accompany a résumé that you submit electronically.
3. Critique the following responses Sonya and Jacqueline each gave in their interviews. Identify each response as poor or good and support your conclusion. For each poor response, prepare a better answer to the interview question.

Question:	How are you with staying later on Thursdays? Would you have a problem with that?
Jacqueline's response:	No, I don't. I don't have any children at this point . . . it is something that I'd definitely like later in about four years.
Question:	There is a certain amount of clerical work involved with the position. Do you think you would have a problem with that?

Jacqueline's response:	That might ruffle my feathers a little bit considering my work experience and where I come from.
Question:	I see that you do some rock climbing on the side. There are some people here who are interested in doing that too.
Jacqueline's response:	I love rock climbing. It's a great workout. I would be interested in organizing a rock climbing event.
Question:	What would you consider to be your weakness?
Sonya's response:	I had a problem with being a team player. I always felt that I could get more done on my own. But in my last job I learned to delegate and learned that by working together you can get more done.
Question:	Where do you see yourself in three years?
Sonya's response:	I'd love to do marketing. I would like to have a high position in marketing, but I'm open. Wherever you need me, I would try to fulfill whatever need you have because I love the company so much.
Question:	What's your biggest accomplishment? What do you bring to the company?
Sonya's response:	I'm a really hard worker and this might sound soft, but I think the most important thing is being kind and getting along with other people.

4. As Jacqueline, prepare five specific questions to ask Robert and Paul at this interview.

5. Identify two positive and two negative communication behaviors of each candidate during the interview.

6. As Sonya or Jacqueline, write a follow-up letter to the interview and address the letter to Robert. Thank him for the hospitality, remind him of your strong points, reiterate your interest in the position and anything you may have learned, allay any negative impressions, and convey your enthusiasm for the company.

A

abstract A summary of a report, specifying the recommendations and the reasons for them. Also called an executive summary.

acknowledgment responses Nods, smiles, frowns, and words that let a speaker know you are listening.

active listening Feeding back the literal meaning or the emotional content or both so that the speaker knows that the listener has heard and understood.

active verb A verb that describes the action of the grammatical subject of the sentence.

adjustment A positive response to a claim letter. If the company agrees to grant a refund, the amount due will be adjusted.

alliteration A sound pattern occurring when several words begin with the same sound.

alternating pattern Discussing the alternatives first as they relate to the first criterion, then as they relate to the second criterion, and so on: ABC, ABC, ABC.

AMS Simplified format A letter format that omits the salutation and complimentary close and lines everything up at the left margin.

analytical report A report that interprets information.

argument The reasons or logic offered to persuade the audience.

assumptions Statements that are not proved in a report, but on which the recommendations are based.

audience benefits Benefits or advantages that the audience gets by using the communicator's services, buying the communicator's products, following the communicator's policies, or adopting the communicator's ideas. Audience benefits can exist for policies and ideas as well as for goods and services.

auxiliary audience People who may encounter your message but will not have to interact with it. This audience includes "read only" people.

average See *mean*.

B

bar chart A visual consisting of parallel bars or rectangles that represent specific sets of data.

behavioral interviews Job interviews that ask candidates to describe actual behaviors they have used in the past in specific situations.

bias-free language Language that does not discriminate against people on the basis of sex, physical condition, race, age, or any other category.

blind ads Job listings that do not list the company's name.

blind copies Copies sent to other recipients that are not listed on the original letter, memo or e-mail.

block format In letters, a format in which inside address, date, and signature block are lined up at the left margin. In résumés, a format in which dates are listed in one column and job titles and descriptions in another. This format emphasizes work history.

blocking Disagreeing with every idea that is proposed.

body language Nonverbal communication conveyed by posture and movement, eye contact, facial expressions, and gestures.

boilerplate Language from a previous document that a writer includes in a new document. Writers use boilerplate both to save time and energy and to use language that has already been approved by the organization's legal staff.

boxhead Used in tables, the boxhead is the variable whose label is at the top.

brainstorming A method of generating ideas by recording everything people in a group think of, without judging or evaluating the ideas.

branching question Question that sends respondents who answer differently to different parts of the questionnaire. Allows respondents to answer only those questions that are relevant to their experience.

bridge (in prospecting job letters) A sentence that connects the attention-getter to the body of a letter.

brochure Booklet (often part of a direct mailing) that gives more information about a product or organization.

buffer A neutral or positive statement designed to allow the writer to bury, or buffer, the negative message.

build goodwill To create a good image of yourself and of your organization—the kind of image that makes people want to do business with you.

bullets Small circles (filled or open) or squares that set off items in a list. When you are giving examples, but the number is not exact and the order does not matter, use bullets to set off items.

business plan A document written to raise capital for a new business venture or to outline future actions for an established business.

businessese A kind of jargon including unnecessary words. Some words were common 200–300 years ago but are no longer part of spoken English. Some have never been used outside of business writing. All of these terms should be omitted.

buying time with limited agreement Agreeing with the small part of a criticism that one does accept as true.

bypassing Miscommunication that occurs when two people use the same symbol to mean different things.

C

case The grammatical role a noun or pronoun plays in a sentence. The nominative case is used for the subject of a clause, the possessive to show who or what something belongs to, the objective case for the object of a verb or a preposition.

central selling point A super audience benefit, big enough to motivate people by itself, but also serving as an umbrella to cover other benefits and to unify the message.

channel The physical means by which a message is sent. Written channels include e-mails memos, letters, and billboards. Oral channels include phone calls, speeches, and face-to-face conversations.

channel overload The inability of a channel to carry all the messages that are being sent.

chartjunk   Decoration that is irrelevant to a visual and that may be misleading.

checking for feelings   Identifying the emotions that the previous speaker seemed to be expressing verbally or non-verbally.

checking for inferences   Trying to identify the unspoken content or feelings implied by what the previous speaker has actually said.

chronological résumé   A résumé that lists what you did in a dated order, starting with the most recent events and going backward in reverse chronology.

citation   Attributing a quotation or other idea to a source in the body of the report.

claim   The part of an argument that the speaker or writer wants the audience to agree with.

claim letter   A letter seeking a replacement or refund.

clip art   Predrawn images that you can import into your documents.

close   The ending of a document.

closed body position   Includes keeping the arms and legs crossed and close to the body. Suggests physical and psychological discomfort, defending oneself, and shutting the other person out. Also called a defensive body position.

closed question   Question with a limited number of possible responses.

closure report   A report summarizing completed research that does not result in action or recommendation.

clowning   Making unproductive jokes and diverting the group from its task.

cluster sample   A sample of all subjects at each of a random sample of locations. This method is usually faster and cheaper than random sampling when face-to-face interviews are required.

clustering   A method of thinking up ideas by writing the central topic in the middle of the page, circling it, writing down the ideas that topic suggests, and circling them.

cognitive dissonance   A theory which posits that it is psychologically uncomfortable to hold two ideas that are dissonant or conflicting. The theory of cognitive dissonance explains that people will resolve dissonance by deciding that one of the ideas is less important, by rejecting one of the ideas, or by constructing a third idea that has room for both of the conflicting ideas.

cold list   A list used in marketing of people with no prior connection to your group.

collaborative writing   Working with other writers to produce a single document.

collection letter   A letter asking a customer to pay for goods and services received.

collection series   A series of letters asking customers to pay for goods and services they have already received. Early letters in the series assume that the reader intends to pay but final letters threaten legal action if the bill is not paid.

comma splice or comma fault   Using a comma to join two independent clauses. To correct, use a semicolon, use a comma with a conjunction, subordinate one of the clauses, or use a period and start a new sentence.

common ground   Values and goals that the communicator and audience share.

communication theory   A theory explaining what happens when we communicate and where miscommunication can occur.

complaint letter   A letter that challenges a policy or tries to get a decision changed.

complex sentence   Sentence with one main clause and one or more subordinate clauses.

complimentary close   The words after the body of the letter and before the signature. *Sincerely* and *yours truly* are the most commonly used complimentary closes in business letters.

compound sentence   Sentence with two main clauses joined by a comma and conjunction.

conclusions   Section of a report that restates the main points.

conflict resolution   Strategies for getting at the real issue, keeping discussion open, and minimizing hurt feelings so that people can find a solution that seems good to everyone involved.

connotations   The emotional colorings or associations that accompany a word.

contact letter   Letter written to keep in touch with a customer or donor.

convenience sample   A group of subjects to whom the researcher has easy access.

conversational style   Conversational patterns such as speed and volume of speaking, pauses between speakers, whether questions are direct or indirect. When different speakers assign different meanings to a specific pattern, miscommunication results.

coordination   The second stage in the life of a task group, when the group finds, organizes, and interprets information and examines alternatives and assumptions. This is the longest of the stages.

counterclaim   A statement whose truth would negate the truth of the main claim.

credibility   Ability to come across to the audience as believable.

criteria   The standards used to evaluate or weigh the factors in a decision.

critical activities   Activities that must be done on time if a project is to be completed by its due date.

critical incident   An important event that illustrates behavior or a history.

crop   To trim a photograph to fit a specific space. Also, photographs are cropped to delete visual information that is unnecessary or unwanted.

culture   The unconscious patterns of behavior and beliefs that are common to a people, nation, or organization.

cutaway drawings   Line drawings that depict the hidden or interior portions of an object.

cycling   The process of sending a document from writer to superior to writer to yet another superior for several rounds of revisions before the document is approved.

D

dangling modifier   A phrase that modifies a word that is not actually in a sentence. To correct a dangling modifier, recast the modifier as a subordinate clause or revise the sentence so its subject or object can be modified by the dangling phrase.

data   Facts or figures used as a basis for reasoning.

decode   To extract meaning from symbols.

decorative visual   A visual that makes the speaker's points more memorable but that does not convey numerical data.

defensive body position   See *closed body position.*

demographic characteristics   Measurable features of an audience that can be counted objectively: age, education level, income, etc.

denotation   A word's literal or "dictionary" meaning. Most common words in English have more than one denotation. Context usually makes it clear which of several meanings is appropriate.

dependent clause   See *subordinate clause.*

descriptive abstract   A listing of the topics an article or report covers that does not summarize what is said about each topic.

deviation bar charts   Bar charts that identify positive and negative values, or winners and losers.

dingbats   Small symbols such as arrows, pointing fingers, and so forth that are part of a typeface.

direct mail   A form of direct marketing that asks for an order, inquiry, or contribution directly from the reader.

direct mail package   The outer envelope of a direct mail letter and everything that goes in it: the letter, brochures, samples, secondary letters, reply card, and reply envelope.

direct marketing   All advertisements that ask for an order, inquiry, or contribution directly from the audience. Includes direct mail, catalogs, telemarketing (telephone sales), and newspaper and TV ads with 800 numbers to place an order.

direct request pattern   A pattern of organization that makes the request directly in the first paragraph.

discourse community   A group of people who share assumptions about what channels, formats, and styles to use for communication, what topics to discuss and how to discuss them, and what constitutes evidence.

divided pattern   Discussing each alternative completely, through all criteria, before going on to the next alternative: AAA, BBB, CCC.

document design   The process of writing, organizing, and laying out a document so that it can be easily used by the intended audience.

documentation   Providing full bibliographic information so that interested readers can go to the original source of material used in a report.

dominating   Trying to run a group by ordering, shutting out others, and insisting on one's own way.

dot chart   A chart that shows correlations or other large data sets. Dot charts have labeled horizontal and vertical axes.

dot planning   A way for large groups to set priorities; involves assigning colored dots to ideas.

E

editing   Checking the draft to see that it satisfies the requirements of good English and the principles of business writing. Unlike revision, which can produce major changes in meaning, editing focuses on the surface of writing.

ego-involvement   The emotional commitment the audience has to its position.

elimination of alternatives   A pattern of organization for reports that discusses the problem and its causes, the impractical solutions and their weaknesses, and finally the solution the writer favors.

ellipses   Spaced dots used in reports to indicate that words have been omitted from quoted material and in direct mail to give the effect of pauses in speech.

emotional appeal   Making the audience want to do what the writer or speaker asks.

empathy   The ability to put oneself in someone else's shoes, to feel with that person.

enclosure   A document that accompanies a letter.

enunciate   To voice all the sounds of each word while speaking.

evaluating   Measuring something, such as a document draft or a group decision, against your goals and the requirements of the situation and audience.

evidence   Data the audience already accepts.

exaggeration   Making something sound bigger or more important than it really is.

executive summary   See *abstract.*

expectancy theory   A theory that argues that motivation is based on the expectation of being rewarded for performance and the importance of the reward.

external audiences   Audiences who are not part of the writer's organization.

external documents   Documents that go to people in another organization.

external report   Report written by a consultant for an organization of which he or she is not a permanent employee.

extranets   Web pages for customers and suppliers.

extrinsic motivators   Benefits that are "added on"; they are not a necessary part of the product or action.

eye contact   Looking another person directly in the eye.

F

feasibility report   A report that evaluates two or more possible alternatives and recommends one of them. Doing nothing is always one alternative.

feedback   The receiver's response to a message.

figure Any visual that is not a table.

five Ws and H Questions that must be answered early in a press release: who, what, when, where, why, and how.

fixed typeface A typeface in which each letter has the same width on the page. Sometimes called *typewriter typeface*.

flaming Sending out an angry e-mail message before thinking about the implications of venting one's anger.

focus groups Small groups who come in to talk with a skilled leader about a potential product or process.

forecast An overview statement that tells the audience what you will discuss in a section or an entire report.

form letter A prewritten, fill-in-the-blank letter designed to fit standard situations.

formal meetings Meetings run under strict rules, like the rules of parliamentary procedure summarized in *Robert's Rules of Order*.

formal report A report containing formal elements such as a title page, a transmittal, a table of contents, and an abstract.

formalization The third and last stage in the life of a task group, when the group makes its decision and seeks consensus.

format The parts of a document and the way they are arranged on a page.

formation The first stage in the life of a task group, when members choose a leader and define the problem they must solve.

freewriting A kind of writing uninhibited by any constraints. Freewriting may be useful in overcoming writer's block, among other things.

frozen evaluation An assessment that does not take into account the possibility of change.

full justification Making both right and left margins of a text even, as opposed to having a ragged right margin.

fused sentence The result when two or more sentences are joined without punctuation or conjunctions.

G

Gantt charts Bar charts used to show schedules. Gantt charts are most commonly used in proposals.

gatekeeper The audience with the power to decide whether your message is sent on to other audiences.

gathering data Physically getting the background data you need. It can include informal and formal research or simply getting the letter to which you're responding.

general semantics The study of the ways behavior is influenced by the words and other symbols used to communicate.

gerund The *-ing* form of a verb; grammatically, it is a verb used as a noun.

getting feedback Asking someone else to evaluate your work. Feedback is useful at every stage of the writing process, not just during composition of the final draft.

glossary A list of terms used in a report with their definitions.

good appeal An appeal in direct marketing that offers believable descriptions of benefits, links the benefits of the product or service to a need or desire that motivates the audience and makes the audience act.

good service or cause A service or cause that fills an identifiable need.

goodwill The value of a business beyond its tangible assets, including its reputation and patronage. Also, a favorable condition and overall atmosphere of trust that can be fostered between parties conducting business.

goodwill ending Shift of emphasis away from the message to the reader. A goodwill ending is positive, personal, and forward-looking and suggests that serving the reader is the real concern.

goodwill presentation A presentation that entertains and validates the audience.

grammar checker Software program that flags errors or doubtful usage.

grapevine An organization's informal informational network that carries gossip and rumors as well as accurate information.

grid system A means of designing layout by imposing columns on a page and lining up graphic elements within the columns.

ground rules Procedural rules adopted by groups to make meetings and processes run smoothly.

grouped bar chart A bar chart that allows the viewer to compare several aspects of each item or several items over time.

groupthink The tendency for a group to reward agreement and directly or indirectly punish dissent.

guided discussion A presentation in which the speaker presents the questions or issues that both speaker and audience have agreed on in advance. Instead of functioning as an expert with all the answers, the speaker serves as a facilitator to help the audience tap its own knowledge.

H

headings Words or short phrases that group points and divide your letter, memo, e-mail or report into sections.

hearing Perceiving sounds. (Not the same thing as listening.)

hidden job market Jobs that are never advertised but that may be available or may be created for the right candidate.

hidden negatives Words that are not negative in themselves, but become negative in context.

high-context culture A culture in which most information is inferred from the context, rather than being spelled out explicitly in words.

histogram A bar chart using pictures, asterisks, or points to represent a unit of the data.

I

impersonal expression A sentence that attributes actions to inanimate objects, designed to avoid placing blame on a reader.

indented format A format for résumés in which items that are logically equivalent begin at the same horizontal space, with carryover lines indented.

independent clause See *main clause*.

infinitive The form of the verb that is preceded by *to*.

inform To explain something or tell the audience something.

informal meetings Loosely run meetings in which votes are not taken on every point.

informal report A report using letter or memo format.

information interview An interview in which you talk to someone who works in the area you hope to enter to find out what the day-to-day work involves and how you can best prepare to enter that field.

information overload A condition in which a human receiver cannot process all the messages he or she receives.

information report A report that collects data for the reader but does not recommend action.

informational dimensions Dimensions of group work focusing on the problem, data, and possible solutions.

informative message Message giving information to which the reader's basic reaction will be neutral.

informative presentation A presentation that informs or teaches the audience.

informative report A report that provides information.

inside address The reader's name and address; put below the date and above the salutation in most letter formats.

interactive presentation A presentation that is a conversation between the speaker and the audience.

intercultural competence The ability to communicate sensitively with people from other cultures and countries, based on an understanding of cultural differences.

internal audiences Audiences in the communicator's organization.

internal document Document written for other employees in the same organization.

internal documentation Providing information about a source in the text itself rather than in footnotes or endnotes.

internal report Reports written by employees for use only in their organization.

interpersonal communication Communication between people.

interpersonal dimensions In a group, efforts promoting friendliness, cooperation, and group loyalty.

interpret To determine the meaning, significance, or importance of a message.

interview Structured conversation with someone who is able to give you useful information.

intranet A Web page just for employees.

intrapreneurs Innovators who work within organizations.

intrinsic motivators Benefits that come automatically from using a product or doing something.

introduction The part of a report that states the purpose and scope of the report. The introduction may also include limitations, assumptions, methods, criteria, and definitions.

J

jargon There are two kinds of jargon. The first kind is the specialized terminology of a technical field. The second is businessese, outdated words that do not have technical meanings and are not used in other forms of English.

judgment See *opinion.*

judgment sample A group of subjects whose views seem useful.

justification report Report that justifies the need for a purchase, an investment, a new personnel line, or a change in procedure.

justified margins Margins that end evenly on the right side of the page.

K

keywords Words used in (1) a résumé to summarize areas of expertise, qualifications, and (2) an article or report to describe the content. Keywords facilitate computer searches.

L

letter Short document using block, modified, or AMS Simplified letter format that goes to readers outside your organization.

letterhead Stationery with the organization's name, logo, address, and telephone number printed on the page.

limitations Problems or factors that constrain the validity of the recommendations of a report.

line graph A visual consisting of lines that show trends or allow the viewer to interpolate values between the observed values.

low-context culture A culture in which most information is conveyed explicitly in words rather than being inferred from context.

M

mailing list The list of names and addresses to which a communication is sent.

main clause A group of words that can stand by itself as a complete sentence. Also called an independent clause.

Maslow's hierarchy of needs Five levels of human need posited by Abraham H. Maslow. They include physical needs, the need for safety and security, for love and belonging, for esteem and recognition, and for self-actualization.

mean The average of a group of numbers. Found by adding up all the numbers and dividing by the number of numbers.

median The middle number in a ranked set of numbers.

memo Document using memo format sent to readers in your organization.

methods section The section of a report or survey describing how the data were gathered.

minutes Records of a meeting, listing the items discussed, the results of votes, and the persons responsible for carrying out follow-up steps.

mirror question Question that paraphrases the content of the answer an interviewee gave to the last question.

misplaced modifier A word or phrase that appears to modify another element of the sentence than the writer intended.

mixed punctuation Using a colon after the salutation and a comma after the complimentary close in a letter.

mode The most frequent number in a set of numbers.

modified block format   A letter format in which the inside address, date, and signature block are lined up with each other one-half or two-thirds of the way over on the page.

modifier   A word or phrase giving more information about another word in a sentence.

monochronic culture   Culture in which people do only one important activity at a time.

monologue presentation   A presentation in which the speaker talks without interruption. The presentation is planned and is delivered without deviation.

multiple graphs   Three or more simple stories told by graphs juxtaposed to create a more powerful story.

Myers-Briggs Type Indicator   A scale that categorizes people on four dimensions: introvert-extravert; sensing-intuitive; thinking-feeling; and perceiving-judging.

N

negative message   A message in which basic information conveyed is negative; the reader is expected to be disappointed or angry.

neutral subject line   A subject line that does not give away the writer's stance on an issue.

noise   Any physical or psychological interference in a message.

nominative case   The grammatical form used for the subject of a clause. *I, we, he, she,* and *they* are nominative pronouns.

nonagist   Refers to words, images, or behaviors that do not discriminate against people on the basis of age.

nonracist   Refers to words, images, or behaviors that do not discriminate against people on the basis of race.

nonrestrictive clause   A clause giving extra but unessential information about a noun or pronoun. Because the information is extra, commas separate the clause from the word it modifies.

nonsexist language   Language that treats both sexes neutrally, that does not make assumptions about the proper gender for a job, and that does not imply that one sex is superior to or takes precedence over the other.

nonverbal communication   Communication that does not use words.

normal interview   A job interview with some questions that the interviewer expects to be easy, some questions that present an opportunity to showcase strong points, and some questions that probe any weaknesses evident from the résumé.

noun–pronoun agreement   Having a pronoun be the same number (singular or plural) and the same person (first, second, or third) as the noun it refers to.

O

objective case   The grammatical form used for the object of a verb or preposition. *Me, us, him, her,* and *them* are objective pronouns.

omnibus motion   A motion that allows a group to vote on several related items in a single vote. Saves time in formal meetings with long agendas.

open body position   Includes keeping the arms and legs uncrossed and away from the body. Suggests physical and psychological comfort and openness.

open punctuation   Using no punctuation after the salutation and the complimentary close.

open question   Question with an unlimited number of possible responses.

opinion   A statement that can never be verified, since it includes terms that cannot be measured objectively. Also called a judgment.

organization   The order in which ideas are arranged in a message.

organizational culture   The values, attitudes, and philosophies shared by people in an organization that shape its messages and its reward structure.

outsourcing   Going outside the company for products and services that once were made by the company's employees.

P

package   The outer envelope and everything that goes in it in a direct mailing.

paired bar chart   A bar chart that shows the correlation between two items.

parallel structure   Putting words or ideas that share the same role in the logic of the sentence or paragraph into the same grammatical form.

paraphrase   To repeat in your own words the verbal content of another communication.

passive verb   A verb that describes action done to the grammatical subject of the sentence.

people-first language   Language that names the person first, then the condition: "people with mental retardation." Used to avoid implying that the condition defines the person's potential.

perception   The ability to see, hear, taste, smell, touch.

performance appraisals   Supervisors' written evaluations of their subordinates' work.

persona   The "author" or character who allegedly writes a document; the voice that a communicator assumes in creating a message.

personal space   The distance someone wants between him- or herself and other people in ordinary, nonintimate interchanges.

personalized   A message that is adapted to the individual reader by including the reader's name and address and perhaps other information.

persuade   To motivate and convince the audience to act or change a belief.

persuasive presentation   A presentation that motivates the audience to act or to believe.

pie chart   A circular chart whose sections represent percentages of a given quantity.

pitch   The highness or lowness of a sound. Low-pitched sounds are closer to the bass notes on a piano; high-pitched sounds are closer to the high notes.

planning All the thinking done about a subject and the means of achieving your purposes. Planning takes place not only when devising strategies for the document as a whole, but also when generating "miniplans" that govern sentences or paragraphs.

polarization A logical fallacy that argues there are only two possible positions, one of which is clearly unacceptable.

polychronic culture Culture in which people do several things at once.

population The group a researcher wants to make statements about.

positive emphasis Focusing on the positive rather than the negative aspects of a situation.

positive or good news message Message to which the reader's reaction will be positive.

possessive case The grammatical form used to indicate possession or ownership. *My, our, his, hers, its,* and *their* are possessive pronouns.

post office abbreviations Two-letter abbreviations for states and provinces.

prepositions Words that indicate relationships, for example, *with, in, under, at.*

presenting problem The problem that surfaces as the subject of discord. The presenting problem is often not the real problem.

primary audience The audience who will make a decision or act on the basis of a message.

primary research Research that gathers new information.

pro-and-con pattern A pattern of organization that presents all the arguments for an alternative and then all the arguments against it.

probe question A follow-up question designed to get more information about an answer or to get at specific aspects of a topic.

problem-solving pattern A pattern of organization that describes a problem before offering a solution to the problem.

procedural dimensions Dimensions of group work focusing on methods: how the group makes decisions, who does what, when assignments are due.

process of writing What people actually do when they write: planning, gathering, writing, evaluating, getting feedback, revising, editing, and proofreading.

progress report A statement of the work done during a period of time and the work proposed for the next period.

proofreading Checking the final copy to see that it's free from typographical errors.

proportional typeface A typeface in which some letters are wider than other letters (for example, *w* is wider than *i*).

proposal Document that suggests a method and personnel for finding information or solving a problem.

prospecting letter A job application letter written to a company that has not announced openings but where you'd like to work.

psychographic characteristics Human characteristics that are qualitative rather than quantitative: values, beliefs, goals, and lifestyles.

psychological description Description of a product or service in terms of audience benefits.

psychological reactance Phenomenon occurring when a reader reacts to a negative message by asserting freedom in some other arena.

purpose statement The statement in a proposal or a report specifying the organizational problem, the technical questions that must be answered to solve the problem, and the rhetorical purpose of the report (to explain, to recommend, to request, to propose).

Q

questionnaire List of questions for people to answer in a survey.

R

ragged right margins Margins that do not end evenly on the right side of the page.

random sample A sample for which each member of the population has an equal chance of being chosen.

recommendation report A report that recommends action.

recommendations Section of a report that specifies items for action.

reference line A *subject line* that refers the reader to another document (usually a numbered one, such as an invoice).

referral interview Interviews you schedule to learn about current job opportunities in your field and to get referrals to other people who may have the power to create a job for you. Useful for tapping into unadvertised jobs and the hidden job market.

release date Date a report will be made available to the public.

reply card A card or form designed to make it easy for the reader to respond to a direct mail letter. A good reply card repeats the central selling point, basic product information, and price.

request To ask the audience to take an easy or routine action.

request for proposal (RFP) A statement of the service or product that an agency wants; an invitation for proposals to provide that service or product.

respondents The people who fill out a questionnaire; also called subjects.

response rate The percentage of subjects receiving a questionnaire who answer the questions.

restrictive clause A clause limiting or restricting the meaning of a noun or pronoun. Because its information is essential, no commas separate the clause from the word it restricts.

résumé A persuasive summary of your qualifications for employment.

résumé blasting Posting your résumé widely—usually by the hundreds—on the Web.

reverse chronology Starting with the most recent events, such as job or degree, and going backward in time. Pattern of organization used for chronological résumés.

revising Making changes in the draft: adding, deleting, substituting, or rearranging. Revision can be changes in single words, but more often it means major additions, deletions, or substitutions, as the writer measures the draft against purpose and audience and reshapes the document to make it more effective.

RFP See *request for proposal.*

rhetorical purpose The effect the writer or speaker hopes to have on the audience (to inform, to persuade, to build goodwill).

rhythm The repetition of a pattern of accented and unaccented syllables.

rival hypotheses Alternate explanations for observed results.

rule of three The rule noting a preference for three short parallel examples and explaining that the last will receive the most emphasis.

run-on sentence A sentence containing several main clauses strung together with *and, but, or, so,* or *for.*

S

sales pattern A pattern of persuasion that consists of an attention getting opener, a body with reasons and details, and an action close.

salutation The greeting in a letter: "Dear Ms. Smith."

sample (*in marketing*) A product provided to the audience to whet their appetite for more.

sample (*in research*) The portion of the population a researcher actually studies.

sampling frame The list of all possible sampling units.

sampling units Those items/people actually sampled.

sans serif Literally, *without serifs.* Typeface whose letters lack bases or flicks. Helvetica and Geneva are examples of sans serif typefaces.

saves the reader's time The result of a message whose style, organization, and visual impact help the reader to read, understand, and act on the information as quickly as possible.

schematic diagrams Line drawings of objects and their parts.

scope statement A statement in a proposal or report specifying the subjects the report covers and how broadly or deeply it covers them.

secondary audience The audience who may be asked by the primary audience to comment on a message or to implement ideas after they've been approved.

secondary research Research retrieving data someone else gathered. Includes library research.

segmented, subdivided, or stacked bars Bars in a bar chart that sum components of an item.

semantics or general semantics The study of the ways behavior is influenced by the words and other symbols used to communicate.

sentence fragment A group of words that are not a complete sentence but that are punctuated as if they were a complete sentence.

sentence outline An outline using complete sentences. It contains the thesis or recommendation plus all supporting points.

serif The little extensions from the main strokes on letters. Times Roman and Courier are examples of serif typefaces.

signpost An explicit statement of the place that a speaker or writer has reached: "Now we come to the third point."

simple sentence Sentence with one main clause.

situational interviews Job interviews in which candidates are asked to describe what they would do in specific hypothetical situations.

skills résumé A résumé organized around the skills you've used, rather than the date or the job in which you used them.

solicited letter A job letter written when you know that the company is hiring.

spot visuals Informal visuals that are inserted directly into text. Spot visuals do not have numbers or titles.

stereotyping Putting similar people or events into a single category, even though significant differences exist.

storyboard A visual representation of the structure of a document, with a rectangle representing each page or unit. An alternative to outlining as a method of organizing material.

strategy A plan for reaching your specific goals with a specific audience.

stratified random sample A sample generated by first dividing the sample into the same proportion of subgroups as exists in the population and then taking a random sample for each subgroup.

stress Emphasis given to one or more words in a sentence, or one or more ideas in a message.

stress interview A job interview that deliberately puts the applicant under stress, physical or psychological. Here it's important to change the conditions that create physical stress and to meet psychological stress by rephrasing questions in less inflammatory terms and treating them as requests for information.

structured interview An interview that follows a detailed list of questions prepared in advance.

stub The variable listed on the side in a table.

subject line The title of the document, used to file and retrieve the document. A subject line tells readers why they need to read the document and provides a framework in which to set what you're about to say.

subjects The people studied in an experiment, focus group, or survey.

subordinate clause A group of words containing a subject and a verb but that cannot stand by itself as a complete sentence. Also called a dependent clause.

summarizing Restating and relating major points, pulling ideas together.

summary abstract The logical skeleton of an article or report, containing the thesis or recommendation and its proof.

summary sentence or paragraph   A sentence or paragraph listing in order the topics that following sentences or paragraphs will discuss.

survey   A method of getting information from a group of people.

T

table   Numbers or words arrayed in rows and columns.

talking heads   Headings that are detailed enough to provide an overview of the material in the sections they introduce.

10-K report   A report filed with the Securities and Exchange Commission summarizing the firm's financial performance.

thank-you note   A note thanking someone for helping you.

threat   A statement, explicit or implied, that someone will be punished if he or she does or doesn't do something.

tone   The implied attitude of the author toward the reader and the subject.

tone of voice   The rising or falling inflection that indicates whether a group of words is a question or a statement, whether the speaker is uncertain or confident, whether a statement is sincere or sarcastic.

topic heading   A heading that focuses on the structure of a report. Topic headings give little information.

topic outline   An outline listing the main points and the subpoints under each main point. A topic outline is the basis for the table of contents of a report.

topic sentence   A sentence that introduces or summarizes the main idea in a paragraph.

transmit   To send a message.

transitions   Words, phrases, or sentences that show the connections between ideas.

transmittal   A message explaining why something is being sent.

truncated code   Symbols such as asterisks that turn up other forms of a keyword in a computer search.

truncated graphs   Graphs with part of the scale missing.

two-margin format   A format for résumés in which dates are listed in one column and job titles and descriptions in another. This format emphasizes work history.

U

umbrella sentence or paragraph   A sentence or paragraph listing in order the topics that following sentences or paragraphs will discuss.

understatement   Downplaying or minimizing the size or features of something.

unity   Using only one idea or topic in a paragraph or other piece of writing.

unjustified margins   Margins that do not end evenly on the right side of the page.

unstructured interview   An interview based on three or four main questions prepared in advance and other questions that build on what the interviewee says.

V

venting   Expressing pent-up negative emotions.

verbal communication   Communication that uses words; may be either oral or written.

vested interest   The emotional stake readers have in something if they benefit from maintaining or influencing conditions or actions.

vicarious participation   An emotional strategy in fundraising letters based on the idea that by donating money, readers participate vicariously in work they are not able to do personally.

visual impact   The visual "first impression" you get when you look at a page.

volume   The loudness or softness of a voice or other sound.

W

watchdog audience   An audience that has political, social, or economic power and that may base future actions on its evaluation of your message.

white space   The empty space on the page. White space emphasizes material that it separates from the rest of the text.

wild card   Symbols such as asterisks that turn up other forms of a keyword in a computer search. See also *truncated code*.

withdrawing   Being silent in meetings, not contributing, not helping with the work, not attending meetings.

wordiness   Taking more words than necessary to express an idea.

works cited   The sources specifically referred to in a report.

works consulted   Sources read during the research for a report but not mentioned specifically in the report.

writing   The act of putting words on paper or screen.

Y

you-attitude   A style of communicating that looks at things from the audience point of view, emphasizes what the audience wants to know, respects the audience's intelligence, and protects the audience's ego. Using *you* probably increases you attitude in positive situations. In negative situations or conflict, avoid *you* since that word will attack the audience.

Chapter 1

1. National Association of Colleges and Employers, "Employers Cite Communication Skills, Honesty/Integrity as Key for Job Candidates," in *News for Media Professionals*, http://www.naceweb.org/press/display.asp?year=2007&prid=254 (accessed May 14, 2007).
2. Peter Coy, "The Future of Work," *BusinessWeek*, March 22, 2004, 50.
3. The National Commission on Writing for America's Families, Schools, and Colleges, "Writing: A Ticket to Work . . . Or a Ticket Out: A Survey of Business Leaders," in *College Board* (2004), 7–8.
4. Anne Fisher, "The High Cost of Living and Not Writing Well," *Fortune*, December 7, 1998, 244.
5. Jeffrey Gitomer, *Jeffrey Gitomer's Little Black Book of Connections: 6.5 Assets for Networking Your Way to Rich Relationships* (Austin, TX: Bard Press, 2006), 128–31.
6. Tom DeMint, "So You Want to Be Promoted," *Fire Engineering* 159, no. 7 (2006): 46; Karen M. Kroll, "Mapping Your Career," *PM Network* 19, no. 11 (2005): 28; Jeff Snyder, "Recruiter: What It Takes," *Security* 43, no. 11 (2006): 70.
7. Claudia MonPere McIsaac and Mary Ann Aschauer, "Proposal Writing at Atherton Jordan, Inc.: An Ethnographic Study," *Management Communication Quarterly* 3 (1990): 535.
8. Eric Krell, "The Unintended Word," *HRMagazine* 51, no. 8 (2006): 52.
9. Alex Cassini, "Not So Cheap after All: Email Storage Costs Continue to Grow," *Docume.nt [sic]* 12, no. 4 (2004): 31; and Pui-Wing Tam, "Cutting Files Down to Size: New Approaches Tackle Surplus of Data," *Wall Street Journal*, May 8, 2007, B4.
10. Daniel Machalaba and Betsy McKay, "Amtrak Cites Communications Failure over Brakes," *Wall Street Journal*, May 12, 2005, B2.
11. The National Commission on Writing for America's Families, Schools, and Colleges, "A Powerful Message from State Government," in *College Board* (2005), 26.
12. The National Commission on Writing for America's Families, Schools, and Colleges, "Writing: A Ticket to Work . . . Or a Ticket Out: A Survey of Business Leaders," 29.
13. Stephen Baker, "A Painful Lesson: E-mail is Forever," *BusinessWeek*, March 21, 2005, 36; Gary McWilliams, "Walmart Details Roehm Firing," *Wall Street Journal*, March 21, 2007, B11; and Peter Waldman and Don Clark, "California Charges Dunn, 4 Others In H-P Scandal; Action Sends Strong Message to Business about Privacy; Precedents for the Web Age?" *Wall Street Journal*, October 5, 2006, A1.
14. Elizabeth A. McCord, "The Business Writer, the Law, and Routine Business Communication: A Legal and Rhetorical Analysis," *Journal of Business and Technical Communication* 5, no. 3 (1991): 173–99.
15. Stephen Ohlemacher, "Media Compete with Breathing for American's Time," *Des Moines Register*, December 15, 2006, D1.
16. William M. Bulkeley, "Better Virtual Meetings: With Pricey Cameras, Plasma Screens, 'Telepresence' Replaces Video-Conferencing," *Wall Street Journal*, September 28, 2006, B1, B5.
17. Peter Engardio, "Let's Offshore the Lawyers," *BusinessWeek*, September 18, 2006, 42.
18. Engardio, "Let's Offshore the Lawyers," 43.
19. Tam, "Cutting Files Down to Size: New Approaches Tackle Surplus of Data," B4.
20. Jared Sandberg, "Employees Forsake Dreaded Email for the Beloved Phone," *Wall Street Journal*, September 26, 2006, B1.
21. Sandberg, "Employees Forsake Dreaded Email for the Beloved Phone," B1.
22. Bullets quoted from Phred Dvorak and Vauhini Vara, "At Many Companies, Hunt for Leakers Expands Arsenal of Monitoring Tactics," *Wall Street Journal*, September 11, 2006, B1.
23. Stephanie Armour, "Employers Look Closely at What Workers Do on Job: Companies Get More Vigilant as Technology Increases Their Risks," *USA Today*, November 8, 2006, 2B.
24. Vauhini Vara, "How Firms' Web-Filter Use Is Changing: Blocking Efforts Target Social and Video Sites; Finding Happy Medium," *Wall Street Journal*, January 16, 2007, B3.
25. Roger Cheng, "I Can See You: Small Businesses and Local Governments Are Finding It's Easier than Ever to Track Their Employees," *Wall Street Journal*, November 11, 2006, R6; and Ellen Nakashima, "Enjoying Technology's Conveniences but Not Escaping Its Watchful Eyes," *Washington Post*, January 16, 2007, A01.
26. Armour, "Employers Look Closely at What Workers Do on Job: Companies Get More Vigilant as Technology Increases Their Risks," 2B; and M. P. McQueen, "Laptop Lockdown: Companies Start Holding Employees Responsible for Security of Portable Devices They Use for Work," *Wall Street Journal*, June 28, 2006, D1.
27. Armour, "Employers Look Closely at What Workers Do on Job: Companies Get More Vigilant as Technology Increases Their Risks," 2B; and M. P. McQueen, "Workers' Terminations for Computer Misuse Rise," *Wall Street Journal*, July 15, 2006, B4.
28. Claes Fornell, "Customer Satisfaction at an All-Time High; Home Depot Makes U-Turn, Best Guy Gains; MetLife Rebounds," in *American Customer Satisfaction Index*, http://www.theacsi.org/index.php?option=com_content&task=view&id=168&Itemid=162 (accessed May 14, 2007).
29. James R. Rosenfield, "Tackling the Tough Topics," *Direct Marketing*, June 2001, 4.
30. Christopher W. Hart, "Beating the Market with Customer Satisfaction," *Harvard Business Review* 85, no. 3 (March 2007): 30–32.
31. "June 2000 Star of the Month," in *Careers: Star of the Month*, http://www.southwest.com/careers/stars/star_June00.html (accessed July 12, 2001).
32. Cate T. Corcoran, "Nordstrom 'Simplifies' Customer Satisfaction," *WWD*, March 22, 2007, 8.
33. Shirley S. Wang, "Health Care Taps 'Mystery Shoppers': To Improve Service, Hospitals and Doctors Hire Spies to Pose as Patients and Report Back," *Wall Street Journal*, August 8, 2006, D1.
34. Mike Bergman, "Nation Adds 2.2 Million Nonemployer Businesses over Five-Year Period," in *Releases: Economic Census*, http://www.census.gov/Press-Release/www/releases/archives/economic_census/001814.html (accessed May 16, 2007).
35. L. D. DeSimone et al., "How Can Big Companies Keep the Entrepreneurial Spirit Alive?" *Harvard Business Review* November–December (1995): 183–92.
36. Christine Uber Grosse, "Managing Communication within Virtual Intercultural Teams," *Business Communication Quarterly* (2002); and Linda H. Heuring, "Patients First," *HRMagazine*, July, 2003, 67–68.

37. Michael Mandel, "What Spending Slowdown? Forget Those Antiquated Government Statistics. U.S. Corporate Investment Is Booming—Just Take a Look Overseas," *BusinessWeek,* April 23, 2007, 30; and Robyn Meredith and Suzanne Hoppough, "Why Globalization Is Good," *Forbes* 179, no. 8 (2007): 64–68.

38. Thomas L. Friedman, *The World Is Flat: A Brief History of the Twenty-First Century,* updated and expanded ed. (New York: Farrar, Straus, & Giroux, 2006), 14.

39. Friedman, *The World Is Flat,* 86.

40. Nanette Byrnes et al., "Reform: Who's Making the Grade: A Performance Review for CEOs, Boards, Analysts, and Others," *BusinessWeek,* September 22, 2003, 80; "On Trial; This Year, the Wheels of Justice May Catch Up to Some Movers and Shakers," *Business Week,* January 12, 2004, 80.

41. Jane Sasseen, "That's Awfully Good Timing: The SEC Takes a Harder Look at Execs Who May Have Backdated to Cut Their Tax Bills," *BusinessWeek,* April 30, 2007, 66.

42. James T. Bond et al., "2005 National Study of Employers: When Work Works," in *Research: Reports,* Families and Work Institute, http://www.familiesandwork.org/site/research/reports/2005NSE.pdf (accessed May 16, 2007).

43. "100 Best Companies, 2006, Aflac," in *Working Mother Magazine,* http://vebranch.rgisolutions.com/web?service=direct/1/ViewTop-ListingPage/dlinkDetails&sp=5&sp=77 (accessed May 16, 2007); "100 Best Companies, 2006, McGraw-Hill," in *Working Mother Magazine,* http://vebranch.rgisolutions.com/web?service=direct/1/ViewTop-ListingPage/dlinkDetails&sp=64&sp=77 (accessed May 16, 2007); and Seema Nayyar. "Focus on the 100 Best—Comeback Moms," in *Working Mother Magazine,* http://vebranch.rgisolutions.com/web?service=direct/1/ViewArticle/Page/&linkFullArticle&sp=67&sp=94 (accessed May 16, 2007).

44. Heuring, "Patients First."

45. Jörgen Sandberg, "Understanding Competence at Work," *Harvard Business Review,* March 2001, 24–28.

46. Coy, "The Future of Work"; Kerry A. Dolan and Robyn Meredith, "A Tale of Two Cities," *Forbes,* April 12, 2004; and Jennifer Reingold, "Into Thin Air," *Fast Company,* April 2004.

47. Eric Abrahamson, "Change without Pain," *Harvard Business Review,* July–August (2000): 75–79; "Change Is Changing," *Harvard Business Review,* April (2001): 125.

48. Max Messmer, "Soft Skills Are Key to Advancing Your Career," *Business Credit* 109, no. 4 (April 2007): 34.

Chapter 2

1. Isabel Briggs Myers, *Introduction to Type* (Palo Alto, CA: Consulting Psychologists Press, 1980). The material in this section follows Myers's paper.

2. Isabel Briggs Myers and Mary H. McCaulley, *Manual: A Guide to the Development and Use of the Myers-Briggs Type Indicator* (Palo Alto, CA: Consulting Psychologists Press, 1985), 248, 251.

3. Jeffrey Zaslow, "Moving On: After a Honeymoon, a Conceptionmoon?" *Wall Street Journal,* November 11, 2006, D2.

4. SRI Consulting Business Intelligence (SRIC-BI), "Global Leader in Psychological Consumer Segmentation Announces System Enhancements to Anticipate the Evolving Marketplace," in *Press Release 18 November 2002,* http://www.sric-bi.com/press/2002-11-18.shtml (accessed May 20, 2007).

5. SRI Consulting Business Intelligence, "Representative VALS™ Projects," in *VALS™ Survey,* http://www.sric-bi.com/VALS/projects.shtml (accessed May 22, 2007).

6. Amy Chozick, "Toyota Tempers Sales View of Lexus Hybrid in U.S.," *Wall Street Journal,* May 19, 2007, A6; and Joseph Weber, "Giving Some Glamour to Grit," *BusinessWeek,* September 18, 2006, 12.

7. "Being Bogusky," *Wall Street Journal,* May 19, 2007, P7; Tamara J. Erickson and Linda Gratton, "What It Means to Work Here," *Harvard Business Review* 85, no. 3 (March 2007): 107; and Samuel Greengard, "Sun's Shining Example," *Workforce Management* 84, no. 3 (2005): 48.

8. Ellen Byron, "Merger Challenge: Unite Toothbrush, Toothpaste: P&G and Gillette Find Creating Synergy Can Be Harder than It Looks," *Wall Street Journal,* April 24, 2007, A1.

9. Moon Ihlwan and Kenji Hall, "New Tech, Old Habits: Despite World-Class IT Networks, Japanese and Korean Workers Are Still Chained to Their Desks," *BusinessWeek,* March 26, 2007, 48–49.

10. Bobby White, "Firms Take a Cue from YouTube: Companies Use Online Video to Reduce Costs, Communicate with Staff," *Wall Street Journal,* January 2, 2007, B3.

11. Ibid.

12. Jeffrey A. Trachtenberg, "Scarcity of Ads Endangers Newspapers' Book Sections," *Wall Street Journal,* March 6, 2007, B1; and Jeffry A. Trachtenberg and Brian Steinberg, "HarperCollins Turns to Web, in a Search for More Romance," *Wall Street Journal,* July 26, 2006, B3.

13. Ellen Byron, "Estée Lauder Tests Web-Ad Waters," *Wall Street Journal,* September 19, 2006, B6.

14. Theresa Howard, "Outdoor Ads Make High-Tech Comeback," *USA Today,* June 21, 2006, 3B.

15. Janet Adamy, "McDonald's Puts Shrek on the Menu," *Wall Street Journal,* May 9, 2007, B3.

16. Emily Steel, "Web-Page Clocks and other 'Widgets' Anchor New Internet Strategy," *Wall Street Journal,* November 21, 2006, B4.

17. "Steamy Hot Line Raises Pulses, Library Funds," *Des Moines Register,* May 9, 2007, 4A.

18. Corey Dade, "R2-D2 Gets Top Billing in Postal Service Promotion," *Wall Street Journal,* March 16, 2007, B3; Laura Petrecca, "Product Placement—You Can't Escape It," *USA Today,* October 11, 2006, 1B; Suzanne Vranica, "Hanger Ads Ensure Message Gets Home," *Wall Street Journal,* March 12, 2007, B4; and Elizabeth Woyke, "A Marriage of Conveyance," *BusinessWeek,* October 30, 2006, 16.

19. Susan Warren, "Spring Break Is a Legal Specialty for Ben Bollinger," *Wall Street Journal,* March 17, 2007, A2.

20. Lev Grossman, "A Game for All Ages," *Time,* May 15, 2006, 39.

21. Sara Silver, "How Match.com Found Love among Boomers: Dating Site Prospers Targeting Older Singles," *Wall Street Journal,* January 27, 2007, A1.

22. Kemba J. Dunham, "Beyond Satisfaction: What Is Customer Service, Anyway? And How Do You Measure It?" *Wall Street Journal,* October 30, 2006, R4.

23. Cecilie Rohwedder, "Store of Knowledge: No. 1 Retailer in Britain Uses 'Clubcard' to Thwart Wal-Mart: Data from Loyalty Program Help Tesco Tailor Products as It Resists U.S. Invader," *Wall Street Journal,* June 6, 2006, A1.

24. Frederick Herzberg, "One More Time: How Do You Motivate Employees," *Harvard Business Review* 65, no. 5 (September–October, 1987): 109–20.

25. Diane Cadrain, "Cash vs. Noncash Rewards," *HRMagazine,* April, 2003, 82–83; and Jennifer Gilbert, "Motivating through the Ages," *Sales & Marketing Management,* November, 2003, 31–40.

26. John Ketzenberger, "Respect, Not Money, Priceless in Cutting Turnover," *Des Moines Register*, November 20, 2006, 3D.

27. Jill Rosenfeld, "Unit of One: Here's an Idea!" *Fast Company*, April 2000, 98.

28. Abraham H. Maslow, *Motivation and Personality* (New York: Harper & Row, 1954).

29. Ellen Byron, "Aiming to Clean Up, P&G Courts Business Customers," *Wall Street Journal*, January 26, 2007, B1.

30. Anne Marie Chaker, "Amid Shortage, States Scramble to Hire Teachers; New Laws Offer Incentives to Lure More People into the Profession," *Wall Street Journal*, August 17, 2006, D1.

31. Jane J. Kim, "Big Banks on Campus: Looking to Lure Lifelong Clients, Firms Dangle Plane Tickets, iPods; Worry over Credit-Card Debt," *Wall Street Journal*, September 6, 2006, D1.

32. Sarmad Ali, "If You Want to Scream, Press . . . : Do Call Centers Have to Be So Infuriating?" *Wall Street Journal*, October 30, 2006, R4.

33. Ryan Chittum, "Price Points: Good Customer Service Costs Money. Some Expenses Are Worth It—and Some Aren't," *Wall Street Journal*, October 30, 2006, R7.

34. Rachel Spilka, "Orality and Literacy in the Workplace: Process- and Text-Based Strategies for Multiple Audience Adaptation," *Journal of Business and Technical Communication* 4, no. 1 (January 1990): 44–67.

Chapter 3

1. Linda Kaplan Thaler and Robin Koval, *The Power of Nice: How to Conquer the Business World with Kindness* (New York: Currency, 2006), 3.

2. David Welch, "Looser Rules, Happier Clients," *BusinessWeek*, March 5, 2007, 62.

3. John A. Byrne, "How to Lead Now: Getting Extraordinary Performance When You Can't Pay for It," *Fast Company*, August 2003, 65.

4. Timothy Aeppel, "Too Good for Lowe's and Home Depot?" *Wall Street Journal*, July 24, 2006, B1, B6.

5. Michael J. Fanuele, "Embrace the Dark Side," *Harvard Business Review* 84, no. 3 (October 2006): 24.

6. Annette N. Shelby and N. Lamar Reinsch, Jr., "Positive Emphasis and You-Attitude: An Empirical Study," *Journal of Business Communication* 32, no. 4 (October 1995): 303–27.

7. Martin E. P. Seligman, *Learned Optimism: How to Change Your Mind and Your Life*, 2nd ed. (New York: Pocket Books, 1998), 96–107.

8. Mark A. Sherman, "Adjectival Negation and the Comprehension of Multiply Negated Sentences," *Journal of Verbal Learning and Verbal Behavior* 15 (1976): 143–57.

9. Jeffrey Zaslow, "In Praise of Less Praise," *Wall Street Journal*, May 3, 2007, D1.

10. " 'Jelly Belly' E-mail Costs Winter Haven Chief of Police His Job," http://www.tampabaylive.com/stories/2006/10/061025jellybelly.shtml (accessed November 2, 2006); and "Winter Haven Police Chief Resigns over Fitness E-Mail," http://www.polkonloine.com/stories/102406/community-news_cop.shtml (accessed November 2, 2006).

11. Stephen C. Dillard, "Litigation Nation," *Wall Street Journal*, November 25, 2006, A9.

12. Margaret Baker Graham and Carol David, "Power and Politeness: Administrative Writing in an 'Organized Anarchy,' " *Journal of Business and Technical Communication* 10, no. 1 (1996): 5–27.

13. John Hagge and Charles Kostelnick, "Linguistic Politeness in Professional Prose: A Discourse Analysis of Auditors' Suggestion Letters, with Implications for Business Communication Pedagogy," *Written Communication* 6, no. 3 (July 1989): 312–39.

14. Priscilla S. Rogers and Song-Mei Lee-Wong, "Reconceptualizing Politeness to Accommodate Dynamic Tensions in Subordinate-to-Superior Reporting," *Journal of Business and Technical Communication* 17, no. 4 (October 2003): 379–412.

15. Brad Edmondson, "What Do You Call a Dark-Skinned Person?" *American Demographics* (October 1993): 9.

16. Robert Bernstein, "More than 50 Million Americans Report Some Level of Disability," in *U.S. Census Bureau: Newsroom: Releases: Aging Population, Children, Miscellaneous*, http://www.census.gov/Press-Release/www/releases/archives/aging_population/ 006809.html (accessed May 11, 2007).

17. Marilyn A. Dyrud, "An Exploration of Gender Bias in Computer Clip Art," *Business Communication Quarterly* 60, no. 4 (December 1997): 30–51.

Chapter 4

1. Robert L. Brown, Jr. and Carl G. Herndl, "An Ethnographic Study of Corporate Writing: Job Status as Reflected in Written Text," in *Functional Approaches to Writing: A Research Perspective*, ed. Barbara Couture (Norwood, NJ: Ablex, 1986), 16–19, 22–23.

2. Matt Reed, "Police Start Phasing Out '10–4,' Other Radio Codes," *Des Moines Register*, November 19, 2006, 12A.

3. U.S. Securities and Exchange Commission Office of Investor Education and Assistance, *A Plain English Handbook: How to Create Clear SEC Discolsure Documents* (Washington, D.C.: 1998).

4. Gerard Braud, "What Does That Mean?" *Communication World* 24, no. 1 (2007): 34.

5. Richard Lederer and Richard Dowis, *Sleeping Dogs Don't Lay: Practical Advice for the Grammatically Challenged* (New York: St. Martin's Press, 1999), 91–92.

6. Linda Flower, *Problem-Solving Strategies for Writing*, 3 ed. (New York: Harcourt Brace Jovanovich, 1989), 38.

7. James Suchan and Robert Colucci, "An Analysis of Communication Efficiency between High-Impact and Bureaucratic Written Communication," *Management Communication Quarterly* 2, no. 4 (1989): 464–73.

8. Hilvard G. Rogers and F. William Brown, "The Impact of Writing Style on Compliance with Instructions," *Journal of Technical Writing and Communication* 23, no. 1 (1993): 53–71.

9. Richard Lederer, "The Terrible Ten," *Toastmaster*, July 2003, 28–29.

10. Robert Frank, "The Wealth Report: Millionaires Need Not Apply; SEC and Others Rewrite the Definition of 'Rich'; The Haves and Have-Mores," *Wall Street Journal*, March 16, 2007, W2.

11. Arlene Weintraub, "Revenge of the Overworked Nerds," *BusinessWeek*, December 8, 2003, 41.

12. Hersch Doby, "Changing the Rules," *Black Enterprise*, April 2000, 23; Mary Ellen Podmolik, "New Rule Raises Stakes for Minority Shop Owners," *Advertising Age*, February 28, 2000, 34.

13. Lisa D. McNary, "The Term 'Win–Win' in Conflict Management: A Classic Case of Misuse and Overuse," *Journal of Business Communication* 40, no. 2 (2003): 144–60.

14. Interoffice memo in a steel company.

15. Quoted by Emery Hutchison, "Things My Mother Never Taught Me about Writing," *Journal of Organizational Communications* (1972): 20.

16. Mary Newton Bruder, *Much Ado about a Lot: How to Mind Your Manners in Print and in Person* (New York: Hyperion, 2000), 51.

17. Philip B. Crosby, *Quality Is Free: The Art of Making Quality Certain* (New York: New American Library, 1979), 79–84.

18. Jaguarad, *Wall Street Journal*, September 29, 2000, A20.

19. Erika L. Kirby and Lynn M. Harter, "Speaking the Language of the Bottom-Line: The Metaphor of 'Managing Diversity,'" *Journal of Business Communication* 40, no. 2 (2003): 28–50.

20. Richard C. Anderson, "Concretization and Sentence Learning," *Journal of Educational Psychology* 66, no. 2 (1974): 179–83.

21. Pamela Layton and Adrian J. Simpson, "Deep Structure in Sentence Comprehension," *Journal of Verbal Learning and Verbal Behavior* 14 (1975); Harris B. Savin and Ellen Perchonock, "Grammatical Structure and the Immediate Recall of English Sentences," *Journal of Verbal Learning and Verbal Behavior* 4 (1965): 348–53.

22. Federal Aviation Administration and Web Content Management Working Group of the Interagency Committee on Government Information, "How To/Tools: Checklist," in *PlainLanguage.gov: Improving Communication from the Federal Government to the Public*, http://www. plainlanguage. gov/howto/quickreference/checklist.cfm (accessed March 31, 2007).

23. Lloyd Bostian and Ann C. Thering, "Scientists: Can They Read What They Write?" *Journal of Technical Writing and Communication* 17 (1987): 417–27; E. B. Coleman, "The Comprehensibility of Several Grammatical Transformations," *Journal of Applied Psychology* 48, no. 3 (1964): 186–90; Keith Rayner, "Visual Attention in Reading: Eye Movements Reflect Cognitive Processes," *Memory and Cognition* 5 (1977): 443–48.

24. Don Bush, "The Most Obvious Fault in Technical Writing," *Intercom*, July/August 2003, 50.

25. Thomas N. Huckin, "A Cognitive Approach to Readability," in *New Essays in Technical and Scientific Communication: Research, Theory, Practice*, ed. Paul V. Anderson, R. John Brockmann, and Carolyn R. Miller (Farmingdale, NY: Baywood, 1983), 93–98.

26. Janice C. Redish and Jack Selzer, "The Place of Readability Formulas in Technical Communication," *Technical Communication* 32, no. 4 (1985): 46–52.

27. James Suchan and Ronald Dulek, "A Reassessment of Clarity in Written Managerial Communications," *Management Communication Quarterly* 4, no. 1 (1990): 93–97.

Chapter 5

1. See especially Linda Flower and John R. Hayes, "The Cognition of Discovery: Defining a Rhetorical Problem," *College Composition and Communication* (February 1980): 21–32; Mike Rose, "Writer's Block: The Cognitive Dimension," published for Conference on College Composition and Communication, 1984; and the essays in two collections: Charles R. Cooper and Lee Odell, *"Research on Composing: Points of Departure,"* (Urbana, IL: National Council of Teachers of English 1978); and Mike Rose, ed., *When a Writer Can't Write: Studies in Writer's Block and Other Composing-Process Problems* (New York: Guilford Press, 1985).

2. Elizabeth Blackburn-Brockmann, "Prewriting, Planning, and Professional Communication," *English Journal* 91, no. 2 (2001):

51–53; and Mark Torrance, Glyn V. Thomas, and Elizabeth J. Robinson, "Individual Differences in Undergraduate Essay-Writing Strategies: A Longitudinal Study," *Higher Education* 39, no. 2 (2000): 181–200.

3. Peter Elbow, *Writing with Power: Techniques for Mastering the Writing Process* (New York: Oxford University Press, 1981), 15–20.

4. See Gabriela Lusser Rico, *Writing the Natural Way* (Los Angeles: J. P. Tarcher, 1983), 10.

5. Rachel Spilka, "Orality and Literacy in the Workplace: Process- and Text-Based Strategies for Multiple Audience Adaptation," *Journal of Business and Technical Communication* 4, no. 1 (January 1990): 44–67.

6. Doris Kearns Goodwin, *Team of Rivals: The Political Genius of Abraham Lincoln* (New York: Simon & Schuster, 2005), 583–87.

7. Jay Greene, "Spell-Cheque Nation," *BusinessWeek*, May 5, 2003, 12.

8. Lynne Truss, *Eats, Shoots & Leaves: The Zero Tolerance Approach to Punctuation* (New York: Gotham Books, 2003), 9–10.

9. Bill Walsh, *Lapsing into a Comma: A Curmudgeon's Guide to the Many Things That Can Go Wrong in Print—and How to Avoid Them* (Lincolnwood, IL: Contemporary Books, 2000), 1.

10. Judith Cape Craig, "The Missing Link between School and Work: Knowing the Demands of the Workplace," *English Journal* 91, no. 2 (2001): 46–50.

11. Dianna Booher, *Cutting Paperwork in the Corporate Culture* (New York: Facts on File Publications, 1986); 23.

12. Susan D. Kleimann, "The Complexity of Workplace Review," *Technical Communication* 38, no. 4 (1991): 520–26.

13. Glenn J. Broadhead and Richard C. Freed, *The Variables of Composition: Process and Product in a Business Setting, Conference on College Composition and Communication Studies in Writing and Rhetoric* (Carbondale, IL: Southern Illinois University Press, 1986), 57.

14. Robert Boice, *Advice for New Faculty Members: Nihil Nimus* (Boston: Allyn & Bacon, 2000), 111–12.

15. N. Ann Chenoweth and John R. Hayes, "The Inner Voice in Writing," *Written Communication* 20 (2003): 99–118.

Chapter 6

1. Linda Reynolds, "The Legibility of Printed Scientific and Technical Information," in *Information Design,* ed. Ronald Easterby and Harm Zwaga (New York: John Wiley & Sons, 1984), 187–208.

2. Eva R. Brumberger, "Visual Rhetoric in the Curriculum: Pedagogy for a Multimodal Workplace," *Business Communication Quarterly* 68, no. 3 (2005): 318–19.

3. Adam Hanft, "Grist: More Power Than Point," in *Inc.,* http://www.inc.com/magazine/20030801/ahanft.html (accessed April 13, 2007); and Matthew L. Wald and John Schwartz, "Shuttle Inquiry Uncovers Flaws in Communication," *New York Times,* August 4, 2003.

4. Bruce Tognazzini, "The Butterfly Ballot: Anatomy of a Disaster," in *Ask Tog,* http://www.asktog.com/columns/042ButterflyBallot.html (accessed April 14, 2007).

5. Charles Kostelnick and Michael Hassett, *Shaping Information: The Rhetoric of Visual Conventions* (Carbondale, IL: Southern Illinois University Press, 2003), 92, 94.

6. Ibid., 206–07.

7. Charles Kostelnick and David Roberts, *Designing Visual Language* (Boston: Allyn & Bacon, 1998), 85–87.

8. George A. Miller, "The Magical Number Seven, Plus or Minus Two: Some Limits on Our Capacity for Processing Information," *Psychological Review* 63, no. 2 (1956): 81–97.

9. Jerry E. Bishop, "Word Processing: Research on Stroke Victims Yields Clues to the Brain's Capacity to Create Language," *Wall Street Journal,* October 12, 1993, A6; and Anne Meyer and David H. Rose, *Learning to Read in the Computer Age,* ed. Jeanne S. Chall, *Reading Research to Practice* (Cambridge, MA: Brookline Books, 1998), 4–6.

10. Karen A. Schriver, *Dynamics in Document Design* (New York: John Wiley & Sons, 1997), 274.

11. Jo Mackiewicz, "What Technical Writing Students Should Know about Typeface Personality," *Journal of Technical Writing and Communication* 34, nos. 1–2 (2004): 113–31.

12. Russell N. Baird, Arthur T. Turnbull, and Duncan McDonald, *The Graphics of Communication: Typography, Layout, Design, Production,* 5th ed. (New York: Holt, Rinehart & Winston, 1987), 37.

13. Philip M. Rubens, "A Reader's View of Text and Graphics: Implications for Transactional Text," *Journal of Technical Writing and Communication* 16, nos. 1–2 (1986): 78.

14. Rolf F. Rehe, *Typography: How to Make It Most Legible* (Carmel, IN: Design Research International), 57, summarizes M. E. Wrolstad, "Adult Preferences in Typography: Exploring the Function of Design," *Journalism Quarterly* 37 (Winter 1960): 211–23.

15. Elizabeth Keyes, "Typography, Color, and Information Structure," *Technical Communication* 40, no. 4 (November 1993): 652.

16. SmartMoney.com. "Market Map 1000," http://www.smartmoney.com/marketmap (accessed April 15, 2007); and Stephen H. Wildstrom, "A Picture Is Worth 1,000 Charts," *BusinessWeek,* January 20, 2003.

17. Monica M. Clark, "Nielsen's 'People Meters' Go Top 10: Atlanta Debut Is Milestone for Device That's Redefining Local TV Audiences' Image," *Wall Street Journal,* June 30, 2006, B2.

18. Gene Zelazny, *Say It with Charts: The Executive's Guide to Successful Presentations,* 4th ed. (New York: McGraw-Hill, 2001), 52.

19. Gerald J. Alred, Charles T. Brusaw, and Walter E. Oliu, *The Business Writer's Handbook,* 8th ed. (New York: St. Martin's Press, 2006), 248–50; William Horton, "The Almost Universal Language: Graphics for International Documents," *Technical Communication* 40, no. 4 (1993): 687; Thyra Rauch, "IBM Visual Interface Design," *The STC Usability PIC Newsletter,* January 1996, 3; and L. G. Thorell and W. J. Smith, *Using Computer Color Effectively: An Illustrated Reference* (Englewood Cliffs, NJ: Prentice Hall, 1990), 12–13.

20. Eric Kenly and Mark Beach, *Getting It Printed: How to Work with Printers & Graphic Imaging Services to Assure Quality, Stay on Schedule, and Control Costs,* 4th ed. (Cincinnati, OH: HOW Design Books, 2004), 68.

21. Ibid., 81, 84.

22. *The Chicago Manual of Style,* 15th ed. (Chicago: University of Chicago Press, 2003); and Edward R. Tufte, *The Visual Display of Quantitative Information,* 2nd ed. (Cheshire, CT: Graphics Press, 2001), 107–21.

23. Thophilus Addo, "The Effects of Dimensionality in Computer Graphics," *Journal of Business Communication* 31, no. 4 (1994): 253–65.

24. Jerry Bowyer, "In Defense of the Unemployment Rate," *National Review Online,* March 5, 2004; Joint Economic Committee, "Charts: Economy," http://jec.senate.gov (accessed August 27, 2004); and Mark Gongloff, "Payroll Growth Disappoints," in *CNN Money,* http://money.cnn.com/2003/12/05/news/economy/jobs/index.htm (accessed April 15, 2007).

25. Tufte, *The Visual Display of Quantitative Information,* 74–75.

26. John Long, "Ethics in the Age of Digital Photography," in *National Press Photographers Association: Educational Workshops,* http://www.nppa.org/professional_development/self-training_resources/eadp_report/index.html (accessed April 15, 2007).

27. Rebecca E. Burnett, *Technical Communication,* 6th ed. (Boston: Thomson-Wadsworth, 2005), 426.

28. Judy Gregory, "Social Issues Infotainment: Using Emotion and Entertainment to Attract Readers' Attention in Social Issues Leaflets," *Information Design Journal* 11, no. 1 (2002–2003): 67–81.

29. Reid Goldsborough, "Substance, Not Style, Draws Hits," in *Philadelphia Inquirer: Personal Computing,* http://findarticles.com/p/articles/mi_kmtpi/is_200405/ai_kepm472154 (accessed April 16, 2007).

30. Kostelnick and Hassett, *Shaping Information,* 160.

31. Jakob Nielsen, "Top Ten Web Design Mistakes of 2005," in *Alertbox,* http://www.useit.com/alertbox/designmistakes.html (accessed April 15, 2007).

32. Jakob Nielsen, "Why You Only Need to Test with 5 Users," in *Alertbox,* http://www.useit.com/alertbox/20000319.html (accessed September 4, 2001).

33. Adapted from Sharon Gaudin, "Study: Personalization Not Secret to E-Commerce," in *IT Management,* http://itmanagement.earthweb.com/ecom/article.php/3091701 (accessed April 15, 2007); Reid Goldsborough, "Substance, Not Style, Draws Hits," in *Philadelphia Inquirer: Personal Computing,* http://findarticles.com/p/articles/mi_kmtpi/is_200405/ai_kepm472154 (accessed April 16, 2007); Robyn Greenspan, "E-Commerce Mainstream, Measurements Lacking," in *Trends & Statistics: The Web's Richest Source,* http://www.clickz.com/showPage.html?page=3338561 (accessed April 16, 2007); Change Science Group, "Winning Credit Card Customers Online: Customer Experience Benchmarks and Best Practices," in *Customer Experience Benchmarking Report Overview,* http://www.changesciences.com/pub/CreditCards/Acquisition/CEBR_WinningCreditCardCustomersOnline_Overview.pdf (accessed April 16, 2007); Davis Neal, "Interview: Good Design Pays Off," in *IT Week,* http://www.itweek.co.uk/itweek/features/2086589/interview-design-pays (accessed April 16, 2007).

Chapter 7

1. Richard Nelson Bolles, *What Color Is Your Parachute: A Practical Manual for Job-Hunters and Career-Changers* (Berkeley: Ten Speed Press, 2007), 209.

2. Anne Fisher, "Does a Résumé Have to Be One Page Long?" in *CNNMoney.com: Fortune: Commentary: Ask Annie,* http://money.cnn.com/2007/03/28/news/economy/resume.fortune/index.htm?postversion=2007032911 (accessed May 30, 2007).

3. Elizabeth Blackburn-Brockman and Kelly Belanger, "One Page or Two? A National Study of CPA Recruiters' Preferences for Résumé Length," *The Journal of Business Communication* 38 (2001): 29–45.

4. David Koeppel, "Those Low Grades in College May Haunt Your Job Search," *New York Times,* December 31, 2006.

5. Phil Elder, "The Trade Secrets of Employment Interviews," paper presented at the Association for Business Communication Midwest Convention, Kansas City, MO, May 2, 1987.

6. Douglas MacMillan, "The Art of the Online Résumé: How to Get Yours Past Electronic Filters that Cull the Herd of Applicants," *BusinessWeek,* May 7, 2007, 86.

7. Katharine Hansen, "Quintessential Careers: Tapping the Power of Keywords to Enhance Your Résumé's Effectiveness," in *Words to Get Hired By: The Jobseeker's Quintessential Lexicon of Powerful Words and Phrases for Résumés and Cover Letters,* http://www.quintcareers.com/printable/resume_keywords.html (accessed May 30, 2007).

8. Dana Mattioli, "Who's Reading Online Résumés? Identity Crooks," *Wall Street Journal,* October 17, 2006, B9.

9. John B. Killoran, "Self-Published Web Résumés: Their Purposes and Their Genre Systems," *Journal of Business and Technical Communication* 20, no. 4 (2006): 425–59.

10. Keith J. Winstein and Daniel Golden, "MIT Admissions Dean Lied on Résumé in 1979, Quits," *Wall Street Journal,* April 27, 2007, B1.

11. Lisa Takeuchi Cullen, "Getting Wise to Lies," *Time,* May 1, 2006, 59.

12. Jon Weinbach, "The Admissions Police," *Wall Street Journal,* April 6, 2007, W1, W10.

Chapter 8

1. Katharine Hansen and Randall Hansen. "The Basics of a Dynamic Cover Letter." In *Cover Letter Resources for Job-Seekers,* Quintessential Careers, http://www.quintcareers.com/cover_letter_basics.html (accessed May 29, 2007).

Chapter 9

1. Thomas Petzinger, Jr., "Lewis Roland's Knack for Finding Truckers Keeps Firm Rolling," *Wall Street Journal,* December 1, 1995, B1.

2. Rachel Emma Silverman, "Covert Job Hunters Need Dress-Code Discretion," in *Home: Job Hunting Advice: Interviewing,* Wall Street Journal: CareerJournal.com, http://www.careerjournal.com/jobhunting/interviewing/20010418-silverman.html (accessed June 5, 2007).

3. Victoria Knight. "More Employers Are Using Personality Tests as Hiring Tools," in *Home: Job Hunting Advice: Interviewing,* Wall Street Journal: CareerJournal.com, http://www.careerjournal.com/jobhunting/interviewing/20060321-knight.html (accessed June 5, 2007).

4. Dana Mattioli, "Sober Thought: How to Mix Work, Alcohol: Taking Cues from Bosses and Clients Can Keep Parties or Meals under Control," *Wall Street Journal,* December 5, 2006, B10.

5. Rachel Emma Silverman, "Great Expectations," *Wall Street Journal,* July 25, 2000, B10.

6. The complete URL citation is: Robert Half Finance & Accounting. "Tell Me about Yourself," in *Press Room: 2005,* http://www.roberthalffinance.com/portal/site/rhf-us/template.PAGE/menuitem.b55c61eb41144dbf9a64e9c302f3dfa0/?javax.portlet.tpst=7658df44c982f2e6fa64e9c302f3dfa0&javax.portlet.prp_7658df44c982f2e6fa64e9c302f3dfa0_releaseId=1577&javax.portlet.prp_7658df44c982f2e6fa64e9c302f3dfa0_request_type=RenderPressRelease&javax.portlet.begCacheTok=com.vignette.cachetoken&javax.portlet.endCacheTok=com.vignette.cachetoken (accessed June 5, 2007).

Chapter 10

1. Diane Brady, "*!#?@ the E-Mail. Can We Talk?" *BusinessWeek,* December 4, 2006, 109.

2. Rogen International, "First International Study on Impact of E-Mail—Tool or Torment?" in *Research: Email,* http://www.rogenint.com/html/s02_article/article_view.asp?id=975&nav_cat_id=159&nav_top_id=56 (accessed April 30, 2007).

3. Gail Fann Thomas and Cynthia L. King, "Reconceptualizing E-Mail Overload," *Journal of Business and Technical Communication* 20, no. 3 (2006): 252–87.

4. David Dawley and William Anthony, "User Perceptions of E-Mail at Work," *Journal of Business and Technical Communication* 17, no. 2 (2003): 170–200.

5. Cristina Zucchermaglio and Alessandra Talamo, "The Development of a Virtual Community of Practices Using Electronic Mail and Communicative Genres," *Journal of Business and Technical Communication* 17, no. 3 (2003): 259–84.

6. MailerMailer LLC, "Email Marketing Metrics Report: January–June (H1) 2006," http://www.mailermailer.com/metrics/TR-H1-2006.pdf (accessed April 30, 2007).

7. Ken Fuson, "Communication about Service Is Key to Patient Satisfaction, Pollster Says," *Des Moines Register,* June 1, 2006, 1A, 4A; and Laura Landro, "Booking Your Medical Office for Safety Checkup," *Wall Street Journal,* November 15, 2006, D3.

8. Gilbert Ross, "Black Box Backfire," *Wall Street Journal,* April 21, 2007, A8.

9. Dinesh Ramde, "Anti-War E-Mail to Soldier Stirs Furor," *Des Moines Register,* January 24, 2007, 5A.

10. Laura Gunderson, "Coupon Isn't Worth Beans at Starbucks," *The Oregonian,* August 31, 2006.

11. Bob Mills, e-mail message to author.

12. Richard Carlson, *Don't Sweat the Small Stuff at Work: Simple Ways to Minimize Stress and Conflict While Bringing Out the Best in Yourself and Others* (New York: Hyperion, 1998), 266.

13. "Lighting a Fire under Campbell," *BusinessWeek,* December 4, 2006, 96; Alison Overholt, "Power Up the People," *Fast Company,* January 2003, 50; Philip Rosedale and Michael Fitzgerald, "How I Did It: Philip Rosedale," *Inc.,* February 2007, 85.

14. Kenneth Blanchard and Spencer Johnson, *The One Minute Manager* (New York: William Morrow, 1982), 19.

15. Knowledge @W. P. Carey, "Customer Rage: It's Not Always about the Money," in *Global Competition through Service,* http://knowledge.wpcarey.asu.edu/index.cfm?fa=viewArticle&id=1143&specialId=27 (accessed February 15, 2007).

16. An earlier version of this problem, the sample solutions, and the discussion appeared in Francis W. Weeks and Kitty O. Locker, *Business Writing Cases and Problems* (Champaign, IL: Stipes, 1980), 40–44.

Chapter 11

1. Daniel Goleman, Richard Boyatzis, and Anni McKee, *Primal Leadership: Learning to Lead with Emotional Intelligence* (Boston: Harvard Business School Press, 2002), 16.

2. Robert I. Sutton, *The No Asshole Rule: Building a Civilized Workplace and Surviving One That Isn't* (New York: Warner Business Books, 2007), 45–48.

3. William Ury, *The Power of a Positive No: How to Say No and Still Get to Yes* (New York: Bantam Books, 2007), 41–42.

4. Peter D. Timmerman and Wayne Harrison, "The Discretionary Use of Electronic Media: Four Considerations for Bad News Bearers," *Journal of Business Communication* 42, no. 4 (2005): 379–89.

5. Susan J. Wells, "From Ideas to Results," *HR Magazine,* February 2005, 54–58.

6. Holly Dolezalek, "Opening Up the Books," *Training,* April 2006, 44.

7. Kitty O. Locker, "Factors in Reader Responses to Negative Letters: Experimental Evidence for Changing What We

Teach," *Journal of Business and Technical Communication* 13, no. 1 (January 1999): 21.

8. Locker, "Factors in Reader Responses ," 25–26.

9. Sharon S. Brehm and Jack W. Brehm, *Psychological Reactance: A Theory of Freedom and Control* (New York: Academic Press, 1981), 3.

10. gap@gap.delivery.net, e-mail message to author, March 8, 2007.

11. hallmark@update.hallmark.com, e-mail message to author, May 8, 2007.

12. Ury, *The Power of a Positive No,* 19.

13. Stephen W. Gilliland et al., "Improving Applicants' Reactions to Rejection Letters: An Application of Fairness Theory," *Personnel Psychology* 54, no. 3 (2001): 669–704; Robert E. Ployhart, Karen Holcombe Ehrhart, and Seth C. Hayes, "Using Attributions to Understand the Effects of Explanations on Applicant Reactions: Are Reactions Consistent with the Covariation Principle?" *Journal of Applied Social Psychology* 35, no. 2 (2005): 259–96.

14. John P. Hausknecht, David V. Day, and Scott C. Thomas, "Applicant Reactions to Selection Procedures: An Updated Model and Meta-analysis," *Personnel Psychology* 57, no. 3 (2004): 639–84.

15. Elizabeth A. McCord, "The Business Writer, the Law, and Routine Business Communication: A Legal and Rhetorical Analysis," *Journal of Business and Technical Communication* 5, no. 2 (1991): 183.

16. Shaun Fawcett, "Resignation Letters: Don't Let Yours Backfire on You," in *Info Blue Book,* http://infobluebook.com/writing/13336.php (accessed February 19, 2007).

17. Kenneth Blanchard and Spencer Johnson, *The One Minute Manager* (New York: William Morrow, 1982), 59.

18. John C. Shaw, Eric Wild, and Jason A. Colquitt, "To Justify or Excuse? A Meta-Analytic Review of the Effects of Explanations," *Journal of Applied Psychology* 88, no. 3 (2003): 444–58.

Chapter 12

1. Pamela Babcock, "Throwing the Switch," *HRMagazine* 48, no. 12 (December 2003): 78.

2. The first and the last are identified by Jay A. Conger, "The Necessary Art of Persuasion," *Harvard Business Review,* May–June 1998, 88.

3. EACA Promotional Marketing Council, "Cyriel (84) Needs a Job," in *European Awards 2006: The Media,* http://www.adforum.com/affiliates/creative_archive/2006/AW888891_PMC/reel_detail2.asp?ID=6684218&TDI=VD16Kqqetr&PAGE=1&bShop=&awcat=&ob=intlevel&awid=(accessed June 11, 2007).

4. Judith H. Dobrzynski, "Unsuccessful Overtures: A New Study Shows Where Orchestras Err in Reaching Out to New Audiences," *Wall Street Journal,* November 4, 2006, P14; and Mark Schoofs, "Novel Police Tactic Puts Drug Markets out of Business: Confronted by the Evidence, Dealers in High Point, N.C., Succumb to Pressure," *Wall Street Journal,* September 27, 2006, A1, A16.

5. Min-Sun Kim and Steven R. Wilson, "A Cross-Cultural Comparison of Implicit Theories of Requesting," *Communication Monographs* 61, no. 3 (September 1994): 210–35; and K. Yoon, C. H. Kim, and M. S. Kim, "A Cross-Cultural Comparison of the Effects of Source Credibility on Attitudes and Behavioral Intentions," *Mass Communication and Society* 1, nos. 3 and 4 (1998): 153–73.

6. Daniel D. Ding, "An Indirect Style in Business Communication," *Journal of Business and Technical Communication* 20, no. 1 (2006): 87–100.

7. Chiqui Cartagena, *Latino Boom! Everything You Need to Know to Grow Your Business in the U.S. Hispanic Market* (New York: Ballantine Books, 2005), 97–98.

8. E. L. Fink et al., "The Semantics of Social Influence: Threats vs. Persuasion," *Communication Monographs* 70, no. 4 (2003): 295–316.

9. G. W. Dudley, J. F. Tanner, and C. A. Fletcher, "What Motivates UK Salespeople to Sell? New University Study Shows Sales Motivation Differs by Country," *PR Newswire,* February 11, 2004.

10. Malcolm Gladwell, *The Tipping Point: How Little Things Can Make a Big Difference* (New York: Little, Brown, 2002), 96–98.

11. Norm Brodsky, "Street Smarts," *Inc.* 25, no. 2 (February 2003): 44–45.

12. Chip Heath and Dan Heath, *Made to Stick: Why Some Ideas Survive and Others Die* (New York: Random House, 2007), 165–68.

13. Used Cardboard Boxes, "The Cheapest, Easiest, and Most Earth-Friendly Way to get Boxes for Packing, Moving, Shipping and Storage," in *Our Company: About Us,* http://www.boomerangboxes.com/ (accessed June 11, 2007).

14. Brian Steinberg, "Kraft Vies for Eyes—and Noses: Ad Play in People Magazine Uses Some Scented Spots to Tickle Readers' Fancy," *Wall Street Journal,* November 13, 2006, B5.

15. Jeffrey Zaslow, "The Most-Praised Generation Goes to Work," *Wall Street Journal,* April 20, 2007, W1, W7.

16. Erin White, "For Relevance, Firms Revamp Worker Reviews," *Wall Street Journal,* July 17, 2006, B1, B5.

17. Robert Guth, "How Microsoft Is Learning to Love Online Advertising," *Wall Street Journal,* November 16, 2006, A1; and Brian Steinberg, "Philips Bets Magazine Readers Need a Reprieve," *Wall Street Journal,* August 1, 2006, B2.

18. Ken Magill, "Email Tops in ROI," in *DM Disciplines: Email, Direct Magazine,* http://directmag.com/disciplines/email/marketing_email_tops_roi/ (accessed June 11, 2007).

19. John D. Beard, David L. Williams, and J. Patrick Kelly, "The Long versus the Short Letter: A Large Sample Study of a Direct-Mail Campaign," *Journal of Direct Marketing* 4, no. 12 (Winter 1990): 13–20.

20. Jeffrey Gitomer, *Little Red Book of Sales Answers: 99.5 Real World Answers That Make Sense, Make Sales, and Make Money* (Upper Saddle River, NJ: Prentice Hall, 2005), 112.

21. Beth Negus Viveiros, "Gifts for Life," *Direct* (July 2004): 9.

22. "Reading Is Fundamental: Stealing the Best Ideas from Leading Fundraisers," *Non-Profit Times* 16, no. 22 (2002): 1–5.

23. Maxwell Sackheim, *My First Sixty-Five Years in Advertising* (Blue Ridge Summit, PA: Tab Books, 1975), 97–100.

Chapter 13

1. Sharon Begley, "Studies Take Measure of How Stereotyping Alters Performance," *Wall Street Journal,* February 23, 2007, B1; and Claude Steele and Joshua Aronson, "Stereotype Threat and Intellectual Test Performance of African Americans," *Journal of Personality and Social Psychology* 69, no. 5 (1995): 797–811.

2. "Financial Facts—Year-End 2006," in *Our Company: Company Information: 3M Facts, 3M,* http://solutions.3m.com/wps/portal/3M/en_US/our/company/information/financial-facts (accessed June 13, 2007); "Google's Moneymaking Machine Cranks Out Another Banner Quarter," in *Financial Headlines,* The Canton Repository, http://www.cantonrep.com/ index.php?ID=349504 (accessed

June 12, 2007); Geraldo Samor, Cecilie Rohwedder, and Ann Zimmerman, "Innocents Abroad? Wal-Mart's Global Sales Rise as It Learns from Mistakes; No More Ice Skates in Mexico," *Wall Street Journal,* May 16, 2006, B1; and "Starbucks Wants 40,000 Stores Worldwide, up from 30,000 Goal," in *October 6, 2006: Business,* International Herald Tribune, http://www.iht.com/articles/ap/2006/10/06/business/NA_FIN_COM_US_Starbucks_Analysts.php (accessed June 12, 2007); and Daniel Workman, "McDonalds Global Sales: Big Mac's International Revenues Sizzle in 2006," in *World Affairs: International Trade: International Trade Leaders: Articles, Suite101,* http://internationaltrade.suite101.com/article.cfm/mcdonalds_global_sales (accessed June 12, 2007).

3. Pete Engardio, "The Future of Outsourcing," *BusinessWeek,* January 30, 2006, 50–58; and Steve Hamm, "Big Blue Shift," *BusinessWeek,* June 5, 2006, 108.

4. Teri Agins, "For U.S. Fashion Firms, a Global Makeover: Tommy Hilfiger Finds Assimilating in Europe Requires a New Look," *Wall Street Journal,* February 2, 2007, A1, A17; Keith Naughton, "The Great Wal-Mart of China," *Newsweek,* October 30, 2006, 50; and Samor, Rohwedder, and Zimmerman, "Innocents Abroad?," B1.

5. Rachel Konrad, "Cisco Shifts Senior Executives to India's Tech Hub," in *Redmond Report: News,* RedmondMag.com, http://redmondmag.com/news/article.asp?editorialsid=8091 (accessed June 13, 2007).

6. Monica Roman, "Coke Calls Up a Veteran," *BusinessWeek,* May 17, 2004, 48; and Eilene Zimmerman, "How I Got Here," *Sales and Marketing Management* 156, no. 5 (May 2004): 63.

7. Carol Hymowitz, "European Executives Give Some Advice on Crossing Borders," *Wall Street Journal,* December 2, 2003, B1.

8. Mark Larson, "More Employees Go Abroad as International Operations Grow," in *Feature,* Workforce Management, http://www.workforce.com/section/09/feature/24/41/22/index_printer.html (accessed June 13, 2007).

9. David Loyn, "Migrants 'Shape Globalised World,'" in *BBC News: Special Reports,* http://news.bbc.co.uk/2/hi/in_depth/6183803.stm (accessed June 13, 2007).

10. Thomas L. Friedman, *The World Is Flat: A Brief History of the Twenty-first Century,* Updated and Expanded ed. (New York: Farrar, Straus and Giroux, 2006), 8.

11. U.S. Census Bureau, "Statistical Abstract of the United States, Table 15: Resident Population by Race, Hispanic Origin, and Single Years of Age: 2005," http://www.census.gov/prod/2006pubs/07statab/pop.pdf (accessed June 11, 2007).

12. U.S. Census Bureau, "Statistical Abstract of the United States, Table 10: Immigrants Admitted by State and Leading Country of Birth: 2005," http://www.census.gov/prod/2006pubs/07statab/pop.pdf (accessed June 11, 2007).

13. Chiqui Cartagena, *Latino Boom! Everything You Need to Know to Grow Your Business in the U.S. Hispanic Market* (New York: Ballantine Books, 2005), 14–15.

14. "About CHIN Radio," in *CHIN: About Us,* http://www.chinradio.com/about.php (accessed June 13, 2006).

15. U.S. Census Bureau, "Statistical Abstract of the United States, Table 15.

16. U.S. Census Bureau, "Statistical Abstract of the United States: Table 52: Language Spoken at Home by State: 2004," http://www.census.gov/prod/2006pubs/07statab/pop.pdf (accessed June 11, 2007).

17. U.S. Census Bureau, "Statistical Abstract of the United States: Table 53: Language Spoken at Home—25 Largest Cities: 2004," http://www.census.gov/prod/2006pubs/07statab/pop.pdf (accessed June 11 2007).

18. "Affluence in Two Cultures," *Hispanic Business,* December 2003, 30–31; and "A Melting Pot with Flavor," *Hispanic Business,* December 2003, 20–21.

19. Julie Bennett, "West Coast Makes Diversity a Corporate Imperative," *Wall Street Journal,* January 30, 2007, B9.

20. Shankar Vedantam, "In Boardrooms, Courtrooms, Diversity Makes Difference," *Cincinnati Post,* January 15, 2007, B2.

21. Patricia S. Parker, "African American Women Executives' Leadership Communication within Dominant-Culture Organizations," *Management Communications Quarterly* 15, no. 1 (August 2001): 42–82.

22. John Webb and Michael Keene, "The Impact of Discourse Communities on International Professional Communication," in *Exploring the Rhetoric of International Professional Communication: An Agenda for Teachers and Researchers,* ed. Carl R. Lovitt and Dixie Goswami (Amityville, NY: Baywood, 1999), 81–109.

23. Françoise Salager-Meyer, María Ángeles Alcaraz Ariza, and Nahirana Zambrano, "The Scimitar, the Dagger and the Glove: Intercultural Differences in the Rhetoric of Criticism in Spanish, French and English Medical Discourse (1930–1995)," *English for Specific Purposes* 22 (2003): 223–47.

24. Kirk R. St. Amant, "Ukraine: A Technical Communication Perspective," *Intercom,* May 2002, 15–17.

25. David Matsumoto, *The New Japan: Debunking Seven Cultural Stereotypes* (Yarmouth, ME: Intercultural Press, 2002), 28–29, 40–41, 144–5.

26. Russell Flannery, "As Easy as $3 \times 7 = 21$," *Forbes* 173, no. 13 (2004): 110.

27. Deborah F. Anderson, "Parlez-Vous Red, White and Blue?" *The Toastmaster,* September 2003, 12–14; and Christina Johansson Robinowitz and Lisa Werner Carr, *Modern-Day Vikings: A Practical Guide to Interacting with the Swedes* (Yarmouth, ME: Intercultural Press, 2001), 132.

28. Robert T. Moran, Philip R. Harris, and Sarah V. Moran, *Managing Cultural Differences: Global Leadership Strategies for the 21st Century,* 7th ed. (Boston: Elsevier, 2007), 341–42.

29. Ibid., 64.

30. Martin J. Gannon, *Understanding Global Cultures: Metaphorical Journeys through 23 Nations,* 2nd ed. (Thousand Oaks, CA: Sage, 2001), 32; and Moran, Harris, and Moran, *Managing Cultural Differences,* 484.

31. Moran, Harris, and Moran, *Managing Cultural Differences,* 579.

32. Ibid.

33. Paul Ekman, Wallace V. Friesen, and John Bear, "The International Language of Gestures," *Psychology Today* 18, no. 5 (May 1984): 64.

34. Gannon, *Understanding Global Cultures,* 13.

35. Edward Twitchell Hall, *Hidden Differences: Doing Business with the Japanese* (Garden City, NY: Anchor-Doubleday, 1987), 25.

36. Sue Shellenbarger, "Time-Zoned: Working around the Round-the-Clock Workday," *Wall Street Journal,* February 15, 2007, D1.

37. Moran, Harris, and Moran, *Managing Cultural Differences,* 445, 78.

38. Malcolm Fleschner, "Worldwide Winner," *Selling Power,* November–December 2001, 54–61.

39. Ira Carnahan, "Presidential Timber Tends to Be Tall," in *Leadership: Compensation: Business in the Beltway,* http://www.forbes.com/compensation/2004/05/19/cz_ic_0519beltway.html (accessed June 13, 2007).

40. Craig Storti, *Old World, New World: Bridging Cultural Differences: Britain, France, Germany, and the U.S.* (Yarmouth, ME: Intercultural Press, 2001), 209.

41. Nick Easen, "Don't Send the Wrong Message," *Business 2.0,* August 2005, 102.

42. Ibid.

Chapter 14

1. Kevin S. Groves, "Leader Emotional Expressivity, Visionary Leadership, and Organizational Change," *Leadership & Organizational Development Journal* 27, no. 7 (2006): 566–83; Ajay Mehra et al., "Distributed Leadership in Teams: The Network of Leadership Perceptions and Team Performance," *The Leadership Quarterly* 17, no. 3 (2006): 232–45; and Kenneth David Stand, "Examining Effective and Ineffective Transformational Project Leadership," *Team Performance Management* 11, no. 3/4 (2005): 68–103.

2. John E. Tropman, *Making Meetings Work,* 2nd ed. (Thousand Oaks, CA: Sage, 2003), 78, 121.

3. Jeswald W. Salacuse, *The Global Negotiator: Making, Managing, and Mending Deals around the World in the Twenty-First Century* (New York: Palgrave Macmillan, 2003), 92.

4. Sari Lindblom-Ylanne, Heikki Pihlajamaki, and Toomas Kotkas, "What Makes a Student Group Successful? Student-Student and Student-Teacher Interaction in a Problem-Based Learning Environment," *Learning Environments Research* 6, no. 1 (January 2003): 59–76.

5. Karen A. Jehn and Elizabeth A. Mannix, "The Dynamic Nature of Conflict: A Longitudinal Study of Intragroup Conflict and Group Performance," *Academy of Management Journal* 44, no. 2 (April 2001): 238–51.

6. Rebecca E. Burnett, "Conflict in Collaborative Decision-Making," in *Professional Communication: The Social Perspective,* ed. Nancy Roundy Blyler and Charlotte Thralls (Newbury Park, CA: Sage, 1993), 144–62; and Rebecca E. Burnett, "Productive and Unproductive Conflict in Collaboration," in *Making Thinking Visible: Writing, Collaborative Planning, and Classroom Inquiry,* ed. Linda Flower, et al. (Urbana, IL: NCTE, 1994), 239–44.

7. Sue Dyer, "The Root Causes of Poor Communication," *Cost Engineering* 48, no. 6 (June 2006): 8–10.

8. Solomon F. Asch, "Opinions and Social Pressure," *Scientific American* 193, no. 5 (1955): 31–35. For a review of recent literature on groupthink, see Marc D. Street, "Groupthink: An Examination of Theoretical Issues, Implications, and Future Research Suggestions," *Small Group Research* 28, no. 1 (1997): 72–93.

9. Jared Diamond, *Collapse: How Societies Choose to Fail or Succeed* (New York: Penguin Books, 2005), 439.

10. Francesca Bariela-Chiappini et al., "Five Perspectives on Intercultural Business Communication," *Business Communication Quarterly* 66, no. 3 (September 2003): 73–96.

11. Kristina B. Dahlin, Laurie R. Weingart, and Pamela J. Hinds, "Team Diversity and Information Use," *Academy of Management Journal* 68, no. 6 (2005): 1107–23; Susannah B. F. Paletz et al., "Ethnic Composition and Its Differential Impact on Group Processes in Diverse Teams," *Small Group Research* 35, no. 2 (April 2004): 128–57; and Leisa D. Sargent and Christina Sue-Chan, "Does Diversity Affect Efficacy? The Intervening Role of Cohesion and Task Interdependence," *Small Group Research* 32, no. 4 (August 2001): 426–50.

12. Salacuse, *The Global Negotiator,* 96–97.

13. Earl H. McKinney Jr. et al., "How Swift Starting Action Teams Get Off the Ground: What United Flight 232 and Airline Crews Can Tell Us about Team Communication," *Management Communication Quarterly* 19, no. 2 (November 2005): 198–237.

14. Jeanne Brett, Kristin Behfar, and Mary C. Kern, "Managing Multicultural Teams," *Harvard Business Review* 84, no. 11 (2006): 84–91.

15. Deborah Tannen, *That's Not What I Meant!* (New York: William Morrow, 1986).

16. Daniel N. Maltz and Ruth A. Borker, "A Cultural Approach to Male-Female Miscommunication," in *Language and Social Identity,* ed. John J. Gumperz (Cambridge: Cambridge University Press, 1982), 202.

17. Marie Helweg-Larson et al., "To Nod or Not to Nod: An Observational Study of Nonverbal Communication and Status in Female and Male College Students," *Psychology of Women Quarterly* 28, no. 4 (2004): 358–61.

18. Tropman, *Making Meetings Work,* 28.

19. Seth Godin, "How to Give Feedback," *Fast Company,* March 2004, 103.

20. Stephen P. Robbins, *Decide and Conquer: Make Winning Decisions and Take Control of Your Life* (Upper Saddle River, NJ: Financial Times Prentice Hall, 2004), 101–5.

21. E. Packard, "Meetings Frustrate Task-Oriented Employees, Study Finds," *Monitor on Psychology* 37, no. 6 (June 2006): 10.

22. Lisa Ede and Andrea Lunsford, *Singular Texts/Plural Authors: Perspectives on Collaborative Writing* (Carbondale, IL: Southern Illinois Press, 1990), 60.

23. Paul Benjamin Lowry, Aaron Curtis, and Michelle Rene Lowry, "Building a Taxonomy and Nomenclature of Collaborative Writing to Improve Interdisciplinary Research and Practice," *Journal of Business Communication* 41, no. 1 (2004): 66–99.

24. Burnett, "Productive and Unproductive Conflict in Collaboration," 239–44.

25. Kitty O. Locker, "What Makes a Collaborative Writing Team Successful? A Case Study of Lawyers and Social Service Workers in a State Agency," in *New Visions in Collaborative Writing,* ed. Janis Forman (Portsmouth, NJ: Boynton, 1991), 37–52.

26. Ede and Lunsford, *Singular Texts/Plural Authors,* 66.

27. Jo Mackiewicz and Kathryn Riley, "The Technical Editor as Diplomat: Linguistic Strategies for Balancing Clarity and Politeness," *Technical Communications* 50, no. 1 (February 2003): 83–95.

Chapter 15

1. For a useful taxonomy of proposals, see Richard C. Freed and David D. Roberts, "The Nature, Classification, and Generic Structure of Proposals," *Journal of Technical Writing and Communication* 19, no. 4 (1989): 317–51.

2. National Institutes of Health, "Award Trends," in *Grants: Awards,* http://grants.nih.gov/grants/award/awardtr.htm (accessed June 16, 2007).

3. Susan J. Wells, "Merging Compensation Strategies," *HRMagazine* 49, no. 5 (May 2004): 66.

4. Ibid.

5. Laura K. Grove, "Finding Funding: Writing Winning Proposals for Research Funds," *Technical Communication* 51 (2004): 25–33.

6. Christine Peterson Barabas, *Technical Writing in a Corporate Culture: A Study of the Nature of Information* (Norwood, NJ: Ablex Publishing, 1990), 327.

7. Palmer Morrel-Samuels, "Getting the Truth into Workplace Surveys," *Harvard Business Review* 80, no. 2 (February 2002): 111–18.

8. See, for example, Public Agenda, "Red Flags," in *Issue Guides: Gay Rights,* http://www.publicagenda.org/issues/frontdoor.cfm?issue_type=gay_rights (accessed June 16, 2007); Pew Forum on Religion and Public Life, "Religious Beliefs Underpin Opposition to Homosexuality," in *Surveys,* http://pewforum.org/docs/index.php?DocID=37 (accessed June 16, 2007).

9. Morrel-Samuels, "Getting the Truth into Workplace Surveys," 116.

10. Morrel-Samuels, "Web Surveys' Hidden Hazards," *Harvard Business Review* 81, no. 7 (July 2003): 16–17; Jakob Nielsen, "Keep Online Surveys Short," in *Alertbox,* www.useit.com (accessed June 16, 2007).

11. Scott Keeter, "The Cell Phone Challenge to Survey Research: National Polls Not Undermined by Growing Cell-Only Population," in *Reports: News Release,* Pew Research Center, http://www.people-press.org/reports/pdf/276.pdf (accessed June 16, 2007).

12. Richard Curtin, Stanley Presser, and Eleanor Singer, "Changes in Telephone Survey Nonreponse over the Past Quarter Century," *Public Opinion Research Quarterly* 69, no. 1 (2005): 87–98.

13. Council for Marketing and Opinion Research, "Recommendations to Improve Respondent Cooperation," in *CMOR: Respondent Cooperation: Tools of the Trade,* http://www.cmor.org/rc/tools.cfm (accessed June 16, 2007).

14. Sharon L. Lohr, *Sampling: Design and Analysis* (Pacific Grove, CA: Duxbury Press, 1999), 3.

15. Cynthia Crossen, "Fiasco in 1936 Survey Brought 'Science' to Election Polling," *Wall Street Journal,* October 2, 2006, B1.

16. Earl E. McDowell, Bridget Mrolza, and Emmy Reppe, "An Investigation of the Interviewing Practices of Technical Writers in Their World of Work," in *Interviewing Practices for Technical Writers,* ed. Earl E. McDowell (Amityville, NY: Baywood Publishing, 1991), 207.

17. Thomas Hunter, "Pulitzer Winner Discusses Interviewing," *IABC Communication World,* April 1985, 13–14.

18. Louise Witt, "Inside Intent," *American Demographics* 26, no. 2 (2004): 34.

19. Suzanne Vranica, "Upfront Deal Turns the Corner; NBC Universal Pact Uses New System Covering Ads Watched via DVR," *Wall Street Journal,* June 14, 2007, B5.

20. Emily Steel, "TV Networks Launch Big Campus Push; New Nielsen System Makes College Students Coveted-Ratings Draw," *Wall Street Journal,* March 5, 2007, B3.

21. Christopher Meyer and Andre Schwager, "Understanding Customer Experience," *Harvard Business Review* 85, no. 2 (February 2007): 116–26.

22. Linda Tischler, "Every Move You Make," *Fast Company,* no. 81 (April 2004): 72.

23. Daniel Kruger, "You Want Data with That?" *Forbes* 173, no. 6 (2004): 58.

24. Shirley S. Wang, "Health Care Taps 'Mystery Shoppers'; To Improve Service, Hospitals and Doctors Hire Spies to Pose as Patients and Report Back," *Wall Street Journal,* August 8, 2006, D1.

Chapter 16

1. Michael Schrage, "Take the Lazy Way Out? That's Far Too Much Work," *Fortune,* February 5, 2001, 212.

2. Michael D. Lemonick, "Medicine's Secret Stat," *Time,* February 26, 2007, 54.

3. Jeffrey Zaslow, "An Iconic Report 20 Years Later: Many of Those Women Married after All," *Wall Street Journal,* May 25, 2006, D1.

4. Nielsen Media Reserach, "Our Measurement Techniques," in *Inside TV Ratings: Meters & Diaries,* http://www.nielsenmedia.com/nc/portal/site/Public/menuitem.55dc65b4a7d5adff3f65936147a062a0/?vgnextoid=096047f8b5264010VgnVCM100000880a260aRCRD (accessed June 17, 2007).

5. "United States: The Ladder of Fame; College Education," *The Economist* 380, no. 8492 (August 26, 2006): 35.

6. Mylene Mangalindan, "Web Ads on the Rebound," *Wall Street Journal,* August 25, 2003, B1, B6; and Michael Totty, "At Last, a Way to Measure Ads," *Wall Street Journal,* June 16, 2003, R4.

7. "Nielsen Explains Male TV Ratings," *Adweek,* December 1, 2003; and Tracie Rozhon, "Networks Criticize Report on Male Viewers," *New York Times,* November 26, 2003, 8.

8. Emily Steel, "Networks Launch Big Campus Push; New Nielsen System Makes College Students Coveted-Ratings Draw," *Wall Street Journal,* March 5, 2007, B3.

9. Jakob Nielsen, "Risks of Quantitative Studies," in *Alertbox,* http://www.useit.com/alertbox/20040301.html (accessed June 18, 2007).

10. Stephen E. Moore, "655,000 War Dead?" *Wall Street Journal,* October 18, 2006, A20.

11. Malcolm Gladwell, *The Tipping Point: How Little Things Can Make a Big Difference* (New York: Little, Brown and Company, 2002), 146; and Steven D. Levitt and Stephen J. Dubner, *Freakonomics: A Rogue Economist Explores the Hidden Side of Everything* (New York: William Morrow, 2005), 119–41.

12. U.S. Department of Transportation, "DOT Announces Historic Low Highway Fatality Rate in 2003," in *In the News: 2004 Press Releases: August 10,* http://www.nhtsa.dot.gov/portal/site/nhtsa/template.MAXIMIZE/menuitem.9fa154a4d39f02e770f6df1020008a0c/?javax.portlet.tpst=16e7334f645825de276eca1046108a0c_ws_MX&javax.portlet.prp_16e7334f645825de276eca1046108a0c_viewID=detail_view&javax.portlet.begCacheTok=token&javax.portlet.endCacheTok=token&itemID=79f433612d89ff00-VgnVCM1000002c567798RCRD&overrideViewName=PressRelease (accessed June 18, 2007); Joseph B. White, "A Turbulent Transition for SUVs: Safety Reports on SUVs and Fuel Laws Paint a Puzzling Picture for Consumers," in *Eyes on the Road,* Wall Street Journal Online, http://online.wsj.com/article/SB109242124890391151-search.html?KEYWORDS=A+Turbulent+Transition+for+SUVs&COLLECTION=wsjie/6month (accessed June 18, 2007).

13. Dan Ackman, "SUVs Deadly to Car Drivers," in *Business: Autos: August 20, 2004,* http://www.forbes.com/business/2004/08/20/cx_da_0820suv.html (accessed June 16, 2007); Daren Fonda, "The Shrinking SUV," *Time* 164, no. 9 (August 30 2004): 65; Danny Hakim, "Safety Gap Grows Wider between S.U.V.'s and Cars," *New York Times,* August 17, 2004, Business/Financial Desk 1.

14. Byron Sharp, "Comparative Quackery," *New Zealand Marketing Magazine,* June 2004.

15. Peter Lynch and John Rothchild, *One Up on Wall Street: How to Use What You Already Know to Make Money in the Market* (New York: Fireside-Simon & Schuster, 2000), 189.

16. Nielsen, "Risks of Quantitative Studies"; and Dan Seligman, "The Story They All Got Wrong," *Forbes* 170, no. 11 (November 25, 2002): 124.

17. Arthur Shapiro, "Let's Redefine Market Research," *Brandweek* 45, no. 25 (June 21, 2004): 20.

18. Brad Cleveland, "Reporting Call Center Activity," *Call Center* 16, no. 12 (December 1, 2003): 36.

19. James Paradis, David Dobrin, and Richard Miller, "Writing at Exxon ITD: Notes on the Writing Environment

of an R&D Organization," in *Writing in Nonacademic Settings* (New York: Guilford, 1985), 300–2.

20. George A. Miller, "The Magical Number Seven, Plus or Minus Two: Some Limits on Our Capacity for Processing Information," *Psychological Review* 63, no. 2 (1956): 81–97.

21. Christopher Marquis, "Reports on Attacks Are Gripping, Not Dry," *New York Times,* June 20, 2004, 27.

Chapter 17

1. Sara Silver, "With Its Future Now Uncertain, Bell Labs Turns to Commerce: Storied Font of Basic Research Gets More Practical Focus Amid Worry over a Merger," *Wall Street Journal,* August 21, 2006, A1.

2. G. Michael Campbell, *Bulletproof Presentations* (Franklin Lakes, NJ: Career Press, 2003), 66–67.

3. Julie Hill, "The Attention Deficit," *Presentations* 17, no. 10 (October 2003): 26.

4. Campbell, *Bulletproof Presentations,* 65.

5. Patricia Fripp, "Want Your Audiences to Remember What You Say? Learn the Importance of Clear Structure," in *Articles: Public Speaking and Presentation Skills Articles,* http://frippandassociates.com/art.clearstructure_faa.html (accessed June 16, 2007).

6. Tad Simmons, "Multimedia or Bust," *Presentations,* 14, no. 2 (February 2000): 44, 48–50.

7. Julie Terberg, "Presentation Visuals Should Complement a Company's Printed Materials," *Presentations* 17, no. 1 (January 2003): 26–27.

8. Marilyn A. Dyrud, "An Exploration of Gender Bias in Computer Clip Art," *Business Communication* Quarterly 60, no. 4 (1997): 30–51.

9. Jennifer Saranow, "Show, Don't Tell: Microsoft and H-P Are Heading to Retail Outlets to Overcome a Big Impediment to Sales: Ignorance," *Wall Street Journal,* March 22, 2004, R-9.

10. Betsy Cummings, "Meeting Masters: Meet Four Companies That Have Managed to Turn Their Sales Meetings into Dynamic, Productive, and Motivational Events," *Sales & Marketing Management* 156, no. 3 (2004): 36–39.

11. David Benady, "Look Who's Talking," *Marketing Week* 27, no. 33 (2004): 35–36.

12. U.S. Census Bureau, "2002 Economic Census," in *Main: Data Sets,* http://factfinder.census.gov/servlet/DatasetMainPage-Servlet?_program=ECN&_submenuId=&_lang=en&_ts= (accessed June 16, 2007).

13. Andy Rooney, "World Has Lost Mental Magician," *Columbus Dispatch,* February 22, 1988, 7A.

14. Chip Heath and Dan Heath, *Made to Stick: Why Some Ideas Survive and Others Die* (New York: Random House, 2007), 7.

15. Heath and Heath, *Made to Stick,* 16–18.

16. Ann Burnett and Diane M. Badzinski, "Judge Nonverbal Communication on Trial: Do Mock Trial Jurors Notice?" *Journal of Communication* 55, no. 2 (2005): 209–24.

17. Judee K. Burgoon, Thomas Birk, and Michael Pfau, "Nonverbal Behaviors, Persuasion, and Credibility," *Human Communication Research* 17, no. 1 (1990): 140–69.

18. Campbell, *Bulletproof Presentations,* 44–45, 126–27.

19. Michael Waldholz, "Lab Notes," *Wall Street Journal,* March 19, 1991, B1; and Dave Zielinski, "Perfect Practice," *Presentations* 17, no. 5 (2003): 30–36.

20. Campbell, *Bulletproof Presentations,* 122.

PHOTO CREDITS

Chapter 1
Page 3, AP Images/NASA/JPL/Caltech
Page 8, © Creatas/Picture Quest
Page 15, © Luca DiCecco/Alamy
Page 17, © STR/AFP/ Getty Images
Page 19, © Digital Vision/Getty Images
Page 20, © Bill Bachmann /The Image Works
Page 24, © Jon Feingersh/zefa/CORBIS
Page 25, Courtesy of McAfee.com
Page 26, © Robert Daly/Getty Images/Stone

Chapter 2
Page 41, AP Images/ WWD
Page 43, Courtesy of the Dow Chemical Company
Page 47 (top), © Jose Luis Pelaez, Inc./CORBIS
Page 47 (bottom), © LWA-Dann Tardif/CORBIS
Page 48, © David M. Russell
Page 59, © NOEK DE GROOT/AFP/Getty Images

Chapter 3
Page 75, Copyright 2007 Donors Choose Inc. Reprinted with permission
Page 82, Courtesy of Ellen Elleman
Page 85, Kitty O. Locker, by permission of Joseph-Beth Booksellers
Page 88, AP Images/Orlin Wagner
Page 94, AP Images/Bill Sikes

Chapter 4
Page 105, Courtesy of Korean Air
Page 119, © Creatas/Picture Quest

Chapter 5
Page 135, © Comstock Images/Jupiter Images

Chapter 6
Page 151, McGraw-Hill Companies Inc, Jill Braaten, photographer
Page 162, Courtesy of the Dow Chemical Company
Page 168, © EVARISTO SA/AFP/Getty Images

Chapter 7
Page 207, AP Images/Harpo Productions, George Burns
Page 217, © Viviane Moos/CORBIS

Chapter 8
Page 243 (top), www.Bank of America.com, Reprinted with permission
Page 243 (bottom), Used with permission, The Procter & Gamble Company, 2007.
Page 255, Reprinted with permission of Bruce Mau Design Inc.

Chapter 9
Page 271, © P. Winbladh/zefa/CORBIS
Page 275 (top left), © T. Kruesselmann/zefa/CORBIS
Page 275 (bottom left), © Jurgen Reisch/Getty Images/ Digital Vision
Page 275 (top middle), © Jack Hollingsworth/Getty Images/ Photodisc
Page 275 (bottom middle), © Rob Lewine/zefa/CORBIS
Page 275 (top right), © imagewerks/Getty Images
Page 275 (bottom right), © David Young-Wolff/PhotoEdit

Page 284, Copyright © Danny Turner. All rights reserved.
Page 287, © Hans Neleman/zefa/CORBIS

Chapter 10
Page 297, © Joe Pugliese Photographs
Page 306, McGraw-Hill Companies Inc, Jill Braaten, photographer
Page 312, Courtesy of Toyota Motor North America, Inc.
Page 312, Courtesy of Toyota Motor North America, Inc.

Chapter 11
Page 335, AP Images/Rick Maiman
Page 346, Reprinted with permission of the Columbus Dispatch
Page 349 (top), Courtesy of State Farm Insurance
Page 349 (bottom), Courtesy, Schwinn Bicycle
Page 351, © Tim Boyle/Getty Images

Chapter 12
Page 369 (left), © CORBIS
Page 369 (middle), © Swim Ink 2, LLC/ CORBIS
Page 369 (right), © Swim Ink 2, LLC/ CORBIS
Page 371, www.rice.edu/wetlands, Reprinted with permission of Linda P. Driskill.
Page 373, Courtesy of Citigroup
Page 385, www.savedaruf.org Reprinted with permission of (c) Olivier Jobard/ SIPA Press
Page 386, Reprinted with permission ©2007, American Heart Association, Inc.
Page 400, © Rhoda Sidney / PhotoEdit

Chapter 13
Page 431, © Matt Stroshane/epa/CORBIS
Page 436, McGraw-Hill Companies Inc, Jill Braaten, photographer
Page 438, AP Images/Itsuo Inouye
Page 440 (left), © Planetpix/Alamy
Page 440 (right), Doctor's Associates, Inc.
Page 444, AP Images/Eugene Hoshiko

Chapter 14
Page 457, AP Images /Fritz Reiss
Page 462, © Ed Honowitz/ Getty Images/Stone
Page 465, © Steve Cole/Getty Images/Riser
Page 468, © Jeff Sciortino Photography
Page 468, © Jeff Sciortino Photography
Page 469 (left), © Keith Brofsky/Getty Images
Page 469 (right), © Leland Bobbe/Getty Images/The Image Bank
Page 475 (left), © Bettmann/CORBIS
Page 475 (right), © Joseph Sohm/Visions of America/CORBIS

Chapter 15
Page 489, McGraw-Hill Companies Inc, Jill Braaten, photographer
Page 493, © Karen Moskowitz Photography
Page 507, © Dwayne Newton/PhotoEdit

Chapter 16
Page 535, McGraw-Hill Companies Inc, Jill Braaten, photographer

Chapter 17
Page 587, © Peter Hvizdak/The Image Works
Page 589, © Image Source Black/Jupiter Images
Page 597, ©Bob Daemmrich /The Image Works